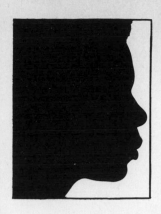

DIRECTORY OF
AFRO-AMERICAN RESOURCES

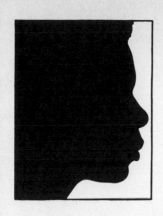

DIRECTORY OF AFRO-AMERICAN RESOURCES

EDITED BY WALTER SCHATZ

RACE RELATIONS
INFORMATION CENTER

R.R. BOWKER COMPANY
NEW YORK & LONDON

Published by R. R. Bowker Co. (A XEROX COMPANY)
1180 Avenue of the Americas, New York, N.Y. 10036

Copyright © 1970 by Xerox Corporation
All rights reserved.
International Standard Book Number: 0-8352-0260-7
Library of Congress Catalog Card Number: 71-126008
Printed and bound in the United States of America.

CONTENTS

PREFACE

Compilation of the *Directory of Afro-American Resources* was started in 1967 as a project of the Southern Education Reporting Service — the predecessor of the Race Relations Information Center — to locate and identify organizations and institutions in the United States which hold materials documenting the history and experiences of black Americans.

Upon its establishment in 1969 as a journalistic research agency and library of contemporary materials on race relations, the Race Relations Information Center assumed responsibility for the project.

The Directory lists 2,108 institutions and 5,365 collections of resource materials. The institutions include college, university, public, governmental and business libraries; federal, state, local and private agencies; and organizations with civil rights programs and responsibilities, or with substantive interests in black America. Also included are listings for numerous radical and extremist groups.

The materials listed consist chiefly of primary source materials and supporting documents. Rare items and secondary source materials are listed where they are held in collections which are physically separate from general library holdings. The Directory does not purport to contain a complete listing of materials and institutions, but it does represent a more extensive coverage in this subject area than is found in earlier reference tools such as encyclopedias, almanacs, handbooks, guides and bibliographies.

Robert F. Campbell
Executive Director
Race Relations Information Center

Nashville, Tennessee 37212

INTRODUCTION

METHODOLOGY

A mailing list of institutions and organizations which either hold collections or which were considered by the editors to be likely to hold collections of materials that document the history of black America was developed during a review of the literature. Over 3,100 secondary sources were consulted, among which were union catalogs, directories, catalog cards, published and unpublished guides to repositories, bibliographies, newspaper, magazine and journal articles.

Questionnaires to serve as a basis for the survey were prepared and pretested during the winter of 1967-68. They were revised, printed and mailed out in several series beginning in early 1968 and continuing through the fall of 1969. Different types of questionnaires were used for different libraries and organizations in order to accommodate dissimilarities in administrative structure, purpose, and kinds of collections.

Questionnaires were sent to the following institutions: 120 traditionally and/or predominantly black colleges and universities; 1,510 college and university libraries; 881 public libraries with annual book funds over $10,000; and approximately 3,000 organizations, associations, and special libraries such as historical societies, business, medical and legal libraries, separatist, segregationist, integrationist, extremist and radical groups, religious orders, churches, urban study centers, publishers, and community and neighborhood organizations. Follow-up mailings were sent to selected institutions.

The questionnaires were supplemented, where practicable, by telephone inquiries, and by personal visits which were conducted by the editorial staff or by persons contracted to investigate the holdings of specific libraries.

During the winter of 1969-70, all information gathered to date was transcribed on coded forms and returned to the individual institutions for verification and corrections. The manuscript was based on replies to this final mailing.

Corrections and additions were made on proofs through the middle of August, 1970, where practical and necessary.

Descriptions of collections differ in completeness and detail depending on the degree of participation by cooperating institutions, or the amount of information obtained from secondary sources. In some instances, listings are included for institutions which did not respond to questionnaires, but where the likelihood of extant collections was high. Where secondary sources were relied upon in the absence of verification, they are used in limited fashion in order to provide skeletal entries.

No attempt was made to list collections held by individual collectors except where photoduplicates or transcripts of such documents were found in the holdings of institutions or organizations. Many small collections are included in the Directory. Inclusion is not based on size or form of holdings. Omission does not represent a judgment that an institution lacks importance, nor should inclusion be interpreted as suggesting the undue importance of an institution or collection.

Special mention is due the National Union Catalog of Manuscript Collections. The NUCMC furnished nearly 1,800 of the 5,365 collections listed in the directory, and provided the editors a model upon which most of the collection citations are based.

DIRECTORY ENTRIES

The book is arranged geographically by state, then by city and by institutions within cities. Each entry carries an alphabetic code to indicate the state in which it is located and a number to indicate position within the state. Specific collections held by an institution are assigned decimal numbers.

For example, the components of the code AL 32.3 refer respectively to the state of Alabama (AL), Stillman College Library, (32), and Negro Collection (.3). This alphabetical-numerical code is carried into the index.

Where supplied by the respondents, or available through secondary sources, the following information is given for each institution listed in the Directory:

1. Name of institution, library or relevant sub-unit followed in parentheses by the acronym or abbreviation used to designate the organization and by the founding date. Inclusion of a sub-unit within a larger entity does not necessarily denote administrative control by the larger entity, since the entries are arranged geographically. For example, an urban study center following the name of a university may mean no more than that the center is located geographically on the campus of the school, possibly in leased quarters.

2. Address and zip code.

3. Telephone: area code followed by the number.

4. Person and title of person directly in charge of the institution, library or facility, or person with whom investigators should correspond relative to use and availability of materials.

5. Services generally available to investigators.

6. Statement of purpose of institution represented. (Such statements are generally omitted for college, university and public libraries, state and federal libraries and archives, and historical societies.)

7. Publications regularly issued, or considered by the editors to have research potential for investigators.

8. Descriptions of collections. The chief elements for each entry are:

   a. Main entry: name of person, family, government agency or other corporate body about which the collection is formed. Where materials were gathered by a collector (person, family, or corporate body), they are entered under the appropriate name. If neither of the above methods of listing is possible, the collection is entered under title, using the name by which it is known, or, if there is none, a title supplied by the editor. Life dates usually follow name of person.

   b. Physical description: general type of material and inclusive dates; and quantity, in terms of items, linear feet of shelf space, reels or feet of microfilm, or in other suitable terms. Notation is made of the form of the materials if they are not originals.

   c. Scope and content: description of the types and groups of materials in the collection, noting their subject matter and the names of the principal persons and corporate bodies with which they deal, and mentioning other special features of the collection. For personal papers, the content note includes brief biographical data. Restrictions on access are noted where known to be other than on-site use.

RESTRICTIONS

Many special libraries provide services to their own organizations exclusively and are not open to the public. In general, where no restrictions are noted, collections are available to qualified researchers, as determined by the respective institutions, for on-site inspection. Materials which are restricted or which are closed to the public are so identified where the information has been supplied to the editors.

In all cases it is advised that investigators inquire of specific institutions prior to visitations in order to confirm or determine current restrictions and availability of materials.

BIBLIOGRAPHY

A bibliography of secondary sources is appended just prior to the main index. This is a selected list of sources which proved valuable to the project staff. Inasmuch as several thousand secondary sources were consulted during the period of investigation it is impossible to list them all. Chiefly, those selected represent publications of a reference or bibliographic nature.

Many numbers of numerous serials were also consulted, as well as histories, autobiographies, biographies, studies, correspondence, organizational files, newspaper and magazine clippings, and so forth.

Inclusion does not mean endorsement, nor does it mean other works in the field are not of value or worthy of investigation, but rather that these cited materials proved fruitful in the preliminary research.

INDEX TO DIRECTORY ENTRIES

This is the main index and contains selected references to subjects, persons, places, and institutions mentioned in the Directory. Each reference has an alphabetical-numerical code which refers to a specific citation in the Directory.

PERSONNEL INDEX

A separate index has been added for purposes of designating those individuals responsible for the supervision and administration of organizations and collections listed in the Directory.

STAFF AND ACKNOWLEDGEMENTS

The survey work and manuscript preparation were carried out by the Race Relations Information Center. In one way or another, most of the members of the Center's staff participated in the planning or execution of the Directory. In addition to its own staff, the Center used the services of outside consultants and contractors.

Staff members of the Center assigned full time to the survey and who held positions of editorial responsibility were Brenda Bell, Patricia Braden, Alex Hurder, Mabel Peterson and Beebe Schatz.

Mary Flad, with the assistance of Mike McLean, was responsible for the design and execution of the index.

Victor Glassberg detailed the holding of the Harvard University libraries.

The largest contribution to the Directory undoubtedly was made by the several thousand persons who responded to the questionnaires and information requests sent them by the Center.

It would be impossible to list all of the persons who have been consulted during the course of the project, or who have materially contributed to it, but special mention must be made of the following persons outside the Race Relations Information Center who helped shape the preliminary work or influenced later efforts of the editor and his staff:

Arna Bontemps, curator, James Weldon Johnson Memorial Collection, Yale University; Frances N. Cheney, associate director, School of Library Science, George Peabody College; Arline Custer, head, Manuscripts Section, Descriptive Cataloging Division, Library of Congress; John W. Davis, formerly special publications director, the Phelps-Stokes Fund; the late Ralph Featherstone, former director of information, Student National Coordinating Committee; Frank Grisham, director, Joint University Libraries, Nashville; Helen-Anne Hilker, interpretive projects officer, Library of Congress; Jean Blackwell Hutson, curator, Schomburg Collection of Negro Literature and History, New York Public Library; Clifton Johnson, director, Amistad Research Center, Dillard

University; David Kaser, director, Cornell University Libraries; Robert Landau, Continental representative, Eurobooks, London, England; Annette Phinazee, dean, School of Library Science, North Carolina Central University; Dorothy B. Porter, supervisor, Negro Collection, Howard University Library; Jessie Carney Smith, university librarian, Fisk University; Henry Lee Swint, professor of history, Vanderbilt University. Principal funding for the Directory came from the Ford Foundation through its grant for the support of Southern Education Reporting Service.

INQUIRIES

Readers' comments, suggestions for improvement of the Directory, or data which may be useful for future editions or revisions are invited. Correspondence should be directed to: Directory of Afro-American Resources, Race Relations Information Center, P.O. 6156, Nashville, Tennessee, 37212.

Walter Schatz
Editor

Nashville, Tennessee
September, 1970

GENERAL ABBREVIATIONS

Admin.	Administrative	Dep.	Deputy	LC	Library of Congress
	Administrator	Dept.	Department	Legis.	Legislative
Adminstr.	Administration	Develop.	Development	Libr.	Library
Admn.	Administrator	Dir.	Director	Librn.	Librarian
Arch.	Archives	Dist.	District	Lit.	Literature
Archit.	Architecture	Div.	Division		
Assoc.	Associate	Docu-		Maj.	Major
Asst.	Assistant	ment.	Documentation	Mem.	Member
Ave.	Avenue	Dr.	Doctor/Drive	Metrop.	Metropolitan
				Mgr.	Manager
b.	born	E.	East	ms/mss	manuscript/
Bd.	Board	Econ.	Economics		manuscripts
Bldg.	Building	Ed.	Education	Msgr.	Monsignor
Blvd.	Boulevard	Emer.	Emeritus		
Bus.	Business	Employ.	Employment	N.	North
Bp.	Bishop	Estab.	Established	n.d.	no date
Br.	Branch	Exec.	Executive	N.E.	Northeast
Brig.	Brigadier	Exp.	Experimental	n.p.	not published
Bur.	Bureau			N.W.	Northwest
		Fed.	Federal	Nat.	National
ca.	circa	fils.	a son (or youth)		
cent.	century	fl.	flourished	Off.	Officer/Office
Chmn.	Chairman	Found.	Foundation		
Cmnr.	Commissioner	ft.	foot/feet	p./pp.	page/pages
Cmt.	Committee			P.O.	Post Office
Co.	Company/County	Gen.	General	photos	photographs
Co-Dir.	Co-Director	Gov.	Governor	ports.	portfolios
Col.	Colonel/Collection			Pres.	President
Comm.	Commission	Hist.	History	Prof.	Professor
Commun.	Community	Hon.	Honorable	Prog./	
Cong.	Congress	Hq.	Headquarters	Progs.	Program/Programs
Consult.	Consultant	Hwy.	Highway	Proj.	Project
Coun.	Council			Pub.	Public
Counsr.	Counselor	Inc.	Incorporated	Publ.	Publications
cu.	cubic	Info.	Information		
		Inst.	Institute	R.G.	Record Group
d.	died			R.R.	Rural Route
Del.	Delegate	Jr.	Junior	Rd.	Road

re	as regards	Sci.	Science	Tel	Telephone
Rels.	Relations	Secy.	Secretary	Treas.	Treasurer
Rep.	Representative	Ser.	Service		
Res.	Research	Serv.	Services	U.S.C.T.	United States
Rev.	Reverend	Soc.	Social		Colored Troops
Regt.	Regiment	South.	Southern	Univ.	University
Rt.	Route	Spec.	Special		
Rt. Rev.	Right Reverend	Sr.	Senior	v.	volume/volumes
		St./Sts.	Street/Streets	V. Chmn.	Vice Chairman
		Sta.	Station	V. Pres.	Vice President
S.	South	Statist.	Statistics	vf	vertical file drawers
S.E.	Southeast	Supt.	Superintendent	vs	versus
S.W.	Southwest	Supvr.	Supervisor		
Sch.	School	Supvry.	Supervisory	W.	West

STATE ABBREVIATIONS

		KS	Kansas	ND	North Dakota
		KY	Kentucky	OH	Ohio
AL	Alabama	LA	Louisiana	OK	Oklahoma
AK	Alaska	ME	Maine	OR	Oregon
AZ	Arizona	MD	Maryland	PA	Pennsylvania
AR	Arkansas	MA	Massachusetts	RI	Rhode Island
CA	California	MI	Michigan	SC	South Carolina
CO	Colorado	MN	Minnesota	SD	South Dakota
CT	Connecticut	MS	Mississippi	TN	Tennessee
DE	Delaware	MO	Missouri	TX	Texas
DC	District of Columbia	MT	Montana (not used)	UT	Utah
FL	Florida	NB	Nebraska	VT	Vermont
GA	Georgia	NV	Nevada	VA	Virginia
HI	Hawaii	NH	New Hampshire	VI	Virgin Islands
ID	Idaho (not used)	NJ	New Jersey	WA	Washington
IL	Illinois	NM	New Mexico	WV	West Virginia
IN	Indiana	NY	New York	WI	Wisconsin
IA	Iowa	NC	North Carolina	WY	Wyoming

DIRECTORY ENTRIES

DIRECTORY ENTRIES

ALABAMA

ALBERTA

AL1   FREEDOM QUILTING BEE (1965). Rt. 1, Box 72, 36720.
Tel 205 573-2225. Miss Mary Brooks.
Freedom Quilting Bee, initiated by the Selma Inter-
Religious Project, is a rural Negro cooperative for the
sale of local crafts.

AUBURN

AL2   ALABAMA COUNCIL ON HUMAN RELATIONS, INC. (1956).
303-A Foster St., 36830. Tel 205 887-3438. Brice
Joyce, Exec. Dir.
The Council, a private agency, works in the areas of
education, employment, housing, voter education, the
administration of justice, and health and welfare. It
operates a small research and information service on
human relations problems in Alabama.
Publ.: Alabama Council Bulletin, monthly newsletter;
Special reports.

.1   Alabama Council on Human Relations, Inc.
Files, 1956- . Records, reports, correspondence,
newsletters, and other papers concerning the activities of the Council.

BIRMINGHAM

AL3   ALABAMA CHRISTIAN MOVEMENT FOR HUMAN RIGHTS.
St. James Baptist Church, 1200 20th St., N. 35207.
Tel 205 251-5342. Rev. C.W. Sewall, Pastor.

AL4   ANTI-DEFAMATION LEAGUE OF B'NAI B'RITH, ALA-
BAMA REGIONAL OFFICE. 1715 City Federal Bldg.,
35203. Tel 205 322-1641. Stuart Lewengrub, Dir.

AL5   BIRMINGHAM PUBLIC LIBRARY (1891). 2020 Seventh
Ave., N. 35203. Tel 205 252-5106. Fant Hill Thornley,
Dir. Interlibrary loan, copying, referrals made.

.1   Rocke, Emma Langdon.
Paintings. 5 items. Watercolor paintings from
Historic Sketches of the South (1941).
.2   Serial Collection.
Publications, 1825- . Included are such newspapers and magazines as Birmingham World
(1940-), Crisis (1910-63), The Liberator (1831-
65, 1929-32), National Anti-Slavery Standard
(1840-71), Negro Worker (1931-37), Negro World
(1926-33), Opportunity (1923-49), Voice of the
Negro (1904-07), and African Repository (1825-92).
.3   Tutwiler Southern History Collection.
Includes material on slavery, the Civil War, Reconstruction, and Negroes.

AL6   BIRMINGHAM PUBLISHING COMPANY (1910), LIBRARY.
130 S. 19th St., 35233. Tel 205 251-5113. F.D.
Harvey, III, Asst. to Pres. Copying, typing, inquiries
answered, referrals made, consultation.
Publishers of books for black clients, especially in
academic and institutional areas.
Publ.: Stepping Stones, periodical bibliography.

.1   Reference library.
ca. 150 items. Includes books, newspapers,
periodicals, mss, correspondence, clippings,
photographs, and memorabilia.

AL7   BIRMINGHAM URBAN LEAGUE. 505 N. 17th St., 35203.
Tel 205 323-8359. Clarence N. Wood, Exec. Dir.

.1   Birmingham Urban League.
Files. Correspondence, minutes of meetings,
studies, financial reports, records, and other
materials dealing with the history, programs and
aims of the League.

AL8   MILES COLLEGE (1905), W.A. BELL LIBRARY. 5500 Avenue G, 35208. Tel 205 786-5281. Mrs. H.R. Patterson,
Librn. Interlibrary loan, bibliographies prepared,
copying.

.1   Afro-American Studies Collection.
ca. 1000 paperbacks. Basic books on the life and
history of black Americans

AL9   NATIONAL CONFERENCE OF CHRISTIANS AND JEWS,
ALABAMA OFFICE. 2026 Second Ave., N. 35203. Tel
205 322-6796. John Edwards, Dir., Ala. Region.

AL10   U.S. EQUAL EMPLOYMENT OPPORTUNITY COMMISSION
(EEOC), BIRMINGHAM REGIONAL OFFICE. 2121
Eighth Ave., 35224. Tel 205 325-3475. Alan J. Gibbs,
Dir.
EEOC investigates and conciliates charges of discrimi-
nation in employment because of race, color, religion,
sex or national origin.
Publ.: EEOC research studies of employment discrimi-
nation.

AL11   WENONAH STATE JUNIOR COLLEGE (1965), LIBRARY.
Rt. 10, Box 486, 35228. Tel 205 788-1666. Mrs.
Johnnie Hunter Copeland, Chief Librn. Interlibrary
loan, inquiries answered.
Publ.: Bibliography of books by and about the Negro,
quarterly.

.1   Martin Luther King, Jr. Memorial Negro Collection.
Includes materials by and about Negroes in all
subject areas, including fiction.

BROWNS

AL12   RESURRECTION CITY, U.S.A. (1968), RESURRECTION
CITY LIBRARY (1969). Rt. 1, Box 125A, 36724. Tel
205 872-7223. Cheryl Buswell.
The City, composed of refugees from the Poor
People's Campaign, is building a new town 16 miles
from Selma, Ala.

.1   Resurrection City, U.S.A.
Miscellaneous, 1968- . Chiefly literature concerning the Poor People's Campaign and its participants. Newspaper and magazine clippings,
photographs, tape recordings, and correspondence
on the history of the refugees of Resurrection City
in Washington, D.C., Northern Virginia, the trek
through the South, and final destination in the Bogue
Chitto community (Browns, Ala.).

FLORENCE

AL13 HANDY HEIGHTS HOUSING DEVELOPMENT AND MU-
SEUM. 35630. Tel 205 764-4311.

.1 Handy, W.C., 1873-1958.
Composer, musician. The museum, in Handy's
restored cabin, houses his piano, trumpet, and
other mementoes.

HAYNEVILLE

AL14 MEDICAL COMMITTEE FOR HUMAN RIGHTS. c/o Lillian
S. McGill, Rt. 1, Box 524, 36040.

HUNTSVILLE

AL15 OAKWOOD COLLEGE (1896), W.H. GREEN MEMORIAL LI-
BRARY (1896). Box 200, 35806. Tel 205 539-9462.
Miss Jannith L. Lewis, Librn.
Publ.: Oakwood College.

.1 Afro-American Heritage collection.
Materials, 17th century- . Microfilm. 131 reels.
Books, newspapers, and mss concerning the Negro
American and his history. See Minnesota Mining
and Manufacturing Company, St. Paul, Minn., for
a full description.
.2 Afro-American Studies Collection.
ca. 1000 paperbacks. Basic books on the life and
history of black Americans.
.3 Oakwood College.
Archives, 1896- .

JACKSONVILLE

AL16 JACKSONVILLE STATE UNIVERSITY, RAMONA WOOD LI-
BRARY. 36265. Tel 205 435-9820. Dr. Alta Millican,
Chmn., Div. of Library and Instructional Media.
Copying.

.1 Facts on Film.
Papers, 1954-67. Microfilm. Contains materials
on civil rights and race relations in the South. See
Race Relations Information Center, Nashville,
Tenn., for a full description.

MOBILE

AL17 MOBILE PUBLIC LIBRARY, TOULMINVILLE BRANCH.
1868 Allison St., 36617. Tel 205 452-3396. Mrs. Virginia Smith, Librn.

.1 Local Negro History Collection.
Papers. Vertical file materials on Negroes in
Mobile and Alabama.

AL18 MOBILE STATE JUNIOR COLLEGE (1965), LIBRARY
(1965). 351 N. Broad St., 36603. Tel 205 433-7476.
Mrs. M.S. Bishop, Librn. Interlibrary loan, copying,
inquiries answered, referrals made.

.1 Negro Collection.
Materials, slavery period- . Books (268 v.),
serials, pamphlets, vf, correspondence, clippings,
films, and photographs, covering all subjects pertaining to Negro Americans.

MONTGOMERY

AL19 ALABAMA ACTION COMMITTEE. 503 Oak St., 36104.
Tel 205 269-1183.

.1 Alabama Action Committee.
Files. Records, reports, correspondence, and
other papers concerning the aims and activities of
the Committee.

AL20 ALABAMA STATE COLLEGE (1874), G.W. TRENHOLM
MEMORIAL LIBRARY (1925). 36101. Tel 205 262-
3581. Elijah Singley, Head Librn. Interlibrary loan,
bibliographies prepared, literature searches, copying,
inquiries answered, referrals made, consultation.

.1 Afro-American Studies Collection.
ca. 1000 paperbacks. Basic books on the life and
history of black Americans.

.2 Materials relating to Negroes.
Papers concerning the following subjects and
organizations: Alabama State Teachers Association, American Council on Human Rights, Association for Study of Negro Life and History, Martin
Luther King, Jr., Memorial Folders, Montgomery
bus boycott (December, 1955-January, 1957), Selma
Montgomery March, and student protest movements in the South (early 1960's).

AL21 ALABAMA STATE DEPARTMENT OF ARCHIVES AND HIS-
TORY (1901), LIBRARY. Washington St. between Bain-
bridge & Union Sts., 36104. Tel 205 269-7783. Milo
B. Howard, Dir.

.1 Coffee, John.
Papers, including materials concerning slavery.
.2 Curry, Jabez Lamar Monroe, 1825-1903.
Papers, 1786-1903. ca. 2500 items. Statesman,
educator, and author. Papers relating to Curry's
activities in the field of education in Alabama, and
with the Peabody Fund, the Slater Fund, and the
Southern Education Board.
.3 DuBose, John Witherspoon, 1836-1918.
Papers, 1857-1917. 3 vf. Planter and author. Correspondence and notes gathered for DuBose's histories, consisting of records, sketches, and chapters for Forty Years of Alabama History, History
of the Canebreak, and other works.
.4 Gould, William P.
"Rules and Regulations for the Management of the
Hill of Howth Plantation." Photostats.
.5 Pickens, Israel.
Family papers. Typescripts, and some originals.
Included are papers pertaining to slavery.
.6 Southern History Collection.
Included is material concerning the Civil War.
.7 Tait, Charles.
Family papers. Includes material pertaining to
slavery.
.8 Torbet, James M.
Plantation diaries. Typescripts.
.9 U.S. Census Bureau.
Manuscript census returns (1860), schedule III for
Alabama, containing information on slaves.
.10 Yancey, William Lowndes, 1814-63.
Papers, 1846-63. 1 vf. Lawyer, orator, and political leader. Correspondence (1864-63), diary
(1861), speeches, and scrapbooks.

AL22 MONTGOMERY PUBLIC LIBRARY (1898). 445 S. Lawrence, 36104. Tel 205 263-4735. Farris J. Martin,
Jr., Dir. Interlibrary loan, bibliographies prepared,
literature searches, copying, typing, inquiries answered, referrals made.

.1 Alabama Imprint Book Collection.
.2 Newspaper collection.
Partial runs of Montgomery Advertiser, Alabama
Journal, and Montgomery Examiner, local newspapers containing information pertaining to
Negroes and race relations in Alabama.
.3 Southern History and Confederacy Book Collection.

NORMAL

AL23 ALABAMA AGRICULTURAL AND MECHANICAL COL-
LEGE (1875), JOSEPH F. DRAKE MEMORIAL LI-
BRARY (1904). P.O. Box 306, 35762. Tel 205 859-
0800. Binford H. Conley, Librn. Interlibrary loan,
bibliographies prepared, copying, typing, inquiries answered, referrals made.

.1 Afro-American Studies Collection.
ca. 1000 paperbacks. Basic books on the life and
history of black Americans.
.2 Facts on Film.
Papers, 1954-67. Microfilm. Contains materials
on civil rights and race relations in the South. See
Race Relations Information Center, Nashville,
Tenn., for a full description.
.3 Negro Collection.
Includes ca. 1300 v. (18 rare titles) by and about
Negroes, primarily belles lettres and history;
serials, vf, theses and dissertations, correspondence, microforms, and art objects.

SELMA

AL24   ALABAMA LUTHERAN ACADEMY (1925), LUTHERAN
SCHOOL LIBRARY (1965). 1804 Green St., 36201.
Tel 205 872-3053. Mrs. Mary B. Gray, Librn.

   .1   Negro Collection.
Materials, ca. 1925- . Books, vf, clippings,
photographs, and sheet music. Covers such
topics as Negroes and labor, education, housing,
public accommodations, entertainment, fair
wages, and religion.

AL25   LAWYERS CONSTITUTIONAL DEFENSE COMMITTEE OF
THE AMERICAN CIVIL LIBERTIES UNION, ALABAMA
FIELD OFFICE. 1015 Griffin St., P.O. Box 956, 36701.

AL26   MEDICAL COMMITTEE FOR HUMAN RIGHTS, SOUTHERN
OFFICE. 1430 First Ave., 36701. Dr. Alvin F.
Pouissant, Southern Field Dir.

AL27   SELMA UNIVERSITY (1878), STONE-ROBINSON LIBRARY
(1959). 1501 Lapsley St., 36701. Tel 205 874-7673.
Mrs. Ira H. Durgan, Librn. Interlibrary loan, inquiries
answered.

   .1   Materials relating to Negroes.
Books, serials, pamphlets, clippings, photographs
by and about Negroes.

AL28   SOUTHERN RURAL RESEARCH PROJECT (SRRP). 802
First Ave., P.O. Box 956, 36701. Tel 205 872-5562.
Mr. U.Z. Nunnally and Miss Dondra Simmons.
A civil rights research and law organization "operating
for the purpose of combating day-to-day racial discrimination by southern-born, southern-bred and
federally salaried employees." SRRP was created to
collect data documenting misuse of federal funds and to
deal with the information by litigation and other means.
Publ.: Annual Report, SRRP Newsletter; monthly
Reports, occasionally.

AL29   SOUTHWEST ALABAMA FARMERS COOPERATIVE ASSO-
CIATION (SWAFCA). 1315-B Jeff Davis Ave., 36701.
Tel 205 872-6227. Joe Johnson, Pres.
SWAFCA is a ten-county farm coop which serves the
needs of black farmers.

TALLADEGA

AL30   TALLADEGA COLLEGE (1869), SAVERY LIBRARY. 35160.
Tel 205 362-2882. Elizabeth Williams, Librn.

   .1   Afro-American Heritage collection.
Materials, 17th century- . Microfilm. 131 reels.
Books, newspapers, and mss concerning the Negro
American and his history. See Minnesota Mining
and Manufacturing Company, St. Paul, Minn., for a
full description.

   .2   Afro-American Studies Collection.
ca. 1000 paperbacks. Basic books on the life and
history of black Americans.

   .3   Alabama State Teachers Association.
Papers, 1882-1912. Minutes of the Association's
meetings.

   .4   Congregational Conference of Alabama Churches.
Papers, 1871-1920. Reports of the Conference.

   .5   Talladega College.
Archives, 1867-1954. ca. 22 ft. Correspondence,
college publications, clippings, and other papers.
The bulk of the collection consists of material relating to the history of Talladega College. Includes
folders on Carol Brice, Sam Coles, Buell Gallagher, Henry Curtis McDowell, and Hale Woodruff.

   .6   Woodruff, Hale.
Paintings. The library has three panels of fres-
coes by Woodruff depicting the Amistad slave
revolt.

TUSCALOOSA

AL31   SELMA INTER-RELIGIOUS PROJECT (SIP) (1965). 810
29th Ave., 35401. Tel 205 758-2301. Rev. Francis X.
Walter, Dir.
SIP is an Alabama-based non-profit corporation serving
the interests of rural poor people in the southwest section of the Alabama Black Belt. It helped found the
Freedom Quilting Bee; provides technical assistance
and contacts for grass roots organizations; sponsors
community education programs among black and white
rural Alabamians; and has recently made available
legal assistance for Movement groups.
Publ.: SIP Newsletter, monthly.

AL32   STILLMAN COLLEGE (1876), WILLIAM H. SHEPPARD LI-
BRARY (1956). 3600 15th St., 35401. Tel 205 752-2548.
Martha L. O'Rourke, Librn. Interlibrary loan, copying,
inquiries answered.

   .1   Afro-American Heritage collection.
Materials, 17th century- . Microfilm. 131 reels.
Books, newspapers, and mss concerning the
Negro American and his history. See Minnesota
Mining and Manufacturing Company, St. Paul,
Minn., for a full description.

   .2   Afro-American Studies Collection.
ca. 1000 paperbacks. Basic books on the life and
history of black Americans.

   .3   Negro Collection.
Books (900 v), serials, pamphlets, vf, sheet
music, sculpture, and paintings. Area of concentration: social sciences.

AL33   UNITED KLANS OF AMERICA INC. P.O. Box 2369, 401
Alston Bldg., 35401. Tel 205 758-2263 (Alston Bldg.).
Robert M. Shelton, Imperial Wizard.
Publ.: The Fiery Cross, monthly magazine.

TUSKEGEE INSTITUTE

AL34   TUSKEGEE INSTITUTE, GEORGE WASHINGTON CARVER
MUSEUM (1938). P.O. Box 40, 36088. Tel 205 727-
8479. Mrs. Elaine F. Thomas, Curator/Dir. Typing,
inquiries answered, referrals made, consultation.
Publ.: Historical Dioramas; Teamwork, Dr. Booker T.
Washington; The Singing Windows at Tuskegee
Institute, B.B. Walcott; Inaugural addresses;
Bulletins by Dr. Carver.

   .1   African Art Collection.
Includes such items as jewelry, swords, daggers,
knives, musical instruments, clothing, baskets,
ornaments, and leather goods.

   .2   African Literature.
Over 300 bound v. and rare pamphlets on South,
Central, and West Coast Africa and more than a
thousand photographs of life in Ghana and Nigeria
in the Etta Moten African Literature Corner.

   .3   Art Gallery.
Contains traveling exhibits of contemporary and
traditional paintings and sculptures, as well as a
permanent collection

   .4   Carver, George Washington, 1864-1943.
Houses Dr. Carver's extensive collection of native
plants, minerals, birds; his products from the
peanut, sweet potato, and clay; the permanent exhibit of vegetables that he had started in 1904; and
his more than 100 paintings.

   .5   Historical Dioramas.
20 items. Dioramas showing the contributions of
the Negro to civilization.

AL35   TUSKEGEE INSTITUTE (1881), HOLLIS BURKE FRISSELL
LIBRARY. 36088. Tel 205 727-8237. Daniel T. Williams, Archivist; Mrs. Annie G. King, Librn. Interlibrary loan, copying, inquiries answered.

   .1   Afro-American Heritage collection.
Materials, 17th century- . Microfilm. 131 reels.
Books, newspapers, and mss concerning the
Negro American and his history. See Minnesota
Mining and Manufacturing Company, St. Paul,
Minn., for a full description.

   .2   Afro-American Studies Collection.
ca. 1000 paperbacks. Basic books on the life and
history of black Americans.

   .3   Calloway, Clinton J.
Papers, ca. 1916-30. 3 vf. Correspondence, reports, and other papers. Included is material concerning Tuskegee's Extension Service and

Tuskegee's role in administering the Rural Schools Programs and Rosenwald Schools.

AL35.4 Carver, George Washington, 1864-1943.
Papers, 1887-1943. 16 vf. Correspondence, reports, documents, affidavits, scrapbooks, special citations, articles, and other papers. In part, copies. Included are letters sent and received, mss containing Carver's personal thoughts and aims, material on experiments and patents, a study by Tuskegee (investigated by Jessie P. Guzman, J. Henry Smith and Bess B. Walcott) on his early life, copies of documents relating to the U.S. Extension Service and the U.S. Department of Agriculture, and reprint articles on Carver's life and work at Tuskegee Institute.

.5 Darnaby, R. S.
Materials, ca. 1890- . Records, schedules, photographs, biographical data, and other papers concerning the history of the Negro and sports. Contains material showing the contributions of the Negro and of Tuskegee to athletics since 1890 and the founding of the Southern Inter-collegiate Athletic Conference (SIAC). Restricted.

.6 Delaney, Sadie Peterson.
Papers. ca. 6 boxes. Chief librarian, Veterans Administration Hospital, Tuskegee, Ala. Collection deals mainly with Mrs. Delaney's activities in the area of bibliotherapy, and includes correspondence and photographs as well as numerous honors and awards.

.7 Derbigny, Irving Anthony.
Correspondence. Vice-president of Tuskegee Institute. Letters sent and received deal with Dr. Derbigny's work at Tuskegee, education in Alabama, higher education in the South, the Carnegie Fund, and the founding and organization of Alpha Kappa Mu National Honorary Society.

.8 Facts on Film.
Papers, 1954-67. Microfilm. Contains materials on civil rights and race relations in the South. See Race Relations Information Center, Nashville, Tenn., for a full description.

.9 Holsey, Albon L.
Correspondence, 1904-47. 16 vf. Member of the Tuskegee Institute faculty, executive secretary of the National Negro Business League, assistant to the president and director of public relations, Tuskegee. Correspondence concerns Holsey's work at Tuskegee Institute and with the National Negro Business League.

.10 Logan, Warren.
Papers. First treasurer of Tuskegee Institute. Correspondence (1901-30), bills, receipts, and other papers concerning the financial matters of the Institute and Logan's role as executor of the Booker T. Washington estate.

.11 Lynching Reports.
A detailed record since 1882 of all known lynchings giving dates, state, race of victims, cause of lynching, and place of lynching. Includes extensive correspondence.

.12 Moton, Robert Russa.
Papers, 1916-35. 111 vf. President of Tuskegee Institute. Chiefly correspondence, relating to the activities of Tuskegee Institute and the role of the Negro in American education, political and business activities, and race relations. Included is material concerning the Negro in World War I, biographical material on Moton, and extensive correspondence pertaining to his interests and activities in the Hampton Institute, National Negro Business League, General Education Board, National Urban League (co-founder), and Council on Interracial Cooperation. Correspondents include such prominent political figures, Negro spokesmen, educational leaders, churchmen, industrialists and philanthropists as George Eastman, William J. Schieffelin, C.C. Ballou, Mary M. Bethune, T.H. Cardoza, Calvin Coolidge, Herbert Hoover, Theodore Roosevelt, Oscar DePriest, Marcus Garvey, W.E.B. DuBois, Thomas A. Edison, T. Thomas Fortune, and C.V. Roman.

.13 Palmer, John R.
Materials. First registrar of Tuskegee Institute. Official and personal correspondence, photo-

graphs, notebooks, interviews of early Tuskegee Institute graduates, materials relating to alumni affairs, and other papers. Collection contains one of the most complete records of the Institute's role in keeping close contact with its graduates.

.14 Patterson, Frederick D.
Papers, 1935-53. President of Tuskegee Institute, president of Phelps-Stokes Fund. Correspondence (1936-41), inventory of speeches (1935-53), mss, statements, publications, and other papers. Collection concerns general education matters of Tuskegee Institute and the South, Negro conferences, and the United Negro College Fund.

.15 Photograph Collection.
ca. 3500 photographs depicting early and contemporary life of Tuskegee Institute and the history of the Negro.

.16 Southern Conference for Human Welfare, Southern Conference Educational Fund, Inc. (SCEF).
Papers. Minutes of executive board meetings, correspondence, financial papers, clippings, booklets, photographs, documents, and mss. Contains material pertaining to civil rights and liberties in the South, to the lives and activities of Carl Braden, Anne Braden, and James A. Dombrowski, and information on the Southern Regional Council, Southern Tenant Farmer's Union, American Peace Mobilization, the CIO, and the National Citizens' Political Action Committee. Also included are files of background materials of the Southern Patriot, publication of SCEF.

.17 Southern Courier
Files, 1965-68. Weekly newspaper. Correspondence, lists of subscribers, articles, information concerning civil rights activities, surveys of Alabama counties and other southern states concerning race relations, pamphlets, clippings, and photographs.

.18 Special Collection Relating to Negro Life and History, Race Relations, and African History.
The Collection was formerly two distinct collections: The Booker T. Washington Collection, which consisted primarily of books, pamphlets, and serials housed as a part of the Library; and the collection formed by the records of Monroe N. Work and the Tuskegee Institute Department of Records and Research. Included in the combined collection are books (ca. 15,000), periodicals and newspapers, pamphlets, theses and dissertations, mss, correspondence, clippings, photographs, and microforms. The Department of Records and Research, and Work materials (ca. 66 vertical files, and 128 boxes) consist chiefly of newspaper clippings and magazine articles relating to the social problems and history of the Negro (1882-1966) and an undetermined amount of correspondence concerning the work of the Department.

.19 Tuskegee Collection.
Materials, ca. 1881- . Miscellaneous materials pertaining to programs and presentations at Tuskegee Institute, and departmental programs; extensive materials on the city of Tuskegee and Macon Co., Ala.; phases of academic life and development at the Institute; and papers concerning the Negro in the South, farmers' conferences and interracial programs.

.20 Washington, Booker Taliaferro, 1856-1915.
Papers, 1885-1915. ca. 82 boxes. Educator, statesman, founder and president (1881-1915) of Tuskegee Institute. Correspondence, printed material by and about Booker T. Washington, speeches, mss, and other papers. Collection contains ms of Washington's Atlanta Exposition or Cotton States exposition speech, extensive student correspondence, material concerning Washington's role on the Committee of Twelve, the personal and business correspondence of Mrs. Booker T. Washington (Margaret Murray) including references to her role in establishing the National Association of Colored Women (1896), and materials concerning publications of the Institute and the National Negro Business League.

.21 Williams, William Taylor Burwell.
Papers, 1902-40. ca. 4 vf. Vice-president of Tuskegee Institute. Correspondence, surveys,

studies, and memorabilia. Materials relating to Hampton Institute, Southern Education Fund, and the Anna T. Jeanes Fund for Negro Rural Schools.

.22 Work, Monroe Nathan, 1866-1945.
Papers, 1908-38. Bibliographer, sociologist, and director, Department of Records and Research, Tuskegee Institute. Correspondence, mss, scrapbooks, and other materials. Includes ms materials for Bibliography of the Negro in Africa and America (1927), and books, periodicals, and papers concerning African history, folklore, anthropology, tribal laws and customs.

AL36   TUSKEGEE INSTITUTE, SOCIAL SCIENCE RESEARCH OFFICE, 36088. Tel 205 727-8011. Eric Krystal.

.1   Tuskegee Institute Department of Records and Research.
Papers, 1 vf. Correspondence of the Department and its director, Mrs. Jessie P. Guzman.

UNIVERSITY

AL37   UNIVERSITY OF ALABAMA LIBRARIES (1831), AMELIA GAYLE GORGAS LIBRARY (1831). Box S, 35486. Tel 205 348-6234. Mrs. Jeanette D. Newsom, Spec. Collections Libbrn. Interlibrary loan, bibliographies prepared, copying, inquiries answered, referrals made, consultation.

.1   Ayers, Harry Mell, 1885-1964.
Papers, 1918-65. ca. 36,960 items. Newspaper editor and publisher, of Anniston, Ala. Correspondence, letters to the editor, editorials, and other papers relating to local, state, and national political campaigns and elections, education, civil rights, and current affairs.

.2   Brookes, Iveson L.
Papers, 1811-1911. ca. 3000 items. Baptist minister and planter. Personal correspondence (702 letters), diaries of his ministry (1827-34), 214 sermons and outlines of sermons, a few thousand receipts for loans and expenses, and two pamphlets which Brookes wrote: A Defence of the South Against the Reproaches and Encroachments of the North (1850), and A Defence of Southern Slavery Against the Attacks of Henry Clay and Alexander Campbell (1851).

.3   Facts on Film.
Papers, 1954-67. Microfilm. Contains materials on civil rights and race relations in the South. See Race Relations Information Center, Nashville, Tenn., for a full description.

.4   Heflin, James Thomas, 1869-1951.
Papers, 1893-1951. 20,000 items. U.S. Representative and Senator from Alabama. Correspondence, speeches, press releases, biographical notes, campaign literature, photos, scrapbooks, and memorabilia. The speeches reflect his attitude on domestic and foreign issues such as segregation, woman suffrage, Presidential campaign of 1928, and Catholicism.

.5   Jemison, Robert, 1802-71.
Papers, 1797-1898. 2214 items. Lawyer, businessman, politician, and planter. Correspondence, 15 letterbooks (1844-69), and other papers concerning Jemison's interests in a plantation, politics, and other business matters. Includes a proclamation to his black people (1865) and a similar proclamation (1827) by his father, William Jemison; correspondence (1871-95) on the settling of his estate; and other materials.

.6   Lull, Cabot, 1835-1925.
Papers, 1832-1925. ca. 740 items. Judge of Elmore Co., Ala. Correspondence, diaries, ledgers, bills, invoices, receipts, contracts, legal and business papers, newspaper clippings, and pictures. Among other subjects, the papers relate to social life in the United States, slavery, Uncle Tom's Cabin, Lincoln's assassination, the underground railroad, and Alabama politics.

.7   Maxwell, Luther H.
Papers, ca. 1920-31. ca. 700 items. Correspondence relating to Maxwell Brothers, a firm of wholesale grocers located in Tuscaloosa, Ala., an

orphans' home, Negro missions, and foreign missions; a postcard collection and personal memorabilia.

.8   Mayfield, Sara, 1905- .
Papers. ca. 3945 items. Author and foreign correspondent. Letters, Negro folk songs and records, plays, novels, short stories, news stories, and articles.

.9   Townsend, Samuel, d. 1856.
Estate papers, 1827-90. ca. 1000 items. Alabama planter. Correspondence, legal documents, and other papers. Primarily concerns the estate Townsend left in 1856 to 40 of his slaves whom he emancipated by a will which was drafted and executed by S.D. Cabaniss, and contested by rival heirs. The estate was liquidated on credit for over $200,000 in 1860, but the war intervened, so the collectible funds were not distributed until the 1870's. Also concerns the education and other affairs of the legatees, their disappointed expectations, and trips on their behalf to Ohio by W.D. Chadicks, and to Kansas by Cabaniss. Includes material on the voided will of Edmund Townsend which left the bulk of his $500,000 estate to his two mulatto children.

AL38   CIVIL LIBERTIES UNION OF ALABAMA. P.O. Box 1972, 35486. Richard Singer, Chmn.

ALASKA

ANCHORAGE

AK1   ALASKA STATE COMMISSION FOR HUMAN RIGHTS (1963). 520 MacKay Bldg., 338 Denali St., 99501. Tel 907 272-9504. Willard L. Bowman, Exec. Dir. Consultation.
State legislative agency empowered to conduct surveys, studies and public education programs; receive and investigate complaints; initiate complaints; conciliate; hold hearings; issue cease-and-desist orders and orders requiring remedial action on behalf of complainant; seek court enforcement of its orders. Its jurisdiction extends to employment (employers, agencies and labor), housing, public accommodations, health facilities, and education.
Publ.: Focus on Human Rights, quarterly newsletter; Annual Report.

.1   Alaska State Commission for Human Rights.
Files, 1963- . Records, correspondence, and reports, including transcript and summary of the Alaska Native Housing Conference (Anchorage, November, 1965), a study of the Pribilof Islands management practices (1965), and reports of equal employment opportunity seminars and human rights conferences (Nome, and Fairbanks, Alaska). Restricted.

ARIZONA

FLAGSTAFF

AZ1   NORTHERN ARIZONA UNIVERSITY, LIBRARY. 86001. Tel 602 523-9011. Librn. Copying, inquiries answered.

.1   Social and Political Action Documents Collection.
Serials, pamphlets, and ephemeral material issued by various right-wing and left-wing groups. Contains material pertaining to segregation, religious prejudices, and social views on race during the late 1950's and early 1960's.

PHOENIX

AZ2   ARIZONA CIVIL LIBERTIES UNION (1959). 7014 N. 16th St., 85020. Tel 602 944-1482. Ted Mote, Exec. Dir.

AZ3   ARIZONA CIVIL RIGHTS COMMISSION (1965). 1623 W.
        Washington St., 85007. Tel 602 271-5263. Wilbur R.
        Johnson, Exec. Dir. Consultation.
        The Commission is a state legislative agency em-
        powered to accept, investigate, and conciliate com-
        plaints in voting, public accommodations and employ-
        ments; conduct surveys, studies and public education
        programs; hold hearings; and recommend legislative
        or other remedial action.

AZ4   NATIONAL CONFERENCE OF CHRISTIANS AND JEWS.
        11 W. Jefferson St., 85003. Tel 602 254-7443. Donald
        A. Eagle, Dir.

AZ5   PHOENIX COMMISSION ON HUMAN RELATIONS (1963).
        332 W. Washington St., 85003. Tel 602 262-6891.
        Henry A. Cabirac, Jr., Dir.
        City agency empowered to gather and disseminate
        data; conduct surveys and studies; serve as an in-
        formation resource; conduct information and education
        programs; and enforce compliance with anti-discrimi-
        nation laws concerning public accommodations and fair
        employment.

AZ6   PHOENIX URBAN LEAGUE (1944). 1515 E. Osborn St.,
        85014. Tel 602 277-5421. Junius A. Bowman, Exec.
        Dir.
        The League works to assist Negroes and other minori-
        ties in their efforts to obtain adequate housing, health,
        educational and cultural opportunities.
        Publ.: Pamphlets, brochures, reports.

        TUCSON

AZ7   ARIZONA PIONEERS' HISTORICAL SOCIETY (1884). 949
        E. Second St., 85719. Tel 602 622-3202. Donald E.
        Phillips, Dir.

        .1 Culin, Beppie.
                Papers, 1850-1900. 325 items. Correspondence,
                bills of sale for slaves, and photos dealing with
                American names and places. Includes 2 letters
                relating to the sale of slaves.
        .2 Miller, William N., b. 1860.
                Papers, 1880-1940. 50 items. Stagecoach driver.
                Letters containing historical information and bio-
                graphical sketches, and reminiscences discussing
                Negro troops in Arizona.

AZ8   TUCSON COMMISSION ON HUMAN RELATIONS (1960). 134
        W. Council St., 85701. Tel 602 791-4235. Leonard L.
        Karter, Exec. Secy.
        City agency empowered to conduct surveys, studies and
        public education programs; to eliminate discrimination
        in places of public accommodation, in employment, in
        housing, and education through investigation, concilia-
        tion, and enforcement. Formerly Mayor's Committee
        on Human Relations.

AZ9   UNIVERSITY OF ARIZONA (1893), LIBRARY. 85721. Tel
        602 884-2101. Robert K. Johnson, Librn. Interlibrary
        loan, bibliographies prepared, copying, typing, inquiries
        answered.

        .1 Arizona Civil Liberties Union.
                Records, 1958-65. 4 boxes. Correspondence, fi-
                nancial reports, minutes of meetings, publications,
                clippings, tape recordings of radio broadcasts, and
                material on various local cases and projects. In-
                cludes papers relating to establishment of the Ari-
                zona Civil Liberties Union as an affiliate of the
                American Civil Liberties Union, operation in con-
                nection with the national civil liberties movement,
                and the Arizona Legislative Co-ordinating Com-
                mittee, an independent ad hoc committee formed to
                encourage passage of constructive State legislation
                in the field of civil rights and liberties.
        .2 Cima, Evelyn L.
                Papers, 1967. 60 pp. Ms of thesis entitled
                "Selected Child-rearing Practices of Lower and
                Middle-class Negro Mothers."
        .3 Davis, Barbara J.
                Papers, 1965. 251 pp. Ms of thesis entitled "Pro-
                motional Techniques Utilized in the Negro Market

for One Hundred Twenty-one National Consumer
Brands."
.4 Finley, Leighton, 1856-94.
        Papers. 1 portfolio. Notebooks and photos re-
        lating to Finley's service as a lieutenant with the
        10th Cavalry, U.S. Army, in Texas and Arizona
        during the Indian wars. Includes "official record"
        of service; two notebooks containing a diary
        (1880-85), financial records, personal memoranda,
        and 40 photos of Apache Indians and military per-
        sonnel at Fort Leavenworth, Kans., Fort Grant,
        Ariz., and Fort Apache, Ariz.

ARKANSAS

        FAYETTEVILLE

AR1   UNIVERSITY OF ARKANSAS (1871), UNIVERSITY LI-
        BRARY (1873). 72701. Tel 501 575-4101. Marvin A.
        Miller, Dir. Interlibrary loan, copying, consultation.

        .1 Brough, Charles Hillman, 1876-1935.
                Papers, 1895-1935. 8 ft. and 6 reels of micro-
                film. Lawyer, educator, author, and Governor of
                Arkansas. Correspondence (ca. 9000 items) in-
                cluding, after 1917, copies of letters by Brough;
                microfilm of 56 scrapbooks (1913-36), of cor-
                respondence, clippings, programs, campaign
                itineraries, lecture tour schedules, speeches,
                resolutions, pamphlets, and other papers con-
                cerning his campaigns, his administration, and
                racial troubles at Elaine, Ark.
        .2 Facts on Film.
                Papers, 1954-67. Microfilm. Contains materials
                on civil rights and race relations in the South. See
                Race Relations Information Center, Nashville,
                Tenn., for a full description.
        .3 Race relations clipping file.
                Newspaper and magazine clippings about Negroes,
                race relations, and desegregation in Arkansas.
        .4 Remmel, Harmon Liveright, 1852-1927.
                Papers, 1879-1927. ca. 7 ft. (7304 items). Busi-
                nessman and Republican Party leader in Arkansas.
                Correspondence and other papers reflecting
                Remmel's political activities; letters concerning
                the Ku Klux Klan.
        .5 Thomas, David Yancey, 1872-1943.
                Papers, 1901-38. 413 items. In part, typescripts.
                Educator, historian. Correspondence, newspaper
                clippings, and pamphlets chiefly relating to
                Thomas' interest in various phases of government.
                Includes papers relating to the Arkansas Coal
                Strike (1914-15), the Elaine race riots (1919-20),
                and race relations.

        FORT SMITH

AR2   CONGRESS OF RACIAL EQUALITY (CORE). 1411 N. 12th
        St., 72901. Ruby Rogers, Secy.

        LITTLE ROCK

AR3   ARKANSAS ARTS CENTER (1963), ELIZABETH PREWITT
        TAYLOR MEMORIAL LIBRARY (1963). MacArthur
        Park, 72203. Tel 501 376-3671. Mrs. Travis McCoy,
        Librn. Interlibrary loan, inquiries answered.

        .1 Reid, John D. collector.
                Materials. ca. 4000 items. Collection of Ameri-
                can jazz, including phonograph records, books,
                periodicals, and memorabilia. Restricted.

AR4   ARKANSAS BAPTIST COLLEGE (1884), LIBRARY. 1600
        and High St., 72204. Tel 501 375-7856.

        .1 Afro-American Studies Collection.
                ca. 1000 paperbacks. Basic books on the life and
                history of black Americans.
        .2 Arkansas Baptist College.
                Archives, 1884- .

AR5   ARKANSAS BLACK HISTORY COMMISSION, SHORTER
        COLLEGE. 72114. James L. Morgan, Dir.

AR6   ARKANSAS COUNCIL ON HUMAN RELATIONS (1954). 1310
        Wright Ave., 72206. Tel 501 376-3541. Elijah Cole-
        man, Exec. Dir.
        The Council, a private agency affiliated with the South-
        ern Regional Council, Atlanta, Ga., has educational
        programs for the improvement of economic, civic and
        racial conditions, and it works to reduce intergroup
        tensions and their causes and to promote intergroup
        understanding. Program areas include housing, educa-
        tion, employment, human relations education, public
        accommodations, and social attitudes.
        Publ.: ACHR Newsletter, 4-6 issues per year

AR7   ARKANSAS HISTORY COMMISSION, STATE ARCHIVES
        (1909). Old State House, West Wing, 300 W. Markham
        St., 72201. Tel 501 374-2917. John L. Ferguson, State
        Historian. Copying, inquiries answered.
        Publ.: Reflections, quarterly periodical.

        .1   Bliss, Calvin Comins, 1823-91.
                Papers, 1841-1906. 2 ft. (600 items). Farmer,
                businessman, member of the Arkansas Infantry
                Volunteers, editor (1864-65) of the Republican
                newspaper Unconditional Union (Little Rock, Ark),
                and Lieutenant Governor of Arkansas. Correspon-
                dence, speeches, accounts, receipts, financial
                statements, vouchers, bills of sale, promissory
                notes, contracts, leases, power of attorney, mili-
                tary records, certificates, reports, legislative bill,
                memoranda, photos, clippings, books, obituary, and
                various land, legal, and other business papers.
                The papers relate chiefly to Bliss' military ser-
                vice, his personal and family affairs, the publica-
                tion of the Unconditional Union, and to Reconstruc-
                tion in Arkansas.
        .2   Brough, Charles Hillman, 1876-1935.
                Scrapbook, 1919. Governor of Arkansas (1917-21).
                Scrapbook of the Elaine, Ark. race riot (1919), with
                illustrations.
        .3   Graves, John William.
                The Arkansas Negro and Segregation, 1890-1903.
                Unpublished M.A. thesis, University of Arkansas,
                1964.
        .4   Gulley, L.C.
                Papers. Official documents and correspondence,
                including references to freedmen, Reconstruction
                politics and economic conditions.
        .5   Miller, Enoch K.
                Papers. 144 items. Included are materials re-
                lating to the work of the Freedmen's Bureau in
                Arkansas (1867-68) in establishing schools, and to
                church work by American Missionary Association
                among freedmen in Arkansas.
        .6   Miscellaneous Arkansas Negro newspapers.
        .7   Murphy, Isaac, and Berry, J.R.
                Papers. Murphy was Governor of Arkansas
                (1864-68); Berry, his son-in-law, was State audi-
                tor (1864-66, 1868-73). Material pertaining to
                Reconstruction politics, government, and social
                and economic conditions.
        .8   Oldham, Kie.
                Papers. Includes correspondence, reports, and
                other items relating to Freedmen Department,
                1865-68.
        .9   Trimble, Robert Wilson.
                Papers. Materials for an unpublished history of
                Arkansas, including some sources on the Civil
                War and Reconstruction.
        .10 Woodruff, William Edward, 1795-1885.
                Papers, 1810-82. 14 ft. (10,000 items). Editor and
                publisher of the Arkansas Gazette, of Arkansas
                Post and later Little Rock, Ark., State treasurer,
                general land and pension agent, and businessman
                and planter. Correspondence, deeds, leases, plats,
                contracts, lists, invoices, statements of account,
                receipts, certificates, affidavits, memoranda, and
                other land, business, and legal papers. Among
                other subjects, the papers relate to the settlement
                of estates for which Woodruff was administrator,
                the hire of slaves, and other affairs relating to the
                Civil War.

AR8   GREATER LITTLE ROCK COUNCIL ON RELIGION AND
        RACE. Pulaski Heights Christian Church, 4724 Hill-
        crest, 72205. Tel 501 663-8149. Rev. Linwood Cole-
        man, Chmn.

AR9   LITTLE ROCK PUBLIC LIBRARY (1910). Seventh and
        Louisiana, 72201. Tel 501 374-1677. Mrs. Alice
        Gray, Acting Librn. Interlibrary loan, literature
        searches, copying, inquiries answered.

        .1   Arkansas File.
                Clippings, 1955-69. Subject areas include Negroes
                and segregation in Arkansas. Material from the
                Arkansas Gazette and Arkansas Democrat. Also
                included is an index of local newspapers for mate-
                rial related to Arkansas.

AR10   NATIONAL CONFERENCE OF CHRISTIANS AND JEWS.
        950 Tower Bldg., Fourth and Center Sts., 72201. Tel
        501 372-5129. William L. Pharr, Dir.

AR11   PHILANDER SMITH COLLEGE, M.L. HARRIS LIBRARY.
        812 W. 13th St., 72203. Tel 501 375-9845. Mrs. Shirley
        Tolefree, Librn.

        .1   Afro-American Heritage collection.
                Materials, 17th century- . Microfilm. 131 reels.
                Books, newspapers, and mss concerning the
                Negro American and his history. See Minnesota
                Mining and Manufacturing Company, St. Paul,
                Minn., for a full description.
        .2   Afro-American Studies Collection.
                ca. 1000 paperbacks. Basic books on the life and
                history of black Americans.

AR12   URBAN LEAGUE OF GREATER LITTLE ROCK (1937). 914
        Gaines St., 72202. Tel 501 374-6432. Mrs. Sylvia
        Hallowell, Acting Dir. Referrals made, consultation.
        Urban League works in the areas of economic develop-
        ment, education, health and welfare, and housing, and
        has a program of community organization in low-
        income areas of the city.
        Publ.: Newsletter, quarterly; Directory of local
                black-owned businesses.

        .1   Urban League of Greater Little Rock.
                Files, 1937- . Records, reports, correspondence,
                and other papers concerning the aims and activi-
                ties of the organization. Included are resource
                materials on race relations and urban problems,
                bibliographies, and film catalogues.

NORTH LITTLE ROCK

AR13   SHORTER COLLEGE (1895), LIBRARY. 604 Locust St.,
        72114. Tel 501 374-6305. Mrs. Joyce Dow, Librn.
        Inquiries answered, referrals made, consultation.

        .1   Shorter College.
                Archives, 1895- . Correspondence, minutes of
                board meetings, financial records, catalogues,
                bulletins, records of admission, and other mate-
                rials dealing with the history and administration of
                the College.

PINE BLUFF

AR14   AGRICULTURAL, MECHANICAL AND NORMAL COLLEGE,
        JOHN BROWN WATSON MEMORIAL LIBRARY (1939).
        71604. Tel 501 535-6700. Mrs. J. Palmer Howard,
        Librn.

        .1   Afro-American Studies Collection.
                ca. 1000 paperbacks. Basic books on the life and
                history of black Americans.
        .2   Facts on Film.
                Papers, 1954-67. Microfilm. Contains materials
                on civil rights and race relations in the South. See
                Race Relations Information Center, Nashville,
                Tenn., for a full description.
        .3   John Brown Watson Memorial Collection.
                Miscellaneous. ca. 1700 v., 30 serials, vf, mss,
                clippings. In part, documents school history and
                contains mss, correspondence, photographs, and

historical objects related to Watson's administration as president of the College. Also includes
general materials by and about Negroes in Arkansas and the South.

CALIFORNIA

ALBANY

CA1   BLACK JOURNALISTS (1969). P.O. Box 6337, 94706. Tel
       415 845-6850.
       Black Journalists is an organization of media workers
       in the San Francisco Bay Area which strives, through
       an independent journal, to analyze and comment on the
       news. They "have charged themselves with a major
       task of bringing truth to journalism and conversely
       truth to the people in the tradition of Douglass, Russ-
       wurm and DuBois."
       Publ.: Ball and Chain Review, monthly.

   .1 Black Journalists.
       Files, 1969- . Correspondence, financial records,
       ms copy of Review articles, and other materials
       pertaining to the activities of the organization and
       its organ, Ball and Chain Review. Restricted.

ALTADENA

CA1a   ALTADENA HUMAN RELATIONS CENTER (1963). 100 N.
       Garfield Ave., 91109. Tel 213 791-1598. William H.
       Boone, Exec. Secy.
       The Committee engages in research and education and
       develops and administers programs in areas of human
       relations, employment, and housing.

BAKERSFIELD

CA2   INTER-GROUP RELATIONS BOARD (1963). City Hall, 1501
       Truxtun Ave., 93301. Tel 805 327-1641. Marian S.
       Irvin, City Clerk.

BELL

CA3   U.S. NATIONAL ARCHIVES AND RECORDS SERVICE
       (1934), FEDERAL RECORDS CENTER (1954). 4747
       Eastern Ave., 90201. Tel 213 268-2548. Benjamin F.
       Cutcliff, Center Mgr. Copying, inquiries answered, re-
       ferrals made, research services.
       The Center accessions, maintains, and disposes of
       records scheduled to be serviced by the Center—all
       federal government agencies located in the 11 southern-
       most counties of California and Clark County, Nevada.
       The Center also provides technical advice and ser-
       vices to the customer agencies in the development and
       installation of improved file and classification sys-
       tems, and microfilm techniques. It also maintains and
       furnishes archival services from the holdings of the
       Center Archives.

   .1 Economic Youth Opportunity Agency (EYOA).
       Records, ca. 1964- . ca. 100 cubic feet. Includes
       works and studies done by local boards; materials
       of various administrative divisions, including the
       Research Division which contains records of Head
       Start and summer youth programs, and of the
       Economic and Youth Opportunity Division. Use
       restricted to EYOA personnel.

BERKELEY

CA4   BAY AREA LIBERTY HOUSE (1968). 1986 Shattuck Ave.,
       94704. Tel 415 845-1886. Mike Brown.
       The Bay Area Liberty House is part of a national
       movement to establish a broad marketing network for
       craft cooperatives in poverty areas, in an effort to
       promote economic independence of poor people of all
       "races."

CA5   BERKELEY ECONOMIC OPPORTUNITY ORGANIZATION.
       3230 Adeline St., 94703. Tel 415 841-9151. Scipio
       Porter, Jr., Dir.

CA6   BERKELEY UNIFIED SCHOOL DISTRICT, OFFICE OF
       HUMAN RELATIONS. 1414 Walnut St., 94709. Tel
       415 841-1422. Kathryne Favors, Dir.
       The Office conducts in-service training of teachers and
       the community.

CA7   (This number not used)

CA8   THE BLACK PANTHER PARTY (1967). 3106 Shattuck Ave.,
       94705. Tel 415 845-0103. Bobby Seale, Chmn.
       The 10-point program and platform of the Party is:
       "1) We want freedom. We want power to determine the
       destiny of our Black Community. 2) We want full em-
       ployment for our people. 3) We want an end to the
       robbery by the capitalist of our Black Community.
       4) We want decent housing, fit for shelter of human be-
       ings. 5) We want education for our people that exposes
       the true nature of this decadent American society.
       6) We want all black men to be exempt from military
       service. 7) We want an immediate end to police bru-
       tality and murder of black people. 8) We want freedom
       for all black men held in federal, state, county and city
       prisons and jails. 9) We want all black people when
       brought to trial to be tried in court by a jury of their
       peer group or people from their black communities, as
       defined by the Constitution of the United States. 10) We
       want land, bread, housing, education, clothing, justice
       and peace." Formerly The Black Panther Party for
       Self Defense.
       Publ.: The Black Panther, weekly newspaper

CA9   FAR WEST LABORATORY FOR EDUCATIONAL RE-
       SEARCH AND DEVELOPMENT (1966). Claremont
       Hotel, 1 Garden Court, 94705. Tel 415 841-9710. Dr.
       John Hemphill, Dir.
       The Laboratory, a federally funded organization, de-
       velops and tests educational products in three major
       programs: in-service teacher education, communica-
       tion, and early childhood education. Products include
       self-contained minicourses to teach skills such as
       questioning, tutoring, and small group instruction; de-
       cision-making information packages that analyze
       alternatives in curriculum and instruction; parent-
       child toy-lending libraries. Also operates responsive-
       environment model training for Head Start and Follow
       Through personnel.

CA10   HUMAN RELATIONS AND WELFARE COMMISSION (1960).
       City Hall, 94704. Tel 415 841-0200. Morton Elkins,
       Spec. Asst.
       The purpose of the Commission is to advise and assist
       other city boards, commissions and departments, and
       private agencies on social welfare needs, standards and
       services; identify and study existing and potential areas
       of interracial friction and tension, and recommend
       corrective measures and offer conferences and con-
       ciliation. The commission issues reports of study and
       research and has subpoena power. Formerly Com-
       munity Welfare Commission.

CA11   MEIKLEJOHN CIVIL LIBERTIES LIBRARY (1965). 1715
       Francisco St., 94703. Tel 415 849-1338. Ann Fagan
       Ginger, Dir. Interlibrary loan, bibliographies pre-
       pared, literature searches, copying, typing, inquiries
       answered, referrals made, consultation, brief writing.
       The Library was founded in honor of Dr. Alexander
       Meiklejohn, a leading American educator and civil
       liberties figure, to establish a collection of research
       materials on civil liberties, due process, civil rights,
       and law of the poor for practicing lawyers, law pro-
       fessors and students, other scholars, and organiza-
       tions.
       Publ.: Mieklejohn Civil Liberties Library Acquisi-
       tions, monthly; Bill of Rights Citator 1955-
       1966 & Holdings of Meiklejohn Library and
       ACLU, 1920-1966.

   .1 Meiklejohn Civil Liberties Library.
       Files of legal cases, books, periodicals, news-
       papers, pamphlets, and clippings. Legal cases

concern equal protection of the law in elections without racial, political, or urban discrimination; jury selection without discrimination; and equal protection of the law in housing, transportation, recreational facilities, dining places, hospitals, government facilities and employment, settling family problems of multi-racial families, and enforcement of federal civil rights acts. The Library has holdings of all publications of the U.S. Civil Rights Commission, and of virtually all state and local human and civil rights agencies, as well as publications of many black organizations and cases and periodicals concerning welfare rights law. Also included are extensive holdings of early civil liberties organizations such as International Labor Defense, International Juridical Association, Constitutional Rights Federation of Michigan, Civil Rights Congress, and the National Lawyers Guild.

CA12   PACIFIC SCHOOL OF RELIGION (1866), CHARLES HOL-BROOK LIBRARY. 1798 Scenic Ave., 94709. Tel 415 848-0528. Oscar Burdick, Librn.

.1   Willey, Samuel Hopkins, 1821-1914.
Correspondence, 1846-74. ca. 200 items. Congregational clergyman, missionary in California, and one of the founders of the University of California. Chiefly Willey's reports to the American Home Missionary Society and replies to his reports. The majority of the letters are by Willey himself and cover the period 1849-62. Among the correspondence are letters dealing with Congregational and Presbyterian church work in California and efforts to prevent the legalization of slavery in California. Correspondents include William Adams, William Alvord, Josiah Bacon, Milton Badger, Henry Ward Beecher, Joseph Augustine Benton, Frederick Billings, S.V. Blakeslee, Isaac Brayton, W.H. Childs, D.B. Cox, John Waldo Douglas, Henry Durant, Israel Edson Dwinell, E.W. Gilman, Charles Hall, Roswell Dwight Hitchcock, Samuel Hopkins, Edward McLean, J. Spaulding, David Spence, George H. Steele, Jason Steele, Andrew L. Stone, Samuel J.C. Swezey, and George Clinton Westcott.

CA13   SOULBOOK. P.O. Box 1097, 94701.
Soulbook is a publication concerned with such subjects as black music and poetry, economics, politics, and anti-imperialism.
Publ.: Soulbook: the Quarterly Journal of Revolutionary Afro-America.

CA14   UNIVERSITY OF CALIFORNIA AT BERKELEY, CENTER FOR REAL ESTATE AND URBAN ECONOMICS (1950), LIBRARY (1950). 260 Stephens Memorial Hall, 94720. Tel 415 642-2491. Nancy Axelrod, Librn. Literature searches, copying, inquiries answered.
The Center is an integral unit of the Institute of Urban and Regional Development at the University. Principal fields of research include urban land economics and real estate practices, including development and operation of land use simulation and forcasting model for the San Francisco Bay Area; development of computer programs for real estate investment analysis and appraising; studies of new communities development; the operation of housing and mortgage markets and the impact of property and income taxation on real estate; and the formulation of national housing goals. Formerly Real Estate Research Program at Berkeley.
Publ.: Annual report; Publications list (Research results published in project reports and professional journals).

.1   Center for Real Estate and Urban Economics Library.
Among holdings are ca. 1600 v., 200 serials, 6000 pamphlets, and 100 student theses, covering topics such as building, finance, housing, land use planning, brokerage, appraisal, public housing, urban renewal, infrastructures, and transportation.

CA15   UNIVERSITY OF CALIFORNIA AT BERKELEY (1868), GENERAL LIBRARY (1868). 94720. Tel 415 845-6000. James E. Skipper, Dir. Interlibrary loan, copying, typing, inquiries answered, referrals made.

.1   Anti-Slavery Propaganda Collection.
ca. 2500 pamphlets. Microcards of originals lo-cated in the Oberlin College Library. See Oberlin College Library, Oberlin, Ohio; or Lost Cause Press (publisher), Louisville, Ky., for more complete description.

.2   Jazz Record Collection.
1920- . ca. 450 discs.

.3   Leigh, Peter Randolph.
Papers, on microfilm, of Leigh's diary and account books.

CA16   UNIVERSITY OF CALIFORNIA AT BERKELEY, INSTITUTE OF GOVERNMENTAL STUDIES, LIBRARY. 109 Moses Hall, University of California, 94720. Tel 415 462-6722. Eugene C. Lee, Dir.
The Institute of Governmental Studies is a research organization and the Library is an integral part of the Institute, serving its research staff, campus students, faculty, and is available for use by local interested groups or individuals.
Publ.: Accessions List, bi-weekly; Research reports; California Public Survey, bi-monthly digest.

.1   Institute of Governmental Studies Library.
Materials, ca. 1920- . Pamphlets, documents, and periodicals. Materials, catalogued in depth, on housing, welfare, planning, minority groups, pressure groups, police, civil disorders, and metropolitan and urban problems.

CA17   UNIVERSITY OF CALIFORNIA AT BERKELEY, SURVEY RESEARCH CENTER (1958), INTERNATIONAL DATA LIBRARY AND REFERENCE SERVICE (1963). 2220 Piedmont Ave., 94720. Tel 415 845-6000. Mrs. Lucy Sells, Librn. Copying, inquiries answered, consultation, coding and data processing.
The Library assists in obtaining, processing and analyzing surveys, and provides assistance in the collection of new survey data. The purpose of the Data Library is to open these studies to wider use in scholarly research and student training, and the Reference Service helps scholars collect original research materials.
Publ.: Articles, monographs, books; Publications List, annually; Annual Report.

.1   Survey Research Center.
Materials. Questionnaires, codes, IBM cards, and magnetic tapes. Copies of domestic and foreign survey studies, covering such topics as attitudes toward governmental welfare programs, racial attitudes, left-wing and right-wing groups, Watts riots, de facto segregation, social work interventions in AFDC families, anti-Semitism (Negro oversample), civil liberties, student rebellion, aid to needy children, fair housing, media habits, and attitudes of Negro families. The Center also maintains a small library of books, periodicals and documents of special relevance to survey research.

CA18   YOUTH COUNCIL FOR COMMUNITY ACTION. 1901 Eighth St., 94710.
The council works to achieve power for the poor and minority groups of West Berkeley.

BEVERLY HILLS

CA19   SAGE PUBLICATIONS INC, LIBRARY. 275 S. Beverly Dr., 90212. Tel 213 274-5979. Sara Miller McCune, Publisher and Pres.
Publ.: Urban Affairs Quarterly; Urban Research News, bi-weekly newsletter; Urban Affairs Annual Reviews.

.1   The library on urban affairs includes material on aspects of racial segregation in cities, urban violence, and poverty. Primarily for editorial reference. Restricted.

CAMARILLO

CA20   ST. JOHN'S SEMINARY, EDWARD L. DOHENY MEMORIAL LIBRARY. Box 38, 93010. Tel 805 482-2755. Francis D. Pansini, Librn.

.1   Doheny, Estelle (Betzold). collector.
     Letters of Presidents of the United States, 1777-
     1947. 104 items. Letters of Presidents, and of a
     few of their wives. Includes 13 letters of Abraham
     Lincoln.

CANYON

CA21   VOCATIONS FOR SOCIAL CHANGE, INC. (1968). 94516.
       Tel 415 376-7743. Staff collective.
       Vocations for Social Change is a decentralized clearing
       house for information on job openings with groups
       working for change in social, political, and economic
       institutions.
       Publ.: Vocations for Social Change, bi-monthly news-
       letter.

CHICO

CA22   CHICO CITIZENS' HUMAN RELATIONS COMMITTEE
       (1964). 1139 Salem, 95926. Mrs. Margery L. Ames,
       Secy.

CLAREMONT

CA23   PROJECT UNDERSTANDING. School of Theology, Clare-
       mont Colleges, 91711. Tel 714 626-3521. Joseph C.
       Hough, Jr., Dir.
       Project Understanding seeks ways to combat and con-
       front racism in the white community.

DALY CITY

CA24   SAN FRANCISCO STATE COLLEGE, THE FREDERIC
       BURK FOUNDATION FOR EDUCATION. 75 Southgate,
       94014. Tel 415 469-2151.
       The Foundation, a non-profit auxiliary which promotes
       the educational services of the College, acts as the
       administrative body for the sponsored grants and con-
       tracts awarded based on faculty proposals. Some of
       these grants and contracts are involved in race-
       related areas directly and indirectly, including Head
       Start, Upward Bound, Project Able, and Teacher
       Corps.

DAVIS

CA25   UNIVERSITY OF CALIFORNIA AT DAVIS (1909), LIBRARY
       (1909). 95616   Tel 916 753-4011. J. Richard
       Blanchard, Librn.

       .1   Anti-Slavery Propaganda Collection.
            ca. 2500 pamphlets. Microcards of originals lo-
            cated in the Oberlin College Library. See Oberlin
            College Library, Oberlin, Ohio; or Lost Cause
            Press (publisher), Louisville, Ky., for more com-
            plete description.
       .2   Pamphlet collection.
            ca. 1900-50. ca. 3500 items. Emphasis is on
            radical political movements.

EAST PALO ALTO

CA26   BLACK LIBERATION PUBLISHERS (1968). P.O. Box
       10242, 94303.
       Black Liberation Publishers supports the concept of
       cooperatives for black collective efforts. It repre-
       sents a coalition of black people with various skills in
       the graphic arts, such as presswork, lithography, and
       camera work. Records confidential.
       Publ.: Teaching aids, course outlines, and other publi-
       cations for Black Studies programs.

CA27   MID-PENINSULA COMMUNITY HOUSE (1963). 2369 Uni-
       versity Ave., 94303. Tel 415 324-0444. Inquiries an-
       swered, referrals made, consultation, organizing ser-
       vices.
       The Mid-Peninsula Community House works to con-
       front and combat racism in the white community.

Publ.: Institutional Racism in American Society - A
Primer; Pamphlets; program descriptions.

CA28   NAIROBI COLLEGE (1969). 94302. Tel 415 323-3169.
       Robert Hoover, Dir.

       .1   Nairobi College.
            Archives, 1969- . Correspondence, minutes of
            board meetings, financial records, bulletins,
            catalogues and other materials dealing with the
            administration and history of the College.

FREMONT

CA29   FREMONT HUMAN RELATIONS COMMISSION (1964). City
       Hall, 94538. Robert A. Nelson, Admin. Asst. to the City
       Mgr.
       The Commission, a local public agency, studies and in-
       vestigates problems of prejudice and discrimination in
       the community, develops and encourages educational
       human relations programs, and seeks to anticipate po-
       tential areas of group tensions.

FRESNO

CA30   CALIFORNIA FAIR EMPLOYMENT PRACTICES COMMIS-
       SION, REGIONAL OFFICE. 2550 Mariposa St., 93721.

CA31   CITY MANAGER'S OFFICE, SPECIAL DEPUTY FOR
       HUMAN RELATIONS. Box 2326, 93721. Tel
       209 266-8031. David R. Jimenez, Spec. Dep.
       The Human Relations Division works to foster
       understanding, respect and good will among all
       racial, religious and nationality groups throughout the
       city; to locate and anticipate potential areas of group
       tensions; to seek to arrive at voluntary solutions to
       community problems by persuasion and conference; and
       to investigate grievances and complaints of citizens in
       regard to discrimination.

HAYWARD

CA32   HUMAN RELATIONS COMMISSION (1964). City Hall, 94541.
       Tel 415 581-2345   Bill Scanlon, City Attorney - Ad-
       visory.

CA33   MECCO ENTERPRISES, INC. (1965). 1335 A St., 94541.
       Tel 415 538-3966. David H. Wellington, Gen. Mgr.
       New Lady is the first nationally circulated monthly
       family service publication specifically serving black
       women. The magazine hopes to serve as a training
       ground for black editorial and managerial personnel,
       and Mecco plans to publish books and booklets on
       specific aspects of black social and economic develop-
       ment.
       Publ.: New Lady, monthly magazine.

HOLLYWOOD

CA34   UNIVERSAL BOOKS (1961). 6258 Hollywood Blvd., 90028.
       Tel 213 467-6867. Jerry B. Weinstein, Owner.
       The company is an antiquarian bookseller and pub-
       lisher specializing in Negro history and Negro litera-
       ture.
       Publ.: Afro-Americana (Bibliography and price guide).

INGLEWOOD

CA35   AMERICAN SOCIETY FOR TRAINING AND DEVELOP-
       MENT. Suite 500, 607 S. Hill St., 90014. Tel
       213 751-1174. Harry L. Bodell, Pres.
       The Society has a program to assist community and
       industrial job training projects for employed ghetto
       residents.

CA36   COMMUNITY STABILIZATION ADVISORY COMMITTEE
       (1966). City Hall, 105 E. Queen St., 90300. Tel
       213 674-7111.
       The Committee advises the City Council on methods to

promote mutual understanding and respect among all groups of people.

CA37   SOUTHWEST REGIONAL LABORATORY FOR EDUCATIONAL RESEARCH AND DEVELOPMENT (1966), LIBRARY (1966). 11300 LaCienega Blvd., 90304. Tel 213 776-3800. Robert W. O'Hare, Div. Head.
The Laboratory is currently involved in communications and problem-solving skills at kindergarten and elementary levels; in research training, instructional management, and quality of education.

LA JOLLA

CA38   CABRILLO FOUNDATION. P.O. Box 1301, 92037. Tel 714 459-1024. John H. Williams, Pres.
Cabrillo Foundation, a community foundation, works toward solving the social and economic problems of minority groups in San Diego County.

CA39   WESTERN BEHAVIORAL SCIENCES INSTITUTE (WBSI) (1959), WBSI LIBRARY. 1150 Siverado, 92037. Tel 714 459-3811. Wayman J. Crow, Pres. and Dir.
WBSI advances human welfare by contributing to man's effort to bring his social and interpersonal relations under greater rational and humanitarian influence; by conducting behavioral science research and programs of action; by seeking to invent approaches that objectively reveal the responsibility for social change. The initial focus is upon three programs which grow out of the past work: Understanding Society, Urban Progress, and Peace and Conflict Resolution. Library and records for use of resident researchers.
Publ.: Studies, bibliography lists, and films.

LONG BEACH

CA40   CALIFORNIA STATE COLLEGE AT LONG BEACH (1949), LIBRARY (1949). 6101 E. Seventh St., 90804. Tel 213 433-0951. Charles J. Boorkman, Librn. Interlibrary loan, inquiries answered.

.1   Anti-Slavery Propaganda Collection.
ca. 2500 pamphlets. Microcards of originals located in the Oberlin College Library. See Oberlin College Library, Oberlin, Ohio; or Lost Cause Press (publisher), Louisville, Ky., for more complete description.

.2   Dumond, Dwight Lowell. collector.
Pamphlets, ca. 1760-1869. ca. 450 items. Anti-slavery propaganda pamphlets.

CA41   LONG BEACH HUMAN RELATIONS COMMISSION (1963). 205 W. Broadway, 90802. B.W. O'Neil, Exec. Asst.
The Commission is an advisory body to the City Council in areas of housing, education, and employment. Formerly Long Beach Human Relations Committee.

LOS ANGELES

CA42   AMERICAN CIVIL LIBERTIES UNION OF SOUTHERN CALIFORNIA. Room 202, 323 W. Fifth St., 90013. Tel 213 626-5156. Eason Monroe, Exec. Dir.

CA43   AMERICAN JEWISH COMMITTEE, WESTERN REGION. 590 N. Vermont Ave., 90004. Tel 213 663-2185. Neil Sandberg, Regional Dir.
The Committee works to combat bigotry and to protect the civil and religious rights of Jews and all men.

CA44   AMERICAN JEWISH CONGRESS, WEST COAST REGION. 590 N. Vermont Ave., 90004. Tel 213 663-8047. Julius M. Cohen, Exec. Dir.

CA45   ANTI-DEFAMATION LEAGUE OF B'NAI B'RITH, CENTRAL PACIFIC REGIONAL OFFICE. 590 N. Vermont Ave., 90004. Tel 213 662-8151. Milton A. Senn, Dir.

CA46   BLACK CONGRESS. 7228 S. Broadway, 90004.
The Congress is an umbrella organization for black community groups.

CA47   BLACK PANTHER PARTY, SOUTHERN CALIFORNIA CENTRAL HEADQUARTERS (1967). 4115 S. Central Ave., 90011. Tel 213 235-4127.
Publ.: Black Panther, weekly newspaper.

CA48   BLUE AND WHITE BUS COMPANY (1968). 210 E. 121st St., 90004. Tel 213 756-5936. Oland Dial, Nat. Asst. Field Mgr.
The Company is a subsidiary of the National Economic Growth and Reconstruction Organization (NEGRO), and operates a public transit system in south central Los Angeles.

CA49   CALIFORNIA COMMITTEE FOR FAIR PRACTICES (1953). Box 74545, 90004. Max Mont, Exec. Secy.
The Committee coordinates State legislative interests of groups concerned with human rights legislation. Major program areas include housing, education, employment, and human relations education.
Publ.: Legislative Memos.

CA50   CALIFORNIA COUNCIL FOR EDUCATIONAL OPPORTUNITY. Suite 745, 5670 Wilshire Blvd., 90036. Tel 213 938-2981. Kenneth S. Washington, Pres.
The Council assists local efforts to increase minority-group enrollment in institutions of higher education throughout the state, and acts as a clearinghouse for information on programs and candidates. The Council includes members involved in public and private higher education, civil rights, governmental and related fields.

CA51   CALIFORNIA FAIR EMPLOYMENT PRACTICES COMMISSION, REGIONAL OFFICE. 322 W. First St., 90012. Tel 213 620-2610

CA52   CALIFORNIA STATE COLLEGE AT LOS ANGELES, BLACK STUDENTS UNION, COMMUNITY RELATIONS CENTER. 4506 S. Western, 90062. Tel 213 224-2015.
The Center is coordinated and staffed by Black Student Union members who plan programs in consumer education, reading dynamics, group interaction and Afro-American history. It also conducts college entrance exams and serves as a counseling office for black students.

CA53   CENTER FOR EXTENDING AMERICAN HISTORY. 2325 Crenshaw Blvd., 90016. Tel 213 733-6645. Hilda G. Finney, Dir.
The Center conducts research in Afro-American history and promotes the teaching and inclusion of black history in textbooks.

CA54   CENTER FOR THE STUDY OF RACIAL AND SOCIAL ISSUES. 5702 Bowesfield, 90016. Tel 213 939-0850. Dr. Charles Thomas.
Among the Center's activities is a consulting service dealing with white racism.

CA55   CHRISTIAN NATIONALIST CRUSADE. Box 27895, 90027.
Publ.: The Cross; The Flag.

CA56   CITY OF LOS ANGELES HUMAN RELATIONS COMMISSION AND BUREAU (1966). Room 700, City Hall, 90012. Tel 213 628-9211. Leon E. Whaley, Exec. Dir.
The Bureau is concerned with specific human relations problems broadly representative of the religious, racial, economic, industrial, labor and professional groups found in the City of Los Angeles. Activities center around housing, education, employment, human relations and education.

CA57   COMMISSION ON THE CHURCH AND RACE (1965). 1411 W. Olympic Blvd., 90015. Tel 213 386-6766. John M. Pratt, Exec. Dir.
The Commission seeks to involve the Protestant Church in Southern California in meaningful action in the racial field; in housing, education, human relations, governmental operations, and social attitudes.

CA58   COMMUNITY RELATIONS CONFERENCE OF SOUTHERN CALIFORNIA. 2131 Second Ave., 90018. Tel 213 293-6275. George L. Thomas, V.Chmn.

CA59   COMMUNITY SERVICE ORGANIZATION, INC. (CSO) (1947). 3285 Stoner Ave., 90066. Tel 213 391-3711. Edmundo

Gonzalez, Nat. Secy. Inquiries answered, referrals made, consultation.
CSO is a federally funded self-help organization concerned with citizenship, immigration and naturalization, voter registration and education. It offers scholarships, credit unions, a buyers' club, and a death benefit society. Its projects include a children's center, health center, citizenship classes and consumer education. Local CSO chapters direct efforts according to needs of local communities and desires of members.
Publ.: Chapter newsletters.

CA60 CONGRESS OF RACIAL EQUALITY (CORE), LOS ANGELES STATE COLLEGE CHAPTER. 1901 W. Santa Barbara, 90062. Tel 213 232-9586. James Newby, Chmn.

CA61 CRENSHAW NEIGHBORS, INC. Suite 505, 3685 Crenshaw Blvd., 90016. Tel 213 293-7550. Mrs. Dorothy Pin, Admin. Dir.
A private organization dedicated to racial integration which operates in areas of fair housing, neighborhood integration, and community education.
Publ.: The Integrator, quarterly journal; Crenshaw Notes, quarterly newsletter.

CA62 EPISCOPAL DIOCESE OF LOS ANGELES. 1220 W. Fourth St., 90054. Tel 213 482-2040. Rev. Canon Nicholas Kouletsis, Canon to the Ordinary on Prog. and Commun. Affairs.

CA63 GOLDEN STATE MUTUAL LIFE INSURANCE COMPANY (1925), LIBRARY (1949). 1999 W. Adams Blvd., 90018. Tel 213 731-1131. Jessie M. Curry, Clerk, Pub. Serv.
The Negro Art collection and the Titus Alexander collection were established to portray an accurate image of historical Negro figures in California, to support and stimulate all aspects of community development, and to create pride in youthful Negro citizens.

.1 Alexander, Titus, d. 1952. collector.
The Alexander collection, Life and History of the Negro, contains chiefly printed works including research materials gathered by Alexander and Miriam Matthews for the study of the subjects depicted in the Alston and Woodruff panels (murals in the Negro Art collection).

.2 Negro Art collection.
Murals, paintings, and sculpture. Basis of the collection is two murals, depicting the Negro's contribution to the growth and development of California. The Charles Alston panel depicts exploration and colonization, 1527-1850; and the Hale Woodruff panel, settlement and development, 1850-1949. Other Negro artists represented include Ron Adams, Charles Alston (b. 1907), Richmond Barthé (b. 1901), William Carter (b. 1909), Alice Gafford (b. 1886), Rose Green, Richard Hung (b. 1935), Daniel Johnson (b. 1938), Jack Jordan (b. 1925), Hughie Lee-Smith (b. 1915), P'lla Mills (1918-1964), Alexander (Skunder) Boghossian (b. 1937), Charles White (b. 1918), Beulah Woodard (1895-1955), and Hale Woodruff (b. 1900).

CA64 GREEN POWER FOUNDATION, INC. 1150 S. San Pedro St., 90015. Tel 213 749-1261.
The Foundation is a non-profit corporation aiming at employing Negroes in Watts, Calif.

CA65 JEWISH FEDERATION-COUNCIL OF GREATER LOS ANGELES, COMMUNITY RELATIONS COMMITTEE (1933). 590 N. Vermont Ave., 90004. Tel 213 663-8484. Joseph Roos, Exec. Dir. Inquiries answered, referrals made.
The Committee is the public relations arm of the organized Jewish community of Greater Los Angeles, its two major functions being: to fight bigotry and work towards development of a climate of public opinion in which all persons are accepted and treated on the basis of their individual value and capacity; and to coordinate locally work done by national human relations agencies similar in nature. Records restricted.
Publ.: Jewish Community Bulletin, semi-monthly memo.

CA66 JEWISH LABOR COMMITTEE. 590 N. Vermont Ave., 90004. Tel 213 662-1148. Max Mont, Field Rep.

CA67 JOIN HANDS (1968). P.O. Box 49955, 90049. Tel 213 472-6889. Mrs. Janice Bernstein, Pres. Inquiries answered, referrals made.
Join Hands is a broad-based citizens movement whose focus is on stimulating members of the majority group to take action in their own community and spheres of influence to bring about racial justice and equality. The organization works through discussion group, educational programs and workshops, neighborhood centers, and a media committee.
Publ.: Join Hands, quarterly newsletter.

.1 Join Hands.
Files, 1968- . ca. 7 vertical files. Records, reports, correspondence, and other papers relating to the aims and activities of the organization. Included are a race relations clipping file, consisting of clippings from major U.S. newspapers and magazines; and a collection of materials from anti-racist groups in U.S.

CA68 LOS ANGELES AREA ECONOMIC DEVELOPMENT AGENCY (1965). 311 W. Manchester Ave., 90003. Robert T. Burroughs, Exec. Dir.
The Agency operates several centers which process and approve applications for loans, provide management training and technical assistance to small business entrepreneurs, disseminate information of value to small businesses, and generate cooperative ventures by minority group businessmen

.1 Los Angeles Area Economic Development Center.
Files. 1965- . Records, reports, correspondence, and other papers concerning the aims and programs of the Agency.

CA69 LOS ANGELES CITY BOARD OF EDUCATION, OFFICE OF URBAN AFFAIRS (1963), URBAN LIBRARY (1967). 450 N. Grand Ave., 90012. Tel 213 628-2284. Edward O. Vail, Supvr. Inquiries answered, referrals made, consultation.
The Urban Library collects and organizes data concerning the school as an institution of the total urban setting.

.1 Urban Library.
Includes books, periodicals and newspapers, pamphlets, vf, theses and dissertations, correspondence, clippings, reports, and studies. Among subjects included are the original study and two follow-ups of the report to the McCone Commission on education; deliberations of Los Angeles Board of Education, Ad Hoc Committee on Equal Educational Opportunity (1963); and all early records and minutes of Los Angeles Youth Opportunity Board and Economic and Youth Opportunity Agency. Correspondence is restricted.

CA70 LOS ANGELES COUNTY COMMISSION ON HUMAN RELATIONS (1958). 1184 Hall of Records, 320 W. Temple St., 90012. Tel 213 618-9211. Herbert L. Carter, Exec. Dir.
The Commission lessens racial and religious prejudice; fosters intergroup understanding and acceptance; cooperates with other community and county agencies; and recommends measures to Board of Supervisors for improvement of human relations. Activities are primarily educational, working with community groups.
Publ.: News and Views, quarterly newsletter.

.1 Los Angeles County Commission on Human Relations.
Files, 1958- . Includes correspondence, reports, studies, and other items of both printed and nonprint nature relating to the whole field of race relations, and in particular to the Los Angeles County area. Restricted.

CA71 LOS ANGELES COUNTY MUSEUM OF NATURAL HISTORY (1913), ARCHIVES, HISTORY DIVISION. 900 Exposition Blvd., 90007. Tel 213 746-0410. William M. Mason, Assoc. Curator of Archives. Copying, inquiries answered, consultation.

.1 The Archives include the abstracted census of 1860, 1870, and 1880 showing names of Los Angeles Negroes; compilation of Negro voters in Los Angeles (1892, 1896, 1898) which consists chiefly of adult males in the Negro community; maps of Los Angeles for the 1890's indicating the homes of all voters; and a card-file index containing each man's name cross-indexed with 1888, 1890, 1897, 1901, and 1905 city directories detailing changes in occupation and residence. Also included are materials collected for an exhibit (1969) on the Negro in America, consisting of photographs (ca. 300, part of which are on local Los Angeles history), documents, lithographs, pamphlets, and other publications.

CA72 LOS ANGELES COUNTY PUBLIC LIBRARY SYSTEM (1913) 320 W. Temple, Box 11, 90053. Tel 213 628-9211. William S. Geller, County Librn. Interlibrary loan, copying, inquiries answered, referrals made.

.1 Governor's Commission on the Los Angeles Riots. California.
Microfilm. 6 reels. Includes transcripts, deposition, consultant's reports, and selected documents concerning the 1964 Watts riots in Los Angeles.

CA73 LOS ANGELES PUBLIC LIBRARY, VERNON BRANCH. 4505 S. Central Ave., 90011. Tel 213 234-0115.

.1 Negro Collection.
ca. 2000 books and 1000 clippings, pictures, and pamphlets relating to Negro life and history.

CA74 LOS ANGELES TECHNICAL SERVICES CORPORATION. 3600 Wilshire Blvd., 90005. Tel 213 385-3557. Edward H. Erath.
The Corporation runs a vocational training center in Watts, Calif., and provides technical advice in the areas of education and manpower training.

CA75 LOS ANGELES URBAN LEAGUE. 2107 W. Washington Blvd., 90018. Tel 213 731-8851. Frank L. Stanley, Exec. Dir.

CA76 NATIONAL CONFERENCE OF CHRISTIANS AND JEWS, SOUTHERN CALIFORNIA REGIONAL OFFICE, 3335 Wilshire Blvd., 90005. Tel 213 385-0491. Robert M. Jones, Exec. Dir.

CA77 OCCIDENTAL COLLEGE (1887), MARY NORTON CLAPP LIBRARY. 1600 Campus Rd., 90041. Tel 213 155-5151. Tyrus G. Harmsen, Librn.

.1 Risdon, F. Ray. collector.
Miscellaneous. Books and pamphlets relating to Lincoln and the Civil War period of American history. Includes some materials about the Negro.

CA78 NATIONAL URBAN LEAGUE, INC., WESTERN REGIONAL OFFICE. 955 S. Western Ave., 90006. Tel 213 737-2840. Henry A. Talbert, Dir.

CA79 SOUTHERN CALIFORNIA LIBRARY FOR SOCIAL STUDIES AND RESEARCH (1963). 1510 W. Seventh St., 90017. Tel 213 934-1484. Jon Greene, Librn. Interlibrary loan, copying.
The Library was established to fill the need for a resource library specializing in radical, progressive and labor literature so that historical as well as contemporary material of the left may be preserved. It also serves the cause of academic freedom; makes source material available to those engaged in the Marxist versus non-Marxist dialog; aids scholars, writers and students to understand the background of the new emerging forces.
Publ.: Catalogs, bibliographies.

.1 Southern California Library for Social Studies and Research.
The Library, specializing in radical, progressive and labor history, contains files of the history of "hundreds of labor and political action groups"; a film section; books (6000 v.); pamphlets (10,000); tape recordings (1000); files of the Los Angeles Civil Rights Congress (1947-53); periodicals; Scottsboro boys case material; Herndon case; Black Panther material; tape recordings of black-brown dialog; Rev. Martin Luther King, Jr's, last address in California on tape three weeks prior to assassination; ephemeral collection of

pamphlets on Communist position on black freedom struggle dating back to early thirties; leaflets; news clippings; and other materials.

CA80 U.S. COMMISSION ON CIVIL RIGHTS, WESTERN FIELD OFFICE. Suite 1739, 312 N. Spring St., 90012. Tel 213 688-3439. Philip Montez, Dir. Inquiries answered, referrals made, consultation.

CA81 UNIVERSITY OF CALIFORNIA AT LOS ANGELES, GRADUATE SCHOOL OF BUSINESS ADMINISTRATION, HOUSING, REAL ESTATE & URBAN LAND STUDIES PROGRAM. 90024. Tel 213 825-3977. Fred E. Case, Dir.
The orientation of the research program is toward economic analysis. Included are research on the real estate markets, on real estate financing, land use, and on public policies affecting real estate, urban blight and renewal, and the relationship between housing and riots (specifically, Watts, 1965). The Program's studies draw upon Los Angeles and other California communities as sources for research data.

CA82 UNIVERSITY OF CALIFORNIA AT LOS ANGELES, INSTITUTE OF GOVERNMENT AND PUBLIC AFFAIRS (1962). Social Sciences 11252, 90024. Tel 213 825-4321. Werner Z. Hirsch, Dir.
The Institute provides the focus, stimulation, and facilities for faculty and researchers who wish to participate in its interdisciplinary programs, which include seminars, conferences, and research. It conducted a study of the Watts riots, and the resultant study of urban poverty is concerned with identifying underlying causes of such riots. The Institute also maintains an urban observatory—a multidisciplinary research effort focused on urban problems, especially those of Los Angeles, Calif. The Institute has developed a selective compilation system of data needed in its own areas of research interest which is available to other universities and research organizations.

CA83 UNIVERSITY OF CALIFORNIA AT LOS ANGELES, LIBRARY (1919), DEPARTMENT OF SPECIAL COLLECTIONS (1946). 120 Powell Library, 90024. Tel 213 825-4988. Wilbur J. Smith, Head, Dept. of Spec. Collections. Copying, inquiries answered, referrals made, consultation.

.1 American Civil Liberties Union of Southern California. Archives, ca. 1935- . Contains correspondence, ephemera, and clippings related to ACLU issues.
.2 Anti-Slavery Propaganda Collection.
ca. 2500 pamphlets. Microcards of originals located in the Oberlin College Library. See Oberlin College Library, Oberlin, Ohio; or Lost Cause Press (publisher), Louisville, Ky., for more complete description.
.3 Extremist Movements Collections.
ca. 10 vf. Literature circulated by civil rights and other social, cultural, and political organizations, pro and con.
.4 Facts on Film.
Papers, 1954-67. Microfilm. Contains materials on civil rights and race relations in the South. See Race Relations Information Center, Nashville, Tenn., for a full description.
.5 Spingarn, Arthur B. collector.
ca. 1800 v. acquired from the owners. Contains biographical and autobiographical studies and items of the Harlem Renaissance in poetry and fiction including works of Langston Hughes, Countee Cullen, and Alain Locke. Included are a few anti-Negro items, and focuses on works by and about American Negroes.
.6 Weintraud, Myman, and Goldberg, William.
Collection of materials on the Socialist Party of the United States.

CA84 UNIVERSITY OF CALIFORNIA AT LOS ANGELES, LIBRARY (1919), SOCIAL SCIENCES MATERIAL SERVICE (1964). A1713A University Library, 90024. Tel 213 825-1897. Mrs. Ann M. Mitchell, Librn. Inquiries answered, referrals made.

.1 The Service contains specialized material in the field of social welfare, industrial relations, and current social issues. Included in the collection are reference books, loose-leaf services, pamphlets (ca. 20,000), newsletters and ephemera. There is also a collection of more than 200 unpublished studies completed as part of requirement for MSW degree; this resource is augmented by the addition of approximately 15 studies annually. Subjects represented in the pamphlet collection include discrimination in employment, equal opportunities in jobs and housing, minorities in labor unions, hardcore unemployed, race relations, poverty, community organization, the socially and culturally disadvantaged, and civil rights. Publications of pressure groups, political parties, and student organizations, including the radical left and the extreme right, are also contained in the Service. Emphasis is on current material.

CA85 UNIVERSITY OF SOUTHERN CALIFORNIA, VonKLEINSMID CENTER, INSTITUTE OF URBAN ECOLOGY (1966). 90007. Tel 213 746-2311. Arthur A. Atkisson, Exec. Dir.
Devoted to improving quality of urban environment through research, graduate education, career training and community information services. Studies include urban anthropology and social pathology.

CA86 UNIVERSITY OF SOUTHERN CALIFORNIA, WESTERN CENTER ON LAW AND POVERTY. University Park, 90007. Tel 213 746-2311. Derrick A. Bell, Jr., Exec. Dir.
The Center is a central legal resource facility which seeks to meet the complex legal needs of the poverty community. Its attorneys provide counseling for the organizations of the poor, seek legal reform through test cases, conduct basic research into law which affects the poor, and provide research and other assistance to neighborhood legal services offices.
Publ.: Quarterly Report

.1 Western Center on Law and Poverty.
Files. Records, correspondence, reports, legal briefs, research data, and other materials concerning the operation and programs of the Center, including information on legal services offices, training seminars in poverty law, research, community counseling, current cases, and other current projects.

CA87 UNIVERSITY OF SOUTHERN CALIFORNIA, YOUTH STUDIES CENTER. University Park, 90007. Tel 213 746-2311. Malcolm W. Klein, Proj. Dir.
The Center has conducted Negro gang studies in south-central Los Angeles.

CA88 URBAN AFFAIRS INSTITUTE, INC. (1967), CENTER ON URBAN AND MINORITY AFFAIRS LIBRARY (1968). 955 S. Western Ave., 90006. Tel 213 737-0660. Neville C. King, Exec. Dir. Interlibrary loan, copying, inquiries answered.
The Institute focuses on current urban problems, and provides internships to graduate students interested in urban affairs and the socio-political organization of minority communities.
Publ.: The Black Politician, journal of current political thought.

CA89 VICTOR GRUEN FOUNDATION FOR ENVIRONMENTAL PLANNING (1968), LIBRARY (1968). 315 N. Beverly Glen Blvd., 90024. Tel 213 474-1196. Claudia Moholy-Nagy, Dir. Bibliographies prepared, literature searches, copying, inquiries answered, referrals made, consultation.
The Foundation supports research and other efforts aimed at improving the human environment. Activities include the collection and organization of research materials for use by scholars and students working on Foundation projects, and community educational programs to help improve lower-income neighborhoods through the interest and involvement of residents of all ages.

CA90 WATTS LABOR COMMUNITY ACTION COMMITTEE (1965). 11401 S. Central Ave., 90059. Tel 213 564-5945. Ted Watkins, Chmn.

The Committee, established after the 1965 riots (Watts, Calif.) by eleven labor unions, has been involved in numerous employment, education, and community improvement programs intended to "change the face of Watts." Current efforts include a community-sponsored relocation program for Watts residents facing relocation as a result of scheduled highway development in the area.

MARIN CITY

CA91 CONGRESS OF RACIAL EQUALITY (CORE). 14 Dutton Court, 94965. Tel 415 332-3755. Doretha Mitchell.

MARTINEZ

CA92 HUMAN RESOURCES COMMISSION (1966). 525 Henrietta St., 94553. Tel 415 228-4400.
The Commission, a local public agency, promotes equality of opportunity for all citizens, protects the rights of all individuals, provides procedures to deal with grievances and channels of communication in the community.

MERCED

CA93 HUMAN RELATIONS COMMITTEE (1963). City Hall, 95340. Tel 209 722-4131. A.R. Schell, City Mgr.

MODESTO

CA94 HUMAN RIGHTS COMMITTEE (1965). Box 642, 95353. Rosemarie Havener, Secy.

NORTHRIDGE

CA95 SAN FERNANDO VALLEY STATE COLLEGE, LIBRARY (1958). 18111 Nordhoff St., 91324. Tel 213 344-4912. Norman Tanis, Librn. Interlibrary loan, copying, typing.

.1 Anti-Slavery Propaganda Collection.
ca. 2500 pamphlets. Microcards of originals located in the Oberlin College Library. See Oberlin College Library, Oberlin, Ohio; or Lost Cause Press (publisher), Louisville, Ky., for more complete description.
.2 Black studies collection.
ca. 2500 v. on the Negro in America.

OAKLAND

CA96 BLACK PANTHER PARTY (1967). P.O. Box 8641, Emeryville Branch, 94608. Tel 415 845-0103.
Publ.: The Black Panther, weekly newspaper.

CA97 COMMUNITY ORGANIZATION FOR URBAN PROGRESS (COUP), 2864 Telegraph Ave., 94609. Tel 415 465-1571. Rev. Joe Barndt.
COUP is organizing in white communities to combat racism, working with cities of the East Bay Area, through community research, political organizing, and organizing around issues.

CA98 COUNTY OF ALAMEDA HUMAN RELATIONS COMMISSION (1964). Room 104M, 1225 Fallon St., 94612. Tel 415 444-0844. Francis B. Jeffrey, Exec. Dir. Inquiries answered, referrals made, consultation.
The Commission does research and gives information to the public concerning problems of discrimination and intergroup relations, acts as a conciliator in crisis situations, investigates complaints, develops programs in the areas of education, housing, and employment, and promotes equality and justice for all members of the community.
Publ.: Alameda County HRC Newsletter, quarterly; Informational memos on special subjects.

CA99 GENERAL AND SPECIALTY CONTRACTORS ASSOCIATION, INC. (1966). 1936 Market St., 94607. Tel

415 832-0474. Ray Dones, Pres. Inquiries answered, referrals made, consultation.
The Association, a non-profit corporation, works to find ways and means of developing jobs in the construction industry for minority workers and other poor people who have been excluded from the industry or who work in it only on a limited basis. Among the programs of the organization is one to assist minority building contractors to undertake large scale construction jobs, especially in inner-city areas, through technical and consulting services.

CA100 OAKLAND MUSEUM, ART DIVISION. Tenth and Fallon Sts., 94607. Tel 415 273-3842. Inquiries answered.

.1 The Art Division's research archives are extensive and organized through artist files. Among black art in the permanent collection of the Art Division are paintings, sculpture, and graphic art by the following artists: J.B.Akoio, Emma Amos, Ralph Arnold, Harrison Branch, Brumsic Brandon, Jr. (6 items), Sylvester Britton, Grafton T. Brown (ca. 2 items, believed to be the first Negro artist in California in the early 1850's, with a specialty of portraying western towns), Eugene A. Burns, Calvin Burnett, Margaret Burroughs, Foyer Cadoo, Arthur Carraway, Yvonne Carter, Eugene Cheltenham, Claude Clark, Sr., Hoyd W. Coleman, Eugenia V. Dunn, Jonathan Eubanks (5 items), Charles Ferguson, Robert Glover, Hugh Harrell, Scotland Harris, Eugene Hawkins, Palmer Hayden, Ben Hazard (8 items), Leroy W. Henderson, Leon Hicks, Elvoyce Hooper, Margo Humphrey (5 items), Richard Hunt, William Jackson, Wilmer James, William N. Johns, Melvin G. Johnson, Milton Johnson, Sargent Johnson, William H. Johnson (19 items), Jack Jordan, Richard Kinney, Anderson Macklin, Philip L. Mason, James McNeil, G. McCullough, William McNeil, Yvonne Meo, E.J. Montgomery (3 items), Norma Morgan, Alvin Pope, Mavis Pusey, Don Pyburn, John Riddle, Charles D. Rogers, Betye Saar, Ernest Satchell, C. Sekoto, Slater Van, Frank E. Smith, William E. Smith, Sylvia Snowden, Laurs Soares, Memo Tessema, Royce H. Vaughan, Ruth G. Waddy (3 items), Charles White, Fred R. Wilson, Charles E. Yates, Hartwell Yeargans.

CA101 OAKLAND MUSEUM, HISTORY DIVISION (1910). Tenth and Fallon Sts., 94607. Tel 415 273-3842. L. Thomas Frye, Acting Curator of Hist. Inquiries answered.
The History Division is seeking to acquire and maintain a collection of material related specifically to the black experience in California and the Far West; and to establish a growing permanent archive which will serve as a resource for the community and for California.

.1 Materials relating to Black History in the West. Miscellaneous. Included are photographs of 19th century California residents and homes; copies of The Elevator, San Francisco black newspaper; "Fifty Years of Freedom," a poster for jubilee songs; and drama, starring Frederick Douglass and John Hall; "The Fifteenth Amendment," lithograph, published by Thomas Kelley (New York, 1870) from original design by James C. Beard; 19th century cast iron toys, products and advertisements; an incomplete list of contracts with early local families and organizations concerned with black history in the immediate Bay Area; and a number of artifacts, photographs, and books on loan from California families.
.2 Shorey, William T.
Artifacts, lithograph, photograph, and documents relating to Shorey, captain of a steam vessel, which sailed from San Francisco harbor, 1918.
3. Sill, William Grant.
20th century. Los Angeles composer and conductor. Pamphlets and programs concerning Sill's works and performances.

CA102 PROJECT UPGRADE. 2315 Valdez St., 94612. Tel 415 465-2445. J. Lamar Childers, Pres.
Project Upgrade operates to give minority craftsmen

with previous construction experience an opportunity to attain journeyman status.

CA103 UNITARIAN UNIVERSALIST PROJECT—EAST BAY, INC. (1967). 1304 Fitzgerald St., 94607. Tel 415 658-4152. George T. Johnson, Dir.
The Project assists in providing economic opportunities for underprivileged persons through vocational guidance and training; coordination of anti-poverty efforts of industry, the community, and government.

OROVILLE

CA104 CONGRESS OF RACIAL EQUALITY (CORE). 3180 Columbia Ave., 95965. Tel 916 534-1022. James Harris.

OXNARD

CA105 COMMISSION ON COMMUNITY RELATIONS (1961). 305 W. Third St., 93030. Tel 805 486-2601. James R. Faulconer, Exec. Secy.

PACOIMA

CA106 CONGRESS OF RACIAL EQUALITY (CORE), SAN FERNANDO VALLEY CHAPTER. Box 695, 91331. Tel 213 896-4142. Leon Garrett, Chmn.

PALM SPRINGS

CA107 CONGRESS OF RACIAL EQUALITY (CORE). Box 2916, 92262. Tel 714 325-3501. Wardell Ward, First V.Chmn.

PASADENA

CA108 AMERICAN FRIENDS SERVICE COMMITTEE (AFSC), COMMUNITY RELATIONS DIVISION, PACIFIC SOUTHWEST REGIONAL OFFICE, RESOURCE CENTER. 980 N. Fair Oaks St., 91105. Tel 213 282-5812. Robert W. Gray, Exec. Secy. Bibliographies prepared, literature searches, copying, typing, inquiries answered, referrals made, consultation.
The Division attacks barriers to adequate housing, education, employment, and economic opportunity; presses for full implementation of government programs; seeks ways for further government and private involvement; works to reverse the growing tension and conflict with enforcement authorities and the system of justice; and educates Americans to the urgency of emerging from our present condition.
Publ.: AFSC Reporter, bi-monthly; Know Your School, monthly; Pamphlets, brochures, reports, studies, bibliography lists.

.1 Community Relations Division.
Files. Correspondence, minutes of meetings, financial records, studies, reports, and other materials pertaining to the history, aims and programs of the Division. Included are materials concerning education, race relations, housing, employment, discrimination, health and welfare and other related subjects.

CA109 HUMAN RELATIONS COMMITTEE (1963). City Hall, 91109. Tel 213 577-4316. William H. Boone, Admin. Asst.

CA110 NATIONAL NEGRO EVANGELICAL ASSOCIATION (NNEA) (1963). 101 E. Claremont, 91103. Marvin L. Printis, Pres.
NNEA is an interdenominational, interchurch organization of congregations, pastors, laymen, evangelists, missionaries, and schools, holding "evangelical, fundamental, and orthodox" views of Christianity. It seeks to advance unity in fellowship and service among Negro evangelicals and groups and to expand their potential.

.1 National Negro Evangelical Association (NNEA).
Files, 1963- . Correspondence, minutes of meetings, financial records, studies, reports, and other materials dealing with the aims, history, and programs of the Association.

CA111 PASADENA CITY SCHOOLS, INTERGROUP EDUCATION.
531 S. Hudson Ave., 91109. Tel 213 795-6981. Raymond J. Pitts, Dir.

PITTSBURG

CA112 PITTSBURG HUMAN RELATIONS COMMISSION. City Hall,
94565. Tel 415 432-6826. Wilbur A. Moser, Chmn.

.1 Pittsburg Human Relations Commission.
Files. Includes records of the Commission as well as a small book and pamphlet library.

REDWOOD CITY

CA113 SAN MATEO COUNTY ECONOMIC OPPORTUNITY COMMISSION (1965). 878 Jefferson Ave., 94063. Tel
415 369-1441. Edward R. Becks, Exec. Dir. Copying, typing, referrals made, consultation.
The Commission functions primarily as a community action organization, but also serves as an advisory agency to the Board of Supervisors on matters pertaining to human resources.
Publ.: EOC Action, newsletter.

RICHMOND

CA114 CONGRESS OF RACIAL EQUALITY (CORE). c/o Savanna
Billo, 3305 Florida Ave., 94804. Tel 415 233-8382.
Samuel Burns, Chmn.

CA115 RICHMOND COMMISSION ON HUMAN RELATIONS (1963).
Room 325, City Hall, 94804. Tel 415 232-1212. H.
Adrian Isabelle, Human Rels. Officer. Referrals made, consultation.
The Commission works to provide advice and assistance to the City Council and citizens in "progressive practices to keep peace and goodwill"; to officially encourage groups and individuals to promote tolerance, goodwill, interfaith and inter-racial harmony.

CA116 RICHMOND PUBLIC LIBRARY. Civic Center Plaza,
94804. Tel 415 234-6632. Rose Mary Towns, City
Librn. Interlibrary loan, bibliographies prepared, literature searches, copying, typing, inquiries answered, referrals made.

.1 Afro-American Culture.
1500 v. Books, magazines, pamphlets by and about the Negro American. Included is material on African history.
.2 Richmond Collection.
Papers. Unpublished papers pertaining to the race problems in Richmond, Calif.; master theses; pamphlets; newspaper clippings of local interest on civil rights; and relevant municipal documents.

RIVERSIDE

CA117 COMMUNITY RELATIONS COMMISSION (1966). Box 868,
92502. Lulamae Clemons, Chmn.

CA118 INLAND AREA URBAN LEAGUE. Suite 244, 3570 Ninth
St., 92501. Tel 714 682-6683. Rossi Elliott, Exec.
Dir.

.1 Inland Area Urban League.
Files. Correspondence, minutes of meetings, financial records, reports, studies, and other materials dealing with the aims, history and programs of the League.

CA119 RIVERSIDE PUBLIC LIBRARY (1879). Seventh and Orange
Sts., 92502. Tel 714 787-7211. Albert Charles Lake,
Libr. Dir. Interlibrary loan, bibliographies prepared, literature searches, copying, typing, inquiries an-

swered, referrals made, consultation, microfilm readers, meeting and seminar room facilities.

.1 Martin Luther King, Jr. Collection.
Miscellaneous. ca. 30 ft. Includes books, records, periodicals, and newspapers pertaining to Negro history and culture.

SACRAMENTO

CA120 CALIFORNIA FAIR EMPLOYMENT PRACTICES COMMISSION, REGIONAL OFFICE. 1020 Eighth St., 95814.
Tel 916 445-9918. Inquiries answered, referrals made, consultation.

CA121 CALIFORNIA STATE ARCHIVES. 1020 O St., 95814. Tel
916 445-4293. W.N. Davis, Jr., Chief of Archives.
Copying, consultation.

.1 The Archives contain bills, resolutions of California
State Legislature on race matters, petitions of the public to the Legislature, case records of State and District courts, social welfare files, and annual reports of county superintendents of schools.
Among these materials are the following:
.2 — California State Legislature.
Papers. Bills, resolutions, and petitions concerning race matters such as immigration of Negroes, enforcement of the fugitive slave law, ratification of the 13th, 14th and 15th Amendments to the U.S. Constitution, testimony of Negroes in court.
.3 — California Supreme Court.
Papers. Case records concerning public school segregation, status of Negro slaves, habeas corpus rights of Negroes, Negro economic enterprise, criminal conduct.
.4 — Sacramento District and County Courts.
Papers. Case records concerning the operation of the anti-testimony law, slavery and servitude, employment of Negroes.
.5 — Secretary of State.
Papers. Articles of incorporation of Negro business, colonization, and social organizations.
.6 — Superintendent of Public Instruction.
Papers. Annual reports of county superintendents of schools containing statistical data on Negro public schools.
.7 — U.S. and California State Censuses.
Papers, 1852-80. Ms population schedules, with race indicated, for the U.S. censuses (1860, 1880), and the special California census (1852).

CA122 CALIFORNIA STATE DEPARTMENT OF EDUCATION, BUREAU OF INTERGROUP RELATIONS (1963). 721
Capitol Mall, 95814. Tel 916 445-4688. Theodore Neff,
Chief, Bur. of Intergroup Rels.
The Bureau advises and assists school districts, upon their request, in the racial and ethnic distribution of pupils to avoid and eliminate de facto segregation and in avoiding racial and ethnic discrimination in employment of certificated personnel.

CA123 CONGRESS OF RACIAL EQUALITY (CORE). 5071 Warwick
Ave., 95820. Tel 916 457-5670. Georgia Bradford,
V.Chmn.

CA124 HUMAN RELATIONS COMMISSION OF THE CITY AND
COUNTY OF SACRAMENTO (1966). Suite 203 B,
1507 21st St., 95814. Tel 916 446-0204. Robert R.
Tyler, Exec. Dir.
The Commission studies, investigates, mediates and holds public hearings on conditions in the City and County which may result in inter-group tensions or discrimination; prepares and disseminates educational and informational material relating to prejudice and discrimination and ways and means of eliminating them; cooperates with other organizations with similar objectives; and cooperates with other private and public agencies in making recommendations to alleviate and forestall inter-group tensions.
Publ.: Human Relations Review, monthly newsletter.

.1   News clippings.
Files, 1968. Clippings from various newspapers and periodicals concerning prejudices, discrimination, and other relevant topics.

CA125   SACRAMENTO CITY-COUNTY LIBRARY (1879/1908). 1930 T St., 95814. Tel 916 449-5651. Miss Dorothy Drake, City-County Librn. Interlibrary loan, bibliographies prepared, literature searches, copying, inquiries answered, referrals made.
A new Martin Luther King Memorial Library will be completed early in 1970, and will contain a collection of Negro history and race relations.

.1   The Sacramento Observer.
Partial run of local weekly newspaper published for Negroes.

SAN ANSELMO

CA126   SAN FRANCISCO THEOLOGICAL SEMINARY (1871), LIBRARY (1871). 2 Kensington Rd., 94960. Tel 415 453-2280. Rev. David E. Green, Librn. Interlibrary loan, copying, typing, inquiries answered.

.1   Martin Luther King, Jr., Memorial Collection.
Books (ca. 1000), periodicals, pamphlets, ms and microforms. A collection of source material in Negro history, the growing collection includes anti-slavery and abolition pamphlets, publications of modern civil rights groups, pro slavery material, and ms sermons (ca. 100) on assassination of Martin Luther King, Jr.

SAN BERNARDINO

CA127   SAN BERNARDINO HUMAN RELATIONS COMMISSION. 536 W. 11th St., 92405. Tel 714 886-9491. James E. Thomas, Dir.

SAN DIEGO

CA128   CALIFORNIA FAIR EMPLOYMENT PRACTICES COMMISSION, REGIONAL OFFICE. 1350 Front St., 92101. Tel 916 232-4361.

CA129   CITIZENS INTERRACIAL COMMITTEE OF SAN DIEGO COUNTY, INC. (1963). 1501 Sixth Ave., 92101. Tel 714 239-0871. Carrol W. Waymon, Exec Dir. Interlibrary loan, bibliographies prepared, literature searches, inquiries answered, referrals made, consultation.
The Committee fosters a community climate in which understanding and relationships among various ethnic, religious and national groups of San Diego can more easily and more naturally take place by taking complaints of all types, assisting in employment, developing public education programs, research, assisting in human relations programs.
Publ.: Newsletter; Special reports, bibliographies, articles, films, and program designs.

.1   Citizens Interracial Committee of San Diego County, Inc.
Files, 1963- . Reports; research data; rosters of local groups; organizations and individuals; catalogues of California colleges; periodicals and other materials pertaining to the Committee's aims, history, and programs.
.2   News clipping file on race relations.
1963- . Clippings pertaining to housing, education, employment, police, and related subjects.

CA130   CITIZENS UNITED FOR RACIAL EQUALITY (CURE) (1968). 502 Robinson Bldg., 520 E St., 92101. Tel 714 279-8809. Referrals made.
CURE works to promote on a community-wide basis the principles of racial equality; to encourage through discussion, news media, individual and group effort the implementation of recommendations; to establish effective lines of communication among, to provide support for, and to provide coordination for the activities of individuals and groups having similar objectives;

and to enlist the aid and support of increasing numbers of citizens toward these ends.
Publ.: CURE, monthly newsletter.

.1   Citizens United for Racial Equality.
Files, 1968- . Records, reports, correspondence, and other papers concerning the aims and activities of the organization.

CA131   CONGRESS OF RACIAL EQUALITY (CORE). Box 14031, 92114. Tel 714 465-8671. George Stevens, Chmn.

CA132   SAN DIEGO PUBLIC LIBRARY. 820 E St., 92101. Tel 714 236-5800. Miss Clara E. Breed, City Librn. Interlibrary loan, copying, inquiries answered.
Publ.: Bibliography lists, leaflets.

.1   Facts on Film.
Papers, 1954-67. Microfilm. Contains materials on civil rights and race relations in the South. See Race Relations Information Center, Nashville, Tenn., for a full description.
.2   Index files.
Short facts taken from newspapers, periodicals, and reference books pertaining to Negroes and "Negro firsts"; pamphlets and pictures concerning integration, segregation, slavery, and Negroes; and phonograph records.

CA133   SAN DIEGO STATE COLLEGE (1897), LIBRARY. 5402 College Ave., 92115. Tel 714 286-6014. Louis A. Kenney, Librn. Interlibrary loan, bibliographies prepared, literature searches, copying, typing, inquiries answered, referrals made, consultation.

.1   Pamphlet file.
Maintained for the School of Social Work. Substantial part of this collection is related to the subject of race and minority problems.

CA134   SAN DIEGO URBAN LEAGUE. Suite 407, Robinson Bldg., 520 E St., 92101. Tel 714 234-3312. John W. Johnson, Exec. Dir.
The League works to improve the social and economic conditions of minorities while promoting equal opportunity for all citizens; to build power, unity, and control in minority communities across the city; to bring about systems change through confrontation wherever inequities exist and to attack basic problems with community coalitions.

.1   San Diego Urban League.
Files. Correspondence, minutes of meetings, financial records, reports, and other materials dealing with the aims, history, and programs of the League. Subjects areas include education, manpower, poverty, economic development, and community development.

SAN FRANCISCO

CA135   AMERICAN CIVIL LIBERTIES UNION OF NORTHERN CALIFORNIA. 503 Market St., 94105. Tel 415 433-2750. Ernest Besig, Exec. Dir.

CA136   AMERICAN DOCUMENTARY FILMS, INC. (1966). 379 Bay St., 94133. Tel 415 982-7475. Sally Pugh, Secy-Treas. Bibliographies prepared.
American Documentary Films is a non-profit corporation for the purpose of producing and distributing films that document and examine social change from a human and independent point of view. The organization seeks to explore the causes and effects of social problems and to stimulate a public search for solutions.
Publ.: Film lists, brochures, position papers, bibliographies; Telegram, occasionally; Films, on such subjects as black liberation, Africa, social issues, poverty, race, draft, welfare, community organizing, and crisis in education.

CA137   AMERICAN FRIENDS SERVICE COMMITTEE (AFSC), COMMUNITY RELATIONS DIVISION, NORTHERN CALIFORNIA REGIONAL OFFICE. 2160 Lake St., 94121. Tel 415 752-7766. Russell F. Jorgensen, Exec. Secy.

CA138 AMERICAN JEWISH COMMITTEE, SAN FRANCISCO BAY AREA OFFICE. 703 Market St., 94103. Tel 415 392-1892. Richard E. Lerner, Area Dir.

CA139 AMERICAN JEWISH CONGRESS, NORTHERN CALIFORNIA DIVISION. 40 First St., 94105. Tel 415 421-7255. Joel Brooks, Exec. Dir. Consultation.
The Congress secures panels of individuals with expertise in various disciplines (businessmen, manufacturers, lawyers, accountants, etc.) who upon request will volunteer their services to assist minority businessmen in setting up and operating various types of business enterprises.

CA140 ANTI-DEFAMATION LEAGUE OF B'NAI B'RITH, CENTRAL PACIFIC REGIONAL OFFICE. 40 First St., 94105. Tel 415 982-4003.

CA141 BAY AREA URBAN LEAGUE (1946). 2400 Sutter St., 94115. Tel 415 567-1835. Percy H. Steele, Jr., Exec. Dir.

.1 Bay Area Urban League.
Files, 1946- . Records, reports, correspondence, and other papers concerning the aims and programs of the League.

CA142 BLACK COMMUNITY RESEARCH AND COMMUNICATIONS PROJECT (1967). Box 15087, 94101. Pleasant Carson, Jr., Dir.
The Project serves as the information resource and propaganda arm of a newly formed organizational/agitational cadre of Bay Area black radicals (unnamed). It aims at pro-community control; armed self-defense; cadre being dedicated to community involvement (black) in all levels of the struggle for liberation; and ruling out integration as a goal and capitalism as an economic means of life. Formerly the research arm of the now defunct Black Nationalist Organization.
Publ.: Roots in Revolt, monthly.

.1 Black Community Research and Communications Project.
Files, 1963-68. Miscellaneous materials on Bay Area black life; civil rights/human rights activities; publications; field reports; staff reports; associate materials on San Francisco Urban Renewal "battles"; extensive materials on San Francisco Black Community Organizing Project; some copies of Fillmore Stand from the Anti-Urban Renewal Organizing Project (limited, 1964-65); and other organizing materials on tenant councils, welfare rights, police brutality, and related subjects. Materials restricted.

CA143 BLACK DIALOGUE (1966). 642 Laguna St., 94102.
Publ.: Black Dialogue, A Black Magazine for Black People, quarterly.

CA144 BLACK DRAFT COUNSELING UNION. 1373 Page St., 94117. Tel 415 863-8786. Inquiries answered, consultation.
The Union feels that the wars against "Third World People" are unjust, racist and should be opposed. It, therefore, counsels on religious, non-religious, due process, and radical discrimination questions; and provides information on alternatives to the draft.

CA145 THE BLACK SCHOLAR. Box 31245, 94131. Tel 415 989-3396. Nathan Hare, Publisher.
Publ.: The Black Scholar, a journal of black studies and research, 10 issues per year.

.1 The Black Scholar.
Files. Correspondence, financial records, studies, reports, and other materials used and collected in preparation for publications.

CA146 CALIFORNIA COMMITTEE FOR FAIR PRACTICES, NORTHERN OFFICE. 2940 16th St., 94103. Tel 415 557-2005.
The Committee coordinates State legislative interests of groups concerned with human rights legislation. Major program areas include housing, education, employment, and human relations education.

CA147 CALIFORNIA FAIR EMPLOYMENT PRACTICES COMMISSION (1959), LIBRARY. Box 603, 455 Golden Gate Ave., 94104. Tel 415 557-2011. Mrs. B.J. Miller, Res. Consult. Inquiries answered, consultation.
The Commission works to eliminate unfair practices in employment and housing through educational and legal methods, community planning and participation, mediation and voluntary action programs.
Publ.: Fair Employment Practice Report, annual; Fair Practice News, semi-monthly; Pamphlets, reports, studies.

.1 California Fair Employment Practices Commission.
Files, 1959- . Includes books, periodicals, newspapers, pamphlets, vf, mss, correspondence, clippings, films, photographs, and tape recordings on civil rights in the fields of education, employment, housing, law, and intergroup relations. It also contains reports from other fair employment agencies, civil rights organizations and human relations units throughout the country.

CA148 CALIFORNIA HISTORICAL SOCIETY (1852), LIBRARY (1920). 2090 Jackson St., 94109. Tel 415 567-1848. James de T. Abajian, Librn. Copying, inquiries answered, consultation.

.1 Western Negro history.
The Society holds mss, pamphlets, photographs, and sheet music concerning the Negro in California and western history.

CA149 CALIFORNIA LABOR FEDERATION, AFL-CIO, LIBRARY. 995 Market St., 94103. Tel 415 781-2838. Mrs. Madeline Alverson, Librn.

.1 Library includes materials on such subjects as labor legislation (including statistics); union movement and activities; social insurance; and civil rights and liberties.

CA150 CALIFORNIA RURAL LEGAL ASSISTANCE (1966). 1212 Market St., 94102. Tel 415 863-4911. James D. Lorenz, Exec. Dir.
The California Rural Legal Assistance gives legal aid to the poor without fee in civil cases in rural California. It is a nonprofit organization funded by the U.S. Office of Economic Opportunity.

CA151 COMMITTEE FOR FAIR RENTS AND TAXES. 380 Sanchez St., 94301. Tel 415 863-2691.

CA152 COUNCIL FOR CIVIL UNITY. 495 Fulton St., 94102. Tel 415 626-7496. Mrs. L. Buchbinder.
The Council coordinates the work of Bay Area fair housing groups which help minority people find housing, force fair housing legislation, and press for improved housing legislation.

CA153 GENERAL AND SPECIALTY CONTRACTORS ASSOCIATION, INC. (1966). 801 McAllister St., 94102. Tel 415 567-8946. Ray Dones, Pres.
The Association, a nonprofit corporation, finds ways and means of developing jobs in the construction industry for minority workers and poor people who have been excluded from the industry or who work in it only on a limited basis.

.1 General and Specialty Contractors Association.
Files, 1966- . Correspondence, minutes of meetings, financial records, and other materials dealing with the aims, history and programs of the Association.

CA154 HUMAN RIGHTS COMMISSION OF SAN FRANCISCO (1964). 1095 Market St., 94102. Tel 415 558-4901. William Becker, Dir.
The Commission functions to assure equal economic, political and educational opportunity, equal accommodations in all business establishments and equal service and protection by public agencies; and to eliminate prejudice and discrimination because of race, religion, color, ancestry or place of birth.
Publ.: Annual reports; Minutes of regular meetings; Special reports (on issues in housing, education,

community relations); <u>Bibliography on Negro Culture and History</u>.

.1   Human Rights Commission of San Francisco.
      Files, 1964- . Records, correspondence, financial
      papers, minutes of meetings, publications, clip-
      pings, tape recordings of meetings, and material
      on various local cases and projects. Included are
      materials on the founding of the Commission, and
      a resource library.

CA155   JEWISH COMMUNITY RELATIONS COUNCIL. 40 First
         St., 94105. Tel 415 982-4000. Earl Raab, Assoc. Dir.

CA156   JEWISH LABOR COMMITTEE, NORTHERN CALIFORNIA
         REGIONAL OFFICE. 2940 16th St., 94103. Tel
         415 621-7742. Regina Forbis, Field Rep.

CA157   JOURNAL OF BLACK POETRY. 1308 Masonic Ave. No. 4,
         94117. Joe Goncalves, Ed.
         Publ.: <u>Journal of Black Poetry</u>, quarterly.

CA158   LIBERTY HOUSE OF SAN FRANCISCO. 160 Belvedere St.,
         94117. Tel 415 564-2944. Steve Keyes.

CA159   M. H. deYOUNG MEMORIAL MUSEUM. Golden Gate Park,
         94118. Tel 415 558-6161. Phillip J. Carlson, Acting
         Dir. Inquiries answered, consultation.
         The Museum operates an educational program for
         minority group children.

CA160   MANAGEMENT COUNCIL FOR BAY AREA EMPLOYMENT
         OPPORTUNITY. 1 Bush St., 94119. Tel 415 391-1190.
         Francis M. Barnes, Pres.
         The Council, composed of business leaders in the area,
         provides job-placement services in an effort to in-
         crease employment opportunities for members of
         minority groups in the San Francisco Bay Area.

CA161   MISSION NEIGHBORHOOD CENTERS, INC. (1894). 2595
         Mission St., 94110. Tel 415 285-3400. Harvey E.
         Gabler, Exec. Dir.
         The Centers are multi-service social welfare centers
         offering services to individuals and families, to
         groups, and to neighbors of the Greater Mission Dis-
         trict.

CA162   MOVEMENT LIBERATION FRONT (1968). 197 Steiner
         St., 94115. Tel 415 552-0896.
         The Movement Liberation Front is a San Francisco Bay
         Area organization of lawyers, law students, and move-
         ment activists doing agitational and educational work
         around legal defense. The organization educates and
         assists other political groups, helping them form their
         own legal defense arms and encouraging them to es-
         tablish communications and cooperate with existing
         legal defense committees.
         Publ.: Pamphlets and other literature concerning legal
               procedure and defense.

CA163   THE MOVEMENT PRESS (1967). 449 14th St., 94103. Tel
         415 626-4577.
         Publ.: <u>The Movement</u>, monthly newspaper.

CA164   MULTI-CULTURE INSTITUTE. 226 Miramar Ave., 94112.
         Tel 415 333-0558.
         The Institute attempts to preserve the ethnic identity of
         minority group children through an educational pro-
         gram.

CA165   NATIONAL ASSOCIATION FOR THE ADVANCEMENT OF
         COLORED PEOPLE (NAACP), WEST COAST RE-
         GIONAL OFFICE (1909). Suite 703, 948 Market St.,
         94102. Tel 415 986-6992. Leonard H. Carter, Regional
         Dir. Bibliographies prepared, literature searches,
         inquiries answered, referrals made, consultation.
         The Association promotes equal and human rights for
         all minorities in the U.S.

      .1   NAACP, West Coast Regional Office.
            Files, 1909- . Records, including books, pam-
            phlets, film strips, and slides by and about black
            people.

CA166   NATIONAL CONFERENCE OF CHRISTIANS AND JEWS
         (NCCJ) (1934). 809 Central Tower Bldg., 703 Market

St., 94103. Tel 415 391-2850. Robert C. DaCosta,
Exec. Dir. Bibliographies prepared, literature
searches, inquiries answered, referrals made, consultation.
NCCJ works, through an educational program, to improve cooperation and understanding among men of all
races and religions who share common civic concerns.
There is special emphasis on police and community
relations, job opportunities for minority groups, workshops for teachers and school administrators, and
youth programs.
Publ.: Annual reports; Periodic newsletter.

.1   National Conference of Christians and Jews.
      Files, 1934- . Included are extensive materials
      and publications in the field of human relations,
      films, and a newspaper clipping file.

CA167   THE NEWSREEL. 450 Alabama St., 94110. Tel
         415 531-2404.
         The Newsreel is a radical film project, making films
         that can be used by organizers and others in the pro-
         cess of building political consciousness and building a
         movement for social change in the U.S.

CA168   PACIFIC PUBLISHING FOUNDATION, INC. (1938). 81
         Clementina St., 94105. Tel 415 292-1602. Al Rich-
         mond, Exec. Ed.
         The Foundation publishes <u>Peoples World</u>, a newspaper
         whose purpose is to treat current events from a Marx-
         ist viewpoint, projecting a socialist alternative, and
         striving to give political expression to a common view-
         point on the Left.
         Publ.: <u>Peoples World</u>, weekly newspaper

CA169   PACT, INC. (1964). 593 Market St., 94105. Tel
         415 956-4840. Everett P. Brandon, Exec. Dir. Inter-
         library loan, consultation.
         PACT was founded to stimulate economic growth and
         provide technical expertise to the minority community.
         Its programs include a business development and
         counseling center, an educational opportunities clearing
         house, and a research and economic consultant
         center.
         Publ.: <u>Newsletter</u>, bi-monthly; Reports and studies;
               <u>Directory of Black Businesses in San Francisco</u>.

      .1   PACT, Inc.
            Files, 1964- . Records, reports, correspondence,
            program plans and evaluations, and other papers
            relating to the programs and aims of the organiza-
            tion.

CA170   SAN FRANCISCO CONFERENCE ON RELIGION AND RACE.
         Room 506, 503 Market St., 94105. Tel 415 392-3189.
         Mrs. Max Semel.

CA171   SAN FRANCISCO NEGRO HISTORICAL AND CULTURAL
         SOCIETY. 1447 Filmore St., 94115. Tel 415 346-9842.
         Mrs. Ethel R. Nance, Librn.

CA172   SAN FRANCISCO PUBLIC LIBRARY (1878). Larkin and
         McAllister Sts., 94102. Tel 417 558-3191. John F.
         Anderson, Librn. Interlibrary loan, bibliographies
         prepared, literature searches, copying, typing, in-
         quiries answered, referrals made.

      .1   Martin Luther King, Jr., Special Collection.
            Materials on black Americans in the San Fran-
            cisco area. Regional black newspapers, family
            papers, scrapbooks, black organizational files,
            tape recorded interviews with people in the San
            Francisco community, and other materials.

CA173   SAN FRANCISCO STATE COLLEGE, COMMUNITY SER-
         VICES INSTITUTE. Hut D, Room 2, 1600 Holloway
         Ave., 94132. Tel 415 469-1188. Sharon Gold and
         Wendy Alfsen.
         The Institute attempts to reeducate and train college
         students so that they may participate intelligently and
         work effectively to end racism in their own com-
         munities.

CA174   U.S. EQUAL EMPLOYMENT OPPORTUNITY COMMISSION,
         SAN FRANCISCO REGIONAL OFFICE. 1095 Market

St., 94111. Tel 415 556-0260. Frank Quinn, Regional Dir.

CA175 URBAN WEST (1967). 593 Market St., 94105. Tel 415 989-5424. John C. Bee, Jr., Ed. and Publisher. Resume referral service to black college students and graduates.
Urban West is a national black-oriented magazine designed to reach black professionals, educators, and students. It is concerned primarily with the problems and issues of urban living from the black man's point of view.
Publ.: Urban West, bi-monthly magazine.

CA176 YOUTH FOR SERVICE (1957). 1160 McAllister, 94115. Tel 415 922-8886. Orville Luster, Exec. Dir.
Youth for Service is an interracial, interfaith organization which enables youth to serve the community by means of volunteer work projects for elderly, sick or handicapped people. It is also the sponsoring agency of the Neighborhood Youth Corps, which provides work experience for unemployed youth.
Publ.: YES Newsletter, bi-monthly.

SAN JOSE

CA177 SAN JOSE HUMAN RELATIONS COMMISSION (1958). City Hall, 95110. Tel 408 292-3141. Mark C. Bihn, Exec. Dir.
The Commission functions to discourage and prevent discriminatory practices; to initiate and investigate complaints; and to hold hearings, make recommendations, and issue reports.

CA178 SAN JOSE PUBLIC LIBRARY. 180 W. San Carlos St., 95113. Tel 408 287-2788. Geraldine L. Nurney, City Librn. Interlibrary loan, bibliographies prepared, copying, typing, inquiries answered, referrals made, business reference, shut-in service.

.1 American Negro Collection.
Books. 500 v. History and literature by and about the Negro.
.2 Lewis, Mary Edmonia, 1845-90.
Materials, including books, periodicals, photographs, newspaper clippings, and correspondence relating to the life and sculpture of Mary Edmonia Lewis.
.3 Negro Art Collection.
Includes 3 marble statues contributed (1873) to the library by artist Mary Edmonia Lewis: "Awake" (Roma 1872), "Asleep" (Roma 1871), and "Lincoln" (1870).

SAN MARINO

CA179 HENRY E. HUNTINGTON LIBRARY AND ART GALLERY. 1151 Oxford Rd., 91108. Tel 213 792-6141. Robert O. Dougan, Librn. Copying, inquiries answered.

.1 Alexander Collection.
Papers, 1848-1939. 35 items. Consists of papers of a freedman who became active in Arkansas politics, and the papers of his son who was the second Negro to graduate from West Point. Included is a journal kept during the march of his cavalry troop in Wyoming, in 1888.
.2 American Tract Society Collection.
Papers, 1864-75. 68 pieces. Scattered correspondence of the Society's agency in Richmond, Va., consisting largely of letters concerning distribution of religious books and tracts, work with freedmen and refugees, prisoners of war, Sunday schools and other juvenile instruction, and gathering funds for rehabilitation.
.3 Blair, Walter D.
Business papers, 1815-81. 144 items. Papers of a Richmond, Va., commission merchant, dealing in wine and liquor, groceries, general merchandise, and the hiring of slaves.
.4 Brock, Robert Alonzo.
Papers, 1582-1914. ca. 50,000 items. Collection of Virginiana, consisting of many groups of family papers, county records, religious and fraternal

records, literary material, and miscellaneous items, including Brock's correspondence.
.5 Bullock, Rufus Brown, 1834-1907.
Papers, 1851-95. 41 items plus press clippings. Republican Governor of Georgia during Reconstruction who resigned and fled the State in 1871 under charges of misgovernment and corruption. Chiefly correspondence between Bullock and his brother, Freeman C. Bullock. The bulk of the papers are for the years 1869-72.
.6 Caplinger, Leonard J.
Papers, 1835-97. 83 items. Illinois farmer and Union soldier. Correspondence of Caplinger with his wife, chiefly relating to his Army service, the siege of Vicksburg, illnesses, hospitalization, dissatisfaction with the war, and anti-Negro attitudes; together with bills, receipts, memoranda, and other papers.
.7 Clarkson, Thomas, 1760-1846.
Papers, 1787-1847. 210 items. British philanthropist. Correspondence, drafts of speeches, and other papers. Includes letters addressed to Clarkson about the abolition of slavery and the slave trade.
.8 Eldridge, James William.
Papers, 1797-1902. ca. 15,000 items. Civil War collection containing letters of many of the most important military and political figures of both the Union and the Confederacy.
.9 Emerson, Ralph Waldo.
Papers, 1821-72, ca. 72 items. Massachusetts essayist, poet, and abolitionist.
.10 Fields, James Thomas, 1816-81.
Papers, ca. 1850-1914. ca. 5074 items. Publisher. Correspondence, literary mss, and other papers. Includes notebooks, scrapbooks, clippings, and other miscellaneous papers of Annie Adams Fields. The letters, mainly addressed to Fields and to his wife are from such writers as Thomas Bailey Aldrich, Ralph Waldo Emerson, Nathaniel Hawthorne, Oliver Wendell Holmes, Henry Wadsworth Longfellow, James Russell Lowell, Harriet Beecher Stowe, and John Greenleaf Whittier.
.11 Grabill, Levi.
Papers, 1861-92. 96 items. 4th Ohio Infantry, and Captain, 22nd U.S. Colored Infantry. Included are photographs, letters and documents, and 2 pocket diaries (1861, 1865),containing details about military affairs and a soldier's life.
.12 Haight, Henry Huntley, 1825-78.
Papers, 1846-85. 508 items. Lawyer and Governor of California. Personal and business papers relating chiefly to the political history of California and to such subjects as land titles in San Francisco, legal proceedings, and the anti-slavery and secession questions.
.13 Higginson, Thomas Wentworth, 1823-1911.
Papers, 1848-1910. 133 items. Congregational minister and author. Correspondence and literary mss. Includes two versions of The Life of John Greenleaf Whittier (1902) and The Life of Birds. Correspondents include Thomas Bailey Aldrich, Oliver Wendell Holmes, James Russell Lowell, Theodore Parker, and John Greenleaf Whittier.
.14 Hill, Lewis.
Papers, 1834-60. 124 items. Forms part of the library's Brock collection. Largely letters addressed to Hill, of Richmond and Fredericksburg, Va., who acted as a commission merchant, bill collector, and agent for hiring out Negro servants.
.15 Hill, Robert.
Business correspondence, 1778-1857. 96 items. Forms part of the library's Brock collection of Virginiana. Business letters to Hill (a commission merchant of Richmond who operated under the firm names of Hill and Dabney, and Robert Hill and Co.) concerning collections, hiring of Negroes, buying of crops, and other matters.
.16 Hooker, Joseph, 1814-79.
Military papers, 1861-64. 3850 items. Army officer. Papers relating to cavalry, preparations for campaigns, picket reports, balloon observers, activities of officers and men in battle and in camp, disciplinary and personnel problems, courts-

martial, civilian relationships, freed slaves, contraband goods, and staff work. Battles represented include Antietam, Chancellorsville, and
Second Malvern Hill.

.17 Lamon, Ward Hill, 1828-93.
Papers, 1848-89. 2409 items. Lawyer. Papers of
Lamon, who was a law partner and close associate
of Abraham Lincoln. Includes copies, in three
large volumes, of William Herndon's source materials for his biography of Lincoln.

.18 Lee family.
Papers, 1722-1892. 150 items. Miscellaneous
letters to and from various members of the Lee
family of Virginia, including Henry Lee and his
son Robert E. Lee. Papers reflect the life and
times through a long period of Virginia history
and culture.

.19 Lee, Fitzhugh, 1835-1905.
Papers, 1863-89. 83 items. Confederate officer
and Governor of Virginia. Miscellaneous documents and letters to and from Lee, mostly for the
period 1886-89, when he was Governor of Virginia.
Many of these papers are petitions praying for
executive clemency. Forms part of the library's
Brock collection.

.20 Lieber, Francis, 1800-72.
Papers, 1815-88. ca. 6000 items. Educator and
publicist. Correspondence and mss of Lieber's
works relating to social and political thought in
the U.S. before and during the Civil War. Some
of the topics emphasized are higher education,
culture of civilization, penology, political science,
constitutional history, and international law.

.21 Macaulay, Zachary, 1768-1838.
Papers, 1787-1888. 1014 items. British philanthropist. Correspondence, journal (1793-99), and
other papers of Macaulay and his family, relating
especially to the anti-slavery movement. Correspondents include Thomas Clarkson, Louis Du-
mont, Hannah More, Baron de Stael, and William
Wilberforce.

.22 Nutt, Rush.
Papers, 1805-1933. 1000 items. Mississippi and
Louisiana planter and physician. Papers of Nutt
and his son relating to cotton culture, manufacture and trade, slaves, plantation affairs, diseases and treatment, the Civil War, construction
of Longwood Plantation house, and litigation over
wills. Includes 29 mss.

.23 Osborn, Luther.
Papers, 1864-65. 392 items. Official papers of
Captain Osborn, Quartermaster, Co. H, 22nd
Regt., U.S. Colored Troops.

.24 Pleasants family.
Papers, 1745-1838. 337 items. Forms part of the
library's Brock Collection. Letters and documents
of a prominent Quaker family of Virginia, containing reference to the family's extensive land
holdings and mercantile and business interests, to
the manumission of slaves, and to the education of
Negroes. Includes epistles, reports, and other
papers relating to the various local Quaker meetings, together with correspondence with Quakers
in Philadelphia and elsewhere.

.25 Rhodes House, Oxford.
Rhodes House Anti-Slavery Papers, 1839-68.
Microfilm. 2 reels. Introduction by H.R. Temper-
ley. (British Records relating to America).

.26 Rust, Horatio Nelson.
Papers, 1799-1906. ca. 1229 items. Nurseryman,
U.S. Indian agent, archeological collector. Includes materials of and relating to John Brown
(1800-59).

.27 Stowe, Harriet Beecher.
Papers, 1853-88. ca. 210 items. Author and abolitionist of Ohio, Massachusetts, and Connecticut.

.28 (This number not used)

.29 Virginia General Assembly.
Papers, 1861-65. 370 items. Contains, among
other topics, discussion of legislation pertaining
to Negro volunteers.

.30 Whittier, John Greenleaf.
Papers, 1832-91. ca. 351 items. Massachusetts
poet and abolitionist.

SAN MATEO

CA180 INTERGROUP RELATIONS ASSOCIATION OF NORTHERN
CALIFORNIA (1966). 511 Verano Court, 94402. Tel
415 344-6544. Louis W. Jones, Exec. Dir.
The Association is an information agency which seeks
to improve communication, and to increase public
awareness of the nature and background of community
problems.
Publ.: Lou Jones Newsletter, monthly.

.1 Intergroup Relations Association of Northern
California.
Files, 1966- . Included are minutes of human relations commissions in Northern California, news
releases, human relations publications, books on
urban problems and affairs, and a small collection
of "fugitive" materials in the human relations
field.

SAN RAFAEL

CA181 MARIN COUNTY FREE LIBRARY (1926). Civic Center Administration Bldg., 94903. Tel 415 479-1100. Bruce
Bajema, County Librn. Interlibrary loan, copying, inquiries answered.

.1 Clement Woodnut Miller (1916-62) Memorial Collection.
Materials. ca. 1100 v., 200 pamphlets, and 4
magazine titles. Congressman from California
(1959-62), organizing member of Marin Chapter,
American Civil Liberties Union. Collection contains materials by and about black people, on
civil liberties and civil rights.

CA182 MARIN COUNTY HUMAN RIGHTS COMMISSION. Civic
Center, Room 341, 94903. Tel 415 479-1100. Robert
B. Brauer, Exec. Officer.
The Commission operates in areas of employment,
education, housing and accommodations; receives and
investigates complaints regarding alleged discrimination; conciliates disputes; and provides advice and
assistance to public and private agencies on matters
relating to human rights.

SANTA BARBARA

CA183 CENTER FOR THE STUDY OF DEMOCRATIC INSTITU-
TIONS, LIBRARY. Box 4068, 93103. Tel 805 969-3281.
Mrs. Mary Kerbrat, Librn.
Publ.: The Center Magazine, bi-monthly.

CA184 UNIVERSITY OF CALIFORNIA AT SANTA BARBARA
(1944), LIBRARY (1944). 93106. Tel 805 961-3466.
Spec. Collections Librn. Interlibrary loan, bibliographies prepared, literature searches, copying,
typing, inquiries answered, referrals made, consultation.

.1 Anti-Slavery Propaganda Collection.
ca. 2500 pamphlets. Microcards of originals located in the Oberlin College Library. See Oberlin
College Library, Oberlin, Ohio; or Lost Cause
Press (publisher), Louisville, Ky., for more complete description.

.2 The William Wyles Collection.
Colonial period-1877. ca. 20,000 items. The Collection includes a growing number of books and
pamphlets relating to slavery in the U.S., the
abolitionist movement, slave narratives, and the
Reconstruction. Also included are Abraham Lincoln materials (ca. 5000 v.), the Westward Movement, regimental histories, and mss, letters, engravings, and autographs of famous individuals of
the period.

SAUSALITO

CA185 CONGRESS OF RACIAL EQUALITY (CORE), MARIN
COUNTY CHAPTER. Box 563, 94965. John Garden-
shire.

STANFORD

CA186 CENTER FOR ADVANCED STUDY IN THE BEHAVIORAL
SCIENCES, INC. 202 Junipero Serra Blvd., 94305.
Tel 415 211-2052. Mrs. Elizabeth W. Calloway, Librn.
Interlibrary loan.

.1 Center for Advanced Study in the Behavioral Sciences,
Inc.
Included in the Center Library are unpublished
mss in the behavioral science fields. The library
and its holdings are private and for the use of the
Center's Fellows only.

CA187 STANFORD UNIVERSITY, HOOVER INSTITUTION ON WAR,
REVOLUTION AND PEACE (1919). 94305. Tel
415 321-2300. Kenneth M. Glazier, Librn. Interlibrary
loan, copying.

.1 America First Committee.
Archives.
.2 American Peace Movement Collection.
Materials comprising the history of the Peace
Movement in the U.S.
.3 Collection on International Communism.
Included is a section on American Communism.
.4 Military collection.
Includes papers of Brigadier General L.R. Boyd,
Commander of the 93rd Division, a Negro unit
which served in the Pacific during World War II.

CA188 STANFORD UNIVERSITY (1891), LIBRARIES (1891). 94305.
Tel 415 321-2300. Julius P. Barcley, Spec. Collections.
Literature searches, copying, inquiries answered,
referrals made.

.1 Civil War and military collection.
Papers, 1851-69. 1 ft. (ca. 850 items). Chiefly
correspondence and diaries of Civil War soldiers
including George Arthur Bailey, 1st Massachu-
setts Infantry and Capt. of Company H, 37th U.S.
Colored Troops; Col. Edward Martindale, served
with 83rd Regt., U.S. Infantry (Colored), 118th
Regt. (Colored) and commanded the Provisional
Brigade, U.S. Colored Troops, 18th Army Corps
and other Negro units; John Wesley Melhorn,
Company C, 10th Virginia Infantry, C.S.A.;
Lemuel E. Newcomb (1838-1921), 11th Regt.,
Maine Volunteer Infantry; and Israel Spenser,
Company A, 136th New York Volunteer Infantry.
The collection also includes papers relating to
the Army service of James Henry Carleton
(1814-23) in California and the Southwest (1851-
65); records of Company M, 4th Illinois Volun-
teer Cavalry (1861-64); and muster rolls of Fort
Duncan, Tex. (1857), and Fort Wayne, Mich. (1869).
Subjects covered include Indian wars, Mountain
Meadows Massacre in Utah, Civil War action in
Arizona and New Mexico, Libby Prison, Delaware
Indians and railroad right-of-way, petition to free
the slaves, Hampton Roads Peace Conference,
sectionalism, and Civil War battles and experiences.
.2 Facts on Film.
Papers, 1954-67. Microfilm. Contains materials
on civil rights and race relations in the South. See
Race Relations Information Center, Nashville,
Tenn., for a full description.
.3 Jones, Herbert Coffin, ca. 1881- .
Papers, 1911-54. ca. 43 ft. (40,000 items). Lawyer and member of the California State Senate
(1913-34) from San Jose, Calif. Correspondence,
documents, pamphlets, clippings and photos, pertaining to Jones' work in the California Senate and
including a considerable amount of material on
legislative actions during the time he was active.
Principal subjects include education, I.W.W., the
Ku Klux Klan, labor, the Mooney case, the Progressive Movement, reapportionment, industrial
rehabilitation and teachers. Principal correspondents include Ralph Arnold, Arthur Hyslop Briggs,
James Middleton Cox, George Creel, Ray Charles
Eberhard, Raymond Leroy Haight, Herbert Hoover,
Hiram W. Johnson, Aimee Semple McPherson,
Frank F. Merriam, Culbert L. Olson, John
Robertson Quinn, Upton Sinclair, Rudolph
Spreckels, and Clement Calhoun Young.
.4 Kane, Thomas Leiper.
Papers, 1845-82. ca. 42 items (including 2
diaries). Pennsylvania abolitionist and Civil
War officer.
.5 Murat, Achille, (Prince), 1801-47.
Papers, 1809-45. ca. 3 ft. (2100 items). Author.
Mainly letters from various members of the
Murat and Bonaparte families to Murat, the son
of Joachim Murat (King of Naples) and Carolina
(Bonaparte) Murat (sister of Napoleon I). Includes
correspondence regarding Murat's attempt to
organize a Belgium Foreign Legion in the 1830's;
ms of his writings on politics, economics,
slavery, and literature; and family papers. The
letters are in French, Italian, and English.
.6 Religion Collection.
Miscellaneous. .5 ft. (26 items). Single items and
small collections pertaining to various religions
or points of religion are written by leaders or
members of certain religious groups. Includes
material on Mormons and Mormonism, the Mor-
mon Battalion, Hebrew printing, Judaism and
pieces of general historical and literary interest.
Also includes Leonard H. Kirkpatrick correspondence with J. Reuben Clark and Joseph Fielding
Smith on Mormons and the Negro.
.7 Shafter, William Rufus, 1835-1906.
Papers, 1863-1904. 3 ft. (ca. 5000 items). Army
officer. Put in command of the 17th U.S. Colored
Infantry on April 19, 1864. Correspondence;
sketches; maps; photos; cartoons; clippings;
broadsides and other printed material; and other
papers chiefly military in nature and predominantly relating to the Spanish American War.
Includes some papers relating to Shafter's career
in the Civil War and on the Texas frontier, the
Congressional Medal of Honor which he was
awarded, and the scandal arising from his con-
troversial actions during the Spanish American
War. Also includes letters and memoranda by
Shafter concerning relations between the American
Expeditionary Force and the Cuban rebels under
Garcia, several Spanish Army documents expressing the Spanish view of American War aims,
and Spanish opinion of the Cuban populace. Correspondents include Russell A. Alger, Henry Clark
Corbin, George Dewey, Calixto Garcia Iniguez,
William McKinley, Nelson A. Miles, Edward O.C.
Ord, Elihu Root, William T. Sampson, and Joseph
Wheeler.
.8 Smith, Lorna. collector.
Papers. 2.5 ft. 98 items. Correspondence,
chiefly to Mrs. Lorna Smith concerning her
work on the Mississippi Summer Project of 1964
and her later help with the efforts of the Student
Non-violent Coordinating Committee, including 29
letters from Stokely Carmichael (1941-) dating
from December, 1964 to May, 1968; an inscribed
book, and 11 scrapbooks of clippings from newspapers, magazines, circulars, folders, conference
advertisements, and programs (July, 1964-April,
1968). Also included is a tape of an address delivered by Carmichael (November 19, 1966) to
the Santa Clara Valley Friends of SNCC. All
items relate directly to Carmichael and to his
role in the Black Power Movement, racial unrest,
and rioting in American cities (as represented by
the press). Included is a copy of Freedom Summer, inscribed by the author Sally Belfrage.
Some of her letters to Mrs. Smith are also found
in the collection, relating her opinions of the
representation Carmichael received in the press.

VALLEJO

CA189 FRIENDSHIP BAPTIST CHURCH, NAACP NEGRO HISTORY
LIBRARY. 1838 Carolina St., 94590. Tel 707 642-1621.

COLORADO

ALAMOSA

CO1   ADAMS STATE COLLEGE OF COLORADO (1921), THE
CENTER FOR CULTURAL STUDIES (1962). 81101.
Tel 303 589-7607. Philip D. Rowley, Dir. Interlibrary
loan, copying, inquiries answered.
The Center's principal areas of interest are human
relations in Colorado, research on Spanish-American
culture, migrant and seasonal workers, the disadvantaged, and programs for improvement of life for
these groups.
> Publ.: Occasional books of research materials regard-
> ing education of the disadvantaged with emphasis
> on migrant workers; Publications list.

CO2   COLORADO CIVIL RIGHTS COMMISSION, REGIONAL OF-
FICE. 721½ Main St, 81101. Tel 303 589-9101.

BOULDER

CO3   UNIVERSITY OF COLORADO, INSTITUTE OF BEHAV-
IORAL SCIENCE. 80304. Tel 303 443-2211. Inquiries
answered.
Research is conducted through various programs and
includes such studies as psychological investigation of
social attitudes with particular reference to relations
between Negroes and whites, and urban adjustments of
Spanish-speaking migrants from rural milieus.

CO4   UNIVERSITY OF COLORADO LIBRARIES (1876), NORLIN
LIBRARY. 80302. Tel 303 443-2211. William H. Webb,
University Bibliographer. Consultation.

   .1   Facts on Film.
Papers, 1954-67. Microfilm. Contains materials
on civil rights and race relations in the South. See
Race Relations Information Center, Nashville,
Tenn., for a full description.

   .2   Social Documents Collection
Serials, vertical files, pamphlets, and ephemeral
material issued by pressure groups. Primary and
secondary research items relating to recent
American social problems; embraces the literature
of dissent with emphasis on extremist statements
to the right and left of the political and social spectrum. Significant portion of materials reflects
rightist views toward segregation. Some material
pertains to religious prejudice, states-rightism,
nazism (Hitlerian and American varieties), and
socialist views on race.

COLORADO SPRINGS

CO5   COLORADO CIVIL RIGHTS COMMISSION, REGIONAL
OFFICE. County Office Building, 27 East Vermijo,
80903. Tel 303 471-0600.

CO6   URBAN LEAGUE OF THE PIKES PEAK REGION (1966).
23 East Pikes Peak Avenue, 80902. Tel 303 634-1525.
John S. Holley, Exec. Dir.

DENVER

CO7   AMERICAN CIVIL LIBERTIES UNION OF COLORADO.
1452 Pennsylvania St., 80203. Tel 303 825-5176.
Dorothy E. Davidson, Exec. Dir.

CO8   ANTI-DEFAMATION LEAGUE OF B'NAI B'RITH,
MOUNTAIN STATES REGIONAL OFFICE (1913), LI-
BRARY. 623 Empire Bldg., 80202. Tel 303 623-7157.
Sheldon Steinhauser, Dir. Consultation.
The League fights against anti-Semitism, discrimina-
tion, prejudice and bigotry; and acts to broaden civil
rights, improve relations among the many groups in
the nation, and achieve equal opportunity for all
Americans.
> Publ.: Books, magazines, periodicals, pamphlets, re-
> prints, films, and plays.

   .1   Collection of intergroup and interreligion materials.
Miscellaneous. ca. 600 items. Books (150), periodicals (250), and films (200) covering the areas of
civil rights, extremism, prejudice, anti-Semitism,
race relations, housing, school desegregation, education and human relations, ethnic and religious
minorities, Jews and Judaism. Restricted.

CO9   CITY AND COUNTY OF DENVER COMMISSION ON COM-
MUNITY RELATIONS (1947). Suite 500, Zook Bldg.,
431 W. Colfax Ave., 80204. Tel 303 297-2621. Minoru
Yasui, Exec. Dir. Inquiries answered, referrals
made, consultation.
County agency created to foster mutual self-respect
and understanding; discourage and prevent discrimination. Services include information about community
resources for education, training and social service
programs, counseling with regard to complaints of
racial, religious, and ethnic group tensions in order to
eliminate discrimination in housing, education, recreation, employment, law enforcement, vocational guidance
and public accommodation.
> Publ.: Highlights, quarterly newsletter; Annual Report;
> Special reports, occasionally.

CO10   COLORADO CIVIL RIGHTS COMMISSION (1957). 312 State
Services Bldg., 1525 Sherman St., 80203. Tel 303
892-2621. James F. Reynolds, Dir.
State agency established in 1951, to investigate complaints of discrimination in the areas of public accommodation, employment, housing; hold hearings; judicial
review; recommend anti-discrimination policies. Has
established an advisory council on school racial matters. Formerly Colorado Anti-Discrimination Commission.
> Publ.: Civil Rights Newsletter, bi-monthly.

CO11   DENVER PUBLIC SCHOOLS, OFFICE OF SCHOOL-COM-
MUNITY RELATIONS (1962). 414 14th St., 80202. Tel
303 266-2255. Gilbert Cruter, Exec. Dir. Interlibrary
loan, bibliographies prepared, inquiries answered,
consultation.
The Office concerns itself with human, intercultural
and intergroup relations, racial-ethnic and socio-
economic factors, and the interrelationships of such
fields between the school and the community.
> Publ.: Voluntary Open Enrollment Bulletin, monthly;
> Human Relations Factor-News and Views:
> Activities and Program in Human Relations
> Area.

CO12   EDUCATION COMMISSION OF THE STATES (1966). 822
Lincoln Tower, 1860 Lincoln St., 80203. Tel 303
255-3631. Wendell H. Pierce, Exec. Dir.
The Commission is a non-profit organization to bring
governors, educators and legislators together for the
improvement of education at the state level.
> Publ.: Compact, bi-monthly magazine; State Leaders
> Directory, annually; ECS Bulletin.

   .1   Education Commission of the States.
Files, 1966- . Records, reports, correspondence,
and other papers concerning the activities of the
Commission.

CO13   LORETTO HEIGHTS COLLEGE (1918), MAY BONFILS
STANTON LIBRARY. 3001 S. Federal Blvd., 80236. Tel
303 922-4142. Joseph W. Sprug, Dir. Interlibrary loan,
bibliographies prepared, literature searches, copying,
typing, inquiries answered, referrals made, consultation.

   .1   Research Center on Women.
Books, periodicals, and other significant English-
language material on women, including material by
and about Negro women.

CO14   METRO DENVER FAIR HOUSING CENTER, INC. (1965).
1525 Josephine St., 80206. Tel 303 399-6655. Robinson
G. Lapp, Exec. Dir. Copying, inquiries answered.
The Center assists minority families to rent or purchase homes in nonsegregated parts of Denver, Col.;
purchases and rehabilitates homes; packages rent supplement projects for non-profit sponsors; runs an in-

formation and education program; does research and development; and community organization work to help low income families gain more control over their own housing problems.
Publ.: *Tempo*, quarterly newsletter.

.1 Metro Denver Fair Housing Center, Inc.
Files, 1965- . Among other urban development and historical materials, a clippings file (July, 1968) on housing in Metro Denver.

CO15 NATIONAL CONFERENCE OF CHRISTIANS AND JEWS, ROCKY MOUNTAIN REGION (1928). Room 305, 821 17th St., 80202. Tel 303 534-4645. Theodore O. Yoder, Dir.

CO16 PARK HILL ACTION COMMITTEE, NORTH EAST PARK HILL CIVIC ASSOCIATION (1962). 2201 Dexter St., 80207. Tel 303 388-0918. Father Rick Kerr, Exec. Dir. Inquiries answered, referrals made, consultation. The Committee seeks to create and maintain a model integrated community by fostering better understanding among persons of different races and ethnic backgrounds; by supporting projects designed to eliminate prejudice; by working for better schools; by working for better cultural and recreational facilities; and by preventing community deterioration.
Publ.: *Park Hill Action News*, monthly newsletter.

.1 Park Hill Action Committee, North East Park Hill Civic Association.
Archives, 1962- . Deposited at the Temple Buell College Library, Denver, Col. Includes materials on fair housing, the Denver school busing controversy, and Operation Park Hill.

CO17 STATE HISTORICAL SOCIETY OF COLORADO (1879), LIBRARY. State Museum, E. 14th St., 80302. Tel 303 892-2305. Mrs. Enid T. Thompson, Librn. Copying, inquiries answered, referrals made, consultation. The Society collects, preserves, and makes available significant materials related to the history of Colorado and its citizens.

.1 Atkins, James A., 1890-1968.
Papers. 100 ft. Humanitarian, author, educator. Books, papers, mss, and documents of one of the pioneer Negro educators of the U.S. Also included are records, documentary material, published and unpublished writings, and personal papers on education, welfare, racism, race relations, police, urban problems, Negro history and biography.
.2 "Ku Klux Klan Kollection."
Papers. Primary materials, including dues and membership records of the Colorado Klan. In part, records restricted until 1990.
.3 Lewis, Junius R.
Papers. Negro miner of Boulder County, Col. Includes the papers from the estate of Henry O. Andrews, attorney.
.4 Materials relating to Negroes.
Books, serials, pamphlets, vertical files, mss, films, phonorecords, sheet music, art, historical objects. Includes contributions of the Negro in Colorado.
.5 Sweet, William Ellery, 1869-1942.
Papers, 1869-1942. ca. 1 ft. Governor of Colorado. Correspondence, diary (1921), telegrams, reports, speeches, campaign publicity and magazine articles, autobiographical materials of Channing Sweet and family, political clippings, and photos, relating among others, to such subjects as prison reform movements, labor rights, and the Ku Klux Klan.
.6 Work Projects Administration (WPA).
Papers, 1930-35. Unpublished materials on Negroes researched by the WPA (1930-35); and unpublished interviews with Negro pioneers (1930-35).

CO18 UNIVERSITY OF DENVER, CENTER ON INTERNATIONAL RACE RELATIONS (1969). 80202. Tel 303 753-1964. George W. Shepherd, Jr., Dir.
The Center provides programs of advanced research and training in comparative race and international relations, including domestic race problems as they affect American policy; and supports and publishes research on race factors in American foreign policy and on the relationship between Africa and black Americans in the United States.

CO19 URBAN LEAGUE OF COLORADO. 1375 Delaware, 80204. Tel 303 623-5201. Sebastian C. Owens, Exec. Dir.

GREELEY

CO20 GREELEY PUBLIC LIBRARY (1877). City Complex Bldg., 80631. Tel 303 353-6123. Esther Fromm, Librn. Interlibrary loan, bibliographies prepared, copying, inquiries answered.

.1 Negro collection.
Subject areas include slavery, Negro history, segregation. Children's books by and about Negroes.

PUEBLO

CO21 COLORADO CIVIL RIGHTS COMMISSION, REGIONAL OFFICE. 407 Thatcher Bldg., Fifth and Main, 81003. Tel 303 545-3520.

CONNECTICUT

BLOOMFIELD

CT1 BLOOMFIELD CONGRESS OF RACIAL EQUALITY. 38 Merriam Ave., 06002. Tel 203 242-8752. Herbert Wright, Chmn.

BRIDGEPORT

CT2 COMMISSION ON HUMAN RIGHTS AND OPPORTUNITIES, SOUTHWEST REGIONAL OFFICE. 20 Yaremich Dr., 06606. Tel 203 374-9423.

CT3 DIOCESE OF BRIDGEPORT, SOCIAL ACTION DEPARTMENT (1964). 389 Kossuth St., 06608. Tel 203 367-3631. Rev. Louis A. DeProfio, Dir.
The Department uses the resources of the Church in promoting civil rights, intergroup harmony and minority group social welfare. Program areas include housing, education, employment, human relations, interreligious affairs, governmental operations, and social attitudes.
Publ.: *Dialogue*, quarterly.

CT4 UNIVERSITY OF BRIDGEPORT, HUMAN RELATIONS CENTER. 06602. Tel 203 384-0711. Abraham E. Knepler.

HARTFORD

CT5 BLUE HILLS CIVIC ASSOCIATION (1962). 711 Blue Hills Ave., 06112. Tel 203 243-0244. David R. Harris, Pres.
The Blue Hills Civic Association seeks to create and maintain an integrated neighborhood.
Publ.: *The Blue Hills News*, monthly newsletter; Pamphlets about the community and its activities.

CT6 CONNECTICUT CIVIL LIBERTIES UNION. Room 312, 721 Main St., 06103. Tel 203 525-1345. Emanuel N. Psarakis, Exec. Dir.

CT7 CONNECTICUT HISTORICAL SOCIETY, LIBRARY (1825). 1 Elizabeth St., 06105. Tel 203 236-5621. Thompson R. Harlow, Dir. Copying, inquiries answered.

.1 Haiti (Republic).
Records, 1796-ca. 1872. ca. 50 items. Haitian official letters and documents (1796-1842), including three of Francois Dominique Toussaint L'Ouverture, one of which is to Tobias Lear, Sept. 17, 1801; Haitian and Jamaican correspondence (1842-ca. 1872) of Hippolyte Daniel de St. Antoine, secretary general of L'Institut d'Afrique de Paris.
.2 Hart, Levi, 1738-1808.
Paper, ca. 1775. 23 pp. Minster, of Preston, Conn.

Ms of ''Some Thoughts on the Subject of Freeing the Negro Slaves in the Colony of Connecticut, humbly offered to the Consideration of all Friends to Liberty and Justice.''

.3 Papers relating to slavery.
Miscellaneous, 1732-1861. 35 items. Documents pertaining to slavery.

.4 Philleo, Calvin Wheeler, 1822-58.
Papers, 1839-79. 4 ft. Lawyer, abolitionist, Free Soil Party leader, and author, of Suffield and Hartford, Conn. Correspondence, diaries, literary mss, memorandum books, and legal papers.

CT8 CONNECTICUT HOUSING INVESTMENT FUND (1966). 75 Pearl St., 06103. Tel 203 524-5993. Maxwell M. Belding, Pres. Inquiries answered, consultation.
The Fund is a program assisting Negroes obtaining homes in scattered locations in the white suburbs of Connecticut.
Publ.: Research reports.

.1 Connecticut Housing Investment Fund.
Records, 1966- . Includes administrative files on the Fund; and books, pamphlets, and other materials on housing and discrimination in housing.

CT9 CONNECTICUT STATE COMMISSION ON HUMAN RIGHTS AND OPPORTUNITIES (1943), LIBRARY (1943). 90 Washington St., 06115. Tel 203 527-6341. Elizabeth Krom, Intergroup Supvr. Interlibrary loan (Conn. only).
State agency having enforcement powers in areas of fair employment and housing and public accommodation, an intergroup education program, affirmative action projects, and a research division. Formerly Connecticut Commission on Civil Rights.
Publ.: Rights, Opportunities Action Report, bi-monthly newsletter; Civil Rights Bulletin, bi-monthly; Various research reports.

.1 Intergroup collection.
Books, periodicals, newspapers, pamphlets, 12 vf, tape recordings, and research materials prepared by the Commission; newspaper and magazine clippings are retained in vf.

CT10 CONNECTICUT STATE LIBRARY (1854). 231 Capitol Ave., 06115. Tel 203 566-4777. Walter T. Brahm, Librn. Interlibrary loan, copying, inquiries answered, referrals made, consultation.

.1 Crandall, Prudence.
Papers, 1869-86. Educator of Negroes and reformer of Connecticut and Illinois.

.2 Nott, Samuel, 1788-1869.
Correspondence, 1850-62. 104 items. Missionary and author. Correspondence relating to Nott's pamphlet Slavery and the Remedy, and other publications.

.3 Smith family.
Papers, 1796-1819. ca. 23 items. Correspondence of Abby Hadassah Smith and Julia Evalina Smith of Connecticut, concerning their careers as abolitionists and feminists.

CT11 HARTFORD COMMISSION ON HUMAN RELATIONS (1964). 550 Main St., 06103. Tel 203 566-3350. Arthur L. Johnson, Exec. Dir.
The Commission fosters mutual understanding and respect and encourages equality of treatment for all racial, religious, and ethnic groups; cooperates with other agencies and organizations having like functions; makes studies and reports; and recommends legislation.

CT12 HARTFORD PUBLIC LIBRARY (1839), ROPKINS BRANCH LIBRARY (1839). 1540 Main St., 06120. Tel 203 525-9121. Edwin G. Jackson, Librn. Interlibrary loan, bibliographies prepared, literature searches, copying, inquiries answered, referrals made, consultation.

.1 Special collection of books by and about the American Negro.

CT13 NATIONAL CONFERENCE OF CHRISTIANS AND JEWS. 983 Main St., 06103. Tel 203 522-4231. Charles T. Sardeson, Dir.

CT14 STOWE-DAY FOUNDATION AND RESEARCH LIBRARY (1941). 77 Forest St., 06105. Tel 203 522-8635. Joseph S. Van Why, Dir. Interlibrary loan, copying, typing, inquiries answered.
The Harriett Beecher Stowe House has been restored and is maintained as a public museum. The Day house is a separate building housing the research library and the administration staff.

.1 Abolition collection.
Pamphlets, ca. 1800-Civil War. ca. 700 items.

.2 Beecher family.
Papers, 1816-96. 183 items. Correspondence between members of the Beecher, Hooker, and Perkins families, and a diary (1901) kept by Isabella (Beecher) Hooker. Family members represented include Edward Beecher (1803-95); Eunice White (Bullard) Beecher (1812-97), author; Harriet (Porter) Beecher; Henry Ward Beecher (1813-87), Congregational minister of the Plymouth Church, Brooklyn, N.Y.; Lyman Beecher (1775-1863), president of Lane Theological Seminary, Cincinnati, Ohio; Thomas Kinnicut Beecher (1824-1907), president of the Connecticut Woman Suffrage Society; John Hooker; and Mary (Beecher) Perkins.

.3 Beecher, Thomas Kinnicut, 1824-1900.
Langdon collection, 1856-89. 86 items. Congregational minister, of Elmira, N.Y. Chiefly correspondence between Beecher and his wife, Julia (Jones) Beecher (1826-1905), including letters from Beecher to members of the Langdon family, especially Mrs. Jervis Langdon (d. 1890), with references to her daughter, Olivia (Langdon) Clemens, wife of Samuel L. Clemens, other letters written while Beecher was visiting the Clemens' home in Hartford, Conn., and letters written by Samuel Clemens and his wife.

.4 Beecher, Lyman, 1775-1863.
The White collection, 1817-53. 176 items. Congregational minister and theologian. Chiefly correspondence (1836-50) written by Beecher to his fellow ministers, and members of his family, especially his son Edward; together with 12 letters by his third wife, Lydia (Beals) Jackson Beecher (1789-1869), her will, a deed for property sold in Brooklyn, N.Y., and other papers.

.5 Garrison, William Lloyd.
Correspondence. Ca. 12 items. Abolitionist. Autographed letters by and to Garrison.

.6 Hooker, Isabella (Beecher), 1822-1907.
Papers, 1839-1901. 978 items. Woman suffragist and reformer. Chiefly correspondence between Mrs. Hooker and her husband, John Hooker (1816-1901), a lawyer, of Hartford, Conn. Includes letters written by John Hooker while on travels through Connecticut as recorder for the State Supreme Court; and letters by Mrs. Hooker from their home at Nook Farm and from the Gleason Water Cure, Elmira, N.Y., containing references to her brother, Thomas K. Beecher, Mr. and Mrs. Jervis Langdon, Harriet Beecher Stowe, Charles Dudley Warner, George H. Warner, and other members of the Warner family.

.7 National Era.
Complete run, June 5, 1851-March 20, 1852. Includes the complete serial (1st appearance) of Uncle Tom's Cabin.

.8 Stowe, Harriet Elizabeth (Beecher), 1811-96.
Papers, ca. 1825-96. 239 items. Author. Letters by Mrs. Stowe to friends, relatives, and publishers, during the course of her career while residing in Cincinnati, Ohio (1832-50), Brunswick, Maine (1852), Andover, Mass. (1853-64), Hartford, Conn. (1864-96), and from her winter home in Mandarin, Fla. (1868-85); journal of travels in Italy (1860); brief biographical account of her childhood, describing the death of her mother, Roxana (Foote) Beecher, wife of Lyman Beecher; draft for part of the novel Agnes of Sorrento (1862) and mss of articles, poems, and other writings.

CT15 TRINITY COLLEGE (1823), DAVID WATKINSON LIBRARY (1857). Summit St., 06106. Tel 203 527-3153. Donald B. Engley, Librn. Interlibrary loan, copying, inquiries answered.

.1 American Negro collection.
Books, pamphlets and other materials on the subjects Negro, Civil War, slavery.

CT16 URBAN LEAGUE OF GREATER HARTFORD. 709 Main St., 06103. Tel 203 522-8163. William J. Brown, Exec. Dir.

.1 Urban League of Greater Hartford.
Records, reports, correspondence, and other papers pertaining to the aims and activities of the organization.

MIDDLETOWN

CT17 WESLEYAN UNIVERSITY, OLIN MEMORIAL LIBRARY (1831). 06457. Tel 203 347-4421. Wyman W. Parker, Librn. Interlibrary loan, bibliographies prepared, literature searches, copying, inquiries answered.

.1 Facts on Film.
Papers, 1954-67. Microfilm. Contains materials on civil rights and race relations in the South. See Race Relations Information Center, Nashville, Tenn., for a full description.

MYSTIC

CT18 THE MARINE HISTORICAL ASSOCIATION, G. W. BLUNT WHITE LIBRARY. Mystic Seaport, 06355. Tel 203 536-2631. Charles R. Schultz, Librn.
Special library of American maritime history, chiefly of the 19th century.

.1 Materials relating to Negroes.
Papers, 19th century. Includes captain's journal and record of voyage (1850's) to Africa of ships chartered by the American Colonization Society. Restricted.

NEW HAVEN

CT19 ANTI-DEFAMATION LEAGUE OF B'NAI B'RITH, CONNECTICUT REGIONAL OFFICE. Suite 3, 1184 Chapel St., 06511. Tel 203 787-4281. Malcolm C. Webber, Dir.

CT20 HUMAN RELATIONS COUNCIL OF GREATER NEW HAVEN, INC. (1950). 89 Howe St., 06511. Tel 203 776-4285. Mrs. Milton Zucker, Exec. Secy.
The Council works toward improving racial, religious, and national origin group relationships within greater New Haven, Conn. Major program areas include housing, education, human relations, and social attitudes.
Publ.: Newsletter, bi-monthly.

CT21 NEW HAVEN COMMISSION ON EQUAL OPPORTUNITIES (1964). 147 Court St., 06510. Tel 203 562-4655. Edward J. Fortes, Exec. Dir. Copying, typing, referrals made.
The Commission promotes mutual understanding and respect, and encourages and assures equality of opportunity without regard for race, color, religion, creed or national origin; conducts programs of education, study, research, investigation and action according to the City statute, and cooperates with other agencies of inter-group relations and equal opportunity. Operates in areas of employment, housing, education and public accommodations.
Publ.: Annual Report; Special reports and studies.

.1 New Haven Commission on Equal Opportunities.
Files, 1964- . 16 vf. Correspondence, clippings, pamphlets, a ms report of the Commission based on its investigation of police activity (Dec., 1965), and other materials concerning the Commission's activities. Restricted.

CT22 NEW HAVEN JEWISH COMMUNITY COUNCIL (1938). 153 Temple St., 06510. Tel 203 865-5181. Benjamin N. Levy, Exec. Dir.
The Council seeks to organize the Jewish community in matters of interest to it and to enhance its relation-

ship with the general community. General areas of community relations include interreligious and intergroup relations, as well as fund-raising.

CT23 URBAN LEAGUE OF GREATER NEW HAVEN (1963). 1 State St., 06511. Tel 203 624-4168. Robert O. Bowles, Exec. Dir.

CT24 YALE UNIVERSITY (1701), STERLING MEMORIAL LIBRARY. 1603A Yale Station, 06520. Tel 203 737-3131. Interlibrary loan, literature searches, copying, inquiries answered, referrals made.

.1 Bacon family.
Papers, 1800-1909. Papers of Leonard Bacon (1802-81), clergyman, educator and writer, pastor of First Church of New Haven, Conn., from 1825-81, prominent abolitionist, and member of the underground railway prior to the Civil War.

.2 Baldwin family.
Papers, 1584-1947. Correspondence and other papers of Roger Sherman Baldwin (1793-1863) relating to the Amistad case (1839-41). Baldwin was later Governor of Connecticut.

.3 Beecher family.
Papers, 1706-1953. 30,000 items. Correspondence, sermons, travel accounts, diaries, newspaper clippings, and other papers of Henry Ward Beecher (1813-87), clergyman, and orator, and of other members of the Beecher family, including Lyman Beecher (1775-1863), clergyman. Includes professional correspondence from H.W. Beecher to leading 19th century clergymen, and letter of Harriet Elizabeth (Beecher) Stowe (1811-96), author, to her brother, as well as some other Stowe material.

.4 Burr, Aaron Columbus.
Papers, 1838-71. Correspondence and other papers relating to an attempt to establish a colony for American Negroes in Belize, Honduras. Both Burr and James Grant were connected with the American Honduras Company.

.5 Donnan, Elizabeth, d. 1955.
Manuscript notes, 1806-63. 2 boxes (ca. 600 items). Professor of economics at Wellesley College. Notes taken from newspapers, ships' logs, and letter books at the Library of Congress; primarily used in Donnan's book Documents Illustrative of the History of the Slave Trade to America.

.6 Embree, Edwin Rogers, 1883-1950.
Papers, 1903-56. ca. 3,000 items. Officer of the Rockefeller Foundation and the Julius Rosenwald Fund and its Division of Human Biology. Personal and other correspondence, family journals (1918-49) of Embree's trips abroad, articles, book reviews, and speeches relating to Embree's books, cultural anthropology, education, medicine, American race relations, religion, and other social sciences.

.7 James Weldon Johnson Memorial Collection of Negro Arts and Letters.
Founded by Carl Van Vechten, the Collection consists of books, periodicals, pamphlets, photographs, objects of art, newspaper clippings, mss, letters, phonograph records, scrapbooks, sheet music, posters and bulletins, concert and theatrical programs, calling cards, handbills, and signatures. The emphasis is on the accomplishments of Negroes in the fields of the fine arts, belles-lettres, and sports in the 20th century. Included in the Collection are such authors and subjects areas as:

.8 —— Burleigh, Henry T.
Contains a large group of inscribed spirituals arranged by Burleigh; mss from the cycle, Passionale, with corrections by James Weldon Johnson, who wrote the words; ms score of the "Prelude to Ouanga."

.9 —— Chesnutt, Charles W.
Complete set of Chesnutt's books, each containing long autobiographical inscriptions.

.10 —— Cullen, Countee.
Manuscript materials include complete series of mss of The Lost Zoo, beginning with Cullen's original notes; typescript of The Medea, con-

taining a prologue and epilogue not included in the published play, and other mss and letters.

.11 —— Handy, W. C.
Published books and sheet music inscribed by the author; letters, photographs, phonograph records, mss and musical scores.

.12 —— Hughes, Langston
Complete set of books with personal inscriptions, songs set to his words, photographs, letters, magazine and newspaper clippings, translations, most of the mss of his poems, books, and plays, and ms correspondence. ca. 5000 items.

.13 —— Johnson, James Weldon.
Complete set of Johnson's books, presentation copies of first editions, with long personal inscriptions; phonograph records, pamphlets, clippings, musical settings of his poems, photographs, and many of his mss and most of his personal correspondence. ca. 10,000 items.

.14 —— McKay, Claude.
Contains ms of Home to Harlem, rare Constab Ballads, and other materials.

.15 —— National Association for the Advancement of Colored People.
Contains most of the pamphlets issued by the NAACP from 1912-42.

.16 —— Sill, William Grant.
Manuscript orchestral score of Still's ballet, "Sahdji," containing comment by Alain Locke and Bruce Nugent.

.17 —— Spingarn, Joel.
Correspondence. Letters from Langston Hughes, James Weldon Johnson, J. Rosamond, and others to Spingarn and to Amy Spingarn.

.18 —— Spirituals and blues.
The Collection is represented by nearly complete holdings of phonograph records of such artists as Bessie and Clara Smith, Paul Robeson, Ethel Waters, Marian Anderson, and Dorothy Maynor.

.19 —— Thurman, Wallace.
Includes an unpublished ms, Aunt Hagar's Children; letters, photographs, and pages of the ms on which Thurman was working when he died.

.20 —— West, Dorothy.
Manuscripts of two short stories.

.21 —— White, Walter F.
Papers. ca. 1000 items. Author of New York, and secretary of the National Association for the Advancement of Colored People. Includes mss of White's works and other materials pertaining to Negroes.

.22 —— Van Vechten, Carl.
Correspondence, mss, association items; photograph collection, ca. 500 photographs of notable Negro personalities made by Van Vechten. ca. 15,000 items.

.23 —— Among other materials in the Collection are: photographs of celebrated paintings by Negroes from the public and private galleries of Europe and America; original paintings, decorations and prints by Charles Sebree, Zell Ingram, Hale Woodruff, Aaron Douglas, and others; books, pamphlets, letters, and association items by authors such as Jean Toomer, George Schuyler, Eric Walrond, Zora Neale Hurston, C.L.R. James, Nella Larsen, Sterling Brown, Georgia Douglass Johnson, Rudolph Fisher, William Stanley Braithwaite, W.E.B. DuBois, Arna Bontemps, Richard Wright, Booker T. Washington, Walter E. Turpin, William Attaway; and books, pamphlets, other materials dealing with the Negro's connection with Communism and the Catholic church, the Negro in art, science, medicine and so forth; anti-slavery pamphlets and slave narratives; and numerous periodicals.

.24 Phillips, Ulrich Bonnell, 1877-1934.
Papers, 1712-1933. Materials, mainly 1790-1865, collected and prepared in connection with his historical studies of the Old South. Includes collected family papers and records, and individual docu-

ments of plantation owners especially in Virginia and Georgia.

.25 Stimson, Henry Lewis, 1867-1950.
Papers, 1870-1950. Includes information in diary and papers relating to Negro troops in World War II when Stimson was Secretary of War.

.26 Stokes, Anson Phelps.
Papers, 1900-39. ca. 50 boxes, 4 vf, and 5 cases. Canon of Washington Cathedral. Includes 76 letter books and other materials pertaining to Negroes.

.27 Todd family.
Papers, 1834-70. Includes papers of John Augustus and Charles Baker Wilder (1852-70), relating to their work with Negro troops during and just after the Civil War. John Wilder (1834-70) was a major in command of the 2nd Regiment, U.S. Colored Troops; Charles Wilder was Superintendent of Contrabands, Fortress Monroe, Va.

.28 Weinberger, Harold.
Papers, 1908-42. 69 boxes. New York lawyer. Materials relating to civil liberties cases.

.29 Woolsey family.
Papers, 1840-1941. 6500 items. Papers relating primarily to Theodore Dwight Woolsey, president of Yale University. Concerns life in New Haven, New York, and Europe, and academic affairs at Yale. Includes correspondence with the American Colonization Society and American Home Missionary Society.

NEW LONDON

CT25   CONNECTICUT COLLEGE (1911), PALMER LIBRARY (1915). 06320. Tel 203 442-1630. Mrs. Mary A. McKenzie, Col. Librn. Copying.

.1   Philleo, Prudence Crandall.
Papers, 1831-86. ca. 50 items. Connecticut and Illinois educator and reformer of Negroes. Materials of the family and other items relating to her career.

NORWALK

CT26   NORWALK CONGRESS OF RACIAL EQUALITY (CORE). 203 Liberty Square, 06854. Tel 203 838-9172. Waverly Yates, Chmn.
Norwalk CORE works for the "liberation of Black peoples from economic deprivation, political disenfranchisement, educational subjugation and military occupation."

STAMFORD

CT27   STAMFORD COMMUNITY COUNCIL (1923). 62 Palmer's Hill Road, 06902. Tel 203 324-3129. Robert Slawson, Exec. Dir.
The Council promotes the general welfare of the community through studying its needs and resources, cooperative planning, and promotion of social improvements. Publ.: Newsletter, bi-monthly.

CT28   STAMFORD HUMAN RIGHTS COMMISSION (1964). Town Hall, Atlantic Square, 06901. Tel 203 348-5841. John T. Brown, Jr., Exec. Dir.
The Commission is a city agency that encourages and brings about mutual understanding and respect among all groups in the city; eliminates prejudice, intolerance, bigotry, discrimination and disorder; and guarantees equal rights. Activities include education, mediation and conciliation.

STONINGTON

CT29   STONINGTON HISTORICAL SOCIETY, LIBRARY. 06378.

.1   Records of Stonington, Conn.
Papers, 1672-1902. 3 ft. (ca. 100 items). In part, transcripts. Materials on the early history of Stonington; military records of the Civil War; autobiographical narrative of a slave (1798); legal papers; and other documents.

STORRS

CT30   UNIVERSITY OF CONNECTICUT, INSTITUTE OF URBAN
        RESEARCH (1963). 06268. Tel 203 429-3311. Karl A.
        Bosworth, Dir. Typing, inquiries answered, referrals
        made, consultation.
        The Institute works to focus the University's resources
        in the area of urban studies and to foster their coordi-
        nation for an effective program of research on urban
        problems. Areas of interest include poverty, community
        action, housing, and reapportionment.
        Publ.: Community Structure Project Series; Urban Re-
        search Reports.

   .1   File of Grants.
        Papers. Materials pertaining to grants available
        from federal, state, and private agencies.
   .2   Newspaper clippings.
        Papers, 1965- . 1 vf and 1 carton. Clippings from
        the Hartford Courant, the Hartford Times, and the
        New York Times pertaining to urban areas and re-
        lated subjects. Areas of interest include urban edu-
        cation, open housing, manpower programs, Connect-
        icut Commission on Human Rights and Opportuni-
        ties, urban unrest and violence, racial integration,
        de facto segregation in schools, job discrimination,
        race relations, Connecticut and national NAACP,
        poverty programs, black studies programs and pro-
        posals, Connecticut's school busing program,
        "Model Cities" programs, and other topics.
   .3   Urban Research Library Collection.
        Miscellaneous. ca. 25 vf. Books (ca. 3000 v.), pam-
        phlets, reports, surveys, bulletins, periodicals, and
        other materials pertaining to racial integration and
        segregation in housing and education, social aspects
        of urban renewal and planning programs, discrimi-
        nation in employment, welfare and poverty pro-
        grams, urban unrest and violence, black economic
        development, civil rights, inner city manpower
        programs, race relations and materials published
        for or by the Connecticut Commission on Human
        Rights and Opportunities. Also includes conference
        and convention materials and reports concerning
        race relations.

CT31   UNIVERSITY OF CONNECTICUT, WILBUR L. CROSS LI-
        BRARY (1881). 06268. Tel 203 429-3311. John P.
        McDonald, Librn. Interlibrary loan, copying.

   .1   Anti-Slavery Propaganda Collection.
        ca. 2500 pamphlets. Microcards of originals
        located in the Oberlin College Library. See Oberlin
        College Library, Oberlin, Ohio; or Lost Cause
        Press (publisher), Louisville, Ky., for more com-
        plete description.

        STRATFORD

CT32   STRATFORD HISTORICAL SOCIETY (1925). 967 Academy
        Hill, 06497. Tel 203 378-0630.

   .1   Slavery Collection.

        WATERBURY

CT33   WATERBURY CONGRESS OF RACIAL EQUALITY. P.O.
        Box 1851, 06720. Horace Green, Chmn.

DELAWARE

        DOVER

DE1   DELAWARE PUBLIC ARCHIVES COMMISSION. Hall of
        Records, 19901. Tel 302 734-5711.

   .1   County records.
        Papers, 1728-1893. Includes indenture and manu-
        mission records.
   .2   Murphy, Thomas G.
        Papers, 1861-1904. 51 items. Clergyman. Cor-
        respondence, journal, military documents, farms

accounts, memorabilia, and other papers. The
bulk of the collection relates to the Civil War.
The correspondence includes letters written by
Murphy to his family while he was chaplain of the
1st Delaware Regiment, and letters written as a
missionary to the freedmen at Amelia Courthouse,
Va.

   .3   Reese, Ann. collector.
        Papers, 1715-1877. 77 items. Chiefly land docu-
        ments including deeds, surveys, and leases for
        lands in Duck Creek, Appoquinimink Creek, and St.
        Georges Hundreds in Kent and New Castle counties,
        Del.; together with apprentice indentures; manu-
        missions and other records concerning slaves;
        business records; personal papers of the Allee,
        Hoffecker, and Peterson families; and other miscel-
        laneous items.

DE2   DELAWARE STATE COLLEGE (1891), WILLIAM C. JASON
        LIBRARY. 19901. Tel 302 734-8271. Gertrude E.
        Winston, Librn.

   .1   Afro-American Studies Collection.
        ca. 1000 paperbacks. Basic books on the life and
        history of black Americans.
   .2   Black studies collection.
        Includes books, newspapers, pamphlets, and peri-
        odicals.
   .3   Delaware State College.
        Archives, 1891- .

        NEWARK

DE3   UNIVERSITY OF DELAWARE, DIVISION OF URBAN
        AFFAIRS (1961). 19711. Tel 302 738-2395. C. Harold
        Brown, Dir.
        The Division conducts analytical research related to
        social, political, and economic problems resulting
        from urbanization, focusing on the adaptation of theoret-
        ical models and concepts to understand the development
        and execution of public policy. Among current research
        projects is a three-year analysis of neighborhood cen-
        ters in Wilmington, Del., measuring the effectiveness of
        neighborhood centers in alleviating the problems of
        ghetto residents.
        Publ.: Studies, reports, surveys.

        WILMINGTON

DE4   CATHOLIC DIOCESE OF WILMINGTON, OFFICE FOR
        INNER-CITY DEVELOPMENT (1965). 1626 N. Union
        St., 19806. E.L. McHugh, Exec. Dir.
        The Office is concerned with community and leadership
        development and development of social action programs.
        It works with other community groups helping urban poor
        people, in programs designed to correct the imbalance
        affecting production, planning and distribution of goods
        and services.

DE5   DEPARTMENT OF LABOR AND INDUSTRIAL RELATIONS,
        DIVISION AGAINST DISCRIMINATION (1961). 506 W.
        Tenth St., 19801. Tel 302 658-9251. C. Robert Burns,
        Exec. Off.
        State agency with jurisdiction in employment; receives
        and investigates complaints, conciliates.

DE6   THE HISTORICAL SOCIETY OF DELAWARE (1866). Old
        Town Hall, Sixth and Market Sts., 19801. Tel 302
        658-9432. Dale Fields, Exec. Dir. Literature searches,
        copying, inquiries answered, referrals made, con-
        sultation.
        Publ.: Delaware History.

   .1   Abolition Society of Delaware.
        Papers, 1801-1916. Minutes of the Acting Com-
        mittee (1801-07, 2 v.), clippings and copies of let-
        ters from Thomas Garrett.
   .2   African School Society, Wilmington, Delaware.
        Papers, 1809-1916. 7 v. Memoranda and accounts.
   .3   Africana School Society.
        Papers, 1819-23. Constitution and minutes.
   .4   Delaware Association for the Moral Improvement and
        Education of the Colored People of the State.

Miscellaneous, 1866-1909. 3 v. Minutes and accounts (1866-96), included are minutes of the annual meetings of the African School Society (1897-1909).

.5   Female African School Society.
Papers, 1833-61. 5 v. Minutes and accounts.

.6   Garrett, Thomas.
Papers, 1700-1866. ca. 75 items. Delaware abolitionist. Materials relating to Garrett's career and his family.

.7   H. F. Brown Collection.
Papers. Contains letters referring to slavery.

.8   Rodney Collection.
Papers. Contains letters referring to slavery.

.9   Young, Pauline. collector.
Collection of newspaper clippings and magazine articles. Contains materials pertaining to the Negro in Delaware.

DE7   NATIONAL CONFERENCE OF CHRISTIANS AND JEWS (NCCJ). 701 Shipley St., 19801. Tel 302 655-0039. Paul Glaeseman, Dir.

DISTRICT OF COLUMBIA

DC1   AFRICAN METHODIST EPISCOPAL CHURCH (1816), DEPARTMENT OF EDUCATION (1884). 1461 Northgate Rd., N.W., 20012. Tel 202 882-1823. Dr. Sherman L. Greene, Jr., Exec. Secy. Inquiries answered, referrals made, consultation.
The Department works to enable Negro graduates to acquire knowledge and skills required for professions and vocations; to qualify Negro graduates for leadership in the struggle of a racially oppressed people for freedom and regard for human dignity irrespective of race or national origin. The Church supports six senior and two junior colleges and two theological seminaries.
Publ.: Reports, studies, and other publications distributed occasionally.

.1   African Methodist Episcopal Church, Department of Education.
Files, 1884- . Correspondence, minutes of board meetings, financial records, and other materials dealing with the support of the following predominantly black colleges, universities and seminaries: Allen University, Columbia, S.C.; Wilberforce University, Wilberforce, Ohio; Daniel Payne College, Birmingham, Ala.; Paul Quinn College, Waco, Tex.; Edward Waters College, Atlanta, Ga.; Kittrell Junior College, Kittrell, N.C.; Shorter Junior College, North Little Rock, Ark.; Payne Theological Seminary, Wilberforce, Ohio; and Turner Theological Seminary, Atlanta, Ga.

DC2   AMERICAN ASSOCIATION OF JUNIOR COLLEGES (1920). 1717 Massachusetts Ave., N.W., 20036. Tel 202 462-4031. Edmund J. Gleazer, Jr., Exec. Dir.
The Association promotes the sound growth of community and junior colleges and helps create in them an atmosphere conducive to learning. Activities directed toward the development of good teaching, suitable curriculums, effective administration, appropriate student guidance services, and communication with local, state, and national communities. A recent project involved the demographic study of Negro access to higher education in metropolitan areas.
Publ.: Junior College Journal, bi-monthly; Federal Affairs Bulletin, occasionally; Occupational Education Bulletin, occasionally.

DC3   AMERICAN ASSOCIATION OF UNIVERSITY PROFESSORS (AAUP). One Dupont Circle, 20036. Tel 202 232-4660. Ralph S. Brown, Jr., Pres. Inquiries answered, consultation.
A recent project of the AAUP is to help predominantly Negro colleges develop written policies and procedures for dealing with the rights and responsibilities of faculty members. A consultant will work with the colleges in preparing written policies covering such matters as

appointment procedures, academic freedom, probationary periods, promotion, tenure, nonreappointment, dismissal procedures, professional ethics and responsibilities, and faculty participation in the decision-making process.
Publ.: AAUP Bulletin, quarterly journal; Academe, newsletter.

.1   American Association of University Professors.
Files. Includes college and university catalogs and faculty handbooks from predominantly Negro colleges with which the Association works.

DC4   AMERICAN CIVIL LIBERTIES UNION, WASHINGTON OFFICE. Suite 501, 1424 16th St., N.W., 20036. Tel 202 483-3830. Lawrence Speiser, Dir.

DC5   THE AMERICAN COLONIZATION SOCIETY (1817). 514 C St., N.E., 20002. Tel 202 544-5700. Charles W. Connelly, Jr., Treas. and Gen. Counsel. Inquiries answered, referrals made.
The Society is a revival of the 19th century organization which was opposed to slavery and helped to return freed slaves to Liberia. The present-day group supports the black American's return to Africa as an alternative to "forced integration" and as a "valve for racial tensions." The Society seeks to educate the public about Marcus Garvey and the black nationalist movement, and to promote student exchange programs, rather than programs of "repatriotism." The organization is governed by a Caucasion board of directors and a segregated Afro-American advisory council.
Publ.: Among the Society's publications are books on African colonization.

.1   American Colonization Society.
Files, 1969- . Records, correspondence, minutes of meetings, and other papers concerning the aims and activities of the organization. Materials restricted.

DC6   AMERICAN COUNCIL ON HUMAN RIGHTS. 1130 Sixth St., N.W., 20001. Tel 202 265-7307. Mrs. Emma Manning Carter, Pres.
The Council works to completely eliminate segregation, exclusion, and any other form of discrimination based on race, religion, or national origin.

DC7   AMERICAN FEDERATION OF LABOR AND CONGRESS OF INDUSTRIAL ORGANIZATIONS (AFL-CIO), DEPARTMENT OF CIVIL RIGHTS (1916). 815 16th St., N.W., 20006. Tel 202 293-5270. Donald Slaiman, Dir. Inquiries answered, consultation.
The Department serves as staff arm to Civil Rights Committee of AFL-CIO; assists in implementation of equal opportunities and non-discrimination policies of AFL-CIO; handles complaints involving any form of union discrimination; helps to set up community civil rights programs; maintains liaison with civil rights groups and government civil rights agencies; staffers serve on equal opportunity workshops at labor schools, appear on panels, and speak to civic groups.
Publ.: Occasional reports, film list, pamphlets, and other informational materials relative to civil rights and equal opportunity.

DC8   AMERICAN FEDERATION OF LABOR AND CONGRESS OF INDUSTRIAL ORGANIZATIONS (AFL-CIO), LIBRARY (1916). 815 16th St., N.W., 20006. Tel 202 628-3870. Mrs. Jean Y. Webber, Librn. Interlibrary loan.
Publ.: The American Federationist, monthly.

.1   American Federation of Labor and Congress of Industrial Organizations (AFL-CIO).
Miscellaneous materials. Books, vertical file materials, journals, newspapers, and other items concerning labor and economics.

DC9   AMERICAN FEDERATION OF TEACHERS, AFL-CIO. Sixth Floor, 1012 14th St., N.W., 20005. Tel 202 737-6141. David Selden, Pres.
The Federation is a national private organization which seeks to improve status of teachers and public education in U.S. Civil rights programs include Freedom Schools

in Mississippi and various conferences on Negro history, especially pertaining to textbooks in elementary and secondary schools.
Publ.: Various pamphlets and articles on problems of racial distortion in textbooks and integration in schools.

DC10 AMERICAN JEWISH COMMITTEE, CENTRAL ATLANTIC AREA. 818 18th St., N.W., 20006. Tel 202 298-8787. Brant Coopersmith, Area Dir.

DC11 AMERICAN JEWISH CONGRESS, NATIONAL CAPITOL REGION. 1346 Connecticut Ave., N.W., 20036. Tel 202 293-5330. Mrs. Murray Foss, Dir.

DC12 AMERICAN SOCIOLOGICAL ASSOCIATION. 1001 Connecticut Ave., N.W., 20036. Tel 202 347-7140. Referrals made, consultation.
The Association is a professional society which answers inquiries in the areas of sociology, criminology, the family, social work, civil rights, and social psychology. Provides consulting, advisory, and referral services.
Publ.: American Sociological Review, bimonthly; Sociology of Education, quarterly journal; Sociology of Sociometry, quarterly journal; The American Sociologist, quarterly; Journal of Health and Social Behavior, quarterly.

DC13 AMERICAN VETERANS COMMITTEE (AVC) INC. (1943). 1333 Connecticut Ave., N.W., 20036. Tel 202 293-4890. Samuel Byer, Nat. Chmn.
AVC is a national organization with a strong civil rights program which has served as a watchdog on integration of regular armed forces, reserves, and National Guard. Veterans claims activities focus on discriminatory situations. Represents veterans with discharge problems.
Publ.: AVC Bulletin, periodically; Special reports.

DC14 AMERICANS FOR DEMOCRATIC ACTION (ADA). 1223 Connecticut Ave., N.W., 20036. Tel 202 265-5771. Leon Shull, Nat. Dir.
The ADA is a national political-action organization concerned with local and national civil rights legislation, education, poverty programs.
Publ.: ADA World, monthly; Congressional Newsletters, bi weekly.

DC15 ANTI-DEFAMATION LEAGUE OF B'NAI B'RITH, DISTRICT OF COLUMBIA-MARYLAND REGIONAL OFFICE. 1640 Rhode Island Ave., N.W., 20036. Tel 202 393-5284. Jason Silverman, Dir.

DE16 APPALACHIAN REGIONAL COMMISSION, DIVISION OF CONTRACT COMPLIANCE AND FEDERAL EMPLOYMENT. 1666 Connecticut Ave., N.W., 20235. Tel 202 967-3106. Alvin Jones Arnett, Spec. Asst. to the Fed. Co-Chmn.
Publ.: Appalachia, bi-monthly.

.1 Division of Federal Employment and Contract Compliance.
Files. Records, correspondence, reports, and other papers concerning equal opportunity in employment and contract compliance.

DC17 ASSOCIATED PUBLISHERS (1921). 1300 Connecticut Ave., N.W., 20001. Tel 202 234-5400. Miss Willie L. Miles, Secy.
Associated Publishers is the publishing agency of the Association for the Study of Negro Life and History.
Publ.: Textbooks and treatises.

.1 Associated Publishers.
Files, 1921- . Correspondence, financial records, books, reports, studies, treatises, and other materials dealing with the Association for the Study of Negro Life and History publications.

DC18 THE ASSOCIATION FOR THE STUDY OF NEGRO LIFE AND HISTORY (1915), LIBRARY (1915). 1538 Ninth St., N.W., 20001. Tel 202 462-0313. Charles H. Wesley, Exec. Dir. Interlibrary loan, bibliographies prepared, literature searches, inquiries answered, consultation.
The Association promotes historical research and

writing; publishes books on Negro life and history; promotes the study of the Negro through schools, colleges, churches, homes, fraternal groups, and clubs; and collects historical mss and materials relating to the Negro people throughout the world.
Publ.: Journal of Negro History, quarterly; Negro History Bulletin, monthly; Monographs, reports, special studies, textbooks, and other publications treating almost every phase of Negro life and history.

.1 The Association for the Study of Negro Life and History. Among the holdings are copies of all Association publications including complete runs of Journal of Negro History (1916- .), and the Negro History Bulletin (1937- .). Also included are books, periodicals, newspapers, pamphlets, mss (including the Carter G. Woodson papers, some of which are deposited in the Library of Congress), clippings, photographs, microforms, art, and historical objects. Restricted.

DC19 BUREAU OF SOCIAL SCIENCE RESEARCH, INC. (1950). LIBRARY. 1200 17th St., N.W., 20036. Tel 202 233-4300. Gloria B. Cooper, Librn. Interlibrary loan, inquiries answered.
The objectives of the Bureau are the development of theory and research methods in the behavioral sciences and the use of the social science methodology in the examination of social problems.
Publ.: BSSR reports and staff papers on minority groups; BSSR Newsletter.

.1 Bureau of Social Science Research, Inc.
Files, 1962- . Books, periodical titles, pamphlets, reports, and staff papers on the subjects of church and desegregation, desegregation and social policy, housing, March on Washington, public school desegregation, public school integration, student disturbance and desegregation, unemployment, and underemployment.

.2 Oral History Project.
Tape recordings. History and analysis of the 1963 March on Washington and of the pre-Washington activities of the Poor People's Campaign, through recorded interviews and other means.

DC20 CATHOLIC UNIVERSITY OF AMERICA, MULLEN LIBRARY, DEPARTMENT OF ARCHIVES AND MANUSCRIPTS. Sixth and Michigan Ave., N.E., 20017. Tel 202 529-6000. Rev. Michael Hall, O.S.B., Archivist.

.1 Haas, Francis Joseph, Bp., 1889-1953.
Papers, 1904-52. 71 ft. Professor of labor economics, arbitrator in labor disputes, and authority on labor relations. Correspondence, writings, speeches, reports, notes, memoranda, press releases, etc. pertaining to Haas's activities as chairman of the President's Committee on Fair Employment Practice during World War II, chairman of the Michigan Committee on Civil Rights, co-chairman of the Council against Intolerance in America, member of the National Recovery Administration, and member of the National Labor Relations Board.

DC21 CENTER FOR APPLIED LINGUISTICS (1959), LIBRARY. (1959). 1717 Massachusetts Ave., N.W., 20036. Tel 202 265-3100. John Lotz, Dir. Bibliographies prepared, copying, inquiries answered, referrals made, consultation.
The Center initially focused on improvement of teaching English as a second language abroad but in 1964 turned major attention to English-language teaching in America. Its Urban Language Study has cast new light on reading and other learning problems of children in deprived city ghettos. The Center helps develop practical guidelines and training resources that will help teachers sort out their own attitudes and values about the native language, and interpret to them new knowledge that is revelant to teaching fundamental language skills.
Publ.: The Linguistic Reporter, bi-monthly; Sociolinguistic and bibliographic studies, handbooks and manuals, and course materials.

DC22 CENTER FOR EMERGENCY SUPPORT. 3515 Idaho Ave., N.W., 20016. Tel 202 462-6883.

The Center works to counteract racism in the white middle-class community and give support to ghetto residents in case of riots and other emergencies.

DC23   CHAMBER OF COMMERCE OF THE UNITED STATES OF AMERICA, COMMUNITY AND REGIONAL DEVELOPMENT GROUP. 1615 H St., N.W., 20006. Tel 202 695-6000. Richard L. Breault, Mgr.
The Group encourages businessmen, Chamber of Commerce and trade and professional associations to learn more about counseling services, loan opportunities, and other such efforts, and to explore ways in which they may cooperate in developing entrepreneurship among minority groups.
Publ.: Case studies showing how local leaders have attacked urban problems.

DC24   THE CHAMBER OF COMMERCE OF THE UNITED STATES OF AMERICA, HUMAN RESOURCES DEVELOPMENT GROUP. 1615 H St., N.W., 20006. Tel 202 659-6100. Reuben D. Siverson, Group Mgr.
The Group, an educational arm of the Chamber, is concerned with civil rights policies affecting employment, and other aspects of management-employee relations.
Publ.: Guide to Civil Rights Act.

DC25   CITIZENS ADVOCATE CENTER (1967). 1211 Connecticut Ave., N.W., 20036. Tel 202 293-1515. Dr. Edgar S. Cahn, Exec. Dir.
The Center functions as a privately funded "ombudsman" to receive complaints and to monitor the administration of federal programs having a direct bearing on the problems of poverty in order to assure that they are implemented fully, forthrightly, and fairly.

DC26   CITIZENS' CRUSADE AGAINST POVERTY (CCAP) (1964), CENTRAL FILES (1965). 2027 Massachusetts Ave., N.W., 20036. Tel 202 293-1220. Richard W. Boone, Exec. Dir. Literature searches, inquiries answered, referrals made.
CCAP is a coalition of concerned individuals and groups committed to work with the poor to attack poverty at its source. While concerned with the development of new strategies and programs to eradicate poverty, most of CCAP's programs are directed to getting resources to poor people with minimum red tape and without sacrificing quality of self-help programs. CCAP's major business is conducted in five areas: national policy recommendations; leadership training for work in low-income areas; advocacy in behalf of the poor and groups representing the poor; technical assistance in behalf of organizations working with and among the poor; and public information.
Publ.: Monthly bulletin.

    .1   Citizens' Crusade Against Poverty.
          Files, 1964- . Includes books, periodical titles, pamphlets, mss, correspondence, and clippings. Correspondence restricted.

DC27   CITYWIDE TENANTS UNION. 2429 Shannon Place, S.E., 20020. Tel 202 581-8414. Harold E. Staley, Dir. Inquiries answered.
The Union works to organize public housing tenants into a viable and effective organization to effect change in the D.C. Housing Authority.

DC28   THE CIVIL RIGHTS DOCUMENTATION PROJECT (CRDP). 1527 New Hampshire Ave., 20036. Tel 202 232-7023. Dr. Vincent J. Browne, Dir.
The CRDP was established by the Fund for the Advancement of Education, to tape interviews with persons who have been significantly engaged in civil rights activities in the U.S. The project also collects materials such as handbills, posters, letters, memoranda, minutes of meetings, and records of civil rights organizations. The interviews cover activities chiefly from 1960. Tapes and transcripts of the tapes are available to researchers under varying restrictions.

    .1   Civil Rights Documentation Project.
          Tape-recorded interviews (May 1, 1967-November 24, 1969) with the following persons;
    .2   — Acevado, Jorge, director of the Economic Opportunity Commission of Santa Clara County, San

Jose, Calif., and spokesman for the Mexican-American community.

.3   — Alexander, Clifford L., Jr., chairman, Equal Employment Opportunity Commission.

.4   — Alexander, Felton S., executive director, Dallas Urban League.

.5   — Alexander, Fred, black city councilman in Charlotte, N.C., also involved in the Charlotte sit-in demonstrations in the early 1960's.

.6   — Alexander, Kelly, North Carolina NAACP president and long-time civil rights fighter in the State.

.7   — Alexander, Sadie T.M., lawyer, Philadelphia, Pa.

.8   — Alexander, Sidney, long-time civil rights activist in Sharkey County, Mississippi, with the Mississippi Freedom Democratic Party.

.9   — Alinsky, Saul, Industrial Areas Foundation, Chicago, Ill.

.10   — Allen, Ernie, co-founder and editor of Soulbook, a black revolutionary magazine.

.11   — Allen, Ivan, mayor, Atlanta, Ga.

.12   — Allen, Michele Paul (Mrs.), leader in the Afro-American Student Movement (ASM) and Nashville SNCC while at Fisk University, and one of the founders of the Black Panther Party of Northern California.

.13   — Allen, Robert, staff writer, The Guardian; and former leader of Afro-Americans for Survival (a black anti-war group), New York, N.Y.

.14   — Amador, Monico, Mexican-American Opportunity Center, Department of Labor, San Jose, California.

.15   — Amerson, Lucius, sheriff, Tuskegee, Ala.

.16   — Anderson, Carl, associate dean of students for Administration and Student Life at Howard University.

.17   — Anderson, Constance E., teacher and teacher trainer, in I.S. 55, Brooklyn, N.Y.

.18   — Anrig, Gregory (Dr.), former director of Equal Opportunities Division of U.S. Dept. of Health, Education, and Welfare.

.19   — Anonymous "A," an anonymous participant in the Washington, D.C., riot (April, 1968).

.20   — Anonymous "B," an anonymous participant in the Washington, D.C., riot (April, 1968).

.21   — Anonymous "C," an anonymous participant in the Washington, D.C., riot (April, 1968).

.22   — Anthony, Paul, executive director, Southern Regional Council.

.23   — Aronica, Louis, director, Metropolitan Fair Housing Council, Washington, D.C.

.24   — Atkinson, Albert B.(Col.), program director for the Eastern Shore, Maryland, Office of Economic Opportunity.

.25   — Aukofer, Frank, reporter, The Milwaukee Journal.

.26   — Austin, Ernest, SCLC staff member and coordinator of the Appalachian leg of the march to Washington (1967).

.27   — Aveilhe, Clyde C., director of student activities, Howard University.

.28   — Ayers, Gary, student activist leader at Howard University.

.29   — Bailey, Peter, staff member, New York office of Ebony magazine, and former personal aide to the late Malcolm X.

.30   — Baker, Ella, special consultant, Southern Conference Educational Fund, Inc., a founder of SNCC, and first staff executive of the Southern Christian Leadership Conference.

.31   — Baldwin, Jesse L., sanitation worker and staunch supporter of the Memphis garbage strike (1968).

.32   — Ballard, Charles, young militant leader of the Invaders, a teen organization in Memphis, Tenn.

.33   — Bancroft, Richard A., civil rights and labor law attorney.

.34   — Barbee, Lloyd, representative from Milwaukee to the Wisconsin State Legislature.

.35   — Barnes, Lois, education chairman, San Francisco branch, NAACP.

.36   — Barnet, Roosevelt, SCLC field secretary in Montgomery; assistant director, Alabama Action Committee.

.37   — Baroni, Father Gino, executive secretary, Archbishop's Committee on Human Relations, Washington, D.C.

DC28.38 — Barry, Marion, first chairman of SNCC, and assistant director, PRIDE, Inc., Washington, D.C.
.39 — Baston, Ruth, associate director, METCO (Metropolitan Council for Educational Opportunity), Boston, Mass.
.40 — Baugh, Howard, police department, Atlanta, Ga.
.41 — Becker, William, director, Human Rights Commission, San Francisco, Calif.
.42 — Bennett, L. Howard, director of civil rights, U.S. Dept. of Defense.
.43 — Bennett, Lerone, senior editor, Ebony magazine.
.44 — Benning, Dwight, member of the Commandos, and the Milwaukee Youth Council.
.45 — Bernhagen, Wayne, A., president, Milwaukee Citizens Civic Voice, and National Civil Alliance.
.46 — Berrigan, Phillip (Rev.), author, and assistant pastor, St. Peter Claver's Church, Baltimore, Md.
.47 — Berry, Edwin, executive director, Chicago Urban League.
.48 — Bevel, James, executive staff member, SCLC.
.49 — Billingsley, Orzell, civil rights lawyer, Birmingham, Ala., and participant in the movement to incorporate all-black towns in Alabama.
.50 — Black, Charles A., chairman of Atlanta protest group.
.51 — Black, Lewis, field director, Alabama Council on Human Relations, Greensboro, Ala.
.52 — Black, Lucille, secretary for membership, NAACP.
.53 — Blackwell, Unita, leader of Mississippi Freedom Democratic Party, and staff member, National Council of Negro Women working with "Project Homes" in Gulfport, Miss.
.54 — Bond, H. Julian, representative to the Georgia State Legislature.
.55 — Boone, Richard (Rev.), SCLC field secretary in Alabama, and executive director, Alabama Action Committee in Montgomery.
.56 — Booth, Mary, SNCC field secretary in Greenwood, Miss., (1961-65), and director of the Greenwood Movement.
.57 — Bowie, Harry, state director of voter education programs, Delta Ministry in Mississippi.
.58 — Braden, Ann, staff member, Southern Conference Educational Fund, and editor of the organization's publication, The Southern Patriot.
.59 — Braden, Carl, executive director, Southern Conference Educational Fund, Louisville, Ky.
.60 — Branton, Wiley A., executive director, United Planning Organization.
.61 — Bremond, Walter, president of the Black Congress.
.62 — Britt, Travis, long-time field worker for SNCC in Mississippi and Alabama; one of the first freedom riders.
.63 — Britton, Harvey, NAACP state field director, Louisiana.
.64 — Brooks, Fred, SNCC leader at Tennessee State University, and organizer of the Liberation School in Nashville.
.65 — Brooks, Lela Mae, vice-chairman, MFDP, Sunflower County, Miss.; and longtime activist in the Sunflower County Movement.
.66 — Brooks, Owen, Mississippi director, Delta Ministry, National Council of Churches.
.67 — Brown, Benjamin D., representative in the Georgia State Legislature.
.68 — Brown, Edward, Citizens Crusade Against Poverty, Washington, D.C.
.69 — Brown, Ewart, president, Student Assembly, Howard University (1967-68).
.70 — Brown, Otis, Jr., chairman, MFDP, and head of the Sunflower Improvement Association and Community Center.
.71 — Brown, Theodore, executive director, Negro American Leadership Conference on Africa.
.72 — Brown, Willie L., member, California State Assembly.
.73 — Browne, John, director of Tuskegee Institute's Community Education Project.
.74 — Bryant, Baxton, executive director, Tennessee Council on Human Relations.
.75 — Bryant, Ethel C., executive assistant to Mayor Sam Yorty of Los Angeles, Calif.
.76 — Buffington, John, chairman, Clay County Community Development Organization; leader in the Mississippi Freedom Democratic Party; former member of SNCC's national executive committee.
.77 — Buford, Kenneth L. (Rev.), NAACP Alabama field director; member of the Tuskegee County Council.
.78 — Burbridge, Thomas N., president, San Francisco branch, NAACP.
.79 — Buskirk, Phillip, head of the legislative committee, Poor Peoples Campaign.
.80 — Butler, Ancusto, leader of grass-roots efforts in Cleveland.
.81 — Cabbage, Charles, community organizer and leading member of the Invaders, Memphis, Tenn.
.82 — Cabera, Y. Arturo, Dept. of Education, San Jose State College; an officer of the Mexican-American Political Association.
.83 — Cableton, Robert, SNCC field secretary in Arkansas.
.84 — Calhoun, John H., community organizer for Economic Opportunity Atlanta, Inc.; political organizer associated with the Republican Party of Georgia.
.85 — Campbell, Robert F., executive director, Southern Education Reporting Service.
.86 — Caplan, Marvin, director, Washington office, Leadership Conference; director, Civil Rights Section, AFL-CIO.
.87 — Carew, Collin, director, New Thing Art and Architecture Center, Washington, D.C.; early SNCC field worker in Mississippi.
.88 — Carliner, David, attorney of Washington, D.C., whose major interest is civil liberties.
.89 — Carter, Hodding, III, editor, Delta-Democrat Times, Greenville, Miss.; a leader of the successful Democratic loyalist challenge group that ousted the "regulars" at the 1968 Democratic National Convention in Chicago.
.90 — Carter, Robert L., general counsel, NAACP.
.91 — Caskin, John L. (Dr.), long-time civil rights activist, Huntsville, Ala.; chairman, National Democratic Party of Alabama.
.92 — Cassell, Charles, long-time civil rights activist, Washington, D.C.; a leader of the Black United Front, and a school board candidate.
.93 — Cayton, Horace R. (Dr.), co-editor of Black Metropolis, with Dr. St. Claire Drake.
.94 — Champion, Newton E., UCLA student chairman, Committee for Black Art and Culture; member, Black Student Union, and Black Athletic Association.
.95 — Chester, William, vice-president, I.L.W. Union in San Francisco.
.96 — Chisolm, Elwood, professor of law, Howard University.
.97 — Clark, Ramsey, Attorney General, U.S. Dept. of Justice.
.98 — Clark, Robert G., Holmes Co., Miss.; first black man elected to the Mississippi Legislature since Reconstruction.
.99 — Clay, William L., U.S. House Representative from St. Louis, Mo.
.100 — Clement, Kenneth (Dr.), campaign director for Carl B. Stokes, black mayor of Cleveland, Ohio.
.101 — Cohen, Wilbur J. (Dr.), former Secretary of U.S. Dept. of Health, Education, and Welfare.
.102 — Coleman, Clarence D., southern regional office, National Urban League.
.103 — Coleman, Milton, student and founder of on-campus alliance of black students, University of Wisconsin, Milwaukee campus.
.104 — Coles, Flournoy, chairman, Interstate-40 Steering Committee, Nashville, Tenn., which is seeking to block the disruption of almost the entire black business community in Nashville by a federal highway.
.105 — Collins, Daniel A. (Dr.), dentist, San Francisco, Calif.
.106 — Comacho, Victor, president, San Marcos Foundation, San Jose, Calif.; leader in the Mexican-American community.
.107 — Comfort, Mark, director, Oakland Direct Action Committee (ODAC); head of the 1200-member

Western contingent of the Poor People's Campaign which traveled to Washington, D.C., during summer of 1968.

DC28.108 — Cook, Harold D. J., "moderate" student leader and vice-president, Student Assembly, Howard University.

.109 — Cookes, Stoney, SCLC staff member in charge of college and youth involvement, and finance officer of Poor People's Campaign.

.110 — Cotton, Douglas M., SNCC field secretary in Mississippi (1961-65).

.111 — Countryman, Peter, founder, Northern Student Movement (NSM).

.112 — Courts, Gus, NAACP leader; head of voter registration drive in Belzoni, Miss.

.113 — Cowan, Pauline, director, Wednesdays in Mississippi (now Workshops in Mississippi) which solicited assistance from persons in New York to aid the Civil Rights Movement in Mississippi.

.114 — Cox, Raymond L., senator, Howard University Student Assembly; president, University Center Council.

.115 — Craft, Juanita, head, youth division, Dallas branch, NAACP.

.116 — Craig, Calvin, Grand Dragon, Georgia Realm, United Klans of America, Knights of the Ku Klux Klan, Atlanta, Ga.

.117 — Cranford, Raymond, farmer and businessman, North Carolina; Klan spokesman, and militant leader of Confederate Knights of the Ku Klux Klan.

.118 — Crenshaw, Cornelia, long-time civic leader in Memphis, Tenn., and one of the leading organizers of the garbage strike and the boycott (1968).

.119 — Cronin, Father John F., author and Catholic leader in civil rights, Baltimore, Md.

.120 — Current, Gloster, director of branches and field administration, NAACP.

.121 — Currier, Theodore, professor of history, Fisk University.

.122 — Dabbs, James McBride, author of several books on the South and former president of the Southern Regional Council.

.123 — Dandridge, Gloria Richardson, leader of Cambridge, Md. protest.

.124 — Daniels, Mercer A., professor of law and law librarian emeritus, Howard University.

.125 — Davidson, Eugene, attorney, realtor, and civil rights leader, of Washington, D.C.

.126 — Davis, Fred, a black member of the Memphis City Council.

.127 — Davis, William R., first Negro to run for the Pennsylvania State Legislature from Philadelphia.

.128 — Day, Noel, co-partner of OSTIE (Organization for Social and Technical Innovation), Boston, Mass.

.129 — Dent, Thomas, director, Free Southern Theater, in New Orleans; poet, writer, and one of the founders of UMBRA magazine, New York City.

.130 — Despres, Leon, lawyer and alderman, Chicago, Ill.

.131 — De Veaux, Jacqueline E., a student sociology major, Tuskegee Institute, Alabama.

.132 — Devine, Annie, a leader of the MFDP and one of three black political candidates to challenge the election and seating of the regular Mississippi congressional delegation in 1965.

.133 — DeWolf, L. Harold (Dr.), dean, Wesley Theological Seminary in Washington, D.C., and principal academic advisor to Dr. Martin Luther King, Jr., while both were associated with Boston University.

.134 — Diamond, Dion T., director, Neighborhood Services Project, United Planning Organization, Washington, D.C.

.135 — Dockery, Richard L., southwest regional director, NAACP (Dallas).

.136 — Drake, St. Clair (Dr.), professor of sociology and anthropology, Stanford University.

.137 — Dunbar, Leslie, executive director, Field Foundation, New York; executive director, Southern Regional Council in Atlanta.

.138 — Duncan, Charles T., corporation counsel, Washington, D.C.

.139 — Durham, W. J., president, Council of Texas Organizations; a lawyer engaged in civil rights cases, including suit filed by Herman Sweatt to open University of Texas law school.

.140 — Durr, Clifton, a white civil rights activist who has a vivid recollection of the days of the Montgomery Bus Boycott.

.141 — Durr, Virginia, wife of attorney Durr and also a participant in the activities that occurred during the Montgomery Bus Boycott.

.142 — Dymally, Mervlyn, member of the California Legislature.

.143 — Edwards, G. Franklin, chairman, Dept. of Sociology, Howard University.

.144 — Eldridge, Tommy, sanitation worker who became an organizer for the Municipal Employees' Union during the garbage strike in Memphis, Tenn. (1968).

.145 — Estrada, Phillip, editor, The Milwaukee Star News.

.146 — Evans, Ronald, militant young black principal of Harlem's P.S. 201.

.147 — Evers, Myrlie, wife of slain Mississippi leader, Medgar Evers.

.148 — Fagan, Maurice B., executive director, Fellowship Commission, Philadelphia, Pa.

.149 — Fanion, Gerald, deputy director, Tennessee Council on Human Relations.

.150 — Farmer, James, national director, CORE; candidate for Congress from Brooklyn, N.Y.

.151 — Fields, John, executive director, U.S. Conference of Mayors, and national coordinator, Urban Coalition, Washington, D.C.

.152 — Fitzhugh, Howard N., vice-president, Pepsi-Cola Company; activist, New Negro Alliance, Washington, D.C.

.153 — Fortune, Hilda, community organizer, college professor; specialist in human relations and sensitivity training; close associate of Mrs. Mary McCloud Bethune.

.154 — Francois, Terry, member of City and County Board of Supervisors of San Francisco; chairman of NAACP (1960-63); former civil rights lawyer.

.155 — Franklin, Harold, first Negro to enroll in Auburn University.

.156 — Freeman, Orville, Secretary, U.S. Dept. of Agriculture (1960-68).

.157 — Gans, Curtis, executive director, Conference of Concerned Democrats, Washington, D.C.

.158 — Gant, Danny, Target City director, CORE, Baltimore, Md.

.159 — Garman, Betty, SNCC fund raiser and staff worker in the South, New York, and Washington offices.

.160 — Gaston, A.C., businessman and NAACP board member, Birmingham, Ala.

.161 — Gibson, John, Program Development Chief, Community Relations Service, U.S. Dept. of Justice.

.162 — Gilmore, Thomas (Rev.), Southern Christian Leadership Conference representative, Greene County, Ala.

.163 — Givens, Cornelius, community organizer, New York Poor People's Campaign; board member, Poor People's Coalition.

.164 — Goff, Regina, director, Programs for the Disadvantaged, U.S. Dept. of Health, Education, and Welfare.

.165 — Goodlett, Carleton B. (Dr.), editor and publisher of the Sun Reporter; active in the World Peace Council.

.166 — Gomillion, Charles G., professor of sociology, Tuskegee Institute.

.167 — Graham, Frank P., president of University of North Carolina.

.168 — Granger, Lester B., former executive secretary, National Urban League.

.169 — Gray, Fred, lawyer in Tuskegee, Ala.

.170 — Gray, Jesse, leader of the Harlem rent strike, New York City.

.171 — Greaves, William, executive producer and co-host for the television program, Black Journal.

.172 — Greeley, Dana (Dr.), president, Unitarian Universalist Association.

.173 — Green, Edith, U.S. House of Representatives, from Oregon.

DC28.174 — Green, Ernest, graduate of Central High School, Little Rock, Ark.; director, Worker's Defense League, New York City.

.175 — Greene, Bill, member, California Legislature; staff member, CORE.

.176 — Griffith, Mahlon, Tennessee State Department of Personnel.

.177 — Griffin, John H., author of Black Like Me.

.178 — Griffin, Noah Webster, regional director, region I (far west and Hawaii), NAACP; leader for equalization of black teachers' salaries in the South in the 1940's.

.179 — Groppi, Father James E., leader, open housing struggle, Milwaukee, Wis.

.180 — Gunn, Richard, lawyer and member of the executive committee, Cleveland NAACP.

.181 — Haley, Frank, civil rights worker in Philadelphia, and Chester, Pa.

.182 — Haley, Richard, associate national director, CORE, and head of Southern regional CORE.

.183 — Halliman, Terrence, civil rights and civil liberties attorney, San Francisco.

.184 — Hamer, Fannie Lou, leader of the MFDP and self-help programs, Sunflower County, Miss.; leader of the delegate challenge at the 1964 Democratic National Convention.

.185 — Hamilton, Charles V., co-author of Black Power, with Stokely Carmichael.

.186 — Hanson, Agnes, parent and member of the governing board of Ocean Hill-Brownsville (N.Y.) School Demonstration Project.

.187 — Harding, Bertram M., director, U.S. Office of Economic Opportunity.

.188 — Harding, Vincent, chairman, Dept. of History, Spelman College, Atlanta, Ga.; leading theorist in the black power, black culture movement; director of the Martin Luther King, Jr., Memorial Center, Atlanta, Ga.

.189 — Hare, Nathan, director, black studies curriculum, San Francisco State College.

.190 — Harris, Michael, president of the freshman class (1967-68), Howard University; political director of Ujama, a student organization at Howard.

.191 — Harris, Patricia R., professor of law, Howard University.

.192 — Harris, Ruth Bates, executive director, Council on Human Relations, Washington, D.C.

.193 — Harris, William H., principal of I.S. 271, Ocean Hill-Brownsville School Demonstration Project, New York City.

.194 — Harrison, William, president, Southwest Alabama Farmers Cooperative Association (SWAFCA); field secretary, Alabama Council on Human Relations; Alabama coordinator, Poor People's Campaign.

.195 — Harville, Agatha, veteran civil rights activist in Selma with SNCC, SCLC, the Medical Committee on Human Rights, and SWAFCA (Southwest Alabama Farmers Cooperative Association, director of day care centers in Selma, Ala.

.196 — Haskins, James (Rev.), vice-president of the Demopolis (Ala.) Civic League.

.197 — Haskins, John, student civil rights activist in Demopolis, Ala.

.198 — Haskins, Kenneth, principal of the Morgan Community School, Washington, D.C.

.199 — Hawkins, Augustus F., U.S. House Representative, Los Angeles, Calif.

.200 — Hayling, Robert B., board member, SCLC; participant in St. Augustine, Fla. demonstrations.

.201 — Hechinger, John, chairman of the Washington, D.C., City Council.

.202 — Hedgeman, Anna Arnold, author; member, executive staff, National Council of Churches.

.203 — Heffernan, Elaine, administrative assistant to Peter Libassi, Office for Civil Rights, U.S. Dept. of Health, Education and Welfare.

.204 — Henderson, Lloyd, chief, education branch, Office for Civil Rights, Dept. of Health, Education and Welfare.

.205 — Henderson, Mae, student, Carleton College, Northfield, Minn.

.206 — Henderson, Thelton E., black attorney, U.S. Dept. of Justice, who worked in the South on civil rights problems for the Kennedy administration (1962-63).

.207 — Henry, Aaron, chairman, Mississippi NAACP.

.208 — Henry, Anthony R., deputy national coordinator, Poor People's Campaign.

.209 — Henry, Clifton W., acting director, U.S. Conference of Mayors, Washington, D.C.; active in the Northern Student Movement.

.210 — Henry, Theodore, NAACP Youth Council leader, Jackson, Miss.

.211 — Hernandez, Aileen C., member, Equal Employment Opportunity Commission; private consultant on labor and employment, San Francisco, Calif.

.212 — Hicks, Robert, vice-president, Bogalusa, La., Voters League, and one of the founders of Deacons for Defense.

.213 — Hirschopf, Philip, civil rights attorney, Alexandria, Va.; founder, Law Student Civil Rights Research Council; general counsel, National Education Association.

.214 — Hobson, Julius, chairman, Associated Community Teams (ACT), Washington, D.C.; plaintiff in the case of Hobson vs. Hansen.

.215 — Hodges, Luther H., Secretary of Commerce, Eisenhower administration; Governor of North Carolina.

.216 — Hoffman, Rufus, public school teacher, Bullock Co., Ala.; treasurer, Southeast Alabama Self-Help Association, Union Springs, Ala.

.217 — Holland, Arthur J., mayor, Trenton, N.J.

.218 — Hollowell, Donald L. director, southern region, U.S. Equal Employment Opportunity Commission.

.219 — Holman, Carl, deputy director, U.S. Commission on Civil Rights, Washington, D.C.

.220 — Horowitz, Larry, administrative assistant to Congressman John Conyers.

.221 — Houck, Thomas E., SCLC staff member and western regional coordinator, Poor People's Campaign.

.222 — Houser, George M., executive director, CORE.

.223 — Horne, Frank S., housing expert, New York City; active consultant during the New Deal era.

.224 — Howe, Harold, II, U.S. Commissioner of Education.

.225 — Huitt, Ralph K., assistant secretary of U.S. Dept. of Health, Education, and Welfare for legislation and congressional relations.

.226 — Hulett, John, director, Lowndes County (Miss.) Community Action Program, and a key man in the Lowndes County Freedom Democratic Party.

.227 — Hurley, Ruby, director, southeast regional office, NAACP.

.228 — Jackson, Ella, member, Lowndes County Co-op, Inc., the Lowndes County Freedom Movement, and the Southwest Alabama Farmers Cooperative Association.

.229 — Jackson, Ellen, director, Operation Exodus, Boston, Mass.

.230 — Jackson, Emory O., editor, The Birmingham World.

.231 — Jackson, Espanol, community organization supervisor, San Francisco, Calif.

.232 — Jackson, H. Ralph, director, minimum salary department of the African Methodist Episcopal Church.

.233 — Jackson, John, Alabama state project director, SNCC.

.234 — Jackson, Matthew, Sr., chairman, Lowndes County Co-op, Inc.; leader, Lowndes County, Miss.

.235 — James, H. Rhett, chairman, Dallas Metropolitan Council, NAACP; leader of sit-ins in Dallas in early 1960's.

.236 — Javitts, Jacob, U.S. Senator from New York, and civil rights advocate.

.237 — Jelinek, Donald, director, Southern Rural Research Project; civil rights lawyer; Alabama attorney, Lawyers Constitutional Defense Committee.

.238 — Jenkins, Esau, community leader, Charleston, S.C.; community organizer, Penn Center, Frogmore, S.C.; and SCLC board member.

.239 — Jenkins, Eunice, SNCC worker, Indianola, Miss., and organizer, Child Development Group of Mississippi.

.240 — Jenkins, Linda, SNCC worker in Indianola, Miss.;

    student, Mississippi Valley State College, Itta Bena, Miss.

DC28.241 — Johnson, Arthur, executive secretary, Detroit branch, NAACP.

.242 — Johnson, Beulah, director, Macon County Community Action Program, Tuskegee, Ala.

.243 — Johnson, Robert E., managing editor, Jet magazine.

.244 — Johnson, Theron, director, northwestern branch, Equal Educational Opportunities Division, U.S. Office of Education.

.245 — Johnson, William A., instructor in political science, Flint Community College, Flint, Mich.; student leader and Hilltop editor at Howard University.

.245a — Jones, Edward, active civil rights worker, member of the Tuskegee Institute Community Education Project, Tuskegee Institute, Ala.

.246 — Jones, James (Rev.), president, Board of Education of the Los Angeles Unified and Junior College Districts; member, McCone Commission; minister, Westminister Presbyterian Church.

.247 — Jones, Joseph C., director, ACCESS; SNCC leader, Washington, D.C.

.248 — Jones, Lewis, research professor of sociology, Tuskegee Institute, Ala.

.249 — Jones, Rachel, SNCC worker and sociology major at Tuskegee Institute.

.250 — Jordan, Vernon, executive director, Voter Education Project, Southern Regional Council, Atlanta, Ga.

.251 — Kastenmeier, Robert W., member, U.S. House of Representatives from Wisconsin.

.252 — Keever, C.M., mayor, Tuskegee, Ala.

.253 — Keller, Rosa, civic leader, New Orleans, La.

.254 — Kennedy, Joseph H., San Francisco Municipal Court.

.255 — Kibbitt, Margaret, MFDP candidate for sheriff, Sunflower Co., Miss.; organizer of quilting cooperatives, Sunflower County.

.256 — King, Annie Mae, long-time civil rights activist, Sunflower County, Miss.

.257 — King, C.B., civil rights lawyer in Alabama and Georgia; attorney for the Albany Movement.

.258 — King, Carole, organizer, Welfare Grievance Committee, Cleveland, Ohio.

.259 — King, Celes, president, Los Angeles NAACP; one of the leaders of the "Young Turks."

.260 — King, Lonnie, chairman, Atlanta protest group; chairman, Young Democrats, Washington, D.C.

.261 — King, Melvin, director, Urban League for Greater Boston.

.262 — King, Slater, vice-president, Albany Movement (1962), and later president.

.263 — Kirchheimer, Rowan P., student, Columbia University; member, Students for a Democratic Society (SDS).

.264 — Kirk, Father David, coordinator, Emmaus House, East Harlem, New York City.

.265 — Klunder, Joann, widow of Rev. Klunder, civil rights worker killed in Cleveland, Ohio.

.266 — Lacy, Shirley, civil rights leader, New Jersey; director of training and technical assistant, Scholarship, Education, and Defense Fund for Racial Equality.

.267 — Landry, Lawrence, national chairman, ACT.

.268 — Lane, Mary, SNCC field secretary, Greenwood, Miss.

.269 — Lawrence, Charles F., Philadelphia Tutorial Service, Philadelphia, Pa.

.270 — Leake, George (Rev.), one of the first black men to run for political office in Charlotte, N.C.; freedom rider.

.271 — Lee, Anthony, plaintiff in Lee vs. Macon County Board of Education, Tuskegee, Ala.

.272 — Lee, George Washington, vice-president, Tri-State Bank of Memphis; leading Republican politican; leader, Elks fraternal organization.

.273 — Leighton, George N., judge, Cook County Circuit Court, Chicago, Ill.

.274 — Leonard, Margaret, early CORE freedom rider, Washington, D.C.

.275 — Lewis, John, third chairman of SNCC.

.276 — Lewis, Rufus, board member, Montgomery (Ala.) Citizens Association.

.277 — Lincoln, C. Eric, professor of sociology, Union Theological Seminary, New York City; author, Black Muslims in America.

.278 — Llorens, David, assistant editor, Ebony magazine.

.279 — Logan, Rayford W., professor emeritus, Howard University.

.280 — Londa, Jeweldean, associate director for health and welfare, National Urban League.

.281 — Looby, Z. Alexander, lawyer with experience in key civil rights cases (Nashville, Tenn.).

.282 — Lopez, Jose, Economic Opportunity Commission, San Jose, Calif.

.283 — Lottman, Michael, managing editor, Southern Courier, Montgomery, Ala.

.284 — Lucas, Robert, chairman, Chicago chapter, CORE; director, north central region, CORE.

.285 — Luster, Hervey P., chairman, western addition area, Action Board of Economic Opportunity Council, San Francisco, Calif.

.286 — Luster, Orville, executive director, Youth for Service, San Francisco.

.287 — Lynch, Walter Gordon, director, Coleman Community Center (New York City); community liaison director, Ocean Hill-Brownsville School Demonstration Project, New York City.

.288 — Mack, John, director, Flint, Mich., Urban League; special assistant to Sterling Tucker; director, Los Angeles Urban League.

.289 — Maier, Henry, mayor, Milwaukee, Wis.

.290 — Major, Reginald, chairman of education committee, San Francisco NAACP; director of educational opportunity program, San Francisco State College.

.291 — Mangrum, Fred, SNCC field secretary in Mississippi.

.292 — Marks, Richard, director, Community Relations Commission, Detroit, Mich.

.293 — Marshall, Joseph, parent, and member of governing board, Ocean Hill-Brownsville School Demonstration Project (New York City).

.294 — Mason, Phillip, Community Relations Service, U.S. Dept. of Justice, Washington, D.C.

.295 — Mays, Benjamin, president emeritus, Morehouse College, Atlanta, Ga.

.296 — Mead, Margaret, noted anthropologist.

.297 — Mcany, George, international president of the AFL-CIO

.298 — Mendoza, Sophie, United People Arriba, San Jose, Calif.

.299 — Mesher, Shirley, civil rights worker and SCLC field representative, Alabama; participant in the Selma (Ala.) movement, voter registration efforts, and Southwest Alabama Farmers Cooperative Association.

.300 — Meredith, James, first Negro to enroll in the University of Mississippi.

.301 — Milgram, Morris, manager, Mutual Real Estate Investment Trust, and leader in building housing developments for interracial occupancy.

.302 — Mitchell, Clarence, Jr., Negro State Senator, Baltimore, Md.

.303 — Mitchell, Edwin H., chairman, Metropolitan Nashville Human Relations Commission.

.304 — Mitchell, William P., executive director, Tuskegee Civic Association, and chairman of the voter franchise committee.

.305 — Moon, Henry Lee, director of public relations, NAACP.

.306 — Moon, Richard (Rev.), Presbyterian university campus minister.

.307 — Moore, Amzie, leader in grass-roots civil rights activities, Mississippi Freedom Democratic Party.

.308 — Moore, Cecil B., president, Philadelphia branch, NAACP.

.309 — Moore, Douglas (Rev.), militant leader in the Washington, D.C., Black United Front; one of the founders of SCLC and SNCC.

.310 — Moore, Ronnie, field secretary, CORE; executive director, Scholarship, Education, and Defense Fund for Racial Equality.

.311 — Morris, Richard, field representative for Senator Mervyn M. Dymally, California Senate.

.312 — Morrisroe, Father Richard, assistant pastor, Holy Name Cathedral, Chicago, Ill.

DC28.313 — Morsell, John, assistant executive director, NAACP.

.314 — Moyer, William H., associate director, Poor People's Campaign.

.315 — Murphy, Alvin, worker with Mexican-Americans through the Catholic Interracial Council, San Jose, Calif.

.316 — Murray, Pauli, member of the faculty, Yale law school.

.317 — Myers, Sherry, Nashville (Tenn.) civil rights activist.

.318 — McClain, Curtis, president, Warehouseman's Union, Local 6, ILWU; chairman, Human Rights Commission, San Francisco, Calif.

.319 — McCoy, Rhody, unit administrator, Ocean Hill-Brownsville School Demonstration Project, New York City.

.320 — McCree, Floyd J., mayor, Flint, Mich.

.321 — McDaniel, Vernon, executive secretary, Negro state teachers' association; NAACP organizer; director of development, Bishop College.

.322 — McDew, Charles F., second chairman of SNCC; consultant with OSTIE, a city planning firm, Cambridge, Mass.

.323 — McDonald, Jimmy, CORE activist.

.324 — McGhee, Silas, SNCC field secretary, Greenwood, Miss.

.325 — McGill, Elzie, founder, Lowndes Co. (Ala.) Co-op, Inc. (1965); leader, Lowndes County Freedom Movement.

.326 — McGill, Elzie (Mrs.), treasurer, Lowndes County Co-op, Inc.

.327 — McGill, Lillian S., field director, Tuskegee Institute Community Education Project; board member, Southwest Alabama Farmers Cooperative Association.

.328 — McKinney, Prentice, member of the Commandos and the Milwaukee Youth Council.

.329 — McKissick, Floyd, national director, CORE; civil rights attorney.

.330 — McKnight, C.A., editor, Charlotte Observer; member of the policy committee, Civil Rights Documentation Project.

.331 — McMillan, Ernest, chairman, Dallas chapter, SNCC.

.332 — Nabrit, James M., president, Howard University.

.333 — Neal, Gaston, co-director, New School for Afro-American Thought, Washington, D.C.

.334 — Nixon, E.D., long-time president of the NAACP in Montgomery, Ala.

.335 — Nixon, John, president, Alabama chapter, NAACP

.336 — Norford, Thomasina J., first full-time black lobbyist on Capitol Hill, while member of Alpha Kappa Alpha Sorority; played major role in desegregating the WAVES and in desegregating the District of Columbia unit of the U.S. Employment Service.

.337 — Offenburger, Thomas Edward, director of department of information, SCLA, Atlanta, Ga.

.338 — Orange, James, coordinator of the eastern section of the Poor People's Campaign; sheriff of Resurrection City.

.339 — Oliveros, Pete, director, San Hidalgo Institute, San Jose, Calif.

.340 — Otey, Inman, leader of activites directed toward fair housing and jobs in Nashville, Tenn.

.341 — O'Boyle, Patrick Cardinal, archbishop of Washington, D.C.

.342 — O'Neal, John, president and founder, the Free Southern Theatre, New York City; SNCC field worker in Mississippi.

.343 — Pacht, Newton, professor of law, Howard University.

.344 — Page, Marion, founder and executive secretary, Albany Movement.

.345 — Parker, J. Allen, president, Alabama Exchange Bank, and member of the City Council, Tuskegee, Ala.

.346 — Parks, Rosa, whose refusal to give up her bus seat led to the Montgomery, Ala., boycott.

.347 — Parris, Guichard, director of public relations, National Urban League.

.348 — Paschall, Eliza, executive director, Metropolitan Atlanta Summit Leadership Congress; leader, Georgia Council on Human Relations.

.349 — Patterson, Eugene, editor, Atlanta Constitution.

.350 — Patton, W.C., director, southern voter registration effort, NAACP.

.351 — Pawley, James A., executive director, Urban League of Essex County, N.J.

.352 — Payne, Nathan, chairman and founder of Orville (Dallas County), Alabama Co-op.

.353 — Peabody, Malcolm E., Jr., director, Inter-Faith Housing Corporation, Boston, Mass.

.354 — Pemberton, John deJ., Jr., executive director, American Civil Liberties Union.

.355 — Pepper, Claude, member, U.S. House of Representatives from Miami, Fla.

.356 — Peters, Joe, benefits coordinator for SCLC; fund raiser, Poor People's Campaign.

.357 — Peterson, James E., administrative assistant to the deputy national coordinator of the Poor People's Campaign.

.358 — Phenix, Roger, Quaker; community black power leader, Johns Island, S.C.

.359 — Phillips, Channing (Rev.), senior minister, Lincoln Congregational Temple, Washington, D.C.

.360 — Phillips, P.B., dean of student affairs, Tuskegee Institute.

.361 — Phillips, Vel, alderman, Milwaukee Common Council.

.362 — Pohlhaus, J. Francis, civil rights attorney and counsel, Washington bureau, NAACP.

.363 — Popham, John N., managing editor, Chattanooga Times, Chattanooga, Tenn.

.364 — Pryor, Downing, chairman, Memphis City Council.

.365 — Puryear, Mahlon, deputy executive director, National Urban League.

.366 — Puryear, Paul, chairman, dept. of political science, Fisk University.

.367 — Ragland, Martha, civil rights worker, Nashville, Tenn.

.368 — Randolph, A. Phillip, president, Brotherhood of Sleeping Car Porters.

.369 — Rauh, Joseph L., Jr., civil liberties lawyer.

.370 — Rawlings, Charles W. (Rev.), director, department of urban affairs, Council of Churches of Greater Cleveland.

.371 — Raymond, George, leader, Mississippi Freedom Democratic Party; freedom rider; chief, CORE forces in Mississippi.

.372 — Reed, Eugene T. (Dr.), leader of the "Young Turk" insurgents within the NAACP.

.373 — Reed, Joe L., executive secretary, Alabama State Teachers Association.

.374 — Reed, Thomas, candidate for mayor of Tuskegee, Ala., and one of the first black candidates to seek election to the Alabama House of Representatives.

.375 — Reese, Frederick (Rev.), civil rights activist in voter registration efforts in Selma, Ala.

.376 — Reid, Herbert, professor of law, Howard University, Washington, D.C.

.377 — Reid, McCann, editor, Tri-State Defender (Memphis, Tenn.), a Negro weekly newspaper associated with the Chicago Defender.

.378 — Reynolds, Raymond J., judge, San Francisco Municipal Court.

.379 — Rich, Marvin, director of community relations, CORE; president of the Scholarship, Education, and Defense Fund.

.380 — Richmond, Isaac (Rev.), community organizer, Beaufort County, S.C.; staff member, Penn Center, Frogmore, S.C., in a program to develop community leaders from the South.

.381 — Rippey, Robert, community organizer, United Planning Organization, Washington, D.C.

.382 — Roberson, Peggy, reporter, Birmingham News.

.383 — Robinson, Cleveland, national president, Negro American Labor Council; international vice-president, Retail and Wholesale Department Store Union, AFL-CIO.

.384 — Robinson, James H., executive director, Operation Crossroads Africa, Inc.

.385 — Robinson, Lewis G., J.F.K. House, Cleveland, Ohio.

.386 — Robinson, Beth, head of J.F. K. House; accused by Cuyahoga (Cleveland) grand jury of participating in the 1966 Hough riot.

.387 — Rogers, Will Henry, Jr., SNCC field secretary in Mississippi and Alabama.

DC28.388 — Romero, Richard, coordinator of the southwest contingent of the Poor People's Campaign, and leader of the Mexican American participants in that campaign (1968).

.389 — Rooke, Elaine L., parent, representative on the governing board, Ocean Hill-Brownsville School Demonstration Project (New York City).

.390 — Rowan, Carl T., author and columnist, Washington, D.C.

.391 — Rudolph, Wilma (Mrs. Robert Eldridge), Olympic champion, winner of three gold medals; administrative analyst, black studies program, UCLA, Los Angeles, Calif.

.392 — Rutherford, John C., administrative coordinator of Resurrection City.

.393 — Salvatori, Henry, campaign manager for Mayor Sam Yorty, Los Angeles (spring, 1969).

.394 — Sanders, Emma, leader, Mississippi Freedom Democratic Party, and a long-time civil rights activist.

.395 — Sampson, Albert (Rev.), SCLC staff member.

.396 — Saunders, Bill, community organizer and staff member, Penn Center, Johns Island, S.C.

.397 — (This number not used).

.398 — Savage, Philip, field secretary, Tri-State NAACP, Philadelphia, Pa.

.399 — Schermer, George, inner-city consultant to the White House.

.400 — Schingle, Frank E., local leader of the John Birch Society, Memphis, Tenn.

.401 — Schneider, Charles, editor, Memphis Press-Scimitar.

.402 — Schwarzchild, Henry, consultant for special projects, the Field Foundation; executive director, Lawyers Constitutional Defense Committee.

.403 — Scott, C.A., publisher, Atlanta Daily World.

.404 — Seale, Bobby, chairman, Black Panther Party.

.405 — Seay, Solomon, Jr., civil rights attorney, Montgomery, Ala., who was deeply involved in the Montgomery bus boycott litigation.

.406 — Seigenthaler, John, editor, Nashville Tennessean; administrative assistant (1961-62) to Attorney-General Robert F. Kennedy.

.407 — Shagaloff, June, education specialist, NAACP.

.408 — Shakow, Patricia Connell, legislative aid to U.S. Senator Jacob Javitts, New York.

.409 — Shannon, Katherine, administrative assistant to the national coordinator, Poor People's Campaign.

.410 — Shores, Arthur, civil rights lawyer, Birmingham, Ala., concerned with desegregation of public education in Alabama.

.411 — Shuttlesworth, Fred L. (Rev.), civil rights activist, Cincinnati, Ohio; pastor, Greater New Light Baptist Church.

.412 — Sias, Henry, Sr., chairman, Mississippi Freedom Democratic Party, Issaquena County; member of delegation which challenged seating of the "regulars" at the 1964 Democratic National Convention.

.413 — Sirles, Charles, community service worker, Economic Opportunity Council, District 4.

.414 — Slainman, Donald, director of civil rights department, AFL-CIO.

.415 — Slarpten, J.R., mayor, Hobson City, Fla.

.416 — Smiley, Glenn E., executive director, Fellowship of Reconciliation.

.417 — Smith, A. Maceo, member of Committee of 14 which led the way in desegregating public accommodations in Dallas; inter-group relations officer, regional office, U.S. Dept. of Housing and Urban Development.

.418 — Smith, Kelly Miller (Rev.), pastor, First Baptist Church, Nashville, Tenn.

.419 — Smith, Lou, director of Operation Bootstrap; staff member of CORE in Philadelphia, Miss., and northeastern U.S.

.420 — Smith, Maxine, executive secretary, Memphis branch, NAACP.

.421 — Smith, Melvin, the only successful Negro MFDP candidate in Issaquena Co., Miss., in November, 1967, elections; elected constable.

.422 — Smith, Robert L.T.S. (Rev.), long-time civil rights activist in the NAACP, Jackson, Miss.

.423 — Smith, S. Edward, director, Maryland Office of Economic Opportunity, Baltimore, Md.

.424 — Smith, Scott B., Jr., executive director, CORE, Englewood (Chicago, Ill.) chapter.

.425 — Smith, Stanley H. (Dr.), chairman, social science division, Tuskegee Institute; consultant for the Civil Rights Documentation Project; member of the Tuskegee City Council, Tuskegee, Ala.

.426 — Speiser, Lawrence, director, Washington, D.C., office, American Civil Liberties Union.

.427 — Spingarn, Arthur B., president, NAACP.

.428 — Stallworth, Edward, director, high school ROTC program, Tuskegee Institute High School.

.429 — Stanford, Gregory, chairman, Students United for Racial Equality, Marquette University, Milwaukee, Wis.

.430 — Stanley, Frank L., Sr., editor-publisher, Louisville Defender, Louisville, Ky.

.431 — Steele, Percy H., Jr., executive director, Bay Area Urban League.

.432 — Stokes, Lewis, lawyer and brother of Carl Stokes, mayor of Cleveland, Ohio.

.433 — Stovall, Charlayne Hunter, among the first Negroes to enroll in the University of Georgia.

.434 — Suarez, Matteo, CORE field secretary, Mississippi.

.435 — Sugarmon, Russel B., Jr., civil rights lawyer who defended demonstrators during the 1960 sit-ins in Memphis, Tenn.

.436 — Sullivan, Leon H. (Rev.), founder and chairman, Opportunities Industrialization Centers, Philadelphia, Pa.

.437 — Sullivan, Neil V. (Dr.), superintendent of Berkeley United School District.

.438 — Taitt, Adelaide L., one of the SNCC activists during the early days of the organization.

.439 — Taylor, William L., staff director, U.S. Commission on Civil Rights, Washington, D.C.

.440 — Thomas, Piri, civil rights leader among the Spanish-speaking minority of Harlem.

.441 — Tijerina, Reis Lopez, one of the leaders of the Mexican-American contingent that participated in the Poor People's Campaign.

.442 — Tillman, Nathaniel P., dean of instruction, Delaware State College, Dover, Del.

.443 — Tillson, John B., treasurer, Protestant Episcopal diocese of Massachusetts.

.444 — Todd, Mollie, civil rights advocate, Nashville, Tenn.

.445 — Tracy, Octavius, director, Upward Bound, University of San Francisco; member, Black Student Union, San Francisco State College.

.446 — Tucker, Sterling, executive director, Washington Urban League.

.447 — Tureaud, A. P., veteran NAACP activist and civil rights attorney, New Orleans, La.

.448 — Turner, Jesse, president, Memphis branch, NAACP.

.449 — Tyus, Wyomie (Mrs. Arthur Simburg), Olympic champion, double gold medal winner; administrative analyst, black studies program, University of California at Los Angeles.

.450 — Unger, Paul, chairman, Cleveland subcommittee, U.S. Commission on Civil Rights.

.451 — Ussery, Wilfred T., national chairman, CORE; president, Black Urban Systems, a consulting firm.

.452 — Vivian, C.T. (Rev.), civil rights activist, SCLC.

.453 — Vorspan, Albert, director, Commission on Social Action of Reform Judaism, Union of American Hebrew Congregations, New York City.

.454 — Waithe, Eldridge, deputy chief inspector, division 6, New York City Police Department.

.455 — Wagner, Frieda, participant in the Poor People's Campaign.

.456 — Walker, A. Maceo, board chairman and president, Universal Life Insurance Company, Memphis, Tenn.

.457 — Walker, Tillie, participant in the Poor People's Campaign.

.458 — Walker, Wyatt Tee (Rev.), participant in the Poor People's Campaign; SCLC.

.459 — Wallace, William (Rev.), co-chairman of the Greenwood (Miss.) Movement in memory of Dr. Martin Luther King, Jr.; SCLC representative in Mississippi; member, loyalist Democratic delegation from Mississippi to the 1968 Democratic convention.

DC28.460 —— Waller, Alfred (Rev.), United Pastors Association, Cleveland.

.461 —— Walmsley, Arthur (Rev.), acting associate director, Department of Christian Social Relations, Executive Council of the Episcopal Church, New York City.

.462 —— Walter, Francis X. (Rev.), director, Selma, Ala., Inter-religious Project, with recollections of the Selma civil rights movement; founder of the Freedom Quilting Bee, a co-op established in Gees Bend, Ala.

.463 —— Warden, Donald, founder, Afro-American Association, San Francisco, Calif.

.464 —— Watkins, Hollis, SNCC field secretary, Mississippi (1961-65).

.465 —— Weaver, Robert C., Secretary, U.S. Dept. of Housing and Urban Development.

.466 —— Welsh, Mike, executive secretary, Southern Student Organizing Committee.

.467 —— Weschsler, Stuart, associate director, Target City, CORE, Baltimore, Md.

.468 —— White, Andrew (Rev.), SCLC, Nashville,

.469 —— Wilcox, Preston, director, Bedford-Stuyvesant Development Services Corporation; observer of the black students revolt during the Columbia University disorders (1968).

.470 —— Wiley, George, executive director, Welfare Rights Organization; associate national director, CORE.

.471 —— Wilkins, Roger, director, Community Relations Service, U.S. Dept. of Justice, Washington, D.C.

.472 —— Wilks, Gertrude, Mothers for Equal Education, Palo Alto, Calif.

.473 —— Williams, James O., eastern regional director, CORE, Philadelphia, Pa.

.474 —— Williams, John A., essayist, journalist, social critic, and author of The Man Who Cried I Am, Night Song, Sissy, and other works.

.475 —— Williams, Rodney E., commanding officer, Community Relations Unit, San Francisco Police Department.

.476 —— Wilmore, Gayraud S. (Rev.), race relations specialist for the Department of Social Justice, United Presbyterian Church.

.477 —— Wilmore, Jacques, director, northeast field office, U.S. Commission on Civil Rights; director of the Commission's Memphis field office.

.478 —— Wirtz, Willard W., Secretary, U.S. Dept. of Labor.

.479 —— Workman, W.D., editor, The State, a South Carolina newspaper, and author of a book supporting the Southern conservative position.

.480 —— Wright, James Skelly, judge, U.S. Circuit Court of Appeals, District of Columbia, who handed down the public school desegregation order in New Orleans, La.

.481 —— Wright, Michael, SNCC coordinator for Macon County, Ala.; student at Tuskegee Institute.

.482 —— Wright, Robert E., SNCC field worker in Alabama and Mississippi; staff associate, Civil Rights Documentation Project.

.483 —— Wurf, Jerry, international president of American Federation of State, County, and Municipal Employees, AFL-CIO.

.484 —— Yancey, P.Q., civil rights worker, Atlanta, Ga.

.485 —— Young, Andrew (Rev.), executive vice-president of SCLC.

.486 —— Young, Pete, newspaperman who is considered an authority on the Ku Klux Klan; played key role in the 1965 confrontation between the United Klans of America and the House Committee on Un-American Activities.

.487 —— Zellner, Bob, Southern Christian Educational Fund.

.488 —— Zinn, Howard, professor of government, Boston University; author of SNCC: The New Abolitionists.

DC29   THE COLLEGE SERVICE BUREAU (1969). 1026 17th St., N.W., 20036. Tel 202 293-6366. George L. Washington, Dir. Copying, typing, inquiries answered, referrals made, consultation. To affiliates only.
The College Service Bureau, supported by the United Negro College Fund and the Phelps-Stokes Fund's Cooperative College Development Program, was established to provide member colleges with a comprehensive service including the latest information and interpretations of federal programs which offer assistance to colleges. Member colleges are, with a few exceptions, those that are historically Negro private and state-supported institutions.

.1   College Service Bureau.
Files, 1969- . Correspondence, minutes of meetings, and other papers concerning the aims and activities of the Bureau.

DC30   THE COMMISSION FOR CATHOLIC MISSIONS AMONG THE COLORED PEOPLE AND THE INDIANS (1877). 2021 H St., N.W., 20006. Rev. J. B. Tennelly, S.S., D.D., Secy. The Commission was established to administer funds collected for the Negro and Indian Catholic missions. The Commission assists in every way possible these missions and schools throughout the United States.
Publ.: Annual Report.

.1   Commission for Catholic Missions among the Colored People and the Indians.
Files, 1877- . Records, reports, correspondence, and other papers concerning the function and activities of the Commission.

DC31   COMMISSIONERS' COUNCIL ON HUMAN RELATIONS (1958). Room 427, Dist. Bldg., 14th and E Sts., N.W., 20004. Tel 202 629-4723. Mrs. Ruth Bates Harris, Exec. Dir. The Council is concerned with employment (private, agencies, and labor), housing, and public accommodations. It advises government agencies; receives and investigates complaints; conciliates; holds public hearings; and runs education programs.

.1   Commissioners' Council on Human Relations.
Files, 1958- . Documentation dealing with the aims, programs, and history of the Council. Includes correspondence, reports, studies, investigations, minutes of meetings, and financial records.

DC32   (This number not used).

DC33   DELTA SIGMA THETA, INC. (1913), DELTA ARCHIVES (1954). 1814 M St., N.W., 20036. Tel 202 338-7727. Mrs. Lynnette Taylor, Exec. Dir.
The Delta Sigma Theta is a public service sorority whose principal purposes and aims are cultural and educational. It engages in public-service programs, and promotes civil rights and social welfare in areas of housing, education, employment, human relations education, public accommodations and social attitudes.
Publ.: The Delta, monthly journal; The Delta Newsletter, monthly.

.1   Delta Sigma Theta, Inc.
Files, 1913- . Includes documentation dealing with the aims, programs, and history of the organization. Correspondence, reports, minutes of meetings, and financial reports are also included. Unavailable to researchers.

DC34   DISTRICT OF COLUMBIA TEACHERS COLLEGE (1954). LIBRARY. 11th and Harvard St., N.W., 20009. Tel 202 629-4598. Imogene J. Byerly, Chief Librn. Interlibrary loan, bibliographies prepared, copying, inquiries answered, referrals made, consultation.

.1   District of Columbia Teachers College.
Archives, 1954- . Included is some source material in the field of education for Negroes in the District of Columbia.

.2   Miner-Wilson Collection.
Materials. Books (ca. 1000 v.), pamphlets, and mss. Primarily collection of rare books and first editions by and about Negroes.

DC35   EDUCATIONAL ASSOCIATES, INC. 1717 Massachusetts Ave., N.W., 20036. Tel 202 483-2600. Sharon A. Isch, Staff Asst.
Educational Associates is a consultant to the Office of Economic Opportunity for Upward Bound.

DC36   EPISCOPAL DIOCESE OF WASHINGTON, DEPARTMENT OF CHRISTIAN SOCIAL RELATIONS   (1798). Church House, Mt. Saint Alban, N.W., 20016. Tel 202 537-0920. Reginald K. Ingram, Sr., Exec. Dir.
The Department works to promote and encourage all

branches of social welfare work in the Diocese of Washington and to serve as an auxiliary to the general and provincial social welfare agencies. Major program areas include housing, education, human relations education, interreligious affairs, social attitudes, and religious instruction.

Publ.: CSR Bulletin, monthly.

DC37   FEDERAL BAR ASSOCIATION, CIVIL RIGHTS COMMITTEE. 1815 H St., N.W., 20006. Tel 202 638-0252. Nathan Lewin, Chmn., Civil Rights Cmt. Service programs for attorneys and the community.
The Association is a national professional organization open to attorneys on the basis of past federal service. The Civil Rights Committee is organized to express interest of the members in civil rights under law and has sponsored nation-wide series of meetings on lawyers' responsibilities for civil rights under law and orientation conference on civil rights legislation.

DC38   FOUNDATION FOR COOPERATIVE HOUSING. 1012 14th St., N.W., 20005. Tel 202 737-3411. Wallace Campbell, Pres.
The Foundation works to stimulate production of non-profit, principally cooperative, low and middle income housing by the following programs: training specialists in the development and management of low and middle income housing, especially nonprofit rental, sales and cooperative; assisting rural communities in the South to develop nonprofit low-cost housing programs using federal mortgage funds available for 50 years at 2 per cent interest; and developing a demonstrative self-help housing project in Charleston, W.Va.

DC39   FRANKLIN DELANO ROOSEVELT FOUR FREEDOMS LIBRARY, B'NAI B'RITH WOMEN (1957). 1640 Rhode Island Ave., N.W., 20036. Tel 202 393-5284. Bernard Neal Klenke, Librn.

.1   The Library includes holdings on such subjects as anti-Semitism, hate groups, and social-economic and liberation movements.

DC40   FREDERICK DOUGLASS INSTITUTE OF NEGRO ARTS AND HISTORY (1966). 316-318 A St., N.E., 20002. Tel 202 547-8690. Warren M. Robbins, Dir.
The Institute sponsors exhibits and lectures reflecting the contributions of the Negro people to the history and culture of the United States, which are also available for use outside of the Institute.
Publ.: Publication list, calendar of Douglass' writings.

.1   Frederick Douglass Institute of Negro Arts and History.
The Institute contains paintings and sculpture by 19th century artists, such as Edward Mitchell Bannister and Edmonia Lewis; books and original furniture of Frederick Douglass; a calendar of the writings of Douglass; and depictions of important personages who by their pioneer efforts and personal achievements have made significant and unusual contributions to the history of America.

DC41   FRIENDS COMMITTEE ON NATIONAL LEGISLATION (FCNL). 245 Second St., N.E., 20002. Tel 202 547-4343. Edward F. Snyder, Exec. Secy.
The Committee is a national private organization which gathers and distributes information and presents views to members of Congress and to Administration. Civil rights, poverty and clearinghouse programs include information in Newsletter, occasional testimony before Committees of Congress, and lobbying activities.
Publ.: FCNL Washington Newsletter, monthly; Action bulletins and staff studies.

DC42   GEORGE WASHINGTON UNIVERSITY, AMERICAN STUDIES PROGRAM. 2108 G St., N.W., 20006. Tel 202 676-6645. R. H. Walker, Dir. Bibliographies prepared, literature searches.
The Department of American Studies is compiling the Rose Bibliography, a computer-stored bibliography of American reform literature published between 1865-1917. It contains comprehensive information concerning Negro life and race relations, covering selected Negro periodicals published during this era.

DC43   GROUP RESEARCH, INC. 1404 New York Ave., N.W., 20005. Tel 202 783-2818.

.1   Group Research, Inc.
Files. Research reports, questionnaires, interviews, leaflets, pamphlets, and other materials relating to investigation of extremist groups in the United States.

DC44   HEALTH AND WELFARE COUNCIL OF THE NATIONAL CAPITAL AREA, INC. (1957). 95 M St., S.W., 20024. Tel 202 554-1333. Isadore Seeman, Exec. Dir. Community planning.
The Council is a private, non-profit organization which plans, develops and coordinates health, welfare, recreation, and related community services for the metropolitan Washington area, working with both public and private agencies; and it studies and seeks to bring to public attention the welfare problems of the community.
Publ.: Newsletter.

DC45   HOUSING OPPORTUNITIES COUNCIL OF METROPOLITAN WASHINGTON (1969). Suite 805, 711 14th St., N.W., 20005. Tel 202 638-5477. James H. Harvey, Exec. Dir. Inquiries answered, referrals made, consultation.
The Council works to make available to black families the same housing options to which white home buyers and apartment renters have access.

DC46   HOWARD UNIVERSITY, BUREAU OF EDUCATIONAL RESEARCH. 20001. Tel 202 387-6100. Walter G. Daniel, Editor-in-Chief.
Publ.: Journal of Negro Education, quarterly.

.1   Bureau of Educational Research.
Files, 1932- . Includes complete run of the Journal of Negro Education; correspondence about, and ms copies of articles run in the Journal.

DC47   HOWARD UNIVERSITY, CENTER FOR COMMUNITY STUDIES, INSTITUTE FOR YOUTH STUDIES. 20001. Tel 202 387-6100. Jacob R. Fishman, Dir.
The Institute operates an inter-disciplinary training center program for personnel working with problems of youth and juvenile delinquency. Specific emphasis is placed on the experimental training of disadvantaged youth for non-professional occupational roles.

DC48   HOWARD UNIVERSITY, FOUNDERS LIBRARY (1867). 2401 Sixth St., N.W., 20001. Tel 202 797-1423. Mrs. Dorothy B. Porter, Supvr, Negro Collection. Interlibrary loan, bibliographies prepared, literature searches, copying, inquiries answered, consultation.

.1   Negro Collection.
Created as "The Moorland Foundation, the Library of Negro Life and History," by the Board of Trustees in 1914, the collection now contains over 100,000 cataloged and indexed items covering the arts, humanities, journalism, social sciences, physical sciences, medicine, and sports. Included are books, periodicals, newspapers, pamphlets, theses and dissertations, mss, correspondence, clippings, photographs, microforms, phonograph and tape recordings, sheet music, memorabilia, and other items. Among the ms collections are the following:

.2   — Anderson, Marian, 1902- .
Papers, 1939. 11 ft. (7,916 items). Singer. Chiefly clippings relating to Miss Anderson and the DAR controversy, together with letters, telegrams, minutes, memoranda, and pictures.

.3   — Ballock, George W.
Papers, ca. 1865-1903. 12 items. Treasurer of Howard University. Account books, cancelled checks, correspondence, pictures, and mss.

.4   — Bethel Literary and Historical Association of Washington, D.C.
Records, 1895-1900. 60 items. Correspondence, minutes, notes, programs, and a history of the Association.

.5   — Brawley, Benjamin Griffith, 1882-1939.
Papers. ca. 300 items. Educator, author, and professor of English at Howard University.

Includes letters, notes, programs, pamphlets,
photographs, newspapers clippings, poems and
essays; and items related to Brawley's father.
Edward McKnight Brawley (11 items).

DC48.6 — Bruce, Blanche Kelso, 1841-98.
Papers, 1870-97. 700 items. Negro politician,
lecturer, and U.S. Senator from Mississippi.
Correspondence, documents, newspaper clippings, family papers, and other material. Most
of the correspondence relates to Bruce's service as Senator (1874-80) and reflects the
political, economic and social conditions in
Mississippi and in the South during Reconstruction. Correspondents include James Hill, John
R. Lynch, P.B.S. Pinchback, and J.J. Spellman.
The material is related to the library's Josephine Wilson Bruce and Roscoe Conkling Bruce
collections.

.7 — Cathcart collection.
Newspaper clippings, given the library by John
W. Cromwell, secretary of the American Negro
Academy.

.8 — Chapman, Charles Edward, 1880- . collector.
Chapman correspondence, 1834-1901. 97
items, in part transcripts. Correspondence of
abolitionists and other individuals. Correspon-
dents include Henry Bowditch, Lewis Hayden,
George W. Julian, J.C. Lovejoy, Samuel Joseph
May, William C. Nell, Edward Philbrick, and
George Putnam.

.9 — Clarkson, Thomas, 1760-1846.
Papers, 1791-1887. 50 items and 1 v., in part
transcripts and microfilm. English philanthropist and abolitionist. Correspondence relating primarily to the abolition of slavery; and
a diary (1791-92) of Clarkson's mission to
America, containing the memorial and petition
of Thomas Peters, free Negro and sergeant in
the Regiment of Guides and Pioneers, serving
in North America under the command of Gen.
Sir Henry Clinton, together with materials on
the efforts of the Sierra Leone Co. to establish
a settlement of free Negroes on the African
coast.

.10 — Cobb, James Adlai, 1876-1958.
Papers, ca. 1917-36. 363 items. Lawyer and
municipal court judge of Washington, D.C.
Correspondence, scrapbooks, newspaper clippings, pictures, and memorabilia. Letters of
endorsement for the position of municipal judge,
recommendations for positions written by and
to Cobb, certificates of appointments, awards
and citations from various organizations.

.11 — Cook, John Francis, d. 1855.
Papers, 1822-92. ca. 60 items, in part transcripts and microfilm copy. Educator and
founder of the Fifteenth Street Presbyterian
Church, Washington, D.C. Correspondence,
diary, newspapers, newspaper clippings, books,
pamphlets, and photographs. Correspondents
include Frederick Douglass and William Lloyd
Garrison.

.12 — Cook, George William, 1855-1931.
Papers. ca. 60 items. Educator, and dean of
the school of commerce and finance at Howard
University. Includes minute book of the Commerical College faculty (1909-12), addresses,
biographical sketches, clippings, correspondence, mss, pictures, poetry, a song and scrapbook. Correspondents include Theodore Roosevelt, Joel E. Spingarn, and W.E.B. DuBois.

.13 — Douglass, Frederick, 1817-95.
Papers. ca. 300 items. Correspondence, ad-
dresses, documents, picture albums, clippings,
poetry, documents, and other papers. Includes
memorabilia. Correspondents include Garrit
Smith, Mordecai W. Johnson, George F. Hoar,
John Van Voorhis, Jeremial E. Rankins, and
Benjamin F. Auld.

.14 — Durker, James Stanley, 1866-1951.
Papers. ca. 393 items. Educator, president of
Howard University (1918-25), and minister. Indentures and other legal papers, correspondence, newspapers (1918), pictures, paintings,

sermons and pastoral prayers, clippings, diaries, and memorabilia.

.15 — Facts on Film.
Papers, 1954-67. Microfilm. Contains ma-
terials on civil rights and race relations in the
South. See Race Relations Information Center,
Nashville, Tenn., for a full description.

.16 — Frazier, E. Franklin, 1894-1962.
Papers. Historian and sociologist. Unavailable until processed.

.17 — Grimké, Angelina Weld, 1880-1958.
Papers, 1887-1958. 13 boxes. Author and
teacher. Correspondence; diaries; mss of
plays, short stories and poems; accounts, receipts, and other financial papers; educational
material such as lesson outlines, school reports and records, notebooks, and official rating
sheets relating to Miss Grimké's ability as a
teacher in the District of Columbia public school
system; memoranda; recipes; addresses; clippings, newspapers, pamphlets, and other printed
matter. Correspondents include Langston
Hughes, Joan Huxtable, Georgia Douglass Johnson, Alain Locke, Martha McAdoo, Emmett
Scott, Ellen B. Stebbins, Butler R. Wilson, Lillie
Buffum Chase Wyman, Cornhill Publishing Co.,
Harper Brothers, Opportunity and Smart Set
magazines. The material is related to the library's Archibald H. Grimké and Francis J.
Grimké collections.

.18 — Grimké, Archibald Henry, 1849-1930.
Papers, ca. 1868-1930. 43 boxes. Lawyer,
editor, author, lecturer, politician, and diplo-
mat. Business, official, and personal cor-
respondence, official papers concerned with
Grimké's service as U.S. consul to Santo
Domingo (1894-98), biographical data, accounts,
speeches, articles, book reviews, memorabilia,
and portraits. Correspondents include Roscoe
Conkling Bruce, Harry T. Burleigh, Anna J.
Cooper, John Cromwell, Mrs. Frederick Doug-
lass, W.E.B. DuBois, Paul Lawrence Dunbar,
J.B. Foraker, Francis J. Grimké, Sarah Moore
Grimké, Sarah Stanley Grimké, James Weldon
Johnson, Martha A. McAdoo, Emery T. Morris,
A.E. Pillsbury, Elizabeth C. Putnam, Joel E.
Spingarn, O.G. Villard, Booker T. Washington,
Angelina Emily (Grimké) Weld, Butler Wilson,
Lillie Buffum Chase Wyman, John Greenleaf
Whittier, American Negro Academy, Associa-
tion for the Study of Negro Life and History,
Committee of Twelve, Cushing Academy, Doug-
lass Memorial House, National Urban League,
U.S. Dept. of the Interior, U.S. Navy Dept., U.S.
State Dept., U.S. War Dept., and the West-
borough State Hospital.

.19 — Grimké, Francis James, 1850-1937.
Papers, 1834-1937. 20 v. and 15 boxes. Pres-
byterian minister, lecturer, and trustee of
Howard University. Chiefly sermons and ad-
dresses (1881-1928) delivered by Grimké as
pastor of the Fifteenth Street Presbyterian
Church in Washington, D.C., some of which are
tributes to Frederick Barbadoes, William Henry
Bruce, Charles W. Chesnutt, John F. Cook,
Louis Alexander Cornish, Thomas Graham
Dorsey, Frederick Douglass, William Lloyd
Garrison, Henry F. Grant, Mrs. Jacobs, John
M. Langston, Martin Luther, Henry P. Montgomery, Charles H. Peters, John B. Reeve,
Theodore Roosevelt, William Warring, George
Washington, and James H. Worden. A few personal papers including a copy of Grimké's will
and letters relating to it, from Carter G. Woodson and Charles A. Booker, executors, to
Grimké's niece, Angelina Grimké; brief biographical sketch on Theodore Dwight Weld;
books on art; and albums of pictures in European galleries, of dried flowers, and of early
photographs. Papers of Grimké's wife,
Charlotte (Forten) Grimké, writer and poet,
include diaries, albums of original poetry by
members of the Forten family, and newspaper
clippings on Robert Purvis, the abolitionist, his

son, C.B. Purvis, of Freedmen's Hospital and Howard University, and the Rev. Anna H. Shaw.

DC48.20 —— Hobson Normal Institute, Parsons, Kansas.
Papers, 1882-96. ca. 29 items. Hobson Normal Institute was established by the Iowa Yearly Meeting of Friends for Colored Students in 1882, to prepare Negro men and women for public life.

.21 —— Home for Destitute Colored Children, Philadelphia, Pa.
Papers. ca. 33 items. Letters, deeds, land titles, memoranda, committee minutes; receipts and note cards from C.F. Harrop.

.22 —— Howard, Oliver Otis, 1830-1909.
Papers, 1850-1906. 5 boxes. Educator, and army officer. Howard was the first president of Howard University (1869-1874); and commissioner of the Bureau of Refugees, Freedmen, and Abandon Lands. Includes correspondence, documents, memorabilia, pictures, articles, mss, addresses, diaries, military orders, and other papers. Correspondents include Abraham Lincoln and J.G. Blaine.

.23 —— Howard University.
Collection of letters from Howard University men in the Armed Forces, 1942-46. 2 ft. (537 items).

.24 —— Howard University.
Papers. ca. 9 boxes. Minutes of trustees (1867-75), executive committee minutes (1867, 1872, 1877), correspondence, plan of organization of Howard Normal and Theological Institute; legal papers, including deeds, leases, and bonds; reports, contracts, and notes of incorporation. Includes correspondence by or related to J.B. Johnson, D.B. Nichols, H.A. Brewster, Charles Brandon Boynton, John H. Combs, E.M. Cushman, A.T. Augusta, Henry H. Garnett, Oliver O. Howard, E. Whittlesley, Shuball Robinson, George W. Ballach, George B. Vashon, J.F. Stockwell, A.L. Barber, S.C. Pomeroy, and John M. Langston.

.25 —— Langworthy, 1864-1932.
Papers, 1916-20. 265 items. Chemist. Correspondence, articles, biographical sketches, memorabilia, and other papers.

.26 —— Lewis, Thomas Narven.
Papers, ca. 1898-1934. 80 items. African scholar and physician. Chiefly letters written by Lewis to Frank Clawson. Samples of the Bassa language, pamphlets pertaining to Storer College, biography of Lewis, other papers, and photographs.

.27 —— Locke, Alain Leroy.
Papers, 1870-1956. 200 boxes. Author and critic, Howard University philosophy professor. Unavailable until processed.

.28 —— Martin, Charles, b. 1850.
Civil War papers, 1864-65. ca 210 items. Soldier. Journal, volunteer lists, general and special orders, blank forms, roll books, muster roll, forms for receipt of clothing, hospital statements, death statements, and poll tax records of Negroes in Louisiana.

.29 —— Miller, Kelly, 1863-1939.
Correspondence, 1914-39. 402 items, in part transcripts. Educator. Relates chiefly to Miller's efforts to establish a National Negro Museum. Correspondents include Edwin Embree, Lloyd Garrison, F.D. Patterson, Julius Rosenwald, William G. Thirkield, and O.G. Villard.

.30 —— Montgomery, William S.
Papers, ca. prior to the Civil War. 12 items. Contains biographical data on William S. and Sarah Montgomery, free persons of color; certificates of marriage; birth and freedom of Richard and Phillis Jenkins; and other papers.

.31 —— Moorland, Jesse Edward.
Papers, 1800-1940. ca. 6000 items. Congregational clergyman of New York.

.32 —— Murray, Freeman Henry Morris, 1859-1950.
Papers. ca. 200 items. Founder, Murray Brothers Printing Company, Washington, D.C. Includes diaries (1884-85, 1885-87, and

1900-02), photographs, transcripts, and other items relating to Horizon magazine, National Association for the Advancement of Colored People, the Niagara Movement, art, and sculpture. Correspondents include W.E.B. DuBois, William Monroe Trotter, and Geraldine Trotter.

.33 —— National Association for the Advancement of Colored People, Washington, D.C. branch.
Papers, ca. 1920-46. 53 boxes. Correspondence, membership papers, clippings, cash books, ledgers, receipts, minutes, financial papers, reports, surveys, legal papers, and periodicals concerning such subjects as lynching, National Negro Congress, education, Citizens' Committee on Race Relations, poll tax, American Council on Race Relations, Fair Employment Practices Commission, housing, Americans for Democratic Action, Congress of Racial Equality, police brutality, armed forces, discrimination, welfare, and relief. Correspondents include Archibald Grimké, Walter White, James E. Scott, Arthur D. Gray.

.34 —— Negro music collection.
Miscellaneous, 1915-35. ca. 200 items. Music mss by Negro composers.

.35 —— Papers relating to slavery and abolition.
Miscellaneous, 1792-1865. ca. 500 items. Letters and documents relating to slavery and abolition.

.36 —— Parker, Theodore, 1810-60.
Papers, 1846-57. ca. 20 items. Abolitionist, teacher. Papers consist of correspondence between Parker and Samuel Gridley Howe.

.37 —— Pinchback, Pinckney Benton Stewart.
Papers, 1867-1901. 2 boxes. Civil War officer, Governor of Louisiana. Unavailable until processed.

.38 —— Pool, Rosey E.
Papers, 1959-61. ca. 759 items. Correspondence, with autobiographical sketches and poems by contributors to Pool's anthology, Beyond the Blues (1963); and some letters concerning another anthology by Pool, I Am the New Negro. Correspondents include Countee Cullen, Waring Cuney, Owen Dodson, Langston Hughes, LeRoi Jones, Ann Petry, Paul Vesey.

.39 —— Promethean Collection.
Papers. ca. 438 items. Application blanks, letters (ca. 150) during World War II from Prometheans (former members of the 2515 SU-AST, Howard University), organization records, financial reports, newsletters, constitution, and receipts.

.40 —— Rankin, Jeremiah Eames, 1828-1904.
Papers. ca. 100 items. Minister, president of Howard University (1889-1903). Includes a few letters, clippings, writings and sermons, book reviews, prose and poetry.

.41 —— Rapier family.
Papers, 1841-83. 90 items, in part transcripts. Correspondence of James Thomas Rapier (1839-84), U.S. Representative from Alabama, John Rapier, Sr., John Rapier, Jr., Richard Rapier, Henry R. Thomas, James P. Thomas, and Sarah Thomas; diary (dating from 1857) of John H. Rapier, journalist, surgeon, and world traveler, containing cash accounts, clippings, and indications of letters written and received; and a Rapier autobiography.

.42 —— Rapier, James Thomas, 1839-84.
Papers, 1856-65. ca. 75 items. Alabama; newspaper correspondent, U.S. Representative.

.43 —— Razaf, Andy (Paul Andreamentania Razafinkeriefo), 1895- .
Papers. 22 items. Grand Duke and nephew of Queen Ranavalona, III, of Madagascar; composer, lyricist. Framed plaques, correspondence, clippings, one record, photograph, scrapbook. Razaf wrote the lyrics for "Hot Chocolates," "Blackbirds of 1930" (Broadway musical), and other lyrics. Includes collection of sheet music by Razaf.

.44 —— Rillieux, Norbert, 1806-94.
Papers. 10 items. Inventor. Includes 6 bio-

graphical typescripts and photostats of articles
that relate indirectly to Rillieux, who helped
revolutionize the Louisiana sugar industry
through his inventions.

DC48.45 — Rock, John S., 1825- ?.
Autograph album. 1 item. Doctor, dentist,
lawyer, justice of the peace, teacher (D.C.
public schools). The album contains autographs of J.M. Langston, Jonathan Gibbs, J.B.
Reeve, Frederick Douglass, J.W.B. Pennington,
Henry Highland Garnett, and others.

.46 — Ruffin, George Lewis, 1834-86.
Papers, 1753-1924. 291 items, in part typescripts and photocopies (negative). Lawyer and
judge. Correspondence, minutes of the Freedman's Lincoln Memorial Association, genealogical and biographical papers of the Ruffin
family, and newspaper clippings on Ruffin's
appointment as judge and on his relationship to
the National Convention of Colored Men. Correspondents include Edward Wilmont Blyden,
George Washington Cable, Samuel Lenox Re-
mond, Florida Ruffin Ridley, John S. Rock, and
George W. Williams.

.47 — Selective Service System.
Newspaper clippings. 18 boxes. The clippings
pertain to World War II, and cover such subjects as armed forces, air corps, army; editorials and special articles, national defense,
navy, race, race relations, selectees (by
military post), veterans, education, employment, Lynn Army Case, National Service.

.48 — Smoot, Maggie Wilson, 1870-1954.
Log book. 1 item. Log book of the travels
(1882-89) of the Fisk Jubilee Singers.

.49 — Spingarn, Arthur Barnett, 1900- .
Papers, 1900-59. ca. 711 items (9 boxes).
Lawyer. Correspondence (371 items), publishers releases, announcements, invitations, programs, book reviews, broadsides, biographical
data, pictures, clippings, and mss.

.50 — Spingarn, Joel Elias, 1875-1939.
Papers. ca. 1069 items, in part, transcripts.
Author, publisher, philanthropist, president of
the National Association for the Advancement
of Colored People. Correspondence; bills,
lists, reports, pictures, and other material on
the Amenia Conference; NAACP papers; constitution, declaration, and other papers of the
Niagara Movement; newspaper clippings; and
an autograph album. The materials are related to the library's Arthur Spingarn collection.

.51 — Summers, Henry Howard.
Papers, 1896-1939. 124 items, in part, transcripts. Methodist minister and educator.
Programs of various African Episcopal
churches which Summers served as pastor or
guest speaker; programs and other papers of
Oberlin College, Payne Theological Seminary,
and Wilberforce University; biography of
Bishop David Henry Sims and notes relating to
his work; and other papers largely concerned
with Summers' activities as student, minister,
and educator.

.52 — Terrell, Mary Church, 1863-1954.
Papers, 1895-1953. 203 items. Negro leader
and author. Correspondence, clippings, newspaper articles, pamphlets, broadsides, and
other printed matter, and other papers chiefly
relating to the National Association of Colored
Women, of which Mrs. Terrell was first national president. Articles about Mrs. Terrell's
husband, District of Columbia Municipal Court
Judge, Robert H. Terrell, copies of minutes
(1935-36) of the Race Relations Federation of
Churches and letters addressed to Olivia
Davidson Washington (Mrs. Booker T. Washington).

.53 — Turner, Edward Walter, 1850-1927.
Papers. 50 items. Teacher, employee of the
Post Office Department, principal of Kittrell
Academy (1884-90), founder of Federation of
Men's Church Clubs of D.C., and participant in
founding Cliff Rock Beneficial Association.

Announcements, documents, periodicals, correspondence, pictures, programs, reports,
memorabilia, and 2 day books (expenditures
1871-72, and travel log 1877).

.54 — Turner, Henry McNeal, Bp., 1834-1915.
Papers, 1889-1915. 46 items. Methodist
clergyman and first commissioned Negro chaplain in the U.S. Army. Chiefly biographical
material. Addresses, petitions, announcements,
programs, memorials, newspapers, newspaper
clippings, and photographs.

.55 — U.S. Colored Troops.
Papers, 1860-65. 430 v. Includes records of
Negro troops in the Civil War.

.56 — Waring, J. Waties.
Papers, 1945-64. ca. 16,000 items. Federal
judge. Contains the personal papers of Waring
including paintings, photographs, plaques, citations, correspondence, mss, typescripts,
speeches, programs, reports, telegrams, post
cards, greeting cards, periodicals, clippings,
memoranda, documents, briefs, pamphlets,
bulletins, and memorabilia.

.57 — Washington, Booker T., 1859-1915.
Correspondence, 1889-92. Contains 12 photo-
static items relating to George Washington
Cable, chiefly letters.

.58 — Whipper, Leigh. collector.
Theatre collection. 7 boxes (ca. 632 items).
Correspondence, programs, announcements,
clippings, broadsides, souvenir programs,
Negro Actors Guild items, Screen Actors Guild,
typescript of Uncle Tom's Castle, invitations,
and pictures.

.59 — White, Jacob C.
Papers, 1857-1914. 2 ft. (447 items). Educator
and Negro leader. Correspondence and memo-
rabilia. Correspondents include Jonathan C.
Gibbs, Richard T. Greener, Chester T. Morris,
William Nesbit, and George B. Vashon.

.60 — Williams, Daniel Hale.
Papers, 1900-40. 5 vf. Illinois surgeon. Unavailable until processed.

.61 — Works Progress Administration.
Papers, 1934-51. 9 boxes (ca. 7,993 items).
Mss and reports of, and correspondence to
assistants and commissioners of the Works
Progress Administration, Harry L. Hopkins,
Alfred E. Smith, Col. Frank, and Col. Harrington, concerning welfare, relief, labor, the
Negro in federal government agencies, defense employment and Negro workers, rural
Negroes and rehabilitation, Negro WPA, and
the Negro and relief. The Administration was
later renamed the Work Projects Administration.

.62 — Wright, Louis T.
Papers, 1898-1950. 8 vf. New York surgeon.
Unavailable until processed.

DC49   HOWARD UNIVERSITY, SMALL BUSINESS GUIDANCE CEN-
TER. Box 533, 20001. Tel 202 797-1731. Dr. Wilford
L. White, Dir.
The Center is establishing an institute for minority
business education and will bring together and evaluate
material on management systems programs and disseminate their findings to interested groups across the
country.

DC50   INSTITUTE FOR AMERICAN DEMOCRACY. 1330 Massachusetts Ave., N.W., 20005. Tel 202 737-1226. Franklin H.
Littell, Chmn.
The Institute is a research and action organization which
promotes the study of extremist groups and supplies the
public with information concerning these groups. Research includes such groups as the Ku Klux Klan, the
John Birch Society, Minute Men and the Citizens Council.

DC51   INSTITUTE FOR SERVICES TO EDUCATION, INC. 1527
New Hampshire Ave., N.W., 20036. Tel 202 232-7175.
Dr. Elias Blake, Jr., Pres.
Publ.: Expanding Opportunities, quarterly newsletter on
the Negro and higher education, formerly pub-
lished by the American Council on Education.

DC52   INSTITUTE ON AMERICAN FREEDOMS (1965). 1901 F St.,
        N.W., 20006. Tel 202 783-4943. Dr. Daniel M. Berman,
        Exec. Dir.
        The Institute conducts research on civil liberties; pub-
        lishes essays on civil liberties problems for mass dis-
        tribution.

        .1 Institute on American Freedoms.
            Files, 1965- . Correspondence, financial records,
            studies, reports, essays, and other materials deal-
            ing with the aims, history, and programs of the In-
            stitute.

DC53   INTERNATIONAL UNION OF ELECTRICAL WORKERS,
        CIVIL RIGHTS COMMITTEE. 1126 16th St., N.W.,
        20006. Tel 202 296-1200.

DC54   JOINT ACTION IN COMMUNITY SERVICE, INC. (JACS).
        Suite 500, 1730 M St., N.W., 20036. Tel 202 223-0912.
        B. J. Roberts, Exec. Dir. Inquiries answered, refer-
        rals made, consultation.
        JACS recruits, organizes and trains local community
        volunteers to offer personal assistance to persons from
        poverty, unemployed or educationally disadvantaged
        backgrounds.
        Publ.: JACS Volunteer, monthly newsletter.

DC55   LAWYERS' COMMITTEE FOR CIVIL RIGHTS UNDER LAW
        (1963). Suite 1001, 1660 L St., N.W., 20036. Tel 202
        464-6618. Robert L. Nelson, Exec. Dir.
        The Committee is an ad hoc committee of lawyers
        established to provide legal assistance to individuals
        who cannot obtain counsel because of civil rights activi-
        ties, to develop educational programs within state and
        local bar associations, and to carry on demonstration
        projects in police-community relations.

DC56   LEADERSHIP CONFERENCE ON CIVIL RIGHTS (LCCR)
        (1950). 2027 Massachusetts Ave., N.W., 20036. Tel 202
        667-1780. Marvin Caplan, Dir., Washington Office.
        The Conference, formerly the National Council for a
        Permanent FEPC: National Emergency Civil Rights
        Mobilization, is a voluntary, non-partisan association of
        autonomous national organizations seeking to advance
        civil rights for all Americans through government ac-
        tion at the national level. Activities include lobbying
        for legislation and working for the enforcement of such
        legislation.
        Publ.: LCCR Memo, bi-weekly; pamphlets; brochures.

        .1 Leadership Conference on Civil Rights.
            Files. Correspondence, minutes of meetings, finan-
            cial records, studies, reports, and other materials
            concerning the aims, programs, and history of the
            Conference.

DC57   LEAGUE OF WOMEN VOTERS OF THE UNITED STATES.
        1730 M St., N.W., 20036. Tel 202 296-1770. Miss Dixie
        Drake, Exec. Secy.
        The League, a national nonpartisan political action
        group, conducts studies of housing, employment and ed-
        ucation. It is also interested in local and state prob-
        lems involving public education, housing, and employ-
        ment. Voters service activities include informing the
        voter of registration and voting procedures, publishing
        and distributing factual material on candidates and bal-
        lot issues, conducting public meetings of candidates for
        elective offices.
        Publ.: Publications list, reports, and pamphlets.

DC58   LIBERTY LOBBY (1955). 300 Independence Ave., S.E.,
        20003. Tel 202 546-5611. Col. Curtis B. Dall, Chmn.,
        Bd. of Policy.
        "Liberty Lobby is a pressure group for patriotism- the
        only lobby registered with Congress which is wholly
        dedicated to the advancement of governmental policies
        based on our Constitution and Conservative principles."
        It was organized "for the purpose of reversing the dan-
        gerous trend toward socialization internally and to de-
        feat the insidious effort to weaken our resistance to
        international Communism."
        Publ.: Liberty Letter, monthly newsletter; Liberty Low-
        down, monthly report; special publications.

DC59   MEDICAL COMMITTEE FOR HUMAN RIGHTS. 3410 Taylor,
        20009. Tel 202 654-3808.

The Committee, a national private organization, provides medical aid to civil rights organizations and
workers. Involved in organizing rural health centers
and mobile health units; active in Mississippi during
summer of 1964 and the Meredith March of June, 1966;
and worked with the Poor People's Campaign, June,
1968.
Publ.: Health Rights, newsletter.

DC60   MUSEUM OF AFRICAN ART (1964). 316-318 A St., N.E.,
        20002. Tel 202 547-0324. Warren M. Robbins, Dir.

        .1 The Museum of African Art contains more than 2000
            works of traditional African sculpture, masks, and
            musical instruments, including a special gallery
            where the influence of African sculpture on the
            modern art of the Western world is demonstrated
            through the juxtaposition of African sculpture and
            Western paintings. The Museum also contains a
            small reference library on African art and culture.

DC61   NATIONAL ALLIANCE OF BUSINESSMEN (NAB) (1968).
        726 Jackson Place, N.W., 20006. Tel 202 395-3000.
        Donald M. Kendall, Chmn.
        NAB is a group of business executives formed to aid
        the federal government in finding jobs for men—chiefly
        black men from the urban ghettos. The program of NAB
        is Job Opportunities in the Business Sector (JOBS),
        which emphasizes job training and job finding.

        .1 National Alliance of Businessmen (NAB).
            Files, 1968- . Records, reports, minutes of meet-
            ings, correspondence and other papers concerning
            the aims of the organization.

DC62   NATIONAL ASSOCIATION FOR COMMUNITY DEVELOP-
        MENT (NACD). 1424 16th St., N.W., 20036. Tel 202
        667-9138. Robert A. Aleshire, Exec. Dir. Copying, in-
        quiries answered, referrals made.
        NACD stimulates and assists in the effort to provide
        equal opportunity through education, job training, neigh-
        borhood organization, agricultural and business develop-
        ment, and programs of special social services. Pro-
        motes professional competence and growth in adminis-
        tration of state and local community development of
        human resources among charitable and educational in-
        stitutions.
        Publ.: Community Development, monthly newspaper;
               NACD News, bi-weekly newsletter; News from
               NACD, bi-weekly newsletter.

        .1 National Association for Community Development
            (NACD).
            Miscellaneous. Subject areas include legal ser-
            vices, rural programs, housing, neighborhood cen-
            ters, VISTA publications, legislative (reference)
            materials, government agency publications and gen-
            eral reference.

DC63   NATIONAL ASSOCIATION FOR THE ADVANCEMENT OF
        COLORED PEOPLE (NAACP), WASHINGTON OFFICE.
        422 First St., S.E., 20003. Tel 202 544-5694. Clar-
        ence Mitchell, Dir.

DC64   NATIONAL ASSOCIATION OF COLORED GIRLS CLUBS
        (NACGC) (1930). 1601 R St., N.W., 20009. Tel 202
        332-8160. Carole A. Early, Hq. Secy.
        NACGC is sponsored by the National Association of
        Colored Women's Clubs "to begin training toward
        moral, mental and material development of its mem-
        bers; to give girls the right conceptions of health,
        beauty, love, home and service."
        Publ.: National Notes.

        .1 National Association of Colored Girls Clubs (NACGC).
            Files, 1930- . Correspondence, minutes of meet-
            ings, financial records, and other materials deal-
            ing with the aims, history, and programs of NACGC.

DC65   NATIONAL ASSOCIATION OF COLORED WOMEN'S CLUBS,
        INC. (1896). 1601 R St., N.W., 20009. Tel 202 332-8160.
        Mrs Carole A. Early, Hq. Secy.
        The Association is a national social and human relation
        group with a legislative program to keep members in-
        formed on matters affecting women and minority groups
        in the areas of education, housing, employment, public

accommodations. Affiliated with the National Council of Women of the U.S. and the International Council of Women of the World.
Publ.: Newsletters, reports.

DC66   NATIONAL ASSOCIATION OF HOUSING AND REDEVELOP-
MENT OFFICIALS. The Watergate Bldg., 2600 Virginia Ave., N.W., 20037. Tel 202 333-5651.
The Association's project areas include employment, housing, urban renewal and metropolitan development.

DC67   NATIONAL ASSOCIATION OF INTERGROUP RELATIONS
OFFICIALS (NAIRO) (1947). 2027 Massachusetts Ave., N.W., 20036. Tel 202 387-7050. Penelope L. Wright, Acting Staff Dir. Inquiries answered, referrals made, consultation.
NAIRO is concerned with improving skills and standards of practice of professionals involved in areas of civil rights, civil liberties, and intergroup relations.
Publ.: Newsletter, bi-monthly; Journal of Intergroup Relations, quarterly; A Directory of Intergroup Relations Agencies, 1969.

.1   National Association of Intergroup Relations Officials.
Files, 1947- . Includes correspondence, minutes of meetings and conferences, financial records, documentation dealing with the aims, history, and programs of the Association.

DC68   NATIONAL ASSOCIATION OF MARKET DEVELOPERS
(NAMD). P.O. Box 2826, 20013. Tel 202 332-4655. Burt E. Jackson, Exec. Dir.
NAMD is a professional, non-profit organization, composed primarily of sales promotion, advertising and public relations officials, which sponsors annual clinics, seminars, and special conferences featuring significant trends and developments affecting the Negro consumer market.
Publ.: NAMD Emphasis.

DC69   NATIONAL ASSOCIATION OF REAL ESTATE BROKERS,
INC. (NAREB). Suite 1111, 1025 Vermont Ave., N.W., 20005. Tel 202 638-1280. Leon Cox, Jr., Dir.
NAREB was organized to establish and maintain ethical standards of professional conduct; to mobilize public sentiment against restrictions on mortgage financing for Negro home owners, and to urge open occupancy and improved housing conditions for minority groups.

DC70   NATIONAL BANKERS ASSOCIATION (NBA). 4812 Georgia
Ave., N.W., 20011. Tel 202 332-9200. B. Doyle Mitchell, Pres.
The Association, which is composed of banking institutions owned, operated or controlled by Negroes, including banks with biracial officers, studies and interprets new and existing banking legislation affecting members, depositors, and business patrons.

DC71   NATIONAL BEAUTY CULTURISTS LEAGUE, INC. 25 Logan
Circle, N.W., 20005. Tel 202 332-2695. Dr. Katie E. Whickam, Pres.
The League, a predominantly Negro organization, seeks to raise the standards of the beauty profession in order to maintain the confidence of the public and distributes informative educational material among its members.

DC72   NATIONAL BUSINESS LEAGUE (NBL) (1900). 3418 Georgia
Ave., N.W., 20010. Tel 202 726-6300. Berkeley G. Burrell, Pres.
NBL, founded by Booker T. Washington, organized to stimulate business and to promote the industrial, commerical and general economic welfare of Negroes in the U.S.; to foster civic and racial pride; to promote inter-racial cooperation in the economic sphere and to encourage national participation in all matters calculated to enhance the economic progress of Negro Americans.
Formerly National Negro Business League.

DC73   NATIONAL CENTER FOR DISPUTE SETTLEMENT OF THE
AMERICAN ARBITRATION ASSOCIATION (1968). 1819 H St., N.W., 20006. Tel 202 659-5650. Willoughby Abner, Dir. Literature searches, copying, inquiries answered, consultation.
The Center was established to apply mediation and arbitration techniques to areas of social conflict. It has

worked with officials in several major cities to include dispute settlement techniques in their Model Cities programs, advised the National Education Association on merging segregated affiliates into an integrated organization, and has begun a formal training program for mediators and arbitrators at Federal City College in Washington, D.C. Projected activities include developing grievance and hearings procedures for public housing tenants, compiling a national panel of impartial persons to serve in community disputes, and expanding a program for public employee collective bargaining.

.1   National Center for Dispute Settlement.
Files, containing complete information on dispute settlement, including literature on arbitration, mediation, and subjects mentioned above.

DC74   NATIONAL CIVIL LIBERTIES CLEARING HOUSE (1948).
Room 217, 1346 Connecticut Ave., N.W., 20036. Tel 202 293-5466. Mrs. Mary Alice Baldinger, Exec. Dir.
The Clearing House, an association of national organizations, seeks to develop public enlightenment and concern, and disseminate factual reports and educational materials on issues of national importance in the fields of civil liberties, civil rights, and intellectual freedom.
Publ.: Civil Liberties Bulletin, bi-monthly.

.1   National Civil Liberties Clearing House.
Files, 1948- . Includes correspondence, minutes of meetings and conferences, documentation dealing with the aims, history, and programs of the organization, reports, studies, and financial records.

DC75   NATIONAL COMMITTEE FOR CHILDREN AND YOUTH.
Room 504, 1145 19th St., N.W., 20036. Tel 202 338-3057. Mrs. Isabella J. Jones, Exec. Dir.
The Committee was organized to provide channels for communication and sharing of information regarding needs and problems of children and youth through cooperation among national voluntary organizations, national and state public agencies, and state committees for children and youth; and through experimental projects, new techniques, unconventional approaches, and training and use of indigenous personnel. It has been involved in civil rights, poverty, and clearinghouse programs.
Publ.: Publications on topic of children and youth.

DC76   NATIONAL COMMITTEE ON HOUSEHOLD EMPLOYMENT.
1346 Connecticut Ave., N.W., 20036. Tel 202 223-5240. Miss Edith Barksdale, Exec. Dir.
The Committee assists local groups with training programs and the organization of self-sustaining enterprises.

DC77   THE NATIONAL CONFERENCE OF CHRISTIANS AND JEWS,
(NCCJ), WASHINGTON NATIONAL OFFICE. 636 Southern Bldg., 20005. Tel 202 737-5353. Leonard P. Aries, V.Pres.

DC78   THE NATIONAL CONFERENCE OF CHRISTIANS AND
JEWS (NCCJ), WASHINGTON REGIONAL OFFICE. 1425 H St., N.W., 20005. Tel 202 628-9141. Donald F. Sullivan, Exec. Dir. Inquiries answered, consultation.
NCCJ is a civic organization engaged in a program intended to help achieve justice and equality of opportunity for all, to bridge the gaps between groups, and to train and prepare leaders for the intergroup relations aspects of urban living. NCCJ's operations in the Washington area include but are not limited to programs in the fields of youth activities, police-community relations, and equal opportunity in employment, housing, and education.

DC79   NATIONAL COUNCIL OF CATHOLIC WOMEN (1919). 1312
Massachusetts Ave., N.W., 20005. Tel 202 659-6810. Miss Margaret Mealey, Exec. Dir.
The Council is a church-affliliated educational organization, interested in education, housing, and social welfare programs.
Publ.: News From the Hill, legislative newsletter; Word, magazine.

.1   National Council of Catholic Women.
Files, 1920- . Records include such subjects as civil rights legislation, equality of educational opportunities, open housing, welfare and relief, employment, race and poverty.

DC80   NATIONAL COUNCIL OF NEGRO WOMEN, INC. (1935).
Suite 832, 1346 Connecticut Ave., N.W., 20036. Tel 202
223-2363. Miss Dorothy I. Height, Nat. Pres.
The Council is a charitable and educational organization
which works to eliminate prejudice and discrimination,
reduce neighborhood tensions, strengthen family life,
and combat juvenile delinquency. Projects include
Workshops in Mississippi, Technical Assistance Housing
Program in Mississippi, Volunteers Unlimited, Woman-
power, voter education and registration.
Publ.: Newsletters, press releases, quarterly publication, special reports on civil rights problems.

DC81   NATIONAL COUNCIL OF THE CHURCHES OF CHRIST IN
THE U.S.A., DEPARTMENT OF SOCIAL JUSTICE. 110
Maryland Ave., N.E., 20002. Tel 202 544-2350.

DC82   NATIONAL EDUCATION ASSOCIATION (NEA), CENTER
FOR HUMAN RELATIONS (1963). 1201 16th St., N.W.,
20036. Tel 202 223-9400. Samuel B. Ethridge, Asst.
Exec. Secy. Bibliographies prepared, inquiries answered, referrals made, consultation, distribution of
materials.
The Center coordinates the human rights efforts of the
internal units of the NEA, the regional field offices, and
the organizations outside the NEA. It develops programs to reduce problems arising from mergers of
local and state NEA affiliates. Formerly the Professional Rights and Responsibilities Committee on Civil
and Human Rights of Educators.
Publ.: Numerous publications on human relations,
equality of educational opportunity, multi-ethnic
teaching materials, and investigation reports involving areas of civil rights concerns.

DC83   NATIONAL LEAGUE OF CITIES AND THE UNITED STATES
CONFERENCE OF MAYORS, NLC-USCM RESEARCH
LIBRARY (1969). Room 1200, 1612 K St., N.W., 20006.
Tel 202 628-3440. Patrick Healy, Exec. Dir. Interli-
brary loan, inquiries answered.
Local government-university alliance is a goal of the
National League of Cities. Mayors and university pro-
fessors are collaborating to develop and test an urban
research and community services system in at least six
metropolitan areas.
Publ.: Nation's Cities, monthly magazine; Reports, con-
ference proceedings, bulletins.

    .1 Urban Affairs Collection.
        Books (ca. 3500) and journals (300), vertical file
        materials (ca. 500 subject catagories) covering all
        major aspects of urban affairs and life.

DC84   NATIONAL MEDICAL ASSOCIATION. 520 W St., N.W.,
20001. Tel 202 232-1604. Samuel C. Smith, Admin.
Secy.
The Association, a professional society predominantly
made up of Negro physicians, supports activities of civil
rights groups through medical services, counsel, and
financial contributions and is concerned with integration
of all medical societies, medical schools, and hospitals.
Publ.: Bi-monthly journal.

DC85   NATIONAL PHARMACEUTICAL ASSOCIATION, INC. (1947).
Howard University College of Pharmacy, 20001. Tel
202 387-6100. Chauncey I. Cooper, Exec. Secy.
The Association promotes and stimulates scientific and
professional interests of Negroes in American pharmacy and encourages sound business operations among
its 2000 members.

    .1 National Pharmaceutical Association, Inc.
        Files, 1947- . Includes correspondence, minutes of
        meetings, financial records, and other documents
        dealing with the history, aims, and program of the
        Association.

DC86   NATIONAL TECHNICAL ASSOCIATION, INC. (NTA). 3310
Georgia Ave., N.W., 20010. Tel 202 882-8815. Raymond
M. Jones, Exec. Dir. and Secy.
NTA collects and disseminates information concerning
the opportunities in architecture, engineering, science
and related fields: seeks to aid and encourage youth in
preparation for these fields of work; promotes interest
in the professions; and breaks down discriminatory
barriers.

    .1 National Technical Association, Inc. (NTA).
        Files. Includes correspondence, minutes of meet-
        ings, financial records, and other materials dealing
        with the aims, history and programs of NTA.

DC87   NATIONAL TENANTS ORGANIZATION. 711 14th St., N.W.,
20005. Tel 202 347-3358.

DC88   NATIONAL UNITED LICENSED BEVERAGE ASSOCIATION,
INC. (ULBA). 1940 Ninth St., 20001. Tel 202 265-3610.
Garland Pinkston, Pres.
ULBA is a trade association composed of licensed retail
establishments engaged in the sale and distribution of
beverages and other products for public consumption.
It seeks to improve customer relations and managerial
operations; pledges to maintain uniformity in commercial usages; and stresses high levels of business
integrity.

    .1 National United Licensed Beverage Association, Inc.
        (ULBA).
        Files. Includes correspondence, minutes of meet-
        ings, financial records, and other documents deal-
        ing with the aims, history, and programs of ULBA.

DC89   NATIONAL URBAN LEAGUE, INC., FIELD SERVICES OF-
FICE. 1424 16th St., N.W., 20036. Tel 202 265-9277
Sterling Tucker, Dir.

    .1 National Urban League, Field Services Office.
        Files. Records, reports, correspondence, and
        other papers pertaining to the programs and aims
        of the National Urban League and its affiliates.

DC90   NATIONAL URBAN LEAGUE, WASHINGTON BUREAU. Suite
624, 777 14th St., N.W., 20005. Tel 202 393-4332. Mrs.
Cenoria D. Johnson, Dir.

DC91   NATIONAL WELFARE RIGHTS ORGANIZATION, POVERTY-
RIGHTS ACTION CENTER (1966). 1762 Corcoran St.,
N.W., 20009. Tel 202 462-8804. Dr. George A. Wiley,
Exec. Dir.
Organization of welfare recipients and other poor people
made up of affiliated local welfare rights organizations
from the entire country. The Poverty-Rights Action
Center, a private, nonprofit, independent group, is responsible for developing the National Welfare Rights
Movement. Goals of NWRO are: jobs or income (decent
jobs for those who can work and adequate income for
those who cannot work); dignity; justice and democracy
for welfare recipients and other low-income persons.
Publ.: NOW, newspaper; Press Packets, weekly mailings which contain press releases, photographs,
news clippings, and other NWRO publications.

DC92   THE NEGRO BIBLIOGRAPHIC AND RESEARCH CENTER,
INC. (1965). 117 R St., N.E., 20002. Tel 202 232-5006.
Beatrice M. Murphy, Dir. Bibliographies prepared.
The Center is a nonprofit, nongovernmental, nonpoliti-
cal organization created to centralize information about
writings on the Negro, and further the knowledge of the
history, achievements, aims, and problems of the race.
Publ.: Bibliographic Survey: The Negro in Print, bi-
monthly.

    .1 Negro Bibliographic and Research Center, Inc.
        Files, 1965- . Correspondence, books, pamphlets,
        newspapers, periodicals, phonograph records, and
        other items concerning the Negro and race prob-
        lems. Closed to researchers.

DC93   NEIGHBORS, INC. (1957), NORTH WASHINGTON NEIGH-
BORS INC. 6400 Georgia Ave., N.W., 20012. Tel 202
726-3454. David Bogucki, Exec. Dir.
The North Washington Neighbors seeks to maintain and
improve their integrated community, to generally promote integrated communities and an open society, and
to combat discrimination and defend civil liberties.
Publ.: Neighbors Ink, monthly newsletter; Annual Report; pamphlets, brochures, and other informational material about housing, and the organization and its activities.

DC94   NEW SCHOOL FOR AFRO-AMERICAN THOUGHT. 2208
14th St., N.W., 20009. Tel 202 387-9653. Gaston Neal,
Organizer.

The New School offers courses in African and Afro-American history, poetry, and literature, dance, drama, the history of jazz and rock 'n roll and speech, diction and vocabulary.

DC95   NEW THING ART AND ARCHITECTURE CENTER (1967). 2335 18th St., N.W., 20009. Tel 202 332-4500. Topper Carew, Dir. Literature searches, inquiries answered, consultation.
The center is a non-profit cultural organization working with inner-city black youths in the arts: film, photography, dance, creative writing, art, ceramics, fashion design.
Publ.: Films and slide series.

.1 New Thing Art and Architecture Center.
Materials. Included are films, photos, papers, children's and adults' writings about the urban black experience, and information on black arts. Restricted.

DC96   NORTHWEST WASHINGTON FAIR HOUSING ASSOCIATION, INC. (1966). 5804 Georgia Ave., N.W., 20011. Tel 202 966-0808. Harry Conn, Pres.

DC97   OMEGA PSI PHI FRATERNITY. 2714 Georgia Ave., N.W., 20001. Tel 202 667-7158. H. Carl Moultrie I, Esq., Nat. Exec. Secy.
Omega Psi Phi is a national fraternity whose Social Association Committee develops civil rights programs involving employment, housing, public accommodations, and political action.
Publ.: The Oracle, quarterly.

DC98   PHILLIPS GALLERY. 1612 21st St., N.W., 20009. Tel 202 387-2151.

.1 Lawrence, Jacob, 1917- .
The Gallery holds 30 of Lawrence's 60 panels on the "Migration of the Negro." The others are in the Museum of Modern Art, New York City.

DC99   POTOMAC INSTITUTE (1961), LIBRARY (1961). 1501 18th St., N.W., 20036. Tel 202 332-5566. Harold C. Fleming, Pres. Consultation.
The Institute is concerned with developing human resources by expanding opportunities for racial and economically deprived minorities through advisory and research services to government and private agencies involved in the development of minority programs. The primary interests are the affirmative responsibility of government and the role of the private sector of national life in upgrading minorities through bold and imaginative programs.
Publ.: Reports and studies on civil rights problems and poverty.
.1 Potomac Institute.
Files, 1961- . Includes documentation dealing with the aim, history, and programs of the Institute. Among papers are correspondence, reports, studies, investigations, and other materials related to race relations. Restricted.

DC100   PRIDE, INC. 1536 U St., N.W., 20009. Tel 202 483-1900. Marion Barry, Co-dir.
PRIDE, Inc., is a black-pride, self-help enterprise to train underemployed persons. Projects of the organization include several gas stations, a car service center, a candy factory, and landscaping service.

.1 PRIDE, Inc.
Files. Records, reports, correspondence, and other papers concerning the aims and activities of the organization.

DC101   RACIAL STUDIES COMMITTEE (1969). 204 Third St., S.E., 20003. Louis R. Andrews, Exec. Dir.
The Committee works to foster interest in the study of race and racial problems among college and high school students by making literature on the subject of race available free and/or at a reduced price to students and groups of students who indicate both the proper interest in and the potential for such studies and by establishing racial study groups on campuses. It seeks to counteract "the total failure of the Liberal approach to peaceful and constructive race relations."

DC102   ST. JOSEPH'S SEMINARY LIBRARY (1893). 1200 Varnum St., N.E., 20017. Tel 202 526-4231. Rev. Robert E. McCall, Librn.

.1 Negrology collection.
Special collection of material by and about Negroes. Restricted.

DC103   SEVENTH DAY ADVENTISTS, DEPARTMENT OF EDUCATION. 6840 Eastern Ave., N.W., 20012. Tel 202 743-0800. Dr. Charles Bittirsch, Secy., Dept. of Educ.

.1 Department of Education.
Files, 1896- . Correspondence, minutes of board meetings, financial records, and other materials relating to the support of Oakwood College, Huntsville, Ala.

DC104   SOUTHERN CHRISTIAN LEADERSHIP CONFERENCE (SCLC), WASHINGTON OFFICE. 812 S St., N.W., 20001. Tel 202 387-3517. Rev. Walter Fountroy, Dir.

DC105   SPONSORS OF OPEN HOUSING INVESTMENT (1964). Room 807, 1914 Connecticut Ave., N.W., 20009. Tel 202 265-9448. Mrs. Anne W. Shull, Admin. Dir.
Sponsors of Open Housing Investment seeks to educate Americans to implement their beliefs in furthering equality when choosing an investment or a home. Formerly the National Committee on Tithing Investment.
Publ.: SOHI Newsletter, periodically.

.1 Sponsors of Open Housing Investment.
Files, 1964- . Records, correspondence, reports, and other materials concerning the operation and activities of the organization, including files on integrated neighborhoods in America.

DC106   STUDENT NATIONAL COORDINATING COMMITTEE (SNCC), WASHINGTON OFFICE. 2204 14th St., N.W., 20009. Tel 202 387-7445. Lester McKinnie, Dir.

DC107   TRINITY COLLEGE, URBAN EDUCATION CENTER (1967). Michigan Ave. and Franklin, N.E., 20017. Tel 202 269-2000.
The Clinical Training Center in the District's Model School Division represents the first section of Trinity's projected Urban Education Center. Teacher trainees in the Trinity program and teachers in the schools will work together in the Center to develop new materials, curricula and techniques geared to inner-city children.

DC108   THE UNITED CHURCH OF CHRIST, COUNCIL FOR CHRISTIAN SOCIAL ACTION (1961), WASHINGTON OFFICE. 110 Maryland Ave., N.E., 20002. Tel 202 543-1517. Tilford E. Dudley, Dir., Washington Office. Inquiries answered, consultation.
The Council assists church instrumentalities and members to maintain familiarity with social issues and government action or inaction, and maintains channels of communication with government representatives and officials and church bodies.
Publ.: Washington Report, semi-monthly newsletter.

.1 Council for Christian Social Action.
Materials. 18 vf and 50 ft. Included are files of clippings and printed materials on such issues as civil rights, civil liberties, urban problems, housing, hunger, Vietnam, foreign aid and development, domestic vs military priorities, taxation, and government appointments. Also included are books, pamphlets, government reports, and transcripts of hearings on civil rights and liberties, poverty, and other related subjects.

DC109   THE UNITED METHODIST CHURCH, BOARD OF CHRISTIAN SOCIAL CONCERNS, DIVISION OF HUMAN RELATIONS. 100 Maryland Ave., N.E., 20002. Tel 202 543-7722. Dr. Earnest A. Smith, Assoc. Gen. Secy. Inquiries answered, referrals made, consultation.
The Division conducts a program of research, education and action centering around the following Christian social concerns: race relations, civil liberties, public policy on education, church and state relations, civic responsibility, labor-management relations, agriculture, conservation, government and private economic policy and practice, technological changes, unemployment,

housing, and such other concerns as the Board may specify.
Publ.: Engage, bi-weekly.

DC110   UNITED METHODIST COMMISSION ON RELIGION AND RACE (1968). 100 Maryland Ave., N.E., 20002. Tel 202 546-1000. Rev. Woodie W. White, Exec. Secy.

DC111   UNITED PLANNING ORGANIZATION (UPO). 1100 Vermont Ave., N.W., 20005. Tel 202 659-1100. Gary Bellow, Dep. Exec.
UPO is designed to improve life in decaying urban neighborhoods through various groups which work on tutoring projects, recreation programs, community-police relations, and negotiations with city agencies for neighborhood improvements.

    .1   United Planning Organization (UPO).
Files. Correspondence, minutes of meetings, financial records, and other material dealing with the aims, history, and programs of UPO.

DC112   U.S. ADVISORY COMMISSION ON INTERGOVERNMENTAL RELATIONS (1959). 726 Jackson Place, N.W., 20575. Tel 202 393-3111. William G. Colman, Exec. Dir. Inquiries answered, referrals made.
The Commission is an independent, permanent, bi-partisan body established by an Act of Congress to provide technical assistance in the review of proposed legislation in areas of public works, mass transportation, urban area problems, administrative controls for federal grant programs, and other areas requiring intergovernmental cooperation.
Publ.: Technical reports, publications list.

    .1   The Commission's library maintains a collection of books, journals, pamphlets, bibliographies, catalogs, and other informations on federal and state aid programs.

DC113   U.S. ATOMIC ENERGY COMMISSION (1946). 1717 H St., N.W., 20545. Tel 301 973-3793. Marion A. Bowden, Asst. to the Gen. Mgr. for Equal Opportunity Progs.

    .1   Equal Employment Opportunity Office.
Files. Records, reports, correspondence, and other papers concerning equal employment programs, contract compliance, Title VI and federal employment in the Commission. Restricted.

DC114   U.S. BUREAU OF THE BUDGET, HUMAN RESOURCES PROGRAMS DIVISION. New Executive Office Bldg. (FOB 7), 20006. Tel 202 395-4742. Richard P. Nathan, Asst. Dir., Bur. of the Budget.

    .1   Human Resources Programs Division.
Files. Correspondence, reports, records, and other papers concerning the operation and programs of the Division. Restricted.

DC115   U.S. CIVIL AERONAUTICS BOARD. 1825 Connecticut Ave., N.W., 20428. Tel 202 382-7631. Albert Schulze, Dir., Equal Employ. Opportunity.

    .1   U.S. Civil Aeronautics Board.
Equal Employment Opportunity files. Records, reports, correspondence, and other papers concerning equal employment opportunity activities of the Board. Restricted.

DC116   U.S. CIVIL SERVICE COMMISSION. 1900 E St., N.W., 20415. Tel 202 632-6111. N. J. Oganovic, Coordinator for Equal Opportunity in Fed. Employ.

    .1   U.S. Civil Service Commission.
Equal opportunity program files. Reports, records, correspondence, and other papers concerning equal opportunity in federal employment.

DC117   U.S. CIVIL SERVICE COMMISSION (1883), LIBRARY. 1900 E St., N.W., 20415. Tel 202 632-4432. Mrs. Elaine L. Woodruff, Librn. Interlibrary loan, bibliographies prepared, literature searches, copying, typing, inquiries answered, referrals made, consultation.
The Commission is the central personnel agency for the executive branch of the federal government. It administers the merit system under the Civil Service Act of

1883 and is responsible for government-wide leadership in personnel management. It is responsible for leadership and supervision of the program for equal employment opportunity in the federal government, including provision for the prompt, fair, and impartial consideration of all complaints of discrimination in federal employment. Under the supervision of the Commission, special programs are conducted to provide training and employment to youth and to the disadvantaged. Other responsibilities of the Commission include voter listing under the Voting Rights Act of 1965, personnel investigations, enforcement of political activity restrictions, and establishing job qualifications standards.

    .1   U.S. Civil Service Commission Library.
Books, pamphlets, reports, magazine articles, background reference material, and other publications. Comprehensive collection of materials on equal opportunity in the federal government, including information on employment programs for minority groups, employment practices, the Negro in professional and executive positions, and minority groups in federal, state and local governments.

DC118   U.S. COMMISSION ON CIVIL RIGHTS (1957), DOCUMENTATION CENTER (reorganized in 1969). 1405 Eye St., N.W., 20425. Tel 202 382-3392. James D. Williams, Dir., Office of Info. Interlibrary loan, bibliographies prepared, literature searches, copying, inquiries answered, referrals made.
The Commission is an independent, bi-partisan, fact-finding agency which investigates violations of civil rights, studies and collects information concerning legal developments constituting a denial of equal protection of the laws under the Constitution; appraises Federal laws and policies with respect to equal protection of the laws; investigates allegations of vote fraud; and acts as a clearinghouse for civil rights information.
Publ.: Civil Rights Directory; annually; Transcripts of hearings and conferences; Civil Rights Digest; Staff reports; State advisory committee reports; Films; Clearinghouse reports, in such areas as school desegregation, mobility in the Negro community, and racial isolation in public schools.

    .1   Documentation Center.
The Center serves as a repository for basic current data on civil rights and other closely related topics: human, intergroup, and community relations; federal programs in civil rights; federal social welfare programs; demographic statistical programs; and the disciplines of the social and behavioral sciences, the humanities, and law as they concern the above topics. Materials include books (ca. 5300 v.), periodicals (274 titles), pamphlets (1500 v.), vf (12), theses and dissertations (200 v.), and correspondence (9 vf).

    .2   —— Facts on Film.
Papers, 1954-67. Microfilm. Contains materials on civil rights and race relations in the South. See Race Relations Information Center, Nashville, Tenn., for a full description.

DC119   U.S. COMMISSION ON CIVIL RIGHTS, MID-ATLANTIC FIELD OFFICE (1969). 1405 Eye St., N.W., 20425. Tel 202 382-2631. Jacob Schlitt, Dir. Inquiries answered, referrals made, consultation.
The Mid-Atlantic Field Office of the Commission on Civil Rights covers the states of Pennsylvania, West Virginia, Virginia, North Carolina, Maryland, and Delaware.
Publ.: State advisory committee reports.

DC120   U.S. COUNCIL FOR URBAN AFFAIRS (1969). 1600 Pennsylvania Ave., N.W., 20500. Tel 202 456-2880. Daniel P. Moynihan, Exec. Secy.
The Council assists the President in the development of a national urban policy, promotes the coordination of federal programs in urban areas, and encourages cooperation between federal, state, and city governments with special concern for maintenance of local initiative and local decisionmaking. It also ensures that policies concerning urban affairs are cognizant of programs affecting urban, suburban, and rural areas, and assists

the President during emergency situations or under conditions threatening the maintenance of civil order or civil rights.

DC121   U.S. DEPARTMENT OF AGRICULTURE. 14th St. and Independence Ave., S.W., 20250. Tel 202 388-4256. William M. Seabron, Asst. to the Secy. for Civil Rights.

    .1   U.S. Department of Agriculture.
Civil rights files. Records, reports, correspondence, and other materials concerning the civil rights activities of the Department. Includes materials pertaining to contract compliance and Title VI. Restricted.

DC122   U.S. DEPARTMENT OF AGRICULTURE, ECONOMIC RESEARCH SERVICE, ECONOMIC DEVELOPMENT DIVISION. 14th St. and Independence Ave., S.W., 20250. Tel 202 388-3693. William C. Motes, Dir.
In cooperation with the Office of Economic Opportunity, the Economic Research Service is conducting an ongoing research program on the problems of rural poverty, including typologies, resources, migration, and factors related to human resources and program development among rural poverty groups. Records restricted.

DC123   U.S. DEPARTMENT OF AGRICULTURE, NATIONAL AGRICULTURAL LIBRARY (1862). 14th St. and Independence Ave., S.W., 20250. Tel 202 388-3434. Foster E. Mohrhardt, Librn.

    .1   National Agricultural Library.
Among the holdings of the library are materials on agricultural societies, organizations, cooperatives, and government institutions; rural sociology; and the economic and sociological aspects of agriculture in general, among many other subjects.

DC124   U.S. DEPARTMENT OF AGRICULTURE, OFFICE OF PERSONNEL. 14 St. and Independence Ave., S.W., 20250. Tel 202 388-3585. Carl B. Barnes, Dir. of Personnel.

    .1   Office of Personnel.
Files. Records, correspondence, reports and other papers, including materials relating to the Equal Employment Opportunity programs and activities of the Department. Records unavailable.

DC125   U.S. DEPARTMENT OF AGRICULTURE, RURAL COMMUNITY DEVELOPMENT SERVICE. 14th St. and Independence Ave., 20250. Tel 202 388-7235. D. R. Matthews, Dep. Adminstr.

    .1   Rural Community Development Service.
Files. Records, correspondence, reports and other materials concerning the operation and activities of the Service in connection with minority groups.

DC126   U.S. DEPARTMENT OF COMMERCE, BUREAU OF THE CENSUS (1902), LIBRARY. Room 2455, Federal Office Bldg. #3 (Mail Address: Bureau of the Census, Washington, D.C. 20233). Tel 301 440-1314. Dorothy W. Kaufman, Librn. Interlibrary loan, bibliographies prepared, literature searches, copying, inquiries answered, referrals made.
The Bureau collects, tabulates, and publishes a wide variety of statistical data and provides statistical information about the people and the economy of the Nation in order to assist the government and the public generally in planning, carrying out, and evaluating their active program.
Publ.: U.S. Census publications; Bureau of the Census Catalog, quarterly, with monthly supplements; Bureau of the Census Library Notes.

    .1   U.S. Bureau of the Census Library.
Among the holdings of the Library are books, pamphlets, serials, a collection of state and local government documents, and a collection of documents from federal agencies and commissions. Much of this material includes information about the non-white population. Race relations materials can be located through specific subject cards in the public catalog.

    .2   —   U.S. Census publications.
Materials, 1790- . From the first census report (1790), which shows the number of slaves by county or similar area, to the latest census and current population surveys, these reports are valuable primary sources of statistics on minority groups. Among subjects covered in current census materials are, for the Negro population, employment, income of families, military participation, mobility, occupation, poverty-non-poverty areas, voter participation, residence, school enrollment, socio-economic status, educational attainment, living conditions and health, and conditions in low-income areas.

DC127   U.S. DEPARTMENT OF COMMERCE, DIVISION OF TITLE VI, CONTRACT COMPLIANCE, FEDERAL EMPLOYMENT AND DIRECT FEDERAL PROGRAMS. 14th and Constitution Ave., N.W., 20230. Tel 202 967-5049. Luther C. Steward, Jr., Equal Opportunity Coordinator.

    .1   U.S. Department of Commerce.
Equal opportunity files. Records, reports, correspondence, and other papers concerning equal employment opportunity programs, title VI, contract compliances and other federal employment programs.

DC128   U.S. DEPARTMENT OF COMMERCE, ECONOMIC DEVELOPMENT ADMINISTRATION. 14th St. and Constitution Ave., N.W., 20007. Tel 202 783-9200. Percy H. Williams, Dir.
The primary function of the Administration is the long-range economic development of areas and regions of substantial and persistent unemployment and underemployment and low-family income. It creats new employment opportunities by developing and expanding facilities and enterprises in such areas and regions.

    .1   Economic Development Administration.
Files. Records, reports, correspondence, program plans and evaluations, and other papers concerning the functions of the Administration.

DC129   U.S. DEPARTMENT OF COMMERCE, OFFICE OF MINORITY BUSINESS ENTERPRISE (1969). 14th St. and Constitution Ave., N.W., 20230. Tel 202 783-9200. A.S. Venable, Dep. Dir.
The objectives of the Office are to provide a central point for all federal assistance programs, to attempt to mobilize private-sector involvement, and to act as an information center for programs in this area.

    .1   Office of Minority Business Enterprise.
Files, 1969- . Records, reports, correspondence, and other papers concerning the programs and aims of the Office.

DC130   U.S. DEPARTMENT OF DEFENSE, DEPARTMENT OF THE ARMY, ARMY LIBRARY (1944). Room 1 A 518, The Pentagon, 20310. Tel 202 695-5346. O.W. Holloway, Dir. Interlibrary loan, bibliographies prepared, literature searches, inquiries answered.

    .1   Army Library.
In the holdings of the Library is a collection of military unit histories, containing materials concerning Negro troops, and extensive military and congressional documents, containing materials pertaining to discrimination in the Armed Forces.

DC131   U.S. DEPARTMENT OF DEFENSE, DIRECTORATE FOR CIVIL DISTURBANCE PLANNING AND OPERATIONS. The Pentagon, 20301. Tel 202 645-6700. Col. William N. Hon, Dir.
The Director of Civil Disturbance Planning and Operations advises the Secretary of the Army and the Chief of Staff on military support in all matters relating to civil disturbances and riot control. Under the command of the Directorate are civil disturbance watch teams, which survey the U.S. for riots and outbreaks of disturbance. The watch teams maintain dossiers on 150 crucial cities in the nation where racial eruptions could occur, including such information as maps, names and telephone numbers of local public and civic leaders, location of utilities and power substations, data on assembly areas for troops, transportation, concentrations of black and other low-income residents and detention centers in addition to conventional jails. Records restricted.

DC132   U.S. DEPARTMENT OF DEFENSE, OFFICE FOR CIVIL
         RIGHTS. The Pentagon, 20301. Tel 202 695-0110. L.
         Howard Bennett, Acting Dep. Asst. Secy. of Defense
         (Civil Rights). Inquiries answered, referrals made,
         consultation.
         The Deputy Assistant Secretary of Defense concentrates
         upon the policy of the Department of Defense programs
         for assuring equality of treatment and opportunity for
         all military and civilian personnel. In performance of
         this function, the Deputy shall be the representative of
         the Secretary of Defense in civil rights matters, give
         direction to programs that promote equal opportunity for
         military and civilian personnel, provide policy guidance
         and review policies, regulations and manuals of the mil-
         itary departments, and monitor their performance
         through periodic reports and visits to field installations.
         Publ.: Reports and studies concerning integration and
                equal opportunities in the Armed Forces.

     .1 Office for Civil Rights.
         Files. ca. 190 cu. ft. Records, reports, correspon-
         dence, and other papers concerning equal opportu-
         nity in the Armed Forces, including material on
         Title VI, contract compliance and federal employ-
         ment. Restricted.

DC133   U.S. DEPARTMENT OF HEALTH, EDUCATION, AND WEL-
         FARE; HEALTH SERVICES AND MENTAL HEALTH
         ADMINISTRATION; NATIONAL CENTER FOR HEALTH
         STATISTICS. 330 Independence Ave., S.W., 20201. Tel
         202 962-3278. Theodore D. Woolsey, Dir.
         The Center provides a factual statistical basis for plan-
         ning national programs designed to advance the health
         and well-being of the American people. Functions and
         responsibilities of the Center include, among many
         others, analysis and interpretation of health data to re-
         flect demographic and socioeconomic factors; stimula-
         tion of expansion of data for analytical studies; the
         development of indexes of health; household surveys to
         obtain data on health and demographic factors related to
         illness, injuries, disability and costs and uses of medi-
         cal services; analysis and interpretation of vital statis-
         tics; and analysis of health resources.
         Publ.: Monthly Vital Statistics Report; Vital and Health
                Statistics Series, studies in a wide range of sub-
                ject areas, many of which include data by race.

DC134   U.S. DEPARTMENT OF HEALTH, EDUCATION, AND WEL-
         FARE, LIBRARY (1953). 330 Independence Ave., S.W.,
         20201. Tel 202 963-3631. Kanardy L. Taylor, Librn.
         Interlibrary loan.

     .1 U.S. Department of Health, Education, and Welfare Li-
         brary.
         Among books, periodicals, reports of public and
         private agencies, and the complete file of Office of
         Education publications, are considerable materials
         relating to Negroes and education, welfare, health,
         and law.

DC135   U.S. DEPARTMENT OF HEALTH, EDUCATION, AND WEL-
         FARE; OFFICE FOR CIVIL RIGHTS (1966), INFORMA-
         TION DIVISION-RESOURCES AND MATERIALS UNIT.
         Room 3210, Regional Office, Bldg. #3, Seventh and D
         Sts., S.W., 20202. Tel 202 962-0740. Mrs. Mary Lou
         Watkins, Librn. Inquiries answered, referrals made.
         The Office for Civil Rights is responsible for the admin-
         istration of departmental policies under Title VI of the
         Civil Rights Act of 1964, which prohibits discrimination
         on account of race, color or national origin in any pro-
         gram or activity receiving federal assistance.
         Publ.: OCR Newsletter.

     .1 Office for Civil Rights.
         Files, 1966- . Records, correspondence, reports,
         and other papers concerning the operation and
         activities of the Office.

     .2 —— Information Division.
         Materials. Included are books, periodicals,
         pamphlets, clippings, films, and materials in
         the general area of civil rights. Clipping files
         (1964- .) are maintained in a variety of cate-
         gories and by state on civil rights progress.
         An area of special strength lies in materials
         (unpublished) related to the implementation of

Titles IV and VI of the Civil Rights Act of 1964.
Use of clipping files restricted.

     .3 —— Facts on Film.
         Papers, 1954-67. Microfilm. Contains materi-
         als on civil rights and race relations in the
         South. See Race Relations Information Center,
         Nashville, Tenn., for a full description.

DC136   U.S. DEPARTMENT OF HEALTH, EDUCATION, AND WEL-
         FARE; OFFICE OF EDUCATION; NATIONAL CENTER
         FOR EDUCATIONAL RESEARCH AND DEVELOPMENT;
         EDUCATIONAL RESOURCES INFORMATION CENTER
         (ERIC) (1965). 400 Maryland Ave., S.W., 20202. Tel 202
         963-1110. Harvey Marron, Dir.
         ERIC is a nationwide decentralized information system
         designed to help advance research and development on
         educational programs and processes and to accelerate
         widespread adoption of research-based educational pro-
         grams. Through a nationwide network of 19 subject
         oriented clearinghouses, material is screened, indexed
         and abstracted and disseminated. The full text of most
         documents processed into the ERIC system is sold by
         the ERIC Document Reproduction Service in both micro-
         fiche and hardcopy form.
         Publ.: Research in Education, monthly abstracting jour-
                nal; Current Index to Journals in Education,
                monthly; Specialized collections including a spe-
                cial Disadvantaged Collection; Clearinghouse
                state-of-the-art papers, newsletters, and bibli-
                ographies.

     .1 Educational Resources Information Center (ERIC).
         The ERIC clearinghouses cover the whole spectrum
         of education. Among the types of materials avail-
         able through ERIC are: from the Clearinghouse on
         the Disadvantaged, research reports and other
         documents on the educational, psychological, social,
         and general development of urban children and
         youth who are socially, economically, or culturally
         disadvantaged; through the Clearinghouse on Voca-
         tional and Technical Education, research documents
         on the general field of vocational and technical edu-
         cation; research reports on formal and informal
         adult and continuing education through the Clearing-
         house for Adult and Continuing Education; and from
         the Clearinghouse on Rural Education and Small
         Schools, research documents on the organization,
         administration, curriculum, innovative programs
         and other aspects of small schools and rural educa-
         tion in general. Current document collection is
         approximately 30,000 documents; 11,300 documents
         were added during fiscal year 1969.

DC137   U.S. DEPARTMENT OF HEALTH, EDUCATION, AND WEL-
         FARE; OFFICE OF EDUCATION; NATIONAL CENTER
         FOR EDUCATIONAL STATISTICS. 400 Maryland Ave.,
         S.W., 20202. Tel 202 963-6901. W. Vance Grant, Spe-
         cialist, Educational Statist.
         The Center collects, analyzes, and disseminates statis-
         tics on education at all levels and provides consulting
         and advisory services on educational data processing to
         the education community.
         Publ.: Directory Public Schools in Large Districts (with
                enrollment and staff, by race); Digest of Educa-
                tional Statistics, annual.

     .1 National Center for Educational Statistics.
         Files. Includes materials concerned with the edu-
         cational opportunities of minority groups and data
         on institutions of higher education attended predom-
         inantly by Negro students and also some statistics
         on the enrollment and educational attainment of
         white and nonwhite persons.

DC138   U.S. DEPARTMENT OF HEALTH, EDUCATION, AND WEL-
         FARE; OFFICE OF EDUCATION; OFFICE OF PRO-
         GRAMS FOR THE DISADVANTAGED. 400 Maryland
         Ave., S.W., 20202. Tel 202 962-5121. Regina Goff,
         Asst. Cmnr.
         The Office of Programs for the Disadvantaged provides
         leadership for and program data on federal educational
         programs for the disadvantaged, concentrating on Office
         of Education and Office of Economic Opportunity pro-
         grams designed for such populations. It formally com-
         municates with the disadvantaged and their representa-

tives to improve knowledge at the local level regarding
relevant Office of Education programs and to receive
constant feedback concerning the operation of these programs.

Publ.: Newsletter - About OE Programs for the Disadvantaged; Descriptions of research and demonstration programs, and programs in job training
and retraining.

.1   Office of Programs for the Disadvantaged.
Files. Included are studies and reports, such as
Recommendations of Grass-Roots Conferences
Sponsored by the Office of the Disadvantaged; Voca-
tional Training, Employment and Unemployment,
containing national trends (1969), profiles of the
states (1969) and profiles of 30 American cities;
Profiles of Fifty Major American Cities; and State
Profiles on School Dropouts, Juvenile Delinquents,
Unemployed Youth and Related Federal Programs
(1966).

DC139   U.S. DEPARTMENT OF HEALTH, EDUCATION, AND WEL-
FARE; OFFICE OF EDUCATION; TEACHER CORPS
(1965). Seventh and D Sts., S.W., 20202. Tel 202 962-
6303. Richard A. Graham, Dir., Teacher Corps. Inquiries answered.
Publ.: Handbooks, guidelines, pamphlets and other materials discriptive of the Teacher Corps.

.1   Teacher Corps.
Files, 1966- . Records, correspondence, reports,
and other papers concerning the operation and activities of the Teacher Corps. Includes materials
about economically disadvantaged youth and education in predominantly black school areas. Restricted. Formerly National Teacher Corps.

DC140   U.S. DEPARTMENT OF HEALTH, EDUCATION, AND WEL-
FARE; SOCIAL AND REHABILITATION SERVICE (1967).
330 Independence Ave., S.W., 20201. Tel 202 963-1110.
Mary E. Switzer, Admn. Inquiries answered, referrals
made, consultation.
The Social and Rehabilitation Service administers the
federal programs providing technical, consultative, and
financial support to states, local communities, other
organizations and individuals in the provision of social
services, rehabilitation, income maintenance, medical,
families and child welfare, and other necessary services
to aged and aging, children and youth, the disabled, and
families in need.

.1   Social and Rehabilitation Service.
Files, 1967- . Records, reports, correspondence,
and other materials relating to the programs administered by the Service, including information
about Aid to Families with Dependent Children, and
medical care programs.

DC141   U.S. DEPARTMENT OF HOUSING AND URBAN DEVELOP-
MENT (HUD), COMMUNITY DEVELOPMENT INFOR-
MATION CENTER (1966). 1626 K St., N.W., 20410.
Tel 202 755-6420. Harrison Knapp, Dir. Inquiries
answered, referrals made, consultation.
The Center is part of a program to provide more direct
service to anyone seeking answers and guidance on
housing and urban affairs from the U.S. Government.
It provides direct contact with the various offices and
programs of the Department of Housing and Urban
Development, and with urban-related activities elsewhere in the federal government. The Center's clearinghouse service is designed to supply technical assistance and information covering all aspects of housing and
urban development. It disseminates the results of research, study and demonstration programs of HUD.

DC142   U.S. DEPARTMENT OF HOUSING AND URBAN DEVELOP-
MENT (HUD), LIBRARY. Seventh and D Sts., S.W.,
20410. Tel 202 755-6376. Mrs. Elsa S. Freeman, Dir.
Interlibrary loan, bibliographies prepared, literature
searches, copying, inquiries answered, referrals made,
consultation.
Publ.: Housing and Planning References, bi-monthly;
Bibliographies, including research on equal opportunity in housing.

.1   U.S. Department of Housing and Urban Development Library.

Contains books, periodicals, newspapers, pamphlets,
theses and dissertations, and films about race relations in connection with housing, city planning, and
urban renewal.

DC143   U.S. DEPARTMENT OF HOUSING AND URBAN DEVELOP-
MENT (HUD), MODEL CITIES ADMINISTRATION (1966).
451 Seventh Ave., S.W., 20410. Tel 202 655-4000.
Walter G. Farr, Dir.

.1   Model Cities Administration.
Files, 1966- . Records, correspondence, reports,
and other materials concerning the operation and
activities of the Administration. Includes information on black neighborhoods in which there are
Model Cities programs.

DC144   U.S. DEPARTMENT OF HOUSING AND URBAN DEVELOP-
MENT (HUD), OFFICE OF THE ASSISTANT SECRE-
TARY FOR EQUAL OPPORTUNITY. 451 Seventh St.,
N.W., 20410. Tel 202 655-4000. Samuel J. Simmons,
Asst. Secy.
The Office of the Assistant Secretary for Equal Opportunity is concerned with equal opportunity in housing, public facilities and employment. The Office administers
the federal fair housing law, works to assure equal employment opportunity practices by the Department and
its contractors, and encourages the development of minority job and business opportunities, as well as assures
equal opportunity in the administration of programs receiving financial assistance from HUD.
Publ.: Educational brochures on fair housing, low-
income housing, and equal employment opportunities.

.1   Office of the Assistant Secretary for Equal Opportunity.
Files. Records, reports, correspondence, and other
papers concerning the civil rights functions of the
Office, including materials arising from investigations under the fair housing law. Restricted.

DC145   U.S. DEPARTMENT OF JUSTICE, BUREAU OF NARCOTICS
AND DANGEROUS DRUGS, LIBRARY. Room 601, 1405 I
St., N.W., 20537. Tel 202 382-5706. Mrs. Jane N. Zack,
Librn. Interlibrary loan, inquiries answered.
The Bureau engages in drug abuse prevention and con-
trol through education and enforcement.

.1   Bureau of Narcotics and Dangerous Drugs Library.
The Library has general and legal collection of materials concerning the history of narcotics and
dangerous drugs, their abuse and control, enforcement, treatment, and international aspects of the
problems; also included is some material relating
to narcotics and drug abuse in the Negro population.

DC146   U.S. DEPARTMENT OF JUSTICE, BUREAU OF PRISONS,
CENTRAL OFFICE LIBRARY. Room 400, 101 Indiana
Ave., N.W., 20537. Tel 202 737-8200. Lloyd W. Hooker,
Librn. Interlibrary loan, inquiries answered.

.1   Central Office Library.
Among holdings are books, periodicals, booklets,
brochures, indexes, and statistical summaries concerning crime and offenders, criminals, juvenile
delinquency, penology, corrections and related subjects, including material on Negro Americans.

DC147   U.S. DEPARTMENT OF JUSTICE, CIVIL RIGHTS DIVISION.
Tenth and Pennsylvania Ave., S.W., 20530. Tel 202 737-
8200. Jerris Leonard, Asst. Attorney Gen.
The Civil Rights Division enforces civil rights laws and
executive orders prohibiting discrimination, authorizes
intervention in cases brought by private litigants involving the denial of equal protection of the laws on account
of race, among other responsibilities.

.1   Civil Rights Division.
Files. Records, reports, correspondence, briefs,
and other legal papers concerning investigations
and court cases conducted by the Division. Restricted.

DC148   U.S. DEPARTMENT OF JUSTICE, COMMUNITY RELATIONS
SERVICE (CRS) (1964). Ninth St. and Pennsylvania
Ave., S.W., 20530. Tel 202 386-6214. Benjamin F.
Holman, Dir.
CRS assists communities in coping with difficulties

arising from intergroup tensions. It also helps communities identify their social problems, develop their own resources for problem-solving, make use of federal programs and services, and encourages minority group participation in decision-making. CRS has worked in the areas of employment, education, model cities and housing, police-community relations, media relations, and crisis aid. Programs are carried out by the Divisions of Field Services and Support Services through five regional offices and 19 field offices.
Publ.: Annual Report.

.1 Community Relations Service.
Files, 1964- . Records, reports, correspondence, studies, and other materials concerning the activities and programs of the Service.

.2 —— Media Library.
Pamphlets, clippings, films, and tape recordings concerning media-community relations and media coverage of racial incidents. Includes press clippings giving examples of different media practices in covering race relations, and programs designed to improve race relations.

DC149 U.S. DEPARTMENT OF JUSTICE; FEDERAL BUREAU OF INVESTIGATION (FBI); FILES AND COMMUNICATIONS DIVISION. Ninth St. and Pennsylvania Ave., S.W., 20535. Tel 202 393-7100. William S. Tavel, Asst. Dir.
FBI has charge of investigating all violations of federal laws with the exception of those which have been assigned by legislative enactment or executive order to another federal agency. Among the matters over which the FBI has jurisdiction are subversive activities, election law and civil rights violations.

.1 Files and Communications Division.
Files. Records, reports, correspondence, and other papers relating to the investigation of civil rights matters and other pertinent subjects. Unavailable to researchers.

DC150 U.S. DEPARTMENT OF JUSTICE, MAIN LIBRARY. Ninth St. and Pennsylvania Ave., S.W., 20535. Tel 202 737-8200. Marvin P. Hogan, Librn.

.1 U.S. Department of Justice Library.
Among the holdings of the Library are books, pamphlets, articles, reports and other materials about civil rights cases and acts.

DC151 U.S. DEPARTMENT OF LABOR. 14th and Constitution Ave., N.W., 20219. Tel 202 961-2003. Jack Howard, Coordinator of Civil Rights Activities.

.1 U.S. Department of Labor.
Civil rights files. Records, correspondence, reports, and other papers concerning civil rights activities of the Department, including material on equal employment opportunity programs and Title VI and contract compliance. Restricted.

DC152 U.S. DEPARTMENT OF LABOR; BUREAU OF LABOR STATISTICS; DIVISION OF ECONOMIC STUDIES. 441 G St., N.W., 20212. Tel 202 961-2913. Dorothy K. Newman, Asst. Chief. Inquiries answered.
The Division of Economic Studies seeks to provide new insights into social and economic issues and to provide leadership in attacking the problems of poverty, unemployment, and underemployment through intensive research. The Division selects and assembles primary data for analysis, and prepares articles, bulletins, and reports for publication.
Publ.: Pamphlets, reports, and other literature.

.1 Division of Economic Studies.
Pamphlets, mss, correspondence, articles, and memoranda concerning black Americans in relation to problems of poverty, unemployment, underemployment, and other related subjects. Correspondence restricted.

DC153 U.S. DEPARTMENT OF LABOR, LIBRARY. 14th and Constitution Ave., N.W., 20210. Tel 202 961-2423. Margaret F. Brickett, Librn. Interlibrary loan, inquiries answered.

.1 U.S. Department of Labor Library.
Among the holdings are books, periodicals, and re-

ports, including an extensive collection of labor union publications. The Library contains materials relating to Negroes in the labor movement, poverty and unemployment among minority groups, and similar subjects.

DC154 U.S. DEPARTMENT OF LABOR; MANPOWER ADMINISTRATION; JOB CORPS. 1111 18th St., N.W., 20210. Tel 202 382-6134. William Mirengoff, Acting Dir.
The Job Corps seeks to increase the employability of young men and women aged 16-21 from low-income families by providing them with education, vocational training, counseling, useful work experience and community involvement through rural or urban centers. Under Department of Labor operation, the training programs emphasize both residential and non-residential components, more local emphasis in recruiting and job placement, and linkages into existing local or regional community agencies and organizations.
Publ.: The Corpsman, national newspaper; Pamphlets, brochures, and program manuals.

.1 Job Corps.
Files, 1965- . Records, correspondence, reports, and other materials relating to the operation and programs of the Job Corps and its centers.

DC155 U.S. DEPARTMENT OF LABOR; MANPOWER ADMINISTRATION; OFFICE OF POLICY, EVALUATION, AND RESEARCH; MANPOWER RESEARCH CLEARINGHOUSE AND UTILIZATION SERVICE. 1730 M St., N.W., 20210. Tel 202 961-3695.
The Office of Policy, Evaluation and Research is interested in manpower development and training programs, including special training programs for hardcore, disadvantaged, unemployed persons; and manpower requirements, resources, and utilization.
Publ.: Manpower Research Projects, annual; Directories, abstracts, bibliographies, and reports.

.1 Manpower Research Clearinghouse and Utilization Service.
Files. The Service maintains an inventory of current manpower research conducted or sponsored by the Labor Department, including the following areas of interest: manpower (social, cultural, educational, and economic aspects); national training programs; unemployment or under-utilization of the nation's youth and of non-white, poorly educated, handicapped, and older workers; employment in chronically depressed communities, regions, and industries; human resources in rural areas, skill shortages, legislation and policy affecting manpower programs and problems.

DC156 U.S. DEPARTMENT OF LABOR; MANPOWER ADMINISTRATION; U.S. TRAINING AND EMPLOYMENT SERVICE (USTES). 14th and Constitution Ave., N.W., 20210. Tel 202 386-6016. Assoc. Adminstr.
USTES responsibilities are related to the administration of a nationwide system of public employment service, and the development of comprehensive work-training and work-experience programs and delivery systems designed to relieve the effects of unemployment and to promote maximum utilization of the nation's manpower. USTES is responsible for administering the Neighborhood Youth Corps, Special Impact Program, Operation Mainstream, New Careers, Work Incentive Program, On-The-Job Training, Job Opportunities in the Business Sector (JOBS), Concentrated Employment Program (CEP), and it assists in the administration of the Model Cities Program

.1 U.S. Training and Employment Service.
Files. Records, reports, correspondence, program plans and evaluations, and other materials relating to the operation and activities of programs administered by the Service.

DC157 U.S. DEPARTMENT OF LABOR, OFFICE OF EQUAL OPPORTUNITY IN MANPOWER PROGRAMS (1965). 14th St. and Constitution Ave., N.W., 20210. Tel 202 961-5084. Arthur A. Chapin, Dir.
The Office of Equal Opportunity in Manpower Programs is responsible for achieving Title VI compliance and maintaining a policy of non-discrimination in federally

assisted programs administered by the Labor Department.

.1   Office of Equal Opportunity in Manpower Programs.
        Files, 1965- . Records, reports, correspondence,
        and other papers concerning the functions of the
        Office.

DC158   U.S. DEPARTMENT OF LABOR, OFFICE OF FEDERAL
         CONTRACT COMPLIANCE (1965). 14th and Constitution
         Ave., N.W., 20210. Tel 202 961-3414. Ward McCreedy,
         Acting Dir.
         The Office administers the executive order which re-
         quires that U.S. Government contractors and subcon-
         tractors (including federally-assisted construction pro-
         jects) take affirmative action to ensure equal employ-
         ment opportunity. Formerly the President's Committee
         on Equal Employment Opportunity.

.1   Office of Federal Contract Compliance.
        Files, 1965- . Records, reports, correspondence,
        and other papers relating to the activities of the
        Office.

DC159   U.S. DEPARTMENT OF LABOR, WOMEN'S BUREAU (1920).
         14th St. and Constitution Ave., N.W., 20210. Tel 202
         961-2036. Mrs. Elizabeth Duncan Koontz, Dir.
         The Women's Bureau develops policies and programs
         to promote the welfare of wage-earning women and to
         encourage the better utilization of womanpower. The
         Bureau serves as the focal point of informed concern,
         policy advice, and leadership, and is the clearinghouse
         and central source of information within the federal
         government on questions relating to development of
         womanpower resources and the economic, legal, and
         civil status of women.
         Publ.: Leaflets, conference reports, bulletins, standards
               and legislation affecting women, fact sheets, re-
               prints, and other materials.

.1   Women's Bureau.
        Files, 1920- . Correspondence, records, reports,
        and other papers concerning the operation and
        activities of the Women's Bureau, including mate-
        rial on Negro women. Restricted.

DC160   U.S. DEPARTMENT OF STATE; AGENCY FOR INTERNA-
         TIONAL DEVELOPMENT (AID); OFFICE OF EQUAL
         OPPORTUNITY. 2201 C St., N.W., 20520. Tel 202 737-
         8582. Mrs. Nira H. Long, Spec. Asst.

.1   Office of Equal Opportunity.
        Files. Records, correspondence, reports, and other
        papers concerning equal employment opportunity
        and other programs of the office.

DC161   U.S. DEPARTMENT OF STATE, EQUAL EMPLOYMENT
         OPPORTUNITY PROGRAM. 2201 C St., N.W., 20520.
         Tel 202 383-8547. Eddie N. Williams, Dir.

.1   Equal Employment Opportunity Program.
        Files. Records, reports, and other papers relating
        to the operation and activities of the Program.

DC162   U.S. DEPARTMENT OF STATE, PEACE CORPS (1961). 806
         Connecticut Ave., N.W., 20525. Tel 202 382-2335.
         Delano E. Lewis, Spec. Asst. to the Dir. for Equal Em-
         ploy. Opportunity.

.1   Equal Employment Opportunity Program.
        Files, 1964- . Records, correspondence, reports
        and other papers relating to equal employment op-
        portunity in the Peace Corps.

DC163   U.S. DEPARTMENT OF THE INTERIOR. G and 18th Sts.,
         N.W., 20240. Tel 202 343-3101. Harry Shooshan, Coor-
         dinator for Departmental Civil Rights Activities.

DC164   U.S. DEPARTMENT OF THE INTERIOR, NATIONAL PARK
         SERVICE, DIVISION OF INFORMATION. Interior
         Bldg., 18th and C Sts., N.W., 20240. Tel 202 737-1820.
         Edwin N. Winge, Chief, Div. of Info. Inquiries an-
         swered, referrals made.

.1   Douglass, Frederick, 1817-95.
        Papers. Included are letters to and by Douglass
        (ca. 1000); records of deeds, bond holdings, mort-
        gages, insurance policies and abstracts of title (ca.

80 items); his speeches, collected in book form and
in individual pamphlets; his personal book collection; the Douglass Monthly newspaper (several
years, bound); North Star newspaper (ca. 14 months,
bound); several assorted issues of various newspapers throughout the country, including the New
National Era; Douglass' personal effects, including
home furnishings and walking canes; sound movie
and slides on his life; his autobiography, Narrative
on the Life of Frederick Douglass (1845); and various books on Douglass. In National Capital Parks -
East Library.

DC165   U.S. DEPARTMENT OF THE INTERIOR, OFFICE FOR
         EQUAL OPPORTUNITY. C St. between 18th and 19th
         Sts., N.W., 20240. Tel 202 343-5693. Edward Shelton,
         Dir.

.1   Office for Equal Opportunity.
        Files. Records, correspondence, reports, and
        other papers concerning equal employment oppor-
        tunity programs, contract compliance, Title VI,
        and other federal employment programs. Re-
        stricted.

DC166   U.S. DEPARTMENT OF THE TREASURY, EQUAL OP-
         PORTUNITY PROGRAM. Pennsylvania Ave. and 15th
         St., N.W., 20220. Tel 202 964-5035. David A. Sawyer,
         Dir.

.1   Office of Equal Opportunity.
        Files. Records, correspondence, reports and other
        papers concerning the equal opportunity programs
        and actions of the Department.

DC167   U.S. DEPARTMENT OF TRANSPORTATION, OFFICE OF
         CIVIL RIGHTS. 400 Seventh St., S.W., 20590. Tel 202
         962-8377. Richard F. Lally, Dir.

.1   Office of Civil Rights.
        Files. Information on the civil rights and equal
        opportunity activities of the Department of Trans-
        portation relating to Department employment prac-
        tices; services rendered to the public; employment
        practices of contractors and subcontractors under
        direct or federally assisted contracts; operation of
        federally assisted activites; and other programs
        and efforts involving Department assistance, par-
        ticipation or endorsement.

DC168   U.S. EQUAL EMPLOYMENT OPPORTUNITY COMMISSION
         (EEOC) (1964). 1800 G St., N.W., 20506. Tel 202 343-
         7691. George W. Draper, III, Exec. Dir. Inquiries an-
         swered, referrals made, consultation.
         The EEOC has a two-fold purpose: to end discrimination
         based on race, color, religion, sex, or national origin in
         all conditions of employment, including hiring or firing,
         wages, terms, benefits, testing procedures, classifica-
         tion, facilities, promotion, training, retraining, and
         apprenticeship; and to initiate and promote affirmative
         action programs to open up new job opportunities for
         minority group members and women at every level of
         employment.
         Publ.: EEOC Research Reports in such areas as job
               training, status and characteristics of the Negro
               workforce, employment opportunities in various
               fields, Negro underemployment and job discrimi-
               nation.

.1   U.S. Equal Employment Opportunity Commission.
        Files, 1964- . Records, correspondence, reports,
        and other papers concerning investigations, educa-
        tion and action programs, and other activities of the
        Commission.

DC169   U.S. FEDERAL COMMUNICATIONS COMMISSION (FCC).
         1919 M St., N.W., 20554. Tel 202 632-6366. Robert V.
         Cahill, Equal Employ. Opportunity Officer.

.1   Office of Equal Employment Opportunity.
        Files, 1964- . Records, reports, correspondence,
        and other papers concerning the equal employment
        programs of the Department.

DC170   U.S. FEDERAL TRADE COMMISSION. Pennsylvania Ave. at
         Sixth St., N.W., 20580. Tel 202 393-6800. John A.

Delaney, Acting Exec. Dir. and Dir. of Equal Employ. Opportunity.

.1 Equal Employment Opportunity Program.
Files, 1964- . Records, correspondence, reports, and other papers concerning equal employment opportunity and other programs such as federal employment, contract compliance, and Title VI.

DC171   U.S. GENERAL SERVICES ADMINISTRATION, CIVIL RIGHTS DIVISION. 18th and F Sts., N.W., 20405. Tel 202 343-9162. David Mann, Dir.

.1   Civil Rights Division.
Files. Records, reports, correspondence, and other papers relating to civil rights matters and activities of the Administration, including material on Title VI, contract compliance, and federal employment.

DC172   U.S. GENERAL SERVICES ADMINISTRATION, NATIONAL ARCHIVES AND RECORDS SERVICE (1934), WASHINGTON NATIONAL RECORDS CENTER. 4205 Suitland Rd., Suitland, Md. (Mailing address: Washington National Records Center, Washington, D.C. 20409). Tel 202 963-6404. James B. Rhoads, Acting Archivist of the U.S.
The National Archives and Records Service is responsibile for selecting, preserving, and making available to the government and the public the permanently valuable noncurrent records of the Federal government and for promoting improved current records management and paperwork practices in federal agencies. It is also responsible for publishing the laws, constitutional amendments, presidential documents, and administrative regulations having general applicability and legal effect, and for the administration of the presidential libraries. Materials in the National Archives are classified according to record group (R.G.).
Publ.: For information concerning ordering instructions for Archive publications, the pamphlet, Publications of the National Archives and Records Service, is available from the Publications Sales Branch, National Archives and Records Service, Washington, D.C. 20408. Among hundreds of Archive bulletins, staff papers, finding aids, preliminary inventories, reference papers, and special lists are found the following publications: Committee on Fair Employment Practice (1962), Data Relating to Negro Military Personnel in the Nineteenth Century (1968), Federal Writers' Project, Work Projects Administration, 1935-44 (1953), A Guide to Documents in the National Archives: For Negro Studies (1947), Guide to Federal Archives Relating to the Civil War (1962), Guide to the Archives of the Confederate States of America (1968), Guide to the Records in the National Archives (1948), Selected List of Documents and Photographs Relating to Negro History (n.d.), Selected Series of Records Issued by the Commissioner of the Bureau of Refugees, Freedmen, and Abandoned Lands, 1865-1872 (1969), Statistical Records Among the Records of the Bureau of Refugees, Freedmen, and Abandoned Lands (1968), The Work of the Civilian Conservation Corps (1914).

.1   R.G. 1, War Labor Policies Board.
Correspondence, 1918. 1 folder. Correspondence between Dr. George E. Haynes, director of the Division of Negro Economics of the Labor Department, and Felix Frankfurter, chairman of the board, deals with interracial relations, the Negro's economic position, and cooperative arrangements between the Division and the U.S. Employment Service.

.2   R.G. 2, National War Labor Board.
Files, 1918-19. One case file relates to a dispute involving Negro employees only: no. 213- Philadelphia Terminal employees (1918). There are also a number of cases in trades and industries employing large numbers of Negroes: express, shipbuilding, longshore work, coal mining, building trades (in the South), tobacco, foundries, and lumber.

.3   R.G. 3, U.S. Housing Corporation.
Records, 1918. 1 folder. Deals with living conditions of Negro war workers.

.4   R.G. 4, U.S. Food Administration.
Records of the Negro Press Section, 1917-18. Includes material indicating the efforts made to reach Negro organizations with material on wartime food conservation.

.5   R.G. 9, National Recovery Administration.
Records, 1933-37. Reports, memoranda, special studies, and other records. Material is divided into three categories: reports and memoranda dealing specifically with Negro problems having a bearing on the NRA program, such as regional wage differentials; special studies and reports on particular trades and industries in which references are made to Negro wages and working conditions, as, for example, studies of the tobacco worker; and studies and other records relating to trades and industries employing large numbers of Negroes, in which there is no explicit reference to Negro problems as such, for example, lumber and timber, tobacco, cotton picking, and the service trades.

.6   R.G. 10, National Commission on Law Observance and Enforcement.
Records, 1929-31. Agency popularly known as the Wickersham Commission. Records include material on discrimination in law enforcement by police agencies in the courts, and in matters of civil and personal rights. The records do not add appreciably to the Commission's published reports.

.7   R.G. 11, General Records of the U.S. Government.
Records, 1778-1945. File of constitutional and statutory enactments and of treaties, including source material on slavery and the slave trade, colonization, emancipation, civil and political rights. Antislave treaties include two with Great Britain —the Webster-Ashburton Treaty (1842) and one in 1870 — and the Statute of Brussels (1890) with the European powers multilaterally. Records relating to the ratification of the 13, 14, and 15th Amendments include correspondence between the Secretary of State and the Governors of the States, and some messages of the Governors to the legislatures. The file of unperfected treaties contains the treaty of December 15, 1863, with the Netherlands concerning the emigration of freedmen to Surinam.

.8   R.G. 12, Office of Education.
Files, 1917-45. Reports, correspondence, schedules, questionnaires, proposals, plans, and financial papers. Material covering activities under federal grants-in-aid, for trade, agricultural, and home economics education (1917-37), educational activities in the Negro Civilian Conservation Corps camps (1934-39), national survey of Negro vocational education and guidance (made with Works Progress Administration assistance, 1936-37), and material relating to engineering, science, and management war training courses offered by a number of Negro colleges and universities at government expense (1941-45).
Files, 1954- . Records of the U.S. Commissioner of Education (Restricted).

.9   R.G. 13, Railroad Labor Boards.
Files, 1898-1934. Case files arising out of the Erdman Act (1898-1913) and before the Board of Mediation and Conciliation (1913-21), the Railroad Labor Board (1920-26) and the Board of Mediation and Conciliation (1926-34) all predecessors of the present National Mediation Board. Considerable amount of material reveals or reflects discriminatory practices against Negroes on the part of employers and of unions.

.10 R.G. 14, U.S. Railroad Administration.
Files, 1917-37. This agency operated the railroad network of the U.S. from 1917 to 1920. Records from this period include material on segregation practices involving passengers, and on discriminations against Negro railroad employees. After 1920, the Administration functioned only as a liquidator of the wartime arrangements between the government and the railroad companies, but it continued to receive, in decreasing quantity, complaints and suggestions about segregation and discrimination matters.

.11 R.G. 15, Veterans Administration.
Files, 1800-1945. Case files, records, reports,

and correspondence. Includes case files covering Negro veterans (or their beneficiaries) who received or applied for pensions, benefits, and the like as a result of the participation in the wars of the U.S. (1776-1918), not arranged by race or color; rehabilitation records (post 1919) deal with the training, placement, and employment of disabled Negro veterans of the war of 1917-18, including a series of reports by N.R.A. Crossland, chief of the Negro Division, dealing with various sections of the country, and reports and correspondence from districts with large Negro populations.

DC172.12 R.G. 16, General Records, Agriculture Department.
Records of the Secretary's office, 1839-1966. Scattered material after 1910 reflects the personnel policy of the Department, and the attitude of individuals of the staff towards the Negro farmer. Includes correspondence with George Washington Carver, with Tuskegee Institute, and with other Negro schools and colleges. Also includes various records on southern farm tenancy (1933-66).

.13 R.G. 21, U.S. District Courts.
Records, 1783-1929. Among the many court records are materials concerning the following districts:

.14 — District of Columbia.
Minutes of the circuit court (1801-63) contain entries on the commitments of fugitive slaves. There are separately filed manumission papers (deeds, wills, affidavits, bills of sale), 1821-62; manumission and emancipation papers (1857-62) relating to voluntary manumissions, emancipation under the act of April 16, 1862, and claims for emancipation filed by slaves whose masters had failed to file schedules under that act; fugitive slave material (1862-63); and case materials dealing with civil rights during the Reconstruction period, and with discrimination, civil and political rights, from Reconstruction to 1929.

.15 — Eastern District of North Carolina.
Records include case materials, from 1791, dealing with slavery; materials, during Reconstruction, pertaining to civil rights, the Ku Klux Klan and other intimidation cases; and case records, to 1911, relating to civil and political rights, discrimination, and similar matters.

.16 — Southern District of New York and Eastern District of Pennsylvania.
Records include, from 1789, case files in admiralty and criminal matters arising out of the slave trade; and materials, during Reconstruction and to 1912, pertaining to civil and political rights, discrimination, and similar matters.

.17 R.G. 24, Bureau of Naval Personnel.
Records of the former Bureau of Navigation. Includes ship's quarterly muster rolls (1860-65) showing name, rating, date and place of enlistment and of birth, etc., and usually including "Negro" or "mulatto" in appropriate cases under "complexion." Personnel files include records of officers who served in the African Squadron.

.18 R.G. 25, National Labor Relations Board.
Files, 1933-41. Case files include disputes in which intimidation, segregation, and discrimination were principal issues; and also many other cases in trades and industries employing large numbers of Negroes: iron and steel, shipbuilding, tobacco, coal mining, longshore work, etc.

.19 R.G. 29, Bureau of the Census.
Records, 1790-1930. Population schedules, or their equivalents, for the census of 1790-1880, inclusive, of 1910, and of 1930, and separate slave census of 1850 and 1860. The slave schedules for the 1860 census give for each slaveholder the number of his slaves; their age, sex, and color; those who were fugitives; the number manumitted; those who were deaf and dumb, blind, insane, or "idiotic"; and the number of slave houses. Also for the 1860 census are photographic copies of printed maps of the Southern states with symbols showing for each county the number of whites, free Negroes, and slaves, as well as agricultural information; and in-

formation on slaves and freedmen on Indian reservations west of Arkansas.

.20 R.G. 32, U.S. Shipping Board.
1 folder, "Labor Conditions - Negro Labor," (1918-19). Contains material dealing with union and employer discrimination and similar matters in the shipbuilding industry during the war of 1917-18 and after, and cross-references to additional material elsewhere among these records.

.21 R.G. 33, Extension Service.
Records, 1889-1939. Includes material not dealing specifically with Negro agricultural problems as such but relating to areas with large Negro agricultural populations. There are also narrative and statistical reports from Negro county agents, home demonstration leaders, and club workers. In 1938 there were about 300 of these workers.

.22 R.G. 35, Civilian Conservation Corps.
Records, 1933-43. Files and photographs. Contains only the files of CCC top management. Administrative, Selection Division, and Public Relations files contain general material on Negro CCC camps, on policy and procedure in selecting Negro enrollees, on results achieved with Negro enrollees, on complaints of discrimination, etc. Photographs (ca. 200) are of activities and training of Negro enrollees under the CCC program. Also included are reports of inspections of Negro camps and racially mixed camps, and records concerning complaints on location of Negro camps.

.23 R.G. 36, Bureau of Customs.
Records. Included are groups of slave manifests for New Orleans (1819-56), and for Savannah, Georgia (prior to 1808); and a time book (1 v.) for mechanics and slaves employed at Fort Morgan, Alabama (1861-62). Other slave manifests are scattered through the records of other ports.

.24 R.G. 41, Bureau of Marine Inspection and Navigation.
Not segregated by race or color, these records include applications for various seamen's certificates (1915-40), and material on the training and recruitment of merchant seamen (1917-34).

.25 R.G. 45, Naval Records Collection, Office of Naval Records and Library.
Records. Correspondence, logbooks, and letterbooks on the African Squadron, and a roll of slaves employed by the engineer office at Charleston, S.C. (1862-64). Included in the material of the African Squadron is considerable correspondence (1819-61) between the Secretary of the Navy and commanding officers of the Squadron, U.S. agents on the Guinea coast, federal executive and judicial officials, the American Colonization Society, and private individuals and firms relating to the seizure of American slaving vessels, their condemnation in the U.S. District Courts, arrangements for shipment of liberated Africans to reception centers at Sherbro Island and along the Liberian coast, the establishment, maintenance, and supply of these centers, the role of U.S. naval vessels in combating the traffic in slaves and in facilitating African and Negro American colonization in Liberia, and the activities of the American Colonization Society and state societies. Separately filed is the letter book (1843-45) of the first commander of the African Squadron, Matthew C. Perry, and the letter book (1847-49) of his successor, William C. Bolton.

.26 R.G. 46, U.S. Senate.
Records, 37th-82nd Congresses. Materials, particularly memorials and petitions of the following Senate standing committees:

.27 — Committee on the District of Columbia.
Petitions and memorials concerning such matters as the employment of freedmen or "contrabands" in the District, opposition to the abolition of slavery in the District, extension of voting irrespective of color, legislation to put all white men who are citizens and residents of the District "upon an equal footing with the Negroes."

.28 — Committee on Education and Labor.
Petition for appropriations to Wilberforce University, Ohio, for the education of freedmen, and the testimony (1883) of Mrs. George R.

Ward dealing with the following subjects: Southern life before the Civil War, Negro superstitions, Negro matrimony, religion among the Negroes, the "scursion nuisance," "service servants," and others.

DC172.29 — Committee on Foreign Relations.
Petitions and memorials asking the recognition of Liberia and "Hayti" (Haiti).

.30 — Committee on the Judiciary.
Petitions and memorials concerning the establishment of a bureau of education (urged by Negro citizens of Wilmington, N.C.), and urging that there be a constitutional amendment to prohibit discriminatory legislation on account of race or color; and copies of proceedings of the State legislature of Texas (1870) concerning the 13th, 14th, and 15th Amendments.

.31 — Committee on Military Affairs and the Militia.
Memorials concerning the equality of Negro troops with white, the status of Negro soldiers, and the memorial of the American Freedmen's Commission on the education of freedmen.

.32 — Committee on the Post Office and Post Roads.
Petitions referred to the committee to allow the New York Caucasian and "all other Democratic papers now excluded from the mails, in all the loyal States, the same privileges now enjoyed by Republican and Abolition papers."

Records and reports of the following Senate select committees:

.33 — Joint Select Committee to Inquire Into the Condition of the Late Insurrectionary States.
This committee gave attention to the "Ku Klux Conspiracy." Originals of the Committee's reports.

.34 — Select Committee on a Bill to Confiscate the Property and Free the Slaves of Rebels.
No records of this committee have been found, but the originals of the resolution referred to the Committee and of the bill reported are available.

.35 — Select Committee on Slavery and the Treatment of Freedmen.
Memorials, including letters and scrolls with signatures and often addresses and occupations, on the following subjects: Liberation of slaves in the seceded states, the abolition of slavery throughout the U.S., the suppression or the reopening of the African Slave Act, advice to "drop the Negro question and attend to the business of the country," the extension of the right of suffrage to freed slaves, the Crittenden resolutions, the disturbed state of the country, and the "suppression of the rebellion." Also included are some petitions for the confiscation of "rebel lands" and their donation to men in the Union service, and the incomplete original of one of the Committee's reports.

.36 — Select Committee to Inquire Into the Facts Attending the Invasion and Seizure of the United States Armory at Harper's Ferry by John Brown and his Companions.
Records of the Committee, including its original report with its journal, correspondence, summonses and returns, newspapers containing items about Richard Realf, and correspondence with the Governor of Virginia about John Brown's papers.

.37 R.G. 48, General Records, Interior Department.
Materials concerning the following divisions and offices:

.38 — Appointments Division.
Records, 1870-1939, contain the personnel files of all Freedmen's Hospital and of some Howard University personnel, and of all Registers of Deeds in the District of Columbia. There is a large amount of biographical material on prominent Negroes, including Daniel Hale Williams, Surgeon-in-Chief at Freedmen's Hospital in the 1890's.

.39 — Office of the Secretary.
Correspondence, 1870-1939. General correspondence files contain material on the admin-

istrative supervision of the Department over Freedmen's Hospital and Howard University in Washington, giving information on the policies and management of these institutions. Correspondence concerning the Office of Education (1918-39) deals generally with the interest of the two offices in Negro education.

.40 — Patents and Miscellaneous Division.
Materials on the Suppression of the slave trade and the colonization of freed Negroes (1854-79), including correspondence between the Department and the President, Congress and various executive departments (1858-72), the U.S. agent for liberated Africans in Liberia (1860-65), the judges and arbitrators of the Mixed Courts of Justice, the American Colonization Society, and other individuals; and contracts, payrolls, and other papers concerning the Department's activities in these areas.

.41 R.G. 55, Danish Government of the Virgin Islands.
Records, 1672-1917. A considerable amount of material (much of it in Danish) deals with slavery and other Negro problems. Included are records concerning the slave insurrections of the middle of the 19th century which led to emancipation in 1848.

.42 R.G. 56, General Records of the Department of the Treasury.
Records of the Office of the Secretary include correspondence from Salmon P. Chase, Secretary of the Treasury, to President Lincoln concerning the Fort Pillow massacre. Records of the following special agencies:

.43 — Third Special Agency (Louisiana, Mississippi, Texas, Arkansas, Alabama, Florida).
Material (1863-65) concerning dealings of the Supervising Special Agent with military officials in regard to freedmen before the establishment of the Bureau of Refugees, Freedmen, and Abandoned Lands.

.44 — Fifth Special Agency (South Carolina, Georgia, Florida).
Records relating to the Sea Islands area of South Carolina, consisting of a sales book of captured, confiscated, or abandoned property; papers relating to the establishment of trade and to supply stores; schedules of appraised, captured or abandoned property; and papers relating to incoming and outgoing shipments and to supplies for families and plantations. The "Port Royal Correspondence" includes descriptions of the earliest means adopted to care for and educate the freedmen in the area.

.45 R.G. 58, Bureau of Internal Revenue
Records, 1862-99. The Commissioner of Internal Revenue administered the Act of Congress of August 5, 1861, for the levying of direct taxes in the states declared to be in insurrection, under which lands were confiscated to be broken up and distributed to former slaves or to persons faithful to the Federal government. Records cover the activities of the Direct Tax Commission for the District of South Carolina and of the Commissioner of Internal Revenue, and include a number of mss, annotated and printed maps, one accompanied by 26 surveyors' field notebooks, which reflect activities of the commissioners in and around St. Helena and St. Luke's parishes, S.C.

.46 R.G. 59, General Records, State Department.
Correspondence, 1774-1942. The diplomatic correspondence, especially from Great Britain and Brazil, contains information on the slave trade; the correspondence of the many Negroes who served in diplomatic and consular capacities, particularly in Haiti, Liberia, Santo Domingo, and Madagascar, and the applications and recommendations filed in connection with their appointment, is a source of biographical information. The miscellaneous correspondence includes letters from the various colonization societies, and material, as late as the early 1900's which reveals a continued interest in Negro colonization and also which concern the restriction of immigration of Negro Americans into other countries. See also, R.G. 84.

DC172.47 R.G. 60, General Records, Justice Department.
Records, 1823-1937. Materials, classified under
the following categories:

.48 — Central Files.
Considerable quantity of material, after 1870,
relating to such subjects as suffrage in Alabama
(1890-92) and South Carolina (1890-91); peonage
(ca. 1900-37); and the Brownsville, Texas, riot
(August, 1906). Certain sub-files (1919-34) relating to Negro problems, consisting of correspondence with U.S. District Attorneys and
Marshals, members of Congress, and individuals and organizations; and material on the
Ku Klux Klan in the 1920's.

.49 — Files, 1952-60.
Contain materials pertaining to race relations
(restricted).

.50 — Papers of the Attorney General.
Letters, chiefly from the President, heads of
departments, members of Congress, and U.S.
District Attorneys and Marshals, together with
drafts of replies and related matter submitted
to the Attorney General. Undetermined quantity of material, under such headings as Slave
Trade (1823-69), Fugitive Slave Law (1853-61),
and, relating to the Negro in the Civil War and
Reconstruction periods, Negroes (1862-70) and
Enforcement Act (1865-70).

.51 R.G. 62, Council of National Defense.
Records, 1916-21. This Council had a Committee
on Labor whose records contain a small amount of
material on Negro employment and manpower resources.

.52 R.G. 69, Work Projects Administration.
Records, 1933-43. Reports, mss, correspondence,
photographs, sound recordings, and motion pictures. Contains reports and mss of experiences by
those artists, musicians, actors and writers employed by the WPA, including records of the WPA
Theatre project which produced 75 plays by Negro
units in several cities. Also included is correspondence concerning the administration of the
agency's Negro education program; recordings of
Negro choirs and a recording for Negro Health
Week; photographs (ca. 100) of Negroes on construction projects, scientific research projects, and
miscellaneous other activities, and pictures of
recreational facilities provided for Negro children;
and a motion picture, "We Work Again," 1936.
Formerly Works Progress Administration.

.53 R.G. 71, Bureau of Yards and Docks.
Records include a muster roll of "contrabands" at
Port Royal, Va., 1863.

.54 R.G. 74, General Records, Labor Department.
The Negro Economics Division of the Secretary's
office is represented by a small report and correspondence files (1919-21) on the activities of the
Division, Negro working conditions, interracial relationships, and developments in Negro business
and agriculture. Other scattered records of the
Secretary's office (1917-33) deal with Negro migration, the Negro in the post-war Reconstruction
period, racial friction, and other matters.

.55 R.G. 75, Office of Indian Affairs.
General records include a good deal of material
(1870-90) on the Negroes who were held as slaves
by the Five Civilized Tribes in Indian Territory,
particularly on the post-Civil War status of such
Negroes in relationship to the tribes which had held
them. Land Division files include papers pertaining to lands of freedmen in Indian Territory.

.56 R.G. 77, Records of the Office of the Chief of Engineers.
Among the records relating to the War Department
are indexes to claims papers of contrabands who
worked on Fort Pickering, Memphis, Tenn., 1862-
63.

.57 R.G. 80, General Records, Navy Department.
Index to these records shows four cards (1897-
1926) on Negroes, one relating to enlistment and recruiting; and 14 cards (1926-42) captioned "Negro."
Included in the general records are photographs
(ca. 35 items) from World War II, among which are
pictures of Negro honor graduates from Naval

Training Stations, and of Negro workmen in small
war plants.

.58 R.G. 83, Bureau of Agricultural Economics.
Records, 1919-40. Correspondence and manuscript
files, including material on Negroes as farmers
generally, on Negro farm tenantry, on Negro migration from southern farms to northern industry, and
on Tuskegee Institute. Also included are photographs (ca. 20 items, 1906-11) of Negro farmers
and tenant farmers, their homes and agricultural
activities in various southern states.

.59 R.G. 84, Foreign Service Posts.
This record group supplements and complements
records in R.G. 59. Included are the following
pertinent materials:

.60 — Records of the U.S. Legation at Monrovia, Liberia.
1856-1935. Included are dispatches sent to and
received from the State Department, circulars,
general files, notes to and from the Liberian
government and officials, instructions to consuls, and miscellaneous correspondence sent
and received. Among the miscellaneous correspondence received are Presidential proclamations relating to suppression of the slave
trade and the American Civil War, the Report
of Commissioners of the USA to Liberia, and
an agreement on the basis of the report to
maintain Liberian independence, integrity and
financial stability.

.61 — Records of the U.S. Consulate General at Monrovia,
Liberia.
Records include dispatches to and from the
State Department, general correspondence, and
miscellaneous letters sent and received. Included are documents pertaining to American
Negro immigration into Liberia, and the American Agent for Liberated Africans; lists of
African slaves recaptured from slavers and a
contract of the American Colonization Society
for their care; and a series of replies to an
inquiry concerning economic opportunities open
to Negro Americans in various American
consular districts.

.62 R.G. 90, U.S. Public Health Service.
Records, 1897-1923. Morbidity reports and studies
in some cases show the incidence of diseases by
race. There is some correspondence of the Venereal Disease Division regarding its own and State
Health Boards' activities among Negroes. Also included is a film (1938), "Three Counties Against
Syphillis."

.63 R.G. 92, Records of the Office of Quartermaster General.
Records pertaining to the Civil War period include
freedmen and riots among the subjects listed, burial
lists of Negro troops, and rolls of persons employed
in a civilian capacity, listing ex-slaves as contrabands.

.64 R.G. 94, The Adjutant General's Office.
Records, primarily during the Civil War period.
Also included are materials concerning Negro participation in the Colonial and Revolutionary wars
and in the militia of various colonies. Among the
general records are the following:

General correspondence and related records,
arranged according to "trunk":

.65 — Trunk 4.
Includes papers concerning the Memphis riots
of 1866.

.66 — Trunk 31.
American Freedmen's inquiry Commission.
Preliminary and final reports, proceedings,
testimony taken (grouped geographically), and
other papers, including names of witnesses, a
file of extracts relating to slavery, and sup-
plemental reports such as The Self-Freedmen
of Canada West (Howe, 1964), and The Emancipated Slave Face to Face with his Old Master,
Valley of the Lower Mississippi (McKaye,
1864).

.67 — Trunk 166.
Opinions of the Solicitor of the War Depart-

ment (May, 1864), concerning the status of a slave if drafted, among other topics.

DC172.68   —— Trunk 189.
Papers concerning the Baltimore riot of April, 1861.

Generals' papers and books:

.69   —— Thomas, Lorenzo.
Papers, April 1, 1863-July, 1864. 2 v. Adjutant General, U.S. Army. Orders, letters and telegrams sent by Thomas. Contains records of Thomas' recruitment and organization of Negro troops in the Mississippi Valley, and lists of the officers selected for commissions in the USCT, as well as problems encountered in assembling Negro regiments.

.70   —— Generals' reports of service.
Reports, ca. 1864-72. Reports of Union general officers of their service during the Civil War. Contains information on recruitment, organization, and use of Negro troops, as recorded by such officers as Casey, Chetlain, Ullmann, and Wild.

.71   —— Military service records.
Muster rolls, and monthly returns for the Regular Army and volunteer units; regimental and company descriptive books for volunteer organizations; registers of enlistment (1798-1914, especially 1863-65); reports of examinations of recruits (1884-1912) and registers of physical examinations (1864-1912); compiled service records of volunteer Union soldiers serving with U.S. Colored Troops; carded medical records for the Regular Army (1821-84, 1894-1912) and for volunteers in the Civil War; registers of discharges for the Regular Army (1861-86). From these records it is possible to determine information relating to troop strength and position, and information relating to individual soldiers.

Also among the general records are found the records of the following branches, divisions, and miscellaneous commissions:

.72   —— Bureau for Colored Troops.
Records, 1863-89. Correspondence, applications for appointment, registers and rosters, register of resignations, and other papers, concerning recruitment, organization and service of Negro units and their officers. Other records include a Negro troop register (1869) showing whether "slave or free on or before April 19, 1861," and record of regiments of U.S. Colored Troops (1863-65). Also included is an 8 volume compilation (1885) containing, in chronological arrangement, copies of official records, state papers, and historical extracts of various kinds relating to the Negro in the military service of the United States to about 1885. Some information on labor conditions is included.

.73   —— Commission Branch.
Records include registers of appointments in the U.S. Colored Troops (1863-66), and copies of letters pertaining to officers for the U.S. Colored Troops (1863).

.74   —— Commission on Corrupt Practices in the South.
Testimony, exhibits, reports and related papers (1864-65), and ms final report (1865). Among the matters investigated were freedmen's affairs.

.75   —— Freedmen's Branch.
Records, 1872-79. Formed after the discontinuance of the Bureau of Refugees, Freedmen, and Abandoned Lands. Correspondence, employee records, reports, financial and legal papers, and bounty records. Materials relate to the functions of the Bureau which were essentially receiving, passing upon, and paying claims of Negro soldiers and sailors or their heirs for bounty, pension, arrears of pay, commutation of rations and prize money.

.76   —— Howard Court of Inquiry.
Testimony, exhibits, and argument of the judge advocate in the inquiry of charges against Brig.

Gen. Oliver Otis Howard of mismanagement of the Disbursing Branch of the Bureau of Refugees, Freedmen, and Abandoned Lands, and of confusion and imperfection in the Bureau's records (1874).

.77   —— Slave Claims Commissions.
Records, 1864-67. Registers of claims, kept by the commissions of Delaware, Kentucky, Maryland, Missouri, Tennessee, and West Virginia.

.78   —— Surgeon General's Office.
Civil War records include a volume of "Accounts of Physicians serving with Freedmen, Refugees, etc., Who Have Been Paid from the Medical and Hospital Appropriation" (1862-64); hospital records for the Regular Army and the U.S. Colored Troops; and Freedmen's Bureau medical records such as monthly returns of commissioned medical officers and physicians employed under contract (1865-69), contracts with female employees (1865-69) and service personnel (1865-70) at hospitals, reports on such service personnel (1868-71), and reports and receipt rolls of Medical Department personnel hired in North Carolina (1866-68).

.79 R.G. 95, Forest Service.
Among these records are the files of Camp Peterboro, N.J., a Negro camp of the Civilian Conservation Corps (1933-42), managed by the Forest Service.

.80 R.G. 96, Farm Security Administration.
Records, 1933-40. Correspondence files indicate that the Administration had the advice of Joseph H.B. Evans on Negro aspects of the resettlement program. Records of the rehabilitation, resettlement, and tenant farm purchase program after the Depression include hundreds of letters from debt-ridden farmers; reports and correspondence describing the resettlement of more than 1700 disadvantaged Negro families; and loan case files and correspondence documenting the farm purchase program which included 2000 southern Negro families by 1940. Also included are records relating to southern farm migratory workers.

.81 R.G. 98, Army Commands.
Records, including materials relating to the following:

.82   —— 25th Army Corps.
Records, 1864-66. 56 registry v. and 20 document boxes. 25th Army Corps was the first Negro army corps.

.83   —— Military districts.
Records, 1867-70. Materials pertaining to the five military districts into which the South was organized during Reconstruction. Records contain information on the status of the Negro; on his protection by law and in the courts; on interracial relationships, including references to the Ku Klux Klan (1868) in the records of the 5th District (Louisiana and Texas); and on the registration of Negro voters.

.84   —— Regular and Volunteer Regiments, Forts, Camps and other Army Posts.
Included in the records of various commands (1866-1942) are records of Negro units. Included is material on the recruiting, organizing, equipping, mustering-in, and mustering-out of Negro soldiers, correspondence concerning their segregation, protests against stationing them in certain localities, and on related subjects. Also included are reports of the Vicksburg Marine (later Freedmen's) Hospital (1863-68).

.85 R.G. 101, Comptroller of the Currency.
Records (1865-1924) of the Freedman's Saving and Trust Company, an institution chartered by the Federal government.

.86 R.G. 102, Children's Bureau.
Records, 1906-30. Scattered references to Negro problems include birth statistics for Charleston, S.C. (1906-12), correspondence on Negro infant and maternal mortality (1929), and on Negro social workers engaged by the Bureau (1930).

.87 R.G. 105, Bureau of Refugees, Freedmen, and Abandoned Lands.

Records, 1865-72. Records include correspondence and reports on all phases of the Bureau's work with the freed Negroes, such as aiding them to settle on the land, furnishing them with the necessities of life including medical care, transporting them when displaced, acting as mediators between them and prospective and actual employers in arranging the terms of labor contracts, giving legal advice and assistance, assisting other agencies in maintaining schools, etc. Records are divided as follows:

DC172.88 — Archive Division.
This Division received and stored the records of the Bureau offices as they were closed. Records include book records of some of the Bureau's divisions.

.89 — Assistant Commissioners' Headquarters.
Records of the Assistant Commissioners Headquarters in the following states: Alabama, Arkansas, District of Columbia, Florida, Georgia, Kentucky, Tennessee, Louisiana, Maryland, Mississippi, Missouri and Arkansas, North Carolina, South Carolina, Texas, and Virginia. The extant records consist chiefly of book records of the Assistant Commissioner's office, the inspector general and disbursing officer, the chief medical officer, the chief quartermaster, the superintendent of education, and the district and subdistrict offices (1865-72). Book records include registers of letters received, letters sent, books, endorsements, orders and circulars, claims records, employment registers, contracts, freedmen's court records, hospital records, registers of complaints, records of persons hired, books showing rations issued, bounty registers, and marriage records. Included for the District of Columbia are records pertaining to Freedmen's Village at Arlington Heights, sick and wounded refugees and freedmen at Freedmen's Hospital, the Industrial School and home schools for freed children, the Commission for the Relief of Destitute Colored Persons. Other subjects covered include the Freedmen's Hospital at New Orleans; lists of orphans at the Freedmen's Hospital Orphan Asylum in New Orleans; complaints received by the Maryland office relating to the apprenticing of Negro children; and similar items for the other states.

.90 — Claim Division.
Included are records of assistance to discharged Negro soldiers and sailors and their families, in the collection of amounts due them (1866-72); and the records of the Prosecution Branch, which are very important for establishing the facts of military service of many individual Negro soldiers and sailors, among which are such items as long lists of names and persons entitled to bounty, pensions claims and pension record books, pay and bounty claims, and claims for prize money, commutation of rations, and substitute money.

.91 — Education Division.
Correspondence. Letters received by the General Superintendent of Education (1866-70) include those from societies and individuals interested in the education of freedmen and from state superintendents of education. Other important records are reports of the state superintendents, schedules of schools and rental accounts received from secretaries of private freedmen's aid societies (1868-70); lists of teachers employed by such organizations as the Friends Freedmen Association of Philadelphia, the American Missionary Society, the Presbyterian Committee on Home Missions; and materials pertaining to the histories of societies interested in freedmen.

.92 — Land Division.
Records concerning the restoration of abandoned property to former owners. Included in the surviving records are copies of letters sent and endorsements; the Division's special orders and circulars; letters received; list of confiscated property; applications and orders for property restoration; and monthly and yearly reports from Assistant Commissioners listing abandoned and confiscated lands in their custody. Each entry in the property registers shows name of owner; description, location, and value of property; date of abandonment, seizure, or confiscation; and by whom and when restored.

.93 — Medical Division.
Correspondence, including copies of letters sent by the Chief Medical Officer (1867-70); copies of his endorsements (1865-71) and letters received from the chief medical officers serving under the Assistant Commissioners in the several states (1866-70); and records containing statistics about the illnesses of freedmen and refugees and the treatment they received.

.94 — Office of the Assistant Inspector General.
This office distributed supplies to destitute persons in the South. Records pertaining to supply functions include press copies of letters sent (1867-68); letters received; and copies of congressional resolutions and War Department orders concerning the relief of the destitute, with associated correspondence (1867).

.95 — Office of the Chief Disbursing Officer.
Among the funds handled by this office were the refugees and freedmen's fund, from which the current expenses of the Freedmen's Bureau were paid until July 1, 1866; "retained" or "irregular" bounty fund; destitute relief fund, for temporary relief of the destitute population of the District of Columbia; and the pay, bounty, and prize money fund, for settlement of moneys due to Negro soldiers, sailors or marines. Records pertaining specifically to the different funds handled include the journal (1865-72) and accounts current (1865-70) of the refugees and freedmen fund, and accounts current of the school fund.

.96 — Office of the Chief Quartermaster.
Records relating to the transportation of refugees and freedmen, and correspondence to Bureau officials and to societies interested in freedmen.

.97 — Records Division.
Includes correspondence, relating to all aspects of Bureau functions, addressed to or received from the Secretary of War, other War Department officials, the Assistant Commissioners in the states in which the Bureau operated, State Governors, and various societies interested in freedmen. Other records include weekly, monthly, and annual abstracts of the Assistant Commissioners (1865-70). Also included are the special field orders issued by Commissioner Howard (Oct. 19-Nov. 6, 1865), register and letters received by Howard; a file of papers relating to the Bureau's operations (1865-68) received from the Executive Mansion in 1874; letters (1867-68) received by T.D. Eliot, chairman of the House Committee on Freedmen's Affairs; papers (1865-70) relating to a claim of Maj. George J. Alden; weekly inspection reports of buildings occupied by Howard University; and a file of letters and affidavits concerning criminal offenses against freedmen in Texas (1868).

.98 R.G. 107, Office of the Secretary of War.
Records, 1791-1942. For the Civil War period, correspondence with officers in the field deals with the recruitment and organization of Negro troops in the federal forces, and to a lesser extent with the problems created by Negroes behind the federal line in the South. Scattered correspondence from the field and from posts (ca. 1900-17) also relates to problems arising out of the presence of Negro troops. To trace records in this group requires knowledge of names, dates, and subjects.

.99 R.G. 108, Headquarters of the Army.
Records, 1827-1903. This material is of the same sort described above, R.G. 107, except that correspondence is between the various army head-

quarters and officers in the field. Also included is correspondence pertaining to civil rights in Florida and the New Orleans riot (1866).

DC172.100 R.G. 109, War Department Collection of Confederate Records.

Records, 1861-65. Materials contain information on the Negro as a source of labor on military works (teamsters, herders, stewards, and cooks) for the Confederate army in the field and in hospitals, and as a source of military manpower by impressment and recruitment. Classified under the following headings:

.101 —— Bureau of Conscription.

Records on the conscription service in Virginia include a record of details of free Negroes made at Camp Lee (1864-65); a register of free Negroes enrolled and assigned, giving age and birthplace, among other information (1864-65); a report on the enrollment of free Negroes; and a register of slaves impressed by enrolling officers (1864-65).

.102 —— Compiled Records.

Documents of the Treasury Department concerning claims for lost property and Negro slaves, among other subjects; records of the Union provost marshal's office including correspondence about the capture of contraband of war and slaves and the disposition of slaves, and lists of Negro laborers; and a file relating to military and civilian personnel (1861-65) including material on slaves.

.103 —— Medical Department.

.103a —— Mobile, Alabama. Engineer Hospital Register of patients (Jan., 1864-Apr., 1865) including slaves and Federal Negro patients.

.104 —— Farmville, Virginia. General Hospital. List of free Negroes and slaves employed and of other employees.

.105 —— Richmond, Virginia.

Records of the following hospitals: Chimborazo General Hospital, registers, memorandum book, and miscellaneous record books giving lists of slaves hired (1862-65); General Hospital 21, list of Negro employees (1862-65); General Hospital 13, register of Union and Negro patients (1863-65); General Hospital 24, record of payment for services and hire of slaves (1863-64).

.106 —— Office of the Quartermaster General, Rolls and Payrolls.

Records include a register of claims (1863-65) by military personnel for Negroes escaped to the enemy; slave payrolls (1861-65), giving period of service and name of owner; an alphabetical name index to payrolls of civilian employees and slaves (1861-65) prepared by Adjutant General's office; record of clothing issued to slaves (Oct. 1863-Dec. 65), giving overseer's name and county, name of slave and owner, and quantity of clothing and other items issued.

.107 —— Ordnance Department.

Macon, Georgia. In the records of the Macon Armory; copies of letters and telegrams sent by the superintendent (1862-65) to owners of slaves hired, among others; records of slaves employed by the master builder (1864); returns of work done (1862-65) by Negro laborers, carpenters, and bricklayers. Among the records of the Macon Arsenal is a record of clothing and shoes issued to detailed soldiers and slaves (1864-65); and, in records pertaining to the Macon Central Laboratory, letters (1862-64) to slaveowners, among others.

.108 —— Regiments, Battalions and Companies.

Records of Kentucky troops include a list of Negroes hired as regimental cooks (1862).

.109 —— Territorial Commands and Armies.

Records of the District of the Gulf include rolls of civilians, Negroes, and detailed men employed by the quartermaster at Mobile (1864-65), and a record of slaves hired (1864-65).

.110 R.G. 110, Provost Marshal General's Bureau.

Proceedings (1862-63) of the provost court of trials of persons charged with violating General Butler's orders, and of applications for the emancipation of slaves. This record group also contains enrollment lists (1863-65) for the national draft, giving residence, age, race, profession, marital status and place of birth.

.111 R.G. 111, Office of the Chief Signal Officer.

Among these records are several silent films, "Occupation of Afrique Sub-Sector, 93rd Division, April 8-July 4, 1918" and "Post Armistice Training, 93rd Division, November 11, 1918-March 11, 1919."

.112 R.G. 115, Bureau of Reclamation.

Records include photographs (ca. 20) of Negro farmers and their agricultural activities, with emphasis on tobacco culture, Georgia, South Carolina, Alabama (1927).

.113 R.G. 118, U.S. Attorneys and Marshals.

Records, 1830-1920. The correspondence files of the U.S. Attorney for the Southern District of Alabama (Mobile), includes a few letters dealing with the laws prohibiting the further importation of slaves (1830-60), and occasional letters dealing with civil rights matters affecting Negroes (1865-1920). Records for the Southern District of New York contain scattered correspondence concerning the enforcement of legislation prohibiting the import of slaves.

.114 R.G. 119, National Youth Administration.

Records, 1935-43. Files (only partial) of the Office of Negro Affairs deal generally with NYA activities in the training of Negroes (including aviation and other defense training), in health programs for Negro youth, in school and college education programs for Negroes, in cooperation with Negro organizations; it includes correspondence, memoranda, reports, statistical tabulations, press releases and other materials. Other branches of NYA have considerable material on the agency's work with Negro youth, including such items as final (historical) reports of state offices, each with a section on Negro youth work, headquarters and state office reports, both on types of activities (as education) with sections on Negro problems and programs; a number of periodical statistical issuances; approved work project plans showing the extent of Negro participation; and student work program plans from Negro institutions and from institutions with a considerable Negro element in their student bodies. Also included are photographs (ca. 300) of activities of Negro boys and girls in various projects, such as shop training, domestic training and scientific training; and a silent film (1939), "Youth Building at Wilberforce."

.115 R.G. 120, American Expeditionary Forces.

Records, 1917-21. This record group is the source of material on Negro participation in World War I and on the history of the units with which Negro soldiers served. Included are records of the various headquarters, posts, and organizations, in France, Germany, and Siberia; strength returns of such organizations; and medical organization records. Individual service records are not included.

.116 R.G. 121.

Contains records of the employment of Negro artists in government art programs during the 1930's.

.117 R.G. 123, U.S. Court of Claims.

Records, 1855-1940. Records include claims on the part of persons seeking some redress for property seized by or in behalf of the Federal government during the Civil War. Some of the claimants can be identified as Negroes; in other cases, notably those involving plantation owners, there is material among the evidentiary papers filed with the claims bearing on slavery and other aspects of plantation economy. See also, R.G. 205.

.118 R.G. 125, Judge Advocate General's Office (Navy).

Records, 1862-1942. Includes court-martial case files, among which there may be presumed to be case files relating to Negro naval personnel. Arranged chronologically.

.119 R.G. 126, Division of Territories and Island Possessions.

This agency continues in the Interior Department functions formerly performed by the State Department and by the War Department (Bureau of Insular Affairs). Files captioned "Negro" exist for Puerto Rico (1898-1935), for Cuba (for the two periods of occupation, 1898-1902 and 1906-09), and for the Philippine Islands.

DC172.120 R.G. 128, Joint Committees of Congress.
Records include material for the following committees:

.121 — Joint Committee on Reconstruction (39th Congress). This record group contains the incomplete ms of the Committee's report, and a few petitions referred to the Committee.

.122 — Joint Select Committee on the Conduct of the War (37th and 38th Congresses). Papers include such subjects as returning slaves, the Fort Pillow massacre, and testimony concerning the operation of the prison known as the "Slave Pen."

.123 — Joint Select Committee to Inquire into the Condition of the Late Insurrectionary States (42nd Congress). This committee focused its attention upon the "Ku Klux Klan Conspiracy." Records include the Committee's journal, incomplete, identified as "Journal of the Kuklux Committee."

.124 R.G. 133, Federal Coordinator of Transportation. Records, 1933-36. Considerable amount of material deals with Negro labor problems in the railroad industry. This material relates to the attitude of white unions toward Negro railroad employees, to employment discriminations on the part of railroads, to efforts on the part of Negroes and of railroad companies to extend the employment opportunities of Negroes, to the relationship of company unions to Negro employment problems, and the like. It includes reports, with related statements, exhibits, and correspondence, basic schedules of investigations, and unsolicited complaints, suggestions and allegations.

.125 R.G. 135, Public Works Administration. Records, 1933-39. Includes photographs (ca. 10) of housing developments for Negroes in Birmingham, Ala., and Miami, Fla., schools constructed for Negro children in Independence, Mo., Chattanooga, Tenn., and Memphis, Tenn. Records concerning World War II farm labor camps.

.126 R.G. 140, Military Government of Cuba. Records, 1898-1903. Includes several files relating to discrimination, and to rumors of a Negro revolution in 1900-01.

.127 R.G. 145, Agricultural Adjustment Administration. Records, 1933-38. Included is material dealing with AAA conferences attended by Negroes, with AAA referenda (in which there was Negro participation), and with AAA educational work carried on among Negroes by Negro employees of the Administration. Records concerning landlord-tenant relations.

.128 R.G. 153, Judge Advocate General's Office (War). Records, 1812-1942. These records are similar in character to those cited under R.G. 125. Records of investigations pertinent to the Civil War include testimony, reports, and correspondence regarding the investigation (by the Provost Marshal, Department of the Missouri) of the activities of the Order of American Knights of the Golden Circle (1864).

.129 R.G. 155, Wage and Hour and Public Contracts Division. Records, 1938-42, of the Wage and Hour Branch. Case files dealing with the establishment of minimum wages in low-paid industries or occupations. Economic data on Negroes are included in the files of the tobacco, gray-iron jobbing foundry, clay products, passenger motor carriers, and pulp and primary paper industries. Among other industries whose case files may be of interest because of the large number of Negroes employed are rubber products manufacturing, lumber and timber products, and Puerto Rico needlework, and fabric and leather gloves. There are also hearings on regulations governing the employers of "red caps" (railroad station porters).

130 R.G. 157, Maritime Labor Board. Records, 1938-42. Included is some material on the employment effect of segregation and discrimination in hiring halls, and on disputes arising out of unwillingness of white seamen to work with Negroes. Some reports discuss the condition of Negro maritime workers, especially longshoremen, in southern ports: wages, hours, working conditions, advancement opportunities, union characteristics, and the attitudes of employers and white co-workers. A large file of collective agreements, while apparently containing no specifically Negro data, may be of interest because of the number of maritime, and especially longshore, unions which have Negro members.

.131 R.G. 164, Office of Experiment Stations. Correspondence, 1902-22. Includes material pertaining to the work of George Washington Carver at the Tuskegee Experiment Station.

.132 R.G. 165, War Department General Staff. Photographs. Included are photographs of military activities of Negroes with the American Expeditionary Forces in Europe during World War I (ca. 300 items); military activities of Negroes in the U.S. during World War I, showing enlistment and training of Negro troops at various army camps, Red Cross activities among Negro soldiers, the return of the 15th Infantry Regiment (Negro) to New York, recreational activities, and portraits of Negroes who received military decorations (ca. 100 items); and photographs and photographic copies of drawings of Negroes in the Civil War, showing Negro companies, contraband camps, slaves, drummerboys, a slave market, Negro cottages, a portrait of the Hon. Robert Smalls, S.C., and miscellaneous scenes showing Negroes (ca. 15 items).

.133 R.G. 171, Office of Civilian Defense. Records, 1940-45. General correspondence files include materials under the classification "Racial Relations." Other headquarters records show similar material specifically Negro in subject. Some interracial material is to be found in regional office files.

.134 R.G. 174, Office of the Secretary of Labor. Records. Included are records (1952-60) containing some material pertaining to Negroes. Restricted.

.135 R.G. 176, Bureau of Human Nutrition and Home Economics. Records, 1917-37. Index indicates studies material for several articles on Negro dietary and other home economics problems.

.136 R.G. 183, U.S. Employment Service. Records, 1933-39. The file of J.A. Oxley, advisor on Negro affairs, and field representative of the USES, includes correspondence, memoranda, conference minutes, and reports on the availability of the USES services to Negro applicants. The reports cover many aspects of the status of Negro labor such as population trends, chief occupations, amount of unemployment, available relief; and evaluate the local activities of the USES. Correspondence is particularly concerned with discrimination in the employment and placement of Negroes. Other files contain complaints of and reports on discrimination in private and relief employment and placement of Negroes, material on segregated USES facilities in southern states, reports on the extent of formal Negro participation in the USES program, and the like. A USES-conducted survey of youth in Maryland (1938-39) is a source of information on the age, sex, education, and experience of Negro youth in that State.

.137 R.G. 186, Spanish Governors of Puerto Rico. Records, 1750-1898. Included is material dealing with slavery to 1873 (the date of emancipation) and with other Negro problems thereafter; and a census of slaves of 1872.

.138 R.G. 202, National War Labor Board. Records, 1941-45, including records of the predecessor National Defense Mediation Board. Records consist of case files in dispute and wage stabilization matters. Cases involving unions having Negro members will contain data on wartime Negro hours, wages and working conditions. Negro workers were particularly numerous in the aircraft, steel, shipbuilding, lumber and rubber industries.

DC172.139 R.G. 204, Records of the Office of the Pardon Clerk.
Records, 1853-1923. The pardon records concern many crimes against the U.S., including engaging in the slave trade and service on board a slaver, and rioting. Records contain petitions, letters of recommendation, character affidavits, correspondence, reports of district attorneys and others, and other materials related to investigation of the cases.

.140 R.G. 205, Court of Claims Section (Justice).
Records, 1868-1942. This record group includes material relating to the defense by the U.S. of the claims described in R.G. 123.

.141 R.G. 207, General Records of the Housing and Home Finance Agency.
Records. 27 ft. Records of predecessor agencies consisting of case files relating to housing projects of the Resettlement Administration and the Farm Security Administration (1934-42); and files of the Federal Public Housing Authority (1945-46).

.142 R.G. 208, Office of War Information.
Records, 1942-45. The Bureau of Intelligence of this agency made studies of Negro and interracial conditions, including a Preliminary Appraisal of the Present Negro Situation (March, 1942), Study of White and Colored Opinions - The Negroes' Role in the War, and White Attitudes Toward Negroes.

.143 R.G. 211, War Manpower Commission.
Records, 1942-45. Records of the Training-Within-Industry Service of the WMC deal with discrimination against Negroes in hiring and in training for defense and war industry, and with efforts to combat such discrimination, and to promote the employment and training of Negroes. There is also general material on discrimination in relation to the program of full manpower utilization, including anti-discrimination activities of Negro organizations, and some documentation of the origin of the Fair Employment Practice Committee (See R.G. 228).

.144 R.G. 212, Committee for Congested Production Areas.
Records, 1943-45. This coordinating agency produced records dealing with critical situations in such matters as workers' housing and transportation, educational and recreational facilities, and similar off-the-job working conditions in a number of war-congested areas with substantial Negro working population, both established and newly attracted by war industry. Examples of war-congested areas for which there are records are Detroit-Willow Run, Mich., Mobile, Ala., Hampton Roads, Va., Charleston, S.C., Knoxville, Tenn., and Muskegon, Mich.

.145 R.G. 215, Office of Community War Services.
Records, 1940-42. Scattered records of this agency deal with recreation, day care of children, health problems, and related matters, as they affected Negro war workers. There is material on segregated service men's centers and war-workers' medical services, and occasional intensive studies of particular areas, such as Norfolk, Va., dealing with the impact of the war and of war industry on the established and the immigrant Negro population.

.146 R.G. 217, Records of the General Accounting Office.
Records relating to the function of the following offices:

.147 — Commissioners on Emancipation in the District of Columbia.
Records include minutes (April 28, 1862-January 14, 1863), petitions, and the original of the Commissioners' final report.

.148 — Offices of Comptrollers and Auditors.
Included are registers of payments for the militia and Negro troops (1863-65); registers of claims under laws providing bounty for capturing slavers (1855-65); accounts concerning the suppression of the slave trade; registers of accounts for transportation of Negro troops (1863-64), and for Army subsistence, including settled accounts of officers assigned to the Bureau of Refugees, Freedmen, and Abandoned Lands; and records of Freedmen's Bureau accounts (1867-82) showing payments made by the Navy Department for money due Negro sailors.

.149 — South Carolina State Direct Tax Commission.
Records include certificates for land bid in by the U.S. and later sold by commissioners to "heads of families of the African race" (1863-65), and applications to purchase land by preemption, filed in response to a circular issued to freedmen of South Carolina, authorizing them to locate on land set aside for them (1864).

.150 R.G. 220, Records of Presidential Committees, Commissions, and Boards.
Records of Hobart Taylor, Jr., executive vice chairman of the President's Committee on Equal Employment Opportunity (1961-65) consisting mainly of correspondence with the White House. Records (1957-60) of U.S. Commission on Civil Rights, records (1955-61) of President's Committee on Government Employment Policy, records of the President's Committee on Government Contracts, and files and records of the National Commission on the Causes and Prevention of Violence, and of the National Advisory Commission on Civil Disorders.

.151 R.G. 228, Committee on Fair Employment Practices.
Records, 1941-46. Case records, reports, studies, memoranda, and reference materials, concerning the Committee's function to secure full use of manpower resources for war production by eliminating racial discrimination in employment. Materials contain information on employment discrimination and the programs of the Committee. Some additional materials on the origins of the Committee are mentioned in R.G. 211.

.152 R.G. 233, Records of the United States House of Representatives.
Records, primarily covering the Civil War and post-Civil War period. In the general records are documents that were tabled rather than referred to committees, such as papers relating to slavery, an amendment to the Constitution to abolish slavery, and to grant to Negro soldiers pay and allowances equal to those of white soldiers. Records of the following committees contain relevant information:

.153 — Committee on Appropriations.
Petitions concerning the commemoration of a half-century of Negro freedom (63rd Congress).

.154 — Committee on Education and Labor.
Book of minutes relating to the investigation of charges against Major General O.O. Howard, Commissioner of the Bureau of Refugees, Freedmen, and Abandoned Lands (41st Cong.).

.155 — Committee on Foreign Affairs.
Petitions and memorials on the slave trade (36th Cong.) and referred papers on the recognition of Liberia (37th Cong.).

.156 — Committee on Freedmen's Affairs.
Records, 1866-79, including records of the Select Committee on Freedmen's Affairs, 1865-66. Records of the 40th Congress include records concerning Maj. Gen. Howard's desire for an investigation of his management of the Bureau of Refugees, Freedmen, and Abandoned Lands; records on freedmen's affairs in Kentucky, Mississippi, North Carolina, Texas, and Virginia; records on the National Freedman's Savings and Trust Co.; petitions and memorials concerning the continuation of the Freedmen's Bureau, emigration to Liberia, and other subjects.

.157 — Committee on Military Affairs.
Records, petitions and memorials concerning, among many other subjects, former slaves employed as servants in the Army of Kentucky, the abolition of slavery, and Negro troops (37th and 38th Cong.); papers concerning the court martial at Raleigh of the Assistant Commissioner for North Carolina of the Bureau of Refugees, Freedmen, and Abandoned Lands (40th Cong.); and report of the Assistant Adjutant General on the Freedmen's Bureau (42nd Cong.).

.158 — Committee on the Judiciary.
Records for the 36th and 37th Congresses include papers concerning slavery in the Terri-

tory of New Mexico; suppression of the foreign slave trade; fugitive slave laws; abolition of slavery in general and in the District of Columbia; the freeing of slaves by purchase; advice to Congress to "drop the Negro question and attend to the business of the country"; repeal of the Fugitive Slave Act; confiscation of the property and liberation of the slaves of persons "supporting the rebellion"; reduction of South Carolina, Georgia, and part of Florida "into territorial condition to be colonized by Negroes freed by force of arms or by acts of Congress"; and similar subjects. Post-war records include papers concerning civil and legal rights, especially of freedmen, and enforcement of Reconstruction acts.

.159 —— Committee on Ways and Means.
Records, 35th-37th Congresses, include papers concerning the suppression of the African slave trade, and advice to drop the "Negro question."

.160 —— Select Committee on Gradual Emancipation.
Papers referred to the Committee, concerning gradual emancipation in the states of Delaware, Maryland, Virginia, Kentucky, Tennessee, and Missouri.

.161 —— Select Committee on Reconstruction.
Committee investigated the "Ku-Klux outrages" in Tennessee. Records deal with problems of Reconstruction.

.162 —— Select Committee on the Confiscation of Rebel Property.
Papers referred to the Committee. Committee reported a bill to "free from servitude the slaves of the rebels."

.163 —— Select Committee on the New Orleans Riots.
There are no records as such, but reports deal with the post-war situation, throwing light on wartime conditions and events.

.164 —— Select Committee to Consider a Bill to Establish a Bureau of Emancipation.
Committee papers and those referred to the Committee.

.165 —— Select Committee to Investigate the Affairs of the Freedman's Savings and Trust Co.
Records, 44th Congress.

.166 —— Select Committee to Investigate the Memphis Riots and Massacres.
There are no records of the Committee as such. Its printed report, with testimony and exhibits appended, depicts the "state of things" in Memphis at the time (1866) and certain conditions during and following the war, including particularly Negro-white relationships and the work of the Freedmen's Bureau.

.167 R.G. 235, Department of Health, Education, and Welfare.
Files of the Secretary (1953-60), containing materials pertaining to Negroes. Restricted.

.168 R.G. 249, Records of the Commissary General of Prisoners.
The records for Richmond, Va., include a register of Negro prisoners (1862-65) which gives information on their status and disposition.

.169 R.G. 267, Records of the Supreme Court of the United States.
Case files, 1792-1915, include Africa-connected cases relating to the slave trade, and cases arising from the civil rights acts adopted after the Civil War and from the Civil War Amendments to the Constitution.

.170 R.G. 316, Social Science Research Council.
Records relating to the Federal Work Relief Program (1935-37). Correspondence and memoranda chiefly of Arthur Whittier Macmahon, John David Millett, and Gladys Ogden; documents; printed and processed issuances of federal, state, and private agencies engaged or concerned with the Federal Work Relief Program; clippings; and the working papers of Gladys Ogden. Materials relate to projects approved and terms of aid; program recommendations and Presidential approvals; State and regional program planning, technological trends and national policy; Negro problems; apprenticeship training; vocational guidance and education; rural resettlement and rehabilitation.

.171 R.G. 365, Treasury Department Collection of Confederate Records.
Records include a register of claims filed on behalf of deceased soldiers (Jan. 3-Nov. 14, 1862), covering claims by others for the hire of slaves, among other things.

.172 R.G. 366, Records of Civil War Special Agencies of the Treasury Department.
Includes records of abandoned property, relating to records of the Freedmen's Bureau.

.173 R.G. 391, Records of the U.S. Regular Army Mobile Unit.
Includes descriptive books of the Regular Army regiments.

.174 R.G. 393, Records of United States Army Continental Commands.
Records, 1821-1920, of military districts and departments, including material relating to the Freedmen's Bureau.

DC173 U.S. GOVERNMENT PRINTING OFFICE. North Capital and H Sts., N.W., 20401. Tel 202 541-2014. Douglas G. True, Equal Employ. Opportunity Officer.

.1 Equal Employment Opportunity Program.
Files. Records, correspondence, reports and other papers concerning equal employment matters and other civil rights activities.

DC174 U.S. INFORMATION AGENCY. 1776 Pennsylvania Ave., N.W., 20547. Tel 202 632-4810. Lionel S. Mosley, Dir. of Equal Employ. Opportunity.

.1 U.S. Information Agency.
Equal Employment Opportunity Files. Includes reports, records, correspondence, and other papers concerning federal employment, and civil rights matters in the Agency.

DC175 U.S. INTERSTATE COMMERCE COMMISSION (ICC), BUREAU OF ENFORCEMENT. Constitution Ave. and 12th St., N.W., 20415. Tel 202 737-9765. Bernard A. Gould, Dir.
Among other powers and responsibilities, the Commission has regulatory authority over discrimination against passengers traveling in interstate or common carriers regulated by the Commission.

.1 Bureau of Enforcement.
Files. Records, correspondence, reports and other papers concerning investigation and enforcement activities relating to discrimination.

DC176 U.S. LIBRARY OF CONGRESS (1800). 10 First St., S.E., 20540. Tel 202 783-0400. L. Quincy Mumford, Librn. of Congress. Interlibrary loan, copying, typing, referrals made, consultation, answers inquiries which cannot be satisfied by libraries in the inquirer's state but declines requests for information for academic exercises, debates, or contests; publication for purchase of union catalogs, LC catalogs, catalog cards, bibliographies, and other guides.
The Library of Congress is the reference library and major research arm of the U.S. Congress and is a reference and research library for other government agencies, other libraries, and the adult public. The holdings of the Library of Congress on June 30, 1969, totaled more than 59,890,000 items, embracing all forms of library materials and pertaining to all aspects of the Nation's cultural heritage. These materials may be consulted by adults in 17 public reading rooms—2 reading rooms for the general book collections, and 15 for specialized materials.
Publ.: For information concerning the detailed use of the Library and for ordering instructions for its publications, the pamphlets, Information for Readers in the Library of Congress, and Library of Congress Publications in Print, are available on request from the Central Services Division, Library of Congress, Washington, D.C. 20504. Among some 350 titles in print are: A Directory of Information Resources in the United States: Federal Government, 1967; Folk Music: A Catalog of Folk Songs, Ballads, Dances, Instrumental Pieces, and Folk Tales of the United States and Latin America on Phonograph Records, 1964; Guide to the Study of the United States of America,

1960; <u>Library of Congress Quarterly Journal</u>; <u>Literary Recordings: A Checklist of the Archive of Recorded Poetry and Literature</u>, 1966; <u>National Register of Microform Masters</u>; <u>National Union Catalog</u>; <u>National Union Catalog of Manuscript Collections</u>; <u>Negro Newspapers on Microfilm</u>; <u>New Serial Titles</u>; <u>Union List of Serials</u>; <u>The Negro in the United States</u>.

Among materials in the Library relating to Negroes are the following collections which are described according to their formats—books, newspapers and unbound serials, mss, photographs and films, and music and sound recordings:

DC176.1   Books.

It is not feasible among book collections of more than 14,846,000 items to detail volumes dealing with or related to the races. The Library's holdings are pre-eminent in American history and politics, bibliography and library science, public documents, and publications of learned societies, among others, and its law collection is possibly the most comprehensive in the world. The book collections include not only monographs (books and pamphlets) but also bound copies of titles published in series (periodicals, learned journals, government documents, etc.). Access to the general book collections is made through the Main Reading Room and the Thomas Jefferson Room. Rareties and unique items are available only in the Library's special reading rooms. Among such materials is:

.2 — Slave Narrative Collection of the Federal Writer's Project.

ca. 10,000 typewritten pages transcribing interviews during the 1930's with former slaves, descendants of slaves, and witnesses to slavery, as well as transcripts of slave laws. May be consulted in the Rare Book Room.

.3   Newspapers and unbound serial publications.

The Library receives more than 1500 newspaper titles and more than 150,000 other serial titles (including government serial publications) from around the world. Of the 1500 newspapers, about 400 are retained on a current basis only; the remainder, of which 225 are published in the United States, are retained permanently. Access to unbound periodicals, journals, and government documents and access to newspapers (whether bound, unbound, or on microfilm) is made chiefly through the reading room of the Serial Division. Bound periodicals become a part of the book collections. Numerous serial titles in the collections are Negro publications, and many others contain materials for Afro-American studies.

.4   Manuscript collections.

The Library of Congress holds some 5000 collections containing a total of more than 29,572,000 ms items relating to American history and civilization. Among them, the following collections are known to contain materials relating to Afro-Americans. Access is through the Manuscript Reading Room.

.5 — Account books collection.

18th-19th century. 112 items. Included are ms volumes concerning plantation life.

.6 — Ambler, John, 1762-1836.

Papers, 1800-62. 68 items. Planter and militia officer. Correspondence and other papers, mostly relating to Ambler's service in the Virginia Militia, especially in the 19th and 2nd Regiments, during the period 1807-22. Correspondents include William H. Cabell, John H. Cooke, Augustine Davis, George Dixon, John S. Pleasants, and George W. Smith.

.7 — American Antislavery Society.

Papers, 1833-40. 1 box.

.8 — American Colonization Society.

Archives, 1816-1965. ca. 190,000 items. The Society was instrumental in removing free Negroes from the United States to Liberia, aided in the manumission of slaves, and in the suppression of the slave trade. Records consist of letterbooks, account books, minutes of proceedings, reports, financial records, and correspondence. Includes material on Liberia, lists of emigrants, correspondence with branch societies, church organizations, prospective colonists, slaveholders, and Society agents in Liberia.

.9 — Ames, Louise (Bates), 1908- .

Papers, 1939-64. 4 ft. (3000 items). Child psychologist and educator. Correspondence; bibliography of Dr. Ames (1935-65); clippings, printed matter, and memorabilia relating to the work of Dr. Ames and her collaborator, Frances Lillian Ilg, as columnists and doctors, and to the Gesell Institute of Child Development. The papers of Dr. Ames and Frances Ilg supplement the comparative studies of Negro and white children in the Gesell papers.

.10 — Arnold, Henry Harley, 1886-1950.

Papers, 1907-50. 110 ft. (85,000 items). Pioneer aviator and U.S. Army officer. Family correspondence (1934-50); general correspondence; notes and mss of articles and speeches; reports; newspaper clippings, and many other materials. Papers relate to, among many other subjects, the policies and events of World Wars I and II, including material concerning the Negro in the military service. Restricted.

.11 — Baker, Ray Stannard, 1870-1946.

Papers, 1836-1946. 61 ft. (ca. 30,000 items), in part photocopies and typescripts. Journalist, author, and biographer of Woodrow Wilson. Diaries, journals, correspondence, memoranda, notebooks; mss, of books, articles, and addresses; scrapbooks, photos., and printed matter. Baker's papers concern his family and early life, his career in newspaper and magazine writing and editing, his books; and includes considerable comment by Baker on the Negro question. Among correspondents are Booker T. Washington, William E.B. DuBois, Jane Addams, and George Foster Peabody.

.12 — Banks, Nathaniel Prentice, 1816-94.

Papers. Army officer. Included in the papers of Banks, a Major General of the Union Army, are materials on the Negro in the Civil War, the labor system instituted by Banks in New Orleans, La., Reconstruction, and 10 letters concerning politics and the New Orleans Massacre of July 30, 1866.

.13 — Barnes, Samuel D.

Papers, 1791-1867. ca. 7 items. Includes diaries, referring to Barnes' work with the Freedmen's Bureau in Mississippi.

.14 — Beecher, Henry Ward, 1813-87.

Papers, 1836-86. 9 ft. (ca. 5400 items). Clergyman. Mainly drafts of sermons (1837-68), together with correspondence (ca. 25 items, 1836-85, including 4 letters by Beecher); notes for speeches and lectures; seminary notes (1836); notebooks (1843-48); ms and galley proof of his work <u>Life of Jesus the Christ</u>; clippings, and scrapbooks. Included are letters concerning the status of Negroes, conditions at Andersonville prison, and the readmission of the seceded states to the Union.

.15 — Beveridge, Albert Jeremiah, 1862-1927.

Beveridge-Lincoln papers, 1788-1928. 15 ft., in part photocopies and transcripts. Political leader, biographer, and historian. Copies of Lincoln documents (correspondence, memoranda, reports, articles, clippings) and photographs used by Beveridge as source material in writing his biography of Lincoln, and the ms of the biography together with voluminous notes and comments by those to whom portions of the text were submitted for criticism. Many of the originals of the Lincoln documents are in the Herndon-Weik and the Lyman Trumbull collection in the Library.

.16 — Birney, James Gillespie, 1792-1857.

Papers, 1830-50. 14 items, 4 v., and 1 reel of microfilm. Anti-slavery leader. Diaries (1830, 1834, 1840-50), notebook and correspondence (1834-35) mainly from Birney to Theodore D. Weld and Gerrit Smith. Relates to slavery, abolition, African colonization, emancipation, and politics of the period. The microfilm, made from papers in the Library's Birney, Elizur Wright, and American Colonization Society collections, consists of letters from Birney to Ralph Randolph Gurley, Gerrit Smith, Theodore D. Weld, Elizur Wright, and others.

DC176.17 — Black, Jeremiah Sullivan.
Papers, 1813-1904. ca. 10,000 items. Attorney General under Buchanan. Contains material relating to Black's enforcement of federal laws affecting the slave trade and fugitive slaves.

.18 — Blair family.
Papers, 1836-1925. 21 ft. (ca. 11,700 items). Correspondence, legal papers, financial papers, biographical and genealogical data, political diary of Montgomery Blair, printed matter, lectures, speeches, military papers, and other papers of Francis Preston Blair, Jr., Francis Preston Blair, Sr., Gist Blair, and Montgomery Blair, relating to the publication of the Washington (D.C.) Globe, the Civil War and Reconstruction, the Dred Scott case, Montgomery Blair's activities as lawyer and Postmaster General in Lincoln's Cabinet, and other papers. Includes correspondence of William Ernest Smith, Thomas Hart Benton, Benjamin F. Butler, Cassius M. Clay, Charles A. Dana, James Buchanan Eads, Samuel Taylor Glover, Andrew Jackson, Samuel Phillips Lee, Whitelaw Reid, Martin Van Buren, and Gideon Welles.

.19 — Breckinridge family.
Papers, 1750-1950. ca. 515,000 items. Includes papers relating to Robert J. Breckinridge, Kentucky Presbyterian clergyman associated with the cause of Negro colonization.

.20 — Brennan, William J., Jr.
Papers, 1956- . ca. 11,000 items. Supreme Court Justice. Included are letters, notes, memoranda, and other papers relating to segregation and civil rights cases. Restricted.

.21 — British and Foreign Anti-Slavery and Aborigines Protection Society.
Archives, 1839-68. Microfilm (2 reels). Micrococopies of part of the Society's paper. Subjects include slavery, and the slave trade. Originals are held in the Rhodes House Library, Oxford, England.

.22 — Brown, John, 1800-59.
Papers, 1801-1928. ca. 300 items, in part transcripts and photocopies. Abolitionist. Letters, telegrams, documents, photographs, clippings, and other items, some by John Brown but most of them relating to him and to his raid on Harper's Ferry. Most of the collection consists of letters and telegrams from various individuals to Gov. Henry A. Wise of Virginia (Oct.-Dec., 1859).

.23 — Browning, Silas W., 1820-88.
Papers, 1779-1890. 59 items. Abolitionist and soldier in the 53rd Massachusetts Volunteer Infantry. Chiefly letters (1862-63) from Browning to his wife and daughters from Mississippi and Louisiana relating to his activities as a hospital steward, the diet and the health of the regiment, conduct of the troops, and conditions in the South.

.24 — Bruce family.
Papers, 1792-1892. 2 ft. (1500 items). Bills, receipts, invoices, notes, and other plantation accounts (chiefly 1800-80) of Charles Bruce (1798-1879), planter, merchant, and State senator of Staunton Hill Plantation, Charlotte Co., Va., and his parents, James and Elvira Bruce.

.25 — Burton, Harold Hitz.
Papers, 1918-63. ca. 12,000 items. Associate Justice of the U.S. Supreme Court (1945-58). Correspondence, notes, and memoranda of Burton and various Justices who served on the Court during Burton's period in office. Included are materials relating to segregation cases in the 1940's and '50's.

.26 — Butler, Benjamin F.
Papers, 1831-96. ca. 190,000 items. Army officer, and originator of the term "contraband," as applied to fleeing slaves. Included are such subjects as his Civil War career, the administration of New Orleans, La., during the Civil War, the enlistment of Negroes into the Union Army from the Department of Virginia and North Carolina, and Reconstruction. Butler was a Major General in the Union Army.

.27 — Cameron, Simon, 1799-1889.
Papers, 1738-1889. ca. 8000 items. U.S. Senator, and Secretary of War. Cameron was a prominent anti-slavery figure during the Civil War period.

.28 — Carnegie, Andrew, 1835-1919.
Papers, 1803-1935. 67,000 items. Industrialist and philanthropist. Correspondence, reports, memoranda, speeches, articles, book files, financial papers, printed matter and other papers (chiefly 1890-1919) relating to all facets of Carnegie's life and concerning such matters as cultural and social interests, economics, libraries, the Negro, the Andrew Carnegie Fund, Carnegie Foundation for the Advancement of Teaching, Carnegie Corporation of New York, and the Carnegie Trust Fund. Among the many correspondents are Charles W. Eliot, Seth Low, Walter Hines Page, Whitelaw Reid, Elihu Root, Carl Schurz, and Booker T. Washington.

.29 — Chandler, Zachariah, 1813-79.
Papers, 1854-99. 2 ft. (1100 items). U.S. Senator from Michigan and Secretary of the Interior. Correspondence, principally letters received, only a few dating after 1879, relating chiefly to the politics of the Civil War and Reconstruction. Reflects the views of the radical, anti-slavery element of the Republican Party when Chandler was serving on the Republican Congressional Committee and the Joint Committee on the Conduct of War, and was chairman of the Committee on Commerce.

.30 — Clarkson, James Sullivan, 1842-1918.
Papers, 1851-1917. ca. 2 ft. (ca. 1200 items). In part, transcripts. Politician, editor, and business executive. Correspondence, speeches, articles, newspapers clippings, and printed matter, relating chiefly to Clarkson's activities in the Republican party and his business interests. Included are materials relating to Clarkson's interest in Negro technicians in Africa, and the education of African students in America. Collection also contains papers relating to his service as surveyor of customs for the Post of New York, during which time he was President Theodore Roosevelt's principal white consultant on the matter of dispensing Negro patronage.

.31 — Clarkson, Levinus.
Papers, 1772-93. 1 box and 1 portfolio. Negro merchant of South Carolina.

.32 — Clay, Henry, 1777-1852.
Papers, 1770-1910. 7 ft. (4500 items). Statesman. Principally correspondence (chiefly 1814-52) plus drafts of Clay's "dispatches and instructions" as Secretary of State. The overwhelming subject of the collection is politics and the papers relate to nearly all phases of Clay's public career, and such subjects as slavery, public lands, and internal improvements.

.33 — Clinch, Duncan Lamont, 1787-1849.
Papers, 1834-59. 4 v. Soldier and Georgia planter. Two letter copybooks (1834-36), order book (1834-36), and ledger (1859) listing slaves at Clinch's plantation, the Refuge, and their dollar value. Mainly Clinch's letters and orders when he commanded American forces at Fort King and other Florida fortifications during the Seminole War (1834-36), to reflecting concern over depredations committed by Indians and Negroes.

.34 — Cockburn, Sir George.
Papers, ca. 1788-1847. 82 v. British admiral. Logbooks, journals, correspondence, and fleet orders. Materials relate in part to cruises to Africa and to the slave trade.

.35 — Coker, Reverend Daniel.
Diary, 1821. Agent of the American Colonization Society. Coker's diary was kept at Foura Bay on the west coast of Africa in 1821.

DC176.36 —— Covode, John, 1808-71.
Papers, 1854-70. ca. 100 items. U.S. Representative from Pennsylvania. Included is the draft of Covode's report on conditions in the Mississippi Valley after the Civil War.

.37 —— Crittenden, John Jordan, 1787-1863.
Papers, 1782-1888. 6 ft. (ca. 2600 items). Lawyer and statesman. Correspondence, legal papers, and some speeches and state papers. Mainly correspondence covering Crittenden's career as Senator, U.S. Attorney General, and Governor of Kentucky (1848-50), and concerning national politics, particularly tariff and banking matters, Texas, Mexico, and slavery.

.38 —— Curry, Jabez Lamar Monroe, 1825-1903.
Papers, 1637-1939. 10 ft. (ca. 3850 items) and 4 reels of microfilm (microcopy of original materials in Alabama Dept. of History and Archives). Alabama statesman, author, clergyman, diplomat, and educator. Diaries, correspondence, printed matter, clippings, memorabilia, notes and memoranda, documents and legal papers, accounts, lectures and sermons, essays, scrapbook, mss. of autobiography, speeches, and articles. Reports and other papers concern the Peabody Education Fund, the John F. Slater Fund for Negro education, the Southern Education Board, Curry's studies on Civil War history and the civic government of the Confederacy. The Diaries (1866-1902) and much of the correspondence (1880-1903) relate to Curry's career as an educator, diplomat, and Baptist minister.

.39 —— Curtis, Benjamin Robbins, 1809-74.
Papers, 1831-79. 450 items. Lawyer, of Massachusetts and Associate Justice of the U.S. Supreme Court. Principally correspondence, with several legal papers, mostly dealing with legal and judicial matters, occasionally touching upon politics. Includes a few papers concerning the Dred Scott case among which are the Roger B. Taney correspondence and a paper by Curtis entitled Some Observations on the Above Correspondence.

.40 —— Delano family.
Papers, 1853-89. ca. 1 ft. (1540 items). Correspondence (largely 1869) and photograph album of Columbus Delano (1809-96), U.S. Representative from Ohio and Secretary of the Interior, and his son John Sherman Delano, businessman. Relates to such subjects as Ohio and national politics, and the purchase of the Archives of the Confederate States of America. Among the correspondents are Henry Ward Beecher, Schuyler Colfax, Roscoe Conkling, Hamilton Fish, Jay Gould, and Whitelaw Reid.

.41 —— Dickinson, Anna Elizabeth, 1842-1932.
Papers, 1860-1932. 12 ft. (ca. 8500 items). Abolitionist, actress, author, and suffragette. Correspondence, speeches, plays, legal and financial documents, newspaper clippings, and other papers, covering such topics as abolition and Negro rights, woman suffrage, Republican party election campaigns, and the theater. Correspondents include Susan B. Anthony, Noah Brooks, Benjamin F. Butler, Oliver Johnson, Wendell Phillips, Theodore Tilton, Whitelaw Reid, and Charles D. Warner.

.42 —— Doar, Stephen D.
Papers, 1851-62. 2 items. Includes plantation accounts.

.43 —— Dr. Bray's Associates.
Mss. 8 boxes. Photocopies. One of the objects of this organization was the support of Negro schools on British plantations. Original mss housed in building of Society for the Propagation of the Gospel in London. Papers include correspondence and a 1729 minute book.

.44 —— Doolittle, James Rood, 1815-97.
Papers, 1858-1929. 136 items, in part transcripts. Judge and U.S. Senator from Wisconsin. Correspondence, speeches, and clippings related to matters concerning Doolittle during the Civil War and Reconstruction period.

.45 —— Douglas, William O.
Papers, 1925- . ca. 105 items. Supreme Court Justice. Included are letters, notes, memoranda, and other papers relating to segregation and civil rights cases. Restricted.

.46 —— Douglass, Frederick.
Papers, 1845-1904. Microfilm, 20 reels. Microcopies of the Frederick Douglass papers that were in the Douglass home in Anacostia, Md.

.47 —— Dutilh and Wachsmuth, Philadelphia.
Records, 1784-1800. ca. 5000 items. Business correspondence, accounts, documents relating to trade with other shipping houses in Europe, America, and the West Indies; and the slave trade. Mainly in French with some Dutch and English.

.48 —— Ewell, Richard Stoddert, 1817-72.
Papers, 1838-96. ca. 200 items. U.S. and Confederate Army officer. Chiefly letters from Ewell to his family and others concerning Army life, the Mexican War, the Civil War, and his imprisonment at Fort Warren, Mass. Includes accounts of the Gettysburg and Peninsular campaigns and the use of Negroes as soldiers by the Confederacy. In part, photocopies.

.49 —— Ewing, Thomas, 1789-1871.
Family papers, 1757-1941. 123 ft. (ca. 94,000 items), in part transcripts. Lawyer, U.S. Senator from Ohio, U.S. Secretary of the Interior and Secretary of the Treasury. Correspondence, diaries, journals, biographical material, genealogical records, legal and military papers, financial papers, drafts and printed copies of speeches, lectures, books, articles, essays, public letters, poems, reports, briefs, notes, autographs, telegrams, scrapbooks, maps, photographs, drawings, printed matter, and memorabilia. The bulk of the collection dates from 1830-1900 and pertains to westward expansion and frontier life, the struggle for freedom in Kansas, the Peace Convention (1861), the assassination of Lincoln, the Johnson administration, Reconstruction, and other subjects.

.50 —— Fessenden, William Pitt, 1806-69.
Papers, 1832-78. 2 ft. (1000 items). Lawyer, politician, and Cabinet officer. Correspondence, telegrams, newspaper clippings, and other related printed matter, reflecting Maine and national politics, abolitionism, financing of the Civil War, Reconstruction, and the impeachment of Andrew Johnson.

.51 —— Fleetwood, Christian Abraham, 1840-1914.
Papers, 1797-1945. 2 ft. (ca. 400 items). Free Negro, soldier, and civic leader. Diaries, correspondence, legal documents, genealogical records, memorabilia, photographs, scrapbook, and printed matter. Subjects dealt with include slavery, Fleetwood's military and civilian career during and after the Civil War, education, nursing, and other civic and social problems of the Negro community, particularly in the District of Columbia, where Fleetwood held various government and business positions. Includes papers of his wife, Sarah Iredell Fleetwood, a nurse, and several members of the family.

.52 —— Floyd, John.
Papers, 1823-32. ca. 30 items. Included is correspondence (ca. 1820-30) bearing on slavery.

.53 —— Foote, Andrew Hull.
Papers, 1838-63. ca. 800 items. Navy officer. The mss of Rear Admiral Foote include two journals (1849-51) kept during a cruise to the African coast in pursuit of slave ships; also includes accounts of sea chases and notes on Liberia and St. Helena.

.54 —— Force, Peter.
Papers, 1812-67. ca. 11,000 items. Printer for the American Colonization Society.

.55 —— Foulke, William Dudley, 1848-1935.
Papers, 1884-1935. 3 ft. (ca. 2100 items).

Lawyer, author, and civic reformer. Correspondence, telegrams, speeches, writings, clippings, and pamphlets, largely concerning Foulke's civic reform activities, particularly those relating to the National Civil Service Reform League, the Ku Klux Klan, and Prohibition; and personal correspondence.

DC176.56 — France, Archives Nationales: Archives de la Marine, series B, 17th-19th centuries. 57,600 items. Photocopies and microfilm made from originals in the Archives Nationales, Paris. Sub-series B-7: Foreign countries, commerce and consulates, letters received, including memoirs and documents relating to the U.S., and containing notes on slavery in America.

.57 — Frankfurter, Felix, 1882-1965. Papers, 1864-1965. ca. 36,000 items. Supreme Court Justice. Included are letters, notes, and memoranda relating to segregation and civil rights cases.

.58 — Friends of Freedom. Record book, 1834-58. Anti-slavery album of contributions from Friends of Freedom.

.59 — Frost, Edward, 1801-68. Papers, 1802-66. 2 ft. (ca. 1500 items). Planter, businessman, jurist, and district attorney for South Carolina. Family correspondence, political, legal and business records, commissions, appointments, wills, estate and plantation accounts, ledgers, and memorabilia relating to Frost's service as district attorney, states rights delegate from Charleston to the State legislature.

.60 — Fulham Palace Archives: Archives of the Bishop of London. Transcripts of American material (chiefly 17th-18th centuries) in this collection. Letters and documents relating to the colonies.

.61 — Gesell, Arnold Lucius, 1880-1961. Papers, 1870-1961. 100 ft. (ca. 90,000 items). Child specialist and director of the Yale Clinic of Child Development. Correspondence, abstracts, addresses, biographical material, charts, clinical records, clippings, contracts, financial papers, genealogical records, lectures, personnel records, photos, reports, scrapbooks, and other papers concerning Gesell's professional life. Includes material relating to his work in the Gesell Institute of Child Development, Yale Clinic of Child Development; Catherine Amatruda, Louise (Bates) Ames, Burton Castner, Frances L. Ilg, and Helen Thompson; the Connecticut Child Welfare Survey; the childhood development of Abraham Lincoln; and comparative studies of the mental and physical development of Negro and white children. Restricted by donor.

.62 — Giddings, Joshua Reed, 1795-1864. Papers, 1839-96. 3 boxes (ca. 900 items). Abolitionist and U.S. Representative. Chiefly correspondence of his son-in-law, George W. Julian, abolitionist and U.S. Representative from Indiana (1845-96).

.63 — Gillette, James Jenkins, d. 1881. Papers, 1857-84. 2 ft. (ca. 2000 items). U.S. Army Commissary of Subsistence and U.S. Commissioner of Claims, Mobile, Ala. Correspondence, military papers, receipts, court records, and docket book, relating to Gillette's military service and his activities as claims' commissioner. Includes papers relating to the U.S. Circuit Court for the Fifth Circuit, the Republican party in Alabama, the elections of 1876 and 1880, the Freedmen's Bureau, and Negro education.

.64 — Great Britain collection. Included are logbooks (1808-40) covering the movement and activities of 61 British naval vessels on the African, West Indian, and North American Stations.

.65 — Greeley, Horace, 1811-72. Papers, 1826-1928. 4 ft. (ca. 1500 items), in part transcripts. Journalist. Correspondence, lectures, autobiography, articles, notes, and speeches by and about Greeley, newspaper clippings, scrapbooks, a notebook, printed matter, and other papers, chiefly 1860-72. Includes material relating to Greeley's early life in New York City as printer and publisher of literary and political newspapers, the slavery issue, and Liberal Republicanism. Among correspondents are Charles A. Dana, John G. Nicolay, and Gerrit Smith.

.66 — Green, Duff, 1791-1875. Papers, 1813-79. 2 ft. (1200 items), in part transcripts. Journalist, politician, and industrial promoter. Correspondence (1826-79), official and legal documents, clippings, and other printed matter. Chiefly letters (1826-44) relating to business affairs, free trade, slavery, Texas, and other political matters.

.67 — Hammond, James Henry, 1807-64. Papers, 1823-75. 10 ft. (5000 items). Governor of South Carolina and U.S. Senator. Correspondence, diaries, scrapbooks, account books, plantation manuals, and printed copies of Hammond's speeches, for the most part reflecting State and national politics in the three decades leading to the Civil War. Among subjects mentioned are states' rights, slavery, the Southern Convention at Nashville, Tenn. in 1850, secession, and nullification. Plantation books (1831-58) include lists of Negroes and notes on management of slaves.

.68 — Harmon Foundation. Papers, 1928-40. ca. 16 file drawers, and numerous cartons. Correspondence, photos, biographical data, and other records. Included are files of correspondence concerning African art, and materials relating to the work of American artists of Negro origin, comprised of biographical data on each artist, photographs of him and his work, and correspondence. Also included is correspondence (ca. 1920-30's) relative to awards for distinguished achievements by Americans of Negro origin in literature, music, industry, science, fine arts, education, and religion.

.69 — Harper, Robert Goodloe, 1765-1825. Papers, 1796-1823. ca. 50 items. A founder and influential member of the American Colonization Society.

.70 — Harrison, Burton. Papers of the Burton Harrison family, 1812-1944. ca. 12,000 items. Includes papers of Jesse Burton Harrison relating to his activities in support of the American Colonization Society.

.71 — Hartz, Edward L. Papers, 1847-1910. ca. 315 items. Union Army officer. Includes journal (1864) containing information on a voyage taken to return Negro colonists from the Ile à Vache, south west of Haiti.

.72 — Hawks, Ester H. Papers, 1856-67. 515 items. Nurse, of Manchester, N.H. Correspondence and other papers relating to the activities of Mrs. Hawks and her husband Dr. J. Milton Hawks in caring for sick and wounded soldiers in various military hospitals during the Civil War and in establishing schools and distributing supplies throughout the South for the National Freedman's Relief Association. Includes numerous letters from her husband and a few from Brig. Gen. Rufus Saxton, military governor of the Dept. of the South.

.73 — Hay, John Milton, 1838-1905. Papers, 1856-1905. 30 ft. and 1 reel of microfilm. In part, photocopies. Microfilm copy of diary and notebooks at Brown University. Statesman, diplomat, author, journalist, and poet. Correspondence and letterbooks, speeches, diaries, notebooks, scrapbook, clippings, printed matter, memorabilia, photos, and memoranda, mainly for the years 1897-1905, when Hay served as Ambassador to Great Britain and as Secretary of State. Earlier papers deal with his legal, literary, and journalistic activities, and with his service as assistant secretary to Abraham Lincoln.

DC176.74 —— Herndon, William Henry, 1818-91.
Herndon-Weik Collection of Lincolniana. ca. 1824-1927. 11 ft. (ca. 4600 items), in part, typescripts of 115 Lincoln letters (1855-65). Lawyer of Springfield, Illinois, and law partner of Abraham Lincoln. Correspondence, legal documents written in whole or part by Lincoln, a campaign notebook in scrapbook form prepared for the debate (1858) with Stephen Douglas and another devoted to slavery; prints, etchings, photos of Lincoln and others, clippings, printed matter, and memorabilia. Includes papers of Herndon concerning Lincoln and his biography of Lincoln; papers (1830-1927) of Jesse William Weik, lawyer of Greencastle, Indiana, and biographer of Lincoln in collaboration with Herndon, the Weik Manuscript Corporation, and other papers of the Corporation. Much of the collection is duplicated in the Ward Hill Lamon papers in the Henry E. Huntington Library, San Marino, California.

.75 —— Hertz, Edward.
Hertz Collection of Lincolniana. 8 boxes. N.Y. lawyer. Includes ms of Hertz' biography of Lincoln.

.76 —— Holmes, George Frederick, 1820-97.
Papers, 1785-1893. ca. 100 items. Editor, scholar, author, and educator. Correspondence relating to Holmes' editorship of the Southern Quarterly Review, to his scholarly articles and an unpublished history of the Civil War; includes remarks upon slavery.

.77 —— Holmes, John Haynes, 1879-1964.
Papers, ca. 1938-64. ca. 50,000 items. Clergyman, associated with the American Civil Liberties Union and with other liberal causes.

.78 —— Howe, Julia Ward, 1819-1910.
Papers, 1861-1917. 2 ft. (ca. 1500 items). Author and reformer. About 30 items of correspondence, together with addresses, articles, lectures, poems, sermons, and other writings by Mrs. Howe, on such subjects as religion, nature, literature, politics, suffrage, the Negro, education, and social work. Part of the material is in the hand of an amanuensis.

.79 —— Huebsch, Benjamin W., 1876-1964.
Papers, 1893-1964. 17 ft. (10,515 items). Publisher. Correspondence, diary (1925-61), financial papers, articles and speeches, literary mss, notebooks, and miscellaneous papers. Includes material relating to Huebsch's work with the American Civil Liberties Union, among many other papers.

.80 —— Jefferson, Thomas, 1743-1826.
Papers, 1651-1856. ca. 50,000 items. Third President of the United States. Contains material relating to slavery.

.81 —— Kapp, Friedrich, 1824-84.
Collection of correspondence, 1842-84. ca. 600 items. In German, primarily transcripts and excerpts of letters by or to Kapp formed by his great-granddaughter, Edith G. H. Lenel, for her doctoral dissertation (1935). German politician, historian and revolutionary; lawyer of New York City and New York State Commissioner of Emigration. Correspondence relating the life and political philosophy of Kapp, including the slavery question.

.82 —— Lambeth Palace Library: Manuscripts of the Archbishop of Canterbury.
Transcripts of American material (1595-18th cent.) in this collection. Letters and other papers relating to colonies, plantations, Indians, and other subjects.

.83 —— Lathers, Richard, 1820-1903.
Papers, 1826-1901. ca. 210 items. Merchant, of Georgetown, S.C., and New York City, and officer in the 31st Regt., South Carolina Militia, who later supported the Union. Correspondence, speeches, circulars, clippings, and other printed matter includes material relating to the Civil War and Reconstruction, local history of South Carolina and New York, political, cultural, social, philanthropic, and religious activities.

.84 —— Latrobe, John Hazlehurst Boneval, 1803-91.
Papers, 1828-50. ca. 26 items. Lawyer and inventor, supporter of the American Colonization Society.

.85 —— Laurens, Henry, 1724-92.
Papers of Henry and John Laurens, 1732-1811. ca. 90 items. Merchant, planter, statesman, of Charleston, S.C. Correspondence, notes respecting diplomatic appointments, diary, and journal fragments. Bulk of the material, dating after 1775, deals mainly with military, political, and diplomatic events of the Revolutionary War, and includes the employment of Negro slaves in the Army, and the war in the South. Correspondents include Alexander Hamilton, John Rutledge, Thomas Bee, Ralph Izard, Baron Holtzendorff, John Lloyd, Mary Laurens, and John Lewis Gervais.

.86 —— Leavitt, Joshua, 1794-1873.
Family papers, 1812-71. 1 ft. (ca. 100 items). Abolitionist, clergyman, and editor. Chiefly letters from Leavitt to his brother, Roger Hooker Leavitt, relating to family affairs, abolition, the Free Soil party, and Joshua Leavitt's editorship of the periodicals The Evangelist, The Emancipator, and The Independent. Correspondents include Samuel Clesson Allen, George Grennell, Jr., and Moses Smith.

.87 —— Lieber, Francis, 1800-1872.
Papers, 1841-72. 250 items. Educator, political scientist, and publicist. Principally Lieber's letters to his friend, Samuel B. Ruggles, trustee of Columbia College, relating to Lieber's writings, political theory, politics, abolitionism, free trade, and his resignation from South Carolina College.

.88 —— Limongi, Felix. collector.
The Felix Limongi collection of papers re Louisiana, New Orleans, slavery, Civil War, and Reconstruction, 1832-80. 240 items. Chiefly legal correspondence, documents, clippings, parts of docket files, and other papers of the New Orleans law firm of Hornor & Benedict (formerly Durant & Hornor) relating to legal problems of slavery, the Civil War, and Reconstruction. Names represented include William S. Benedict, Thomas Jefferson Durant, and Joseph P. Hornor.

.89 —— Lincoln, Abraham, 1809-65.
Papers, 1833-1916. 41 ft. (ca. 40,000 items). U.S. President. Correspondence and other papers, mainly letters addressed to Lincoln during his Presidency. Includes some 1200 items preserved by John G. Nicolay in his capacities as Lincoln's secretary and editor of the writings; 2 drafts of the Gettysburg Address, the letter of condolence from Queen Victoria to Mrs. Lincoln, and a very small amount of material about Lincoln, 1865-1916. Correspondents include Nathaniel Banks, Edward Bates, Montgomery Blair, Benjamin Brewster, Salmon P. Chase, Schuyler Colfax, David Davis, Ulysses S. Grant, John Hay, Andrew Johnson, Reverdy Johnson, George B. McClellan, George G. Meade, Edwin D. Morgan, John G. Nicolay, William Rosecrans, William H. Seward, Horatio Seymour, Caleb B. Smith, James Speed, Edwin M. Stanton, Charles Sumner, Lyman Trumbull, Lew Wallace, Elihu B. Washburne, and Gideon Welles.

.90 —— Logan family.
Papers, 1847-1923. 61 ft. (46,000 items). Correspondence, legal and military papers, drafts of speeches, articles and books, scrapbooks, maps, memorabilia, photographs, and printed matter, chiefly 1860-1917. Most of the material concerns John Alexander Logan (1826-86) Union Army officer and U.S. Representative and Senator from Illinois, and relates to the military, political, and social history of the Civil

War and post-war period on such subjects as Reconstruction, and the impeachment of Andrew Johnson.

DC176.91 —— Lowndes, William, 1782-1822.

Papers, 1787-1842. 1 ft. (ca. 100 items). Planter and U.S. Representative from South Carolina. Correspondence, journals, notes, and memoranda. The bulk of the correspondence is between Lowndes and Charles Cotesworth Pinckney and between Lowndes and his wife, Elizabeth (Pinckney) Lowndes. The journals contain descriptions of day-to-day operations of Lowndes' plantations.

.92 —— McCulloch, Hugh, 1808-95.

Papers, 1855-94. 600 items. Banker, financier, Comptroller of the Currency, and Secretary of the Treasury. Primarily correspondence with some speeches, reports, and other related material, chiefly 1863-69. Subjects mentioned include finance, currency, Reconstruction, enfranchisement of Negroes, and politics.

.93 —— McKaye, James M., 1805-88.

Papers, 1862-1953. 53 items. Business executive and member of the U.S. American Freedmen's Inquiry Commission which was appointed by President Lincoln to gather data for the Emancipation Proclamation. Correspondence (1862-63) of the Commission, an incomplete autobiography (1822-55), newspaper clippings, and other papers. Correspondents include James N. Gloucester, Samuel Gridley Howe, Robert Dale Owen, Edwin M. Stanton, Charles Sumner, and William J. Wilson.

.94 —— McLean, John, 1785-1861.

Papers, 1817-61. 8 ft. (ca. 3500 items). U.S. Representative from Ohio, Postmaster General, and Supreme Court Justice. Correspondence, legal briefs, financial data, docket book (ca. 1820), printed matter, a file of reports, opinions, and briefs arranged by case name, and other papers relating to such subjects as Whig party, secession trends, slavery, and McLean's dissent in the Dred Scott case. Correspondents include James Buchanan, John C. Calhoun, Salmon P. Chase, Thomas Ewing, James Madison, Richard Rush, Daniel Webster, and Thurlow Weed.

.95 —— McPherson, Edward, 1830-95.

Papers, 1738-1936. 23 ft. (ca. 18,000 items). Editor, political cyclopedist, statistician, and U.S. Representative from Pennsylvania. Correspondence; family, financial, and estate papers, genealogy, and family history; records (1856-88) of the U.S. House of Representatives; a speech, article, and book file; scrapbooks, and other papers; on such subjects as national and local Republican party politics and campaigns, and the Reconstruction period.

.96 —— Madison, James, 1751-1836.

Papers, 1723-1859. ca. 12,000 items. Fourth President of the United States. Contains material relating to slavery.

.97 —— Mangum, Willie Person, 1792-1861.

Papers, 1771-1906. 7 ft. (ca. 5000 items). Judge, U.S. Senator, and Representative from North Carolina. Correspondence, notes, diaries, speeches, legal papers, memoranda, bills, receipts, and printed material, concerning local, southern, and national politics, the Whig party in the South, the Mangum plantation, and economic and social conditions in North Carolina.

.98 —— Mann, Mary Tyler (Peabody), 1806-87.

Papers, 1863-76. 75 items. In part, transcripts and photocopies of originals in Antioch College, Yellow Springs, Ohio. Educator and wife of Horace Mann. Correspondence, newspapers, clippings, and printed matter. Includes letters from Mrs. Mann's niece, Maria R. Mann, while stationed at the Freedmen's Camp, Helena, Ark., to the Rev. William L. Ropes, and to her family.

.99 —— Mason, Alexander Macomb, 1841-97.

Papers, 1871-98. 51 items. Resident of Washington, D.C., and Bey of Massaua, Eritrea. Official letters to Mason, diplomatic papers, orders, reports, articles, and other papers relating to the Egyptian Sudan and Ethiopia expeditions in search of oil and water, in which Mason participated in the service of the Khedive of Egypt under the command of Generals Charles Stone and Charles Gordon. Includes material relating to the slave trade.

.100 —— Milton, George Fort, 1894-1955.

Papers, 1828-1963. ca. 30,000 items. Editor, historian, and public official. Correspondence, reports, printed matter, and other papers. Materials pertaining to lynching, to Milton's Eve of Conflict and Age of Hate, to his membership (1930-33) on the Commission on Interracial Cooperation, and the Southern Commission on the Study of Lynching.

.101 —— Miner, Myrtilla, 1815-64.

Papers, 1839-64. 2 ft., in part photocopies. Correspondence, documents, notes, pamphlets, clippings, photographs, and other papers relating to Miss Miner's efforts in the establishment and maintenance of a school for Negro girls in Washington, D.C. The bulk of the papers were assembled by Lester G. Wells, whose unfinished biography of Miss Miner is included. Correspondents include Samuel Rhoads, Benjamin Tatham, and members of the Miner family. The school, Miner's Teachers College, later became affiliated with Howard University.

.102 —— Mitchell, Samuel Chiles, 1864-1948.

Papers, 1903-13. 8 ft. (ca. 5000 items). Professor and college president. Family and general correspondence; ms, typescript, nearprint, and printed copies of speeches, articles, and lectures; a small file of poetry and financial papers; reports, records, and memoranda relating to the administration of the Peabody Education Fund. The bulk of the collection dates from 1908-13 while he was president of the University of South Carolina. Subjects represented include education in the South.

.103 —— Monroe, James, 1758-1831.

Papers, 1758-1839. ca. 5000 items. Fifth President of the United States. Included is material pertaining to slavery.

.104 —— National Association for the Advancement of Colored People.

Records, 1909-59. ca. 1.5-2 million items. Correspondence, clippings, legal briefs, trial transcripts, speeches, articles, and other printed and unprinted materials, principally 1919-59, recording the growth and development of the Association, minutes of the meetings of the board of directors and of the executive committee, office diaries, employment records, financial records including special funds for the Sweet Case, data on life memberships, publicity records including the activities of the Speakers' Bureau. Treated are such subjects as discrimination in business and government, segregation in schools, government, and private establishments, lynchings, mob violence, race riots, antilynching measures, suppression of the Negro vote in the South, labor disputes, unions, politics, "Birth of a Nation," Garvey Movement, armed forces, Pan Africanism, Ku Klux Klan, Spingarn Medal, American Civil Liberties Union, and providing extensive background on Negro life in urban and rural America, especially in the 1930's. Concern with Negro welfare outside the U.S. is also covered, specifically in the files relating to Haiti, the Virgin Islands, and the Pan-African Congress. Includes correspondence and other material relating to the Association's branches, mainly for the period 1910-39, and reflecting civil rights infringements and violations, local grievances, requests for advice on legal matters and other local matters. Branch files consist of records from Montgomery, Ala., District of Columbia, Baltimore, Md., Chicago, Ill., New York City, and from the states of Alabama, California, Idaho, Illinois, Maryland, Mississippi, New

York, Pennsylvania, Ohio, Rhode Island, and South Carolina. Other material relating to the Association is found in the records of the Scottsboro Defense Committee; personal papers of Thurgood Marshall; extensive official, as well as some personal, correspondence of such NAACP officers as Robert Bagnall, Charles Houston, Addie Hunton, James Weldon Johnson, Daisy Lampkin, E. Frederick Morrow, William Pickens, Herbert Seligman, Walter White, and Roy Wilkins; and official correspondence of Roy Nash, Mary White Ovington, Charles E. Russell, John R. Shillady, Arthur Spingarn, Joel Spingarn, Moorfield Storey, Oswald G. Villard, and William E. Walling. Additions to this collection are expected.

DC176.105 — National Urban League.
Records, 1910-60. ca. 250 vf (ca. .5 million items). All phases of League activity are reflected in the collection. Included are the League's general correspondence, memoranda to United States Presidents, minutes of the meetings of the board of trustees, clippings, official and personal correspondence of officers, League publications, financial records, and membership files. Among other subjects treated are adoptions, Beaux Arts Ball, industrial relations, employment discrimination, vocational training, urbanization, migration, urban welfare and relief, International Conference on Social Welfare, White Citizens Councils, freedom rides, housing, and education. Public opinion of the League and its social involvement can be traced through many scrapbook items. Restricted.

.106 — National Urban League, Southern Regional Office.
Records, 1912-64. ca. 122 ft. (ca. 85,000 items). Correspondence, reports, minutes of meetings, speeches, articles, memoranda, notes, surveys, and miscellaneous material, chiefly 1943-61. Includes personal papers (1912-19) of the Office's first director, Jesse O. Thomas, and records for the years of his tenure (1919-43) chiefly concerned with his activities on behalf of the office and with its financial operations; personal papers (1930-46) of Nelson C. Jackson, director, 1946-53; and articles by Jesse O. Thomas, William Y. Bell, Jr. (director, 1944-46), and Nelson C. Jackson on many issues relating to Negroes in the South from the 1920's to the 1950's. Subjects include the Office's founding in 1919, its subsequent role as the coordinating body of the League in 13 Southern and Border states, the growth and development of local affiliates in southern cities, the reaction of local affiliates to the needs of the Negro community, difficulties in staffing branches with qualified personnel, the relationship of administrative and other department personnel in the national office to the staff of the Southern Office, employment trends of Negroes in the South, budgetary considerations concerned primarily with financing national programs, and the Atlanta School of Social Work. Correspondents include Harry Alston, Blanche A. Beatty, William Y. Bell, Jr., Clarence Coleman, George Edmund Haynes, T. Arnold Hill, Albion Holsey, John Hope, C.B. Hosmer, Nelson C. Jackson, Eugene Kinckle Jones, Robert Moton, A.M. Neeley, Franklin O. Nichols, Guichard Parris, Mahlon Puryear, Ann Tanneyhill, Jesse O. Thomas, Julius A. Thomas, Forrest B. Washington, L. Hollingsworth Wood, and Whitney M. Young, Jr. Additions to this collection are expected. Open to investigators under restrictions accepted by the Library.

.107 — Nicolay, John G., 1832-1901.
Papers, 1859-1913. 1 v. and 16 boxes. Private secretary and biographer of President Lincoln. Includes notes, diaries, letters, scrapbooks relating to Lincoln's administration, and correspondence of Nicolay's daughter Helen with Robert Todd Lincoln. 1873-1913.

.108 — Niebuhr, Reinhold, 1892- .
Papers, 1913-66. 12 ft. (ca. 5600 items). Theologian. Correspondence, speeches, sermons, articles, book reviews, typescripts of books and articles, biographical material, bibliographies, photographs, and memorabilia, relating to Dr. Niebuhr's interest in the Delta Cooperative Farm project, Hillhouse, Miss. (1935-43), the Committee on Economic and Racial Justice of the Socialist Party of Tennessee (1935-38), and other social agencies. Includes papers (1952-63) of June Bingham and the ms of her biography of Niebuhr, Courage to Change (1961). Niebuhr's correspondents include Jacques Barzun, James Bryant Conant, George Sherwood Eddy, Felix Frankfurter, Robert Maynard Hutchins, Margaret Mead, Arthur Meier Schlesinger, Sr., and Paul Tillich.

.109 — Ogden, Robert C.
Papers, 1862-1923. ca. 9000 items. Merchant, president of the board of trustees, Hampton Institute, and a trustee of Tuskegee Institute. Subjects include promotion and stimulation of white and Negro education in the South, especially late 19th and early 20th century.

.110 — Olmsted, Frederick Law, 1822-1903.
Papers, 1822-1903. 20 ft. (ca. 24,000 items), in part photocopies of originals in the Kansas State Historical Society collections. Landscape architect and author. Correspondence, letter books, journals, notebooks, financial records, contracts, drafts of reports, speeches, lectures, articles, essays, scrapbooks, newspaper clippings. Includes material on landscape architecture, design, planning, slavery, the New England Emigrant Aid Society, and Free Soil party.

.111 — Parker, Theodore, 1810-60.
Papers, 1832-63. 1 box and 150 items. Unitarian minister and abolitionist, of Massachusetts.

.112 — Patterson, Robert Porter, 1891-1952.
Papers, 1940-51. 5 ft. (2800 items). Lawyer, jurist, and Secretary of War. Correspondence, memoranda, reports, typed and near-print copies of speeches covering the period when Patterson was Assistant Secretary (1940), Under Secretary (1940-45), and Secretary of War (1945-47). Bulk of the correspondence and memoranda (1940-47) concerns war time production, procurement, logistics, allocation, soldier morale, reorganization of the Army, the Air Force, and segregation in the armed forces.

.113 — Peabody, George Foster, 1852-1938.
Papers, 1894-1937. 30 ft. (ca. 25,000 items). Banker and philanthropist. Correspondence and other papers reflecting Peabody's activities in the Democratic party, banking interests, and his many special interests such as Negro welfare, the development of education in the South. Includes correspondents and papers by and about Newton D. Baker, Nicholas G.J. Ballanta-Taylor, Wade Chance, Staughton Cooley, Arthur W. Milbury, Walter H. Page, Louis F. Post, William G. Rice, Franklin D. Roosevelt, Edward M. Shepherd, John A. Slade, Woodrow Wilson, and Booker T. Washington. Among other subjects are Howard University, Hampton Institute, and the Negro Rural School Fund.

.114 — Perea, Beverly Harrison, 1851-1915.
Military service scrapbook, 1876-1915. 45 items. Officer, of 24th Infantry Regt., U.S. Army, and first Negro officer to be buried in Arlington National Cemetery. Correspondence, commissions, special orders, clippings, memorabilia, and other papers, relating to Perea's military career and the controversy over his burial.

.115 — Perry, Matthew C.
Papers, 1843-45. 3 boxes. Navy officer. Early participant in the establishment of Liberia and first commander of the African Squadron.

DC176.116 — Pershing, John Joseph, 1860-1948.
Papers, 1882-1949. 172 ft. (ca. 127,000 items). U.S. Army officer. Correspondence, diaries, notebooks, speeches, statements, orders, drafts, maps, scrapbooks, clippings, picture albums, posters, photographs, miscellaneous printed matter, and memorabilia covering Pershing's career in the Indian campaigns, in Cuba, and other military expeditions. Includes preparatory data and drafts for Pershing's book, and for his unpublished memoirs; family correspondence; and materials relating to his death. Pershing served as a first lieutenant in the 10th Cavalry Regiment, and acquired the nickname "Black Jack Pershing."

.117 — Personal Papers.
Scattered through these miscellaneous personal papers are references to slavery, such as in Miscellaneous, G: Edmund P. Gaines to Governor A.B. Roman (New Orleans, November 16, 1831); Miscellaneous, J: Roger Jones to (Colonel Duncan A. Clinch?) (Washington, March 17, 1829); Miscellaneous, M: Alexander Macomb to Nathan Morse (Washington, October 12, 1831).

.118 — Phillips family.
Papers, 1832-1914. 9 ft. (7000 items). Correspondence, letter books, legal record books, journals, dockets, notebooks, and an unpublished autobiography of Philip Phillips, relating chiefly to the law practice of Philip Phillips and his son, William Hallet Phillips, both of whom practiced before the Supreme Court. Among other items, the Philip Phillips papers concern the slave trade, the repeal of the Missouri compromise and the passage of the Kansas-Nebraska bill; and the William Hallett Phillips papers, the lynching at Hahnville, La.

.119 — Pickens, Francis Wilkinson, 1805-69.
Papers of Francis W. Pickens and Milledge L. Bonham, 1837-1920. 1 ft. (ca. 400 items). Correspondence, reports, resolutions, military papers, applications for office, petitions, administrative papers, memoranda, and newspaper clippings (1837-66 and 1917-20) relating to Pickens and Milledge Luke Bonham (1930-90), Governors of South Carolina. The bulk of the collection dates from 1860 to 1864 and relates mainly to the governorship (1860-62) of Pickens, the governorship (1862-65) of Bonham, the Civil War, memorials of free Negroes volunteering services to the State of South Carolina, papers relating to a transfer of Negroes to Haiti in 1861, report of the Committee of the Georgetown District for removal of slaves, December, 1862, and correspondence and orders regarding free Negroes captured in arms in 1863.

.120 — Presbyterian Church in the U.S.A.
Washington City Presbytery records, 1823-1936. 4 ft. Records of the Presbytery of the District of Columbia (1823-66), of the Presbytery of the Potomac (1858-70), of the Presbyterian Church in the U.S.A. and of the Presbytery of the Potomac (1858-70), of the Presbyterian Church in the U.S. (Southern) which united to form the Presbytery of Washington City in 1870; together with the records (1870-1936) of the Presbytery of Washington City. Includes correspondence, minutes, reports, ordinations, committee appointments, church assessments, ministerial appointments, death notices of clergy, and material relating to other ecclesiastical matters; together with "The church and the civil war (Negro churches)".

.121 — Randolph, William B.
Papers, 1774-1869. ca. 1000 items. Includes plantation account books.

.122 — Reavis, Turner.
Papers, 1842-90. 1 item. Account book, Alabama.

.123 — Roberts, Jonathan, family.
Papers, 1734-1944. ca. 5000 items. Materials relating to a family of free Negroes that moved from North Carolina to a community in Indiana, later known as "Roberts Settlement." Includes

a notebook (1734-1813), a scrapbook with financial papers, memoranda, genealogies, correspondence, legal papers, and clippings.

.124 — Roune, d'Ossier.
Papers, 1891-1902. 1 box. French administrative agent in Santo Domingo. Included is correspondence with Toussaint l'Ouverture, general and liberator of Haiti.

.125 — Ruffin, Edmund, 1794-1865.
Diary, 1856-65. 14 v. Agriculturist and publisher. Diary detailing Ruffin's activities and opinions as an experimentalist in agriculture, anti-unionist, and slavery advocate and describing plantation life on his Virginia estates at Marlbourne and Beechwood; travels and social gossip relating to the area between Amelia Co. and Richmond, Va.; Ruffin's views on county, State Confederate, and Union politics. Includes copies of letters, holograph maps, pamphlets, clippings, and fragmentary essays.

.126 — Russell, Charles Edward.
Papers, ca. 1900-40's. ca. 6000 items. Author, journalist, diplomat, and politician. Materials include correspondence and mss of Russell reflecting his liberal viewpoint of such subjects as economic and social reform.

.127 — Sanborn, Franklin Benjamin, 1831-1917.
Papers, 1852-79. 121 items. In part, transcripts (handwritten) of letters. Author, journalist, and abolitionist. Chiefly college essays (1852-55); correspondence (1857-72) with Gerrit Smith, and correspondence (1877-79) with Octavius Brooks Frothingham concerning Frothingham's biography of Smith (1878).

.128 — Sanger, Margaret.
Papers, 1913-61. ca. 115,000 items. Advocate of planned parenthood. Includes a "Clinical Research Bureau File" containing information on the Harlem Clinic.

.129 — Schofield, John McAllister, 1831-1906.
Papers, 1837-1906. 38 ft. (30,000 items), in part transcripts made for Schofield (ca. 1897) from originals in the War Dept. Archives for purposes of preparing his memoirs. Army officer and public official. Correspondence, diary (1863), journals (1876-91), military papers, memoranda, reports, dispatches, financial records, court-martial papers, mss and notes of speeches, articles, and a memoir, maps, memorabilia, and printed matter. The bulk of the collection dates between 1862-95; includes Reconstruction in Virginia under Schofield (1866-68).

.130 — Selfridge, Thomas Oliver, 1836-58.
16 boxes. Naval officer on duty with the African Squadron, 1858.

.131 — Sheridan, Philip Henry, 1831-88.
Papers, 1853-88. 53 ft. (ca. 18,000 items), in part transcripts from War Dept. records. Army officer. Correspondence, letter books, telegrams, endorsements, reports, orders, field dispatches, speeches, citations, financial records, scrapbooks, a draft of Sheridan's personal memoirs, and memorabilia. Concerns the Civil War, the Reconstruction, Mexican border troubles, Indian wars, and military administration. Related material is found in the Library's Daniel O. Drennan collection.

.132 — Shiner, Michael.
Diary, 1813-65. 186 pages. Negro resident of the District of Columbia, who appears to have been employed at the Washington Navy Yard. Contains accounts of important events and happenings in Washington.

.133 — Shufeldt, Robert Wilson.
Papers, 1836-1910. ca. 15,000 items. Naval officer, served in African Squadron (1849). Collection includes copies of reports made by Shufeldt on various African countries while on a cruise (ca. 1878) to advance American commercial interests, and records of his activities as an arbitrator in a boundary dispute between Liberia and Sierra Leone. Also included are papers of Shufeldt's son, Mason Shufeldt, comprised of correspondence, reports, and other

writings that relate to an exploring expedition led by the younger Shufeldt into Africa in 1890, in connection with the World's Columbia Exposition.

DC176.134 —— Schurz, Carl, 1829-1906.
Papers, 1842-1932. 55 ft. (ca. 23,000 items). Army officer, statesman, and journalist. Correspondence, speeches, articles, newspaper clippings, printed matter, and scrapbooks, chiefly 1860-1906. Subjects include Liberal Republicanism, civil service reform, and the Hayes administration, in which Schurz served as Secretary of the Interior, 1877-81. Correspondents include Rutherford B. Hayes, Abraham Lincoln, Moorfield Storey, Ida Tarbell, and others.

.135 —— Simpson, Matthew
Papers, ca. 1835-85. ca. 35 boxes. Bishop of the Methodist Episcopal Church, antislavery advocate, and counselor of many prominent public figures. Correspondence, letterbooks, speeches, sermons, and other papers.

.136 —— Slave Papers.
Miscellaneous group of mss which accumulated during the earlier years of the Manuscript Division under the title of Slave Papers. Included are such items as slave appraisals, mortgages, accounts of Negroes recovered from bondage, certificates of emancipation, birth certificates of slaves, bonds for behavior, papers relating to the slave ship Wanderer, autobiography of a slave, and letters from Liberia.

.137 —— Society for the Propagation of the Gospel in Foreign Parts.
Records, 1701-?. Microfilm, of original records in London. The Society focused its missionary activity on the American colonies until the Revolutionary War. Records contain letters from missionaries, supporters of the Society, civil officials in the colonies, and those seeking its assistance. Missionary activities among the Negroes and the effects of slavery are among subjects mentioned.

.138 —— Spaatz, Carl, 1891- .
Papers, 1915-53. ca. 115,150 items. General, U.S. Army. Contains material relating to the Negro in the armed forces during World War II. Restricted.

.139 —— Spingarn, Arthur Barnett, 1878- .
Papers, 1911-64. 288 ft. (37,000 items). Lawyer and a founder of the National Association for the Advancement of Colored People. Correspondence, legal files, minutes of the board of directors, reports, a file of Crisis material, printed matter, and legal, estate, and financial papers of the NAACP, and miscellaneous files relating to the New York State Social Hygiene and Tuberculosis Association, and Manhattan Council, New York State Committee Against Discrimination (1950-54). Includes outline of a study of Negro troops in World War II, an autograph collection of ca. 77 letters, and list by States of all licensed Negro notaries public in the 1860's. Names represented include Clarence Darrow, W.E.B. DuBois, Thurgood Marshall, and Moorfield Storey. Restricted.

.140 —— Squier, Ephraim George, 1821-88.
Papers, 1841-84. 5 ft. (4000 items). Archeologist, diplomat, and businessman. Correspondence, business records, mss of writings, a bibliography of Squier's writings (1876), and other papers relating to his interest in archeology and ethnology. Includes material concerning the American Ethnological Society; the New York Anthropological Society; his numerous writings in the anthropological and ethnological field; together with mss and drafts of articles. Squier's papers were used by William R. Stanton to develop an account of scientific attitudes toward race in America (1815-59). Among Squier's correspondents were Josiah Clark Nott, and George R. Gliddon.

.141 —— Stanton, Edwin McMasters, 1814-69.
Papers, 1831-70. 10 ft. (ca. 7600 items). Lawyer and U.S. Attorney General and Secretary of War. Correspondence, essays, and drafts of reports. The bulk of the collection dates from the Civil War and stresses Stanton's role as Secretary of War. Major correspondents include most of the cabinet members and ranking government officials during Stanton's tenure; other correspondents include George Bancroft, Henry Ward Beecher, Charles Dana, William Lloyd Garrison, Francis Lieber, Harriet Beecher Stowe, and Lyman Trumbull.

.142 —— Stephens, Alexander Hamilton, 1812-83.
Papers, 1784-1886. 25 ft. (ca. 7000 items). Lawyer, journalist, author, and statesman; Governor of Georgia, member of both Houses of Congress, and Vice-President of the Confederate States of America. Correspondence, mss of autobiography and journal (1834-37), telegrams, memoranda, legal documents, and clippings. Chiefly letters received, including those from Stephens' slaves, and dealing with plantation matters, philanthropy, and local affairs, as well as with such national and sectional questions as slavery, the Texas issue, political parties, states' rights, Compromise of 1850, Kansas-Nebraska bill, Dred Scott decision, secession, formation and operation of the Confederate Government, the Civil War and Reconstruction, campaign of 1876, education, and other social, economic, literary, and political matters. Correspondents include Francis P. Blair, Joseph E. Brown, Fitzwilliam Byrdsall, Henry Cleveland, Howell Cobb, Augustus H. Garland, John B. Gordon, Paul H. Hayne, William H. Hidell, Henry R. Jackson, Herschel V. Johnson, Richard Malcolm Johnston, Lucius Q.C. Lamar, James R. Randall, J. Henley Smith, Robert Toombs, James Waddell, and Ambrose R. Wright.

.143 —— Stephenson, Nathaniel Wright, 1867-1935.
Papers, 1922-30. 3 ft. Historian and college professor. Galley and page proofs and a few notes for Stephenson's biography of Nelson W. Aldrich (1930); notes and revised drafts or final near-print copies of 22 scenarios prepared or edited by Stephenson for The Chronicles of America educational motion picture series; and notes for other possible scenarios relating to abolition, the underground railroad, the Negro in the Civil War, the Methodist schism, and the Reconstruction period.

.144 —— Stevens, Thaddeus, 1792-1868.
Papers, 1813-69. 5 ft. (2750 items). Lawyer and U.S. Representative from Pennsylvania. General and official correspondence, legal, business, and financial papers, ms and printed copies of Stevens' speeches, clippings, and other printed matter, chiefly when Stevens was in Congress and relating to the Civil War, Reconstruction, family and business affairs. Among correspondents are John Binney, Salmon P. Chase, Horace Greeley, William Nesbit, William B. Reed, and Simon Stevens.

.145 —— Storey, Moorfield,
Papers, 1850-1929. ca. 4000 items. Lawyer, author, supporter of liberal causes. Included in the papers is one of the "missing" journals of Ralph Waldo Emerson, in which Emerson discusses the subject of slavery. Correspondents include James Weldon Johnson, Joel E. Spingarn, and Walter White.

.146 —— Styron, William.
Papers, 1951- . ca. 35 items. Author. Holograph draft of The Confessions of Nat Turner (1967), including extra and rejected pages, and the original typescript as well as the author's corrected galleys, the editor's galleys and the printer's galleys. Restricted.

.147 —— Taft, Robert Alphonso, 1889-1953.
Papers, 1900-53. ca. 682,000 items. Included are materials relating to Army and Navy matters, some of which involve the Negro; and separate files on the Negro and on civil rights. Restricted.

DC176.148 — Tappan, Benjamin, 1773-1857.
Papers, 1795-1900. 6 ft. (3650 items), in part photocopies of originals owned by the Ohio Historical Society. Jurist and U.S. Senator from Ohio. Principally correspondence, with some legal and business papers, relating to Ohio and national politics (primarily Jacksonian), antislavery, family matters. Among principal correspondents are John Gould Anthony, Ethan Allen Brown, Joseph N. Neef, John Sloan, E.W. Whittlesey, and several members of the Tappan family.

.149 — Tappan, Lewis, 1788-1873.
Papers, 1812-72. ca. 3 ft. (5200 items). Merchant and antislavery leader. Correspondence, journal, and other papers. Includes a diary kept by Tappan while attending the antislavery conference in London (1843), correspondence concerning the antislavery societies with which Tappan was associated, autobiographical notes, a scrapbook and other material relating to the Tappan family and its genealogy, and a handwritten speech written by John Quincy Adams on the Amistad case. Principal correspondents include John Quincy Adams, James Gillespie Birney, Jonathan Green, Samuel Dexter Hastings, William Jay, Theodore Sedgwick, Joseph Sturge, Arthur and Benjamin Tappan, and John Greenleaf Whittier.

.150 — Taylor, Zachary, 1784-1850.
Papers, 1814-1931. 631 items. U.S. President. Correspondence, military papers, an autobiographical account (ca. 1826), documents relating to Taylor's estate and to the management of the plantation Fashion in Louisiana by Taylor's son Richard, and a small amount of material about Taylor.

.151 — Terrell, Mary Church, 1863-1954.
Papers, 1886-1954. 20 ft. (ca. 11,800 items). Negro leader and author. Correspondence, diaries, literary mss, clippings, notebooks, datebooks, miscellaneous printed matter, photographs, and memorabilia. Includes typescripts and mss of Mrs. Terrell's autobiography, A Colored Woman in a White World, as well as articles, speeches, short stories and poetry. The clippings, mostly by or about Mrs. Terrell, deal with politics, rights of women, desegregation in the District of Columbia, and related topics. Correspondents include Jane Addams, Mary McLeod Bethune, Carrie Chapman Catt, Ruth Hanna McCormick, and Booker T. Washington.

.152 — Terrell, Robert Heberton, 1857-1925.
Papers, 1880-1925. 3 ft. (ca. 2500 items). Teacher, lawyer, and judge. Correspondence, speeches, scrapbooks, pamphlets, articles, books and other miscellaneous printed matter relating Terrell's interests in Negro education and welfare, courts, and politics, to his career as a member of the Washington Board of Trade and high school principal, and to his service on the municipal bench of the District of Columbia. Correspondents include Frederick Douglass, William McKinley, Theodore Roosevelt, Elihu Root, Booker T. Washington, and Woodrow Wilson.

.153 — Thompson, Ambrose W.
Papers, 1874-1960. 26 ft. (ca. 12,300 items). Businessman, and inventor. Business and family correspondence, letter books, memoranda, reports, statistical tables, patent papers, stocks and bonds, drawings, maps, and printed matter, including material on the Chiriqui Improvement Company, and other companies in which Thompson was interested. The Chiriqui Improvement Company's lands in Central Panama were often proposed during the Civil War for the colonization of freed Negroes.

.154 — Thornton, William.
Papers, 1742-1812. ca. 3400 items. Inventor, architect, and member of the American Colonization Society. Included are a number of mss on the subject of Negro colonization.

.155 — Trist, Nicholas Philip.
Papers, 1783-1873. 44 v., and 11 boxes. Consul at Havana, Cuba, and special agent in Mexico. Contains information on the slave trade.

.156 — Trumbull, Lyman, 1813-96.
Papers, 1843-94. 13 ft. (ca. 4500 items). U.S. Senator from Illinois. Chiefly letters (1855-72) received by Trumbull on political matters, together with a few drafts or copies of replies. Subjects include the elections of 1856, 1860, 1866, and 1872, Illinois state politics, the Kansas-Nebraska bill, secession, the Civil War, Reconstruction, the civil rights bill, and the Liberal Republican movement of 1872.

.157 — Underwood, John Curtis, 1809-73.
Papers, 1856-98. 140 items. Lawyer, planter, and U.S. District Court judge, of Virginia. Chiefly correspondence (1857-72) received by Underwood and relating to the Republican Party, political matters, abolition, the Civil War, Reconstruction, Virginia, and judicial matters. Correspondents include Benjamin F. Butler, Salmon P. Chase, Lydia Maria Child, Horace Greeley, Hinton R. Helper, William H. Seward, Harriet Beecher Stowe, Alfred H. Terry, Charles Sumner, and Elihu B. Washburne.

.158 — Van Buren, Martin, 1782-1862.
Papers, 1787-1868. ca. 6000 items. Eighth President of the United States. Included is material pertaining to slavery.

.159 — Wade, Benjamin Franklin, 1800-78.
Papers, 1832-81. 6 ft. (ca. 3500 items). Lawyer, U.S. Senator from Ohio, and Republican party leader. Chiefly political correspondence (1852-69); together with some personal letters from Wade to his wife and parents, letters relating to his law practice and business, printed speeches, maps, and business papers. Subjects include Ohio and national politics, the elections of 1860, 1864, and 1868, secession, the Civil War, the Congressional Committee on the Conduct of the War, emancipation, Reconstruction, Negro suffrage, and the impeachment of Andrew Johnson. Correspondents include James A. Briggs, Salmon P. Chase, Jacob D. Cox, H. Winter Davis, William Dennison, John W. Forney, James A. Garfield, Joseph H. Geiger, William A. Goodlow, Adam Gurowski, Abraham Lincoln, R.F. Paine, Donn Piatt, William S. Rosecrans, William H. Seward, Green Clay Smith, Edwin M. Stanton, and Charles Sumner.

.160 — Washburn, Israel, 1813-83.
Papers, 1838-1908. 1 ft. (300 items). Lawyer, U.S. Representative, and Governor of Maine. Principally correspondence concerning politics in Maine during the early years of the Civil War and such national events as the Kansas-Nebraska act, the presidential elections of 1856 and 1860, the formation of the Republican party and the Civil War.

.161 — Washington, Booker Taliaferro, 1859?-1915.
Papers, 1882-1942. 443 ft. (ca. 300,000 items). Educator, author, leader in the advancement of the Negro race. Eleven large correspondence series, with mss of books, articles, and speeches, printed matter, scrapbooks, reports and documents. Photographs. Much of the material relates to Tuskegee Institute, Hampton Institute, the National Negro Business League, and the General Education Board. Important correspondents include William H. Baldwin, Wallace Buttrick, Andrew Carnegie, George Washington Carver, James C. Clarkson, James H. Dillard, Frederick Douglass, William E.B. DuBois, Charles W. Eliot, T. Thomas Fortune, Hollis B. Frissell, Abraham Grant, Leigh Hunt, Seth Low, Fred R. Moore, Robert R. Moton, E. Gardiner Murphy, Robert C. Ogden, Walter Hines Page, George F. Peabody, John D. Rockefeller, Theodore Roosevelt, Julius Rosenwald, Emmett J. Scott, Anson Phelps Stokes, William Howard Taft, Victor H. Tulane, and Oswald Garrison Villard.

DC176.162 —— Weld, Theodore Dwight, 1803-95.
Papers, 1836-88. 21 items. Abolitionist. Includes correspondence with Angela Grimké Weld.

.163 —— Welles, Gideon, 1802-78.
Papers, 1777-1911. 30 ft. (ca. 15,000 items). Editor, politician, and Secretary of the Navy. Correspondence, diaries, and scrapbooks; together with notes of Henry B. Learned relating to Welles. Subjects include Welles' career in Connecticut and national politics and the conduct of the Lincoln administration. Correspondents include Montgomery Blair, Salmon P. Chase, John A. Dahlgren, Richard Mentor Johnson, and J.J.R. Pease.

.164 —— West Indian and slave trade papers.
1671-1790. 380 sheets. Photocopies of originals in Rigsarchiv, Copenhagen. Miscellaneous transcripts of official records relating to the Danish West Indies (1700-90) and transcripts relating to the slave trade in the Danish West Indies and finances (1671-1763).

.165 —— Western Antislavery Society.
Papers, 1845-57. 2 v.

.166 —— Wilson, Henry, 1812-75.
Papers, 1851-75. ca. 200 items. U.S. Senator from Massachusetts and Vice President of the U.S. Chiefly letters received; together with copies of some outgoing correspondence, relating to state and national politics, abolition, the Civil War, Reconstruction, patronage, and the organization of the Army. Correspondents include George A. Ashmun, Nathaniel P. Banks, Benjamin F. Butler, Cassius M. Clay, Schuyler Colfax, Neal Dow, William Lloyd Garrison, Adam Gurowski, Joseph Hooker, John Jay, Benson J. Lossing, Theodore Parker, Garrit Smith, Charles Sumner, Elihu B. Washburne, Thurlow Weed, and Richard Yates.

.167 —— Wiltberger, Christian.
Diary, 1821. Missionary. Wiltberger's diary (1821) relates to events of a voyage to Liberia with a shipload of colonists, and to missionary activities in Liberia.

.168 —— Woodson, Carter Godwin, 1875-1950. collector.
Carter G. Woodson collection of Negro papers and related documents, 1796-1931. 6 ft. (ca. 5000 items). Correspondence, diaries, addresses, legal documents of the 19th century, and clippings, relating to Negro history, the "Journal of Negro Life and History," appointments to federal office, race relations, discrimination, employment opportunities, state and national politics, and business. Includes papers of John T. Clark, Whitfield McKinley, and Benjamin T. Tanner. Correspondents include John E. Bruce, George Washington Carver, William D. Crum, Frederick Douglass, Christian A. Fleetweed, T. Thomas Fortune, Richard Theodore Greener, Henry Cabot Lodge, John R. Lynch, Medill McCormick, Hiram Revels, Theodore Roosevelt, Julius Rosenwald, Emmett J. Scott, Melville E. Stone, Benjamin R. Tillman, Booker T. Washington, Col. Charles Young, and Thomas W. Higginson.

.169 —— Wright, Elizur, 1804-85.
Papers, 1817-1910. 7 ft. (2500 items). Reformer, actuary, and publisher. Family, general and business correspondence, clippings, account book (1828-32), ms books and writings, a membership book (1836-37) of the Auxiliaries of the American Anti-Slavery Society and scrapbooks. The bulk of the collection concerns 19th century politics, religion, and movements, the American Anti-Slavery Society, abolition, antimasonry, free thought, and Wright's translations, books, and other publications. Among correspondents are, D.M. Bennett of the Truth Seeker, William Birney of the National Liberal League, Edward Bossage, George S. Boutwell, Salmon P. Chase, Charles Anderson Dana, J.N. Danforth, E.B. Foote, Jr., of the National Defense Association, William Lloyd Garrison, Horace Greeley, Amos A.

Phelps, Wendell Phillips, William Henry Seward, Gerrit Smith, Henry Brewster Stanton, Lewis Tappan, George Vaughan, F.B. Wakeman, and Theodore Dwight Weld.

.170 Pictorial collection.
Pictorial materials in the Library of Congress encompass more than 3 million photographic negatives, prints, stereographs, and slides; some 40,000 posters; more than 176,000 artists' prints and drawings; some 97,000 reels of motion-picture film; and other items. Among the graphic and photographic collections containing resources for Afro-American studies and available through the Prints and Photographs Reading Room are the following:

.171 —— American Colonization Society Collection.
ca. 1840-1913. ca. 550 photographs and a number of pictorial items. Pictures of Americans connected with the Society; pictures of Liberians; and scenes in Liberia and other parts of West Africa.

.172 —— Bain, George Grantham. collector.
ca. 1898-1916. ca. 120,000 photographs. Portraits (chiefly of Americans) and news pictures from Bain's news-picture agency.

.173 —— Farm Security Agency-Office of War Information.
1935-45. ca. 75,000 photographic items. Pictures documenting many aspects of life in the U.S. (1935-45) with emphasis on farming and selected industries, rural and small-town life, selected cities, individual agricultural workers, family case histories, and civilian activities during World War II.

.174 —— Harmon Foundation.
Materials, chiefly 20th cent. Several hundred items, in process of cataloging. Etchings, lithographs, and other artists' prints by American and African Negroes; documentation of the Harmon Foundation's activities in health and recreation.

.175 —— Johnston, Frances Benjamin. collector.
ca. 1888-1930. ca. 10,000 photographic items. Documentary photographs of historic American architecture, coal mining in Pennsylvania, a shoe factory in Massachusetts, Hampton Institute in Virginia, Carlisle Indian School in Pennsylvania, Tuskegee Institute, and life in the White House during several administrations; portraits.

.176 —— Lomax collections.
1930's. ca. 1000 photographic items. Pictures, made by John A. Lomax, his son Alan Lomax, and perhaps others, of folk singers, folk dancers, children at play, and prisoners in the southern U.S.; scenes of daily life.

.177 —— National Association for the Advancement of Colored People.
ca. 1909-59. Several hundred photographic items, in process of cataloging. Pictures documenting the Association's activities, portraits, news photographs, and other pictorial items.

.178 —— Texas Centennial Exposition.
1936. ca. 125 negatives and 300 photoprints. Included are pictures of exhibits in the Hall of Negro Life.

.179 —— Ulmann, Doris. collector.
1920-35. ca. 200 photographs. Pictures of rural inhabitants of the upland regions of the southern U.S., featuring local crafts and customs, scenery, portraits.

.180 —— Van Vechten, Carl. collector.
1930's-60's. ca. 1240 photographic items. Portraits of public figures, among them portraits of about 150 prominent Negro actors, singers, authors, and others.

.181 —— The Library's archival collection of motion pictures contains some 35,000 titles representing theatrical feature films and newsreels, documentary and educational films, short subjects, and television films (news, documentaries, and entertainment). Among these motion pictures are a number of feature films produced since the

1940's which deal with Negro life in the U.S. or which feature all-Negro casts; a number of television documentaries dating from the late 1950's to the present and dealing with civil rights, urban problems, etc.; and a small number of educational and documentary films from earlier years involving Negroes in the U.S. Films may be viewed in the Motion Picture Section for research purposes. Appointments should be made in advance.

.182 Music and sound recordings of music and speech. The Library's holdings include more than 3,277,000 items of music and more than 266,000 sound recordings on discs, tapes, and wires. Sound recordings include not only music but also poetry, literature, speeches, and oral history. Access to these recordings is made through the Recorded Sound Section in the Music Division. Appointments are requested.

Among sound recordings of interest in Afro-American studies are more than 1500 discs and 70 tape-reels containing folk music and folk tales of Negro Americans, recorded by John and Alan Lomax, Melville Herskovits, Herbert Halpert, John Henry Faulk, Willis James, Harry Oster, Bruce Jackson, Fisk University, the Hampton Institute, and others.

DC177   U.S. NATIONAL ADVISORY COUNCIL ON THE EDUCATION OF DISADVANTAGED CHILDREN (1965). 1900 E St., N.W., 20415. Tel 202 382-1613. F. Dana Payne, Acting Dir.
The Council was established by the Elementary and Secondary Education Act of 1965, for the purpose of reviewing the administration and operation of the provisions of Title I of the Act, including its effectiveness in improving the educational attainment of educationally deprived children.
Publ.: Annual Report.
.1   U.S. National Advisory Council on the Education of Disadvantaged Children.
Files, 1965- . Records, correspondence, reports, and other papers concerning the functions of the Council.

DC178   U.S. NATIONAL AERONAUTICS AND SPACE ADMINISTRATION. 400 Maryland Ave., S.W., 20546. Tel 202 962-4463. Bernard Moritz, Coordinator of Civil Rights Activities.
.1   Office for Civil Rights.
Files. Records, correspondence, reports and other papers concerning equal employment opportunity programs, contract compliance, Title VI, and other matters relating to civil rights.

DC179   U.S. NATIONAL COMMISSION ON URBAN PROBLEMS. Room 640, 806 15th St., N.W., 20005. Tel 202 382-8226. Richard W. O'Neill, Chmn., Hearings and Progs. Cmt.
The Commission conducts hearings on zoning and land use; building and housing codes; the impact of federal, state, and local taxation; local revenue problems; urban renewal; public housing, cooperative housing, technical aspects of housing, and the effect of highways and other public works on urban environment.

DC180   U.S. NATIONAL FOUNDATION ON ARTS AND HUMANITIES, OFFICE OF CONTRACT COMPLIANCE. 1800 G St., N.W., 20506. Tel 202 382-6363. Charles B. Ruttenberg, Gen. Counsel. Copying, inquiries answered, referrals made, consultation.
.1   Office of Contract Compliance.
Files. Records, correspondence, reports and other papers concerning contract compliance, Title VI, and related subjects. Restricted.

DC181   U.S. NATIONAL LABOR RELATIONS BOARD (NLRB). 1717 Pennsylvania Ave., N.W., 20570. Tel 202 382-5263. Clarence S. Wright, Dir. of Equal Employ. Opportunity. Inquiries answered.
.1   U.S. National Labor Relations Board.
Files, 1966- . Records, correspondence, reports and other papers relating to the Board's internal

administration of the government-wide equal employment opportunity program. (Normally records kept for 2 or 3 years). Limited use.

DC182   U.S. NATIONAL LABOR RELATIONS BOARD (NLRB) (1935), LIBRARY (1947). 1717 Pennsylvania Ave., N.W., 20507. Tel 202 382-4329. Mrs. Lempi L. Wickline, Librn. Interlibrary loan, bibliographies prepared, literature searches, referrals made.
Publ.: Bibliographies, of labor law and industrial relations.
.1   U.S. National Labor Relations Board Library.
The Library contains books, pamphlets, and other materials concerning that area of race relations which deals with labor and management as it relates to the Labor Management Relations Act, 1947. Included is material concerning fair employment practices.

DC183   U.S. NATIONAL SCIENCE FOUNDATION, OFFICE FOR EQUAL OPPORTUNITY. 1800 G St., N.W., 20550. Tel 202 632-5998. Howard S. Schilling, Dir. of Equal Employ. Opportunity.
.1   Office for Equal Opportunity.
Files. Records, correspondence, reports, and other papers concerning equal employment opportunity and other civil rights matters.

DC184   U.S. OFFICE OF ECONOMIC OPPORTUNITY (OEO) (1964), LIBRARY (1965). Room 223, 1200 19th St., N.W., 20506. Tel 202 382-6046. Theodore Cutler, Chief Librn. Interlibrary loan, bibliographies prepared, copying, inquiries answered, referrals made.
The OEO was established to mobilize the human and financial resources of the nation to combat poverty in the United States. OEO administers nation-wide programs, including urban and rural community action programs, special impact programs, work and training for youth and adults, and VISTA (Volunteers in Service to America).
.1   U.S. Office of Economic Opportunity.
Files, 1965- . Correspondence, reports, records, program plans and evaluations and other materials concerning the operation and activities of the Office and its programs.
.2   — U.S. Office of Economic Opportunity Library.
Books (20,000), periodicals (300 titles), pamphlets, newspapers, 4 vf, research reports, statistical data, and other materials relating to poverty, its causes, effects and possible elimination. The holdings are particularly strong in the areas of minority groups, public welfare, and education of the disadvantaged. Included are OEO research reports (ca. 600), statistical profiles of 3135 counties in the U.S. and state and local area files.

DC185   U.S. OFFICE OF ECONOMIC OPPORTUNITY (OEO), OFFICE OF CIVIL RIGHTS. 1200 19th St., N.W., 20506. Tel 202 382-6246. Maurice A. Dawkins, Asst. Dir. for Civil Rights.
.1   Office of Civil Rights.
Files, 1964- . Records, correspondence, reports, evaluations and other papers relating to the civil rights policies, directives and procedures for OEO. Includes material relating to research and evaluation, community relations, education, and contract compliance.

DC186   U.S. OFFICE OF EMERGENCY PREPAREDNESS. Executive Office Bldg. Annex, 604 17th St., N.W., 20504. Tel 202 395-5890. Mordecai M. Merker, Civil Rights Coordinator.
.1   U.S. Office of Emergency Preparedness.
Files. Records, correspondence, reports and other papers concerning equal employment opportunity, contract compliance, Title VI, and federal employment.

DC187   U.S. POST OFFICE DEPARTMENT, OFFICE OF EQUAL EMPLOYMENT OPPORTUNITY (1967). 1200 Pennsyl-

vania Ave., N.W., 20260. Tel 202 961-7643. Dr. Charles
H. Thomas, Jr., Dir. Inquiries answered, referrals
made, consultation.
The Office functions to assure an affirmative action
Equal Employment Opportunity Program throughout the
Post Office Department's field service as well as Headquarters in Washington, D.C., and it works to utilize
fully all qualified minorities and to assist in upgrading
the skills of all employees.

.1 Office of Equal Employment Opportunity.
Files, 1967- . Records, correspondence, reports
and other papers relating to equal opportunity programs and practices of the Department, especially
concerning employment.

DC188 U.S. PRESIDENT'S ADVISORY COUNCIL FOR MINORITY
ENTERPRISE (1969). 923 15th St., N.W., 20005. Tel
202 638-0056. Alan Steelman, Dir. Inquiries answered,
referrals made.
The Council was established to help the government
provide financial support, ideas, and technical assistance for its minority-business program. It is compiling a report on how to stimulate urban enterprise, and
has established five task force committees in the areas
of business opportunities, management and technical
assistance, expanded participation (community-based
corporations), finance, and national strategy.

DC189 U.S. PRESIDENT'S COMMITTEE ON EQUAL OPPORTU-
NITY IN HOUSING (1962). 451 Seventh St., S.W., 20410.
Tel 202 755-7252. Walter W. Gusey, Staff Dir.
The Committee was established to supervise and coordinate the activities of various governmental departments
and agencies in preventing discrimination in housing and
related facilities they own or operate, and in housing
and related facilities assisted by programs they administer; also to encourage educational programs to eliminate the causes of discrimination in housing and related
facilities provided with federal assistance.

.1 U.S. President's Committee on Equal Opportunity in
Housing.
Files, 1962- . Records, reports, correspondence,
and other papers relating to the activities of the
Committee.

DC190 U.S. PRESIDENT'S COUNCIL ON YOUTH OPPORTUNITY
(1967), RESEARCH AND PUBLIC AFFAIRS. 801 19th
St., N.W., 20006. Tel 202 382-2381. John M. Hein,
Dir. of Res. and Pub. Affairs. Consultation.
The Council was formed to coordinate youth opportunity
programs of employment, education, recreation, and
health services. It is charged with assuring effective
program planning for summer, and other youth programs, strengthening the coordination of such programs among federal departments and agencies and
evaluating their effectiveness, and encouraging state,
local, and non-profit, and other private organizations to
participate fully in efforts to enhance youth opportunity.
Publ.: Bibliography on Youth Programs (1968).

.1 President's Council on Youth Opportunity.
Files, 1967- . Records, correspondence, reports,
evaluations, and other papers concerning the functions of the Council. Restricted.

.2 —— Research and Public Affairs.
Pamphlets, correspondence, films, photographs, and tape recordings about youth programs and opportunity, including material on
black American youth. Restricted.

DC191 U.S. SMALL BUSINESS ADMINISTRATION (SBA), OFFICE
OF EQUAL OPPORTUNITY (1964). 1441 L St., N.W.,
20416. Tel 202 382-5064. Edward S. Dulcan, Dir.

.1 Office of Equal Opportunity.
Files, 1964- . Records, correspondence, reports,
and other papers concerning equal employment
opportunity, contract compliance and Title VI.

DC192 U.S. SMALL BUSINESS ADMINISTRATION (SBA), OFFICE
OF MINORITY ENTERPRISE (1953). 1441 L St., N.W.,
20416. Tel 202 383-3111. Asst. Adminstr. for Minority
Enterprises.
SBA aids, counsels, assists and protects the interests of

small business. Programs include the improvement of
management skills of small business owners, potential
owners and managers, and research studies of the economic environment, as well as assistance programs
through loans. Under "Operation Business Mainstream," it has a program which coordinates its services to give maximum thrust to its Minority Enterprise
programs. This operation is conducted by the Office of
the Assistant Administrator for Minority Enterprises.

.1 Office of Minority Enterprise.
Files, 1953- . Records, correspondence, reports,
plans and other papers concerning minority entrepreneurship, including materials relating to black-
owned businesses in the U.S.

DC193 U.S. SMITHSONIAN INSTITUTION (1846). Tenth and Constitution Ave., N.W., 20560. Tel 202 381-5382. Interlibrary
loan, copying, inquiries answered, referrals made,
consultation.
The Smithsonian Institution Libraries provide specialized information and related services to universities, research and government agencies, and individual
scholars, principally, in the fields of aeronautics,
American biography, American history, anthropology,
astronautics, astrophysics, botany, ecology, mineralogy,
museology, oceanography, paleobiology, tropical biology,
and zoology.

.1 Among the permanent exhibits of the Institution are ca.
20 displays in the Museum of History and Technology pertaining to Afro-American achievements.
Included are 2 cases on "African Backgrounds and
the Beginning of Negro Slavery," a diorama on the
Survey of the Federal Territory, an exhibit on
human rights, and a full-size reproduction of a
Maryland tenant house depicting how poor Negro
tenant farmers lived in the 19th century. Temporary exhibits have included one planned and constructed by students from Fisk University called
"Color Me Mankind," and a display of the paintings of Captain Buck on the anti-slavery trade.
The Museum also maintains an Afro-American
history bibliography, consisting of photographs
(ca. 1500) and "a fairly extensive data file on
bibliographical and biographical resources."

DC194 U.S. SMITHSONIAN INSTITUTION, NATIONAL GALLERY
OF ART (1937). Sixth St. and Constitution Ave., N.W.,
20565. Tel 202 737-4215. Inquiries answered, referrals
made, extension services.

.1 Index of American Design.
35 watercolor renderings of Negro handicrafts from
southern plantations. Mostly anonymous. Includes
furniture, costumes, ceramics, and metal.
.2 Johnston, Joshua.
"The Westwood Children," oil portrait. Black
American portrait artist, active between 1796-1824.
.3 Morgan, Norma, 1928- .
"David in the Wilderness," engraving, 1956.
.4 Williams, Walter, 1920- .
"Fighting Cock," color woodcut, 1957.

DC194a U.S. SMITHSONIAN INSTITUTION, NATIONAL PORTRAIT
GALLERY. Eighth and F Sts., N.W., 20565. Tel 212
628-1810. Marvin S. Sadik, Dir.

.1 National Portrait Gallery.
Among the holdings of the Gallery is a collection of
31 paintings of Afro-American subjects produced
for the Harmon Foundation, by Laura Wheeler
Waring and Betsy Graves Reyneau, and a piece of
sculpture by William Artis.

DC195 U.S. SMITHSONIAN INSTITUTION, SCIENCE INFORMATION
EXCHANGE (1948). 1730 M St., N.W., 20036. Tel 202
381-5513. Monroe Freeman, Dir. Inquiries answered.
The Exchange is a clearinghouse for information on
current scientific research actually in progress, in all
fields of the physical, life, behavioral, social and
engineering sciences. It is concerned only with records
of research planned or actually in progress; does not
receive progress reports or other forms of published
research results; but provides notices of research projects upon request.

.1 Science Information Exchange.
Abstracts of research in psychological, social and sociological studies and demonstration projects, and in the area of social (including educational) services for the culturally and economically deprived. The research includes such subjects as pre-college programs for students from low-income families; prejudice and other interracial attitudes of Negro youth; community advisory services on racial problems; intellectual stimulation of culturally deprived infants; community and job development; effects of relocation on families from urban renewal areas; sources of differential effects of desegregated schooling; improving the reading and writing skills of culturally disadvantaged college students; development of moral attitudes and the influence of ethnic group membership; structure of English used by Negro speakers; motivation of Negro college students; community action programs, migratory worker programs; socio-cultural dynamics in psychopathology; and many other related topics.

DC196 U.S. SUPREME COURT, OFFICE OF THE CLERK. One First St., N.E., 20543. Tel 202 393-1640. Charles Hallam, Librn.

.1 Office of the Clerk.
Files of Supreme Court Cases, including cases pertaining to school desegregation, discrimination in employment, public accommodations, voting rights, and other civil rights matters. Also included is information concerning judicial practice and procedures before the Supreme Court, status of pending cases, and calendar of cases and activities of the Court. Records restricted.

.2 The Supreme Court also maintains a library, including materials concerning legislative histories of federal acts, the use of which is restricted to members admitted to practice before the Court, attorneys for federal agencies, and members of Congress.

DC197 U.S. VETERANS ADMINISTRATION, OFFICE OF EQUAL EMPLOYMENT OPPORTUNITY. Vermont Ave. and H St., N.W., 20420. Tel 202 389-2381. Irene Parsons, Asst. Adminstr. for Personnel and Dir. of Equal Employ. Opportunity.

.1 Office of Equal Employment Opportunity.
Files, 1964- . Records, reports, correspondence, and other papers concerning equal employment opportunity.

DC198 UNITED STATES CATHOLIC CONFERENCE, SOCIAL ACTION DEPARTMENT. 1312 Massachusetts Ave., N.W., 20005. Tel 202 659-6660. John Cosgrove, Dir.
The Department, a national service group to Bishops, is interested in social action, race relations, peace, employment, and migrant labor. It coordinates national Catholic efforts in the areas of social action and development. Formerly The National Catholic Welfare Conference.
Publ.: Task Force on Urban Problems, newsletter, 10 issues per year.

DC199 UNITED STATES CONFERENCE OF MAYORS (1932). 1612 H St., N.W., 20006. Tel 202 638-6966. John J. Gunther, Exec. Dir. Inquiries answered, referrals made.
The Conference of Mayors provides assistance to local officials in solving complex urban human relations problems and in establishing programs to ease racial tensions.

.1 United States Conference of Mayors.
Files, 1964- . Records, correspondence, reports and other papers concerning the programs and activities of the Conference.

DC200 UNITED STATES NATIONAL STUDENT ASSOCIATION (NSA) (1947), INFORMATION CENTER. 2115 S St., N.W., 20008. Tel 202 387-5100. Charles F. Palmer, Pres.
Bibliographies prepared, literature searches, inquiries answered, referrals made, consultation.
NSA, an association of student governments, operates programs dealing with student participation in university affairs as they relate to communities, drug studies, a student government information office, Center for Educational Reform, Community Action Curricula Program, Tutorial Assistance Center, and a legal rights program.
Publ.: NSA Newsletter, bi-weekly; Edcentric, bi-weekly newsletter of the Educational Reform Center.

DC201 URBAN AMERICA, INC. (1965). 1717 Massachusetts Ave., N.W., 20036. Tel 202 265-2224. William L. Slayton, Pres.
Urban America, an independent, nonprofit organization, is concerned with stimulating public policies and private actions to improve the quality of life in the nation's cities. Its programs are carried out by five centers: The Urban Policy Center which undertakes research and issues reports on matters of public policy relating to American cities; The Urban Design Center is concerned with the impact of physical improvements on the appearance and workings of the city, and consults with public and private clients on the design and planning process; The States Action Center assists state governors on urban problems; The Nonprofit Housing Center provides technical and professional assistance to nonprofit sponsors of low- and moderate-income housing, and to business and citizens' organizations in formation of development funds and corporations; The Urban Information Center produces the publications and maintains a reference service for the press and the 80 local citizens' organizations affiliated with Urban America.
Publ.: CITY, bi-monthly magazine; Chronicle, monthly news supplement to CITY; The Architectural Forum, monthly journal; Special publications.

DC202 THE URBAN COALITION (1967), LIBRARY. 2100 M St., N.W., 20037. Tel 202 293-7625. John W. Gardner, Chmn. Interlibrary loan, inquiries answered.
The Coalition includes prominent businessmen, civil rights, labor, religious and civic leaders who seek to alleviate the crisis in the nation's urban centers through all-out attacks on the unemployment problem. It supports employment programs by the private sector represented in the Coalition. The Coalition's Task Force on Private Employment works with businessmen to design and promote innovative programs for the recruitment, training, and private employment of the hard-core unemployed in ghetto areas. It urges national housing and improved education programs, and assists local communities in organizing coalitions to solve local problems.
Publ.: Report, monthly newsletter; Action Report; Special publications; Monthly Monitor, a digest of newsclips on the activities of Coalitions; Program case studies and other reports.

.1 Urban Coalition Library.
Books (ca. 300 v.), pamphlets and periodicals (ca. 1000), newspapers and files of newspaper and periodical clippings, relating to urban affairs. Restricted.

DC203 THE URBAN INSTITUTE (1968). 2100 M St., N.W., 20037. Tel 202 223-1950. William Gorham, Exec. Dir.
The Institute is a government-supported independent corporation created to work with cities to develop plans of actions for overcoming their urban problems; study problems common to cities and advance ideas on how they can be solved; make independent evaluations of the effectiveness of federal, state, and local programs; serve as a center or clearinghouse for knowledge and research about urban problems.
Publ.: A Directory of Urban Research Centers (1970).

DC204 WASHINGTON CENTER FOR METROPOLITAN STUDIES (1959), LIBRARY (1967). Room 202, 1717 Massachusetts Ave., N.W., 20036. Tel 202 462-4868. Mrs. Janice Lessel, Librn. Interlibrary loan, copying, inquiries answered, referrals made.
The Center is a non-profit corporation established under the sponsorship of the five universities of Maryland and Virginia. It has three major program areas: public service; interuniversity activities; and independent urban research. The Center maintains its own program of policy and basic research on Washington and problems of urbanism in general.

Publ.: Reports, studies, proposals, investigations, lectures, pamphlets, and newsletter.

.1 Washington Center for Metropolitan Studies Library. Contains books (ca. 5000), magazines and newsletters (ca. 100), government documents, maps, and vertical file materials relating to urban affairs in general and in the Washington metropolitan area affairs specifically. Subjects include urban sociology (communities, life in urban areas, works on the city and the "urban crisis," race relations, ethnic and minority groups, citizen participation and housing), urban economics, local government, city and regional planning, land use and open space, new towns, transportations, urban growth and development. Includes a continuing bibliography of masters' theses and doctoral dissertations completed in Washington area universities and dealing with urban topics. In part, unavailable to researchers.

DC205 WASHINGTON JOURNALISM CENTER (1965). 2401 Virginia Ave., N.W., 20037. Tel 202 338-4100. Julius Duscha, Dir.
The Center conducts fellowship programs for experienced journalists, and recruits Negroes for careers in journalism.

DC206 WASHINGTON URBAN LEAGUE, INC. (1938), LIBRARY. 1424 16th St., N.W., 20036. Tel 202 265-8200. John E. Jacob, Acting Exec. Dir. Inquiries answered, referrals made.
The League works, through interracial cooperation, to aid in the development of a secure and exemplary American democracy by assisting communities to ameliorate conditions and solve problems arising out of racial inequities within the fields of job development and employment, education and youth incentives, housing and health and welfare.
Publ.: Equality, newsletter; Annual Report; Reports on League projects.

.1 Washington Urban League, Inc.
Records, 1960-69. 28 vf. Minutes of meetings, correspondence, project reports, clippings, testimony before government agencies and materials on various local cases and projects in which the League was involved.

.2 Washington Urban League, Inc. Library.
Miscellaneous. 36 ft. and 4 vf. Books, reports, magazine articles, newspaper clippings on racial and urban problems (both local and national).

DC207 WOMEN'S INTERNATIONAL LEAGUE FOR PEACE AND FREEDOM, WASHINGTON OFFICE (1915). 120 Maryland Ave., N.E., 20002. Tel 202 546-8840. Patricia A. Samuel, Legis. Dir.
The League was founded during World War I, with Jane Addams as its first president, to establish by peaceful means those political, economic, social and psychological conditions which can assure peace and freedom.
Publ.: The Washington Newsletter, monthly; The Action Bulletin, monthly; Miscellaneous papers.

DC208 ZETA PHI BETA SORORITY, INC. 1734 New Hampshire Ave., N.W., 20009. Tel 202 387-3103. Mrs. Emma J. Dewberry, Exec. Secy.
The Sorority's programs include leadership development, human and civil rights, youth and adult leadership programs and social and welfare projects.
Publ.: The Archon (to membership).

FLORIDA

CORAL GABLES

FL1 INTER-FAITH AGENCY FOR SOCIAL JUSTICE. 1215 Mariola Court, 33134. Tel 305 661-9069. Mrs. Milton Margulis.

FL2 UNIVERSITY OF MIAMI (1926), OTTO G. RICHTER LIBRARY (1926). Box 8214, 33124. Tel 305 285-3551. Archie L. McNeal, Dir. Interlibrary loan, copying, typing.

.1 Facts on Film.
Papers, 1954-67. Microfilm. Contains materials on civil rights and race relations in the South. See Race Relations Information Center, Nashville, Tenn., for a full description.

DAYTONA BEACH

FL3 BETHUNE-COOKMAN COLLEGE (1904), HARRISON RHODES MEMORIAL LIBRARY (1904). Second St., 32015. Tel 904 255-1401. Martha M. Berhel, Head Librn. Interlibrary loan, copying, inquiries answered, referrals made.

.1 Afro-American Studies Collection.
ca. 1000 paperbacks. Basic books on the life and history of black Americans.

.2 Bethune-Cookman College.
Archives, 1923-   Formed from a merger of the Daytona Educational and Industrial School for Negro Girls and Cookman Institute. Correspondence, minutes of board meetings, financial records, bulletins, catalogues, records of admission, and other materials dealing with the history and administration of the school. Restricted.

.3 Bethune, Mary McLeod, 1875-1955.
Papers. Educator; administrator of the Division of Negro Affairs, National Youth Administration (NYA); founder of Bethune-Cookman College; president of the National Council of Negro Women; recipient of the Spingarn Award (1935); and head of the "Black Cabinet." Documents and private papers concerning her career as an educator, civil rights leader, and intimate friend of the Roosevelts and other prominent Americans. Restricted.

.4 Afro-American Heritage collection.
Materials, 17th century- . Microfilm. 131 reels. Books, newspapers, and mss concerning the Negro American and his history. See Minnesota Mining and Manufacturing Company, St. Paul, Minn., for a full description. Restricted.

.5 Negro and African Collection.
Books (ca. 1200), periodicals, newspapers, pamphlets, clippings, art, photographs, tape recordings, phonograph records. Collection contains items by and about Negroes in all subject areas. Restricted.

DUNNELLON

FL4 CONGRESS OF RACIAL EQUALITY (CORE). P.O. Box 771, 32630. John Welsey Bostick, Chmn.

FORT LAUDERDALE

FL5 CHRISTIAN CONSTITUTIONAL EDUCATION LEAGUE, INC. P.O. Box 9013, 33310. Tel 305 565-6858. Helen M. Wolf, Editor.
Publ.: The White Sentinel, monthly.

GAINESVILLE

FL6 UNIVERSITY OF FLORIDA (1853), P.K. YONGE LIBRARY. 32601. Tel 904 376-3261. Margaret Knox Goggin, Acting Dir. of Libraries. Interlibrary loan, bibliographies prepared, literature searches, copying, typing, inquiries answered.

.1 Florida History Collection.
Unique materials concerning minority ethnic and racial groups in Florida, including the Negro. Includes books, newspapers, mss, microforms. Restricted.

JACKSONVILLE

FL7 AFRO-AMERICAN INSURANCE COMPANY (1901). 101 E. Union St., 32202. Tel 904 356-0441. I.H. Burney, II, Pres.

FL8 EDWARD WATERS COLLEGE (1866), H.Y. TOOKES LIBRARY (1945). 1658 Kings Rd., 32209. Tel 904 353-9335. Mrs. Olga L. Bradham, Head Librn. Bibliographies prepared, literature searches, inquiries answered, referrals made.

  .1 Afro-American Studies Collection.
      ca. 1000 paperbacks. Basic books on the life and history of black Americans.
  .2 Negro collection.
      Books (ca. 500), serials, pamphlets, films, phonorecords, art, and other general materials.
  .3 Edward Waters College.
      Archives, 1866- .

FL9 JACKSONVILLE URBAN LEAGUE (1947). 829 Pearl St., 32202. Tel 904 356-8336. Clanzel Brown, Exec. Dir. The League, a non-profit social service agency, utilizes the methods of community organization to secure equal opportunity for all citizens in the areas of employment, education, housing, health and welfare, and economic development. The basic philosophy and objective of the Urban League is to help the disadvantaged person to help himself. To accomplish this task, it collects and analyzes its findings, evaluates the results, mobilizes the community resources to focus attention on racial problems and develops programs toward their solutions.
Publ.: Newsletter, semi-annual; Economic Development Survey.

  .1 Jacksonville Urban League.
      Files, 1947- . Correspondence, minutes of meetings, financial records, reports, studies, and other materials dealing with the aims, history and programs of the League.

MIAMI

FL10 AMERICAN CIVIL LIBERTIES UNION OF FLORIDA. 502 Olympia Bldg., 33131. Tel 305 373-2052. Florence Diffenderfer, Exec. Dir.

FL11 AMERICAN JEWISH COMMITTEE, FLORIDA AREA (1906). 701 DuPont Plaza Center, 33131. Tel 305 373-4749. Walter Zand, Dir. Inquiries answered, referrals made, consultation.
The Committee combats bigotry, protects civil and religious rights of people, and seeks improved human relations for all men everywhere.

FL12 ANTI-DEFAMATION LEAGUE OF B'NAI B'RITH, FLORIDA REGIONAL OFFICE. 907 Seybold Bldg., 33132. Tel 305 373-6306. Arthur N. Teitelbaum, Dir.

FL13 COMMUNITY RELATIONS BOARD. Dade County Courthouse, 33130. Tel 305 377-5345. H.B. Sissel, Exec. Dir.

FL14 CONGRESS OF RACIAL EQUALITY (CORE). P.O. Box 6096, 33123. Peter Christiansen, Co-Chmn.

FL15 FLORIDA COUNCIL ON HUMAN RELATIONS (1956). 1221 N.W. 43rd St., 33142. Tel 305 661-5598. August H. Vanden Bosche, Exec. Dir.
The Council works to counteract prejudice and discrimination in the areas of housing, education, employment, human relations education, social attitudes through the State and 20 local councils. This private agency is affiliated with the Southern Regional Council, Atlanta, Ga.
Publ.: Open Doors, bi-monthly.

FL16 FLORIDA MEMORIAL COLLEGE (1892), JONATHAN SEWELL LIBRARY. 15800 N.W. 42nd Ave., 33054. Tel 305 625-4141. Leroy Thompson, Head Librn.

  .1 Afro-American Studies Collection.
      ca. 1000 paperbacks. Basic books on the life and history of black Americans.
  .2 Florida Memorial College.
      Archives, 1892- . Correspondence, minutes of board meetings, financial records, records of admission, and other materials dealing with the history and administration of the College.

FL17 METROPOLITAN DADE COUNTY COMMUNITY RELATIONS BOARD (1963). 1401-D Courthouse, 33130. Tel 305 377-5345. Robert H. Simms, Exec. Dir. The Board is a public intergroup relations agency which works to foster mutual understanding, tolerance and respect among all economic, social, religious and ethnic groups; makes studies, recommendations; cooperates in development of educational programs with other organizations and leaders.

FL18 NATIONAL CONFERENCE OF CHRISTIANS AND JEWS, INC. 906 Dupont Plaza Center, 33131. Tel 305 373-7658. Frank J. Magrath, Dir.

FL19 NEGRO EDUCATIONAL REVIEW. c/o Florida Memorial College, 15800 N.W. 42nd Ave., 33054. Tel 305 625-4141. Irving Scott, Editor.
Publ.: Negro Educational Review, quarterly journal.

  .1 Negro Educational Review.
      Files. Correspondence, financial records, subscription lists, studies, reports, and other materials dealing with the publication of the journal.

FL20 URBAN LEAGUE OF GREATER MIAMI, INC. (1943). 395 N.W. First St., 33128. Tel 305 377-3681. T. Willard Fair, Exec. Dir.
Formerly, Negro Service Council.

NORTH MIAMI

FL21 AMERICAN JEWISH CONGRESS, SOUTHEAST REGION. Suite 11B, 1190 N.E. 125th St., 33161. Tel 305 891-3141. Yosef I. Yanich, Dir. Copying, typing, inquiries answered, referrals made, consultation. The Congress is a voluntary membership organization of American Jews who work to foster the unity and creative survival of the Jewish people; help Israel develop in freedom, security and peace; combat anti-Semitism and all forms of racism; promote the cause of world peace; preserve and extend the democratic way of life; protect religious liberty and separation of church and state; oppose Communism, Facism and all forms of totalitarianism; and advance civil rights and civil liberties to achieve full equality in a free society.

  .1 American Jewish Congress.
      Files. Includes current clippings, publications of all kinds devoted to human relations problems, and other materials pertaining to the activities of the Congress.

ST. AUGUSTINE

FL22 ST. AUGUSTINE HISTORICAL SOCIETY (1883), LIBRARY. 271 Charlotte St., 32084. Tel 904 829-5514. Luis R. Arana, Librn. Interlibrary loan, typing, inquiries answered, referrals made, consultation.

  .1 Miscellaneous papers pertaining to slavery.

ST. PETERSBURG

FL23 CONGRESS OF RACIAL EQUALITY (CORE). $1905\frac{1}{2}$ 11th Ave. S., 33712. Tel 813 867-1027. W.C. Banks, Chmn.

SARASOTA

FL24 SARASOTA PUBLIC LIBRARY (1940). 701 Plaza de Santo Domingo, 33577. Tel 813 955-4903. Mrs. Betty W. Service, Head Librn. Interlibrary loan, literature searches, inquiries answered.

  .1 Vertical file collection.
      Contains sections on Negroes, social problems, civil rights, and the Office of Economic Opportunity.

TALLAHASSEE

FL25 FLORIDA AGRICULTURAL AND MECHANICAL UNIVERSITY (1887), SAMUEL H. COLEMAN MEMORIAL LI-

BRARY (1947). Box 78, 32307. Tel 305 222-8030.
Nicolas E. Gaymon, Dir. of Libraries. Interlibrary
loan, copying, inquiries answered, consultation.
Publ.: Catalog of the Negro Collections in the Florida
Agricultural and Mechanical University Library
and the Florida State University Library (1969).

.1 Afro-American Studies Collection.
    ca. 1000 paperbacks. Basic books on the life and
    history of black Americans.
.2 Florida Agricultural and Mechanical University.
    Archives, 1887- . Correspondence, minutes of
    board meetings, records of admission, bulletins,
    catalogs, financial records, and other materials
    dealing with the history and administration of the
    University.
.3 Negro Collection.
    Miscellaneous, 1840- . Books (ca. 8000 v.);
    serials (ca. 40 titles); pamphlets; 2 vf; clippings;
    photographs; microforms; phonorecords; film-
    strips. Subjects include: race relations in com-
    munication, religion, economics, athletics; inter-
    national affairs, business; prejudices and apathies;
    segregation and education; discrimination; sex and
    racism; civil rights; Black Muslims; interaction of
    ethnic and racial groups; Negroes in politics; Ne-
    gro suffrage; sociological studies; patterns of
    race relations in the South; riots; moral conditions
    of Negroes; folk beliefs and folklore; slavery; the
    Negro in medicine, music, art, literature, religion,
    science, sports, armed forces, law, politics; and
    Reconstruction.

FL26   FLORIDA STATE UNIVERSITY (1857), ROBERT M.
       STROZIER LIBRARY (1857). 32306. Tel 904 599-3290.
       N. Orwin Rush, Dir. Interlibrary loan, copying,
       typing, inquiries answered.
       Publ.: Catalog of the Negro Collections in the Florida
       Agricultural and Mechanical University Library
       and the Florida State University Library (1969).

.1 Bird family.
    Bird-Ulmer family papers, 1851-1922. 55 items.
    Photocopies made in 1964 from originals in the
    possession of Mrs. Daniel B. Bird, Monticello,
    Fla. Correspondence, land deeds, tax papers,
    political and other speeches, estate papers, divi-
    sion of land, division of slaves with values as-
    signed, and other papers of the Bird and Ulmer
    families of Jefferson Co., Fla., especially the
    Monticello area. The papers relate chiefly to the
    plantations, Bunker Hill, Nacossa, and Freelawn.
.2 Davis, Preston & Company.
    Thomas Jacob Oglesby collection, 1766-1850. 621
    items. Personal and business correspondence,
    legal and other papers of a firm of general mer-
    chants of Lynchburg and Bedford, Va. (operated by
    Smithson H. Davis and Bowker Preston) who
    traded in cotton, tobacco, wheat, and hides and
    skins, and purchased and hired out slaves to
    farmers.
.3 Facts on Film.
    Papers, 1954-67. Microfilm. Contains materials
    on civil rights and race relations in the South. See
    Race Relations Information Center, Nashville,
    Tenn., for a full description.
.4 Hollingsworth, John, 1773-1841.
    Papers, 1768-1887. 520 items. Owner and opera-
    tor of the Mount Vernon Plantation, Jefferson Co.,
    Fla. Agreements, tax receipts, bills, production
    lists of slaves, accounts, statements for tuition
    and board for children, doctor bills, railroad
    bills of lading, express receipts, promissory
    notes, lists of sale of slaves, and other papers,
    relating chiefly to the operation of a Florida
    cotton plantation.

TAMPA

FL27   COMMISSION OF COMMUNITY RELATIONS (1964). Room
       806, Citizens Bldg., 33602. Tel 813 228-7388. Charles
       I. Jones, Admn.
       The Commission works to better race relations so-
       cially, economically and educationally.

.1 Commission of Community Relations.
    Files, 1964- . Records, correspondence, reports,
    and other papers concerning the aims and pro-
    grams of the Commission.

FL28   TAMPA URBAN LEAGUE   2102 W. Main St., 33607. Tel
       813 251-1881. Mrs. Augusta E. Marshall, Exec. Dir.

.1 Tampa Urban League.
    Files. Correspondence, minutes of meetings, fi-
    nancial records, studies, reports, and other mate-
    rials dealing with the aims, history, and programs
    of the League.

FL29   UNIVERSITY OF SOUTH FLORIDA, LIBRARY (1960). 4202
       Fowler Ave., 33620. Tel 813 974-2721. Mrs. Mary
       Lou Harkness, Dir. of Libraries. Copying, typing, in-
       quiries answered.

.1 Facts on Film.
    Papers, 1954-67. Microfilm. Contains materials
    on civil rights and race relations in the South. See
    Race Relations Information Center, Nashville,
    Tenn., for a full description.

GEORGIA

ALBANY

GA1   ALBANY STATE COLLEGE (1903), MARGARET ROOD
      HAZARD LIBRARY. Hazard Dr., 31705. Tel 912 435-
      3411. Guy C. Craft, Head Librn.

.1 Afro-American Studies Collection
    ca. 1000 paperbacks. Basic books on the life and
    history of black Americans
.2 Negro Literature Collection.
    ca. 550 books. Most are by black authors. Collec-
    tion contains all the published works of Rev.
    Martin Luther King, Jr. and of Dr. Joseph Holly,
    former president of Albany State College; and
    some materials about black culture and history.

GA2   ALBANY URBAN LEAGUE, INC. (1968). 316 W. Broad
      Ave., 31702. Tel 912 435-6172. William Waymer,
      Exec. Dir. Copying, typing, inquiries answered, re-
      ferrals made, consultation.
      The League works toward the movement of Albany's
      minority group members into the mainstream of
      American life.
      Publ.: Quarterly newsletters and annual reports.

.1 Albany Urban League.
    Files, 1968- . Records, reports, correspondence,
    and other papers concerning the programs of the
    organization.

AMERICUS

GA3   KOINONIA PARTNERS (1942). Rt. 2, 31709. Tel
      912 924-7253. Millard Fuller.
      An integrated Christian community isolated from the
      surrounding white community where residents do agri-
      cultural and community improvement work in coopera-
      tion with local black residents. Their course of action
      is directed at communicating, instructing, and applying.
      Formerly Koinonia Farms.
      Publ.: Quarterly newsletter.

ATHENS

GA4   UNIVERSITY OF GEORGIA, ILAH DUNLAP LITTLE ME-
      MORIAL LIBRARY. 30601. Tel 404 542-2716. William
      Porter Kellam, Dir.

.1 Barrow, David Crenshaw, 1815-99.
    Papers, 1817-1915. ca. 5 ft. (3886 items). Planter,
    politician, Army officer, and educator. Correspon-
    dence, diaries, bills, receipts, deeds, account
    books, plantation records, and church records.
    Includes overseer's letters and records concerning
    his plantation, letters and other material on the

Civil War, and material on the social history of
Georgia, 1850-80. Correspondents include David
C. Barrow, Jr., James Barrow, Pope Barrow,
Howell Cobb, and Wilson Lumpkin. The material
is related to the library's collection of University
presidents' papers.

.2 Facts on Film.
Papers, 1954-67. Microfilm. Contains materials
on civil rights and race relations in the South. See
Race Relations Information Center, Nashville,
Tenn., for a full description.

.3 Farrow, Henry Patillo, 1834-1907.
Papers, 1855-1937. ca. 4600 items. Lawyer, and
attorney general of Georgia. Correspondence,
documents, broadsides, pamphlets, newspapers,
clippings, and pictures reflecting Georgia politics
during and after Reconstruction. Political correspondents include James Atkins, Madison Bell,
Joseph E. Brown, Alfred E. Buck, Rebecca (Latimer) Felton, Dr. William H. Felton, John B.
Gordon, Z.B. Hargrove, James Longstreet, and
Emory Speer.

.4 Georgia and Southern Authors.
Mss of both black and white Georgia and Southern
authors.

.5 Jones, Charles Colcock, 1831-93.
Papers, 1757-1905. ca. 2 ft. (1337 items). Lawyer, mayor of Savannah, Ga., Confederate soldier,
and historian. Correspondence and other papers,
of Jones and his parents, Charles C. Jones, Sr.,
and Mary Sharpe Jones; and a journal (1864-65) of
William B. Hodgson. Includes materials concerning plantation life in Liberty County, Ga., in the
Civil War, the defense and occupation of Savannah,
and Georgia history in general.

GA5 UNIVERSITY OF GEORGIA, INSTITUTE OF COMMUNITY
AND AREA DEVELOPMENT (1961). University Libraries, 30601. Tel 404 542-3350. E.E. Melvin, Dir.
Consultation.
The Institute works to strengthen and expand the services of the University to communities and areas on
their problems and adjustment needs. University
faculty members take charge of program aspects such
as business and economic research, community organization, recreation.
Publ.: Studies and reports.

GA6 UNIVERSITY OF GEORGIA, SCHOOL DESEGREGATION
EDUCATIONAL CENTER (1967). College of Education,
30601. Tel 404 542-3354. Dr. Morrill M. Hall, Dir.
The Center attacks instructional and administrative
problems related to school desegregation. It works
with teachers, students and administrators in this area.
The Center also initiates action in certain areas to
work on these problems, such as sponsoring a series
of graduate courses for teachers with emphasis on
administrative problems of school desegregation.

GA7 UNIVERSITY OF GEORGIA, SOCIAL SCIENCE RESEARCH
INSTITUTE (1960). 30601. Tel 404 542-1806. Homer
C. Cooper, Dir.
The Institute administers, coordinates and facilitates
interdisciplinary research in social sciences at the
University, particularly basic studies in the various
disciplines concerned with human affairs and the increasing impact of change on the people and culture of
the South.

.1 Social Science Research Institute.
Files, 1960- . Correspondence, reports, studies,
and other materials dealing with the aims, history
and programs of the Institute.

ATLANTA

GA8 AMERICAN CIVIL LIBERTIES UNION OF GEORGIA. 5
Forsyth St., N.W., 30303. Tel 404 523-5398.

GA9 AMERICAN CIVIL LIBERTIES UNION, SOUTHERN RE-
GIONAL OFFICE. 5 Forsyth St., N.W., 30303. Tel
404 523-2721. Charles Morgan, Jr., South. Regional
Dir.

.1 American Civil Liberties Union, Southern Regional
Office.
Files. ca. 10 vf. Includes 15 legal cases (briefs
and related material) on jury discrimination in
Alabama, penal desegregation and other legal
cases.

GA10 AMERICAN FEDERATION OF LABOR - CONGRESS OF IN-
DUSTRIAL ORGANIZATIONS (AFL-CIO), DEPART-
MENT OF CIVIL RIGHTS, SOUTHERN OFFICE. Suite
1422, 40 Marietta St., N.W., 30303. Tel 404 525-9549.
Elmer T. Kehrer, Dir.

GA11 AMERICAN FRIENDS SERVICE COMMITTEE (AFSC), AT-
LANTA OFFICE (1961). Room 502, 41 Exchange Place,
S.E., 30303. Tel 404 523-6628. Noyse Collinson, Dir.

.1 American Friends Service Committee.
Files. Included are school desegregation task
force papers, including 3 years of field reports
from workers on Louisiana, Mississippi, Alabama,
Georgia, and the Carolinas; and other papers
centered around such topics as economic trends
in the U.S. relative to AFSC objectives in changing
community structure, the employment on merit
project - break color line, an open housing project, Alabama and South Carolina community relations projects of developing concepts for quality
education, and economic harassment in the South.
Restricted.

GA12 AMERICAN JEWISH COMMITTEE, SOUTHERN REGION.
100 Edgewood, 30303. Tel 404 523-8451. Charles F.
Wittenstein, Dir.

.1 American Jewish Committee.
Files. Materials on extremism in the South, including analysis and perspectives on such groups
as the Ku Klux Klan and the White Citizens Council. Restricted.

GA13 ANTI-DEFAMATION LEAGUE OF B'NAI B'RITH, SOUTH-
EASTERN REGIONAL OFFICE (1945). 41 Exchange
Place, S.E., 30303. Tel 404 523-3391. Stuart Lewengrub, Dir. Consultation.
The league attempts to preserve and translate into
greater effectiveness the ideals of American democracy. Its programs have been directed in particular to
combating discrimination against minorities, to fighting
the threat of all forms of totalitarianism, and to promoting intercultural understanding and cooperation
among all the religious faiths in America.
Publ.: Research project reports, staff and field reports.

.1 Anti-Defamation League Collection.
Papers and pamphlets, 1952- . 44 vf. Contains
staff and field reports, and research project reports, from the Southern Regional Office; pamphlets and books published by the main office in
New York City. Research projects include a study
of racial discrimination in college admissions.
The collection also contains numerous papers and
pamphlets by and about the Ku Klux Klan, White
Citizens Council, left-wing and right-wing organizations, and extremist groups. Restricted.

.2 Audio-visual library.
Films, including many concerning race relations.
Some have been produced by the Anti-Defamation
League; others have been acquired from other
sources. Available for purchase or rental.

GA14 ATLANTA CITIZENS' COUNCIL. Henry Grady Bldg.,
30303. Tel 404 525-2230. Jack W. Callaway, Pres.
The Council's library is restricted to the use of research members and editorial staff of the organization.

GA15 ATLANTA HISTORICAL SOCIETY (1926), MARGARET
MITCHELL MEMORIAL LIBRARY (1949). 3099 An-
drews Dr., N.W., 30305. Tel 404 261-6055. Franklin
M. Garrett, Dir. Copying, inquiries answered.
Publ.: The Atlanta Historical Bulletin, quarterly.

.1 The Atlanta Historical Society contains materials on
such subjects as the Atlanta Campaign (Civil War),

U.S. Civil War history, Atlanta history, the Southern states, and Georgia history.

GA16   ATLANTA MUNICIPAL COMMUNITY RELATIONS COM-
MISSION (1966). 1203 City Hall, 30303. Tel
404 522-4463. Nat Welch, Exec. Dir.

GA17   ATLANTA PUBLIC LIBRARY, WEST HUNTER BRANCH.
1116 Hunter St., S.W., 30314. Tel 404 728-3912.
Carlton C. Rochell, Dir. Bibliographies prepared,
literature searches, copying.

.1   Negro collection.
Materials. ca. 1000 items. Books, newspapers,
and ephemera by and about black Americans. Sub-
jects include the Negro in the Armed Forces and
Negroes in Atlanta. Included is the Atlanta Daily
World (on microfilm, 1931- .).

.2   Negro Progress in Atlanta, Georgia Collection.
Extensive materials on Negroes in Atlanta, 1950-
60, made available through the Mrs. Annie W.
McPheeters Index (1964).

.3   Southern History Collection.
Contains some items on the history of blacks,
especially in Georgia, on the Civil War, and Reconstruction.

GA18   ATLANTA UNIVERSITY CENTER, PHYLON. 233 Chestnut
St., 30314. Tel 404 523-6431. Tilman C. Cothran, Editor.
Phylon is a quarterly journal devoted exclusively to
scientific, scholarly articles on race and culture. It is
designed to appeal to the scholar, scientist and general
reader.
Publ.: Phylon, A Review of Race and Culture, quarterly
journal.

GA19   ATLANTA UNIVERSITY (1867), TREVOR ARNETT LI-
BRARY (1929). 273 Chestnut St., S.W., 30314. Tel
404 523-6431. Gaynelle Barksdale, Chief Librn. Interlibrary loan, bibliographies prepared, literature
searches, copying, inquiries answered, referrals made,
consultation.

.1   Negro collection.
Materials, early 18th century- . Books (ca.
12,000), mss (ca. 4500), newspaper and periodical
titles, pamphlets, (ca. 1000), stamps, memorabilia,
and 48 vf of photographs, clippings, and other
ephemeral material. Collection contains material
on the history of black Americans since the Civil
War, on the Civil War, slavery, Africa, and the
colonization of Liberia and Sierra Leone by Negro
Americans. It also contains mss, first editions,
and published works of black artists, musicians,
poets, and writers.

.2 — Afro-American Heritage collection.
Materials, 17th century- . Microfilm. 131
reels. Books, newspapers, and manuscripts
concerning the Negro American and his history. See Minnesota Mining and Manufacturing
Company, St. Paul, Minn., for a full description.

.3 — Anderson, Trezzvant.
Papers, early 1960's. ca. 300 ms items. Includes articles and correspondence written by
him when in Georgia.

.4 — Association of Southern Women for the Prevention
of Lynching (ASWPL).
Papers, 1930-41. ca. 11,576 items. Organizational records, correspondence, clippings,
brochures, and pamphlets which include publications of the organization. ASWPL, a part of
the Commission on Interracial Cooperation's
program, made exhaustive case studies of
lynchings and maintained a continuing program
against their occurrence.

.5 — Atlanta University Archives.
Papers, 1870-1948. Correspondence, mostly
in the category of monies pledged, designated,
and spent. There are subdivisions of various
presidential papers.

.6 — Brown, John, 1800-59.
Papers, 1814-1932. 87 items. Abolitionist.
Chiefly correspondence, together with bonds
written and signed by Brown, a sketch of the

Haymaker Plot drawn by him, an order
signed by General Robert E. Lee, who im-
prisoned Brown, and two diaries and papers in
a wallet of Judge Richard Parker, who sen-
tenced him to death. Over half of the collection consists of Brown's letters (1826-49) to
his business partner, Seth Thompson; a second
large group of letters (1857-58) is from
Franklin Benjamin Sanborn, friend and biographer, to Brown. Includes letters from
Brown to his second wife, Mary Anne (Day)
Brown, to his cousin, the Rev. Luther Humphrey, and to David Hudson and Mrs. George
L. Stearns; and letters from Brown's sons,
Jason, John, and Oliver Brown, his father,
Owen Brown, and his uncle, Abiel Brown.

.7 — Bumstead, Horace.
Papers, 1875-1907. 1 box. Congregational
minister, president of Atlanta University.

.8 — Clarkson, Thomas, 1760-1846.
Papers, 1785-1929. 42 items. English abolitionist. Chiefly correspondence together with
two copies of Clarkson's "Anno liceat invitos
in servitutem dare," a journal relating to his
visit to France after the fall of the Bastille; a
ms by Mrs. Dickinson, wife of the Rector of
Wolferton; four silhouettes; an annotated copy
of the New Testament (1826 edition), and other
papers. Includes 17 letters from Clarkson
and his wife, Catherine (Buck) Clarkson, by
Sir Robert Forsyth Scott, master of St. John's
College, Cambridge, relating to a ms of a
Clarkson essay.

.9 — Commission for Interracial Cooperation.
Papers, 1906-44. 61,967 items. Records,
correspondence, clippings, and brochures.
Materials concern the Commission's programs in the areas of legal justice, prevention of lynching, educational facilities, housing and living conditions, recreational facilities, economic justice, equality of traveling
facilities, and welcoming returning black
soldiers of World War I; department, state,
district, county, and local conferences on the
matter of race relations; and such persons as
Will Alexander, M. Ashley Jones, and Mary
McLeod Bethune.

.10 — Countee Cullen Memorial Collection.
Papers, late 19th century- . ca. 3250 items.
Correspondence, literary mss, poems, articles, notes, post cards, proofs, theater bills
and programs, music and concert programs
and bills, newspaper and magazine reviews,
books, periodicals, art programs and bills,
reprints, pamphlets and broadsides, advertisements and critical notices. Chiefly collected by Harold Jackman. Emphasis is upon
contemporary life. Persons represented include Samuel Howard Archer, president of
Morehouse College, James Baldwin, Richmond
Barthe, sculptor, Arna Bontemps, Gwendolyn
Brooks, Countee Cullen, Owen Dodson, Angelina Grimké, William Christopher Handy, composer, Langston Hughes, Georgia Douglas
Johnson, Claude McKay, Eslanda Goode Robeson, Paul Robeson, actor, Charles Sebree, Era
Bell Thompson, Leigh Whipper, and Clarence
Cameron White, composer. The collection is
described in "An Annotated Bibliography of
the Dated Manuscripts in the Countee Cullen
Memorial Collection" by Lola B. Evans, an
Atlanta University thesis, 1959, and in "The
Countee Cullen Memorial Collection at Atlanta University." by Wallace Van Jackson,
published in Crisis, May, 1947, pp. 140-142.

.11 — Facts on Film.
Papers, 1954-67. Microfilm. Contains mate-
rials on civil rights and race relations in the
South. See Race Relations Information Center,
Nashville, Tenn., for a full description.

.12 — Foreman, Clark.
Papers. 5 vf and 3 boxes of materials on the
fight against the poll tax. Included is correspondence containing information concerning

the operation of the Southern Conference for Human Welfare, the background of the NEC report, Henry Wallace, and other politicians.

GA19.13 — Freedmen's papers.
Miscellaneous, 1867. A ledger of contracts between freedmen and employers.

.14 — Hamilton, Grace Towns.
Papers. 500 items. Daughter of George A. Towns, one of the first graduates of Atlanta University; member, Georgia State Legislature. Included is material concerning her association with the YWCA; the Atlanta Urban League; Adult Education Extension Work; voter education; improvement, expansion and desegregation of public school facilities; housing; planning and construction of the Hugh Spalding Pavilion of Grady Hospital; and the board of trustees of Meharry Medical College.

.15 — Hope, John.
Papers, 1868-1936. 1183 items. Correspondence, records, pamphlets, and clippings, chiefly 1929-36. Material is centered around Hope's presidency of Morehouse College and Atlanta University. Included is material concerning the affiliation of Spelman, Morehouse, and Atlanta University; building program; the board of trustees; financial budget control; the Negro Ministers Institute; and speeches, personal letters, and articles written by Hope, as well as honors and awards to him, and the material gathered for the Ridgely Tarrance biography of Hope.

.16 — Lincoln, C. Eric.
Author and educator. Collection contains 718 ms items on Black Muslims and race relations. It also contains correspondence subsequent to his book, The Black Muslims in America (1961).

.17 — McDuffie, Elizabeth and Irvin.
Papers, ca. 1930-45. Elizabeth McDuffie was the first Negro woman to live in the White House. Irvin McDuffie was a valet of Franklin D. Roosevelt. Materials concern Roosevelt's campaigns for presidency, his years in the White House, and the McDuffie's part in the struggle for civil rights for Negroes. The collection is uncataloged.

.18 — Negro American Artists Collection.
1942- . ca. 300 items. Paintings, sculpture, and prints, collected annually through an art show held by Atlanta University. Some of the major artists represented are Charles White, Jacob Lawrence, Calvin Burnett, Elizabeth Catlett, John Wilson, William Artis, and Hal Woodruff.

.19 — Negro Business Project.
Papers, 1944-45. 3665 items. Correspondence, surveys, reports, and studies pertaining to the project. Content covers years 1830-1947. Project was a study of Negro businesses in 12 cities to discover courses which would be helpful in graduate business schools. Results of this project helped shape the graduate course in business at Atlanta University. 12 cities used in the survey subsequently became local chapters of the National Negro Business League. Collection contains primarily raw data and statistical information.

.20 — Neighborhood Union.
Papers, 1908-61. 738 unbound ms items and related printed matter, 9 bound ms v., 20 pictures, and 1 plaque. Chiefly 1920-30. Correspondence, records, and printed matter tracing the founding and activities of one of the earliest private social welfare agencies in Atlanta, Ga.

.21 — Sheet Music Collection.
Manuscripts. ca. 442, including 83 mss in the Maud Cuney Hare Collection.

.22 — Hare, Maud Cuney, 18??-1936.
Papers, ca. 1900-1936. 83 mss, and numerous photographs and clippings. Concert pianist, lecturer, and writer. The collection contains rare music mss, autographed photographs, programs, and biographies of noted musicians. Composers represented are Dett (10 mss), W.C. Handy (10 mss), M.C. Hare (9 mss), Diton, Burleigh, J.R. Johnson, C.C. White, Will M. Cook, Gussie Davis, Edwin Hill, S.W. Jamieson, Coleridge-Taylor, Consuelo B. Cook, Joseph Cotter, Justin Elie, E.A. Hackley, Justin Holland, Nora Douglas Holt, Henry Mather, Gerald Tyler, and others. There are also 10 mss of minstrel songs in the collection, and photographs of Marian Anderson, Kemper Harreld, Harry Burleigh, Carl Diton, Noble Sissle, and W.C. Handy.

.23 — Slaughter, Henry P. collector.
Papers, early 19th century-1946. 8828 items. Books and pamphlets (7035 v.), 70 folders of clippings, 180 portraits, over 200 letters, 71 prints, 233 pieces of sheet music, and over 200 famous signatures. Sold to the library in 1946 by Henry P. Slaughter. Slaughter's interest as a collector centered around the acquisition of slavery literature. The books in the collection are devoted to slavery and slave trials, the life of John Brown, American statesmen who have been connected with the Negro, activities of the Ku Klux Klan, and contemporary and 19th century writings by and about Negroes. They include the works of Paul Lawrence Dunbar, including the first editions of his poems, autographed copies of Phyllis Wheatley's poems, and 34 Frederick Douglass items containing slave narratives used as weapons by the abolitionists. Books are also on Africa, Haiti and Cuba, comprising histories, travelogues, and narratives, and include the works of Haitian writers in poetry and prose. Clippings include files of anti-lynching papers, and clippings and materials on Monroe Trotter, editor of The Boston Guardian. The collection also contains 442 mss with emphasis on slavery and the early history of the Negro in the United States, including slave papers, and letters of abolitionists. The famous signatures include those of 19 presidents and 13 members of Lincoln's cabinet.

.24 — Southern Conference for Human Welfare.
Papers, 1938-48. 15,478 items. Organizational records, correspondence, and clippings. Major work of the Conference was the fight against the poll tax. Material is chiefly concerned with the North Carolina and Washington, D.C., chapters of the Conference, and includes papers pertaining to Clark Foreman, Mrs. Virginia Durr, and Mary McLeod Bethune.

.25 — Southern Regional Council (SRC).
Papers, 1944- . The Atlanta University Negro Collection is a depository for Southern Regional Council papers. The collection now contains only the publications of SRC.

.26 — Tanner, Henry O., 1859-1937.
Painter. 9 mss, letters by Tanner, prints and albums.

.27 — Thayer Lincoln Collection.
Papers. 350 items. ca. 1830-65. Donated by Mrs. Anna Chittendon Thayer. Correspondence, pamphlets, books, contemporary news accounts, numerous photographs, handbills, cartoons, White House chinaware, Lincoln coins, and other "association items."

.28 — Towns, George Alexander, 1870-1961.
Papers, 1867-1961. ca. 1340 items. Correspondence, poems, plays, essays, lectures, and notes relating to Atlanta University, Harvard University, and Fort Valley State College. Includes material and notes written by Towns as a student and teacher and correspondence with James Weldon Johnson, writer and diplomat, William N. Seaver, librarian at Massachusetts Institute of Technology, and Atlanta

University presidents, faculty, and alumni, and Harvard classmates. The collection contains 855 mss on Atlanta University, the Negro in Altanta and Georgia, and activities of Harvard classmates.

.29 —— Tuttle Collection.
Papers. 851 items. Materials concerning slavery.

.30 —— Ware, Edward Tevichell.
Papers, 1902-19. 16,645 items. President of Atlanta University. Correspondence, records, pamphlets, and clippings, chiefly 1907-14. Contains letters of recommendation, monies pledged, and student business transactions.

.31 —— Wynes, Charles E.
Papers. 7 mss of books and articles on the Negro in Virginia.

GA20   ATLANTA URBAN LEAGUE, INC. (1920). Suite 310, 75 Piedmont Ave., N.E., 30303. Tel 404 521-2355. Lyndon A. Wade, Exec. Dir. Inquiries answered, referrals made, consultation.
The League encourages, assists and engages in such activities and kinds of work which will lead toward the improvement of underprivileged persons in Metropolitan Atlanta. It works to discover unmet community needs in education, employment, housing, health, and welfare, and to encourage and develop such types of programs for meeting those needs; to promote the improvement of interracial understanding and cooperation; and to employ the techniques of effective community organization in the discovery, the correction and the prevention of conditions out of which racial tension, poverty, and disorder arise.

.1 Atlanta Urban League.
Files, 1920- . Correspondence, minutes of meetings, financial records, studies, reports, and other materials dealing with the aims, history, and programs of the League.

GA21   BLACK METHODISTS FOR CHURCH RENEWAL, INC. (1968). 1532 Gordon St., S.W., 30310. Tel 404 758-8118. Cain H. Felder, Exec. Dir.
Black Methodists for Church Renewal is an organization of black Methodist ministers and lay people who are united in their belief in black power as the response to racism in the United Methodist Church and in American society, and who seek to bring about renewal in the church at all levels. Formerly National Conference of Negro Methodists.
Publ.: Findings of Black Methodists for Church Renewal; Now, newsletter.

.1 Black Methodists for Church Renewal.
Files, 1967- . Records, correspondence, minutes of meetings, reports, and other papers concerning the aims and programs of the organization. Included are newspaper clipping files, position papers and task force reports. Files of National Conference of Negro Methodists (1967-Feb., 1968) are also included.

GA22   CLARK COLLEGE, GEORGE SMITH KEENEY LIBRARY. 240 Chestnut St., S.W., 30314. Tel 404 524-7883. Mrs. Fannie Barnes, Librn.

.1 Afro-American Heritage collection.
Materials, 17th century- . Microfilm. 131 reels. Books, newspapers, and mss concerning the Negro American and his history. See Minnesota Mining and Manufacturing Company, St. Paul, Minn., for a full description.

.2 Afro-American Studies Collection.
ca. 1000 paperbacks. Basic books on the life and history of black Americans.

GA23   COUNCIL OF JEWISH WOMEN, LOCAL EDUCATION PROJECT. Jewish Community Center, 1745 Peachtree St., N.W., 30309. Tel 404 875-7881.

GA24   COUNCIL ON LEGAL EDUCATION OPPORTUNITY (CLEO) (1967). 863 Fair St., S.W., 30314. Tel 404 755-6648. Melvin D. Kennedy, Exec. Dir. Interlibrary loan, referrals made, consultation.
The Council works to expand and to enhance the op-

portunities to study and practice law for members of disadvantaged groups - chiefly Negroes, American Indians, and Ibiro-Americans. It also provides financial assistance, counseling, and other aid to these students; and seeks to support those law schools serving primarily the needs of minority students. CLEO attempts to serve as a clearinghouse of materials on all subjects within or related to its purpose.
Publ.: Periodic newsletter; memoranda, reports and other documents.

.1 Council on Legal Education Opportunity.
Files, 1967- . Memoranda, reports, and other documents concerning the programs of CLEO, law school and legal programs, and on other subjects related to legal education and minority groups.

GA25   EMORY UNIVERSITY (1836), ASA GRIGGS CANDLER LIBRARY. 30322. Tel 404 377-2411. Guy R. Lyle, Dir.

.1 Babb, John D.
Family papers, 1862-65. 205 items. Sergeant in Company B, 5th Maryland Regt., Volunteer Infantry, U.S.A., and officer in Company D. Correspondence of Babb with his parents, John Babb, Sr., and Wealthy H. Babb, and his sister, Agnes Babb, relating to his experiences during the Civil War in Maryland, Virginia, West Virginia, and Libby Prison, the divided allegiance of the people of Baltimore, and the emancipation of the Negro.

.2 Battey, Robert, 1828-95.
Papers, 1810-94. 173 items. Surgeon. Correspondence, receipts, notes, excerpts from ledgers and cashbooks, and other papers, mostly letters of Battey and other members of the family. Concerns medicine and surgery, interviews with physicians on trips to Europe and America, slavery, conditions during the Civil War and Reconstruction, family problems and other personal matters.

.3 Darling, Charles B., d. 1864.
Correspondence, 1861-64. 91 items. Soldier. Mostly letters of Darling to his father, J.M. Darling, while serving in the 1st Regt. of New York Dragoons (originally called the 130th Infantry, then the 19th Cavalry) in Virginia, including material on recruiting, war news and rumors, marches, movement by train, camp sites and camp life, food, quarters, officers, chaplains, southern whites and Negroes, Rebel officers and men, the countryside, destruction of southern homes and farms, and confidence in Abraham Lincoln and Ulysses S. Grant.

.4 Fogle, Theodore Turner, 1834-64.
Papers, 1851-65. 205 items. Officer in Company G, 2nd Regt., Georgia Volunteer Infantry. Correspondence and miscellaneous papers, chiefly relating to Fogle's Civil War experiences in Virginia. Subjects include slavery, Confederate hospitals, the battles of Sharpsburg, Second Bull Run, Gettysburg, and Chickamauga, the Columbus guards, and the blockade.

.5 George, E.H. collector.
Papers, 1804-1932. 74 items. Correspondence, deeds, and other business and legal papers, dealing with land, slaves, stock certificates, and other property in Georgia and Kentucky, including land deeded to Asbury College, Wilmore, Ky.

.6 Georgia Collection I, 1779-1960.
Papers relating to Georgia politics and government. 132 items. Chiefly letters of Georgian political figures concerned with routine political and personal matters; Includes "Proceedings (1960) of the Georgia Legislative Committee Leading up to the Integration of the Schools." Persons represented include Howell Cobb, William Harris Crawford, William Crosby Dawson, John B. Gordon, and Thomas Butler King.

.7 Long, Nimrod W.E.
Confederate soldier letters, 1860-65. 58 items. Confederate soldier, plantation owner, State legislator, and merchant of Perote, Pike Co., Ala. Letters from Long, a member of Company B, 51st Regt., Alabama Cavalry, to his wife, Queen Long, who ran the plantation in his ab-

sence. Much of the correspondence is concerned with advice about planting, harvesting, care of crops, livestock and farm tools, and the discipline of Negroes, and with camp life, food, clothing, morale, discipline, officers, and civilians.

.8 Palmer, Charles Forrest.
Miscellaneous. ca. 15,000 items, and 2000 v. Personal papers, books and other printed materials pertaining to slum clearance, low-cost housing, town planning, and related topics. Includes letters; documents from government officials, commission heads, and other public officials; diaries; photographs; reports; pictures; objects of art; and printed materials, which include official documents from wartime to the present. Palmer served as President Franklin D. Roosevelt's defense housing coordinator (1940-42). Housed in the Robert W. Woodruff Library at Emory University.

.9 Pitts, Thomas Henry, 1834-71.
Pitts-Craig correspondence, 1856-75. 80 ft. of microfilm (248 items). Officer in Company I, 3rd South Carolina Regt., and resident of Clinton, S.C., Calhoun, Ga., and St. Louis, Mo. Correspondence between Pitts and his future wife relating to the first Battle of Bull Run, the Seven Days' Battle, the Sharpsburg Campaign, and Reconstruction.

.10 Thiot family.
Papers, 1756-1865. 194 items. Correspondence, land and title papers, notes, accounts, slave receipts, statements, estate papers and other material concerning the movement of the family and slaves from Jamaica to Georgia, the purchase and operation of the plantation Knoxborough by Charles Thiot (d. ca. 1810) and Charles Thiot, Jr.; and the Civil War service of Charles Henry Thiot (1822-65) with the Chatham Artillery and the 1st Regt. of Georgia Infantry. Much of the material before 1804 is in French or Spanish.

.11 Wilson, Alpheus Waters, Bp., 1834-1916.
Papers, 1854-1916. 124 items. Methodist clergyman. Correspondence of Wilson with his wife, Susan B. Wilson, notebook, copy (1914) of the Discipline of the Methodist Episcopal Church South, and a sermon. Subjects include church affairs, conditions in Baltimore during the Civil War, and slavery.

GA26   EPISCOPAL SOCIETY FOR CULTURAL AND RACIAL UNITY (1961). 5 Forsyth St., 30303. Tel 404 525-7975. Rev. Albert R. Driesbach, Jr., Exec. Dir.
ESCRU works to eliminate racial, color and class barriers in the church, its camps, conferences, schools, colleges, hospitals, and other institutions. The organization supports anti-discrimination activities and community organizing. Local chapters determine their own priorities.
Publ.: ESCRU Newsletter, bi-monthly.

.1 Episcopal Society for Cultural and Racial Unity.
Papers, 1961- . 6 vf. Books, pamphlets, papers, correspondence, and records of the organization. Subjects include the church and race, a study of Negro clergy, jury selection, and employment discrimination. The files also contain staff and field reports.

GA27   FEDERATION OF SOUTHERN COOPERATIVES. 52 Fairlie St., N.W., 30303. Tel 404 524-6098. Charles Prejean.
The Federation makes available to membership, training, technical help, education and marketing information. It serves low-income, grass-roots cooperative enterprises or organizations.

GA28   GEORGIA CONGRESS OF COLORED PARENTS AND TEACHERS (1921). 201 Ashby St., N.W., 30314. Tel 404 523-6717.
The Georgia Congress is the local arm of the National Congress of Colored Parents and Teachers.
Publ.: Georgia Family.

GA29   GEORGIA COUNCIL OF HUMAN RELATIONS. 5 Forsyth St., N.W., 30303. Tel 404 525-6468. John L. McCown, Exec. Dir.

The Council works throughout Georgia to devise, develop and publicize techniques and programs of youth and adult education to counteract prejudice and discrimination based on race, religion, nationality, or ethnic group origin; and to awaken interest in and stimulate local and state-wide community groups to constructive and democratic attitudes toward problems of intergroup living. The major program areas are housing, education, employment, human relations education, public accommodations, governmental operations, social attitudes, welfare rights, legal rights, police-community relations, tutorials, biracial books, youth, and voter registration.
Publ.: Georgia Council Newsletter, monthly.

GA30   GEORGIA DEPARTMENT OF ARCHIVES AND HISTORY (1918). 330 Capitol Ave., S.E., 30334. Tel 404 522-0010. Miss Carroll Hart, Dir. of Archives. Bibliographies prepared, literature searches, copying, typing, inquiries answered, referrals made, consultation.

Adjutant General's Office Collection.

.1 —— National Guard Riot Duty.
Papers, 1903-11. 95 pp. Records of the National Guard's actions to prevent lynchings and to quell riots. Includes materials about attempted lynchings in Monroe, Elberton, Hawkinsville, Preston, Bainbridge, and Columbus (14 pp.); about a lynching at Lawrenceville (1 page); about a lynching at Statesboro (67 pp.); and about the 1906 Race Riot in Atlanta (13 pp.).

.2 —— Negro Companies in the National Guard.
Papers, ca. 1895-1905. ca. 225 pp. Correspondence, returns, training reports, and inspection reports, for the 4 Negro companies in the National Guard.

Executive Department Collection.

.3 —— Campbell, Tunis G.
Papers, ca. 1872. 92 pp. Documents containing evidence from a contested election for State Senator from McIntosh County in 1872, between Tunis G. Campbell, a black man, and Hiram Maddox, a white man. The material ranges from testimony offered to voters' lists.

.4 —— Negro Insurrection, 1875.
Papers, ca. 1875. 42 pp. Transcript of the trial of some Negro members of an "equal rights" association who were charged with insurrection in 1875. The document was a special report to the Governor on the trial which was held in the Superior Court of Johnson County.

Legislative Documents Collection.

.5 —— Campbell, Tunis.
Papers, ca. 1871. 324 pp. Documents dealing with testimony concerning Campbell's "inflammatory" speeches to Negroes in Darien in 1871, his activities as judge in the case of ship Captain John Erwin, and his purchase and subsequent resale of some plantation property.

.6 —— Campbell, Tunis G., Jr.
Papers, ca. 1865-76. 12 pp. Negro member of the Georgia House of Representatives from McIntosh County. Testimony from legislative investigation of Campbell, who was arrested in an Atlanta opera house for disorderly behavior. Because of immunity granted House members, the arrest prompted a legislative investigation.

.7 —— Mitchell County Riot, 1868.
Joint Committee Report, ca. 1868. 3 pp. Concerns disturbance in Camilla, Ga., 1868. Includes a newspaper description of events.

Manuscripts Collection.

.8 —— African Slave Case.
Papers, 1818-22. ca. 425 pp. Correspondence, depositions, slave manifests, and court proceedings. This collection concerns the charges leveled at William B. Mitchell, Indian

agent in the Creek Nation. He was charged
with being party to the illegal importation of
slaves into Georgia.

.9 —— Ku Klux Klan.
Papers, 1871-72. 56 pp. Correspondence,
affidavits, and court proceedings. Contains a
printed copy of the proceedings of a court of
enquiry held at Cartersville (Bartow County)
on June 20, 1871, to inquire about the murder
of a freedman, George Wright, by several
white men. Also contains correspondence and
affidavits sent to the Governor in 1871 and
1872 requesting that a pardon be granted to
Henry Drummond who was one of the men
tried and convicted in the case of George
Wright.

.10 —— Negroes in Georgia.
Papers, ca. 1798-1920. 140 pp. of mss, 2
pamphlets, and 1 article. Loose papers and
documents related to Negroes in Georgia. Although the earliest one is dated 1798, and
there are a few scattered items up to 1860,
most of the collection relates to the Reconstruction period with a few pieces dated in the
early twentieth century.

.11 —— Reconstruction.
Papers, 1865-76. Collection contains many
documents which discuss the plight of the Negro and his relation to the whites (ca. 284 pp.).
Most of the items concern the election of 1868,
and some of the fraudulent election practices
committed by both Democrats and Republicans.
There are some references to the Ku Klux
Klan.

Microfilm Library Collection.

.12 —— Cobb, Thomas Reed Rootes.
Book, 1858. 1 v., 358 pp. On microfilm.
Cobb's An Inquiry into the Law of Negro
Slavery in the United States of America. To
Which is prefixed An Historical Sketch of
Slavery. Savannah: W. Thorne Williams.

.13 —— Jones, John J.
Papers, ca. 1835-65. 1 reel of microfilm.
Deeds, receipts, and other records relating to
slavery and the use of slave labor by the Confederate States of America.

.14 —— Newspaper and Periodicals Collection.
Papers, 1901-36. Newspapers and periodicals
on microfilm. Includes The Kourier, 1924-36,
official organ of the headquarters of the Ku
Klux Klan, published monthly in Atlanta, Ga.
(3 reels of microfilm; original in the Library
of Congress); and Voice of the People, 1901-
04, a newspaper published in Atlanta by the
Colored National Emigration Association (1
reel of microfilm).

Official Records of Georgia Counties Collection.

.15 —— Free Persons of Color Registers.
Papers, ca. 1780-1864. ca. 25 reels of microfilm. Registers usually include name, age,
occupation (sometimes), property, and white
sponsor; available for 21 counties.

.16 —— Indentures of Apprenticeship.
Papers, ca. 1866-1900. 15 reels of microfilm. Primarily indentures of freed Negroes; available for 15 counties.

.17 —— Records of Slave Trials, 1813-43.
Papers, 1813-43. ca. 10 reels of microfilm. Records of slave trials; available for
ca. 10 counties.

.18 —— Slave Requisitions.
Papers, ca. 1800-45. ca. 15 reels of microfilm. Affidavits of persons bringing slaves
into the State; available for ca. 15 counties.

.19 Schedule of Slave Owners, 1850 and 1860.
Papers. 10 reels of microfilm. Official records
of the U.S. Bureau of the Census; Schedule of
Slave Owners, 1850 and 1860; available for all
Georgia counties.

Special Collections.

.20 —— Gardner, James.
Papers, 1867-73. Miner and businessman

from Columbia County, Ga. Correspondence
and plantation accounts. In this collection of
his papers are seven letters written to Gardner from J.P. Carroll, an attorney in
Charleston, S.C. in 1873. They deal with the
presence of Negro lawyers in Southern courts.
There are also some plantation accounts at
least part of which deal with handling freedmen in 1867.

.21 —— Northen, William Jonathan.
Papers, 1872-1912. Governor of the State of
Georgia, 1890-94. Collection of Northen's
private papers, including some 137 pp. of
material relating to the Negro in the South.
These pages consist of letters, pamphlets, a
copy of a speech, and an article. The collection also contains six scrapbooks of newspaper clippings and personal correspondence,
some of which pertains to the Negro.

.22 —— Segregation Collection.
Papers, ca. 1956-60. 206 items. Broadsides,
cartoons, newspaper clippings, newspapers,
pamphlets, public correspondence, speeches
and tracts, and some other items. Collection
deals with states' rights, integration, segregation, politics, communism, and racism from
the viewpoint of the political right-wing. Most
of the items fall within the period 1956-60.

GA31 GEORGIA TEACHERS AND EDUCATION ASSOCIATION
(GTEA) (1918). 201 Ashby St., N.W., 30314. Tel
404 522-7512. Horace E. Tate, Exec. Secy. Inquiries
answered, referrals made, consultation.
The Association is a State-wide professional association of Negro educators in Georgia and is an affiliate of
the National Education Association, the American
Teachers Association, and the National Council of Officers of State Teachers Associations.
Publ.: GTEA Herald, quarterly; GT&EA Reporter,
quarterly.

.1 Georgia Teachers and Education Association.
Files, 1918- . Included are unpublished studies on
teacher displacement and materials on salary discrimination. Restricted.

GA32 INTERDENOMINATIONAL THEOLOGICAL CENTER (1957),
LIBRARY (1957). 671 Beckwith St., S.W., 30314. Tel
404 522-1744. Wilson N. Flemister, Librn. Interlibrary loan, bibliographies prepared, literature
searches, copying, inquiries answered, referrals made.
Publ.: Subject bibliographies on various aspects of the
Afro-American experience.

.1 The Library's collection consists of papers, mainly
from the 19th century or before, on the Negro in
America, with special focus on Negro religious
history. Possibly the most comprehensive archives
in the United States in the field of Negro religious
history. The collection is divided into Africana,
papers on Negro church history, and papers on slavery and anti-slavery propaganda. In part, restricted.

.2 Africana Collection.
Materials on Africa collected in connection with
the Stewart Missionary Foundation at Gammon
Seminary, Atlanta, Ga. Many items were purchased in the late 19th century from American and
foreign booksellers. The collection is uncataloged.

.3 Negro Church History Collection.
Papers, 19th century. Books, newspaper and periodical titles, correspondence, records, minutes,
reports, journals, and other papers. The collection contains minutes, reports, journals, and other
papers of the annual and general conferences, association meetings and conventions of the A.M.E.,
C.M.E., Methodist, Baptist, and A.M.E. Zion
churches; and also reports of the American Missionary Association and the Freedmen's Aid Society (M.E. Church). The collection contains partial runs of the following periodicals: A.M.E.
Church Review, the Christian Index (C.M.E.), The
A.M.E. Zion Quarterly Review, The Star of Zion
(A.M.E. Zion), The Christian Recorder (A.M.E.),
The American Missionary (A.M.E.), The Southwestern Christian Advocate (M.E.), The (Atlanta)

Methodist Advocate (M.E.), The African Repository (American Colonization Society) and The
Liberia Bulletin, Missionary Seer (A.M.E. Zion),
The Messenger (C.M.E.), The Christian Educator
(M.E.), Journal of Religious Education of the
A.M.E. Church, and The Central Christian Advo-
cate (Methodist, C.J.). Collection contains the
most complete holdings of The (Atlanta) Methodist
Advocate in the United States, with 7 full years
complete (1870, 1871, 1872, 1875, 1876, 1881, 1882)
and 2/3 to 3/4 of the remaining years except for
1869. The Methodist Advocate was published in
Atlanta from 1869-1882, edited most of the time by
Erasmus Q. Fuller. It contains extensive source
materials on the M.E. Church in the South after the
Civil War; the problems of sectional and national
Methodism; the difficulties and failure of "church
reconstruction" in the South; the social and political, as well as religious aspects of Reconstruction;
racial adjustments, problems and finally separation in the Southern work of the M.E. Church. The
Negro Church History Collection contains 10 ms
collections, consisting of the papers and correspondence of organizations and individuals important in the history of the Gammon Seminary. The
ms collections contain correspondence by and to
numerous important American Methodist leaders,
including Bishops Thoburn, Goodsell, Fowler,
Luccock, Bashford, Warren, Foss, Cranston,
Hughes, Hartzell, Mallalieu, Jones, McIntyre,
David Moore, McDowell, McConnell, Hamilton,
Quayle, Walden, Candler, Haygood, and others.
There are some letters from A.M.E leaders
Benjamin Tanner and Henry M. Turner; A.M.E.
Zion Bishop Clinton; and other outstanding Negro
leaders, such as editor Thomas Fortune, Booker
T. Washington, the poet C.W. Chesnutt, and
educator-churchman I. Garland Penn, and nu-
merous college presidents in Negro Methodist
schools in the South. The ms collections are as
follows:

.4 — Atkinson, L.D.
        Papers. President of Gammon Seminary.
.5 — Bowen, J.W.E.
        Papers. President of Gammon Seminary and
        Negro Methodist leader.
.6 — Freedmen's Aid Society and Southern Education
        Board.
        Papers. 105 bound letter books and 6 vf.
.7 — Gammon Seminary Historical Papers.
        Papers of Gammon Seminary, Atlanta, Ga.
        Since 1957 Gammon has been a part of the
        Interdenominational Theological Center.
.8 — King, Willis J.
        Papers, while president of Gammon Seminary.
.9 — M.E. Church Mission in the South During Recon-
        struction.
        Papers, 1865-67. Letters and reports con-
        cerning early post-Civil War work among
        freedmen; the organization of the M.E. Church
        in Georgia and Alabama; the opposition of the
        white South and the M.E. Church, South; his-
        tory of the attempt at "church reconstruction"
        under native Southerners and Northern mis-
        sionaries, such as J.H. Caldwell, A.S. Lakin,
        J.W. Yarbrough, and James Chalfant.
.10 — Soule, Francis Asbury.
        Papers, ca. 1845-60. 3 sermon books.
        Minister of the Methodist Episcopal Church,
        South, as of 1845. Sermons were on subjects
        such as the dangers of Catholicism, missions,
        temperance, and an attack on the Fugitive
        Slave Law.
.11 — Stewart Missionary Foundation.
        Papers.
.12 — Thirkield, W.P.
        Papers. President of Gammon Seminary and
        Howard University, and Methodist Bishop.
.13 — Watters, Philip M.
        Papers. President of Gammon Seminary.
.14 Slavery and Anti-Slavery Propaganda Collection.
        Papers, 1788-1890. ca. 200 items. Books, pam-
        phlets, newspaper and periodical titles, sermons,
        speeches, and memoirs. The collection consists

primarily of anti-slavery literature, but contains
some pro-slavery propaganda. Subjects represented include history of slavery in the United
States and Britain, slavery and the M.E. Church,
slavery and science, slavery and the Bible,
slavery and skin color, the African slave trade,
narratives of the sufferings of slaves, slavery
during the Civil War, history of the abolition of
slavery in Britain, and materials about Charles
Sumner, Lunsford Lane, Father Henson, Frederick
Douglass, W.L. Garrison, W. Phillips, and John
Brown.

GA33   MARTIN LUTHER KING, JR. MEMORIAL CENTER (1968),
        LIBRARY PROJECT. 671 Beckwith St., S.W., 30314.
        Tel 404 524-1956. Vincent Harding, Dir. Copying, in-
        quiries answered.
        The Library Project of the Center collects materials
        of organizations and individuals involved in the Civil
        Rights Movement (1954-), and arranges, indexes, and
        preserves these materials so that they may be used by
        scholars to write the history of the Movement. Mate-
        rials will become available on a restricted basis after
        September, 1970. Other programs of the Center in-
        clude the Institute of the Black World - a community of
        black scholars who are concerned with the develop-
        ment of academic research in the experiences of black
        people, development of new materials and methods for
        the teaching of black children, and development of a
        Black Policy Studies Center.

        Clippings File.
            Clippings from newspapers and periodicals, ca.
            1954- . File includes the following collections:
        .1 — Bond, Mrs. Horace Mann. collector.
                News clippings, ca. 1954-68. Collection con-
                tains articles on civil rights movement in At-
                lanta; on Julian Bond, member of Georgia
                House of Representatives, and son of Mrs.
                H.M. Bond; and on Dr. Horace Mann Bond,
                professor at Atlanta University.
        .2 — Coca-Cola Company. collector.
                Newspaper clippings, April-May, 1968. Arti-
                cles on Rev. Martin Luther King, Jr. and
                American civil rights movement written dur-
                ing the 10 days between King's assassination
                and funeral, from newspapers collected by
                Coca-Cola Co. offices and plants all over the
                world.
        .3 — Lewis, Lillian M. collector.
                Clippings, ca. 1960-68. Contains articles on
                John Lewis, chairman (1963-66) of Student
                Nonviolent Coordinating Committee; on SNCC;
                and on the civil rights movement in the South.
        .4 — Martin Luther King, Jr. Memorial Center. col-
                lector.
                Clippings, 1968- . Articles on Afro-American
                life and activities clipped from 70 newspaper
                and periodical titles.

        .5 Dexter Avenue Baptist Church.
                Papers, 1854- . Records, correspondence, and
                other papers dating from the founding of Mont-
                gomery, Ala., church where Martin Luther King,
                Jr. was pastor, 1955-60.
        .6 Forman, James, 1929- .
                Tape recordings, ca. 1960-68. Civil rights leader.
                Collection contains interviews concerning Student
                Nonviolent Coordinating Committee; and speeches
                of James Forman, executive secretary of SNCC,
                1963-66.
        .7 Harding, Vincent.
                Papers, ca. 1961- . Civil rights leader and
                teacher. Large collection of correspondence,
                records, pamphlets, broadsides, clippings, and
                other papers. Collection falls into four periods:
                (1) Harding's work in Atlanta as a lay minister for
                Mennonite Church and director of Mennonite
                House, an organization involved in education and
                work with the poor, 1961-63; (2) his work in the
                civil rights movement in Montgomery, Selma, and
                Birmingham, Ala., and Albany, Ga., 1963-65, in-
                cluding his participation in training program at
                Antioch College for civil rights workers who came
                South in summers of 1963 and 1964; (3) as teacher
                and head of history department at Spelman College,

Atlanta University, 1965-69; and (4) as director
of Martin Luther King, Jr. Memorial Center in Atlanta, 1968- .

.8 King, C.B.
Papers, ca. 1961-64. Attorney in Albany, Ga.
Collection contains court records of cases arising
from Albany Movement, 1962.

.9 King, Coretta (Scott).
Papers, ca. 1955-69. Civil rights leader and wife
of Rev. Martin Luther King, Jr. Correspondence,
clippings, and other papers of Mrs. King. Includes
correspondence and condolences on death of her
husband.

.10 King, Martin Luther, Jr., 1929-68.
Papers, ca. 1950-68. Baptist clergyman, author,
and civil rights leader. Correspondence, personal
and family papers relating to King's early life, ca.
1950-55; his work as pastor of Dexter Avenue Baptist Church, Montgomery, Ala., 1955-60; his work
with Montgomery Improvement Association, 1955-
60, and Montgomery bus boycott, 1955-56; as co-
pastor with his father of Ebenezer Baptist Church,
Atlanta, Ga., 1960-68; winning Nobel Peace Prize,
1964; his work as president of Southern Christian
Leadership Conference, 1957-68, and involvement
in civil rights campaigns, including Memphis,
Tenn., sanitation workers' strike, 1968, during
which he was shot and killed. Collection contains
papers, chiefly from 1962-68, and some papers
from before 1955.

.11 King, Slater.
Papers, ca. 1960-68. Businessman in Albany, Ga.
Small collection of personal papers dealing with
his insurance agency, and correspondence with his
family and his brother, C.B. King. Subjects include the Albany Movement, 1962.

.12 Levin, Thomas.
Papers, ca. 1964-66. Psychiatrist. Papers, clippings, and correspondence relating to Levin's
work as director of Child Development Group of
Mississippi, an early federal Head Start program
under Office of Economic Opportunity. Papers
concern organizing the program and problems with
people and government agencies.

.13 Martin Luther King Speaks.
Tape recordings, ca. 1960- . ca. 1000 tapes. In-
cludes speeches of Martin Luther King, Jr., Ralph
Abernathy, Andrew Young, and other officials of
Southern Christian Leadership Conference. Col-
lection is duplicate of SCLC radio program,
"Martin Luther King Speaks," in New York City.

.14 Medical Committee for Human Rights.
Papers, ca. 1964-66. Correspondence and records
of group of physicians, including Dr. Thomas
Levin, who went to Mississippi in 1964 to work
with black people and civil rights movement.

.15 Montgomery Improvement Association.
Papers, 1955- . Records, correspondence, pamphlets, broadsides, clippings, court records, and
transcripts of trials. Some on microfilm. Collection contains materials of Martin Luther King,
Jr.; Ralph D. Abernathy; Dr. Anderson, president;
E.D. Nixon; and attorney, Fred D. Gray. Includes
following collection:

.16 —— Gray, Fred D.
Papers, 1955-68. Attorney and clergyman.
Court records and transcripts of trials. On
microfilm. Includes records of his suit to end
segregation of buses in Montgomery, Ala.,
1955-56, and other civil rights cases.

.17 Northern Student Movement.
Papers, 1964. Organization of students who came
to Mississippi and other Southern states as civil
rights workers in summer, 1964. Papers are
chiefly organizational materials. Includes papers
of William Strickland.

.18 Photograph Collection.
Photographs, 1954- . Depicts the civil rights
movement, chiefly in the South, with photographs
contributed by staff photographer of Southern
Christian Leadership Conference, and by major
news services and magazines.

.19 Southern Christian Leadership Conference.
Papers, 1957- . Atlanta-based civil rights orga-

nization. Large collection consisting of correspondence, records, clippings, pamphlets, broadsides, photographs, and other papers. Papers reflect SCLC's involvement in civil rights movement, including Alabama sit-in movement, 1960;
Freedom Rides, 1961; Albany Movement, 1962;
March on Washington, 1963; SCLC's "long hot
summer" campaign for civil rights, 1964; demonstrations in Selma, Ala., 1965; SCLC voter
registration drives in Virginia, North Carolina,
South Carolina, Georgia, Florida, Alabama, and
Louisiana, 1965; Chicago civil rights campaign,
1965; SCLC resolution opposing Vietnam war
adopted at annual convention in Jackson, Miss.,
1965. Other SCLC campaigns mentioned include
Chicago fair housing drive, and demonstrations in
Cicero, Ill., 1966; Birmingham voting rights
marches, 1966; voting rights demonstrations in
Grenada, Miss., 1966; march to Jackson, Miss.,
led by Martin L. King, Jr. after the wounding of
James Meredith, 1966; Memphis sanitation
workers' strike, 1968; assassination of Rev. Martin
Luther King, Jr., president of SCLC, 1968; Poor
People's Campaign, 1968; and the Charleston, S.C.,
hospital workers' strike, 1969. Collection con-
tains papers of leaders of SCLC, including Rev.
Martin L. King, Jr., Rev. Ralph D. Abernathy, Rev.
Andrew Young, Rev. Jesse H. Jackson, Rev. James
Bevel, Rev. Fred Shuttlesworth, Hosea Williams,
and Rev. Wyatt T. Walker.

GA34   MOREHOUSE COLLEGE, MOREHOUSE COLLEGE READ-
ING ROOM. 223 Chestnut St., S.W., 30314. Tel 404
523-5071. Mrs. Jesse Ebanks, Librn.

.1 Afro-American Heritage collection.
Materials. 17th century- . Microfilm. 131 reels.
Books, newspapers, and mss concerning the Negro
American and his history. See Minnesota Mining
and Manufacturing Company, St. Paul, Minn., for a
full description.

.2 Afro-American Studies Collection.
ca. 1000 paperbacks. Basic books on the life and
history of black Americans.

GA35   MORRIS BROWN COLLEGE (1881), LIBRARY. 643 Hunter
St., N.W., 30314. Tel 404 525-7831. Mrs. Victoria W.
Jenkins, Head Librn. Interlibrary loan, copying, typing,
referrals made.

.1 Afro-American Heritage collection.
Materials, 17th century- . Microfilm. 131 reels.
Books, newspapers, and mss concerning the Negro
American and his history. See Minnesota Mining
and Manufacturing Company, St. Paul, Minn., for a
full description.

.2 Afro-American Studies Collection.
ca. 1000 paperbacks. Basic books on the life and
history of black Americans.

.3 Human Relations Collection.
Books. ca. 125 v. Books by and about Negroes.
Subjects include race relations, black history, and
Afro-American literature.

GA36   NATIONAL ASSOCIATION FOR THE ADVANCEMENT OF
COLORED PEOPLE (NAACP), SOUTHEAST REGIONAL
OFFICE. Room 107, 859½ Hunter St., N.W., 30314. Tel
404 688-8868. Mrs. Ruby Hurley, Regional Dir.

GA37   NATIONAL ASSOCIATION OF STATE UNIVERSITIES AND
LAND-GRANT COLLEGES, OFFICE FOR ADVANCE-
MENT OF PUBLIC NEGRO COLLEGES (OAPNC)
(1968). Suite 577, 805 Peachtree St., N.E., 30308. Tel
404 874-8073. Herman B. Smith, Jr., Dir. Inquiries
answered, referrals made, consultation.
OAPNC was established as an operating staff office of
the National Association of State Universities and Land-
Grant Colleges to assist the nation's 34 public Negro
colleges in increasing their share of financial support
provided by private voluntary agencies including
corporations and foundations.
Publ.: Investment in Opportunity; Fact Book on Public
Negro Colleges; Newsletter.

.1 Office for Advancement of Public Negro Colleges
(OAPNC).
Files, 1968- . Records, minutes, correspondence,

and other materials including college catalogs, bulletins, and news releases of public Negro colleges.

GA38 NATIONAL CONFERENCE OF CHRISTIANS AND JEWS, GEORGIA REGION. 40 Marietta St., N.W., 30303. Tel 404 688-7510. A. Wilson Cheek, Dir.

GA39 NATIONAL CONGRESS OF COLORED PARENTS AND TEACHERS (NCCPT) (1926). 201 Ashby St., N.W., 30314. Tel 404 524-1792. Mrs. E.R. Gay, Pres. NCCPT works to promote the betterment and improvement of the educational process of all Negro children in the elementary and secondary schools in some southern states.
Publ.: Our National Family, semi-annual magazine.

.1 National Congress of Colored Parents and Teachers (NCCPT).
Files, 1926- . Correspondence, financial reports, minutes of meetings, publications, and other materials concerning various projects of the NCCPT.

GA40 NATIONAL SHARECROPPER'S FUND. 5 Forsyth St., N.W., 30303. Tel 404 522-3697. Leonard E. Smith, South. Dir.
Publ.: Special literature on rural economic development.

GA41 NATIONAL URBAN LEAGUE, INC., SOUTHERN REGIONAL OFFICE (1925). Suite 417, 136 Marietta St., N.W., 30303. Tel 404 688-8778. Clarence D. Coleman, Dir.
The League works to conduct, support and evaluate programs to end poverty among blacks; sponsors training programs to raise the employment potential of black people with little education, black high school graduates and college dropouts as well; provides support to strengthen the programs of its affiliate organizations; and makes studies and evaluations of community organizing and anti-poverty programs.
Publ.: Bread and Butter, weekly newsletter.

.1 National Urban League, Inc., Southern Regional Office.
Files. Books, pamphlets, papers, publications of the League and its affiliates, including field and visit reports on economic and social conditions of blacks in cities in the South and studies of black community organization in the South. In part, restricted.

GA42 ORGANIZATION OF BLACK COLLEGES (1969). c/o Clark College, 30314. Tel 404 524-7762. Dr. Vivian W. Henderson, Chmn.
The Organization of Black Colleges is an association of 111 predominantly Negro colleges which seeks a stronger voice in policy decisions affecting higher education, and more financial support from federal and private sources.

.1 Organization of Black Colleges.
Files, 1969- . Records, correspondence, reports, and other papers concerning the founding and activities of the organization.

GA43 ST. MARTIN'S COUNCIL ON HUMAN RELATIONS. 3110 Ashford Dunwoody, N.E., 30319. Tel 404 237-2203.

GA44 SOUTHEASTERN EDUCATION LABORATORY. 3450 International Blvd., 30354. Tel 404 766-0951. Dr. Kenneth W. Tidwell, Exec. Dir.
The Laboratory, a federal regional education laboratory, works to eliminate educational deprivation among the culturally and educationally disadvantaged through special programs developing teaching-learning tools for school children.

GA45 SOUTHERN ASSOCIATION OF COLLEGES AND SCHOOLS (1895). 795 Peachtree St., N.E., 30308. Tel 404 875-8011. Dr. Felix C. Robb, Exec. Dir. Accreditation.
The Association is concerned with the assessment and improvement of institutional quality in 11 Southern states. It administers the Education Improvement Project (EIP).
Publ.: Proceedings, annual report; Clearinghouse.

.1 Southern Association of Colleges and Schools.
Files. Records, reports, correspondence, and other papers concerning the activities of the organization, including materials pertaining to EIP.

GA46 SOUTHERN CHRISTIAN LEADERSHIP CONFERENCE (SCLC) (1957). 334 Auburn Ave., N.E., 30303. Tel 404 522-1420. Rev. Ralph Abernathy, Pres.
The Conference is a national civil rights group organized around affiliate organizations that operate out of Negro churches and civic organizations. Its program includes non-violent direct action, voter registration, citizenship schools, selective buying campaigns, economic development, slum tenement unions, and cooperatives.
Publ.: Reports, newsletters.

.1 Southern Christian Leadership Conference (SCLC).
Files, 1957- . Correspondence, records, papers and taped speeches of Martin Luther King, Jr., and tape-recorded interviews concerning the activities of the organization.

GA47 SOUTHERN EDUCATION FOUNDATION (SEF) (1867). 811 Cypress St., N.E., 30308. Tel 404 875-0279. Dr. John A. Griffin, Exec. Dir.
SEF assists Negroes in the South through education to become full and participating members of the region of which they are a part.
Publ.: Studies of higher education opportunities for southern Negroes.

.1 Southern Education Foundation (SEF).
Files, 1867- . Includes studies of the role and functions of predominantly Negro colleges, produced by individual colleges in cooperation with the SEF.

GA48 SOUTHERN EDUCATION PROGRAM, INC. 859½ Hunter St., N.W., 30314. Tel 404 525-6042. Lawrence Rushing, Dir. Inquiries answered, referrals made.
The Program is a non-profit recruitment clearinghouse, placing black teachers in 94 black colleges.

GA49 SOUTHERN REGIONAL COUNCIL (SRC) (1944), LIBRARY. 5 Forsyth St., 30303. Tel 404 522-8764. Mrs. Bernice S. Morrison, Librn. Literature searches, inquiries answered, consultation.
The Council works in areas of housing, education, employment, human relations, education, social attitudes, voter education, community organization, labor education, prison reform and judicial reform, and cooperates closely with Councils of Human Relations in the eleven southeastern states, to attain equal opportunities for people of the South.
Publ.: New South, quarterly magazine; Field Activities Newsletter; Voter Education Project Newsletter; Special reports; South Today, monthly.

.1 Civil Rights Collection.
Miscellaneous, 1944- . Books (ca. 800 v.); pamphlets (280 4 inch bins or ca. 90 ft.); 132 vf of newspaper and magazine clippings and publications of other organizations. The books contain information on Negro history, Southern history, civil rights and civil liberties issues. SRC publications and the background materials in the collection deal with social issues such as Black Power; black youth in Atlanta; prisons in Arkansas, Mississippi, Louisiana, and other states; starvation of blacks in Mississippi; Atlanta housing and residential patterns for the black population; slums and ghettos; race-related violence; the effects of Negro voting; census reports; racial discrimination by the federal courts; history of the Southern Regional Council (1944- .); state commissions on human relations; Negro veterans of World War II; and peonage.

Other subjects include economic issues such as the U.S. Minimum Wage law; welfare programs; the Memphis garbage strike (1968); economic status of Negroes; Negro employment opportunities in Houston, Tex., Atlanta, Ga., Chattanooga, Tenn., and other cities; the civil rights issues such as school desegregation (1954- .); University of

Mississippi riots (1962); "massacre" of black students at Orangeburg, S.C. (1968); desegregation of Albany, Ga.; and agricultural issues such as rural education; migrant farmers; black farmers in South Carolina and other states; and federal farm programs affecting Negroes in the South. The collection is kept up to date with clippings from 20 newspapers daily, 20 magazines weekly, and papers from community and voter registration organizations, publications of the Center for the Study of Democratic Institutions, the Citizens' Council, SNCC, Negro colleges, scholastic journals, law reviews, student organizations, and church groups.

.2 Facts on Film.
Papers, 1954-67. Microfilm. Contains materials on civil rights and race relations in the South. See Race Relations Information Center, Nashville, Tenn., for a full description.

.3 Ku Klux Klan Collection.
Papers, 1944- . Books, pamphlets, newspaper clippings, notes, mss, posters, and pictures, concerning the revival of the Ku Klux Klan after World War II.

.4 Oral History Project.
Tape-recorded interviews. Interviews with black political candidates in the South by Julian Bond.

GA50 SOUTHERN REGIONAL EDUCATION BOARD (SREB) (1948), LIBRARY. 130 Sixth St., N.W., 30313. Tel 404 875-9211. E.F. Schietinger, Assoc. Dir. for Res. Interlibrary loan, inquiries answered, consultation. SREB works to improve institutions of higher education and mental health in the South through work with educators and legislators in the 15 Southern states: Alabama, Arkansas, Florida, Georgia, Kentucky, Louisiana, Maryland, Mississippi, North Carolina, Oklahoma, South Carolina, Tennessee, Texas, Virginia, and West Virginia.
Publ.: State Legislation Affecting Higher Education in the South, annually; Regional Action, quarterly; Mental Health Briefs, quarterly; Financing Higher Education, occasionally.

.1 Institute for Higher Educational Opportunity.
Files, 1967- . Materials on Negro colleges and opportunities for education for Negroes in the South, which has developed from the Higher Education Opportunity Project.

.2 Southern Regional Education Board (SREB).
Miscellaneous, 1948- . ca. 5000 items. Books, pamphlets, and papers. Materials concern higher education and mental health in the South. Contains limited materials on black colleges; and statistical studies made by SREB which include data on black schools.

GA51 SPELMAN COLLEGE (1881), LIBRARY. 350 Leonard St., S.W., 30314. Tel 404 688-5765. Mrs. Mexico Mickelbury, Librn.

.1 African Collection.
ca. 2000 items. Books, papers, poems, phonograph records. Subject areas are Afro-American and African history; literature and music by black authors and musicians.

.2 Afro-American Heritage collection.
Materials, 17th century- . Microfilm. 131 reels. Books, newspapers, and mss concerning the Negro American and his history. See Minnesota Mining and Manufacturing Company, St. Paul, Minn., for a full description.

.3 Afro-American Studies Collection.
ca. 1000 paperbacks. Basic books on the life and history of black Americans.

GA52 STUDENT NATIONAL COORDINATING COMMITTEE (SNCC) (1960). 360 Nelson St., S.W., 30313. Tel 404 688-0331. H. Rap Brown, Nat. Dir. SNCC organizes black people to gain power over their own lives and communities, and provides national coordination of organizing activities. Formerly Student Nonviolent Coordinating Committee.

.1 Student National Coordinating Committee (SNCC).
Files, ca. 1962- . Materials reflect the civil

rights movement in the South, and include correspondence, records, pamphlets, and publications of SNCC. Includes runs of SNCC Newsletter, The Voice, The Nitty-Gritty, The Afro-American, and Watts Line Report. Records restricted.

GA53 UNITED CHURCH WOMEN OF GEORGIA, RACE EDUCATION PROJECT. 201 Washington St., S.W., 30308. Tel 404 524-3887. Mrs. Jack May, State Chmn.

.1 United Church Women of Georgia, Race Education Project.
Files. Materials on race, labor, international relations, especially in the South and in Georgia.

GA54 UNITED NEGRO COLLEGE FUND, INC., REGION V AND GEORGIA STATE OFFICES (1944). Suite 509, 87 Walton St., N.W., 30303. Tel 404 523-6171. James E. Bullard, Regional Dir.
The Fund is a federation of 36 private predominantly Negro colleges organized to make joint annual appeal for national support for its members' scholarship and financial aid programs, to upgrade faculty salaries, teaching equipment, libraries, and the development of remedial programs.

GA55 U.S. COMMISSION ON CIVIL RIGHTS, SOUTHERN FIELD OFFICE. Room 362, Citizens Trust Bank Bldg., 75 Piedmont Ave., 30303. Tel 404 526-4391. Bobby Doctor, Dir.
The Southern Field Office covers Kentucky, Tennessee, South Carolina, Georgia, Mississippi, Alabama, Louisiana, and Florida.

GA56 U.S. DEPARTMENT OF HEALTH, EDUCATION AND WELFARE, OFFICE OF THE SECRETARY, OFFICE FOR CIVIL RIGHTS, REGION IV. 50 Seventh St., N.E., 30323. Tel 404 526-5087. Samuel L. Younge, Dep. Dir.

GA57 U.S. DEPARTMENT OF HOUSING AND URBAN DEVELOPMENT (HUD), HUD REGION III LIBRARY. Peachtree St. and Seventh Bldg., 30303. Tel 404 526-5339. Patricia Cook, Librn. Interlibrary loan.
The Library is for HUD staff use. Materials restricted.

GA58 U.S. EQUAL EMPLOYMENT OPPORTUNITY COMMISSION (EEOC), ATLANTA REGIONAL OFFICE (1965). 1776 Peachtree St., N.W., 30309. Tel 404 526-5581. Donald L. Hollowell, Regional Dir.
The Commission investigates complaints of discrimination, and if it finds they are justified, seeks a full remedy by the process of conciliation; and promotes programs of voluntary compliance by employers, unions and community organizations to put the idea of equal employment opportunity into actual operation. Records restricted.
Publ.: U.S. EEOC Annual Report; Pamphlets, brochures, posters.

GA59 U.S. OFFICE OF ECONOMIC OPPORTUNITY, SOUTHEAST REGIONAL OFFICE. 101 Marietta, N.W., 30303. Tel 404 526-6068.

GA60 URBAN LABORATORY IN EDUCATION, EDUCATION IMPROVEMENT PROJECT. 55 Walnut St., S.W., 30314. Tel 404 577-4524. Sidney H. Estes, Dir.

GA61 YOUNG WOMEN'S CHRISTIAN ASSOCIATION (YWCA), NATIONAL BOARD, SOUTHERN REGIONAL OFFICE. 41 Exchange Place, S.E., 30303. Tel 404 525-4658. Miss Rosetta Gardner, South. Regional Dir.
YWCA meets the recreational and spiritual needs of women and girls. It conducts tutorial programs, and has engaged in community action programs such as voter registration. The student branch of the YWCA (Student Christian Association) combats social isolation on the campus and in the community, and poverty.

.1 Young Women's Christian Association, National Board, Southern Regional Office.
Papers, ca. 1945- . Records, correspondence, mailings to members, reports and studies. Contains complete records of the voter registration project operated in the South until 1966; completed

questionnaires and papers from a self-audit to determine the progress of integration in the YWCA and Student Christian Association (1946-1947). Restricted.

AUGUSTA

GA62 THE COURIER PUBLISHING COMPANY. Suite 500, 500 Bldg., 30902. Tel 404 722-3748. Roy V. Harris. Publ.: *Augusta Courier*, weekly.

GA63 PAINE COLLEGE (1882), WARREN A. CANDLER LIBRARY (1947). 30901. Tel 404 722-4471. Miss Helen E. Gilbert, Librn. Interlibrary loan, bibliographies prepared, literature searches, inquiries answered, referrals made.

.1 Afro-American Heritage collection.
Materials, 17th century- . Microfilm. 131 reels. Books, newspapers, and mss concerning the Negro American and his history. See Minnesota Mining and Manufacturing Company, St. Paul, Minn., for a full description.
.2 Afro-American Studies Collection.
ca. 1000 paperbacks. Basic books on the life and history of black Americans.
.3 Walker-Gilbert Collection.
Collection contains books on Negro history (ca. 200 v.) and other subjects. The books on Negro history date from 1837-1910 and describe slavery in the South, the abolitionists, the Negro's religious problems, economic conditions of the Negro, histories of the development and early growth of Negro churches in America, and the life of the Negro during the latter half of the 19th century.

EAST POINT

GA64 U.S. NATIONAL ARCHIVES AND RECORDS SERVICE, FEDERAL RECORDS CENTER LIBRARY (1951). 1557 St. Joseph Ave., 30044. Tel 404 526-7474. James O. Hall, Supvry. Archivist. Literature searches, copying, inquiries answered, consultation, microfilming. The Archive stores records for federal agencies which are required by law to preserve them; and stores records of archival value for the use of historians.

.1 Archival Collection.
Records of 92 Federal agencies, 1716- . 500,000 cu. ft. Microfilm and other archival records and federal court Records from the southeastern states: Alabama, Florida, Georgia, North Carolina, Mississippi, South Carolina, and Tennessee. In part, restricted. Includes the following collections:
.2 — Circuit Courts Collection.
Papers, 1789-1911. 1955 cu. ft. Judicial records from the southeastern region. Minute books, docket books, execution docket books, and case files. Papers represent criminal, civil and equity cases involving breach of contract, property settlements, and appeals of District Court decisions. Early cases frequently involve slaves. Later cases sometimes concern the civil rights of Negroes.
.3 — Civil Commission Records, 1863-64. Memphis, Tennessee.
Papers, 1863-64. 2 cu. ft. A minute book, dockets, and final record books of the Civil Commission, Memphis, Tenn. This Commission was established by the U.S. Army under Special Order 247 to hear all suits brought by citizens loyal to the Federal Government.
.4 — Confederate States, 1861-65.
Papers, 1861-65. 26 cu. ft. Records from the District Courts in Atlanta, Knoxville, Mobile, Montgomery, New Bern, Oxford, Pensacola, Raleigh, Savannah, Tallahassee, and Wilmington. Minute books; judgment, sequestration, and garnishment dockets; and case files; including hearings on criminal, civil, admiralty and equity cases. Contains extensive material dealing with matters arising as a result of the Civil War.

.5 — District Courts Collection.
Papers, 1789-1965. 34,955 cu. ft. Judicial records from the southeastern region. Dockets, minutes, journals, abstracts of judgment, indexes, and case files. Contains adjudication of admiralty and bankruptcy matters, and various actions brought by the United States, and minor criminal violations prior to 1911. Thereafter jurisdiction expanded to include matters previously handled by the Circuit Courts. Contains records of civil rights and school desegregation cases in the states of Alabama, Florida, Georgia, North Carolina, Mississippi, South Carolina, and Tennessee.
.6 — Federal Population Censuses, 1850 and 1880.
Seventh Census, 1850. 75 rolls of microfilm. Tenth Census, 1880. 225 rolls. Schedules for the states of Alabama, Florida, Georgia, North Carolina, Mississippi, South Carolina, and Tennessee only. In addition to the filmed records there are name indexes to the 1880 Federal population schedules for the states of Alabama, Florida, Georgia, and Mississippi (partial) on Soundex coded cards. 112 cu. ft.
.7 — U.S. Attorney's Records, 1861-1964.
Papers, 1861-1964. 5440 cu. ft. Records from the southeastern region. The bulk of these records consists of civil and criminal case files, 1950-64; a small volume of precedent cases, and 7 v. of civil and criminal proceedings, 1861-1907. Contains records from cases involving the civil rights of Negroes and desegregation of schools.

FORT VALLEY

GA65 FORT VALLEY STATE COLLEGE (1895), HENRY ALEXANDER HUNT MEMORIAL LIBRARY (1925). 31030. Tel 912 825-8281. Homie Regulus, Librn. Interlibrary loan, bibliographies prepared, copying. Publ.: Quarterly newsletter.

.1 Afro-American Studies Collection.
ca. 1000 paperbacks. Basic books on the life and history of black Americans.
.2 Negro History and Literature Collection.
Books, periodical and newspaper titles, theses and dissertations. ca. 2500 items. Library plans to build up holdings with special regard to federal legislation, 1954 to date; and to add sculpture, paintings and music to the Collection.

SAVANNAH

GA66 GEORGIA HISTORICAL SOCIETY (1839). W.B. Hodgson Hall, 501 Whitaker St., 31401. Tel 912 234-1585. Lilla M. Hawes, Dir. Interlibrary loan, inquiries answered, referrals made, consultation, limited amount of research for members. The Society collects, preserves and diffuses information relative to the State of Georgia in particular, American history generally, and maintains a historical library for the use of its members and others.

.1 The Society holds books, pamphlets, mss, clippings, and sheet music pertaining to the Negro in the South in various collections. Included are such items as slave manifests and bills of sale, plantation journals, and sheet music. Among collections containing relevant materials are the following:
.2 — Chatham County Registers of Free Persons of Color.
Books, 1826-64. 4 v.
.3 — City of Savannah Register of Free Persons of Color.
Book, 1860-63. 1 v.
.4 — Potter, James.
Papers, 1828-31. 1 v. Plantation journal of Argyle Plantation containing rosters of slaves and daily work reports.
.5 — Sheet music pertaining to the Negro in the South.
Miscellaneous. Various collections contain published and unpublished items pertaining to

the Negro in the South. Among the unpublished
materials at the Society are: "The Island
Lullaby," lyrics by Mary Cabaniss and music
by Rita Crofut (6 pp.); ditto copies of songs
(12 titles), lyrics and music, as sung by the
Negroes on Daufuskie Island, S.C; and typed
copies of 10 additional songs, lyrics only.

.6 — Telfair family.
Papers, 1772-1875. 7 v. and 25 boxes. Includes papers of Edward Telfair (Georgia
planter, member of Continental Congress, and
Governor), and letterbooks and account books
with entries pertaining to sales of slaves.

.7 — Wayne-Stites-Anderson families.
Papers, 1791-1875. 25 v. and 11 boxes. Contains papers of Richard Wayne (South Carolina
and Georgia commission merchant), James
Moore Wayne (Georgia, U.S. Representative
and Supreme Court Justice), Richard M.
Stites (Georgia lawyer), and George W.
Anderson (Georgia, Confederate Army officer,
cotton factor, and planter). Includes plantation books from Beverly and Berwick plantations (1874-76, 2 v.) containing daily account
of work done by hands.

GA67   NATIONAL STATES RIGHTS PARTY (NSRP) (1948). Box
6263, 31405. Tel 404 355-4271. Edward R. Fields,
Nat. Secy.
The Party works "to awaken the American people to
the Inequality of man."
Publ.: The Thunderbolt, monthly tabloid newspaper.

.1   National States Rights Party.
Files. Books, pamphlets, and NSRP publications
covering such subjects as white supremacy,
eugenics and race, civil rights, riots, race and
social revolution.

GA68   SAVANNAH STATE COLLEGE (1890), A.H. GORDON LI-
BRARY. 31404. Tel 912 354-5717. A.J. McLemore,
Librn. Interlibrary loan, bibliographies prepared,
literature searches, copying, inquiries answered, consultation.

.1   Afro-American Studies Collection.
ca. 1000 paperbacks. Basic books on the life and
history of black Americans.

.2   Facts on Film.
Papers, 1954-67. Microfilm. Contains materials
on civil rights and race relations in the South. See
Race Relations Information Center, Nashville,
Tenn., for a full description.

.3   Negro Collection.
Books (ca. 1250), pamphlets, periodical and newspaper titles, correspondence, and clippings (20
scrapbooks). Materials by and about black Americans. Collection contains 49 microfilm reels of
the Savannah Tribune, oldest Negro newspaper in
continuous existence.

GA69   TELFAIR ACADEMY OF ARTS AND SCIENCES. 121
Barnard, 31401. Tel 912 232-1177.

.1   Telfair Plantation Records.
Materials, containing information pertaining to
slavery.

HAWAII

HILO

HI1   DEPARTMENT OF LABOR AND INDUSTRIAL RELATIONS,
ENFORCEMENT DIVISION, FIELD OFFICE. 9 Ship-
man St., 96720. Tel 808 561-7391.

HONOLULU

HI2   AMERICAN CIVIL LIBERTIES UNION OF HAWAII. 2500
Pali Hwy., 96817. Tel 808 595-6681. Wallace
Fukunaga, Pres. Consultation.

HI3   DEPARTMENT OF LABOR AND INDUSTRIAL RELATIONS,
ENFORCEMENT DIVISION (1964). 825 Mililani St.,
96813. Tel 808 548-2211. Robert K. Hasegawa, Dir.
The Department, a state agency, operates in areas of
employment discrimination (employers, agencies, and
labor), and is empowered to receive and investigate
complaints, hold public hearings, issue cease-and-
desist orders, and seek court enforcement of its
orders.

LIHUE

HI4   DEPARTMENT OF LABOR AND INDUSTRIAL RELATIONS,
ENFORCEMENT DIVISION, FIELD OFFICE. Circuit
Court Bldg., 96766. Tel 808 245-4091.

WAILUKU

HI5   DEPARTMENT OF LABOR AND INDUSTRIAL RELATIONS,
ENFORCEMENT DIVISION, FIELD OFFICE. 54 S.
High St., 96793. Tel 808 244-4322.

ILLINOIS

CARBONDALE

IL1   SOUTHERN ILLINOIS UNIVERSITY, COMMUNITY DE-
VELOPMENT SERVICES: COMMUNITY STUDIES UNIT.
62901. Tel 618 453-2491. Ernest K. Alix, Dir.
The Community Studies Unit is the research arm of
Community Development Services, which engages in
applied, evaluational, and theoretical research. The
Unit maintains working relationships with various departments of the University by keeping researchers
posted on research needs and opportunities in the
southern Illinois area, by lending limited financial
support to researchers, and by using researchers as
technical consultants when needed.

IL2   SOUTHERN ILLINOIS UNIVERSITY (1869), DELYTE W.
MORRIS LIBRARY (1874). 62903. Tel 618 453-2681.
F.S. Randall, Dir. Interlibrary loan, copying, in-
quiries answered, referrals made.

.1   Facts on Film.
Papers, 1954-67. Microfilm. Contains materials
on civil rights and race relations in the South. See
Race Relations Information Center, Nashville,
Tenn., for a full description.

.2   Schroeder, Theodore A., 1867-1954.
Papers. Correspondence, mss, legal records.
Constitutional lawyer, and founder with Lincoln
Steffens of the Free Speech League, a forerunner
of the American Civil Liberties Union. Included in
the Free Speech League files are extensive corre-
spondence with such figures as Anthony Comstock,
Samuel Gompers, Eugene V. Debs, Margaret
Sanger, John Dewey, H.L. Mencken, Arthur Garfield
Hays, G. Stanley Hall, Emma Goldman, W.E.B. Du-
Bois, Maynard Shipley, and others associated with
political and social movements of the first half of
the 20th century. In addition to thousands of letters, the collection contains notes and mss of
Schroeder's writings, and records of legal cases
in which he was involved.

CHAMPAIGN

IL3   UNIVERSITY OF ILLINOIS AT URBANA-CHAMPAIGN,
NEGRO CURRICULUM DEVELOPMENT PROJECT
(1968). 404 E. Staughton St., 61820. Tel 217 333-1000.
Daniel Dixon, Dir.
The Project is concentrating on an oral history of the
activist struggle for civil rights among black Ameri-
cans, with emphasis on the contributions of the Student
Nonviolent Coordinating Committee.

.1   Negro Curriculum Development Project.
Files, 1968- . Includes correspondence, minutes

of meetings, financial records, studies, investigations, reports, and other documents dealing with the history, aims, and programs of the Project.

IL4   URBAN LEAGUE OF CHAMPAIGN COUNTY, INC. (1910). 29½ Main St., 61820. Tel 217 356-1364. Vernon L. Barkstall, Exec. Dir. Literature searches, copying, typing, inquiries answered, referrals made, consultation.
The League's purpose is to eliminate racial segregation and discrimination in American life; and to give guidance and help to Negroes and other economically disadvantaged groups so that they may share equally the responsibilities and rewards of full citizenship.
Publ.: Reporter, annual newsletter; Annual reports, pamphlets, brochures.

.1   Champaign County Urban League.
Files, 1910- . Correspondence, minutes of meetings, financial records, studies, reports, and other materials dealing with the aims, history, and housing, health and education, job development and employment, and education and youth incentive programs of the League.

CHICAGO

IL5   AFRICAN METHODIST EPISCOPAL ZION CHURCH, BOARD OF CHRISTIAN EDUCATION. 128 E. 58th St., 60605. Rev. James W. Eichelberger, Dir.

.1   African Methodist Episcopal Zion Church, Board of Christian Education.
Files. Correspondence, minutes of board meetings, financial records, and other materials relating to the Board's support of the following predominantly black colleges: Livingstone College, Salisbury, N.C.; Lomax-Hannon College, Greenville, Ala.

IL6   AFRO-AM PRESS, DIVISION OF AFRO-AM BOOKS, INC. (1969). 133 S. Racine Ave., 60607. Tel 312 421-6060. David C. Ross, Jr., Publisher.
Afro-Am Press has as its primary goal the facsimile publishing of out-of-print works in the field of Afro-American history and culture. It does not restrict itself to facsimile publishing and is not necessarily a reprint house.

IL7   ALPHA KAPPA ALPHA (1908). 5211 S. Greenwood Ave., 60615. Tel 312 684-1282. Mrs. Carey B. Preston, Exec. Secy.
National Negro sorority founded at Howard University, Washington, D.C. It is the oldest college-based sorority founded by Negro women. The sorority's programs include scholarship grants; Negro heritage; the operation of a Job Corps Center in Cleveland, Ohio; a leadership school; distribution of information about federal statutes affecting welfare, housing and employment; and voter education and registration campaigns.
Publ.: The Ivy Leaf, quarterly magazine; Heritage Series, brochures on contemporary Negro men and women in various professions.

.1   Alpha Kappa Alpha.
Files, 1922- . Includes organization records, brochures and pamphlets, correspondence, and complete run of the Ivy Leaf (1922- .).

IL8   ALPHA PHI ALPHA. 4432 S. Parkway, 60655. Tel 312 373-1819. Laurence T. Young, Exec. Secy.
A national Negro fraternity with a program of political action and education; and sponsor of an annual citizenship week to encourage voter registration.
Publ.: The Sphinx, monthly magazine.

IL9   AMERICAN CIVIL LIBERTIES UNION, ILLINOIS DIVISION. Room 400, 6 S. Clark St., 60603. Tel 312 636-5564. Jay Miller, Exec. Dir.

IL10   AMERICAN FREEDOM OF RESIDENCE FUND (AFRF) (1960). 176 W. Adams St., 60603. Tel 312 588-1666. Charles Benton, Chmn. of the Bd.
AFRF contributes funds "to provide educational, research, legal, and financial assistance to help guaran-

tee the right of all citizens to live where they choose," and disseminates information on open occupancy.
Publ.: AFRF News, occasionally.

.1   American Freedom of Residence Fund (AFRF).
Files, 1960- . Correspondence, minutes of meetings, financial records, studies, reports, and other materials dealing with the aims, history, and programs of AFRF.

IL11   AMERICAN FRIENDS SERVICE COMMITTEE, INC., CHICAGO REGIONAL OFFICE. 407 S. Dearborn St., 60605. Tel 312 427-2533. Kale Williams, Exec. Secy.

IL12   AMERICAN JEWISH COMMITTEE, MIDWEST REGIONAL OFFICE. Suite 712, 105 W. Adams St., 60603. Tel 312 782-2444. Joel Ollander, Regional Dir.

IL13   AMERICAN JEWISH CONGRESS, COUNCIL OF GREATER CHICAGO AND MIDWEST REGION. 105 W. Adams St., 60603. Tel 312 332-7355. Mrs. Perry Sachs, Acting Dir.

IL14   AMERICAN MEDICAL ASSOCIATION (AMA) (1847), ARCHIVE-LIBRARY DEPARTMENT. 535 N. Dearborn St., 60610. Tel 312 527-1500. Susan Crawford, Dir. Interlibrary loan, bibliographies prepared, literature searches, copying, inquiries answered, referrals made, consultation.
AMA works to further the art and science of medicine and the health of the public.

.1   The Library attempts to collect all materials related to race and the medical profession, except for clinical materials regarding race. Subjects include race relations in the medical profession, race and professional medical organizations, history of medicine, and medical socio-economics.

IL15   AMERICAN SECURITY COUNCIL (1955), LIBRARY. 123 N. Wacker Dr., 60606. Tel 312 263-2784. William K. Lambie, Jr., Admin. Dir. Research services for member companies and government agencies only.
The Council is a non-profit research and education organization which deals with national security problems. It has conducted several studies in the area of the changing strategic military and naval balance between the United States and the U.S.S.R.; and is currently sponsoring a study commission, in conjunction with the Institute for American Strategy, on meeting revolutionary challenges to America, such as those posed by the Black Panthers, Students for a Democratic Society, and other organizations.

.1   American Security Council.
Contains more than 6,000,000 index cards concerning revolutionary activity in America; an up-to-date file of periodical and newspaper clippings about radical organizations; and books (6000) on national security matters. Restricted.

IL16   ANTI-DEFAMATION LEAGUE OF B'NAI B'RITH, MIDWEST REGIONAL OFFICE. 222 W. Adams St., 60606. Tel 312 782-5080. A. Abbot Rosen, Dir.
Publ.: A.D.L. New Materials Bulletin, bi-monthly; Catalogs, pamphlets.

.1   Race Relations Publications Collection.
Books, pamphlets, reprints, films. Materials published on the problems of Negroes in contemporary America. Subjects include civil rights, prejudice, race relations, housing and school desegregation, education and human relations, the black family, black history, and a bibliography of black history and literature.

IL17   ARCHDIOCESE OF CHICAGO SCHOOL BOARD, CENTER FOR URBAN EDUCATION (CUE) (1964). 2401 W. Walton St., 60622. Tel 312 486-2170. Librn.
CUE works to provide continuous in-service education for the teachers of the inner city.
Publ.: CUE News.

.1   Urban Education Collection.
Books, pamphlets, reports, and contemporary studies. Collection concerns the education of the urban child. Special emphasis is given to black

history, and the educational problems of urban
black children.

IL18   ART INSTITUTE OF CHICAGO (1901). S. Michigan Ave. at
        Adams St., 60603. Tel 312 236-7080. Ruth E. Schone-
        man, Librn.

        The Institute holds paintings and sculpture by Negro
        artists. Among those represented are the follow-
        ing:

        .1 —— Hunt, Richard.
                    Sculpture. 1 item. Sculptor. Sculpture en-
                    titled "Hero Construction."
        .2 —— Perkins, Marion, 1908- .
                    Sculpture. 1 item. Sculptor. Sculpture en-
                    titled "Man of Sorrows."
        .3 —— Tanner, Henry Ossawa, 1859-1937.
                    Painting. 1 item. Artist. Painting entitled
                    "The Two Disciples at the Tomb."

IL19   BLACK WOMEN'S COMMITTEE FOR THE CARE AND
        PROTECTION OF OUR CHILDREN, GWENDOLYN
        BROOKS LIBRARY. 4521 S. Oakenwald, 60653. Tel
        312 548-9402.
        Publ.: BWC (Black Women's Committee) News.

        .1 Gwendolyn Brooks Library.
                Includes books, pamphlets, periodicals concerning
                black history.

IL20   BUREAU ON JEWISH EMPLOYMENT PROBLEMS (1937).
        22 W. Monroe, 60603. Tel 312 726-9817. Sidney H.
        Silverman, Acting Dir.
        The Bureau seeks to eliminate discrimination against
        Jews and other minority groups in employment
        practices; investigates complaints and works with in-
        dustry, labor, employment and government agencies to
        develop fair employment procedures; conducts re-
        search regarding the Jewish labor market, occupational
        distribution, and other related areas.

IL21   CATHOLIC INTERRACIAL COUNCIL OF CHICAGO (1946).
        21 W. Superior St., 60610. Tel 312 337-1025. John
        Hatch, Exec. Dir.
        The Council is an independent organization of Catholic
        lay men and women, serving the metropolitan Chicago
        area to promote civil rights for black people and other
        minority groups.
        Publ.: Witness, bi-monthly membership newsletter.

        .1 Race Relations Collection.
                ca. 250 books and other publications concerning
                Negroes and race relations. Council file mate-
                rials (1946-1963) have been donated to the Chicago
                Historical Society.

IL22   CENTER FOR RESEARCH LIBRARIES (1949). 5721 Cottage
        Grove Ave., 60637. Tel 312 955-4545. Gordon R. Wil-
        liams, Dir. Interlibrary loan, copying.
        The Center houses and services little used research
        materials for member libraries; and purchases mate-
        rials for cooperative use.

        .1 Africana.
                Books, periodicals, newspapers, archives (on mi-
                crofilm) of publications and mss originating in
                Africa, or relating to Africa, particularly south of
                the Sahara and the Republic of South Africa. The
                material is collected under the Cooperative Afri-
                cana Microform Project (CAMP). Restricted to
                member libraries.
        .2 American Negro newspapers collection.
                Newspapers, 1965- . 17 titles. Contains
                newspapers published by and about Negroes in
                America. In part, microfilm. Restricted to mem-
                ber libraries.

IL23   CHICAGO BOARD OF EDUCATION, BOARD OF EDUCATION
        LIBRARY. Room 846, 228 N. LaSalle St., 60601. Tel
        312 332-7800. Mary I. Byrne, Librn. Interlibrary
        loan.
        Publ.: Pamphlets, bibliography lists.

        .1 Chicago Board of Education.
                Archives, 1863- . Includes proceedings of the
                Board (1873- .); annual reports of superintendents

(1863- .); and selected reports by the Board.
Among subjects included are race relations in
Chicago schools.

IL24   CHICAGO COMMISSION ON HUMAN RELATIONS (1947).
        211 W. Wacker Dr., 60606. Tel 312 744-4100. James
        E. Burns, Dir.
        The Commission secures the furnishing of equal ser-
        vices to residents of Chicago; trains city employees to
        use methods of dealing with intergroup tensions which
        develop respect for equal rights and which result in
        equal treatment without regard to race, color, creed,
        national origin or ancestry; has subpoena authority;
        conducts investigations; holds public hearings; recom-
        mends to the Mayor suspensions and revocations of
        licenses; and may initiate complaints.
        Publ.: Human Relations News of Chicago, monthly
            newsletter.

        .1 Chicago Commission on Human Relations.
                Papers, 1943- . Correspondence, records, com-
                plaints, pamphlets and publications of the Com-
                mission. Files reflect the problems of blacks in
                Chicago and the role of the Human Relations Com-
                mission (1947- .) and of its predecessor, Mayor's
                Committee on Race Relations (1943-47).

IL25   CHICAGO COMMISSION ON YOUTH WELFARE (1958). 185
        N. Wabash, 60601. Tel 312 744-4000. Charles P.
        Livermore, Exec. Dir.
        The Commission cooperates with the Mayor, City Coun-
        cil, City departments, agencies and officials in formu-
        lating and carrying into effect a comprehensive pro-
        gram of youth welfare involving all public and voluntary
        agencies engaged in providing services to youth; car-
        ries out programs in the areas of housing, education,
        employment, human relations, interreligious affairs,
        social attitudes, and community organization.
        Publ.: CYW Newsletter, monthly.

IL26   CHICAGO CONFERENCE ON RELIGION AND RACE. 21 W.
        Superior St., 60610. Tel 312 641-1030. Eugene J.
        Callahan, Exec. Dir.
        An organization to promote racial cooperation and in-
        tegration. It has operated a housing program since
        1965 that has helped nonwhite families obtain housing
        in integrated neighborhoods, in some cases by financing
        homes or by purchasing them for later resale.

IL27   CHICAGO ECONOMIC DEVELOPMENT CORPORATION
        (1965). 343 S. Dearborn St., 60604. Tel 312 939-3044.
        Garland C. Guice, Exec. Dir. Referrals made, con-
        sultation.
        The Corporation aids small businesses, especially in
        ghetto areas. Formerly Chicago Small Business Op-
        portunities Corporation.
        Publ.: Studies, reports on retailing in low-income
            areas.

IL28   CHICAGO HISTORICAL SOCIETY (1856), LIBRARY (1856).
        North Ave. and Clark St., 60614. Tel 312 642-4600.
        Miss Margaret Scriven, Chief Librn.
        Publ.: Chicago History, semi-annual journal.

        Manuscript Division.
        .1 —— Adams, Cyrus Hall, III, 1909- .
                Papers, 1962-68. 15 ft. Correspondence, re-
                ports and various ms and printed materials
                relative to Adams' service as a member of the
                Chicago Board of Education (1962-68). Many
                of these materials concern racial matters in
                the Chicago Public Schools. Unavailable.
        .2 —— Adams, John Quincy, 1767-1848.
                Papers, 1838. 4 pp. Washington, D.C. Ad-
                dressed to Arnold Buffum, Philadelphia, Pa.,
                concerning Texas question, presidential
                candidates, and abolitionists.
        .3 —— Aldrich, James Franklin, 1853-1932.
                Letterbooks, 1831-1918. Contains letters of
                William Pitt Kellogg to Frank Aldrich con-
                cerning problems of Negroes in St. Louis, Mo.
        .4 —— Aldridge, Ira Frederick, 1805-67.
                Papers, 1867. 2 pp. Papers from Paris to
                Messers Givvon and Company in New York,
                giving authority to make engagements in New

York City; lists repertoire. Also includes letter to an unidentified person forwarding an agreement for bookings; anticipates unfavorable reception in New York.

IL28.5 — American Colonization Society.
Records, 1820-58. ca. 110 items. Correspondence and other papers, including account sheets, the constitution of the Society, instructions to its agents, letters of introduction from the Board of Managers, materials on formation of auxiliary societies, on the importance of suppressing the slave trade, on the African settlements, and on fund-raising measures. Correspondents include Eli Ayres, E. Bacon, Elias B. Caldwell, Ralph Randolph Gurley, Harry D. Hunter, Joseph King, J. Macaulay, John Mason, Smith Thompson, and Thomas Tyson.

.6 — Andrews, Richard.
Paper, 1759. 1 p. New London, Conn. Deed of sale for Negro slave called Calloway to Asher Isaacs, witnessed by John and Elizabeth Burr.

.7 — Angle, Paul McClelland, 1900- . collector.
Bloody Williamson papers, 1875-1951. ca. 1500 items and 8 reels of microfilm. In part, photocopies. Correspondence, newspaper and magazine articles, court testimony, scrapbooks, newspapers, pamphlets and other papers gathered by Angle in preparation for his book, Bloody Williamson, published in 1952. The material pertains to lawlessness and violence in Williamson County, Ill., chiefly during the 1920's, and involves coal mine strikes and violence, prohibition enforcement and attendant gangsterism, family feuds, and the Ku Klux Klan. Includes copies of scrapbooks (13 v.) compiled by Oldham Paisley relating to the Herrin Massacre and its aftermath; and microfilm copies of the Illinois Miner (1922-29).

.8 — Arnold, Richard D.
Papers, 1864. 2 pp. Mayor of Savannah, Chatham County, Ga. License to Garrison Frayser to preach in Third African Church. Signed also by N.B. Knapp and John Williamson, justices of inferior court of Chatham County, and by S. Landrum and D.G. Daniell and M.F. Willis, ministers of Sunbury Baptist Church.

.9 — Augur, Abraham, ca. 1724-98.
Paper, 1777. 1 p. New Haven, Conn. Receipt for 25 francs for Negro slave from Joshua Chandler, sold by State for forfeit.

.10 — Avery, George Smith, 1835-1923.
Papers, 1860-65. 181 items (92 letters by Avery, 89 to him). Letters from Capt. George S. Avery (of the 12th Illinois Infantry and the 3rd Missouri Cavalry) to his wife and her letters to him; provide an account of his views on the War, slavery, and Army life and service; and presents home-front feelings; material on the 3rd Missouri in Arkansas and Missouri, with some battle commentary.

.11 — Baker, Edward Dickinson, 1811-61.
Paper, 1850. 1 p. Washington, D.C. Addressed to Henry Asbury, Quincy, Ill. Slavery question and his personal stand on it; comment on choice for judge.

.12 — Baker, H.
Paper, 1864. 1 p. Augusta, Ga., received of E. Steadman, eight thousand dollars for the purchase of two Negro slaves; one, about twenty years old and her son, about eight years old; " warrant them sound and healthy to date.''

.13 — Barletlett, Reuben.
Paper, 1848. 1 p. St. Louis, Mo. Contains information concerning Barletlett's runaway slave.

.14 — Bartlett, Napoleon B.
Papers, 1864. 4 pp. Letters (July 22, 1864) by, to, and about Pvt. Napoleon Bartlett, Company C, 76th Illinois Infantry, mentioning fighting among Negroes in regiment.

.15 — Bassett, Richard, 1746-1815.
Paper, 1809. 1 p. Addressed to Nehemiah Tilton concerning the marriage of a freedman, Henry Fox, to one of Tilton's slave women, Sarah.

.16 — Beauregard, Pierre G.T.
Papers, 1863. 3pp. Papers from Barnwell District, S.C. to General Beauregard suggesting impressment of idle free Negroes for work on Charleston and coastal defense. Recommends appointment of James M. Canter and Sidney W. Garvin to handle the matter, and endorsement of verso by Beauregard and Gov. Bonham. Also includes Special Order No. 244 from Charleston, S.C. by order of Gen. Beauregard giving authorization and specifications for Lt. Col. A.F. Browning's impressment of free and slave labor; signed by Otey and endorsed by Gov. Bonham.

.17 — Benson, A.G.
Letter, 1861. 3 pp. Addressed to Abraham Lincoln, dated New York, Oct. 31, 1861, making suggestions for new tariff laws and also ways of ending the war by public proclamation of universal emancipation throughout the land.

.18 — Benton, Thomas Hart, 1782-1858.
Papers, 1850? 23 pp. Incomplete ms of speech given in U.S. Senate on the abolition of slavery in Mexico and the illegality of slavery in California and New Mexico.

.19 — Bissell, William Henry.
Papers, 1850. 4 pp. Washington, D.C. Letter addressed to Hon. William Martin, concerning slavery question, stability of the Union, admission of California to the Union, and slavery's effect on party lines.

.20 — Blanchard, Rufus, 1821-1904.
Book, 1858. 1 v. Subscription book for Blanchard's Northwestern Quarterly magazine, with autographs and addresses of subscribers, including Abraham Lincoln; plus ms abolitionist verse, and newspaper clippings regarding the magazine. (Volume inscribed as presented to William Bross by Blanchard, Chicago, Ill., February, 1884.)

.21 — Brennan, Sebastian Bauman.
Papers, 1863-66. 20 items. Routine administrative orders, accounts, correspondence, etc. relative to the management of the 84th Infantry Regt., U.S. Colored Troops.

.22 — Brotherhood of Sleeping Car Porters.
Papers, 1925-69 (primarily 1925-45). 10 ft. Correspondence, membership records and other papers (7 ft.) of the Chicago Division of the BSCP, including a good deal of significant A. Philip Randolph correspondence during the 1920's, and correspondence and other items relative to Fair Employment Practices legislation during the 1940's; plus 3 ft. of archival records (1938-56) of the Brotherhood's International Ladies Auxiliary, much of them being correspondence of the Auxiliary's president, Mrs. Halena Wilson, and convention reports.

.23 — Brown, John, 1800-59.
Papers, 1842-1910. ca. 95 items. Correspondence, other papers and printed matter of and about the abolitionist. Letters by Brown, which comprise about a third of the collection, include letters to his sisters written shortly before his execution, letters concerning his activities in Kansas, a letter concerning payment for pikes to be used in the Negro uprising, Brown's last written statement before ascending the scaffold, and a note listing his terms for peace in Kansas. Printed matter includes a copy of the "Provisional Constitution and Ordinances for the People of the U.S.," submitted by Brown to a convention of followers and friends at Chatham, Canada (May, 1858), which was found in his home at the time of his capture, and the Bible used by Brown while awaiting trial. Other papers include information of his father's estate;

family reminiscences, many of them contemporary; Annie Brown Adams' comments on her father, chiefly on his life at the Kennedy farm prior to Harper's Ferry; letters of sympathy for Brown written by Frank Sanborn, O.G. Villard, O.P. Anderson and John Parr; a lecture by Sanborn on Brown (1857), a poem by William E. Channing entitled "Burial of John Brown"; letters from Governors Chase, Wise and Hicks concerning the trouble with Brown's forces in 1859. The Brown papers are related to the library's Judge Richard Parker papers.

IL28.24 — Bryant, Dabney S.
   Paper, 1852. 1 p. Louisville, Ky. Bill of sale to Dunlop and Hathaway for Negro slave, witnessed by Andrew Hawes.

.25 — Buckner, Simon Bolivar, 1823-1914.
   Papers, 1862. 3 pp. Albany, N.Y. Letter addressed to Dr. Sprague. Includes a poetic extract on "the virtue of freedom and bondage of slavery."

.26 — Bullard, E.E.
   Papers, 1856. 2 pp. Chicago, Ill. Letter addressed to Mr. Ormsby, concerning Stephen Douglas's speech, Fremont's election, abolition of slavery, Illinois unification against slavery in the North, southern Illinois unification for slavery.

.27 — Butler, Benjamin Franklin, 1818-93.
   Papers, 1865. 1½ pp. A farewell to the soldiers of the Army of the James; and to the Negro troops of the Army of the James (January 8, 1865) from the Headquarters, Dept. of Virginia and North Carolina.

.28 — Butler, William.
   Papers, 1862. 3 pp. Letter to Jesse K. Dubois and Butler from W.H. Powell in Joliet, Ill., concerning draft quota and abolitionists.

.29 — Calhoun, John Caldwell, 1782-1850.
   Papers, 1848. 4 pp. Washington, D.C. Letter to Hon. W. Lumpkin concerning Democratic and Whig parties, abolitionist, "incidents injurious to the South," including appointments by Polk and other matters.

.30 — Cantwell, Daniel Michael, 1914- .
   Papers, 1934-65. 7 ft. Correspondence and other papers of Monsignor Cantwell (Chaplain of the Catholic Council of Chicago, Friendship House and the Catholic Council on Working Life) relative to his activities and to the involvement of Roman Catholic clergy and laity in race relations and other social action matters, including a good many items on racial discrimination in housing. The Cantwell papers are related to the library's holdings of the Catholic Interracial Council of Chicago, Friendship House, the Catholic Council on Working Life and the Catholic Adult Education Center.

.31 — Carey, Archibald James, Jr., 1908- .
   Papers, chiefly 1942-66. 22 ft. Correspondence and other records mainly relative to Rev. Carey's service as Chicago Third Ward Alderman (1947-55) and as vice-chairman (1955-57) and chairman (1957-61) of the President's Committee on Government Employment Policy; plus lesser amounts of material concerning his ministerial career in the African Methodist Episcopal Church and his service during 1953 as a member of the United States Delegation to the United Nations.

.32 — Carter, Robert, 1728-1804.
   Papers, 1775-95. ca. 7 items. Request to Rev. Mr. Gibern to baptize a Negro child, John, born August 6, 1775; Extract from deed recorded in the Northumberland District Court, Va.; emancipation of Primus, aged 22 years, from slavery (January 2, 1792); statement of manumission (August 1, 1791) of slaves Dinah, Hall, and Judith; extract from deed recorded in Northumberland district court; emancipation from slavery of Daniel, aged 44 years, according to a law entitled "an act to authorize the manumission of slaves" enacted in the General Assembly for the Commonwealth of Virginia, in the year 1782; and indentures (1795) for the transfer of Carter's slave, Louisa, to George Evans as apprentice until Jan. 1, 1800, "when she is to be freed."

.33 — Catholic Interracial Council of Chicago.
   Archives, 1945-64. 32 ft. Correspondence, reports, studies, financial records, and other ms, mimeograph and printed records of the Council's efforts to improve race relations, particularly to ending discriminatory practices in housing, employment and education, both within and without the church. The Interracial Council papers are related to the library's Father Cantwell and Friendship House collections.

.34 — Chew, Benjamin, 1722-1810.
   Papers, 1770. 2 pp. A list of Chew's Negroes at Whitehall, Pa.

.35 — Chicago Commons.
   Archives, 1894-1966. 23 ft. Board minutes, correspondence, reports, neighborhood census data and other working papers of Chicago Commons, a social settlement (estab. in 1894) in the West Town community area of the city. Collection particularly strong as regards attitudes and social conditions in an ethnically and racially changing neighborhood.

.36 — Chicago Woman's Club.
   Book, 1927. 1 v. Board minutes and other records, including a 1927 "Negro in Art Week" scrapbook, which contains approximately 50 original letters from prominent people relative to the Chicago Woman's Club's Negro in Art Week project (November 16-23, 1927).

.37 — Chinn, Thomas.
   Paper, 1817. 1 p. Bill of sale to William Kerner for Negro slave Milly, witnessed by Hugh Frazer, with notice of record in Harrison Co., Ky. (May 24, 1817) by William Moore.

.38 — Chouteau, Pierre.
   Papers, 1809, 1819. 2 pp. St. Louis, Mo. Sale of a mulatto woman by Pelagie Chouteau to Pierre Chouteau; document, signed by S. Labbadie, witnessed by M.P. Leduc and Sarpy (March 11, 1819). Pierre Chouteau recorded on the same document the sale of "the mulatress" to Genevieve Beauvais; witnessed by Leduc.

.39 — Citizens of New Orleans, Louisiana.
   Papers, 1848-51. 7 items. Includes orders for release of slaves from municipal prison.

.40 — Civil War Bill.
   Papers, 1866. 3 items. Printed document. "An act to protect all persons in the United States in their civil rights, and furnish the means of their vindication" plus certification signed by William H. Seward and forwarding letter by Edward Jordan to Henry S. Fitch.

.41 — Claiborne, A.S.
   Paper, 1836. 1 p. A bill of sale for 44 Negro slaves.

.42 — Clarkson, David J.
   Papers, 1834. 2 pp. Claiborne Co., Tenn. Bill of sale for Negro girl Peggy, aged 9 years, to Hugh Graham.

.43 — Clay, Cassius Marcellus, 1810-93.
   Papers, 1844, 1847, 1862. 6 pp. Includes a letter to Hubert P. Main, Bridgefield, Conn., from St. Petersburg, Russia, concerning compliance with request for an autograph, expression of sentiment that "Liberation and slavery cannot coexist: one, or the other must die"; a letter to Jabez D. Hammond, Cherry Valley, Otsego City, N.Y. from Lexington, Ky., concerning slavery; a letter to Horace Greeley concerning his reception at Lexington.

.44 — Clinton, DeWitt, 1769-1828.
   Paper, 1825. 1 p. A pardon given to Patrick Smith, a Negro, convicted of grand larceny.

IL28.45 — Clough, Allen B.
Papers, 1852-64. 12 items. Letters, mainly from Tolono and Sadorus, Ill., and Vincennes, Ind. (1859-64) to his brother Andrew in Yonkers, N.Y. Comments on life in Illinois, law practice and real estate profits there. Criticism of abolitionists, Lincoln, and Negroes. Criticism (Aug. 21, 1860 letter) of Lincoln's skill as a lawyer; and claim (in an 1860 letter) that Lincoln told Clough that he had no doubt of Douglas defeating him for President.

.46 — Cochran, Samuel.
Paper, 1820. 1 p. Brownsville, Jackson Co., Ill. Certificate for removal of two Negro servants from Randolph to Jackson Co. Signed also by T. Nash, clerk of the County Commissioner's Court of Jackson County. Note of Cochran's assignment of rights and interests in above mentioned Negroes.

.47 — Coit, Thomas Winthrop.
Papers, 1874. 2 pp. Correspondence mentioning practices of slavery by Puritans, fugitive slaves, fugitive slave laws, and other topics.

.48 — Coles, Edward, 1786-1868.
Correspondence, 1809-58. ca. 100 items. Chiefly letters by Coles (private secretary to President James Madison and Governor of Illinois) to Mr. and Mrs. James Madison on historical and personal matters, furnishing commentary on Illinois and national affairs, including slavery in the U.S. and Illinois.

.49 — Confederate States of America Army.
Papers, 1863-64. 2 pp. Impressment receipt given to William S. May by Thomas P. Williamson, impressment agent, for slaves and other property received; valuation of provisions and forage correct. Impressment from the Headquarters, Department of the Gulf, Alabama, for one slave, State of Alabama; signed by Thomas P. Williamson, impressment agent.

.50 — Congress of Racial Equality (Chicago Chapter).
Papers, 1956-66. 2 ft. Minutes, memoranda, reports and other records of the Chicago Chapter of CORE, including items from CORE chapters in various parts of the U.S., and from other Chicago civil rights organizations, the Chicago Urban League, in particular.

.51 — Conway, Joseph.
Papers, 1815. 3 pp. Includes indenture papers for a Negro woman, Lucey, to Robert Chesney.

.52 — Cooke, Flora Juliette, 1864-1953.
Papers, 1804-1960. 14,500 items and 20 packages. Professional and personal papers relative to the admission of Negro students into the Francis W. Parker School during the 1940's; relative to Miss Cooke's dispute with Senator Bilbo of Mississippi over his 1945 filibuster against the Fair Employment Practices Commission legislation; and other subjects.

.53 — Counselbaum, Stella Levinkind.
Papers, 1944-69. ca. 350 items. Correspondence, chiefly incoming letters congratulating Mrs. Counselbaum on awards given her for her human and race relations and intergroup work; articles by and about Mrs. Counselbaum; award certificates, biographical data, and other materials.

.54 — Crawford, William Harris, 1772-1834.
Paper, 1816. 1 p. Washington, D.C. To Messrs. Gales and Seaton, editors of the National Intelligencer, advertising for a "cook and boy."

.55 — Cuffe, Paul, 1759-1817.
Paper, 1813. 1 p. Paper from Westport to Perry Locks in Boston acknowledging Locks' letter; chance of conveying letters to land; and assurances of interest in Negroes.

.56 — Davis, Corneal A.
Papers, chiefly 1957-67. 3 ft. Sundry correspondence, speeches and other papers, chiefly concerning Davis' service as a Representative from Chicago in the Illinois General Assembly and his role as chairman of the American Negro Emancipation Centennial Commission in Illinois.

.57 — Davis, David, 1815-86.
Papers, 1815-1921. 9 ft. In part, photostatic copies of Davis mss in the Illinois State Historical Library in Springfield, Ill., and of Davis and other items in various repositories across the country. The materials were gathered by Willard L. King for his biography, Lincoln's Manager, David Davis (Harvard University Press, 1960). Correspondence, legal documents, speeches, articles, etc. relative to the personal, legal and political life of David Davis, lawyer, Abraham Lincoln's 1860 Presidential campaign manager; U.S. Supreme Court Associate Justice (1862-77), and U.S. Senator from Illinois (1877-83). Includes considerable Lincoln and Supreme Court material; information on political, social and economic conditions in Illinois and the nation; abolitionist and slavery items; papers relative to the Civil War, the War with Mexico, and the American, Democratic, Free Soil, Know Nothing and Republican parties, particularly the last named.

.58 — Davis, Hector and Company.
Books, 1857-65. 2 v. Richmond, Va. Ledgers containing record of slave sales; cost price, selling price, doctor and food bills, advertising, profits on sale, commission, and other materials.

.59 — De Blanc, Louis.
Papers, 1796. 4 pp. Natchitoches, La. Certified copy of manumission of slave, "mulatress," belonging to Jean B. Grappe.

.60 — Delassus, Charles Dehault.
Papers, 1803. 2 pp. St. Louis, Mo. Concerns the purchase by a mulatto, Pelagie, of her freedom; document signed by Delassus, Chouteau, Valois and Hortiz.

.61 — Demotte, Thomas H.
Papers, 1864. 5 items. Holly Springs and Waterford, Miss. Materials addressed to John Aiken, receipted orders for beef for Negro Union regiments dated for August, 1864.

.62 — Despres, Leon Mathis, 1908- .
Papers, 1955-68. 6 ft. and 14 reels of microfilm. Carbon copies (6 ft.) of outgoing Aldermanic correspondence (1955-67) of Leon M. Despres, Chicago Fifth Ward Alderman since 1955, plus microfilm copies of related press clippings (1953-68). The collection provides considerable information on the Hyde Park, Woodlawn and South Shore communities represented by Despres in the Chicago City Council.

.63 — Dewey, Charles Schuveldt, 1882- .
Papers, 1943. 20 items. Letters, speeches, printed items, and other items relative to the House Committee on Un-American Activities' demand for the removal of William Pickens, a Negro, from the Treasury Department staff. Pickens was accused of membership in and association with Communist front organizations.

.64 — DeWolf, Calvin.
Papers, 1838-47. 5 items (14 pp.). Chicago, Ill. Addressed to his brother James in Austinburg, Ohio, concerning personal affairs, the abolition movement, and mercantile business in Chicago.

.65 — Dickinson, Richard H.
Miscellaneous papers, 1841-61. ca. 25 items. Richmond, Va. Auctioneer. Chiefly letters to Dickinson regarding sale of Negroes, and a letter of presentation from Sidney Corning Eastman (January 29, 1917).

.66 — Dillingham, Paul, 1799-1891.
Papers, 1848. 4 pp. Includes references to the extension of slavery into the territories; belief in power of Congress to exclude slavery from Territories; southern feeling that Gen. Cass would veto any act of Congress excluding

slavery from territories, passage of bill excluding slavery from Oregon and its signing by southern president, and other relevant topics.

IL28.67 — Dorivcourt, Antoine.
Paper, 1851. 1 p. Notary public of New Orleans, La. Concerns claim of R.G. Labarre, lien holder on note of Dorivcourt for 15 year old female slave.

.68 — Douglass, Frederick, 1817-95.
Paper, 1895. 1 p. Introduction for Mr. Smith of Chicago and his invention for preservation of southern food products, addressed to Booker T. Washington.

.69 — Dyer, E.G.
Papers, 1884. 15 pp. Burlington, Wis. Letter to Zebina Eastman, Gainesville, Fla., concerning slaves held in Wisconsin by prominent settlers from Kentucky and Virginia; escape of Caroline Quarles by way of Chicago and Detroit; abolitionists; and Dyer's family.

.70 — Eastman, Zebina, 1815-83.
Papers, 1840-83. ca. 360 items. Letters to Eastman (1842-83) from leading abolitionists, concerning abolitionist activities, attitudes and publications, and the 1874 Anti-Slavery Reunion in Chicago (335 items, 45 of which are in the J. Frank Aldrich papers). Plus various account books (26 v., 1840-55) dealing with the business aspects of Eastman's abolitionist newspapers, the Genius of Liberty, the Western Citizen, and the Free West.

.71 — Eaton, Lucien.
Paper, 1864. 2 pp. St. Louis, Mo. Addressed Willard P. Hall, Acting Governor of Missouri. Entreats Hall to heed petition advocating pardon of three prisoners jailed for aiding slaves to escape, plus Hall's endorsement on disposition of matter.

.72 — Edwards, Ninian, 1775-1833.
Papers, n.d. Materials concerning Illinois, Kentucky, and national political scene and governmental papers, including Edwards' undated notes (ca. early 1800's) for a pro-slavery speech.

Papers, 1829. 2 pp. Addressed to Ninian Edwards, Vandalia, Ill., enclosing copy of communication from Mr. Vaughn to the State Department relative to extradition from Canada of Paul Vallad and mulatto slave stolen by him from an Illinois citizen. Materials come from President Martin Van Buren, Washington, D.C.

.73 — Elgin, A.M.
Paper, 1864. 1 p. Mobile, Ala. State and county taxes for the year ending March, 1864, receipted by H.T. Gains, tax collector. Contains references to slavery.

.74 — Elk Grove Congregational Church.
Papers, 1846. Resolution against slavery (February 13).

.75 — Fardon, Thomas.
Papers, 1754. 3 pp. Bill of sale for two Negroes, signed by Thomas Fardon and Andrew Gautier, New York, 1754; and bill of sale from Rumbouts, Dutchess Co., N.Y., for two Negroes to Abraham Fardon, witnessed by John Gibson and Jacobus Fardon and attested by Jacobus Fardon (February 13, 1772), whose statement is notarized by Andrew Gautier.

.76 — Fitzpatrick, John, 1872-1946.
Papers, 1890-1965. 6 ft. Papers, chiefly correspondence received by Fitzpatrick as president of the Chicago Federation of Labor and as organizer for the American Federation of Labor, including about 75 items (mainly 1919-30) dealing with Negroes, chiefly in the working force.

.77 — Flower family.
Papers, 1824-46. 43 items. Letters from various members of the Flower family in Albion, Ill., to Edward Flower in England, with some of them concerning Negro emancipation.

.78 — Flower, George, 1788-1862.
Diaries, 1814-17. 3 v. V. 1 (July 7-September 9, 1814, 212 pp.) contains material relevant to the agriculture and labor conditions; v. 2 (June 11-December 14, 1816, 211 pp.) contains materials about Flower's trip to U.S., New York, Philadelphia, Pa. and Ohio; and v. 3 contains materials concerning Cincinnati, Ohio, Kentucky, Nashville, Tenn., Virginia, Maryland, Washington. All the volumes contain materials concerning slavery in the U.S.

.79 — Frankel, Julius.
Books, 1788-1860. 3 v. 96 indentures, bills of sale, legal opinions, pleas, and other materials relative to slavery in Kentucky.

.80 — Friendship House.
Papers, 1937-63. 8 ft. Correspondence, reports, minutes and other records of Friendship House, a national Catholic interracial movement, which seeks to provide opportunities to discuss and study racial problems and to work for their solutions. The first Friendship House was opened in Harlem (1938); chapters soon appeared in other cities, with a Chicago House opened in 1942. Although the Chicago House is the only one now in operation, the movement still functions on a national basis. Most of the papers concern the operation of Chicago FH on the local level and as national headquarters of the movement. Also significant materials relative to the Shreveport, La., Friendship House and to the publication, financing and distributing of FH publication, Community. The papers also include smaller groups of materials dealing with Friendship Houses in New York City, Portland, Ore., and Washington, D.C. The collection is related to the Library's Father Daniel M. Cantwell papers.

.81 — Frothingham, Octavius Brooks, 1822-95.
Papers, 1857. 3 pp. Jersey City, N.J. Addressed to J.P. Leavitt; concerning his rise in popularity "due to the mighty idea of Freedom, whose rushing wings have lifted me with many others out of the dust and made me flutter in its wake."

.82 — Grand Army of the Republic, Department of Illinois, George H. Thomas Post.
Papers, 1861-66. 11 pp. Collection of informative sheets concerning the Civil War veterans, some being personal narratives, were individually catalogued such as Hiram Bixby's, who served as enlisted man and officer, containing anecdotal comments on service with the 5th Massachusetts Militia, 1861; 14th U.S. Infantry, 1862-64; and the 36th Infantry U.S. Colored Troops, 1864-66.

.83 — Gaines, Irene McCoy, 1900?-1964.
Papers, 1893-1964. 3 ft. Correspondence and other papers of Mrs. Gaines, a social worker, clubwoman, civil leader, and Republican party candidate for local office in Chicago. Items relative to civil rights, political and social matters in the Negro community from the 1920's thru 1964. Many of these materials concern her service as president of the National Association of Colored Women's Clubs, Inc., and as president of the Chicago Council of Negro Organizations. Also includes a small significant lot of articles by and correspondence (1904-19) of Mrs. Gaines' uncle, George W. Ellis, secretary of the American Legation to the Republic of Liberia and as an assistant corporation counsel in Chicago.

.84 — Gallagher, James.
Papers, 1837. 1 p. Certified transcript of manumission papers of slaves of David A. Smith, Lawrence County, Ala., signed by Wiley Gallaway, clerk.

.85 — Garlock, William Bryan, 1842-1928.
Papers, 1921. 17 pp. "The Rise, Progress and Culmination of the Abolition Party in the United States and What It Accomplished," copy of an essay read before the McLean County, Ill., Historical Society (September 3, 1921).

IL28.86 — Gaston, William, 1778-1844.
Papers, 1819. 3 pp. Savannah, Ga. Papers to Messrs. Charles W. Karthaus & Co., Baltimore, Md., mentioning delay in privateer case; chance of selling Gobel's claim to McKinne; slaves to be removed to South Carolina; prices; statistics on exports from Savannah (October-December, 1818).

.87 — Grant, Ulysses Simpson, 1822-85.
Paper, 1859. 1 p. President of U.S. An instrument emancipating slave William, from St. Louis, Mo., attested by Stephen Rice.

.88 — Greater Lawndale Conservation Commission.
Papers, 1954-64. 12 ft. Correspondence, minutes, reports, newsclippings, financial records and other papers of the GLCC, an organization devoted to the conservation, rehabilitation and redevelopment of the North Lawndale community area of Chicago, which was the site of rioting during 1965 and 1966, and following the murder of Dr. Martin Luther King, Jr., in 1968.

.89 — Griffith, Dr. David J.
Papers, 1862-64. 3 v. and ca. 204 pp. Civil War medical records, mostly in Tennessee. Includes a copy of General Orders and Circular (Washington, D.C.) to medical directors concerning respectively, employment of Negro medical personnel, and care of wounded Negro troops.

.90 — Gurley, Ralph Randolph, 1797-1872.
Papers, 1859. 2 pp. Washington, D.C. Addressed to Hon. W.H. Seward, U.S. Senate; concerning U.S. Government, Liberia, and slaves.

.91 — Hall, Samuel, 1695-1776.
Paper, 1771. 1 p. Wallingford, Conn. Receipt to Amos Hotsford for sale of Negro named Prudence, cost 50 francs. Witnessed by Joshua Chandler and Damaris Hall.

.92 — Hamlin, Hannibal, 1809-91.
Papers, 1849. 2 pp. Hampden, Ill. Paper to Hon. W.P. Haines concerning slavery, and political outcomes in "old York."

.93 — Harrison, James.
Papers, 1785. 1 p. Inventory and valuation of sundry effects belonging to Robert Carter at the Old Ordinary plantation.

.94 — Hilliard, Raymond Marcellus, 1907-1966.
Papers, 1922-66. 63 ft. Correspondence and other papers of Raymond M. Hilliard relative to his career as a private and public welfare administrator in New York City (1948-53) and as director of the Cook County Department of Public Aid (1954-66); plus a large lot of correspondence, reports, newsclipping scrapbooks and other working papers (primarily 1922-58) of the Cook County Department of Public Aid. Many of these papers involve Negroes as public welfare recipients.

.95 — Hoge, Robert Perry, 1821-89.
Papers, 1862-63. 17 pp. Civil War diary, by member of Illinois Infantry, 104th Regt., giving account of battles and camp sites in the South; and comments on increased strength given to South because of Emancipation Proclamation.

.96 — Hunter, John.
Paper, 1836. 1 p. Russel Co., Ala. Bill of sale for Negro slaves sold to John Page; witnessed by Samuel Crannell and W.W. Beattie.

.97 — Hunter, Samuel.
Paper, 1827. 1 p. Summerville, Fayette Co., Tenn. Addressed to the editor of the Illinois Gazette, Shawny Town, Ill. Notice to be inserted in Gazette advertising for three runaway slaves.

.98 — Huntington, Jeremiah, 1743-1818.
Paper, 1764. 1 p. Norwich, Conn. Deed of sale for Negro girl Sylvia to Christopher Leffingwell, witnessed by Ebenezer Case and Joshua Prior, Jr.

.99 — Illinois church collection.
Records, 1695-1834. 3 v. Transcript copies of records of baptisms, marriages, deaths and burials (some of them involving Negroes) at the Immaculate Conception parish in Kaskaskia (1695-1834), St. Anne's parish in Fort Chartres (1721-65) and at St. Joseph's parish in Prairie du Rocher (1761-98).

.100 — Immaculate Conception Parish, Kaskaskia, Illinois.
Records, 1695-1834. Records of baptisms, marriages, and deaths of Negroes in Illinois.

.101 — Jackson, Samuel.
Papers, 1802-04. 3 pp. Deed of sale from Robert Hays to John Donelson for slave witnessed by Thomas Harney and Hinckey Pettway. Material addressed to Gen. Andrew Jackson near Nashville, Tenn., concerning slave deals and other business.

.102 — Johnston, J.R.
Paper, 1857. 1 p. Hamilton Co., Tenn. Addressed to Henry Gotcher; receipt for $850 for Negro male, Rufus; receipt for $1250 for Negro woman and her three children.

.103 — Jones, John, 1817-79.
Miscellaneous, 1844-1905. 5 items. Jones, a 19th century merchant, was the first Negro elected to public office in Chicago (the Cook County Board of Commissioners) and a member of the Chicago Board of Education. The materials consist of a scrapbook of newsclippings on Negro affairs, abetted by some of Jones' handwritten reflections; "Certificates of Freedom" issued to Jones and his wife, 1844; and 2 covering letters from the Jones family.

Papers, 1955. Washington, D.C. Letter to Illinois Historical Society at Chicago, giving some biographical details about the grandmother of Miss Theodora L. Purnell, Mary Jones, and offering a portrait of her to the Society, also includes a letter to H. Maxson Holloway, of the Society, in which Miss Purnell gives the dates of birth and death of her grandmother.

.104 — Keith, Sir William, 1680-1749.
Paper, 1725. 1 p. Paper to Thomas Biles, from Philadelphia, Pa., giving authorization of Jeremiah Langhorne, William Biles, Anthony Burton, Thomas Watson, John Hall, and Christopher Vansandt as trial justices for Negro offenders.

.105 — Kendrick, John F., 1874- .
Papers, 1959. 2 v. (346 pp.). Ms of book, Midsummer Picnic of '98, (unpublished, 1959); which describes and evaluates work of Negro troops of 24th U.S. Infantry, and 8th Illinois Infantry in Cuban campaign of Spanish-American War.

.106 — Kimberly, Edmund Stoughton.
Papers, 1851. 2 pp. Albany, Athens Co., Ohio. Addressed to Dr. E.S. Kimberly from H.W. Stimson concerning his activities since leaving Chicago, and an abolition center.

.107 — Kirk, John.
Letter books, 1852-71. 8 v. Contains materials concerning business and private letters of John Kirk, an agent for various hardware manufacturers in Pennsylvania, Ohio, and Chicago, Ill. Frequent references to slavery question; "hard times" during Civil War period, religious exhortations, mentions of preaching in private letters, and references to movement for colonization of Negroes, in letters dated March 6th and 13th 1853 (v. 1); May 26, 1853 (v. 2).

.108 — La Garciniere, Fagot.
Paper, 1766. 1 p. St. Genevieve. Declaration (1766) of La Garciniere that he is not responsible for the two Negroes that Casaud is sending to Illinois to go to Monsieur de Vaugines.

.109 — Lambert, David, 1740-1815.
Paper, 1773. 1 p. Milford, Newhaven Co., Conn. Deed of sale to Amos Botsford, for a Negro girl.

.110 — Lamon, Ward Hill, 1828-93.
Papers, 1862. 2 pp. Addressed to Gen. William Orme in Washington, D.C. regarding an

article which appeared in the Chicago Tribune, hostilities between the President and abolitionists, the preparation by abolitionists to attack Mrs. Lincoln, and appointments to U.S. Supreme Court.

IL28.111 — Longfellow, Henry Wadsworth, 1807-82.
Papers, 1852. 4 pp. Cambridge, Mass. Letter to Harriet Beecher Stowe concerning inability to furnish slavery poem for her volume: "a bad poem is worse than no poem, and does more harm than good to any cause." Includes congratulations on Uncle Tom's Cabin, "one of the greatest triumphs rendered in literary history, to say nothing of the higher triumph of its moral effect."

.112 — Losee, James.
Paper, 1795. 2 pp. Bill of sale for Negro man named Potter to John Moore by Losee of South Hemstead, witnessed by Thomas Lambert Moore and John Skidmore. Also includes indenture terms between John Moore and Potter, signed by Moore and Potter.

.113 — Lovejoy, Elijah Parrish, 1802-37.
Papers, 1835. 3 pp. Correspondence to Gerrit Smith concerning conditions in a slave state, the effects of slavery on people, the Onserver, and other topics.

.114 — Lovejoy, Owen, 1811-64.
Papers, 1838. 3 pp. New York City, N.Y. Letter to Lovejoy's mother, Mrs. Elizabeth G. Lovejoy, of Old Towne, Maine. Personal and family matters, views on memoir of the Rev. Elijah P. Lovejoy, and various abolitionist publications.

.115 — Lowe, Walter L., 1900- .
Papers, 1933-68. 140 items. Correspondence and other papers of Walter L. Lowe, Chicago insurance broker and Negro community leader, including texts of articles and speeches by Lowe on racial discrimination.

.116 — Luquet, Charles.
Papers, 1859. 4 pp. New Orleans, La. Sale of slave by Charles Luquet to Charles Weiss.

.117 — Lyman, David.
Papers, 1779. 1 p. A request addressed to Col. Henry Jackson, Newtown, Mass. for prevention of reenlistment of Lyman's slave, Fortune, in Jackson's regiment (June, 1779), and concerning Negro troops.

.118 — Mather, Thomas.
Papers, 1820-22. 5 pp. Letter from Kaskaskia, Ill., to Mather, Vandalia, Ill. written by Nathaniel Pope (1774-1860) on such subjects as State loan office and insurance of notes, "Missouri struggle" in Congress, relief claim of C. and T. Pullit, William H. Brown, and the extension of slavery to territories in the U.S. Also includes a petition to the citizens of Randolph Co., Ill., to Senator Samuel Crozier and Representatives John McFerron, Thomas Mather, and Raphael Widen urging alteration of present state constitutions, and containing references to slavery in Illinois and the U.S.

.119 — Max Straus Jewish Community Center.
Papers, 1941-69. 10 ft. Correspondence, board minutes, reports and other records (mainly from the 1950's and 1960's) of Max Straus Center, which was opened in the Albany Park area of Chicago in 1941.

.120 — Merrilies, John.
Diaries of the Civil War. 3 v. Lieutenant, 1st Regiment, Illinois Light Artillery. Descriptions of Merrilies' service in the Mississippi Valley, around Vicksburg, and in Mississippi and Tennessee, including an account of the performance of Negro troops in action against Confederate forces commanded by Forrest, containing high praise for their courage and tenacity.

.121 — Merryweather, George, 1846-1924.
Papers, 1862. 4 pp. Letters, including statement (in letter of September 17, 1862) that "New England Abolitionists talk the most of

giving one's life for his country & they are the last to think of doing it."

.122 — Miller, Sarah C., 1833-1917.
Papers, 1896. 9 pp. Centre Point, Tex. Correspondence to brother "Ned" (Edward G. Mason), describing the old Southwest: "camel-corral used (1850's) to provide transportation over Great American desert and reclaim it for the South & slavery...."

.123 — Mitchell, Arthur W., 1883-1968.
Papers, 1898-1968. 30 ft. Correspondence and other papers of Arthur W. Mitchell, primarily relative to his service as a Representative from Illinois in the U.S. House of Representatives from January 1935 thru January 1943. Mitchell, the first Negro Democrat to serve in the House, was elected from the second U.S. Congressional district in Chicago, the seat formerly being held by Oscar DePriest and currently by William L. Dawson. In addition to their local and national political significance, the papers also concern Mitchell's role as director of the Western Division of the Colored Voters of the Democratic National Campaign Committee in 1936. Restricted.

.124 — Morton, Sterling, 1885-1961.
Papers, 1959. 11 pp. "The Illinois Reserve Militia during World War I and After" by Sterling Morton (December 4, 1959), an article centering around the 1919 Chicago Race Riots, particularly the roles played by the Illinois National Guard (in which Morton served as a captain), the Chicago police, and Governor Lowden.

.125 — Mott, Lucretia, 1793-1880.
Paper, 1875. 1 p. Addressed to Dr. A.M. Ross concerning aiding escape of slaves; "the real abolitionists were far from cold or indifferent to the labors of those not connected with us, but our principles forbade the use of arms and our funds were always drawn upon to the utmost to supply the travel through the 'underground railroad.'"

.126 — Munn, John, 1805-?
Miscellaneous. 40 v. and 27 photos. Includes comments on the Emancipation Proclamation (September 23, 1862), and abolitionists.

.127 — Murray, James Cunningham, 1917- .
Papers, 1959-67. 6 ft. Correspondence and other papers mainly relative to Murray's service as Chicago 18th Ward Alderman (1959-67), representing the Bogan area of the city. Some of the materials concern white citizen's views on racial matters, particularly the open occupancy question and the integration of Chicago's public schools.

.128 — Nash, Solomon.
Papers, 1788. 2 pp. Inventory of sundries at Old Ordinary Farm, Westmoreland Co., Va., belonging to Robert Carter.

.129 — Near North Side Property Owners Association, Chicago, Ill.
Papers, 1936. 2 pp. Letter to the Chicago Historical Society stating: "We are sending you herewith some information concerning the work planned to prevent colored occupancy in the Near North Side area south of Chicago Avenue through ... a property owners agreement ...."

.130 — Needham, Arnold T.
Papers, 1864. 8 pp. Woodville, Ala. Addressed to Rev. William Western Patton, D.D., concerning a visit to Chicago, school for Negro slaves, "Negro's need of education and explanation of Scriptures," and military occupation.

.131 — Negro and ministrel songs.
Miscellaneous. ca. 100 titles. Songs by and about Negroes, among which are the following: "Bonja Song" (ca. 1820); "Coal Black Rose" (ca. 1827); "Cornfield Green" (second series, Old Dan Emmit's Original Banjo Melodies, 1844); "Dandy Jim From Carolina" (1843);

"Get Along Black Man!" (n.d.); "Haverly's Grotesque March" (1878); "How Are You Green-Backs!" (n.d.) "I'm Sailing on de Old Canal" (1846); "Jimmy Crow" (1828); "Johnny's Equal Is Not Here" (1858); "Old Dan Tucker" (1843); "Whar Did You Come From" (1840); "Zip Coon" (ca. 1834).

IL28.132 — Negro newspapers.
Miscellaneous, 1882- . 7 titles. Among newspapers are the following: Broad Ax (August 31, 1895-September 10, 1927); Chicago Bee (7 issues, 1938-42); Chicago Defender (1909- .); Daily Defender (February 1956- .); Chicago Whip (scattered editions, 1919-31); Chicago World (2 issues, March 2, 1935 and August 17, 1935); and The Conservator (scattered issues, 1882-86).

.133 — New France.
Papers, 1769-70, 1805. 3 items. Bill of sale of Negro slave by David Williams to Antoine Bienvenu (October 5, 1769); bill of sale of slave from Joseph Liberville to Antoine Bienvenu, signed by Liberville using nickname, Jason, fils (January 25, 1770); and bill of sale of mulatto, Joseph, by Antoine Bienvenu to Henry Bienvenu (November 25, 1805).

.134 — Noble, James, ca. 1790-1831.
Paper, 1820. 1 p. Washington, D.C. Addressed to Gen. R. Hannah, Brookville, Ind. concerning public lands, Missouri slave question in Congress.

.135 — Osgood, Joseph.
Papers, 1778. 2 pp. Papers from Salem, Mass., including a bill to Nathl. Appleton for medical services for a Negro woman.

.136 — Parker, Richard, 1810-1897.
Papers, 1796-1882. 134 items. Lawyer, judge and U.S. Representative. Correspondence, a diary (1869), bankbook, records of slave transactions, receipts, 6 charges to a grand jury, printed material, and other papers concerning legal and political matters, particularly Parker's handling of the trial of John Brown, Parker's career and the Parker family. The material is related to the Library's John Brown papers.

.137 — Parkway Community House.
Papers, 1937-57. 1 ft. Correspondence, board minutes, financial data and other papers (1937-49 and 1955-57) of Parkway Community House (Horace R. Cayton, director), a social settlement serving the Grand Boulevard, Washington Park, Hyde Park and Kenwood community areas of Chicago.

.138 — Patton, William Weston, 1821-89.
Papers, 1862-66. ca. 265 pp. Miscellaneous Civil War materials containing a memorial to Abraham Lincoln in Chicago protesting slavery, plea for national emancipation; a sermon on the "Observation in the Border Slave States" (Oct. 18, 1863); assassination of President Lincoln; and other topics.

.139 — Payne, John.
Papers, 1861. 3½ pp. Cavelle, near Cape Palmas, Liberia, to his brother William L. Payne, concerning non-arrival of supplies, and the effect on the South of reopening the African slave trade.

.140 — Percy, Charles Harting, 1919- .
Papers, 1958. Correspondence and other papers chiefly relative to Percy's roles in Republican party fund-raising and in the formulation and expression of basic party principles, culminating in the 1960 Republican National Platform; includes a Bell and Howell Company inter-office memorandum of July 3, 1958 addressed to Percy on the Company's policy on hiring members of minority groups.

.141 — Pierce, Franklin, 1804-69.
Papers, 1850. 4 pp. Addressed to Hon. Jeff Davis, Washington, D.C. from Pierce, President of the U.S., concerning need of leader to fight abolition.

.142 — Piernas, Pedro.
Papers, 1771. 2 pp. St. Louis, Mo. Manumission of Indian slave Pierrot with history of his ownership by Francois Daire and others. Signed also by Daire, his mark, and Labuniere, witness.

.143 — Pierpont, John, 1785-1866.
Paper, 1861. 1 p. West Medford, Ill. Addressed to Hubert P. Main; "to rid the world of slavery, bitter fruit, cut down the tree and dig up every root."

.144 — Pike, Charles B.
Papers, 1800. 3 pp. Fort Pickering, Chickasaw Bluff, Ga. Paper from Zebulon Pike (d. 1834) to Dd. Henley, concerning Negro slaves claimed by Cherokees, once owned by John Pettegrew.

.145 — Procter, Addison Gilbert, 1838-1925.
Papers, 1920. 40 pp. "The Slave-Holding Indians" an address delivered by Procter at the Chicago Historical Society (December 9, 1920), concerning the Cherokee Indians during the Civil War; interview with Lincoln which dealt with the demand for the removal of Gen. Blunt over the meat scandal in the Army of the Frontier.

.146 — Ralston, John.
Paper, 1803. 1 p. List of slaves from the estate of Jane Owen and owned by Ralston and Stephen Redden, and the term of years each had to serve from February 28, 1803.

.147 — Randolph, Edmund, 1753-1813.
Papers, 1790. 1 p. Paper from New Kent court-house to His Excellency the Governor of Virginia (Richmond); pleading for Negro condemned to death for stealing, with the belief in misinterpretation of law in the case.

.148 — Rawlins, John Aaron, 1831-69.
Papers, 1863. 4 pp. Materials pertaining to Major General U.S. Grant, suggestion of recommendation for promotion of Sherman, McPherson, George Thomas, and others, policy for retaliation against Confederate treatment of blacks, and criticism heard of General Nathaniel Banks and other officers.

.149 — Reavis, Logan Uriah.
Papers, 1859, 1863, 1865. 15 pp. Letter from Richard Yates (1813-73) to William Jayne concerning repeal of Missouri Compromise, retribution; letter from Chauncey Ives Filley (1829-?) addressed to Marshal Phillips, Mayor's Office, St. Louis, Mo., concerning slave shipments in Missouri; and letter to Richard Yates from J.R. Underwood, Belleville, Ill., concerning black codes in Illinois.

.150 — Ridgely, R.
Paper, n.d. 1 p. List of slaves and sundries conveyed to W. Morris by R. Ridgely or Amos Long.

.151 — Roach, George.
Papers, 1802. 1 p. Shenandoah Co., Va. Addressed to Robert Carter regarding slavery; "I believe you to be a good man and the poor man's friend; I want you to try me and if I won't do, discharge me; if you will give me a chance to live, the favor will never be forgotten."

.152 — Roberts, John M.
Papers, n.d. Roberts', of Morton, Tazewell County, Ill., written account of the activities of an anti-slavery group; formation of the society; underground railway established from St. Louis about 1842; list of speakers at meetings.

.153 — Roberts, Joseph Jenkins, 1809-76.
Papers, 1853. 1 p. Correspondence from Monrovia, Liberia, to Rev. John Morris Penso concerning colonization, Liberia, and the operation of the Methodist mission.

.154 — Roboards, L.C., and brothers.
Book, 1863-65. 1 v. Records of commission and consignment sales of Negroes and household goods at Lynchburg, Va.

IL28.155 —— Ross, William H.
　　　　　　Papers, 1859-65. 30 items. Letters (chiefly from Mississippi and Tennessee) from Corporal Ross of the 40th Illinois Infantry to his family in Vandalia. Significantly mentioned are the Battles of Shiloh and Corinth, Miss., and the attitudes of Ross and other Union soldiers to the emancipating and arming of Negroes.

.156 —— Roy, Antoine.
　　　　　　Papers, 1804. 2 pp. St. Louis, Mo. Manumission of slave named Catherine, by her owner, Antoine Roy; document signed also by M.P., Leduc, Mozzell and Amos Stoddard.

.157 —— St. Anne's Parish, Fort Chartres, Illinois.
　　　　　　Book, 1721-65. 1 v. (96 pp.). Copy of Parish Register listing births, baptisms, marriages, deaths, and burials; includes an index of names of parishioners as mentioned in the Register of Negroes in Illinois.

.158 —— St. Joseph's Parish, Prairie du Rocher, Ill.
　　　　　　Papers. 250 pp. Ms copies of Parish records listing births, deaths, baptisms, marriages, and burials (in French).

.159 —— Saunders, Theodore D.
　　　　　　Papers, 1949-67. 3 times (4 pp.). Contract (March 28, 1949) for appearance of Theodore D. "Red" Saunders' band at the DeLisa Night Club; photocopy of Martin Luther King, Jr.'s letter of July 11, 1966 to Saunders; telegram from Alderman Ralph Metcalfe to Saunders, June 23, 1967.

.160 —— Scott, Henry Bruce.
　　　　　　Papers, 1865. 1 p. Appointment of C.N.W. Cunningham as captain of the 28th Regiment, U.S. Colored Troops (January 2, 1865), from Headquarters, Dept. of Virginia and North Carolina, Army of the James.

.161 —— Sears, Sarah.
　　　　　　Paper, 1776. 1 p. New Haven, Conn. Deed of sale to Amos Botsford for Negro girl. Witnessed by Eliam Raymond and Benjamin Jarvis.

.162 —— Simon, Seymour F., 1915- .
　　　　　　Papers, 1927-66. 4 ft. Papers relative to Simon's service as president of the Cook County (Illinois) Board of Commissioners, including correspondence (1 ft.) and other data (1965-66) on the admission of Negro patients to Cook County Hospital and of Negro students to the Cook County School of Nursing.

.163 —— Slavery collection.
　　　　　　Papers, 1849-60. 16 items. Documents concerning sale of slaves, their descriptions and prices. All documents in French.

.164 —— Slavery songs.
　　　　　　Miscellaneous. ca. 30 titles. Songs pertaining to slavery in the U.S., among which are the following: "The Contrabands Jubilee" (1862); "Eliza's Flight" (1852); "The Fugitive's Song" (1845); "Juney at the Gate" (1850); "Old Abe Has Gone and Did It, Boys" (1862).

.165 —— Smith, Robert W.
　　　　　　Paper, 1855. 1 p. Mobile, Ala. Receipt for $775 paid by N. Robinson for a female slave.

.166 —— Smith, Samuel, 1752-1859.
　　　　　　Paper, 1782. 1 p. Indenture between William Hannah, Baltimore, and Samuel Smith, of the same county, for Negro woman.

.167 —— Social settlements. Chicago, Ill. Abraham Lincoln Center.
　　　　　　Papers, 1938-67. 220 items. Minutes of meetings of the board of trustees plus some treasurer's reports and a few other related records.

.168 —— Stephens, Alexander, 1812-83.
　　　　　　Papers, 1854. 4 pp. Washington, D.C. Letter to Issac Kirkpatrick, containing references to the Nebraska Bill, slavery, U.S. Congress, and other related topics.

.169 —— Stotesbury, William.
　　　　　　Papers, 1865. 4 pp. Fishkill Landing. Account (August 15, 1865) of Stotesbury's confinement by the Confederates in Negro jails in the South, living conditions, and treatment of prisoners. Stotesbury was a Union Navy officer captured while attempting to destroy the ram Albermarle.

.170 —— Strachan, Robert G.
　　　　　　Paper, 1847. $\frac{1}{2}$ p. Petersburg, (?). Receipt for $725 for purchase of two Negro slaves; made out to Col. R.M. Harrison; signed by Robert Strachan.

.171 —— Street, Joseph M.
　　　　　　Paper, 1820. 1 p. Shawanoe Town, Ill. Notice of runaway Negro named London.

.172 —— Stringfellow, John Henry, d. 1905.
　　　　　　Papers, 1858. 2 pp. Atchison, Kans. Letter to Henry Alexander Wise in praise for his attitude on Kansas question; Virginia's attitude; intention of moving to Culpeper Co., Va.

.173 —— Sumner, Charles, 1811-74.
　　　　　　Papers, 1862. 3 pp. Boston, Mass. Addressed to Major ?, commenting on proclamation of Act of Congress; necessity of providing employment for slaves coming within northern lines.

.174 —— Swift, Heman.
　　　　　　Paper, 1774. 1 p. Cornwall, Litchfield Co., Conn. To Daniel Rexford ordering the return of runaway slave to Amos Bochford (New Haven, Conn.) with Rexford's bill for expenses added.

.175 —— Taliferro, William.
　　　　　　Paper, 1732. 1 p. Inventory and appraisement of Negroes belonging to the estate of Robert Carter, in obedience to an order of the Carolina County Court, signed also by John Callette, Jr. and William Daniel.

.176 —— Tanner, Henry.
　　　　　　Papers, n.d. 1 v. Ms copy of the <u>Martyrdom of Lovejoy</u>; an account of the life, trials and perils of Rev. Elijah Lovejoy, who was killed by a pro-slavery mob at Alton, Ill., on the night of Nov. 7, 1837; by an eyewitness.

.177 —— Taylor, Lea Demarest, 1883- .
　　　　　　Papers, 1901-67. 10 ft. Includes correspondence and other items (scattered through the collection) dealing with Negro life in the U.S., mainly in Chicago, particularly with discriminatory conditions confronting Negroes.

.178 —— U.S. Custom House, Franklin, La.
　　　　　　Papers, 1858. 2 pp. Manifest of slaves on board steamer Matagorda of New Orleans, La., bound from Port of Franklin to Port of Galveston, Tex. One slave listed on manifest: 11-year old Henry, owned by W.R. Parker, plus certification that this is true copy of original manifest on file in custom house office.

.179 —— Vallandigham, Clement Laird, 1820-71.
　　　　　　Papers, 1862. 2 pp. Addressed to A.D. Fener from Vallandigham in Dayton, Ohio, and containing anti-abolitionist comments.

.180 —— Valle, Felix.
　　　　　　Papers, 1838. 2 pp. St. Genevieve. To Pierre Menard; containing information concerning the sale of a slave by G. Beauvais to A. Chouteau.

.181 —— Virginia Central Railroad Co.
　　　　　　Paper, 1864. $\frac{1}{2}$ p. Promissory note by Company to O.Hl Pettus, for quarterly payments for hire of a slave, named Alex, who was to be employed on the Virginia Central Railroad.

.182 —— Ward, Joseph.
　　　　　　Paper, 1811. 2 pp. Correspondence from President John Adams commenting on the abolition of slavery, the St. Domingo conflict where "bloodshed and piracy will accompany the growth of Negroes," the altruism of the English toward slavery, and other topics.

.183 —— Washington family.
　　　　　　Papers, 1754, 1785, 1797. 4 pp. Letter to Mrs. Hannah Washington, Bushfield, Va., concerning the slave John, family news and messages from Bushrod Washington (1762-1829); bill of sale (1797) to William Augustine Washington for Negro Adam, witnessed by William Rice; bill of sale from Westmoreland

Co., Va., for Negro named Daniel to William Augustine Washington, witnessed by William Brown; and a division of the Negroes made and agreed to between Col. George Lee and the brothers of the deceased Maj. Lawrence Washington, indorsed to brother by George Washington.

.184 — Washington, George.
Paper, 1790. 1 p. Westmoreland Co., Va. Account of Negroes owned by Mrs. Hannah Lee Washington.

.185 — Weinstein, Jacob Joseph, 1902- .
Papers, 1939-1968. 1 ft. Correspondence and other sundry personal papers (chiefly 1948-68) of Jacob J. Weinstein, Rabbi of K.A.M. Temple, Chicago (1939-68); and invocations delivered by him (1942-68).

.186 — Welters, Edward A.
Papers, 1942-59. 65 items. Miscellany, chiefly letters to Welters, a member of the Illinois General Assembly (1945-47). Includes correspondence with Richard J. Daley, Dwight Green, Edmund K. Jarecki, Edward J. Kelly, Paul Powell, and Adlai Stevenson; and several letters of the People Welfare Organization of Chicago, of which Welters was the chairman.

.187 — Wheeler, Arthur Dana, 1861-1912.
Papers, 1905. 36 pp. Sundry letters, documents, memorial volumes and other materials. Includes ms of Wheeler's The Future of the American Negro.

.188 — White, William (Rev.).
Papers, 1827. 3 pp. Papers from Philadelphia, Pa., regarding a missionary society, Negro organizations; feuds among Negroes, and instruction of Negro children.

.189 — Willard, Samuel.
Papers, 1885. 8 pp. Washington, D.C. Addressed to Samuel Willard from William Birney (1819-1907) denying Garrison's influence on his father, criticizing Garrison, and referring to Amasa Walker. Later correspondence comments further on Walker, his father, and Garrison.

.190 — Williams, Judy.
Papers, 1887. 2 pp. Macon Co., Ala. Indenture of Judy Williams' two sons to Jesse J. Jordan for the year 1888.

.191 — Wimbish, Christopher C., 1892-1962.
Papers, 1870-1962. 1 ft. Correspondence and other miscellaneous papers of Christopher C. Wimbish, a Negro, including some items concerning his service, as an Illinois State Senator (1940's and 1950's), and a few letters he wrote during the First World War. Assorted Wimbish family papers and photographs accompany the Christopher C. Wimbish items.

.192 — Woodhull, J.
Papers, 1855. 1 p. Manifest of slaves to be transported on board the steamer "Florida," from A.W. Parker, Savannah, Ga.

.193 — The Woodlawn Organization.
Papers, 1963-66. 39 items. Mimeograph and ms materials relative to the activities of the Organization; plus information on Manpower Training Programs.

.194 — Wormeley, Eleanor.
Papers, 1813. 2 pp. Richmond, Va. Receipt for $1159 from James Fox for 3 slaves, with Josa Chew, her attorney signing for her. Witnessed by George D. Nicholson, on reverse side is Fox's deed of same slaves to Mrs. Wormeley for same sum (March 10, 1813).

.195 Museum Exhibits.
Portraits, memorabilia, furniture, and other displays. Portraits of two distinguished Chicago Negroes, both by Aaron E. Darling, are exhibited. One is of John Jones (1811-79), who settled in Chicago in 1845 and became a successful businessman and the first Negro to hold elective office in Cook County, as a county commissioner (1871-75). The other is of Mary Richardson Jones, a worker for the repeal of the Illinois Black Laws, and for improved conditions for Negroes in Illinois. Among the museum exhibits are a diorama that traces Lincoln's career and his interests in the slavery question; a replica of the cabin built prior to 1790 by Jean DuSable, Chicago's pioneer settler; numerous exhibits related to the days of slavery; memorabilia of the abolitionist, John Brown, and the table on which Robert E. Lee signed the surrender document at Appomattox Courthouse; and 3 oil paintings (ca. 1850-53) depicting slaves and slave marts.

.196 Print and Photograph Department.
Miscellaneous. Materials mainly in the period of the Civil War. 20th Century Negro material in the files mainly consists of: items on race riots and slum housing in the city; a few photographs of noteworthy Chicago Negroes; personal and archival photos from individuals and organizations, whose papers are in the Society's manuscript collections, such as Congressman Arthur W. Mitchell, Monsignor Daniel M. Cantwell, the Catholic Interracial Council of Chicago, Friendship House, Negroes in the Civil War. 20 ferrotypes (tintypes) of unidentified Negroes in Civil War clothing; lithographs, engravings of slave traffic on the coast of Africa; chromolithograph; gravure; negatives of photographs of riots and Negroes in the theater; and a number of photographs, among which are housing lived in by Negroes just before such housing was cleared for construction of housing projects in Chicago (1940's). Broadsides (ca. 300, 1800's-1960's) of various sizes pertaining to the following subjects and persons: Freedman's Bureau; Black Muslims; slaves and slave marts; John Brown; Negro soldiers; contrabands; Emancipation Proclamation; abolitionist and anti-slavery movement; Elijah Muhammad; Negroes in athletics; NAACP; various riots in the U.S.; school integration and desegregation; SNCC; march on Washington; CORE; Negroes in politics; Martin Luther King, Jr.; Christian Buyers League to Stop Integration; James Farmer; housing; education; and other topics.

IL29   CHICAGO PUBLIC LIBRARY (1873). 78 E. Washington St., 60602. Tel 312 236-8922. Dr. Alex Ladenson, Acting Chief Librn.

.1   Civil War Museum Collection, G.A.R. Memorial Hall. Materials relating to the Civil War, 1861-65. ca. 200 items. Included in the collection are items relating to slavery and abolitionists; anti-slavery tract (n.d.) of the American Reform Tract and Book Society; copper slave tags used to identify trade of slaves for public auctions (Charleston, 1826-56); slave whip; song sheets, including "The Fugitive Song" and "The Negro Emancipation Song"; notice posted for runaway slave (June 25, 1861); broadside of slave song, "Dandy Jim of Caroline"; ms bill of sale for 3 slaves for $2500 (at Kansas, April 26, 1861); and broadside, "Rev. Elijah Parish Lovejoy ... A Martyr to Liberty ... " (Boston, n.d.).

IL30   CHICAGO PUBLIC LIBRARY, GEORGE CLEVELAND HALL BRANCH (1932). 4801 S. Michigan Ave., 60615. Tel 312 536-2275. Donald F. Joyce, Head Librn., Hall Br. Interlibrary loan, bibliographies prepared, literature searches, copying, inquiries answered, referrals made, consultation, film programs, children's programs, writers' workshop.

The following materials relating to Negroes are restricted, in part.

.1   — Chicago Negro Union Catalog.
Index to materials on the Negro in the principal libraries of Chicago. Catalog was completed by the W.P.A. Omnibus Library Project, June, 1940. It includes books, magazine articles, reports, bulletins, theses and other unpublished material. Catalog consists of 75,000 cards with full catalog entries, annotations, and many analytics. It is arranged in dictionary style, using a specially prepared

list of subject headings suitable for the
literature concerning the Negro.

.2 —— Hughes, Langston, 1902-67.
Papers. Typescripts of The Big Sea (first
draft, n.p., n.d.) and Not Without Laughter
(n.d., n.p.), and author's proofs of The Big Sea
(June, 1940).

.3 —— Special Negro Collection.
Books (4000 v.), periodical titles, pamphlets,
clippings, and other materials by and about
black people. The books are divided into fiction and non-fiction, the fiction including
representatives of almost every novel published by a Negro in the United States; most
copies are autographed. Under non-fiction
the collection is very strong in Negro sociology, education, and history. The collection
contains complete runs of the following periodicals: Crisis, Negro History Bulletin,
Phylon, Journal of Negro History, Journal of
Negro Education, Color, Our World, and
Opportunity; and also a special file on black
people in Illinois consisting of pamphlets,
clippings and other papers, collected chiefly
between 1938-40, on the history of the Negro
in Illinois since statehood.

.4 —— Works Project Administration, Illinois Writers'
Project.
Files, "The Negro in Illinois," 1938-40. Intention of the Project was apparently to create
research information files on the Negro in
Illinois from early times to the late 1930's as
revealed through written and oral sources.
Material in the files represents transcribed
parts of books, newspaper articles, periodical
articles, and transcribed interviews of then-
living early Negro settlers in Illinois.

.5 —— Wright, Richard, 1908-60.
Papers. Typescripts of Blueprint for Negro
Literature (18 pp., n.d., n.p.) and Big Boy
Leaves Home (48 pp., n.d., n.p.).

IL31   CHICAGO PUBLIC SCHOOLS, BUREAU OF HUMAN RELA-
TIONS. Board of Education, 228 N. LaSalle St., 60601.
Tel 312 332-7800. Gar Muller, Staff Mem.

IL32   CHICAGO STATE UNIVERSITY, ORAL HISTORY RE-
SEARCH PROJECT. 500 N. Pulaski Rd., 60624. Tel
312 224-3900. Henry (Skip) Simmons, Dir.
The Project is concerned with the overall history of the
growth of Chicago in areas of business, industry, politics; growth and development of black communities in
Chicago and the black Americans' movement into and
within the city of Chicago.

.1   Oral History Research Project.
Files. Includes correspondence, minutes of meetings, financial records, studies, investigations,
reports, and other documents dealing with the
aims, history, and programs of the Project.

IL33   CHICAGO TENANTS UNION. 3543 W. Jackson Blvd., 60624.
Tel 312 826-4900.

IL34   CHICAGO URBAN LEAGUE, RESEARCH OFFICE. 4500 S.
Michigan Ave., 60653. Tel 312 285-5800. Sanford
Sherizen, Res. Dir. Inquiries answered, referrals
made, consultation.
The League is a voluntary city-wide organization working to improve race relations and reduce race-based
discrimination through methods of research, education,
community organization, and interracial cooperation.

.1   Urban League Research Collection.
Books (ca. 1500 v.), periodical titles, pamphlets
(ca. 350), and clippings (ca. 2500). Stress is on
forms of institutional racism. Race relations
materials are of a general nature and represent
current social science research.

IL35   THE CHRISTIAN CENTURY FOUNDATION (1908). 407 S.
Dearborn St., 60605. Tel 312 427-5380. Alan Geyer,
Pres. of Found. and Editor of Christian Century.
The Foundation works to relate the Christian gospel to
the whole range of human experiences, through raising

and commenting on civil, social and cultural issues.
Publ.: The Christian Century, weekly journal; The
Christian Ministry, bi-monthly journal.

.1   The Christian Century Foundation.
Files, 1908- . Included are mss of articles concerning religion and race, racial disturbances,
black power and economic development, and other
such subjects.

IL36   CITY OF CHICAGO, DEPARTMENT OF URBAN RENEWAL
(DUR) (1947), DEPARTMENT OF PUBLIC INFORMA-
TION. 320 N. Clark St., 60610. Tel 312 744-4000.
Lewis W. Hill, Cmnr. Copying, inquiries answered,
referrals made, consultation.
DUR works to eradicate and redevelop slum and
blighted vacant areas and conserve urban residential
areas.
Publ.: Annual Report; Renewal Review, monthly news-
letter.

.1   Department of Urban Renewal.
Papers, ca. 1947- . Minutes of meetings, correspondence, maps, and other materials relating to
urban renewal. Contains some materials from
predecessor organizations, the Chicago Land
Clearance Commission and the Community Conservation Board; information on various DUR
project areas, records of land transactions; and
various incompleted miscellaneous files on several
other City of Chicago departments, such as Board
of Education and Department of Development and
Planning.

IL37   COMMITTEE FOR INDEPENDENT POLITICAL ACTION
(CIPA). 1517 Howard St., 60626. Amy Kesselman.
CIPA works to organize communities around demands
for radical change.

IL38   COMMITTEE FOR ONE SOCIETY (1968). 40 N. Ashland,
60607. Tel 312 243-2205. Mrs. Susan Tobias, Res.
Dir. Copying.
The Society researches and acts on institutional white
racism; collaborates to support black groups when appropriate, feasible and practical; and develops training programs to overcome white racism. Affiliated
with the Urban Training Center.

.1   Committee for One Society.
Files. 4 vf. Correspondence, articles, newspaper
clippings, annual reports of corporations, studies,
community surveys, and other papers. Materials
relate to institutional racism and to the activities
of the Committee.

IL39   COMMUNITY RENEWAL SOCIETY (1882). 116 S. Michigan
Ave., 60603. Tel 312 236-4830. Donald L. Benedict,
Exec. Dir.
The Society was founded by the Congregationalists
(United Church of Christ) for the renewal and
strengthening of religious programs in the Chicago
metropolitan area, to work with all low-income migrant
groups in the areas of employment, human relations,
social attitudes, education, and housing, and provide
technical assistance to neighborhood groups in Chicago's Model Cities areas.

IL40   THE ECUMENICAL INSTITUTE (1954). 3444 Congress
Parkway, 60624. Tel 312 722-3444. Mrs. Joyce
Townley, Dir.
The Institute does research on economic, political,
educational and social problems of the ghetto; and conducts a general inner-city renewal program involving
tutoring children, courses in Negro heritage for pre-
school children, legal aid, and health services.

IL41   ENGLEWOOD URBAN PROGRESS CENTER. 839 W. 64th
St., 60621. Tel 312 873-9600. Rachel Ridley, Exec.
Dir.

IL42   FAIR EMPLOYMENT PRACTICES COMMISSION (FEPC)
(1961). 160 N. LaSalle St., 60601. Tel 312 346-2000.
Walter J. Ducey, Exec. Dir. Inquiries answered, consultation.
The Commission seeks to eliminate discrimination in

employment practices and to work for equal employment opportunity for all persons.
Publ.: Annual Report.

.1 Fair Employment Practices Commission.
Files, 1959- . Records, correspondence, reports, and other papers concerning the operation of the Commission. Included are records of the Illinois Committee for Equal Job Opportunities (1959-61), consisting of correspondence, records, of meetings, reports on sub-committees, strategy papers, and newspaper clippings.

IL43 FRANK LONDON BROWN NEGRO HISTORY CLUB. c/o Chatham YMCA, 1021 E. 83rd St., 60617. Tel 312 828-3133. Francis Ward, Chmn.
The Club is a voluntary association of persons interested in promoting the teaching of the history and culture of African-Americans.

.1 African-American Pictorial Exhibit.
Posters, paintings, photographs, books, pamphlets. The materials illustrate and describe the history of black people in America.

IL44 FRIENDSHIP HOUSE (1938). 4233 S. Indiana Ave., 60653. Tel 312 624-7700. Betty Plank, Dir.
Friendship House is a law group working for racial justice, housing, child care; and to encourage communication between groups, especially between white and black people, by holding weekend conferences, week-long study programs, and workshops for members of the professions; by distributing educational materials; by providing a Speakers Bureau; and through programs for the home and community. Friendship House has published Community magazine since 1941. Available from Friendship House is a series of tape recordings of such persons as Jesse Jackson, Martin Luther King, Jr., C.T. Vivian, and James Groppi.
Publ.: Community, monthly magazine.

.1 Friendship House.
Files. Correspondence, records, staff reports, brochures, and other materials concerning the operation and activities of the organization. Records, 1938-63, are held at the Chicago Historical Society, and include a complete run of Community magazine.

IL45 HISTORICAL PICTURES SERVICE (1956). 2753 W. North Ave., 60647. Tel 312 486-6575. Joseph Karzen, Dir.
Copying, inquiries answered, referrals made, consultation, research and supply of photocopies.
The Service maintains a file of pictures covering "every important person, place, thing, and event in history."

.1 Historical Pictures Service.
Files. ca. 1,650,000 items, of which ca. 20,000-60,000 are pictures of important persons and events in race relations and black history. Included are photographs, engravings, drawings, paintings, cartoons, and caricatures.

IL46 HMH PUBLISHING COMPANY, INC. (1953), LIBRARY. 919 N. Michigan Ave., 60611. Tel 312 642-1000. Karen D. Halsne, Librn. Copying, typing, inquiries answered, referrals made.
Publ.: Playboy, monthly magazine.

.1 HMH Publishing Company.
Files. Includes material concerning civil rights and the black man used in articles for Playboy magazine. Books, periodical titles, clippings, correspondence, and art work. In part, restricted.

IL47 HYDE PARK - KENWOOD COMMUNITY CONFERENCE. 1525 E. 53rd St., 60615. Tel 312 288-8343. Sharon Jeffry, Acting Exec. Dir.
The Hyde Park - Kenwood Community Conference is a neighborhood association which seeks to maintain and improve an integrated community.
Publ.: Pamphlets and other informational materials on the Conference, its programs, urban problems, integrated communities, and community programs.

IL48 ILLINOIS COMMISSION ON HUMAN RELATIONS (1943). 160 N. LaSalle St., 60601. Tel 312 346-2000. Roger W. Nathan, Exec. Dir.
The Commission works for the elimination of discrimination through activities in housing, education, human relations education, public accommodations, governmental operations and police-community relations.
Publ.: Biennial Report.

IL49 INDUSTRIAL AREAS FOUNDATION (IAF). 8 S. Michigan Ave., 60603. Tel 312 236-1931. Saul Alinsky, Exec. Dir.
IAF exists to study the characteristics and problems of American industrial areas, and to aid in the development of programs for the solution of these problems.

IL50 INSTITUTE FOR JUVENILE RESEARCH (1909), LIBRARY (1928). 907 Wolcott, 60612. Tel 312 341-7323. Elaine A. Harriston, Librn.
The Research Program of the Institute is concerned with the scientific study of children and adolescents, including both normal and abnormal processes.
Publ.: News and Notes; Research Profile; Research reports.

.1 Institute for Juvenile Research Library.
Research report files, 1964- . Reports and reprinted articles from journals and books. Studies of achievement and non-achievement among lower-class Negro children, including such topics as the correlates of achievement and under-achievement in urban Negro children and their school-age siblings; the relation of personality, family, social network and achievement; the early elementary school record as a predictor of high school achievement; and the determinants of achievement and under-achievement. Restricted.

IL51 INTEGRATED EDUCATION ASSOCIATES (1963). 343 S. Dearborn St., 60604. Tel 312 922-8361. Meyer Weinberg, Editor. Inquiries answered, referrals made, consultation.
Integrated Education Associates disseminates information on current educational practices toward minority group children: black, Spanish-speaking, Indian, and Appalachian white. The sources of the information range from scholarly and journalistic to generalized, impartial observation. Included are comments on the minority group experience by many individuals of varying ethnic backgrounds.
Publ.: Integrated Education, bi-monthly magazine; School Integration, a bibliography; Readers, reports, and bibliographies in education, Afro-American history, and related subjects.

.1 Chicago school integration movement.
Materials. Books, periodicals, pamphlets, vf, theses, mss, and correspondence (ca. 2000 items) about school integration in the Chicago area, including material pertaining to the school work of the Coordinating Council of Community Organizations. Correspondence restricted.

.2 Daily newspaper clipping file.
1963- . Detailed clippings on the Chicago school integration movement, mounted and arranged chronologically. Also includes clippings on New York school integration, based primarily on the New York Times.

.3 School integration in the United States.
Clippings and reports on school integration in various parts of the United States, primarily in the North and West.

IL51a INTERNATIONAL BLACK WIRE. 4340 S. Cottage Grove Ave., 60653. Tel 312 684-3366. Al Saladin, Editor-in-Chief.
International Black Wire is "an organ dedicated to directing 30,000,000 Blacks to the halls of deliverance." Its publication policy is to "weigh the evidence, check for their authenticity and also grant exposure to those small grass root organizations which are co-related with our endeavor and that being to serve in the best interest of the Black community."
Publ.: International Black Wire, bi-monthly tabloid newspaper.

IL52   INTERRELIGIOUS COUNCIL ON URBAN AFFAIRS. Room
        1006, 116 S. Michigan, 60603. Tel 312 641-1545. Rev.
        Shelvin J. Hall, Exec. Dir.
        The Council researches and evaluates major com-
        munity organizations and organizing efforts in the Chi-
        cago area and issues as they affect these organiza-
        tions, such as public education, police power and
        Model Cities program; develops recommendations and
        priorities on urban needs; conducts training sessions
        and seminars on topics of urban concern; and coordi-
        nates support of organizing efforts and distributes
        information about such efforts and the needs of the
        Chicago area. The research of the Council is, at
        present, available only to its member bodies.

IL53   JEWISH LABOR COMMITTEE, ILLINOIS REGIONAL OF-
        FICE. 431 S. Dearborn St., 60605. Tel 312 939-2087.
        David Schacter, Field Rep.

IL54   JOHNSON PUBLISHING COMPANY, LIBRARY (1949). 1820
        S. Michigan Ave., 60616. Tel 312 225-1000. Mrs.
        Lucille Phinnie, Librn.
        Publ.: Ebony, monthly magazine; Tan, monthly maga-
            zine; Jet, weekly magazine; Black World (for-
            merly Negro Digest), monthly magazine.

        .1 Contemporary Negroes.
            Extensive vertical file materials by and about the
            Negro today, with emphasis on his relation to busi-
            ness, religion, science, sports, and politics, and
            including biographical information about outstand-
            ing persons in these fields.
        .2 Negro newspapers.
            Complete files of the major black newspapers in
            the United States.
        .3 Photograph collection.
            ca. 400,000 photographs of people and events in
            Negro history.

IL55   JOIN COMMUNITY UNION. 4441 N. Clifton, 60640. Tel
        312 334-8040.
        Publ.: The Firing Line, weekly newspaper.

IL56   LEADERSHIP COUNCIL FOR METROPOLITAN OPEN
        COMMUNITIES (1966). 155 N. Wacker Dr., 60606. Tel
        312 236-9850. Edward L. Holmgren, Exec. Dir.
        The Council initiates and promotes educational and ac-
        tion programs for fair housing practices in the Chicago
        area.
        Publ.: Newsletter, monthly; Research reports relative
            to housing.

IL57   THE LOST FOUND NATION OF ISLAM IN THE WILDER-
        NESS OF NORTH AMERICA, MUHAMMAD'S
        MOSQUE NO. 2 (1930). 5335 S. Greenwood Ave., 60615.
        Tel 312 684-8823. Abass Rassoull, Nat. Secy.
        The "Black Muslims" (Lost Found Nation) believe in the
        separation of the "so-called Negroes and the so-called
        white Americans," and in the right to establish a
        separate state under Allah. The Muslim program in-
        cludes equality of opportunity, freedom for all "Be-
        lievers of Islam" in federal prisons, an end to police
        brutality, the teaching of Islam without hindrance or
        suppression, and the education of all black children by
        their own teachers. Activities and enterprises include
        Muslim farms in Alabama, Georgia, and Michigan,
        business and residential properties in the Chicago
        area, and the University of Islam in Chicago, Detroit,
        New York, Washington, Atlanta, and Los Angeles.
        Publ.: Muhammad Speaks, weekly newspaper.

IL58   LOYOLA UNIVERSITY, CENTER FOR RESEARCH IN
        URBAN GOVERNMENT (1965). 820 N. Michigan Ave.,
        60611. Tel 312 944-0800. Phil Doyle, Dir.
        The Center gathers data for use by urban governmental
        agencies in research and development efforts. In addi-
        tion, it occasionally publishes studies of current po-
        litical and governmental problems in the Chicago area.

IL59   LUTHERAN HUMAN RELATIONS ASSOCIATION OF AMER-
        ICA, INC., CHICAGO PROJECT. 5046 S. Greenwood,
        60615. Tel 312 924-4466. Rev. George Hrbek, Dir.

IL60   McCORMICK THEOLOGICAL SEMINARY, INSTITUTE ON
        THE CHURCH IN URBAN-INDUSTRIAL SOCIETY
        (1966). 800 W. Belden Ave., 60614. Tel 312 549-3700.

Marshal L. Scott, Dir. Inquiries answered, consultation.
The Institute, which is located on the campus of Mc-
Cormick Theological Seminary, is an information and
advisory center on urban and industrial ministries
which provides resources and world-wide consultation
in the field of urban missions, coordinates the exchange
of information on literature in the field of urbanization
and industrialization, and which acts as a research
center for persons in the Chicago area. Collections of
the Institute are held in the McGraw Memorial Library
of McCormick Theological Seminary.

IL61   MUSEUM OF AFRICAN AMERICAN HISTORY (DuSABLE
        MUSEUM OF AFRICAN AMERICAN HISTORY) (1961).
        3806 S. Michigan Ave., 60653. Tel 312 536-8910.
        Margaret Burroughs, Dir.
        The Museum collects and preserves artifacts and
        works pertaining to African-American history and
        educates the public about this history. The Museum
        dates from the early 1940's when the National Negro
        Museum and History Foundation was begun. The
        present museum opened in 1961 as the Museum of
        Negro History, but in 1966 the name changed to the
        Museum of African American History.
        Publ.: Afro-American Heritage calendar, annually;
            Black history kit, containing biographical bro-
            chures, maps, pictures, and other educational
            materials; Books concerning Afro-American
            history and culture.

        .1 Art and Artifact collection.
            ca. 300 items, excluding photographs. Paintings,
            sculpture, photographs, and artifacts of Ameri-
            cans of African descent. Included are a $200
            wanted poster for an escaped slave, statues of
            famous blacks, and artifacts such as bowls and
            containers. Artists represented include Marion
            Perkins, Charles White Richmond Barthé, Syl-
            vester Britton, Selma Burke, Margaret Bur-
            roughs, Elizabeth Catlett, Edward Christmas,
            Eldzive Corlov, Eugene Edaw, Robert Glover,
            Leon N. Hicks, Robert Jones, Herman Ring,
            Clifford Lee, Anna McCullough, Ramon Price,
            William Edward Scott, Lawrence Taylor, Al
            Tyler, Garret Whyte, and John Wilson.
        .2 Library collection.
            Materials by and about black Americans, including
            books (ca. 8000 v.), periodicals, mss, and a news-
            paper clipping file covering all aspects of Negro
            life and culture. Mss include notebooks and diary
            of Captain Harry Dean; other collections have not
            been cataloged.
        .3 Record collection.
            ca. 500 78 rpm records. Includes recordings of
            Bessie Smith and Bert Williams, among others.
        .4 Tape recording collection.
            Tapes include speeches, statements, and inter-
            views with such persons as W.E.B. DuBois, Mal-
            colm X, Lorraine Hansberry, James Baldwin,
            Ronnie Fair, Charles White, and interviews with
            old settlers of Chicago.

IL62   NATIONAL ASSOCIATION FOR THE ADVANCEMENT OF
        COLORED PEOPLE (NAACP), SOUTHSIDE CHICAGO
        BRANCH OFFICE. Room 635, 407 S. Dearborn St.,
        60605. Tel 312 922-6781. Edward J. McClellan, Urban
        Prog. Dir.

IL63   NATIONAL BAPTIST CONVENTION, USA, INC. 3101 S.
        Parkway, 60616. Tel 312 546-0148. Rev. J.H. Jack-
        son, Pres.

IL64   NATIONAL BLACK LIBERATION ALLIANCE (1968). 75 E.
        35th St., 60616. Tel 312 842-0198. Robert L. Lucas,
        Chmn. Typing, inquiries answered, community orga-
        nizing.
        The Alliance promotes, supports, and advances the in-
        terests of black people at local, state and national
        levels; develops economic power to attain an indepen-
        dent black economy; develops leadership and utilizes
        to best advantage the political power inherent in the
        black community; and furthers the educational, cul-
        tural, and social interests of black people to fight
        racism and to prevent the genocide and destruction of

black people. Formerly Congress of Racial Equality. Publ.: Black Liberator Newspaper.

.1 National Black Liberation Alliance.
Records, 1960- . Reports, correspondence, minutes of meetings, and other papers concerning the establishment of the Alliance, and its activities. Contains records of predecessor organization, Chicago Congress of Racial Equality, 1960-68 (6 boxes), including correspondence, financial reports, minutes of meetings, publications, clippings, and material on various local and national cases.

IL65   NATIONAL CATHOLIC CONFERENCE FOR INTERRACIAL JUSTICE (NCCIJ). 1307 S. Wabash Ave., 60605. Tel 312 341-1530. James T. Harris, Jr., Exec. Dir.
A National federation of Catholic human relations and urban organizations. The Conference provides services and does research in the areas of education, housing, medicine, and employment. Programs include Project Equality, in which religious institutions use their influence and resources to encourage fair employment, and a medical project aimed at ending discrimination in medicine and meeting health needs of minority groups. Also conducts research on effective means of church involvement in urban problems with emphasis on low-income housing or slum improvement, and on church activities in the ghetto.
Publ.: Commitment, bi-monthly house organ; Project Equality News, monthly newsletter.

.1 National Catholic Conference for Interracial Justice.
Materials. Documentation (ca. 1960- .) dealing with the aims, programs and history of the Conference, including correspondence, reports, studies, minutes of meetings, and financial records; and books and materials concerning the field of human rights with emphasis on Roman Catholic thought in this area.

IL66   NATIONAL CONFERENCE OF CHRISTIANS AND JEWS (NCCJ), CHICAGO REGION. 203 N. Wabash Ave., 60601. Tel 312 236-9272. Gerald A. Renner, Exec. Dir. Consultation.
Publ.: Bibliographies on intergroup relations.

IL67   NATIONAL FUNERAL DIRECTORS AND MORTICIANS ASSOCIATION, INC. (NFDMA). 730 E. 63rd St., 60621. Tel 312 363-5757. Jenifer W. Renfro, Pres.
NFDMA, an organization of black morticians, seeks to promote the art and science of the mortuary profession and to interpret local and national legislation affecting funeral directors and morticians.

IL68   NATIONAL INSURANCE ASSOCIATION (NIA) (1921). 2400 S. Michigan Ave., 60616. Tel 312 842-5125. Charles A. Davis, Exec. Dir.
NIA was organized to raise the standards and practices of the 11,000 participating members; to contribute to total health and insurance education of the nation; and to build public confidence in insurance companies owned and operated by Negroes.
Publ.: Pilot, bi-monthly magazine; Annual proceedings.

.1 National Insurance Association (NIA).
Files, 1927- . ca. 200 items. Includes correspondence, minutes of meetings, financial records, and other material dealing with the aims, history, and program of the Association; and files of the Pilot (18 v.).

IL69   NATIONAL NEWSPAPER PUBLISHERS ASSOCIATION (NNPA) (1940). 2400 S. Michigan Ave., 60616. Tel 312 225-2400. John H. Sengstacke, Pres.
The Association is a national professional society, composed of 70 daily and weekly Negro newspapers published in the United States. The Association conducts consumer surveys and marketing research campaigns to determine the extent of reader education, circulation coverage and public reaction to editorial policies and news content of member publications. It also initiates action programs, disseminates information, and supports other phases of the civil rights movement.

IL70   NATIONAL OPINION RESEARCH CENTER (1941), LIBRARY AND DATA ARCHIVES (1941). 6030 S. Ellis Ave., 60637. Tel 312 684-5600. Patrick Bova, Librn. Inter-library loan, copying, inquiries answered, referrals made, provides data from sample surveys.
NORC is a sociological research center affiliated with the University of Chicago, utilizing the survey method, primarily to study problems of society, to build theory and to advance methodology. The Library and Data Archives service the collected data for outside users, and make available documents reporting on data analysis and data for secondary analyses.
Publ.: Bibliographies and inventories of studies, and publications in social research.

.1 Library and Data Archives.
1942- . Original sample survey data from studies concerned with race relations, such as white attitudes toward Negroes, decision-making in urban school systems, and integrated neighborhoods. Data in punched card or tape format, also completed questionnaires, field records and tabulations. Studies include a Detroit race opinion survey after a riot (1943); racial tension in Baltimore (1948); tension barometer, a comparison of attitudes to measure interracial tension (1950); racial problems - white attitudes toward Negroes (1942); cross-sectional study of educational, political and Negro questions (1943); Memphis Negroes and the war (1942); the Negro looks at the war (1942); the Negroes' role in the war (1943); the Negro protest movement (1963); desegregation in the public schools; and racial strife in New York's Bedford-Stuyvesant Area. Restricted.

IL71   NEGRO PRESS INTERNATIONAL (1964). 5708 S. State St., 60621. Tel 312 324-6320. J.H. Randall, Managing Dir.
News-gathering and distribution agency maintaining library for reference purposes.

.1 Negro Press International.
Files. ca. 16 vf. Restricted.

IL72   THE NEWBERRY LIBRARY (1887). 60 W. Walton St., 60610. Tel 312 943-9090. Lawrence W. Towner, Dir. and Librn. Copying, inquiries answered.
Privately endowed research institution in the humanities, available without charge to qualified users.

.1 Francis Driscoll Sheet Music Collection.
Collection includes holdings of abolition songs and minstrel songs.
.2 Nineteenth Century American Fiction Collection.
Large holdings of novels depicting the Negro are included in this collection.
.3 Slavery and the abolitionist movement.
Collection of first editions of book and pamphlet literature relating to slavery, the abolition movement, and the Civil War, together with modern monographic secondary material.

IL73   NORTHEASTERN ILLINOIS STATE COLLEGE, CENTER FOR INNER CITY STUDIES (1966), LIBRARY (1967). 700 E. Oakwood Blvd., 60653. Tel 312 373-3050. Dorothy W. Robinson, Librn. Bibliographies prepared, inquiries answered, consultation.
The Center seeks to eradicate misconceptions concerning the disadvantaged minorities in America, and to instill proper attitudes and values, and provide the proper tools which will allow those who work with disadvantaged minorities to function positively and creatively in meeting the needs of inner-city dwellers.
Publ.: Inner City Issues, quarterly.

.1 Center for Inner City Studies Library.
Materials. ca. 3200 items. Books (ca. 2600 v.), periodicals, newspapers, pamphlets, vertical file materials, theses and dissertations, clippings, films, microforms, phonograph records. Collection focuses on the causes and effects of disadvantagement, with special emphasis in the areas of education and social welfare.

IL74   (This number not used).

IL75 ORGANIZATION OF BLACK AMERICAN CULTURE (OBAC), WRITERS' WORKSHOP (1966), THE HOYT W. FULLER LIBRARY (1969). 77 E. 35th St., 60616. Tel 312 329-9116. Carolyn Rodgers, Librn.
The Writers' Workshop of OBAC seeks to encourage the highest quality of literary expression reflecting the Black Experience, and to establish and define the standards by which creative writing which reflects the Black Experience is to be judged. The Fuller Library is a community resource, designed to meet the community's need for information, education and entertainment, relevant to their real situations and in line with their hopes.
Publ.: NOMMO, literary quarterly; OBAC Newsletter.

.1 Hoyt W. Fuller Library.
Books by and about Africans and Afro-Americans, their history, literature, and art; and current American and Third World periodicals.
.2 Writers' Workshop.
Files. Records of the organization and mss by members of the group.

IL76 PROVIDENT HOSPITAL (1893), LIBRARY. 426 E. 51st St., 60615. Tel 312 285-5300.
Provident Hospital is the first training school for Negro nurses in the United States, founded by Dr. Daniel Hale Williams who performed the first successful operation on the human heart in 1893.

.1 Provident Hospital.
Files, 1893- . Correspondence, minutes of board meetings, financial records, mss of reports written by Dr. Daniel Hale Williams, records of admissions to nursing school and other material pertaining to the administration and history of the Hospital.

IL77 SOUTH SHORE COMMISSION (1954). 7134 S. Jeffery Blvd., 60649. Tel 312 667-7276. Julian Klugman, Exec. Dir. Copying, typing, inquiries answered, referrals made, consultation.
The South Shore Commission is involved in a "managed integration" effort through its tenant referral service, youth guidance work, and education in race relations and police-community relations. It serves as a clearing house for information concerning crime, housing, and other matters of interest to the South Shore community of Chicago, Ill.
Publ.: The South Shore Scene, monthly newspaper.

IL78 STUDENTS FOR A DEMOCRATIC SOCIETY (SDS). 1608 W. Madison St., 60612. Tel 312 666-3874. Michael Klonsky, Nat. Secy.
SDS is a national radical movement whose program centers on economic, social, institutional and cultural change in America. It carries on activities concerned with peace, education, employment, housing, social welfare, student power, black power, and draft resistance, including supporting the black liberation struggle and developing community union organizations in poor areas, both black and white.

IL79 TRAVELERS RESEARCH PUBLISHING CO., INC. (1942). 8034 S. Prairie Ave., 60619. Tel 312 483-2891. Clarence M. Markham, Jr., Publisher and Editor.
Publ.: The Negro Traveler and Conventioneer, monthly magazine.

.1 Travelers Research Publishing Co., Inc.
Files, 1942- . Records, reports, correspondence, mss of articles, and other papers concerning the Negro Traveler and Conventioneer.

IL80 UNITED MORTGAGE BANKERS OF AMERICA, INC. (UMBA) (1962). 840 E. 87th St., 60619. Tel 312 994-7200. Dempsey J. Travis, Pres.
UMBA is a black mortgage banking organization founded to bring together persons interested in the mortgage banking business, to exchange information and establish educational programs to enable Negroes to enter the field.

.1 United Mortgage Bankers Association (UMBA).
Files, 1962- . Includes correspondence, minutes of meetings, financial records, and other docu-

ments dealing with the aims, history, and programs of UMBA.

IL81 U.S. COMMISSION ON CIVIL RIGHTS, MIDWEST FIELD OFFICE. Federal Office Bldg., 219 S. Dearborn St., 60604. Tel 312 353-7371. Clark G. Roberts, Dir.

IL82 U.S. DEPARTMENT OF HEALTH, EDUCATION AND WELFARE; REGIONAL OFFICE FOR CIVIL RIGHTS. 226 W. Jackson, 60606. Tel 312 353-5453. Fred Cioffi, Acting Dir. Inquiries answered, referrals made.

IL83 U.S. EQUAL EMPLOYMENT OPPORTUNITY COMMISSION, CHICAGO REGIONAL OFFICE. U.S. Court House and Federal Office Bldg., 219 S. Dearborn St., 60604. Tel 312 353-7550. Elmer W. McLain, Regional Dir.

IL84 U.S. NATIONAL ARCHIVES AND RECORDS SERVICE (1934), FEDERAL RECORDS CENTER (1969). 7201 S. Leamington Ave., 60638. Tel 312 353-5720. Bruce C. Harding, Chief, Regional Archives Br. Copying, inquiries answered.
The Center selects, preserves, and services those records of federal agencies located in Wisconsin, Illinois, Indiana, Ohio, Michigan, and Kentucky which are deemed to be of archival value. Materials are classified according to Record Group (R.G.), and are, in part, restricted.

.1 R.G. 21, U.S. District Courts.
Records, 1789-1959. 5816 cu. ft. Case files and entry books for federal courts in Region 5.
.2 R.G. 381, Office of Economic Opportunity.
Records, 1965-67. 87 cu. ft. Records and materials about the development and operation of the Office of Economic Opportunity and the programs which it administers.
.3 R.G. 390, Neighborhood Youth Corps.
Records, 1864-66. 65 cu. ft. Records and materials about the development and operation of the Neighborhood Youth Corps, a program under the Economic Opportunity Act of 1964. Also included are some records of the Job Corps Center. Permission of agency required for use.

IL85 UNIVERSITY OF CHICAGO, CENTER FOR URBAN STUDIES (1963). 5852 S. University Ave., 60637. Tel 312 643-0800. Jack Meltzer, Dir.
The Center functions as both a research and a teaching unit. It provides a focus for urban research in progress throughout the University, and has a research program of its own. Areas of interest include housing, evaluation of urban planning programs, anti-poverty programs, and urban renewal.
Publ.: Reports, studies, surveys.

IL86 UNIVERSITY OF CHICAGO, DEPARTMENT OF SOCIOLOGY, COMMUNITY AND FAMILY STUDY CENTER. 1126 E. 59th St., 60637. Tel 312 643-0800. Donald J. Bogue, Dir.
The Community and Family Study Center conducts research and publishes and distributes the reports of the Interuniversity Social Research Committee about race and ethnic relations in the Chicago area.
Publ.: Research reports.

.1 Community and Family Study Center.
Books, reports, questionnaires, interviews, tables, and other materials used in compiling the series of monographs on race relations published by the Community and Family Study Center. Subjects found in the completed reports include attitudes toward integration, civil rights and the civil rights movement; civil rights and militancy; interracial misunderstanding and divided leadership; social distance and ecology; segregation and local government in relation to public planning and action; and findings and interpretations about race and education in Chicago.

IL87 UNIVERSITY OF CHICAGO (1891), LIBRARY. 1116 E. 59th St., 60637. Tel 312 643-0800. Herman H. Fussler, Librn. Interlibrary loan, copying.

The following materials are restricted, in part.

.1 Burgess, Ernest.
   Papers. Sociologist. Includes materials on urban problems.

.2 Butler, Edward Burgess, 1853-1928. collector.
   Butler-Gunsaulus collection, 16th-20th centuries. 2 ft. Chiefly letters relating to American history, collected by Butler and Frank Wakely Gunsaulus (1856-1921). Represented in the collection are Henry Ward Beecher, John Brown, William Cullen Bryant, George Washington Cable, Ulysses S. Grant, Horace Greeley, Abraham Lincoln, Roger B. Taney, Stephen A. Douglas, Ralph Waldo Emerson, William H. Seward, and Charles Sumner.

.3 Cook, Orator Fuller, 1867-1949.
   Papers, 1891-1945. 33 folders. Botanist and college president. Correspondence, business material, publications, photos, and other papers about Liberia; Liberian folklore; the College of Liberia, of which Cook was president; colonization societies; missionaries in Liberia; and botanical collections and specimens for donation.

.4 Douglas, Stephen Arnold, 1813-61.
   Papers, 1835-61. ca. 23 ft. (ca. 16,000 items). U.S. Senator from Illinois. Mostly letters (1855-61) written to Douglas.

.5 Facts on Film.
   Papers, 1954-67. Microfilm. Contains materials on civil rights and race relations in the South. See Race Relations Information Center, Nashville, Tenn., for a full description.

.6 Lewis, Fielding, 1763?-1834.
   Business records, 1790-1834. ca. 1500 items. Legal documents, tax receipts, inventories, and other papers dealing with the management of Lewis' plantation "Weyanoke," along the James River, Charles City County, Va.

.7 Lincoln Historical Collection, 1608-1918.
   2 ft. Papers relating to Abraham Lincoln and his family, including 40 papers of Lincoln, and letters and documents of his grandfather, father, wife, and sons, together with papers of leaders and participants in affairs before, during, and after the Civil War.

.8 Oldroyd, Osborn Hamiline, 1842-1930.
   Papers, 1818-1930. 5 ft. Historian. Correspondence, scrapbooks, clippings (1827-1910) concerning Lincoln's life and the Civil War, and memorabilia relating to Oldroyd's published works, his collection of Lincolniana, the G.A.R., and Woman's Relief Corps.

.9 Poetry.
   Records, 1912-60. 32 ft. Correspondence, business papers, and mss submitted to the editors. Contains poems and letters of major American poets, including black poets Countee Cullen and Langston Hughes.

.10 Rosenwald, Julius, 1862-1932.
   Papers, 1862-1930. 33 ft. (ca. 30,000 items). Businessman and philanthropist of Chicago. Correspondence; memoranda; speeches; scrapbooks containing clippings, letters, and memorabilia; and other papers relating to Rosenwald's civic and philanthropic activities, including his work with the Planning Commission, and Provident Hospital.

.11 Schilling, George A. b. 1850.
   Papers, 1887-1936. 2 ft. (5 v. and 4 folders). Labor leader. Correspondence, notes, drafts of speeches, pamphlets, and newspaper clippings concerning the Haymarket Riot and the Knights of Labor, among other subjects. Correspondents include William Jennings Bryan.

.12 Wirth, Louis.
   Papers. Sociologist. Includes materials on urban problems.

IL88 UNIVERSITY OF CHICAGO, POPULATION RESEARCH CENTER AND CHICAGO COMMUNITY INVENTORY (1947). 1413 E. 60th St., 60637. Tel 312 643-0800. Philip M. Hauser, Dir. Inquiries answered, consultation.
The long-range interest of the Center is continued study of population and human ecology on the international, national, and local level. The Center provides technical services to research agencies, business firms, civic groups, and community agencies. The library is maintained primarily for Center research staff and class use.
Publ.: Studies, reports, surveys of the present research staff, as well as those from PRC research projects and CCI contracts for statistical services.

IL89 UNIVERSITY OF ILLINOIS AT CHICAGO CIRCLE, CENTER FOR URBAN STUDIES (1967). Box 4348, 60680. Tel 312 663-8722. William L. Garrison, Dir.
The Center for Urban Studies, oriented toward a multidisciplinary approach to the investigation and solution of urban problems, conducts research and seminar programs about, among other topics, problems of education within and for urban environments, urban planning and urban renewal, and the policies and activities of state and local governments.

IL90 UNIVERSITY OF ILLINOIS AT CHICAGO CIRCLE, LIBRARY (1946). P.O. Box 8198, 60680. Tel 312 663-2716. Robert J. Adelsperger, Spec. Collections Librn.
Copying, inquiries answered, referrals made, consultation.

.1 Aldis family.
   Papers, 1872-1954. 6 ft. Papers of Arthur Taylor Aldis (1861-1934), and his son, Graham Aldis (1895- .). Correspondence, reports, lists, minutes, speeches, proceedings, resolutions, bylaws, memoranda, statements, agenda, press releases, questionnaires, receipts, atlases, post cards, notes, petition, fact sheets, clippings, and published material, relating to the activities of Arthur Taylor Aldis as a civic leader, realtor, and philanthropist, his son Graham Aldis, and to Aldis and Company. Also included are minutes, reports, and general information on the activities of the Metropolitan Housing Council of Greater Chicago, the Chicago Land Clearance Commission, federal housing programs, the erection of low-rent housing, the Noland Land Bill (H.R. 12397) of 1919, financial support for charitable, social, and educational institutions, human relations, and the campaign to secure national legislation to prohibit acts of violence against Negroes. Other materials concern the Illinois State Housing Board from the Chicago Land Clearance Commission.

.2 American Friends Service Committee, Chicago Regional Office.
   Papers, 1934-68. 73 ft. Papers pertaining to the philosophy, organization, and activities of the Quakers, including material on labor, education, morality, civil liberties, capital punishment, United Nations, nuclear testing, Gandhi and India, foreign policy of the U.S., immigration, international cooperation, colonialism, discrimination and segregation, economics, Europe, Asia, Africa, and disarmament.

.3 Chicago Conference on Religion and Race.
   Papers, 1967- . .05 ft. Reports, press releases, newsletters, pamphlets, and leaflets. Included are materials pertaining to open housing, religion's role in racial crises, unemployment, and the activities of the National and Chicago Conference on Religion and Race.

.4 Chicago Urban League.
   Papers, 1932-62. 13 ft. Correspondence, proposed programs, memoranda, minutes, agendas, lists, published material, job specifications, photos, press releases, invitations, appraisal sheets, clippings, agreements and drafts of agreements, financial records, announcements, unpublished histories, manuals, notes of conferences and interviews, constitutions and drafts of constitutions, schedules, test scores, and statistical activities, and annual reports of the League pertaining to the activities, personnel, and finances of the Chicago branch; discrimination in employment by Chicago's industry; general policies and practices of the National Urban League; community organizations and League-sponsored activities in Chi-

cago's Negro neighborhoods; vocational guidance conferences for Chicago's Negro youth; and disturbances at Chicago housing projects for Negroes. Also included are minutes of meetings; memoranda; publications; correspondence; announcements; agendas; press releases; monthly, financial, and annual reports of other related organizations.

IL90.5 Chicago Woman's Aid Society.
Papers, 1892-1967. 9.5 ft. Correspondence, annual reports, minutes, bulletins, clippings, notes, and programs pertaining to naturalization, planned parenthood, public health and school administration, race relations, child studies, and summer recreational activities.

.6 Duncan-Maxwell Young Men's Christian Association.
Papers, 1958-67. .05 ft. Memoranda, photos, lists, pamphlets, leaflets, minutes, reports, and programs pertaining to urban renewal projects for the Roosevelt-Halsted area; Camp Duncan, a summer camp for neighborhood children; and the activities and program of the Duncan-Maxwell YMCA center.

.7 Firman House, Chicago, Illinois.
Papers, 1957-66. .05 ft. Reports, constitution, pamphlets, clippings, fliers, and leaflets pertaining to the activities, personnel policies, and programs of the House. The activities concern the maintenance of the Christian Neighborhood House, Fuller Park Area, and the Robert R. Taylor Homes. The House was founded in 1872, as a Congregational Church Mission and Sunday School. Later, under joint Congregational and Presbyterian auspices, the Presbytery of Chicago moved the agency to its present location, 53rd Street. Firman House provides for the maintenance of a Christian Neighborhood House which seeks to improve the social, moral, educational, economic, and spiritual welfare of the people.

.8 Fort Dearborn Project, Chicago, Illinois.
Papers, 1948-59. 4 ft. Correspondence, financial records, photos, reports, minutes, published material, questionnaires, state congressional legislation, proceedings, legal documents and articles of incorporation pertaining to the purpose and achievements of the Fort Dearborn Project Committee, including by-laws, reports, financial records, minutes, and architectural designs of the project; reports on population, housing characteristics, and traffic survey of the Near North Side, the need for the central loop location of government buildings, a consolidated federal courthouse and landing sites for helicopters, controversy over enacting state and city legislation creating a public building commission and its constitutionality, the federal government aiding states financially to eliminate urban blight and the slums, and urban renewal projects in Michigan, New York, Ohio, Pennsylvania, and Texas; correspondence relative to opposition of realtors and business leaders to the Project, coordinating the plans of private developers in creating new residential areas for the Near North Side and Hyde Park communities (Chicago, Ill.) and establishing a linking underground subway system in the "loop."

.9 Gary Urban League.
Papers, 1910-65. 12 ft. Correspondence, reports, and other materials pertaining to urban redevelopment plans for Gary, Ind.; economic conditions of minority groups; race relations; and the activities of the Gary League in particular, the National Urban League, and other Urban Leagues in the U.S.

.10 Greater Lawndale Conservation Commission.
Papers, 1955-67. 5 ft. Reports, fliers, correspondence, lists, memoranda, newsletters, and minutes pertaining to their programs, organization and auxiliary agencies concerned with urban renewal schools, health facilities, and the status of the southside Chicago community.

.11 The Hyde Park Neighborhood Club, Chicago, Illinois.
Papers, 1909-66. .5 ft. Memoranda, reprints, fliers, announcements, and schedules of the Club (1958-66); reports on the study of treatment cases served through the Hyde Park Youth Pro-

ject and cooperating agencies (February, 1961), volunteers in services to youth and families (1965), after-school study centers (1964); and building a new Hyde Park Neighborhood Club.

.12 Illinois Commission on Employment of Youth.
Records, 1934-62. 7 ft. Correspondence, annual reports, speeches, reports, financial records, statistics, published material, by-laws, lists, Illinois State and congressional bills, minutes, surveys, questionnaires, memoranda, and other papers, relating to the activities of the Commission and to the establishment of standards for youth employment and certification, the securing of protective child labor legislation, especially for pinsetters and caddies, youth and work camps, hard-to-reach youth, and migratory labor in Illinois and Minnesota.

.13 Illinois Commission on Human Relations.
Papers, 1963-66. .05 ft. Reports, leaflets, and lists pertaining to local fair housing ordinances in Illinois; curriculum resource materials, race prejudice; and suburban Chicago residential desegregation (1966).

.14 The Illinois Humane Society.
Papers, 1879-1953. 143 ft. Case records, some correspondence, and annual reports concerning the Society's investigation of cases of cruelty to animals and children and subsequent court action instituted by the Society. The bulk of the Society's papers are in the Illinois State Historical Library in Springfield, Ill.

.15 Jane Dent Home for Aged Colored People.
Papers, 1898-1955. .5 ft. Annual reports (1898-1955), directory, programs, and minutes (1921-27) of the Home pertaining to the relief of old Negro people, without regard to creed.

.16 National Lutheran Council, Division of American Missions.
Papers, 1942-66. 2.3 ft. Founded 1942, the Division was the successor to the Lutheran Home Mission Council of America. Materials on the Christian approach to Jewish people; race relations in the U.S.; migratory labor; mission workers on Indian reservations; housing for minorities; nonsegregated housing; Dr. Martin Luther King, Jr.; immigration service committee; urban and rural church planning; education and desegregation; and other related subjects.

.17 Negro History Pamphlet Collection.
1807-71. Annual reports, pertaining to the New England Anti-Slavery Society, abolitionists, American slavery, the fugitive slaves and negotiations with Great Britain, John Brown and other related subjects. In addition, the collection contains speeches on the above subjects by Benjamin Wade, William H. Seward, Charles Sumner, Henry Clay, Thomas Hart Benton, Schuyler Colfax, Thomas Corwin, John Bell, George S. Boutwell, F.T. Frelinghuysen, William Lloyd Garrison, Horace Mann, Henry Wilson, and many others.

.18 Negro Literature Collection.
Miscellaneous. ca. 100 items. Books, pamphlets, broadsides of current black writing published by private or underground presses and consisting largely of poetry by blacks.

.19 North Shore Summer Housing Project, Chicago, Illinois.
Papers, 1965-66. .05 ft. Mimeograph material pertaining to the open housing project where North Shore realtors were asked to give equal service and treatment to all homeseekers in order to sell on a nondiscriminatory basis.

.20 Olander, Victor A., 1873-1949.
Papers, 1873-1949. 24 ft. Secretary-treasurer of the Illinois State Federation of Labor from 1914; secretary-treasurer of the Seamen's International Union of America (1925-36); and director-secretary of radio station WCFL, Inc., until 1946. Papers pertaining to the activities of the Illinois Federation of Labor including relations between labor and management, the injunction-limitation bill (1915-26), the Henrici Waitresses Case (1914), Taft Vale Case (1919), and others; Illinois Constitutional conventions; the Thirteenth Amendment (involuntary servitude) and its relation to military

conscription; legal powers of school boards (1939-46); race riots in East St. Louis, Ill. (1917); and the Chicago Housing Committee (1926-27). Another segment of the Olander papers is on file at Chicago Historical Society.

.21 Pamphlet collection.
1908-64. Pamphlets pertaining to the economic conditions of the South, racial desegregation and integration, urban problems, the Communist and the Negro, and the Ku Klux Klan.

.22 Payne, Aaron.
Papers, 1943-66. .05 ft. Lawyer, assistant prosecutor, assistant corporation counsel for the city of Chicago, and arbitrator for the Illinois Industrial Commission. Clippings, correspondence, speech, and photos, pertaining to the civil liberties cases of Nat King Cole, Mr. and Mrs. Eddie Mallory, and others; urban renewal projects; and correspondence with Richard H. Cain, Abraham L. Marovitz, Otto Kerner, Ralph H. Metcalfe, Olander W. Wilson, and Richard J. Daley.

.23 Phillis Wheatley Home for Girls, Chicago, Illinois.
Papers, 1963-66. .05 ft. By-laws, leaflets, fliers, programs, certificates, and reports. The Home was established (1906) to maintain a home to safeguard and protect young Negro women who arrived in Chicago as strangers, to surround them with Christian influences, and to aid them in securing employment.

.24 Rich, Adena Miller, 1888-1967.
Papers, 1881-1966. 7 ft. Jane Addams' successor as head resident of Hull-House, Chicago (1935-37); an authority on immigration and public welfare; founder and director until 1954, of the Immigrants' Protective League; and one of the founders of the Illinois League of Women Voters. Correspondence, clippings, notes, calling and greeting cards, invitations, lists, personal histories, announcements, reprints, photographs, programs, addresses, resolutions, published material, annual reports, studies, and year books pertaining to social hygiene; immigration and naturalization questions; public welfare in the State of Illinois; prenatal care in Chicago; the Cook County, Ill., prison system (1922); the appointment of Mrs. Rich to the head residency of Hull-House; Julia Lathrop (1858-1932) as president of the Illinois League of Women Voters; and the 1939 and 1940 White House Conference on ''Children in a Democracy''; the career of Jane Addams (1860-1935); the International Conference on Social Work at Frankfurt, Germany (1932); Mrs. Rich's activities and work at Hull-House, with specific emphasis on the years she was head resident; the restoration of Hull-House as a historical monument.

.25 Sierra Leone Colonial Government Collection.
Papers, 1792-1825. 16 items. Ms items pertaining to the public and private papers of British officials in Sierra Leone reflecting the establishment and growth of the colony; the geographic and ethnological descriptions of Sierra Leone and neighboring territories; and the attempted suppression of the West African slave trade. Sierra Leone, on the West African coast, was established by the British (1787) for the purpose of resettling former slaves.

.26 Slavery collection.
Miscellaneous. ca. 1750's through Civil War. ca. 325 v. Materials on various aspects of slavery, with particular emphasis on the early British, American, and French anti-slavery movements. Includes abolitionist tracts, committee and society reports, speeches, slave-trade statistics and accounts, personal narratives, descriptions of voyages and expeditions, and official government documents.

.27 Student Nonviolent Coordinating Committee, The Chicago SNCC Freedom Center.
Papers, 1964-65. 5 ft. Mimeographed material relating to the purpose and activities of the Chicago SNCC Freedom Center, including the war on poverty program; the housing problem; the direct action projects; and the programs of the youth council.

.28 The Travelers Aid Society of Chicago.
Papers, 1914-61. 6.5 ft. Correspondence, memoranda, lists, agendas, minutes, articles of incorporation, salary scales, financial records, tally sheets, constitutions, by-laws, manuals, case histories, reports, and published material of the Travelers Aid Society pertaining to aiding new immigrants to Chicago, Ill.; assisting old travelers in terminals and railroad stations; locating relatives of runaway children; the financing and personnel practices of private social work agencies; the work of United Service Organization, Inc., National Travelers Aid Society of New York City, and Grant Hospital, Chicago, Ill. These papers also include minutes, programs, annual reports and published material of other related organizations.

.29 United Service Employees Union, Local 329.
Papers, 1941-61. 8 ft. Correspondence, minutes, legal and financial records, and statistical reports pertaining to the growth and internal operations of the United Service Employees Union; disputes within the Union's international organization; organizational drives in Chicago's food and other industries; and the association of the local with various civil liberties and rights groups. Sidney Lens, leader of Local 329, has involved the local with such organizations as the NAACP and the Chicago Committee for the Defense of Labor Victims of France.

.30 Wabash Young Men's Christian Association.
Papers, 1931-58. 1.5 ft. Papers pertaining to the Association's activities and programs consist of photos, minutes, published material, reports, clippings, and scrapbooks. The Wabash YMCA serves a predominantly Negro community.

.31 Young Men's Christian Association of Chicago, Illinois.
Papers, 1940. .05 ft. Notebook containing information on the history, development, and structure of the YMCA of Chicago.

IL91 URBAN RESEARCH CORPORATION (1968). 5464 S. Shore Dr., 60615. Tel 312 955-3050. John Naisbitt, Pres.
The Corporation researches and publishes information concerning urban economic and social development. Its services are especially directed to meeting the needs of: (1) corporations which are interested in participating in the effort to improve and stabilize urban conditions; (2) educational institutions, particularly universities, which require information and services as part of curricula and in their own efforts to identify solutions to urban problems; (3) federal, state and municipal government agencies which develop programs to cope with the increasingly complex urban problems; and (4) foundations and private social institutions. The company's Education Division helps large city school systems to plan and organize experimental urban-oriented programs for primary and secondary education.
Publ.: Urban Crisis Monitor, weekly information service on urban affairs; Urban Enterprise, biweekly newsletter on minority economic development; Training the Hardcore, 12 v. manual for program design and training; Reports, guidelines, studies, and other papers concerning urban problems.

.1 Urban affairs data bank.
The data bank classifies into more than 200 catagories information on contemporary urban conditions throughout the U.S., and serves as the basis for research projects and Corporation publications.

IL92 URBAN TRAINING CENTER FOR CHRISTIAN MISSION (1965). 40 N. Ashland Ave., 60607. Tel 312 829-1272. Richard S. Gordon, Pres.
The Center trains ministers, black and white, from all denominations for effective action on urban problems, and provides fellowships and internships for black ministers.

IL93 W ADVERTISING AGENCY (1968). 757 W. 79th St., 60620. Tel 312 994-0988. Donald C. Walker, Pres. Copying, inquiries answered, referrals made, consultation.

W Advertising Agency compiles and distributes a
telephone directory which lists black-owned or operated businesses, non-profit organizations and agencies
which are considered beneficial to the black community, and emergency numbers of police and fire departments and hospitals located in the black areas of
Chicago.
Publ.: Black Book Directory, annually.

IL94   W.E.B. DuBOIS CLUB. 180 N. Wacker Dr., 60606. Jarvis
        Tyner, Nat. Chmn.

IL95   THE WOODLAWN ORGANIZATION (TWO). 1135 E. 63rd
        St., 60637. Tel 312 288-5840. E. Duke McNeil, Pres.,
        and Leon Finney, Dir.
        TWO, a grass-roots neighborhood organization com-
        posed of 115 block clubs, civic groups, tenant associa-
        tions, welfare unions, and church organizations, is
        concerned with neighborhood improvement through
        self-help efforts in housing, schools, consumer prac-
        tices, social welfare, civil rights, community mainte-
        nance, and health. TWO seeks to develop self-
        determination on the part of the residents of the pre-
        dominantly Negro community, who have cooperated and
        participated in voter registration campaigns, anti-slum
        drives, education, on-the-job training, community
        clean-up campaigns, and community indictment of the
        public schools for deliberate segregation tactics.

IL96   YOUNG MEN'S CHRISTIAN ASSOCIATION (YMCA) OF
        METROPOLITAN CHICAGO (1858). 19 S. LaSalle St.,
        60603. Tel 312 222-8150. John O. Root, Gen. Exec.
        Inquiries answered, consultation.
        The YMCA works to "aid in the development of Chris-
        tian standards of living, conduct, and life purpose in its
        members and constituency."
        Publ.: Viewpoint Magazine; Annual Report.

        .1 Young Men's Christian Association of Metropolitan
            Chicago.
            Files. Annual meeting speech texts; annual re-
            ports; news clippings; Viewpoint articles concern-
            ing racism, black pride, and related subjects; and
            informational materials concerning urban prob-
            lems, equal opportunities in employment and edu-
            cation, and black entrepreneurship. Research re-
            quests should be addressed to the Divisional Di-
            rector for Urban Action, YMCA of Metropolitan
            Chicago.

IL97   YOUNG WOMEN'S CHRISTIAN ASSOCIATION (YWCA) OF
        METROPOLITAN CHICAGO (1866). 1001 N. Dearborn
        St., 60610. Tel 312 944-4380. Joan P. Brown, Dir. of
        Human Rels. Inquiries answered, referrals made,
        consultation.
        The YWCA brings together women of diverse experi-
        ences and faiths in order that they might gain deeper
        understanding and relationships, and to work for
        peace, justice, freedom and dignity for all people. It
        conducts community planning and participation projects
        in the areas of housing, education, employment, and
        human relations education, and offers technical assis-
        tance to "indigenous" community organizations.
        Publ.: Progress, 8 issues per year.

DeKALB

IL98   NORTHERN ILLINOIS UNIVERSITY (1899), SWEN FRANK-
        LIN PARSON LIBRARY (1942). 60115. Tel 815 753-
        1094. Clyde C. Walton, Dir., Univ. Libraries. Interli-
        brary loan, bibliographies prepared, literature
        searches, copying, typing, inquiries answered, refer-
        rals made, consultation. The various services are of-
        fered on a limited basis.
        Publ.: A Student Guide to Black Studies.

        .1 Black Studies collection.
            Reprints, microfilm, and microcards. Includes
            Negro newspapers on microfilm photoduplicated by
            the Library of Congress (1953); the Oberlin Col-
            lege Library of Slavery Pamphlets (1776- .) on
            microcards; the American Periodical Series
            (1800-50) on microfilm; and the British Parlia-
            mentary Papers on the Slave Trade in reprint,
            (1810-60).

        .2 Facts on Film.
            Papers, 1954-67. Microfilm. Contains materials
            on civil rights and race relations in the South. See
            Race Relations Information Center, Nashville,
            Tenn., for a full description.

EAST ST. LOUIS

IL99   CONGRESS OF RACIAL EQUALITY (CORE). 541 Veronica
        Place, 62201. Tel 618 271-8377. Omar Canty, Jr., Dir.

IL100   URBAN LEAGUE OF MADISON AND ST. CLAIR COUNTIES.
        c/o Mr. William Boyne, Metro East Journal, 425
        Missouri Ave., 62201. Tel 618 874-7440. William
        Boyne, Dir.

        .1 Urban League of Madison and St. Clair Counties.
            Files. Correspondence, minutes of meetings, fi-
            nancial records, studies, reports, and other mate-
            rials dealing with the aims, history, and programs
            of the League.

EDWARDSVILLE

IL101   SOUTHERN ILLINOIS UNIVERSITY, EDWARDSVILLE CAM-
        PUS (1957), LOVEJOY LIBRARY (1965). 62025. Tel
        618 692-2711. John C. Abbott, Dir. Interlibrary loan,
        copying, inquiries answered, referrals made, consulta-
        tion, audio visual materials.

        .1 Anti-Slavery Propaganda Collection.
            ca. 2500 pamphlets. Microcards of originals lo-
            cated in the Oberlin College Library. See Oberlin
            College Library, Oberlin, Ohio; or Lost Cause
            Press (publisher), Louisville, Ky., for more com-
            plete description.
        .2 Loosley Civil War collection.
            Papers. ca. 100 items. Letters of Edwin Loosley,
            DuQoin, Ill., private in the Union Army, 81st Divi-
            sion. "Informative and lively accounts" of Civil
            War activities, including a description of the 81st's
            part in the Vicksburg campaign.
        .3 Negro newspapers collection.
            Microfilm copies of various Negro newspapers.
        .4 Radical literature collection.
            Miscellaneous, 1945- . Pamphlets, leaflets,
            magazines, newspapers, books, and other mate-
            rials from radical organizations with leftist or
            rightist leanings. Deals with the struggles of
            black people and movements such as Garveyism,
            non-violent protest and Black Power, and includes
            material by other ethnic minorities as well as
            extremist groups.

EVANSTON

IL102   EVANSTON HUMAN RELATIONS COMMISSION (1961).
        1806 Maple Ave., 60201. Tel 312 475-3100. Stephen
        W. Graves, Acting Exec. Dir.
        The Commission encourages understanding, tolerance,
        responsibility and cooperation among all groups and
        individuals in the Evanston community and conducts
        programs in the areas of housing, education, employ-
        ment, human relations and social attitudes. Formerly
        Evanston Community Relations Commission.
        Publ.: Director's Notes, bi-monthly.

IL103   NATIONAL MERIT SCHOLARSHIP CORPORATION (NMSC),
        NATIONAL ACHIEVEMENT SCHOLARSHIP PRO-
        GRAM. 990 Grove St., 60201. Tel 312 869-5100.
        Hermon Dunlap Smith, Chmn.
        NMSC works to identify, honor, and encourage superior
        academic achievement through the awarding of college
        scholarships to outstanding Negro students selected in
        national competition.

IL103a NORTHWESTERN UNIVERSITY, CENTER FOR URBAN AF-
        FAIRS (1968). 2040 Sheridan Rd., 60201. Tel 312 492-
        3395. Raymond W. Mack, Dir.
        The Center coordinates the University's scholarly
        activities in the area of urbanism; studies, through an
        interdisciplinary approach, methods of dealing with

urban problems and of developing community laboratories; and initiates new teaching, research, and policy studies for the University curriculum. Some of the interdisciplinary programs, in cooperation with the city of Chicago, are a research analysis of institutional racial discrimination in Chicago, a linking of the University's medical clinics with a legal aid clinic, and a planning study of black entrepreneurship in the ghetto.

IL104   NORTHWESTERN UNIVERSITY (1851), LIBRARY (1856). 1937 Sheridan Rd., 60201. Tel 312 492-5217. Thomas R. Buckman, Univ. Librn. Interlibrary loan, bibliographies prepared, literature searches, copying, inquiries answered.
Publ.: Catalog of the African Collection, Northwestern University Library (1962, 2 v.); Joint Acquisitions List of Africana (JALA), bi-monthly.

.1   Melville J. Herskovits Library of African Studies. Miscellaneous. ca. 50,000 items. Books, periodicals, newspapers, archival materials, mss, maps, phonograph records, photographs, and language tapes. Material about Africa, with strong holdings in anthropology, art, economics, geography, health and hygiene, history, law, political science, psychology, sociology, and language and linguistics. Among the collections are the following:

.2   — Church Missionary Society.
Archives, 1799-1910. Microfilmed copy of records pertaining to Africa.
.3   — Herskovits, Melville J.
Papers, 1927-63. 57 vf. Anthropologist and author. Closed until 1988.
.4   — Presbyterian Historical Society, Philadelphia, Pa.
Records, 1843-54. Records of Commodore Matthew Perry, first commander of the African Squadron sent to suppress the slave trade, including microfilmed section of U.S. National Archives relating to Africa, such as the consular reports and letter books.
.5   Wright, Richard.
Papers. Ms of Black Power.
.6   Ephemeral Literature of Modern Radical Movements. Materials. Contains a limited, but growing collection of materials concerning radical black organizations such as the Black Panthers.

IL105   NORTHWESTERN UNIVERSITY, MEDILL SCHOOL OF JOURNALISM, URBAN JOURNALISM CENTER. 60201. Tel 312 492-5328. I.W. Cole, Dir.
The Center works to help local news media discharge their responsibility of bringing about public understanding of urban problems, in order that the public may make intelligent decisions in the solving of these problems. The Center has studied and reported on several large cities in terms of their cultural, political, social, and physical environments, including in some cases an analysis of racial problems. Studies are available for Pittsburgh, Indianapolis, Minneapolis, Denver and Seattle.
Publ.: Studies, reports.

JACKSONVILLE

IL106   MacMURRAY COLLEGE (1846), HENRY PFEIFFER LIBRARY. 62650. Tel 217 245-6151. Victoria E. Hargrave, Librn. Interlibrary loan, copying, typing, inquiries answered.

.1   Martin Luther King, Jr. Memorial Collection. Miscellaneous. ca. 200 items. Contains materials pertaining to Afro-American history, biographies of famous Negroes, and writings by Negroes, past and present.

MACOMB

IL107   WESTERN ILLINOIS UNIVERSITY, MEMORIAL LIBRARY. 61455. Tel 309 899-3521. Donald S. MacVean, Dir. Interlibrary loan.

.1   Facts on Film.
Papers, 1954-67. Microfilm. Contains materials on civil rights and race relations in the South. See

Race Relations Information Center, Nashville, Tenn., for a full description.

NORMAL

IL108   ILLINOIS STATE UNIVERSITY AT NORMAL (1857), MILNER LIBRARY. 61761. Tel 309 453-2213. Joe W. Kraus, Dir.

.1   Livingston Collection on Intergroup Relations.

PEORIA

IL109   PEORIA COMMISSION ON HUMAN RELATIONS (1961). Room 404, 419 Fulton, 61602. Tel 309 673-3763. Valeska S. Hinton, Exec. Secy.
The Commission investigates reports of civil rights violations; encourages equal opportunity in employment, housing, public accommodations and education; and attempts to educate the community and create understanding and channels of communication within it.
Publ.: Human Relations Here and There, quarterly newsletter.

IL110   PEORIA CONFERENCE ON RELIGION AND RACE. 2508 N. Sheridan Rd., 61604. Tel 309 688-8501. Rev. Clark E. Taylor, Dir. of Urban Work.

IL111   TRI-COUNTY URBAN LEAGUE (1964). 209 N. Franklin St., 61602. Tel 309 673-7474. Frank Campbell, Exec. Dir.

RIVERSIDE

IL112   ALLIANCE FOR FIRST AMENDMENT FREEDOMS (1963). P.O. Box 48, 60546. Tel 312 482-7234. Charles Frederick, Exec. Secy. Literature searches, inquiries answered, referrals made.
The Alliance collects, cards and presents information on First Amendment and civil rights cases, and points out to the general public specifically what their First-Amendment and civil rights are.
Publ.: Bulletins, occasionally.

.1   Alliance for First Amendment Freedoms.
Files, 1963- . Records, reports, and other extensive file materials regarding court cases involving First Amendment or civil rights; collection of major publications of civil rights organizations (1963- .); and some additional newsletters, bulletins, and newspapers (1963- .). Restricted.

SPRINGFIELD

IL113   FAIR EMPLOYMENT PRACTICES COMMISSION (FEPC), REGIONAL OFFICE. 103 Centennial Bldg., 62706. Tel 217 525-2000.

IL114   ILLINOIS COMMISSION ON HUMAN RELATIONS (1965). 105 E. Monroe, 62706. Tel 217 525-2964. Ivan R. Levin, Dep. Dir. Bibliographies prepared, typing, inquiries answered, referrals made, consultation.
The Commission seeks to eliminate discrimination based on race, religion or national ancestry through activities in the areas of housing, education, public accommodations, human relations education, governmental operation, and police-community relations.

IL115   ILLINOIS STATE ARCHIVES (1921). Spring St., 62706. Tel 217 525-4866. Theodore J. Cassady, Asst. State Archivist.

.1   Adjutant General's Office, State of Illinois.
Files. Contains the muster books of 29th Infantry Regiment, U.S.C.T.

IL116   ILLINOIS STATE HISTORICAL LIBRARY (1889). Old State Capitol Complex, 62706. Tel 217 525-4836. William K. Alderfer, State Historian. Interlibrary loan, bibliographies prepared, literature searches, inquiries answered, referrals made, consultation.
Publ.: The Journal of the Illinois State Historical Society, quarterly.

.1 Banks, Nathaniel P.
    Papers, 1840-94. ca. 2300 items. Governor of
    Massachusetts, U.S. Representative, railroad
    executive, Civil War officer.

.2 Griffin, John A., 1842-1902.
    Papers, 1860-69. 396 items. Union Army soldier.
    Diary (1862-63) kept as a private in Company D,
    17th Illinois Infantry, and correspondence, in-
    cluding letters from soldiers in the 53rd U.S.
    Colored Infantry.

.3 Hinch, Benjamin P.
    Correspondence, 1838-56. 102 items. Postmaster
    at New Haven, Ill., and member of the 19th Illinois
    General Assembly. Letters include those from
    Hinch's brother, H. Hinch in St. Francisville, La.,
    concerning his term of mayor of St. Francisville
    during the 1830's, flatboatmen, rioting among the
    Irish, fears of Negro insurrections, and economic
    and social conditions in West Feliciana Parish, La.

.4 Papers relating to Abraham Lincoln.
    Among collections containing materials of Lin-
    coln's political career, personal associates and
    his biographers are the following:

.5 — Abraham Lincoln Association.
    Files, 1909-52. ca. 5000 items. Correspon-
    dence about Lincoln with collectors, writers,
    and artists and the recollections of persons
    associated with Lincoln.

.6 — Beveridge, Albert J.
    Papers, 1924-26. ca. 60 items. U.S. Senator
    and Lincoln biographer. Materials concerning
    Lincoln's biography.

.7 — Commissioners' Court Records, Sangamon
    County, Illinois.
    Papers, 1821-40. 4 v. Materials which cover
    the period of Lincoln's residence in New
    Salem, Ill.

.8 — Hay, John Milton.
    Papers, 1856-1905. ca. 700 items. Lincoln's
    secretary and biographer, poet, diplomat,
    Secretary of State. Includes notes and other
    materials of his collaboration on a Lincoln
    biography with John G. Nicolay.

.9 — Hay, John Milton and Stuart, John T.
    Papers, 1817-91. ca. 500 items. Materials of
    Milton Hay (Illinois legislator and lawyer) and
    John T. Stuart (law partner of Lincoln, Black
    Hawk War officer, U.S. Representative).

.10 — Hayne, William.
    Papers, 1855-1911. ca. 60 items. Physician,
    friend of Lincoln.

.11 — Henry, Anson J.
    Papers, 1852-65. ca. 23 items, and 1 v.
    Physician to Lincoln and his wife, surveyor.

.12 — Lincoln, Abraham.
    Papers, 1809-65. ca. 6200 items. Originals
    and photostat copies. Lincoln's papers con-
    cerning his career.

.13 — Lincoln, Mary Todd.
    Papers, 1848-80. ca. 128 items. Wife of
    Abraham Lincoln.

.14 — National Lincoln Monument Association.
    Records, 1865-95. 1 v. and ca. 3000 items.
    Papers concerning the erection of the Lincoln
    Monument at Springfield, Ill.

.15 — Nicolay, John G.
    Papers, 1886-90. ca. 5800 items. Lincoln's
    biographer. Materials concerning the life of
    Lincoln.

.16 — Stevens, Frank E. collector.
    Miscellaneous, 1821-70. ca. 400 items.
    Materials concerning the Black Hawk War,
    Lincoln, and Douglas.

.17 — Swett, Leonard.
    Papers, 1847-90. ca. 100 items. Illinois
    lawyer, friend of Lincoln.

.18 — Weik, Jesse W.
    Papers, 1828-1929. ca. 1000 items.
    Lincoln biographer.

.19 — Welles, Gideon.
    Papers, 1860-61. ca. 30 items. Newspaper
    editor, Secretary of Navy.

IL117 SPRINGFIELD HUMAN RELATIONS COMMISSION (1948).
    Room 208, Municipal Bldg., 62701. Tel 217 525-0676.
    Mrs. Glenn Kniss, Exec. Dir.
    The Commission investigates complaints, seeks con-
    ciliation, and promotes better understanding among all
    groups and peoples in the community.

IL118 SPRINGFIELD URBAN LEAGUE, INC. Suite 2, 322½ S.
    Sixth St., 62701. Tel 217 522-8411. Comer L. Cox,
    Exec. Dir.

.1 Springfield Urban League.
    Files. Correspondence, minutes of meetings, fi-
    nancial records, studies, reports, and other mate-
    rials dealing with the aims, history, and programs
    of the League.

URBANA

IL119 ERIC CLEARINGHOUSE ON EARLY CHILDHOOD EDUCA-
    TION (1967). 805 W. Pennsylvania Ave., 61801. Tel
    217 333-1386. Brian W. Carss, Dir. Bibliographies
    prepared, literature searches, copying, typing, in-
    quiries answered, referrals made, consultation.
    The Clearinghouse will act as an information analysis
    center for educational practitioners and researchers
    in the field of early childhood education. It will also
    prepare periodic non-technical summaries and in-
    terpretative discussions of current research for Head
    Start and similar operations.
    Publ.: Bibliographies, occasional papers, pamphlets.

.1 ERIC (Educational Research Information Center)
    Clearinghouse on Early Childhood Education.
    Files, ca. 1963- . ca. 170 items. Microfilm.
    Articles, pamphlets, speeches, surveys, reports,
    and other documents concerning racial and mi-
    nority group problems, with emphasis on education.

IL120 UNIVERSITY OF ILLINOIS AT URBANA-CHAMPAIGN, BU-
    REAU OF COMMUNITY PLANNING (1934). 1202 W.
    California, 61801. Tel 217 333-0790. Eric C. Freund,
    Dir.
    The Bureau works to aid in community problem-
    solving through providing public services and activities
    to stimulate public interest and action in planning, re-
    search in the field of urban and regional planning, and
    assisting communities in formulating effective planning
    policies.

IL121 UNIVERSITY OF ILLINOIS AT URBANA-CHAMPAIGN
    (1867), LIBRARY (1867). 61803. Tel 217 333-0790.
    Robert B. Downs, Dean of Library Admin. Interlibrary
    loan, copying, typing, inquiries answered, referrals
    made.

.1 Baskette Collection of Freedom of Expression.
    Miscellaneous, 16th century- . ca. 10,000 v.
    Books, periodicals and pamphlets. Restricted.

.2 Facts on Film.
    Papers, 1954-67. Microfilm. Contains materials
    on civil rights and race relations in the South. See
    Race Relations Information Center, Nashville,
    Tenn., for a full description.

.3 Garner, James Wilford, 1871-1938.
    Papers, 1830-1942. 3 ft. Professor of political
    science at the University of Illinois. Correspon-
    dence; mss on the Civil War, Abraham Lincoln,
    among others; reprints of publications relating to
    Reconstruction in Mississippi; and other reprints,
    addresses, and memorabilia. Restricted.

.4 Johnston, Wayne Andrew, 1897-1967.
    Papers, 1945-67. ca. 9 ft. President of the Illi-
    nois Central Railroad and member and president
    of the board of trustees of the University of Illi-
    nois. Correspondence, reports, and memoranda,
    relating chiefly to university affairs, including the
    W.E.B. DuBois Club, and racial discrimination on
    campus. Restricted.

.5 Lee, Albert, 1874-1948.
    Papers, 1920-42. 3 ft. Chief clerk of the presi-
    dent's office (University of Illinois). Correspon-
    dence, programs, notes, and memoranda, relating
    to Negro students, Negro Masonic organizations,

the African Methodist Episcopal Church, and related topics. Restricted.

.6 Randall, James Garfield, 1881-1953.
Papers, 1903-53. 6 ft. Professor of history at University of Illinois. Correspondence; mss of writings, notes; drafts, proofs, and finished copies of monographs; and other records and documents. Mss include Civil War and Reconstruction (1937). Also in the collection are comments (1935-36) of Earl M. Coulter, Roy F. Nichols, James L. Sellers, Fred A. Shannon, Charles S. Sydnor, and others on Randall's ms of Civil War and Reconstruction, and material relating to historical subjects, particularly Abraham Lincoln, the Civil War, and Reconstruction. Restricted.

.7 Tiebout, Harry M.
Papers, 1941-63. ca. 3 ft. Professor of philosophy at the University of Illinois. Correspondence, photos, newspaper clippings, pamphlets, handbills, reprints, news releases, newsletters, and affidavits, concerning racial discrimination in newspaper advertising, housing, Illinois Union facilities, McKinley Hospital, restaurants, theaters, public recreational facilities, university and community employment, barbershops, fraternities and sororities, and the organization of student-faculty-community groups to oppose discrimination. Groups represented include the Champaign-Urbana branch and the University of Illinois chapter of the NAACP, and the Student-Community Interracial Committee. Restricted.

.8 U.S. Congress. House
Memorials and petitions from the Illinois country, 1803-20 93 items. Photocopies. Memorials, petitions and other communications to the House of Representatives, chiefly from people in the Illinois country on the separation of Illinois from Indiana Territory, land grants and titles, and slavery. Restricted.

WAUKEGAN

IL122 LAKE COUNTY URBAN LEAGUE (1967). 309 Washington St., 60085. Vernon L. Barkstall, Exec. Dir. Referrals made, consultation.

IL123 WAUKEGAN PUBLIC LIBRARY (1898). 128 N. County St., 60085. Tel 312 623-2041. Ruth W. Gregory, Librn. Interlibrary loan, bibliographies prepared, literature searches, copying, inquiries answered, referrals made.

.1 Charles Morrison Memorial Collection.
Miscellaneous. ca. 250 items. Secondary material on human relations for boys and girls.

WHEATON

IL124 WHEATON COLLEGE, LIBRARY (1860). 501 E. Seminary Ave., 60187. Tel 312 628-5102. June Weitting, Acting Librn. Interlibrary loan, copying.

.1 Blanchard, Jonathan, 1811-92.
Papers, 1831-91. ca. 200 items. Presbyterian minister, abolitionist, and president of Knox College, Galesburg, Ill., and Wheaton College, Wheaton, Ill. Correspondence, diaries, and sermons, relating to education, Biblical exposition, the Midwest before and after the Civil War, and antilodge, antislavery, and reform movements, Restricted.

WILMETTE

IL125 NORTH AMERICAN BAHA'I, OFFICE FOR HUMAN RIGHTS (NABOHR) (1968). 112 Linden Ave., 60091. Tel 312 268-4397. Juliette B. Buford, Dir. Inquiries answered. The Office was established to promote International Human Rights Year (1968) and human rights programs of the Baha'i faith in North America.
Publ.: NABOHR Newsletter; Reports concerning International Human Rights Year.

INDIANA

ANDERSON

IN1 ANDERSON URBAN LEAGUE (1926). 631 Citizens Bank Bldg., 46016. Tel 317 642-4971. William B. Harper. Exec. Dir.

BLOOMINGTON

IN2 INDIANA UNIVERSITY, DEPARTMENT OF FINE ARTS, COMMITTEE FOR THE DEVELOPMENT OF ART IN NEGRO COLLEGES (CDANC) (1964). 47405. Tel 812 332-0211. Albert Elsen, Co-Chmn.
CDANC represents professionals from various branches of the art world, including teachers, critics, art historians, museum and gallery personnel, painters, sculptors, publishers who serve as an advisory rather than fund-raising group, and operates mainly through semi-autonomous subcommittees. It aids in development of art in predominantly Negro colleges, inquires into actual teaching conditions and policies, coordinates activities affecting art teaching in colleges, gathers and disseminates information, and creates contacts between Negro art departments and qualified advisers, and serves as arranger for historian-consultant programs and summer teaching institute.

.1 Committee for the Development of Art in Negro Colleges (CDANC).
Files, 1964- . Correspondence, minutes of meetings, financial records, studies, reports, and other materials dealing with the aims, history, and programs of CDANC.

EAST CHICAGO

IN3 HUMAN RELATIONS COMMISSION (1966). 4225 Indianapolis Blvd., 46312. Tel 219 398-4200. Leo A. Miller, Exec. Dir.
The Commission works to promote equality of opportunity for all citizens; to promote understanding, respect and good will; to provide procedures to deal with grievances and channels of communication; to prevent violence and reduce tensions; to facilitate orderly social change; to serve as a source of objective information. Formerly, Fair Employment Practice Commission (1951).

ELKHART

IN4 ELKHART URBAN LEAGUE. 209 S. Second St., 46514. Tel 219 522-3350. Simon P. Montgomery, Exec. Dir.

.1 Elkhart Urban League.
Files. Correspondence, minutes of meetings, financial records, studies, reports, and other materials dealing with the history, aims and programs of the League.

EVANSVILLE

IN5 MAYOR'S COMMISSION ON HUMAN RELATIONS (1949). Room 133, Civic Center Complex, 47708. Tel 812 426-5474. Mrs. Janet R. Walker, Exec. Dir.
The Commission works to see that all citizens have equal rights. Program areas include housing, education, employment, human relations, public accommodations, social attitudes, police-community relations, communication.
Publ.: Annual Report; Reverberations, monthly; Brochures, reports.

IN6 UNIVERSITY OF EVANSVILLE, IGLEHEART CENTER FOR THE STUDY OF URBAN AFFAIRS (1968). Box 329, 47701. Tel 812 479-2377. Richard C. Hall, Dir. Interlibrary loan, copying, inquiries answered.
The Center seeks to develop academic programs that will acquaint undergraduate students of professional objectives with the realities of urban life. The local

community will be used as a laboratory in conducting research on contemporary urban problems. The Center also provides consulting and research services to the public and governmental agencies of Evansville and environs, utilizing the resources of the University and faculty.
Publ.: Reports and studies.

.1 Urban Affairs Collection.
Subject areas include housing and employment problems as affected by race.

IN7   WILLARD LIBRARY. 21 First Ave., 47710. Tel 812 425-5591. Marcia Wheeler, Librn.

.1 Slavery Collection.

FERDINAND

IN8   ST. BENEDICT COLLEGE AND CONVENT OF THE IMMACULATE CONCEPTION (1867), ST. BENEDICT COLLEGE LIBRARY (1946). 47532. Tel 812 367-1411. Sister Mary Angela Sasse, Librn. Interlibrary loan, bibliographies prepared, literature searches, copying, typing, inquiries answered, referrals made, consultation.

.1 Area Race Relations Clipping Collection.
Newspaper clippings, 1966- . News relating to race relations around Ferdinand, Ind. Restricted.
.2 Elementary School Textbook Collection.
Current textbooks. Collection demonstrates the increasing representation of Negroes in the illustrations of elementary school textbooks. Restricted.

FORT WAYNE

IN9   FORT WAYNE PUBLIC LIBRARY (1895). 900 Webster St., 46802. Tel 219 742-7241. Fred J. Reynolds, Head Librn. Interlibrary loan, bibliographies prepared, literature searches, copying, typing, inquiries answered, taping facilities.

.1 American Negro Collection.
History and literature by and about the Negro. 45 v.
.2 Microfilm Serial Collection.
Pittsburgh Courier, 1923-68; Colored American, 1840-41; Crisis, 1935-63; Liberator, 1831-65; Negro Worker, 1931-37; Negro World, 1926-33; New York Age, 1905-60; Opportunity, 1936-49.

IN10   FORT WAYNE URBAN LEAGUE, INC. (1920). 227 E. Washington Blvd., 46802. Tel 219 422-4776. Charles Redd, Exec. Dir. Copying, typing, inquiries answered, referrals made, consultation.
The League offers services in the areas of education, housing, employment, health, family and welfare.

.1 Fort Wayne Urban League, Inc.
Files, 1920- . Correspondence, minutes of meetings, financial records, reports, studies, and other materials dealing with the aims, history, and programs of the League.

IN11   LINCOLN NATIONAL LIFE INSURANCE COMPANY (1905). LINCOLN NATIONAL LIFE FOUNDATION LIBRARY-MUSEUM (1928). 1301 S. Harrison St., 46801. Tel 219 742-5421. Dr. R. Gerald McMurty, Dir. Interlibrary loan, literature searches, copying, typing, inquiries answered, speakers available.
A research library and museum dedicated to the collection and preservation of information contributing to a better understanding of the growth and achievements of Abraham Lincoln.
Publ.: Lincoln Lore, monthly bulletin.

.1 Lincoln Archives Autograph Collection.
Correspondence and papers, ca. 1800-1900. Original writing and documents of Lincoln (80 items); letters addressed to Lincoln (219 items); thousands of letters relating to Lincoln, over 500 by people who knew him; and letters and documents of Lincoln's ancestors, father, wife and children.

.2 Lincoln Archives Kentucky Records Collection.
Records, 1780-1865. 1200 original mss; thousands of records copied from original entries in Kentucky courthouses.
.3 Lincoln Archives Microfilm Collection.
Papers, ca. 1800-65 (on microfilm). Contains copies of The Lincoln Papers, 18,350 documents in the Library of Congress; of the Herndon-Weik Collection, records and reminiscences by and about Lincoln, located in the Library of Congress; of the Herndon-Lamon collection; Kentucky records; newspaper titles from Vincennes, Ind. (1807-28) and Louisville, Ky. (1832-43); and church and genealogical records.
.4 Lincoln Museum Broadsides Collection.
Broadsides, ca. 1830-65. ca. 1500 items. Political posters, addresses, ballots, caricatures.
.5 Lincoln Museum Original Photographs Collection.
Photographs in cabinet and carte-de-visite size. Also 119 Lincoln photographs arranged in chronological order, made from original negatives or contemporary photographic prints.
.6 Lincoln Museum Paintings Collection.
Oil paintings. 28 items. Original studies depicting various human interest episodes in Lincoln's life. Contains paintings by Pruett Carter, Dean Cornwell, J.C. Leyendecker, Frederic Mizen, Berney Lettick, Ken Riley, C.C. Beall, and others.
.7 Lincoln Museum Prints Collection.
Prints of Lincoln. 6000 items. Engravings, woodcuts, etchings, lithographs and pictures by modern reproductive processes.
.8 Lincoln Museum Sculpture and Medals Collection.
Sculpture and medals, ca. 1860- . 1235 items. 235 busts, statuettes, masks and plaques. 1000 Lincoln medals.
.9 Lincolniana Association Book Collection.
400 v. Books similar to those Lincoln read, including one with Lincoln's signature.
.10 Lincolniana Book Collection.
Books and pamphlets. 10,000 v. Exclusively about Lincoln.
.11 Lincolniana Clippings Collection.
Clippings, ca. 1850- . 100,000 pp. (76 steel files). Reference to 5000 specific subjects relating to Lincoln.
.12 Lincolniana Collateral Publications Collection.
Books and pamphlets, ca. 6000 v. Biographies of Lincoln's associates; histories of the communities where he lived; reminiscences of men who knew him, and discussions on political subjects.
.13 Lincolniana Periodicals Collection.
ca. 7500 magazine articles on Lincoln, 1850- . Newspaper titles, ca. 1830-65. Complete files of leading historical magazines which have featured Lincoln articles.
.14 Thompson, Richard Wigginton, 1809-1900.
Papers, ca. 1830-65. 575 items. Lawyer, politician, and author. Secretary of the Navy under Rutherford B. Hayes. Contains information on political life in Indiana during Lincoln's day.

IN12   MAYOR'S COMMISSION ON HUMAN RELATIONS (1952). 300 E. Berry St., 46802. Tel 219 743-0178. Carl A. Benson, Exec. Secy.
The Committee works to study problems of group relationships within the city, particularly as they relate to the government; to advise mayor, city council, and all city departments, agencies, and officials for the betterment of intergroup relationships within the community; and to provide beneficial training for city employees. Has compliance powers through agreement with Indiana Civil Rights Commission.
Publ.: Newsletter, bi-monthly.

GARY

IN13   GARY COMMISSION ON HUMAN RELATIONS (1965). Municipal Bldg., 401 Broadway, 46402. Tel 219 884-2461. Charles H. King, Jr., Exec. Dir. Inquiries answered, consultation.
The Commission seeks to assure equal opportunity in housing and employment for people for all races; to en-

force the municipal anti-discrimination ordinance; and to recommend ways to make it more effective.

.1 Human Relations Collection.
Papers, pamphlets, books, clippings, tape recordings. Contains staff studies of local situations and problems; clippings from local newspapers; formal papers in complaint cases; tape recordings of public hearings.

IN14 INDIANA CIVIL RIGHTS COMMISSION, REGIONAL OFFICE (1965). 572 Rutledge, 46404. Tel 219 883-8015. Eugene A. Luening, Consult. Bibliographies prepared, inquiries answered, referrals made, consultation. The Commission works to effectuate the public policy of the State as it is legislated in the Indiana Civil Rights Act; investigate charges; and undertake affirmative action programs.
Publ.: Annual Reports; Pamphlets and brochures.

.1 Intergroup Relations, Race, Social Change collection. Miscellaneous. Contains books ca. 600 v.), pamphlets (100 titles), newspaper clippings, reports, surveys, files, records, tape recordings, films and other materials pertaining to the Commission.

IN15 INFO. 1649 Broadway, 46407. Tel 219 882-5591.
Publ.: Info, black ethnic weekly.

IN16 URBAN LEAGUE OF GARY. Suite 309, 1649 Broadway, 46407. Tel 219 886-9139. George R. Coker, Exec. Dir.

.1 Urban League of Gary.
Files. Correspondence, minutes of meetings, financial reports, studies, reports, and other materials dealing with the aims, history and programs of the League.

GREENCASTLE

IN17 DePAUW UNIVERSITY AND UNITED METHODIST CHURCH (1837, 1766), ARCHIVES (1951). Roy O.West Library, 46135. Tel 317 653-9721. Miss Eleanore Cammack, Archivist. Literature searches, copying, typing.
Publ.: Annual Report; Circuit Writer, annual newsletter.

.1 Quarterly Anti-Slavery Magazine, 1835-37.

INDIANAPOLIS

IN18 ANTI-DEFAMATION LEAGUE OF B'NAI B'RITH, INDIANA REGIONAL OFFICE (1955). 108 E. Washington St., 46204. Tel 317 637-4026. Robert Gordon, Dir. Referrals made, consultation.

IN19 BUTLER-TARKINGTON NEIGHBORHOOD ASSOCIATION. 5227 N. Cornelius, 46208. Tel 317 283-5183. Mrs. Carolyn Hawkins, Pres.
The Association seeks to conserve and improve the integrated community.
Publ.: Butler-Tarkington Newsletter, monthly; Pamphlets on the Association and its programs.

IN20 CHRISTIAN CHURCH (DISCIPLES OF CHRIST), INC., BOARD OF HIGHER EDUCATION. 222 S. Downey Ave., 46219. Tel 317 353-1491. Dr. William L. Miller, Jr., Pres. Referrals made, consultation.
The Board interprets the concerns and issues in higher education to the Church and seeks the counsel of the Church concerning ways the institutions with which it carries on work can fulfill its mission; assists member institutions in achieving and maintaining academic excellence; calls upon them to demonstrate high ethical standards in their relations to all institutions of higher education; supports the autonomy of the institutions, and assists them in developing programs appropriate to their institutional purposes.

.1 Board of Higher Education.
Files. Correspondence, minutes of board meetings, financial records, and other materials relating to the Board's support of the following predominantly black colleges: Jarvis Christian College, Hawkins, Tex., Tougaloo College, Tougaloo, Miss.

IN21 CITY OF INDIANAPOLIS COMMISSION ON HUMAN RIGHTS (1953). Room 1742, City-County Bldg., 46204. Tel 317 633-3200. J. Griffin Crump, Exec. Dir.
The Commission works to eliminate sources of conflict between racial, cultural, and ethnic groups. Activities in areas of housing, education, employment, human relations, public accommodations, interreligious affairs, governmental operations, police-community relations. Compliance powers in relation to open occupancy ordinance and fair employment practices.
Publ.: Newsletter, quarterly; Annual Report.

IN22 INDIANA AND INDIANAPOLIS JEWISH COMMUNITY RELATIONS COUNCIL (1946). 615 N. Alabama, Room 412, 46204. Tel 317 637-2473. Norman Sider, Exec. Dir. Inquiries answered, referrals made, consultation. The Council formulates plans and policy on community relations matters; conducts public education programs; and acts as an advisory group for local Jewish organizations working in areas of intergroup and community relations. It maintains a small intergroup relations collection of books and pamphlets.

IN23 INDIANA CIVIL LIBERTIES UNION. 423 Board of Trade Bldg., 46204. Tel 317 635-4056. Craig Eldon Pinkus, Exec. Dir.

IN24 INDIANA CIVIL RIGHTS COMMISSION (1961). 1004 State Office Bldg., 100 N. Senate Ave., 46204. Tel 317 633-4855. C. Lee Crean, Jr., Exec. Dir.
The Commission seeks to provide equal opportunity and to eliminate segregation of the races in employment (private, public agencies and labor), education, housing and public accommodations. The Commission has power to conduct surveys, studies and public education programs; to create advisory bodies; to receive and investigate and to initiate complaints; to conciliate; to hold hearings (with subpoena power); to issue cease and desist orders requiring remedial action on behalf of complainants; and to seek court enforcement of its orders.
Publ.: Annual Report.

IN25 INDIANA HISTORICAL SOCIETY (1933), WILLIAM HENRY SMITH MEMORIAL LIBRARY. 140 N. Senate Ave., 46204. Tel 317 633-4976. Caroline Dunn, Librn. Inquiries answered.

.1 Mills, Caleb, 1806-79.
Papers, ca. 200 items. Educator. Includes Civil War letters relating to Negro troops; Civil War correspondence of Mills' son, Benjamin, and Benjamin Mills' diary (1864-65).
.2 Miscellaneous printed and ms material on Negroes, principally of Indiana. Ms items indexed. Also includes a card file of miscellaneous references.

IN26 INDIANA STATE LIBRARY (1825). 140 N. Senate, 46204. Tel 317 633-6730. Miss Marcelle Foote, Dir. Interlibrary loan, bibliographies prepared, copying, inquiries answered, referrals made.

.1 Anti-slavery papers. (Items scattered throughout library holdings.)
Papers, ca. 1800-65. Papers, newspapers and newsletters, correspondence, records, legal papers, and minutes of meetings. Contains minutes of the Neel's Creek Anti-Slavery Society of Jefferson County, Ind. (1839-45); records of the Henry County Female Anti-Slavery Society, of Spiceland, Ind. (1841-49); publications of the executive committee of the State Anti-Slavery Society (1841); anti-slavery newspapers (1842-48); the preamble, constitution, and papers of the Anti-Slavery Society of Hanover College and Indiana Theological Seminary (1836); a publication of the Society of Friends, Indiana Yearly Meeting (1853); proceedings of the Indiana Convention, assembled in Milton, Ind., to organize a state anti-slavery society (1838); legal papers in the South Bend fugitive slave case, the case of David Powell and family, slaves of John Norris of Boone County, Ky., involving the right to a writ of habeas corpus after being apprehended (1851).
.2 Colfax, Schuyler, 1823-85.
Papers, 1778-1926. 300 items. Newspaper pub-

lisher, U.S. Representative from Indiana, and Vice President of the U.S. Letters regarding personal business and political questions, including references to slavery.

 .3 Hamilton, Allen.
   Papers, 1817-99. 6000 items. Banker, Indian agent, and member of the Indiana Constitutional Convention of 1850. Letters regarding banking questions, legislation, the Constitutional Convention, and other matters, including references to slavery.

 .4 Julian, George W.
   Papers, 1778-1902. 1600 items, including 2 journals. Lawyer, abolitionist, and U.S. Representative. Materials contain references to slavery.

IN27 INDIANAPOLIS URBAN LEAGUE (1965). Suite 814, Underwriters Bldg., 445 N. Pennsylvania St., 46204. Tel 317 639-5391. Sam H. Jones, Exec. Dir.
  The League is a community service agency organized to ameliorate conditions and/or solve problems arising out of racial inequities. It concentrates on problems and opportunities in employment and training, housing and family life, education and youth development, recreation and leisure time activities, and general health and welfare. Includes research fact-finding, interpretation and public education, demonstration, and projection of future problems and goals.
  Publ.: Urbanews, quarterly newsletter.

 .1 Indianapolis Urban League.
   Files, 1965- . Correspondence, minutes of meetings, financial records, reports, studies, and other materials dealing with the aims, history and programs of the League.

IN28 NATIONAL CONFERENCE OF CHRISTIANS AND JEWS (NCCJ). 108 E. Washington St., Room 1501, 46204. Tel 317 924-5731. Thomas H. Barnett, Dir. Bibliographies prepared.
  NCCJ is a civic organization engaged in a nationwide program of intergroup education.

IN29 NATIONAL INSTITUTE ON RELIGION AND RACE (1963), LIBRARY (1964). Catholic Seminary Foundation of Indianapolis, 4545 N. Michigan Rd., 46208. Tel 317 925-9095. Alfred Whitelock, Librn. Interlibrary loan, copying, typing, inquiries answered.
  The Institute seeks to increase the influence of religion by ending racial bias and religious injustice; to conduct projects in leadership training, economic education and cultural enrichment; to foster improvement in living conditions of Negro neighborhoods and integration; to provide support for local councils on religion and race.
  Publ.: Studies in Religion and Race, annual; Newsletter, bi-weekly.

 .1 Religion and Race Collection.
   Books (ca. 2000), periodicals, pamphlets, mss, correspondence, and tape recordings on religion and race, including material relevant for Afro-American studies.

LAFAYETTE

IN30 PURDUE UNIVERSITY LIBRARIES (1874). 47907. Tel 317 749-2571. John H. Moriarty, Dir. Interlibrary loan, bibliographies prepared, literature searches, copying, typing, inquiries answered, referrals made.
  The development of a basic collection of book and non-book materials suitable for a Black Cultural Center is in progress. It will include documentary, historical, and selected contemporary works on such subjects as psychological and socio-economic-political aspects, and artistic contributions of Afro-Americans.

 .1 Facts on Film.
   Papers, 1954-67. Microfilm. Contains materials on civil rights and race relations in the South. See Race Relations Information Center, Nashville, Tenn., for a full description.

 .2 Tape recordings.
   Included are tape recordings (18 tapes) of the Last Citizen Series, produced by radio station WBAA and Louis Schneider, professor of sociology at Purdue, covering such topics as prejudice, color and race, migration and urbanization, the city and the worker, Negro crime, intimidation, protest, and defense; recordings from the City Lecture Series, containing historical information and discussions by Budd Schulberg, Albert Mayor, Jonathan Kozol, Paul Goodman, Dick Gregory and some Black Panthers; and a partial collection of historical music, including folk songs, Negro work songs, spirituals, and the Negro in jazz.

MARION

IN31 MARION URBAN LEAGUE, INC. (1942). 1221 W. 12th St., 46952. Tel 317 664-3933. Henry G. Curry, Exec. Dir.

 .1 Marion Urban League, Inc.
   Files, 1942- . Correspondence, minutes of meetings, financial records, reports, studies, and other materials dealing with the aims, history and programs of the League.

NOTRE DAME

IN32 UNIVERSITY OF NOTRE DAME, MEMORIAL LIBRARY (1873). 46556. Tel 219 284-7317. James W. Simonson, Dir.

 .1 Facts on Film.
   Papers, 1954-67. Microfilm. Contains materials on civil rights and race relations in the South. See Race Relations Information Center, Nashville, Tenn., for a full description.

RICHMOND

IN33 EARLHAM COLLEGE (1847), LILLY LIBRARY (1847). National Rd., W., 47374. Tel 317 962-6561. Evan Ira Farber, Librn. Interlibrary loan, bibliographies prepared, literature searches, copying, inquiries answered.

 .1 Morris, Homer Lawrence, 1886-1951.
   Papers, 1908-51. 12 ft. Economist and educator. Correspondence, notes for speeches, reports to and from Morris, student notebooks from Earlham College, Indiana University, and Columbia University; outlines of courses taught at Penn, Hunter, and Earlham Colleges and Fisk University; and ms and typewritten copies of Morris' work Plight of the Bituminous Coal Miner. Unpublished guide to part of the collection in the library.

 .2 Quaker archives.
   Papers. Minutes, reports, financial documents, correspondence, biographical sketches, reminiscences, clippings, maps and photos relating to Quaker organizations and individuals, especially in the midwest. Contains materials on anti-slavery movements; the underground railroad in Indiana; Quaker statements and positions relating to race generally.

 .3 Society of Friends, Indiana Yearly Meeting.
   Records, 1821-1920. 8 v. and 1 folder. Correspondence, minutes, and other papers, including memorials of deceased Friends (1821-46) of the Indiana Yearly Meeting, a catalog (1848) of its library, minutes (1821-68) of its Committee on the Concerns of People of Colour, minutes (1864-65) of its Executive Committee on Freedmen, a minute book (1886-98) of the Kerr City, Fla., Monthly Meeting (attached to the Indiana Yearly Meeting), a copy-book of correspondence and a treasurer's book (both 1857-80) of the Indiana Bible Association of Friends, and correspondence (1920) relating to meetings in Oregon.

SOUTH BEND

IN34 NATIONAL CONFERENCE OF CHRISTIANS AND JEWS (NCCJ). 103 W. Wayne, 46601. Tel 219 232-7166. Jack DeLong, Dir.

IN35   SOUTH BEND HUMAN RELATIONS AND FAIR EMPLOY-
        MENT PRACTICES COMMISSION (1966). 214 N. Main
        St., 46601. Tel 219 284-9295. George V. Neagu, Exec.
        Dir.
        The Commission promotes equality of opportunity,
        understanding, respect, and good will among all citi-
        zens; provides procedures to deal with grievances and
        channels of communication; encourages community
        cooperation to reduce tensions; facilitates orderly so-
        cial change; serves as a source of objective informa-
        tion. It can impose financial penalty if employment
        discrimination is found; housing and other complaints
        can be taken to public hearing and finding.

IN36   SOUTH BEND PUBLIC LIBRARY. 122 W. Wayne St.,
        46601. Tel 219 288-4413. Roger B. Francis, Dir.
        Interlibrary loan, copying, inquiries answered.

    .1 Local History Collection.
        Books, pamphlets, transcripts, newspaper titles,
        and clippings, ca. 1922- . Contains National Urban
        League study of blacks in South Bend (1958); tran-
        script of Board of Public Safety hearings on civil
        disorders (3 v., 1967), and the Report of the Board
        of Public Safety (1967); transcript of Citizens Fair
        Housing Committee hearing on discrimination in
        housing (1963); clippings (ca. 1 ft.) from South
        Bend newspapers on Negro biographies, health,
        housing, music, publications, societies and organi-
        zations (ca. 1925- .).

IN37   SOUTH BEND URBAN LEAGUE. 625 Sherland Bldg., 105
        E. Jefferson Blvd., 46601. Tel 219 288-8389. Cassell
        Lawson, Exec. Dir.
        The League works to eliminate discrimination and
        poverty in American life; attempts to give black
        people the same life chances that other Americans
        have; uses the community organizations process in
        creating a more viable black community through eco-
        nomical, political, and social agencies; is concerned
        about the internal growth of the black family unit; and
        works to build ghetto power.

    .1 South Bend Urban League.
        Files. Correspondence, minutes of meetings, fi-
        nancial records, studies, reports, and other mate-
        rials dealing with the aims, history, and programs
        of the League.

TERRE HAUTE

IN38   NEGRO AMERICAN LITERATURE FORUM. School of Edu-
        cation, Indiana State University, 47809. Tel
        812 232-6311. John F. Bayliss, Editor.
        The Forum seeks to arouse interest in the instruction
        of Negro American literature through popularizing this
        area of studies among teachers at all levels of educa-
        tion, and to encourage scholarly debate and research.
        Publ.: Negro American Literature Forum, quarterly
        magazine.

VALPARAISO

IN39   LUTHERAN HUMAN RELATIONS ASSOCIATION OF AMER-
        ICA (LHRAA) (1953), LIBRARY. Valparaiso University,
        46383. Tel 219 462-0331. Rev. Karl Thiele, Assoc.
        Exec. Secy. Interlibrary loan, bibliographies prepared,
        literature searches, copying, inquiries answered.
        LHRAA works to help the Church assert leadership in
        the area of intercultural and interracial relations by
        alerting the Church to its problems and opportunities,
        by conducting workshops and institutes, and by working
        with individuals, organizations and other groups.
        Publ.: The Vanguard, monthly; Books and pamphlets on
        race relations.

    .1 Race Relations Collection.
        Books (ca. 600), periodical and newspaper titles,
        pamphlets, theses and dissertations, and clippings
        (ca. 3 vf) on race relations and the Church's role.
    .2 Schulze, Andrew.
        Papers, ca. 1925-54 (on microfilm). Lutheran
        minister and author. Memoirs, sermons, corre-
        spondence, awards, and collected materials, in-

cluding Schulze's sermon on communicant integration (1937); records from his work in Chicago,
St. Louis, and Columbus, Ohio; notes on experiences in Albany, Ga. and Winston-Salem,
N.C.; and his book My Neighbors of Another Color.
Collection contains papers of the Chicago Lutheran Society for Better Race Relations, Lutheran Ladies' Aid for Negro Missions, and the
Bulletin and Institute papers of the St. Louis Lutheran Society for Better Race Relations. Also
materials on race relations attitudes; interracial
marriage and miscegenation; histories of Negro
missions; discrimination and rejection of Negroes;
salaries of Negro workers; and importation of
slaves.

IOWA

AMES

IA1   IOWA STATE UNIVERSITY OF SCIENCE AND TECH-
        NOLOGY, LIBRARY. 50010. Tel 515 294-4111. Robert
        W. Orr, Dir.

    .1 Iowa State History Collection.
        Papers, 1858-1965. ca. 15 ft. Includes corre-
        spondence (1889-1931) of Louis Hermann Pammel,
        botanist, conservationist, and professor at Iowa
        State College, containing correspondence with his
        student, George Washington Carver, and papers
        relating to the Iowa State Soil Conservation Com-
        mittee, Iowa State Park Commission, and Iowa
        Academy of Science.

DES MOINES

IA2   AMERICAN FRIENDS SERVICE COMMITTEE, COMMUNITY
        RELATIONS DIVISION, NORTH CENTRAL REGIONAL
        OFFICE. 4211 Grand Ave., 50312. Tel 515 274-0453.
        Cecil E. Hinshaw, Exec. Secy.

IA3   DES MOINES COMMISSION ON HUMAN RIGHTS (1956).
        Armory Bldg., E. First and Des Moines St., 50309.
        Tel 515 283-4284. Perry W. Hooks, Exec. Dir.
        The Commission studies problems of relationships of
        various races, colors, creeds, and nationalities living
        within the community and assists the city government
        on problems involving discrimination in employment,
        housing, and public accommodations.
        Publ.: Highlights on Human Rights, quarterly; Annual
        Report.

IA4   DRAKE UNIVERSITY (1881), COWLES LIBRARY. 28th and
        University Ave., 50311. Tel 515 271-2198. Dr. George
        J. Rausch, Jr., Dir. of Libraries. Interlibrary loan,
        copying, inquiries answered, consultation.

    .1 Griffing Memorial collection.
        ca. 2000 v. Established in 1946, the collection
        emphasizes materials promoting harmonious re-
        lations among nations and peoples. Includes many
        titles on minority groups and race relations.

IA5   IOWA CIVIL LIBERTIES UNION. 1101 Walnut St., 50309.
        Tel 515 282-0923. Herbert Kelly, Exec. Secy.

IA6   IOWA CIVIL RIGHTS COMMISSION (1965). State Capitol
        Bldg., 50319. Tel 515 281-5129. Alvin Hayes, Jr.,
        Exec. Dir.
        The Commission is a state agency operating in areas
        of employment, housing, public accommodation, and
        empowered to enforce Iowa statutes concerning dis-
        crimination, hold hearings, conduct research into
        problems of intergroup relations, study and make
        recommendations for job opportunity and training, and
        issue cease and desist orders.
        Publ.: Annual report; Iowa Civil Rights Reporter,
        quarterly newsletter; Leaflets and brochures.

    .1 Iowa Civil Rights Commission.
        Files, 1965- . Research reports, newsletters,

federal government publications, annual reports, census materials and reports, newspaper clippings file, books and periodicals.

IA7   IOWA DEPARTMENT OF HISTORY AND ARCHIVES, IOWA HISTORICAL LIBRARY (1892). E. 12th St. and Grand Ave., 50319. Tel 515 281-5472. Lida Lisle Greene, Librn. Copying, inquiries answered.
Publ.: Annals of Iowa.

.1 Todd, John, 1818-94.
Papers. 5 items and 2 v. Congregational minister and abolitionist. Correspondence and other papers, including some material on John Brown. Persons mentioned include Nathaniel Bradley Baker, John F. Cook, Mr. Maxon, Joseph Smith, and Aaron Stevens.

IA8   NATIONAL CONFERENCE OF CHRISTIANS AND JEWS. Room 707, 309 Sixth Ave., 50309. Tel 515 244-7227. Earl S. Kalp, Dir.

INDIANOLA

IA9   SIMPSON COLLEGE (1891), DUNN LIBRARY. 50125. Tel 515 961-2748. William W. Garton, Librn. Interlibrary loan, bibliographies prepared, copying, typing, inquiries answered.

.1 Simpson College.
Archives. Includes material (chiefly photographic) pertaining to the two years that George Washington Carver spent at Simpson (1890-91). Photographic material restricted.

IOWA CITY

IA10 UNIVERSITY OF IOWA, IOWA URBAN COMMUNITY RESEARCH CENTER (1960), LIBRARY (1963). Macbride Hall, 52240. Tel 319 353-4745. Lyle W. Shannon, Acting Dir. Consultation, Research training.
The long-range interest of the Center is to stimulate research in urban sociology, to disseminate original research in the monograph series, and to disseminate the results of other studies that have been published in professional journals.
Publ.: Monograph series; Reprint series of articles by associates of the Center; Publications list.

.1 The Iowa Urban Community Research Center has a data bank of IBM cards for most of the studies that have been conducted by its associates and their graduate students. Available to qualified staff and graduate students who wish to conduct further analyses.

IA11 UNIVERSITY OF IOWA LIBRARIES (1855). 52240. Tel 319 353-4450. Leslie W. Dunlap, Dir. Copying, inquiries answered.

.1 Facts on Film.
Papers, 1954-67. Microfilm. Contains materials on civil rights and race relations in the South. See Race Relations Information Center, Nashville, Tenn., for a full description.
.2 Social Documents collection.
Materials, 1948- . ca. 275 ft. and 5 vertical files. Serial and non-serial newspaper, magazine, newsletter, and pamphlet materials. Collection consists chiefly of publications of right-wing organizations, including the American Nazi Party, National States Rights Party, National Renaissance Party, United Klans of America, and the Christian Constitutional Education League, Inc. A few left-wing civil rights and black militant publications are included, such as the New Crusader, Muhammed Speaks, and the Southern Patriot. Collection also consists of publications of conservative religious organizations with strong political interests.
.3 Strong, George W.
Papers, 1863-1908. 40 items. Commanding officer of Company H, 1st Regiment of Tennessee Infantry, African Descent, later the 59th Colored Infantry Regiment, 16th Corps, 1863-65. Correspondence, memos, orders, supply lists.

MOUNT PLEASANT

IA12 IOWA WESLEYAN COLLEGE (1842), ARCHIVES (1963). 52641. Tel 319 385-2211. Louis A. Haselmayer, Dir. of Archives. Copying, inquiries answered.

.1 Archival and alumni records.
Information on the first Negro students who were graduated from Iowa Wesleyan College 1885, 1887, 1891.
.2 Iowa Conference Historical Society of the United Methodist Church.
Records, 1844- . Records of all Iowa Methodist Conference actions on slavery, abolition, and freedmen's organizations. Includes materials of the Methodist Episcopal, Methodist Protestant, Evangelical and United Bretheren churches.
.3 Mount Pleasant newspapers.
ca. 1861-1900. References to activities of Negro social and church groups in the Mount Pleasant community and to the admission of the first Negro students to the local school system (March 1867).

WATERLOO

IA13 WATERLOO COMMISSION ON HUMAN RIGHTS (1967). 400 E. Sixth St., 50703. Tel 319 232-6521. M. Peter Middleton, Exec. Dir.
The Commission attempts to eliminate and prevent discrimination and prejudice in human relations in the areas of housing, employment, education and police-community relations by studying and analyzing problems, making recommendations to the mayor and the city council, and by initiating human relations education programs. Formerly Mayor's Commission on Human Relationships.

KANSAS

ABILENE

KS1   U.S. GENERAL SERVICES ADMINISTRATION, NATIONAL ARCHIVES & RECORDS SERVICE (1961), DWIGHT D. EISENHOWER LIBRARY (1961). 67410. Tel 913 263-4751. John E. Wickman, Dir. Copying, inquiries answered, referrals made.
The Library is a repository for all papers, books and memorabilia of General Dwight D. Eisenhower, including material collected by Eisenhower and members of his administration concerning such subjects as equal employment opportunity, civil rights, school desegregation, the Civil Rights Acts of 1957 and 1960, and discrimination in the Armed Forces.

KANSAS CITY

KS2   COMMISSION ON HUMAN RELATIONS (1962). City Hall, 805 N. Sixth St., 66101. Tel 913 371-3300. Mrs. Jean Pavela, Exec. Dir.
The Commission investigates complaints in the areas of housing, education, employment, public accommodations, human relations; conducts research and programs to educate the public; and administers the city ordinance on city government contracts, public accommodations, and fair housing.
Publ.: Annual Report; Pamphlets, brochures.

KS3   CONGRESS OF RACIAL EQUALITY (CORE). c/o Carl Randolph, 940 Greeley Ave., 66101. Tel 913 342-8237. Carl Randolph, Chmn.

LAWRENCE

KS4   KANSAS CIVIL LIBERTIES UNION. 600 Louisiana Ave., 66044. Tel 913 843-4081. James Seaver, Chmn.

KS5   UNIVERSITY OF KANSAS, CENTER FOR REGIONAL STUDIES. 210 Summerfield Hall, 66044. Tel 913 864-2700. David L. Huff, Dir.
The Center is an interdisciplinary research organiza-

tion whose general purpose is to contribute toward a better understanding of the process of growth and development in regional and urban areas. In addition to research in the area of methodological issues, the Center is completing a behavioral study to determine why bias exists in locational decisions against declining and depressed areas.

KS6 UNIVERSITY OF KANSAS LIBRARIES (1866). 66044. Tel 913 864-3601. David W. Heron, Dir. Interlibrary loan, copying.

.1 Abolitionist Pamphlets.
ca. 100 items.

.2 Highland and Iowa Point, Kansas, Papers, 1826-1941.
425 items. In part, transcript (typewritten) of Irvin's diary made from the original in the Kansas State Historical Society. Business correspondence and other papers of John Bayless, co-founder of Highland, Kans., and president of the Highland Town Company; copy of the diary (1841-42) and other papers of Samuel W. Irvin, missionary, Highland Mission; and receipts for purchases of slaves and other papers of William Patton, pioneer of Iowa Point, Kans.

.3 Hughes, Langston, 1902-67.
Poet. Collection of books and materials by and about Hughes.

.4 Josephson Collection.
ca. 1920-60. ca. 7500 items. Pamphlets, newsletters, booklets, and other materials, with emphasis on American communist and socialist movements.

.5 Miller, Josiah, 1828-70.
Papers, 1845-1903. 114 items. Lawyer, probate judge of Douglas County, Kans., publisher (with R.G. Elliott) of the newspaper, Kansas Free State, member of the Kansas State Senate, and U.S. Army officer. Correspondence, business papers, cashbook, and list of subscribers of the Kansas Free State, among other items.

.6 Robinson, Charles, 1818-94.
Papers, 1836-1909. 435 items and 6 scrapbooks. First governor of the State of Kansas. Correspondence, documents, and addresses, mainly of the period 1854-61, when Robinson was resident agent for the New England Emigrant Aid Company and Free-State leader; and scrapbooks made by Mrs. Robinson containing clippings about Robinson, J.H. Lane, John Brown, and other men prominent in early Kansas history.

.7 Wilcox Collection of Contemporary Political Ephemera.
ca. 1960- . ca. 1000 items. Leaflets, pamphlets, flyers, periodicals, books, and recordings concerning organizations of the left and the right.

PITTSBURG

KS7 KANSAS STATE COLLEGE OF PITTSBURG (1903), PORTER LIBRARY (1903). 66762. Tel 316 231-7000. John Carralda, Dir. of Libraries. Interlibrary loan, bibliographies prepared, copying, typing, inquiries answered, consultation.

.1 Haldeman-Julius Memorial Collection.
ca. 1920-46. ca. 150 items. Mss, notes, correspondence, proof sheets, newspaper clippings, brochures, and books. The collection includes the ms materials of Marcet and E. Haldeman-Julius for "The Negro Student in Kansas," a study of the colleges and universities of Kansas (1926-28), consisting of interview notes, correspondence with Negro students, college and university teachers and administrators, officers of the NAACP, and interested citizens, the proofsheets and the ms in various stages of revision, and pertinent newspaper clippings and brochures; the ms of "Dixie: A Story of Violence in the Central South," by Marcet and E. Haldeman-Julius, a novel published as Violence (Simon and Schuster, 1929); and 20 Little Blue Books and Big Blue Books dealing with Negro rights (1923-46).

TOPEKA

KS8 HUMAN RELATIONS COMMISSION (1963). Room 54, City Hall, 66603. Tel 913 235-9261. Allen J. Correll, Exec. Dir.
The Commission investigates cases of discrimination against racial, religious or ethnic groups or their members, encourages mutual understanding and equality of treatment. The Commission has a library and an intensive educational program, including books and films.

KS9 KANSAS COMMISSION ON CIVIL RIGHTS (1961). State Office Bldg., 66612. Tel 913 296-3206. Homer C. Floyd, Dir. Inquiries answered.
The Commission administers the Kansas Act Against Discrimination, and works to eliminate and prevent discrimination in all employment relations and in all places of public accommodation through an educational program and a compliance program to investigate and resolve complaints. It provides consultants on race relations, assistance in filing complaints of discrimination, materials on human relations, speakers on civil rights, and films concerning intergroup relations. The Commission maintains a small book and film library.
Publ.: The Docket, monthly newsletter; History of Minority Groups in Kansas, series of reports; Report of Progress.

KS10 KANSAS STATE HISTORICAL SOCIETY (1875), ARCHIVES DEPARTMENT. Tenth and Jackson Sts., 66612. Tel 913 296-3251. Robert W. Richmond, State Archivist. Copying, inquiries answered.
Publ.: The Kansas Historical Quarterly.

.1 Brown, John, 1800-59.
Papers, 1849-1916. 37 books, 66 pamphlets, 13 v. of clippings, several hundred letters, and mss. Abolitionist.

.2 Freedman's Relief Association.
Papers, 1879-81. 4 v. and 1 box. Material concerning the activities of the Association and its recipients.

.3 Higginson, Thomas Wentworth, 1823-1911.
Papers, 1855-60. 169 items. Abolitionist, soldier, and clergyman. Correspondence, telegrams, accounts, bills, receipts, and other papers relating chiefly to Free-State emigration to Kansas, aid to settlers, and border troubles.

.4 Hinton, Richard Josiah, 1830-1901.
Papers, 1850-1901. 4 ft. Journalist, author, and Union Army officer. Correspondence, journal (1856), notebooks, and other papers. Correspondence includes letters chiefly relating to John Brown and his followers, to Richard Realf whose poems Hinton published with a memoir, and to the cooperative movement and socialism in which Hinton was interested, together with Civil War letters, and 29 letters from Realf. Also includes notes on Realf, fragments and copies of his poems, and his testimony before the Harpers Ferry investigating committee.

.5 Montgomery, James.
Letters, ca. 1859-71. ca. 80 items. Radical abolitionist, and lieutenant in the Union Army. Letters received and sent by James Montgomery, including information on Montgomery's role in the movement to arm Negroes at the beginning of the Civil War, and on his relations with Kansas Senator James H. Lane, Charles Jennison, George L. Stearns, all abolitionists, and Kansas Governor Charles Robinson.

.6 Robinson, Charles.
Papers, 1848-1911. ca. 10 ft. Governor of Kansas. Contains material concerning Robinson's activities during the Civil War, and information pertaining to the friction among Senator James H. Lane and his lieutenants, Charles Jennison and James Montgomery in their move to assemble Negro regiments (1862).

.7 Stearns, George L.
Correspondence, ca. 1850-65. ca. 1 ft. Boston ship chandler and abolitionist. Contains some papers relating to Stearns' activities with John

Brown in the late 1850's, and material relating to
the disagreements of abolitionists James Lane,
Charles Jennison, and James Montgomery concerning Negro regiments in the Civil War (1862).

.8   Van Horn, Benjamin.
Ms, ca. 1900. ca. 30 pages, typescript. Horn's
autobiography, including a description of his recruitment of Negro troops for Senator James
Lane and General James G. Blunt, and an account
of his activities as lieutenant and captain of Company I, 1st Kansas Colored Volunteers.

KS11   TOPEKA INTERFAITH COUNCIL FOR RACIAL JUSTICE.
c/o Most Pure Heart of Mary Church, 3601 W. 17th
St., 66604. Tel 913 233-8957. Rev. Robert Fitz-
Gerald, Secy.

WICHITA

KS12   HUMAN RELATIONS COMMISSION. 104 S. Main St., 67202.
Tel 316 262-0611. Floyd L. Hansen.

KS13   NATIONAL CONFERENCE OF CHRISTIANS AND JEWS
(NCCJ). Room 309, 105 S. Broadway, 67202. Tel
316 264-8136. Maurice Terry, Dir. Consultation.

KS14   OFFICE OF HUMAN RESOURCE DEVELOPMENT. City
Bldg. Annex, 104 S. Main St., 67202. Tel 316 262-0611.
William E. Knox, Coordinator.

KS15   WICHITA STATE UNIVERSITY, ABLAH LIBRARY. 67208.
Tel 316 683-7561. C. Edward Carroll, Librn.

.1   Garrison, William Lloyd, 1805-79.
Papers and autographed letters, 1814-79. 1200
items. Letters to and from important public
figures, concerning slavery, abolition, family life
and politics.

KS16   WICHITA STATE UNIVERSITY, CENTER FOR URBAN
STUDIES, LIBRARY (1958). 67208. Tel 316 683-7561.

KS17   WICHITA URBAN LEAGUE. 1405 N. Minneapolis, 67214.
Tel 316 262-2463. Hugh Jackson, Exec. Dir.

.1   Wichita Urban League.
Files. Correspondence, minutes of meetings,
financial records, studies, reports, and other
materials dealing with the aims, history and programs of the League.

WINFIELD

KS18   KANSAS WEST CONFERENCE OF THE UNITED METHOD-
IST CHURCH, ARCHIVES AND HISTORY LIBRARY.
Southwestern College, 67156. Tel 316 221-0097. Ina
Turner Gray, Dir. Copying, inquiries answered.
Formerly Central Kansas Conference of the Methodist
Church, Methodist Historical Society Depository.

.1   See, A.N., ca. 1840-1920.
Autobiography, published 1920. Microfilm. A.N.
See was a pioneer Methodist preacher in Northwest Kansas, who, before going to Kansas,
preached and taught in Covington and Oxford, Ga.
(1867). Book contains accounts of his work in
Georgia, his experiences teaching school, which
included Negroes, his attempts on election day to
insure that the Negroes would not be cheated out
of their vote, and threats and harassment by
members of the Ku Klux Klan.

XAVIER

KS19   SAINT MARY COLLEGE (1923), LIBRARY (1858). 66098.
Tel 913 682-5151. Sister Mary Mark Orr, Head Librn.
Interlibrary loan, bibliographies prepared, literature
searches, copying, inquiries answered, referrals made,
consultation.
The Archival and Special Collections Division collects
material relating to and showing the influence of Negroes, American Indians, Mexican-Americans and their
bearing on the founding of the Sisters of Charity of

Leavenworth in 1858 and their subsequent work to 1968
as educators, social workers, nurses, and missionaries,
particularly in the city and county of Leavenworth, the
territory and State of Kansas, and the territory and
State of Montana

.1   Craig Collection of Americana.

.2   —— Marsteller family.
Papers, 1810-54. 6 items. Collection includes disposition and value of slaves belonging to the Horton Williams estate (1810), slave
indenture paper (1824), receipt for rental of
Negroes (1838), disposition of a slave belonging to Richard Hays (1841), list of slaves given
to the Hays family (1844), and a circuit court
certification that a runaway slave belongs to
Samuel A. Marsteller (1854).

.3   —— United States History, 1783-1864.
Slave papers, 1824-65. 8 items. Material
about the sale and treatment of slaves, including a bill of sale for Negro woman and
child (1824), account of money loaned to Negroes (1854), the sale of slaves (1857), a letter
by William Pillow on the sale of slaves (1857),
payment ($650) for a girl between G.R. John-
son and E.L. Wilie, and a bill of $118 to John
W. Keeson from A.G. Edmondson for treatment of slaves (1862).

.4   —— United States History, 1865-1917.
1865. 1 item. Labor contract with freedmen.

.5   Ross Collection of Americana.

.6   —— Fields, Maurice Colfax.
Papers, 1915-38. 102 items. Negro poet.
Letters, display material, books, articles,
photograph, transcript, and questionnaire.
Materials by and about Maurice C. Fields and
other Negro poets and authors, among which
are a photograph of Maurice C. Fields and
letters by him; letters of Mrs. Pearl Palmer,
mother of Maurice Fields; the works of
Fields; articles on Fields, including a thesis,
The Life and Poetry of Maurice C. Fields, by
Sister Agnes Eugenia Finn, S.C.L.; letters and
transcript from Brooklyn College; letters
from teachers and friends of Fields; letters
from Negro poets, artists, and teachers, and
from sisters, priests, publishers, and libraries; a questionnaire answered by Elizabeth Monigue Maginn; literature by Negroes;
poems by Frances McNamara; and miscellaneous letters.

.7   —— Meyer, Father Prosper, O.S.B. (Edward), 1912-61.
Papers. 10 items. First Kansas Negro or-
dained a Catholic priest. Typescript, clippings, photographs, and memorial cards.

.8   —— Negroes.
83 items. Reference books, bibliographies,
periodicals, pamphlets and leaflets, autographs, and clippings, including clippings on
Negroes of Leavenworth.

.9   —— Shorter, Rt. Rev. Msgr. Joseph A., 1863-1936.
Materials. ca. 1000 items. Founder, pastor,
and Superior of Guardian Angel Church,
School, Home for Orphan Girls, and Farm
Home for Orphan Boys. Msgr. Shorter devoted more than 50 years to the pastoral care
of Negroes of the Leavenworth (Kansas) Diocese. This collection contains his library and
letters and clippings found in his books and
periodicals.

KENTUCKY

BEREA

KY1   BEREA COLLEGE, LIBRARY. 40403. Tel 606 986-3781.
Mrs. Dorothy Crowder, Librn.

.1   Papers relating to anti-slavery in the U.S.
Miscellaneous, 1842-1925. Included are papers of

the following leaders in the movement for the abolition of slavery and the education of Negroes.

.2 — Clay, Cassius Marcellus.
Papers. ca. 53 items. U.S. Minister to Russia.

.3 — Fairchild, Edward Henry.
Papers. ca. 58 items. Presbyterian clergyman, Oberlin College (Ohio) official, president of Berea College.

.4 — Fee, John G.
Papers. ca. 774 items. Presbyterian clergyman, founder of Berea College.

.5 — Frost, William G.
Papers. President of Berea College.

.6 — Goodell, William.
Papers. Editor and reformer of New York and Rhode Island.

.7 — Rogers, John A. R.
Papers. Congregational clergyman, teacher at the predecessor of Berea College.

.8 — Smith, Gerrit.
Papers. Philanthropist, U.S. Representative from New York.

.9 — Tappan, Lewis.
Papers. Merchant and abolitionist of New York and Massachusetts.

BOWLING GREEN

KY2 WESTERN KENTUCKY UNIVERSITY (1907), MARGIE HELM LIBRARY. 42101. Tel 502 745-3951. Sara Tyler, Dir. of Library Serv. Interlibrary loan, literature searches, copying, inquiries answered.

.1 Anti-Slavery Propaganda Collection.
ca. 2500 pamphlets. Microcards of originals located in the Oberlin College Library. See Oberlin College Library, Oberlin, Ohio; or Lost Cause Press (publisher), Louisville, Ky., for more complete description.

.2 Research collection.
Miscellaneous materials. Mss (diaries, wills, letters from Liberia); music; broadsides; minutes and publications of religious organizations; journals, such as African Repository, v. 6-50 (1830-74), and Kentucky Colonization Society reports and publications; and books published 1840-60.

FRANKFORT

KY3 KENTUCKY COMMISSION ON HUMAN RIGHTS (1960). 26 Capitol Annex Bldg., 40601. Tel 502 564-3550. Galen Martin, Exec. Dir. Copying, typing, inquiries answered, referrals made, consultation.
The Commission, an independent agency within the executive branch, functions to safeguard all individuals within the state from discrimination because of race, color, religion and national origin in connection with employment and public accommodations. Commission has jurisdiction over employers of eight or more, over public accommodations, education, and real estate transactions. It has enforcement powers including subpoena; cease-and-desist orders; temporary injunctions to require posting of notices; initiation of complaints; record keeping and reporting; and fines for retaliation against a complainant.
Publ.: Human Rights News, bi-monthly newsletter; Surveys, studies and reports.

.1 Kentucky Commission on Human Rights.
Materials on race relations in Kentucky. Books (ca. 100), periodicals and newspapers, pamphlets, correspondence (29 vf), and newspaper clippings (1 vf). Surveys, studies and reports on Negro employment in Kentucky government and industry; apartment desegregation, and property values in changing neighborhoods; school pairing plans; and race relations law.

KY4 KENTUCKY STATE COLLEGE (1886), BLAZER LIBRARY (1886). E. Main St., 40601. Tel 502 564-5852. James R. O'Rourke, Sr., Librn. Interlibrary loan, bibliographies prepared, literature searches, copying, typing, inquiries answered.

.1 Afro-American Studies Collection.
ca. 1000 paperbacks. Basic books on the life and history of black Americans.

.2 Jones, Paul W.L., Collection.
Small collection of books by and about Negroes.

.3 Negro Life and History Collection.
Historical and literary works from the mid-19th century to the present. Books (ca. 2000), pamphlets (400), photographs, periodicals, newspapers, clippings (2 vf), films, microforms, tape and phonograph records. Complete runs of Pittsburgh Courier and Ebony on microfilm.

LEXINGTON

KY5 LEXINGTON - FAYETTE COUNTY HUMAN RIGHTS COMMISSION (1967). City Hall Annex, 227 N. Upper St., 40507. Tel 606 252-3079. Gregory E. Shinert, Exec. Dir.
The Commission works to eliminate discrimination against individuals and groups in employment, public accommodations and housing; to enforce the ordinances and resolutions of the City and County; and to act as a conciliator among all economic, social, religious, ethnic and racial groups. The Commission receives and initiates complaints, investigates and conciliates, holds public hearings, issues orders, and negotiates. It has enforcement powers in employment, public accommodations and housing, through the circuit court. Formerly the Lexington Human Rights Commission, founded in 1963.
Publ.: Sincerely Yours, bi-monthly newsletter.

KY6 UNIVERSITY OF KENTUCKY (1865), MARGARET I. KING LIBRARY (1912). 40506. Tel 606 258-9000. Stuart Forth, Dir. Interlibrary loan, copying, inquiries answered.

.1 Anti-Slavery Propaganda Collection.
ca. 2500 pamphlets. Microcards of originals located in the Oberlin College Library. See Oberlin College Library, Oberlin, Ohio; or Lost Cause Press (publisher), Louisville, Ky., for more complete description.

.2 Buckner family.
Papers, containing material relating to slavery.

.3 Clay, Cassius Marcellus, 1846-1913.
Correspondence, 1871-1913. 2 ft. (ca. 2120 items). Farmer, stockbreeder, and member of the Kentucky State Legislature. Correspondence (chiefly 1890-95) and other papers concerning the gubernatorial election of 1895, the Farmer's Alliance, the question of free silver, the tobacco war, and the University of Kentucky.

.4 Facts on Film.
Papers, 1954-67. Microfilm. Contains materials on civil rights and race relations in the South. See Race Relations Information Center, Nashville, Tenn., for a full description.

.5 Gibson family.
Gibson-Humphrey family papers, 1840-1955. ca. 400 items. Kentucky family which spread to Mississippi and Louisiana. Correspondence and other papers. Includes material about the effect of the Civil War and Reconstruction on life in the deep South and Kentucky; and about Sarah Humphreys' activities in the Kentucky Equal Rights Association.

.6 Gordon family.
Correspondence, 1771-1924. 2 ft. (1266 items). Correspondence of John Gordon, Georgia farmer, of his wife Sarah and their ten children. The bulk of the material relates to Neal McDougal Gordon who for 30 years was pastor of a Presbyterian church in Jessamine Co., Ky. Contains materials dealing with the Civil War and with the colonization of Negroes in Liberia.

.7 Lindley family.
Papers, 1810-1941. 3 ft (1215 items and 78 v.). Correspondence, diaries, account books, ms textbooks, and scrapbooks of a family of North Carolina Quakers that moved to Indiana about 1811 because it disapproved of slavery.

.8 McCue, John Marshall, 1816-90.
Papers, 1833-89. ca. 200 items. Justice of the

peace and prominent citizen of Augusta Co., Va.
Correspondence, diaries, account books, and
genealogical notes. Contains information on John
Brown's preparation for his raid on Harpers
Ferry, and includes 95 letters from John Daniel
Imboden, Confederate general, on the Civil War
and the industrial development of southwest
Virginia. The material is related to the Library's
James Blythe Anderson papers.

.9 Shelby family.
Papers, containing material relating to slavery.

.10 Stevenson, John White, 1812-86.
Papers, 1877-85. ca. 2 ft. Governor of Kentucky
and U.S. Senator. Letter books and diaries.
Among other subjects, the letter books contain information on Kentucky State politics, particularly
in the Reconstruction period.

.11 Troutman family.
Business records, 1729-1885. 546 items. Correspondence and business papers (chiefly 1816-85) of
the descendants of John Michael Troutman of Nelson Co., Ky., concerning farming operations in
Kentucky and the deep South. Includes letters relating to the family's efforts to regain money lost
when slaves joined the Union Army. The material
is related to the Library's Dicken-Troutman family
papers.

.12 Troutman, Francis, 1820-81.
Papers, 1816-1945. 6 ft. (2972 items and 51 v.).
Lawyer, farmer, and stockbreeder of Bourbon and
Henry Counties, Ky. Correspondence (both family
and business) and business records of Troutman,
of his wife, Anna, and of his father-in-law George
D. Dicken. Contains material relating to Troutman's successful prosecution of a fugitive slave
case in Michigan; his representation of his father-
in-law who was accused of blockade running during
the Civil War, and includes land indentures (1816-
39) of Dicken. Family correspondence reflects the
life of the period.

.13 Wilson, Samuel Mackay, 1871-1946. collector.
Papers. Virginia court records, 1743-1871.
309 items. Miscellaneous records, most of them
from courts in Augusta County, containing a
broadside advertising a reward for a runaway
slave, and other papers.

KY7 URBAN LEAGUE OF LEXINGTON-FAYETTE COUNTY
(1968). 629 Georgetown, 40508. Tel 606 233-1562.
Walter M. Brown, Exec. Dir. Inquiries answered, referrals made, consultation.
The League, an interracial social welfare agency, is
dedicated to equalizing the life results of Negro Americans and other disadvantaged people. It is concerned
with bringing about change in the institutions and systems which have reinforced and perpetuated a cycle of
dependence. Its projects and programs are designed to
solve problems in health and welfare, education, housing, employment, and economic development, and include a Youth Service Bureau, Success Motivation
Center, Center for Economic Development, and a
Secretarial Training Program.
Publ.: Annual Report.

.1 Urban League of Lexington-Fayette County.
Files, 1968- . Correspondence, minutes of meetings, financial records, studies, reports, and other
materials dealing with the aims, history and programs of the League.

LOUISVILLE

KY8 THE FILSON CLUB, INC. (1884), LIBRARY (1884). 118 W.
Breckenridge St., 40203. Tel 502 582-3727. Miss
Evelyn R. Dale, Acting Curator. Copying, inquiries
answered.
The Filson Club, Inc. is a Kentucky historical society,
organized for collecting, preserving and publishing
historical material, especially that pertaining to Kentucky, Ohio River Valley, and early Virginia material.
Publ.: The Filson Club History Quarterly; Historical
monographs and other publications.

.1 Abell, G.W.
Paper, 1860. 1 item. Bill of sale of Negro girl,
July 20, 1860, to Daniel McCulloch. Restricted.

.2 Anderson, Charles, 1814-95.
Papers. 1 box (ca. 165 pp.). A memoir, The Story
of Soldier's Retreat, which contains material concerning slavery in the U.S. and Kentucky, fugitive
slaves, and Negro's social life and customs. Restricted.

.3 Associate Reformed Presbyterian Church.
Papers, 1849, 1852-54, 1856-67. 30 items. Minutes of Presbytery of Kentucky concerning opposition of the Rush Creek congregation to the discussion of slavery and kindred topics (September 17,
1864); and "report ordered to be prepared (August
24, 1866) on the duty of the Presbytery to the
Colored people in their bounds." Restricted.

.4 Baker, Alfred K., 1810-?.
Papers, 1833-63. 1 v. and 36 items. Contains a
bill of sale for Negro woman (August 11, 1848),
and other materials on slavery in Kentucky. Restricted.

.5 Ballard, (Andrew Jackson).
Papers, 1852. Inventory of the slaves and per-
sonal estate of Thomas J. Ballard, appraised by
R.D. and William Waters by order of the Shelby
County, Ky., Court (December 14, 1852). Re-
stricted.

.6 Ballard, Fanny Thruston, 1826-96.
Papers, 1852-99. Letters to her old maid-servant,
Cecelia (1852-59); article by R.C. Ballard Thruston
containing copies of the above letters (1899); and
letters from Cecelia to R.C. Ballard Thruston
(1896-99). Some materials reveal conditions of
slaves and data concerning fugitive slaves. Restricted.

.7 Beech Creek Baptist Church, Shelby County, Kentucky.
Minute book, 1825-40. 1 v. (273 pp.). Contains a
list of members, including "black members."
Restricted.

.8 Bethel Baptist Church, Shelby County, Kentucky.
Minute books, 1809-1911. 3 v. List of members,
including Negroes. Restricted.

.9 Bibb family.
Papers, 1760-1887. 5 boxes. Contains material
concerning slavery in the U.S., and in Kentucky.
Restricted.

.10 Blair, Alexander.
Paper, 1828. 1 p. Contemporary copy of deed of
emancipation of a slave. Restricted.

.11 Boyd, Lucinda (Rogers), 1838-1913.
Papers. 92 pp. Typewritten copy of ms for The
Naptha Lamp, a novel concerning slavery. Re-
stricted.

.12 Breckinridge, Robert Jefferson, 1800-71.
Papers, 1845-52. 1 box (108 items). Includes
promissory notes for the hire of Negro slaves
owned by Breckinridge in 1853 and 1857. Restricted.

.13 Breckinridge, Virginia (Hart) Shelby, 1809-59.
Papers, 1827-59. 10 boxes. Correspondence containing material pertaining to slavery in Kentucky. Restricted.

.14 Brown, Orlando, 1801-67.
Papers, 1780-1898. 1178 items. Lawyer, author
and public official. Correspondence, articles,
genealogical records, and other papers. Includes
family correspondence of the Brown and Watt
families; correspondence connected with the
Commonwealth, a Frankfort, Ky., newspaper of
which Brown was proprietor and editor; correspondence with Orlando Brown, Jr., at Yale and
during his military service during the Civil War;
records of the building of the Orlando Brown
house in Frankfort in 1835; papers relating to the
presidential campaigns of William Henry Harrison
and Zachary Taylor; papers (1780-1837) of Brown's
father, Senator John Brown, and of Orlando Brown,
Jr., and other papers. Included are a letter to
Brown (1856) in New Haven, Conn., from Frankfort,
Ky., mentioning a "backlist of free negroes who
were notified to leave town"; paper concerning
meeting of trustees (1848) called for the purpose
of inquiring into the permits of the "Free people of

Color,'' with names and ages; letter from Mathew Watts (slave) to Mrs. Elizabeth Brown, Frankfort, Ky. (1837), his mistress, asking to come to see her and not remain hired in Virginia; 2 letters of Garnett Duncan (slave) to Orlando Brown (1841), wishing consent of Brown to marry his slave Letitia, and later writing about his wife; letters (1831-59) of Alice Watts Saunders to her sister, Mrs. Elizabeth Brown, and to other relatives, containing references to slavery in Virginia; a petition of James B. Townsend, for the Commonwealth, to the Senate and House of Representatives for the removal to Africa of emancipated slaves, and a letter by Robert Brown (a runaway slave) to ''Mille,'' but sent to ''Mr. Lander Brown,'' (1854, from Canada), offering to pay Mr. Brown $750 for his wife and child.

KY8.15 Buffalo Lick Baptist Church, Shelby County, Kentucky.
Minute book, 1805-38. 1 v. (158 pp.). Contains list of members including three ''Persons of Colour.'' Restricted.

.16 Christianburg Baptist Church, Christianburg, Shelby County, Kentucky.
Papers, 1810-75. 1 v. (124 pp.). List of members containing ''coloured members,'' (1810-73). Restricted.

.17 Churchill family.
Papers, 1797. Included is a letter by John McClure of Jefferson Co., Ky., to Henry Churchill, concerning the sale of a Negro man named Will (August 29, 1797). Restricted.

.18 Clark, Edmund.
Papers, 1801-75. Included are mortgage on land and Negroes by James Stephens and Mary Bird, his wife, of Spottsylvania Co., Va., to Jonathan Clark to secure a debt; papers from the Circuit Clerk's office, Morganfield, Union Co., Ky. (1818-19), pertaining to Fitzhugh vs. Gilchrist, concerning the ownership of two slave girls, part of the estate of Edmund Clark; and letters to Dennis Fitzhugh (1807-18) regarding these two slave girls.

.19 Clark, Issac, 1787-1868.
Papers, 1807-71. ca. 1073 items. Farmer of Jefferson County, Ky. Letters (40 items, 1807-68), accounts (688 items, 1812-69), and other papers. Papers include orders for the impressment of Clark's Negroes to work for the Louisville and Nashville Railroad in 1863. Material is related to the repository's Jonathan Clark papers in the Clark-Hite collection. Restricted.

.20 Clark, Meriwether Lewis, 1809-81.
Family records, 1853. 102 pp. Compiled by Meriwether Lewis Clark. Contains lists of slaves and horses owned and other references to slavery in the U.S. Restricted.

.21 Clark, William, 1795-1879.
Papers, 1811-79. ca. 1125 items. Physician, farmer, and manufacturer of hempen products. Correspondence and other papers. Included are bills of sale for Negroes (1829-48).

.22 Clay, Cassius Marcellus, 1810-1903.
Papers, 1844-1907. ca. 3 ft. U.S. Minister to Russia, lawyer, and abolitionist, of Kentucky. Letters, including those written by Clay to his wife and children while he served as Minister to Russia (1862-69); newspaper clippings containing his letters (1852-85) and speeches (1853-95) about anti-slavery and U.S. politics; a typewritten copy of his speech at Moscow (1866); a ms of an article, ''Labor and Capital'' (1866); and clippings of his magazine articles (1832-66). Includes some correspondence of Clay's wife, Mary Jane (Warfield) Clay, and his daughter, Mary Barr Clay, with some letters to Mary Barr Clay from Susan B. Anthony, Alice Stone Blackwell, Lucy Stone, and other suffragists. A scrapbook made by Mary Barr Clay contains newspaper clippings about the Civil War. Restricted.

.23 Cravens, T.R.
Family papers, 1804-78. 1 box. Includes bill of sale for 5 Negro slaves (January 21, 1833), and other references to slavery in Kentucky. Restricted.

.24 Croghan family.
Papers. Includes inventory (5 pp., photostat) of the personal estate and slaves of Dr. John Croghan (1790-1849) of Locust Grove, near Louisville, Ky. (1849). Restricted.

.25 Crutchfield, James Stapleton, 1800-72.
Papers, 1827-63. 31 items. Includes deed from R.A. Crutchfield to J.S. Crutchfield for his interest in slaves (February 16, 1829), and other references to slavery in Kentucky. Restricted.

.26 Daveiss, Joseph Hamilton, 1774-1811.
Papers, 1786-1855. 277 items. Kentucky lawyer. Correspondence, legal papers, land papers (1786-1806), statements of account (1797-1811), commissions, and estate papers. Correspondence (1797-1811) relates chiefly to Kentucky lands and Negroes, Daveiss's opposition to Aaron Burr, his removal from office as U.S. attorney for the District of Kentucky in 1807, publication of his pamphlet vindicating his conduct, and authorship of a bill before Congress for arming and disciplining the militia of the U.S. in 1811. Also includes papers of Samuel Daveiss (1775-1856). Restricted.

.27 Dowd, Almeron.
Letters, 1845. 2 items. Letters (dated August 23 and 30, 1845), discussing slavery and abolition, Cassius M. Clay and the True American. Restricted.

.28 Downs, George F., 1814-1908.
Memorandum book, 1846-64. 1 v. (112 pp.). Includes records of the division of 15 Negroes made December 10, 1850. Restricted.

.29 Durrett, Reuben Thomas, 1824-1913.
Papers, 1821-1931. 30 ft. (12,580 items). In part, transcripts. Lawyer, editor, and author. Personal and legal correspondence (1847-1913); letters to Durrett as editor of The Louisville Courier and as president of the Filson Club; mss of books, articles, lectures, editorials, orations, and addresses; papers relating to the Filson Club; and papers acquired through Durrett's law practice, including pension claims of Negro soldiers who served in the Civil War, and miscellaneous legal papers. Also included is Uncle Zeke's sermon on the proclamation of the mayor of Louisville, Ky., showing among other things how slavery is to be rooted out of the land (9 pp.). Restricted.

.30 Ellis, James Tandy.
Paper, 1942. 1 p. Typewritten. A letter to Samuel J. Boldrick, Ghent, Ky. (January 17, 1942) in regard to his writings, objections of eastern Negroes to Negro stories and Negro dialect. Restricted.

.31 Filson Club, Louisville, Kentucky.
Diaries and journals, 1770-1920. 76 v., 23 items, and 5 microfilm reproductions. In part, transcripts (typewritten) and photocopies (negative and positive). Includes many military diaries concerning service in American wars, including the Civil War, and diaries about pioneer travel, especially from Virginia to Kentucky and on the Ohio and Mississippi Rivers. Contains information about pioneer life in Kentucky, surveying, farming, exploring, Indians, religious and social life, slavery, government service, States' rights, and the Know-Nothing party. Restricted.

.32 Garvin, S.
Memorandum book, 1846-63. 1 v. (20 pp.). Includes a record of slaves. Restricted.

.33 Green, Norvin, 1818-93.
Papers, 1839-92. 6 ft. Physician, legislator, and business executive. Correspondence, letter press books, accounts and tax receipts (1840-77); accounts for medical services (1842-51); bills, notebooks, and an address before a medical society. Collection includes papers relating to slavery (1847-64). Restricted.

.34 Green, Willis, d. 1862 and Green, Lafayette.
Papers, 1818-93. 3 boxes. Includes miscellaneous legal papers (1826-55) concerning slavery in Kentucky. Restricted.

.35 Grigsby family.
Papers, 1818-84. ca. 5241 items. Papers of Susan Preston (Shelby) Grigsby of Traveller's

Rest, near Danville, Ky.; her father, Alfred Shelby (1804-32), youngest son of Gov. Isaac Shelby of Kentucky; her husband, General John Warren Grisby, C.S.A., and other relatives. Includes papers of the allied Gibson family of Louisiana, and the Hart and Wallace families of Kentucky. Included are slavery documents, and a ms on slave labor in Kentucky by an unknown writer. Restricted.

KY8.36 Halsey, Edmund T. collector.
Papers. Included are the papers of George Claiborne Thompson (1778-1856), farmer, slave owner, and member of the Kentucky Legislature, of Shawanee Springs, Mercer Co., Ky., including correspondence and papers containing references to slavery in Kentucky; letters of Letitia Thompson Vance (130 items, 1844-55, 1871, 1873), including letters from her father George Claiborne Thompson, containing comments on farming, politics, and his slaves, especially his letter of July 14, 1853, about whipping slaves; bill of sale to Letitia Thompson Vance, for a "Negro boy named Dick, aged between 25 and 30 years" (1863); papers of William L. Vance consisting of letters (1848-63), including one accompanied by a bill of sale (1859) for a Negro man named Milo, and a receipt and memorandum book (1853-61) containing list of Negroes belonging to the estate of his father-in-law, George C. Thompson; and a resolution adopted by the Legislature of Kentucky in 1846 providing for the gift of a gun to Jack Hart, slave and "pioneer of the African race in Kentucky," to replace one that was lost at the Battle of Blue Licks. Restricted.

.37 Hickman, Richard Baylor, 1865-1949. collector.
Papers, 1780-1897. ca. 138 items. Autograph letters, commissions, deeds, minutes of meetings, and miscellaneous documents. Includes receipt of John Denny to John Guthrie for "three people of colour" whom Guthrie obtained for him by law in Mississippi, Jan. 1, 1828. Restricted.

.38 Hinde, Thomas S., 1734-1828.
Papers, 1827. 4 pp. Papers to Thomas Noble Lindsey, of the Engineer Corps, Wabash and Maumee Route, Fort Wayne, Ind., from New Port, Ky. (July 2, 1827), "requesting that by runaway Negroes, Juda and Betsey be taken up...." Restricted.

.39 Hord, William.
Account-book, 1798-1823. 1 v. (121 pp.). Contains a list of Negroes taken to Kentucky and births of Negro children. Restricted.

.40 Howard, Thomas C.
Papers, 1780-1844. 3 boxes. Includes letters (1806-40) containing references to slavery in Kentucky. Restricted.

.41 Hunt, John Wesley, 1772-1849.
Papers, 1792-1849. ca. 1994 items. Merchant, farmer, and hemp manufacturer, of Lexington, Ky. Correspondence, statements of account, bills of lading and receipts for tobacco, warehouse receipts for tobacco; bills of sale for Negroes (1826-43). Correspondence covers Hunt's partnership with Harry Heth at Richmond in 1793, and his later partnerships with Abijah Hunt (1795-1800) and with a son, in Lexington, Ky. Correspondence relates to the buying and selling of tobacco, hemp, cotton, linen, ginseng, saltpeter, gunpowder, iron, whisky, salt, slaves, horses, and mules, among other things. Restricted.

.42 Ingram, Jeremiah.
Papers, 1796-1832. 1 box. Contains bills of sale for Negro children (1804-05), and references to slavery in Virginia and Kentucky. Restricted.

.43 Jacob, John Jeremiah, 1778-1852.
Papers, 1806-51. 6 boxes. Includes letters (1806-07, 1816) and slavery documents (1813-46), pertaining to slavery in Kentucky. Restricted.

.44 Jeffrey, Alexander, 1815-99.
Papers, 1835-99. 6 ft. Business executive. Correspondence (1835-99), personal and family accounts (1846-99), land papers, and tax receipts. Includes papers concerning slavery in Kentucky.

.45 Jeffrey, Rosa Vertner Johnson, 1824-94.
Papers, 1855-92. 148 items and 1 v. Poetess.

Correspondence, poems and legal papers, including a release of a claim against Mrs. Jeffrey for sale of a Negro woman who proved to be "unsound" (1862), powers of attorney, statement of cotton captured at Vicksburg, Miss., in 1864 from Mrs. Jeffrey's plantation, "Canton Place," claim against the U.S. for damage to the residence of Mrs. Elizabeth Vertner during the Civil War. The correspondence, chiefly literary, contains some family letters including those of her husband, Alexander Jeffrey, describing Lexington, Ky., during the Civil War. Also contains papers (1853-62) of Claudius M. Johnson (1818-61), including a bill of sale from Archibald P. Williams of Franklin Co., Ky., to Johnson for a Negro girl named Lucky (1853). Restricted.

.46 Joyes family.
Papers, 1780-1928. 6 ft. Papers of a Louisville, Ky., family including Patrick Joyes (1750-1806), merchant and landowner; his son, Thomas Joyes (1789-1866), an officer in the War of 1812, surveyor, and landowner; his grandson, Patrick Joyes (b. 1826); Chapman Coleman (d. 1850), commission merchant and marshal of the U.S. Kentucky district. Includes correspondence (1783-1868) relating in large part to Thomas Joyes' land transactions, the litigation arising therefrom, and the management of his landed property. The papers of Chapman Coleman include correspondence (1823), fee bills (1831-43), statements of account, bills of sale for slaves (1823-37), land papers concerning land in Bath and Mason Counties, Ky., Frankfort and Louisville, Ky., Louisiana and Mississippi. Papers of Patrick Joyes consist of correspondence containing family news, financial discussions, and political comments. Restricted.

.47 Kentucky census records.
Miscellaneous, 1810-90. Microfilm. Kentucky census records (1810-80) from the National Archives; special census for Kentucky (1890); special census of manufactures for Kentucky and Indiana (1820- .). Restricted.

.48 Kentucky newspapers.
Extensive collection of Kentucky newspapers and some out-of-state papers with material pertaining to slavery, Negroes, and relevant subjects. Restricted.

.49 King family.
Papers, 1789-1850. 1 box. Contains manumission papers of a female slave, (January 30, 1841), and other materials pertaining to slavery in Kentucky. Restricted.

.50 Kinkead, Cleves, 1882-1955.
Papers. Includes notebook (1925) containing list of books on medieval history and slavery with notes and comments by Kinkead. Restricted.

.51 Love, James Young, 1797-1876, and Love, Thomas.
Papers, 1785-1820. 1 box. Contains slave certificates (April 14, 1842). Restricted.

.52 McConochie, James Robert, ca. 1786-1853.
Papers, 1812-69. 1 box (191 items). Includes bills of sale, notes, hiring agreements (1817-53) and other materials pertaining to slavery. Restricted.

.53 McElroy, William Thomas, 1829-?.
Journal, 1852-68, 1889, 1901-05. 1 v. Includes McElroy's notes on his decision to preach in a slave state. Restricted.

.54 Meriwether, William, 1757?-1814.
Papers, 1780-1818. 1 box. Includes slavery documents (1795, 1801) and references to slavery in Kentucky. Restricted.

.55 Miles and Hynes, Murfreesboro, Tennessee.
Day-book, 1820-21. 1 v. (21 pp.). A mutilated day-book (January 13, 1820-February 17, 1821) containing references to slavery in Tennessee. Restricted.

.56 Miller, Howard, 1832-?.
Diaries, 1857-67; 1878-88. 3 v. Diaries containing material concerning slavery and the freeing of slaves in Kentucky. Restricted.

.57 Miscellaneous papers.
Contains papers pertaining to slavery and Negroes in the United States, among which are certificates (1811) of freedom of Negroes in the City and

County of New York; article (16 pp.) by Mary Katherine Rogers Clay (1844-?), " 'Old Captain,' or the founder of the first colored church of Kentucky"; a letter (2 pp., copy, 1869) by Samuel Langhorne Clemens (1835-1910), mentioning having seen in Hartford a portrait by Inman of a Negro prince who befriended a party of American and English gentlemen traveling in Africa in 1790 and who was later sold into slavery and discovered by one of the party in Louisville in 1820; constitution (copy) of the Danville (Ky.) Colonization Society and proceedings of meetings (1829-35), including list of members; letter (July 11-12, 1864) from the citizens of Hawesville (65 signatures) to General Stephen Burbridge, commander of the District of Kentucky, seeking the discharge of 3 men who were arrested in connection with an attack made on the steamer "Science No. 2" on June 19th when newly enlisted Negro slaves were being embarked; will (typewritten copy) of Sarah Winston Syme Henry (d. 1785) in which she bequeaths mourning rings, Negroes, tobacco and wearing apparel to sons John Syme, William and Patrick Henry, daughters, and grandchildren; a letter of L. Lawes, Jefferson Co., Ky. (1812) to William Lawes, Princess Ann, Somerset Co., Md., in which he discusses the "return of Captain Funk from New Orleans where he sold Gabe for only $280," and the fact that "Negroes are cheaper in New Orleans than in Kentucky," among other personal matters; a bill of sale for a slave of John Lewis (1846); will (1843) of Slingsby Linthicum (d. 1848) bequeathing slaves to members of his family; and a letter (3 pp., 1826 sic 1862?) of Charles Anderson Wickliffe (1788-1869) to Ed. M. Harvey (?) in reply to the question "Should Congress have abolished slavery in the District of Columbia?" Restricted.

KY8.58 Morgan, C.C., and Company.
Papers, 1853-80. 2 boxes. Includes two cancelled checks for purchase of Negroes (1858-59). Restricted.

59 Newburg Christian Church, Newburg, Kentucky.
Church book, 1836-91. 1 v. (141 pp.). Includes list of names of "Black members of Newburg Church." Restricted.

.60 Nicholasville, Kentucky.
Minute book of trustees, 1824-42. 1 v. (243 pp.). Includes by-laws adopted in 1824 relative to slaves and free Negroes, and an order for the whipping of slaves. Restricted.

.61 Otter, John D.
Papers, 1832-86. 22 items and 1 v. Includes bill of sale for Negro woman and two children (Nov. 20, 1846). Restricted.

.62 Owens, William.
Papers, 1851-55. 6 items. Papers of William Owens, Jr. of Logan Co., Ky., including deed to him from Mary Miller for land in Logan County (Jan. 9, 1851); receipts from William Owens, Sr., and Nancy Hamblin for proceeds of land and slaves (Jan. 16, 1851, and August 8, 1851); bill of sale from William Owens, Sr., to William Owens, Jr., for a Negro slave (Aug. 12, 1851); bill of sale from James B. Anderson for 3 slaves (Dec. 24, 1855). Restricted.

.63 Parrish, C.H.
Ms. 1 p., and clipping. To Rev. C.E. Craik, Dean, Christ Church Cathedral, Louisville, Ky. Eckstein Norton University, Cane Spring, Bullitt Co., Ky. (Feb. 2, 1900). Concerning Negroes. Restricted.

.64 Personal papers in small groups.
Includes papers pertaining to slavery and Negroes, among which are papers (1789-1836) of Botts and Hedges families including bill of sale for a Negro boy (1833) and bill for medical services for Negro slaves (1833-35); Crist-McCormick-Hessey papers (1809-52, 24 items) including bills of sale for Negroes (1808-52); letters (1832, 1836-40) of John Irwin (1809-89) containing references to slavery in Kentucky; a letter of W. Edwin Russell from Paris, 1919, to Sylvester Andrew Russell, Lebanon, Ky., discussing the attitude of the French toward their Negroes and new ideas of Negro

Americans about equality; and papers (1841-69) of Mr. and Mrs. Silas Sisson.

.65 Pirtle, Alfred, 1837-1926.
Papers, 1847-1924. 6 ft. Kentucky historian. Correspondence (1847-1923), including a volume of Civil War letters; a journal (1859-62), containing references to Negroes; and Pirtle's writings for magazines and newspapers on local and State history.

.66 Pirtle family.
Papers of the Pirtle and Rogers families, 1797-1875. 62 items. Mainly papers of Judge Henry Pirtle (1798-1880) of Louisville, Ky., and of Dr. Coleman Rogers (1781-1855). Papers include letters (1801-36) to Gen. James Taylor of Newport, Ky., and a letter (1829) from Martin Van Buren to William T. Barry about the return of Taylor's fugitive slaves from Canada. Restricted.

.67 Pleasant Grove Baptist Church, Jefferson County, Kentucky.
Minute book, 1805-84. 1 v. (308 pp.). Contains references to the exclusion of Negro membership (1868). Restricted.

.68 Pleasanthill, Kentucky.
Shaker village records, 1815-1917. 40 v. Journals, account books, a "mill book," covenant book, hymnbooks, and a cookbook. Includes lists of members, records of removals of members from one family or society to another, and of deaths of members; proceedings of church meetings, family meetings, and union meetings; description of rites and some account of doctrines; records of farming and building operations and other activities, and weather records. Included in journals are references to Negroes.

.69 Pope, William Hamilton, 1803-66.
Papers, 1830-66. 1 box. Includes slavery documents. Restricted.

.70 Porter, Lemuel C., 1810-87.
Diary, June 3, 1848-Sept. 2, 1862. 1 v. (99 pp.). Contains references to slavery in Kentucky. Restricted.

.71 Prather, Thomas, d. 1823.
Papers, 1801-38. 47 items. Includes slavery documents, 1823-26. Restricted.

.72 Read-Sutherland families.
Papers. Includes papers (3 items) of John Sutherland (d. 1818) of Nelson Co., Ky., including his will, disposing of land and slaves; and a receipt of Philip Read (d. 1829) pertaining to slavery (1812).

.73 Reed, Demcy.
Bill of sale for slaves, 1801. Restricted.

.74 Rudd, James, 1789-67.
Account book, 1830-60. 1 v. Account book kept by Rudd, farmer, land and slave owner of Louisville, Ky., containing record of cash received for hire of slaves, some of whom worked on steamboats, (1839-60); list of slaves owned (1853 and 1858); accounts with tenants of real property (1832-56); and other records. Restricted.

.75 Shelby, Isaac, 1750-1826.
Papers, 1760-1839. ca. 175 items. In part, transcripts (typewritten) and photocopies (negative). Governor of Kentucky. Correspondence, accounts, and land and legal papers of Shelby, and some other papers. Issac Shelby correspondence (1777-1823) concerns Kentucky politics, and slave stealers, among other topics. Collection also contains legal papers in the case of James Parberry's heirs v. Isaac Shelby concerning the ownership of a slave (1799-1819). Restricted.

.76 Short, Charles Wilkins, 1794-1863.
Papers, 1811-69. 9 ft. Physician, teacher, and botanist. Correspondence (1813-49) with Short's uncle, William Short of Philadelphia; family and business correspondence (1818-22); diary (1860) kept at "Hayfield" in Louisville; memoranda of letters written and received (1816-60); account book, commonplace book, notebooks and drawings. Correspondence of Charles Short with his uncle, William Short, contains references to slavery in Kentucky. Also included is a letter of Catherine Matilda Strader (Mrs. William) Short (April 6, 1869) to William Short, near Elizabeth-

town, Ky., telling of Short's father travelling on omnibus from Elizabethtown to Louisville with the Lieutenant Governor of Louisiana (Oscar J. Dunn?), a Negro, who made application in Washington to be sent as Minister to the Court of St. James, and of Short's hopes that this Negro will gain precedence over Horace Greeley who applied for the same position; and a letter by John Hedges (1816) to Dr. C.W. Short, concerning, among other matters, the sale of a Negro slave, Betty, who was one of 50 slaves mortgaged by John Churchill, grandfather of Mary Henry Churchill Short. Restricted.

.77 Skipwith, Peyton.
Letter, n.d. 1 p. To Thomas Churchill, Middlesex County, offering to buy 40 or 50 slaves which were advertised in Davis' paper of January 24. Restricted.

.78 State University, Louisville, Kentucky.
Receipts, 1891. 2 pieces. Concerns Negro education. Restricted.

.79 Summers, Benjamin Franklin, d. 1853?
Account-book, 1838-59. 1 v. 391 pp. Entry of pills sold to Henry Walker, "Free Negro," August 7, 1841. Restricted.

.80 Sutton family.
Papers, 1796-1831. 2 boxes. Includes bill of sale for slaves sold to John Sutton, II, in 1817. Restricted.

.81 Taylor, Edmund Haynes.
Papers, 1818-73. 6 boxes. Kentucky banker, treasurer of Kentucky Colonization Society. Restricted.

.82 Taylor, Francis, 1747-99.
Diary, 1786-92. Microfilm. Contains references to slavery in Virginia. Restricted.

.83 Taylor, James, 1769-1848.
Papers, 1774-1888. 1706 items. Papers of General James Taylor, farmer, land speculator, and officer of the Kentucky Militia, and of his son, James, Jr., lawyer. Includes miscellaneous papers relating to lands in Ohio and Kentucky; correspondence, deeds, and agreements (1774-1883); papers (1856-73) of Barry Taylor regarding farming and personal affairs; papers (1782-1815) of Maj. David Leitch; letters and documents; miscellaneous family letters and papers; and other materials. Included are a bill of sale for slaves; a reference to a Negro boy hired by James T. Eubanks for "bearing off brick, packing away and setting kills," July 1, 1812; and a letter from David G. Devon (Georgetown, Brown Co., Ohio, May 20, 1842) concerning abolitionists and the freeing of Negroes. Restricted.

.84 Taylor-Barbour-Crutchfield families.
Papers. Includes receipts and bond from the estate of William Berry Taylor (1768-1836) containing information on slavery in Kentucky. Restricted.

.85 Terrell, Chiles, 1780-1851.
Papers, 1799-1865. 1 box, 77 items. Includes deeds of trust (1828-29), and contract (1828), pertaining to slavery in Kentucky. Restricted.

.86 Thompson, George, 1749-1830?
Papers, 1829-30. 4 items. Deed of gift for 48 slaves, June 22, 1830. Restricted.

.87 Thruston, Charles William, 1796-1865.
Papers. Included are bills for the sale or hire of Negro slaves, notices of runaway slaves, slavery documents, a letter from Thruston, Bruckner, and John Thruston (Jefferson Co., Ky., Nov. 2, 1800) to Charles Thruston regarding the reuniting of a family of Negro slaves, and a contract (1790) for the exchange of Negro slaves. Among slavery documents and bills are a bill of J. Reed (1831) for a coffin for a Negro; bill of Thomas Jefferson to C.W. Thruston (1834) including item "Nov. 18, to repr. negro collar"; receipt (1836) of James Shockley to C.W. Thruston for 44 hogs heads with a penciled note, probably by C.W. Thruston, "meat for negroes"; and receipt (1836) from Richard Oldham "for maintaining in jail a negro boy." Restricted.

.88 Thurman, Edward C., 1882-1950.
Papers. Contains documents on slavery, including bills of sale, slave rental contracts, and printed advertisement of slaves for sale. Includes letter of John Clarke Young (1803-57) to Rev. Charles Hodge, professor of Biblical theology, Princeton, N.J. (184?) discussing the attitude toward slavery in Kentucky. Restricted.

.89 Torian, William.
Bill of sale for a slave, 1864. Restricted.

.90 Wallace family.
Papers, 1764-1884. 310 items. Papers of the Wallace family of King George Co., Va., Crittenden Co., Ky., and Louisville, Ky., consisting of correspondence, wills, and legal records, including records of Negroes belonging to the estate of Thomas Wallace (1819-29). Contains correspondence of Lt. Thomas Wallace, 6th Kentucky Cavalry, Morgan's Division, Confederate Army, with his parents, Mr. and Mrs. Arthur Hooe Wallace, and with his brother and sisters, while serving in the army and as a prisoner of war at Camp Chase and Johnson's Island, Ohio (1860-65). Restricted.

.91 Walton, James Orvin, 1843-?.
Letters, 1864-65. 1 v., typewritten copies. Includes references concerning the use of Negroes in South Carolina. Restricted.

.92 Williams, Wesley, d. 1925.
Autograph collection. 35 items. Contains references to slavery in Kentucky. Restricted.

KY9   KENTUCKY CIVIL LIBERTIES UNION (KCLU) (1955). 809 Center Bldg., 40202. Tel 502 583-8421. Suzanne K. Post, Chmn. Inquiries answered, referrals made, legal counsel.
The KCLU provides legal counsel in cases involving infringement of civil liberties, and works to effect changes in legislation.
Publ.: Newsletter.

.1 Kentucky Civil Liberties Union.
Files, 1962- . Records pertaining to membership activity, requests for legal services, board actions, committee reports, and press coverage.

KY10   KENTUCKY COMMISSION ON HUMAN RIGHTS, LOUISVILLE OFFICE (1960). 600 W. Walnut St., 40203. Tel 502 583-2775. Copying, typing, inquiries answered, consultation.
The Commission enforces the law which prohibits discrimination in places of public accommodation, places of employment of eight or more employees, and in real estate transactions.

KY11   THE LINCOLN FOUNDATION, INC. (1946). 230 Heyburn Bldg., 40202. Tel 502 585-4733. J. Mansir Tydings, Exec. Secy. Referrals made, consultation.
The Foundation is the successor to Lincoln Institute of Kentucky which became a state-operated institution. The endowment funds of the school were retained by the Foundation and are used to promote equality and opportunities for the Negroes of Kentucky. Among the Foundation programs are Youth Speaks, Inc., a forum dealing with contemporary issues and whose members are also involved in community volunteer services; consulting services to local boards of education for development of teacher guides and bibliographies for courses in Afro-American history; and a black theater workshop involving local professional actors and technical personnel of Actors Theater of Louisville and youth and adults in four black ghetto areas of the city.

KY12   LOST CAUSE PRESS (1955). 1140-1146 Starks Bldg., 40202. Tel 502 584-8404. Nancy and Charles Farnsley, Pres. and Secy-Treas.
Lost Cause Press has published, on microcard, collections of books and pamphlets, most of which were originally published in the 19th century. Among the microcard collections are the Anti-Slavery Propaganda Collection in the Oberlin College Library, and the Dumond Collection of Slavery pamphlets in the Long Beach State College Library.
Publ.: Lost Cause Press: Microcard Collection, monthly catalogue of new publications.

.1 Anti-Slavery Propaganda Collection.
Consists mainly of American anti-slavery propa-

ganda published before January 1, 1863. ca. 2500 pamphlets. On microcards. The Collection covers annual reports; proceedings; constitutions; platforms and addresses of anti-slavery societies - the moral and humanitarian argument and religious aspects of the controversy; slavery and the law; the economic argument against slavery; anti-colonizationism; vindication of the Negro race; vindication of abolitionist principles; collections of speeches and writings of anti-slavery men; the moderate anti-slavery point of view; travelers' observations of slavery; slave narratives; biographies of leaders of the Anti-Slavery Movement; children's literature, poetry, songs, anthologies and gift books; newspapers and periodicals; the anti-slavery controversy in politics; slavery and the Civil War; the pro-slavery reply to the Anti-Slavery Movement; and the British Anti-Slavery Movement.

.2 Dumond Collection of Slavery Pamphlets.
Pamphlets. ca. 700 items. On microcards. Literature written and circulated by those active in the anti-slavery movement.

KY13 LOUISVILLE FREE PUBLIC LIBRARY, WESTERN BRANCH (1905). 602 S. Tenth St., 40203. Tel 502 584-5526. Mrs. Ruth M. Harry, Br. Librn. Interlibrary loan, bibliographies prepared, copying, inquiries answered, referrals made, consultation.

.1 Anti-Slavery Propaganda Collection.
ca. 2500 pamphlets. Microcards of originals located in the Oberlin College Library. See Oberlin College Library, Oberlin, Ohio; or Lost Cause Press (publisher), Louisville, Ky., for more complete description.

.2 Cotter, Joseph S., Sr.
Papers, 1920-43. ca. 1 vf. Unpublished and published poems, essays, songs, short stories and plays, and lesson plans of Joseph S. Cotter, Sr., principal of S. Coleridge-Taylor Coloured School, Louisville, Ky.

.3 Negro History Collection.
Material by and about Negroes. 3 vf, 100 phonograph records, and ca. 2000 v. Books, periodicals and newspapers, pamphlets, theses and dissertations, and clippings.

KY14 LOUISVILLE HUMAN RELATIONS COMMISSION. 601 W. Jefferson, 40202. Tel 502 585-2251. Mark Alter.

KY15 LOUISVILLE URBAN LEAGUE. 209 W. Market St., 40202. Tel 502 583-4835. Charles T. Steele, Exec. Dir.

KY16 NATIONAL CONFERENCE OF CHRISTIANS AND JEWS (NCCJ). 429 W. Walnut St., 40202. Tel 502 583-0281. Raymond K. LeRoux, Regional Dir.
NCCJ seeks to promote better human relations in the community through workshops, discussions, and other educational programs.

KY17 SIMMONS BIBLE COLLEGE (1879), LIBRARY (1900). 1811 Dumesnil St., 40210. Tel 502 776-1443. Mrs. Gertrude H. Lively, Librn. Inquiries answered, consultation.

.1 Simmons Bible College.
Archives, 1879- . Correspondence, minutes of board meetings, financial records, bulletins, catalogs, records of admission, and other materials dealing with the history and administration of the College. Formerly Simmons University.

KY18 SOUTHERN BAPTIST THEOLOGICAL SEMINARY (1859), JAMES P. BOYCE MEMORIAL LIBRARY. 2825 Lexington Rd., 40206. Tel 502 897-4806. Dr. Leo T. Crismon, Librn. Interlibrary loan, copying, typing, inquiries answered, referrals made.

.1 Southern Baptist Theological Seminary, Southeastern States Collection.
Papers relating to Baptists in the Southeastern States, 1770-1952. 1 ft. and 1 reel of microfilm. In part transcripts (typewritten). Minutes of several Baptist churches; a thesis (1952) by Creighton M. Oliver entitled South Carolina Baptists and the Slavery Issues; and Materials Toward a History of the Baptists, compiled by Morgan Edwards (1722-95).

.2 Sheet music collection.
Materials, 19th century. Included are spirituals (ca. 100), minstrels (ca. 20), and books (ca. 30), of Negro slave, work, and camp songs.

KY19 SOUTHERN CONFERENCE EDUCATIONAL FUND (SCEF) (1938). 3210 W. Broadway, 40211. Tel 502 774-3331. Carl Braden, Exec. Dir.
SCEF works to end poverty and racial injustice in the South by helping people of all colors to organize; to inform people of activities to these ends through a newspaper and publications, to oppose war as an instrument of national policy and to end the draft. SCEF works with community groups and other civil rights organizations. It gives staff and financial assistance on education, social welfare, voter registration, and community organizing.
Publ.: Southern Patriot, 10 issues per year.

.1 Southern Conference Educational Fund (SCEF).
Files. Books, pamphlets, clippings, photographs, and recent SCEF records and papers. SCEF papers more than two years old are sent to the Wisconsin Historical Society; other SCEF papers are on deposit at Tuskegee Institute, Tuskegee Institute, Ala., and at the University of Tennessee, Knoxville, Tenn.

KY20 UNIVERSITY OF LOUISVILLE (1798), LIBRARY. 2301 S. Third St., 40208. Tel 502 636-4621. Dr. Wayne S. Yenawine, Dir. of Libraries. Interlibrary loan, copying, inquiries answered, referrals made, consultation.

.1 Afro-American Library.
Books. ca. 500 v.

.2 Anti-Slavery Propaganda Collection.
ca. 2500 pamphlets. Microcards of originals located in the Oberlin College Library. See Oberlin College Library, Oberlin, Ohio; or Lost Cause Press (publisher), Louisville, Ky., for more complete description.

.3 Facts on Film.
Papers, 1954-67. Microfilm. Contains materials on civil rights and race relations in the South. See Race Relations Information Center, Nashville, Tenn., for a full description.

.4 Harlan, John Marshall, 1883-1911.
Papers, 1854-1915. ca. 8 ft. (ca. 1500 items). Associate Justice, U.S. Supreme Court. Correspondence, daybooks, account books, briefs, dockets, legal records, newspaper clippings, and other papers, relating chiefly to Harlan's activities as Supreme Court Justice, including his positions on civil rights, income tax, and trusts, and his activities in the Republican party and the Presbyterian Church.

KY21 UNIVERSITY OF LOUISVILLE, SOUTHERN POLICE INSTITUTE (1951), LIBRARY (1967). 40208. Tel 502 636-4534. David A. McCandless, Dir., South. Police Inst.

.1 Southern Police Institute Library.
The Library contains books concerning federal and state laws including U.S. Supreme Court decisions, and a limited collection of materials with race relations topics.

KY22 UNIVERSITY OF LOUISVILLE, URBAN STUDIES CENTER (1966). Gardencourt Campus, Alta Vista Rd., 40205. Tel 502 897-5161. Joseph F. Maloney, Dir. Inquiries answered, referrals made, consultation.
The primary interests of the Center are activities which relate to the solution of contemporary problems of urban life. Its instructional program is pointed towards higher education in community development. Its research-action programs are aimed at fulfilling the needs of potential, as well as actual, urban residents. Its service activities are directed towards involvement of and assistance to citizens in governmental and community participation.

.1 Urban Studies Center.
Included are papers (1966-68) of the Louisville CAP Agency Study, an intensive study of the local federal government anti-poverty program; and materials pertaining to "A Family Mobility, Man-

power and Community Development System," a
project to develop pre-operational plans for developing New Communities to solve the problems
of rural and urban poverty, to be completed late
1971.

MOREHEAD

KY23 MOREHEAD STATE COLLEGE, JOHNSON CAMDEN LI-
BRARY (1922). 40351. Tel 606 784-4181. Ione M.
Chapman, Librn.

.1 Anti-Slavery Propaganda Collection.
ca. 2500 pamphlets. Microcards of originals located in the Oberlin College Library. See Oberlin
College Library, Oberlin, Ohio; or Lost Cause
Press (publisher), Louisville, Ky., for more complete description.
.2 Facts on Film.
Papers, 1954-67. Microfilm. Contains materials
on civil rights and race relations in the South. See
Race Relations Information Center, Nashville,
Tenn., for a full description.

LOUISIANA

BATON ROUGE

LA1 LOUISIANA COMMISSION ON HUMAN RELATIONS, RIGHTS,
AND RESPONSIBILITIES (1965). P.O. Box 44095, State
Capitol Bldg., 70804. Tel 504 389-6136. Mrs. Pattie
Peterson, Exec. Secy.
The Commission advises the Governor and provides
leadership throughout Louisiana in the area of human
relations. It also encourages citizens to involve themselves in human relations problems through meaningful
communication.

.1 Race relations clippings collection.
Newspaper clippings, 1965- . 4 vf. Subjects include race relations and allied fields.

LA2 LOUISIANA COUNCIL ON HUMAN RELATIONS. 7986 Scenic
Hwy., 70807. Tel 504 775-4048.

LA3 LOUISIANA STATE LIBRARY (1925). P.O. Box 131, Third
St., 70821. Tel 504 389-6651. Sallie Farrell, State
Librn. Interlibrary loan, bibliographies prepared, literature searches, copying, inquiries answered, referrals made, consultation.

.1 Louisiana State Library.
The Library contains a large collection of materials pertaining to Louisiana and Louisianians. Included are books and vertical file materials relating to histories of the Negro in Louisiana, and to
individual Negro leaders, authors, and artists.

LA4 LOUISIANA STATE SOVEREIGNTY COMMISSION. State
Capitol Bldg., 70804. Tel 504 389-6601.

LA5 LOUISIANA STATE UNIVERSITY AND AGRICULTURAL
AND MECHANICAL COLLEGE (1860), LIBRARY (1860).
70803. Tel 504 388-2217. Theodore N. McMullan, Dir.
Interlibrary loan, copying, inquiries answered.

.1 Anti-Slavery Propaganda Collection.
ca. 2500 pamphlets. Microcards of originals located in the Oberlin College Library. See Oberlin
College Library, Oberlin, Ohio; or Lost Cause
Press (publisher), Louisville, Ky., for more complete description.
.2 Department of Archives and Manuscripts.
Miscellaneous, 1750- . 2,500,000 items. Mss;
public, university and business archives. Collection area spans the Lower Mississippi Valley and
includes extensive holdings of Civil War materials
and Negro history materials. Among the ms collections containing references to slavery are the following:
.3 —— Butler family.
Papers.

.4 —— Butler, Thomas W.
Papers.
.5 —— Capell family.
Papers. Includes papers of Eli J. Capell.
.6 —— Gillespie family.
Papers. Includes papers of James A. Gillespie.
.7 —— Jenkins family.
Papers. Typescripts and some originals. Includes papers of John C. Jenkins.
.8 —— Lance, Samuel J.
Papers. Letters and papers of the Lance family, including Confederate letters and records.
Contains some material pertaining to the Negro
in the Civil War.
.9 —— Liddell family.
Papers. Includes papers of St. John R. Liddell.
.10 —— Marston family.
Papers. Includes papers of Henry Marston.
.11 —— Minor, William J.
Papers.
.12 —— Pré Aux Cleres Plantation.
Record books.
.13 —— Pugh, Alexander Franklin.
Diaries. Typescripts.
.14 —— Weeks family.
Papers. Includes papers of David Weeks.

.15 Facts on Film.
Papers, 1954-67. Microfilm. Contains materials
on civil rights and race relations in the South. See
Race Relations Information Center, Nashville,
Tenn., for a full description.
.16 Louisiana Collection.
Miscellaneous. Books, journals, maps, sheet music
photographs, parish and municipal documents, vertical file of clippings and pamphlets. Subjects include Louisiana biography and history, and materials written by Louisianians. Collection is also a
depository for Louisiana state documents.

LA6 SOUTHERN UNIVERSITY AND AGRICULTURAL AND
MECHANICAL COLLEGE (1880), LIBRARY (1928).
South. Br. Post Off., 70813. Tel 504 775-6300. Mrs.
Camille S. Shade, Head Librn. Interlibrary loan, bibli-
ographies prepared, literature searches, copying, in-
quiries answered, referrals made, consultation.

.1 Afro-American Studies Collection.
ca. 1000 paperbacks. Basic books on the life and
history of black Americans.
.2 Facts on Film.
Papers, 1954-67. Microfilm. Contains materials
on civil rights and race relations in the South. See
Race Relations Information Center, Nashville,
Tenn., for a full description.
.3 Negro Life and History Collection.
Books, 1850- . ca. 3000 v. Books by and about Negroes.

GRAMBLING

LA7 GRAMBLING COLLEGE OF LOUISIANA, A. C. MEMORIAL
LIBRARY. P.O. Box 3, 71245. Tel 318 247-3761. Mrs.
Mary Watson Hymon, Head Librn. Interlibrary loan,
bibliographies prepared, literature searches, copying,
inquiries answered, referrals made.

.1 Afro-American Studies Collection.
ca. 1000 paperbacks. Basic books on the life and
history of black Americans.
.2 Facts on Film.
Papers, 1954-67. Microfilm. Contains materials
on civil rights and race relations in the South. See
Race Relations Information Center, Nashville,
Tenn., for a full description.
.3 Louisiana collection.
Materials. Contains a limited amount of material
on Negroes in Louisiana.

LAFAYETTE

LA8 SOUTHERN CONSUMERS EDUCATION FOUNDATION (1964).
P.O. Box 3005, 425 General Mouton St., 70501. Tel 318
232-1126. Rev. A.J. McKnight, C.S.Sp., Dir.

The Foundation seeks to assist the development of co-operatives in Louisiana.

LA9   SOUTHERN COOPERATIVE DEVELOPMENT PROGRAM.
P.O. Box 3005, 204 Gauthier Rd., 70501. Tel 318 232-9206. Father A.J. McKnight.
The Program works primarily to organize black people into cooperatives: agricultural, handicraft, self-help housing, consumer co-ops and several credit unions. It is a part of the Federation of Southern Cooperatives, Atlanta, Ga.

LA10 UNIVERSITY OF SOUTHWESTERN LOUISIANA, LIBRARY.
70506. Tel 318 233-3850. Kenneth E. Toombs, Dir.

.1 Southwestern Archives and Manuscript Collection.

.2 —— Watson family.
Dalton Watson papers, 1793-1930. ca. 1 ft. (ca. 2000 items. Correspondence, plantation records, and other papers, chiefly 1820-60 and 1890-1920, relating to the Montgomery, Smylie, Watson, and Young families, of Port Gibson, Miss., and Waterproof, La. Persons represented include the Rev. James Smylie (ca. 1790-1850) and J. W. Watson (ca. 1865-1921).

.3 —— Williams, David Reichard, 1890-1960.
Papers, 1912-60. ca. 15 ft. (20,000 items). Architect and administrator for federal housing programs. Correspondence, plans, reports, and photos, relating to Williams' activities with the resettlement program of the Federal Emergency Relief Administration and the National Youth Administration and other housing programs. Includes many New Deal and regional photographs.

NATCHITOCHES

LA11 NORTHWESTERN STATE COLLEGE OF LOUISIANA (1884).
RUSSELL LIBRARY (1884). College Ave., 71457. Tel 318 357-6471. Donald L. McKenzie, Librn.

.1 Cloutier family.
Papers, 1725-1941. ca. 500 items. Originals and microfilm copy of collection. Correspondence, diary, deed, plats, maps, land papers, speech, plantation books, accounts, bills of sale for slaves, promissory notes, inventory, bills of lading, bills, receipts, financial report and statements, estate papers, lists of slaves, military papers, diploma, school papers, notebooks, birth and death records for Natchitoches and Natchitoches Parish, La., programs, newspapers and newspaper clippings, books, magazines, and other papers relating to the Natchitoches area of Louisiana. Subjects include the cotton trade and the Civil War. Names represented include Louis Alexandre Buard, Suzette (Mrs. L.A.) Buard, Emile Cloutier, Emmanuel Cloutier, Jean Baptiste Cloutier, Vernon Cloutier, Emile Hertzog, Henry Hertzog, Aurore (Mrs. Benj.) Metoyer, Benjamin Metoyer, and the Buard and Cloutier families.

.2 Facts on Film.
Papers, 1954-67. Microfilm. Contains materials on civil rights and race relations in the South. See Race Relations Information Center, Nashville, Tenn., for a full description.

NEW ORLEANS

LA12 AMERICAN CIVIL LIBERTIES UNION (ACLU) OF LOUISIANA. 606 Common, 70113. Tel 504 522-0617. Alan Helseth, Exec. Dir.

LA13 ANTI-DEFAMATION LEAGUE OF B'NAI B'RITH, SOUTH CENTRAL REGIONAL OFFICE. 535 Gravier St., 70130. Tel 504 522-9534. A.I. Botnick, Dir.

LA14 COMMUNITY RELATIONS COUNCIL OF GREATER NEW ORLEANS (1960). 2140 St. Bernard Ave., 70119. Tel 504 949-2250. Revius O. Ortique, Jr., Pres. Consultation.
The Council, affiliated with the Southern Regional

Council, Atlanta, Ga., works to bring about a community climate of "mutual understanding and respect among all peoples."

LA15 CONSERVATIVE SOCIETY OF AMERICA. P.O. Box 4254, 7817 Green St., 70118. Tel 504 865-1450. Kent Courtney, Nat. Chmn.

.1 Conservative Society of America.
Materials published by the Society include topics such as civil rights and politics from a conservative perspective.

LA16 DILLARD UNIVERSITY, AMISTAD RESEARCH CENTER (1966). 70122. Clifton H. Johnson, Dir. Interlibrary loan, copying.
The Center maintains an archives department for the collection of manuscripts and other source materials, and promotes research projects in the study of Negro life and history.
Publ.: Selected bibliography.

.1 Adams, Inez, ?-1967.
Papers, ca. 1920-64. ca. 3000 items. Professor of anthropology, Fisk University and Brooklyn College. Correspondence, personal papers, mss, and other materials, including notes relating to her travels in Africa.

.2 American Home Missionary Society.
Archives, ca. 1817-1902. ca. 200,000 items. Multi-denominational society which established missions and schools throughout the U.S. and Canada; later sponsored by Congregational church as the Congregational Home Missionary Society; forerunner of United Church of Christ Board for Homeland Ministries. Reports, financial statements, contracts, clippings, and correspondence of field ministers from most of the states to headquarters in New York. Among numerous subjects discussed relating to local conditions and church matters, correspondence reflects the dichotomy between ministers serving churches with slave-holding members and those with abolitionist congregations. Correspondence from southern states and elsewhere documents the successful efforts of the Society to aid and educate southern blacks during the period of civil conflict, ca. 1855-75.

.3 American Missionary Association.
Archives, 1839-1879. 53 ft. (ca. 150,000 items). Correspondence, constitutions, circulars, proclamations, pamphlets, photos., and other papers relating to the Civil War, African slavery, abolition, the Underground Railroad, the colonization of Africa, Negro education, Reconstruction, Fisk University, and the Ku Klux Klan. Includes the constitution of the American Freedman's Aid Commission; a journal kept by H.M. Ladd while exploring in Africa for a suitable location for a mission; correspondence of John G. Fee, E.H. Fairchild and Mattie E. Anderson relating to Berea College; and the correspondence of Lewis and Arthur Tappan with and for the American Missionary Association. Other persons represented include Samuel C. Armstrong, Henry Ward Beecher, Lyman Beecher, Thomas K. Beecher, Gail Borden, John Bowring, Salmon P. Chase, Erastus M. Cravath, Charles G. Finney, Clinton B. Fisk, James A. Garfield, William Lloyd Garrison, Parke Godwin, Oliver O. Howard, John Jay, William Jay, Owen Lovejoy, Isaac Pendleton, Anson G. Phelps, William H. Seward, Gerrit Smith, Adam K. Spence, Henry B. Stanton, and Charles Sumner.

.4 Barnett, Claude A.
Papers. Director, Associated Negro Press. Restricted.

.5 Beard, Augustus Field, 1833-1934.
Papers, 1923-35. 190 items. Congregational minister; corresponding secretary, American Missionary Association, 1886-1903; author. Chiefly correspondence (1923-35), speech (1930), short memoir (n.d.) and clippings (1929-33). Outgoing letters are chiefly to Rev. Frederick Leslie Brownlee (1883-1962) and his wife, Ruth. Among subjects discussed are the publication program of the American Missionary Association; reunions and alumni

of Yale University, including William Pickens and
Henry Lee de Forest; teachers and past and present
conditions of institutions associated with the Association, including Cotton Valley School, Fisk University, LeMoyne College, Talladega College, and
Tougaloo College.

.6 Bethune, Mary McLeod, 1875-1955.
Papers, ca. 1919-50. ca. 1200 items.

.7 Brownlee, Frederick Leslie, 1883-1962.
Papers, ca. 1900-62. ca. 60,000 items. Executive
secretary (1928-48) of the American Missionary
Association. Correspondence, clippings, photographs, and mss of books and articles. Includes
correspondence from August Field Beard, executive
secretary (1890-1920) of the Association.

.8 Cartwright, Marguerite Dorsey.
Papers, ca. 30,000 items. Social worker, educator, and diplomat. Correspondence and other materials dealing with her career as newspaper correspondent, lecturer, and teacher. Subjects discussed include the Negro theater, the United Nations, the Negro press, the Peace Corps and
Africa. She is the author of the book, The Negro on
the American Stage.

.9 Dudley, Edward R.
Papers. Judge, president of Borough of Manhattan (N.Y.). Restricted.

.10 Hedgeman, Anna Arnold.
Papers. Civil rights leader. Restricted.

.11 Jones, Lewis.
Papers, ca. 1940-67. ca. 1500 items.

.12 Lee, George W.
Papers. Vice president of Atlanta Life Insurance
Company, prominent in Benevolent Orders of the
Elks, and Republican leader in Tennessee and in the
nation. Scrapbooks and a ms copy of his life as
recorded by the History Project of Memphis State
University. Lee is also the author of Beale Street
Where the Blues Were Born. Persons mentioned
are W.C. Handy and Ed (Boss) Crump of Memphis,
Tenn.

.13 Long, Herman H.
Papers, ca. 1940-66. ca. 75,000 items. College
president, and former director of the Race Relations Department, Fisk University.

.14 Race Relations Department, American Missionary
Association.
Archives, 1942- . ca. 100,000 items. Correspondence, notes and studies, pamphlets, clippings, lectures, and other papers pertaining to the history of
twenty-five (25) annual institutes of race relations
and the activities in race relations during the tenure of Herman Long, John Hope II, Lewis W. Jones,
and others.

.15 Valien, Preston and Bonita.
Papers, ca. 1935-60. ca. 75,000 items. Former
instructors at Fisk University. Preston Valien
served as assistant commissioner of education,
U.S. Department of Health, Education, and Welfare.

.16 Voorhees, Lillian Welch, 1898- .
Papers, 1917-68. 163 items. Playwright; professor of English, speech, and drama at Tougaloo College (Tougaloo, Miss.), Talladega College (Talladega, Ala.), and Fisk University (Nashville, Tenn.).
Correspondence and teaching contracts (1917-67),
abstract of doctoral dissertation (1925), ms plays,
undated poem, programs, clippings, newspaper, and
periodical articles. Chiefly personal letters (1945-
64) from Rev. Frederick Leslie Brownlee (1883-
1962), secretary-emeritus of the American Missionary Association, and his wife, Ruth (1882-1966),
to Miss Voorhees and her mother, Mrs. Emma W.
Voorhees, including comments on Brownlee's work
at the John C. Campbell Folk School, Brasstown,
N.C. (1953-60) and Berea College, both associated
with the Association. Persons mentioned include
W.E.B. DuBois, Charles S. and Maria A.B. Johnson,
Rev. William Faulkner, Mary E. Spence, and
Stephen J. Wright. Ms plays include "An' De Walls
Came Tumblin' Down" (dramatization of poem by
Paul Lawrence Dunbar) and a dramatization with
music of Longfellow's Hiawatha, by Miss Voorhees
and Olivia Hunter; "Amistad" by Owen Dodson;
"Six Yesteryears," historical pageant about Talla-

dega College (1927); and "Black Monday's Children," by Floria Demby Maddox (1960).

.17 Wells, Eric S.
Papers. Restricted.

.18 Yepez, Dorothy.
Papers, ca. 1935-69. ca. 4000 items. Philanthropist and art gallery owner.

LA17 DILLARD UNIVERSITY (1930), WILL W. ALEXANDER LI-
BRARY (1930). 2601 Gentilly Blvd., 70122. Tel 504
943-8861. Nicholas E. Gaymon, Librn. Interlibrary
loan, inquiries answered.

.1 Afro-American Heritage collection.
Materials, 17th century- . Microfilm. 131 reels.
Books, newspapers, and mss concerning the Negro
American and his history. See Minnesota Mining
and Manufacturing Company, St. Paul, Minn., for a
full description.

.2 Afro-American Studies Collection.
ca. 1000 paperbacks. Basic books on the life and
history of black Americans.

.3 Facts on Film.
Papers, 1954-67. Microfilm. Contains materials
on civil rights and race relations in the South. See
Race Relations Information Center, Nashville,
Tenn., for a full description.

.4 History of Negroes - Past and Present.
ca. 500 books, newspaper and periodical titles, 3 vf.
Subjects include slavery and abolition, Reconstruction, and the history of Negroes in Louisiana.

.5 Negroes in New Orleans.
Newspaper titles and card index. Index to articles
on Negroes in New Orleans, 1850-65.

.6 Negro Musicians and Composers.
Papers. Mss and published works, phonograph records, tapes, microfilm, and books. Subjects include
classical and popular music, church music, swing,
and jazz; biography of Negro musicians; and the
history of Negro contributions to music.

LA18 FREE MEN SPEAK, INC. P.O. Box 4223, 70118. Tel 504
865-1613. Phoebe Courtney, Managing Editor.
Free Men Speak, Inc., works to defeat "Socialist and
Communist influences that pervade the thinking and the
policies of the federal government and the two major
parties."
Publ.: The Independent American, bi-monthly newspaper.

LA19 KNIGHTS OF PETER CLAVER (1909). 1821 Orleans Ave.,
70116. Tel 504 944-0208. Wallace L. Young, Jr., Exec.
Secy.
The Knights of Peter Claver is a Catholic fraternal
organization named for St. Peter Claver, a 17th century
Jesuit who did missionary work among Negro slaves in
South America. The organization, which contributes to
civil rights activist groups as well as to charity, was
founded because Catholic Negroes felt a need for a fraternal brotherhood.
Publ.: The Claverite, bi-monthly.

LA20 LAWYERS CONSTITUTIONAL DEFENSE COMMITTEE OF
THE ROGER BALDWIN FOUNDATION OF ACLU, INC.,
SOUTHERN OFFICE. 606 Common St., 70130. Tel 504
523-1797. George M. Strickler, Jr., Staff Counsel.
The Committee provides legal services to the civil
rights movement.

LA21 NATIONAL ASSOCIATION FOR THE ADVANCEMENT OF
COLORED PEOPLE (NAACP). 1821 Orleans Ave.,
70116. Tel 504 944-0278. Wallace L. Young, Jr., Pres.
Inquiries answered, referrals made, consultation.
The New Orleans branch of the NAACP works to improve the political, educational, social and economic
status of minority groups; to eliminate racial prejudice;
to keep the public aware of the adverse effects of racial
discrimination; and to take all lawful action to secure
its elimination.

.1 National Association for the Advancement of Colored
People.
Files, 1962- . Records of the organization. Hold-
ings prior to 1956 were destroyed in 1956 when the

State of Louisiana enjoined the organization from
operating because the assocation refused to submit
a list of membership for fear of reprisals to individuals.

LA22   NATIONAL BAR ASSOCIATION, INC. 2140 St. Bernard
       Ave., 70119. Tel 504 949-2250. Revius O. Ortique, Jr.,
       Pres.
       The Association, a national professional organization of
       Negro attorneys, seeks to assure legal representation in
       the South for Negro citizens, to aid Negro law students,
       and to work for equal access for Negroes to the Ameri-
       can Bar.
       Publ.: Bulletins, issued to members.

LA23   NATIONAL CATHOLIC CONFERENCE FOR INTERRACIAL
       JUSTICE, SOUTHERN FIELD SERVICE. 8017 Palm St.,
       70125. Tel 505 482-5792. John P. Sisson, Dir.

       .1   Southern Field Service Files.
            Papers, 1962- . ca. 20 vf. Clippings and corre-
            spondence which deal with social action in the
            South, especially as relates to the Catholic dioceses
            and organizations; extensive coverage of all the
            civil rights organizations; various state, city, and
            county human relations groups; and specialized ef-
            forts such as farm cooperatives and self-help
            housing. Restricted.

LA24   NATIONAL CONFERENCE OF CHRISTIANS AND JEWS
       (NCCJ). 611 Gravier St., 70130. Tel 504 522-3760.
       Joseph P. Murphy, Dir.

LA25   NATIONWIDE HOTEL ASSOCIATION, INC. (NHA). P.O. Box
       10283, 70121. Tel 504 835-3161. Ellis L. Marsalis,
       Pres.
       NHA works to improve the facilities and services of its
       members to provide better accommodations for per-
       manent guests and travelers.

       .1   Nationwide Hotel Association, Inc. (NHA).
            Files. Includes correspondence, minutes of meet-
            ings, financial records, and other documents dealing
            with the aims, history, and programs of the Associ-
            ation.

LA26   NEW ORLEANS JAZZ MUSEUM AND ARCHIVES (1961). 340
       Bourbon St., 70116. Tel 504 525-3760. Mrs. James B.
       Byrnes, Dir. Inquiries answered, referrals made, con-
       sultation.
       The Museum seeks to present the history of the growth
       of jazz, to tell the story of the great jazz men, and to
       spread information about jazz all over the world. It
       prepares traveling exhibits, arranges tours by jazz
       bands, and narrates programs on jazz music.
       Publ.: Films, records, coins, photographs, color slides,
            posters, and club magazine.

       .1   Exhibit Room Jazz Collection.
            Instruments, records, photographs, sheet music,
            jazz sculpture and paintings, and 10 half hour pro-
            grams of recorded rare music. Most items were
            donated by the musicians who used them. Subjects
            portrayed by the collection include the evolution of
            the banjo (a typical African instrument refined into
            a tool of jazz); Storyville (New Orleans' prostitution
            district from 1897 to 1917) including material on
            the early jazz pianist, Jelly Roll Morton, early
            white bands such as the Original Dixieland Jazz
            Band, and Louis Armstrong. Photographs of many
            musicians and jazz groups are displayed.
       .2   Foreign Jazz Posters.
            Posters and photographs. Collection of materials
            illustrating jazz groups and advertising perfor-
            mances.
       .3   Rare Recordings Collection.
            Phonograph records and tapes, ca. 1900- . ca.
            3000 items. Collection contains rare items from
            the history of jazz.

LA27   NEW ORLEANS PUBLIC LIBRARY. 219 Loyola Ave., 70140.
       Tel 504 523-4602. M.E. Wright, Jr., Librn. Bibliogra-
       phies prepared, literature searches, copying, inquiries
       answered, referrals made, consultation.

Art and Music Division.

.1   Jazz Music Research Collection.
     Phonograph recordings, ca. 1900- . ca. 2000
     items. Items reflect the history of jazz.
Louisiana Division

.2   Louisiana State Document Collection.
     Depository for printed state documents, ca. 1830- .
.3   Manuscript Archives Collection of City of New Orleans.
     Papers, ca. 1750- . Included are lists of Negroes
     on the chain gang; lists of free Negroes from before
     the Civil War; New Orleans ordinances; dockets of
     suits brought against free Negroes from other
     states; emancipations; manumissions and passes.
.4   Newspaper Collection Card Index.
     Newspaper articles (ca. 1804- .) on Negroes in
     Louisiana can be located through card index.

LA28   SOUTHERN LEGAL ACTION MOVEMENT (SLAM) (1968).
       P.O. Box 50435, 70115. Connie Hodes, Dir.
       SLAM is a non-political organization through which
       southern lawyers and law students express public opin-
       ions and political analysis, with some non-lawyer par-
       ticipation. Its major function is to spread legal infor-
       mation on such subjects as the First Amendment; civil
       rights law; military law; poverty law, including housing
       and welfare law; and selective service law.
       Publ.: SLAM, monthly.

       .1   Southern Legal Action Movement (SLAM).
            Files, 1968- . Includes correspondence, minutes of
            meetings, financial records, studies, investigations,
            reports, notes for publications, and other materials
            dealing with the aims, history, and programs of the
            Movement.

LA29   TENANTS UNION OF NEW ORLEANS (1968). 2526 Mazant
       St., 70117. Tel 504 944-4736. Shirley Lampton, Exec.
       Dir.
       The Union, an organization of tenants living in the
       various public housing projects in the Greater New Or-
       leans area, as well as those interested in the improve-
       ment of low-income housing generally, is dedicated to
       the protection and the advancement of the security,
       health, and sanitary conditions of the housing in which
       persons with low income must live.

LA30   TULANE UNIVERSITY (1884), HOWARD-TILTON MEMO-
       RIAL LIBRARY (1940). Freret and Newcomb Place,
       70118. Tel 504 865-7711. Dr. John H. Gribbin, Dir. of
       the Univ. Library. Interlibrary loan, copying, inquiries
       answered, referrals made if necessary.

       .1   Archive of New Orleans Jazz.
            Materials, ca. 1900- . Papers, photographs, tapes,
            and phonograph records. The Archive contains
            taped interviews of jazz musicians and personali-
            ties (ca. 500); photographs of Negro social organi-
            zations and their annual parades, and Negro funer-
            als; phonograph records (ca. 5000); sheet music (ca.
            5000); clippings and posters (ca. 7 vf.). The col-
            lection portrays the history of jazz to the present.
       .2   Farar, Benjamin.
            Papers, 1773-1826. 58 items. Planter. Personal
            and business correspondence (mostly 1820-26) con-
            cerning life in New Orleans and on Laurel Hill
            Plantation, in Adams County, Miss., and 2 land
            grants (1773-90).
       .3   Mercer, William Newton, 1792-1879?.
            Papers, 1829-54. 351 items. Physician, planter,
            and banker. Correspondence (mostly 1835-41), and
            other papers. Includes business and personal let-
            ters from friends describing life, politics, and
            business in Natchez, Miss., and reporting cotton
            and corn planting, shipping, troubles with overse-
            ers, treatment of slaves, and epidemics, on Mer-
            cer's Laurel Hill, Ellis Cliffs, and Ormonde planta-
            tions in Adams County, Miss.; and letters (1837-41)
            from A. & J. Dick & Co., a New Orleans shipping
            firm, concerning cotton sales, prices and ship-
            ments.
       .4   Louisiana Historical Association Collection.
            Collection contains a record book of the Nachitoches
            Parish enrolling office, containing descriptive lists

and reports of slaves and conscripts enrolled,
(1864-65).

.5 Louisiana and Southern History Collection.
Books, mss and photographs. Contains material
relating to the role of Negroes in Louisiana and
southern history.

.6 Saxon, Lyle, 1891-1946.
Papers, 1784-1945. 3297 items and 7 v. Author.
Personal and business correspondence, diaries,
literary mss, clippings (mostly articles written by
or about Saxon and reviews of his books), scrapbooks, source notes, photos, and other papers. The
bulk of the material dates from 1929-45 and consists largely of letters to Saxon, some of which are
fan mail. Includes a record of the sale of a slave,
an old map, material (1888-95) relating to Mrs.
Elizabeth Lyle Saxon and her work in the woman
suffrage movement, a scrapbook (1908-10) of
Andrew J. Lyle, mss written by Saxon's friends and
prepared by W.P.A. projects.

.7 School integration.
Papers, 1954- . Leaflets and broadsides (ca. 20
boxes) representing positions for and against integration of schools in the South.

LA31 TULANE UNIVERSITY, URBAN STUDIES CENTER (1968).
70118. Tel 504 865-7711. Carl L. Harter, Exec. Dir.
The goals of the Center are to establish a coordinated,
interdisciplinary program at Tulane for the training of
specialists in metropolitan and urban affairs and planning; to encourage and to facilitate the conduct of urban
research at Tulane and to help cope with the urban
problems of metropolitan New Orleans.
Publ.: Metropolitan New Orleans Urban Affairs Bibliography.

LA32 U.S. EQUAL EMPLOYMENT OPPORTUNITY COMMISSION,
NEW ORLEANS REGIONAL OFFICE. 33 St. Charles
St., 70130. Tel 504 527-2725. Glenn Clasen, Area Dir.

LA33 URBAN LEAGUE OF GREATER NEW ORLEANS. 1821
Orleans Ave., 70116. Tel 504 947-5504. Clarence L.
Barney, Exec. Dir.

.1 Urban League of Greater New Orleans.
Files. Correspondence, minutes of meetings, financial records, reports, studies, and other materials dealing with the aims, history, and programs
of the League.

LA34 WHITE WORLD DISTRIBUTING COMPANY (WWDC) (1969).
4618½ Conti St., 70119. Alvin N. Gray.
WWDC is a "White Man's specialty shop" which caters
exclusively to the white man's interest. It supplies
goods and services pertinent to the advancement of the
"White Cause."

LA35 XAVIER UNIVERSITY OF LOUISIANA (1915), LIBRARY
(1937). 3912 Pine St., 70125. Tel 504 482-0917. Sister
Mary Stanislaus Dalton, SBS, Librn. Interlibrary loan,
bibliographies prepared, literature searches (limited),
copying, inquiries answered, referrals made (limited),
consultation.
Publ.: Bibliographies; Xavier Studies, journal, occasional articles on race relations.

.1 Afro-American Studies Collection.
ca. 600 paperbacks. Basic books on the life and
history of black Americans.

.2 Afro-American Heritage collection.
Materials, 17th century- . Microfilm. 131 reels.
Books, newspapers, and mss concerning the Negro
American and his history. See Minnesota Mining
and Manufacturing Company, St. Paul, Minn., for a
full description.

.3 Brice, Albert G.
Book, 1858. 1 v. Diary of a Louisiana lawyer relating to Negro Americans.

.4 Gayarré, Charles E.A.
Papers, 1888. Correspondence of Gayarré (Louisi-
ana lawyer and historian) pertaining to the Negro
American.

.5 Negro History Collection.
Books (ca. 4500 v.), periodical and newspaper titles.
The collection contains material on Negro life, cul-

ture and history, on Negroes in Louisiana, and
school desegregation in Louisiana and New Orleans.

.6 Negro Slave Manumission Reports.
Papers, 1832-1957. ca. 5500 items. Collection
deals with slave ships arriving, generally, in the
ports of Louisiana, Texas, and Mississippi (1832-
57). Reports tell who the slaves were, where they
came from, and who was to receive them.

.7 Rare Book Room Negro Collection.
Books (ca. 300 v.) published between 1840 and 1900.
Collection contains many first editions of books
about the Civil War and Reconstruction.

.8 Records relating to Negroes.
Papers, 1733-1808. Photostat copies. Registers of
baptism, marriage and burial of free persons of
color.

RUSTON

LA36 LOUISIANA POLYTECHNICAL INSTITUTE (1895), PRES-
COTT MEMORIAL LIBRARY. 71270. Tel 318 257-
0211. Sam A. Dyson, Dir. of Libraries.

.1 Facts on Film.
Papers, 1954-67. Microfilm. Contains materials
on civil rights and race relations in the South. See
Race Relations Information Center, Nashville,
Tenn., for a full description.

SHREVEPORT

LA37 CENTENARY COLLEGE (1825), LIBRARY (1825). 71104.
Tel 318 861-2431. Charles W. Harrington, Head Librn.
Copying, inquiries answered, consultation.

.1 Louisiana Conference of the United Methodist Church.
Records, 1847- . ca. 8 vf and 10 shelves. Contains
materials on slavery and the role of the Negro in
the Methodist Church in Louisiana.

LA38 SOUTHERN UNIVERSITY, SHREVEPORT-BOSSIER CITY
CAMPUS, LIBRARY (1966). 3050 Cooper Rd., 71107.
Tel 318 424-6552. Miss Martha Ashmon, Reference
Librn. Interlibrary loan, copying, inquiries answered.

.1 Negro Collection.
Books (ca. 400), newspapers and periodicals, photo-
graphs (ca. 150), tapes, and phonograph records.
Materials by and about Negroes.

MAINE

AUGUSTA

ME1 DEPARTMENT OF LABOR AND INDUSTRY. Room 413,
State Off. Bldg., 04330. Tel 207 623-4511. Miss
Marion E. Martin, Cmnr.
The Department is a state agency empowered to re-
ceive and investigate complaints in areas of employment
discrimination.

BRUNSWICK

ME2 BOWDOIN COLLEGE (1794), HAWTHORNE-LONGFELLOW
LIBRARY. 04011. Tel 207 725-8731. Arthur Monke,
Librn. Interlibrary loan, copying, typing, inquiries an-
swered.

.1 Howard, Oliver Otis, 1843-1910.
Papers, ca. 100,000 letters received, 62 letter-
press volumes of outgoing correspondence, 12
boxes of addresses and essays, 20 scrapbooks.
Founder and president of Howard University, 1869-
72. Material relating to the founding of Howard
University, Howard's work as commissioner of the
Freedmen's Bureau, 1865-72, and his various western Indian assignments, 1872-82, including peace
commissioner to the Apaches under Cochise, 1872,
and the campaign against the Nez Percé under Chief
Joseph, 1877.

.2 The Portrayal of the Negro in American Painting, 1710-1963.
Archives of the largest exhibit on this subject, held at Bowdoin College Museum of Art, 1964. Includes correspondence with scholars, curators, lenders, and descriptions and photos of many paintings not used.

PORTLAND

ME3 MAINE CIVIL LIBERTIES UNION (1968). P.O. Box 1062, 04104. Tel 207 774-5444. Orlando E. Deloqu, Pres. Consultation, legal services.

.1 Maine Civil Liberties Union.
Files, 1968- . Records, reports, correspondence, legal briefs, and other papers concerning the activities and court cases of the Union.

ME4 MAINE HISTORICAL SOCIETY (1822), LIBRARY (1822). 485 Congress St., 04111. Tel 207 774-9351. Gerald Morris, Dir. and Librn. Interlibrary loan, literature searches, copying, inquiries answered, referrals made, consultation.

.1 Loyal Legion Library collection.
Pamphlets. ca. 200 items. Concerning slavery and anti-slavery.

MARYLAND

ABERDEEN

MD1 HAMILTON COURT IMPROVEMENT ASSOCIATION, INC. (HCIA) (1969). P.O. Box 68, 21001. Tel 301 272-5311. Clarence Davis, Exec. Dir.
HCIA is designed to serve the needs of the black community in Aberdeen, Md., and surrounding areas on issues of education, employment and housing.
Publ.: David Walker Journal, monthly.

.1 Hamilton Court Improvement Association, Inc. (HCIA)
Files, 1969- . Correspondence, minutes of meetings, reports, studies, investigations, financial records, and other documents dealing with the aims, history, and program of the Association.

ANNAPOLIS

MD2 MARYLAND HALL OF RECORDS (1935), MARYLAND HALL OF RECORDS COMMISSION LIBRARY (1935). Box 828, College Ave. and St. John's St., 21404. Tel 301 268-3371. Morris L. Radoff, Archivist.

.1 Baltimore, Prince George's, and Talbot County Records.
Papers, ca. 1830-60. Microfilm. Will books, inventories, and administrator's accounts.
.2 Brooke family.
Green collection, 1733-1923. ca. 2 ft. Surveys, deeds, family bills, farm account books, and other account books of a planter family of Montgomery County, Md.
.3 Certificates of freedom.
Papers, 1805. Records of certificates issued by the clerk of the county court to free Negroes, attesting that the bearer had furnished satisfactory proof of his freedom. The certificates include name of Negro, brief physical description, name of former owner, if any, and date issued.
.4 List of free Negroes.
Papers, 1832. Census of free Negroes taken by the sheriff and delivered to the clerk of the county court as required by Chapter 281 of the Acts of 1831. This was part of the movement to colonize the free Negroes of Maryland in Liberia.
.5 Manumissions.
Papers. Record of Negro slaves set free by owners. The procedure for doing so was first regulated by Chapter 1 of the Acts of 1752, which required that deeds of manumission be recorded among the records of the clerk of the county court.

In most counties they were entered in the Land Records. Chapter 67 of the Acts of 1796, repealed and reenacted the laws relating to Negroes. It required, among other things, that manumissions be enrolled in a good and sufficient book, regularly alphabeted by the names of both parties.
.6 Slave statistics.
Papers. Register of slaves in each county on November 1, 1864, made under the provisions of Chapter 189 of the Acts of 1867. It gives name of owner, name of slave, age, sex, physical condition, time of servitude, if enlisted or drafted into military service, regiment and compensation paid owner. It is arranged alphabetically by name of owner within each election district.
.7 Taylor family.
Papers, 1725-1824. 72 items. Personal and business papers of a plantation family of Calvert County, Md.

BALTIMORE

MD3 ACTIVISTS FOR FAIR HOUSING, INC. 2316 W. North Ave., 21216. Tel 301 669-6034. Sampson Green, Chmn.
Activists is a civil rights organization involved in research and agitation for fair housing practices in the Baltimore area.
Publ.: Research reports concerning the exploitation of the Negro community in housing practices.

MD4 AMERICAN CIVIL LIBERTIES UNION (ACLU), MARYLAND BRANCH. 1231 N. Calvert St., 21202. Tel 301 685-5195. Mrs. Fred Robin, Exec. Dir.

MD5 AMERICAN FRIENDS SERVICE COMMITTEE (AFSC), COMMUNITY RELATIONS PROGRAM, MIDDLE ATLANTIC REGIONAL OFFICE. 319 E. 25th St., 21218. Tel 301 467-9100. Ted Robinson, Exec. Dir.

MD6 AMERICAN JEWISH CONGRESS, MARYLAND STATE COUNCIL. 5113 Park Heights Ave., 21215. Tel 301 542-7020. Tamar Paul, Secy.

MD7 BALTIMORE COMMUNITY RELATIONS COMMISSION. 210 N. Calvert St., 21202. Tel 301 752-2000. David L. Glenn, Dir.
The Commission investigates cases of racial discrimination, and initiates community relations programs to help eliminate tension situations. Formerly Equal Employment Opportunity Commission; Equal Opportunity Commission.
Publ.: Community Relations Newsletter, monthly.

MD8 BALTIMORE NEIGHBORHOODS, INC. (1959). 32 W. 25th St., 21218. Tel 301 243-6007. George B. Laurent, Exec. Dir.
Conducts programs to maintain racially mixed neighborhoods and to create new housing opportunities for minority groups through education, checking on governmental agencies, a house listing service, and fighting panic selling.

MD9 BALTIMORE URBAN LEAGUE. 1150 Mondawmin Concourse, 21215. Tel 301 523-0706. Furman L. Templeton, Pres.

MD10 CONGRESS OF RACIAL EQUALITY (CORE). 832 N. Gay, 21205. Tel 301 732-5432. James Griffin, Chmn.

MD11 COPPIN STATE COLLEGE (1900), LIBRARY (1900). 2500 W. North Ave., 21216. Tel 301 523-1111. Mrs. Hilda B. Clark, Librn.

.1 Afro-American Studies Collection.
ca. 1000 paperbacks. Basic books on the life and history of black Americans.

MD11a COUNCIL FOR EQUAL BUSINESS OPPORTUNITY. 1102 Mondawmin Concourse, 21215. Tel 301 669-2863. Benjamin Goldstein, Dir.
The three main programs of the Council are subcontracting with major industrial firms in Baltimore; building a construction program designed to help Negroes get in construction, general contracting and sub-

contracting; and starting a small business investment company to provide venture capital for black entrepreneurs.

.1 Council for Equal Business Opportunity.
    Files. Records, reports, correspondence, and other papers concerning the programs of the Council.

MD12 ENOCH PRATT FREE LIBRARY. 400 Cathedral St., 21201. Tel 301 685-6700. Edwin Castagna, Dir. Literature searches, inquiries answered.
      Publ.: The Blacklist, annotated reading list.

.1 American Negro Poetry Collection.
    Restricted.
.2 Negro History Collection.
    Materials on Negro history, including slavery. Restricted.

MD13 THE JOHNS HOPKINS UNIVERSITY, INSTITUTE OF SOUTHERN HISTORY (1966). 21218. Tel 301 467-3300. David Donald, Dir.
      To encourage scholarly research and creative thinking about the history of the South and its relevance to current educational and social problems. In addition to offering regular undergraduate and graduate training in Southern and Negro history, the Institute conducts several programs, including an Experienced Teacher Fellowship Program in Southern history for college and secondary school teachers, and the sponsorship of specialized seminars and public lectures by leading Southerners.

MD14 THE JOHNS HOPKINS UNIVERSITY (1876), MILTON S. EISENHOWER LIBRARY (1876). 21218. Tel 301 467-3300. John H. Berthel, Librn. Interlibrary loan, bibliographies prepared, literature searches, copying, typing, inquiries answered, referrals made, consultation.

.1 Birney, William. collector.
    ca. 1000 titles. Pamphlets, books, and newspapers. General William Birney, Union Army officer, son of James G. Birney, candidate for the presidency (1840, 1844). The collection, representing the history of slavery, includes minutes of the first general Abolition Convention (1794) and many succeeding meetings down to 1827; memorials presented to Congress (1790-91); the "Kentucky Protest" speech of Rev. David Rice in the Kentucky Constitutional Convention, 1792; Torrey's "Portraiture of Domestic Slavery," 1817; reports and circulars of the American Anti-Slavery Society, the Maryland Colonization Society, among others; literature concerning the political and religious controversies, 1835-65; a file of Osborn's Philanthropist, 1817-18; six volumes of Benjamin Lundy's paper, The Genius of Universal Emancipation; five volumes of the Philanthropist, edited by J. G. Birney, which later became the National Era.
.2 Facts on Film.
    Papers, 1954-67. Microfilm. Contains materials on civil rights and race relations in the South. See Race Relations Information Center, Nashville, Tenn., for a full description.

MD15 THE JOHNS HOPKINS UNIVERSITY, RESEARCH AND DEVELOPMENT CENTER FOR THE STUDY OF SOCIAL ORGANIZATION OF SCHOOLS (1966), THE J.H.U. RESEARCH AND DEVELOPMENT LIBRARY. 3505 N. Charles St., 21218. Tel 301 467-3300. Miss Audrey Y. Smallwood, Secy.
      The Center studies various organizational and administrative arrangements and scheduling, the racial and socio-economic integration of schools' informal social structures among students and teachers, organizational patterns throughout school systems, and the relations between levels of education. Continuing research focuses on the problem of school desegregation and its effects on students of varying racial and ethnic backgrounds.
      Publ.: Research reports.

.1 Race relations collection.
    Papers concerning race relations and school desegregation, including studies about differences of economic, social and political indicators between Negroes and whites, and studies of the effects of school desegregation on the attitudes and behavior of Negro and white students.

MD16 JOSEPHITE FATHERS. 1130 N. Calvert St., 21202. Tel 301 727-3386. Rev. Peter E. Hogan, Dir.

.1 Josephite Fathers.
    Archives, 1871- . Papers of the Superior Generals of the Josephite Fathers (1893- .), including papers pertaining to the Mill Hill Fathers, an English order with which the Josephite Fathers were originally associated. Includes correspondence of the Superior Generals; materials concerning work with Negro communities and the first Negro Catholic parishes in Maryland, Delaware, District of Columbia, Tennessee, Florida, Alabama, Mississippi, Texas, Louisiana, Massachusetts, Michigan, North Carolina, South Carolina, and Virginia; and newspaper clippings from Negro and Catholic newspapers, concerning the Negro in the Catholic Church. The collection is one of the "prime sources in the U.S." for materials concerning Negroes and the Catholic Church.

MD17 MARYLAND COMMISSION ON HUMAN RELATIONS. 301 W. Preston St., 21201. Tel 301 383-3010. Treadwell O. Phillips, Exec. Dir.
      The Commission works to administer the public accommodations and fair employment practices laws, and to encourage good interracial relations. Formerly Maryland Commission on Interracial Problems and Relations.
      Publ.: Newsletter.

MD18 MARYLAND COMMISSION ON NEGRO HISTORY AND CULTURE (1969). Room 305, Jackson Towers, 1123 N. Eutaw St., 21201. Tel 301 728-1110. Franklin C. Showell, Exec. Dir.
      The Commission is conducting a study of proposals to create a better understanding and knowledge of black history and culture. It conducts surveys concerning the collection, preservation and dissemination of materials dealing with black history, and is examining the possibility of establishing a center of black history and culture.

.1 Maryland Commission on Negro History and Culture.
    Files, 1969- . Records, reports, questionnaires, and survey research data concerning the preservation of black history materials, and other aims and activities of the Commission.

MD19 MARYLAND HISTORICAL SOCIETY (1844), LIBRARY (1844). 201 Monument St., 21201. Tel 301 685-3750. P. William Filby, Librn. and Asst. Dir. Copying, typing, inquiries answered.
      Publ.: Manuscript Collection of the Maryland Historical Society (1968).

.1 Baltimore Normal School.
    Records, 1867-1908. 5 v. Minutes of the board of trustees of the Baltimore Normal School for the education of Negro teachers; executive committee minutes, and records of receipts and expenditures.
.2 Bond family.
    Papers, 1749-1866. 1 ft. Correspondence, land surveys, leases, deeds, indentures, inventories, accounts, ledger, medical account book, daybooks, other financial records, and other papers of John Bond, of Fells Point, Md., Thomas Emerson Bond, physician, abolitionist, and editor of Christian Advocate & Journal, Thomas Bond, lawyer and son of John Bond, and other members of the Bond family. Includes genealogical material on the Bond, Fell, and McCulloch families and minutes and accounts of the Fountain Company, which was formed to exploit minerals in Frederick Co., Md. Some of the papers relate to the settlement of John Bond's estate.
.3 Bond, Hugh Lennox, 1826-93.
    Papers, ca. 1850-73. 37 items, 1 v., and 1 box. Covers three Bond collections: Bond Civil War scrapbook (1861-65); Bond papers (1870-73); Bond-McCulloch family papers (1859-70). Federal judge in North Carolina during Ku Klux Klan threats and

leader of the Know-Nothing party in Baltimore. Correspondence, genealogical material on the Brickhead, Bond, and McCulloch families, scrapbooks, clippings, published reports on the Ku Klux Klan trials (1872), and other papers, relating to family history, the Civil War, slavery and Reconstruction, and the Ku Klux Klan trials.

MD19.4 Buchanan, Robert Christie, 1811-78.
Papers, 1811-90. ca. 1 ft. Army officer. Military correspondence, letters for the Adams family of Boston, letters from Buchanan to his mother and sister, commissions, orders, and other documents relating to his career. Subjects include the Civil War and service in Louisiana (1868-70) dealing with Ku Klux Klan affairs.

.5 Charitable organizations' papers, 1865-1956.
14 v. and 1 envelope. In part, transcripts (handwritten). Minute book (1894-1904) of the Mountain Lake Park Auxiliary of the Woman's Foreign Missionary Society of the Methodist Episcopal Church, Lake Park, Md.; records (1865-82) of Emily Albert, treasurer of the Union Orphan Asylum (later Nursery & Child's Hospital), Baltimore, including receipts, expenditures, and items relating to benefit performances; correspondence and other papers of the Elizabeth King Ellicott Fund, Inc., relating in part to donations to the Y.M.C.A. for an addition to a Baltimore branch for Negroes and to the Provident Hospital, of Baltimore, which was primarily devoted to the care of Negro patients; and mss of "Charities and corrections of Maryland," a chapter in Maryland book (1893) by David Isiah Green.

.6 Civil War.
Papers, 1860-93, 1910. 218 items, and 26 v. In part, transcripts (handwritten). Correspondence, constitutions, lists of members and record books of military units, diaries, histories, other papers, poems, songs, cartoons, scrapbooks, and memorabilia of the Civil War and its aftermath, chiefly as it affected Maryland and Marylanders (mostly Unionists). Subjects include the occupation of Baltimore by Federal troops; letters from prisoners, wounded men, and other soldiers describing campaigns and military life; the stand of religious denominations, especially the Methodist church on secession, slavery, and the position of the churches in the South.

.7 Ford's Theatre, Washington, D.C.
Papers, 1865-1903? 1 box. Letters, notes, articles, and newspaper clippings relating to Lincoln's assassination, of the trial, and of Mary Surratt's hanging. Persons represented include Edwin Booth, John Wilkes Booth, Edward Spangler, Edwin Stanton, and John T. Ford, owner and manager of Ford's Theatre in Washington and in Baltimore at the time of Lincoln's death.

.8 Ingle, Edward, 1861-1924.
Papers, 1883-ca. 1925. ca. 2 ft., 102 items, and 13 v. In part, transcripts (typewritten). Journalist. Correspondence with Woodrow Wilson relating to the tariff, income tax, and other current affairs; letters received as managing editor of the Manufacturer's Record, a Baltimore paper, chiefly from James R. Randall and Gustavus M. Pinckney, lawyer, of Charleston, S.C., relating to public affairs, conditions in the South, the Ogden movement, and Negro labor; other correspondence; and clippings of articles relating to ecclesiastical and business affairs, book reviews, news reports, essays, and editorials.

.9 Johnson, Reverdy, 1796-1876.
Papers, 1846-76. ca. 450 items. In part, transcripts. U.S. Senator from Maryland. Correspondence, affidavits, drafts of letters from Johnson to General Benjamin F. Butler, commander of the Department of the Gulf of New Orleans, and to consuls and firms, and other documents relating to Johnson's work (1862) as U.S. Commissioner to settle a conflict between Butler and the consuls and merchants of New Orleans; together with miscellaneous correspondence, bills, and receipts from the Citizens' Bank of Louisiana. Other names represented include William H. Seward.

.10 Latrobe family.
Papers, 1796-1947. ca. 3 ft. and 31 v. In part,

transcripts. Includes three collections: Latrobe collection (1796-1853); Mrs. Bamble Latrobe collection (1801-99); and Latrobe papers (1816-1947). Correspondence, diaries and journals, speeches, articles, mss of poetry and other writings, legal notebook, sketchbooks, accounts of printed matter, newspaper clippings, and other papers of Benjamin Henry Latrobe (1764-1820), architect and engineer, his sons, Benjamin Henry Latrobe, Jr. (1806-78) and John Hazelhurst Boneval Latrobe (1803-91), and Osmun Latrobe (d. 1939). Includes diary and journal describing J.H.B. Latrobe's activities in various states, the Civil War diary and letters of Osmun Latrobe, the mss of John Edward Semmes' book, J.H.B. Latrobe, His Life and Times (1917), and material relating to the Maryland State Colonization Society, the colonization of Liberia, and the American Colonization Society. Correspondents include Charles Carroll, Robert G. Harper, Samuel Hazelhurst, James S. Howard, William O. Hugart, Washington Irving, Thomas Jefferson, Reverdy Johnson, Charles Hazelhurst Latrobe, Charles J. Latrobe, Julia Latrobe, Maria Eleanor Latrobe, Mary Elizabeth Latrobe, Charles Shaler, Moses Sheppard, Roger B. Taney, Zachary Taylor, Daniel Webster, and S.D. Wyeth. The Latrobe collection, and the Mrs. Bramble Latrobe collection are restricted.

.11 Law, Thomas, 1756-1834.
Papers, 1792-1834. 46 items and 1 v. In part, transcripts. Correspondence relating to an expedition to examine land in Western Pennsylvania, and the Negro problem. Includes the letter book of John Law and correspondence with General James Wilkinson relating to his involvement in Aaron Burr's proposed uprising. Correspondents include B. Beaumer, John C. Calhoun, and Dudley Selden.

.12 Lloyd family.
Papers, 1660-1890. 10 ft., 19 boxes, and 500 items. Documents, receipts, letters, and other materials addressed to Edward Lloyd, V, Governor of Maryland. Farm journals, 18th and 19th centuries; land papers, late 17th and 18th centuries; personal and business correspondence, 18th and 19th centuries, of the Lloyd family of Wye House, Talbot County, Md. Farm journals show crops planted and harvested, livestock, race horses, slaves, and other possessions on the farm. This abstract includes the Lloyd collection, and the Lloyd papers.

.13 Maryland State Colonization Society, 1827-1902.
Records, 1827-71. 30 ft. (84 v. and 5 boxes). Correspondence, financial records, manumission books and copies and extracts of documents and wills freeing slaves, pamphlets, and a complete set (1835-61) of the Maryland Colonization Journal. Includes material relating to the work of John H. B. Latrobe, Dr. James Hall, and John Brown Russwurm, Governor of Maryland in Liberia, a colony which was incorporated into the Republic of Liberia.

.14 Michael, Charles Wesley, 1884-1952.
Papers, 1659-1909. ca. 4 ft. In part, transcripts. Employee of the Department of Internal Revenue, insurance agent, and resident of Bel Air, Md. Correspondence of Michael; letters, deeds, maps, and other papers relating to the Michael family of Harford County, Md.; and correspondence of the Osburn family. Subjects include family affairs, runaway slaves, and local politics.

.15 Patterson, William, 1752-1835.
Papers, 1770's-1838. ca. 75 items, 4 v., and 1 package. In part, transcript (handwritten). Merchant, of Baltimore. Business correspondence, receipt books, will, and other papers of Patterson, relating to shipping matters, plantation affairs, ground rents, other financial affairs, and his children's education. Correspondents include Dolley (Payne) Madison, General Samuel Smith, General Otho Holland Williams, and others, and indentures and other papers signed by John Armstrong, minister to France.

.16 Preston, William P., 1811-80.
Papers, 1778-1886. ca. 6240 items, 9 v. and 1 box. Criminal lawyer, of Baltimore. Correspondence, diaries, deeds, indentures, wills, copies of court proceedings, warrants, proceedings (1833-35) of

the Moot Court of the Friday Evening Club, scrapbooks, and other papers of Preston. Subjects include the failure of the Bank of Maryland, the Know-Nothing party, slavery, and legal cases.

.17 Pringle, Mark U., d. 1826.
Correspondence, 1796-98, 1811-18. Letterbook (2 v.). In part, transcripts (handwritten). Businessman, of Baltimore. Business correspondence relating to prices, insurance, commodities, trading opportunities, management of a farm on the Sesquehanna River, agricultural improvements, slave labor, lumber trade, and other business matters.

.18 Richardson, Levin, 1758-1865.
Papers, 1831-61. 41 items. In part, transcripts. Shipbuilder, landowner, State legislator, and resident of Church Creek, Dorchester County, Md. Correspondence relating to shipbuilding by the Richardson brothers, land in Dorchester County, shipment of merchandise, local politics, Church Creek, and Loomtown Academy government. Includes letters written by Richardson while in the State legislature and letters from James L. Dorsey describing the Baltimore riot of April 19, 1861, and slaves Dorsey held.

.19 Ridgely family.
Papers, 1732-1900. ca. 9 ft. and 106 v. In part, photocopies. Correspondence, accounts, bills, receipts, land grants, shipping accounts and records, bonds, powers of attorney, agreements, other legal papers, logbook (1756-58) of Charles Ridgely (1733-1790); ledgers, daybooks, memorandum books, account books, and other papers of Charles Ridgely, Nicholas G. Ridgely, John Ridgely, Elijah Ridgely, Samuel Sterrett, and other members of the Ridgely family. Subjects include the construction and furnishing of "Hampton" near Towson, Md., slave buying, Margaret Ridgely's mission in Liberia, and land purchases. Other names mentioned include Samuel Chase, Reverdy Johnson, William Pinkney. The materials cover the following five collections: Ridgely papers (1733-1884); Ridgely family papers (1759-1900); Ridgely material (1827-1921); Ridgely papers (1740-1880); and Ridgely papers (1733-1858).

.20 Stockbridge, Henry, 1856-1924.
Papers, 1860-1928. 25 items and 21 v. In part, transcripts (handwritten). Lawyer, judge, and U.S. Representative, of Baltimore. Correspondence, certificates, and scrapbooks of clippings, speeches, articles, reports, and other papers, relating to Stockbridge's career, to the Maryland Historical Society, and to the Civil War and Reconstruction, especially in Baltimore and Maryland. Includes letters received (1928) by Enos S. Stockbridge, lawyer and regent of the University of Maryland. Henry Stockbridge's correspondents include Enoch Pratt.

.21 Trimble, Isaac Ridgeway, 1802-88.
In part, transcripts. Civil engineer, Confederate officer, and resident of Baltimore. Correspondence and other papers relating to the Baltimore riot of April 19, 1861, the mission of Col. Francis J. Thomas, adjutant general of volunteer forces to Virginia, to obtain supplies from Virginia authorities for the defense of Baltimore, and control of volunteer forces for police and preservation of order in Baltimore. Includes many letters of instruction from Charles Howard, president of the Board of Police of Baltimore. This abstract also covers the Trimble Papers.

.22 Williams, Edwin Anderson, 1878-1948.
Papers, 1749-1960. 4 v. and 2 boxes. In part, transcripts. Cashier, auditor, and authority on Virginia genealogy. Correspondence, diary (1749-51) of William Chancellor of Philadelphia while serving as ship's physician on a slaving expedition to Africa, bills, receipts, and other family papers. Includes a continuation of Williams' "Plain facts about some Virginians" and an index to it.

.23 Williams, Otho Holland.
Papers, 1773-1839. 1515 items and 1 v. In part, photocopies (positive). Revolutionary Army officer from Maryland and naval officer and collector for the Port of Baltimore. Papers relating to Revolutionary War battles, the beginnings of the federal

government, life in Baltimore and western Maryland, and correspondence, including with Light Horse Harry Lee and George Washington. These materials include the following collections: Otho Holland Williams accounts (1773-96); Holland Williams papers (1781-1839); Williams record book (1780-81).

.24 Wright, William H. De Courcy, 1796-1864.
Correspondence, 1829-46. ca. 50 items. In part, transcripts (handwritten). Coffee merchant, of Baltimore, and U.S. consul to Rio de Janeiro. Correspondence while serving as consul, relating to the African slave trade, trade between South America and the U.S., the shipment of merchandise, and the business affairs of Maxwell, Wright and Company. Correspondents include Solomon B. Davies, Daniel Giraud, R. M. Hamilton, Reverdy Johnson, Edward Livingston, Martin Van Buren, and Henry A. Wise

MD19a   MORGAN STATE COLLEGE, COLLEGE LANGUAGE ASSOCIATION (1957). 21212. Tel 301 323-2270. Therman B. O'daniel, Editor.
Publ.: CLA Journal, quarterly.

MD20   MORGAN STATE COLLEGE (1867), SOPER LIBRARY (1939). Hillen Rd. and Cold Spring Lane, 21212. Tel 301 323-2270. Walter Fisher, Dir.

.1 Afro-American Studies Collection.
Ca. 1000 paperbacks. Basic books on the life and history of black Americans.

.2 Facts on Film.
Papers, 1954-67. Microfilm. Contains materials on civil rights and race relations in the South. See Race Relations Information Center, Nashville, Tenn., for a full description.

.3 Forbush, Bliss. collector.
Miscellaneous. Trustee of Morgan State College. Collection contains books, pamphlets, articles, clippings, and other papers about Quaker and slavery history.

.4 Henson, Matthew J.
Papers. Member of Admiral Peary's expedition to the North Pole.

.5 Murphy, Carl, 1801-1967. collector.
Personal library. 1800 v. Publisher of the Baltimore Afro-American newspaper, historian, and chairman of the board of trustees of Morgan State College. First edition and out-of-print books, primarily relating to Negro life and history.

.6 Negro Collection.
Books by and about the Negro; papers and memorabilia of such persons as Emmett P. Scott, secretary to Booker T. Washington, and Arthur J. Smith, associated with the Far East Consular Division of the State Department.

.7 Scott, Emmet P.
Papers, 1900-51. ca. 3000 items. Materials pertaining to the history of the Negro.

MD21   MORGAN STATE COLLEGE, URBAN STUDIES INSTITUTE (1963). Cold Spring Lane and Hillen Rd., 21212. Tel 301 254-6870. Dr. Homer E. Favor, Dir.
The Institute conducts research on urban affairs, with particular reference to local community, including studies on unemployment in inner-city of Baltimore, training program for unemployed workers on Maryland's eastern shore, urban poverty, urban renewal and segregated housing; provides advice and counsel to community organizations; and assists in formulation of their programs.
Publ.: Biennial Report; Monographs of research studies.

.1 Urban Studies Institute.
Files, 1963- . Correspondence, financial records, reports, studies, a collection of monographs and other publications pertinent to Baltimore area, and other materials dealing with the aims, history, and programs of the Institute.

MD22   MOUNT PROVIDENCE JUNIOR COLLEGE (1829), LIBRARY. 701 Gun Rd., 21227. Tel 301 247-0448. Sister Mary Pius, O.S.P., Librn.
The College is conducted by the Oblate Sisters of Provi-

dence, the oldest community of Negro Sisters in the U.S. The Order was founded in Baltimore, Md., in 1829 by Rev. Father Joubert, a Sulpician priest, who, with four Negro Sisters, opened a small school for Negro children in Baltimore, Md., in 1829.

.1 Negro History Collection.
ca. 250 items. Books, by or about the Negro, pamphlets, magazines, newspaper clippings, and periodicals, among which are files of the Negro History Bulletin, Oblate, The Journal of Negro Education, and the Journal of Negro History. Subjects include Catholic education, religion, and race relations. Unavailable to researchers.

MD23 NATIONAL CONFERENCE OF CHRISTIANS AND JEWS (NCCJ), MARYLAND REGIONAL OFFICE. 300 Equitable Bldg., 21202. Tel 301 539-2660. Jacob Cunningham, Exec. Dir.

MD24 UNITED METHODIST HISTORICAL SOCIETY OF THE BALTIMORE ANNUAL CONFERENCE, INC. (1855), LOVELY LANE MUSEUM (1855). 2200 St. Paul St., 21218. Tel 301 889-4458. Rev. Edwin Schell, Exec. Secy. Interlibrary loan, literature searches, copying, typing, inquiries answered, referrals made, consultation. The Society engages in the gathering, preservation and dissemination of Methodist history.

.1 Baltimore Annual Conference of the Methodist Episcopal Church.
Archives, 1784- . Includes books, periodicals, pamphlets, vf, mss, on such subjects as anti-slavery and manumission.
.2 Washington Annual Conference of the Methodist Church.
Archives, 1864-1965. Includes books, periodicals, pamphlets, vf, mss, and an index (ca. 3000 entries) of local and travelling preachers.

MD25 WILLIAM L. MOORE FOUNDATION (1963). 433 E. 25th St., 21218. Tel 301 235-6845. Norman V.A. Reeves, Chmn. Inquiries answered, referrals made, consultation, speakers bureau.
The Foundation works to disseminate information about black Americans to the total community through its library and various programs.

.1 Materials pertaining to Afro-Americans.
Miscellaneous. Books (ca. 3000 v.) about or written by Afro-Americans, newspaper and magazine clippings on prominent figures and problems in the black community.

BETHESDA

MD25a RESOURCE MANAGEMENT CORPORATION, BLACK BUYER SURVEY. 7315 Wisconsin Ave., 20014. Tel 301 657-1810. W.E. Reynolds, V.Pres. Consultation, Market Research.
The Black Buyer is a semiannual survey of 2000 Negro heads of households in 25 SMSA's throughout the U.S. "This study constitutes the largest continuing sample of the urban Negro available in the nation." In addition to consumer information for various clients, the Black Buyer has yielded information relating to Negro leadership, major issues facing the black community, data on the black soldier, and business aspirations of the urban Negro.
Publ.: The Black Buyer Bulletin, occasionally; Surveys and studies, by subscription.

.1 Black Buyer Survey.
Files. Correspondence, financial records, studies, reports, survey research data, and materials dealing with the findings and activities of the Survey. Also included are secondary data concerning the black consumer. Restricted.

BOWIE

MD26 BOWIE STATE COLLEGE (1867), THOMAS G. PULLEN LIBRARY. 20715. Tel 301 262-3350. Lillian M. Gary, Librn. Copying.

.1 Negro Collection.
ca. 1000 v. Books by and about Negroes.

COLLEGE PARK

MD27 UNIVERSITY OF MARYLAND, DEPARTMENT OF HISTORY, THE BOOKER T. WASHINGTON PAPERS PROJECT (1967). 20742. Tel 301 454-2843. Louis R. Harlan, Editor.
The Project is working toward publication of a selection of the correspondence and other papers of Booker T. Washington.

.1 Booker T. Washington, 1856-1915.
Papers, 1860-1915. Chiefly, photocopies. Speeches, letters, and some incoming correspondence of Washington describing Negro life and affairs of his period. Unavailable for research.

MD28 UNIVERSITY OF MARYLAND. McKELDIN LIBRARY. 20742. Tel 301 454-3011. Howard Rovelstad, Dir. Interlibrary loan, copying, inquiries answered.

.1 Anti-Slavery Propaganda Collection.
ca. 2500 pamphlets. Microcards of originals located in the Oberlin College Library. See Oberlin College Library, Oberlin, Ohio; or Lost Cause Press (publisher), Louisville, Ky., for more complete description.
.2 Facts on Film.
Papers, 1954-67. Microfilm. Contains materials on civil rights and race relations in the South. See Race Relations Information Center, Nashville, Tenn., for a full description.
.3 Materials relating to Negroes.
Miscellaneous. Books and a considerable number of papers relating to the Negro problems in Maryland prior to 1960; small collection of material on the French West Indies; and material concerning the slave trade.

FORT HOLABIRD

MD29 U.S. ARMY INTELLIGENCE SCHOOL LIBRARY (1949). Tallmadge Hall, 21219. Tel 301 527-5215. John Y. Cole, Jr., Chief, library branch.

.1 U.S. Army Intelligence School Library.
Materials in the area of political science, generally of intelligence interest, including extremism in the U.S.

OXON HILL

MD30 PRINCE GEORGE'S COUNTY MEMORIAL LIBRARY, OXON HILL BRANCH LIBRARY. 5450 Oxon Hill Rd., 20021. Tel 301 248-3900. Margaret Thrasher, Curator. Bibliographies prepared, literature searches, copying, inquiries answered, referrals made.
Publ.: Selective List of Government Publications About the American Negro, annually.

.1 Sojourner Truth Collection.
Materials. Books, periodicals, documents, sheet music, films, recordings, and other materials concerning the history, accomplishments and problems of the Negro American, including current books as well as rare and unique historical items. Collection contains, among other materials, slave narratives; first editions of works by Negro authors; early works by and about the Negro American for children (ca. 1890-1920); sheet music from the Harlem Renaissance period; and materials concerning Sojourner Truth (slave, evangelist, abolitionist, and campaigner for women's rights and temperance), including Olive Gilbert's Narrative of Sojourner Truth (1850 and 1884) and Gilbert Vale's Fanaticism (1835).

PRINCESS ANNE

MD31 MARYLAND STATE COLLEGE (1886), LIBRARY (1886). 21853. Tel 301 651-2200. Jason C. Grant, III, Head Librn. Interlibrary loan, bibliographies prepared, copying, typing, inquiries answered, referrals made, consultation.

.1   Afro-American Studies Collection.
         ca. 1000 paperbacks. Basic books on the life and
         history of black Americans.
.2   Facts on Film.
         Papers, 1954-67. Microfilm. Contains materials
         on civil rights and race relations in the South. See
         Race Relations Information Center, Nashville,
         Tenn., for a full description.
.3   John Bailey Negro Collection.
         ca. 1700 items. Materials by and about Negroes,
         among which are fiction, nonfiction, reference
         books, pamphlets, phonograph records, microfilm,
         newspapers (including the Pittsburgh Courier,
         1923-66), magazines, and first editions of rare
         books by Negro authors. Restricted.
.4   Materials pertaining to Negroes.
         Miscellaneous. Books (ca. 800 v.); periodical and
         newspaper titles; pamphlets (ca. 250); 3 vf; clip-
         pings pertaining to Maryland State College; micro-
         forms (ca. 250); phonograph records; and a Mary-
         land Collection (Negro) containing ca. 100 v. Re-
         stricted.

TOWSON

MD32   HUMAN RELATIONS COMMISSION OF BALTIMORE
         COUNTY. County Office Bldg., 21402. Tel 301 494-
         3117. Edgar L. Feingold, Exec. Dir.

MASSACHUSETTS

AMHERST

MA1   HAMPSHIRE INTER-LIBRARY CENTER, INC. (HILC) (1951).
         c/o Univ. of Massachusetts, 01002. Tel 413 545-2620.
         Jackson Lethbridge, Dir. Interlibrary loan, copying.
         The Center was established to provide a jointly-owned
         research collection to supplement the holdings of the li-
         braries of the participating institution. Membership in-
         cludes Amherst College, Mount Holyoke College, Smith
         College, University of Massachusetts, and Forbes Li-
         brary of Northampton, Massachusetts.
         Publ.: Annual Report; A Guide to the Hampshire Inter-
              Library Center.

.1   Facts on Film.
         Papers, 1954-67. Microfilm. Contains materials
         on civil rights and race relations in the South. See
         Race Relations Information Center, Nashville,
         Tenn., for a full description.
.2   Newspaper collection.
         Newspapers, ca. 1800- . Microfilm. Included are
         the Pittsburgh Courier (1923- .), Opportunity (1923-
         31, v. 1-9), Atlanta Constitution (1868-1918), Coun-
         tryman (1862-65, v. 1-21), Southern Confederacy
         (1861-65, Atlanta, Ga.), and Gate City Guardian
         (1861, Atlanta).
.3   U.S. Congress.
         Bills and Resolutions, 1801-72. 7th-42nd Congress.
         Microfilm.

MA2   JONES LIBRARY. Amity St., 01002. Tel 413 253-3101.
         William F. Merrill, Dir.

.1   Field family.
         Correspondence, 1848-61. 185 items. Letters
         from Charles Kellogg Field (1803-80), lawyer and
         State legislator of Windham County, Vt.; and letters
         from his daughter Julia Kellogg Field (1829-90)
         describing her life as a teacher in Smithfield, Va.,
         including comments on social life and slaves (1855-
         60).

MA3   UNIVERSITY OF MASSACHUSETTS, BUREAU OF GOVERN-
         MENT RESEARCH. 01002. Tel 413 545-0111. Irving
         Howards, Dir.
         The Bureau conducts research in a wide range of gov-
         ernmental areas, including metropolitan problems, pub-
         lic administration, educational research, and minority
         group problems. In addition, staff members serve as
         consultants to local and state officials on such programs
         as public health reorganization and antipoverty projects.

MA4   UNIVERSITY OF MASSACHUSETTS, LIBRARY. 01002. Tel
         413 545-0111. David M. Clay, Dir. of Libraries. Inter-
         library loan, copying, inquiries answered.
         Publ.: Selected Negro Reference Books and Bibliogra-
              phies, annotated guide.

         The University Library has important holdings of li-
         brary materials on the subjects of the Negro and race
         relations, including books, periodicals, and microform
         collections.
.1   Anti-Slavery Pamphlet Collection.
         360 items. Miscellaneous publications on a variety
         of topics relating to anti-slavery movements.
         Mostly U.S. material published in the first half of
         the 19th cent. Calendar and index available. Re-
         stricted.
.2   Facts on Film.
         Papers, 1954-67. Microfilm. Contains materials
         on civil rights and race relations in the South. See
         Race Relations Information Center, Nashville,
         Tenn., for a full description.

BELMONT

MA5   THE JOHN BIRCH SOCIETY, INC. (1958). 395 Concord Ave.,
         02178. Tel 617 489-0600. Robert Welch, Founder.
         The Society seeks to learn the truth about the commu-
         nist "menace" and take some positive concerted action
         to prevent its spread. Since 1961, the Society has
         "worked steadily to expose and oppose Communist
         hands in the so-called civil rights movement."
         Publ.: American Opinion, monthly magazine; Review of
              the News, weekly magazine; Books, pamphlets,
              brochures, and other printed material concerning
              such subjects as the Society, communism, civil
              rights, Negroes, and the U.S. Supreme Court.

.1   John Birch Society.
         Files, 1958- . Records, reports, correspondence,
         and other papers concerning the aims and activities
         of the organization.

BEVERLY

MA6   BEVERLY HISTORICAL SOCIETY, INC. (1891). 117 Cabot
         St., 01915. Tel 617 922-1186. Ruth H. Hill, Librn.
         Historian. Inquiries answered.

.1   Materials relating to Negroes.
         Papers. Included are Kidnapping from the Soil, ad-
         dress by unknown person, Faneuil Hall, Boston,
         Mass., Sept. 24, 1846; The Slave Question, The
         Democracy of Connecticut, speech by C.M. Inger-
         soll of Conn. delivered before the House of Rep-
         resentatives, March 31, 1852; The Constitution of
         the Anti-Slavery Society of Salem, Mass., by Cyrus
         Pitt Grosvenor, 1824; Rev. Dr. Richard Furman's
         Exposition of the Baptists relative to the Colored
         Population of the United States in a Communication
         to the Governor of South Carolina, 1823; Anti-
         Slavery Record, v. 2, May 1836; 12th Annual Re-
         port, Massachusetts Anti-Slavery Society, 1852;
         Slavery, a lecture delivered before the Lyceum in
         Attleborough, Mass., Jan. 4, 1838, by Rev. Benja-
         min Ober, Pawtucket, Mass.; Monthly Offering, v. 1
         #5; The African Repository and Colonial Journal
         (bound) 1835-62, 1865.

BOSTON

MA7   ACTION FOR BOSTON COMMUNITY DEVELOPMENT
         (ABCD), MINORITY BUSINESS OPPORTUNITIES. 150
         Tremont, 02108. Tel 617 742-5600. Riva Poor, Dir.,
         MBO.
         Minority Business Opportunities, a division of ABCD,
         helps businessmen of minority groups with their busi-
         ness problems and aids in the formation of new busi-
         nesses. The organization has also organized free man-
         agement courses for businessmen in conjunction with
         the Roxbury Business Development Corporation, and is
         developing a program which will provide capital and

trained personnel for community-owned businesses in poor areas.

MA8   AMERICAN CONGREGATIONAL ASSOCIATION (1853), CONGREGATIONAL LIBRARY (1853). 14 Beacon St., 02215. Tel 617 523-0470. Dwight L. Cart, Librn. Interlibrary loan, literature searches, copying, typing, inquiries answered, referrals made.
Publ.: Bulletin of the Congregational Library, quarterly.

.1   Abolition and slavery.
Materials, 1660- . Books, pamphlets, and other papers relating to the abolition controversy and the attitudes of ministers and churches in New England toward slavery and abolition, including works of Richard, Increase, Cotton, and the Minor Mathers.

.2   General Council of the Congregational and Christian Churches of the United States.
Archives, 1865-1964. 65 ft. Correspondence, minutes, reports, financial records, resolutions, printed matter, and other papers relating to the national activities of the Congregational Christian Churches, the General Council, the American Board of Commissioners for Foreign Missions, the Board of Home Missions, the Council for Social Action, and the Missions Council. The bulk of the correspondence is that of Dr. Douglas Horton. Research access restricted.

.3   Newspapers.
Included are the Guardian (Boston, 1902-04, 1-3, microfilm), Congregationalist and Herald of Gospel Liberty (Boston, 1816-1934), American Missionary (New York, 1857-1934, 1846-63 incomplete).

.4   State Congregational Conference.
Reports, 1800- .

.5   Torrey, Charles Turner, 1813-46.
Papers, 1837-44. 47 items. Abolitionist, journalist, and clergyman. Correspondence and 7 sermons, concerning abolition and Torrey's imprisonment in Baltimore, 1844, for anti-slavery activities. Includes the report of a committee of William Lloyd Garrison, Amos Augustus Phelps and Edmund Quincy on a new anti-slavery paper and a letter introducing Salmon P. Chase to Torrey's prison warden. Correspondents include Nehemiah Adams, George Bourne, John Codman, Myron Holley, Joshua Leavitt, Ellis Gray Loring, William Henry Seward, S.E. Sewall, Gerrit Smith, Richard Salter Storrs, Nathaniel Willis, and Leonard Woods.

.6   Trotter, William Monroe.
Papers.

MA9   AMERICAN FRIENDS SERVICE COMMITTEE (AFSC), COMMUNITY RELATIONS DIVISION, NEW ENGLAND REGIONAL OFFICE. 48 Inman St., 02139. Tel 617 864-3150. Robert Lyon, Exec. Secy.

MA10   AMERICAN JEWISH COMMITTEE, NEW ENGLAND REGIONAL OFFICE. 72 Franklin St., 02110. Tel 617 426-7415. Philip Perlmutter, Regional Dir.

MA11   AMERICAN JEWISH CONGRESS, NEW ENGLAND REGION. 72 Franklin St., 02110. Tel 617 542-0265. M. Jacob Joslow, Dir.

MA12   ANTI-DEFAMATION LEAGUE OF B'NAI B'RITH. 72 Franklin St., Suite 504, 02110. Tel 617 542-4977. Sol Kolack, Dir.

MA13   BOSTON ATHENAEUM (1807). 10½ Beacon St., 02108. Tel 617 227-0270. Walter Muir Whitehill, Dir. and Librn. Interlibrary loan, literature searches, copying, inquiries answered.

.1   Confederate States imprints.

.2   Materials pertaining to Negroes.
Miscellaneous. Includes primary sources, books, pamphlets, and other items relating to the Negro. Many of the books concern Negro education, Negro participation in the War of 1812, annual reports of concerned organizations, and Negro suffrage.

.3   Whittier, John Greenleaf.
Papers, 1837-89. ca. 53 items. Poet and abolitionist, of Massachusetts. Correspondence relating to his career.

MA14   BOSTON PUBLIC LIBRARY (1852). Copley Square, 02117. Tel 617 536-5400. Philip J. McNiff, Dir. and Librn. Interlibrary loan, copying, inquiries answered.

.1   Anti-slavery collection.
Papers, ca. 1820-1900. Correspondence, mss, books, pamphlets, account books, records, clippings, daguerreotypes, and miscellaneous memorabilia. The collection includes correspondence of William Lloyd Garrison (6000 letters), Samuel May, Jr. (500 titles, 1834-70), A.A. Phelps (3000 titles), and Weston family (3000 titles); mss by and about British and American abolitionists, John Brown, David and Lydia Maria Child, Thomas Clarkson, J.B. and Mary Estlin, the Grimké sisters, T.W. Higginson, Loring Moody, Edumond Quincy, Lysander Spooner, George Thompson, Richard Webb, William Wilberforce, Elizur Wright and H.C. Wright; Liberator account books (20 v.); miscellaneous records of American, Massachusetts, and New England Anti-Slavery Societies (8 v.); material relating to freedmen's schools (especially those involving Lydia Chace and Ednah Dow Cheney) and to fugitive slaves (especially Anthony Burns); 6 bundles of contemporary newspaper clippings collected by Samuel May, Jr., on slave trade; books and pamphlets relating to abolitionist movement from the libraries of Wendell Phillips and Theodore Parker; daguerreotypes of abolitionists; music, especially spirituals; and miscellaneous memorabilia, e.g. pike used by John Brown, wood engravings used for Liberator masthead, and inkstand used at anti-slavery convention, Philadelphia, 1833. Also in the collection are a number of rare broadsides from 1821 satirizing the Negro's celebration of the abolition of slavery.

.2   Anti-Slavery Propaganda Collection.
ca. 2500 pamphlets. Microcards of originals located in the Oberlin College Library. See Oberlin College Library, Oberlin, Ohio; or Lost Cause Press (publisher), Louisville, Ky., for more complete description.

.3   Benjamin P. Hunt Library.
Manuscripts, volumes, and charts relating to the West Indies and slavery. ca. 700 items.

.4   Facts on Film.
Papers, 1954-67. Microfilm. Contains materials on civil rights and race relations in the South. See Race Relations Information Center, Nashville, Tenn., for a full description.

.5   Higginson, Thomas Wentworth.
Papers, 1854-1909. ca. 250 items. Abolitionist, Civil War officer, social reformer, and author, of Massachusetts. Material relating to Higginson's career and activities.

.6   King, Thomas Starr.
Papers, 1834-77. ca. 30 v. Minister, of Massachusetts and California. Includes some of King's sermons.

.7   Mather family.
Papers, 1632-89. ca. 7 v. Massachusetts family. Includes materials of Richard Mather, Increase Mather, and Cotton Mather, relating to Negroes.

.8   Negro newspapers.
Newspapers, 1828- . 65 titles. Microfilm. Representative collection of Negro newspapers, national and local (New England), beginning with a complete file of Freedom's Journal (March 16, 1826-March 28, 1829).

.9   Oakes, Ziba B.
Papers, 1854-58. 652 items. Broker, of Charleston, S.C., dealing in Negroes and real estate. Correspondence and other papers relating to the slave trade in Charleston, S.C., and other parts of the South, Oakes' farm, runaway slaves, and yellow fever, among other topics. Correspondents include F.C. Barber, Augusta, Ga., Burch, Kirkland & Company, Montgomery, Ala., Thomas Limehouse, of Goulding and Summerville, S.C., A.J. McElveen, Sumterville, S.C., William Wright, Savannah, Ga., and Wylly & Montmollin, Savannah, Ga.

.10   Parker, Theodore.
Papers, 1832-58. ca. 8 v. Theologian, abolitionist and publicist, of Massachusetts. Materials relating to anti-slavery.

MA15 BOSTON UNIVERSITY, HUMAN RELATIONS LABORATORY.
270 Bay State Rd., 02115. Tel 617 262-4300. Kenneth
D. Benne, Dir. Interlibrary loan.
The Laboratory is concerned with the range of human
relations from inter-personal relations to community
relations. Its areas of responsibility include instruction
(seminars and field service projects), research (basic
and applied), and community service (short-term and
long-term training programs and consultation with
particular agencies involved in intergroup problems).
Also in the program of the Center are annual faculty
conferences, the provision of voluntary groups designed to support self-examination, and a "living-in"
summer workshop.

.1   Joseph G. Brin Memorial Collection of Human Relations
Literature.
Miscellaneous. ca. 1200 items. Books, reprints,
journals, and other interdisciplinary materials concerning the field of human relations.

MA16 BOSTON UNIVERSITY (1870), MUGAR MEMORIAL LI-
BRARY. 771 Commonwealth Ave., 02215. Tel 617 353-
3725. Howard B. Gotlieb, Chief, Spec. Collections.
Copying, typing, inquiries answered.

.1   Barrett, Oliver Roger, 1873-1950.
Papers. 2 boxes. Lincoln scholar. Correspondence, and other papers by Lincoln scholars.
.2   Bartlett, Truman Howe, b. 1835.
Papers, 19th-20th cent. 3 boxes. Personal correspondence and correspondence with Lincoln scholars, and papers relating to Abraham Lincoln's visit
to New Hampshire. Correspondents include Mathew
Brady, Robert Todd Lincoln, Frederick Meserve,
John G. Nicolay, E.A. Robinson, and Ida M. Tarbell.
.3   Beecher, John.
Papers. Poet, educator.
.4   Bullard, Frederic Lauriston, 1866-1952.
Papers, 19-20th cent. 18 ft. Lincoln scholar.
Correspondence, notebooks, and clippings pertaining to Abraham Lincoln.
.5   Chalmers, Alan Knight, 1897- .
Papers, 1916-65. 20 ft. Congregational minister,
professor, and civil rights worker, of New York and
Boston. Correspondence, sermons, speeches, articles, proof sheets of writings, memorabilia, clippings, photos, and other papers. Includes Chalmers' papers as chairman of the Scottsboro National Defense Committee, as president of the
NAACP legal fund, as minister of the Broadway
Tabernacle Church, New York City, and other
churches, and professor at Boston University School
of Theology. The correspondence includes letters
from the men indicted in the Scottsboro case and
from outstanding liberal figures in politics, religion and the arts.
.6   Cloete, Stuart, 1897- .
Papers, 1952-65. ca. 1800 items. Author, of South
Africa. Correspondence, holographs and typescripts of Cloete's works in various drafts, clippings, and other papers. Much of the personal correspondence reflects contemporary South African
opinion on race problems.
.7   East, P. D., 1921- .
Papers, 1956-65. 14 ft. Newspaper editor of Petal
Paper, Petal, Mississippi. Personal and business
correspondence (ca. 2000 items), typescripts of
East's writings, business records of the Petal Paper, photos, reviews, and clippings. Includes 92
letters from Sarah Patton Boyle and 168 from John
Howard Griffin.
.8   Hincks, Edward Winslow, 1830-94.
Papers, 1856-80. ca. 300 items. U.S. Army officer. Correspondence; communications, including
holograph and printed orders to and by Hincks while
he was serving in the 8th and 19th Massachusetts
Volunteer Militia and the 25th and 40th Massachusetts Infantry during the Civil War; and material
relating to Hincks' work during the Reconstruction
period in North Carolina. Includes orders (some
from the field) and letters from Generals Benjamin
F. Butler, Nelson A. Miles, and others; and correspondence of Hincks with Henry Wilson, chairman
of the Military Affairs Committee of Congress,

concerning Hincks' military service and the political activities of General Butler.
.9   Kennedy, Jay Richard.
Papers.
.10 Killens, John Oliver.
Papers. Author.
.11 King, Martin Luther, Jr., 1929-68.
Papers, 1956-61. 30 ft. Baptist clergyman, author,
and Negro civil rights leader. Personal and business correspondence relating to King's work as
president of the Southern Christian Leadership Conference in Atlanta, Ga.; correspondence of King with
Senator Paul Douglas, Medgar Evers, Bayard
Rustin, and others; records of awards and honors in
connection with King's work in civil rights; and records of the various civil rights campaigns, including
the Montgomery, Ala., bus boycott.
.12 Kunstler, William M.
Papers. Attorney, American Civil Liberties Union;
author.
.13 Lincoln, Abraham, 1809-65.
Stone collection of Lincoln letters, 1860-65. 95
items. Letters by Lincoln, collected by Edward
Carleton Stone.
.14 North, Sterling, 1906- .
Papers, 1952-64. ca. 1 ft. Author and editor.
Correspondence, mss of writings, financial records, and other items concerning the publication of
North's works beginning with his book Abe Lincoln,
Log Cabin to White House (1956).
.15 Stevens, Shane.
Papers.
.16 Willis, George H.
Papers, 1863-66. ca. 125 items. Union officer.
Papers relating to Willis' Civil War military service with the 40th Massachusetts Infantry, the African Brigade of North Carolina Volunteers commanded by Edward A. Wild, and the 118th Colored
Infantry Regiment. Includes orders, commissions
and supply records for 118th Regiment while Willis
was quartermaster.
.17 Yerby, Frank, 1916- .
Papers, 1954-64. ca. 150 items. Author. Correspondence with publishers; holographs and typescripts, in various drafts, of 52 of Yerby's published and unpublished works; and proof sheets.

MA17 CIVIL LIBERTIES UNION OF MASSACHUSETTS. 3 Joy
St., 02108. Tel 617 227-9459. Luther Knight McNair,
Exec. Dir.

MA18 HARVARD UNIVERSITY, BAKER LIBRARY, GRADUATE
SCHOOL OF BUSINESS ADMINISTRATION. Soldiers
Field Rd., 02163. Tel 617 868-1020. Kenneth E.
Carpeter, Curator, Kress Library; Robert W. Lovett,
Curator, Manuscript Div. Interlibrary loan, literature
searches, copying, typing, inquiries answered, refer-
rals made.

.1   Kress Library of Business and Economics.
Among the holdings relating to black American and
African topics are reports, brochures, and government documents on the activities of the Royal African Company; books and pamphlets on early British, French and Portuguese colonization, commerce, and the slave trade and slavery, especially
in the West Indies.
Manuscripts Division.
.2   — Account books in Spanish and relating to Spanish
enterprises, 1752-1803.
7 v. Among records of other businesses is an
account book (1752-58) of the Spanish Royal
Company, Cuba, which engaged in slave
trading.
.3   — DeWolf, James, 1764-1837.
Papers. 3 v. and 1 box. Slave trader of
Bristol, R.I.
.4   — Donations for education in Liberia.
1 v., 1860-65. Boston, Mass.
.5   — Garrison, William Lloyd, 1874-?
Letter books, 1903-21. ca. 2 ft. (11 v.). Businessman, of Boston, Mass., and grandson of
William Lloyd Garrison, the abolitionist. Let-

ters, chiefly of a personal nature, relating to
family affairs and other matters.

.6 —— Lopez, Aaron, 1731-1782.
Papers. 4 v. Merchant and slave trader of
Newport, R.I.

.7 —— Miscellaneous business records.
Records of several merchants and trading
firms which did business in Africa during the
19th century, among which are the papers of
B.S. Pray and Company which traded in South
Africa, 1868-1928 (645 v., 57 boxes, 9 cases).

MA19   HARVARD UNIVERSITY, HARVARD CENTER FOR POPU-
LATION STUDIES LIBRARY (1965). 665 Huntington
Ave., 02115. Tel 617 734-3300. Wilma E. Winters,
Librn. Interlibrary loan, copying.

.1 Library
Books, periodicals, reports, files, and other materials about all aspects of population, including education and ethnic groups. Use restricted to members of Center and students.

MA20   INTERFAITH HOUSING CORPORATION (1966). 120 Boylston
St., 02116. Tel 617 426-9808. Malcolm E. Peabody, Jr.,
Dir.
The Corporation is an interreligious organization
formed to work for non-profit low and moderate income
housing in the Boston area.

MA21   JEWISH COMMUNITY COUNCIL OF METROPOLITAN
BOSTON (1943). Suite 406, 72 Franklin St., 02110. Tel
617 542-7525. Robert E. Segal, Exec. Dir.
The Council seeks to maintain the dignity and integrity
of Jewish life and to carry out intergroup educational
programs for the Jewish community and the entire Boston area. The Council conducts programs in the areas
of housing, employment, education, human relations,
interreligious affairs, social attitudes, anti-Semitism,
civil liberties, the State of Israel, and church-state
relations.

MA22   MASSACHUSETTS COMMISSION AGAINST DISCRIMINATION
(1946). 39 Boylston St., 02116. Tel 617 727-3990. Walter H. Nolan, Exec. Secy.
The Commission is a permanent, administrative-adjudi-
cative agency under the Massachusetts Executive Department, with powers to issue cease-and-desist orders
and to seek court enforcement of its orders. Its purpose
is to eliminate discrimination in employment, housing,
public accommodations, and education. It conducts educational programs and creates advisory bodies in seeking to fulfill this purpose. Formerly the Fair Employment Practice Commission.

.1 Massachusetts Commission Against Discrimination.
Files, 1946- . Records, reports, and other materials relating to actions and programs of the Commission.

MA23   MASSACHUSETTS HISTORICAL SOCIETY LIBRARY (1791).
1154 Boylston St., 02216. Tel 617 536-1608. Stephen T.
Riley, Dir.

.1 Andrew, John A.
Papers, 1772-1896. 14 v. and 24 boxes. Lawyer,
abolitionist, and Governor of Massachusetts. Contains materials relating to Negroes and anti-slavery.

.2 Barry, Charles Cushing, 1806-88.
Papers, 1834-1906. ca. 50 items. Bank cashier, of
Boston. Treasurer's accounts and a notebook of
minutes of meetings (1834-38) of the Pine Street
Anti-Slavery Society of Boston of which Barry was
secretary and treasurer; together with correspondence and documents (1855-80) relating to the purchase of the freedom of the slave Anthony Burns
with which Barry was involved as administrator and
personal contributor.

.3 Brown, John, 1800-59.
Papers, 1859-85. 1 v. and 1 box. Abolitionist, of
Pennsylvania, New York, Kansas. Consisting of
papers relating to Brown's career and activities.

.4 Goodale, Warren, b. 1836.
Papers, 1847-65. 66 items. Army officer. Letters
from Goodale to his children while serving with the

11th Massachusetts Battery, 9th Army, in Virginia,
and with the 14th U.S. Colored Infantry Volunteers
in Virginia and Texas, describing his daily life,
duties as cannoneer, duties in charge of Negro
troops, and other military activities.

.5 Howe, Samuel Gridley.
Papers, 1838-74. 1 box. Educator of blind, reformer, and abolitionist from Massachusetts. Includes materials relating to Howe's career, anti-
slavery and Negroes.

.6 Jackson, Francis.
Papers, 1691-1844. 1 box. Reformer, president of
the Anti-slavery Society, of Massachusetts. Includes material relating to Jackson's career.

.7 Liberia College collection.
Papers, 1842-1927. ca. 35 boxes. Letters, letter
books, mss, receipts and pamphlets, including some
materials from the Massachusetts Colonization Society.

.8 Massachusetts Colonization Society.
Papers, 1842-1911. 1 box. Records of the organization's activities among Negroes.

.9 May, Samuel, 1810-99.
Papers, 1825-1912. ca. 375 items. Unitarian
minister, of Leicester, Mass. Correspondence, diaries, sermons, and notebooks of Samuel May and
Caroline F. Putnam. Letters of Miss Putnam describe her administration of the Holley School, a
charitable school for black people at Lottsburgh,
Va., problems of antislavery agents, the local
scene, and the work of Abigail Kelley Foster and
Sallie Holley. May's papers relate to his schooling
at Harvard College and his ministry.

.10 Mitchell, Henry Hedge.
Papers, 1861-80. 53 items. Correspondence, busi-
ness receipts, and other documents concerning
Mitchell's military service as surgeon with the 39th
Massachusetts Volunteers and the North Carolina
Colored Troops, among other activities.

.11 New England Freedman's Aid Society.
Papers, 1862-73. 10 v. Records relating to Negroes and the activities of the Society.

.12 Quincy, Edmund.
Papers, 1822-86. 2 boxes. Author and abolitionist,
from Massachusetts. Materials relating to anti-
slavery.

.13 Sargent, Winthrop, 1753-1820.
Papers, 1772-1948. ca. 2000 items. In part, transcripts (typewritten) of originals in possession of
the Ohio Historical Society. Revolutionary Army
officer, Ohio Company agent, secretary of the
Northwest Territory, and governor of the Mississippi Territory. Personal, business, and official
correspondence and papers relating to the Sargent
estate, to Sargent's plantations near Natchez, and
the Congressional investigation of Sargent's administration of the Mississippi Territory and his dismissal, among other military business, and family
matters.

MA24   METROPOLITAN COUNCIL FOR EDUCATIONAL OPPOR-
TUNITY. 178 Humboldt Ave., 02121. Tel 617 427-1545.
The Council assists in the integration of the Boston
school system by transporting children from the black
Roxbury area to predominantly white suburban schools.

MA25   MILITARY ORDER OF THE LOYAL LEGION OF THE
UNITED STATES (1901), MASSACHUSETTS COMMAND-
ERY LIBRARY. Copley Square Hotel, 47 Huntington
Ave., 02216. Tel 617 536-9000. Preston S. Lincoln,
Esq., Curator/Librn. Copying.
The Legion "was organized to preserve the results of
the War from nullification by Confederate subversive
agents and their sympathizers in the North." It is car-
ried on today by descendants of Union officers, many of
them veterans of World Wars I, II, and Korea and Viet
Nam. The Legion's Museum and Library rooms are
administered by the Boston Division, University of
Massachusetts. Formerly the Union Officer Veteran
Association of the U.S. Civil War.

.1 Massachusetts Commandery Library.
Books, photographs, regimental histories, ordnance,
and other papers and mementos. Included are

books (ca. 6000) and pictures (ca. 36,000, many
made by Brady and Gardiner) concerning the Civil
War; and the private library of General Draper,
consisting of Civil War books and pamphlets (1000
v.), containing much Confederate literature. Open
by appointment only.

MA26   NATIONAL CONFERENCE OF CHRISTIANS AND JEWS
(NCCJ). 73 Tremont St., 02108. Tel 617 523-7510.
Frank E. McElroy, Dir.

MA27   UNITARIAN UNIVERSALIST ASSOCIATION, DIVISION OF
SOCIAL RESPONSIBILITY. 25 Beacon St., 02108. Tel
617 742-2100. Dr. Homer A. Jack, Dir. Inquiries
answered.
The Division works in the areas of civil rights, education, employment, housing, public accommodations,
voting problems, and poverty.
Publ.: SR Newsletter; Washington Memo; Xchange Newsletter (on black-white relations); UN Memo.

.1   Division of Social Responsibility.
Records, 1964- . Records and scrapbook of Selma-
Montgomery March, 1965; "To Bear Witness" photo
essay; files of involvement in legislative efforts in
Civil Rights Bills of 1964, 1965, and 1968; files on
civil rights broken down into housing, voting, education, jobs, and other topics; and a series of special
reports (5 titles) on the Black Caucus Controversy.

MA28   U.S. DEPARTMENT OF HEALTH, EDUCATION, AND WEL-
FARE; OFFICE FOR CIVIL RIGHTS, REGION I. John
F. Kennedy Fed. Bldg., 02203. Tel 617 223-6397. John
G. Bynoe, Regional Civil Rights Dir.
The Office for Civil Rights administers the anti-discrimination provision of the Civil Rights Act of 1964
for the Department of HEW. The Office has the goal of
eliminating discrimination in every facility in this
country that receives federal assistance, including
schools, colleges, universities, hospitals, nursing
homes, and other social service facilities and state
agencies.

MA29   U.S. GENERAL SERVICES ADMINISTRATION, NATIONAL
ARCHIVES AND RECORDS SERVICE, JOHN F. KEN-
NEDY LIBRARY, INC. 122 Bowdoin St., 02108. Tel 617
742-1777. Mary L. Maloney, Asst. Admin.
The Library, a division of the National Archives, will
house a complete record of the life, the times, and the
administration of the 35th President.

.1   John F. Kennedy Library.
Personal papers of John Fitzgerald Kennedy, 1917-
63, 35th President of the United States; and copies
of public records of the Kennedy Administration.
Original mss (ca. 14,900,000 pages), microfilm
copies of mss (ca. 2,500,000 pages), oral history
interviews (ca. 600), books and other printed items
(ca. 12,000), museum objects (ca. 10,500), photographs (ca. 73,000), motion pictures (ca. 860,000
ft.), and sound recording tapes and discs (ca. 1000).
Included are many documents relating to civil
rights.

MA30   ZION RESEARCH FOUNDATION (1920), LIBRARY (1923).
Boston University, 771 Commonwealth Ave., 02215.
Tel 617 353-3724. Miss Wilma Corcoran, Librn. Interlibrary loan, bibliographies prepared, copying, inquiries answered.

.1   Alma Lutz Collection on Church and Slavery.
Pamphlets and books on the attitude of churchmen
toward slavery, primarily in the U.S.

BROOKLINE

MA31   NEGRO COLLEGE COMMITTEE ON ADULT EDUCATION
(NCCAE) (1958). 138 Mountfort St., 02148. Peter E.
Siegle, Exec. Secy.
NCCAE is a project to help provide southern Negro col-
leges with adult education personnel trained to develop
continuing education programs for their community. It
was organized by the Center for the Study of Liberal
Education for Adults.

.1   Negro College Committee on Adult Education (NAACE).
Files, 1958- . Correspondence, minutes of meetings, financial records, studies, reports, and other
materials dealing with the aims, history, and programs of the Committee.

MA32   PUBLIC LIBRARY OF BROOKLINE (1857). 361 Washington
St., 02146. Tel 617 734-0100. Theresa A. Carroll,
Librn. Interlibrary loan, inquiries answered.

.1   Materials pertaining to anti-slavery.
Miscellaneous. Materials include annual reports of
the American Anti-Slavery Society (v. 1-7, 27;
1834-40, 1861); pamphlets of anti-slavery tracts
(1860-62) from the American Anti-Slavery Society
(1 v.); anti-slavery pamphlets (v. 2-8, 1845-52);
Anti-Slavery Record (v. 3; 1837); The Liberty Bell,
by Friends of Freedom (12 v., incomplete run, 1839-
58); Annual Report (2 v., 1832-52), Massachusetts
Anti-Slavery Society; Non-Slaveholder (3 v., 1847,
1849-50); and other reports, studies, books and
periodicals concerning anti-slavery.

CAMBRIDGE

MA33   CAMBRIDGE CENTER FOR SOCIAL STUDIES, INC. 42
Kirkland St., 02138. Tel 617 868-1210. Rev. James J.
McGinley, S.J., Dir.
Among its other research activities, the Center is con-
ducting a study of the social responsibility of manage-
ment, unemployment, employment discrimination, urban
economy, and labor arbitration and mediation.
Publ.: Publications list.

MA34   CIVIC UNITY COMMITTEE (1945). 57 Inman St., 02139.
Tel 617 876-6800. Mrs. Zoya Slive, Exec. Dir. Inquiries answered, referrals made, consultation.
The Committee is the official unit of the City of Cambridge for analyzing and evaluating the problems of minority groups in the area. It plans and conducts programs designed to encourage understanding and cooperation among all groups in Cambridge. The Committee
was formerly the Cambridge Committee for Racial and
Religious Understanding.

MA35   CIVIL DISORDER RESEARCH INSTITUTE (1969). P.O. Box
185, Harvard Square Sta., 02138. Tel 617 266-2398.
Ronald A. Gray, Publisher.
The Institute is a private organization which collects,
researches, analyzes and verifies data relating to civil
disorders in the U.S. The chief program of the Institute
is the publication of Civil Disorder Digest, a summary
of all available information on disorders precipitated by
racial and political conflicts, high school and university
issues, sabotage, and labor disputes where violence
occurs.
Publ.: Civil Disorder Digest, biweekly newsletter.

MA35a   CIVIL LIBERTIES LEGAL DEFENSE FUND, INC. (CLLDF)
(1967). 2 Bow St., 02138. Tel 617 864-8680. John G.S.
Flym, Esq., Staff Counsel.
The CLLDF is a legal defense organization which
undertakes projects to increase the on-going availability of competent legal defense for those who dissent—
minority communities, student activists or uninvolved
spectators at demonstrations. The issues are the war,
justice for black people, and fair trials for "con-
spirators."

MA36   COMMUNITY LEGAL ASSISTANCE OFFICE (1966), LI-
BRARY. 235 Broadway, 02139. Tel 617 492-6250.
Paul Newman, Chief Attorney. Copying, typing, inquiries answered, referrals made, consultation.
The Office is operated by Harvard Law School to provide legal services to people who cannot afford private
attorneys.
Publ.: Pamphlets on such subjects and welfare and legal
rights.

.1   Community Legal Assistance Office Library.
Books, periodicals, vertical file materials, and
theses and dissertations dealing specifically with
the legal aspects of civil rights issues.

MA37 EDUCATION DEVELOPMENT CENTER, INC. (1967), LI-
      BRARY OF THE SOCIAL STUDIES CURRICULUM
      PROGRAM. 15 Mifflin Place, 02138. Tel 617 868-
      5800. Peter B. Dow, Dir.
      The result of a merger of Educational Services Incor-
      porated (1958) and the Institute for Educational Innova-
      tion (1966), the Education Development Center was
      formed as a non-profit institution to operate the New
      England regional educational laboratory and programs
      in curriculum development and reform. The Social
      Studies Curriculum Program is interested in developing
      materials that will engage students in the fundamental
      problems of human society and its history. It has pro-
      duced an Afro-American unit for use in the study of
      black history.

MA38 HARVARD UNIVERSITY, GRADUATE SCHOOL OF EDUCA-
      TION, OFFICE OF FIELD ACTIVITIES (1968). 221
      Longfellow Hall, Appian Way, 02138. Tel 617 868-7600.
      George B. Thomas, Dir.
      The Office is concerned with problems of educational
      inadequacy and inequality, predominantly in urban, but
      also in rural areas. It attempts to match needs articu-
      lated by community people with the gamut of Harvard
      Graduate School of Education student/faculty, research/
      training interests. The goal is to try to meet existing
      needs with existing resources and through that process
      of direct contact to improve the general quality of re-
      sources available to those whose lives are immediately
      and daily touched by present inequalities.

MA39 HARVARD UNIVERSITY, HARVARD COLLEGE LIBRARY,
      HOUGHTON LIBRARY (1942). 02138. Tel 617 868-7600.
      William H. Bond, Librn. Copying, typing, inquiries an-
      swered, referrals made, consultation.
      Publ.: Afro-American Studies: A Guide to Resources of
          the Harvard University Library (preliminary edi-
          tion, 1969).

      Manuscript Collection.

.1 — American Board of Commissioners of Foreign
       Missions.
       Papers, ca. 1830-1960. In part, copies. Cor-
       respondence between Board of Commissioners
       and missionaries, diaries, reports, photo-
       graphs, and mss indexed in separate bound
       volume. Collection includes much material
       on Africa.
.2 — American Freedman's Inquiry Commission.
       Papers, ca. 1862-3. 1 box. Mss containing
       information on the condition of ex-slaves,
       statistics, taxes, suggestions for treatment,
       among other topics.
.3 — Armistead, Wilson.
       1848. Tribute to the Negro, a 2-page state-
       ment.
.4 — Bailey, Gamaliel, 1807-59.
       Papers, ca. 1830-55. Mss and correspon-
       dence, including a letter about the Quarterly
       Anti-Slavery Magazine (1830).
.5 — Baker, Ray Stannard, 1870-1946.
       Letters, 1901-29, in various ms collections.
       Liberal author and civil rights advocate.
.6 — Banks, Nathaniel P., 1816-94.
       Papers, ca. 1850-70. Union General and
       Governor of Massachusetts. Numerous let-
       ters and mss, including a ten-page statement
       on the ability of freedmen to support them-
       selves (1864).
.7 — Beecher, Henry Ward.
       Papers, 1850-87. ca. 61 items. Massachu-
       setts, Indiana, New York; congregational
       clergyman and abolitionist.
.8 — Benezet, Anthony, 1713-84.
       Letters, 1776. Quaker pamphleteer and anti-
       slavery advocate.
.9 — Birney, James G., 1817-88.
       Letter, 1882. Abolitionist, politician.
.10 — Borgman, Albert Stephens, 1890-?. collector.
       18th and 19th cent. Autographs. 4 boxes.
       Collection contains letters from William
       Lloyd Garrison, Wendell Phillips, and Joel
       Chandler Harris, among others.
.11 — Braithwaite, William Stanley, 1878-1962. collector.
       Collection of autographs, 1897-1929. 28

boxes. Writer, anthologist. Includes letters
from Countee Cullen, James Weldon Johnson,
Langston Hughes, Claude McKay, and Alain
Locke, and poems by J.W. Johnson and Alain
Locke.
.12 — Brown, John, 1800-59.
       Papers, ca. 1850-80. Abolitionist leader.
       Various mss, including letters by and about
       John Brown and his raid, and documents con-
       cerning the raid, including lists of names.
.13 — Buffum, Arnold, 1782-1859.
       Papers, 1839-59. 18 items. Collection in-
       cludes an 18-page statement on slavery and
       newspaper clippings (n.d. 184?)
.14 — Cable, George Washington, 1844-1925.
       The Grandissime: A Story of the New Orleans
       Creoles, 1879. 734 pp. Southern liberal.
.15 — Champion, Rev. George.
       Journals, 1834-37. 2 v. The journals concern
       Champion's voyage from Boston to Cape Town
       (1834-35) and his activities as missionary to
       the Zulus (1835-37).
.16 — Channing, William Ellery, 1780-1842.
       Correspondence. 3 boxes. Unitarian clergy-
       man and liberal leader. Correspondence in-
       cludes letters to and from the leading liberals
       of Channing's time.
.17 — Child, Lydia Maria (Francis), 1802-80.
       Papers, 1845-80. Included in the collection
       are many letters about anti-slavery matters.
.18 — Clarke, James Freeman, 1810-88.
       Personal and family papers. 11 boxes. Uni-
       tarian clergyman and anti-slavery advocate.
       Collection includes letters from Booker T.
       Washington, Harriet Beecher Stowe and
       Charles Sumner, among others.
.19 — Cowper, William, 1731-1900.
       Poems. Includes a sonnet (n.d.) of anti-
       slavery interest by Cowper, and another anti-
       slavery sonnet by William Hayley (n.d.).
.20 — Davis, Edward Morris, 1811-88.
       Collection of letters received, 1834-54. 1 v.
       Letters include many of anti-slavery interest.
.21 — Dearborn, Frederick M. collector.
       Collection of military and political Ameri-
       cana. ca. 18 boxes. Collection includes 10
       boxes of Confederate Civil War papers and 8
       boxes of Union Civil War papers.
.22 — Dix, Dorothea Lynde.
       Papers, 1826-86. 1 v., 35 boxes, and 600
       items. Social reformer and abolitionist.
.23 — Douglass, Frederick 1817?-95.
       Various letters in different collections, ca.
       1850-86. Black abolitionist, author.
.24 — Downing, George T.
       Correspondence, 1866. 3 pp. Black protest
       leader. Includes letter to Charles Sumner pro-
       testing segregation in U.S. Senate gallery
       seatings.
.25 — DuBois, William Edward Burghardt, 1868-1963.
       Various letters in different collections. Black
       scholar, author, and civil rights leader.
.26 — Dunbar, Paul Laurence, 1872-1906.
       Letters, in various collections. Black poet.
.27 — Eaton, John.
       Manuscript, 1863. 19 pp. Unpublished report
       on freedmen.
.28 — Emerson, Charles Chauncy, 1808-36.
       Lecture on Slavery, 1835. 26 pp. ms. For-
       merly attributed to Ralph Waldo Emerson.
.29 — Emerson, Ralph Waldo, 1803-82.
       Papers, 1825-82. ca. 11,000 items. Poet,
       abolitionist, of Massachusetts. Includes 10,000
       letters to Emerson and his family, hundreds of
       personal letters, 140 v. journals, and literary
       mss. Restricted.
.30 — Facts on Film.
       Papers, 1954-67. Microfilm. Contains mate-
       rials on civil rights and race relations in the
       South. See Race Relations Information Center,
       Nashville, Tenn., for a full description.
.31 — Freedman's Aid Society.
       Daily journal, 1869-71. 1 v., 360 pp.
.32 — Fuller, Margaret (Marchioness Ossole).
       Papers, 1662-1870. 23 boxes and 100 items.

Materials of the Fuller family, including 49
letters to Emerson.

MD39.33 — Garrison family.
Papers. 7 boxes. Collection includes much
correspondence between Wendell Phillips Garrison and William Lloyd Garrison, Sr., 1857-
79.

.34 — Goodell, William, 1792-1878.
Various letters, including one letter (1837)
about Quarterly Anti-Slavery Magazine, and
one letter (1840) also about anti-slavery
matters.

.35 — Hall, Hugh.
Barbados letter book, 1716-20. Ms copy. 270
pp. and index. Includes references to Barbados
slavery.

.36 — Hammond, Eli Shelby.
Description of slave life on a plantation before
the Civil War. Pencil notes on three note pads
(1895), written in response to request of Hammond's son for recollections of ante-bellum
plantation life.

.37 — Harris, Joel Chandler, 1848-1908.
Letters, in different collections. Popularizer
of the Uncle Remus tales.

.38 — Higginson, Thomas Wentworth, 1823-1911.
Papers, in different collections. Reformer,
soldier and author. Included are Higginson's
diaries, 1863-1911 (47 v.); memoranda of military duty; one folder of "Negro Songs," ca.
1865; correspondence with Booker T. Washington, William Lloyd Garrison, Sr., William
Lloyd Garrison, Jr., Wendell Phillips, and
others; and materials about John Brown and
his Harper's Ferry raid (ca. 1878-1910).

.39 — Hoar, George Frisbie, 1826-1904. collector.
Autographs. 2 boxes. Collection includes one
letter from Toussaint L'Ouverture (1800); letter from Charles Sumner (1860); notes for
autobiography by Wendell Phillips; and lines
on Wendell Phillips by Daniel Webster.

.40 — Holmes, John Haynes, 1879-?.
Correspondence, in various collections. In
part, copies. Liberal leader.

.41 — Howard, Oliver Otis, 1830-1909.
Letters, in various collections. ca. 1863-1908.
Commissioner of the Freedman's Bureau.

.42 — Howe, Julia Ward.
Papers, 1827-1910. 60 v., 15 boxes, and ca.
1000 items. Abolitionist. Papers pertaining
to anti-slavery.

.43 — Howe, Mark Antony DeWolf, 1864-1960.
Correspondence, ca. 1890-1954. 35 boxes.
Writer. Collection includes correspondence
with numerous 20th century liberals such as
Moorfield Storey and Oswald Garrison Villard.

.44 — Howe, Samuel Gridley, 1801-76.
Correspondence, ca. 1840-70. Reformer.
Correspondents include 19th century liberal
figures Charles Sumner, Oliver Wendell
Holmes, and Thomas Wentworth Higginson.

.45 — Jay, John, 1745-1829.
Correspondence, in various collections, 1778-
1829. Political leader and anti-slavery advocate.

.46 — Johnson, Andrew, 1808-75.
Correspondence, in various collections, 1850-
68. President of the U.S.

.47 — Kossuth, Lajos, 1802-94.
Correspondence, ca. 1850-70. Hungarian
revolutionary leader and liberal. Letters include one on slavery.

.48 — Ku Klux Klan.
Documents. Included are a letter threatening
an abolitionist (18??) and two framed Klan
charters (1920, 1928).

.49 — Lea, Henry Charles, 1825-1909.
Book reviews, 1865. Writer, publisher of
North American Review. Two reviews
of books dealing with slavery, both published
in the North American Review.

.50 — The Liberator, ed. William Lloyd Garrison.
Bound v., 1860's. Bound in with the newspaper copies in some volumes are various

broadsides, statements and fragments of anti-
slavery interest.

.51 — Lincoln, Abraham, 1809-65.
Correspondence, in various collections.
President of the U.S.

.52 — Lincoln, William.
Writ of execution for public sale of slave,
1770. 1 p.

.53 — Lindsay, Vachel, 1879-1931.
Original ms of poem "The Congo." 4 sheets.
Poet.

.54 — Locke, Alain, 1886-1954.
Letters and poems, in various collections.
Critic and chronicler of the "Harlem
Renaissance."

.55 — Longfellow, Henry Wadsworth, 1807-82.
Papers. Poet. Collection includes letters to
Longfellow (66 boxes), among which are letters from Charles Sumner, 1837-74 (402 letters) and a letter from Wilson Armistead about
anti-slavery matters; and a "Boston Hymn" by
Ralph Waldo Emerson, 1863, in celebration of
the Emancipation Proclamation.

.56 — McKim, James Miller, 1810-74.
Correspondence, in various collections, ca.
1850-80. 10 letters. Abolitionist leader.

.57 — McLain, W.
Letters, 1854. 3 pp. Concerning suppression
of slave trade.

.58 — Miles, Henry.
Papers and correspondence, 1826-80. 2 boxes.
Quaker leader, liberal. Letters, documents,
and other materials about Quakers and anti-
slavery matters.

.59 — Moore, Samuel Preston.
Certified ms copy of manumission certificate,
1776.

.60 — Moton, Robert Russa, 1867-?.
Correspondence, in various collections.
Second president of Tuskegee Institute.

.61 — Mott, Lucretia, 1793-1880.
Papers. 4 items, including letters and frag-
ments relating to anti-slavery matters.
Quaker leader and abolitionist.

.62 — Norton, Charles Eliot, 1827-1900.
Papers, ca. 1845-1908. 44 boxes. Professor
of history of fine arts, Harvard University.
Correspondents include Booker T. Washington,
Charles Sumner, Thomas Wentworth Higgin-
son, and Wendell Phillips.

.63 — Owen, Robert Dale, 1801-77.
"A Bill to Emancipate Persons of African
Descent...," 1862. 6 pp. American re-
former.

.64 — Page, Walter Hines, 1855-1918.
Papers. ca. 34 boxes. Journalist and diplomat. Letters, diaries, and other materials,
"American Period," including correspondence
with members of the Garrison family, and 21
items from or about Booker T. Washington.

.65 — Palfrey, John Gorham, 1796-1881.
Family papers, ca. 1760-1881. 150 boxes.
Unitarian clergyman, historian. Collection includes 148 letters from Charles Sumner and
199 letters to Charles Sumner, 1836-73; correspondence, ca. 1830-70, with Thomas Wentworth Higginson, Harriet Beecher Stowe, numerous Free Soil parties, and Wendell
Phillips; and correspondence of interest concerning the free-soil question and anti-slavery
with J.R. Giddings, Ellis Grey, and Ebeneezer
Rockwood Hoar.

.66 — Parsons, Theodore, and Pearson, Eliphalet.
"Forensic Dispute" re slavery, 1773. Tran-
scription of the dialogue, 39 pp.

.67 — Parton, James, 1822-91.
Correspondence. 8 boxes. Collector and
writer. Collection includes correspondence
with Booker T. Washington and Harriet
Beecher Stowe, ca. 1863-91.

.68 — Pascal, Paul.
Correspondence, ca. 1830s. 5 folders. Letters from Pascal, a New Orleans slave dealer,
to B. Raux in Norfolk, Va., including bills of

sale from Raux to customers and financial accounts, among other business papers.

MD39.69 —— Phillips, Wendell, 1811-84.
Correspondence, in various collections, ca. 1840-80. Abolitionist leader.

.70 —— Pickard-Whittier Papers.
Correspondence, ca. 1832-1914. 19 boxes. John Greenleaf Whittier, 1807-92, poet, and Samuel T. Pickard, 1829-1915, biographer. Includes correspondence, 1890-1901, with Booker T. Washington and one letter to Mrs. Booker T. Washington; and 45 letters, 1846-74, by John Greenleaf Whittier to Charles Sumner.

.71 —— Provisional National Progressive (Party) Committee.
Official Report of Proceedings, 3 August, 1912. Typed carbon copy. 266 pp. Report includes debate on the question of voting rights of blacks.

.72 —— Robeson, Paul, 1898- .
Two letters in different collections. Black actor.

.73 —— Roosevelt, Theodore, 1858-1919.
Papers. Extensive collection. President of the U.S.

.74 —— Russel, le Baron.
Report on the condition of ex-slave refugees in Union Army, 1862. 19 pp., plus 4-page addendum. Also 1862 covering letter for Russel's report.

.75 —— Sanborn, Franklin Benjamin, 1831-1917.
Materials. 1 box. Many copies of originals in the Boston Public Library. Collected materials about John Brown and the Harper's Ferry raid.

.76 —— Shaw, Sarah Blake (Sturgis), 1815-1902.
Correspondence. 1 box. Included are 156 letters from Lydia Maria Child, 1838-80, with much of anti-slavery interest.

.77 —— Siebert, Wilbur Henry, 1866-?.
Materials. Compiler and historian. 45 v. Materials collected for his study The Underground Railroad. Mss, typescripts, and newspaper clippings. Indexed and compiled by states of the Union.

.78 —— Slavery papers.
ca. 1800-63. 1 box. Mss, bills of sale, advertisements for sale, legal certificates, U.S. Army "contraband" passes, and other papers.

.79 —— Slavery papers.
Legal documents concerning slave sale and apprenticeship, 1796, 1804, 1829. 3 items.

.80 —— Smith, Gerrit, 1797-1874.
Correspondence, in various collections. 17 letters. Abolitionist leader.

.81 —— Smith, Joseph H.
Negro folk songs, ca. 1920's. 1 folder. Collection includes typed words to twelve songs, plus some fragments, some printed songs, and explanatory letters.

.82 —— Sparks, Jared, 1789-1866. collector.
Materials. Copies, with some originals. Catalogued in 18 card-file drawers. Collection covers primarily the American revolutionary period, but also contains some material from colonial times through mid-19th century. ca. 60 listings under headings "Slavery," "Negroes," and "Abolitionists." Sparks was president of Harvard University.

.83 —— Spingarn, Joel, 1875-?.
Correspondence, in different collections. Liberal and civil rights advocate.

.84 —— Stone, Dr. C.
Records. 1 v. Free-Soil Roll, 1852-53, a list of Free-soil voters in Boston.

.85 —— Stone, Brigadier General C. P.
General Orders No. 16, re fugitive slaves.

.86 —— Storey, Moorfield, 1845-1929.
Correspondence, in various collections. Liberal spokesman.

.87 —— Sumner, Charles, 1811-74.
Papers. 152 boxes, partially indexed by box. U.S. Senator and abolitionist. Contains ex-

tensive information of anti-slavery interest. See Charles Sumner auto-file for Sumner works not included in this collection, e.g.: Charles Sumner, Report made to the Senate for the repeal of all fugitive slave bills (1866), and The Crime Against Kansas (1856). Also see separate catch-all box of Charles Sumner material, including one 12-page letter to H.J. Peirce, 1861, giving Sumner's views on slavery.

.88 —— Tappan family.
Papers, primarily personal letters, in various collections. Abolitionist family, including Arthur Tappan (1786-1865), president of American and Foreign Anti-Slavery society, and Lewis Tappan (1788-1873).

.89 —— Toussaint L'Ouverture (Pierre Dominique), 1746-1803.
Papers, ca. 1790-1803. 15 items. In part, facsimile. Haitian revolutionary leader. Letters and documents in French, and two English newspaper clippings.

.90 —— Treat, John Henry.
"Republican Speeches and Political Facts," 1857. 1 v., 42 pp. Concerns politics and the slave question.

.91 —— Trotter, William Monroe.
Letters. Black radical leader and editor of the Boston Guardian, which was begun in 1901.

.92 —— Truth, Sojourner, 1797-1883.
Letter, 1876. Abolitionist, preacher, and lecturer, born a slave.

.93 —— Villard, Oswald Garrison, 1872-1949.
Papers. 80 boxes. Civil rights advocate, liberal, author, and editor of the Nation. Collection includes correspondence with all major figures and many minor ones about civil rights issues, NAACP, and other related topics.

.94 —— Wadsworth, Brigadier General J.S.
"Report on Inspection of Colored Troops and Colored Refugees in the Mississippi Valley...," 1863. 23 pp.

.95 —— Ward, Samuel Gray, 1817-1907.
Correspondence, ca. 1830-1907. 7 boxes. Correspondents include Charles Sumner, Thomas Wentworth Higginson, et al.

.96 —— Washington, Booker Taliaferro, 1856-1915.
Letters, in various collections. Founder of Tuskegee Institute and black leader.

.97 —— West Indies.
Records, 1680-1725. 1 v., 836 pp. Acts, reports, petitions, opinions, and other documents containing numerous references to the slave question.

.98 —— Wheatley, Phillis, 1753?-94.
Poem, 1772.

.99 —— The White Ethiopian.
British play, ca. 1640. Author unknown. 278 pp. Photostatic copy of the original British Museum ms.

.100—— White, Newman Ivy. collector.
"Negro songs and Folklore," 1916 and 1919. 3 v., 351 songs. Volumes include the original mss of contributors, typewritten copies of mss, and analyses.

.101—— White, Walter.
Letters, in different collections, ca. 1930-40. President of NAACP.

.102—— Whitney, Henry Austin.
Letter, 1863, and telegram about the Emancipation Proclamation.

.103—— Woolman, John, 1720-72.
Two letters, 1745 and 1758. Quaker leader and anti-slavery advocate.

.104—— Wright, Elizur, 1803-85.
Letters, ca. 1830-70. Anti-slavery advocate.

.105 Theatre Collection.
Records, portraits, clippings, pamphlets, programs, sheet music, reviews, and other materials about the American theatre. The Collection includes items relevant to the black man such as photos, engravings, and lithographs of performers,

including Paul Robeson and Ira Aldridge; printed material on the "Black Theater," including newspaper clippings, both biographical and reviews; 1 box of materials relating to performances of Uncle Tom's Cabin, including playbills, letters and prompt books; 14 folio boxes of broadsides, advertisements, photos, journals, sheet music, and histories concerning minstrels (ca. 1860- early 1900's); 8 boxes of cabinet photos of minstrels; contemporary clippings about performers such as Aldridge and Robeson; and a collection of playbills and broadsides, filed by performer.

MA40   HARVARD UNIVERSITY, HARVARD COLLEGE LIBRARY, WIDENER LIBRARY. 02138. Tel 617 868-7600. Douglas W. Bryant, Univ. Librn.

.1   Document Division.
Among its holdings the document division has four Afro-American newspapers on microfilm: the Chicago Defender (1965- .), the Pittsburgh Courier (1923- .), the Baltimore Afro-American (1893- .), and the Bay State Banner (1965- .). Also, as a depository library for U.S. government publications, the division has basic research documents published by the government about Afro-Americans in the U.S., including congressional debates and hearings on education, slavery, emancipation, civil rights, discrimination, and urban affairs; speeches of presidents and cabinet members; statistical reports; and publications on various aspects of American life, such as Negro Population, 1790-1915.

.2   Facts on Film.
Papers, 1954-67. Microfilm. Contains materials on civil rights and race relations in the South. See Race Relations Information Center, Nashville, Tenn., for a full description.

.3   The Negro in the United States, pre-1865.
Materials, classified in the general holdings. Includes collection of pamphlets (ca. 200) dealing with slavery and the Abolition Movement; a collection of slave autobiographies; source material on the Underground Railroad; and material on the Abolition Movement, including such sets of documents as the Reports of the Massachusetts Anti-Slavery Society, and files of journals such as The Non-Slaveholder and the Quarterly Anti-Slavery Magazine.

.4   The Negro in the United States, since 1865.
Materials, classified in the general holdings. Primarily works covering recent aspects of Afro-American history, including periodicals and journals such as the Negro Yearbook, the Journal of Negro History, Crisis, Phylon, and the Negro History Bulletin.

MA41   HARVARD UNIVERSITY, HARVARD PROGRAM ON REGIONAL AND URBAN ECONOMICS (1966). 235 Littauer Center, Harvard Center, 02138. Tel 617 868-7600. John F. Kain, Dir.
The Harvard Program on Regional and Urban Economics is a teaching program at both the undergraduate and graduate level and a program of research on regional and urban economics. Major areas of current research include changes in metropolitan structure and ghetto labor markets, determinants of North-South migration, the prospects of southern economic development, and ghetto unemployment and low income.
Publ.: Interim and final reports on completed research.

MA42   HARVARD UNIVERSITY, LAW SCHOOL LIBRARY (1817). Langdell Hall, 02138. Tel 617 868-7000. Earl C. Borgeson, Librn. Interlibrary loan, copying.

.1   Law Library.
Among its holdings the library has a large collection of legal publications of interest for Afro-American studies, including publication in the categories of civil rights, laws about slavery and servitude, poverty in its legal context, discrimination, and civil procedure; publications on the legal context of civil rights and poverty, such as public assistance handbooks and pamphlets for the poor issued by the U.S. government; and a reserve collection of current court decisions on law and poverty.

MA43   HARVARD UNIVERSITY, UNIVERSITY HEALTH SERVICES. 75 Mount Auburn St., 02138. Tel 617 491-2800.
The University Health Services provide health care for the University Community and conduct research in areas relating to physical and mental health. Among its research activities is a series of systematic studies on minority groups conducted by Dr. Robert Coles. These studies have centered on the impact of social and political conflict, particularly racial, on the lives of the affected children and their families, especially among Appalachian and migrant worker families, southern children, black and white, and Mexican-Americans. A recent grant enabled an exploration of the conditions in the home, school, and neighborhood that affect the child's mind, his development, his aspirations and actions.

.1   University Health Services.
Records. Reports, questionnaires, and other research data relating to studies of minority groups.

MA44   MASSACHUSETTS INSTITUTE OF TECHNOLOGY AND HARVARD UNIVERSITY, JOINT CENTER FOR URBAN STUDIES (1957). 66 Church St., 02138. Tel 617 868-1410. Mrs. Aubrey Brown, Librn.
The Center was established to stimulate and facilitate research in urban and regional affairs and the creation of a link between research and policy applications. It provides an interdisciplinary setting and enhanced communication for faculty and students from the two parent institutions, encourages interest in urban and regional studies among other scholars in Cambridge, and draws additional talent to the area. Basic research projects have been conducted in such fields as the politics and government of American cities, urban design and the image of the city, housing and urban renewal, urban history, and urban social structure and migration.
Publ.: Books, monographs, reports.

.1   Joint Center for Urban Studies Library.
Original research data, journal subscriptions, and reports by the Center's research staff.

MA45   ORGANIZATION FOR SOCIAL AND TECHNICAL INNOVATION (OSTI). 264 Third St., 02142. Tel 617 547-7515. Dr. Donald A. Schon, Dir.
OSTI is a social science consulting agency for urban problems.
Publ.: Reports and brochures.

MA46   RADCLIFFE COLLEGE (1881), ARTHUR & ELIZABETH SCHLESINGER LIBRARY ON THE HISTORY OF WOMEN IN AMERICA (1943). 3 James St., 02138. Tel 617 868-7600. Jeannette B. Cheek, Dir. Interlibrary loan, bibliographies prepared, literature searches, copying, typing, inquiries answered, referrals made.

.1   Anthony, Susan Brownell, 1820-1906.
Papers, 1815-1944. 2 boxes. Reformer and suffragist. Diaries, letters, speeches, family papers, and photos. Names and subjects represented include Carrie Chapman Catt, Anna Howard Shaw, antislavery, the Canajoharie Academy, social life and customs of New England and New York State, temperance, and women's suffrage.

.2   Beecher family.
Papers, 1850-1946. 3 boxes. Correspondence, diaries, and photos of James C. Beecher (1828-86), his wife Frances (Johnson) Beecher Perkins (b. 1832) and their adopted twin daughters, Mary Frances (Beecher) Beecher (d. 1952) and Margaret (Beecher) Ward. Includes Civil War correspondence of Beecher, who commanded the 1st North Carolina Colored Volunteers, and a few letters by other members of the Lyman Beecher family. Persons represented include Catharine Beecher, Thomas K. Beecher, William Gillette, Isabella Beecher Hooker, Henry Orlando Marcy, Harriet Beecher Stowe, and Charles Dudley Warner.

.3   Beecher family.
Papers of the Beecher and Stowe families, 1798-1956. 16 boxes. Correspondence, miscellaneous writing, clippings, and memorabilia. Includes Lyman Beecher Stowe's correspondence and re-

search on Charlotte Perkins Gilman and Charlotte Cushman, and a bibliography of the Beecher family. Names represented include Henry Ward Beecher (1813-87), James C. Beecher (1828-86), George Eliot [pseud] (1819-80), Oliver Wendell Holmes (1809-94), Florence Nightingale (1820-1910), Harriet Beecher Stowe (1811-96), Harriet Beecher Stowe II (b. 1836), Lyman Beecher Stowe (b. 1880), and many other members of the Beecher and Stowe families.

.4 Blackwell family.
Papers, 1835-1933. 10 boxes and 1 package. Correspondence, diaries, reminiscences, biographical and autobiographical material, photos, and memorabilia relating to three generations of the Blackwell family, headed by Samuel Blackwell. Subjects represented include the American Colonization Society and antislavery, among others.

.5 Brown, Charlotte (Hawkins) 1883-1961.
Papers, 1906-48. 4 boxes. Negro educator. Correspondence, speeches, memorabilia and biographical material. Includes the charter, constitution, reports of the president, student publications and photos, and other materials relating to the Palmer Memorial Institute, Sedalia, N.C., founded by Dr. Brown, protege of Alice Freeman Palmer. Persons represented include Maria Baldwin, Mary McLeod Bethune, Samuel A. Eliot, James Weldon Johnson, and Mary B. Talbert.

.6 Butcher, Beatrice Bowen.
Papers, 1936. 70 pp. Microfilm. M.A. thesis entitled "The Evolution of Negro Women's Schools in the United States." Original in Howard University.

.7 Cabot family.
Papers, 1786-1945. 13 boxes. Letters, diaries, travel journals, and other papers of four generations of the Cabot family of Boston, centering on James Elliott Cabot (1821-1903), of the Harvard class of 1840. Extends back to Thomas Handasyd Perkin's letters and records of the slave, tea, and spice trade (1786-1840).

.8 Child, David Lee, 1794-1874.
Letters, 1837-57. 7 items. Letters to Ellis Gray Loring, Anna Loring, Lydia Maria Child concerning personal matters, slavery and sugar manufacture. Letters in various collections.

.9 Child, Lydia Maria (Francis), 1802-80.
Letters, 1828-79. 343 items. Letters to Ellis Gray Loring, Anna Loring Dresel, Louisa Loring, Charles S. Francis, Henrietta Sargent, Abigail Williams May, Francis Jackson Garrison and others, concerning personal matters and slavery. Also a biographical sketch of Mrs. Child by Abigail Williams May. Letters in various collections.

.10 Connecticut Committee for Equal Rights.
Papers, 1943-54. 6 boxes. Records, correspondence, and other material relating the Committee's activities.

.11 Fields, Emma L.
Papers, 1948. 117 pp. Microfilm. Typewritten copy of the M.A. thesis entitled "The Women's Club Movement in the United States, 1877-1900." Original in Howard University.

.12 Foster, Abigail (Kelley), 1810-87.
Letters, 1859-86. 4 items. Abolitionist. Letters to William Lloyd Garrison, Mrs. Robinson and others concerning slavery. In various collections.

.13 Harper, Frances Ellen Watkins, 1825-1911.
Poems, edited with a biographical and critical introduction, and bibliography, by Theodora Williams Daniel (M.A. thesis, 1937). Microfilm. 257 pp. Original in Howard University.

.14 Harreld, Claudia (White).
Typed mss of the recorded reminiscences (1952) of Mrs. Harreld, first woman graduate of Spelman College, Ga.

.15 Hatter, Henrietta R.
Papers, 1939. 76 pp. Microfilm. Typewritten M.A. thesis entitled "History of Minor Teachers College."

.16 Holt family.
Holt-Messer family papers, 1838-1960. 5 file boxes. The Holt family papers consist largely of the papers of Joseph Burt Holt (1828-99); his wife, Julia Evelyn Rollins Holt (1829-95); and their

daughter, Emily Burt Holt (1854-1934). Includes extensive personal and family correspondence, and official documents connected with Joseph and Julia Holt's philanthropic work with various governmental agencies in Mississippi. The Messer family papers includes portraits of Frederick Douglass and his son.

.17 Howe, Julia (Ward) 1819-1910.
Papers, 1869-1910. 9 v. and 1 box. Author and reformer. Correspondence, addresses, scrapbooks of newspaper articles, and other papers, showing Mrs. Howe's interest in abolition, woman suffrage, women's clubs, and many other causes. Includes material relating to her poem, Battle Hymn of the Republic, and to the Hesperian, the Peacemaker, Woman's Journal, Woman's Tribune, and the Association for the Advancement of Women.

.18 Knox, Maryal, 1879-1955.
Papers, 1880-1956. 1 box. Social worker. Correspondence, reports, biographical material, and photos relating to Miss Knox's settlement work, particularly in East Harlem area where she was honored for 50 years' service in 1952. Includes material relating to Jay Knox.

.19 League of Women for Community Service, Boston, Massachusetts.
Volumes, 1918-21; 1924-38. 3 v. Boston Negro women's organization.

.20 Loring family.
Correspondence, 1828-1919. 4 boxes. Over 700 letters of members of the Loring family, including Ellis Gray Loring, abolitionist (1802-58), his wife Louisa (Gillman) Loring (1797-1868), their daughter Anna (1830-96), wife of Otto Dresel (1826-90), and their children Louise Loring Dresel (b. 1864) and Ellis Loring Dresel (1865-1925). Others represented in the collection include Lydia Maria Child, Dorothea Lynde Dix, William Lloyd Garrison, Julia Ward Howe, Charles Sumner, and Angelina Grimké Weld.

.21 May family.
May Goddard family papers, 1766-1904. 2 boxes and 2 v. Correspondence, diaries, documents, account books, photos, and memorabilia of the May and Goddard families of New England. Includes the papers of Abigail Williams May (1829-88), Boston reformer and one of the first woman members of the Boston School Committee, containing letters from prominent suffragists, abolitionists, and authors. Persons represented include Louisa May Alcott, Ednah Dow Cheney, Julia Ward Howe, Frederick Warren Goddard May (1821-1904), Samuel May (1810-99), Samuel Joseph May (1797-1871), Elizabeth Stuart Phelps, and Lucy Stone.

.22 Riverdale Children's Association.
Papers, 1956. 2 folders. Contains typescript (43 pp.) of the history of the Association, founded in 1836 as the Colored Orphan's Asylum, written by Elizabeth Leonard. Also includes the 120th anniversary celebration booklet.

.23 Smith, Julia Hamilton, b. 1885.
Typed mss of recorded reminiscences.

.24 Stokes, Olivia, and Caroline Phelps Stokes.
Papers, in various collections. Anti-slavery advocates.

CONCORD

MA47   CONCORD FREE PUBLIC LIBRARY (1865). 129 Main St., 01742. Tel 617 369-2309. Edward J. Diffley, Librn.

.1 Brown family.
Papers, ca. 1854-82. ca. 40 items. In part, photocopies. Correspondence of the family of John Brown (1800-59). Contains letters by Brown, concerning his work and news of his family, including one to Franklin Benjamin Sanborn (1831-1917) about joining his cause; letters by Sarah Brown, his daughter, to John Brown, Jr., and Sanborn, chiefly concerning raising money for her mother, Mrs. John Brown; letters of Sanborn, including 28 letters (1854-60) to Theodore Parker containing frequent references to Brown; autographed ms by John Brown, Jr., John Brown of Osawatomie: a History

Not an Apology; John Brown, Jr.'s discharge certificate (1855) from Headquarters, Kansas Volunteers; and a programme (November 22, 1882) of
entertainment in aid of John Brown's widow.

.2   Emerson, Ralph Waldo.
Papers, 1835-73. ca. 45 items. Essayist and poet,
of Massachusetts. Much of the material concerns
slavery, abolition, and the Civil War.

MEDFORD

MA48   MEDFORD HISTORICAL SOCIETY. 402 Main St., 20155.
Laura H. Smith, Librn.

.1   Slave trade.
Papers, 1759-69. Letters and business papers relating to the slave trade.

MA49   TUFTS UNIVERSITY (1852), LIBRARY. 02155. Tel 617 628-
5000. Joseph S. Komidar, Univ. Librn. Copying, typing,
inquiries answered, referrals made.

.1   Ryder Collection of Confederate Archives.
Collection includes 455 morning reports of prisoners in the Richmond, Va., military prisons, showing numbers of Negroes on hand, received, or
transferred each day.

MA50   TUFTS UNIVERSITY, LINCOLN FILENE CENTER FOR
CITIZENSHIP AND PUBLIC AFFAIRS (1963), INTER-
GROUP RELATIONS CURRICULUM (CURRICULUM
IMPROVEMENT PROJECT/OEO) (1965). 02155. Tel
617 628-5000. John S. Gibson, Dir. Bibliographies
prepared, copying, consultation.
The Office of Education sponsored project develops
teaching strategies and instructional materials for use
at the elementary school level in order to improve
teaching and learning about intergroup relations, and
provides an extensive in-service program for teachers.
Publ.: The Intergroup Relations Curriculum: A Program
for Elementary School Education; and photographs and films for use with the curriculum.

.1   Intergroup Relations Curriculum Improvement Project.
Materials and records. Collection includes books
and readings for children in the area of intergroup
relations; instructional materials for use in the
elementary school grades to help young people
develop concepts and discover ideas in the curriculum materials; portfolios developed in the process
of using the intergroup relations curriculum; and
film, audiotapes of class sessions, and evaluation
data. Restricted.

NEW BEDFORD

MA51   MASSACHUSETTS COMMISSION AGAINST DISCRIMINA-
TION, FIELD OFFICE. 22 Union St., 02740. Tel 617
997-3191.

MA52   NEW BEDFORD FREE PUBLIC LIBRARY (1852). Box C
902, Pleasant St., 02741. Tel 617 999-6291. Frances
Ann Bold, Dir. Interlibrary loan, copying.

.1   Cuffe, Paul, b. 1759.
Papers. Negro shipbuilder, businessman and
Quaker who transported Negroes to Sierra Leone.
Log book, letters, and other documents relating to
Cuffe's activities.

NEWTON

MA53   EDUCATION DEVELOPMENT CENTER (1967), LIBRARY.
55 Chapel St., 02160. Tel 617 969-7100. Judith Currie,
Asst. in Publ. Literature searches, inquiries answered.
The Center, a merger of Educational Services Incorporated (1958) and the Institute for Educational Innovation
(1966), was formed as a non-profit institution to operate
the New England regional educational laboratory and
programs in curriculum development and reform.
Among many other projects, ESI has produced a
television-based course of study for schools on the subject of racial tension and conflict in America entitled
One Nation, Indivisible?

MA54   SWEDENBORG SCHOOL OF RELIGION (1867), LIBRARY.
48 Sargent St., 02158. Tel 617 244-0504. Marian J.
Kirven, Librn. Interlibrary loan, inquiries answered,
referrals made.
The Swedenborg School of Religion (formerly New
Church Theological School) prepares men for the min-
istry, particularly in the Church of New Jerusalem
(Swedenborgian) denomination.

.1   Swedenborg School of Religion.
Archives. Materials by or about Emanual Swedenborg (1688-1772), Swedish scientist and religious
teacher, and about the Church of the New Jerusalem,
a denomination based on Swedenborg's religious
system. Included in the collection are sermons and
lectures (ca. 1840- .) written by New Church members about slavery and race problems.

NORTHAMPTON

MA55   FORBES LIBRARY (1894). 20 West St., 01060. Tel 413 584-
8550. Oliver R. Hayes, Librn. Interlibrary loan, copying, inquiries answered, referrals made.

.1   Northampton, Massachusetts Young Men's Institute.
Records, 1846-72. 4 v. Records of meetings of the
executive committee (1846-49); secretary's records
(1846-72); and a volume of letters and papers
(1852-60). Includes letters from the following lec-
turers at the Institute: Louis Agassiz, Phineas T.
Barnum, Henry Ward Beecher, George Washington
Bethune, Horace Bushnell, George B. Cheever,
Cassius M. Clay, George William Curtis, Ralph
Waldo Emerson, Edward Everett, Henry Giles,
Horace Greeley, Oliver Wendell Holmes, Sr., Mark
Hopkins, Thomas Starr King, Wendell Phillips,
John Godfrey Saxe, Bayard Taylor, John Todd, Ed-
win Percy Whipple, and Robert Charles Winthrop.

MA56   SMITH COLLEGE (1871), WILLIAM ALLAN NEILSON LI-
BRARY (1909), SOPHIA SMITH COLLECTION (1942).
01060. Tel 413 584-2700. Marcia W. Bradley, Dir.,
Sophia Smith Collection. Interlibrary loan, copying,
inquiries answered, referrals made, consultation.
Publ.: Pamphlets, concerning the Sophia Smith Collection.

.1   The Sophia Smith Collection seeks to preserve and
organize material on the social and intellectual
history of women from the earliest records to the
contemporary, from all countries.

.2   —— Brewer, Vivion Mercer (Lenon).
Papers, 1956-66. 5 ft. In part, transcripts
(typewritten) and photocopies. Correspondence, committee papers, agenda, minutes,
memoranda, newsletters, background material
surveys, newspaper advertisements, pamphlets, articles, segregationist material, clippings, and other papers, relating to Mrs.
Brewer's work to open the schools of Arkansas during the integration crisis of 1958 and
to maintain progress in subsequent years. Includes material on the Women's Emergency
Committee to Open Our Schools, the Little
Rock (Ark.) School Board, Democratic pri-
maries, bond issues, referendums, integration in other areas, national news-magazine
coverage, and sympathetic organizations.

.3   —— Clark, Kate (Upson) 1851-1935.
Papers, 1862-1935. 2 ft. Author and lecturer. Correspondence, diaries, notes for
articles and lectures, and other papers relating to family and business matters. Includes an unpublished ms, The Affair of William Strickland and Company, an account of
charges (1856-58) of abolitionist connivance
by a bookselling firm in Mobile, Ala., in which
Mrs. Clark's father, Charles Upson, was a
business associate.

.4   —— Garrison, William Lloyd, 1838-1909.
Family papers, 1830-1967. 70 ft. Businessman and reformer of Boston, Mass. Correspondence, diaries, speeches, photos, clippings, articles, printed matter, scrapbooks,
and memorabilia, relating to the activities

and interests of the Garrison, Wright, and Mott families of Boston, Auburn, N.Y., New York City, Philadelphia, and England, to abolition, freedmen's societies, women's rights and suffrage, free trade, the single tax, immigration problems (especially Chinese), and anti-imperialism. Correspondents and persons represented include Susan Brownell Anthony, Alice Stone Blackwell, Henry Brown Blackwell, Maria Weston Chapman, Agnes Garrison, Eleanor Garrison, Ellen Wright Garrison, Francis Jackson Garrison, Frank Wright Garrison, George Thompson Garrison, Wendell Phillips Garrison, William Lloyd Garrison (1805-79), William Lloyd Garrison (1838-1909), Henry George, Margaret Storrs Gierson, Daniel Kiefer, Lucretia Coffin Mott, Wendell Phillips, Parker Pilsbury, Elizabeth Cady Stanton, Lucy Stone, Theodore Dwight Welt, David Wright, and Martha Coffin Pelham Wright.

.5 — Harris, Julia Florida (Collier) 1875- .
Papers, 1921-55. 1 ft. Author and journalist. Correspondence, articles, and mss of published and unpublished writings of Mrs. Harris. The correspondence concerns chiefly the journalistic work relating to social and civic improvement of Mrs. Harris and her husband, Julian La Rose Harris, with the Columbus, Ga., Enquirer-Sun and the Chattanooga (Tenn.) Times. Correspondents include George Washington Carver.

.6 — Howland, Isabel.
Papers, 1888-1903. 1 ft. (502 items). Woman suffrage worker and reformer. Correspondence and other papers of Isabel Howland in her position as corresponding secretary of the Association for the Advancement of Women and of the New York State Woman Suffrage Association. Subjects include women's suffrage, women's rights, and other reform movements such as the battle for abolition of slavery. Persons represented include Susan B. Anthony, Alida Avery, Alice Stone Blackwell, Carrie Chapman Catt, William Lloyd Garrison, Adele Hutchinson, Anna Howard Shaw, Elizabeth Cady Stanton, Lucy Stone, Booker T. Washington, and Frances E. Willard.

.7 — Negro women.
Materials. Information on Negro women, their education, organizations, and contributions generally. Includes papers of the National Association of Colored Women and the National Council of Negro Women, and an index to pertinent material in periodicals.

.8 — New England Hospital.
Records, ca. 1820-1955. 15 ft. Correspondence, business and financial papers, circulars, rules, memoranda, minutes of physicians' meetings, photos, scrapbooks, application materials from women medical students seeking internships, and other papers relating to the early history of a Boston teaching hospital, emphasizing the history of medical education for women and the fields of gynecology, obstetrics, and pediatrics. Includes several hundred letters collected for autograph value for sale at 19th century fundraising fairs; these letters relate to the social history of the period, woman suffrage, social services, abolition, freedmen's education, literature, and Civil War relief. Names chiefly represented include Alice Stone Blackwell, Elizabeth Blackwell, Thomas Wentworth Higginson, Julia (Ward) Howe, Elizabeth Palmer Peabody, Lucy Stone, and John Greenleaf Whittier.

.9 — Slavery.
Miscellaneous materials. ca. 3 ft. Includes reports (1830's-60's) of Female Anti-slavery Societies, mainly in New England; and some material on freedmen's schools and relief societies, largely run by women, during and after the Civil War.

.10 — Starr, Ellen Gates, 1859-1940.
Papers, 1840's-1940. Co-founder and organizer of Hull House, worker for labor legislation and reform, religious writer, and fine bookbinder. Correspondence with Jane Addams during their college days at Rockford College in Illinois, family and personal correspondence, and other papers.

.11 — Stowe, Harriet Beecher.
Correspondence.

.12 — Van Kleeck.
Papers, 1922-57. ca. items. New York; social research worker, director of social studies of Russell Sage Foundation. A large collection of correspondence and material relating to her pioneer work in social research.

NORTHBOROUGH

MA57   NORTHBOROUGH HISTORICAL SOCIETY (1906), GALE MEMORIAL LIBRARY. Main St., 01532. Mrs. David H. Benton, Curator. Typing.

.1   Northborough, Massachusetts.
Miscellaneous papers, 1766-1966. 4 ft. Correspondence and diaries of the Rev. and Mrs. Joseph Allen with their family in Hingham, Mass., and other clergymen relating to church affairs, slavery, temperance, schools, and town affairs; other personal correspondence; historical essays; estate papers of Samuel Goodenow and others; and other papers relating to Northborough and vicinity.

NORTON

MA58   WHEATON COLLEGE (1834), LIBRARY (1923). 02766. Tel 617 285-7722. Miss Hilda F. Harris, Librn. Interlibrary loan, literature searches, copying, inquiries answered, referrals made.

.1   Blanchard, Jonathan, 1811-92.
Papers, 1831-91. ca. 200 items. Presbyterian minister, abolitionist, and president of Knox College, Galesburg, Ill., and Wheaton College, Wheaton, Ill. Correspondence, diaries, and sermons, relating to education, Biblical exposition, the Midwest before and after the Civil War, and anti-lodge, anti-slavery, and reform movements.

NORWOOD

MA59   NORTH AMERICAN FEDERATION OF THE THIRD ORDER OF ST. FRANCIS, ACTION FOR INTERRACIAL UNDERSTANDING. 575 Neponset St., 02062. Tel 617 762-4139. Ralph E. Fenton, Nat. Exec. Dir.

ROXBURY

MA60   CONGRESS OF RACIAL EQUALITY (CORE), BOSTON CHAPTER. 373 Bluehill Ave., 02119. Tel 617 445-9458. Carri Turnbow.

MA61   FAIR HOUSING, INC. (1961). 94 Seaver St., 02121. Tel 617 445-5900. Mrs. Albert M. Sacks, Exec. Dir. Inquiries answered, consultation.
Fair Housing seeks to eliminate prejudice and discrimination in housing opportunities; and maintains a neighborhood housing service in Roxbury where it assists persons subject to discrimination in obtaining sales or rental housing in greater Boston, and persons who are homeless or living in substandard dwellings in obtaining standard accommodations.
Publ.: Reports.

MA61a   NATIONAL CENTER OF AFRO-AMERICAN ARTISTS, MUSEUM. 122 Elm Hill Ave., 02119. Tel 617 442-8820. Edmund B. Gaither, Curator.

MA62   URBAN LEAGUE OF GREATER BOSTON, INC. 100 Warren St., 02119. Tel 617 445-9450. Melvin H. King, Exec. Dir.

.1   Urban League of Greater Boston, Inc.
Files. Records, reports, correspondence, program
plans and evaluations, and other papers concerning
the aims and activities of the organization.

SALEM

MA63   ESSEX INSTITUTE (1848), JAMES DUNCAN PHILLIPS LI-
BRARY. 132 Essex St., 01970. Tel 617 744-3390.
Mrs. Charles A. Potter, Librn. Interlibrary loan,
copying, typing, inquiries answered, referrals made,
consultation.
The Institute was formed from the merger of the Essex
Historical Society and the Essex County Natural His-
tory Society.
Publ.: The Essex Institute Historical Collections, quar-
terly journal.

.1   American Negro History.
ca. 14,000 entries on the following subjects: Slavery, slave trade, fugitive slaves, abolitionists, African colonists, and Negroes. Includes materials
such as letters (ca. 200) of members of the Salem
Anti-Slavery Society (1849-61).
.2   Bates, William B.
Journal, 1845. Captain of the Richmond. Journal
includes full account of trading conditions in the
ports of Mozambique and of the effects of British
measures against the slave trade from this area.
.3   Lopez, Aaron, 1731-82.
Papers, 1764-69. 1 envelope. Merchant and slave
trader of Newport, R.I.
.4   Peabody, George Foster.
Papers, 1830-57. ca. 140 boxes. Merchant, financier, philanthropist; of Massachusetts, District of
Columbia, and Maryland. Included is material pertaining to the slave trade.
.5   Whittier, John Greenleaf.
Papers, 1824-91. ca. 27 v. Poet and abolitionist,
of Massachusetts.

MA64   PEABODY MUSEUM OF SALEM (1799), PHILLIPS LI-
BRARY. 161 Essex St., 01970. Tel 617 745-1876.
Mrs. Paul E. Andrews, Librn. Interlibrary loan,
copying, inquiries answered, referrals made, consultation.
The Museum maintains collections for display and study
in the areas of maritime history, ethnology of the Pacific and Far East, and the natural history of Essex
County, Mass. Also available to qualified persons are
study collections and the Phillips Library of manuscript
and printed books, documents, ship plans, charts, maps
and photographs.
Publ.: The American Neptune, quarterly journal of maritime history.

.1   Herald.
Ship logbook, 1801-09. Included in the Herald's
logbook is an account of Cape Town and Mauritius
is a description of the condition of the slave population.
.2   Ionia.
Ship logbooks, 1859-60, 1863. Includes information concerning business arrangements between
legitimate traders and slave merchants on the
West African coast.
.3   Shepard, Michael.
Papers, 1836-53. Letter collection contains information on commercial affairs for the entire East
African area and includes accounts of the freeing
of slaves in the French possessions.

SOUTH HADLEY

MA65   MOUNT HOLYOKE COLLEGE, WILLISTON MEMORIAL LI-
BRARY (1840). 01075. Tel 413 536-4000. Mrs. Anne
C. Edmonds, Librn.

.1   Beecher family.
Papers, 1822-94. ca. 41 items. Papers of Lyman
Beecher, a Presbyterian clergyman and abolitionist
of Connecticut, Massachusetts, and Ohio, and his
family.

SPRINGFIELD

MA66   CATHOLIC SCHOLARSHIPS FOR NEGROES, INC. (1946).
254 Union St., 01105. Mrs. Roger L. Putnam, Pres.
The Corporation provides scholarships for Negro
students based on need. The scholarships are not
limited to Catholics.

MA67   GROUP INVESTIGATION ASSOCIATES (GIA) (1964). Box 21,
01101. Tel 413 732-0439. Kenneth G. Conley, Res. Dir.
Literature searches, copying, inquiries answered.
GIA is an information-gathering and political research
organization concerned primarily with the extent,
causes, and dangers of Neo-Nazi, Fascist, and racist
manifestations prevalent among certain political groups.
GIA maintains an information center and conducts an
advisory service for those interested in researching
extremist groups.
Publ.: GIA Newsletter.

.1   Group Investigation Associates.
National Information Center files. 1935- . Pamphlets, leaflets, newspaper clippings, recordings,
films, reports, and other research data about extremist organizations in the U.S. Available from
the center are tape recordings, such as an interview with the Minute Men Raiders and excerpts
from speeches of George Lincoln Rockwell; films
of the Ku Klux Klan and the American Nazi Party;
samples of extremist literature; and printed reports on right-wing organizations.

MA68   HUMAN RELATIONS COMMISSION (1961). Room 426, City
Hall, 01103. Tel 413 736-2711. Douglas B. Jenkins,
Jr., Dir. Interlibrary loan, inquiries answered, referrals made.
The Commission seeks to relieve intergroup tensions,
increase opportunities for minority groups, investigate
complaints, and to educate the community in the area of
human relations.
Publ.: Annual Report.

.1   Human Relations Commission.
Small collection of books, pamphlets, reports,
newspaper and magazine clippings, and related
materials concerning human relations, especially in
the Springfield area.

MA69   MASSACHUSETTS COMMISSION AGAINST DISCRIMINA-
TION, FIELD OFFICE. 145 State St., 01103. Tel 413
739-2145. David Burres, Cmnr.

MA70   SPRINGFIELD COLLEGE, COMMUNITY TENSIONS
CENTER (1958). 01109. Tel 413 787-2100. Miriam F.
Hirsch, ACSW Coordinator. Consultation.
The Center provides training and consultative services
in human relations, education, community planning and
participation, and mediation.

MA71   URBAN LEAGUE OF SPRINGFIELD. 84-86 Hillman St.,
01103. Tel 413 739-4793. Thomas R. Lawrence, Jr.,
Exec. Dir.

.1   Urban League of Springfield.
Files. Correspondence, minutes of meetings, financial records, studies, reports, and other materials dealing with the aims, history, and programs
of the League.

WALTHAM

MA72   AMERICAN JEWISH HISTORICAL SOCIETY (1892). 2
Thornton Rd., 02154. Tel 617 891-8110. Nathan M.
Kaganoff, Librn.

.1   Diamond, David, 1898-1968.
Papers, 1928-68. 6 boxes (ca. 3000 items). Contains correspondence relating to Diamond's legal
and political career and materials concerning the
American Civil Liberties Union, and civil rights
and anti-discrimination legislation, among many
other subjects.
.2   Felsenthal, Bernhard, 1822-1908.
Papers, 1856-1920. 800 items. Rabbi. Primarily,
correspondence in English, German, Hebrew, and
French about religious matters, including ref-

erences to B'nai B'rith and the anti-slavery issue in the Fremont campaign of 1856.

.3 Jacobs, Phillip, d. 1818.
Collection, 1760-1832. 2 cartons (200 items). Contains correspondence, receipt books, business records, and other papers. Included in the business records is a bill of sale for a Negro slave.

.4 Kohler, Max James, 1871-1934.
Papers, 1888-1934. 11 ft. Historian, lawyer, and Jewish communal leader. Correspondence, reports, notes, scrapbooks, and other papers. Correspondents include the American Civil Liberties Union, the American Jewish Commitee, B'nai B'rith, the National Conference of Christians and Jews, and the Union of American Hebrew Congregations Board of Delegates on Civil Rights.

.5 Leeser, Isaac, 1806-68.
Papers, 1820-66. 1 carton (141 items). Letters and articles in ms to Leeser containing references to, among many other subjects, slavery and the Civil War.

.6 Lopez, Aaron, 1731-82.
Papers, 1752-94. 14 cartons (6869 items). Merchant and slave trader of Newport, R.I.

.7 Sheftall, Mordecai, 1735-95.
Papers, 1761-1873. 3175 items. Among ms materials are miscellaneous letters and papers of the Sheftall family, including correspondence concerning claims against the U.S., bills of sales for slaves, copies of public documents, and private correspondence.

.8 Weill, Milton, 1891- .
Papers, 1941-46. 1 carton (244 items). Chiefly correspondence, memoranda, and speeches to the National Jewish Welfare Board, the Anti-Defamation League of B'nai B'rith and other organizations.

MA73   BRANDEIS UNIVERSITY, LEMBERG CENTER FOR THE STUDY OF VIOLENCE (1966). 02154. Tel 617 894-2605. John P. Spiegel, Dir.
The Center conducts research on the causes and consequences of collective violence. Currently research is directed to violence arising from rapid social change and the polarization of attitudes in regard to the admission of minority groups - blacks, Puerto Ricans, students, and women - into the decision-making and opportunity structures of the social system. Attention is also given to the development of an integrated theory of collective violence embracing cultural, political, sociological, psychological and biological factors.
Publ.: Riot Data Review, newsletter; Confrontation, newsletter; Monographs, documentary film series.

.1 Payne, George L., 1876-1968.
Papers, 1926-1946. 6 folders. Unitarian minister active in civil rights efforts in Boston, Mass.

.2 Riot Data Clearinghouse.
Collects and analyses information about civil disorders. The data, taken from primary and secondary sources, are organized according to time, place, precipitating event, cause of the disturbance, number and type of participants, number of law enforcement officers, number arrested, injured, killed, and the amount of damages. Includes books, pamphlets, clippings, and tape recordings.

.3 Tape recordings.
Recordings of meetings and conferences (ca. 40), and of interviews (ca. 450). Interviews with "decision-makers" in 10 cities (Boston, San Francisco, Cleveland, Pittsburgh, Dayton, Akron, Nashville, Birmingham, New Orleans, Atlanta) in which political styles of the city government have been compared with respect to race-related hostility. These consist of black and white government officials, business, civil rights, church and labor leaders. Use restricted to persons having a bona fide research interest.

WELLESLEY

MA74   WELLESLEY COLLEGE (1875), LIBRARY. 02181. Tel 617 235-0320. Helen M. Brown, Librn. Interlibrary loan, bibliographies prepared, literature searches, copying, inquiries answered.

.1 Elbert Collection.
1773-1930's. Ella Smith Elbert, B.A., Wellesley, 1888, collector. Books (ca. 750), pamphlets (ca. 100); tracts on slavery, abolition and the Reconstruction period in the U.S.; autobiographical material, such as memoirs, letters, journals, and other personal narratives, written prior to the abolition of slavery, by men and women, both black and white. Although the earliest printed item is an edition of Phillis Wheatley, Poems on Various Subjects, 1773, the bulk of the collection consists of works published between 1830-90.

.2 Whitney, Anne, 1821-1915.
Papers, 1835-1915. 12 ft. (ca. 3000 items). Sculptor. Correspondence, poems, diaries, engagement books, pictures and clippings, among other personal papers. Among the correspondents is Booker T. Washington.

WILLIAMSTOWN

MA75   ROPER PUBLIC OPINION RESEARCH CENTER (1946). Williams College, 01267. Tel 413 458-5500. Philip K. Hastings, Dir. Search and retrieval, analysis, data set reproduction.
Publ.: Newsletter, quarterly.

.1 Roper Public Opinion Research Center.
The Center contains computer tapes of more than 7000 studies conducted in the U.S. since 1936, and will tabulate replies to questions asked on any of 74 major subjects covering all or any segment of descriptive information regarding the respondents' age, sex, race, education, income and geographic location. About one-third of the studies in the data bank are American; the remaining come from 65 other countries. In addition to standard demographic information about the respondents, the studies contain attitudinal and behavioral information.

WORCESTER

MA76   AMERICAN ANTIQUARIAN SOCIETY (1812). 185 Salisbury St., 01609. Tel 617 755-5221. Marcus A. McCorison, Dir. and Librn. Copying, inquiries answered.
Publ.: Proceedings of AAS, semi-annually.

.1 Agard, Charles W., 1848-1913.
Papers. 6 boxes. Notes and papers on ships, shipping, the slave trade, whaling, and the Civil War.

.2 American Antiquarian Society, Worcester, Massachusetts.
Papers. 1 box. Relating to the anti-slavery movement in Massachusetts, 1834-57.

.3 Chase, Lucy.
Papers, 1824-1902. 2 boxes. Quaker, educator of Negroes, of Massachusetts. Includes slave dealer's papers (1846-64), and letters and papers from President Jefferson Davis' offices after the fall of Richmond, Va.

.4 Foster family.
Papers, 1836-1921. ca. 400 items. Correspondence of Stephen Symonds Foster (abolitionist, temperance and woman suffrage advocate) and his wife, Abigail Kelley Foster (abolitionist, feminist, of Massachusetts) concerning slavery, abolition, and related subjects.

.5 Negro newspapers.
Newspapers. Includes such rare Negro newspapers as Rights of All, and the Colored American.

.6 Papers relating to slavery.
Miscellaneous, 1834-57. 1 box. Papers relating chiefly to the anti-slavery movement in Massachusetts.

MA77   HOLY CROSS COLLEGE, DINAND MEMORIAL LIBRARY. College St., 01610. Tel 617 793-3371. James M. Mahoney, Librn.

.1 O'Flynn, Richard, 1829-1905. collector.
Papers, 1840-1905. 2 ft. (115 items). Correspondence, scrapbooks, and other papers collected by O'Flynn relating to the Irish and their descendants

in Worcester, Mass. Includes correspondence and official papers of Horace E. James, chaplain of the Massachusetts 25th Regiment, and later superintendent of Negro affairs, District of North Carolina.

MA78   WORCESTER HISTORICAL SOCIETY, INC. (1875). 39 Salisbury St., 01608. Tel 617 753-8278. Mrs. Elizabeth Cassidy, Dir.

.1   Anti-slavery societies.
Records, 1835-65. 3 v. and 2 items. Materials pertaining to anti-slavery societies in Worcester, Mass.

.2   Foster family.
Papers, 1837-93. ca. 118 items. Papers of Abigail Kelley Foster, known as Abby Kelley, and her husband, Stephen Symonds Foster, relating to their careers and work as abolitionists and women suffrage advovcates.

MICHIGAN

ANN ARBOR

MI1   AMERICAN FRIENDS SERVICE COMMITTEE, MICHIGAN AREA COMMITTEE. 1414 Hill St., 48104. Tel 313 761-8283. Ralph Kerman, Mich. Area Prog. Secy.
The AFSC is a corporate expression of Quaker faith and practice. It attempts to relieve human suffering and to find non-violent solutions to conflicts, and works for a world society that is non-violently ordered, in which men are neither debased or exploited for any reason.

MI2   ANN ARBOR HUMAN RELATIONS COMMISSION (1957). 100 N. Fifth Ave., 48103. Tel 313 761-2400. David C. Cowley, Dir.
The Commission investigates problems and situations of discrimination, coordinates private organizations concerned with human relations, disseminates information and educational materials, and makes recommendations to the City Council.

MI3   UNIVERSITY MICROFILMS, XEROX EDUCATION GROUP. 300 Zeeb Rd., 48106. Tel 313 761-4700.
University Microfilms is a company of the Xerox Corporation which, among other things, publishes Dissertation Abstracts and makes available copies of doctoral dissertations in all fields. Copies of research may be obtained in the broad areas of education, psychology, black history, minority groups, urban planning, race relations, prejudice, civil rights, discrimination, etc.
Publ.: Dissertation Abstracts, monthly; American Doctoral Dissertations, annually; Bibliographies, including A Bibliography of Doctoral Research on the Negro, 1933-1966 (1969), and A Working Bibliography on the Negro in the United States (1969).

.1   University Microfilms.
Included are periodical backfiles on microfilm, including such 19th century serials as The Liberator, African Repository, and such 20th century serials as Phylon, Negro History Bulletin and Journal of Negro History; ca. 1000-1500 dissertations on the Negro in America; ca. 1000 dissertations on Africa; and several hundred out-of-print books on the Negro in America.

MI4   UNIVERSITY OF MICHIGAN, DEPARTMENT OF SOCIOLOGY, CENTER FOR RESEARCH ON SOCIAL ORGANIZATION. 48104. Tel 313 764-7487.
The Center is a research and training branch of the Department of Sociology which collects material on complex or formal social organizations.
Publ.: Working paper series; Reprint series.

.1   Center for Research on Social Organization.
Files. Research reports (ca. 800), journal and periodical titles (ca. 4000), punch cards (400,000), magnetic computer tapes (40), file-card abstracts, government documents, field notes, inter-

views, questionnaires, and work sheets dealing with original research conducted by the Center. Approved researchers may have access to the collection.

MI5   UNIVERSITY OF MICHIGAN, ENVIRONMENTAL SIMULATION LABORATORY (1968). 611 Church St., 48104. Tel 313 763-0258. Richard D. Duke, Dir. Inquiries answered.
The Laboratory conducts research in the areas of urban policy formation, urban problems, and applications of computer technology to both of the former. Emphasis is on urban management systems and the development of a laboratory community for urban research. The Laboratory has developed an extensive file on the socioeconomic characteristics of the Ann Arbor, Mich., metropolitan area with the aim of making Ann Arbor a laboratory community. The work in this area has at least three prime objectives: first, to provide better understanding of the community and how its various components interact; second, to develop devices to train the urban decision-maker in the implications and effective use of the new electronic systems; and third, to achieve some ability to predict the major activities of a community.

.1   Environmental Simulation Laboratory.
Files, 1968- . Records, reports, statistical analyses, studies, and other research data.

MI6   UNIVERSITY OF MICHIGAN, GENERAL LIBRARY (1838). 48104. Tel 313 764-9356. Frederick H. Wagman, Dir. Interlibrary loan, bibliographies prepared, literature searches, copying, typing, inquiries answered, consultation.

.1   The library has strong collections in anti-slavery literature (ca. 1125 titles, including history of slavery in the U.S., anti-slavery movements, and the Emancipation Proclamation), and Negro American literature, as well as extensive holdings in the areas of Negro history, segregation in education, discrimination, and related topics.

.2   —— Facts on Film.
Papers, 1954-67. Microfilm. Contains materials on civil rights and race relations in the South. See Race Relations Information Center, Nashville, Tenn., for a full description.

.3   —— Labadie Collection.
Materials. ca. 1600 items. Joseph Labadie, anarchist, original collector. Books, pamphlets, periodicals, clippings, mss, tape recordings, phonograph records, and other materials. Collection of material on radical economic and reform movements, including publications of numerous minority political groups, social protest movements, monetary reform movements, labor movement history, and civil liberties groups, among which are many rare and unique items. Collection contains letters on Negro participation in radical labor unions, and some papers of Ben Fletcher, Negro leader of the International Workers of the World.

M17   UNIVERSITY OF MICHIGAN, INSTITUTE FOR SOCIAL RESEARCH (1946), LIBRARY (1965). 48104. Tel 313 763-2167. William G. Jones, Dir. of Library Serv.
The Institute seeks to acquire data on social behavior utilizing scientific methods. Underlying this aim is the faith that scientific methods, in particular the use of quantitative measurement linked with developing theory, can make a major contribution to knowledge about social relationships and human behavior.
Publ.: An index of staff publications, as well as other brochures, is available without charge from the Publications Division of the Institute.

.1   Institute for Social Research Library.
Staff publications in the general areas of minorities and race relations, including topics such as discrimination practices in industry, aspirations of Negro college students, drinking behavior among Negro college students, and attitudes of Negroes toward whites.

MI8   UNIVERSITY OF MICHIGAN, INSTITUTE OF PUBLIC
       POLICY STUDIES (1914). 1516 Rackham Bldg., 48104.
       Tel 313 764-3490. John P. Crecine, Dir.
       Research projects of the Institute include studies of
       urban growth patterns, urban land use, effects of riots
       on community attitudes, racial discrimination, political
       behavior in the city, public health programs, and race
       relations.
       Publ.: Discussion papers, such as Alienation and Po-
           litical Behavior, and The Meaning of Black
           Power.

MI9   UNIVERSITY OF MICHIGAN, MICHIGAN HISTORICAL
       COLLECTIONS (1935). 160 Rackham Bldg., 48104.
       Tel 313 764-3482. Robert M. Warner, Dir. Copying,
       inquiries answered, referrals made.

.1   American Home Missionary Society.
       5 reels of microfilm. 1825-47.
.2   Bingham, Kinsley Scott, 1808-61.
       Papers, 1820-1909. ca. 600 items. Governor and
       U.S. Representative and Senator from Michigan.
       Correspondence and papers of the Bingham and
       Warden families dealing with family affairs,
       politics, and the Civil War, among other matters.
       Includes a letter from Henry S. Dinn about
       slavery and the Civil War.
.3   Carlisle family.
       Papers, 1860-1945. 3 ft. Correspondence and
       other papers of Daniel Carlisle's family of
       Buchanan, Mich. Includes letters written by Han-
       nah Carlisle while she was a nurse in Kentucky,
       later as a teacher with the Freedmen's Bureau
       during the Civil War.
.4   Chandler, Elizabeth Margaret, 1807-34.
       Correspondence, 1793-1933. 155 items. Author,
       and departmental editor of the Genius of Uni-
       versal Emancipation. Letters written by Miss
       Chandler, her brother, Thomas Chandler, and their
       aunts, Ruth Evans and Jane Howell, mainly 1830-
       44, relating to pioneer life in Michigan, family af-
       fairs, Quakers, anti-slavery agitation, and other
       topics of national interest; and correspondence re-
       lating to this collection.
.5   Chase, Lew Allen, 1879-1957.
       Papers, 1820-1955. ca. 200 items and 1 v. Pro-
       fessor of history at Northern Michigan College.
       Correspondence (1895-1955) dealing with Chase's
       work and family affairs, and other papers. In-
       cludes nine letters (1927) between James Cochran
       and Chase on southern and northern attitudes
       toward Negroes and a ms entitles Personal Recol-
       lections of the Civil War, by D.A. Chase.
.6   Comin, John, 1869-1947.
       Papers, 1894-1945. 120 items and 21 v. Presby-
       terian clergyman and stated clerk of the Michigan
       Synod. Correspondence (1897-1945) and other
       papers dealing with the Presbyterian Church,
       U.S.A. Includes ms of Comin's book The Synod of
       Michigan and the Slavery Question.
.7   Darling, Robert B.
       Papers, 1911-53. 54 items. Chauffeur for Chase
       S. Osborn, Governor of Michigan. Correspon-
       dence, primarily with Governor Osborn; driver's
       licenses; letter of recommendation; and other
       papers.
.8   Davenny, Wilson Imbrie, 1859-1917.
       Papers, 1879-1917. 6 ft. Spanish-American War
       veteran, journalist, and political leader. Cor-
       respondence, scrapbooks, personal accounts, and
       miscellaneous papers. Correspondents include
       Charles W. Fairbanks, Samuel W. Smith, and
       Booker T. Washington.
.9   Detroit Urban League.
       Records, 1917-51. 15 ft. (12 boxes). Correspon-
       dence, minutes, reports, financial statements, and
       other records covering the activities of the League
       and its director, John C. Dancey, detailing many
       facets of the life of the Negro in the depression,
       World War II, including the 1943 race riots, and
       the postwar period. Includes material on employ-
       ment, housing, racial conflict, elections, strikes,
       crime, welfare, Negro churches, and other orga-
       nizations concerned with the Negro such as the
       NAACP.

.10   Detroit race riot.
       Scrapbook, 1943. 1 v. Scrapbook of Detroit race
       riot recounting daily events as reported in Detroit
       metropolitan newspapers.
.11   Dunn, Newell Ransom, 1818-1900.
       Papers, 1835-1900. 18 ft. and 39 v. Free Will
       Baptist clergyman in New Hampshire, Ohio,
       Kansas, and Michigan, and professor and presi-
       dent of Hillsdale College, Hillsdale, Mich. Cor-
       respondence and other papers of Dunn, including
       mention of his antislavery and Republican party
       activities. Includes Civil War letters from his
       sons, Francis Wayland Dunn (1843-74) and Newell
       Ransom Dunn (1841-63); and 19 diaries of Francis
       Wayland Dunn (1860-70) which include his activi-
       ties as a soldier in the 64th Illinois Infantry during
       the Civil War.
.12   Foster, Theodore, 1812-65.
       Papers, 1835-62. 40 items and 5 v. Co-editor of
       the Signal of Liberty, editor of the Lansing State
       Republican, and superintendent of the State Indus-
       trial School for Boys in Lansing, Mich. Account
       books (4 v.) containing subscription lists for the
       Signal of Liberty; 20 antislavery papers con-
       sisting of mss on the Liberty party, the Coloniza-
       tion Society, the slave trade and other aspects
       of slavery; a scrapbook; and other papers re-
       lating to philosophical, sociological, and religious
       topics.
.13   Grand Rapids Urban League and Brough Community
       Association.
       Records, 1943-61. ca. 3 ft. Correspondence,
       minutes, reports, newsletters, and other papers
       relating to the activities of the Association and the
       Negro community of Brough in Grand Rapids, Mich.
.14   Gregg, Phineas.
       Papers, 1849-1925. 1 ft. Physician. Three deeds,
       docket books, and marriage records of members
       of the Saunders Colony of freed slaves in Calvin
       Township, Cass Co., Mich., among whom Gregg
       worked; incomplete reminiscences of this Negro
       settlement by Gregg's son, William C. Gregg; an
       incomplete biography of Abdulah, a Moslem
       neighbor of William Gregg; and a ms (1925) by
       Frank C. Gregg.
.15   Haviland, Laura Smith, 1808-98.
       Papers, ca. 1879-96, 1933. 13 items. Anti-slavery
       and temperance spokesman. Included is a scrap-
       book with material on Rasin Institute; biographical
       sketch (1933) of Laura Haviland written by Adda
       Camburn Church; correspondence and miscellanea.
.16   Historical Records Survey. Michigan.
       Records, 1936-41. 195 ft. and 1 v. In part, tran-
       scripts. Correspondence; rough drafts of guides;
       field reports of workers; transcripts of land
       patents and board of supervisor's proceedings
       from many Michigan counties and townships, used
       in compiling the Inventory of County Archives; and
       other materials, including a History of the Negro
       in Michigan. Many of the proceedings date back to
       the 1850's.
.17   Hutchins, Harry Burns, 1847-1930.
       Papers, 1908-30. President of the University of
       Michigan. Included is a letter (May 1, 1917) from
       W.E.B. DuBois concerning Negro students at the
       University of Michigan.
.18   Kosten, Edward A., d. 1954
       Papers, 1913-54. ca. 200 items. Labor official of
       Grand Rapids, Mich. Correspondence, dues book,
       radio scripts, and other materials relating to
       Michigan labor unions, the aged, job discrimina-
       tion, the Community Chest, and school integration
       in Grand Rapids.
.19   Louis, Joe, 1914-
       Scrapbooks and newspaper clippings, 1935-41.
       93 v. Boxer.
.20   Lowe, Berenice Bryant.
       Papers, ca. 1937-64. ca. 175 items. Collected by
       Mrs. Stanley Lowe of Battle Creek, Mich. Con-
       tains materials concerning Margaret Nickerson
       Martin of Jackson, Mich., amateur writer and poet
       in the 1930's and 1940's, and on Sojourner Truth,
       free Negro abolitionist who settled in Battle Creek
       in 1867.

.21 Moulton, Charles Henry, 1838-1916.
Papers, 1861-1914. 83 items. Correspondence
and miscellaneous papers. Includes 76 letters
describing, among other things, the attitude of the
people of Baltimore and New Orleans toward the
occupying troops and his own attitude toward Negroes.

.22 Murphy, George, 1894-1961.
Papers, 1911-61. 15 boxes and 1 v. Judge of the
Recorder's Court in Detroit, Mich. Correspondence, legal briefs, grand jury findings and public
hearings, newspaper clippings, and other materials concerning Detroit politics (1935-61), the
grand jury investigation of Detroit Street railways
(1936), arbitration of labor disputes (1936-41), investigation of the Charles Street housing project in
Detroit (1939-40).

.23 Muskegon, Michigan, Urban League.
Papers, 1943-61. 12 boxes. Reports and minutes.

.24 Norris, Mark, 1796-1862.
Papers, 1815-91. ca. 2 ft. and 1 v. Businessman,
of Ypsilanti, Mich. Correspondence of Norris, his
wife, Roccina B. Norris, his son Lyman D. Norris,
and other members of the Norris and Whittelsey
families concerning, among many other subjects,
Dred Scott and the Civil War.

.25 Osborn, Jefferson, 1824-?
Correspondence, 1851. 2 items (Photostat). Correspondence of Osborn and D.T. Nicholson of Calvin Co., Mich., concerning financial aid for a
court case to aid fugitive slaves, including a list
of contributors.

.26 Perry.
Autobiographical sketch, undated, of Perry, a free
Negro who escaped from kidnappers and settled in
Cass Co., Mich.

.27 Reed, Seth, 1823-1924.
Papers, 1848-1923. 61 items and 2 v. Methodist
clergyman. Correspondence; a diary of Reed's
service as a member of the U.S. Christian Commission in Tennessee and Alabama, in which he
discusses wartime destruction, slavery and education of slaves, hospitals, and aid to soldiers; and
a sermon delivered the Sunday after Lincoln's
assassination.

.28 Signal of Liberty.
Files. ca. 1840-48. Michigan antislavery newspaper. Complete run.

.29 Social Justice.
Files. ca. 1930-42. Edited by Father Couglin.
Complete run.

.30 Spalding, Wilbur F.. 1834-64.
Papers, 1862-64. 58 items. Photocopies made
from originals owned by Lyle Walsh. 57 letters
from Spalding written to his wife while serving
with Company I, 6th Michigan Infantry, during the
Civil War, describing the Siege of Port Hudson,
and expressing his unhappiness with Army life and
the conduct of the war.

.31 Sweet, Ossian H.
Transcript, 1925-26. 1 reel, microfilm. Transcript of testimony in Recorder's Court of the city
of Detroit in the case of The People vs. Ossian
Sweet, Gladys Sweet, et al.

.32 Taylor family.
Papers, 1827-1908. ca. 3 ft. and 18 v. Correspondence of the Taylor family, particularly of Barton
Taylor, Methodist clergyman, dealing with family
affairs and religious matters, especially the
Methodist church; and sermons, articles, and addresses on various topics, including slavery.

.33 Thomas, Nathan Macy, 1803-87.
Papers, 1818-89. ca. 2 ft. and 4 v. Quaker, abolitionist, and physician of Mt. Pleasant, Ohio and
Schoolcraft, Mich. Correspondence of Thomas
with his wife, Pamela S. Thomas, his children,
Ella Thomas, Malcolm Thomas, and Stanton
Thomas, and with relatives, friends, public
leaders, abolitionists and publishers dealing
largely with family affairs, the Liberty party, and
particularly with anti-slavery activities; an autobiography of Thomas; addresses; essays; a petition; and miscellaneous papers. Correspondents
include James G. Birney, Erastus Hussey, Lucius
Lyon, S.B. Thayer, Jesse Thomas (father of

Nathan), Jesse Thomas (brother of Nathan), Jonathan Thomas, and Seymour B. Treadwell.

.34 Treadwell, Seymour Boughton, 1795-1867.
Papers, 1818-69. ca. 400 items. Editor of the
Michigan Freeman. Chiefly correspondence of
Treadwell, his son, Jefferson Treadwell, and other
members of the family; addresses; clippings;
broadsides; and land records. The correspondence
covers personal and business affairs; firsthand
views of the South and slavery in 1859-60, the anti-
slavery movement in Michigan and elsewhere, the
Hamilton Institute of New York, temperance, and
politics. Correspondents include John P. Cleveland, George W. Eaton, Arthur L. Porter, Gerrit
Smith, Alvan Stewart, Charles H. Stewart, Electa
Maria Sheldon Stewart, Samuel N. Sweet, and
Jerome Treadwell.

.35 Trowbridge, Luther Stephen, 1836-1912.
Papers, 1842-90. ca. 200 items. Civil War officer. Chiefly correspondence and other papers
of Trowbridge, major general in the 10th Cavalry
during the Civil War, and of other members of
his family.

.36 Vandercook, Roy C., 1873-1960.
Papers, 1900-57. 200 items and 2 vols. Michigan
State police commissioner, National Guard commander, and businessman. Diary (1920) kept while
Vandercook was police commissioner, in which he
recorded notes on the "red" raids of the 1920's
and of Alexander J. Groesbeck; order book (1905-12)
for the 1st Battery of Artillery, Michigan National
Guard; and newspaper clippings and correspondence dealing with the National Guard, the copper
strike of 1913-14, the Jackson prison riot of 1912,
and Woodbridge N. Ferris' inauguration.

.37 Walker, Moses L.
Papers, 1926-50. 59 items. Member of Detroit
NAACP. Correspondence concerning civil rights
and local politics.

.38 Writer's Program, Michigan WPA.
Miscellaneous material on the Negro American.
61 boxes.

MI10 UNIVERSITY OF MICHIGAN, SCHOOL OF MUSIC, LI-
BRARY. North Campus, 48108. Tel 313 764-2512.
Wallace S. Bjorke, Music Librn. Interlibrary loan,
copying, inquiries answered.

.1 Phonorecord Collection.
ca. 1000 recordings of ethnic music, including
blues and Negro spirituals.

MI11 UNIVERSITY OF MICHIGAN (1817), WILLIAM L. CLEM-
ENTS LIBRARY (1923). S. University Ave., 48104.
Tel 313 764-2347. Howard H. Peckham, Dir. In-
quiries answered.
Publ.: Annual report.

.1 Birney, James Gillespie, 1792-1857.
Papers, 1816-57. 7 ft. (ca. 1700 items). In part,
photocopies. Antislavery leader. Correspondence
and personal business papers, mostly concerned
with Birney's activities in such groups as the
American Colonization Society, the American Anti-
slavery Society, and the Liberty party, and with
the publication of the Philanthropist, an anti-
slavery journal. The chief correspondent was
Theodore D. Weld. Other important correspondents include Gamaliel Bailey, Guy Beckley, William Birney, James M. Buchanan, Theodore
Foster, Seth Merrill Gates, William Goodell,
Beriah Green, Ralph Randolph Gurley, Joshua
Leavitt, Henry Brewster Stanton, Lewis Tappan,
Elizur Wright, Jr., and John Clarke Young. Restricted.

.2 Brinley family.
Papers, 1822-88. 8 ft. Business, family, and
bibliographical correspondence of George Brinley,
Boston merchant; and of his son George Brinley,
Hartford businessman and collector of rare Americana. The father's papers include correspondence with agents, friends, and churchmen, reflecting the political upheavals, business panics,
and antislavery sentiment of the time. Important
correspondents include James T. Austin, Francis
Brinley, E.B. Corwin, William Croswell, S.G.

Drake, Samuel F. Haven, Theron Metcalf, Jacob B. Moore, Bernard Quaritch, Stephen Salisbury, William C. Stimpson, James Hammond Trumbull, and George Savage White. Restricted.

.3 Dauphin County, Pennsylvania.
Slave Records, 1788-1825. 1 item, 49 pp. Record book containing statements granting freedom to Negro slaves, in accordance with an act passed by the legislative assembly of Pennsylvania, in 1788. Restricted.

.4 Facts on Film.
Papers, 1954-67. Microfilm. Contains materials on civil rights and race relations in the South. See Race Relations Information Center, Nashville, Tenn., for a full description.

.5 Lovejoy, Owen, 1811-64.
Papers, 1828-1948. 200 items. U.S. Representative from Illinois, minister, and abolitionist. Letters, family deeds, anti-slavery pamphlets, newspaper clippings, and commemorative brochures by or about Lovejoy. An important correspondent is Elijah P. Lovejoy, Sr. Restricted.

.6 Marshall, Henry Grimes, 1839-1918.
Letters, 1862-65. Union soldier and officer. Letters from Marshall to his family describing, among other events, action before Petersburg and Richmond while he was captain of a Negro regiment, the 29th Connecticut Volunteers. Relates details of camp life, rumors, opinions of officers and conduct of the war, in addition to reports of engagements with the Confederate Army. Letters from July to Oct. 1865, are from Brownsville, Tex., where Marshall's unit was sent after the war. Restricted.

.7 Wayne, Anthony, 1745-1796.
Papers, 1783-1853. 3 ft. (877 items). Army officer. Included is correspondence related to his business affairs involving the management of his Georgia rice plantations, and to the settling of his estate after his death. Restricted.

.8 Weld family.
Papers, 1822-98. 4 ft. (ca. 1200 items). Correspondence, diaries, notebooks and other papers of Theodore Dwight Weld, his wife Angelina Grimké Weld, her sister Sarah Moore Grimke and his son Charles Stuart F. Weld, relating to religious questions, the American Anti-slavery Society, and movements for social reform. 350 of the letters pertaining to the anti-slavery movement were published in Letters of Theodore Dwight Weld, Angelina Grimké Weld and Sarah Grimké, 1822-44, edited by Gilbert H. Barnes and Dwight L. Dummond (1934). Important correspondents, of whom the most significant is Charles Stuart, are Lydia Maria Francis Child, Charles Grandison Finney, Beriah Green, Henry Brewster Stanton, Sereno Wright Streeter, Lewis Tappan, James Armstrong Thome, and Elizur Wright, Jr. Restricted.

MI12 UNIVERSITY OF MICHIGAN-WAYNE STATE UNIVERSITY, INSTITUTE OF LABOR AND INDUSTRIAL RELATIONS, PEOPLE AND POVERTY LIBRARY (1966). 405 S. Fourth St., 48103. Tel 313 764-9477. Beverly Sumpter, Librn.
Publ.: People and Poverty, bi-monthly journal, formerly, Poverty and Human Resources Abstracts; Policy Papers in Human Resources and Industrial Relations.

.1 People and Poverty Library.
ca. 5000 items. Books, periodicals, pamphlets, dissertations, mss and other papers and reports which are cited in People and Poverty. Collection covers poverty and related manpower aspects, including material on the education of the disadvantaged, especially vocational and job training programs; the war on poverty and other government programs; descriptive material on minority group characteristics and their surrounding conditions; and papers focusing on policy trends with respect to poverty and manpower.

MI13 WHITE PANTHER PARTY (1969). 1510 Hill St., 48104. John Sinclair, Minister of Information.
The White Panther Party's 10 point program is based on the belief that "the only solution to the problems of the people of the earth now is through the establishment of a free economy throughout the world in which the only consideration is the needs of the people all the time."

BATTLE CREEK

MI14 BATTLE CREEK AREA URBAN LEAGUE. 182 W. Van Buren St., 49014. Tel 616 965-2336. Milton J. Robinson, Exec. Dir.

.1 Battle Creek Area Urban League.
Files. Correspondence, minutes of meetings, financial records, reports, studies, and other materials dealing with the aims, history, and programs of the League.

MI15 MICHIGAN CIVIL RIGHTS COMMISSION, REGIONAL OFFICE (1964). 65 W. Michigan, Suite 629, 49014. Tel 616 962-9342.

BENTON HARBOR

MI16 BENTON HARBOR PUBLIC LIBRARY (1899). 213 E. Wall St., 49022. Tel 616 926-6139. Thomas E. Alford, Library Dir. Interlibrary loan, copying, inquiries answered.

.1 Martin Luther King, Jr. Collection.
ca. 200 contemporary books concerning black history.

MI17 MICHIGAN CIVIL RIGHTS COMMISSION, REGIONAL OFFICE (1964). Suite 402, Fidelity Bldg., 49022. Tel 616 927-1221. Lawrence E. Crockett, Dist. Exec. Copying, typing, inquiries answered, consultation. Publ.: Newsletter.

DEARBORN

MI18 DEARBORN PUBLIC LIBRARY (1921), HENRY FORD CENTENNIAL LIBRARY. 16301 Michigan Ave., 48126. Tel 313 271-1000. Rollin P. Marquis, Chief Librn. Interlibrary loan, bibliographies prepared, literature searches, copying, inquiries answered, referrals made.

.1 Negroes in Michigan.
Materials, including newspaper clippings (ca. 293), chiefly from local newspapers, regarding race relations in the city of Dearborn; and pamphlets on Negroes in Michigan, the Detroit race riots, and other related topics.

DETROIT

MI19 AFRO-AMERICAN CULTURAL DEVELOPMENT FOUNDATION. 12818 Linwood, 48238. Tel 313 869-5550.

MI20 AMERICAN CIVIL LIBERTIES UNION (ACLU) OF MICHIGAN. 808 Washington Boulevard Bldg., 48226. Tel 313 961-4662. Ernest Mazey, Exec. Dir. Inquiries answered, referrals made, consultation. ACLU is a national, non-profit, non-partisan voluntary association concerned with matters of constitutional rights and liberties. Publ.: Civil Liberties Newsletter, quarterly.

MI21 AMERICAN JEWISH COMMITTEE, MICHIGAN-INDIANA AREA. 163 Madison Ave., 48226. Tel 313 965-3353. Sherwood Sandweiss, Dir.

MI22 AMERICAN JEWISH CONGRESS, MICHIGAN REGIONAL OFFICE. 163 Madison Ave., 48226. Tel 313 965-3319. Betty Malos, Dir.

MI23 ANTI-DEFAMATION LEAGUE OF B'NAI B'RITH, MICHIGAN REGIONAL OFFICE. Suite 120, 163 Madison Ave., 48226. Tel 313 962-9686. Richard Lobenthal, Dir.

MI24 ARCHIVES OF AMERICAN ART (1954), LIBRARY. 5200 Woodward Ave., 48202. Tel 313 833-2199. W.E. Woolfenden, Dir.

.1 Pippin, Horace, 1888-1946.
    Papers. 1 folder. Mss of writings and one letter,
    reflecting the life of a Negro primitive painter.
    Includes four separate fragments, one of them
    illustrated, describing Pippin's life at the front in
    WW I, and an autobiographical letter expressing
    his views on art. These documents were used by
    Selden Rodman for his book, Horace Pippin; a Ne-
    gro Painter in America (1947).

MI25 ASSOCIATION FOR THE STUDY OF NEGRO LIFE AND
      HISTORY, DETROIT BRANCH. 5401 Woodward Ave.,
      48202. Tel 313 321-1701.

      .1 Association for the Study of Negro Life and History.
          Files. Records, reports, speeches, correspon-
          dence, and other papers relating to the interests
          and activities of the organization.

MI26 COMMISSION ON COMMUNITY RELATIONS (1943). Fourth
      Floor, 150 Michigan Ave., 48226. Tel 313 963-9550.
      Curtis E. Rodgers, Secy.-Dir. Inquiries answered, re-
      ferrals made, consultation, provide speakers, loan
      films, etc.
      The Commission investigates claims of discrimination
      practices in areas of housing, employment, and ac-
      commodations. It also cooperates with other agencies
      in human relations education programs. Formerly
      Mayor's Interracial Committee.
      Publ.: Highlights, monthly; Meeting the Issues,
          monthly; Confrontation, monthly.

MI27 DETROIT HISTORICAL SOCIETY. 5401 Woodward Ave.,
      48202. Tel 313 321-1701. Miss Gail M. Artner, Urban
      Hist. Curator. Inquiries answered, referrals made.
      Publ.: Society Bulletins.

      .1 The Society's Negro History Collection relates De-
          troit's history through artifacts concerning local
          personalities and events. Most archival mate-
          rials are transferred to the Burton Historical Col-
          lection of the Detroit Public Library.
      .2 — Mahoney, Charles H., 1886-1966.
          Materials. Founder and president of Great
          Lakes Mutual Life Insurance Company, attor-
          ney, first Negro American full delegate to the
          United Nations (1954). Collection includes
          some 60 artifacts of personal memorabilia;
          honorary degrees; certificates of aptitude, of
          achievement, of membership; merit awards
          and testimonies, relating to Mahoney's activi-
          ties, work, and involvement in the Detroit City
          Plan Commission (1918-22), the Wayne County
          Board of Supervisors (1922-32), and the Michi-
          gan Labor Commission (1939-47), as well as
          the above-mentioned positions.
      .3 — Mumford, Orville G.
          Membership card to "Detroit Heirloom and
          Culture Society," issued to Mumford June 1,
          1954, signed by President Fred Hart Williams
          and Secretary Ilene Keats.
      .4 — Smith, Alexander, Jr.
          Oil portraits, 1950's. 8 items. Detroit Negro
          artist. Portraits of Otis Smith, Sugar Ray
          Robinson, William Oliver, Joe Louis, Walter
          Harding, Willis Graves, Charles Diggs, Cora
          Brown.
      .5 — Tolan, Thomas Edward, Jr., 1909-67.
          Collection includes 62 medals, trophies, loving
          cups and miscellaneous items, among which
          are awards won by Tolan in track and field
          events at the University of Michigan (1925-30)
          and the Olympic games at Los Angeles (1932).

MI28 DETROIT INSTITUTE OF ARTS, RESEARCH LIBRARY.
      5200 Woodward Ave., 48202. Tel 313 831-0360. Fran-
      cis Warren Peters, Librn.

      .1 Permanent collection.
          Included in the collection are paintings and other
          works by three Negro artists: Robert S. Duncan-
          son, Jacob Lawrence, and Hughie Lee-Smith.

MI29 DETROIT PUBLIC LIBRARY (1865). 5201 Woodward
      Ave., 48202. Tel 313 321-1000. Charles M. Mohr-

hardt, Dir. Interlibrary loan, copying, typing, inquiries answered, referrals made, consultation.
Publ.: Negro in America (A selected list of recent
    books), annual.

.1 Azalia Hackley Collection.
    Materials related to Negroes in music and the
    performing arts. In honor of a pioneer Detroit
    music educator who created scholarships for
    talented young Negro musicians, including Kemper
    Harreld, Clarence Cameron White, Nathaniel Dett
    and others. Books (ca. 750 v.) on Negroes in the
    performing arts, a collection of clippings (18 file
    drawers), musical scores (1400) and phonograph
    records (1525) of popular songs by Negro com-
    posers and lyricists, including special collections
    of Duke Ellington and Bert Williams. Restricted.
.2 Burton Historical Collection.
    Materials. Books, pamphlets, periodical and
    newspaper titles, documents, diaries, mss, and
    other papers. Collection of Americana including
    source materials on the history of Michigan, De-
    troit, the Great Lakes Region and the Old North-
    west. Materials contain extensive resources in
    the field of local and regional Negro history. Re-
    stricted. Among the collections containing papers
    concerning slavery and Negro history are the
    following:
.3 — Dutilh family.
    Correspondence, 1755-1874. 5 boxes. Letters
    in French, English, Spanish, German, and
    Dutch, of members of the Dutilh family in
    France, Holland, England, Smyrna, and West
    Indies, Philadelphia, and other places. Sub-
    jects represented include plans for con-
    struction of slave dwellings, among many
    other topics.
.4 — Emmons, Halmer H., 1814-77.
    Papers, ca. 1816-85. 207 v. Lawyer, of De-
    troit, and U.S. Circuit Judge for Michigan,
    Ohio, Kentucky, and Tennessee. Correspon-
    dence, and other legal papers, including mate-
    rial concerning railroad activities and contro-
    versies, Emmons' efforts to stop Confederate
    activity in Canada during the Civil War, and
    postwar and Reconstruction conditions,
    particularly in Tennessee.
.5 — Harrow family.
    Papers, 1779-1891. 22 v. In part, tran-
    scripts (typewritten). Papers of the Harrow
    family of St. Clair County, Mich., including
    material relating to slavery.
.5a — Hastings, Eurotas P., 1791-1866.
    Papers, 1808-1919. 10 boxes and ca. 7 v.
    Businessman and banker, of Detroit. Includes
    materials relating to the activities, particu-
    larly in Michigan, of the American Board of
    Home Missions, the American Board of Com-
    missioners of Foreign Missions, and the
    American Tract Society, to anti-Catholic and
    anti-slavery movements.
.6 — Lambert, William.
    Papers. Included are deeds of manumission
    of slaves; papers of Benjamin Willoughby, a
    free Negro of Detroit; and other miscella-
    neous items.
.7 — Michigan Chronicle, Detroit.
    Emancipation Proclamation essay contest,
    1963. 2 boxes.
.8 — Scofield, Abishai.
    Papers, 1802-60's. 111 items. Correspon-
    dence, indentures, and receipts of the Scofield
    family of New York State. The correspon-
    dence relates to family matters, antislavery
    agitation in Madison Co., N.Y., and work
    among Negroes at Berea College and Camp
    Nelson, in Kentucky. Correspondents include
    the American Missionary Association and John
    G. Fee.
.9 — Williams, Fred Hart, -1961.
    Papers. Writer, descendant of old Detroit
    Negro family. Ms of Detroit Heritage (A His-
    tory of Negroes in Detroit), 1957, a collec-
    tion of biographies of prominent Detroit Ne-
    groes, written by Williams and Hoyt Fuller.

.10 —— Witherell, Benjamin Franklin Hawkins, 1797-1867.
Papers, 1781-1924. 5 v. and 2 boxes. Lawyer,
judge, and Michigan State Legislator. Legal
papers, correspondence, and other items.
Mentioned are the Negro riots of 1833.

MI30 DETROIT PUBLIC SCHOOLS, INTERCULTURAL RELA-
TIONS DEPARTMENT. 5057 Woodward Ave., 48202.
Tel 313 833-7900. George Henderson, Asst. Dir.

MI31 DETROIT URBAN LEAGUE (1916). 208 Mack St., 48201.
Tel 313 832-4600. Mrs. Anne A. Lewis, Dir., Spec.
Serv. and Res.
The League works for community betterment through
interracial cooperation, especially in the areas of job
development and employment, health and welfare, education and youth incentives, veterans' affairs, and
housing. Its collection of books on Negro life and history is available to schools, community centers,
churches, public libraries, and other organizations.
Publ.: Reports and surveys concerning such topics as
the 1967 Detroit riot, low-income Detroit Negro
families, and life styles and social attitudes of
middle-income Negroes and whites in Detroit.

.1 Detroit Urban League Collection on Negro Life and
History.
Books (ca. 500 v.) by and about Negroes, including works about fine arts, literature, biography,
social studies, history, religion, education, anthropology, and current revolution.
.2 Detroit Urban League.
Files, 1950- . Records and mss. Files, 1916-50,
have been deposited with the Michigan Historical
Collections, University of Michigan.

MI32 EPISCOPAL SOCIETY FOR CULTURAL AND RACIAL
UNITY, DIOCESE OF MICHIGAN. 4800 Woodward,
48202. Tel 313 832-4400.

MI33 GREATER DETROIT COMMITTEE FOR FAIR HOUSING
PRACTICES. Room 705, Fine Arts Bldg., 58 W. Adams
St., 48226. Tel 313 962-4248. Rev. Charles Butler,
Chmn.

MI34 INTER-FAITH CENTERS FOR RACIAL JUSTICE, INC.
10344 Puritan Ave., 48238. Tel 313 345-4350. William
T. Downs, Exec. Dir.
The Centers comprise a network in the Detroit metropolitan area and seek to organize people to confront racial issues in whatever form they may emerge. The
Centers mobilize interested individuals and organizations which are committed to the attainment of racial
justice. Frequently this takes the form of developing
support in white communities for black-initiated demands in the political and economic spheres.
Publ.: Newsletter, monthly; Issue-centered publications, irregularly.

.1 Each Center maintains a basic library of written and
audio-visual material concerning racial issues.
In addition, each Center compiles additional data
about the community in which it is located, and
conducts on a continuing basis, education for action programs and maintains files of these program materials.

MI35 INTERNATIONAL AFRO-AMERICAN MUSEUM, INC.
(1965). 1549 W. Grand Blvd., 48206. Tel 313 899-2576.
Dr. Charles H. Wright, Pres. Copying, typing, inquiries answered, referrals made, consultation.
The Museum seeks to give creative, visual expression
and understanding to the people of America as to the
true roles and contributions of the Negro to the building
of this country, and to correct the distortion of the
black man's rich cultural heritage in Africa. It maintains a mobile museum, as well as an African art and
history exhibit.
Publ.: International Afro-American Museum, quarterly
newsletter.

.1 Museum collection.
Artistic displays, maps, documents, newspaper
items, pictures, letters, recordings, and artifacts of significance and relevance to the history

of the Afro-American's struggle for freedom. Includes skins, drums, statues, paintings, and maps.
.2 Oral History Project.
Tape recordings. ca. 30. Recordings of the life
stories of elderly Negroes and other persons
whose experiences illuminate some facet of Negro
history, including local Negro artists.

MI36 MERRILL-PALMER INSTITUTE OF HUMAN DEVELOP-
MENT AND FAMILY LIFE (1927), EDNA NOBLE WHITE
LIBRARY. 71 E. Ferry Ave., 48202. Tel 313 875-7450.
Margaret A. Downey, Librn. Interlibrary loan.
The Institute is dedicated to the study and better
understanding of man, from infancy to old age. It is
particularly concerned with knowledge of the things
that promote good human relationships within the
family and in the community. The Institute educates
students from all over the world in the broad area of
human behavior, promotes research in the physical,
social, and mental aspects of human development, and
disseminates information.
Publ.: Merrill-Palmer Quarterly of Behavior and
Development.

MI37 METROPOLITAN DETROIT COUNCIL OF CHURCHES,
COMMISSION ON RACE AND CULTURAL RELATIONS.
63 Colombia E., 48201. Tel 313 962-0340. Rev. G.
Merrill Lenox, Exec. Dir.

MI38 METROPOLITAN FUND, INC. 211 W. Fort St., 48226. Tel
313 961-7887. Mrs. Kenneth J. Myles, Admin. Asst.
The Metropolitan Fund is a non-profit corporation
which develops research and action on metropolitan
problems. In cooperation with the New Detroit Committee it produced the Progress Report of the New Detroit Committee, a blueprint for action on Detroit's
urban problems. In the past, the Metropolitan fund has
received grants to help support the improvement of
interracial communications, including the establishment of suburban action centers and the production of
a documentary film about the tensions of the black
community; and grants for inner-city development
programs in the areas of education for school dropouts, job placement for inner-city high school graduates, and summer school programs in the Detroit public schools.

MI39 MICHIGAN CIVIL RIGHTS COMMISSION (1964), LIBRARY.
1100 Cadillac Square Bldg., 48226. Tel 313 212-1810.
Dalpat K. Daya, Dir., Res. and Planning. Interlibrary
loan, literature searches, copying, typing, inquiries
answered, consultation.
The Commission, a state agency, is mandated to protect the civil rights of the people of Michigan. Its
jurisdiction includes equal protection of the laws in the
areas of employment, education, housing, and public
accommodations. Formerly the Fair Employment
Practices Commission.
Publ.: Newsletter, monthly; Directory of Civil Rights
and Human Relations Agencies in Michigan
(1967); Brochures, posters, and reports.

.1 Commission Library.
Books (ca. 1000), periodical titles (40), newspaper
titles (4), pamphlets (ca. 600), and vf (ca. 6) about
civil rights issues, including annual reports of
other state agencies and a collection of current
statements about civil rights problems.

MI40 MICHIGAN ECONOMIC OPPORTUNITIES OFFICE. 7310
Woodward, 48207. Tel 313 871-5344. Raymond O.
Hatcher, Dep. Dir.

MI41 MICHIGAN EDUCATION ASSOCIATION, HUMAN RELA-
TIONS COMMISSION. 11736 Royal Grand, 48239.
Tel 313 533-9541. Boyd Bosma, Chmn.

MI42 MICHIGAN EMPLOYMENT SECURITY COMMISSION,
EQUAL EMPLOYMENT OPPORTUNITY SECTION
(1933). 7310 Woodward Ave., 49202. Tel 313 872-4900.
Mrs. Geraldine Bledsoe, Chief.
The Section seeks to eliminate discrimination in employment throughout the state. It works with other
human relations organizations and mediates and nego-

tiates with the Michigan Civil Rights Commission.
Publ.: The Messenger, monthly.

MI43   MICHIGAN LABOR COMMITTEE FOR HUMAN RIGHTS.
163 Madison Ave., 48226. Tel 313 962-7195. Jack
Carper, Dir.

MI44   NATIONAL ASSOCIATION FOR THE ADVANCEMENT OF
COLORED PEOPLE, DETROIT BRANCH (1912). 242
E. Warren Ave., 48201. Tel 313 831-5525. William H.
Penn, Sr., Exec. Secy.
Publ.: Newsletters; News releases.

MI45   NATIONAL CONFERENCE OF CHRISTIANS AND JEWS
(NCCJ). 150 W. Boston Blvd., 48202. Tel
313 869-6306. Robert M. Frehse, Dir.

MI46   NATIONAL HOUSEWIVES' LEAGUE OF AMERICA (1933).
539 Melbourne, 48202. Nannie E. Black, Secy.
The League is made up of Negro women seeking to
strengthen the economic base of their communities
through a program of positive support for businesses
owned and operated by Negroes, and for firms which
employ Negroes; aids stores in financial difficulty by
increased purchasing; conducts tours of businesses;
sponsors high school essay contest on business and
economics.
Publ.: Bulletin, quarterly.

.1   National Housewives' League of America.
Files, 1933- . Correspondence, minutes of meetings, financial records and other materials dealing
with the aims, programs and history of the League.

MI47   NEWS AND LETTERS COMMITTEES (1955). 415 Brainard
St., 48201. Tel 313 833-1989. Olga Domanski, Bus.
Mgr.
News and Letters Committees was formed as a part of
the search by workers, black people, youth and women
for a totally new way of life under which man can be
free to guide his own destiny. The publication of News
and Letters provides a means of communication among
working people on their common problems, aspirations,
ideas and needs.
Publ.: News and Letters, monthly newsletter; Pamphlets.

.1   News and Letters Committees.
Files, 1955- . Complete run of News and Letters,
records, pamphlets, articles, and mss published in
News and Letters.

MI48   PEOPLE AGAINST RACISM (PAR). 5705 Woodward Ave.,
48201. Tel 313 871-2222. Frank Joyce, Dir.
PAR is a Detroit based organization which seeks to
eliminate racism through education and direct action
programs.

MI49   R.L. POLK AND COMPANY. 431 Howard St., 48226. Tel
313 961-9470. Walter Gardner, Pres.
R.L. Polk & Co. is a private data-gathering service.
Among its many projects is one giving sociological
profiles of entire cities, which can provide urban
statistical data about slum and riot areas.

MI50   RADICAL EDUCATION PROJECT (REP) (1966). Box
561-A, 48232. Tel 313 825-2922. Inquiries answered,
referrals made.
REP is a research, education and publication center
for the radical left. It serves as a channel for discussion and publication among people who seek to be
active workers for social change throughout their
lives.
Publ.: Something Else, newsletter issued irregularly.
Formerly Radicals in the Professions.

.1   Radical Education Project.
Files, 1966- . Records, reports, pamphlets, and
other materials about the politics of the radical
left. Literature is available from REP on the
following subjects: political economy; imperialism;
the Third World; the Black Colony; labor; the educational institution; book critiques; power structure
research; movement perspectives; and women's
liberation.

MI51   ROMAN CATHOLIC ARCHDIOCESE OF DETROIT, COM-
MUNITY AFFAIRS DEPARTMENT (1966). 305 Michigan Ave., 48226. Tel 313 963-3680. Msgr. Thomas J.
Gumbleton, Dir.
The Community Affairs Department plans programs
and activities for the improvement of intergroup relations within the Archdiocese of Detroit in the areas of
housing, education, human relations education and social attitudes. Formerly the Archbishop's Committee
for Human Relations (1961).

MI52   TRADE UNION LEADERSHIP COUNCIL (TULC) (1958).
8670 Grand River Ave., 48204. Tel 313 898-1020.
Robert Battle, III, Pres.
TULC, affiliated with Negro American Labor Council,
seeks increased leadership and job opportunities for
Negroes.
Publ.: The Vanguard, monthly newsletter.

.1   Trade Union Leadership Council (TULC).
Files, 1958- . Correspondence, minutes of meetings, financial records, reports, studies, and other
materials dealing with the aims, programs and
history of the Council.

MI53   UNITED AUTOMOBILE WORKERS (UAW), FAIR PRAC-
TICES DEPARTMENT (1946). 8000 E. Jefferson St.,
48214. Tel 313 926-5000. William H. Oliver, Co-Dir.
The primary function of the Fair Practices Department is to handle discrimination cases in UAW plants.
It is the contact agent between UAW, other international unions and organizations such as the NAACP and
the Urban League. The Department also acts as a
watchdog on the international union and its locals'
policy regarding civil rights matters and promotes
civil rights legislation. Other activities include the
sponsorship of conferences on civil rights on a state-
wide or regional basis every two years.
Publ.: Monthly bulletin on civil rights developments in
locals; Fair Practices Fact Sheet, quarterly.

MI54   UNIVERSITY OF DETROIT, CENTER FOR HUMAN RELA-
TIONS (1954), LIBRARY. 4001 W. McNichols Rd.,
48221. Tel 313 342-1000. Dr. Tibor Payzs, Dir.
The Center conducts research on human relations and
political science, including studies on person-to-
person, person-to-group, and group-to-group relations
in the family, church, community, economic and social
groups, and school; provides educational instruction,
community services; conducts workshops, seminars,
forums and institutes.

.1   Center for Human Relations.
Files, 1954- . Correspondence, financial records,
studies, reports, and other materials dealing with
the aims, history, and programs of the Center.
Maintains a library on human relations.

MI55   UNIVERSITY OF DETROIT (1877), LIBRARY. 4001 Mc-
Nichols Rd., 48221. Tel 313 342-1000. Rev. Robert
Kearns, S.J., Dir. Interlibrary loan, copying, inquiries
answered.

.1   Afro-American Heritage collection.
Materials, 17th century- . Microfilm. 131 reels.
Books, newspapers, and mss concerning the Negro
American and his history. See Minnesota Mining
and Manufacturing Company, St. Paul, Minn., for a
full description.

.2   Materials relating to Negroes.
Miscellaneous. Vertical file materials, including
such subjects as civil rights, Detroit-community
relations, discrimination in housing, Negroes, and
race problems.

MI56   UNIVERSITY OF DETROIT, URBAN STUDIES INSTITUTE
(1964). 4001 W. McNichols Rd., 48221. Tel 313 342-
1000. Joseph M. Althoff, Dir.
The Institute conducts research on urban problems and
related social phenomena, including studies on urban
conservation, community organization, Catholic population and current social issues; provides field experience for professional development of students of
the University; and acts as consultant for local community organizations.

.1 Urban Studies Institute.
Files, 1964- . Correspondence, financial records, studies, reports, and other materials dealing with the aims, programs and history of the Institute.

MI57 WAYNE STATE UNIVERSITY, CENTER FOR URBAN STUDIES (1967). 5229 Cass Ave., 48202. Tel 313 577-2114. Bertram M. Gross, Dir. Bibliographies prepared, inquiries answered, consultation.
The Center's primary purpose is the promotion of interdisciplinary study in the University's approach to solving the problems of urban living. With this approach, the Center assists students, faculty, administrators and staff in extending and improving the University's involvement in urban affairs. Primarily funded by Wayne State University, the Center is concerned with education, research, community services and international urban studies.

.1 Center for Urban Studies.
Files, 1967- . Records, reports, questionnaires, interviews, statistical data, and other research materials concerning urban problems. Includes information relative to the Detroit riots in the form of tape recordings, photographs, interviews, studies, and other materials.

MI58 WAYNE STATE UNIVERSITY (1868), LIBRARY. 5210 Second St., 48202. Tel 313 833-2400. G. Flint Purdy, Librn. Interlibrary loan, copying, inquiries answered.

.1 Afro-American collection.
ca. 700 v. Books by black authors.
.2 Facts on Film.
Papers, 1954-67. Microfilm. Contains materials on civil rights and race relations in the South. See Race Relations Information Center, Nashville, Tenn., for a full description.
.3 Labor Archives.
Collection of archival materials of labor groups, much of which is concerned with the position of Negro workers and progress in the movement for economic equality.
.4 Ross, Harry, 1901- .
Papers, 1912-62. 6 ft. International representative of the United Automobile Workers of America and member of the Union's Fair Practices and Anti-discrimination Dept. Correspondence, press releases, notes, and clippings, pertaining to labor unions of the automobile industry, particularly the Ford Motor Company and the Dodge Division of the Chrysler Corporation. Correspondents include the Rev. Charles Coughlin, William Green, John L. Lewis, Frank Morrison, Frances Perkins, and Rolland J. Thomas.

EAST LANSING

MI58a MICHIGAN STATE UNIVERSITY, CENTER FOR URBAN AFFAIRS. Owen Graduate Center, 48823. Tel 517 355-1855. Dr. Robert L. Green, Dir.
The Center's primary function is to develop the University's potential for helping to solve urban problems and to meet urban needs.
Publ.: Urban Affairs Today, bimonthly newsletter.

MI59 MICHIGAN STATE UNIVERSITY, INSTITUTE FOR COMMUNITY DEVELOPMENT AND SERVICES, OFFICE OF HUMAN RELATIONS (1966). Kellogg Center, 48823. Tel 517 355-0100. Dr. Duane L. Gibson, Dir. Consultation.
The Institute serves as a bridge between the University and community by defining social problems and bringing in resources to deal with the problems with local actions and expansion of their own capabilities.
Publ.: Reports, proceedings, concerning such subjects as employment opportunity, Negro leadership, and community conflicts.

MI60 MICHIGAN STATE UNIVERSITY (1855), LIBRARY. 48823. Tel 517 353-8700. Richard E. Chapin, Dir. Interlibrary loan, copying, inquiries answered, referrals made.
Publ.: University Library, newsletter.

.1 Anti-Slavery Propaganda Collection.
ca. 2500 pamphlets. Microcards of originals located in the Oberlin College Library. See Oberlin College, Oberlin, Ohio; or Lost Cause Press (publisher), Louisville, Ky., for more complete description.
.2 Facts on Film.
Papers, 1954-67. Microfilm. Contains materials on civil rights and race relations in the South. See Race Relations Information Center, Nashville, Tenn., for a full description.
.3 Jewell T. Stevens Collection.
Material about Abraham Lincoln.
.4 U.S. Commission on Civil Rights.
Reports, 1957-date.
.5 U.S. Congress.
Hearings and reports of various committees dealing with civil rights.
.6 U.S. Congress.
Congressional reports before and after the Civil War, on slavery, the Ku Klux Klan, and related topics.

MI61 MICHIGAN STATE UNIVERSITY, SCHOOL OF LABOR AND INDUSTRIAL RELATIONS (1957), LIBRARY (1957). 48823. Tel 517 353-8706. Mrs. Martha Jane Soltow, Librn. Interlibrary loan, bibliographies prepared, literature searches, copying, typing, inquiries answered, referrals made.

.1 School of Labor and Industrial Relations Library.
Miscellaneous. Pamphlets, newspapers, periodicals, annotated bibliographies, and special reference works. Included are pamphlet files (ca. 200 vf) covering such subjects as industrial relations (including labor unions, labor history, discrimination, and labor economics), organization and management, personnel policies and personnel management, industrial psychology (including human relations, employee attitudes and motivation); newspapers and periodicals from all major U.S. unions as well as many foreign and international; and a collection of materials (1960's, 2 vf) pertaining to the Negro American, consisting of pamphlets, periodicals, reprints, and other materials of current interest, primarily in the area of discrimination in employment (restricted).

MI62 MICHIGAN STATE UNIVERSITY, SCHOOL OF POLICE ADMINISTRATION AND PUBLIC SAFETY, NATIONAL CENTER ON POLICE AND COMMUNITY RELATIONS (1965), BRENNAN MEMORIAL LIBRARY (1966). 403 Olds Hall, 48823. Tel 517 353-3374. Louis A. Radelet, Dir. Bibliographies prepared, literature searches, inquiries answered, referrals made, consultation.
The Center provides services designed to achieve closer cooperation in human relations within the community. For law enforcement bodies across the country it provides educational and instructional courses for the improvement of police-community relations as well as publishes manuals and other literature in this field; and provides consultation for police and community agencies in developing programs for common action. The Center also conducts an annual National Institute on Police-Community Relations, and maintains a small, focused research library chiefly for student and faculty use.
Publ.: Bibliography in Police-Community Relations and annual supplement.

FLINT

MI63 FLINT HUMAN RELATIONS COMMISSION (1963). 1204 Harrison St., 48503. Tel 517 238-5641. Robert H. Atwood, Dir. Inquiries answered, referrals made, consultation.
The Commission investigates and conciliates complaints of discrimination, promotes understanding among various groups, and generally seeks to prevent tension and keep open lines of communication within the community. The Commission has committees which work in the areas of education, housing, employment, information, community organization and services, and tension control.
Publ.: Annual Report; Periodic studies.

MI64   MICHIGAN CONFERENCE OF NAACP BRANCHES. 2918 N.
        Saginaw St., 48505. Tel 313 238-2421. Inquiries an-
        swered, referrals made, consultation.
        The Conference is a coordinating body for NAACP
        branches in Michigan.
        Publ.: Monthly newsletter.

        .1 Michigan Conference of NAACP Branches.
            Files. Civil rights materials, posters, books,
            pamphlets, and file material on housing, educa-
            tion, and legal service.

MI65   THE MOTT FOUNDATION (1926), LIBRARY. 510 Mott
        Foundation Bldg., 48503. Tel 313 767-5050. James W.
        Pirie, Librn.
        The Mott Foundation seeks to increase the strength and
        stature of character in individuals and, through citizens
        working effectively together, thereby strengthen the
        free enterprise system. The Foundation conceives, re-
        searches, tests and demonstrates programs in the
        areas of education, including adult education, race re-
        lations, physical fitness, crime and delinquency preven-
        tion, health, family life, and vocational guidance; com-
        munity planning and service, including housing, public
        transportation, recreation, and urban data; programs in
        conjunction with the public schools, and programs in
        fair housing and spiritual development; and in the train-
        ing of leadership in community involvement.
        Publ.: Annual Report; Brochures.

        .1 Mott Foundation.
            Files, 1935- . Records and reports of projects
            funded by the Foundation, including statistical
            analyses and indicators of success and effective-
            ness in the community of Flint.

MI66   URBAN LEAGUE (1943). Room 1016, Metropolitan Bldg.,
        48502. Tel 313 239-2195. Milton J. Robinson, Dir.

GRAND RAPIDS

MI67   GRAND RAPIDS DEPARTMENT OF COMMUNITY RELA-
        TIONS (1955). City Hall, Room 305, 35 Lyon St., N.E.,
        49502. Tel 616 456-3027. S. David Bogucki, Acting
        Dir.
        The Department of Community Relations seeks to
        foster mutual understanding and discourage discrimi-
        nation in the city of Grand Rapids. It cooperates with
        other governmental agencies and private organiza-
        tions in human relations programs and makes studies
        and investigations in the area of discriminatory prac-
        tices. The Department makes recommendations to the
        City Commission.

MI68   GRAND RAPIDS URBAN LEAGUE, INC. (1943). 252 State
        St., S.E., 49502. Tel 616 459-3281. Paul Phillips,
        Exec. Dir.

MI69   MICHIGAN CIVIL RIGHTS COMMISSION, REGIONAL OF-
        FICE (1964). 1214 Madison, S.E., 49507. Tel 616
        245-2218. Curtis Strader, Dist. Exec. Copying,
        typing, inquiries answered, referrals made, consulta-
        tion.

HIGHLAND PARK

MI70   McGREGOR PUBLIC LIBRARY (1919). 12244 Woodward
        Ave., 48203. Tel 313 867-0988. Helen E. Pratt, Librn.
        Interlibrary loan, copying, inquiries answered.

        .1 McGregor Public Library.
            Included in the general holdings are a large book
            collection about Negroes; a collection of clippings
            and pamphlets on Negroes and race relations,
            particularly concerning southeastern Michigan; a
            picture file; and recordings of Negroes.

JACKSON

MI71   MICHIGAN CIVIL RIGHTS COMMISSION, REGIONAL OF-
        FICE (1964). Suite 601, 180 W. Michigan, 49201. Tel
        517 787-4490.

KALAMAZOO

MI72   COMMUNITY RELATIONS BOARD OF KALAMAZOO (1957).
        641 Gull St., 49006. Tel 616 345-7111. Edward E.
        Ferguson, Dir.
        The Board is appointed by the city government and has
        compliance powers in housing and employment.
        Publ.: Annual Report.

MI73   KALAMAZOO LIBRARY SYSTEM, KING MEMORIAL COL-
        LECTION OF BLACK CULTURE (1969). 315 S. Rose
        St., 49006. Tel 616 342-9837. Mark Crum, Dir.

        .1 Martin Luther King, Jr., Memorial Collection.
            Books, films, records, and other materials on the
            heritage, culture, and contributions of black people
            to the world.

MI74   W.E. UPJOHN INSTITUTE FOR EMPLOYMENT RESEARCH
        (1945). 300 S. Westnedge Ave., 49007. Tel 616 343-
        5541. Harold C. Taylor, Dir.
        The Institute conducts research into the causes and
        effects of unemployment, manpower problems, and
        measures for the alleviation of unemployment. It also
        serves as a publication outlet for studies done by staff
        members and research associates.
        Publ.: Business Conditions in Kalamazoo, quarterly
            report; Series of reports on employment and
            unemployment, unemployment insurance, and
            Michigan economy.

        .1 W.E. Upjohn Institute for Employment Research.
            Files, 1945- . Includes mss, correspondence,
            publications, research reports, and other data on
            such subjects as employment and unemployment,
            economic and business enterprise, public policy,
            and the Michigan economy. Closed to researchers.

MI75   WESTERN MICHIGAN UNIVERSITY (1903), DWIGHT B.
        WALDO LIBRARY (1903). 49001. Tel 616 383-1847.
        Peter Spyers-Duran, Dir. of Libraries. Interlibrary
        loan, copying, typing.

        .1 Ann Kercher Memorial Fund Collection of Africa.
            ca. 30,000 v. Primarily a collection of social sci-
            ence materials on Africa, but contains some
            emphasis on the relationship between Africans and
            the Negro American.
        .2 Facts on Film.
            Papers, 1954-67. Microfilm. Contains materials
            on civil rights and race relations in the South. See
            Race Relations Information Center, Nashville,
            Tenn., for a full description.
        .3 Randall Frazier Memorial Fund Collection on Negro
            Materials.
            ca. 10,000 v. Literature by Negro Americans,
            and historical, sociological and other materials
            about the Negro American.

LANSING

MI76   GREATER LANSING URBAN LEAGUE (1966). 601 N.
        Capitol Ave., 48933. Tel 517 487-3608. Exec. Dir.
        Referrals made.
        The League is a voluntary, non-profit, social and
        community organization agency whose goal is equal
        life chances for all persons. It works through fact
        finding, negotiation, education, interracial coopera-
        tion and community organization in the areas of re-
        search, economic development and employment, hous-
        ing, health and welfare, and community organization.

        .1 Greater Lansing Urban League.
            Files, 1966- . Records, reports, correspondence,
            and other papers pertaining to the aims and
            activities of the organization.

MI77   LANSING HUMAN RELATIONS COMMITTEE (1963). 4th
        Floor, City Hall Bldg., 48933. Tel 517 372-5000.
        Richard D. Letts, Dir. Bibliographies prepared, in-
        quiries answered, referrals made, consultation.
        The Committee works to promote amicable relations
        among the racial and cultural groups within the com-
        munity; to take appropriate steps to deal with condi-
        tions which strain relationships; and to assemble,

analyze and disseminate authentic and factual data relating to interracial and other group relationships.

.1 Lansing Human Relations Committee.
Files, 1963- . Records and reports of the organization; collection of pamphlets and periodicals published by such groups as the Urban League, Office of Economic Opportunity, and the NAACP; a file of local newspaper clippings concerning human relations issues in the Lansing area; low-cost housing brochures; and records on the Field Representative (Detached Workers) Program.

MI78 MICHIGAN CIVIL RIGHTS COMMISSION, REGIONAL OFFICE (1964). 1116 S. Washington Ave., 48913. Tel 517 373-3590.

MI79 MICHIGAN DEPARTMENT OF EDUCATION, BUREAU OF LIBRARY SERVICES (1828), MICHIGAN STATE LIBRARY. 735 E. Michigan Ave., 48913. Tel 517 373-1594. Francis X. Scannell, State Librn. Interlibrary loan, bibliographies prepared, literature searches, copying, inquiries answered, referrals made, consultation.
Publ.: Bibliographies.

.1 Anti-slavery materials.
Tracts and pamphlets. ca. 200 items. Included are abolitionist anti-slavery tracts and Freedman's Bureau reports.

.2 19th Century Periodical Collection.
Among this collection are significant periodicals such as the African Repository and Colonial Journal, Washington, 1827-37.

.3 The Negro in Michigan.
Primarily published material relating to the black experience in Michigan and race relations in the state. Collection includes newspaper clippings, brochures, histories and biographies; state and local government reports on race relations and the Detroit riots of 1833, 1863, 1943, and 1967; and student papers and theses, such as The Civil and Political Status of the Negro in Michigan and the Northwest before 1870 (1935), Slavery in Early Detroit (1938), and A Century with the Negroes of Detroit: 1830-1930 (1949).

MI80 MICHIGAN HISTORICAL COMMISSION (1913), STATE ARCHIVES AND LIBRARY (1913). 3405 N. Logan St., 48918. Tel 517 373-0510. Dennis R. Bodem, State Archivist. Interlibrary loan, literature searches, copying, inquiries answered, referrals made, consultation.
Publ.: Numerous published finding aids, pamphlets, filmstrips and paintings.

.1 Census Records for Michigan.
Special schedules of the Federal census (1850-80); and population and special schedules of state census (1864-94) enumerating individuals, indicating race, and place of origin.

.2 Del Rio, James Cohen, 1924- .
Papers, 1956- . 4 ft. State legislator (1965- .) of Detroit, Mich., 24th District. Includes material concerning Del Rio's role in obtaining equal opportunity in housing, employment, and education for citizens of Michigan.

.3 Executive Office, State of Michigan.
Records, 1943-48. Harry F. Kelly (1943-46), and Kim Sigler (1947-48). Includes items on the Detroit race riot.

.4 Executive Office, State of Michigan.
Records, 1810-1910. Includes material of criminal cases concerning minorities; and riots.

.5 Fair Employment Practices Commission.
Records, 1955-63. Among other materials are 100 photographs.

.6 "Hate" literature collection.
Small quantity of "hate" literature (both religious and racial) which circulated during the 1960 Presidential campaign.

.7 Michigan Association of Colored Women's Clubs.
Biographic sketches and photographs of leading Negro club women throughout Michigan, chiefly of the 1960's.

.8 Michigan Military Establishment, 1838-1943.
Records, including ms records of the First Mich-

igan Colored Troops (102nd U.S. Colored Infantry), 1860's, and Race Riot in Detroit, 1943.

.9 Office of Secretary of State, State of Michigan.
Records. Includes items concerning race riots of the 19th century.

.10 Records of the Office of Attorney General (1919-63).
Includes items relating to riots; discrimination in housing, business firms, advertising of tourist and resort facilities; and removal of public officials.

MOUNT PLEASANT

MI81 CENTRAL MICHIGAN UNIVERSITY (1892), CLARKE HISTORICAL LIBRARY (1955). 48858. Tel 517 774-3010. John Cumming, Dir. Copying, typing, inquiries answered.

.1 Abolitionist and slavery materials.
Miscellaneous, 1824-1968. ca. 249 items. Collection of miscellaneous items concerning slavery and anti-slavery activities. Included are abolitionist newspapers, books and pamphlets on the underground railroad and slavery, and a Michigan slave bill.

.2 "The Negro as the Butt of Humor."
Miscellaneous, 1857, 1864, 1870's-1880's. ca. 52 items. Collection of cartoons, caricatures, and advertising literature in which the Negro is portrayed stereotypically.

.3 Sewall, Henry, 1752-1846.
Letters, 1784-1866. 79 items. Army officer and government employee, of Augusta, Maine. Mostly correspondence from Sewall to his son, William Sewall (1797-1846), in Boston, Mass., and Illinois. Concerns opinions held on government and slavery, among other subjects. Includes 3 letters to his son William concerning slavery: one depicting his views on slavery, sacred music and religion (November 10, 1826); one concerning religion, slavery, temperance societies (December 12, 1834); one telling his gladness that William "has done with slavery," (November 20, 1835).

MUSKEGON

MI82 NATIONAL BAR ASSOCIATION. Michigan Theater Bldg., 49441. Tel 616 722-6369. Charles E. Waugh, Pres. A National professional association of Negro attorneys concerned with legal representation in the South for Negro citizens, aid to Negro law students, and equal access to the American Bar.
Publ.: Periodic bulletins to members.

MI83 URBAN LEAGUE OF GREATER MUSKEGON. 500 W. Muskegon Ave., 49441. Tel 616 722-6994. Thomas Dowdell, Exec. Dir.

.1 Urban League of Greater Muskegon.
Files. Correspondence, minutes of meetings, financial records, reports, studies, and other materials dealing with the aims, history and programs of the League.

MUSKEGON HEIGHTS

MI84 MICHIGAN CIVIL RIGHTS COMMISSION, REGIONAL OFFICE (1964). 10 E. Sherman, 49444. Tel 616 739-7168.

NILES

MI85 NILES PUBLIC LIBRARY (1903). 620 E. Main St., 49120. Tel 616 683-8545. Mrs. Anne Frese, Head Librn. Interlibrary loan, bibliographies prepared, copying.
Publ.: Bibliographies on human rights and Negro heritage.

.1 Jones, Joe
Negro artist. Oil painting "Lumber Mill Near Rockland."

.2 Underground Railroad.
Secondary source material on the Michigan underground railroad. Newspaper clippings, inter-

views, and photocopy of two pages from the diary
of Zachariah Schugart of Vandalia, Mich. (1843),
containing lists of slaves who travelled the underground railroad.

PONTIAC

MI86   MICHIGAN CIVIL RIGHTS COMMISSION, REGIONAL OF-
        FICE (1964). Suite 2, 84 Auburn, 48058. Tel 313 334-
        4978.

MI87   PONTIAC AREA URBAN LEAGUE. 132 Franklin Blvd.,
        48053. Tel 313 335-8730. Clarence Barnes, Dir.

ROCHESTER

MI88   OAKLAND UNIVERSITY (1957), KRESGE LIBRARY (1959).
        Squirrel and Walton Rds., 48063. Tel 313 338-7211.
        W. Royce Butler, Univ. Librn. Interlibrary loan,
        copying, inquiries answered.

        .1   Martin Luther King, Jr., Memorial Collection.
             Books on the historical, social and economic
             aspect of the Negro. ca. 250 v.

SAGINAW

MI89   HUMAN RELATIONS COMMISSION (1958). 1320 S. Wash-
        ington, 48601. Tel 517 753-5411. David B. Rogers,
        Coordinator.
        The Commission works to prevent discriminatory
        practices, conducts programs of community education
        and information, and investigates and studies com-
        plaints and problems in Saginaw.

MI90   MICHIGAN CIVIL RIGHTS COMMISSION, REGIONAL OF-
        FICE. Suite 310, 126 N. Franklin, 48606. Tel 517 754-
        8421.

YPSILANTI

MI91   EASTERN MICHIGAN UNIVERSITY, INSTITUTE FOR COM-
        MUNITY AND EDUCATIONAL RESEARCH. 209 Pearl
        St., 48197. Tel 313 483-6100. Ralph V. Smith, Dir.
        The Institute is an interdisciplinary social science re-
        search institute which studies problems such as
        curriculum planning and racial integration.

MINNESOTA

DULUTH

MN1   NATIONAL CONFERENCE OF CHRISTIANS AND JEWS
        (NCCJ). 10 E. Superior St., 55802. Tel 218 722-5777.
        Mrs. Elvira T. Johnson, Dir.

MINNEAPOLIS

MN2   ANTI-DEFAMATION LEAGUE OF B'NAI B'RITH, MINNE-
        SOTA-DAKOTAS REGIONAL OFFICE. 303 Gorham
        Bldg., 127 N. Seventh St., 55403. Tel 612 335-3277.
        Monroe Schlactus, Dir.

        .1   The League's Library for research and reference in
             the field of civil rights includes materials on
             anti-Semitism, the black American, the Indian
             American, and on the radical right and its
             organizations.
        .2   Anti-Defamation League.
             Files. Included are all of the League's publica-
             tions, Congressional reports on housing and civil
             rights, books, pamphlets (ca. 300), Minnesota
             State Reports on housing and civil rights, and the
             University of Minnesota's Training Center publica-
             tions.

MN3   CITY OF MINNEAPOLIS, COMMISSION ON HUMAN RELA-
        TIONS, AND DEPARTMENT OF CIVIL RIGHTS (1967).
        Room 415, WCCO Bldg., 625 Second Ave., S., 55402.

Tel 612 330-7736. Robert Benford, Dir., Dept. of Civil
Rights. Inquiries answered, referrals made, consultation.
The Commission carries out the policies of the City in
the field of human relations, while the Department
coordinates the activities and provides all administrative services and functions for the Commission. Together, they promote civil rights and enforce ordinance
provisions which provide for equality of opportunity and
prohibiting discriminatory practices with respect to
employment, labor union membership, housing accommodations, property rights, education, public accommodations, and public services. Formerly Minneapolis Fair Employment Practices Commission,
Mayor's Commission on Human Relations.
Publ.: Brochures and leaflets.

        .1   Minneapolis Commission on Human Relations.
             Files, 1967- . Records and intergroup relations
             collection. ca. 150 books, and 3 vf. Includes fi-
             nancial and personnel records; case files; cor-
             respondence; Departmental and Commission activi-
             ties reports; history of the establishment (1967) of
             Minneapolis Ordinance on Civil Rights, the Com-
             mission and the Department; clippings and papers
             concerning intergroup relations; and clippings and
             papers of local poverty and intergroup relations
             agencies and events. Restricted.

MN4   GRAVES MINORITY REPORT. 204 W. Franklin Ave.,
        55404. Tel 612 339-2915. Charles R. Graves, Editor.
        The Report is a weekly newsletter covering various
        programs for minority groups including what churches,
        foundations, non-profit groups, and civil rights groups
        are doing, but chiefly dealing with government efforts.
        Publ.: Graves Minority Report, weekly newsletter.

MN5   JEWISH COMMUNITY RELATIONS COUNCIL OF MINNE-
        SOTA (1939). 211 Produce Bank Bldg., 55403. Tel
        612 338-7816. Samuel L. Scheiner, Exec. Dir.
        The Council carries on educational programs and
        activities to disseminate information on human rela-
        tions, group relations. Formerly the Minnesota
        Jewish Council.

MN6   JEWISH LABOR COMMITTEE, MINNESOTA REGIONAL
        OFFICE. 211 Produce Bank Bldg., Seventh St. and
        First Ave. N., 55403. Tel 612 338-7816. Louis E.
        Lerman, Field Rep. Typing, inquiries answered,
        consultation.
        The Committee works in close cooperation with human
        rights committees officially appointed by Central Labor
        Bodies of the AFL-CIO in Minnesota. It conducts an
        educational campaign against bigotry and discrimina-
        tion, largely within the labor movement.

        .1   Jewish Labor Committee.
             Materials. Included are publications for distribu-
             tion, movies and slides for loan, and newspaper
             and magazine clippings on human relations.

MN7   MINNESOTA CIVIL LIBERTIES UNION. 925 Upper Mid-
        west Bldg., 55401. Tel 612 333-2534. Lynn S. Castner,
        Exec. Dir.

MN8   MINNESOTA COUNCIL ON RELIGION AND RACE (1964).
        Suite 300, Pick Nicollet Hotel, Washington Avenue on-
        the-Mall, 55401. Tel 612 336-3392. Sally Lou Todd,
        Exec. Secy.
        Educational and charitable organization which con-
        ducts interreligious programming in the areas of civil
        and human rights. Sponsors Project Equality in Minne-
        sota, program of the National Catholic Conference for
        Interracial Justice.
        Publ.: Fair Housing Briefs, semi-monthly journal.

MN9   NATIONAL CONFERENCE OF CHRISTIANS AND JEWS
        (NCCJ). 527 Second Ave. S., 55402. Tel 612 336-5365.
        J. Lloyd Evans, Dir.

MN10   UNIVERSITY OF MINNESOTA, LIBRARY. 55455. Tel 612
        373-3082. Edward B. Stanford, Dir. of Libraries.

        .1   Miscellaneous theses concerning the Negro.
             Theses and dissertations, ca. 1920-61. Included
             are such topics as the Negro in Minnesota, social
             adjustment in integrated neighborhoods, the

lynching of three Negroes in Duluth (1920), racial conflict in Minneapolis and St. Paul (1932), discrimination in employment in Minneapolis and St. Paul (1950), the Governor's Interracial Committee of Minnesota, employment status and opportunities for Negroes in St. Paul (1954), and the educational status of Negro children in Minneapolis schools (1926). Also included is History of the St. Paul Urban League (1947), by Whitney Young, Jr.

MN11   UNIVERSITY OF MINNESOTA, SOCIAL WELFARE HISTORY ARCHIVES CENTER (1964). 55455. Tel 612 373-4420. Clarke A. Chambers, Dir. Copying, inquiries answered, referrals made, consultation.
To collect, preserve, and make available to scholars the historical records of national voluntary welfare associations and leaders in the fields of social service and social reform.

.1   American Social Health Association.
Records, ca. 1906-64. 125 ft. Materials concerning venereal disease, sex education, prostitution, and narcotics addiction, and the relation of housing, recreation, and sanitation, to vice.

.2   Baden Street Settlement, Rochester, New York.
Records, 1901-66. 5 ft. In part, microfilm made from original materials in possession of the Baden Street Settlement. Subjects include casework, child care, day care, education of the underprivileged, employment, immigrants, race problems, recreation, settlement and government programs, social action, social work, and urban renewal.

.3   Five Towns Community House, Lawrence, Long Island, New York.
Records, 1907-65. 15 ft. Records relative to the work of the settlement, which functioned in a racially mixed area with clients from varying income groups. Correspondence, minutes, reports, financial records, and extensive group work records showing racial interaction and attitudes.

.4   Hopkirk, Howard William, 1894-1963.
Papers, 1927-63. ca. 500 items. Social worker. Correspondence, articles, speeches, Study of Southern Presbyterian Orphanages (1927), and other papers, relating to child welfare, church-related child welfare, cottage mothers, foster home care, juvenile delinquency, Negro children and step-parents.

.5   Kennedy, Albert J., 1879-1968.
Papers, ca. 1915-60. 12 ft. Settlement house pioneer. Includes material on origin and programs of settlements in Chicago, New York, and Philadelphia; and material for a 1964 interracial study.

.6   National Federation of Settlements and Neighborhood Centers.
Records, 1891-1965. ca. 30 ft. Materials relating to the national organization, its city federations, and its more than 280 settlement houses, with information on its annual conferences and activities, including such subjects as Americanization, civil liberties and rights, community centers, federal welfare programs, the Great Depression, housing, and immigrants. Individuals represented include Jane Addams, Gregory Bellamy, Charles Cooper, John L. Elliott, Irving M. Kriegsfield, John McDowell, Lillie M. Peck, Mary K. Simkhovitch, Graham and Lea D. Taylor, Lillian Wald, Robert A. Woods, and others.

.7   National Florence Crittenton Mission.
Records, 1895-1959. 6.25 ft. Material on Mission homes throughout the country in their care of unwed mothers, including material on admission policies and homes for Negro unwed mothers.

.8   National Urban League.
ca. 1920-65. 7 ft. Pamphlets, publications of the League and other welfare associations.

.9   Survey Associates.
Records, 1891-1952. Administrative, financial, and editorial records of the Survey and Survey Graphic magazines. Individuals represented include Rossa B. Cooley, Edwin R. Embree, Bruno Lasker, Ben B. Lindsey, Alain Locke, George Foster Peabody, Graham Romeyn Taylor, Oswald Garrison Villard, Lillian D. Wald, and other prominent 20th century welfare figures. Subjects

and organizations include Harlem, Negro social workers, the "New Negro," race relations, the National Conference of Social Work, the Penn Normal, Agricultural, and Industrial School, Chicago Commission on Race Relations, the Julius Rosenwald Fund, and other topics bearing on welfare broadly conceived.

.10   United Neighborhood Houses of New York.
Records, 1898-1961. 45 ft. Settlement papers dealing with immigration and Americanization, adult education, civil liberties, consumer protection, housing, labor, Negroes in New York City, recreation, unemployment, etc. Persons represented include Jane Addams, Roger Baldwin, Helen M. Harris, Stanley M. Isaacs, Albert J. Kennedy, Joseph R. McCarthy, and Lillian D. Wald.

MN12   UNIVERSITY OF MINNESOTA, TRAINING CENTER FOR COMMUNITY PROGRAMS (1963). Room 231, Clay School, 55455. Tel 612 373-2851. Arthur M. Harkins, Dir.
The Center seeks to develop educational programs for workers confronted with problems of juvenile delinquency and to reduce inequity and lack of opportunity for the nation's poor. Projects include Low Income Persons' Educational Opportunities Program, Organized Labor's Employment Opportunity Program.

MN13   URBAN LEAGUE. 1016 Plymouth Ave., N., 55411. Tel 612 521-2278. Gleason Glover, Exec. Dir.

MN14   THE WAY - OPPORTUNITIES UNLIMITED, INC. (1966), 1913 Plymouth Ave., N., 55411. Tel 612 522-4394. The Way is a community service organization involved in housing, education, employment, human relations, interreligious affairs, and social attitudes.

NORTHFIELD

MN15   CARLETON COLLEGE (1867), LIBRARY. 55057. Tel 507 645-4431. Robert K. Bruce, Col. Librn. Interlibrary loan, copying, inquiries answered.

.1   Phonograph Record Collection.
ca. 2000 records. Jazz and related music of Negro origins. Restricted.

MN16   CARLTON COLLEGE, RADICAL RESEARCH CENTER (1969). 55057. Tel 507 645-4431. Robert Stilger, Nat. Dir. Inquiries answered, referrals made.
The Center indexes publications for a national index of publication of the alternative or critical press. It has set up a network of local indexers; publishes a quarterly listing on topics such as education, the draft, racism, and women's liberation. Center also provides a data check service on particular topics, articles, or authors.
Publ.: Alternative Press Index, quarterly listing of articles by topic.

.1   Radical Research Center.
Files, 1969- . Included are issues of all publications being indexed by the Center, and files of names and organizations which are active in various phases of the Movement and radical politics.

MN17   NORTHFIELD PUBLIC LIBRARY. 55057. Tel 507 645-7626. Mrs. Constance Doty, Librn.

.1   Scofield, John L.
Papers, 1832-88. ca. 60 items. Civil War surgeon. Contains materials relating to a Negro hospital in Memphis, Tenn.

MN18   ST. OLAF COLLEGE (1925), NORWEGIAN-AMERICAN HISTORICAL ASSOCIATION ARCHIVES. 55057. Tel 507 655-5621. Lloyd Hustvedt, Exec. Secy. Interlibrary loan, copying.

.1   Johnson, John A., 1832-1901.
Papers, 1854-1966. ca. 1577 items. Manufacturer of farm machinery and journalist, of Madison, Wis. Correspondence, articles, pamphlets, reports, notes, and other papers, relating largely to the farm machinery business. Includes material re-

lating to the Civil War, slavery, and the public school system.

.2 Norwegian-American Immigration and Pioneer Life, 1801-1966.
709 items. In part, transcripts. Correspondence, diaries, family histories, biographies, account books, reports, photos, and other papers, relating to the Civil War, and slavery, among other subjects.

.3 Norwegian-American Letters, 1807-1956.
1330 items. Chiefly transcripts and photocopies from Norwegian-American newspapers, made ca. 1928 by Theodore C. Blegen. Letters and articles by Norwegian-Americans from various states transcribed from the Norwegian-American press of the U.S. Includes material relating to the Civil War, politics, and slaves, among others.

.4 Torgerson, Torger A., 1838-1906.
Papers, 1837-1936. 118 items. In part, transcript. Lutheran minister, of Lake Mills, Iowa. Church records, histories of congregations served by Torgerson, and an article on slavery, among other items.

ST. PAUL

MN19 THE CENTER FOR URBAN ENCOUNTER (1966). 2200 University Ave., 55114. Tel 612 644-5020. Rev. William Grace, Exec. Dir. Typing, inquiries answered, referrals made, consultation.
The Center provides "action-reflection experiences in social change for the church leadership of the Twin Cities to enable this constituency to become agents of systemic social change."
Publ.: Annotated bibliography on issues in current social change; Volunteer Ministry Involvement Opportunities; Newsletter, bi-monthly.

.1 Center for Urban Encounter.
Materials. ca. 35 periodical titles, 300 books and pamphlets, and reprints concerning the role of church in social issues. Also included is a file of newspaper clippings on local events.

MN20 CITY OF ST. PAUL, DEPARTMENT OF HUMAN RIGHTS (1967). 1731 City Hall, 55102. Tel 612 223-4288. Louis H. Ervin, Dir.
The Department fosters equal opportunity in employment, housing, public accommodations, public services, and education.
Publ.: Annual reports and informational pamphlets.

MN21 MINNESOTA DEPARTMENT OF HUMAN RIGHTS (1967), MARTIN LUTHER KING, JR. MEMORIAL LIBRARY ON HUMAN RELATIONS (1968). 60 State Office Bldg., 55101. Tel 612 221-2931. Frank C. Kent, Cmnr. Bibliographies prepared, literature searches, copying, inquiries answered, consultation, loan privileges.
The Department has jurisdiction over public services, educational institutions, employment, housing, and public accommodations. Conducts surveys, studies, and public education programs; advises state and local government agencies; receives and investigates complaints; holds hearings; and issues cease-and-desist orders with power to seek court enforcement. Maintains library which serves as the official state collection of research materials on race relations.
Publ.: Annual Report; Brochures and leaflets concerning the law and areas of jurisdiction.

.1 Martin Luther King, Jr. Memorial Library on Human Relations.
Contains books, periodicals, newspapers, pamphlets, files, and clippings.

MN22 MINNESOTA HISTORICAL SOCIETY (1849). 690 Cedar St., 55101. Tel 612 221-2747. Lucile M. Kane, Dir. Interlibrary loan, copying, inquiries answered.
Publ.: Minnesota History, quarterly journal; Minnesota History News; Numerous finding aids.

Audio-Visual Library.

.1 — Photograph collection.
ca. 200 items. Some materials on the Negro in Minnesota, mostly after the period of settlement.

Manuscript Department

.2 — Adelphia Club, Minneapolis and St. Paul, Minnesota.
Papers, 1899- . Negro civic and social club. Histories, clippings about the club and its functions, and material on the 50th anniversary celebration.

.3 — Bailey, Everett Hoskins, 1850-1938.
Papers, ca. 2500 items and 8 v. Banker. Correspondence, diaries, maps, memoranda, legal papers, genealogical material, school papers and newspaper clippings. Family papers include a diary (1851) of Frederick A. Jones, Mrs. Bailey's father, containing descriptions of school teaching in Mississippi and steamboat trips up the Mississippi and Ohio Rivers, views on slavery, and family data, among other items.

.4 — Bassett, Joel Bean, 1817-1912.
Papers, 1859-76. 86 items. Mainly correspondence and accounts kept by Bassett as Chippewa Indian agent in Minnesota (1865-69). Includes letters from George Bonga and Henry B. Whipple and data on Chief Hole-in-the-Day. The letters by Bonga were published in the Journal of Negro History, volume 12 (January, 1927) pp. 41-54.

.5 — Baxter, Luther Loren, 1832-1915.
Papers, 1853-1911. 1 box. Judge. Correspondence and Baxter's routine reports as an officer in Minnesota regiments during the Civil War. Includes a letter on the freedmen in Mississippi and letters by Horace Austin, Andrew Chatfield, William R. Merriam, and Knute Nelson in regard to local politics in Minnesota.

.6 — Benjamin, John, 1823-1902.
Papers, 1840-1951. ca. 3 ft. Correspondence, biographical and genealogical data, journals, ledgers, receipts, deeds, newspaper clippings, memorabilia, and printed matter relating to John Benjamin and his family. The correspondence is concerned with the conflict in Kansas over slavery just prior to the Civil War, Kansas land values, and other subjects.

.7 — Bishop, Judson Wade.
Papers, 1856-1917, 1949. 2 boxes. Letters, newspaper clippings and other papers of the family of Judson Wade Bishop of St. Paul, Minn. Includes two volumes of correspondence (November 4, 1856-January 6, 1865), which deals with Bishop's experiences during the Civil War; and gives detailed information on the action engaged in by the Regiment in Kentucky, Tennessee, Mississippi, Alabama, the battles of Chicamauga, Chattanooga, Missionary Ridge, Atlanta, and Savannah; camp life and army routine, the weather, crops, army food, clothing, condition of life among the civilian population in the South, the use of Negroes by the northern troops, and Bishop's reaction to military campaigns and to Lincoln's Emancipation Proclamation.

.8 — Bowler, James Madison, 1838-1916.
Papers, 1856-1930. ca. 1000 items. Printer, teacher, and politician. Chiefly correspondence between Bowler and his wife Elizabeth (Caleff) Bowler during the Civil War when he was a member of the 3rd Minnesota Regiment. The letters give details on camp life, marches, and army routine and relate to the Battle of Murfreesboro, the Vicksburg campaign, the occupation of Little Rock, Ark., the 113th U.S. Colored Infantry (of which Bowler was in charge, 1865-66), and Reconstruction work in the South. Includes Civil War letters from Bowler's relatives in Maine reflecting antiwar sentiment, letters from Bowler's brother, Joseph, a member of the 22nd and 11th Maine Infantry Regiments, giving information on the actions of those regiments in the Virginia

campaigns; treasurer's checks and a deed to
Nininger City, Minn. signed by Ignatius
Donnelly; a list of scholars in the Nininger
school kept by Bowler (1861); and newspaper
clippings relating to Bowler's career.

MN22.9 —— Brill, Edith.
Scrapbook, 1937-53. <u>Progress of the Recognition of the Rights of the Negro in the United
States</u>. Collection of pamphlets and clippings
showing the trend to a favorable press coverage toward the Negro, including items concerning social, political, and military matters, along with Urban League activities, Fair
Employment Practice Commission literature,
conferences on race questions, and discrimination. Most of the clippings are from Minnesota newspapers.

.10 —— Brin, Fanny (Fligelman), 1884- .
Papers, 1896-1958. 10 ft. (ca. 12,500 items).
Teacher and resident of Minneapolis. Correspondence, reports, minutes, speeches,
articles, news releases, circular letters,
posters, broadsides, pamphlets, and newspaper clippings relating to the social welfare
organizations, the peace societies, the
women's organizations, and the Jewish
groups in which Mrs. Brin was active. Includes letters from Jewish refugees and
material on anti-Semitism and Palestine.
Organizations represented include American
Jewish Committee, American Youth Congress,
International Assembly of Women, National
Conference of Christians and Jews, National
Council of Jewish Women, World Peace
Foundation, and World Youth Congress, among
others.

.11 —— Clapp, George Christopher.
Papers, 1853, 1862-1968. 1 box. Materials
concerning Clapp's Civil War experiences,
when he was mustered into Company K,
7th Minnesota Regiment (August 19, 1862);
his experiences in the Sibley Expedition
of 1863; and his going South and spending the
rest of the war in Tennessee and Kentucky.

.12 —— Densmore, Benjamin.
Papers, 1797-1952. ca. 7 boxes. Correspondence, school reports, essays, maps, diaries,
poetry and song books of the Densmore and
allied families. Material concerning western
migration, schools, politics, religion, the Civil
War, the Sibley Expedition into Dakota (1863),
social and economic conditions; and genealogical charts of the Densmore and Fowle families.

.13 —— Donnelly, Ignatius, 1831-1901.
Papers, 1850-1909. ca. 38 v. and 95 boxes.
Politician and reformer. Correspondence,
diaries, memorandum books, notebooks, personal account books, address books, scrapbooks, and other papers, reflecting Donnelly's
career as townsite speculator at Nininger,
Minn., politician, Lieutenant Governor
of Minnesota, U.S. Representative, member of
the Minnesota Senate and House, and national
leader in third-party movements. The correspondence relates to the development of
Nininger, Minn., the Granger movement,
Horace Greeley's presidential campaign,
Donnelly's newspaper, the <u>Anti-Monopolist</u>,
local politics, the Farmers' alliance, and the
Populist party. A variety of topics are mentioned, such as nativism, slavery, Indian affairs, Reconstruction, Catholicism, civil service reform, the tariff, agricultural societies
and fairs, the Shakespeare-Bacon controversy,
journalism, land policies, lyceums, and
Donnelly's extensive lecturing. Includes a
daybook for the Representative (1895) and one
for the <u>Anti-Monopolist</u> (1876-77). Correspondents include George L. Becker, Clarence P.
Carpenter, Cushman K. Davis, Everett W.
Fish, Dr. Thomas Foster (1818-1903), Horace
Greeley, Harlan P. Hall, Joseph A. Leonard,
Andrew R. McGill, William W. Mayo, Frank J.
Mead, Daniel D. Merrill, Stephen Miller,
Thomas M. Newson, John Nininger, Randolph

M. Probstfield, Daniel Rohrer, and John H.
Stevens.

.14 —— Edward F. Waite Neighborhood House, Minneapolis.
Records, 1922-62. 11 ft. (ca. 12,500 items).
Correspondence, histories of the house, minutes of the board of directors, financial data,
reports, newspaper clippings, and other papers
relating to summer camps and other activities
of the House. Includes information on child
care facilities, school and lunch programs,
care of mentally retarded children, adult
education, housing, family life, urban renewal, and social and economic problems relating to the American Indian population of
Minneapolis; and material relating to the
American Association of Group Workers, the
American Association of Social Workers, the
Minneapolis Council of Social Agencies,
Minneapolis Federation of Settlements, National Association of Social Workers, National
Federation of Settlements, Southern Minnesota
Chapter of the National Association of Social
Workers, and Twin City Federation of Settle-
ments.

.15 —— Eggleston, Edward.
Papers, 1856-66. 67 items. Photostat copy.
Correspondence and other papers relating to
Edward Eggleston's life in Minnesota. The
correspondence relates to the Minnesota
years of Eggleston as a circuit rider, reformer, Methodist minister, Bible agent,
teacher, lecturer, journalist, librarian, novelist, and historian; and interchanging ideas
with other early eminent Methodist clergymen
regarding the annual Methodist conferences,
and general church politics which reveals the
clergy's attitudes toward contemporary issues such as slavery, post-war Negro
suffrage, and teaching theology.

.16 —— Farnum, Reuben, 1835-1918.
Papers, 1864-65. 2 folders including 82 items.
Served in Mississippi and in the Georgia and
Carolina campaigns as a member of the forces
under the command of General Sherman at the
Battle of Atlanta and the march from Atlanta
to Savannah. Materials consist of letters (ca.
75, 1864-65) describing the routine activities
of military life and includes many comments
on rations, illnesses, and medical care of the
troops; remarks on the Negroes serving in the
Union army.

.17 —— Folsom, William Henry Carman.
Papers, 1836-1944. 9 boxes. Papers of Folsom (lumberman, general store proprietor,
legislator, sometime preacher and temperance lecturer, speculative businessman,
manufacturer, real estate dealer, regional
historian, and conscientious citizen) and his
family, including correspondence with the
Wymans of Maine, his wife's family.

.18 —— Gillis, John A., 1840-?.
Diaries, 1861-69. 1 box. Diaries kept by
Gillis as a member of Company K, 64th Regiment, Ohio Infantry, during the Civil War and
after his return to Bucyrus, Ohio, relating to
campaigns, life in the camps, political opinions, slavery, the assassination of Abraham
Lincoln, incidents in Gillis' personal life, the
presidency of Andrew Johnson, the election of
U.S. Grant, local politics, Gillis' appointment
as mail agent, activities of the G.A.R., and
social life in Bucyrus.

.19 —— Gilman, Robbins.
Papers, 1699-1952. 94 boxes. Papers, documents, correspondence, and other materials
on family affairs, intellectual and ethical development, and leadership and participation in
religious, social welfare, cultural and business organizations. In part, restricted.

.20 —— Glenn family.
Papers, 1842-1919. ca. 100 items. Letters to
Andrew W. Glenn from his sons, Harry W. and
Horace H.; a volume (1842-70) kept by mem-
bers of the McMillan family containing, among
other items, two letters (1868-69) written by

Aggie Wallace from a school in Nashville, Tenn., describing southern attitudes towards northern teachers and the activities of the KKK.

MN22.21 —— Greater Minneapolis Interfaith Fair Housing Program, Minneapolis, Minnesota.
Papers, undated, 1946-67. 38 boxes. Materials pertaining to the Program (first called the Greater Minneapolis Interfaith Fair Housing Project) which was formally constituted as an experimental program in desegregated housing; pertaining to fair housing institutes, publication of fair housing pledges, support of open occupancy legislation, personal contact, and several other means being employed. Restricted.

.22 —— Hale, William Dinsmore.
Papers, 1819-1913. 21 boxes (144 v., 1 reel microfilm, and ca. 2000 items). Correspondence and miscellaneous papers growing out of the career of William D. Washburn (1876-1902); correspondence and other data on crop prospects of the U.S. and foreign countries, with particular reference to Minnesota and North Dakota; letters by William D. Washburn and others on Minnesota politics (1878, 1884, 1892-93), Hale family letters and accounts containing information on social and economic conditions (1870-1913).

.23 —— Hallie Q. Brown House, St. Paul, Minnesota.
Papers, 1938-63. 32 items. Correspondence and miscellaneous papers (1940-63) relating to the Hallie Q. Brown settlement house. A paper prepared by I. Myrtle Carden in 1938, contains information on the St. Paul Negro community with emphasis on economic and cultural opportunities of Negroes and the activities of the settlement house. Correspondence for 1947 concerns the visit of Dr. Hallie Q. Brown to the settlement house for its 18th anniversary celebration. A 1962 report prepared by F. J. Davis concerns the relocation of families forced to move as a result of the construction of the St. Anthony-Rondo Freeway. Several printed brochures describe the program and activities of the house. Also included in the collection is a facsimile of a letter from Abraham Lincoln to Major Ramsey (October 17, 1861).

.24 —— Hathaway, Clarence A.
Papers, 1928-40. 1 box, 1 reel tape recording. Fifteen transcripts of speeches delivered by Clarence Hathaway.1933-40, and ms of a book written by Hathaway entitled The American Negro and the Churches (1928); and other materials concerning his career with the Socialist party and the American Communist party, his activities in the labor movement, and as editor of the official American Communist newspaper The Daily Worker (1934-39).

.25 —— Herrick, Henry Nathan, 1832-86.
Papers, 1851-1956. ca. 500 items and 7 v. Baptist minister. Correspondence, diaries (1857-70), sermons, genealogical data, newspaper clippings and Civil War discharge papers. The bulk of the correspondence consists of letters (1864-65) written by Herrick as chaplain with the 5th Minnesota Regiment to his wife in Minneapolis. Although the letters place great emphasis on religion in army life they also contain descriptions of travel on troop ships, war damage, civilian life, Negro troops, army food and hospitals, battles, and marches.

.26 —— Jewish Community Relations Council of Minnesota.
Papers, undated, 1922-67. 63 boxes. Newspaper clippings, reports, magazine articles, publications, and some correspondence relating to the investigative activities of the Jewish Community Relations Council of Minnesota.

.27 —— Kohlsaat, Reimer, 1810-68.
Papers, 1834-1941. 500 items and 4 v. Storekeeper and farm manager. Correspondence, diary, essays, family histories, and printed matter of Kohlsaat and his family. Includes letters relating to Kohlsaat's son giving information on the outbreak of the Civil War and other events, letters from other members of the family giving data on reactions to slavery, religion and other matters.

.28 —— Larson, Louise E. collector.
Papers, 1857-1916. ca. 500 items. Correspondence and printed matter collected by Louise E. Larson and Henrietta (Larson) Town, both of Winona, Minn. The correspondence relates to election campaigns, political appointments, the Civil War, the Spanish-American War, Negro suffrage, and an epidemic in Chicago (1866). Correspondents include such Minnesota and national political figures as: Tams Bixby, Alexander Bull, Joseph G. Cannon, Cushmen K. Davis, Edward Eggleston, William W. Folwell, John Hay, Andrew R. McGill, William R. Marshall, William R. Merriam, Stephen Miller, Knute Nelson, John S. Pillsbury, Alexander Ramsey, Theodore Roosevelt, James A. Tawney, Samuel R. VanSant, Gideon Welles, and William Windom.

.29 —— Ludden, John Dwight, 1819-1907.
Papers, 1774-1906. 8 boxes. Correspondence, account books, memorandum books, sermons (1847-56), Massachusetts land deeds (1794-1848), maps and plats of towns and townships in North Dakota and Minnesota. Includes letters (1894-1904) from Booker T. Washington and his wife acknowledging gifts to the Tuskegee Institute.

.30 —— McGill, Andrew Ryan.
Papers, 1794-1931. 11 boxes. The personal and family papers of Governor Andrew Ryan McGill which deal largely with McGill's political career, family history, and legal problems involving land, mortgage and insurance problems.

.31 —— Mayo, Charles Edwin, 1827-99.
Papers, 1851-98. ca. 500 items. Businessman, customs employee, and secretary and president of the Minnesota Historical Society. Chiefly autographs of prominent 19th century political leaders; together with two amateur handwritten literary newspapers. One of them (1856-58), edited by Mayo, gives data on social activities in St. Paul, the weather, arrival of steamboats, births, marriages, and deaths in the community, sessions of the Minnesota legislature, fires, accidents, lyceum meetings, and the founding of the St. Paul Y.M.C.A. and the St. Paul Public Library, and includes essays and poems. Important names represented include Jean L.R. Agassiz, Thomas F. Bayard, Frank P. Blair, Edward W. Bok, Frederika Bremer, Salmon P. Chase, William A. Croffut, Caleb Cushing, Richard H. Dana, Dorothea L. Dix, Frederick Douglass, Cyrus W. Field, Albert Gallatin, Elbert Hubbard, Edward Augustus, Duke of Kent, the Marquis de Lafayette, Horace Mann, David D. Porter, Thomas B. Reed, Carl Schurz, Alexander H. Stephens, Cornelius Vanderbilt, and John E. Wool.

.32 —— Minnesota Annals.
Collection of items assembled by the WPA Writer's Project, 1852-87. Newspaper clippings, primarily of St. Paul and Minneapolis, notes, surveys, and other materials. Included are accounts of contrabands coming to Minnesota and of attempts to establish and maintain a school for Negro children in St. Paul during the Civil War period; an ethnological survey of South St. Paul, notes on early Negro life in Minnesota; and material concerning the Pilgrim Baptist Church.

.33 —— Minnesota League of Women Voters.
Records, 1919-60. 22 ft. (1800 items and 22 v.). Correspondence, by-laws, reports, minutes, accounts, speeches, circulars, broadsides, and other printed matter, relating to

memorial funds, conventions, meetings, and study programs of the League. Study topics include foreign policy, governmental reorganization, civil rights, home rule in Washington, D.C., taxes, housing, labor relations, public health, the Minnesota Legislative Research Council, school district reorganization, voter services, library service, and candidate questionnaires. Includes a letter from Elizabeth Cady Stanton and one from Susan B. Anthony.

MN22.34 — Miscellaneous interviews.
Interviews concerning the Negro in Minnesota. Included are interviews with Sally Brown Dover, born a slave, and her daughter, Mamie M. White, who migrated to Minnesota in 1881; Edward S. Hall, who arrived in St. Paul in 1900; and Joseph Evan Johnson (b. 1868). Interviews contain information on such subjects as miscegenation during the period of slavery; racial problems of a mulatto family in a predominantly white city; John Brown, whose death Mrs. Dover witnessed; and various St. Paul organizations, including the Hallie Q. Brown Community House, Pilgrim Baptist Church, the Urban League, NAACP, St. James A.M.E. Church, lodges, and other Negro social and civic clubs.

.35 — Montgomery, Thomas, 1841-1907.
Letters, 1862-67. 1 reel of microfilm (149 items) made from originals lent by Charles Montgomery. Union soldier. Letters written by Montgomery to his family in Cleveland, Minn., while serving in the Civil War as a corporal in Company K, 7th Regiment, Minnesota Infantry, and as a captain in Company I, 65th Regiment, and Company B, 67th Regiment, U.S. Colored Infantry, relating to the Sioux Indian outbreak in 1862, to General Henry H. Sibley's punitive expedition against the Sioux, to the treatment of Indian prisoners, to plans for Negro education and citizenship, to the treatment of Negroes after the War, and to a proposed Negro farming colony in the St. Peter Land District, Minn. Includes information on lower Mississippi River floods in 1865, methods of combating smallpox and cholera, Masons, national politics, religious activities of Negro soldiers, and descriptions of Baton Rouge, New Orleans, Port Hudson, La., Vicksburg, Miss., St. Louis, and the region around Mankato and Minneopa Falls in Blue Earth County, Minn.

.36 — Neill, Edward Duffield, 1823-93.
Papers, 1827-1930. 13 v. and 8 boxes. Presbyterian minister, educator, historian. Correspondence, notes, scrapbooks, newspaper clippings, and other papers gathered by Neill as a student at Amherst and Andover, a home missionary in Illinois, a minister in St. Paul, the founder of churches in Minnesota, State superintendent of education and chancellor of the University of Minnesota, chaplain of the 1st Minnesota Volunteer Infantry and of the Philadelphia hospitals during the Civil War, American consul at Dublin, professor and president of Macalester College, and a historian of Minnesota and colonial America, especially Virginia and Maryland. Includes letters (1864-66) to Lincoln and Andrew Johnson, obtained by Neill in the capacity of private secretary to the two presidents, relating to appointments, the election of 1864, the colonization of slaves, pardons, and the English attitude toward the American Civil War. Correspondents include Matthias W. Baldwin, George L. Becker, Cushman K. Davis, Lyman C. Draper, Dr. Thomas Foster (1818-1903), James A. Froude, John Hay, James J. Hill, Charles Macalester, Samuel J.R. McMillan, William R. Marshall, Stephen Miller (1816-81), John G. Nicolay, Francis Parkman, John S. Pillsbury, Alexander Ramsey, Henry M. Rice, Lawrence Taliaferro, Reuben G. Thwaites, and Justin Winsor.

.37 — Nichols, Henry M.
Papers, 1843-62. 2 boxes. Diaries (1846-60) kept by Nichols, describing his work as a school teacher and a preacher in Massachusetts, his journey to Minnesota, his activities as an agent of the Northampton colony, and his career as a home missionary and minister at St. Anthony, Stillwater, and Minneapolis; letters from relatives in Connecticut and Massachusetts concerning social life and family affairs; sermons by Nichols and addresses before Lyceum and Y.M.C.A. groups, revealing his attitude toward slavery; and his ms of the Chronicles of Stillwater.

.38 — Nicols, John, 1811-73.
Papers, 1818-69. 1 box. Correspondence and diaries (1862, 1864, 1869) kept by Nicols in St. Paul concerning personal and business matters and his activities as a regent of the University of Minnesota and as a member of the Minnesota legislature. Includes letters written by a Maryland woman (1847) discussing slavery, and notes kept by Nicols on the Civil War and on a trip to Washington, D.C., in 1864. Other correspondents were William R. Marshall and Henry H. Sibley.

.39 — Northfield Lyceum.
Records, 1856-63. 6 reels of microfilm. Constitution, bylaws, and minutes of the meetings of a debating society which also maintained a reading room and a circulating library. Includes discussions of the Dred Scott decision, the extension of slavery, state loans to railroads, and Minnesota's admission to the Union.

.40 — Noyes, Frank Wright.
Papers, 1802-1964. 2 boxes. Included are data relating to the Lucien Warner family which gives information on Lucien's marriage, on schools in Clauseville and on cotton growing in Alabama (1859); and a letter from Noyes to his wife concerning his trip through the southern U.S., southern treatment of Negroes, and information on southern industrial growth.

.41 — Paige, Mabeth (Hurd).
Papers, 1943-58. 50 items. Member of the Minnesota legislature. Correspondence, speeches, and printed matter. The printed material includes a reprint of an article on the 1958 school desegregation crisis in Little Rock, Ark.

.42 — Phyllis Wheatley Settlement House, Minneapolis.
Records, 1924-63. 7 ft. (ca. 8000 items). Correspondence, minutes of the board of directors, reports, budgets, financial records, personnel records, newspaper clippings, and printed matter, relating to financial and personnel matters; activities of the House such as summer camps; social work agencies and organizations; the N.A.A.C.P., Urban League, and other Negro organizations; public housing; human rights organizations and commissions; and other settlement houses in Minneapolis and St. Paul.

.43 — Protestant Episcopal Church in the U.S.A., Provinces. Northwest.
Records, 1914-42. 2 boxes. Correspondence, journals, synod reports, minutes of meetings, programs, clippings, constitution, and notes relating to missions maintained by the church, women's auxiliary activities, a survey of the Negro population in the Northwest, religious education in schools for the deaf, young people's work, members of the clergy, and committee assignments.

.44 — Ramsey, Alexander.
Papers, 1775-1965. 61 boxes. Details the career of Ramsey and his family (1840's-1965). Papers consist of correspondence, newspaper clippings, printed materials, invitations, calling cards, greeting cards, deeds, financial papers, diaries, scrapbooks, school essay books and lecture note books, journals,

ledgers, and similar types of volumes. Correspondence contains information on Minnesota politics, national politics, the Republican party, the Civil War, social life in Minnesota and Washington, D.C.

MN22.45 — Reed, Axel Hayford.
Papers, 1861-65. 1 box. Diaries (4 v.) kept by Axel H. Reed, a lieutenant in Company K, 2nd Minnesota Regiment. The diaries contain entries concerning marches, skirmishes, camp life, and Reed's views on the war, Negroes, slavery, the conduct of the war, and the military leaders.

.46 — Robinson, Mortimer.
Papers, 1859-74. 1 reel of microfilm. Letters written by Robinson from Minneapolis, Minn. (1859), and by soldiers in the Civil War, and a brief diary kept by Robinson describing his trip South with the 6th Minnesota Regiment (1864). Letters are copied into a volume that recorded the minutes of meetings of the Hennepin County Anti-Slavery Society. The Society appointed a committee to visit the state legislature to urge the passage of a stringent personal liberty bill and the amendment of the state constitution to provide equal suffrage.

.47 — Shedd, Charles.
Papers, 1857-1933. 1 reel of microfilm. Correspondence, undated (1859-70?), and genealogical data relating to the Charles Shedd family. The letters give data on Shedd's work and his reactions to the pre-Civil War crises, and his espousal of the southern cause after the outbreak of the war. Other letters (1862-63) were written to Mrs. Alden by Charles Richmond, while a member of Company C, Second Minnesota Regiment, which tell of army life, military campaigns in Mississippi, Alabama, and Tennessee.

.48 — Smalley, Palemon Jared.
Papers, 1863-1944. 1 box. Correspondence (1863-1912); newspaper clippings (1890-1944); articles, autobiography, and other papers of Palemon J. Smalley, St. Paul newspaperman and political leader. Includes letters written to Smalley from many prominent political leaders throughout the country, dealing with Smalley's activities as secretary of the Minnesota Democratic State Central Committee, the party's stand on tariff revision, particularly in relation to the passage of the Wilson Tariff Reform Bill. Among the correspondents are Jefferson Davis, President of the Confederacy, Grover Cleveland, Elihu Root, and Booker T. Washington.

.49 — Smith, Samuel George.
Papers, 1891, 1893. 1 box (ca. 104 items). Correspondence compiled by Samuel George Smith which includes letters (ca. 52, 1891) received by Smith in reply to his questionnaire which he sent to prominent St. Paul citizens. The writers give their opinions on civic improvement. Some letter writers include: John Q. Adams (editor of the Negro newspaper, The Appeal), Henry A. Castle, Moses E. Clapp, Ignatius Donnelly, Andrew R. McGill, William R. Marshall, and Alexander Ramsey. Subjects include St. Paul civic improvement and Negroes in Minnesota.

.50 — Southworth family.
Papers, 1852-1917. 150 items and 2 volumes. Correspondence includes, in part, information on civilian life during the Civil War, and reactions to Lincoln's emancipation policies, and Civil War letters (1862) from Eli Southworth, a member of Company A, 4th Minnesota Regiment.

.51 — Staples, George Howard.
Papers, 1882-1950. 1 box. Correspondence (1882-1938), diaries, and other papers of the family of George Howard Staples, pioneer settlers in Mendota Township, Dakota County, Minn. The papers include mss by members of

the Staples family which are: "Genealogy of the Lincoln-Dayton-Staples Family" (1738-1930, 16 typed pp.); "Autobiography of George H. Staples," (5 pp.); and "Samuel Staples Narrative" (11 typed pp.) which is reminiscence of Samuel Cole Staples, giving information on his early life in Maine; and his experiences in the South at the outbreak of the Civil War.

.52 — Steefel, Genevieve Fallon, 1899- .
Papers, ca. 1923-62. ca. 17 ft. (ca. 17,500 items). Correspondence, notes, records, reports of organizations, newspaper clippings, published materials, and other papers, relating to organizations in which Mrs. Steefel, wife of Professor Lawrence D. Steefel, of the University of Minnesota, was active. Among those represented are the American Council on Race Relations; Fair Employment Practices Commission; First Unitarian Society of Minneapolis; Highlander Folk School, Monteagle, Tenn.; League of Women Voters; Mayor's Council on Human Relations; Minneapolis Family and Children's Service; Unitarian Service Committee. Correspondents include Joseph H. Ball, John A. Blatnik, the Rev. Arthur Foote, Hubert H. Humphrey, Walter H. Judd, William B. Pearson, Robert C. Weaver, Luther W. Youngdahl, and the Rev. Reuben K. Youngdahl.

.53 — Taliaferro, Major Lawrence.
Papers, ca. 1820-40. Contain allusions to slavery.

.54 — Wade, Edward P.
Papers, 1869-1900. 48 items. Messenger at the Minnesota Capitol. Personal correspondence, fire insurance policies for Wade's home in St. Paul, and articles of incorporation of the Africo-American Social Club (1884) and of the John Brown Monument Association (1895), both of St. Paul.

.55 — Wier, Roy William, 1888-1963.
Papers, ca. 1920-63. ca. 3 ft. (ca. 3000 items). State legislator and U.S. Representative from Minnesota. Correspondence, newspaper clippings, voting records, and other papers, including material on federal aid to education, the House Committee on Un-American Activities, and school desegregation in Washington, D.C. Correspondents include Carl R. Gray, Eric G. Hoyer, Hubert H. Humphrey, P. Kenneth Peterson, and Edward J. Thye.

.56 — Willey, Austin.
Papers, 1827-96. 44 items, 1 reel of microfilm. Editor for 20 years of first anti-slavery paper in Maine; lecturer and author; worked for anti-slavery cause and prohibition; editor of Advocate of Freedom, Liberty Standard, Portland Inquirer (1838-57); and a Free Soil Republican. Material on anti-slavery and prohibition activities in Maine and Minnesota, with a few letters from men like Neal Dow, John Greenleaf Whittier, and Lewis Clark, the George Harris of Uncle Tom's Cabin; and newspaper clipping concerning Willey at the time he left Maine (1855) and letters (1855-56, 4 items) recommending him.

.57 — Williams family.
Papers, 1792-1965. ca. 3 ft. (ca. 2000 items). Correspondence, diaries, genealogical material, newspaper clippings, and other papers, relating to the families of Thomas Hale Williams (1813-1901) and Samuel McKeehan Williams (1845-1930), operators of a book and stationery store in Minneapolis. Correspondents include Thomas H. Williams, who was also founder and librarian of the Minneapolis Athenaeum, writing of Elijah Lovejoy's anti-slavery activities and of territorial Minnesota; his parents Thomas and Ruth (Hale) Williams, and his brothers and sister, Nathan, Stephen, and Mary, who wrote of family matters and of antislavery and

temperance movements. Diarists include Samuel McK. Williams, and his family, Edward H. Williams, J.C. Williams, Louise Williams, Ruth J. Williams, and Sarah (Hale) Williams.

.58 — Williams, Howard Yolen, 1889- .
Papers, 1924-52. 19 ft. Minister and political leader. Correspondence, minutes of meetings and other materials relating to such organizations as the League for Independent Political Action, the Farmer Labor Political Federation, the Farmer Labor Party of Minnesota, the Union for Democratic Action. The papers contain information on the many political protest groups of the 1930's and on such issues as organized labor, minority problems, and race relations. Correspondents include Harry E. Barnes, Louis F. Budenz, John Dewey, Paul Douglas, Felix Frankfurter, Lynn L. Frazier, William Green, the La Follettes, Ernest Lundeen, Gerald P. Nye, Henrik Shipstead, Norman M. Thomas, Rexford G. Tugwell, and Oswald G. Villard.

.59 — Wright family.
Papers, 1785-1955. ca. 4 ft. Correspondence, diaries, legal papers, and other papers of the George Burdick Wright family. The pre-Civil War letters contain information on events leading to the War, including slavery, the attack on Charles Sumner by Preston Brooks, elections, and other events. The Civil War correspondence of Thomas William Clarke, a member of the 29th Regiment, Massachusetts Infantry, contains much material on battles engaged in by the regiment, changes in command in the Union army, civilian attitudes toward the War, and the activities of the Freedmen's Bureau.

MN23 MINNESOTA MINING AND MANUFACTURING COMPANY (3M COMPANY). 3M Center, 55101. Tel 612 733-7297. W. Doug McLuen, Div. Publicist.
3M International Microfilm Press, in its Specialized Film Library, has an arrangement to microfilm and sell materials from the New York Public Library and the Schomburg Collection of Negro Literature and History. Among the books, periodicals and newspapers in this Afro-American Heritage series (131 reels of microfilm) are The Crisis (November, 1910-68), The Story of Benjamin Banneker, Works of Frederick Douglass, The Life and Works of Paul Dunbar, Freedom's Journal (1827-29), The Imperial Night Hawk (March, 1923-November, 1924), The Liberator, The Messenger (1917-28), National Standard (1840-71), The Negro Worker (1931-37), Southern Workman (1897-1939), and Voice of the Negro (1904-07).

MN24 MINNESOTA STATE ARCHIVES COMMISSION, ARCHIVES AND RECORDS SERVICE. 117 University Ave., 55101. Tel 612 221-2506. Dr. Franklin W. Burch, State Archivist. Records accessible for research.

.1 Governor's Human Rights Commission.
Records, 1957-60. ca. 1 ft. Correspondence, reports, and information received, concerning housing, civil rights and related areas.

MN25 ST. PAUL PUBLIC LIBRARY (1882). 90 W. Fourth St., 55102. Tel 612 224-3383. J. Archer Eggen, Dir. of Libraries. Interlibrary loan, bibliographies prepared, copying, typing, inquiries answered, referrals made, consultation.

.1 Clipping file.
ca. 1923- . Clippings on Negroes taken primarily from St. Paul and Twin City newspapers, including information on housing, open occupancy, and the Urban League, among other subjects.

MN26 ST. PAUL URBAN LEAGUE (1923). 401 Selby Ave., 55101. Tel 612 224-5771. Lawrence H. Borom, Exec. Dir. Inquiries answered, referrals made, consultation, services in community welfare, employment, housing, and research.
The League is a private, non-profit, community service agency dedicated to equalizing life results for black people and other minorities with white people in this society, and to ending white racism.
Publ.: Newsletter, monthly; Black business directory; Reports and studies.

.1 St. Paul Urban League.
Files, 1923- . Correspondence, financial records, minutes of meetings, clippings, photographs, and race relations materials, including books (ca. 250 v.) and recordings concerning black history.

MISSISSIPPI

BAY ST. LOUIS

MS1 ST. AUGUSTINE'S SEMINARY (1920), HOUSE LIBRARY (1922). 39520. Tel 601 467-6414. W. Howard Johnson, Librn.
St. Augustine's was founded (1920) in Greenville, Miss., by missionaries of the Society of the Divine Word who originally came to the South to establish mission chapels and schools for Negroes.

.1 Negro Collection.

CLARKSDALE

MS2 COAHOMA JUNIOR COLLEGE (1949). Route 1, Box 616, 38614. Tel 601 627-7433. Benjamin F. McLaurin, Pres.

.1 Coahoma Junior College.
Files, 1949- . Includes correspondence, minutes of board meetings, records of admission, financial records, and other materials pertaining to the history and administration of the College

GREENVILLE

MS3 DELTA MINISTRY PROJECT (1964). Box 457, 38701. Tel 601 334-4587. Owen H. Brooks, Dir. Copying, typing, inquiries answered, consultation.
The Project is working in Mississippi on the problems of prejudice and of the dispossessed, through meeting immediate human needs, economic development, public responsibility, education, and community organization.
Publ.: Delta Ministry Reports, bi-monthly.

.1 Delta Ministry Project.
Files, 1964- . Papers and correspondence for Mississippi civil rights activities including newspaper clippings (ca. 50 cartons), plus current files.

HATTIESBURG

MS4 UNIVERSITY OF SOUTHERN MISSISSIPPI. LIBRARY. Box 53, Southern Station, 39401. Tel 601 266-7011. James Hanson, Spec. Collections Librn.

.1 Anti-Slavery Propaganda Collection.
ca. 2500 pamphlets. Microcards of originals located in the Oberlin College Library. See Oberlin College Library, Oberlin, Ohio; or Lost Cause Press (publisher), Louisville, Ky., for more complete description.

.2 Editorial Cartoon Collection.
ca. 1965- . ca. 1500 items. Editorial cartoons. Includes samples by John T. McCutcheon of the Chicago Tribune, Daniel E. Holland of the Tribune, James J. Dobbins of the Boston Herald, Herc Ficklin of the Dallas Morning News, Joe Parrish of the Chicago Tribune, Arthur B. Poinier of the Detroit News, Edmund S. Valtman of the Hartford Times, L.D. Warren of the Cincinnati Enquirer, Richard Q. Yardley of the Baltimore Sun, and other national and local cartoonists. Bob Howie, cartoonist for the Jackson (Miss.) Daily News, is the collection's chief contributor.

.3   Facts on Film.
Papers, 1954-67. Microfilm. Contains materials
on civil rights and race relations in the South. See
Race Relations Information Center, Nashville,
Tenn., for a full description.

HOLLY SPRINGS

MS5   MISSISSIPPI INDUSTRIAL COLLEGE (1905), LIBRARY.
38635. Tel 601 252-3411. Miss Annie R. Montgomery,
Librn.

.1   Afro-American Studies Collection.
ca. 1000 paperbacks. Basic books on the life and
history of black Americans.

MS6   RUST COLLEGE (1866), MAGEE MEMORIAL LIBRARY
(1891). 38635. Tel 601 252-4661. Wilfred T. Mayfield, Dir. of Res. and Projs.

.1   Afro-American Studies Collection.
ca. 1000 paperbacks. Basic books on the life and
history of black Americans.

ITTA BENA

MS7   MISSISSIPPI VALLEY STATE COLLEGE (1950), LIBRARY
(1952). 38941. Tel 601 254-2321. Mrs. Clara L.
Bedenfield, Librn. Interlibrary loan, copying, typing.

.1   Afro-American Studies Collection.
ca. 1000 paperbacks. Basic books on the life and
history of black Americans.
.2   Negro Collection.
Books (ca. 460 v.), newspapers, clippings, periodicals, and vertical file materials concerning the
Negro.

JACKSON

MS8   CHILD DEVELOPMENT GROUP OF MISSISSIPPI (CDGM)
(1965). Vincent Blvd., 39205.
CDGM began as an U.S. Office of Economic Opportunity
financed Head Start project headed by a few white psy-
chologists and educators. It was an attempt to intro-
duce radical innovation concerning the education of
children in poor black communities in Mississippi and
was run by indigenous people.

MS9   THE CITIZENS COUNCILS OF AMERICA. 315-352 Plaza
Bldg., 39201. Tel 601 352-4456. W. J. Simmons, Dir.
Publ.: The Citizen, monthly magazine; Also speeches,
pamphlets, reprints, etc.

MS10   EDUCATION AND TRAINING FOR COOPERATIVES. P.O.
Box 3345, 39207. Tel 601 355-1920. Ian Tomlin, Dir.
The Cooperative works to encourage cooperative movement, including all aspects of cooperative activity and
training in special skills and crafts.

MS11   JACKSON STATE COLLEGE (1877), LIBRARY. Founder's
Room, 1325 Lynch St., 39217. Tel 601 948-8533. Mrs.
Ernestine A. Lipscomb, Librn.

.1   Afro-American Studies Collection.
ca. 1000 paperbacks. Basic books on the life and
history of black Americans.
.2   Portraits and rare books collection.

MS12   LAWYERS' COMMITTEE FOR CIVIL RIGHTS UNDER LAW.
223 N. Farish St., 39201. Tel 601 948-5400. Lawrence
Aschenbrenner, Chief Counsel.

MS13   LAWYERS CONSTITUTIONAL DEFENSE COMMITTEE OF
THE ROGER BALDWIN FOUNDATION OF ACLU, INC.
P.O. Box 3568, 603 N. Farish St., 39202. Tel 601
948-4191. Armand Derfner, Chief Staff Counsel.

.1   Lawyers Constitutional Defense Committee of the
Roger Baldwin Foundation of ACLU, Inc.
Files, 1965- . Legal material on civil rights
cases in Mississippi.

MS14   LIBERTY HOUSE, POOR PEOPLE'S CORPORATION (1965).
P.O. Box 3468, 39207. Tel 601 352-8302. Larry Rand,
Mgr.
The Corporation works to provide jobs through hand-
craft cooperatives for poor people in Mississippi.

MS15   MILLSAPS COLLEGE, ORAL HISTORY PROJECT. 39210.
Tel 601 354-5201. John Quincy Adams, Dir.
The Project is concerned with the history and development of the State of Mississippi and places emphasis
upon the civil rights struggles and the development and
movement of Negroes in the State

MS16   MISSISSIPPI COUNCIL ON HUMAN RELATIONS (1965),
COUNCIL LIBRARY (1968). 302 First Federal Bldg.,
39201. Tel 601 948-0878. Kenneth L. Dean, Exec. Dir.
Inquiries answered, referrals made, consultation.
The Council promotes education in areas of human re-
lations and related social problems. Affiliated with
Southern Regional Council, Atlanta, Ga.
Publ.: Interpreter, quarterly newsletter.

MS17   MISSISSIPPI DEPARTMENT OF ARCHIVES AND HISTORY
(1902). War Memorial Bldg., P.O. Box 571, 39205.
Tel 601 352-5001. Charlotte Capers, Dir. Copying,
inquiries answered, referrals made.
Publ.: Annual Report; Index of Alfred H. Stone Collection on the Negro and Cognate Subjects, and
other finding aids.
.1   Abbey, Richard, 1805- .
Papers, 1843-91. ca. 665 items. Yazoo County,
(Miss.) cotton planter and Methodist minister.
Many papers relate to Abbey's service with the
Publishing House of the Methodist Episcopal
Church, South, of which he was special agent to
prosecute claims against the U.S. Government for
property destroyed during the Civil War.
.2   Alcorn, James Lusk, 1816-94.
Papers of James L. Alcorn and family, 1839-1906.
ca. 55 items. Coahoma County planter, statesman,
and political leader of Mississippi during the Reconstruction era. Chief coverage is for the period
1850-79, during which Alcorn was planter, military
officer, Governor, and U.S. Senator. The diary
covers part of 1863-64, and relates to Alcorn's
military service.
.3   Ames, Adelbert, 1835-1933.
Papers, 1874-1929. ca. 36 items. Union Army officer; military and civilian Governor during the
Reconstruction period in Mississippi. Miscellaneous correspondence, chiefly dealing with public
affairs during Ames' period in office. Of interest
is the correspondence with E. Benjamin Andrews,
president of Brown University, discussing the historical significance of Ames' administration. One
letter to Ames, signed "M," gives "secret" information on the Vicksburg riot of 1874.
.4   Clark, Charles, 1811?-1877.
Papers of Charles and Frederick Clark, 1810-92.
ca. 233 items and 24 v. Personal and business
papers and plantation records of Charles Clark,
Confederate brigadier general and wartime
Governor of Mississippi, and his son Frederick
Clark, lawyer. The correspondence mainly
covers 1860-79, and includes copies of 5 letters
from Charles Clark to Andrew Johnson (1865-66),
2 from William Yerger (1862-65), 1 from Alexander M. Clayton (1869), and correspondence concerning State property turned over to the Union
Army in 1865. There are 24 volumes of accounts,
records, notes, and correspondence, containing in
part: execution docket of Charles Clark (1836-40);
several volumes of plantation diaries and accounts
of Doro Plantation in Bolivar County kept by overseers J.B. Flowers, H.T. Cassity, Samuel J.
Dickey, William B. Farrar, and A.D. Sailor, and
by Mrs. Charles Clark; plantation book of Burnside
Plantation (W.E. Montgomery) (1859-65) and of
Doro Plantation (1879-80); book of miscellaneous
plantation records and newspaper clippings of the
Civil War (1810-66); book listing slaves and accounts of ante bellum and post bellum periods;
and suit book (1870-74) and Doro Plantation accounts (1885-88).

MS17.5 Dunbar, William, 1749-1810.
Papers, 1776-1812. ca. 34 items and 7 v. In part, photocopies. Explorer, geologist, and meteorologist, of Adams County. Correspondence, diary, journals, letter books, and scientific papers. Some of the correspondence is with Thomas Jefferson. The volumes contain, in part, a journal, Transactions on the Plantation of William Dunbar (1776-80), letter book (mutilated; 1802-05), and letter book (1805-12).

.6 Dupree, H.T.T., b. 1882.
Plantation account books, 1878-1900. ca. 4 v. Accounts of a Hinds County planter and physician, who farmed near Raymond, Miss. The ledgers cover all or parts of the years 1878-81, 1886-87, 1891-94, and 1894-1900.

.7 Finch, Anslem J.
Papers. Includes letters (4) from George Washington Carver to Dr. Finch, dated March 24, 1924; September 24, 1927; March 3, 1928; and February 23, 1929. Also includes one letter from Mary McLeod Bethune to Dr. Finch dated June 27, 1942.

.8 Ford, John.
Papers of John Ford and family, 1818-1944. ca. 145 items. Early settler in Mississippi, pioneer in Mississippi Methodism, and leader in public affairs of the Mississippi Territory and the State in its infancy. Documents, letters, and business papers of Ford and his descendants. Includes items pertaining to the estate of W.M. Rankin, division of property, slaves, and monies. There are minutes of trustees of the school at Fordsville (1858).

.9 Gordon, Robert.
Diaries of Robert and James Gordon, 1851-76. ca. 6 v. In part, typescripts. Four diaries of Robert Gordon, prominent planter of Pontotoc County, covering the years 1851, 1853, 1857, and 1858. Two diaries (1873 and 1876) of his son, James Gordon, planter, State legislator, Confederate Army officer, author, and U.S. Senator from Mississippi.

.10 Hamilton, Charles D.
Papers, 1858-70. ca. 875 items. Planter, of Grand Gulf, Miss., who had extensive business interests in Louisiana. Some letters are from Henry W. Allen, with whom Hamilton was associated in the Allendale plantation near Baton Rouge; B. Stevens, who was connected with Allendale; and from William Phillips, who rented the "Conner Farm" in Louisiana.

.11 Hughes, Henry.
Papers, 1837-59. 16 v. and 10 items. Writer and apologist for slavery. Materials concerning slavery, abolitionist movement, Negroes and related subjects.

.12 Killona Plantation.
Records, 1836-ca. 1886. ca. 3 v. Journals, including cotton book and business book, of Holmes County plantation, for the year 1836 and the period ca. 1868-86. The records, kept by Jorden Bailey, the plantation manager, reflect farming practices in the Acona neighborhood, in the hill portion of Holmes County.

.13 McLaurin, Anselm Joseph, 1848-1909.
Papers, 1832-ca. 1909. ca. 47 items and 6 v. In part, transcripts. Lawyer and statesman, of Brandon, Rankin County; Governor of Mississippi and U.S. Senator. Scrapbooks pertaining to the family contain miscellaneous letters, broadsides, pictures, and clippings; many of the latter concern the Senator's political career and his death. Papers of family members include several bills of sale for slaves, among them one for slaves bought from Duncan McLaurin of Simpson Company by Daniel and John D. McLaurin in 1847.

.14 Magruder, James Trueman, 1786-1830.
Papers, 1780-1831. 2 items and 5 v. Merchant seaman and planter, of Maryland and Jefferson County, Miss. Some materials are: plantation account book presenting farming operations and social activities at Mount Ararat Plantation, near Church Hill, Miss.; ms (1828) by Magruder's son, Alexander Leonard Covington Magruder, advo-

cating prohibition of the importation of slaves for sale in Mississippi.

Mississippi.

.15 —— Cemetery records, 1862-1938. 1 v. and 1 reel of microfilm. In part, typescript. The records of Greenwood Cemetery, Jackson, Miss., include a list of burials, 1823-60; a register of lots sold, 1862-1915; register of white, Negro, and pauper burials, 1872; of white burials, 1872-97; and of Negro burials, 1893-98. The roster of cemeteries in Monroe County (compiled by W.A. Evans and associates in 1938) contains indexes of the cemeteries and of family names.

.16 —— Federal population census, 1816-80. Includes slave schedules for 1850 and 1860.

.17 —— Miscellaneous papers, 1785-1953. ca. 1390 items. In part, transcripts and photocopies. Chiefly correspondence (personal and business); miscellaneous papers. Most of the material relates to the period of the Civil War. Contains information chiefly on military personages and activities; on routine action in the offices of Governors and Senators, on church work and schools; and also scattered information on lawsuits, slaves, and politics. Among those represented are Theodore G. Bilbo, Albert G. Brown, J.E. Brown of Blue Mountain, James Brown of Oxford; Callaway family, John F.H. Claiborne of Pontotoc; Foster Freeland and Freeman Freeland, of Holly Springs. and Ellen Steele Satterfield, of Laurel.

.18 —— Official records, 1810-1947. 100 items, 36 v. and 1 reel of microfilm. In part, typescripts and photocopies. Official correspondence, record books, daybook, cashbook, fee book, land deed book; tax records, court records, court docket, briefs; receipts, plantation notes; journal, minutes, annual report, constitution; inventory of archives, indexes, directory, list of names; radio scripts, translations of documents, maps, and miscellaneous papers. Persons and institutions prominently mentioned are Adams County Poorhouse; Board of Inspectors, Mississippi State Penitentiary; circuit courts of Jefferson and Sunflower counties; M.A. Clark, James J. Collier; Commissioners of Direct Taxes for District of Mississippi; Anthony Foster of Sardis, Miss.; Hinds County Jail, and School Board; Leflore County Courts; Fleming Moore, justice of the peace; Orphans Court, Madison County; George B. Power; probate courts of Attala and Choctaw counties; Will Purvis, defendant in various Mississippi courts; Rankin County court, and supervisors: A.J. Smith, justice of the peace; U.S. District Court; Warren County sheriff and tax collector; and Works Progress Administration: Adult Education and Nursery School Project, Civil Works Administration for Mississippi, Federal Emergency Relief Administration, and Mississippi Writers' Project.

.19 —— Plantation records, 1818-65. 45 items and 8 v. Plantation books, cashbook, and miscellaneous documents pertaining to Nanechehaw plantation of Charles B. Allen; to Aventine plantation in Adams County, owned by Thomas R. Shields; to Brooksdale farm in Amite County of the Rev. Hamilton McKnight; to Artornish and Loch Leven plantations in Adams County owned by James Brown of New York City; to Nailer plantation, kept by Dan Burnet of Port Gibson as administrator of Francis Nailer's estate; to plantations of Levin Covington in Adams County, of William R. Elley in Washington County, of Thomas E. Helm, Jackson, Miss.; of Belmont plantation in Claiborne County, kept by L.W. Montgomery; and to two unidentified plantations, one of which is near Holly Springs, Marshall County. Also includes minutes of the Adams Athenaeum, March 1825-October 1826; and records of lands owned by Brown in Chicasaw,

Choctaw, Lafayette, Oktibbeha, and Yalobusha Counties, Miss. Contains material on cotton picking, Negroes, plantation life, and family history.

MS17.20 — Records, 1920-24, of State Improvement Bond Commission. 5918 items. Correspondence, minutes, financial records, and other materials of the Commission, which was established for supervising expenditures of funds appropriated for permanent improvements to State buildings. Includes material relating to Alcorn Agricultural and Mechanical College.

.21 Osborn, Samuel George.
Plantation account books, 1892-1938. 3 v. Accounts of a Learned, Hinds County, Miss., planter. In part, closed to investigators until 1968.

.22 Panther Burn Plantation, Percy, Mississippi.
Records, 1859-82. 2 v. Account books kept by John Willis. The 1859 entries are in a blank "Cotton plantation record and account book" by Thomas Affleck. It includes daily records of passing events, record of cotton picked, and inventories.

.23 Quitman, John Anthony, 1799-1858.
Papers, 1812-60. 2532 items, 4 v. and 1 reel of microfilm. In part, typescripts and microcopy of original mss in Alderman Library, University of Virginia. Planter, lawyer, Mexican War officer, and political leader, of Natchez, Miss. Correspondence, military papers and records, bills, receipt notes, legal papers, scrapbook, plantation accounts, and family papers. Much material relates to the political controversies of the time, particularly the slavery question. Other papers concern Quitman's service as Masonic grand master in Mississippi, and his interest in filibustering expeditions involving Cuba and Nicaragua. The plantation accounts reflect the affairs of Springfield Plantation, Adams County, Miss. The scrapbook contains clippings relating to the American or Know Nothing party, the Southern Rights Union, Henry S. Foote, and the "Democracy of Mississippi" platform.

.24 Rollins, Bertie (Shaw).
Papers, 1821-1951. 386 items. In part, transcripts. Writer and historian, of Aberdeen, Monroe County, Miss. Typewritten and ms copies of letters and records concerning the town and county. Includes, among other items, contracts between planters and freedmen.

.25 St. Philip's Episcopal Church, Kirkwood, Miss.
Records, 1848-88. 2 v. Vestry minutes and parish register of the church, which was located in Madison County at a village near the home of Gov. William McWillie. The parish register contains a list of rectors, historical sketch, and articles of association of the parish, as well as a list of communicants, baptism, marriages, confirmations, and funerals. A separate list contains similar data for Negro members.

.26 Sessions, Joseph F., b. 1838.
Papers, 1861-65. 169 items. Confederate Army officer, lawyer, and public official, of Brookhaven, Miss. Correspondence, orders, reports, and other military papers, reflecting Sessions' service in various army units. A document of August 1865 contains an agreement between Sessions and his freedmen, and a letter of December 1865 gives a partial account of his military service. There are 2 circulars issued by the Freedmen's Bureau in 1865.

.27 Sharkey, Clay, b. 1844.
Papers, 1867-1931. 155 items. Confederate Army veteran, farmer, merchant, and State legislator, of Jackson, Miss., and Washington County, Miss. Correspondence and essays, including about 124 autobiographical accounts relating details of ante bellum plantation life in Hinds and Leake Counties, and events of Sharkey's Civil War service.

.28 Sizer, Henry E.
Papers, 1844-67. 44 items. Bills of sale for slaves, together with 3 letters and a newspaper clipping. The slaves were bought by agents of Sizer in New Orleans, Richmond, and Nashville.

.29 Snodgrass, John.
Papers of John Snodgrass and family, 1814-77. 25 items and 4 v. Planter, of Claiborne County, Miss. Correspondence, business papers, and account books. The papers mainly cover the period 1833-77, with no papers dating from the 1860's. There are 2 plantation account books covering 1814-32 and 1819-26 respectively. There are several letters of John Snodgrass' wife, Margaret. Other correspondents include Joseph B. Ard, Emma Snodgrass, E.P. Snodgrass, and T.H. Snodgrass.

.30 Stone, Alfred Holt, 1870-1955.
Papers, 1933-55. 167 v. Member of board of trustees of Dept. of Archives and History (Nov. 1, 1933-May 11, 1955), chairman of State Tax Commission (May 1, 1932-May 11, 1955). History and literature by and about the Negro.

.31 Stuart family.
Papers of the Stuart, Mayes, and Dimitry families, 1840-1948. 1811 items and 36 v. Diaries, journals, correspondence, business papers, pictures, notes, literary and historical mss, newspaper clippings, scrapbooks, land records, notebooks, and other papers. Chiefly the papers of the family of Oscar J.E. Stuart, of Summit; the family of Robert B. Mayes, lawyer and probate judge of Yazoo City or Yazoo County; and the family of John Bull Smith Dimitry, Confederate veteran, author, historian, and journalist, of New Orleans. Grouped in 3 files: correspondence, mss, and clippings. The largest group of letters dates from the 1860's. The mss are, in part, the reminiscences of Florence B. Carson about Vicksburg, Miss., and Oasis Plantation, Coahoma County, Miss. Among the 36 v. are Memoirs of Vicksburg, by F.B. Carson; Oasis, A Mississippi Plantation 50 Years Ago, by F.B. Carson; and These Were My Homes, by F.B. Carson.

.32 Stuart, Oscar J.E.
Papers of Oscar J.E. Stuart and family, 1848-1909. 195 items and 4 v. Lawyer, of Summit, Pike County, Miss. Diaries, correspondence, and broadsides, concerning Stuart and members of his family. The diaries (1850-62) were kept by Ann L. Hardeman, sister-in-law of Stuart. The letters reflect conditions during the ante bellum period, the Civil War, and Reconstruction. Among the correspondents are Stuart's sons, James H. Stuart, Oscar E. Stuart, and Edward Stuart, all of whom served in the Confederate forces.

.33 Sykes, Columbus.
Papers, 1851-97. 242 items and 8 v. Lawyer, Confederate veteran, and planter, of Aberdeen, Miss. Correspondence, accounts, notebooks, plantation records, and papers of members of Sykes family. Among the items are the plantation records of Mrs. E.P. Sykes (1866), G.A. Sykes, Bardstown Junction, Ky. (1883-90), and a journal-daybook of E.P. Barbour (1896-97).

.34 Taylor, Lewis L.
Business records, 1836-40. 85 items. Merchant, of Jackson, Miss. Miscellaneous business papers. An item of interest is a receipt given by Abram Womack to Taylor for payment for 12 slaves.

.35 Vick family.
Papers of the Vick and Phelps families, 1810-1906. 185 items. Papers and documents of the families of Burwell Vick; his sons, Henry W. Vick and Gray J. Vick; and A.J. Phelps, of Nitta Yuma Plantation in Washington County, Miss. Includes a Mississippi Territory indenture (1810), lists of Negroes sold or mortgaged to the Bank of the U.S. (1834-49), the wills of Burwell Vick and Gray J. Vick, and correspondence between A.J. Phelps and George C. Harris regarding plantation boundary lines.

.36 Wade, Walter.
Plantation diaries, 1834-54. 2 v. Physician, and owner of Ross Wood Plantation, Jefferson County, Miss. Entries pertaining to plantation management, lists of slaves, records of cotton picked, accounts, and miscellaneous information regarding the plantation.

.37 Walthall, William T., 1820-99.
Papers, 1803-1955. 9921 items and 119 v. Confederate veteran, journalist, and diplomat, of Mobile, Ala. and Vicksburg, Miss. Business, personal, legal, and military correspondence; diaries, memoranda, clippings, and other papers of the Walthall family, including A.C. Walthall, F.H. Walthall, Flora B. Walthall, Maud Walthall, and William T. Walthall, written at Mobile, Ala., Pensacola, Fla., Vicksburg, Miss., and Virginia. Relates in part to Walthall's work as newspaper editorial writer for the Mobile Tribune and Mobile Register, and to the Commission on Inter-racial Cooperation, and its successor the Southern Regional Council. Correspondents include Wirt Adams, Jefferson Davis, J.W. Door, J.A. Early, W. Preston Johnston, Edward Livingston, and Raphael Semmes.

MS18   MISSISSIPPI FREEDOM DEMOCRATIC PARTY (1964). 507½ Farish St., 39202. Lawrence Guyot, Dir.

.1 Mississippi Freedom Democratic Party.
Records, ca. 1964-66. Correspondence, pamphlets, speeches, legal documents, surveys, and other publications relating to the majority of the programs and organizational techniques initiated by the Mississippi Freedom Democratic Party between 1964 and 1966. Materials are listed under the headings of: party structure, administration, organizing material; legal suits, and programs; other organizational groups; economics; agriculture; county reports, containing specific information on party structure and programs for 50 out of the 82 counties in the State of Mississippi. Subjects include Mississippi food program, welfare complaints, politics, Democratic National Committee, voter registration, reapportionment, congressional challenge (1965), convention challenge (1964), Mississippi Democratic Conference, Mississippi Freedom Labor Union, Brooklyn Freedom Democratic Party Movement, and the Free Southern Theater.

MS19   MISSISSIPPI STATE SOVEREIGNTY COMMISSION. 407 New Capitol, 39209. Tel 601 354-6085.

MS20   SOUTHERN MEDIA. 117 W. Church St., 39202. Tel 601 352-9109. Doris Derby and Jesse Morris, Directors.
Southern Media produces films of southern cooperatives.

.1 Mississippi Freedom Democratic Party.
Tape recordings.
.2 Council of Federated Organizations (COFO).
Tape recordings.

MS21   URBAN LEAGUE OF GREATER JACKSON. 119 N. Farish St., 39201. Tel 601 948-5267. Fred Nolan, Exec. Dir.

.1 Urban League of Greater Jackson.
Files. Correspondence, minutes of meetings, financial records, studies, reports, and other materials dealing with the aims, history and programs of the League.

LEXINGTON

MS22   SAINTS JUNIOR COLLEGE (1918). P.O. Box 419, 39095. Tel 601 834-1741. Arenia C. Mallory, Pres.

.1 Saints Junior College.
Archives, 1918- . Includes correspondence, minutes of board meetings, financial records, records of admission, and other documents dealing with the history and administration of the College.

LORMAN

MS23   ALCORN AGRICULTURAL AND MECHANICAL COLLEGE (1871), LIBRARY. Box 762, 39096. Tel 601 437-5151. Mrs. E.Y. Hendricks, Librn.

.1 Afro-American Studies Collection.
ca. 1000 paperbacks. Basic books on the life and history of black Americans.

NATCHEZ

MS24   NATCHEZ JUNIOR COLLEGE (1885). 1010 N. Union Extension, 39120. Tel 601 445-9702. LeVander Kinds, Pres.

.1 Natchez Junior College.
Archives, 1885- . Includes correspondence, minutes of board meetings, records of admission, financial records, and other documents dealing with the history and administration of the College.

OKOLONA

MS25   OKOLONA COLLEGE. 38860. A.P. Wilburn, Pres.

.1 Okolona College.
Archives. Correspondence, minutes of board meetings, financial records, bulletins, catalogs, records of admission, and other materials relating to the history and administration of the College.

PINEY WOODS

MS26   PINEY WOODS COUNTRY LIFE SCHOOL (1910). 39148. Tel 601 845-6616. Laurence C. Jones, Pres.

.1 Piney Woods Country Life School.
Archives, 1910- . Includes correspondence, minutes of board meetings, financial records, records of admission, and other documents dealing with the history and administration of the School.

PRENTISS

MS27   PRENTISS NORMAL & INDUSTRIAL INSTITUTE (1907). 39474. Tel 601 792-4735. Mrs. J.E. Johnson, Pres.

.1 Prentiss Normal and Industrial Institute.
Archives, 1930- . Includes correspondence, minutes of board meetings, financial records, records of admission, bulletins, catalogs, and other documents dealing with the history and administration of the Institute.

STATE COLLEGE

MS28   MISSISSIPPI STATE UNIVERSITY (1878), MITCHELL MEMORIAL LIBRARY. P.O. Drawer 5408, 39762. Tel 601 325-4225. George R. Lewis, Dir. Interlibrary loan, copying, inquiries answered, consultation.

Among the Library's collections are materials which, in part, are closed to researchers.
.1 Cavett, E.D., 1845-1919.
Swann-Cavett papers, 1884-1929. 486 items. Soldier, Grand Cyclops of Noxubee (Miss.) Ku Klux Klan, deputy U.S. tax collector of Mississippi, and State legislator. Family correspondence (1884-1927) of Mrs. Allie (Cavett) Swann, Cavett's daughter. Includes pamphlets and reprints opposing woman's suffrage; statements and receipts; legal papers including deeds, and abstract of title; and newspaper clippings by and about Cavett.
.2 Church Records.
Papers, 1819-1957. Mississippi Baptist Church records (1819-1957); Mississippi Methodist Church records (1833-1955); Mississippi Primitive Baptist Church records (1819-1950); Mississippi Presbyterian Church records (1832-1949). Contains church rolls, minutes, and other records, showing Negro membership in white churches before and after the Civil War.
.3 Cox, A. Eugene.
Papers, 1934-68. ca. 9536 items. Former resident director of Providence Cooperative Farm in

Holmes County, Miss., and former employee of National Council of Churches. Correspondence, published material, newspaper clippings, and other items pertaining mostly to racial problems in the South. Covers such topics as the Citizens Councils, Mississippi State Sovereignty Commission, National Council of Churches and related organizations, farm labor unions, and cooperative farms.

.4 Darden family.
Papers, 1835-1944. 476 items. Personal correspondence and business and legal papers of John W., John J., Thomas L., and Putnam Darden and others; bills of sale for slaves and horses; and cotton accounts.

.5 Facts on Film.
Papers, 1954-67. Microfilm. Contains materials on civil rights and race relations in the South. See Race Relations Information Center, Nashville, Tenn., for a full description.

.6 Hobbs family.
Papers, 1835-1935. ca. 25,000 items. Correspondence, statements of account, and other material concerning the Brookhaven, Miss., Weekly Leader edited by B.T. Hobbs. After his death in 1910, the Leader was edited and managed by Mrs. Lena Menger Hobbs and Paul Hobbs. Also includes correspondence regarding Mississippi politics (1887-1932), the prohibition movement in Mississippi (1886-1912), the Anti-White Cap Movement in Lincoln County (1902-09), and other papers.

.7 Mississippi Integration.
Miscellaneous. ca. 6 vf and bound materials. Publications, literature, speeches, broadsides, special editions, reprints, "hate sheets," clippings, concerning the many phases of integration and the civil rights struggle in Mississippi, including phonotapes (418 titles) of Citizens Council radio program entitled "Citizens Council Forums."

.8 Mississippi State University, State College, Mississippi, 1888-1963.
500 items. Correspondence, speeches, notes, articles, clippings, and other papers of persons connected with the University. Most of the papers relate to the University but other subjects include the election of John F. Kennedy and integration on the campus.

.9 Phi Alpha Theta Collection.
Miscellaneous. ca. 2 ft. Collected by the Mississippi State University history fraternity. Vertical file material on state politics, especially minority groups; right- and left-wing organizations and literature; campus issues, such as dissent, ROTC, and Viet Nam.

.10 Randolph, Edward Brett, 1792-1848.
Randolph-Sherman papers, 1813-1947. 1 reel of microfilm (negative), 215 items. Microfilm made in 1960 from originals owned by Mrs. T. Bailey Hardy, Columbus, Miss. Officer and sutler in the War of 1812, participant in the Seminole campaign, planter of Lowndes County, Miss., and Receiver of Public Moneys for District Lands, Columbus, Miss. Correspondence (1813-1947) of Randolph, his wife, relatives, and friends; his account of his part in the War of 1812; his protests (1844) against the Methodist Episcopal Church Schism; and other materials. Randolph manumitted 21 slaves in 1836.

.11 Rice, Nannie Herndon, 1886-1963.
Papers, 1824-1963. 7539 items. In part, typescripts. Librarian at Mississippi State University. Correspondence, diaries, bills of sale of slaves, and rent and labor contracts. Papers of Miss Rice describe Meadow Woods, the Rice plantation in Oktibbeha County, Miss. Other papers include those of Miss Rice's parents, John W. Rice and Augusta (Hopkins) Rice, her brother, Arthur H. Rice, physician and planter, of Oktibbeha County, Miss., and others, relating to the Civil War, Reconstruction, the Mississippi Legislature, and other subjects.

.12 Rollins, Bertie (Shaw).
Papers, 1821-1957. 295 items. In part, transcripts (handwritten) and photocopies. Author and historian, of Aberdeen, Miss. Family correspondence (1848-1905) relating to life in Monroe County, Miss., and to Confederate campaigns; articles and illustrations by Jack Knox of the Nashville Banner; clippings and papers concerning Monroe County; five scrapbooks of clippings on local and family history; register (1865) of contracts by planters and freedmen; Monroe County court minutes (1821).

.13 Ross, Holt Edgar, 1897-1968.
Papers, 1916-66. 357 items. In part, typescripts. Lawyer and representative for labor union, of Mississippi and New Orleans. Correspondence, articles, poems, and speeches by Ross, newspaper clippings, photos, and other papers, chiefly relating to Ross' efforts in behalf of the International Longshoremen's Association, International Hod Carriers', Building, and Common Laborers' Union, American Federation of Labor, and Congress of Industrial Organizations, together with material on Ross' trip to the Trade Union Congress, Blackpool, Eng., 1944, and a trip to Puerto Rico to review labor problems. Correspondents include Dwight D. Eisenhower, Alfred A. Force, Robert S. Green, William Green, and others.

.14 Ross, Isaac, 1760-1836.
Estate papers, 1845-89. 276 items. Plantation owner from Jefferson County, Miss., whose will provided for the manumission of his slaves and their return to Liberia if they so desired. Correspondence, business and legal records concerning Isaac Ross Wade (grandson of Isaac Ross) and the Isaac Ross Estate, Jefferson County, Miss. Included are correspondence and records of transactions with the American Colonization Society.

.15 Shaw, Thompson B., 1706-1054.
McKell papers, 1818-1931. 459 items. Plantation owner, of Jefferson County, Miss. Personal and family correspondence (1818-98); eight Civil War letters, chiefly civilian, and business papers relating to the plantation.

.16 Sheldon, George Lawson, 1870-1960.
Papers, 1928-61. 5512 items. In part, typescripts. Nebraska State senator, and Governor, State legislator of Mississippi, and leader of the "Lily White" Republican party of Mississippi. Correspondence, legal papers, speeches, poetry, and newspaper clippings, together with county, State, and national records (1932-61) of the Republican party of Mississippi, largely relating to efforts to unseat the Howard-Redmond delegates, the Negro faction, at national conventions and in party patronage. Correspondents include Thomas L. Bailey, Charles H. Blewitt, Mike Sennett Conner, Charles U. Gordon, Pat Harrison, Herbert Hoover, Robert H. Lucas, Clayton Rand, Lamont Rowlands, Harrison E. Spangler, Nelson Taylor, Mildred S. Topp, Hugh White, and J.A. White.

.17 Williams family.
Papers, 1823-1906. 192 items. Correspondence (1879-99) of Campbell A. Williams from Louisiana, Central America, and Millsaps College (Jackson, Miss.), and share crop contracts (1895-99).

TOUGALOO

MS29 FREEDOM INFORMATION SERVICE. Box 120, 39174. Tel 601 355-1511. Jan Hillegas, Dir.
Conducts research and writing on Mississippi politics, economics, power structure, etc. for Mississippi Newsletter and miscellaneous brochures.

MS30 TOUGALOO COLLEGE (1869), EVA HILLS EASTMAN LIBRARY (ca. 1910). 39174. Tel 601 982-4342. Mrs. Jeannetts C. Roach, Librn. Interlibrary loan, literature searches, inquiries answered.

.1 Afro-American Heritage collection.
Materials, 17th century- . Microfilm. 131 reels. Books, newspapers, and mss concerning the Negro American and his history. See Minnesota Mining and Manufacturing Company, St. Paul, Minn., for a full description.

.2 Afro-American Studies Collection.
ca. 1000 paperbacks. Basic books on the life and history of black Americans.

.3   American Negro Collection.
      Miscellaneous. ca. 1500 v. History and literature
      by and about the Negro.
.4   Ross Collection.
      Miscellaneous, late 18th century- . ca. 1000
      items. Includes books, pamphlets, periodicals and
      clippings, chiefly on the economic, political and so-
      cial life of Africa.

UTICA

MS31   UTICA JUNIOR COLLEGE (1903), WILLIAM H. HOLTZ-
        CLAW MEMORIAL LIBRARY (1951). 39175. Tel 601
        885-2311. Christine N. Stevens, Librn.

.1   Utica Junior College.
        Archives, 1903- .

VICKSBURG

MS32   OLD COURTHOUSE MUSEUM. 39180. Tel 601 636-0741.
        Mrs. Eva W. Davis, Dir.

.1   Vicksburg and Warren County Historical Society.
        Ms collection, 1803-1900. ca. 150 items and 200 v.
        In part, transcripts. Correspondence, diaries,
        scrapbooks, receipts for slaves, genealogical
        materials, and other papers concerning Vicksburg
        and the South, particularly during the Civil War.
        Includes letters written during the siege of
        Vicksburg.

WEST POINT

MS33   MARY HOLMES JUNIOR COLLEGE (1892). 39773. Tel
        601 494-2576. John Walton, Pres.

.1   Mary Holmes Junior College.
        Files, 1892- . Includes correspondence, minutes
        of board meetings, financial records, admission
        records, and other documents concerning the ad-
        ministration and history of the College.

MISSOURI

CLAYTON

MO1   ST. LOUIS COUNTY COMMISSION ON HUMAN RELATIONS
        (1964). Fourth Floor, County Courthouse, 7900 For-
        syth, 63105. Tel 314 863-6360. Myron Schwartz,
        Cmnr.
        The Commission was established by ordinance and is
        appointed to enforce the County Public Accommoda-
        tions Code, and to "foster mutual self-respect gen-
        erally among the various groups in St. Louis County."

.1   St. Louis County Commission on Human Relations.
        Files, 1964- . Correspondence, legal documents,
        and other materials relating to the enforcement of
        anti-discriminatory laws.

COLUMBIA

MO2   STATE HISTORICAL SOCIETY OF MISSOURI (1898). Hitt
        and Lowry Sts., 65201. Tel 314 443-3165. Dr. Richard
        S. Brownlee, Dir. and Secy. Interlibrary loan, copying,
        inquiries answered, referrals made, consultation.
        Publ.: Missouri Historical Review; quarterly journal.

.1   Applegate, Lisbon, 1803-75.
        Papers, 1819-99. 3461 items and 19 v. Merchant,
        surveyor, and county judge, of Chariton County,
        Mo. Correspondence and business papers, chiefly,
        1840-80. Includes correspondence relating to the
        Civil War in Missouri, the hire and sale of Negro
        slaves, economic problems, and land matters; the
        San Francisco Vigilance Committee, and the effect
        of the Civil War on citizens of California.
.2   Breckenridge family.
        Papers, 1750-1960. ca. 11 ft. In part, tran-

scripts. Chiefly correspondence (1900-50) between the compiler of the collection, James M.
Breckenridge, and descendants of the Breckenridge
and Breckenridge and related families; biographical sketches, copies of documents establishing
military service dates of various family members, sermons, letters, printed speeches, pamphlets, accounts of slave sales, and other papers.
Persons represented include Alexander Breckenridge (1789-1859), William C.P. Breckenridge
(1837-1904), General James Breckinridge (1763-
1833), John Breckinridge (1760-1806), John C.
Breckinridge (1821-75), the Reverend Robert J.
Breckinridge (1800-71), Samuel M. Breckinridge
(1828-91), and the Reverend William L. Breckinridge (1803-76); families included are the Bryan,
Clark, Cowan, Gamble, Keele, Kerr, Preston,
Schaurtes, Wells, Wilcox, and Willoughby
families.
.3   France, Charles B., 1835-95.
        Papers, 1857-90. 1 box. Banker, of St. Joseph,
        Mo. Correspondence, diaries, and other papers.
        Letters to France relate primarily to business
        and family matters and the Civil War, religion,
        reaction in California to Lincoln's assassination,
        Reconstruction, and the freed Negroes in the area
        of Mobile, Ala.
.4   Guitar, Odon, 1825-1908.
        Papers, 1836-1903. 253 items. Lawyer and Union
        Army officer, of Boone County, Mo. Correspon-
        dence, military papers, and accounts. Material
        bulks largest for the years, 1862-64. Correspon-
        dence relates to the Civil War in Missouri, south-
        ern sympathizers, guerrilla bands and raids, the
        emancipation of slaves, problems involved in pro-
        tecting the freed Negro, and the enlistment of Ne-
        groes in the Union Army.
.5   Leonard, Abiel, 1797-1863.
        Papers, 1786-1933. 3114 items and 51 v. Farmer,
        lawyer, and justice of the Missouri Supreme Court.
        Correspondence of Leonard and members of his
        family, of Howard County, Mo. concerning his law
        practice, land investments, state and national poli-
        tics, economic conditions, Negro slavery, emanci-
        pation of slaves, the Kansas-Nebraska Act, Mor-
        mons in Missouri, secession of the southern
        states, nullification, the Civil War, New Madrid
        (Mo.) land claims; legal papers containing notes
        on cases during Leonard's general law practice,
        opinions on cases tried while he was a justice of
        the Missouri Supreme Court, and information on
        the New Madrid land claims cases. Correspon-
        dents include William H. Ashley, David Bates, Ed-
        ward Bates, William V.N. Bay, Hamilton Gamble,
        Henry S. Geyer, Peyton R. Hayden, David S.
        Lamme, Nathaniel Leonard, Reeves Leonard, John
        Miller, Joel R. Poinsett, Benjamin H. Reeves,
        James S. Rollins, and George C. Sibley.
.6   Negro Associations Collection.
.7   —— Ancient Order of United Workmen.
        Proceedings of the Supreme Lodge, Ancient
        Order of United Workmen, 17th stated meet-
        ing, 1889.
.8   —— Brothers and Sisters of Purity.
        Minutes of Grand Lodge United Order,
        Brothers and Sisters of Purity, 1901.
.9   —— Grand United Order of Odd Fellows.
        Includes journal of proceedings of general
        meetings, 1889, 1902, 1904; subcommittee of
        management quarterly circular, 1903-11; and
        journal of proceedings of meetings of District
        Grand Lodge No. 8 of Missouri and jurisdic-
        tion, 1906, 1907, 1910, 1912, 1913, 1914, 1915,
        1916, 1917. Also contains journal of proceed-
        ings of the General Meeting Grand United
        Order of Odd Fellows, 1906; and proceedings
        of the annual session of the District Grand
        Lodge No. 8, 1906, 1907, 1910.
.10   —— Grand Order of the Orient.
        The Improved and Perfected Ritual and
        Declarations of Principles and Purposes of the
        Grand Order of the Orient, Empire of the
        Orient.

MO2.11 —— Heroines of Jericho.
Proceedings of the Annual Communication of the Grand Court of the Heroines of Jericho for the State of Missouri and its jurisdiction, 1888, 1894, 1895, 1897-1900, 1902-04, 1914, 1917.

.12 —— Independent Order of Odd Fellows.
Includes constitutions of Grand Subordinate Encampments of the State of Missouri, adopted 1881, amended to 1888; proceedings of the Annual Communication of the Sovereign Grand Lodge of the Independent Order of Odd Fellows, 1894, 1897, 1901, and 1903.

.13 —— Knights and Daughters of Tabor.
Official proceedings of the Knights and Daughters of Tabor International Order of Twelve for the jurisdiction of Missouri, 1894-97, 1902-04; proceedings of the fifth annual session of the Grand Temple and Tabernacle, Independent Order of Seven, 1887; proceedings of the 15th annual session of the National Grand Temple and Tabernacle, 1887; ritual of the Order, Keokuk, Iowa, 1889; articles of association, constitution, rules and regulations, of the Independent Order of Seven, 1883, 1888; Chief Grand Mentor's annual message, 29th annual grand session, Grand Temple and Tabernacle, jurisdiction of Missouri, Mexico, Co., 1916; The Taborian Voice, Vol. 1, Nos. 2, 5, 6, 7, 8, and Vol. 2, No. 1, (1915-16); organization and proceedings of the first, second, and third annual sessions of the Dual Grand Lodge of the Independent Order of Good Templar of the State of Missouri, 1881; proceedings of the organization of the State Grand Temple and Tabernacle for Missouri and jurisdiction, 1887-93, 1901-14; and official proceedings, M.W. Grand Lodge A.F. and A.M. for the State of Missouri and jurisdiction, held at St. Louis, Mo., 1890-1926.

.14 —— Knights of Pythias.
Official proceedings of Knights of Pythias, 1898, 1899, 1907, 1911, 1915, 1916, 1917, 1926; third biennial report of S.W. Starks, Supreme Chancellor to the Supreme Lodge, 1905; and constitutions of subordinate lodges, 1898.

.15 —— Knights Templar.
Official proceedings of the United Grand Commandery of Knights Templar, 1887-89, 1891-95, 1914.

.16 —— Ladies' Pleiades.
Ritual of the Ladies' Pleiades Council, containing the degrees, lectures, password, signs, etc., together with the burial ceremonies and installations of officers, as adopted by the Supreme Grand Lodge of the U.S.A., revised and arranged by Mrs. Fannie B. Cole, 1884.

.17 —— Order of Calanthe.
Minutes of the Annual Session of the Grand Court of Missouri Order of Calanthe, 1911.

.18 —— Order of Galilean Fishermen.
Minutes of the annual session of the Supreme Grand Tabernacle Order of Galilean Fishermen, both north and south of Mason's and Dixon's Line, 1882.

.19 —— Royal Arch Masons.
Official proceedings of the Grand Royal Chapter of the State of Missouri and its jurisdiction, 1885, 1887-90, 1892, 1893, 1901; and the constitution of the Grand Royal Chapter of Missouri and jurisdiction as revised and approved at the Annual Convocation, 1890, 1905, Hannibal, Mo.

.20 —— Royal Sons and Daughters of Douglass.
Official proceedings of the annual session of the Grand Convention of Royal Sons and Daughters of Douglass, State of Missouri and jurisdiction, 1904.

.21 —— Royal Tribe of Joseph.
By-laws of Benner Lodge, No. 57, Sedalia, Mo., adopted April, 1896; and constitution and laws of the Royal Tribe of Joseph, governing the Supreme, Grand and Subordinate lodges, 1896.

.22 —— United Brothers of Friendship.
Proceedings of the biennial session of the National Grand Lodge, United Brothers of Friendship and National Grand Temple, Sisters of the Mysterious Ten of America, 1884, 1886, 1888; and proceedings of the annual session of the Grand Lodge of the United Brothers of Friendship of the State of Missouri, 1885, 1886, 1890-1930.

.23 —— United Grand Chapter, Order of the Eastern Star.
Proceedings of the annual communication of the United Chapter for the State of Missouri and its jurisdiction, 1900-04; proposed amendments to constitution of Grand Chapter; and in the Kansas City Court of Appeals, March term, 1902, Statement, Additional Abstract of Record and Brief for Respondents, Lexington, Mo., 1902, the Grand Chapter Order of Eastern Star for Missouri and jurisdiction appelant, vs. the United Grand Chapter of the Order of Eastern Star for Missouri and jurisdiction.

.24 —— United Party to Virtue.
Ritual of the Grand Independent Order of the United Party of Virtue, Free and Excellent of America, 1891

.25 —— United Sons of Protection.
The journal of proceedings of the Annual Session of the Grand Lodge of the United Sons of Protection, 1878.

.26 —— Wise Men of the U.S.A.
Uniform by-laws and Rules of Order for the Government of the Subordinate Lodges, Wise Men of the U.S.A., 1883; and ritual of the Wise Men, initiatory, first, second, and third degrees, composed of rules, laws and regulations relating to the election, obligation and installation, also, explanatory lectures, signs, pass-words, and key to the private works of the lodge, as prepared and arranged by Rev. R. Rush, Supreme Archon, and Rev. B.W. Steward, 1882.

.27 Negro Churches Collection.

.28 —— African Methodist Episcopal.
Program of the District Conference, Sunday School Convention and Normal and Theological Institute of the Hannibal Presiding Elder District of the North Missouri Conference of the African Methodist Episcopal Church, 1901-02; minutes of the session of the Missouri Annual Conference of the African Methodist Episcopal Church, 1893, 1904; and proceedings of the North Missouri Annual Conference of the African Methodist Episcopal Church, 1883, 1884, 1886, 1892, 1893, 1896-1900, 1902-08, 1914.

.29 —— Baptist.
Minutes of the 22nd annual session of the Berean Missionary Baptist Association, 19th annual session of the Berean Sunday School Convention, and the 5th annual session of the Woman's Home, Foreign Missionary and Education Convention, held with the Compton Hill Baptist Church, St. Louis, Mo., 1899; minutes of the 23rd annual session of the Missouri Baptist State Convention and the Missouri Baptist Women's Home, Foreign Missionary and Educational Convention, held with the Tabernacle Baptist Church, St. Louis, Mo., 1912; minutes of the annual meeting of the Central District Baptist Association, of Missouri, 1894-96, 1904; journal of the proceedings of the 14th annual session of the Baptist General Association of the Western States and Territories, 1887; minutes of the 22nd annual meeting of the Free Will Baptist Association, of Western Missouri, 1890; proceedings of the 12th annual session of the Kansas Baptist State Convention and the W.H. and F.M. Convention, 1903; minutes of the Missouri Baptist Convention, 1900; minutes of the Northwestern and Southern Baptist Convention, 1864; proceedings of the annual session of the Mount Carmel Baptist Association, 1900, 1902-

03, 1916; minutes of the annual session of the Mount Carmel Baptist Sunday School Convention, 1902-03; minutes of the annual meeting of the Mt. Zion Baptist Association, 1897; minutes of the annual meeting of the Mt. Zion Baptist Sunday School Convention and the Ministerial and Deacons Union, 1901; annual statistical report to the National Baptist Convention, Austin, Tex., 1904; minutes of the annual meeting of the 2nd District Baptist Sunday School Convention, 1887; journal of the proceedings of the annual meeting of the North Missouri Baptist Sunday School Convention, 1886, 1887, 1894, 1895, 1901, 1902, 1904, 1911; minutes of the annual meeting of the North Missouri Baptist Association, 1883; minutes of the 3rd anniversary of the 1st district of the North Missouri Baptist Association, 1876, 1884, 1888; proceedings of the annual session of the Shiloh District Baptist Association and the Women's Home, Foreign Missionary and Educational Convention, 1904; minutes of the annual session of the 3rd District Baptist Association, 1901-1904; proceedings of the annual meeting of the Union Missionary Baptist Association of Missouri, 1889, 1895, 1896; minutes of the organization of the Western Colored Baptist Convention, 1853; and journal of the annual session of the Free Baptist Western Missouri Association Sunday School Convention and Women's Missionary Convention, 1907.

.30 — Christian.
Minutes of the annual convention of the 2nd Christian Church of Missouri, 1887, 1900, 1903, 1904.

.31 Negro Newspaper Collection.
Newspapers, ca. 1890-1968. In part, microfilms. Newspapers include the Kansas City American (1928-33), Kansas City Call (1919, 1922-1931, 1934-66), Liberator (1903), Rising Sun (1903-07), Kansas City Sun (1914-24), from Kansas City; the Western Messenger (1914-17), from Jefferson City; the St. Louis Advance (1908), St. Louis American (1949-66), American Eagle (1905), St. Louis Argus (1916-66), from St. Louis; the Sedalia Times (1901-16) from Sedalia; and the American Negro (1890), from Springfield, Mo.

.32 Rollins, James Sidney, 1812-88.
Papers, 1830-1938. 13 boxes. Microfilm copy (negative) of 33 letters (1870-85) of Rollins to Carl Schurz, from the Schurz papers in the Library of Congress. Lawyer, railroad organizer, State legislator, and U.S. Representative from Missouri (1862-64). Chiefly correspondence (1830-85) and other papers concerning Rollins' law practice, business interests, and personal and family matters. Other topics include state and national politics, bills introduced in the state legislature, economic conditions, the Civil War, the emancipation of slaves, Reconstruction and "Bourbon" democracy. Correspondents include William Ashley, Edward Bates, Thomas Hart Benton, George Caleb Bingham, Frank P. Blair, Jr., Benjamin G. Brown, C.F. Burnam, Cassius M. Clay, Thomas T. Crittenden, Alexander W. Doniphan, Odon Guitar, and Carl Schurz.

.33 Smith, Thomas Adams, 1781-1844.
Papers, 1798-1864. 1747 items. Army officer. Correspondence and seven letter books (1812-31) concerning the War of 1812, especially in Florida and New York, problems with the Indians and runaway slaves in Florida; politics; and sale of public lands. Correspondents include William Ashley, David Barton, John C. Calhoun, William Clark, William H. Crawford, Thomas Flournoy, William Henry Harrison, Andrew Jackson, Stephen H. Long, Thomas Pinckney, David Todd, and James Wilkinson.

.34 Starr, Frederick, 1826-67.
Papers, 1850-63. 30 items and 12 folders of clippings. Presbyterian clergyman, of Weston, Mo. Correspondence, broadsides, pamphlets, and newspaper clippings relating to the settlement of

the Kansas and Nebraska territories, border conflicts, abolition vs. slavery, politics of Kansas and Missouri, Indian affairs, public land sales, claims, and prices, popular sovereignty, squatters' rights, religion on the frontier.

MO3   UNIVERSITY OF MISSOURI (1839), BUSINESS AND PUBLIC ADMINISTRATION RESEARCH CENTER (1959). 65201. Tel 312 449-9251. Robert Paterson, Dir. Bibliographies prepared, copying, typing, inquiries answered, consultation.
The Center conducts research in two major areas: urban affairs, and international development. There are four categories into which the research is organized: (1) Public affairs programs, which include urban studies; (2) Resource development programs, which include manpower and population studies and transportation studies; (3) Administration programs which include systems analysis studies and intergovernmental studies; and (4) the Opinion Survey Program.
Publ.: Business and Government Review, bimonthly journal; Special publications.

.1   Business and Public Administration Research Center. Miscellaneous, 1959- . Current titles in economics, accounting, business management, political science, and government affairs. Records restricted.

MO4   UNIVERSITY OF MISSOURI LIBRARY, WESTERN HISTORICAL MANUSCRIPTS COLLECTION. 65201. Tel 314 449-9128. Richard S. Brownlee, Dir. Inquiries answered.

.1   Atchison, David Rice, 1807-86.
Papers, 1837-1953. 5 v. and 19 folders. U.S. Senator from Missouri. Correspondence, miscellaneous papers, and volumes containing accounts, records of daily events, and ideas on politics. The correspondence mentions the Civil War, political parties, and conditions after the war. Correspondents include Jefferson Davis, Edward Everett, Stephen W. Kearny, Richard M. Johnson, Nathaniel Lyon, James M. Mason, Andrew H. Reeder, and George G. Vest.

.2   Belwood and Ezell families.
Papers, 1850-1936. ca. 1600 items. Correspondence and other papers of the Belwood and Ezell families of Kentucky, Missouri, and Texas, including 2 diaries of Mary Belwood (1870-72), a diary of her son John Ezell (1906). Correspondence contains opinions of the role of Kentucky in the Civil War (1861), comments on radical rule in Missouri and Texas during Reconstruction, and other subjects.

.3   Brady, Thomas A., 1902-1964.
Papers. Includes material on the admission of Negroes to the University of Missouri.

.4   Brown, James.
Correspondence, 1856-66. 1 folder and microfilm. Typescripts and microfilm, made from originals temporarily deposited by Homer M. Brown. Correspondence of James Brown and other members of the Brown family, including references to the hiring of slaves, activities of Robert E. Lee, Civil War incidents, monetary and political conditions of the period, crops, and slave desertions.

.5   Burt, Franklin.
Papers, 1843-1903. 3 v. and 5 folders. Papers of a tax assessor of Callaway County, Mo., including a diary (1859-72) recording routines of farm life; and an assessor's book (1858) listing landowners and slaves.

.6   Cahoon, Benjamin Benson.
Correspondence, 1842-89. 67 folders. Correspondence of a lawyer and land agent of Fredericktown, Mo., relating mainly to Cahoon's activities in the Republican party (1878-81) and to his law practice. Includes references to Ulysses S. Grant, Frank P. Blair, Jr., B. Gatz Brown, and the rights of Negroes in the educational system of Missouri. Correspondents include Henry Ziegenheim, Carl Schurz, G.A. Moser, T.B. Whitledge, Thomas C.

Fletcher, D. Pat Dyer, Newton Crane, and an
anti-third term committee in Missouri, headed by
John B. Henderson.
MO4.7 Congress of Racial Equality. Columbia, Mo., Chapter.
Records, 1959-64. ca. 500 items. Correspondence, constitutions, minutes, membership lists,
and papers relating to integration in Columbia,
Mo., and at the University of Missouri.
.8 Corby family.
Papers, 1804-1905. 3 v. and 49 folders. Papers
of a pioneer family of St. Joseph, Mo. including,
in part, bills of sale for slaves.
.9 Decker, Perl D., 1875-1934.
Papers, 1897-1939. 3 v. and 53 folders. Correspondence, speeches, and scrapbooks of a Missouri lawyer and U.S. Congressman, relating to
prohibition, women's suffrage, the Ku Klux Klan,
and other political and social issues.
.10 Donnelly, Phil M., 1891-1961.
Papers, 1944-57. 125 ft. Lawyer and Governor of
Missouri. Personal, political, and legal correspondence, departmental correspondence,
speeches, newspaper clippings, and books, relating
especially to Donnelly's two terms as Governor.
Includes, in part, material relating to segregation
and integration and their effect on Negro education
in Missouri.
.11 Gaines family.
Papers, 1851-76. 3 folders. Typescripts and
microfilm. Letters to Miss Lou Bell and Mrs.
Jennie Bell Gaines from relatives and a Confederate soldier, held prisoner at Johnson's
Island, Ohio. Some of the topics discussed are
freed Negroes, cholera, and indentures.
.12 Gano, John Allen, b. 1805.
Papers, 1794-1948. 120 folders. Disciples of
Christ minister. Correspondence, newspapers,
and other documents. Chiefly letters to Gano
telling of family life in Kentucky, his father-in-
law's plantation in Louisiana, Civil War difficulties, and giving information on economic,
social, and political developments in Missouri.
.13 Givens, Spencer H.
Papers, 1816-1911. 35 folders. Justice of the
Peace of Cooper County, Mo. Correspondence
(family and business), and bills of sale for a
slave. Includes one paper of Levin Cropper.
.14 Hickman-Bryan families.
Papers, 1796-1920. 3 v. and 297 folders. Correspondence, accounts, legal documents, and
miscellaneous business papers of the Hickman
family in Missouri and Louisiana and the Bryan
family in Kentucky and Missouri, including papers
of David M. Hickman, David H. Hickman, John L.
Hickman, Thomas H. Hickman, Thaddeus B. Hickman, Sarah Hickman, and John H. Bryan. Includes
records of sales of land and Negroes, and other
items.
.15 Hyde, Arthur Mastick, 1877-1947.
Papers, 1886-1949. 1765 folders. Governor of
Missouri and U.S. Secretary of Agriculture. Correspondence, clippings, pamphlets, and other
papers relating to numerous aspects of national
politics, state politics and administration, and
miscellany. Persons and organizations named include, D.L. Wilson, Charles Nagle, William E.
Borah, Jesse W. Barrett, Calvin Coolidge, Herbert
Hoover, Frederick D. Gardner, Jewell Mayes,
Herbert S. Hadley, Warren G. Harding, Seldon P.
Spencer, James A. Reed, Gifford Pinchot, Alfred
E. Smith, Henry A. Wallace, the State Fish and
Game Dept., the Ku Klux Klan, Lincoln University,
Mo., the National Association for the Advancement
of Colored People, the University of Missouri, and
others.
.16 Killian, Joseph C., 1825-95, and Charles A., 1852-
1936.
Papers of Joseph C. Killian and Charles A. Killian,
1821-1935. ca. 285 items. Lawyer of Perryville,
Mo. Correspondence, diary (1869), and legal
papers of Killian; together with correspondence,
and other legal papers of his son, Charles A.
Killian, also a lawyer of Perryville, Mo. Includes
papers relating to national affairs, education,
slave traffic, and Mississippi riverboats.

.17 Larwill family.
Papers, 1794-1947. 34 folders. Correspondence
and other papers of William C. Larwill of Devon-
shire, England, and Wooster, Ohio, and his sons
Joseph Larwill, surveyor and land agent, and John
Larwill, political leader. Includes numerous letters from William Patterson relating to politics of
the Jackson era, price lists and other data on the
New Orleans market, and papers on the Ku Klux
Klan in Ohio.
.18 McEulen, Elmore L.
Letters, 1944-45. 2 folders. Letters and A.P.O.
weekly bulletin sent to William G. McNeel by
Private McEulen while serving in San Francisco
with the 9206 Technical Service Unit T.C. of
Army Post Office Detachment. The letters discuss McEulen's duty in the A.P.O., Negro re-
placements, the election and absentee ballots,
President Truman, and war news in Europe.
.19 Missouri, Columbia.
Official records, 1901. 313 pp. Contains Social
and Economic Census of the Colored Population,
1901.
.20 Shanks, Charles. collector.
Civil War scrapbooks, 1850-65. 2 v. Newspaper
clippings relating to the Civil War and to the
period immediately prior to it. Includes discussions of slavery problems, states' rights issue,
People's party national convention, peace over-
tures of the North and South, military arrests of
civilians, and speeches and articles by military
leaders of the day.
.21 Shaw, Milton.
Papers, 1824-1921. 5 folders. Typescripts.
Letters from Rutherford County, Tenn., Fairview,
Ky., and Lockwood, Mo., discussing slaves and
other matters.
.22 Sheppard family.
Correspondence, 1844-77. 6 folders. Typescripts
and microfilm, made from originals owned by
Charles Sheppard. Correspondence of the Sheppard, Williams, and related families of Pennsylvania, Ohio, Tennessee, Missouri, California, and
England, relating to religion, banking, mercantile
activities, slaves, loans, and personal affairs.
.23 Smith, Thomas Adams.
Papers, 1777-1919. 11 folders. In part, photocopies, Correspondence and other papers of a
physician and landowner of Saline Co., Mo., including letters from Smith to his wife Kate and a
record of births, deaths, sales, and other pertinent
items in the lives of 180 slaves, covering the years
1777-1864.
.24 Snoddy, Daniel F.
Papers, 1817-61. 8 folders. Typescripts and microfilm. Correspondence and other papers of
Daniel F. Snoddy of Saline County, Mo., and other
members of the Snoddy family. Includes letters
from relatives in various southern states, and
bills of sale for slaves.
.25 Squatter Sovereign.
Newspaper, 1855-57. Newspaper of Atchison,
Kans.
.26 Swain, Warren.
Papers, 1820-42. 6 folders. Seaman and trader.
Principally a diary recording events and observations during a voyage to New Orleans and the return trip to Boston (1820-21), with daily entries,
and information on plantations, Negroes, and other
subjects.
.27 Tate family.
Papers, 1786-1871. 7 folders. Correspondence
and other papers of the Tate family of Kentucky
and Missouri, including a bill of sale for a Negro
woman.
.28 Tucker (D.M. and J.H.), Fulton, Mo.
Records, 1833-1902. 3 v. and 40 folders. Records
of a general store including slave records.
.29 University of Missouri, Agricultural Extension Service.
Records, 1912-59. Contains material on Negro
workers in the Extension Service.
.30 University of Missouri, President's Office.
Papers. Contains material on the admission of
Negroes to the University of Missouri. Relevant
materials also in the Thomas A. Brady papers.

.31 White, John R.
   Record book, 1846-60. Slave record book contains
   names and relevant information on White's slave-
   holdings.

DIAMOND

MO5   U.S. NATIONAL PARK SERVICE, GEORGE WASHINGTON
      CARVER NATIONAL MONUMENT, RESEARCH LI-
      BRARY (1954). Box 38, 64840. Tel 314 325-4584.
      David L. Hieb, Supt. and Terry E. Maze, Historian.
      Copying, typing, inquiries answered.
      The Carver National Monument, the first national
      monument to honor a Negro, contains a museum with
      the scientist's discoveries, personal belongings, and
      objects related to the area at the time he lived there.
      The monument is located on the land where the scien-
      tist spent his childhood.

   .1 Carver, George Washington, 1860-1943.
       Materials on life and work of Carver. Includes
       books (ca. 100), archives, documents, tapes, slides,
       and pictures.

INDEPENDENCE

MO6   U.S. GENERAL SERVICES ADMINISTRATION, NATIONAL
      ARCHIVES AND RECORDS SERVICE, HARRY S TRU-
      MAN LIBRARY (1957). 24 Highway at Delaware, 64050.
      Tel 816 252-1144. Philip C. Brooks, Dir. Interlibrary
      loan, bibliographies prepared, copying, inquiries an-
      swered, consultation.
      The Library collects and provides reference service
      for material relating to the career and administration
      of President Truman and to the office of the President.

   .1 Matthews, Francis P., 1887-1952.
       Papers, 1932-52. 25 ft. Businessman and govern-
       ment official. Correspondence, memoranda, re-
       ports, speech files, appointment schedules, news-
       paper clippings files, publications, and other mate-
       rials, relating to Matthews' career as chairman of
       the Douglas County, Nebr., Democratic Central
       Committee; as Supreme Knight, Knights of Colum-
       bus; as chairman of the Committee on Socialism
       and Communism, U.S. Chamber of Commerce; as
       chairman of the Executive Committee on National
       Catholic Community Service; as a member of the
       President's Committee on Civil Rights.
   .2 Nash, Philleo.
       Files, 1946-52. 11 ft. Special assistant to Presi-
       dent Truman for problems of minority groups.
   .3 President's Commission on Internal Security and Indi-
       vidual Rights.
       Records, 1951. 3 ft. Correspondence, adminis-
       trative files, minutes of meetings, records relating
       to executive sessions, records of the Commission's
       general counsel, and newspaper clipping files.
   .4 President's Commission on Migratory Labor.
       Records, 1950-51. 5 ft.
   .5 President's Committee on Civil Rights.
       Records, 1946-47. 13 ft. General correspondence
       and administrative records; correspondence with
       government departments and agencies, Committee
       members, individuals, institutions, and private
       organizations; records relating to meetings, hear-
       ings, and staff interviews; statements of witnesses
       appearing before the Committee; records relating
       to reports and recommendations of the Committee
       and its subcommittees; and a reference file.
   .6 President's Committee on Equality of Treatment and
       Opportunity in the Armed Services.
       Records, 1949-50. 4 ft. Correspondence, records
       of meetings, reports, memoranda, publications,
       newspaper clipping files, and other materials.
   .7 Truman, Harry S, 1884- .
       Files, 1945-52. ca. 7 ft. White House papers of
       President Truman relating to race relations.

JEFFERSON CITY

MO7   LINCOLN UNIVERSITY (1866), INMAN E. PAGE LIBRARY.
      65101. Tel 314 636-8121. Mrs. Freddye B. Ashford,

Librn. Interlibrary loan, bibliographies prepared,
literature searches, copying, typing, inquiries answered, referrals made, consultation.

   .1 Afro-American Studies Collection.
       ca. 1000 paperbacks. Basic books on the life and
       history of black Americans. Restricted.

MO8   MISSOURI COMMISSION ON HUMAN RIGHTS (1957). 314
      E. High St., 65101. Tel 314 635-7961. Richard E. Risk,
      Acting Exec. Dir.
      The Commission is a permanent, independent agency,
      appointed for purposes of research, investigation, con-
      ciliation, subpoena, issuing cease-and-desist orders,
      and seeking court enforcement in the areas of employ-
      ment, public accommodations and education where dis-
      crimination is practiced.
      Publ.: Progress, bimonthly newsletter.

KANSAS CITY

MO9   AMERICAN CIVIL LIBERTIES UNION (ACLU) OF WEST-
      ERN MISSOURI. 5100 Rockhill Rd., 64110. Tel 816
      842-3564. Eleanore Blue, Secy.

MO10 CIVIL RIGHTS ADVISORY COMMISSION OF THE JACKSON
      COUNTY COURT (1963). 12th and Oak, 64106. Tel 816
      221-8500. Mrs. Gail W. Achtenberg, Coordinator.
      Copying, typing, inquiries answered, referrals made,
      consultation.
      The Commission serves in a fact-finding and advisory
      capacity to the judges of the Jackson County Court and
      makes recommendations to the Court in matters related
      to: the integration of facilities, programs, and services
      of all county institutions; equal employment opportuni-
      ties in the hiring and promotion practices of all county
      offices; and other related public human relations work.
      Formerly the Jackson County Civil Rights Commission.

   .1 Civil Rights Advisory Commission of the Jackson
       County Court.
       Miscellaneous, 1963- . Clippings of relevant mate-
       rial, primarily local; minutes; and other records
       of activities of the Commission. Restricted.

MO11 COUNCIL FOR UNITED ACTION. 1610 E. 12th St., 64106.
      Tel 816 921-6500. Michael Miller, Staff Dir.
      The Council is a Negro organization formed to aid the
      poor, and works in a variety of areas: consumer wel-
      fare, housing, employment, schools, poverty, and
      youth.

MO12 COUNCIL ON RELIGION AND RACE. 3210 Michigan, 64109.
      Tel 816 924-7500. Maurice Culver, Dir.

MO13 GEORGE WASHINGTON CARVER NEIGHBORHOOD CEN-
      TER. 3407 E. 36th St., 64113. Tel 816 921-5564. Mrs.
      Ann Jacobson, Proj. Dir. Bibliographies prepared,
      literature searches, typing, inquiries answered, refer-
      rals made, consultation, develop programs using audio-
      visual materials in the community.
      The Center offers day care, youth services, adult
      groups, community organization, and information and
      referral. The Center's Committee for Negro History
      is a first step in developing interest in Negro heritage,
      art, literature, drama, and music.

MO14 GREATER KANSAS CITY CIVIL LIBERTIES UNION. 5100
      Rockhill Rd., 64110. Tel 816 276-1650. Miss Eleanore
      Blue, Secy.

   .1 Greater Kansas City Civil Liberties Union.
       Files. Records, reports, correspondence, legal
       briefs, and other papers concerning the activities
       and court cases of the Union.

MO15 INSTITUTE FOR COMMUNITY SERVICES (1949). 301 E.
      Armour Blvd., 64101. Tel 816 753-6524. Paul H. Bow-
      man, Dir. Inquiries answered, consultation.
      The Institute is an independent social science research
      institute which conducts research programs in five
      main areas: public affairs, education, social services,
      aging, health, and mental health. Over 300 research
      reports have been published.

MO16   JEWISH COMMUNITY RELATIONS BUREAU, INFORMA-
        TION CENTER (1940). 1211 Walnut St., 64106. Tel
        816 421-5808. Sidney Lawrence, Dir. Bibliographies
        prepared, inquiries answered, consultation.
        The Organization seeks to expand the understanding of
        cultural pluralism and maintains programs aimed at
        combatting prejudice, discrimination and bigotry.

    .1 Jewish Community Relations Information Center.
        Files, 1940- . Books (ca. 300 v.); pamphlets (ca.
        3700); mss, correspondence, clippings, phono-
        graph records and films covering such subjects as
        human relations research; combatting anti-Semi-
        tism; racial conflict; attitudes involving bigotry,
        prejudice, discrimination in housing, education,
        employment, social discrimination, public accom-
        modation; inter-faith understanding; law and law
        enforcement involving civil rights and liberties;
        church-state separation; concerns of Jewish com-
        munity with Israel, Soviet Union; Neo-Nazism; ex-
        tremism of right and left in white and black com-
        munity organization; urban affairs; techniques of
        community organization; white working class and
        the "Reacting Americans"; relations of the Jewish
        community with other minority racial, religious
        and ethnic groups.

MO17   KANSAS CITY COMMISSION ON HUMAN RELATIONS, DE-
        PARTMENT OF HUMAN RELATIONS (1951). 26th
        Floor, City Hall, 64106. Tel 816 274-1432. Alvin L.
        Brooks, Dir. Bibliographies prepared, literature
        searches, copying, inquiries answered, referrals made,
        consultation, speaker available; plan programs.
        The Commission is a city agency which recommends
        means of eliminating prejudice, discrimination and
        tension; receives and investigates complaints; initiates
        and conducts voluntary surveys; and holds hearings.
        Publ.: Pamphlets, book lists, reports.

    .1 Kansas City Commission on Human Relations, Depart-
        ment of Human Relations.
        Files, 1951- . 6 boxes. Records, correspondence,
        clippings, reports, surveys, and business records.

MO18   MISSOURI COMMISSION ON HUMAN RIGHTS, FIELD OF-
        FICE. 615 E. 13th St., 64106. Tel 816 274-6491.

MO19   NATIONAL ASSOCIATION FOR THE ADVANCEMENT OF
        COLORED PEOPLE (NAACP), REGION IV. 2704
        Prospect Ave., 64128. Tel 816 923-3641. Julius E.
        Williams, Dir.

MO20   NATIONAL CONFERENCE OF CHRISTIANS AND JEWS
        (NCCJ) (1928). 916 Walnut St., 64106. Tel 816 221-
        0688. John E. Lathrop, Exec. Dir. Interlibrary loan,
        consultation.
        The Conference acts to promote cooperation among
        Protestants, Catholics, and Jews, and works to elimi-
        nate intergroup prejudices.

    .1 National Conferences of Christians and Jews.
        Files, 1928- . Contains books, periodicals, pam-
        phlets, correspondence, and films, relating to race
        relations.

MO21   NELSON-ATKINS ART GALLERY (1933), ART REFERENCE
        LIBRARY. 4525 Oak, 64111. Tel 816 561-4000. Mrs.
        Caroline P. Brennan, Librn.
        The Library is for the use of curators, museum staff,
        graduate students and professors.

        Among the holdings of the Gallery are a collection of
        African sculpture and works by the following black
        artists:
    .1 Binford, Julian.
        Drawing, 1936-41. 1 item. Artist. A drawing en-
        titled "Preaching Deacon."
    .2 Lawrence, Jacob.
        Watercolor, 1945. 1 item. Artist. Watercolor en-
        titled "Home Chores."

MO22   PANEL OF AMERICAN WOMEN. 210 Westpoint Rd.,
        64108. Tel 816 531-8933. Mrs. Paul Brown, Nat.
        Coordinator.
        The Panel consists of groups of women in several U.S.

and Canadian cities who present panel-type programs
to church, school, and civic groups discussing their
personal experiences in meeting bias and prejudices
they or their children have met in schools, housing,
employment and other situations. Their aim is to promote understanding among people.

    .1 Panel of American Women.
        Files. Correspondence, minutes of meetings, fi-
        nancial records, and other materials dealing with
        the aims, programs, and history of the Panel.

MO23   U.S. EQUAL EMPLOYMENT OPPORTUNITY COMMISSION,
        KANSAS CITY REGIONAL OFFICE (1966). 911 Walnut
        St., 64106. Tel 816 374-5779. Charles Clark, Regional
        Dir. Inquiries answered, referrals made, consultation,
        Title VII enforcement.

MO24   UNIVERSITY OF MISSOURI AT KANSAS CITY (1963), CEN-
        TER FOR THE STUDY OF METROPOLITAN PROB-
        LEMS IN EDUCATION (1965). Nelson House, 515 Brush
        Creek Blvd., 64110. Tel 816 276-2718. Daniel U.
        Levine, Dir. Local loans.
        The Center conducts research on metropolitan educa-
        tion.
        Publ.: Reports, studies.

    .1 Center for the Study of Metropolitan Problems in Edu-
        cation.
        Books, periodicals, pamphlets, syllabi, and other
        materials concerning principally the areas of equal
        opportunity in education, curriculum materials for
        the teaching of Negro history and civil rights is-
        sues in elementary and secondary schools, and
        curriculum materials appropriate for teaching dis-
        advantaged students in elementary and secondary
        schools. Restricted.

MO25   URBAN LEAGUE OF KANSAS CITY (1920). 916 Walnut,
        64106. Tel 816 471-0550. Lounneer Pemberton, Dir.
        Inquiries answered, referrals made, consultation.
        Publ.: Annual Report; Newsletter.

NORMANDY

MO26   THE AFRO-AMERICAN BIBLIOGRAPHIC RESEARCHER
        (1969). 3344 Lucas Hunt Rd., 63121. Gladys Marie
        Sturgis, Dir.
        The Afro-American Bibliographic Researcher is a re-
        search service which compiles and publishes a biblio-
        graphical sourcebook, Professional Guide to the Afro-
        American in Print, which gives a descriptive listing of
        current books by and about the Afro-American, as well
        as a listing of additional sourcebooks, periodicals and
        organizations.
        Publ.: Professional Guide to the Afro-American in
        Print: A Bibliography of Current Works by and
        about the Black Man of America, semiannual.

ST. ANN

MO27   CENTRAL MIDWESTERN REGIONAL EDUCATIONAL
        LABORATORY, INC. (CEMREL) (1966), EDUCATIONAL
        MATERIALS CENTER. 10646 St. Charles Rock Rd.,
        63074. Tel 314 429-3535. Jan Pope, Asst. Librn. In-
        terlibrary loan, literature searches, copying, inquiries
        answered, referrals made, consultation.
        The Laboratory works to develop comprehensive cur-
        ricula in mathematics and aesthetic education for all
        children, K-12, and instructional techniques and mate-
        rials for children with learning disabilities. It is also
        concerned with encouraging the use of exemplary new
        social studies curriculums and establishing a center for
        the dissemination of new science curricular materials.
        Publ.: CEMREL Newsletter; Special publications, pub-
        lication list.

    .1 Educational Materials Center.
        Miscellaneous, 1966- . Limited collection of
        books, pamphlets, reports, emphasizing mathe-
        matics, aesthetic education, learning disabilities.
        Some material on culture, sociology, intergroup
        relations, general education.

ST. LOUIS

MO28   AMERICAN CIVIL LIBERTIES UNION (ACLU) OF EASTERN
        MISSOURI. 3910 Lindell, 63108. Tel 314 534-1246.
        Mrs. Evelyn Schreiber, Secy.
        Publ.: Liberties, quarterly.

MO29   AMERICAN JEWISH COMMITTEE, WEST CENTRAL AREA.
        Suite 1068, 818 Olive St., 63101. Tel 314 621-2519.
        Morton W. Ryweck, Exec. Dir.

MO30   AMERICAN JEWISH CONGRESS, SOUTHWEST REGION.
        Room 204, 7803 Clayton Rd., 63117. Tel 314 725-7170.
        Alexandra Orgel, Dir.

MO31   ANTI-DEFAMATION LEAGUE OF B'NAI B'RITH, MIS-
        SOURI-SOUTHERN ILLINOIS REGIONAL OFFICE.
        Suite 1104, 721 Olive St., 63101. Tel 314 231-7323.
        Melvin I. Cooperman, Dir.
        Publ.: Publication lists, brochures, reports.

MO32   CATHOLIC ARCHDIOCESE OF ST. LOUIS, COMMISSION
        ON HUMAN RIGHTS (1963). 4445 Lindell Blvd., 63108.
        Tel 314 533-1887. Rt. Rev. Francis M. Doyle, Exec.
        Secy. Inquiries answered, referrals made, consulta-
        tion.
        The Commission is established to use all the resources
        of the Catholic Church to improve living conditions of
        all residents of our inner city and to change the attitude,
        mentality, and conscience of the white community.
        Publ.: Human Rights, bimonthly; Pamphlets, sermon
        outlines, reprints, and program guides.

MO33   CITY ART MUSEUM OF ST. LOUIS. Forest Park, 63110.
        Tel 314 721-0067. Emily S. Ryan, Curator.

   .1   Duncanson, Robert S.
            Painting. Negro artist. Oil painting entitled
            "View of St. Anne's River, Canada."

MO34   CONCORDIA HISTORICAL INSTITUTE (1847). 801 De Mun
        Ave., 63105. Tel 314 721-5934. Aug R. Suelflow, Dir.
        Interlibrary loan, bibliographies prepared, copying,
        inquiries answered, referrals made.
        The Institute collects material on American Luther-
        anism and serves as the archives depository for the
        Lutheran Church-Missouri Synod.
        Publ.: Concordia Historical Institute Quarterly; His-
        torical Footnotes, newsletter; Regional Archi-
        vist, periodically; Bulletins.

   .1   Evangelical Lutheran Synodical Conference of North
        America. Missionary Board.
            Records, 1906-53. 24 ft. (ca. 15,000 items). In
            part, typescripts. Correspondence, minutes, fi-
            nancial records, reports, and other records, re-
            lating to the Board's missionary activities among
            Negroes in the South, to Immanuel Lutheran Col-
            lege in Greensboro, N.C., to Alabama Lutheran
            Academy and College in Selma, Ala., to Piney
            Woods Country Life School in Piney Woods, Miss.,
            and to the missionary work among Ibesikpo
            tribes in Nigeria. Includes reports on negotiations
            with the Qua Iboe Mission, on the work of Henry
            Nau, on the establishment of a central hospital,
            and on the Nigerian Lutheran Seminary. Re-
            stricted.
   .2   Lutheran Church-Missouri Synod. Board of Home Mis-
        sions in North and South America.
            Records, 1853-1962. ca. 25 ft. In part, type-
            scripts and photocopies. Correspondence, finan-
            cial records, minutes, reports, printed matter, and
            other papers, relating to the missionary activities
            carried on by the Board, its predecessors and by
            its various committees and commissions, including
            in part, Board for Colored Missions, Board for
            Home Missions in North America, foreign mis-
            sions, Home Mission Builders and Planning Com-
            mittees, Rural Commission and Rural Life Insti-
            tute, Urban Advisory Committee, Urban Church
            Planning Committee, Urban Institute, and Com-
            mittee on Home Missions in Rural and Urban
            Areas. Restricted.
   .3   Lutheran Church-Missouri Synod. Districts. Western.
            Records, 1855-1955. 7 ft. (ca. 10,500 items). Con-
            tains minutes, essays and proceedings from meet-
            ings, conferences of western district groups of the

Lutheran Church-Missouri Synod; also, includes
files of the Western District Mission Board,
mainly correspondence and reports (1926-55) relating to congregations and preaching stations, including North Little Rock, London, Mena, and
Little Rock (Negro Missions) in Arkansas. Restricted.

MO35   CONGRESS OF RACIAL EQUALITY (CORE). 5532 Natural
        Bridge, 63108. Tel 314 423-1454. Bill Bailey, Chmn.

MO36   GREATER NEIGHBORHOOD ASSOCIATION OF UNIVERSITY
        CITY, MISSOURI (1967). c/o Alan C. Kohn, 411 N.
        Seventh St., 63101. Tel 314 621-8575. Kenneth Hyman,
        Pres. Consultation.
        The Association acts as a planning and coordinating
        body for local neighborhood associations in the St.
        Louis area. The local associations are concerned with
        problems of integration and neighborhood improve-
        ment, and are encouraged by the city government as
        opportunities for citizens to participate in the govern-
        ing of their own neighborhoods. Records closed to
        researchers.
        Publ.: Periodic newsletters.

MO37   GREATER ST. LOUIS COMMITTEE FOR FREEDOM OF
        RESIDENCE. 5868½ Delmar, 63112. Tel 314 727-4128.
        James H. Sporleder, Exec. Dir.

MO38   JEWISH COMMUNITY RELATIONS COUNCIL OF ST.
        LOUIS. Suite 419, 722 Chestnut St., 63101. Tel 314
        241-2584. Norman A. Stack, Exec. Dir.
        The Council works to provide and support educational
        programs concerned with a better understanding of re-
        ligious freedom and other basic liberties; democratic
        inter-group attitudes; equality of opportunity without
        regard to race, religion or ethnic origin; and the role
        of Judaism as a source and support for the traditions of
        American democracy and justice.
        Publ.: News from the JCRC, irregular journal.

   .1   Jewish Community Relations Council of St. Louis Li-
        brary.
            Books, periodicals, reprints, pamphlets, news
            clippings, films, and correspondence on the sub-
            jects of race, race relations, inter-group educa-
            tion, segregation, integration, and related issues.

MO39   THE LUTHERAN CHURCH, MISSOURI SYNOD, BOARD OF
        HIGHER EDUCATION. 210 N. Broadway, 63102. Tel
        314 231-6969. Rev. Arthur M. Ahlschwede, Dir.

   .1   Board of Higher Education.
            Files. Correspondence, minutes of board meet-
            ings, financial records, and other materials re-
            lating to the Board's support of the Alabama Lu-
            theran Academy & College, Selma, Ala.

MO40   MISSOURI HISTORICAL SOCIETY (1866), ARCHIVES (1866).
        Jefferson Memorial Bldg., 63112. Tel 314 726-2622.
        Mrs. Frances H. Stadler, Archivist. Copying, inquiries
        answered.
        Publ.: The Bulletin, quarterly.

   .1   Bates family.
            Papers, 1754-1851. ca. 2000 items. In part, type-
            scripts and photocopies. Correspondence, letter
            books, business and legal papers, poems, and edi-
            torial papers, of Edward and Frederick Bates of
            Virginia and Missouri, and of other members of the
            family, including Barton, Onward, and Tarleton
            Bates. Contains material on Missouri politics,
            and the Reconstruction.
   .2   Bissell, William Henry, 1811-60.
            Papers, 1824-61. ca. 220 items. Governor and
            U.S. Representative from Illinois. Correspon-
            dence, diary, speech, and other articles. Letters,
            primarily from statesmen and politicians, relate
            to Bissell's speech (1850) on the question of
            slavery.
   .3   Broadhead, James Overton, 1819-98.
            Papers, 1802-1906. ca. 900 items. In part, type-
            scripts. Lawyer, minister to Switzerland, and U.S.
            Representative from Missouri. Correspondence
            (relating to the emancipation question and the
            silver question), legal papers and notes, Civil War
            data, and copies of some of Broadhead's many

speeches. Includes memoranda relating to Missouri politics and government; rough drafts of lectures, articles, and legal notes; and other materials.

.4 Chamberlin, T.W. collector.
Chamberlin collection, 1661-1945. ca. 100 items. In part, typescripts. Newspaper clippings, World War I letters, and typewritten records of material on the Dred Scott case.

.5 Conway, Joseph, 1763-1830.
Papers, 1798-1922. ca. 60 items. Pioneer of St. Louis County, Mo. and Indian fighter. Chiefly 1798-1881; in part, bills of sale of Negroes.

.6 Cook, Fannie (Frank), 1893-1949.
Papers, 1881-1949. ca. 4 ft. Author and lecturer. Correspondence, literary papers, biographical data, scrapbooks, notebooks, pamphlets, clippings, periodicals, and other printed material reflecting Mrs. Cook's interest in the southeast Missouri sharecroppers, inter-racial problems, labor movements, and relief conditions. Includes mss of Mrs. Palmer's Honey (winner of the George Washington Carver award, 1946), Storm Against the Wall (1948), The Long Bridge (1949), the unpublished William Beaumont, and numerous short stories.

.7 Church papers, 1727-1962.
2 ft. Papers containing historical information relating to churches in early St. Louis and other parts of Missouri; names of ministers in the Missouri Conference of the Methodist Episcopal Church, who refused to become identified with the Methodist Episcopal Church, South, when the schism (1845) occurred in Columbia, Mo.; and other items.

.8 Diamant, Henry A. collector.
Henry A. Diamant collection, 1805-75. ca. 100 items. Chiefly bills, deeds, governors' appointments of justices of the peace; legal papers; slave emancipation papers, and other items.

.9 Eliot, William Greenleaf, 1811-87.
Papers, 1841-1961. ca. 125 items. In part, photocopies. Unitarian clergyman, of St. Louis, Mo. Correspondence relating to the Civil War, slavery; clippings; and miscellaneous items. Correspondents include Barton Bates, Edward Bates, Hudson E. Bridge, Salmon P. Chase, Edward Everett, John C. Fremont, John M. Forbes, Hamilton R. Gamble, Ulysses S. Grant, Henry W. Halleck, Winfield S. Hancock, John B. Henderson, Ethan A. Hitchcock, Abraham Lincoln, Joseph J. Reynolds, John McAllister Schofield, William T. Sherman, James E. Yeatman, and Charles Zagonyi.

.10 Elliott, Newton G., 1812-77?
Papers, 1834-1909. ca. 600 items. Justice of the peace, sheriff of Howard County, Mo., and State legislator. Correspondence relating to slave papers, and other subjects.

.11 Emmons family.
Papers, 1796-1938. ca. 200 items. In part, land and slavery papers of Benjamin L. Emmons I, Missouri State legislator, Benjamin L. Emmons, II, and also Benjamin L. Emmons, III, who engaged in the abstracting business in St. Charles, Mo., and was the local historian.

.12 Florida plantation papers.
Miscellaneous, 1847-98. Overseers' reports, plantation journals, and other documents pertaining to the operation of two middle Florida plantations.

.13 Green, John, 1835-1913.
Papers, 1855-1956. 5 ft. Physician, of St. Louis, Mo. Correspondence, journals (1858-72), records and notes, writings, and printed pamphlets of Dr. Green, his wife, Hattie (Jones) Green, and his daughter, Elizabeth Green, relating to the People's Art Center for Negroes in St. Louis, and other items.

.14 Hempstead, Stephen, 1754-1831.
Papers, 1754-1927. ca. 150 items. Revolutionary soldier from New London, Conn., who moved to St. Louis, Mo., in 1811. Letter book (1805-30), correspondence of the Stephen Hempstead family and early religious leaders, diary (1787-1831), and other materials. Includes four letters from Manuel Lisa, farm tasks and occupation of Hempstead's

slaves, and information on the establishment of missions in the Missouri Territory.

.15 Lant, John A.
Papers, 1830-97. ca. 100 items. Journalist, of Toledo, Ohio, and Tarrytown, N.Y. Correspondence, drafts of lectures and written articles, and printed material, relating to laboring people, remedies for evil, slavery, scientific reconstruction of society, and other subjects.

.16 MacKenzie, Kenneth, 1797-1861.
Papers, 1796-1918. ca. 1500 items. Fur trader, organizer of the Columbia Fur Company, member of the firm of Chouteau and MacKenzie, an associate of Pierre Chouteau, Jr. and Company, commission merchant, and an investor in lands in Missouri, Illinois, and Minnesota. Business, personal, and family correspondence; bills of sale (1828-41) for slaves; and other items.

.17 Slavery papers.
Miscellaneous. Letters and documents about slavery, bills of sale, manumission papers, records of hiring out of slaves, and related materials.

.18 Smith, Luther R., 1860-1910.
Papers. Correspondence and miscellaneous papers of Judge Luther R. Smith, captain in Union Army, judge of Circuit Court of Alabama during Reconstruction period. Correspondence is concerned with operation of plantations during post-war era, contains correspondence describing Ku Klux Klan influence in Alabama politics and depredations of Klan in area.

.19 Snyder, John F.
Papers, 1847-88. Correspondence concerning slavery and Negroes.

.20 Sublette papers.
Miscellaneous, 1848-54. Collection containing several documents and letters concerning runaway slaves, charges for apprehension and keep of same; accounts with B.M. Lunch, slave dealer, about charges.

.21 Tiffany, P. Dexter.
Papers. Large collection of official St. Louis County documents, including bonds of free Negroes, fines and sentences imposed on unlicensed free Negroes, records of runaway slaves, and a list, printed in 1841, and updated yearly in ms until 1859, of free Negroes licensed by the St. Louis County Court.

MO41   NATIONAL ASSOCIATION FOR THE ADVANCEMENT OF COLORED PEOPLE (NAACP). 1259 N. Kingshighway, 63113. Tel 314 361-3020. Ina Boon, Exec. Secy.

MO42   NATIONAL ASSOCIATION OF MARKET DEVELOPERS.
c/o Falstaff Brewing Corporation, 5050 Oakland Ave., 63110. Tel 314 863-9249. Allen L. McKellar, NBL Task Force Del.
The Association is a professional association of men and women, most of them black, who provide marketing and community relations services for major corporations primarily in the consumer-goods fields, and for various public service institutions and agencies. It is the sponsor of Operation Intercom, a program to improve the two-way flow of operationally useful information between establishment or organizations and organizations within black and other major ethnic communities.

.1 National Association of Market Developers.
Files. Records, reports, correspondence, and other papers concerning the functions of the organization.

MO43   NATIONAL CONFERENCE OF CHRISTIANS AND JEWS (NCCJ). Room 915, 721 Olive St., 63101. Tel 314 241-5103. Virgil L. Border, Dir.

MO44   NATIONAL URBAN LEAGUE, INC., MIDWESTERN REGIONAL OFFICE. Chemical Bldg., 721 Olive St., 63101. Tel 314 421-6393. M. Leo Bohanon, Regional Dir.

MO45   PRESBYTERIAN INTERRACIAL COUNCIL (PIC) (1963). 1570 Chambers Rd., 63136. Tel 314 869-5850. Roger A. Harless, Exec. Secy.

PIC is interested in implementing the teachings of the church on race relations.
Publ.: _Now_, quarterly newsletter.

.1 Presbyterian Interracial Council (PIC).
Files, 1963- . Correspondence, minutes of meetings, financial records, reports, studies, and other materials dealing with the aims, programs and history of the Council.

MO46   ST. LOUIS COUNCIL ON HUMAN RELATIONS (1953). 1230 Market St., 63101. Tel 314 453-3301. W.J. Decatur, Exec. Secy.
The Council serves as the administering agency for local fair housing, employment and public accommodations laws; receives, investigates, and conciliates complaints; holds hearings; and makes studies, surveys, and investigations.

MO47   ST. LOUIS PUBLIC LIBRARY (1865). 1301 Olive St., 63103. Tel 314 241-2288. Paxton P. Price, Librn. Interlibrary loan, bibliographies prepared, literature searches, copying, typing, referrals made.

.1 Current titles on black America.
This collection consists of multiple copies of over 1400 titles being used by the Community Service Department for the development of its work in the black poverty areas of St. Louis, Mo.
.2 Julia Davis Collection.
Books, pamphlets, monographs, and mss. Subjects represented include race relations; Negroes in art, music and the theatre; and biographical sketches on local Negro teachers, clergymen, and other prominent figures. Initial support for the collection given by Davis, a St. Louis, Mo. school teacher.

MO48   ST. LOUIS UNIVERSITY, CENTER FOR URBAN PROGRAMS (1968). 221 N. Grand Blvd., 63103. Tel 314 535-3300. George D. Wendel, Dir. Copying, inquiries answered, referrals made, consultation.
The Center coordinates the resources of universities, city agencies, and businesses in solving problems of the St. Louis area.

.1 Urban Studies Collection.
Miscellaneous, 1968- . Books (ca. 200 v.), miscellaneous reports, journals and clipping files concerning the metropolitan problems in general. Restricted.

MO49   ST. LOUIS UNIVERSITY, HUMAN RELATIONS CENTER FOR TRAINING AND RESEARCH (1952), HUMAN RELATIONS LIBRARY (1956). 221 N. Grand St., 63103. Tel 314 535-3300. Rev. Trafford P. Maher, S.J., Dir., Human Rels. Center. Bibliographies prepared, inquiries answered, consultation.
The Center offers a degree program for training teachers, hospital administrators, agency directors, etc., and services the community in human relations projects.
Publ.: _Proceedings_, annually, 1958-1968.

.1 Human Relations Library Collection.
Materials, ca. 16,000 items. Includes books (ca. 2500), periodicals, newspapers (20), pamphlets (ca. 2000), vf, theses, mss, correspondence and clippings (ca. 10,500), relating to employment, housing, integration, the culturally disadvantaged, health services, civil rights and liberties, history of state, local and federal human rights commissions.

MO50   UNIVERSITY OF MISSOURI AT ST. LOUIS, CENTER FOR COMMUNITY AND METROPOLITAN STUDIES (1965). 8001 Natural Bridge Rd., 63121. Tel 314 453-5273.
The Center coordinates research, training, and community service projects in the St. Louis metropolitan area. Research activities include such projects as the development of a critical bibliography of economic development information sources for the three-State Ozark Region Commission, a sample survey of businessmen in one of the declining business districts of St. Louis, and a socio-economic study of Kinloch, Mo., an all-Negro incorporated city. The Center has developed a clearinghouse function chiefly for socioeconomic materials on the St. Louis metropolitan area.

MO51   URBAN LEAGUE OF ST. LOUIS, INC. 4401 Fair Ave., 63115. Tel 314 389-0040. Lawrence Borom, Exec. Dir.

.1 Urban League of St. Louis, Inc.
Files. Records, reports, correspondence, and other papers concerning the programs and aims of the organization.

MO52   WASHINGTON UNIVERSITY, INSTITUTE FOR URBAN AND REGIONAL STUDIES (1961). 246 McMillan Hall, 63130. Tel 314 361-0900. Charles L. Leven, Dir.
The scope and content of the Institute's program is primarily determined by the urban research interests of the faculty at Washington University. The Institute hopes to enrich the training of scholars studying urban phenomena and to make contributions to the understanding of urban and regional processes and policies, both in St. Louis and elsewhere in the nation and the world.
Publ.: _Reviews in Urban Economics_.

MO53   WASHINGTON UNIVERSITY, JOHN M. OLIN LIBRARY. Lindell and Skinker Blvds., 63130. Tel 314 863-0100. William H. Kurth, Assoc. Dir. Interlibrary loan, bibliographies prepared, copying, typing, inquiries answered, referrals made.

.1 Duncan, Robert Edward, 1919- .
Papers, 1949-67. 229 items. Poet and dramatist. Correspondence, poems, proofs, notes, copy of Duncan's _A Book of Resemblances_ (1966), and other papers, relating to his personal life, his other works, works and writing of LeRoi Jones, other literary figures, and publishing. Correspondents include Jess Collins, LeRoi Jones, Henry Wenning, Auerhelm Press, San Francisco, Calif., and Meriden Gravure Company, Meriden, Conn. Other persons represented include Robert Creeley, Denise Levertov, Charles Olson, Stan Persky, Diane di Prima, Jack Spicer, and George Stanley.
.2 Negro Newspaper Collection.
Newspapers. On microfilm; newspapers filmed by the Library of Congress Photoduplication Department and listed in A.S. Pride's pamphlet _Negro Newspapers on Microfilm_. Included is the _St. Louis Argus_, _East St. Louis Crusader_, and _The St. Louis Sentinal_.

MO54   WASHINGTON UNIVERSITY, THE SOCIAL SCIENCE INSTITUTE. 63130. Tel 314 863-0100. Muriel W. Pumphrey, Dir.
The Institute sponsors a broad spectrum of faculty research projects, a number of which are in the area of urban affairs. Topics of urban affairs research projects in 1967 have included among others, social and community problems in public housing areas, analysis of methods for identifying residential blight, a description of the patterns of social organization characteristic of an urban white poor population, and a proposal for ways to motivate school children from disadvantaged areas.

UNIVERSITY CITY

MO55   UNIVERSITY CITY COMMISSION ON HUMAN RELATIONS (1960). 6801 Delmar Blvd., 63130. Arnold Wilson, Exec. Secy.
The Commission, which works to foster friendly relations among the various segments of the population of University City, has powers of compliance in public accommodations, and employment.

NEBRASKA

LINCOLN

NB1   NEBRASKA CIVIL LIBERTIES UNION (1967). 6300 A St., 68510. Tel 402 489-4029. Charles S. Stephen, Jr., Pres. Inquiries answered, referrals made, consultation.
The Union works to further the objectives of the na-

tional American Civil Liberties Union and to advance
the causes of civil liberties in the State of Nebraska,
including those rights secured by the Constitution of the
U.S. and of the State of Nebraska; and to promote the
observance of the rights of free speech, free press, free
assemblage, equality before the law and other civil
liberties.
Publ.: Newsletter, occasionally.

.1 Nebraska Civil Liberties Union.
    Files, 1967- . Correspondence, newsletters, com-
    munication from ACLU, board minutes, publications
    and other materials concerning the activities of the
    Union.

NB2 NEBRASKA EQUAL EMPLOYMENT OPPORTUNITY COM-
     MISSION (1965). P.O. Box 4862, State Capitol Bldg.,
     68509. Tel 402 473-1624. Reid E. Devoe, Exec. Dir.
     State commission to fight discrimination in hiring and
     firing. Can conduct investigations and pass upon
     charges of unlawful employment practices; hold public
     hearings; issue cease-and-desist orders.

NB3 NEBRASKA STATE HISTORICAL SOCIETY (1878), LI-
     BRARY (1878). 1500 R St., 68508. Tel 402 432-2793.
     Mrs. Louise Small, Librn. Literature searches,
     copying, inquiries answered, referrals made, consulta-
     tion.
     Publ.: Nebraska History, quarterly journal.

.1 Day, (Mrs.) Lee.
    Letters. Relates experiences of her father,
    Charles Spease, and other Negro homesteaders in
    Nebraska.
.2 Gere family.
    Papers, 1819-1954. ca. 5400 items. Correspon-
    dence, diaries, biographies, genealogies, and printed
    matter, relating to the Civil War, Nebraska poli-
    tics, Table Rock, Neb., and World War I. Corre-
    spondents include W.J. Bryan, David Butler, Willa
    Cather, Clement Chase, J.W. Dawes, R.W. Furnas,
    James H. Garfield, Horace Greeley, and others.
.3 Kliese, August F.
    Correspondence, 1863-66. ca. 600 items. Union
    Army officer with the 22nd Wisconsin Infantry,
    Company E, and the 17th U.S. Colored Infantry,
    Company E. Correspondence relating to the rec-
    ords of the Quartermaster's Department, Company
    E, 17th U.S. Colored Infantry, stationed at Gallatin,
    Tenn.
.4 Malone, Robert T., 1891-1963
    Papers, 1930-63. 8 ft. Director of the Division of
    Employment Security, Nebraska Department of
    Labor in Lincoln, Neb. Correspondence, records
    and speeches (1947-49), addresses (1939-48), notes
    (1957-58), and other papers relating to housing, the
    National Council of Catholic Women, and the Na-
    tional Union for Social Justice in Lincoln, the Lin-
    coln Urban League, and the American Interprofes-
    sional League.
.5 Malone, Robert T., 1891-1963
    Papers, 1925-63. 7 ft. (ca. 5000 items). Public
    official, of Lincoln, Neb. Correspondence, ad-
    dresses by Malone and others, and other papers re-
    lating to social and welfare legislation, race rela-
    tions and other aspects of community development
    in Nebraska, and particularly Lincoln. The addres-
    ses relate generally to activities of the Catholic
    Church in relief and social work. Other topics in-
    clude housing and unemployment compensation. In-
    cludes a chronological outline of social legislation
    in Nebraska (1935), with indices, by Hattie P. Wil-
    liams. Organizations represented include Human
    Relations Committee, National Conference of
    Christians and Jews, National Union of Social Jus-
    tice, and Urban League. Correspondents include
    Charles D. Ammon, C.M. Baker, Frank Bane, H.L.
    Blackledge, M.J. Blue, R.B. Brega, K.O. Broady,
    Ralph G. Brooks, Edward R. Burke, Hugh Butler,
    E. Glenn Callen, R.E. Campbell, Terry Carpenter,
    James V. Casey, G.V. Casler, R.L. Cochran, J.P.
    Colbert, Oren S. Copeland, Charles S. Coughlin,
    Robert B. Crosby, Carl T. Curtis, Edward J.
    Dugan, E.C. Eppley, T.A. Filipi, F.E. Fitzgerald,
    Dwight Griswold, Clarence E. Haley, Leland R.
    Hall, William F. Haycock, J.B. Hillers, James

Keller, Lloyd W. Kelley, Vincent B. Kinney, Al-
bert Kjar, A.T. Lobdell, Henry C. Luckey, Ray
McConnell, Charles F. McLaughlin, Clyde W.
Malone, Chet B. Marshall, Lloyd J. Marti, Eugene
P. Mullany, John Painter, C. Petrus Peterson, Val
Peterson, F.C. Radke, Walter R. Raecke, James M.
Reinhardt, Neil Rooney, Fred A. Seaton, John P.
Senning, Arthur M. Schlesinger, Melvin L. Shakes-
peare, A.Q. Schimmel, Alois Slepicka, Glenn E.
Smith, Anna Smrha, Frank A. Stech, Willard E.
Townshend, and Kenneth S. Wherry.
.6 Nebraska State Farmers' Alliance.
    Records, 1874-1920. 5 ft. Correspondence, re-
    ports, receipts, vouchers, petitions, 24 volumes of
    ledgers, mailing lists, and pamphlets of the State
    Farmers' Alliance; notes of Luna E. Kellie, state
    secretary, including biographical sketches; mss of
    The Farmers Alliance and the Nebraska Independ-
    ent (1918) by Charles Q. DeFrance and James
    Thompson Kellie (1920) and The Farmers Alliance
    in Nebraska, a History of Its Later Period from
    1894-1904 by Miss Kellie; minutes (1890-92) of the
    Alliance of Norman, Neb., and correspondence and
    reports (1893-95) of local Alliances. Correspon-
    dents include William V. Allen, William P. Bricker,
    Elsie Buckman, Jay Burrows, O. Cravath, W.F.
    Dale, Helen Goff, J.L. Leonard, George Lynn, W.A.
    McKeishan, W.S. Morgan, John H. Powers, Asa
    Taylor, J.M. Thompson, and S. Edward Thornton.
.7 Watkins, Albert, 1848-1923.
    Papers, 1890-1923. ca. 1200 items. Historian.
    General correspondence and research notes relat-
    ing to the business management and publication of
    the Illustrated History of Nebraska (1905-13), and
    to Watkins' activities with the Nebraska State
    Historical Society, and southern Negro problems.
    Correspondents include Clarence S. Paine and
    Jacob North and Company, printers.

OMAHA

NB4 ANTI-DEFAMATION LEAGUE OF B'NAI B'RITH, PLAINS
     STATES REGIONAL OFFICE. 537 Securities Bldg.,
     68102. Tel 402 341-3575. Harold Adler, Dir.

NB5 CONGRESS OF RACIAL EQUALITY (CORE). 1624 Evans,
     68110. Tel 402 453-0998. Rev. R.E. McNair, Chmn.

NB6 NATIONAL CONFERENCE OF CHRISTIANS AND JEWS
     (NCCJ). 608 Omaha Nat. Bank Bldg., 68102. Tel 402
     556-3065. Dr. Neil B. Danberg, Dir.

NB7 NEBRASKA NEGRO HISTORICAL SOCIETY, INC. (1965),
     LIBRARY (1965). 2934 N. 24th St., 68110. Tel 402 451-
     4538. Alice E. Station, Chmn., Library Cmt. Inquiries
     answered, referrals made.
     The Society works to identify, restore, preserve, and
     display Negro history in the State of Nebraska.

.1 Negro History Collection.
    ca. 350 items. Includes books, theses and dis-
    sertations, correspondence, clippings, and photo-
    graphs.

NB8 OMAHA HUMAN RELATIONS DEPARTMENT AND BOARD.
     Room 404, Interim City Hall, 68102. Tel 402 341-8122.
     Joe N. Williams, Human Relations Dir.
     City agency which advises elected officials on enforce-
     ment of laws prohibiting discrimination, and institutes
     educational programs on equal rights.

NB9 OMAHA PUBLIC LIBRARY (1877). 1823 Harney St., 68102.
     Tel 402 342-4766. Frank E. Gibson, Library Dir.
     Interlibrary loan, copying, inquiries answered.
     Publ.: Bibliographies.

.1 Delta Sigma Theta Collection on Negro History and
    Culture.
    ca. 1000 books on Negro life and history. Estab-
    lished by a gift from Delta Sigma Theta, a black
    national women's service sorority.

NB10 OMAHA URBAN LEAGUE. 312 Karback Bldg., 209 S. 15th
      St., 68102. Tel 402 342-7648. Jack Claytor, Exec. Dir.

.1 Omaha Urban League, Inc.
Files. Records, reports, correspondence, and other papers concerning the aims and activities of the organization.

NB11 UNIVERSITY OF NEBRASKA, THE URBAN STUDIES CENTER. 68105. Tel 402 553-4700. Wayne Wheeler, Dir.

NEVADA

LAS VEGAS

NV1 NATIONAL CONFERENCE OF CHRISTIANS AND JEWS (NCCJ) (1958). Suite D, 2140 Paradise Rd., 89105. Tel 702 735-4047. Dr. Lloyd D. McNeil, Exec. Dir. Literature searches, inquiries answered, referrals made, consultation.
NCCJ is a civic organization servicing Las Vegas and Reno, Nev., and dedicated to the ideals of brotherhood and justice as the standard of practice in human relationships among all people.

NV2 AMERICAN CIVIL LIBERTIES UNION OF NEVADA (1966). 1267 Douglas Dr., 89102. Tel 702 870-3797. Robert Throckmorton, Chmn.

NV3 NEVADA COMMISSION ON EQUAL RIGHTS OF CITIZENS (1961). State Bldg., Room 100-B, 215 E. Bonanza, 89101. Tel 702 385-0104. Tyrone K. Levi, Exec. Secy. Inquiries answered, referrals made, consultation.
The Commission, a legislative agency, works to enforce fair employment practice and public accommodations laws, by court order if necessary. It has the power to study and investigate problems arising between groups in the State of Nevada which may result in discrimination or prejudice because of race, religion or other discriminatory conditions; and formulate and carry out programs of education and disseminate information with the object of discouraging and eliminating any such prejudice or discriminations.

.1 Nevada Commission on Equal Rights of Citizens.
Files, 1961- . Vertical files containing correspondence, records of all cases, biennial reports to the Governor and Legislature, minutes of Commission meetings, budget and financial records, publications and news clippings; CBS news film of the Chicago and Watts riots; 14 v. of transcript of the public hearings in the case of NAACP versus 13 Strip and Downtown Hotels and Casinos and the Culinary and Teamsters' Union.

RENO

NV4 NEVADA COMMISSION ON EQUAL RIGHTS OF CITIZENS, FIELD OFFICE (1967). 560 Mill St., 89501. Tel 702 784-6355. Victor A. Morton, Asst. Secy. Referrals made, consultation.
The Commission works to do away with discrimination in the areas of race, color, religious creed and national origin.

NV5 UNIVERSITY OF NEVADA (1874), NOBLE H. GETCHELL LIBRARY, SPECIAL COLLECTIONS DEPARTMENT (1963). 89507. Tel 702 784-6538. Robert D. Armstrong, Spec. Collections Librn. Copying, inquiries answered, referrals made.

.1 American Civil Liberties Union of Nevada.
Archives, 1966- .
.2 Benedict, Russell G. collector.
Papers. ca. 2000 items. Includes books, clippings, pamphlets and other materials on race relations. Titles of files relevant to Negro studies are: Civil Rights; Communism; Reformist Left; New and Misc. Left; Old Left; Attitudes toward Negroes and Black Power Groups; Institutions and Issues; Negro Rightists, Black Muslims; Rightwing Columnists; Rightwing Organizations and Leaders; Nevada; Racism; additional material on riots not yet cataloged. Also included are various titles on the

"Negro inferiority" claim, on the Citizens Councils, on "Aryan-Race" theories, tax-supported state segregationist groups, the "vermin" press, and foreign racism or Facism. Approximately 175 racist organizations (not all specifically anti-Negro) are represented in the collection.

.3 Hulse, James W.
Papers, 1964-66. ca. 1 ft. Materials from membership on Nevada Commission on Equal Rights of Citizens.
.4 Human Relations Action Council.
Papers, 1968- . ca. 6 in. University of Nevada faculty-student group. Includes records, minutes, resolutions, and other materials relating to the activities of the group.
.5 Literary Collection.
Includes books, pamphlets, periodical contributions, translations, and other materials by American authors, including items (ca. 600) by four black writers: James Baldwin, Ralph Ellison, Langston Hughes, and Richard Wright.
.6 National Association for the Advancement of Colored People, Reno-Sparks Branch.
Records, 1958-61. ca. 1 ft.
.7 Nevada Commission on Equal Rights of Citizens.
Hearings, 1964. ca. 1 reel. On microfilm.
.8 Scott, Eddie.
Reno civil rights leader. An oral history of Scott's career.

NEW HAMPSHIRE

CONCORD

NH1 NEW HAMPSHIRE HISTORICAL SOCIETY (1823). 30 Park St., 03302. Tel 603 225-3381. Literature searches.
Publ.: Historical New Hampshire, quarterly magazine.

.1 Chandler, William Eaton, 1835-1917.
Papers, 1829-1917. 22 ft. (ca. 25,000 items). Lawyer, politician, U.S. Senator, from Concord, N.H. Correspondence, family records, diaries, documents, articles, speeches, and newspaper clippings, relating to Chandler's political career. Includes material on the cotton courts in Mississippi, and the prosecution of Civil War claims in England, and other subjects relating to his career. Correspondents include such people as Louis D. Brandeis, William J. Bryan, Benjamin F. Butler, Winston Churchill (author, 1871-1914), James A. Garfield, William L. Garrison, Horace Greeley, Robert M. La Follette (1855-1925), Whitelaw Reid, Theodore Roosevelt, Benjamin R. Tillman, and Booker T. Washington.
.2 Farmer, John, 1789-1838.
Correspondence, 1806-39. 5 boxes (ca. 1700 items). Antiquarian, secretary of New Hampshire Historical Society, and of the New Hampshire Anti-Slavery Society. Includes some correspondence with antislavery leaders, including Wendell Phillips and John Greenleaf Whittier.
.3 Greeley, Horace.
Papers, 1850-72. 1 Envelope. Editor of New York Tribune, U.S. Representative from New York.
.4 Hale, John Parker, 1806-73.
Papers, 1818-79. 6 ft. (ca. 5000 items). Lawyer, U.S. Senator, candidate for President on Free-Soil ticket (1852), ambassador to Spain. Correspondence, a few letterbooks, scrapbook, copies of speeches. Much of the correspondence relates to the anti-slavery movement before the Civil War.
.5 Kimball, Joseph Horace, 1813-38.
Papers, 1831-38. 23 items. Editor, Herald of Freedom, Concord, N.H. Diaries, correspondence, writings relating to the anti-slavery movement. Includes diary of a 6-months trip to Antigua, Barbados and Jamaica to investigate the effects of emancipation in the British West Indies, 1837. Kimball made the trip with James A. Thome as an agent for the American Anti-Slavery Society.
.6 Newspaper collection.
Included are Herald of Freedom, 1835-46 (incomplete), published bi-weekly by the Anti-Slavery So-

ciety, Concord, N.H., Granite Freeman, 1844-47, published weekly, Concord, N.H., Christian Freeman and Family Visitor, 1847-54, and other newspapers containing anti-slavery materials.

.7 Parrott, Enoch Greenleafe, 1815-79.
Letter, Jan. 29, 1844. 20 pages. Naval officer, U.S.S. Saratoga. Letter, written to Parrott's brother from Madeira, gives a full and vivid account of a punitive expedition made against settlements on the coast of Africa.

.8 Whittier, John.
Papers, 1860-91. 1 box. Poet and abolitionist of Massachusetts.

DOVER

NH2 DOVER PUBLIC LIBRARY. 73 Locust St., 03820. Tel 603 742-3513. Mildred E. Morrison, Librn.

.1 Dover, New Hampshire.
Papers, 1640-1967. ca. 350 items. Civil War letters (1862-64) of Stephen M. Thompson and reminiscences (1890) relating in part to the underground railway operated by local Quakers, especially in Lee, N.H.; miscellaneous letters; diary (1861-64) of Adoniram Littlefield; journals (1810-65) of Enoch Place; minutes of the Free Will Baptist Church, Dover, N.H. (1843-1901); the Unitarian Society (1827-1925).

HANOVER

NH3 DARTMOUTH COLLEGE, BAKER LIBRARY. 03755. Tel 603 646-1110. Edward Connery Lathem, Librn. of the Col. Interlibrary loan, copying, typing, inquiries answered, consultation.

.1 Facts on Film.
Papers, 1954-67. Microfilm. Contains materials on civil rights and race relations in the South. See Race Relations Information Center, Nashville, Tenn., for a full description.

.2 Hale, John P.
Papers. Included is material pertaining to the abolition period.

JAFFREY

NH4 JAFFREY PUBLIC LIBRARY. Box 385, 03452. Tel 603 532-7301. Mrs. Evelyn Ruffle, Librn.

.1 Fortune, Amos, 1710?-1801.
Papers, ca. 1770-1801. Slave, freeman by own purchase, founder of Jaffrey Social Library (1795). Included are Fortune's freedom papers and many receipts for sale of leather from his tannery.

NEW JERSEY

ASBURY PARK

NJ1 BETHUNE JONES (1930). 321 Sunset Ave., 07712. Tel 201 775-4853. Bethune Jones, Publisher.
Bethune Jones publishes From the State Capitals, a reporting service designed "to meet the needs of those aware of the importance of developments in state capitals." Various publications cover such areas as planning, financing and construction of publicly-aided housing, slum clearance, urban redevelopment and renewal, financing and administration of general public-assistance, medical assistance, and welfare programs.
Publ.: From the State Capitals; Racial Relations, monthly report.

EAST ORANGE

NJ2 CLEARING HOUSE OPPORTUNITIES FOR INTEGRATING COMMUNITIES (CHOICE) (1963). 589 Central Ave., 07018. Gail Willitts, Dir. Inquiries answered, referrals made, consultation.

CHOICE assists any home or apartment seeker (chiefly non-white families) to attain the home of his choice in the nine northern counties of New Jersey, and is sponsored by the Essex County Urban League and the New Jersey Committee Against Discrimination in Housing.
Publ.: The Workshop, 8-10 issues per year.

ELIZABETH

NJ3 CITY COMMISSION ON HUMAN RELATIONS (1950). 316 Irvington Ave., 07208. Tel 201 354-7030. Hubert U. Barbour, Jr., Exec. Dir.
The Commission recommends to the Mayor and governing body policies, precedures and educational programs that will aid in eliminating all types of discrimination; and effectuates through positive action the guarantee of equal rights for all.

NJ4 CONGRESS OF RACIAL EQUALITY (CORE). 856 E. Jersey St., 07201. Tel 201 355-6674. Arthur Johnson, Chmn.

NJ5 UNION COUNTY URBAN LEAGUE (1945). Community Serv. Center, 692 Bayway, 07202. Tel 201 351-7200. Leroy R. Coles, Jr., Exec. Dir.

.1 Union County Urban League.
Files, 1945- . Correspondence, minutes of meetings, financial records, studies, reports, and other materials dealing with the aims, history, and programs of the League.

ENGLEWOOD

NJ6 URBAN LEAGUE FOR BERGEN COUNTY (1918). 28 Van Brunt St., 07631. Tel 201 568-4988. John O. Crawley, Exec. Dir.
Formerly the Urban League of Englewood, N.J.

ESSEX FELLS

NJ7 THE NEW SOCIETY (1968). Box 114, 07021. John Sullivan, Ed.
"TRUD! is a racist-revolutionary periodical dedicated to the establishment of a Pan-Caucasian state, reaching from the Urals to the California coast." It seeks "to engender a renewed sense of racial and cultural pride within the Caucasian family of nations, to protect and sustain our biological and spiritual identity, knowing that miscegenation on an ever-increasing scale would eventually result in the genocide of the Caucasian people."
Publ.: TRUD!, monthly magazine.

.1 The New Society.
Files, 1968- . Records, correspondence, issues of TRUD, and ms of articles concerning race and racism.

GLASSBORO

NJ8 GLASSBORO STATE COLLEGE, SAVITZ LIBRARY. 08028. Tel 609 881-8400. Magdalena Houlroyd, Curator, Stewart Collection. Interlibrary loan, copying, inquiries answered, consultation.
Publ.: Books on the Negro, Slavery, Abolitionists, and Related Topics in the Stewart Collection of the Savitz Library (1964).

.1 Stewart Collection.

.2 — Abolition Collection.
1760-1837. 40 items. Includes the Constitution of the Pennsylvania Society for Promoting the Abolition of Slavery (1788) and the Constitution of the New Jersey Society for promoting the Abolition of Slavery.

.3 — New Jersey Abolition Society.
Papers. ca. 40 items. Includes minutes (1797-1804) and lists of Negroes from various places in South Jersey (1798-99).

.4 — Newspapers.
11 items. Camden Union Recorder, Camden, N.J. (scattered issues, 1918-20), and Atlantic

City Herald, Atlantic City, N.J. (Mar. 16, 1929).

.5 — Quaker Collection.
Materials. Includes manumission papers for Negroes held by Quakers, chiefly in Salem County, 1777 (43 items); and books (ca. 30) on slave trade and slavery, with emphasis on the Quaker view point in the late 18th century.

MADISON

NJ9   DREW UNIVERSITY (1866), ROSE MEMORIAL LIBRARY (1938). Madison Ave., 07940. Tel 201 377-3000. Dr. Arthur E. Jones, Jr., Dir. Interlibrary loan, literature searches, copying, typing, inquiries answered, referrals made, consultation.

.1   Slavery Collection.
Books (ca. 1200), and pamphlets (ca. 3000). Contains materials on Civil War, Reconstruction, slavery in the U.S., slavery and the church, and slavery and the Methodist Church.

MONTCLAIR

NJ10   MONTCLAIR PUBLIC LIBRARY (1893). 50 S. Fullerton Ave., 07042. Tel 201 744-0500. Arthur Curley, Dir. Interlibrary loan, copying, inquiries answered.

.1   Afro-American Collection.
Books. ca. 3000 v. Contains books about the cultural heritage and contemporary concerns of black Americans.

MORRISTOWN

NJ11   MORRIS COUNTY URBAN LEAGUE, INC. Washington St. and Schuyler Place, 07960. Tel 201 539-2121. Richard D. Martin, Exec. Dir.

NEW BRUNSWICK

NJ12   RUTGERS - THE STATE UNIVERSITY, LIBRARY (1766). 08901. Tel 201 247-1766. Donald A. Sinclair, Curator of Spec. Collections. Copying.
Publ.: The Negro and New Jersey; a Checklist of Books, Pamphlets, Official Publications, Broadsides, and Dissertations, 1754-1964, in the Rutgers University Library (1965).

.1   African Association of New Brunswick, New Jersey.
Records, 1817-24. Minutes and constitution. The Association, with white and Negro members, was formed to support the African School (Parsippany, N.J.), founded 1816 by the Presbyterian Synod of New York and New Jersey to educate Negro teachers and preachers. Included are vouchers and certificates of owners permitting their slaves to join the Association; also unrelated clippings (1846-53) concerning politics.

.2   Brinckerhoff, Isaac W., III, 1821-1910.
The Port Royal Gazette, 1862-63. 140 pp. Ms periodical recording Brinckerhoff's experiences and observations as a Freedman's Bureau superintendent of plantations near Beaufort, S.C. (March, 1862-Jan., 1863) and St. Augustine, Fla. (Feb., 1863). The writer, Baptist clergyman formerly associated with the American Tract Society (New York), describes conditions under Union military occupation, and especially the circumstances of the liberated slaves. Library also has Brinckerhoff's 252-page autobiography.

.3   Brown, John Mason, 1801-?
Diary, 1825-38. 3 v. Storekeeper, of Quaker background, Salem, Mass. Diary describes social, family, business, and local affairs, visits to nearby places and to Philadelphia, and a Salem fugitive slave case (1834-35).

.4   How family.
Papers, 1800-20th century. 7 boxes. Papers of Mrs. and Mrs. Samuel Blanchard How of New Brunswick, N.J., their son, Henry K. How of San

Antonio, Tex., and his wife, Mary Kinnan How, Blanche How, Ann S. Kinnan, George Kinnan, John Kinnan, and Lucinda (Shaw) Kinnan, and her sister, Nancy Shaw. Papers of Samuel B. How, a Presbyterian clergyman, include personal and theological correspondence (1810-67), much of which relates to his anti-abolition pamphlet, Slaveholding Not Sinful (1855), about the Negro question and the political climate, North and South, immediately before the Civil War.

.5   McKeag family.
Papers, 1827-1939. 7 items and 4 v. Bonds for slaves, releases, indentures, a record of real estate transactions (1911-31), and other papers of the McKeag family of New Brunswick, N.J.

.6   Middlesex County, N.J.
Records, New Brunswick, N.J., 1800-44. 2 v. Register of black children, 1804-44; and record of slave manumissions, 1800-25.

.7   New Brunswick Colonization Society.
Records, 1838-54. 1 folder. Records, including constitutions, with subscriptions of members; minutes, 1838-39 and 53-54.

.8   Piscataway Township, N.J.
Records, 1805-07. 1 folder. Certificates of abandonment for Negro children born of slave parents.

.9   Sherman, Adelbert C.
Papers, 1864-1908. 162 items. Correspondence, receipts, bills, and other personal papers, together with Civil War papers, including the reports, rolls, and returns of personnel and equipment of Company G, 28th U.S. Colored Infantry in which Sherman served as captain (1864-66) in Virginia and Texas. Places mentioned include Maine and Massachusetts.

.10   Smith, Miles C.
Papers, 1826-1930. 14 folders. Resident of New Brunswick, N.J. In part, certificates and release (1821-25) concerned with the manumission of a slave, Henry Compton; diaries (1836-41) of Hatfield Smith; and clippings and miscellaneous papers.

.11   Still, Peter.
Papers, 1798-1875. 57 items. Correspondence, chiefly letters received relating to a campaign to purchase Still's wife and family held as slaves in Alabama, and the publication of his biography (1850-75); memo book of funds collected (1853-54); Still family record (1798-1821). Places mentioned are Burlington, N.J., and Philadelphia, Pa.

.12   Van Liew family.
Van Liew-Voorhees family papers, 1777-1859. 102 items. Papers of the Van Liew-Voorhees family of Franklin Township and Somerset County, N.J., including bills, receipts, bonds, and other papers of John D. Van Liew for 1777-1832, Abraham J. Voorhees for 1817-49, Henry Vroom DeMott for 1834-73, and Matilda Voorhees DeMott. John D. Van Liew's papers include slave sale bills among other items.

.13   Whitney, Henry, 1844-?
Civil War journal, April 23-Oct. 30, 1864. 133 pages. Lieutenant, 45th Regiment, USCT. Whitney's journal, sent in sections to his parents, Mr. and Mrs. Bennett Whitney, Bridgeport, Conn., gives accounts of his recruitment of Negro soldiers in West Virginia (while stationed at Clarksburg), of delivering Negro recruit detachments from Camp Case, Va., to various regiments, and of behavior of Negroes and southern whites. Also included are details about the Free Military School for Applicants for Command of Colored Troops (Philadelphia) and Whitney's former fellow students there.

.14   Wilberforce, William.
Letterbook. 1 v. English philanthropist, member of Parliament and abolitionist.

NJ13   RUTGERS-THE STATE UNIVERSITY, URBAN STUDIES CENTER (1966). 137 Church St., 08901. Tel 201 247-1766. John E. Bebout, Dir.
The Center seeks to help the University relate to urban society; to help the state and its communities deal with urban problems; and to contribute to knowledge about urban life.
Publ.: Books, monographs, articles.

NJ14   URBAN LEAGUE OF GREATER NEW BRUNSWICK (1945).
       114 New St., 08901. Tel 201 247-9066. Joseph H.
       Wyke, Exec. Dir.
       The League is working to build the internal strength
       and power of the black and poor communities and to
       simultaneously accelerate the equalization of life re-
       sults between black and white.

NEWARK

NJ15   AMERICAN CIVIL LIBERTIES UNION (ACLU) OF NEW
       JERSEY. Room 203, 45 Academy St., 07102. Tel 201
       642-2084. Stephen M. Nagler, Exec. Dir.
       The ACLU works for the protection of constitutional
       rights through legal action in defense of civil liberties
       and through education to expand understanding and ac-
       ceptance of the rights guaranteed in the Bill of Rights.
       Publ.: Civil Liberties Reporter.

NJ16   AMERICAN JEWISH COMMITTEE, NEW JERSEY AREA.
       10 Commerce Court, 07102. Tel 201 242-1633. Sydney
       Kellner, Area Dir.

NJ17   AMERICAN JEWISH CONGRESS, NEW JERSEY REGION.
       17 William St., 07102. Tel 201 623-4754.

NJ18   ANTI-DEFAMATION LEAGUE OF B'NAI B'RITH, NEW
       JERSEY REGIONAL OFFICE. 24 Commerce St.,
       07102. Tel 201 623-6241. Robert Kohler, Dir.

NJ19   GREATER NEWARK URBAN COALITION, INC. P.O. Box
       130, 07101. Tel 201 624-7475. Gustav Heninburg,
       Pres.
       The Coalition was established to implement agreement
       on neighborhood development made between the State of
       New Jersey and residents of Newark's Central Ward in
       the aftermath of the Newark riots of July, 1967. The
       agreement includes plans for the ward's redevelop-
       ment, construction of a medical school, provision of
       health services, training, and employment programs,
       relocation of families, and citizen involvement in the
       Model Cities program.

NJ20   NATIONAL CONFERENCE OF CHRISTIANS AND JEWS
       (NCCJ), INC., NEW JERSEY REGION (1928). Room
       1102, 790 Broad St., 07102. Tel 201 642-6025.
       Howard J. Devaney, Dir. Bibliographies prepared,
       inquiries answered, referrals made, educational pro-
       grams.
       NCCJ promotes justice, amity, understanding and co-
       operation among Protestants, Catholics, and Jews, and
       works to analyze, moderate and finally eliminate inter-
       group prejudices.
       Publ.: Brochures and reports.

NJ21   NEW JERSEY DEPARTMENT OF LAW AND PUBLIC
       SAFETY, DIVISION ON CIVIL RIGHTS (1945). 1100
       Raymond Blvd., 07102. Tel 201 648-2700. James H.
       Blair, Dir. Bibliographies prepared, inquiries an-
       swered, referrals made, consultation.
       The Division is an executive agency with full powers to
       issue cease-and-desist orders and affect affirmative
       relief in areas of employment, housing, and public ac-
       commodations. The Division also enforces the prohibi-
       tion of discrimination in employment on public con-
       tracts. Formerly a part of the Department of Educa-
       tion, Division against Discrimination.
       Publ.: Equal Opportunities, 6 issues per year; Annual,
           quarterly, and monthly reports.
       .1 Division on Civil Rights.
           Contains books, pamphlets, mss, correspondence,
           clippings, films, and tapes in the area of civil
           rights covering employment, the draft, discrimi-
           nation, housing, Negro history, and other subjects.

NJ22   NEW JERSEY HISTORICAL SOCIETY (1845). 230 Broadway,
       07104. Tel 201 483-3939. Edith O. May, Librn. Copy-
       ing, inquiries answered.
       .1 New Jersey Historical Society Library.
           Contains books, pamphlets, vertical file materials,
           mss, and clippings relating to Negroes and Jackson
           whites. Includes a large number of 19th century

pamphlets on slavery and the American Colonization Society.

NJ23   NEWARK HUMAN RIGHTS COMMISSION. City Hall, 07102.
       Tel 201 643-6300. John T. Barnes.

NJ24   THE NEWARK MUSEUM ASSOCIATION LIBRARY (1926).
       43-49 Washington St., 07101. Tel 201 642-0011. Helen
       Olsson, Library Asst. Inquiries answered.
       .1 Tanner, Henry Ossawa.
           Painting. Painter and son of a bishop of the Afri-
           can Methodist Church. Entitled "The Good Shep-
           herd."
       .2 White, Charles W.
           Painting. Contemporary Negro artist. Entitled
           "Sojourner Truth and Booker T. Washington."
       .3 Woodruff, Hale A.
           Painting. Contemporary Negro artist. Entitled
           "Poor Man's Cotton."

NJ25   NEWARK PUBLIC LIBRARY. 5 Washington St., 07101. Tel
       201 624-7100. James E. Bryan, Dir. Interlibrary loan,
       copying, inquiries answered, referrals made.
       Publ.: Intergroup Relations List, monthly typed list for
           city agencies.
       .1 Facts on Film.
           Papers, 1954-67. Microfilm. Contains materials
           on civil rights and race relations in the South. See
           Race Relations Information Center, Nashville,
           Tenn., for a full description.
       .2 Negro Art.
           Contains phonograph records, biographies of Negro
           musicians and artists, original art works, and a
           picture file of famous Negroes.
       .3 Negro in New Jersey.
           Includes books, pamphlets, periodicals, and files on
           the Negro in New Jersey.
       .4 Newark Rebellion of 1967.
           Includes clippings, documents, and books on the
           Newark rebellion.

NJ26   URBAN LEAGUE OF ESSEX COUNTY. 58 Jones St., 07103.
       Tel 201 623-1780. James A. Pawley, Exec. Dir.
       .1 Urban League of Essex County.
           Files. Correspondence, minutes of meetings, fi-
           nancial records, studies, reports, and other mater-
           ials dealing with the aims, history, and programs
           of the League.

PATERSON

NJ27   PATERSON FREE PUBLIC LIBRARY (1885). 250 Broad-
       way, 07501. Tel 201 279-4200. Leo Fichtelberg, Dir.
       Interlibrary loan, bibliographies prepared, copying,
       inquiries answered, referrals made.
       Publ.: Book lists and bibliographies.
       .1 Negro history collection.
           Books (ca. 600) concerning Negro history, slavery
           in the U.S., civil rights, integration, and selected
           books by Negro authors.

PLAINFIELD

NJ28   PLAINFIELD HUMAN RELATIONS COMMISSION (1957).
       City Hall, 07060. Tel 201 754-6690. David W. Sullivan,
       Acting Exec. Dir.
       The Commission is a city agency which develops and
       coordinates programs designed to improve community
       relations, advises the mayor, and deals with questions
       of discrimination through conciliation.

PRINCETON

NJ29   EDUCATIONAL TESTING SERVICE (1947), CARL CAMP-
       BELL BRIGHAM LIBRARY (1952). 08540. Tel 609
       921-9000. Priscilla M. Kahn, Librn.
       Educational Testing Service is a nonprofit organization
       that conducts testing programs, publishes tests and
       related materials, engages in research, and provides

advisory services to education, government, and the professions.

.1 Carl Campbell Brigham Library.
Contains materials on tests and measurements and related materials in education and psychology, and the archives for Educational Testing Service. Includes some materials in research bulletins on testing culturally different groups, the effects of class and race on responsiveness to approval and disapproval, validity of tests on Negro and white students in integrated colleges, and other subjects relating to race.

NJ30 PRINCETON UNIVERSITY, COUNCIL OF HUMAN RELATIONS (1953). Green Hall, 08540. Tel 609 452-4524. Dr. Marvin Bressler, Chmn.
The Council conducts research in the social sciences, including interdisciplinary studies on human relations, resources and organization.

.1 Council on Human Relations.
Files, 1953- . Correspondence, financial records, studies, reports, and other materials dealing with the aims, history, and programs of the Council

NJ31 PRINCETON UNIVERSITY (1756), HARVEY S. FIRESTONE LIBRARY. 08540. Tel 609 452-3180. William Dix, Librn. Interlibrary loan, copying, typing, inquiries answered, referrals made.

.1 American Negro Collection.
Materials, ca. 1865- . 22 vf. Collection includes pamphlets; city, state, and federal reports; literature from churches and political parties; interracial organizations; unbound serials, and newspapers. Restricted.

.2 —— Facts on Film.
Papers, 1954-67. Microfilm. Contains materials on civil rights and race relations in the South. See Race Relations Information Center, Nashville, Tenn., for a full description.

Manuscripts Division

.3 —— A.T. Jeanes Foundation.
Papers of the Negro Rural School Fund.

.4 —— Adamic, Louis, 1899-1951.
Papers. ca. 60 cartons. Author. Papers include extensive notes on minority groups in the U.S.

.5 —— American Bible Society.
Papers.

.6 —— American Civil Liberties Union.
Archives. ca. 2000 items. Correspondence, albums, clippings, and other papers, dating from 1912, relating to civil liberties cases of concern to the organization.

.7 —— Baggalay, Richard.
Papers, ca. 1874. Attorney general. Relates to the suppression of the slave trade.

.8 —— Baker, Ray Stannard (David Grayson, pseud.).
Papers, 1918-19. Massachusetts; journalist, author. Mainly papers collected by Stannard.

.9 —— Baruch, Bernard.
Papers.

.10 —— Faulkner, William, 1897- .
Papers. 3 boxes. Author. Correspondence, literary documents, and related papers. Includes typescripts, with autograph corrections, of Faulkner's contributions to periodicals. Among these are "By the People"; "Freedom, American Style"; and "If I Were a Negro."

.11 —— Freedom House.
Papers, 1940. 100 boxes. Materials concerning the history and administration of the House.

.12 —— Gibbons, Herbert, 1880-1934.
Papers. 15 boxes. Foreign correspondent, and traveler in Africa. Author of The New Map of Africa (1916).

.13 —— McAneny, George.
Papers.

.14 —— Rush, Richard.
Papers.

.15 —— Stockton, Robert Field, 1795-1866.
Papers. 12 boxes. Naval officer, and agent of the American Colonization Society who negotiated for the Society's first foothold on the Liberian coast in 1821.

NJ32 PRINCETON UNIVERSITY, SCHOOL OF ARCHITECTURE AND URBAN PLANNING, RESEARCH CENTER FOR URBAN AND ENVIRONMENTAL PLANNING (1966). 08540. Tel 609 452-3748. Robert Geddes, Dean, Sch. of Archit. and Urban Planning.
The Center's research projects are intended to help in the resolution of planning problems currently faced by communities and regions. The Center has two objectives: (1) to provide a setting for urban and environmental planning studies, and (2) to relate social, economic, and political factors to physical planning as the basis for broader, more reliable planning methods. Its activities include individual and joint efforts of faculty members, research staff, and participating students.

SOUTH ORANGE

NJ33 SETON HALL UNIVERSITY, CENTER FOR URBAN RESEARCH AND ENVIRONMENTAL STUDIES (1966). 07079. Tel 201 642-8500. Bernard J. Stuck, William J. Doerflinger, Co-directors.
The Center conducts basic and contract research regarding urban and regional problems, and disseminates the findings of basic research through reports. Past research projects have included an economic base study of Newark, N.J., and an administrative study of public and private agencies engaged in urban renewal in Newark. The Center sponsors a program examining the political problems of urbanization in New Jersey, and a community attitude study for the Police Department of Elizabeth, N.J.

TRENTON

NJ34 NEW JERSEY DEPARTMENT OF COMMUNITY AFFAIRS. P.O. Box 2768, 08625. Tel 201 292-6212. Gregory R. Farrell, Dir., Off. of Econ. Opportunity. Inquiries answered.
In its effort to help solve urban problems, the Department's Office of Economic Opportunity has (1) provided training, counseling and educational programs for rural and urban unemployed poor, under-educated adults and high school dropouts, released county prisoners, narcotics addicts and disadvantaged youths; (2) assisted local legal services offices in administrative and legal matters involving the disadvantaged—programs including "Street Academies" for the educationally deprived and Community Day Care Centers for the children of mothers on welfare.
Publ.: Community, monthly newsletter; New Jersey Planning Topics, quarterly magazine; Office of Legal Services Clearinghouse Report, biweekly.

NJ35 NEW JERSEY DEPARTMENT OF LAW AND PUBLIC SAFETY, DIVISION ON CIVIL RIGHTS, TRENTON OFFICE (1945). 52 W. State St., 08608. Tel 609 292-4605. Inquiries answered, referrals made, consultation.

NJ36 TRENTON FREE PUBLIC LIBRARY. 120 Academy St., 08629. Tel 609 392-7188. Miss Veronica F. Cary, Dir. Interlibrary loan, bibliographies prepared, literature searches, copying, typing, inquiries answered, referrals made, consultation.

.1 New Jersey Sentinel.
Newspaper, 1880-82. Bound copy and microfilm. Weekly Negro newspaper (v. I, no. 8, June 26, 1880-v. III, no. 19, Nov. 13, 1882).

NJ37 UNITED PROGRESS, INC. 143 E. State St., 08603. Tel 609 392-2161. Donald J. Cogsville, Exec. Dir.
United Progress is working on a two-year program to integrate the Action Bound program, which uses outdoor weekend activities to help inner-city boys experience the kind of confidence in themselves that keeps them from dropping out of school.

NEW MEXICO

ALBUQUERQUE

NM1   HUMAN RIGHTS COMMISSION OF NEW MEXICO (1969).
1015 Tijeras N.W., 87102. Tel 505 842-3122. Bryon
L. Stewart, Exec. Dir.
The Commission adopts, promulgates, amends, and
repeals rules and regulations to eliminate discrimination in employment, public accommodations or the
acquisition of housing accommodations and real
property; endeavors to eliminate prejudice; encourages
an educational program and voluntary advisory groups
to study problems of discrimination in all fields; seeks
and enlists the cooperation and contributions and grants
of individuals and foundations; and submits annually a
written report of all activities.

.1   Human Rights Commission of New Mexico.
Files, 1969- . 4 vf. Contains correspondence,
minutes of meetings, newspaper clippings, pamphlets, posters and material on various cases and
projects dealing with discrimination in employment,
housing, real property, public accommodations and
EEOC affirmative action project.

NM2   NATIONAL CONFERENCE OF CHRISTIANS AND JEWS
(NCCJ). 10500 Love Ave., N.E., 87112. Tel 505 299-
6213. Mrs. Cecelia B. Daniel, Dir.

NM3   NEW MEXICO CIVIL LIBERTIES UNION. 131 La Vega,
S.W., 87105. Tel 505 877-5286. John L. Walker, Exec.
Dir. Inquiries answered, referrals made, consultation.
The Union works for the defense of all citizens' constitutional and other civil rights in the areas of free
speech, press and assembly; police community problems; racial discrimination, especially in public accommodations, housing; racism in public school education
(black, Mexican-American, and Indian), county jail and
State prison conditions.
Publ.: NMCLU, bimonthly newsletter.

.1   New Mexico Civil Liberties Union.
Files. Correspondence, newspaper clippings on
activities, minutes of board meetings, case files
on police harassment and physical brutality, legal
briefs and filing papers in major legal cases.

NM4   U.S. EQUAL EMPLOYMENT OPPORTUNITY COMMISSION
(EEOC), ALBUQUERQUE AREA OFFICE (1965). Suite
1000, First Nat. Bank Bldg., 5301 Central N.E., 87108.
Tel 505 843-2061. Tom E. Robles, Area Dir.
EEOC investigates and conciliates complaints of dis-
crimination in employment based on race, creed, color,
national origin, or sex, under Title VII of the Civil
Rights Act of 1964.
Publ.: Pamphlets and posters concerning equal em-
ployment opportunities.

SANTA FE

NM5   NEW MEXICO FAIR EMPLOYMENT PRACTICES COMMIS-
SION (1949). 137 E. DeVargas St., 87501. Tel 505 827-
2722. Richard J. Rodriguez, Exec. Secy.
The Commission, a permanent, departmental agency,
works to eliminate discrimination in employment; has
powers to issue orders to cease and desist and to com-
ply with terms of agreement.
Publ.: Annual Report.

NEW YORK

ALBANY

NY1   ALBANY AREA URBAN LEAGUE. 91 State St., 12207. Tel
518 463-3121. Lawrence Burwell, Exec. Dir.

.1   Albany Area Urban League.
Files. Correspondence, minutes of meetings, financial records, reports, studies, and other materials dealing with the aims, history, and programs
of the Urban League.

NY2   ALBANY INSTITUTE OF HISTORY AND ART, LIBRARY
(1791). 125 Washington Ave., 12210. Tel 518 463-4478.
Kenneth H. MacFarland, Librn. Copying, inquiries answered, referrals made, consultation.
The Institute's research library is for use by the staff
and those seriously interested in research in the history
of the Albany area and American art, particularly New
York State art.
Publ.: Annual Report.

.1   Van Zandt, Gerrit.
Papers, 1723-1831. 488 items. Bills for household
commodities and property, together with some
slave deeds.

NY3   ALBANY INTERRACIAL COUNCIL, ARBOR HILL COMMU-
NITY CENTER (1928). 2 N. Lark, 12210. Tel 518
463-4439. Paul E. Richardson, Dir.
The Council seeks to develop better intergroup relations
in the community, and conducts a program of recreation
and education designed to improve the attitudes and conditions under which members of the community work
and live.

NY4   NEW YORK STATE DEPARTMENT OF EDUCATION, DIVI-
SION OF INTERCULTURAL RELATIONS IN EDUCA-
TION. State Campus Bldg., Washington Ave., 12226.
Tel 518 474-2121.

NY5   NEW YORK STATE, DIVISION OF HUMAN RIGHTS. Alfred
E. Smith Office Bldg., Box 7010, 12225. Tel 518 474-
2705. Salvatore J. Amato, Regional Dir.

NY6   NEW YORK STATE LIBRARY, MANUSCRIPT AND HISTORY
SECTION. Education Bldg., 12224. Tel 518 474-5958.
Juliet Wolohan, Librn.

.1   Butler, Benjamin Franklin.
Papers, 1780-1858. 6 boxes. Chiefly correspondence relating to Butler's career as a New York
lawyer, U.S. Attorney General, and Secretary of
War.

NY7   STATE UNIVERSITY OF NEW YORK AT ALBANY, GRADU-
ATE SCHOOL OF PUBLIC AFFAIRS, LOCAL GOVERN-
MENT STUDIES CENTER (1962). Sayles Hall, 179
Partridge St., 12203. Tel 518 472-3350. Inquiries answered.
The Center functions as a clearinghouse on metropolitan
problems and as a research and publications center. It
maintains an extensive collection of documentary materials on urban problems and, as a clearinghouse, re-
sponds to inquiries from all over the world for data on
these problems.
Publ.: Metropolitan Area Digest, bimonthly report on
metropolitan developments; Metropolitan Area
Annual; Monograph series on public policy issues.

NY8   STATE UNIVERSITY OF NEW YORK AT ALBANY, UNIVER-
SITY LIBRARY (1844). 1223 Western Ave., 12203. Tel
518 457-8542. Alice T. Hastings, Librn.

.1   Facts on Film.
Papers, 1954-67. Microfilm. Contains materials
on civil rights and race relations in the South. See
Race Relations Information Center, Nashville,
Tenn., for a full description.

BRONX

NY9   CONGRESS OF RACIAL EQUALITY (CORE), BRONX CHAP-
TER. 1301 Boston Rd., 10456. Tel 212 991-1950. Sol
Herbert, Chmn.

NY10   NATIONAL CONFERENCE OF CHRISTIANS AND JEWS
(NCCJ). 332 E. 149th St., 10451. Tel 212 993-2122.
Mrs. Margaret Schwarz, Dir.

BRONXVILLE

NY11   BRONXVILLE PUBLIC LIBRARY. 201 Ponfield Rd., 10708.
Tel 914 337-7680. Ellenor K. Luce, Dir.

.1   Ralph J. Bunche Memorial Collection.
Books by and about Negroes.

NY12   SARAH LAWRENCE COLLEGE, INSTITUTE OF COMMU-
NITY STUDIES (1965). 10708. Tel 914 337-0700. Bert
A. Swanson, Dir.
The Institute conducts research and engages in community services activities, including consultation and
workshops. Among the projects of the Institute are an
analysis of the participation of parents, community, and
school officials in the integration controversies of the
New York City public school system; the administration
of the Sarah Lawrence Upward Bound program; and an
analysis of housing decision-making in New York City.

BROOKLYN

NY13   AFRICAN-AMERICAN TEACHERS ASSOCIATION. 1064
Fulton St., 11238. Tel 212 789-3700. Jul' Gilbert,
Exec. Secy.
The Association works to bring quality education to
black communities in New York, seeks to end the op-
pression of black children in schools, and promotes job
advancement for black men and women through its College Placement Center, evening school, Saturday Academy, demonstrations, seminars, and research programs.
Publ.: African-American Teachers Forum, bimonthly
newsletter.

NY14   BEDFORD-STUYVESANT RESTORATION CORPORATION.
144 Ralph Ave., 11233. Tel 212 443-5800. John Doar,
Exec. Dir., Develop. and Serv. Corp.

     .1   Bedford-Stuyvesant Restoration Corporation.
Files. Records, reports, correspondence, and
other papers concerning the operation of the organization.

NY15   BLACK NEWS. 10 Claver Place, 11238. Tel 212 941-6150.
Jim Williams, Editor.
"Black News is a New Community publication. It was
formed in order to encourage a new awareness and involvement among our people. Our main concern is to
agitate, educate, organize. If we don't do these things,
then we ain't doin' nothin'."
Publ.: Black News, bi-weekly magazine, "a third world
Black Publication."

NY16   BOARD OF EDUCATION OF THE CITY OF NEW YORK,
OFFICE OF INTERGROUP EDUCATION (1961). 110
Livingston St., 11201. Tel 212 596-5030. Lynette V.
Tucker, Acting Dir. Interlibrary loan, referrals made,
consultation.
The Office conducts programs and activities in the area
of intergroup relations among pupils, staff, schools and
communities. Included in the activities are in-service
courses for staff, parent workshops, pupil and staff exchange programs, and the maintenance of a resource
center.
Publ.: Bridges to Understanding, quarterly bulletin; Occasional publications.

     .1   Resource center.
Books, periodicals, pamphlets, clippings, pictures,
films, filmstrips, videotapes, and recordings concerning intergroup education.

NY17   THE CITY UNIVERSITY OF NEW YORK, BROOKLYN COL-
LEGE (1930), LIBRARY (1930). Bedford Ave. and Ave. H,
11210. Tel 212 780-5342. Prof. H.G. Bousfield, Librn.
Interlibrary loan, copying, typing, inquiries answered,
referrals made, consultation.

     .1   Facts on Film.
Papers, 1954-67. Microfilm. Contains materials
on civil rights and race relations in the South. See
Race Relations Information Center, Nashville,
Tenn., for a full description.

NY18   THE BROOKLYN MUSEUM (1897), ART REFERENCE LI-
BRARY. 188 Eastern Parkway, 11238. Tel 212 638-
5000. Margaret B. Zorach, Librn. Copying.
Publ.: Monthly calendar and exhibition catalog.

     .1   Brooklyn Museum.
Among the Museum's collection are several works
by Negro artists, including paintings such as "Fu-

neral Sermon," by Jacob Lawrence, "Speracedes
France," by Lois Mailoux Jones, "Before the
Storm," by Richard Mayhew, and "Shoe Shine," by
Ernest Crichlow. The Library contains some ref-
erence material concerning Negro art.

NY19   BROOKLYN PUBLIC LIBRARY (1892). Grand Army Plaza,
11238. Tel 212 789-1212. Miss L. Tudiver, Chief, Soc.
Science Div. Interlibrary loan, copying, inquiries answered, referrals made.

     .1   Afro-American History collection.
Books (ca. 2000 v.) on slavery and Negroes in the
U.S., with some material on Negroes in other
countries.
     .2   Anti-Slavery Propaganda Collection.
ca. 2500 pamphlets. Microcards of originals
located in the Oberlin College Library. See Ober-
lin College Library, Oberlin, Ohio; or Lost Cause
Press (publisher), Louisville, Ky., for more com-
plete description.
     .3   Civil War collection.
Books (ca. 12,000 v.) on all aspects of the Civil
War. In the Library's History Division.
     .4   Facts on Film.
Papers, 1954-67. Microfilm. Contains materials
on civil rights and race relations in the South. See
Race Relations Information Center, Nashville,
Tenn., for a full description.
     .5   Slavery collection.
Included are books and a collection of fugitive slave
pamphlets, some of which are unique in the U.S.

NY20   CATHOLIC CHARITIES, DIOCESE OF BROOKLYN, SOCIAL
ACTION DEPARTMENT (1946). 191 Joralemon St.,
11201. Tel 212 596-8400. Rev. Robert P. Kennedy, Dir.
The Department works for better intergroup relations
through educational and action programs in the fields of
poverty, race and housing.
Publ.: Social Action Newsletter, monthly.

     .1   Social Action Department.
Files. Included are materials concerning the history of Church involvement with the Welfare Rights
Movement and early history of the Brooklyn Welfare Movement, notes on the development of Project
Equality in the metropolitan area, and records of
local Opportunities Industrialization Center (OIC)
and Interfaith Citywide Coordinating Committee
Against Poverty.

NY21   CENTRAL BROOKLYN NEIGHBORHOOD COLLEGE. 21
Saint James Place, 11205. Tel 212 622-5026.
The College is a community-run education program,
serving the black and Puerto Rican communities of
central Brooklyn. The College teaches needed skills
and provides guidance and counseling for entrance into
employment and higher education. It also seeks to expand employment and college opportunities for members
of the community.

NY22   JOINT APPRENTICESHIP PROGRAM OF THE WORKERS
DEFENSE LEAGUE-A. PHILIP RANDOLPH EDUCA-
TIONAL FUND (1964). 1520 Bushwick Ave., 11207. Tel
212 443-1250. Ernest Green, Nat. Dir. Referrals
made.
The Program recruits, tutors and places minority
males in the apprenticeship programs of the building
and construction trades. Formerly the Workers Defense League Apprenticeship Program.
Publ.: Joint Apprenticeship Training catalogs of opportunities in New York, Cleveland, and Boston, annually.

NY22a   M.F. PUBLICATIONS (1969). 269 Utica Ave., 11213. Tel
212 756-5100. Talib M. Zobier, Editor.
Publ.: Etcetera, monthly magazine.

NY23   NATIONAL CONFERENCE OF CHRISTIANS AND JEWS
(NCCJ). 105 Court St., 11201. Tel 212 858-0468. Ralph
D. King, Dir.

NY24   NATIONAL WELFARE RIGHTS ORGANIZATION, BROOK-
LYN WELFARE ACTION COUNCIL. 1002 Bushwick
Ave., 11221. Tel 212 491-1504. Jon Kaufman.

NY25   NEW YORK STATE, DIVISION OF HUMAN RIGHTS, RE-
        GIONAL OFFICE. 15 Lafayette Ave., 11201. Tel 212
        852-0313. Arthur W. Stern, Regional Dir.

NY26   PHI BETA SIGMA FRATERNITY, INC. (1914). 1006 Carroll
        St., 11225. Tel 212 493-5425. William E. Doar, Jr.,
        Nat. Exec. Secy.
        Phi Beta Sigma is a national predominantly Negro fra-
        ternity. It has a human relations program directed by
        the national social action committee, which supplies
        study guides and other education material to local chap-
        ters. The Education and Scholarship Program makes
        loans to members attending colleges and universities on
        the undergraduate and graduate level, and encourages
        education in business and other fields. Bigger and Bet-
        ter Business and education for that purpose is one of
        the Fraternity's oldest programs.
        Publ.: Crescent, semiannually; Sigma Journal, period-
             ically.

NY27   PRATT INSTITUTE, DEPARTMENT OF CITY AND RE-
        GIONAL PLANNING, PRATT CENTER FOR COMMU-
        NITY IMPROVEMENT (1964). 244 Vanderbilt Ave.,
        11205. Tel 212 622-2200. George M. Raymond, Dir.
        The Center provides information and technical assis-
        tance in housing, planning, urban renewal, education
        and related subjects. The Center's program is es-
        sentially one of urban action, and its goals include the
        creation of an institutional and government framework
        within which the community's problems can be solved.
        Publ.: Pratt Planning Papers, quarterly; Reports and
             studies, on subjects such as child care and social
             planning; Community Information Manual.

        BUFFALO

NY28   ANTI-DEFAMATION LEAGUE OF B'NAI B'RITH, WESTERN
        NEW YORK REGIONAL OFFICE. 291 Delaware Ave.,
        14202. Tel 716 853-6108. Louis H. Glickman, Exec.
        Dir.

NY28a   BLACK ACADEMY PRESS, INC. 3296 Main St., 14214. Tel
        716 836-6240. S. Okechukwu Mezu, Editor.
        "Black Academy Review is an interdisciplinary quar-
        terly publication devoted to the defense and edification
        of the black civilization in all its dimensions and varia-
        tions."
        Publ.: Black Academy Review: Quarterly of the Black
             World.

NY29   BUFFALO AND ERIE COUNTY HISTORICAL SOCIETY. 25
        Nottingham Court, 14216. Tel 716 873-9644. Walter S.
        Dunn, Jr., Dir. Interlibrary loan, copying, inquiries
        answered.
        Publ.: Niagara Frontier, quarterly journal; Newsletter.
        .1   Negro newspapers collection.
             1967- . 2 titles. Two local Negro newspapers: The
             Challenger (weekly); and The Buffalo Criterion
             (weekly).
        .2   Wilkeson, Samuel, 1781-1848.
             Papers. President of the American Colonization
             Society, 1838-41, and editor of its organ, the Afri-
             can Repository.

NY30   BUFFALO AND ERIE COUNTY PUBLIC LIBRARY. Lafay-
        ette Square, 14203. Tel 716 856-7525. Joseph B.
        Rounds, Dir. Interlibrary loan, copying, inquiries an-
        swered.
        .1   Materials pertaining to Negroes.
             Miscellaneous. Books (ca. 600 v.) pertaining to
             slavery; books and periodicals (4500 v.) pertaining
             to Negro history, culture, literature, art and music;
             rare books and pamphlets on American Colonization
             Society and Liberia; pamphlets on early political
             activities of Negroes (ca. 200 items); and other
             materials in the rare book room.
        .2   Theodore Tilton Collection.
             Papers. ca. 25 items. Ms letters written to Tilton
             by leading abolitionists; including Frederick Doug-
             lass.

NY31   BUFFALO COMMISSION ON HUMAN RELATIONS (1965).
        1502 City Hall, 14202. Tel 716 856-4200. Sidney Har-
        ris, Exec. Dir.
        The Commission promotes equality of treatment for all
        groups and works to prevent discrimination in areas of
        housing, employment, and public accommodations; it
        makes investigations and studies in the field of human
        relations. Formerly the Board of Community Relations.
        Publ.: Human Relations Report, bimonthly.

NY32   THE BUFFALO FINE ARTS ACADEMY, ALBRIGHT-KNOX
        ART GALLERY (1862). 1285 Elmwood Ave., 14222. Tel
        716 882-8700. Gordon M. Smith, Dir.

        .1   Albright-Knox Art Gallery.
             Among the holdings of the gallery are a gouache,
             "Going to Work" (1943), by Jacob Lawrence, and
             "Self Portrait" (1941), by Horace Pippin.

NY33   BUFFALO URBAN LEAGUE, INC. 234 Jefferson Ave.,
        14204. Tel 716 854-7625. Nelson H. Nichols, Jr.,
        Exec. Dir.

        .1   Buffalo Urban League, Inc.
             Files. Records, reports, correspondence, program
             plans and evaluations, and other papers concerning
             the aims and activities of the organization.

NY34   NEW YORK STATE, DIVISION OF HUMAN RIGHTS, RE-
        GIONAL OFFICE. 125 Main St., 14203. Tel 716 842-
        4456. Victor Einach, Regional Dir.

NY35   STATE UNIVERSITY OF NEW YORK AT BUFFALO, OF-
        FICE OF URBAN AFFAIRS. 14222. Tel 716 837-2000.
        Gordon Edwards, Dir.

NY36   UNIVERSITY OF BUFFALO FOUNDATION. 3435 Main St.,
        14214. Tel 716 837-2000.
        Publ.: Urban Education, quarterly journal about the
             problems of city schools.

        COOPERSTOWN

NY37   NATIONAL BASEBALL HALL OF FAME AND MUSEUM
        (1939). Main St., 13326. Tel 607 547-9988.

        .1   National Baseball Hall of Fame and Museum.
             Among the Museum's collection is considerable
             material about Negro baseball players and their
             achievements. Included is memorabilia of Jackie
             Robinson, Willie Mays, Roberto Clemente, and
             Frank Robinson, along with many others.

NY38   NEW YORK STATE HISTORICAL ASSOCIATION (1899), LI-
        BRARY (1899). Lake Rd., 13326. Tel 607 547-2533.
        John F. Guido, Librn. Interlibrary loan, copying,
        typing, inquiries answered.
        Publ.: New York History.
        .1   Stewart, Alvan.
             Papers, 1829-49. ca. 1 box. Correspondence and
             biographical materials relating to Stewart's career
             as a lawyer and antislavery reformer of New York.

        ELMIRA

NY39   CHEMUNG COUNTY COMMISSION ON HUMAN RELATIONS
        (1965). Federation Bldg., 14901. Tel 607 733-6828.
        Philip J. Davis, Exec. Dir.
        The Commission investigates and takes action to allevi-
        ate incidents of racial tension and conflict, conducts ed-
        ucational programs and conferences for the public in
        attempts to open opportunities for minority groups and
        to resolve discrimination and racial tension. Formerly
        the Mayor's Commission on Human Relations, Elmira.

        FAR ROCKAWAY

NY40   AMERICAN JEWISH CONGRESS, SOUTH SHORE DIVISION.
        Room 400, 1600 Central Ave., 11691. Tel 212 793-2626.
        Leona Schwab, Dir.

FLUSHING

NY41   THE CITY UNIVERSITY OF NEW YORK, QUEENS COL-
LEGE, INSTITUTE FOR COMMUNITY STUDIES (1967).
153-10 61 Rd., 11367. Tel 212 445-7500. Marilyn
Gittell, Dir.
The Institute maintains a program of research and
evaluation which consists of recording and study of efforts at community involvement in schools. Through its
staff and through referral to other agencies, it assists
school decentralization projects in curriculum, legal,
fiscal, administrative-managerial matters, community
organization, and public information.
Publ.: Community, monthly newsletter; Community Issues, monographs on topical urban issues.

GREAT NECK

NY42   AMERICAN JEWISH CONGRESS, NORTH SHORE OFFICE.
445 Northern Blvd., 11021. Tel 516 466-4650. Stanley
Greenberg, Dir.

HEMPSTEAD

NY43   AMERICAN JEWISH COMMITTEE, LONG ISLAND AREA.
144 N. Franklin St., 11550. Tel 516 538-2460. Harold
Applebaum, Area Dir. Inquiries answered, referrals
made, consultation.
Publ.: Annual Report.

.1   American Jewish Committee.
Files. Records, correspondence, minutes, and
other papers concerning the activities of the Committee.

NY44   HOFSTRA UNIVERSITY, CENTER FOR BUSINESS AND UR-
BAN RESEARCH (1966). 11550. Tel 516 560-0500.
Harold Wattel, Dir., Problems of Negro Enterprises.
The Center is a research institute concerned with the
problems of the urban and suburban environment. It is
seeking to refine methods for making employment pro-
jections at the county level, techniques which are important for manpower and retraining planning of the
antipoverty program. Formerly the Bureau of Business
and Community Research (1954).

HYDE PARK

NY45   U.S. GENERAL SERVICES ADMINISTRATION, NATIONAL
ARCHIVES AND RECORDS SERVICE (1934), FRANKLIN
D. ROOSEVELT LIBRARY (1939). Albany Post Rd.,
12538. Tel 914 229-8114. James E. O'Neill, Dir.
Copying, typing, inquiries answered, referrals made,
consultation.
The Library makes available the papers, books, photographs, audio-visual materials, and museum objects of
and about President Franklin D. Roosevelt, Mrs. Franklin D. Roosevelt, many of their associates and organizations. Available to serious researchers upon written
application.
Publ.: The Era of Franklin D. Roosevelt: A Selected
Bibliography of Periodical and Dissertation
Literature (1967).

.1   Roosevelt, Anna Eleanor, 1884-1962.
Papers, 1933-57. 1000 ft. New York; chairman of
the United Nations Commission on Human Rights,
U.S. representative to the United Nations General
Assembly. Chiefly her correspondence, 1933-45.
.2   Roosevelt, Franklin Delano, 1882-1945.
Papers, 1535-1945. 3600 cu. ft. Material from
Presidential years, 1933-45, includes items relating to race relations generally, segregation, anti-
lynching legislation, and the Negro in the armed
services.
.3   U.S. Advisory Committee on Education.
Records, 1936-39. 13 ft. Correspondence, memoranda, abstracts and transcripts of conferences,
notes, statements, reports, and special studies relating to the work of the Committee. The 17 staff
studies produced relate to such topics as vocational
guidance, federal participation in education, vocational rehabilitation, rural education, and Negro
education.

.4   Williams, Aubrey Willis, 1890-1965.
Papers, 1930-59. 21 ft. Social worker, editor,
publisher, and government official. Correspondence, memoranda, reports, speech and article
drafts, and newspaper clippings concerning Williams' work as executive director, Wisconsin Conference of Social Work, and other positions. Includes material relating to Williams' role in civil
rights.

ITHACA

NY46   CORNELL UNIVERSITY, LIBRARY (1865). 14850. Tel 607
275-5181. David Kaser, Dir. Interlibrary loan, copying.

.1   Anti-slavery collection.
Materials. ca. 10,000 items, plus large collection
of uncounted mss. Books, pamphlets, letters, documents, newspapers, and other mss concerning the
history, conditions, and abolition of slavery. The
foundation of the collection is the Samuel J. May
archives, purchased from the abolitionist in 1870.
Included in the collection are several complete
runs of rare abolitionist newspapers, a large body
of underground railroad materials, antislavery
materials of Gerrit Smith, and letter books of the
Freedmen's Aid Society. Available for on-site reference in the Rare Book Room.
.2   Collection of Regional History and University Archives.
Among the holdings are found the following collections containing materials relating to Negroes.
.3   — Abell family.
Papers, 1797-1936. Includes letters (January
26, 1833) from Thomas Pothecary to Dr. William Abell telling of his life in Kentucky and of
his unwillingness to settle there permanently
because of his disapproval of slavery.
.4   — Agricultural Economics Library Donation.
Papers, 1732-1908. Deeds (3 items) for sales
of Negro women (1732, 1758, 1784), Albany,
N.Y., bought by the Van Schaick family.
.5   — Ayres, Sidney. collector.
Yates County area papers, 1779-1919. Includes
one sheet of notes dated October 4, 1842, about
petition for withdrawal from the Wesleyan
Church, Penn Yan, N.Y., by several parishioners because of the church's attitude toward
slavery; also records and resolution offered
denouncing spiritualism.
.6   — Barbour-Parker family.
Letters, 1833-55. Letter (January 14, 1837)
from L.S. Parker to Miss Fanny Barbour,
mentions servant girl, born a slave, adopted by
wealthy family as their heir. Comment on
slavery in general.
.7   — Beckwith, Abijah, 1784-1875.
Journal, 1848-75. In a long essay entitled
"Our Nation, Slavery: Its Worst Evil," Beckwith describes slavery in the U.S., the public
attitude towards the Fugitive Slave Law, and
national excitement over the Compromises of
1820 and 1850, documenting his predictions that
slavery must inevitably decline and that the
South would be defeated in the event of a civil
war.
.8   — Beecher, Thomas Kinnicut, 1824-1900.
Papers, 1844-98. ca. 6 ft. (ca. 2600 items).
Congregational clergyman. Correspondence,
printed matter, and other papers. Chiefly
drafts, outlines, and notes for sermons delivered by Beecher as pastor of the Independent
Congregational Church, Elmira, N.Y. Includes
three letters to Beecher from his brother,
Henry Ward Beecher, 14 letters from Lyman
Beecher to his son James, and one letter from
Samuel L. Clemens to Mrs. Julia Beecher.
.9   — Beekman, Town of.
Records, 1772-1835. Records of annual town
meetings, votes received by candidates for
various local and state positions and for the
U.S. Congress, the town's vote concerning the
New York State Constitution of 1822, town laws;
material pertaining to organization, accounts,

and reports of school districts; and certificates of manumission and names of newborn slaves. Microfilm copies.

NY46.10 —— Berry family.
Papers, 1812-1917. 35 v and 3 boxes. Correspondence, diaries, accounts and other papers concerned with the diverse activities of the related families of Berry, Nearing, and Osborn of Onondaga Co., N.Y., and the Waterbury family of Livingston Co., N.Y. Subjects mentioned include slavery.

.11 —— Braithwaite, William Stanley Beaumont, 1878-1962.
Literary papers, 1916-62. ca. 3 ft. Poet, critic, and editor. Literary correspondence (1160 items), mss of Braithwaite's works, outlines for projected works, and typescripts of the works of many leading poets collected by Braithwaite for his anthologies. Correspondents include James Donald Adams, Joseph Auslander, Louis Bromfield, Bliss Carman. Bennett Cerf, William E.B. DuBois, James Gould Cozzens, Robert Frost, Robert Hillyer, Marianne Moore, Maxwell Perkins, and Booker T. Washington.

.12 —— British and Foreign Anti-Slavery Society.
Paper, January 2, 1841. 1 item. Letter from J.W. Tredgold, secretary of the British and Foreign Anti-Slavery Society for the Abolition of Slavery and the Slave Trade Throughout the World, to H.B. Stanton, handing him a copy of the resolutions of the committee of the Society commending him for valuable services rendered to the cause of abolition while in England.

.13 —— Brockett, Frank S. collector.
Brockett collection, 1773-1890. 183 items. In part, transcripts (typewritten). Collection includes lists from The Old Town book (1773-1816) which contains names of slave owners.

.14 —— Burr, George Lincoln, 1857-1938.
Papers, 1862-1938. 33 boxes and 3 storage cases. University professor, historian, and librarian. Correspondence, diaries, notes, and other papers. Correspondents include Ida Tarbell, Oswald Garrison Villard, and Booker T. Washington.

.15 —— Cantine family.
Papers, 1803, 1831. 2 items. Will of John Cantine of Marbletown, Ulster County, in which he bequeathed land in Tioga, Greene, and Ulster Counties and granted freedom to his slaves (1803); will of Charles Cantine of Caroline, Tompkins County (signed 1831, certified 1836).

.16 —— Civil War covers.
Miscellaneous. Pictorial covers or envelopes relating to many phases of the Civil War. The main categories into which they fall are: political cartoons, usually anti-South; commemorative; patriotic. Among the many items are northern cartoons, anti-Beauregard, Jeff Davis, South, and Negro "Contraband," southern currency, England's part in the Civil War, and other related topics.

.17 —— Civil War period pamphlets.
Miscellaneous, 1862-65. Proceedings of the National Convention of Colored Men, held in the City of Syracuse, N.Y. (October 4-7, 1864); with the "Bill of Wrongs and Rights," and the "Address to the American People."

.18 —— Clemons, Alfred.
Papers, 1822-54. 34 items, 28 v, and 3 boxes. Army officer, builder, and constable of Buffalo, N.Y. Includes reports relating to fugitive slaves.

.19 —— Cooper, Roswell D., 1877-1954.
Papers, 1784-1954. 1 box and 1 reel of microfilm. Agriculturist. Correspondence and other papers. Correspondence contains some comments on a visit to a slave pen in St. Louis (1861), among other topics.

.20 —— Corson, Hiram, 1828-1911.
Papers, 1852-1946. Rev. Hall Harrison (1837-1900), supports Corson in a dispute with the

Baltimore Gazette concerning educational policy in Maryland's public schools, September 9, 1869. The letter is very brief; additional information in mounted newspaper clippings. Much of the debate revolves around the treatment of slavery in Maryland school-books.

.21 —— Crandall, Albert Rogers.
Papers, ca. 1861-1912. 26 items. In these Civil War letters written from encampments in Virginia to his cousins in Alfred Center, N.Y., Crandall depicts the life of a soldier in the 23rd Regiment, N.Y. Volunteers, including descriptions of marching, standing guard, bivoacking, the battles of Fredericksburg (1862) and Rappahannock Station (1863), the hostility of southern women, "contraband" Negro children in camp, and a Negro "camp meeting"; asks about happenings at home; comments on the draft, the Virginia countryside, and the laziness of its inhabitants who lack the Yankee energy to utilize its resources; praises both McClellan and Burnside (citing their popularity among the troops) and Lincoln's Christian attitude towards the enemy; criticizes both the abolitionists' vindictiveness towards the South and the dismissal of McClellan, which he blames on northern politicking; reveals prejudice against the Irish; approves Negro slavery and dreads to think of Negroes emigrating North. Also, a pamphlet (19 pp., 1912) from the 30th Annual Reunion of the 23rd Regiment, N.Y. Volunteers.

.22 —— Cushman, Robert Eugene, 1889- . collector.
Papers, 1940-50. 19 boxes. Correspondence, notes, and printed matter relating to civil liberties in the U.S., collected with the support of a Rockefeller Foundation grant for the study of the "relation of civil rights to the control of subversive activities."

.23 —— Dalley family.
Papers, 1883-1908. 1 box. Correspondence and other papers pertaining to Francis Kernan Dalley's law practice in Ithaca, N.Y., and to the pension claim of a Negro Civil War veteran.

.24 —— Facts on Film.
Papers, 1954-67. Microfilm. Contains materials on civil rights and race relations in the South. See Race Relations Information Center, Nashville, Tenn., for a full description.

.25 —— Fowler family.
Fowler and Wells families' papers, 1838-1901. Correspondence, articles, and other papers relating to the practice of phrenology. Correspondents include Susan B. Anthony, Sarah Grimké, Horace Mann, and Elizur Wright.

.26 —— Fraser, Helen Anderson, 1902- .
Papers, 1918-62. ca. 4 ft. Diaries (1918-54), correspondence, reports, newsletters, press releases, programs, posters, and other items pertaining to Miss Fraser's interest in the Albany Inter-Racial Council, the New York State Commission Against Discrimination, Unitarian Church work, folklore studies, and many other civic and cultural activities. Restricted.

.27 —— Gallwey, Sydney Hollingsworth, 1921- .
Miscellaneous, 1959, 1960, 1962. Paper presented (January 30, 1962) before the Ithaca Council for Equality at St. John's Church entitled "Early Slaves and Freemen of Tompkins County." A biographical sketch of Peter Webb (b. ca. 1792-d. 1866), born in slavery in Virginia and brought to Tompkins County by the Speed family in 1805. Webb obtained his freedom in 1818 after which he married and made his home in the Ithaca area (16 pp. pamphlet). Also includes the author's impressions of his visit to the Brown Farm at North Elba, N.Y., with comments on the life and career of Brown (July 28, 1959, 10 pp. pamphlet).

.28 —— Gould family.
Papers, ca. 1823-69. 6 v. and 1 reel of micro-

film. Contains letters (1862-68) from John Stanton Gould (1810-74), New York State legislator, mentioning his interest in the antislavery movement, among other subjects.

NY46.29 — Gould, Stephen Wanton, 1781-1838.
Diaries, 1823-32. Entry (December 12, 1825), describes the embarkation of a number of Negroes whose ultimate destination was Liberia, where they were to settle under the auspices of the American Colonization Society.

.30 — Greig, John.
Papers, 1794-1870. John C. Adams, associated with William Adams, in a letter to Greig, discusses the tariff, slavery, and John C. Calhoun, and urges that it is essential to split the South from the West in the political struggles of the day (January 8, 1846).

.31 — Griffith, Owen.
Letters, 1856, 1863. 3 items. In a letter (1856) to his brother, Griffith describes his job, high prices in Racine, and the recent Wisconsin gubernatorial election; in two letters (March, 1863) to his brother from the headquarters of the 22nd Regiment of Wisconsin Volunteers near Nashville, Tenn., Capt. Griffith comments on army life, some battle experiences, and Union deserters, thinks the Administration is "honest" and doing its best to crush the "unholy rebellion," mentions southerners' efforts to reclaim "contraband" Negroes from the Union ranks, denounces southern slaveholders, a General Gilbert, Copperheads, and the State of Kentucky, and states that if Fremont had had his way "this whole thing could have been put down long before this."

.32 — Hallett, Samuel.
Papers, 1834-64. 25 items and 2 v. In part, microfilm. Banker. Correspondence, diaries, and other papers. The diaries contain descriptions of antislavery meetings in Exeter Hall, among other subjects.

.33 — Hathaway family.
Papers, 1827-1910. 214 items. Letters and papers of Henry B. Hathaway and other members of a Quaker family interested in temperance, abolition, and education, who lived mainly in Watkins Glen, Schuyler Co., N.Y.

.34 — Hatheway family.
Papers, 1852-ca. 1857. Includes an uncounted number of letters from Miss Elizabeth Dorothea Hatheway (1823-1908) of Solon, Cortland County, N.Y., written to members of her family in the North during the years when she taught in the South, first at an Episcopal Boarding School in Ashwood, Maury County, Tenn., then at another church boarding school, and later as governess to Miss Helen Johnstone, whose mother owned "Annandale," a large plantation about sixteen miles from Jackson, Miss. Letters include descriptions of cotton picking and other aspects of plantation life, mention of her work giving religious instruction to the Negroes, and comments on slavery in general.

.35 — Henry W. Sage collection.
Papers, 1836-1919. Letter to the Rev. Henry Wilson, secretary of the African Colonization Society of Brooklyn, concerning $500 borrowed from Sage (August 7, 1867).

.36 — Howard, Harrison.
Papers, 1848-86. 720 items and 3 v. Secretary of the Peoples' College Association. Correspondence, clippings, and other papers relating to the Peoples' College movement. Correspondents include Henry Ward Beecher, Horace Greeley, and Gerrit Smith.

.37 — Howland, Emily, 1827-1929.
Papers, 1797-1838. 2 ft. and 8 boxes. Educator, reformer, philanthropist. Largely Miss Howland's incoming letters (ca. 1850-1929) which report alleged fraudulent solicitations for support of the Negro refugees in Canada (1852), discuss the misuse of Quaker aid to

contrabands in the U.S. (1863), tell of the trials of those attempting to establish schools for escaped slaves and freedmen in the South (1864-71), are critical of the workings of the Freedmen's Bureau (1866) and discuss life at Oberlin College including a recounting of President Charles Grandison Finney's opinion of John Brown and other abolitionists (ca. 1860-61); also occasional communications regarding a northerner's scheme for colonizing Northumberland County, Va., the woman suffrage movement in New York State, the temperance crusade, the Universal Peace Union and National Arbitration League of Washington, and women's higher education in Great Britain. Among the correspondents are Lillie Devereux Blake, Mary E. Bowman, Gulielma Breeds, Emma V. Brown, Phoebe Hathaway, S. Salley Holley, Henry Ince, J.R. Johnson, Alfred H. Love, E. Nash, Elsie Peabody, L.W. Stibbins, and Julia A. Wilbur. Also, papers of the related Howland and Talcot (Tallcott) families (1797-1932), including correspondence concerning the Hicksite controversy and the influence of Wilburism in the Scipio, N.Y., Meeting and elsewhere in the Society of Friends. The boxes include letters (ca. 1800, 1832-1928), to Emily Howland from her family, friends, and business acquaintances; letters (ca. 300, 1907-28) from persons concerned with Negro schools and other educational institutions which she helped to found or in which she was interested (includes nine letters from Booker T. Washington, 1894-1909); and other materials.

.38 — Hull, Charles Henry, 1864-1936.
Papers, ca. 1850-1945. Thirtieth Annual Report of the Philadelphia Female Anti-Slavery Society, Philadelphia, Pa., 1864. Also includes letter of Jacob Gould Schurman to Hull, concerning the "negress in the dormitory problem," September 30, 1914.

.39 — Ingersoll, Thomas Jefferson, ca. 18 ?-18 ?.
Letters, 1834-61. In letter from Cheneyville, La., to Massachusetts relatives, Ingersoll calls slavery an evil, but takes a states' rights, anti-abolitionist position, May 9, 1842; mentions flourishing position of overseers, wages they command, June 19, 1846; gives views on Kansas-Nebraska bill, supports popular sovereignty, April 27, 1854.

.40 — Krueger, June and Gilbert. collectors.
Letters, 1861-65. Letter (December 15, 1865), Shreveport, La., from C.L. Beebe to Lavinia Obreham, concerning a recent one hundred mile march; encampment and duty with Negro troops; reactions of Union Army troops to use of Negroes and soldiers' opinion on Negro suffrage; number of casualties. Microfilm.

.41 — Ledyard family.
Papers collected by Helen Lincklaen Fairchild, 1793-1916. 6 items, 30 v. and 5 reels of microfilm. Microfilm copies of originals in the possession of the Remington estate. Correspondence and other papers of the Ledyard family of Cazenovia, N.Y. Collection contains business and personal letters with references to local politics and slavery, among other topics; and miscellaneous papers pertaining to the American Colonization Society and the Oneida County Anti-slavery Society.

.42 — Lovejoy, Elijah P.
Broadside, November 7, 1837. "The Last Speech to the Citizens of Alton" by Rev. Lovejoy, who was murdered in defense of "The Liberty of the Press," containing references to anti-slavery.

.43 — McCall family.
Papers, 1749-1924. Contains Ansel J. McCall's correspondence with James F. Chamberlain (1837-63) and James S. McLaury (1837-98), both Union College classmates. One letter of C. Augusta Sheldon, cousin of Ansel (November 18, 1884); also will of James Faulkner,

Steuben County, N.Y., makes references to slaves (November 17, 1812).

NY46.44 — McElheny family.
Papers, 1846-1907. ca. 100 items. These family papers include diaries (1853-55, 1855-63), kept by Thomas J. McElheny and his wife Adelaide (Ada) Taber, concerning their daily activities in Dryden, N.Y., news of friends and relatives, some travel within the state, and church attendance and also containing many comments on political and social phenomena such as the defeat of Fremont and the election of Buchanan in 1856, the problem of local drunkenness (1859), the "murder" of John Brown, the slavery question, the nomination and election of Lincoln, South Carolina secession threats and the need for the North to hold firm, the murderer Rulloff, the sermon of a Negro clergyman from Syracuse and his unsuccessful attempt to raise money for fugitive slaves (December 23, 1860), the Civil War, the election of Seymour (1862) and other topics and materials.

.45 — Mattison, H.
"The Impending Crisis of 1860; or the Present Connection of the Methodist Episcopal Church with Slavery, and Our Duty in Regard to It," by H. Mattison of the Black River Conference. New York: Mason Brothers, No. 46 Walker Street, 1859. 136 pp. pamphlet.

.46 — Morgan, Edwin Barber, 1806-81.
Papers, 1849-54. 302 items. U.S. Representative from New York. Papers concerned principally with elections in the 25th Congressional District of New York in 1850, when Morgan, Whig candidate on a platform of high protectionism, free soil, and the repeal of the Fugitive Slave Law, was defeated by the Loco-Foco candidate, Thomas Y. How.

.47 — Morrill, Justin Smith, 1810-98.
Papers, 1814-1937. 4 ft. Statesman and financier. Correspondence, drafts of speeches, pamphlets and other printed matter, mainly relating to the Civil War and Reconstruction, and the status of the freed Negro.

.48 — Nolen, John, Sr.
Papers. Plans and maps. The city planner, John Nolen, planned numerous new towns in Florida during the land boom of the 1920's. Since these were complete towns being planned, it can be seen that there is a district and identified Negro section with its own schools, park and business section bounded from the rest of town by industry, railroad lines, etc. The most striking example is Venice, Fla., where Harlem Village has streets named Hampton, Armstrong, Lincoln, and Tuskegee.

.49 — Pamphlets pertaining to Negroes.
Miscellaneous. American Slavery As It Is: Testimony of a Thousand Witnesses, published by the American Anti-Slavery Society (1839, 224 pp.); Sixth Annual Report of the Colonization Society of the City of New York (1838, 46 pp.); and Shall Slavery Be Extended?, a speech by Hon. W.A. Sackett, of New York (March 4, 1850, 8 pp.), concerning the President's message communicating the Constitution of California.

.50 — Parker, Addison B., 1869-1944.
Papers, ca. 1873-1944. 6 v. and ca. 130 items. Civic leader; member of the Republican State Committee; deputy secretary of State of New York, 1915-20; Grand Patriarch, I.O.O.F., and publisher of the Lodge Record. Papers of the Parker family of Watertown include six clippings scrapbooks and photograph albums, mainly relating to Parker's civic, political, and fraternal duties, but also containing family photos; ca. 120 letters (December 1917-April 1919) from his son, 2nd Lieutenant Fred M. Parker, relating to his experiences with the Motor Transportation Corps of the A.E.F., and referring to the service of Negro soldiers; and related printed material.

.51 — Pfeiffer, Dorothy S. collector.
Hill, Atkinson, Fleming family papers, 1774-1916. ca. 2 ft. Business and personal correspondence and miscellaneous papers of the Hill, Atkinson, Fleming, Greene, and Popham families of Scarsdale, N.Y., and Bellows Falls, Vt. Includes a letter from Charles Carmer to his sister while in military service in Washington, D.C., in which he comments on the capture of a runaway slave; and a bill of sale and receipt (1808) for purchase of Negro slaves in Georgia.

.52 — Pratt family.
Papers, 1758-1903. The bulk of this material (1853-1903, 43 items), is made up of letters received by Horace L. Edgar Pratt, a Protestant Episcopal rector on Staten Island, and pertain in some way to that denomination; a Civil War draft exemption certificate issued to John A. Kernochan, September 10, 1863, and miscellaneous ms and printed items. The remainder consists of Queens County documents mainly pertaining to Joseph Lawrence and relatives and including a slave bill of sale (1770).

.53 — Rawlins, James Hyndford.
Journal, 1873. Account of visit to a public school for Negro children in Cincinnati, November 14, 1873, and Howard University in Washington, D.C., November 20, 1873.

.54 — Richmond, Juda L., 1807-68.
Family papers, 1844-62. 1 reel microfilm. Diary (January 30-December 7, 1844) in which Richmond describes his activities as a Baptist preacher in Forestville, N.Y., and neighboring town; also makes an attack on the institution of slavery, entry of July 4th.

.55 — Risley, Elijah, 1787-1870.
Letter, February 11, 1850. Photostat copy. Member of Congress from Western New York. Letter to General Risley, Washington, D.C., from Orris Crosby, Belvidere, Boone County, Ill., concerning a claim against the federal government; in commenting on the question of the extension of slavery into the territories, Crosby remarks, "Slavery can not exist in our new Territories...Negroes know enough to run away. They also know enough to make good and even pious Mexicans and Britons but they never can be Americans."

.56 — Rogers, Publius Virgilius, 1824-95.
Papers, 1850-1918. Includes a pamphlet The Doom of Slavery in the Union-Its Safety, 1860.

.57 — Schurman, Jacob Gould, 1854-1942.
Papers, 1878-1942. Letterbook #27 contains a copy of President Schurman's letter of April 5, 1911, p. 683, to various university presidents requesting information on their dormitory housing policies in regard to Negro women; also, copy of his letter to Mrs. Martin, adviser of women, Sage College, on the same subject (April 10, 1911, pp. 693-4).

.58 — Selden family.
Papers, 1785-1857, 1914, 1920. Photostat. In a letter to George W. Gale, William J. Selden describes the island of St. Croix, commenting on the excellent highway system, the abundance of meats, fruits, and other foodstuffs, the weather, churches, slavery, and the living conditions, education, and customs of the Negro population, Dec. 30, 1839.

.59 — Shelton family.
Papers, 1783-1934. 337 items. Chiefly correspondence between members of the interrelated Tappan, Brewster, Tomlinson, and Shelton families, emphasizing religious, missionary, and educational experiences. Includes letters (1827) from Anne Tappan at Catherine Beecher's school, Hartford, Conn.; letters (1834) from Lucy Tappan, a teacher at a religious academy in Detroit, relating to local conditions, Catherine Beecher, and nativist fears; letters from Joseph Tomlinson, Jr. (1851-52), in New York City containing detailed comments on American sympathy for Cuban insur-

rectionists, a meeting for Negro colonization, the preaching of Henry Ward Beecher, and a Democratic-Republican Loco-Foco meeting.

NY46.60 — Shoemaker collection.
Miscellaneous, 1861-66. Marine Sergeant Shoemaker, in a series of letters written home to his parents in Pennsylvania during the Civil War, reflects the sentiments of the Marines on the slavery issue. Especially revealing are his comments on slavery in Washington, D.C., March 9, 1862, the northern copperheads, in a letter written from San Francisco, Cal. (June 2, 1863); and his suggestion that the slaves be brought into the Union ranks to join the actual fighting against their masters, from Washington, D.C. (January 11, 1862).

.61 — Sizer family.
Papers, 1811-71. 34 items and 1 v. Scrapbook of political editorials and correspondence (1839-63) by Thomas J. Sizer, largely from the Buffalo Daily Republic and the Buffalo Commercial Advertiser, with slavery as a particular subject; and other papers.

.62 — Slave bill of sale.
1808. Public vendue, Steuben County, female Negro child.

.63 — Smelzer family.
Papers, 1811-1941. Virgorous disapproval of the abolition movement is expressed by E.S. Buck, Chappell Hill, Washington County, Texas, in a letter to a New York State resident (January 1, 1860).

.64 — Smith, Gerrit.
Pamphlets, 1847-48. Speech of Gerrit Smith made at the National Convention of the Liberty party, on the character, scope, and duties of the Liberty party, at Buffalo, N.Y. (October 21, 1847).

.65 — Smith, Goldwin.
Papers, 1823-1912. Letter from Alex Cornwall (Washington, D.C.) containing notes on the position of the Negro in the U.S., March 6, 1890. Letter of Goldwin Smith to Lord Mount Stephen suggesting that an appropriate charitable foundation would be industrial education for the American Negro; praise of Hampton Institute (February 2, 1901). Letter of George K. Holmes, Chief, U.S. Dept. of Agriculture Division on Foreign Manufactures, to Smith, correcting Smith's statement that white men could not cultivate sugar cane and cotton, commenting on the economic position of the Negro, the problem of the Negro in the South, April 27, 1903.

.66 — Spalding, Lyman A.
Papers, 1815-69. ca. 320 items. Quaker merchant, reformer, and abolitionist, of Lockport, N.Y. Correspondence, printed matter, and other papers illustrating the intellectual history of western New York and antislavery sentiment in the North.

.67 — Stebbins, Amanda.
Letters, 1833-40. Miss Stebbins, Ithaca, N.Y., writes her sister, Sarah Stebbins, South Wilbraham, Mass. (August 28, 1835), mentions abolition; (May 4, 1837) mentions Gerrit Smith lecture a few days earlier at Presbyterian Church and the formation of an anti-slavery society.

.68 — Stuart, Lyman. collector.
Papers, 1806-81. Thomas Johnson of Jefferson, Md. (?), writes to his father-in-law that slaves are "selling 80 head for $65,000." He also comments that he would not sell a slave unless the slave wished to be sold and to agree on who his master shall be (March 22, 1837). Letter of John and George Coventry discuss Negro conditions in the West Indies (October, 1822-July, 1832). Letters to Hester R. Hopkins discuss an anti-slavery society at Auburn, N.Y., and Negro bondage in the South, 1836.

.69 — Taber family.
Papers, 1827-1906. Letter (December 25, 1856) from Henry Gifford of Elkader, Iowa, to S.D. Taber mentioning Presidents James Buchanan and Franklin Pierce and Kansas coming in as a free state.

.70 — Tape recording of Afro-American Lecture Series.
Tape recording and transcripts, 1968. Proceeding of symposia (speeches and panel discussions) including the following subjects: "Slavery and Racial Prejudice," (October 29, 1968); "Manpower Programs in the Ghetto: Private Business With Pride," (December 6, 1968); "Can White Bureaucracy Bring About Black Progress?" (November 1, 1968); "Racism in a White Society." (September 14, 1968); and "The Modern State Against the Blacks," (December 12, 1968).

.71 — Tubman, Harriet.
Miscellaneous. Printed materials including Bishop W.J. Walls', Harriet Tubman, an account of her work in the Underground Railroad and later as a spy and nurse for the Union forces (17 pp. pamphlet); Souvenir Program - Dedication of the Harriet Tubman Home, Auburn, N.Y. (April 30, 1953); Program - Third Annual Pilgrimage to the Harriet Tubman Home, Auburn, N.Y. (October 14, 1955); and a postcard showing a Harriet Tubman quilt design.

.72 — Turner family.
Papers, 1799-1891. 703 items. Largely letters written by members of the related Turner, Baker, and Wheeler families describing activities as they moved southward and westward from Massachusetts and New York. Letters (1824-71) from Marshall Wheeler relate to his activities as a clerk in Shelbyville, Ky., as a farm owner in Carthage, Ill., as the proprietor of a merchandising business at Quincy, Ill., and his life as a merchant, plantation and slave owner, and stock producer at Sabine and Cold Springs, Tex.

.73 — Vanderpoel.
Papers, 1837. 7 pp. pamphlet. "Speech of Mr. Vanderpoel, of New York, on the Resolution Declaring That Slaves Have No Right to Petition Congress;" delivered in the House of Representatives (February 11, 1837).

.74 — White, Andrew Dickson, 1832-1918.
Papers, 1845-1918. 102 ft. Educator and diplomat. Correspondence; mss of speeches, articles and books, and other papers. Correspondents include Ray Stannard Baker, Catherine Beecher, Henry Ward Beecher, Roscoe Conklin, Horace Greeley, Robert G. Ingersoll, Whitelaw Reid, Elihu Root, Carl Schurz, Gerrit Smith, Anson Phelps Stokes, Jr., Ida M. Tarbell, and Henry Villard. The White papers contain two letters from an A.L. Willard to White that are anti-slavery in content: January 5, 1854 (asks how to free slave population in the South and asks if he should contact the underground railroad); January 1, 1855 (was in North Carolina during the winter and reports his dislike of Kansas-Nebraska bill). In letters to White, March 13, 1854, May 15, 1854, and July 1, 1854, a J.W. Coit reports on the reaction in Andover, Mass., to the Kansas-Nebraska act and reports on the "Burns affair" in Boston. The papers for the period through 1874 contain at least three letters from a Charles M. Bliss to White reporting the reaction in Connecticut to the Kansas-Nebraska act. The letters are dated May 29, 1854; July 9, 1854; and June 8, 1854. In the July 9 letter, Bliss reports that Connecticut has passed or is passing an "act for the Defense of Liberty" which is directed at the Fugitive Slave Law and 'kidnappers." The White papers also contain a letter from a H.T. Thompson to Samuel J. May, Nov. 18, 1863. The letter is written from Nashville, Tenn. Thompson requests information on how the ex-slaves fare in Canadian climate after being freed through underground railroad. Thompson reports widespread opinion in border states that emancipation will result in

destruction or expatriation of Negro race ("that they may be as the Indians in short."). He also reports that Nashville is surrounded by camps, homes have been confiscated, occupation forces seem to be accepted by natives, and that slaves are being enlisted in northern armies. A letter from Alford Huzer to White containing a few remarks about Negroes to Summerville, S.C. (July 4, 1904); a petition of Archibald James and sixty other Negro citizens of the City of Rochester, N.Y., requests that they be allowed equal use of the common schools by right of their position as citizens and tax payers (February, 1867).

.75 — White, Ernest I. collector.
Family papers. Letters (December 4, 8, 1859) commenting that workers from the North, imported into Virginia to work in the salt mines, have been threatened by indignant slaveholders because of their abolitionist views. Also includes a letter to Hamilton White from salt manufacturers in Virginia: "It is rather a peculiar thing here now. The publick mind is considerable excited on the Harper's Ferry affair and we anticipate some difficulty in getting Negroes to do our work... We cannot depend upon white labour." (November 29, 1859).

.76 — White, William Pierrepont. collector.
Papers, 1728-1939. 60 ft. Correspondence, deeds, accounts, maps, surveys, pamphlets, and other papers reflecting the westward and southward movement of the White and related families. The early papers relate to the White family of Middletown, Conn., and include information on slave sales. Includes a contract in regard to disposition of a runaway Negro slave belonging to Hugh White, (March 26, 1793); transfer of a "Negro wench" from Peter Waggoner to Hugh White (February 22, 1797); resolution of the free holders of Oneida County respecting the limitation of slavery (December 24, 1819). In a letter to his father-in-law, Hugh White, E.D. Walcott mentions the purchase of a Negro man "24 years of age and a very able stout fellow for which I paid $550 Dollars" (January 28, 1825).

.77 — Wilder, Burt Green.
Papers, 1841-1925. Correspondence between Wilder and Miss Margaret Ware Deland (1857-1945), dated October 17 and 21, 1914 and May 13 and 16, 1915, in which Miss Deland expressed her views on the evils of miscegenation and Wilder argued against them. Includes correspondence, newspaper clippings, pamphlets, and other printed material pertaining to Negro soldiers and their service in the Civil War. The Wilder papers include a special file devoted to the records of the 54th and 55th Massachusetts Infantry and the 5th Massachusetts Cavalry, military regiments containing companies of Negro troops. In the regular correspondence file is a newspaper clipping from the Boston Transcript (January, 1898) titled "The Bravest Colored Soldier," relating the exploits of Sergeant William Carney, a Negro soldier who served in Company C of the 54th Massachusetts Regiment; and a letter from John Edward Bruce to Wilder (January 11, 1913), containing Bruce's comments on the Negro as a soldier. Includes a letter from Edward Bradford Titchener (1867-1927) expressing his views on miscegenation, dated May 21, 1915.

.78 — Willers, Diedrich.
Papers, 1826-1927. Draft of a political speech (written after Civil War, ca. 1865) by Rev. Willers during a meeting of the Democratic party of Seneca County. The speech is in behalf of Horatio Seymour, Hoffman, and the Democratic party in general. The Republican government is accused of heavy taxation, unnecessary armed forces, unjust action against the white population of the Southern States, helping Negroes to be citizens who already try to be assembly-men, judges, etc.

.79 — Woodruff, Mrs. Percy.
Woodruff collection, 1789-1938. 1496 items. Correspondence and other papers of a number of related families of Preston, Chenango Co., N.Y. Kaercher family papers include letters (1846-50) to Kaercher when he was a minister at Peninsula and Burton, Ohio, commenting on education, economic and social conditions; and Kaercher's correspondence during the Civil War with the Women's Central Association of Relief; 3 boxes of sermons with a few antimasonic and antislavery items; and commissions from and reports to the American Home Missionary Society. Pamphlet issued by the American Board of Commissioners for Foreign Missions (20 pp.), contains two letters from ministers defending the acceptance of contributions from slave owners.

NY47   CORNELL UNIVERSITY, OFFICE OF REGIONAL RESOURCES AND DEVELOPMENT (1965). 14850. Tel 607 256-1000. Oliver C. Winston, Dir.
The program envisioned by the Office of Regional Resources and Development is a pioneering effort in demonstrating how a university, such as Cornell, can employ its vast resources of talent, knowledge, imagination and leadership in assisting in the long-range development of a region of which it is an important part.

JAMAICA

NY48   NATIONAL CONFERENCE OF CHRISTIANS AND JEWS (NCCJ), QUEENS REGION (1954). 92-32 Union Hall St., 11433. Tel 212 657-3620. Herman Ebeling, Dir. Inquiries answered, referrals made, consultation.
NCCJ is a civic organization engaged in a nationwide program of intergroup education. It has enlisted people of all backgrounds, who without compromise of conscience or of their distinctive and important religious and racial identities work together to build better relationships.
Publ.: Newsletter, quarterly; NCCJ Report; Pamphlets.

NY49   QUEENS BOROUGH PUBLIC LIBRARY. 89-11 Merrick Blvd., 11432. Tel 212 739-1900. Harold W. Tucker, Dir.

.1   Carter G. Woodson Reference Collection.
Books. ca. 175 v. Books by and about black men in America, including 120 books on the history of the Negro American.

KATONAH

NY50   JOHN JAY HOMESTEAD, JAY LIBRARY (1959). 10536. Tel 914 232-5651. Lewis C. Rubenstein, Curator of History.

.1   Anti-Slavery pamphlet collection.
Pamphlets. Materials concerning anti-slavery matters, pamphlets of William Jay and John Jay, II.

KINDERHOOK

NY51   COLUMBIA COUNTY HISTORICAL SOCIETY LIBRARY (1936). 12106. Tel 518 684-4055. Mary L. Thomas, Librn.

.1   Van Alstyne family.
Papers, 1667-1833. 145 items. In part, transcript. Conveyances of land, leases, agreements, contracts, sales of Negro slaves, and other papers.

MARYKNOLL

NY52   CATHOLIC FOREIGN MISSION SOCIETY OF AMERICA (MARYKNOLL) (1911), MARYKNOLL INFORMATION LIBRARY. 10545. Tel 914 941-7590. Mrs. Carla Quijano, Librn. Copying, typing, inquiries answered. The Maryknoll Information Library serves the edi-

torial department in the publication of <u>Maryknoll Maga-zine</u> and other Maryknoll publications.
Publ.: <u>Maryknoll Magazine</u>, monthly.

.1   Race relations information.
     Materials, 1960- . ca. 300 items and 8 file
     drawers. Books, pamphlets, and clippings. Also
     included is a collection of news releases from
     religious organizations of all denominations, such
     as B'nai B'rith and Religious News Service. The
     library subscribes to numerous African and Afro-
     American periodicals.

MINEOLA

NY53   NATIONAL CONFERENCE OF CHRISTIANS AND JEWS
       (NCCJ), NASSAU-SUFFOLK REGION (1962). 212 Front
       St., 11501. Tel 516 747-0933. Herman Ebeling, Dir.
       Inquiries answered, referrals made, consultation.

MOUNT VERNON

NY54   THE CITY OF MOUNT VERNON, COMMISSION ON HUMAN
       RIGHTS (1963). City Hall, 10550. Tel 914 668-2000.
       Mrs. Vida H. Byas, Exec. Dir.
       The Commission investigates incidents of tension and
       conflict, conducts educational programs and studies in
       human relations, and generally works to foster mutual
       respect and understanding among all groups. Formerly
       the Mayor's Committee on Intergroup Relations.
       Publ.: <u>Equal Rights</u>, quarterly newsletter.

NY55   MOUNT VERNON PUBLIC LIBRARY. 28 S. First St., 10550.
       Tel 914 668-1840. Emanuel Dondy, Dir. Interlibrary
       loan, bibliographies prepared, copying, inquiries an-
       swered.

.1   George Edmund Haynes Memorial Collection.
     Materials. In memory of George Edmund Haynes,
     Negro sociologist and teacher. ca. 150 v. Collec-
     tion includes complete set of the Arno (1968) re-
     prints of Negro literature, and partial runs of
     <u>Crisis</u>, <u>Journal of Negro Education</u>, <u>Journal of
     Negro History</u>, <u>Negro History Bulletin</u>, and <u>Phylon</u>.

NEW ROCHELLE

NY56   GLENWOOD LAKE ASSOCIATION. 271 Storer Ave., 10801.
       Tel 914 235-1855. Dr. Alvin I. Kosak, Pres.
       The Association works to maintain neighborhood inte-
       gration. Records restricted.
       Publ.: <u>The Backfence</u>, irregular newsletter.

NEW YORK

NY57   A. PHILIP RANDOLPH EDUCATIONAL FUND. 260 Park
       Ave. S., 10010. Tel 212 533-8000. Bayard Rustin,
       Exec. Dir.
       The Fund carries on a program of education, voter
       registration and civil rights action. It conducts ap-
       prenticeship training for minority youths seeking jobs
       in the building trades, and holds conferences on the
       problems of race and poverty. In addition, the Fund
       has published analyses on problems relating to the
       civil rights struggle.
       Publ.: Pamphlet series.

NY58   A. PHILIP RANDOLPH INSTITUTE. 217 W. 125th St.,
       10027. Tel 212 666-9510. Bayard Rustin, Exec. Dir.
       The Institute was formed to raise economic issues that
       underlie the civil rights movement. It prepares educa-
       tional materials for all civil rights groups.
       Publ.: Pamphlets, conference programs.

.1   Randolph, Asa Philip, 1889- .
     Papers.

NY59   ACTION TRAINING COALITION (ATC). c/o MUST, 235 E.
       49th St., 10017. Tel 212 753-8462. Randy Nugent,
       Pres. and Nat. Coordinator. Bibliographies prepared,
       literature searches, copying, inquiries answered,
       referrals made.
       ATC works to combat racism in the white community,

to establish and maintain high standards for action
training, and to develop common strategies for social
change. Occasional papers, reports, case studies and
process interpretations are on file with the central
library service of the Institute of the Church in Urban
Industrial Society, 800 West Belden Ave., Chicago, Ill.
60614.

NY60   AFRAM ASSOCIATES, INC. (AAI) (1968). 103 E. 125 St.,
       10035. Tel 212 876-9255. Preston Wilcox, Pres.
       AAI serves as a consultant-enabler in the areas of
       public and higher education, community development,
       staff development and charrettes, conference planning
       and management, materials development and inter-
       organizational coordination. It is in the process of
       developing an Action Library, a vehicle designed to
       circulate new ideas, unpublished statements and action-
       oriented proposals to those who are usually unreached
       by professional journals, national periodicals and the
       like.
       Publ.: <u>Selected Bibliography on White Institutional
       Racism</u> (1969); Publications list.

NY61   AFRO-AMERICAN RESEARCH INSTITUTE, INC. 244 E.
       46th St., 10017. Tel 212 986-5939. Daniel H. Watts,
       Editor-in-chief.
       The Institute publishes <u>Liberator</u>, a magazine of black
       opinion and analysis of trends in Afro-American com-
       munities, and in Africa, Asia, and Latin America.
       Publ.: <u>The Liberator</u>, monthly magazine.

NY61a AFRO-AMERICAN STUDIO FOR ACTING AND SPEECH
       (1966). 15 W. 126th St., 10027. Tel 212 534-9608.
       Ernie McClintock, Dir.
       Theatrical training and productions for and about
       black people.

.1   Afro-American Studio for Acting and Speech Library.
     Miscellaneous. Books (ca. 400 v.), unpublished
     playscripts, newspaper clippings, and magazines.
     Relates chiefly to black theatre.

NY62   ALFRED P. SLOAN FOUNDATION (1934). 630 Fifth Ave.,
       10020. Tel 212 582-0450. Madelyn E. Perkins, Librn.
       The Foundation makes grants-in-aid to educational and
       charitable institutions of recognized standing. In the
       area of race relations it works chiefly to support the
       efforts to expand and strengthen educational opportuni-
       ties for Negroes and disadvantaged youth. Among
       programs supported are the Cooperative College Devel-
       opment Program and National Medical Fellowships.
       Publ.: <u>Annual Report</u>.

.1   Alfred P. Sloan Foundation.
     Files, 1934- . Records, correspondence, reports
     and other papers concerning the operation of the
     Foundation and programs funded by it. Restricted.

NY63   AMALGAMATED PUBLISHERS, INC. (API). 310 Madison
       Ave., 10017. Tel 212 682-5452. Arthur Ralph, Eastern
       Sales Mgr.
       API serves as the national representative and official
       selling agent for 60 Negro member newspapers in the
       U.S.

NY64   AMERICAN ACADEMY OF ARTS AND LETTERS LIBRARY
       (1930). 633 W. 155th St., 10032. Tel 212 286-1480.
       Alyce Nash, Librn. Inquiries answered.
       The Library contains the works of the members and
       books concerning those members. Open to scholars by
       appointment.
       Publ.: Proceedings; Yearbooks.

.1   Baldwin, James, 1924- .
     Papers. ca. 20 items. Writer. Includes corre-
     spondence relating to the Institute of Arts and
     Letters, and transcript of remarks given at a
     dinner meeting, April, 1964, and newspaper clip-
     pings.
.2   Correspondence collections, 1874- .
     Materials. ca. 5400 items. Correspondence of
     authors, painters, sculptors, composers, historians,
     and others, chiefly relating to the American Acad-
     emy of Arts and Letters and to the National Insti-
     tute of Arts and Letters. Correspondents repre-
     sented by more than twenty items include William
     E.B. DuBois.

.3   Ellison, Ralph, 1914- .
        Papers. Writer. Included are correspondence (56
        items) relating to Institute affairs, and newspaper
        clippings (1966-67).
.4   Higginson, Thomas Wentworth, 1823-1911.
        Papers, 1884-1911. 40 items. Author. Correspon-
        dence chiefly relating to the National Institute of
        Arts and Letters and the American Academy of
        Arts and Letters, and mss of Higginson's poems.
        Names prominently mentioned are Julia Ward Howe
        and Edith Wharton.
.5   Hughes, Langston, 1902-67.
        Papers. Writer. Included are correspondence (34
        items) relating to the Institute of Arts and Letters,
        typed ms of "Sorrow for a Midget" (6 drafts), lec-
        ture programs, playbills, book lists, published
        songs and librettos, and an appreciation of Carl Van
        Vechten.
.6   Lawrence, Jacob, 1917- .
        Papers. Writer. Included are correspondence (56
        items) relating to Institute affairs, and newspaper
        clippings (1966-67).

NY65   AMERICAN CIVIL LIBERTIES UNION (ACLU) (1920), LI-
        BRARY AND ARCHIVES (1920). 156 Fifth Ave., 10010.
        Tel 212 675-5990. Edward A. Lewin, Chief of Library
        and Arch. Inquiries answered, referrals made, consul-
        tation.
        The ACLU works to maintain and advance civil liberties
        including the freedom of association, press, religion,
        and speech, and the rights to the franchise, to due pro-
        cess of law, and to equal protection of the laws for all
        people throughout the U.S. and its possessions. The Li-
        brary and Archives provides information to the ACLU
        staff and to outside requests for research in civil liber-
        ties.
        Publ.: Civil Liberties, monthly newspaper; Annual Re-
            port; Inventory of Race Relations Archives,
            yearly; Pamphlets, reports, and news releases.

    .1   American Civil Liberties Union Archives.
            1912- . Books, pamphlets, vf, theses, mss, corre-
            spondence, clippings, records, and other materials
            classified under Equality Before the Law. The col-
            lection includes correspondence, records of min-
            utes, and working papers of the Equality Committee
            of the ACLU National Board, and of legal cases in
            which the ACLU has been involved. Among subjects
            mentioned are race relations, education, employ-
            ment, housing, public accommodations, voting
            rights, private organizational discrimination, court
            procedings, welfare recipients, and indigents. The
            Princeton University Library holds the ACLU
            archives, 1914 to four years prior to any current
            date.

NY66   AMERICAN COUNCIL FOR NATIONALITIES SERVICE
        (ACNS) (1918). 20 W. 40th St., 10018. Tel 212 279-
        2715. J. Frank Dearness, Exec. Dir. Inquiries an-
        swered, referrals made, consultation.
        ACNS is a national, non-profit organization which pro-
        motes understanding and cooperation between the many
        nationality and racial groups in the U.S., and assists
        immigrants to adjust to American life and become fully
        participating citizens. ACNS has 36 member agencies
        which provide services for immigrants and conduct pro-
        grams in intergroup relations, international understand-
        ing, and public education in conjunction with the national
        press and radio. Formed by merger of the Common
        Council for American Unity and the American Federa-
        tion of International Institutes.
        Publ.: Out of Many..., quarterly newsletter; Pamphlets,
            news releases, and bibliographies.

    .1   American Council for Nationalities Service.
            Files. Historical material and agency records are
            housed in the Immigration Archives, University of
            Minnesota.

NY67   AMERICAN DOCUMENTARY FILMS, INC. (1966). 336 W.
        84th St., 10024. Tel 212 799-7440. Henry Hoffmann,
        Distribution Dir. Bibliographies prepared.
        American Documentary Films is a non-profit corpora-
        tion which produces and distributes films that document
        and examine social change from a human and indepen-

dent point of view. The organization seeks to explore
the causes and effects of social problems and to stimulate a public search for solutions.
Publ.: Bibliography of films dealing with lives of black
    people; Film lists, brochures, and fliers; Posi-
    tion papers on political, social, and cultural is-
    sues.

.1   American Documentary Films.
        Films for distribution include subjects such as
        black liberation, capitalism and domestic protest,
        the labor movement and its relation to current
        movement for social change, black communism,
        ghetto housing, poverty, welfare, community orga-
        nizing, and other social issues.

NY68   AMERICAN FEDERATION OF LABOR-CONGRESS OF
        INDUSTRIAL ORGANIZATIONS, CIVIL RIGHTS COM-
        MITTEE. 218 W. 40th St., 10022. Tel 212 889-6464.

NY69   AMERICAN FILM INSTITUTE (THE COMMUNITY FILM
        WORKSHOP COUNCIL). 26 W. 56th St., 10019. Tel 212
        247-0945.
        Among many other activities, the Institute conducts on-
        the-job training of black apprentices in film production
        skills.

NY70   AMERICAN FRIENDS SERVICE COMMITTEE (AFSC), COM-
        MUNITY RELATIONS DIVISION, NEW YORK METRO-
        POLITAN REGIONAL OFFICE. 15 Rutherford Place,
        10003. Tel 212 777-4600. Regional Dir.

NY71   AMERICAN INSTITUTE FOR MARXIST STUDIES (1964),
        LIBRARY (1964). 20 E. 30th St., 10016. Tel 212 689-
        4530. Herbert Aptheker, Dir. Bibliographies prepared,
        inquiries answered, consultation.
        The Institute seeks to bring Marxism, broadly defined,
        into the consciousness of U.S. scholarship, and to assist
        in the development of Marxian scholarship.
        Publ.: Newsletter, bimonthly; Occasional papers, bibli-
            ographies, monograph series, and historical
            series.

    .1   American Institute for Marxist Studies Library.
            The Library contains 7000 v. and bound periodicals
            in the area of Marxism and radicalism, and the
            papers of Elizabeth Gurley Flynn.

NY72   THE AMERICAN INSTITUTE OF ARCHITECTS (AIA), NEW
        YORK CHAPTER (1867). 20 W. 40th St., 10018. Tel
        212 565-1866. Mrs. Margot Henkel, Dir., Admin. and
        Finance.
        The New York Chapter, A.I.A., and the Architects' Re-
        newal Committee in Harlem (ARCH) co-sponsor a
        training program in architecture. Inquiries should be
        addressed to ARCH, 221 W. 116th St., New York, N.Y.
        10026.

NY73   AMERICAN JEWISH COMMITTEE (AJC) (1906), BLAUSTEIN
        LIBRARY (1939). 165 E. 56th St., 10022. Tel 212 751-
        4000. Harry J. Alderman, Library Dir.; Bertram H.
        Gold, Exec. V.Pres. Literature searches, inquiries
        answered, consultation.
        AJC is a national human relations agency devoted to
        intergroup understanding and the protection of civil
        liberties and human rights. The Institute of Human Re-
        lations serves as the national headquarters and as a
        center for research and education in the field of human
        relations.
        Publ.: AJC Newsletter, bimonthly; American Jewish
            Year Book, yearly; Commentary, monthly maga-
            zine; Recent Additions to the Library, monthly;
            Articles of Interest in Current Periodicals,
            monthly.

    .1   The Blaustein Library has materials on all aspects of
            intergroup relations and Jewish community rela-
            tions, including such topics as prejudice and dis-
            crimination, hate movements, civil rights and civil
            liberties, intergroup education, interreligious af-
            fairs and church-state problems, and religious,
            racial, and ethnic groups in American society. The
            holdings include books and pamphlets (ca. 40,000),
            ca. 1000 periodical and newspaper titles, and 50 vf.
            Open to qualified persons with permission.

.2 — American Jewish Committee Archives.
Files, 1906- . Records, reports, documents and other materials concerning the American Jewish Committee.

NY74   AMERICAN JEWISH CONGRESS, COMMISSION ON LAW AND SOCIAL ACTION (1918). 15 E. 84th St., 10028. Tel 212-879-4500. Joseph B. Robison, Dir. Inquiries answered, consultation, legal advice.
The Commission is a national human relations organization offering community education programs. It is especially concerned with religious liberty, racial and religious equality and freedom of expression.

NY75   AMERICAN JEWISH CONGRESS (1918), INFORMATION CENTER ON JEWISH-NEGRO RELATIONS (1970). 15 E. 84th St., 10028. Tel 212 879-4500. Libby Adelman, Dir. Inquiries answered, referrals made, consultation.
The Center collects, collates, and makes available to interested individuals and organizations all published materials dealing with activities in the area of Jewish-Negro relations.

.1   Information Center on Jewish-Negro Relations.
Files, 1970- . Included are reports, studies, press releases, newspaper and periodical articles, pamphlets, books, and other material pertaining to Jewish-Negro relations and activities, and a file of organizations actively working in this area.

NY76   AMERICAN JEWISH CONGRESS (1918), LIBRARY. 15 E. 84th St., 10028. Tel 212 879-4500. Will Maslow, Exec. Dir.
The Congress, a voluntary membership organization of American Jews, works to foster the unity and creative survival of the Jewish people, combat anti-Semitism and all forms of racism, combat and extend the democratic way of life, protect the rights and status of Jews everywhere, and advance civil rights and civil liberties to achieve full equality in a free society for all Americans.
Publ.: Congress Bi-Weekly; Judaism, quarterly.

.1   American Jewish Congress Library.
The Library includes materials on civil liberties, civil rights, discrimination, and church-state relations.

NY77   AMERICAN NEGRO LEADERSHIP CONFERENCE ON AFRICA. Suite 305, 15 E. 40th St., 10016. Tel 212 685-2260. Theodore E. Brown, Dir.
The Conference is an association sponsored by organizations having an interest in African affairs.

NY78   THE AMERICAN NUMISMATIC SOCIETY (1858). Broadway and 156th St., 10032. Tel 212 286-3030. Interlibrary loan, copying, inquiries answered.

.1   American Numismatic Society.
Collection of anti-slavery coins, medals and tokens. ca. 70 items. Chiefly 19th cent. American and English.

NY79   AMERICAN NURSES ASSOCIATION (1896). 10 Columbus Circle, 10019. Tel 212 582-7230. Mrs. Margaret F. Carroll, Dep. Exec. Dir. (Civil Rights Program). Inquiries answered.
The Association is a national professional organization of nurses whose program includes national, state and local activities directed toward equal opportunities within the nursing profession and the total community. Through their education program the Association distributes materials on federal civil rights policies involving health facilities.
Publ.: ANA in Action, quarterly newsletter; American Journal of Nursing, quarterly; Capitol Commentary, legislative newsletter; Economic Security News; Report to Members, biennial.

.1   American Nurses Association, Intergroup Relations Program.
Files, 1946- . Minutes and reports of committee meetings, reports and procedings of conventions, testimony before Congressional committees, correspondence, communications to state and district nurses associations and to membership, administrative reports on intergroup program, materials

on the Mary Mahoney Award, photographs, bulletins of State Nurses Association, and other materials.

NY80   AMERICAN SOCIETY OF AFRICAN CULTURE (AMSAC) (1956), LIBRARY (1956). Room 938, 101 Park Ave., 10017. Tel 212 683-6121. Elinor Bowles, Librn. Bibliographies prepared, inquiries answered.
The Society seeks to provide an understanding of the validity of African and Afro-American cultural contributions as a basis for mutual respect between Americans and Africans and between Africans and other citizens of the world. The Society is composed primarily of scholars, writers, and artists of African descent.
Publ.: African Forum, quarterly journal; AMSAC Newsletter, monthly.

.1   AMSAC Library.
Contains books, periodicals, and other materials on African literature and culture, the Negro American, and international relations. ca. 2000 v.

NY81   ANTI-DEFAMATION LEAGUE OF B'NAI B'RITH (1913), JACOB ALSON MEMORIAL LIBRARY (1939). 315 Lexington Ave., 10016. Tel 212 689-7400. Miss Marjorie Schloss, Librn. Interlibrary loan, copying.
The League is the educational and human relations arm of B'nai B'rith, a Jewish service organization. The League seeks to eliminate the defamation of Jews and other religious groups and to advance understanding among all groups. It develops extensive resource materials for community education programs and conducts research on anti-Semitism and intergroup relations. Audio-visual and printed resource materials are available from the League.
Publ.: Christian Friends Bulletin; ADL Bulletin, 10 issues per year; Facts; Rights; Law; Discriminations Report; Research Bulletin on Intergroup Relations, annually; Fact Finding Report; Research and Evaluation Report; Law Notes.

.1   Jacob Alson Memorial Library.
Contains extensive materials pertaining to fair employment practices, housing, and education.

NY82   ANTI-DEFAMATION LEAGUE OF B'NAI B'RITH, NEW YORK REGIONAL OFFICE. 315 Lexington Ave., 10016. Tel 212 689-7400. Morris S. Sass, Dir.

NY82a   ARCHITECTS' RENEWAL COUNCIL IN HARLEM (ARCH). 221 W. 116th St., 10026. Tel 212 666-9130.
ARCH, a black advocacy planning group of trained professionals, and the New York Chapter, American Institute of Architects, co-sponsor training programs in architecture.

NY83   ARTISTS CIVIL RIGHTS ASSISTANCE FUND. 342 W. 84th St., 10024. Tel 212 362-9821. Mrs. Warren Miller, Exec. Dir.
The Fund was formed to collect money from artists to be distributed to action groups.

NY84   BEHAVIORAL PUBLICATIONS. 2852 Broadway, 10025. Tel 212 662-3101.
Publ.: Community Mental Health Journal, bimonthly.

.1   Behavioral Publications.
Research files. Includes monographs and studies on such topics as indigenous non-professionals, workers' mental health, and the busing of Negro children.

NY84a   BLACK ECONOMIC RESEARCH CENTER (BERC) (1969). 112 W. 120th St., 10027. Tel 212 666-0310. Robert S. Browne, Dir.
BERC "is a privately funded, non-profit organization of black persons who are interested in focusing their attention and skills on the economic aspects of the black condition with a view toward discovering more effective ways to win for the black man his full measure of dignity, security, power, and economic well-being."
Publ.: The Review of Black Political Economy, 3 issues per year.

.1   Black Economic Research Center.
The Center houses a small collection of articles and data relating to black economic development.

NY85   BLACK THEATRE. The New Lafayette Theater, 200 W. 135th St., 10030. Tel 212 283-7350.
Publ.: Black Theater, bimonthly.

NY86   BLOOMINGDALE NEIGHBORHOOD CONSERVATION ASSOCIATION (1959). 868 Amsterdam Ave., 10025. Tel 212 865-7300. Florence Hirschman, Dir.
The Association works, in cooperation with the Building Department, for neighborhood improvement through enforcement of the Housing Code, and operates a free, integrated pre-school program, recreational programs, and parent education programs.

NY87   BOARD OF MISSIONS OF THE UNITED METHODIST CHURCH, NATIONAL DIVISION (1784). 475 Riverside Dr., 10027. Tel 212 749-0700. J. Edward Carothers, Assoc. Gen. Secy. Consultation.
The Board works to develop both the black parish and the black community through community organization and various aids for economic development.
Publ.: World Outlook, magazine; Response, magazine.

NY88   BROTHERHOOD-IN-ACTION (BIA) (1965), LIBRARY. 560 Seventh Ave., 10018. Tel 212 594-0350. Norman H. Perlstein, Exec. Dir. Consultation.
BIA is a non-profit, non-sectraian organization which seeks to further intergroup progress and understanding, by offering program services and facilities to qualified intergroup relations agencies for conferences and training programs.
Publ.: Human Relations Conference Summaries, semi-annually; BIA-NAIRO Directory of Intergroup Relations Agencies (1969).

.1   BIA Library.
Contains ca. 2500 items, including books, periodical titles, pamphlets, theses and dissertations, correspondence, clippings and tape recordings on such subjects as race relations, human and intergroup relations. Primarily for use in conference, consultation, and research efforts of the BIA staff. Restricted, in part.

NY89   BROTHERHOOD OF SLEEPING CAR PORTERS (1925). Suite 710, 103 E. 125th St., 10035. Tel 212 348-2245.

.1   Brotherhood of Sleeping Car Porters.
Files, 1925- .

NY90   BUREAU OF LABOR SERVICES, ECONOMIC DEVELOPMENT ADMINISTRATION, MAYOR'S COMMITTEE ON EXPLOITATION OF WORKERS (1957). 225 Broadway, 10007. Tel 212 566-4778. Harry Stiefel, Dir. Inquiries answered, referrals made, consultation.
The Committee was established to prevent exploitation of workers, to assist exploited workers, and to settle grievances and adjust complaints on job related problems. It deals with all types of exploitation, including minority group discrimination.
Publ.: Pamphlets pertaining to employment.

NY91   CARNEGIE CORPORATION OF NEW YORK (1911). 437 Madison Ave., 10022. Tel 212 753-3100. Alan Pifer, Pres.
The Corporation is a philanthropic foundation created for the advancement and diffusion of knowledge and understanding. Its program includes the support of educational and scientific research, publications, professional and scholarly societies and associations, fine arts, library service and educational institutions. The foundation often makes grants to organizations and institutions concerned with aiding Negroes in higher education, civil rights, black history and culture, legal aid, and problems of education.

NY92   CATHOLIC BOARD FOR MISSION WORK AMONG THE COLORED PEOPLE (1907). 335 Broadway, 10013. Tel 212 226-6843. Benjamin M. Horton, Dir.
The Board supports Sisters' teaching programs among Negroes.
Publ.: Our Colored Missions, monthly.

.1   Catholic Board for Mission Work Among the Colored People.
Files, 1907- . Correspondence, minutes of meet-

ings, financial records, and other materials dealing with the activities of the Board.

NY92a   CATHOLIC INTERRACIAL COUNCIL OF NEW YORK (1932). Suite 2207, 55 Liberty St., 10005. Tel 212 732-5417. Arthur D. Wright, Exec. Dir.
The Council works to foster interracial justice by educating the public to the prospects, situations, contributions and capabilities of black Americans.
Publ.: Interracial Review, monthly magazine.

.1   Catholic Interracial Council of New York.
Files, 1932- . Correspondence, reports, minutes, and other papers concerning the aims, history, and programs of the Council. In part, restricted.

NY93   CENTER FOR URBAN EDUCATION (1965), LIBRARY. 105 Madison Ave., 10016. Tel 212 889-7277. Daniel Wood, Chief Librn. Interlibrary loan, bibliographies prepared, inquiries answered, referrals made.
The Center is an educational research and development corporation chartered by the New York State Board of Regents and contracted as a regional educational laboratory by the U.S. Office of Education. It designs, tests, develops, and introduces new curricular programs into metropolitan-area schools; emphasis also is on programs that seek ways to increase more effective community involvement in urban school system.
Publ.: The Urban Review, bimonthly; The Center Forum, monthly.

.1   Center for Urban Education Library.
Contains some 16,000 titles (including 700 professional journals and periodicals), with emphasis on urban education, sociology, and psychology.

NY94   CHARTER GROUP FOR A PLEDGE OF CONSCIENCE (1964). P.O. Box 356, Cathedral Sta., 10025.
The Charter Group seeks commitments of local citizens to a "pledge of conscience" which "recognizes the responsibility of the white community for racial discrimination and for overcoming conditions caused by it." The Group is concerned with discriminatory practices in housing, schools, employment, and other fields.

.1   Charter Group for a Pledge of Conscience.
Files, 1964- . Correspondence, minutes of meetings, financial records, studies, and other materials dealing with the aims, programs and history of the Group.

NY95   CHRISTIANITY AND CRISIS, INC. (1941). 537 W. 121st St., 10027. Tel 212 662-5907. Wayne H. Cowan, Editor.
Christianity and Crisis, Inc., was founded for the purpose of publishing Christianity and Crisis, a Christian journal of opinion. Articles are often concerned with the black-white dilemma and the Christian response, social, political, racial, economic and international issues.
Publ.: Christianity and Crisis, bimonthly journal.

.1   Christianity and Crisis, Inc.
Files, 1941- . Records, correspondence, a complete run of Christianity and Crisis; published articles concerning religion and race, black power and economic development, civil rights, problems of the inner city, riots, and other related subjects.

NY96   CITIZENS FOR LOCAL DEMOCRACY. 15 W. 44th St., 10036. Tel 212 661-0577. J.L. Shapiro, Exec. Dir.
The Citizens for Local Democracy was founded in response to the need and demand by citizens for community self-government. It seeks to give local citizens the power to control, through locally elected representatives, their own institutions.
Publ.: "Contemporary Affairs," a series of pamphlets

NY97   THE CITY UNIVERSITY OF NEW YORK, CITY COLLEGE, BLACK SCIENCE STUDENTS ORGANIZATION. 133rd St. and Convent Ave., 10031. Tel 212 621-2607. Paul B. Simms, Pres.
The activities of the Organization have included a Conference on Black Students in Medicine and the Sciences to discuss admission standards in medical schools and to suggest new methods and criteria for selection, to

dispel myths that have been perpetrated on the black student concerning medical school, and to inform black students of opportunities and new programs in the field of medicine.

.1 Black Science Students Organization.
Files. Records, reports, correspondence, and other papers concerning the aims and activities of the organization, including material from the National Conference on Black Students in Medicine and the Sciences, such as proposals, evaluations, and copies of speeches delivered.

NY98 THE CITY UNIVERSITY OF NEW YORK, HUNTER COLLEGE, URBAN RESEARCH CENTER (1962). 790 Madison Ave., 10021. Tel 212 879-2100. Prof. Paul Davidoff, Acting Dir.
The Center conducts research on urban and metropolitan affairs, including studies on urban bureaucracies, economics of urban housing and medical care, urban renewal, urban political behavior, intergovernmental and intergroup relations, urban ecology and urban juvenile delinquency; plans and coordinates urban research projects on urban problems; functions as the College's liaison agent with governmental and social agencies; and holds interdisciplinary seminars on specific urban problems.

.1 Urban Research Center.
Files, 1962- . Correspondence, financial records, reports, studies, and other materials dealing with the aims, history, and programs of the Center.

NY99 COLUMBIA UNIVERSITY, BUREAU OF APPLIED SOCIAL RESEARCH (1937). 605 W. 115th St., 10025. Tel 212 280-4050. Judith Barton, Librn. Interlibrary loan, copying, inquiries answered, referrals made, consultation.
The Bureau serves as a research laboratory of the Department of Sociology, and facilitates social research by students and faculty of other departments of the University.
Publ.: The Bureau Reporter, monthly newsletter.

Materials pertaining to urban problems.
.1 Caplovitz, David.
The Merchants of Harlem: A Study of Small Business in a Black Community by David Caplovitz, Lois Sanders, Bernard Levenson, and Joan Wilson. This report (1969), based on interviews with 125 black and 106 white businessmen in Central Harlem and 53 in Bay Ridge, a white middle-class area, is a descriptive comparison of the black vs. white merchants in Harlem, and of Harlem merchants in general vs. the Bay Ridge merchants.

.2 Clarke, Stevens H.
Application of Electronic Computer Techniques to Racial Integration in School Systems by Stevens H. Clarke and Julius Surkis. This report (1967) describes in detail a computerized system for assigning students to schools to maximize racial integration while minimizing time and cost. Using the computer system, MINTRAN-MPS/3600, a table of assignment of students to school buildings is drawn up which places each student in a school with a minimum of total daily student transportation time subject to certain constraints.

.3 Fogelson, Robert.
Who Riots? A Study of Participation in the 1967 Riots by Robert Hill and Robert Fogelson. Analyzing police blotters of people arrested in racial disorders in the U.S. in 1967, this report (1968) develops a profile of riot participation in terms of characteristics such as age, sex, race, birthplace, previous arrest records, formal offense and employment status, and attempts to test the adequacy of the "riffraff theory" of riot participation.

.4 Glaser, William A.
"Some Problems Confronting Harlem" by William A. Glaser and Robert Hill. A series of questions designed to guide a community planning conference. Subject headings: physical planning, economic, education, culture, health and citizen participation. Series designed in 1964.

.5 Jaffe, A.J.; Adams, Walter; and Meyers, Sandra G.
Negro Higher Education in the 1960's, a book compiled in 1968.

.6 Lenihan, Kenneth.
A Research-Demonstration Program to Protect Low-Income Consumers, an action program (1963) to prevent exploitation of low-income consumers in purchase of major durables, as well as an evaluative research design.

.7 Nash, George.
The Community Patrol Corps: A Descriptive Evaluation of the One-Week Experiment. This report (1968) describes and evaluates the one-week experiment of the Community Patrol Corps (made up of male residents between the ages of 18-30) patrolling areas of Harlem. The participants and their experiences are presented as well as the response to the Corps from the community, press, police, and city officials.

.8 Nash, George.
"Harlem Views Columbia University" by George Nash and Cynthia Epstein. An article published in 1968.

.9 Nixon, Julian.
The Negro Consumer, a review (1962) of the economic position and consumer behavior of Negro Americans outside the South. Bibliography included.

NY100 COLUMBIA UNIVERSITY, COLUMBIA UNIVERSITY LIBRARIES, DEPARTMENT OF SPECIAL COLLECTIONS. 10027. Tel 212 280-2231. Kenneth A. Lohf, Librn. for Rare Books and Manuscripts. Copying.

.1 Alexander Gumby Collection on the American Negro.
Materials, ca. 1800-1952. 140 v. and 25 boxes. Newspaper clippings, pictures, extracts from periodicals, and ms letters and documents, relating to all phases of Negro life in America. The material, majority of which covers 1910-50, is arranged in bound volumes under such headings as "The Negro in Bondage," "The Negro as Soldier," "Breaking the Bonds of Slavery," "The Negro in Stamps," "Lynching," and "The South." Outstanding individuals, such as Booker T. Washington, George Washington Carver, Joe Louis, Paul Robeson, and Josephine Baker have single volumes devoted to them.

.2 Anti-Slavery Propaganda Collection.
ca. 2500 pamphlets. Microcards of originals located in the Oberlin College Library. See Oberlin College Library, Oberlin, Ohio; or Lost Cause Press (publisher), Louisville, Ky., for more complete description.

.3 Bancroft, Frederic, 1860-1945.
Papers, ca. 1890-1930. ca. 15,000 items. Historian. Correspondence, documents, notes, articles, speeches, scrapbooks, notebooks, page proofs, clippings, tear sheets, pamphlets, books and other printed matter, and photos. Includes notes and various other source materials for Bancroft's books which deal with the Negro, the South, the Civil War, and the life and work of Carl Schurz.

.4 Berol, Alfred C., 1892- . collector.
American Revolutionary letters and documents, collected by Alfred C. and Madeleine Rossin Berol, 1650-1830. 182 items. Letters and documents, chiefly 1775-80, relating to the American Revolution, or to the persons who figured in it. Includes 16 letters of Henry Laurens, a South Carolina planter, and of his son, John Laurens, among which is a "manumission letter" (1776) written by Henry Laurens to his son.

.5 Conway, Moncure Daniel, 1832-1907.
Letters. Author, Unitarian minister, and abolitionist.

.6 Coss, John Jacob, 1884-1940.
Papers, 1912-40. ca. 850 items. Professor of philosophy at Columbia University. Correspondence, addresses, articles, mss of writings, and notebooks, relating to Columbia University matters, and to the Rosenwald Fund for Negro Education.

.7 Facts on Film.
Papers, 1954-67. Microfilm. Contains materials on civil rights and race relations in the South. See Race Relations Information Center, Nashville, Tenn., for a full description.

.8 Gay, Sydney Howard, 1814-88.
    Papers, ca. 1775-1900. 85 boxes. Journalist,
    author, and abolitionist. Correspondence, reports
    (in letter form) from Gay's reporters at the front
    during the Civil War, diaries, journals, and note-
    books. Includes correspondence of Mrs. Gay, of
    Walter, Sarah and Allan Gay, and of other members
    of the Gay family. Other correspondents include
    William C. Bryant, Horace Greeley and Charles
    Sumner.

.9 Griffing, Josephine Sophie White, 1814-72.
    Papers, 1862-72. 53 items and 2 v. Social re-
    former. Letters written to Mrs. Griffing relating
    to her interests in the emancipation of Negroes, the
    temperance movement, and woman's suffrage;
    scrapbook of clippings about her life and activities;
    and other material. Correspondents include Henry
    Ward Beecher, Anna Dickinson, Horace Greeley,
    Lucretia Mott, William H. Seward, Charles Sumner,
    and John Greenleaf Whittier.

.10 Jay, John, 1745-1829.
    Papers, 1715-1862. ca. 3000 items. Statesman and
    Chief Justice of the U.S. Supreme Court. Corre-
    spondence and other papers of John Jay and the Jay
    family. Includes manumission documents which re-
    veal Jay's interest in the abolition of slavery.

.11 Kelley family.
    Papers, 1681-1936. 1800 items. Correspondence,
    documents, and photos of the Kelley family, of
    Philadelphia. Members of the family most promi-
    nent in the collection are Albert Kelley, Caroline B.
    Kelley, Florence Kelley (1859-1932), who was
    active in the field of social legislation and a resi-
    dent at Hull House in Chicago and at the Henry
    Street Settlement in New York, John Bartram
    Kelley, Margaret Dana Kelley, Nicholas Kelley, and
    William Darrah Kelley (1814-90). Includes 20
    letters (1900-31) to Florence Kelley from Jane
    Addams.

.12 Lindsay, Samuel McCune, 1869-1960.
    Papers, ca. 1889-1950. 6 v. and 153 boxes. Cor-
    respondence, lecture notes, and reports, relating to
    social legislation, prohibition, labor, housing, and
    related topics.

.13 Minor, Robert, 1884-1952.
    Papers, 1907-52. 15,000 items. Journalist, car-
    toonist, and a founder of the Communist movement
    in the U.S. Notes, speeches and articles relating
    to Minor's work as a writer for the Communist
    party and the Daily Worker (New York). Subjects
    include the South and Negro rights, the organization
    and policies of the Communist party from the
    1930's through the postwar period, the agrarian re-
    form movement, and the Communist trials of 1949-
    53. Extensive clippings and pamphlets cover the
    entire domestic political scene and reflect the
    whole of Minor's career.

.14 New York City Suffrage Committee of Colored Citizens.
    "The Principia," prepared by the Suffrage Com-
    mittee in 1860.

.15 New York State Convention of Colored Men.
    Minutes, 1854.

.16 Norman, Dorothy, 1905- .
    Papers, 1923-60. 1700 items. Journalist. Corre-
    spondence, much of which pertains to Mrs. Nor-
    man's column in the New York Post (1940's); re-
    ports, pamphlets, and clippings on a wide range of
    social and political topics: health, population
    control, civil liberties, education, delinquency,
    race relations, and other related subjects. Orga-
    nizations represented include the Americans for
    Democratic Action, the American Civil Liberties
    Union, the Liberal party, the United Nations and
    the National Urban League.

.17 Polanyi, Karl, 1886-1964.
    Papers, 1944-64. ca. 3000 items. Professor of
    economic history at Columbia University. Lecture
    notes, mss of writings, notes, and other papers.
    Includes notes and drafts of his various writings,
    among which is Dahomey and the Slave Trade.

.18 Plimpton, George Arthur, 1855-1936. collector.
    Plimpton mss collections, ca. 17th cent.-1936.
    Collection of papers divided into five parts. The
    slavery collection (1650-1869) contains 153 letters,
    documents, broadsides, and pamphlets on slavery,
    chiefly relating to the southern U.S. in the 19th
    cent., with some items bearing on slavery in the
    17th and 18th cent. in England.

.19 Slavery collection, 1200-1883.
    Materials. 118 items. Letters and papers relating
    to slavery and to the slave trade in England and
    America. Includes a charter on vellum relating to
    a slave or bondsman in England in the late 12th
    cent. and a group of police reports for New Orleans
    (Aug.-Nov., 1883) concerned with Negroes sentenced
    to the chain gang.

.20 Stokes, James Graham Phelps, 1872-1960.
    Papers, 1884-1950's. 85 boxes. Philanthropist
    and publicist. Correspondence, journals, diaries,
    financial records, and other papers relating to the
    numerous social, sociological, political, civic, and
    philanthropic organizations with which Stokes was
    associated. Prominent among them are the Ameri-
    can Alliance for Labor and Democracy, Constitu-
    tional Democracy Association, Legal Aid Society,
    National Security League, Outdoor Recreation
    League, Prison Association of New York, Socialist
    Democratic League and National Party, and the
    YMCA.

.21 United States Civil War papers, ca. 1850-75.
    Papers. ca. 1300 items. Correspondence, docu-
    ments, miscellaneous material, and photos relating
    to the Civil War and the men who fought in it,
    chiefly of the Union Army. In most instances the
    letters are addressed to some close relative and
    record the daily life on the battle field, in camp, or
    in prison. Includes the military and civil records
    of the St. Francis River Command of the Arkansas
    Eastern District, relating to the problems of ship-
    ping, smuggling, blockade running, and Negro
    troops on this section of the Mississippi River.

.22 Villard, Oswald Garrison.
    Papers, 1850-1910. 20 boxes. New York journal-
    ist, editor. Papers relating to John Brown.

NY101 COLUMBIA UNIVERSITY, FACULTY HUMAN RIGHTS COM-
       MITTEE (1966). Dept. of Slavic Languages, 10027. Tel
       212 280-1754. Dr. Robert Belknap.
       The Committee seeks to protect the human and civil
       rights of the members of the Columbia University com-
       munity. Among other activities, it supports an ethnic-
       ally and economically integrated and balanced com-
       munity on Morningside Heights where the University is
       located, works for an increased enrollment and re-
       cruitment of black students and faculty members, and
       supports the right of University employees to collective
       bargaining and unionization.
       Publ.: The Community and the Expansion of Columbia
            University (1967); Statements and reports.

NY102 COLUMBIA UNIVERSITY, ORAL HISTORY RESEARCH OF-
       FICE (1948). Butler Library, 10027. Tel 212 280-2273.
       Louis M. Starr, Dir. Bibliographies prepared, litera-
       ture searches, copying, typing, inquiries answered,
       referrals made, consultation, will research Collection
       for a moderate fee in response to bona fide inquiries/
       requests.
       The Office was established to collect, by means of
       tape-recorded interviews, primary source material that
       would not otherwise exist.
       Publ.: Annual Reports; The Oral History Collection
            (1964), descriptive catalog.

    .1 Civil Rights in Alabama.
        Material about the civil rights movement in
        Tuscaloosa, Ala., in 1964. Includes interviews
        with leaders and participants, and transcripts of
        two mass meetings and interviews with residents
        expressing widely varying attitudes. 259 pp. of
        transcript copy.

    .2 Negro Leaders Project.
        Memoirs by Samuel Battle, William S. Braithwaite,
        W.E.B. DuBois, Lester Granger, E.R. McKinney,
        Benjamin McLaurin, George Schuyler, and Roy
        Wilkins. Other pertinent material is to be found
        throughout the rest of the collection.

NY103 COLUMBIA UNIVERSITY, SCHOOL OF LAW, COLUMBIA
       SURVEY OF HUMAN RIGHTS LAW (1967). P.O. Box
       35, 435 W. 116th St., 10027. Tel 212 280-2640.
       The Survey, established by a group of Columbia Law

School students, deals with creative legal analyses of contemporary human rights problems, such as individual rights and liberties, criminal law and procedure, the rights of the poor, and the protection of emerging "new property" rights.
Publ.: Columbia Survey of Human Rights Law, semiannually.

NY104 COLUMBIA UNIVERSITY, SCHOOL OF SOCIAL WORK, CENTER FOR RESEARCH AND DEMONSTRATION (1956). 2 E. 91st St., 10028. Tel 212 427-5391. Dean Samuel Finestone, Dir.
The Center conducts research on social welfare problems, including studies on child welfare, community activities and social work manpower, and demonstration of service programs.
Publ.: Monographs and project reports.

.1 Center for Research and Demonstration.
Files, 1956- . Correspondence, financial records, reports, studies, and other materials dealing with the aims, history, and programs of the Center.

NY105 COLUMBIA UNIVERSITY, SCHOOL OF SOCIAL WORK (1898), LIBRARY (1949). 2 E. 91st St., 10028. Tel 212 876-6300. Gracy Joyce Bermingham, Librn.

.1 The Library contains the material from the discontinued Russell Sage Foundation Library. The Sage Foundation over a long period of time gave grants to certain organizations specifically serving the interests of Negroes.

NY106 COLUMBIA UNIVERSITY, TEACHERS COLLEGE, ERIC INFORMATION RETRIEVAL CENTER ON THE DISADVANTAGED (1964). Room 1206, Graduate Center, 10027. Tel 212 870-4200. Edmund Gordon, Dir. Literature searches, inquiries answered, referrals made. ERIC was established by the U.S. Office of Education to make the educational community aware of what is taking place within it. The ERIC Information Retrieval Center on the Disadvantaged works to further educational opportunity for the disadvantaged by improving the exchange of research and resource information among those concerned with that information. The Center receives, evaluates, and makes available literature and data about socially, economically, or culturally disadvantaged urban children and youth.
Publ.: IRCD Bulletin, bimonthly; ERIC-IRCD Urban Disadvantaged Series, irregular; Bibliographies, reviews, and position papers.

.1 ERIC Information Retrieval Center on the Disadvantaged.
Materials, 1964- . ca. 40,000 items. Books, periodicals, reports, journal articles, book articles, conference papers, manuals, speeches, pamphlets, and other documents, including the U.S. Equal Educational Opportunity Programs collections (ca. 2000 items), and the ERIC microfiche collection (30,000 items). Subject areas covered by the holdings include the effects of disadvantaged environments; the academic, intellectual, and social performance of disadvantaged children and youth; programs and practices which provide learning experiences designed to compensate for the special problems and build on the characteristics of the disadvantaged; and programs and practices related to economic and ethnic discrimination, segregation, desegregation, and integration in education. Restricted.

NY107 COLUMBIA UNIVERSITY URBAN CENTER (1967). 206 Lewisohn Hall, Columbia University, 10027. Tel 212 280-5004. Franklin H. Williams, Dir.
The Center supports Columbia University's sensitivity and commitment to urban and minority affairs, and seeks to broaden and deepen its competence and capacity to deal with them. It supports teaching and research efforts, and initiates on-going programs in urban and minority affairs, including community projects in such areas as education, health, cultural enrichment, housing, recreation, employment and economic development.
Publ.: Annual Report.

.1 Columbia University Urban Center.
The Center library contains ca. 500 v. on urban and

ethnic studies, and University and minority issues such as economic development, admissions, housing, social welfare; 30 tape recordings, magazines, pamphlets, newspaper clippings on urban affairs, 15 periodical titles, and 10 newspaper titles which are not generally retained in university libraries. Also included are mailing lists, films, and selected programs.

NY108 COMMISSION ON SOCIAL ACTION OF REFORM JUDAISM. 838 Fifth Ave., 10021. Tel 212 249-0100. Albert Vorspan, Dir. Bibliographies prepared, copying, inquiries answered, referrals made, consultation.
The Commission is a national human relations organization, an affiliation of the Union of American Hebrew Congregations and the Central Conference of American Rabbis. It coordinates education efforts on the local level.
Publ.: Counsel, periodic bulletin.

NY109 COMMUNITY COUNCIL OF GREATER NEW YORK, BUREAU OF COMMUNITY STATISTICAL SERVICES. 225 Park Ave., 10003. Tel 212 777-5000.
The Bureau collects statistical data and other information about demographic characteristics and health and social welfare programs in New York City.
Publ.: Demographic and socio-economic studies.

.1 Bureau of Community Statistical Services.
Files. Statistical data, reports, surveys, tabulations, and other research material. Includes card files by neighborhoods of the city on current health and welfare resources covering group work and recreation programs, day-care services for children, public and parochial schools, and churches and synagogues. The public may have access to non-confidential data by appointment.

NY110 COMMUNITY COUNCIL OF GREATER NEW YORK, INFORMATION BUREAU (1928). 225 Park Ave. S., 10003. Tel 212 777-5000. L.V. Oresen, Dir. Referrals made.
The Bureau is a clearinghouse for information about health and social welfare agencies in New York City. It keeps a calendar of events and benefits sponsored by such organizations. The Bureau provides the public with information on the location and the services of public and voluntary organizations working in the fields of health and social welfare.
Publ.: Directory of Social and Health Agencies in New York City.

.1 Information Bureau.
Files. Information about social welfare and health organizations in New York City and the services they provide.

NY111 COMMUNITY DEVELOPMENT FOUNDATION (1959). 345 E. 46th St., 10017. Tel 212 697-0264.
The Foundation is a non-profit, "self-help" organization which supplies technical advice and small interest-free loans, and works for higher employment and the prevention of violence in the community.

NY112 CONGRESS OF RACIAL EQUALITY (CORE) (1943). 200 W. 125th St., 10027. Tel 212 281-9650. Roy Innis, Nat. Dir.
CORE is a national human relations organization which initiates non-violent direct action to end discrimination in education, housing, employment, and public accommodations, and to improve the lives of black people by focusing on the needs of the total black community. CORE conducts several economic development, job training, health and education projects in major cities. Among these projects is the Target City Youth Training Program which trains underemployed or unemployed men and women to be service station operators and secretaries, with the goals of development of resocialization, education, entrepreneurship, black leadership and self-determination.
Publ.: CORElator, bimonthly newsletter; Press releases, reports and special pamphlets.

.1 Congress of Racial Equality.
Files, 1943- . Records and reports of the operation and activities of CORE.

NY113   CONGRESS OF RACIAL EQUALITY (CORE), NEW YORK
        OFFICE. 307 W. 125th St., 10027. Tel 212 864-8809.
        Victor Solomon, Chmn.
        Publ.: Rights and Reviews: A Magazine of the Civil
        Rights Movement in America.

NY114   COUNCIL ON INTERRACIAL BOOKS FOR CHILDREN, INC.
        (1964). 9 E. 40th St., 10016. Tel 212 532-7780. Brad-
        ford Chambers, Chmn. Bibliographies prepared, in-
        quiries answered, consultation.
        The aim of the Council is to encourage the writing,
        production, and effective distribution of books to fill the
        needs of ethnic minority and urban poor children. The
        Council publishes a bulletin with articles about and re-
        views of children's books, offers cash awards for the
        best children's books by Negroes, Spanish Americans
        and American Indians, and offers guidance to authors
        whose work has merit but who need professional help.
        It also features representative art work by Negro illus-
        trators of children's books.
        Publ.: Interracial Books for Children, quarterly bulletin;
        Newsletter; Book lists.

NY115   DOVER PUBLICATIONS, INC., LIBRARY. 180 Varick St.,
        10014. Tel 212 255-3755. John Grafton, Asst. to the
        Pres. Copying, inquiries answered.
        Dover Publications is a reprint publisher which issues,
        among many other publications, a series of reprints in
        the Negro interest.

        .1 Pictorial archives.
            Photographs and pictures, pre-1900. ca. 25,000
            items. Portraits of famous Americans, including
            Negro Americans. Restricted to staff use.

NY115a EARL G. GRAVES PUBLISHING COMPANY, INC. 295
        Madison Ave., 10017. Tel 212 889-8220. Pat Patter-
        son, Editor.
        Black Enterprise seeks to analyze and disseminate in-
        formation that would be of help to black businessmen
        as well as to provide them a forum for their ideas,
        ambitions, and expressions.
        Publ.: Black Enterprise, monthly magazine.

NY116   ENCAMPMENT FOR CITIZENSHIP, INC. (1946). 2 W. 64th
        St., 10023. Tel 212 787-2714. Douglas C. Kelley, Exec.
        Dir.
        Encampment for Citizenship is a non-sectarian, non-
        partisan, non-profit organization which conducts a six-
        week summer leadership training program for young
        people of diverse backgrounds who have an interest in
        public affairs, such as community development, tutoring,
        politics, civil rights, poverty, cooperatives, intern-
        national relations, etc.
        Publ.: Summer Projects, 2-3 issues per year.

NY117   THE EPISCOPAL CHURCH, DIVISION OF COLLEGE AND
        UNIVERSITY WORK. 815 Second Ave., 10017. Tel 212
        867-8400. Rev. Edwin G. Bennett, Dir.

        .1 Division of College and University Work.
            Files. Correspondence, minutes of board meetings,
            financial records, and other materials relating to
            the Division's support of the following predomi-
            nantly black colleges: St. Augustine's College,
            Raleigh, N.C.; St. Paul's College, Lawrenceville,
            Va.; and Voorhees Junior College, Denmark, S.C.

NY118   THE EPISCOPAL CHURCH, EXECUTIVE COUNCIL, EX-
        PERIMENTAL AND SPECIALIZED SERVICES. 815
        Second Ave., 10017. Tel 212 867-8400. Mrs. Muriel
        Webb, Dir.
        Experimental and Specialized Services, the social
        action agency for the Episcopal Church, is concerned
        with programs in the areas of civil rights, intergroup
        relations and social welfare activities.

NY119   EPISCOPAL DIOCESE OF NEW YORK, DEPARTMENT OF
        CHRISTIAN SOCIAL RELATIONS (1935). 1047 Amster-
        dam Ave., 10025. Tel 212 749-1150. John V.P. Lassoe,
        Jr., Dir.
        The Department seeks to stimulate and help Episcopal
        churches and other churches in the New York area to
        engage in programs of social action and education.

NY120   FIFTEENTH STREET PREPARATIVE MEETING OF THE
        RELIGIOUS SOCIETY OF FRIENDS (1681), LIBRARY
        (ca. 1830). 15 Stuyvesant Square W., 10003. Tel 212
        777-8866. John L.P. Maynard, Convenor of the Cmt.
        Inquiries answered.
        The Society is a religious one for the spiritual comfort
        and growth of its members.

        .1 Biographies.
            Biographies of several Friends who were active in
            the abolitionist movement.
        .2 Brown, John, 1800-59.
            Correspondence.
        .3 Underground Railroad.
            Miscellaneous. Books and pamphlets, including a
            collection of stories for children about the railroad.

NY121   FLOYD B. McKISSICK ENTERPRISES, INC. 360 W. 125th
        St., 10035. Tel 212 666-3983. Floyd B. McKissick,
        Pres.
        McKissick Enterprises seeks to stimulate and support
        black economic development. A major project is the
        development of Soul City, a planned industrial commu-
        nity in Warren County, N.C. Other projects include
        Thunder and Lightning Publishing Company, Metropoli-
        tan Human Resources Consortium, and Black Drama
        Productions, Inc.

NY122   THE FORD FOUNDATION (1936), LIBRARY (1953). 320 E.
        43rd St., 10017. Tel 212 573-5000. Clifford R. Johnson,
        Librn.
        The Foundation seeks to serve the public welfare, to
        identify problems of national importance and to under-
        write efforts, mainly of an educational nature, toward
        their solution. Since 1945, the Foundation has made
        large grants to programs involving the Negro American,
        which represent two types of support: that committed to
        specific Negro problems, and that committed to general
        community problems involving Negroes. The areas in
        which grants have been made are undergraduate educa-
        tion, equal career and employment opportunities, com-
        munity development (including primary and secondary
        education for the disadvantaged), delinquency prevention
        and control, and civil rights and race relations.
        Publ.: Grants and Projects Related to the Development
        of the American Negro (n.d.); Annual Report.

        .1 Ford Foundation.
            Files, 1936- . Records and reports of the opera-
            tion of the Foundation and of programs funded
            through the Foundation. Restricted.

NY123   FOUNDATION FOR RESEARCH AND EDUCATION IN
        SICKLE CELL DISEASE. 423 W. 120th St., 10027. Tel
        212 222-8500. Richard Campbell, Dir.
        The Foundation conducts research in sickle cell anemia,
        "an incurable hereditary disease that seriously afflicts
        one in 50 Negro Americans and affects one in 10 to a
        lesser extent . . . The disorder occurs almost exclu-
        sively among Negroes because the mutant gene that
        causes it emerged during the course of evolution in the
        African population."

NY124   FREEDOMWAYS ASSOCIATES, INC. (1959). 799 Broadway,
        10003. Tel 212 477-3985. Ester Jackson, Managing
        Editor.
        Publ.: Freedomways: A Quarterly Review of the Negro
        Freedom Movement.

        .1 Freedomways Associates, Inc.
            Files, 1959- .

NY125   GENERAL EDUCATION BOARD (1902). 111 W. 50th St.,
        10020. Tel 212 265-8100.
        The Board, now defunct, was established to promote
        education in the U.S. without discrimination because of
        race, sex or creed. Over the years the Board made
        large grants for the improvement of educational oppor-
        tunities for Negroes, both through the development of
        public schools and through grants to Negro colleges and
        fellowships to their faculty members. The funds of the
        Board were exhausted in 1964.

        .1 General Education Board Archives.
            1902-64. Records and reports of the operation of
            the Board and of the institutions and organizations

funded by it. The archives, which are held by the Rockefeller Foundation, are closed to the public.

NY126 HARLEM SCHOOL OF THE ARTS, INC. (1964). St. Nicholas Ave. and W. 141st St., 10031. Tel 212 283-4541. Dorothy Maynor, Dir.
The School is a non-sectarian, integrated center for the training of children, teenagers and adults, designed primarily for the enrichment of the lives of the underprivileged. Instruction is offered in a variety of fields: music, ballet and modern dance, drama and art.
Publ.: Newsletter, quarterly; Pamphlets, reports.

NY127 HARLEM YOUTH OPPORTUNITIES UNLIMITED, INC. - ASSOCIATED COMMUNITY TEAMS (HARYOU-ACT). 2444 Seventh Ave., 10030. Tel 212 281-9400.
HARYOU-ACT, Inc., develops participation in local planning through community improvement; operates after-school study centers, arts and culture workshops; employment bureaus, Head Start centers, neighborhood and community service centers, chiefly in the Harlem area.

NY128 HARMON FOUNDATION, INC., DIVISION OF VISUAL EXPERIMENT LIBRARY (1922). 140 Nassau St., 10038. Tel 212 267-4357. Mary B. Brady, Dir.
The Division Library is a film and picture library serving church and educational groups, social service organizations, libraries, governmental agencies, and other groups.

NY129 HUMAN RESOURCES ADMINISTRATION (1966). 222 Church St., 10013. Tel 212 433-4808. Mitchell I. Ginsberg, Adminstr.
The Administration was established to merge the efforts of the antipoverty program, welfare programs, and related agencies under one administration, in order to provide a comprehensive strategy for attacking New York's problems of poverty and human waste. The Administration plans, conducts, coordinates, and evaluates programs in the areas of community action and development, manpower and career development, social and youth services and public assistance, and rehabilitation and preventive services in drug addiction. It includes the Community Development Agency and the Council Against Poverty, the Manpower and Career Development Agency, the Department of Social Services, the Youth Services Agency and the Addiction Services Agency.
Publ.: Human Resources Administration Newsletter, monthly; Council Against Poverty Bulletin, bi-monthly; Neighborhood Youth Corps Staff Notes, monthly; The Welfarer, monthly.

NY130 INDUSTRIAL RELATIONS COUNSELORS, INC. (1926), LIBRARY. 1271 Ave. of the Americas, 10020. Tel 212 757-4600. Margaret B. Boyle, Librn. Interlibrary loan.
Industrial Relations Counselors, Inc., seeks to advance the knowledge and practice of human relationships in industry, commerce, education and government.

.1 Industrial Relations Counselors, Inc.
Miscellaneous. Limited collection of materials on equal employment opportunity.

NY130a INSTITUTE OF JAZZ STUDIES. 108 Waverly Place, 10011. Tel 212 254-0331. Marshall W. Sterns, Exec. Dir.

.1 Institute of Jazz Studies.
Library includes phonograph records (ca. 15,000), books (ca. 1000 v.), and 16 vertical files of newspaper clippings, photographs, jazz magazines, unpublished mss., films, and jazz memorabilia. By appointment.

NY131 INSTITUTE OF PUBLIC ADMINISTRATION. 55 W. 44th St., 10036. Tel 212 661-2540.
The Institute is an independent, non-profit center for research and education in public administration and governmental policy. Research projects in urban affairs have included studies in New York City of programs, organizational arrangements, and methods of financing improvements in the areas of human resources and housing and neighborhood improvement; administration and evaluation of a new technique of tenement rehabilitation through installation of pre-

fabricated units; and a study of requirements for and supply of cultural facilities in urban centers.

NY132 INTERRACIAL COUNCIL FOR BUSINESS OPPORTUNITY FUND, INC. 110 E. 23rd St., 10010. Tel 212 228-5440. John T. Patterson, Nat. Dir.
The Council was created by the Urban League and the American Jewish Congress to help minority groups establish and expand their own businesses. Volunteer consultants provide counsel on business methods and assistance in finding funds. The Council has supported a study of the economic redevelopment of Harlem, making a survey and catalog of business firms and institutions in the area and inventories of job skills and industrial buildings.

NY133 INTERRELIGIOUS FOUNDATION FOR COMMUNITY ORGANIZATION (IFCO) (1967). 211 E. 43rd St., 10017. Tel 212 986-5727. Rev. Lucius Walker, Jr., Exec. Dir.
IFCO coordinates community organization, community development and training efforts of its 24 member organizations, which includes groups and a civic foundation.
Publ.: IFCO Newsletter.

.1 Interreligious Foundation for Community Organization.
Files, 1967- . Includes staff and consultants field reports on projects funded in urban and rural areas.

NY134 JEWISH LABOR COMMITTEE (1959), WILLIAM GREEN HUMAN RELATIONS LIBRARY (1959). 25 E. 78th St., 10021. Tel 212 535-3700. Emanual Muravchik, Dir.
The Committee works with the labor movement and the American Jewish community in seeking to bring a realization that civil rights and the status of minorities are central to the program of organized labor, and that the progress of the American working class is tied to the condition of its most deprived minorities.

.1 The William Green Human Relations Library.
Contains books, journals and periodicals, government documents, union convention proceedings, and microfilmed theses and dissertations in the area of labor and human rights, particularly the American labor movement, civil rights, and minority problems. Open to the public by appointment.

NY135 THE JOHN LaFARGE INSTITUTE (1964). 106 W. 56th St., 10019. Tel 212 586-4221. Rev. Thurston N. Davis, S.J., Dir.
The Institute is an interreligious conference center that continues the work of the Jesuit priest and interracial pioneer for whom it is named. It conducts conferences on urban, interracial and ecumenical questions.

NY136 JOINT SCHOOLS COMMITTEE FOR ACADEMIC EXCELLENCE NOW (1962). 545 W. 126th St., 10027. Tel 212 283-8744. Janet F. Karlson, Pres.
The Committee, which represents Harlem families, co-operates with local PTA groups to "obtain quality integrated education for all youngsters in New York City." The Committee is concerned with accurate portrayal of minority groups in school textbooks, and is working to develop basal readers and social studies texts.

.1 Joint Schools Committee for Academic Excellence Now.
Files, 1962- . Correspondence, minutes of meetings, financial records, reports, studies, and other materials dealing with the aims, programs and history of the Committee.

NY137 LABOR RESEARCH ASSOCIATION (1927), LIBRARY (1927). 80 E. 11th St., 10003. Tel 212 473-1042. Harriet Levine, Off. Mgr. Inquiries answered, referrals made.
The Association conducts investigations and studies of social, economic and political questions in the interest of the labor and progressive movement, and issues these findings in the form of reports, articles, bulletins, pamphlets, and books.
Publ.: Economic Notes, monthly bulletin.

.1 Labor Research Association.
Files, 1927- . Records of the organization, mss, research data, and published reports. The Association Library contains holdings in the areas of

labor and labor problems, social conditions, anti-war action, the Negro in the U.S., civil rights, and civil liberties.

NY138　LAW CENTER FOR CONSTITUTIONAL RIGHTS (1966). 588 Ninth Ave., 10036. Tel 212 265-2500. Morton Stavis, Admin. Counsr.
The Law Center is a non-profit corporation which has developed extensive affirmative litigation techniques in the field of civil rights and civil liberties. It disseminates litigation materials to lawyers throughout the country and provides training for young members of the bar seeking to engage in this type of work. In the course of its work, attorneys associated with the Center have represented various people and organizations in the Movement, including such organizations as the Black Panthers, Students for a Democratic Society, the Student National Coordinating Committee, anti-war protestors, and anti-draft groups.

NY139　LAW STUDENTS CIVIL RIGHTS RESEARCH COUNCIL, INC. (1963), RESEARCH FILES (1964). 156 Fifth Ave., 10010. Tel 212 989-2522. Reynaldo P. Glover, Dir.
The Council seeks to further social change through the use of the laws as one instrument. It assists lawyers and organizations working to end discrimination and poverty and to provide legal services to the poor. Other programs include recruiting Negroes for law school, development of programs of lay advocacy for welfare cases, and curriculum reform in law schools.
Publ.: LSCRRC, newsletter.

　.1　Research files.
Miscellaneous, 1963- . ca. 1100 items. Includes legal memos, legal briefs, and general legal research useful to lawyers and law students working in the area of race relations.

NY140　LAWYERS' CONSTITUTIONAL DEFENSE COMMITTEE OF THE AMERICAN CIVIL LIBERTIES UNION (1964). 156 Fifth Ave., 10010. Tel 212 989-7530. Henry Schwarzschild, Exec. Dir.
The Committee was founded by the chief legal officers of the several national, civil-rights, civil-liberties, religious and intergroup relations organizations. Its purpose and function is to provide free legal services to the civil rights movement and the Negro community in the Deep South through staff and volunteer attorneys.
Publ.: LCDC Docket.

　.1　Lawyers' Constitutional Defense Committee.
Files, 1964- . Materials concerning legal cases and other activities and operations of the Committee. Restricted.

NY141　LEADERSHIP CONFERENCE ON CIVIL RIGHTS (LCCR), NEW YORK OFFICE (1953). 20 W. 40th St., 10018. Tel 212 667-1780. Roy Wilkins, Chmn. Inquiries answered, consultation.
The Conference is a federation of 126 national organizations (religious, labor and nationality) interested in promoting passage of civil rights legislation and in otherwise advancing cause of equality of citizenship. Formerly the National Council for a Permanent FEPC: National Emergency Civil Rights Mobilization.
Publ.: LCCR Memo; Pamphlets and brochures.

　.1　Leadership Conference on Civil Rights.
Files, 1953- . Correspondence, minutes of meetings, financial records, studies, reports, and other materials dealing with the aims, programs, and history of the Conference.

NY142　LEAGUE FOR INDUSTRIAL DEMOCRACY (1905). 112 E. 19th St., 10003. Tel 212 254-5865. Tom Kahn, Exec. Dir.
The League is a national membership organization dedicated to increasing political, social and economic democracy. It works to educate the public in the areas of civil rights, trade unions, student and cooperative movements through the publication of pamphlets, articles, and books. The members of the League seek a society free of racism, totalitarianism, exploitation and privilege.
Publ.: News Bulletin, quarterly; Looking Forward, occasional papers.

　.1　League for Industrial Democracy.
Files, 1905- .

NY143　LONG VIEW PUBLISHING COMPANY (1922), DAILY WORLD LIBRARY (1922). 299 Broadway, 10007. Tel 212 924-2523. Mrs. Sarah Paul, Librn. Inquiries answered.
Long View Publishing Company publishes Daily World (formerly The Worker), a daily newspaper which presents events from a Marxist point of view.
Publ.: Daily World, daily newspaper.

　.1　Daily World Library.
Contains books, periodicals, newspapers, pamphlets, vf, clippings, and photographs in the area of race relations, primarily to provide source material for staff writers.

NY144　LOTT CAREY BAPTIST FOREIGN MISSION CONVENTION (1897). Convent Ave. Baptist Church, 420 W. 145th St., 10031. Tel 212 286-0222. Rev. Dr. M.L. Wilson, Pres.
The Convention is an organization of members of various black Baptist denominations who are committed to living among peoples of different cultures and to aiding evangelistic work in foreign countries through financial support.

　.1　Lott Carey Baptist Foreign Mission Convention.
Files, 1897- . Records, correspondence, reports, and other papers concerning the aims and activities of the Convention.

NY145　LUTHERAN CHURCH IN AMERICA, BOARD OF SOCIAL MINISTRY (1963). 231 Madison Ave., 10016. Tel 212 532-3410. Carl E. Thomas, Exec. Secy. Interlibrary loan, bibliographies prepared, literature searches, copying, typing, inquiries answered, referrals made, consultation.
The Board seeks to stimulate and develop the social concern and ministry of the Lutheran Church in America. The Board engages in many activities, including consultation and conferences, study and research, and publication, in the areas of civil and international affairs, intergroup relations and economic concerns, and social welfare issues.
Publ.: Study packets, pamphlets and brochures.

　.1　Board of Social Ministry.
The Library of the Board contains books, periodicals, reports, newspapers, pamphlets, theses and dissertations, mss, correspondence, and photographs relating to race problems, especially ghetto conditions, education and employment. The Library is primarily for the use of writers and consultants of the Board.

NY146　MARTIN LUTHER KING SPEAKS-SCLC RADIO (1965). Suite 32 G, 260 Audubon Ave., 10033. Tel 212 568-6782. William S. Stein, Producer-director.
SCLC (Southern Christian Leadership Conference) Radio prepares news and regularly scheduled programs for radio station, featuring blacks. It is the plan of the agency to obtain and preserve the tapes of Martin Luther King, Jr. and other prominent blacks in politics, entertainment, and other professions. The ultimate goal of the agency is to set up an audio history of blacks.

　.1　Martin Luther King Speaks-SCLC Radio.
Miscellaneous. Materials pertaining to the operations of the agency and tapes made by various blacks for radio broadcasts which include speeches, sermons, discussions, and other forms of communication. Among the persons on tape are Martin Luther King, Jr., Ralph Abernathy, Lerone Bennett, James Bevel, Andrew Young, Ralph Ellison, James Baldwin, Harry Belafonte, Sidney Poitier, Richard Hatcher, LeRoi Jones, Hosea Williams, C.L. Franklin and many others.

NY147　MEDICAL COMMITTEE FOR HUMAN RIGHTS (MCHR) (1964). 501 Fifth Ave., 10017. Tel 212 661-2933. Dr. T.G.G. Wilson, Exec. Dir.
The Committee provides medical aid, supports biomedical careers for minority and ghetto residents, and works for the liberalization of the medical profession.
Publ.: Health Rights, newsletter.

NY148 METROPOLITAN APPLIED RESEARCH CENTER (MARC).
60 E. 86th St., 10019. Tel 212 628-7400. Kenneth B.
Clark, Dir.
The Center is concerned with civil rights and urban
problems, especially in low-income, minority group
neighborhoods. Projects of the Center include an investigation of welfare services for minority group
children, and a fellowship program to bring civil rights
leaders and social science scholars into closer working
relationships on problems and policies involving social
change. The Center also acts as a national clearing
house for information about black elected officials.

NY149 METROPOLITAN MUSEUM OF ART (1870). Fifth Ave. at
82nd St., 10028. Tel 212 879-5500.

.1 Alston, Charles Henry.
2 items. "Painting" (1950), oil; and print entitled
"Barn and Tree."
.2 Barthé, Richmond, 1901- .
Sculpture, 1941. 1 item. Bronze sculpture entitled
"Boxer."
.3 Bearden, Romare, 1914- .
Paintings. 2 items. Watercolors entitled "Golgotha." (1945), and "The Woodshed" (1969).
.4 Bradley, Peter.
Print. 1 item. Entitled "Mutsumi Maki."
.5 De Knight, Avel.
Painting, 1967. 1 item. Watercolor entitled
"Mediterranean."
.6 Hunt, Richard, 1935- .
Sculpture. 1 item. Welded steel sculpture entitled
"Peregrine Forms."
.7 Johnston, Joshua, 1796-1824.
Painting. 1 item. Oil entitled "Edward and Sarah
Rudder."
.8 Lawrence, Jacob, 1917- .
3 items. Gouache on paper, entitled "Pool Parlor"
(1942), and "Blind Beggars;" and a watercolor
(1945) entitled "The Shoemaker."
.9 Majors, William.
Print. 1 item. Entitled "Arno I."
.10 Parks, Gordon.
Photographs.
.11 Pippin, Horace, 1888-1946.
Painting, 1946. 1 item. Oil entitled "Victorian
Interior."
.12 Van DerZee, James.
Photographs.
.13 White, Charles, 1918.
Etchings.

NY150 MOBILIZATION FOR YOUTH. 214 E. Second St., 10009.
Tel 212 677-0400. Bertram M. Beck. Exec. Dir.
Mobilization for Youth is an experimental organization,
based in a ghetto area, seeking to determine whether or
not delinquency can be reduced by offering legitimate
employment. Programs include a demonstration project
on the effect of youth-administered social services and
social action, and an employment program in new health
occupations in low-income areas.

NY151 MUSEUM OF MODERN ART (1929). 11 W. 53rd St., 10019.
Tel 212 956-6100. Referrals made.

.1 The Museum of Modern Art has drawings, prints, paint-
ings, sculpture, and photographs by Afro-American
artists, including Gordon Parks, Roy De Caraba,
William Majors, Jacob Lawrence, Romare Bearden,
Junius Redwood, Selma Johnson Street, Norma
Morgan, Richard Hunt, Thomas Sills, Daniel LaRue
Johnson, and Mildred Thompson. Works of Jacob
Lawrence include 30 panels from his series "The
Migration of the Negro." The Museum also main-
tains a photograph and slide archive, and a film
library which contain materials relating to Afro-
Americans.

NY152 MUSEUM OF THE CITY OF NEW YORK (1923), LIBRARY
(1932). 1220 Fifth Ave., 10029. Tel 212 534-1672.
Albert K. Baragwanath, Librn. Copying, inquiries answered.

.1 Miscellaneous collection, 1646- .
ca. 3000 items. Papers on various topics relating
to New York. Subjects mentioned include apprenticeship papers, social events, financial matters, citizenship paper, schools and colleges, the
Fire and Police Departments, insurance, legal matters, politics, real estate, ships and shipping, societies and organizations, sports, slavery, and
wills. The period most heavily represented is the
19th century. Restricted.
.2 Theater and music collection.
Portraits, photographs, playbills, scene designs,
and costumes, many of which deal with the Negro
on the New York stage. Includes materials relating
to the careers of such performers as Paul Robeson,
Count Basie, Cab Calloway, Louis Armstrong,
Marian Anderson, Leontyne Price, Rudolph Dunbar,
Duke Ellington, Canada Lee, Richard B. Harrison,
Janet Collins, Lawrence Winters, Hilda Simms,
Gordon Heath, Louis Jordan, Jimmie Lunceford,
Noble Sissle, William Grant Sill, Dean Dixon Roland
Hayes, Edward Matthews, Aubrey Pankey, Kenneth
Spencer, William Warfield, Dorothy Maynor, Carol
Brice, Ann Brown, Todd Duncan, Robert McFerrin,
Mattiwilda Dobbs, and others. Restricted.

NY153 MUTUAL REAL ESTATE INVESTMENT TRUST (1965). 30
E. 42nd St., 10017. Tel 212 687-6550. Morris Milgram,
Mgr.
The Trust was organized to provide investors with an
opportunity to own an interest in properties, primarily
apartment buildings, to be open to all people. M-REIT
has bought and integrated apartment buildings in New
York, New Jersey, Virginia, and Illinois.

NY154 NAACP LEGAL DEFENSE AND EDUCATIONAL FUND
(1939). 10 Columbus Circle, 10019. Tel 212 586-8397.
Jack Greenberg, Director-Counsel.
The Fund is an organization, independent of the NAACP,
which operates as the major legal arm of the civil rights
movement. It represents the Southern Christian Leadership Conference, the Congress of Racial Equality,
Student National Coordinating Committee, and the
NAACP, as well as individual citizens. Its attorneys
handle cases in the areas of housing, education, employment, health, public accommodations, and the defense of civil rights workers against illegal arrests and
harassment. Programs include a legal campaign to
establish new civil rights precedents in courts; lawyer
training institutes; scholarship for Negro students; provision of personnel to aid parents in school desegregation; and a legal information and community service
division to provide simple information about rights
under the law.
Publ.: Docket Report; Report, quarterly; Newsletters,
annual reports, education literature, and fact-
finding memoranda.

.1 Facts on Film.
Papers, 1954-67. Microfilm. Contains materials
on civil rights and race relations in the South. See
Race Relations Information Center, Nashville,
Tenn., for a full description.
.2 Legal Defense and Educational Fund.
Files, 1939- . Correspondence, reports and other
legal papers relating to the activities of the Fund.
Access restricted.

NY155 NATIONAL AFRO-AMERICAN BUILDERS, INC. c/o
NAACP, 1790 Broadway, 10019. Tel 212 245-2100.
Robert W. Easley, Dir.
A multi-city organization composed of minority con-
tractors' associations in major cities, organized to pool
resources and to help bonding.

NY156 NATIONAL ASSEMBLY FOR SOCIAL POLICY AND DEVEL-
OPMENT, INC. (1945, reorganized 1968). 345 E. 46th
St., 10017. Tel 212 687-8300. C.F. McNeil, Exec. Dir.
The Assembly is an association of national organizations, local, state, and regional planning bodies, and
individual citizens working together to improve the social health and unity of the nation. The Assembly seeks
to advance national social policy through documenting
needs and resources, giving technical consultation,
communicating needs to those in a position to bring
about change, developing and adapting educational pro-

grams in areas of social concern, and coordinating the activities and concerns of various organizations. Formerly the National Social Welfare Assembly.
Publ.: Annual Report; Memo to Members; Reports and pamphlets in such areas as racial factors in casework services, racial discrimination, civil rights, and the urban crisis; Report from Washington.

.1 National Assembly for Social Policy and Development. Files, 1945- . Records, correspondence, reports, and other materials relating to the operation and activities of the Assembly.

NY157 NATIONAL ASSOCIATION FOR AFRICAN AMERICAN EDUCATION (NAAAE). 103 E. 125th St., 10035. Tel 212 876-9255. Preston Wilcox, Chmn.
NAAAE is an organization of black persons who are active in the educational liberation and survival of black people. The overall objective of the organization is to change or create new educational systems and processes in order to insure the immediate and long-range survival of the black community. NAAAE is concerned with the re-education of the black teacher, the development of meaningful curricula and a meaningful language, community control of the black school, and practical alternatives to the public school structure, among other related areas. Services include a speakers bureau, a research and information center, and program development.
Publ.: Pamphlets.

.1 National Association for African American Education. Files. Includes proceedings of the 1st Conference of the National Association of Afro American Educators held in Chicago, Ill., (June 8, 9, 10, 1968); report of the National Organization Planning Committee of NAAAE held in St. Louis, Mo. (August, 1968); and proceedings of the 2nd National Conference of the National Association for African American Education in Atlanta, Ga. (August 20-24, 1969).

NY158 NATIONAL ASSOCIATION FOR THE ADVANCEMENT OF COLORED PEOPLE (NAACP) (1909). 1790 Broadway, 10019. Tel 212 279-1400. Roy Wilkins, Exec. Dir.
NAACP is a national civil rights organization which seeks to improve the political, educational, social and economic status of minority groups, to eliminate racial prejudice, to keep the public aware of the adverse effects of racial discrimination and to take lawful action to secure its elimination. Activities include lobbying for civil rights legislation, voter registration drives, and direct action programs. NAACP also maintains an education field staff to provide services related to integration and quality education in local schools, as well as legal, housing and labor departments.
Publ.: The Crisis, monthly magazine; Press releases, brochures, pamphlets; Annual Report.

.1 National Association for the Advancement of Colored People.
Files, 1909- . The records of the organization are deposited annually in the Manuscript Division of the Library of Congress.

NY159 NATIONAL ASSOCIATION OF NEGRO MUSICIANS (NANM) (1923). P.O. Box 191, Colonial Park Sta., 10039. Leroy H. Boyd, Exec. Secy.
NANM is an organization of amateur and professional musicians and others interested in music, that works to foster a larger public appreciation for and education in good music, and to resist the desecration of Negro spirituals.

.1 National Association of Negro Musicians (NANM). Files, 1923- . Correspondence, minutes of meetings, financial records, and other materials dealing with the aims, history, and programs of the Association.

NY160 NATIONAL ASSOCIATION OF SOCIAL WORKERS. 2 Park Ave., 10016. Tel 212 686-7128. Joseph P. Anderson, Exec. Dir.
The Association seeks to promote quality and effectiveness of social work practices in the U.S. It conducts legislative and clearinghouse programs in civil rights,

poverty, and other social welfare areas.
Publ.: Social Work; NASW News; Abstracts; Washington Memorandum.

NY161 NATIONAL COMMITTEE AGAINST DISCRIMINATION IN HOUSING (1950). 323 Lexington Ave., 10016. Tel 212 685-8911. Edward Rutledge, Exec. Dir.
The Committee is an organization of groups and individuals seeking to eliminate all forms of discrimination and segregation in housing. It conducts research, develops educational materials and programs, and offers technical assistance and counsel on community activities, as well as furnishes up-to-date information on anti-discriminatory housing laws and ordinances throughout the nation.
Publ.: Trends in Housing, bimonthly newsletter; Reports and studies.

.1 National Committee Against Discrimination in Housing. Files, 1950- . Records, reports, correspondence, and memoranda concerning the activities of the Committee.

NY162 NATIONAL COMMITTEE OF NEGRO CHURCHMEN, INC. (1966). 354 Convent Ave., 10031. Tel 212 862-9628. Rev. J. Metz Rollins, Acting Exec. Secy.
The Committee was established to provide a national vehicle for moving forward toward the ecumenical unity of black clergy and laity and toward the empowerment of the Afro-American Community.
Publ.: Newsletter, monthly.

NY163 NATIONAL COMMITTEE ON EMPLOYMENT OF YOUTH OF THE NATIONAL CHILD LABOR COMMITTEE. 145 E. 32nd St., 10016. Tel 212 683-4545. Miss Jean Dulaff, Librn. Inquiries answered, referrals made.
The Committee seeks to provide more and better employment opportunities, training, and educational opportunities for the nation's youth. Particular attention is given to youth with special employment problems, such as school dropouts, slow learners, members of minority groups, children of migrant workers, and children from low-income families.
Publ.: New Generation, quarterly. Formerly American Child.

.1 National Committee on the Employment of Youth. The Library of the Committee contains relevant materials on specific aspects of youth programs involving race relations.

NY164 NATIONAL CONFERENCE OF CHRISTIANS AND JEWS (NCCJ), NEW YORK REGIONAL OFFICE. 43 W. 57th St., 10019. Tel 212 688-7530. Paul G. Barker, Dir.

NY165 NATIONAL CONFERENCE OF CHRISTIANS AND JEWS (NCCJ) (1928), PAULA K. LAZRUS LIBRARY OF INTERGROUP RELATIONS (1955). 43 W. 57th St., 10019. Tel 212 688-7530. Dr. Bernhard E. Olson, Supvr. Bibliographies prepared, inquiries answered, referrals made, consultation.
NCCJ is a civic organization engaged in a nation-wide program of intergroup education. It seeks to build better relationships among people of all religions, races and nationalities.
Publ.: NCCJ Newsletter, quarterly; Dialogue, quarterly; Books for Brotherhood, annual bibliography; Paperbacks in Intergroup Relations, annual bibliography.

.1 Paula K. Lazrus Library of Intergroup Relations. ca. 6000 items. Includes books, periodicals, newspapers, and vf on such subjects as Negroes, race relations, civil rights, intergroup education, Jews and intergroup relations, Catholics and intergroup relations, and Protestants and intergroup relations.

NY166 NATIONAL CONFERENCE OF CHRISTIANS AND JEWS (NCCJ), POLICE-COMMUNITY RELATIONS PROGRAMS. 43 W. 57th St., 10019. Tel 212 688-7530. Joseph R. Harris, Dir.

NY167 NATIONAL COUNCIL OF JEWISH WOMEN, INC. (1893). 1 W. 47th St., 10036. Tel 212 246-3175. Miss Hannah Stein, Exec. Dir.
The Council is involved in social action, community

services of all kinds, and conducts education and action programs in poverty, peace and Jewish affairs. Projects include legislative action in support of civil rights laws; recruiting, screening and community projects for the Women's Job Corps; fact-finding and community education in areas of housing, job and consumer problems of the poor, and volunteer service in Head Start, and participation in Women in Community Service (WICS).
Publ.: Council Woman, bimonthly; Council Platform.

NY168 NATIONAL COUNCIL OF NEGRO WOMEN, INC., FIELD OFFICE. 884 Third Ave., 10022. Tel 212 355-0205.

NY169 NATIONAL COUNCIL OF THE CHURCHES OF CHRIST IN THE U.S.A., DELTA OPPORTUNITIES CORPORATION (1965). 475 Riverside Dr., 10027. Tel 212 870-2200.
The Corporation, partially supported by the National Council, was established by a group of Negro and white Mississippians to provide jobs and low-income housing in the Delta area. Among its projects is a training and self-help housing program for dispossessed farm workers.

.1 Delta Opportunities Corporation.
Files, 1965- . Correspondence, records, and reports of the operation and activities of the organization.

NY170 NATIONAL COUNCIL OF THE CHURCHES OF CHRIST IN THE U.S.A., DIVISION OF CHRISTIAN LIFE AND MISSION, COMMISSION ON RELIGION AND RACE (1963). 475 Riverside Dr., 10027. Tel 212 870-2131.
The Commission seeks to focus the concern, conviction, resources, and action of the member communions on issues of religion and race. Some of the Commission's activities have included the organization of the National Committee of Negro Churchmen, and education programs in the South in voter registration, literacy, and citizenship.
Publ.: Commission reports; Other literature such as a statement on black power, and information on Metropolitan Rural Development for Equal Opportunity.

NY171 NATIONAL COUNCIL OF THE CHURCHES OF CHRIST IN THE U.S.A., DIVISION OF CHRISTIAN LIFE AND MISSION, DEPARTMENT OF SOCIAL JUSTICE. 475 Riverside Dr., 10027. Tel 212 870-2439. David Ramage, Jr., Chmn., Dept. of Soc. Justice.
The Department serves as a resource to church groups affiliated with the National Council of Churches. Its national programs include a Technology and Human Values Project, whose anti-poverty task force provides assistance to self-organization of the poor and economic development for equal opportunity; a commission on social welfare; and educational programs for reconciliation in racial problem areas.
Publ.: Information Service, biweekly; Briefings from the Department of Social Justice, monthly.

NY172 NATIONAL COUNCIL OF THE CHURCHES OF CHRIST IN THE U.S.A., DIVISION OF CHRISTIAN LIFE AND MISSION, THE MIGRANT MINISTRY. 475 Riverside Dr., 10027. Tel 212 870-2298. Rev. William E. Scholes, Dir. of Field Serv.
The Migrant Ministry, operating in 38 states, seeks to point out the problems of migratory farm workers, to coordinate concerns in migrant legislation, to help migrant workers overcome the poverty cycle, and to eliminate discrimination and exploitation of these workers. Programs include vocational training, job placement, medical clinics and adult literacy classes.

NY173 NATIONAL COUNCIL OF THE CHURCHES OF CHRIST IN THE U.S.A., RESEARCH LIBRARY. 475 Riverside Dr., 10027. Tel 212 870-2565. Constant H. Jacquet, Jr., Dir.

.1 Research Library.
Contains over 8000 books, 150 current periodicals, 150 microfilm reels, many reports and staff papers. The major emphasis is placed on the role of the church in society and on the social sciences related to religion, including psychology, sociology, eco-

nomics and political science. Library is open by appointment to staff members of church organizations and academic persons.

NY174 NATIONAL COUNCIL OF WOMEN OF THE U.S. 345 E. 46th St., 10017. Tel 212 697-1278. Mrs. Eve R. Dyrssen, Exec. Dir.
The Council serves as a clearinghouse, coordinator, catalyst, and resource in matters that affect all society but are of special interest to women. The Council is composed of thirty women's organizations. It has arranged workshops and conferences on civil rights.

NY175 NATIONAL COUNCIL OF YMCAs OF THE U.S.A. (1851), YMCA HISTORICAL LIBRARY (1880). 291 Broadway, 10007. Tel 212 349-0700. Virginia Downes, Librn. Interlibrary loan, bibliographies prepared, literature searches, copying, typing, inquiries answered, referrals made.
The Council collects material of documentary significance on the work of the YMCAs in the U.S. and elsewhere; unites the historical background and the current developments of the Movement in a working center for research of YMCA and related subjects; preserves the unique documents which are the heritage of the YMCAs of North America and makes them available to YMCA personnel and others for reading and reference; and effects correlation with the libraries, archives and historical records of other YMCAs.
Publ.: Annual Library reports and occasional interpretive articles.

.1 Historical records of the YMCA of the U.S.A.
Records, 1851- . Books, pamphlets, theses and dissertations, mss, correspondence, photographs, and historical objects. Many local records contain material on programs with non-white groups. Also included are materials (ca. 9 stack shelves) concerning the national program on interracial work, and non-YMCA materials on race; and large archival collection of biographies and biographical background material about early black YMCA leaders. Restricted.

NY176 NATIONAL COUNCIL ON CRIME AND DELINQUENCY (NCCD), INFORMATION CENTER (1907). 44 E. 23rd St., 10010. Tel 212 254-7110. J. Robert Weber, Dir. Interlibrary loan, bibliographies prepared, literature searches, inquiries answered, referrals made, consultation.
The Information Center provides reference and document services and acts as a clearinghouse for research, information and literature on probation, parole, correctional institutions, juvenile and family courts, and the prevention and treatment of crime and delinquency. The National Council has conducted a juvenile court study, a juvenile institutions project, and a study on correctional training and manpower.
Publ.: Information Review on Crime and Delinquency, bimonthly; Crime and Delinquency, quarterly; Selected Highlights of Crime & Delinquency Literature, bimonthly; Journal of Research in Crime and Delinquency, semiannually.

NY177 NATIONAL COUNCIL ON CRIME AND DELINQUENCY (1907), LIBRARY. 44 E. 23rd St., 10010. Tel 212 254-7110. Miss Arminé Dikijian, Librn. Interlibrary loan, bibliographies prepared, literature searches, inquiries answered, referrals made, consultation.

.1 The Library of the National Council on Crime and Delinquency contains materials on crime and delinquency among racial groups, and the etiology of such offenses. Also included in the holdings is a strong collection of materials on law enforcement, with particular emphasis on police-community relations.

NY178 NATIONAL ECONOMIC GROWTH AND RECONSTRUCTION ORGANIZATION (NEGRO). c/o Dr. T.W. Matthew, 409 Edgecombe Ave., 10032. Tel 212 657-4000. Dr. T.W. Matthew, Dir.
NEGRO is a civil rights, self-help group which owns and operates, among other enterprises, the Blue and White Bus Company of Jamaica, N.Y., and the Interfaith Hospital, an addict treatment center also in Jamaica.

NY179   NATIONAL EMERGENCY CIVIL LIBERTIES COMMITTEE
         (1951). 25 E. 26th St., 10010. Tel 212 683-8120. Edith
         Tiger, Dir.
         The Committee was formed by dissident members of
         the American Civil Liberties Union and involves itself
         in New Left social and political controversies. The
         Committee works with student groups, draft resisters,
         the poor, victims of police malpractices and convicts
         by providing legal aid.
         Publ.: Rights, bimonthly.

         .1   National Emergency Civil Liberties Committee.
              Files, 1951- . Includes correspondence, minutes of
              meetings, financial records, investigations, and
              other documents dealing with the aims, history, and
              plans of the Committee.

NY180   NATIONAL FEDERATION OF SETTLEMENTS AND NEIGH-
         BORHOOD CENTERS (1911). 232 Madison Ave., 10016.
         Tel 212 679-6110. Margaret E. Berry, Exec. Dir. In-
         quiries answered.
         The Federation is the national spokesman and liaison
         for member agencies in the U.S.
         Publ.: Pamphlets, reports, and studies on such topics
              as race relations in settlement programs, civil
              rights and social welfare, housing and urban re-
              newal, and integrated education.

         .1   National Federation of Settlements and Neighborhood
              Centers.
              Files, 1911- . Includes program reports from
              member agencies, under subjects such as commu-
              nity control, black theater and arts programs, work
              on white racism, housing, race relations, youth
              groups and others; research data used by Dr. St.
              Clair Drake in his study Race Relations in a Time
              of Rapid Social Change; and data used in compiling
              workbook for Conference on Violence funded by
              National Institute of Mental Health.

NY181   NATIONAL JEWISH COMMUNITY RELATIONS ADVISORY
         COUNCIL (1944). 55 W. 42nd St., 10036. Tel 212 564-
         3450. Isaiah M. Minkoff, Exec. Vice-Chairman. In-
         quiries answered.
         The Council is a coordinating council of national and
         local Jewish community relations groups.
         Publ.: Reports of Plenary Session, annually.

NY182   NATIONAL MEDICAL ASSOCIATION. 421 Hudson St.,
         10014. Tel 212 247-4122.
         Publ.: Journal of the National Medical Association.

NY183   NATIONAL MEMORIAL AFRICAN BOOKSTORE (1934). 101
         W. 125th St., 10027. Tel 212 662-6860. Lewis H.
         Michaux, Founder and Pres.
         The Bookstore is "dedicated to disseminating informa-
         tion by and about Blacks. Here you will find all the
         facts about all the blacks all over the world. Know your
         heritage and human rights so you can walk in dignity and
         live in the light of life—for if a people knoweth not what
         they are worth, they can not know what's their share in
         life—and have to take the crumbs that are left from
         other people's table. So write in or come in for a new
         head dress that won't rub off in bed, but will abide with
         you until you are dead. We boast the only Black peoples
         Hall of Fame."

         .1   Materials pertaining to blacks.
              Books. ca. 200,000 v. of Afro-American history
              and literature.

NY184   NATIONAL NEGRO EVANGELICAL ASSOCIATION. P.O.
         Box 32, 10035. George M. Perry, Nat. Pres.
         The Association is an interdenominational organization
         of clergy and lay people, involved in inner-city pro-
         grams, including counseling services and the support of
         a singing group seeking to reach people through music.

         .1   National Negro Evangelical Association.
              Files. Records, reports, correspondence, and
              other papers concerning the operation and activities
              of the Association.

NY185   NATIONAL NEGRO INDUSTRIAL AND ECONOMIC UNION.
         150 Fifth Ave., 10011. Tel 212 691-7060.

NY186   NATIONAL OFFICE FOR THE RIGHTS OF THE INDIGENT
         (NORI). 10 Columbus Circle, 10019. Tel 212 586-8397.
         Jack Greenberg, Director-Counsel.
         NORI, under the sponsorship of NAACP Legal Defense
         and Educational Fund, Inc., plans and coordinates legal
         actions affecting rights of the poor. The principal task
         of the Office is making precedents in courts dealing
         with poverty law, especially in the areas of welfare
         laws, excessive consumer credit rates, consumer
         frauds, slum housing, public housing, protection of
         migrant workers, and rights of the indigent in criminal
         prosecution. It also conducts conferences on problems
         in poverty laws, and retains experts in various fields
         for advice and participation in conferences and litiga-
         tion.
         Publ.: Newsletter, annual reports, educational litera-
              ture, and fact-finding memoranda.

NY187   NATIONAL SCHOLARSHIP SERVICE AND FUND FOR
         NEGRO STUDENTS (NSSFNS) (1948). 1776 Broadway,
         10019. Tel 212 757-8100. Hugh W. Lane, Pres. In-
         quiries answered, referrals made, consultation.
         NSSFNS is a non-profit organization established to as-
         sist black high school juniors and seniors in obtaining
         college admission and financial aid by means of a col-
         lege advisory and referral service. It also maintains a
         limited scholarship fund to which counselled students
         who do not receive sufficient aid from colleges can ap-
         ply for supplementary assistance after all other finan-
         cial aid resources have been utilized.

NY188   NATIONAL SHARECROPPERS FUND (NSF) (1937). 112 E.
         19th St., 10003. Tel 212 473-0284. Fay Bennett, Exec.
         Dir. Inquiries answered, referrals made.
         NSF provides technical assistance to poverty-stricken
         people in rural areas; serves as an information center
         on issues related to rural poverty; conducts a Southern
         Rural Project, under contract with the Office of Eco-
         nomic Opportunity, to develop training programs for the
         hard-core rural poor; in conjunction with the Southern
         Regional Council and state councils on human rela-
         tions, operates the Rural Advancement Project, a coop-
         erative program; lobbies for legislation favorable to the
         rural poor through its tax-exempt subsidiary, The Rural
         Advancement Fund of the NSF; carries on field pro-
         gram, educational and charitable work.
         Publ.: Annual Report on the Condition of Farm Workers
              and Small Farmers in U.S.A.; Rural Advance,
              quarterly; Informational bulletins and pamphlets.

         .1   National Sharecroppers Fund.
              Files, 1937- . 1 vertical file of clippings, several
              vertical files of correspondence and reports.

NY189   NATIONAL TRADE UNION COUNCIL FOR HUMAN RIGHTS
         (NTUC) (1956). 25 E. 78th St., 10021. Betty Kaye
         Taylor, Exec. Secy.
         NTUC works to guide and direct a civil rights program
         carried on with and through the organized trade union
         movement; cooperates with state and city central labor
         bodies in establishing local programs and activities in
         the field of civil rights. Formerly the Jewish Labor
         Committee (JLC) National Trade Union Council.

         .1   National Trade Union Council for Human Rights (NTUC).
              Files, 1956- . Correspondence, minutes of meet-
              ings, financial records, reports, studies, and other
              materials dealing with its sponsor - the Jewish
              Labor Committee - and the aims, history, and
              programs of NTUC.

NY190   NATIONAL URBAN LEAGUE, EASTERN REGIONAL OF-
         FICE. 420 Madison Ave., 10017. Tel 212 751-0300.
         Alexander J. Allen, Dir.

NY191   NATIONAL URBAN LEAGUE, INC. (1910), EUGENE
         KINCKLE JONES LIBRARY (FORMERLY THE RE-
         SEARCH LIBRARY) (1921). 55 E. 52nd St., 10022. Tel
         212 751-0300. Mrs. L. Lucille Chappelle, Res. Asst.
         Bibliographies prepared, inquiries answered, referrals
         made.
         The League is a community service agency using the
         tools and methods of social work to secure equal oppor-
         tunity for Negroes and other disadvantaged minorities.

It is non-partisan and inter racial in its leadership and staff. The League works in the areas of economic development and employment, education, health and welfare, and housing. Programs and activities include Operation Equality, a fair housing program to help minority families find desirable integrated housing; Project Enable, a parent education and neighborhood action program to help parents in poverty areas improve situations in which they rear their children; on-the-job training; a national skills bank; and other projects.

Publ.: Urban League Newsletter, bimonthly; National Urban League Annual Report; Report to Business, bimonthly; Selected Bibliography on the Negro, periodically.

.1 Eugene Kinckle Jones Library.
The Library of the Urban League contains books, theses and dissertations, mss, historical objects, pamphlets and magazine articles, and a clipping file of newspaper articles, dealing with human and race relations. Major holdings of the Library are community studies on the social and economic conditions of minority population (1940-67) in various cities, among which are Seattle, Wash. (1943), Miami, Fla. (1943), Gary, Ind. (1944), Houston, Tex. (1945), Kansas City, Mo. (1946), Los Angeles, Calif. (1947), New Orleans, La. (1950); and studies made under the League's Community Relations Project (1944-47) in similar cities. The Library also contains source materials prepared by research scholars who have written about the agency and its programs.

.2 National Urban League.
Files, 1960- . Correspondence, minutes, memoranda, scrapbooks, research and documentary material. Includes papers relating to the operation and activities of the Urban League; facts and statistics about Negro life; and materials pertaining to such subjects as industrial relations, housing, urban renewal, education, health and welfare. Files, 1910-1960, are held in the Manuscript Division of the Library of Congress, and contain material on the above subjects.

NY192 NEGRO ACTION GROUP, INC. (NAG). 611 E. Sixth St., 10009. Tel 212 254-7050. Frederick Lewis, Dir.
NAG is a social-services organization which maintains a library, conducts child-care centers, education programs, and other cooperative programs designed to aid the Negro community.
Publ.: NAG's Bag, bimonthly newsletter.

.1 Negro Action Group, Inc.
Files. Includes reports, studies, minutes of meetings, financial reports, library materials, and other papers and materials dealing with the aims, programs, and activities of the Group.

NY193 NEGRO ACTORS GUILD OF AMERICA, INC. 1674 Broadway, 10019. Tel 212 245-4343. Valdo Freeman, Admin. Secy.
The Guild is a welfare organization which assists members of the theatre. It also furnishes information when possible about the theatre and its people.
Publ.: Newsletter occasionally.

NY194 NEGRO AMERICAN LABOR COUNCIL. 13 Astor Place, 10003. Tel 212 662-4700. Cleveland Robinson, Nat. Pres.
The Council is a national association of Negro trade union members working to eliminate discrimination in employment and in unions. The Council, committed to the militant trade union movement, works in cooperation with official labor bodies.
Publ.: Bulletins.

NY195 NEGRO BOOK CLUB, INC. 160 W. 85th St., 10024. Tel 212 362-8349. L. Alexander Brooks, Dir. of Publications.
The Club is the publisher and compiler of the Guide to African American Books, a bibliography of books in print by and about black Americans. Included in the Guide is information about records, visual aids, maps, film strips, and art.

Publ.: Guide to African American Books; Negro Book Club Newsletter.

NY196 NEGRO ENSEMBLE COMPANY. 1545 Broadway, 10036. Tel 212 247-4770. Douglas Turner Ward, Artistic Dir.
The Ensemble is a training and production company which assists minorities in gaining access into and experience in the theatrical arts.

NY197 NEGRO HISTORY ASSOCIATES, INC. (1964). Box 583, Manhattanville Sta., 10027. Tel 212 638-3983. M.A. Harris, Curator. Consultation.
The Associates collect rare materials pertaining to the Negro; research, particularly to locate descendants of famous persons to acquire memorabilia; produce film-strips; and present exhibitions on the Negro for schools, teacher training and other occasions; and sell photos from library of 3000 photos useful to writers, publishing concerns and other interested persons.

.1 M. A. Harris Collection.
Miscellaneous. ca. 300 items. Documents, photographs, drawings, newspapers, stamps, coins, medals, and other items. Collection traces Negro participation in American life and is divided into the following sections: Colonial years, Revolutionary War, Slavery and Anti-Slavery, the Civil War, Reconstruction, and contemporary history. Included are such items as a family Bible belonging to Jonathan C. Gibbs, a Negro who served as superintendent of education and secretary of state of Florida following the Civil War; an etching of Barzillai Lew, a fifer in the Revolution; and material on Mary Black, a Negro woman accused of witchcraft in the Salem, Mass., trials. Restricted.

NY198 NEGRO LABOR COMMITTEE. 312 W. 125th St., 10027. Tel 212 864-3295. L. Joseph Overton, Dir.
The Committee, composed of labor organizations, seeks to organize and guide Negro workers into legitimate trade unions, and to achieve solidarity of all workers, regardless of race.

NY199 NEGRO PRESS PHOTO SERVICE, INC. 120 E. 32nd St., 10016. Tel 212 689-8975.

NY200 NEW SCHOOL FOR SOCIAL RESEARCH, CENTER FOR NEW YORK CITY AFFAIRS (1965). 70 Fifth Ave., 10011. Tel 212 675-1260. Henry Cohen, Dir.
The Center is an educational unit of the New School for Social Research devoted entirely to the study and improvement of the New York metropolitan region. Through programs of education, information and research, it seeks to make a contribution toward a broader understanding of the New York area. The Metropolitan Information Service of the Center collects and maintains information concerning organizational and research activities which pertain to New York City. The Community News Service, staffed by black and Puerto Rican journalists, provides daily news coverage of New York's minority communities.
Publ.: City Almanac, bulletin; Community News Service reports.

NY201 NEW YORK CITY COMMISSION ON HUMAN RIGHTS (1955). 80 Lafayette St., 10013. Tel 212 566-5597. Simeon Golar, Chmn. Bibliographies prepared, copying, typing, inquiries answered, referrals made.
The Commission enforces the City Human Rights Law, and seeks to eliminate and prevent discrimination in employment, places of public accommodation, resort or amusement, in housing accommodations and commercial space, because of race, creed, color or national origin. Formerly the Commission on Intergroup Relations.
Publ.: CCHR 50/50 Reporter, bimonthly.

.1 Commission on Human Rights.
Files, 1955- . Records and reports of the operation and activities of the Commission, and pamphlets, research reports, and reports of conferences such as New York City's Racial Distribution (Goldblatt, 1959), Negroes in New York (Cromien, 1961), Bias in the Building Industry, 1963-67, Report on Three Demonstration Projects in the City Schools, 1968, and Community Values and Conflicts.

NY202 NEW YORK CITY HOUSING AND DEVELOPMENT ADMIN-
       ISTRATION, DEPARTMENT OF RELOCATION (1963).
       2 Lafayette St., 10007. Tel 212 566-6500. Earl A.
       Rawlins, Cmnr.
       The Administration provides and maintains tenant
       relocation services for residential and commercial
       tenants being displaced by governmental action, such as
       through urban renewal programs. Formerly the Bu-
       reau of Relocation in Department of Real Estate.

NY203 NEW YORK CITY HOUSING AUTHORITY, OFFICE OF COM-
       MUNITY AFFAIRS, INTERGROUP RELATIONS DIVI-
       SION (1958). 250 Broadway, 10007. Tel 212 433-4144.
       David W. Holland, Chief, Intergroup Rels. Div.
       The Division investigates and takes action on incidents
       of racial tension in housing developments and/or com-
       plaints of discrimination in housing; conducts training
       for staff and tenants in human relations; participates in
       studies of site selection, analyzing community prob-
       lems, educational and social facilities; cooperates with
       other community relations organizations in implement-
       ing programs to improve racial and intergroup rela-
       tions; and consults with other Authority departments on
       human relations and community problems.

NY204 NEW YORK CITY MISSION SOCIETY (1812). 105 E. 22nd
       St., 10010. Tel 212 674-3500. Rev. David Barry, Exec.
       Dir.
       The Society is a Protestant-sponsored organization
       which carries on activities in the areas of education,
       employment, and interreligious affairs. It administers
       the Interfaith City-Wide Coordinating Committee
       Against Poverty, which is sponsored by and worked in
       Protestant, Catholic, and Jewish neighborhood institu-
       tions.
       Publ.: Reporting to Our Friends, 3 issues per year.

NY205 NEW YORK CIVIL LIBERTIES UNION, INC. 156 Fifth Ave.,
       10010. Tel 212 929-6076. Aryeh Neier, Exec. Dir.

NY206 NEW YORK HISTORICAL SOCIETY (1804). 170 Central
       Park W., 10024. Tel 212 873-3400. James Gregory,
       Librn. Copying, inquiries answered.

       .1 Beekman, Gerard, 1719-97.
               Papers, ca. 100 v. Papers of Beekman, a New York
               merchant involved in the slave trade, and of his
               descendants.
       .2 Brown, James F.
               Papers, 1829-64. 10 v. Negro gardener at Fish-
               kill, N.Y. Diaries, receipt book, and notebook.
       .3 Clarkson, John, 1764-1828.
               Journals, 1791-92. 2 v. British naval officer and
               Governor of Sierra Leone. Journals of Clarkson's
               missions to America (1791-92) and to Africa (1792)
               relating to the slave trade.
       .4 Greeley, Horace.
               Papers, 1846-70. ca. 61 items. New York; editor
               of New York Tribune, U.S. Representative.
       .5 Holley, Myron, 1779-1841.
               Letters, 1799-1840. 41 items. Abolitionist.
       .6 Kentucky papers, 1787-1863.
               ca. 100 items. Miscellaneous papers relating to
               the disposition of slaves in Kentucky, particularly
               in Lincoln and Fayette Counties. Includes inven-
               tories and appraisements of estates, deeds of gift
               and bills of sale.
       .7 Massachusetts Anti-Slavery Society.
               Records, 1850-58. ca. 100 items. Correspondence
               and other papers. Includes petitions to the Massa-
               chusetts Legislature, resolutions, donations to the
               Liberator, and a list of fugitive slaves aided by the
               Vigilance Committee. Persons whose names ap-
               pear frequently are William Lloyd Garrison,
               Francis Jackson, Ellis Gray Loring, Wendell Phil-
               lips, Edmund Quincy, and Samuel E. Sewall.
       .8 New York Society for Promoting the Manumission of
           Slaves.
               Records, 1786-1849. 11 v. Accounts, minutes,
               indentures, and other papers.
       .9 Papers relating to slavery, 18th-19th century.
               7 boxes. Correspondence and business papers on
               the slave trade, together with writings and reports
               of individuals about slavery. Includes letters from
               Jacobus Van Cortlandt and Philip Livingston &

Sons on the slave trade in the first half of the 18th
century; papers of Dutilh and Wachsmith (1 v., 1
folder), 18th and 19th century Philadelphia shipping
merchants.
       .10 Riot of 1834, New York City.
               Correspondence concerning the protection of the
               people during the riot of 1834 in New York City. 53
               items.
       .11 Sharp, Granville, 1735-1813.
               Papers, 1768-73. 3 v. Transcripts. British aboli-
               tionist. Letters to Sharp about slavery, its evils,
               and its legal aspect; Sharp's copy of the case of
               Lewis, a Negro, vs. Stappleton, his master (London
               1771); and Sharp's copy of the case of James
               Somerset, a Negro slave from Virginia (1772).
       .12 Slavery Collection.
               Books and pamphlets, ca. 1790-Reconstruction. ca.
               500 books and 20,000 pamphlets.
       .13 Smith, Gerrit, 1797-1874.
               Letters, 1834-74. 45 items. Reformer.
       .14 Society for the Prevention of the Absconding and Abduc-
            tion of Slaves, Richmond, Va.
               Papers, 1833. 1 v. Minutes of the Society.
       .15 Spooner, Lysander, 1808-87.
               Correspondence, 1845-62. 2 boxes. Lawyer from
               Boston. Correspondence concerning slavery.
       .16 Taylor, John W., 1784-1854.
               Correspondence, 1813-33. 7 boxes. U.S. Repre-
               sentative from New York and anti-slavery leader.

NY207 NEW YORK PUBLIC LIBRARY (1895). Manuscript Division,
       Fifth Ave. and 42nd St., 10018. Tel 212 790-6338.
       Gerald D. McDonald, Keeper of Manuscripts. Copying,
       typing, inquiries answered.
       Publ.: Dictionary catalog and other finding aids.

       .1 Beecher, Henry Ward, 1813-97.
               Papers, 1860-64. 126 pieces. Congregational
               clergyman and abolitionist.
       .2 Child, Lydia Maria Francis.
               Papers, 1838-43. 62 items. Author and abolition-
               ist.
       .3 Facts on Film.
               Papers, 1954-67. Microfilm. Contains materials
               on civil rights and race relations in the South. See
               Race Relations Information Center, Nashville,
               Tenn., for a full description.
       .4 Greeley, Horace, 1811-72.
               Papers, 1836-72. 5 boxes. Political leader, aboli-
               tionist, and editor of the New York Tribune.
       .5 Griswold, B.
               Miscellaneous papers. Included in this collection
               is a description of the early years of Liberian
               colonization.
       .6 Hunter, Maurice.
               Scrapbooks. New York City African model.
       .7 Lincoln, Abraham, 1809-65.
               Papers, 1847-65. 4 boxes. 16th President of the
               U.S.
       .8 McKim, James Miller.
               Papers, 1866-67. 1 v. Abolitionist, of Pennsyl-
               vania, New Jersey and New York.
       .9 Smith, Gerrit.
               Papers, 1819-74. Philanthropist and abolitionist.
       .10 Toussaint L'Ouverture (Pierre Dominique), 1743-1803.
               Papers (several thousand). Ms and letters relating
               to Toussaint, Haitian general and liberator.
       .11 Van Vechten, Carl.
               Papers, ca. 1900- . 60 ft. Novelist, music critic
               and philanthropist. Collection of mss, correspon-
               dence and rare editions, with scattered references
               to the Negro.
       .12 Weaver, Aaron Ward, 1832-1919.
               Papers. ca. 75 items. Served with the African
               Squadron, 1857-59

NY208 NEW YORK PUBLIC LIBRARY (1895), COUNTEE CULLEN
       REGIONAL BRANCH. 104 W. 136th St., 10030. Tel 212
       281-0700. Interlibrary loan, bibliographies prepared,
       inquiries answered, referrals made, consultation.
       The Regional Branch Library houses the North Manhat-
       tan Library Project, designed to show what increased
       library services can do in a deprived area.

       .1 Douglas, Aaron, 1899- .
               Black artist. Four murals depicting stages in the
               history of the Negro in America.

.2   James Weldon Johnson Memorial Collection.
       Books, ca. 250. Collection of books for children
       that give an unbiased, accurate, well-rounded pic-
       ture of Negro life in all parts of the world.

NY209 NEW YORK PUBLIC LIBRARY (1895), LIBRARY AND MU-
       SEUM OF THE PERFORMING ARTS. 111 Amsterdam
       Ave., 10023. Tel 212 799-2200. Dr. Robert Henderson,
       Chief.

.1   The Library of the Performing Arts has material on the
       Negro in music, theatre, dance and the films, and
       its Reference Department contains a large amount
       of U.S. Negro material in its special collections.

NY210 THE NEW YORK PUBLIC LIBRARY, 135th STREET
       BRANCH, SCHOMBURG COLLECTION OF NEGRO LIT-
       ERATURE AND HISTORY (1925). 103 W. 135th St.,
       10030. Tel 212 794-4000. Mrs. Jean Blackwell Hutson,
       Curator. Copying, inquiries answered, referrals made,
       consultation.
       Publ.: Dictionary Catalog of the Schomburg Collections
              of Negro Literature and History (1962, 1968);
              Harlem: A Bibliography; The Negro: A Bibli-
              ography.

.1   The Schomburg Collection is a reference and research
       library devoted to the life and history of Afro-
       Americans. The nucleus of this Collection is the
       private library assembled by Arthur A. Schomburg,
       a Puerto Rican of African descent, purchased by
       the Carnegie Corporation of New York and pre-
       sented to the New York Public Library. The Col-
       lection provides books of black authorship, literary
       and historical works, and magazines, pamphlets,
       mss, photographs, pictures, prints, newspaper
       clippings, playbills, programs, broadsides, sheet
       music, tape and phonograph recordings, and films.

.2   — Aldridge, Ira, 1807?-67.
       Papers. ca. 21 items. Shakespearean actor.
       Scrapbook of playbills, photos, and letters,
       chiefly of Amanda Ira Aldridge (1866-1956),
       his daughter.

.3   — Allen, Cleveland G.
       Papers, ca. 1925-53. ca. 80 items. Lecturer,
       newspaperman, and writer. Includes corre-
       spondence, lectures, and "Allen's National
       News Bureau," chiefly concerning the annual
       Harriet Beecher Stowe birthday pilgrimage.

.4   — Art collection.
       Oil Paintings. ca. 108. Included are works by
       the following black American artists: Victor
       Amerino, Alvarez, Edward M. Bannister, Rich-
       mond Barthé, Eugenie Baizerman, J.I. Brah-
       min, E.H. Bischoff, William Ernest Braxton
       (16 items), J. Califano, Claude Clark, E.
       Simms Campbell, R. Coleman, Moses T.
       Cross, Bundy, Aaron Douglas, Chester Danes,
       Gilbert Goraleigh, Blanche Grambs, J.W.
       Hardrick, Hirschfeld, Agnes Hart, Theodore G.
       Haupt, William Jackson, Lois M. Jones, Malnin
       Gray Johnson (7 items), Lavedo, Carl V. Lind,
       Ben Earl Looney, Helga Meyer, Archibald J.
       Motley, Jr., Elizabeth Olds, C.M. Parenzuela,
       Richard Reid, Lillian Richter, Earle Richard-
       son, H. Rivers, Donald Reid, W.J. Russell,
       Augusta Savage, William E. Scott, Georgette
       Seabrooke, Charles Sebree, Albert Alexander
       Smith, M. Schulman, H.O. Tanner, Louise B.
       Terry, Carole Weinstock, Charles White, E.
       Wilson, Pastor Argudin, and T. Auguste.
       Etchings, lithographs, engravings, and water
       colors; works by Negro artists and of Negro
       subjects.

.5   — Autograph letter collection.
       Hundreds of autographed letters, including
       those of Bessie A. Buchanan, W.E.B. DuBois,
       T. Thomas Fortune, Amy Jacques Garvey,
       William Lloyd Garrison, Kelly Miller, R.R.
       Moton, Walter White, and Carter Woodson.

.6   — Bearden, Bessye J., -1943.
       Papers. Journalist, deputy collector of
       Internal Revenue, political and civic leader in
       Harlem (1920's-30's), and mother of Romare
       Bearden, artist. Included are correspondence,
       newspaper clippings, speeches, and other
       items.

.7   — Boyd, Rubic.
       Papers, 1935. A 25-part series of articles on
       Paul Laurence Dunbar released by Associated
       Negro Press.

.8   — Braithwaite, William Stanley, 1878-1962.
       Papers, 1952-54. ca. 5 items. Includes mss,
       poems, and correspondence.

.9   — Broderick, Francis L.
       Papers. 2 boxes, 4 notebooks, 1 folder. Notes
       made from the W.E.B. DuBois papers and used
       in Broderick's doctoral dissertation at Har-
       vard University. Later published as W.E.B.
       DuBois, Negro Leader in a Time of Crisis
       (1959).

.10   — Bruce, John Edward, 1856-1924.
       Papers, 1872-1920's. ca. 1300 items. Writer,
       publisher, and first president of the Negro So-
       ciety for Historical Research. Correspon-
       dence, pamphlets, essays, poems, plays, an
       autobiography (6 pages, 1875), and other mss.
       Includes material relating to Bruce's early
       life as a slave; his newspaper work and the
       publications which he founded (The Argus; The
       Sunday Item, 1880; The Chronicle; the Grit,
       1884; Weekly Standard, 1908; and edited (The
       Commonwealth, Baltimore, 1884; and Howards
       American Magazine, 1896-1901); his involve-
       ment in Marcus Garvey's "Back to Africa"
       movement; the African Society (London), the
       Order of African Redemption (Liberia); the
       African Methodist Episcopal Zion Church; the
       New York State Negro exhibit at the Tennessee
       Centennial Exposition (1899); and the Negro So-
       ciety for Historical Research. Among his cor-
       respondents are Charles W. Anderson, Senator
       Blanche K. Bruce, W.E.B. DuBois, James K.
       Vardaman, Cole Blease, Marcus Garvey, Wil-
       liam H. Ferris, and Alexander Crummell.

.11   — Braxton, William Ernest.
       Papers, 1925. 2 items. One letter and exhibi-
       tion list of his oils, pastels, and drawings.

.12   — Citizen's Protective League, New York.
       Papers, 1900. ca. 10 items. Correspondence
       and press releases, concerning the New York
       City race riot in 1900.

.13   — Civil Rights Congress (CRC).
       Papers, 1946-ca. 1956. ca. 138 boxes.
       Formed from a merger of the International
       Labor Defense and the Federation for Constitu-
       tional Liberties. Correspondence, press re-
       leases, clippings, photographs, tapes, phono-
       discs, film, and trial transcripts. Collection
       includes cases, correspondence and publica-
       tions (2 boxes) of the CRC Prisoner's Relief
       Committee; correspondence and publications
       (2 boxes) of the CRC Law Letter Department
       and Literature Department; clippings and
       other materials (10 boxes) of the Communist
       Party of the U.S.A. concerning the "Trial of
       the 12" (1949); materials (6 boxes) concern-
       ing legal cases and special projects of the
       New York Civil Rights Congress, including
       papers relating to the Trenton Six (194?); and
       clippings, publications, and correspondence
       (10 boxes) of the Citizens Emergency Defense
       Conference. Other subjects and persons in-
       clude Sam Kanter, Nat Ross, W.L. Patterson,
       the Smith Act, Brownell vs. CRC, Oklahoma
       vs. Eli Jaffee, and the House Committee on
       Un-American Activities.

.14   — Civil War Collection.
       Papers, 1864. ca. 51 items. Includes forage
       abstracts, requisitions, and requisition receipts
       for the 55th Regiment, USCT, and the 2nd, 6th,
       and 7th Regiments, USHA, at Fort Pickering.

.15   — Colmand, Henry.
       Papers, ca. 1863-68. ca. 88 items. First
       Lieutenant, Union Army. Includes 96th In-
       fantry Regiment, USCT, military orders, pay-
       roll receipts, survey requisitions, transfers,
       and other papers.

.16   — Crummell, Alexander, 1819-98.
       Papers, ca. 1837-90's. ca. 668 items. Epis-
       copal minister, scholar, and founder of the
       American Negro Academy. Correspondence,

sermons, addresses, mss, and other papers. Includes material relating to Crummell's ministry, his study in England, his life and work (20 years) in Liberia, the founding of St. Luke's Church in Washington, D.C. (1873), and the founding of the American Negro Academy (1897). Correspondents (256 letters) and persons mentioned include Charles L. Reason, Paul Laurence Dunbar, R.S. Rust, E.E. Smith, William H. Morris, the African Emigration Society, Foreign Missions of the New York Protestant Episcopal Church, James McCune Smith, Lemuel Haynes, Henry Highland Garnet, Bishop Onderdonk (of the Epsicopal General Theological Seminary), William and John Jay, John W. Cromwell, Archibald and Francis Grimké, Kelly Miller, and others.

NY210.17 —— Cullen, Countee, 1903-46.
Papers, ca. 1924-41. ca. 9 items. Ms poems, correspondence, and miscellaneous papers.

.18 —— Douglass, Frederick, 1817-95.
Papers. ca. 5 items.

.19 —— DuBois, William Edward Burghardt, 1868-1963.
Papers, ca. 1911-32. ca. 19 items. Includes correspondence, and a lecture ms (1949) paying tribute to Dr. Carter G. Woodson.

.20 —— Dunbar, Paul Laurence, 1872-1906.
Papers, 1890's-1900's. ca. 99 items. Chiefly correspondence of Dunbar and his wife, Alice Ruth Moore Dunbar, to their literary agent, Paul R. Reynolds.

.21 —— Facts on Film.
Papers, 1954-67. Microfilm. Contains materials on civil rights and race relations in the South. See Race Relations Information Center, Nashville, Tenn., for a full description.

.22 —— Federal Writers' Project.
Negroes of New York material. Research material, including biographical sketches, on such subjects as education, religion, history, housing, Marcus Garvey, political life, organizations, music, theatre, films, health, policemen and firemen, the Negro press, slavery and sports; and various drafts of this material published as The Negro in New York: An Informal Social History (1967), edited by Roi Ottley and William J. Weatherby.

.23 —— Fitzgerald, Robert G., 1840-1919.
Papers. Diary, family papers, sketches, and other items. Given to the Schomburg Collection by Pauli Murray, granddaughter of Fitzgerald, after the publication of her book Proud Shoes: The Story of an American Family (1956).

.24 —— Fleetwood, Christian A.
Papers, 1860's-1931. Sergeant-Major, 4th Regiment, USCT; Congressional medal of honor winner as a result of action at Chapman's Farm, Richmond, Va., September 24, 1864. Includes portrait photographs (1860's), news clippings about the 10th Cavalry in the Indian Wars, manumission papers, and bulletins of the American Interracial Peace Committee (1929-31).

.25 —— Friendship House of Harlem.
Papers, ca. 1953-55. ca. 3 vf. Includes correspondence, housing complaints, rent protests, press releases, pamphlets, and brochures; and field notes and other materials concerning the United Neighborhood Houses of New York questionnaire "Families who have relocated from public improvement sites."

.26 —— Garrison, William Lloyd, 1805-79.
Papers, ca. 19 items. Abolitionist.

.27 —— Greener, Richard Theodore, 1844-1923.
Papers, ca. 1870's-1910's. ca. 7 items. First Negro graduate of Harvard University, and professor at the University of South Carolina. Includes letters and mss.

.28 —— Hammon, Jupiter, ca. 1720-ca. 1800.
An address to the Negroes in the State of New York. Poet.

.29 —— Harlem on My Mind.
Photocopies. ca. 300 items. Exhibited at the Metropolitan Museum of Art, New York City,

1968. Photographs, newspaper articles, and documents used to depict the history of Harlem (1900-68). Included are pictures of everyday scenes, clubs and organizations, musicians and entertainers, sports figures, literary and political figures, and current events.

.30 —— Haynes, Lemuel, 1753-1833.
Sermons, ca. 1805-21. Negro minister of a white congregation in Rutland, Vt., for thirty years before the Civil War.

.31 —— Hughes, Langston, 1902-67.
Papers. Contains several folders of mss, including ms of The Weary Blues, and a few letters.

.32 —— Humane Brotherhood.
Minutebook, 1843. 1 item. "Proceeding Book of Human Brotherhood," including minutes and proceedings of the Brotherhood.

.33 —— International Labor Defense.
Papers, ca. 1931-50. ca. 6 vf. Correspondence, minutes, financial reports, legal documents, clippings, photographs, press releases, mss and other papers. Included is material concerning politics, labor, the Scottsboro Defense, papers and mss of the defense committee for the Thomas Mooney trial, and copies of the Labor Defender.

.34 —— Johnson, Oakley C., 1890- .
Papers, ca. 1946-68. ca. 3 ft. (ea. 4000 items). Professor, journalist, and civil libertarian. Correspondence, pamphlets, speeches, financial materials, school and student publications, legal cases, press releases, clippings, mss, reports, and other papers. Contains materials concerning Johnson's teaching at Talladega (Alabama, 1946-47), Dillard University (Louisiana, 1947-51), and Tillotson College (Texas, 1951-52); a "Study of Unequal Justice in Louisiana" (1950-51, Carnegie Grant-in-Aid); the Louisiana Civil Rights Congress, of which Johnson was executive secretary (1949-51), including papers concerning the Trenton Six, Ray Brooks, the Ocie Jugger-Paul Washington case, the Progressive party and the Young Progressive party; writings on civil liberties and segregation; Marxism; the House Committee on Un-American Activities investigation of Johnson's activities; and a report of an extended trip through the South (1957).

.35 —— Kennedy, Stetson.
Papers, ca. 1940. ca. 3 ft. Journalist. Correspondence, memos, interviews, clippings, press releases, photographs, and other materials. Includes Ku Klux Klan documents (originals and photocopies), materials concerning the Klan in Tennessee and California, Klan inheritance, Klan law, interviews of Klan members by Kennedy, the American Shores Patrol, and anti-union work of the Klan.

.36 —— Locke, Alain, 1886-1954.
Papers, ca. 1930's. ca. 10 items. Writer and critic. Correspondence, mainly with Mrs. C.A. Latimer; and other papers.

.37 —— Lydenberry, Harry M.
Papers. ca. 25 items. Letters, and a ms of an article on Paul Laurence Dunbar, among other papers.

.38 —— Lyons and Williamson family.
Papers, 1783-1957. ca. 200 items. Includes autobiographical ms of Maritcha Rémond Lyons; and photographs, letters, memorabilia, and legal papers of Harry A. Williamson, Mary Joseph Marshall Lyons, Albro Lyons, and Theresa Lyons Bunell.

.39 —— McClendon, Rose.
Papers, 1923-34. 2 v. Black New York actress during the 1920's and 30's. Reviews, pictures, programs, congratulatory messages, and notices connected with the career of Rose McClendon. V. 1 (1923-34) includes press notices of the stage productions of the plays Rosanne, Deep River, In Abraham's Bosom and Porgy; v. 2 (1931-33) includes press notices of the stage productions of the plays House of Connelly, Never No More, Black Souls, Brain

Sweat, Roll, Sweet Chariot, Panic, and the CBC program John Henry.

NY210.40 — McKay, Claude, 1890-1948.
Papers, 1924-46. 35 items. Poet. Miscellaneous correspondence, and mss.

.41 — Miscellaneous letters and papers.
Papers, ca. 1757-1940's. ca. 65 items. Letters, sermons, reports, receipts, and other papers. Represented are Phillis Wheatley, William Wells Brown, Frederick Douglass, Grace Douglass, Hilary R.N. Johnson, William H. Brooks, Victor Sejour, Richard Hill, and others.

.42 — Miscellaneous manuscripts.
Manuscripts, 1716-1941. Addresses, poems, selections from books, sermons, official proclamations, reports, wills, certificates of freedom, slave sales, and many letters. Included are materials pertaining to the following persons; Cole Blease, Edward Blyden, J.W.E. Bowen, William Wells Brown, Nannie Burroughs, William Ellery Channing, Thomas Clarkson, Marcus Garvey, Hannibal Hamlin, Hubert Harrison, James Weldon Johnson, John W. Cromwell, Martin R. Delany, James H. Dillard, Henry Highland Garnet, General Leclerc, Toussaint L'Ouverture, Daniel Murray, P.B.S. Pinchback, Ignatius Sancho, Victor Sejour, Granville Sharpe, Carter G. Woodson, T. Thomas Fortune, Frederick Douglass, William Lloyd Garrison, and Alexander Dumas.

.43 — Moore, Fred R., 1857-1943.
Papers, ca. 1908. ca. 4 items. Harlem leader, editor and publisher of the New York Age newspaper, minister to Siberia, and member of the board of the Dunbar National Bank in Harlem. Legal papers, including certificate of incorporation for the Moore Publishing and Printing Company, New York City.

.44 — Myrdal, Gunnar.
Manuscripts. 81 typescript v. of field notes and memoranda used by Myrdal in writing An American Dilemma (1944), a study of the Negro in America, sponsored by the Carnegie Corporation. Among the persons who prepared research memoranda on special subjects are Richard Sterner, Arnold Rose, Ralph J. Bunche, Guy B. Johnson, Paul H. Norgren, Dorothy S. Thomas, Doxey A. Wilkerson, M.F. Ashley-Montagu, Sterling Brown, J.G. St. Clair Drake, E. Franklin Frazier, Melville J. Herskovits, Charles S. Johnson, Otto Klineberg, Ira De A. Reid, and Louis Wirth.

.45 — Music collection.
Phonodiscs, 1920-present. Phonodiscs of music composed or performed by black people, including spirituals, jazz, classical, and rhythm and blues.

.46 — National Association of Colored Graduate Nurses.
Files, 1908-51. ca. 60 items. Included are the Association's publications, scrapbook, programs, and press releases.

.47 — National Negro Congress.
Files, 1933-47. ca. 46 ft. (ca. 67,200 items). Correspondence, statements, documents, statistics, speeches, reports, financial papers, resolutions, photographs, and other materials. The collection is comprised of the pre-Congress records (1933-35), including files of the Negro Industrial league (1933) and the Joint Committee on National Recovery (1933-35); the files of each sucessive executive secretary of the Congress (John P. Davis, 1935-42, Edward E. Strong, 1943, Thelma Dale, and Revels Clayton, 1945-47); materials pertaining to the Negro Labor Victory Committee (1942-45), including Negro Freedom Rally files, union records, and records of Charles A. Collins and M. Moran Weston; financial records; and mss and publications. Among the many subjects and correspondents represented are the Ku Klux Klan, Howard University, American Peace Mobilization, American Youth Commission, Maury Maverick, George B. Murphy, Jr., Dorothy Kelso Funn, Ruth Jett, Adam Clayton

Powell, Jr., NAACP, National Youth Administration, police brutality, Max Yergan, anti-lynching bill, Citizen's Committee to End Discrimination at Horn and Hardart, Congress of Industrial Organizations, employment discrimination, fair employment practices committee, Southern Negro Youth Conference, housing, Kill the Klan Committee, March on Washington (1943), Africa, Democratic party, job study, military equality, political action, Urban League, Emergency Jobs Conference, National Council of Negro Women, school strikes, American Council on Race Relations, American Crusade to End Lynching, Armed Forces, Association for the Study of Negro Life and History, Civil Rights Congress, Georgia Lynching Campaign, National Citizens' Political Action Committee, National Council of American-Soviet Friendship, Southern Conference on Human Welfare, United Automobile Workers, New York State Committee to Abolish the Poll Tax, U.N. Commission on Human Rights, Theodore Bilbo, Harry S Truman, B'nai B'rith, Communist Political Association, Freedom Fighters Committee, voter registration, Henry A. Wallace, and many other persons and organizations. Also included is correspondence with the various state councils and with labor unions; and such Congress publications as Action, Congress View, Congress Vue, Monthly Letter, and National Negro Congress News.

.48 — National Urban League, Department of Promotion and Publicity.
Papers, ca. 1950's-60's. Pamphlets, news clippings, memos, press releases, and ephemeral materials on such subjects as employment, race relations, housing, anti-discrimination laws, and health and welfare; card file of key mailings; and pledge cards for the "March on Washington for Jobs and Freedom" (1963).

.49 — Negro newspapers.
ca. 400 newspaper titles, 1827-1969. On miccrofilm. Included are such papers as the California Eagle, Cleveland Gazette, the Savannah Tribune, Freedom's Journal, The Colored American, The Liberator, National Anti-Slavery Standard, and The Negro Worker.

.50 — "Negro Week" collection.
Papers, 1940. ca. 500 items. Correspondence and other documents relative to "Negro Week" at the New York World's Fair (1940). Bills, drafts of speeches, minutes of meetings, press releases, photographs, passes, radio scripts, telegrams, and many letters. Included is the typescript of The Negro in the Building of America. Persons mentioned include Marian Anderson, Justice Jane Bolin, Francis Bosworth, Willie Bryant, Gene Buck, George Washington Carver, General B.O. Davis, Commissioner Hubert T. Delaney, Geraldyn Dismond, Aaron Douglas, W.E.B. DuBois, Todd Duncan, Ella Fitzgerald, W.C. Handy, Roland Hayes, The Julius Rosenwald Fund, Alain Locke, Hattie McDaniels, Dorothy Maynor, Judge Myles Paige, A. Philip Randolph, Paul Robeson, Bill Robinson, Eleanor Roosevelt, the Southernaires, Maxine Sullivan, Channing Tobias, Ethel Waters, Walter White, Paul Williams, Walter Winchell, and Richard Wright, as well as many Negro college presidents, scholars, fraternity presidents, and labor leaders.

.51 — Negro World Digest.
Papers, 1939-41. ca. 9 ft. (850 items). Monthly literary magazine (July-Dec., 1940). Correspondence, articles intended for publication, office notes and memos, and permit material. Primarily correspondence inquiring into the potential services offered by the publication.

.52 — Peters, Solomon.
Will, 1694. 1 item. Certified copy of Peters' will.

NY210.53 — Photograph collection.
ca. 15,000 items (10,000 of which are unavailable until processing). Represents items
received from the Office of War Information,
Works Progress Administration, International
Labor Defense, Farm Security, the Amsterdam
News, and the New York Urban League.

.54 — Pickens, William, 1881-1954.
Papers, 1905-54. ca. 6 ft. (ca. 21,000 items).
Educator, writer, dean of Morgan College
(1918-19), and field secretary for the National
Association for the Advancement of Colored
People (1920-42). Correspondence, editorials,
financial records, and other papers. Correspondence relates to lectures, the selective
service system (member of the Appeals Board
of Draft Board #5, New York City, 1937-41),
and Pickens' activities as director of the Interracial Section of the Savings Bond Division of
the Treasury Department (1942-51), and family
matters. Editorial materials include essays,
editorials, mss, news releases, clippings and
correspondence relating to, among other subjects, Marcus Garvey, the Ku Klux Klan, and
lynching.

.55 — Rayner, John B., 1850-1918.
Papers. Microfilm. Teacher, minister, and
populist organizer in Texas (1894-98) for the
People's party. Correspondence, newspaper
clippings, and other items.

.56 — Reason, Patrick.
Papers, ca. 1830-60's. ca. 20 items. Includes
indentures, genealogy of the Reason family,
photographs, and sketches by his son, Charles
Reason.

.57 — Revels, Hiram Rhoades, 1822-1901.
Papers, 1870-1901. Originals and on microfilm. Preacher, president of Alcorn College
(Mississippi), and first Negro Senator (1870).
Included are scrapbook of clippings, programs,
photographs, letters and notes covering his
activities.

.58 — Rising Sons of Liberty.
Minutebook, 1875. 1 item. "Constitution of
the Rising Sons of Liberty of the City of Manchester, Virginia."

.59 — Robeson, Paul, 1898- .
Papers, ca. 1943-50's. ca. 17 boxes. Press
releases, passport materials, mss, and materials pertaining to performances. Includes
correspondence, clippings, and photographs
pertaining to the World Peace Council and the
Council on African Affairs. Restricted.

.60 — Schomburg, Arthur A., 1874-1938.
Papers, ca. 1904-38. 6.7 ft. (ca. 8000 items).
Writer, collector, and curator; organizer and
secretary of the Negro Society for Historic Research, and president of the American Negro
Academy. Correspondence, mss and typescripts by various authors. Collection contains
materials relating to the Schomburg Collection,
and Schomburg's interests and activities as
historian, bibliophile, curator and private citi-
zen. Correspondents include Henrietta Buck-
master, Thomas Dewey, W.E.B. DuBois, W.C.
Handy, Langston Hughes, Charles S. Johnson,
Claude McKay, J.A. Rogers, The Honorable
Stenio Vincent (President of Haiti), Walter
White, Carter G. Woodson, and many others.
Among authors represented in the ms collec-
tion are John Steward, John Edward Bruce,
Nancy Cunard, Henry B. Wilkinson, Willis N.
Huggins, Laphin H. Dolph, Robert S. Dixon,
William H. Ferris, Claude McKay, James
Tamplin Laing, E.W. Gaillard, Grace E.
Walker, Daisy C. Reed, Ira Aldridge, Lemuel
L. Foster, D.B. Fulton, Jack Thorne, Moses
Ashley, and Francis Williams.

.61 — Seldon, Benjamin F.
Papers, ca. 1921-43. ca. 363 items. Correspondence (1938-43) and personal letters
(1921-30).

.62 — Shaw, Adele Marie.
Papers, ca. 1886. Includes a ms for The

American Negro, and 3 letters from Walter H.
Page, editor, Doubleday and Page.

.63 — Slavery and abolition collections.
Papers, 1700-1890's. ca. 100 items. Letters,
slave sales, passes, certificates of registry,
manumission papers, wills, speeches, and
other papers. Includes letters from William
Lloyd Garrison, Theodore Weld, Frederick
Douglass, William Wilberforce, Thomas Clarkson, and Granville Sharpe; and materials relating to the Amistad mutiny (1839) and other
slave cases, the Underground Railroad, the
Haitian Revolution, lynching, miscegenation,
political parties, the slave trade, the African
Congress, the Black Star Line, Free Masonry,
labor unions, Liberia, the Fisk Jubilee Singers, Sherman's march to the sea, life in Harlem, the Ku Klux Klan, education, Negro literary societies. Negro congressman, Negro
"society", and abolition efforts. Other persons and publications mentioned include
Angelina and Sarah Grimké, Denmark Vesey,
Nat Turner, Freedom's Journal, David Walker's Appeal, and Frederick Douglass' Paper.

.64 — Smythe, Hugh, 1913- .
Papers, 1942-63. ca. 5 ft. (ca. 600 items).
Educator, author, and diplomat. Correspondence, mss, materials relating to Smythe's
professional activities, and papers of his wife,
Mabel Murphy Smythe, and of W.E.B. DuBois.
Included is correspondence pertaining to a
Nigerian research trip (1957); ms materials
(articles, books, book reviews and speeches)
pertaining to Africa, The New Nigerian Elite
(1960), Japan, and race relations in America;
and materials concerning Smythe's academic
activities, his interests in United Nations affairs, Crossroads Africa (field director,
1959-60), and civil rights activities. Papers
of Mabel Murphy Smythe include personal
memorabilia, correspondence, mss; and research material on segregation in education,
used to prepare the Brown vs. Board of Education case (1954) for the U.S. Supreme Court.
W.E.B. DuBois papers (1890-1944) contain correspondence, speeches, articles, and mss, including Race Relations in the United States
(1948) and Economic Illiteracy (1947).

.65 — Sutton, Peters.
Ms of The Negro and Race Integrity.

.66 — Tape Recording Collection.
ca. 240 tapes. Interviews, speeches, readings,
recordings of meetings, and documentary re-
cordings. The Collection contains tapes by
Herbert Aptheker, Osceola Archer, Byron
Baer, James Baldwin, Jack Barnes, Ross
Barnett, David Berkman, Arna Bontemps,
George Breitman, Gavin Bushell, Emile
Capouya, Robert C. Chapman, Alice Childress,
John Henrik Clarke, Albert Cleague, Horace
Clayton, W. Montague Cobb, John Conyers, Os-
sie Davis, Clifton DeBerry, James DeLoach,
Thomas Dent, W.E.B. DuBois, Dwight Lowell
Dumond, P.D. East, Ralph Ellison, James
Farmer, George Grief, John Howard Griffin,
Fannie Lou Hamer, John Hammond, Lorraine
Hansberry, Milton Henry, Nat Hentoff, Nora
Hicks, Herbert Hill, Langston Hughes, Harold
Jackman, LeRoi Jones, Elayne Jones Kaufman,
Kenneth Kaunda, Alfred Kazin, John O. Kil-
lens, Martin Luther King, Jr., Sidney Kingsley,
Franz J.T. Lee, Mr. and Mrs. Lemmon
(Brownsville, Tenn.), R.W.B. Lewis, Louis
Lomax, Malcolm (Little) X (11 tapes), Mrs.
Z.K. Mathews, Gertrude McBrown, James
Meredith, Howard Meyer, Charles Morgan, Jr.,
Frederick O'Neal, Douglas Pugh, Saunders
Redding, William Reed, Grant Reynolds, An-
drew Robinson, Phillip Rose, Bayard Rustin,
John Scott, Evelyn Sell, James Shabazz, Ed
Shaw, Charles Sims, Lillian Smith, Mildred
Stock, William Styron, Wilbert Tatum, Ernest
Thomas, Jackie Vaughn, Robert Vernon,
Brenda Wolcott, Wyatt Tee Walker, Solomon

Wangboje, Dave Weber, Milton P. Webster, Hilda Weiss, Robert Williams, William Worthy, J. Skelly Wright. The tapes cover such subjects as the Democratic party, Brotherhood of Sleeping Car Porters, Puerto Rican problems in New York, Committee Against Jim Crow in the Army, freedom movement in Mississippi, Marxism, Committee for the Schomburg Collection, Africa, Racism, Militant Labor Forum, Haryou-Act, Freedom Democratic party, Freedom Now party, Deacons for Self Defense, abolitionist movement, White Citizens Council, Robert Gould Shaw, March on Washington (1963), Freedom Schools, Mississippi Freedom Summer (1964), James Chaney, Asilomar Negro Writers Conference, Watts, housing, African theatre, Black Muslim movement, Tent City, On Guard, Fayette County, Tennessee, Radio Free Dixie, Hazel Brannon Smith, Southern Conference Educational Fund, Mississippi Delta blues music, and de facto segregation.

.67 —— Typescripts, galleys, and mss.
Many of these items comprised the "Birth of a Book Exhibit," first organized in 1940 to show the process from original ms to published v. Among the authors represented are Herbert Aptheker, Sally Belfrage, Arna Bontemps, William Stanley Braithewaite, Henrietta Buckmaster, George Washington Carver, Countee Cullen, Frederick Douglass, St. Clair Drake, W.E.B. DuBois, Ralph Ellison, Howard Fast, the Federal Writer's Project, Lorenzo Greene, John Hope Franklin, W.C. Handy, MacKinley Helm, Melville Herskovitz, Rockham Holt, Langston Hughes, Charles S. Johnson, Alain Locke, Rayford Logan, Albert Murray, Herbert R. Northroup, Roi Ottley, Saunders Redding, William Attaway, Anna Curtis, and Dorothy Sterling.

.68 —— Tubman, Harriet, 1820-1913.
Materials. ca. 150 items. Underground railroad conductor. Included are correspondence, photographs, abolitionists' petition, interviews, newspaper clippings, her Civil War record, pension claim, pamphlets, magazine articles, and an obituary of her in a Toronto newspaper. Collected by Earl Conrad, author of Harriet Tubman (1943).

.69 —— United Sons of Providence.
Minutebook, 1843. 1 item. Minute book of the United Sons of Providence, Manchester, Va.

.70 —— Washington, Booker Taliaferro, 1856-1915.
Papers. ca. 1864-1913. ca. 108 items. Chiefly correspondence of Washington and his wife to Miss Emily Howland concerning her financial assistance to Tuskegee Institute, conditions of Negroes in the U.S. and other political and social comments. Other correspondents include F.J. Garrison (ca. 30 letters), William Lloyd Garrison, Quincy Ewing, Theresa H. Garrison, and William Hayes Ward.

.71 —— Wheeler, Gerald E. collector.
Papers. ca. 30 items. Includes correspondence, clippings, and other miscellaneous items collected by Wheeler for his master's thesis on Hiram R. Revels.

.72 —— Whipper, Leigh, 1877- .
Papers. Broadway and film actor. Included are playbills, newspaper clippings, correspondence, programs, poetry, some of his writings for radio and the theatre, and other items.

.73 —— Winks, Robin W.
Materials. ca. 5 boxes and 4 folders. Professor at Yale University. Research notes and documents on the Negro in Canada, for his forthcoming book on Negroes in Canada.

.74 —— Williams, Egbert Austin, 1875-1922.
Scrapbooks. 2 v. Black comedian. V. 1 consists of anecdotes, jokes, axioms, proverbs, and funs and puns compiled for Williams by Alex Rogers (dated 1918); v. 2 consists entirely of song lyrics (1918). Also included are

some books inscribed to Williams from his library.

.75 —— Williamson, Harry A., 1875-1965. collector.
Library on Negro masonry, late 19th century - present. ca. 1000 items. Books, minutes of meetings, periodicals and publications of various mason organizations.

.76 —— Wright, Richard.
Papers. Mss, typescripts, photostats, and photographs. Author and playwright. Includes original typescript of Wright's Native Son, original ms of an unpublished novel entitled Monument to Memory, the second draft of Long Dream (1958), the original typescript of Wright's biography by Constance Webb published in 1968, a mimeographed copy of the screenplay of Native Son written by Wright and Pierre Channel, produced (1958) in Argentina, photographs once belonging to Wright, and photostatic copies of many of Wright's personal papers.

NY211   NEW YORK STATE, DEPARTMENT OF LABOR, DIVISION OF EMPLOYMENT (1935), RESEARCH LIBRARY (1935). 370 Seventh Ave., 10001. Tel 212 563-7660. Alfred L. Green, Exec. Dir. Bibliographies prepared, inquiries answered.
The Division administers the State Employment Service as well as the Unemployment Insurance Program in New York State. It also participates in the Manpower Development Training Act (MDTA) program, the State Training Act (SMA) and employment-related poverty programs. The Research Unit of the Division conducts special studies in the area of employment and unemployment.
Publ.: Operations, monthly; Employment Review, monthly; Manpower Trends, monthly.

.1   Research Library.
Miscellaneous. Books (10,000 v.) including reference v.; periodicals (ca. 400 titles) including general, documentary, and trade union publications; ca. 380 vf. of materials which includes pamphlets, documents, and reports. Restricted.

NY212   NEW YORK STATE, DIVISION OF HOUSING AND COMMUNITY RENEWAL, REFERENCE ROOM. 393 Seventh Ave., 10001. Tel 212 971-1651. Hugo J. Forde, Senior Clerk. Interlibrary loan, referrals made.

.1   Reference Room.
Books, reports, pamphlets, and other materials concerning housing, urban renewal and related subjects.

NY213   NEW YORK STATE, EXECUTIVE DEPARTMENT, DIVISION OF HUMAN RIGHTS (1945), REFERENCE LIBRARY (1950). 270 Broadway, 10007. Tel 212 488-5372. Simon Fediuk, Librn. Interlibrary loan, bibliographies prepared, literature searches, copying, inquiries answered, referrals made, consultation.
The Division is a permanent executive agency which investigates and takes action on complaints in the areas of employment, housing, education, and public accommodations. Formerly the New York State Commission for Human Rights.
Publ.: Library Accessions Annotated, bimonthly; Bibliographies on housing and urban renewal, education, employment, and related subjects.

.1   Human Rights Reference Library.
ca. 5500 items. Books, periodicals, newspapers, pamphlets, vf, theses and dissertations, correspondence, clippings, photographs, microfilm, and historical objects. Most of the collection is dedicated to intergroup relations, especially concerning Negroes, Jews, Puerto Ricans, and other ethnic groups. Also included are publications and materials relating to most state agencies on civil rights in the U.S. and Canada, and most private and church organizations.

NY214   NEW YORK UNIVERSITY, DEPARTMENT OF PSYCHOLOGY, RESEARCH CENTER FOR HUMAN RELATIONS. Washington Square, 10003. Tel 212 598-1212.
The Center places emphasis on applied research, consultation, and a summer workshop in the area of

human relations. Studies conducted by the Center include one of test motivation of Negro college students.

.1 Research Center for Human Relations.
Files. Records, reports, research data, and other materials pertaining to the operation and research of the Center.

NY215 NEW YORK UNIVERSITY, GRADUATE SCHOOL OF SOCIAL WORK, CENTER FOR THE STUDY OF UNEMPLOYED YOUTH. 853 Broadway, 10003. Tel 212 598-2614. Stanley Sadofsky, Dir.
The Center engages in a variety of activities designed to contribute to knowledge of the multiple problems faced by unemployed youth and to assist in the planning and administration of programs for such youth. The program of the Center consists of research, including a study of changes in work attitudes and performance of youth in the Neighborhood Youth Corps; the development of curriculum material for training those involved in youth work; technical assistance for the Comprehensive Employment Programs and Scheuer nonprofessional programs; and training programs.
Publ.: Research reports, monographs, and other pamphlets.

.1 Center for the Study of Unemployed Youth.
Files. Records, reports, research data, and other materials pertaining to the operation and research of the Center.

NY216 NEW YORK UNIVERSITY, NEW CAREERS DEVELOPMENT CENTER, NEW CAREERS TRAINING LABORATORY (1967). 184 Fifth Ave., 10010. Tel 212 598-7644. Frank Riessman, Dir. Inquiries answered, referrals made, consultation.
The Center and the Laboratory are both organized to develop and plan more effective human service system delivery (health, education, welfare, and community development services), and to train trainers and key cadre with particular emphasis upon the utilization of persons lacking formal skills and training. Special concern is focused on minority groups both as recipients of these services and as employees of these agencies.
Publ.: New Careers Newsletter; Reports, studies, and pamphlets concerning new careers.

.1 New Careers Development Center.
Collection of materials on new careers programs in health, education, mental health, social services, police and corrections, and related areas.

NY217 NEW YORK UNIVERSITY, SCHOOL OF EDUCATION, INSTITUTE FOR DEVELOPMENTAL STUDIES (1958), DATA AND REFERENCE LIBRARY (1965). 239 Greene St., 10003. Tel 212 677-3960. Charlotte Monks, Librn.
The Institute is a complex research, evaluation, demonstration and training program concerned with specifying what the learning disabilities of the disadvantaged child are, what causes them, what can be done to overcome them, and how the school as a system can be oriented to meet the needs of these children.

.1 Institute for Developmental Studies.
Files, 1958- . Records, reports, research data, and other materials relating to the operation and research activities of the Institute.

NY218 NEW YORK UNIVERSITY, SCHOOL OF LAW, ARTHUR GARFIELD HAYS CIVIL LIBERTIES PROGRAM (1958). 40 Washington Square, S., 10003. Tel 212 598-2555. Norman Dorsen, Dir. Inquiries answered, consultation.
The Program conducts research in critical areas of constitutional law, provides practical assistance to action organizations in the field of human rights, and trains law students for public and professional service in civil liberties and civil rights.
Publ.: Research papers, court briefs, articles for law reviews.

.1 Arthur Garfield Hays Civil Liberties Program.
Files, 1958- . Records, reports, research data, legal briefs and papers, and other materials relating to the operation and research activities of the Program.

NY219 NEW YORK UNIVERSITY LIBRARIES (1835). Washington Square. Tel 212 598-2485. Charles F. Gosnell, Dir. of Libraries.

.1 Facts on Film.
Papers, 1954-67. Microfilm. Contains materials on civil rights and race relations in the South. See Race Relations Information Center, Nashville, Tenn., for a full description.

NY220 NEW YORK UNIVERSITY LIBRARIES, TAMINENT LIBRARY. 7 E. 15th St., 10003. Tel 212 598-3708. Dorothy Swanson, Librn. Interlibrary loan, copying, inquiries answered.
Publ.: Taminent Library Bulletin, irregular.

.1 The Library has material relating chiefly to the history of labor and the radical movement in the U.S. and various Socialist, Communist, and labor leaders in the U.S. Persons and organizations included are:

.2 — American Socialist and labor organizations.
Papers, 1872-1926. 105 v. Included are minutes and letter books of various American Socialist and labor organizations.

.3 — Claessens, August.
Papers, 1919-55. ca. 720 items. Author, lecturer, teacher, Socialist assemblyman, of New York.

.4 — Debs, Eugene V.
Papers, 1898-1920. ca. 2500 items and 20 v. Labor leader, Socialist of Indiana.

.5 — Hillquit, Morris.
Papers, 1907-56. ca. 500 items. Socialist leader of New York.

.6 — Lee, Algernon.
Papers, 1896-1952. ca. 4500 items and 15 v. Socialist, director of the Rand School of Social Science.

.7 — London, Meyer.
Papers, 1910-56. ca. 3600 items and 5 v. Lawyer, Socialist, U.S. Representative of New York.

.8 — Rand School of Social Science.
Papers, 1906-56. 82 v. and ca. 21,000 items. Records of the former Rand School of Social Science and its Meyer London Memorial Library.

NY221 THE NEWSREEL. 322 Seventh Ave., 10001. Tel 212 565-4930.
Newsreel is a nation-wide organization of activists committed to film as a means of stimulating radical social change. It produces and distributes documentary films, including ones such as an interview with Huey Newton, a Black Panther in jail; and the Ocean-Brownsville, N.Y., teacher's strike.

NY222 NEWSWEEK, INC., LIBRARY (1933). 444 Madison Ave., 10022. Tel 212 421-1234. Ted Slate, Chief Librn. Inquiries answered.
Publ.: Newsweek, weekly magazine.

.1 Newsweek has written extensively on the subject of race relations, but its resources and collections, much of which is based on confidential information, are available for staff use only.

NY223 NORTHSIDE CENTER FOR CHILD DEVELOPMENT, INC. (1946). 31 W. 110th St., 10026. Tel 212 369-6464. Dr. Mamie Phipps Clark, Exec. Dir.
Northside Center provides educational, psychiatric, psychological, and social services to children and their families. It works to realize human potential, to prevent delinquency, to unify and strengthen the family and to serve the whole community. Programs include remedial reading and arithmetic; psychiatric, psychological and psychiatric casework therapy; volunteer projects; community education, through Chapter Two of the Union of Concerned Parents; and research concerning remedial reading and family services, needs, and treatment.
Publ.: Parent to Parent, newsletter published by Parents Council of Northside Center.

NY224 THE PANEL OF AMERICANS, INC. (1942). 2061 Broadway., 10023. Tel 212 724-4325. Gladys Harburger, Exec. Dir.
The Panel works to develop programs of education to counteract prejudice and discrimination and to stimulate constructive community attitudes and insights into problems of intergroup living in America.
Publ.: Panel of Americans Newsletter, quarterly.

NY225 PHELPS-STOKES FUND (1911), EDITORIAL RESEARCH LIBRARY (1964). 22 E. 54th St., 10022. Tel 212 421-1801.
The Fund was established to foster education for Negroes in America and Africa and the American Indian, and to secure housing for low-income groups in New York City.
Publ.: Negro Facts and Figures, biennially.

.1 Editorial Research Library.
Files, 1964- . 26 vf. Includes correspondence; ca. 2000 research monographs, pamphlets, government publications, and periodical articles; ca. 150 theses and dissertations; books; and a newspaper clipping file. Materials cover all aspects of contemporary Negro American urban and rural life: population and migration, housing, health, education, employment, income, social welfare dependency, crime and juvenile delinquency, civil rights, civil disorder, politics. The principal aim of the library is to keep abreast of trend data which measure the changing economic, social and cultural condition of the Negro in the U.S. Restricted.
.2 Phelps-Stokes Fund.
Archives, 1911- . Records, reports, correspondence, and other papers relating to the operation of the Fund and to the programs funded by it. Restricted.

NY226 PLANNED COMMUNITIES, INC. (PC) (1958). Room 1708, 41 E. 42nd St., 10017. Tel 212 687-6318. Morris Milgram, Chmn. of Bd. Inquiries answered, consultation.
PC is a private company established to demonstrate to the housing industry that integrated housing works by buying apartment houses, not in minority group neighborhoods, and opening them to all. PC founded and manages the Mutual Real Estate Investment Trust (MREIT), which was organized also to show that integrated housing works on a business basis. Formerly Modern Community Developers.
Publ.: Annual Report.

.1 Planned Communities, Inc.
Files, 1958- . Extensive materials and records of Deerfield freedom-of-residence battle (1959-63), and freedom-of-residence struggles in other areas, as well as materials on the history of housing integration. Much of this material, including extensive library on housing integration and allied subjects, is at the home of Morris Milgram, 5 Longford St., Philadelphia, Pa.

NY227 PLANNERS FOR EQUAL OPPORTUNITY (PEO). 76 Reade St., 10007. Miss Sidney Abbott, Exec. Secy.
PEO is an organization of professional and grass-roots planners whose aim is to democratize the planning profession. Programs and policies are aimed at involving minority persons in planning schools and agencies and insuring local control of such programs as Model Cities.
Publ.: Equalop, quarterly newsletter.

NY228 PROTESTANT EPISCOPAL CHURCH, EXECUTIVE COUNCIL (1919), HENRY KNOX SHERRILL MEMORIAL LIBRARY. 815 Second Ave., 10017. Tel 212 867-8400. Rev. R.C. Martin, Jr., Assoc. Dir. of Exp. and Specialized Serv. Inquiries answered, referrals made, consultation.
The General Convention Special Program was established by the Episcopal Church in 1967, to put some of the financial and professional resources of the Executive Council at the disposal of indigenous groups of poor people for the sake of self-determination and the development of bases of power and influence in their communities.
Publ.: Reports of various cases, evaluations, and stories about client groups of poor people.

NY229 PUBLIC AFFAIRS COMMITTEE (1935). 381 Park Ave. S., 10016. Tel 212 683-4331. Maxwell S. Stewart, Secy. and Editor.
The Committee seeks to help educate the American public on vital economic and social problems, particularly through concise and interesting pamphlets dealing with such problems.
Publ.: Public Affairs Pamphlet; and annual reports.

NY230 RADIO CORPORATION OF AMERICA, URBAN AFFAIRS AND COMMUNITY RELATIONS DEPARTMENT. 30 Rockefeller Plaza, 10020. Tel 212 265-5900. Samuel M. Convissor, Dir.
The Department, among other activities and programs, publishes a community relations newsletter to alert business executives across the country to potential social, civic and business problem situations, and to propose action to avoid them; is responsible for initiating and developing programs to be undertaken by the Corporation in the community relations and urban areas.
Publ.: RCA Community Relations Newsletter, monthly; Booklets and speeches concerning urban affairs.

NY231 THE REAL GREAT SOCIETY, INC. 130 E. Seventh St., 10009. Tel 212 533-6600. Carlos Garcia, Pres.
Through a grant, the Society has supported the training of unemployed young men in basic construction skills, while developing five vest-pocket parks in East Harlem.

NY232 RENEWAL MAGAZINE (1962). 235 E. 49th St., 10017. James R. McGraw, Editor.
Publ.: Renewal, monthly magazine.

.1 Renewal Magazine.
Files, 1963- . Records, correspondence, mss, and other papers. Included are mss of articles concerning such subjects as black power, riots, ghettos, black economic development, racial dissent in the church, black theology.

NY233 ROMAN CATHOLIC ARCHDIOCESE OF NEW YORK, APOSTOLATE OF HUMAN RELATIONS (1967). 34 W. 134th St., 10037. Tel 212 759-1400. Msgr. Gregory L. Mooney, Dir.
The Apostolate seeks to develop awareness, understanding and action in the field of human relations on the part of Catholic leadership.

NY234 SCHOLARSHIP, EDUCATION AND DEFENSE FUND FOR RACE EQUALITY, INC. (SEDFRE) (1962). 164 Madison Ave., 10016. Tel 212 532-8216. Ronnie M. Moore, Exec. Dir.
SEDFRE is a national organization which works to develop leadership programs and community organization techniques, engages in voter registration and provides scholarship assistance to students who have demonstrated leadership in civil rights activities. SEDFRE also conducts a Technical Assistance Program which provides systematic services for newly elected Negro officials, such as school board members.
Publ.: Newsletter, bimonthly.

NY235 SOUTHERN CONFERENCE EDUCATIONAL FUND, (SCEF) NEW YORK OFFICE. Suite 412, 799 Broadway, 10003. Tel 212 864-7100.

NY236 THE TEACHERS INCORPORATED. 35 Market St., 10002. Tel 212 267-5470. Roger Landrum, Pres.
The Teachers Incorporated is a non-profit private corporation dedicated to educational change; trains and locates teachers in school districts where critical educational and political issues are at stake, such as community control, curriculum, or workable integration. Projects are operated in New York City, Washington, D.C., Chapel Hill, N.C., and are initiated in collaboration with communities.
Publ.: Reports of programs, project descriptions, posters, newsletters.

NY237 TIME, INC., BUREAU OF EDITORIAL REFERENCE, LIBRARY (1930). Time and Life Bldg., Rockefeller Center, 10020. Tel 212 556-3991. Peter Draz, Librn.

.1 The library of Time, Inc., is a general library with extensive clipping and report files including such subjects as Negroes, urban problems, civil disorders and riots, civil rights, race relations, and discrimination. Restricted to staff use only.

NY238   UNION LEAGUE CLUB (1863), LIBRARY. 38 E. 37th St., 10016. Tel 212 685-3800. Margaret E. Lippencott, Librn.

   .1   Union League Club Library.
Miscellaneous. Contain materials pertaining to the Civil War and Reconstruction.

NY239   UNION THEOLOGICAL SEMINARY (1836), LIBRARY (1836). 3041 Broadway, 10027. Tel 212 662-7100. Robert F. Beach, Librn. Interlibrary loan.

   .1   Student Interracial Ministry.
Archives. ca. 12 ft. Materials reflecting the work of the Ministry.

NY240   UNITED CHURCH OF CHRIST, COMMISSION FOR RACIAL JUSTICE (1963). Room 93, 287 Park Ave. S., 10010. Tel 212 475-2121. Charles E. Cobb, Exec. Dir.
Publ.: Pamphlets.

NY241   UNITED CHURCH OF CHRIST, COUNCIL FOR CHRISTIAN SOCIAL ACTION (1957). 289 Park Ave. S., 10010. Tel 212 475-2121. Dr. Lewis I. Maddocks, Exec. Dir.
The Council provides and publishes information and literature on social issues, and formulates programs of social education and action for the United Church of Christ. The Council was formed by merger of the Council for Social Action, Congregational Christian Churches and the Commission on Social Action, Evangelical and Reformed Church.
Publ.: Social Action, magazine.

NY242   UNITED CHURCH OF CHRIST, UNITED CHURCH BOARD FOR HOMELAND MINISTRIES, DIVISION OF HIGHER EDUCATION AND THE AMERICAN MISSIONARY ASSOCIATION. 287 Park Ave. S., 10010. Tel 212 475-2121. Rev. Wesley Hotchkiss, Dir.
The Division is the educational wing of the United Church Board for Homeland Ministries. It includes the work of the American Missionary Association (founded in 1846) which is primarily concerned with the rights and development of minority groups in American society. American Missionary Association archives are located at the Amistad Research Center, Dillard University, New Orleans, La.
Publ.: The Journal, monthly magazine.

   .1   Division of Higher Education & American Missionary Association.
Files. Correspondence, minutes of board meetings, financial records, and other materials relating to the Division's support of the following predominantly black colleges and universities: Fisk University, Nashville, Tenn.; LeMoyne-Owen College, Memphis, Tenn.; Talladega College, Talladega, Ala.; Huston-Tillotson College, Austin, Tex.; Tougaloo College, Tougaloo, Miss.; and Dillard University, New Orleans, La.

NY243   UNITED NEGRO COLLEGE FUND (1944). 55 E. 52nd St., 10022. Tel 212 751-0700. Vernon Jordan, Exec. Dir.
The Fund was founded to help improve the quality of the educational programs at private Negro colleges. Money raised by the Fund is used for scholarships, teacher salaries, books, laboratory supplies and equipment. A current program of the Fund is to provide member institutions with microfilmed copies of material from the Schomburg Collection of Negro Literature and History.
Publ.: Pamphlets, brochures.

   .1   United Negro College Fund.
Files, 1944- . Records, reports, correspondence, documents, and other papers relating to the operation of the Fund.

NY244   UNITED PRESBYTERIAN CHURCH IN THE U.S.A., BOARD OF NATIONAL MISSIONS. 475 Riverside Dr., 10027. Tel 212 870-3041. Rev. J. Forest Burns, Dir.

   .1   Board of National Missions.
Files. Correspondence, minutes of board meetings, financial records, and other materials relating to the support of the following predominantly black colleges: Barber-Scotia College, Concord, N.C.; Johnson C. Smith University, Charlotte, N.C.; Knoxville College, Knoxville, Tenn.; and Mary Holmes Junior College, West Point, Miss.

NY245   UNITED PRESBYTERIAN CHURCH IN THE U.S.A., BOARD OF NATIONAL MISSIONS, DIVISION OF CHURCH AND RACE. 475 Riverside Dr., 10027. Tel 212 870-2200. Dr. Gayraud S. Wilmore, Jr., Chmn.
The Division works to insure that Church boards, agencies, Synods, Presbyteries, and churches are taking steps to further racial justice, including the employment and investment policies of church bodies, as well as action to provide equality in society as a whole.
Publ.: Religion and Race Memo.

   .1   Division of Church and Race.
The Division holds ca. 100 books, mss, correspondence, and photographs, concerning race relations.

NY246   U.S. COMMISSION ON CIVIL RIGHTS, NORTHEAST FIELD OFFICE. Room 313, 26 Federal Plaza, 10007. Tel 212 264-0400. Jacques Wilmore, Dir.
The Northeast Field Office handles the affairs of the Commission for the states of Connecticut, Delaware, Maine, Massachusetts, New Hampshire, New Jersey, New York, Pennsylvania, Rhode Island, and Vermont.

NY247   U.S. EQUAL EMPLOYMENT OPPORTUNITY COMMISSION, NEW YORK REGIONAL OFFICE. Suite 1306, 26 Federal Plaza, 10007. Tel 212 736-8787. Jack J. Olivero, Regional Dir.

NY248   U.S. SMALL BUSINESS ADMINISTRATION (SBA), NEW YORK AREA OFFICE. Room 3930, 26 Federal Plaza, 10007. Tel 212 264-4390. Kenneth W. Smallwood, Equal Opportunity Coordinator.
An arm of the SBA's "outreach" program, the Equal Opportunity Coordinator attempts to make all Negro businesses and prospective businessmen aware of SBA's financial assistance and economic opportunity loan programs.

NY249   U.S. NEGRO WORLD. Box 595, Manhattanville Sta., 10027.
Publ.: U.S. Negro World Press Directory, annually.

NY250   UNIVERSITY PLACE BOOK SHOP (1932). 840 Broadway, 10003. Tel 212 254-5998. William French, Mgr.
The Shop has an extensive collection of pamphlets and books by and about the Afro-American, for sale.
Publ. The Negro, semiannual catalog; Books by Negro Authors, semiannual; Africa, semiannual catalog.

NY251   URBAN CORPS NATIONAL DEVELOPMENT OFFICE (1968). 250 Broadway, 10007. Tel 212 964-5552. Michael B. Goldstein, Dir. Inquiries answered, referrals made, consultation.
The Urban Corps is a program designed to provide college students with the opportunity to perform important work in the public service. The National Development Office serves as a catalyst to encourage and assist cities in the development of their own Urban Corps programs, tailored to the specific needs of the community.
Publ.: Catalog of Urban Corps Programs, quarterly; Urban Corps National News, bimonthly; Urban Corps Document Series.

   .1   Urban Corps National Development Office.
Files, 1968- . Records, reports, studies and other papers relating to the operation of the Office and to Urban Corps programs across the U.S.

NY252   URBAN LEAGUE OF GREATER NEW YORK. 204 W. 136th St., 10030. Tel 212 751-0300. Eugene S. Callendar, Exec. Dir.
Publ.: 40 Acres and a Mule, bimonthly.

NY253   W.C. HANDY MUSIC PUBLISHING COMPANY (1917). 1650 Broadway, 10003. Tel 212 247-7755.
The firm was founded by W.C. Handy, and is now managed by Handy's son and daughters.

NY254   W.E.B. DUBOIS CLUBS OF AMERICA. 34 W. 17th St., 10011. Tel 212 929-2010.

.1   W.E.B. DuBois Clubs.
     Files.

NY255 WHITE AMERICANS TO SUPPORT BLACK LIBERATION.
       Room 408, 857 Broadway, 10003.
       White Americans to Support Black Liberation was
       formed "to support and defend black liberation organi-
       zations and black militants financially, morally, and
       loyally," and "to give aid and comfort to the black
       community by supplying food, medicine and other
       items, to be available during and after attacks on the
       community."

NY256 WORKERS DEFENSE LEAGUE (WDL) (1930's). 112 E. 19th
       St., 10003. Tel 212 254-4953. Robert Joe Pierport,
       Admin. Secy.
       WDL is a human rights organization which promotes
       equality in employment, labor unions, and the courts;
       and fights racial, economic, and political exploitation
       through legal investigations and trials.
       Publ.: Pamphlets.

   .1 Workers Defense League.
       Files, 1930's- . Includes correspondence, minutes
       of meetings, financial records, studies, investiga-
       tions, and other material dealing with the aims,
       history, and programs of the League.

NY257 YESHIVA UNIVERSITY, POLLACK LIBRARY. Amsterdam
       Ave. and 186th St., 10033. Tel 212 568-8400. Solomon
       Zeides, Librn. Interlibrary loan, copying.

   .1 The Pollack Library holds materials relative to all
       areas of Afro-American studies in "extensive and
       intensive strength."

NY258 YIVO INSTITUTE FOR JEWISH RESEARCH, LIBRARY AND
       ARCHIVES. 1048 Fifth Ave., 10028. Tel 212 535-6700.
       Dina Abramowicz, Librn.

   .1 American Jewish Congress.
       Papers, 1915- . 13 folders. Included are records
       of the organization.

NY259 YOUNG MEN'S CHRISTIAN ASSOCIATION (YMCA), NA-
       TIONAL BOARD, COMMITTEE FOR INTERRACIAL
       ADVANCE. 291 Broadway, 10007. Tel 212 349-0700.
       Leo B. Marsh, Asst. Exec. Dir.
       The Committee was formed to further racial integra-
       tion in the YMCA and to work in the area of special
       racial problems. Programs include developing action
       plans concerning social welfare problems, studies, and
       intercultural programs.
       Publ.: Reports, newsletters and other interpretive data;
       Selected Readings on Civil Rights and Racial Is-
       sues, semiannually.

NY260 YOUNG WOMEN'S CHRISTIAN ASSOCIATION (YWCA), NA-
       TIONAL BOARD (1858), LIBRARY (1959). 600 Lexing-
       ton Ave., 10022. Tel 212 753-4700. Elizabeth Norris,
       Librn. Interlibrary loan, bibliographies prepared, lit-
       erature searches, copying, inquiries answered, refer-
       rals made, consultation.
       YWCA seeks to further the mental, spiritual and physi-
       cal development of girls and young women.
       Publ.: Pamphlets and resource materials for commu-
       nity action groups and interracial activities.

   .1 Young Women's Christian Association, National Board.
       Archives, 1858- . ca. 6 vf. Historical records of
       YWCA race relations; interclassified with other
       historical documents in YWCA archives; national
       records; unpublished reports; correspondence;
       survey studies; dissertations; interviews; photo-
       graphs; published magazine articles; partial rec-
       ords of Phillis Wheatley branches and other local
       Negro branches; books and pamphlets (ca. 300) on
       contemporary civil rights and race issues in the
       U.S.; and all YWCA published materials on race
       subjects, especially policy statements, civil rights
       action and recommendations. Subject areas in-
       clude: integration of Negro and white women in the
       total YWCA program (1893-1931); interracial work
       on college campuses, including the South (1900- .);
       and World War I hostess clubs, segregated, for

work with Negro military personnel (1918). Restricted.

NY261 YOUNG WOMEN'S CHRISTIAN ASSOCIATION (YWCA), NA-
       TIONAL BOARD, OFFICE OF RACIAL JUSTICE. 600
       Lexington Ave., 10022. Tel 212 753-4700. Dorothy I.
       Height, Dir., Off. of Racial Justice.
       The Office monitors the National YWCA Board and gives
       direction to local associations in the area of racial
       justice; keeps the national office and local organizations
       abreast of developments in civil and human rights; en-
       courages action toward racial justice both in the YWCA
       and in all aspects of community life. Formerly Office
       of Racial Integration.

NEWBURGH

NY262 EPIPHANY APOSTOLIC COLLEGE (1889), LIBRARY.
       Windsor Highway, Box 390, 12553. Tel 914 562-4350.
       Rev. Gordon P. Hughes, Librn. Interlibrary loan.

   .1 Civil War collection.
       Books (ca. 476 v.).
   .2 Negrology collection.
       Books (ca. 862 v.). History and literature by and
       about the Negro.

NIAGARA FALLS

NY263 CITY OF NIAGARA FALLS, COMMISSION ON HUMAN RE-
       LATIONS (1964). City Hall, 14302. Tel 716 285-7811.
       J. Wesley Acosta, Jr., Exec. Dir.
       The Commission receives and investigates complaints
       of discrimination; conducts educational programs to
       better intergroup relations in the community; conducts
       surveys and studies; and develops plans for eliminating
       discrimination through conferences, conciliation and
       persuasion.

NYACK

NY264 FELLOWSHIP OF RECONCILIATION (1915), SHADOWCLIFF
       LIBRARY. Box 271, 10960. Tel 914 358-4601. Johanna
       Bosch, Librn., Researcher. Literature searches, in-
       quiries answered.
       The Fellowship is an international organization which
       works to end war and to mitigate its consequences, in
       the belief that love and compassion provide the only
       genuine basis for healthy human relationships. The
       group seeks to find nonviolent solutions to race con-
       flicts, industrial disputes and other situations in which
       fear and hatred might lead to violence.
       Publ.: Fellowship, magazine; Current Issues.

   .1 Fellowship of Reconciliation.
       Files, 1915- . Records, correspondence, reports
       of seminars and conferences, and other materials
       concerning the aims and activities of the organiza-
       tion. Restricted.

ONEIDA

NY265 MADISON COUNTY HISTORICAL SOCIETY. 13421. David
       Goff, Dir. Inquiries answered, referrals made, consul-
       tation.

   .1 Smith family.
       Papers, 1764-1874. ca. 100 items. Papers of
       Peter Smith (New York merchant and landowner)
       and his son Gerrit Smith (New York philanthropist,
       abolitionist, U.S. Representative). Includes papers
       relating to anti-slavery. Restricted.

PURCHASE

NY266 MANHATTANVILLE COLLEGE (1841), BRADY MEMORIAL
       LIBRARY (1841). 10577. Tel 914 946-9600. Sister
       Elizabeth O'Connor, Librn. Copying.

   .1 Martin Luther King, Jr., Collection.
       ca. 1200 v. Books and periodicals, concerning the
       history of the Negro and race relations in general.

Collection contains over 100 v. on slavery in the
U.S., including original slave accounts, memoirs,
and accounts of the underground railroad. Many v.
are first or early editions. Restricted.

ROCHESTER

NY267 AMERICAN BAPTIST HISTORICAL SOCIETY (1853). 1106
S. Goodman St., 14620. Tel 717 473-1740. Rev. Edward
C. Starr, Curator. Consultation.
The Society collects materials by, about, and against the
Baptist position. The reference library contains works
on all aspects of Baptist life and work, including Negro
Baptists.

NY268 CITY OF ROCHESTER, DIVISION OF COMMUNITY RELA-
TIONS (1964). 365 Public Safety Bldg., 14614. Tel 716
454-4000. Mrs. Sophie G. Divers, Dir. Inquiries answered, referrals made, consultation.
The Division was created to encourage and promote
equality of opportunity for all members of the community, and to act as a liaison between the administration
and the community in all things that will assure the
democratic process. Formerly the Office of Community Services.

NY269 FIGHT (FREEDOM-INTEGRATION-GOD-HONOR-TODAY)
(1966). 86 Prospect St., 14608. Tel 716 436-9880.
FIGHT was developed as a community organization by
Saul Alinsky and sponsored by the Rochester Area
Council of Churches to create equal employment opportunities, job-training and hiring programs for Negroes.

NY270 ROCHESTER PUBLIC LIBRARY. 115 South Ave., 14604.
Tel 716 546-6990. Harold S. Hacker, Dir. Interlibrary
loan, copying, inquiries answered, consultation.

.1 O'Rielly, Henry, 1806-86.
Papers, 1826-78. 2000 items. Author and pioneer
in the erection of telegraph lines. Correspondence,
memoranda, and other papers, including material
relating to the Negro troops from New York State
in the Civil War. Correspondents include Horace
Greeley, Gerrit Smith, Salmon P. Chase, Whitelaw
Reid, and William H. Seward.

NY271 UNIVERSITY OF ROCHESTER, CENTER FOR THE STUDY
OF GROUP RELATIONS. 14627. Tel 716 275-2121.
The Center trains students in the area of intergroup
relations, group relations research, and community
service.

NY272 UNIVERSITY OF ROCHESTER (1850), RUSH RHEES LI-
BRARY. River Campus Sta., 14627. Tel 716 275-4461.
John R. Russell, Dir.

.1 Facts on Film.
Papers, 1954-67. Microfilm. Contains materials
on civil rights and race relations in the South. See
Race Relations Information Center, Nashville,
Tenn., for a full description.

.2 Gannett, William Channing, 1840-1923.
Papers, 1850-1944. 24 ft. Unitarian clergyman.
Correspondence, diaries, financial papers, hymns
and hymnals, lectures, articles, Sunday school les-
sons, clippings, and printed matter. Includes a collection of Unity magazines (1878-1928), and letters
relating to the western Unitarian controversy, the
education of the freedmen at Port Royal, S.C. during the Civil War, Unity magazine, among other
subjects. Correspondents include Jane Addams,
Abigail May Alcott, Susan B. Anthony, Ezra Stiles
Gannett, Samuel Longfellow, Elihu Root, Alphonso
and William Howard Taft, Booker T. Washington,
Frank Lloyd Wright, and many Unitarian leaders.

NY273 URBAN LEAGUE OF ROCHESTER, INC. (1965). 80 Main
St. W., 14614. Tel 716 325-6530. Laplois Ashford,
Exec. Dir.

SCHENECTADY

NY274 CONGRESS OF RACIAL EQUALITY (CORE). 944 Strong St.,
12307. Tel 518 393-5656. Joseph Allen, Chmn.

NY275 SCHENECTADY COUNTY HISTORICAL SOCIETY (1905),
LIBRARY AND ARCHIVES. 32 Washington St., 12305.
Tel 518 374-0263. H.A. McConville, Curator.

.1 American Colonization Society.
Papers. Relating to the Society and to Liberian
colonization.

NY276 UNION COLLEGE (1795), SCHAFFER LIBRARY (1795).
12308. Tel 518 346-8751. Edwin K. Tolan, Librn.
Copying, inquiries answered.

.1 Lewis, Tayler, 1802-77.
Papers, 1832-70. 56 items. Orientalist, author,
and professor at Union College. Correspondence,
diary (1892), mss of Lewis' books, articles, and
essays, and other papers. Includes correspondence relating to antislavery and the Civil War.

.2 Yates, Andrew, 1772-1844.
Papers, 1792-1844. ca. 600 items. Congregational
clergyman and educator at Union College and
Chittenango Polytechnic Institute, Madison County,
N.Y. Correspondence, sermons, lectures on moral
philosophy, and notes on education, government, law
and slavery. The bulk of the collection consists of
sermons delivered by Yates in Schenectady, Albany,
Troy, Chittenango, and other nearby areas in New
York and East Hartford, Conn.

SYRACUSE

NY277 HUMAN RIGHTS COMMISSION OF SYRACUSE AND ONON-
DAGA COUNTY. 211 City Hall, 13202. Tel 315 473-
4695. Millicent Allewelt, Exec. Dir.

NY278 SYRACUSE UNIVERSITY, CARNEGIE LIBRARY. 13210.
Tel 315 476-5541. Jack T. Ericson, Head, Manuscript
Div. Interlibrary loan, copying, inquiries answered,
referrals made, consultation.

.1 Bank of the United States, Charleston, South Carolina.
Bill of sale. 1 p. Bill of sale, March 5, 1827, of 5
Negroes, three males and two females, "with the
future increase and issue of the females," to Edward R. Pinckney, for $1136. Printed form com-
pleted in holograph.

.2 Becker, Frank J. 1899- .
Papers, 1924-64. 48 ft. U.S. Representative from
New York. Correspondence, bills, memoranda,
published copies of many of Becker's speeches,
printed matter, and other papers, relating to committee work and legislation, the Armed Services
Committee, immigrants, and civil rights.

.3 Bogert, John A. b. 1836.
Family correspondence, 1862-66. 50 items.
Marble worker and Union officer, of New York
City. Chiefly letters written by Bogert to his parents, Mr. and Mrs. Jacob C. Bogert, and his
brother Willie, while he was a private in the 9th
New York Volunteer Infantry, a lieutenant and
captain in the 127th New York Infantry, provost
marshal of Beaufort, S.C., and lieutenant colonel
of the 103rd Regiment, U.S. Colored Infantry.

.4 Bontemps, Arna Wendell, 1902- .
Papers, 1939-61. 12 ft. Author and librarian.
Correspondence; mss of various versions of
Bontemps' books, a musical, plays, reports, songs,
and speeches; photos; and published materials.
Correspondents include Nelson Algren, Countee
Cullen, W.C. Handy, and Clare Booth Luce.

.5 Braithwaite, William Stanley Beaumont, 1878-1962.
Literary papers, 1916-62. ca. 3 ft. Poet, critic,
and editor. Literary correspondence (1160 items),
mss of Braithwaite's works, outlines for projected
works, and typescripts of the works of many leading poets collected by Braithwaite for his anthologies. Correspondents include James Donald
Adams, Joseph Auslander, Louis Bromfield, Bliss
Carman, Bennett Cerf, William E.B. DuBois, James
Gould Cozzens, Robert Frost, Robert Hillyer, Marianne Moore, Maxwell Perkins, and Booker T.
Washington.

.6 Chapman family.
Papers, ca. 1841-1954. 8 ft. (3250 items). Correspondence, documents and other personal papers of

the Chapman family of Onondaga and Madison
Counties, N.Y. Includes 1100 letters of Nathan
Randall Chapman concerning anti-slavery sentiments, the Baptist Church and the local history of
Fayetteville, N.Y.; 100 letters of Nathan Chapman
relating to anti-slavery feeling, local politics,
farming, social life, and civic matters; and letters
of Jermain Wesley Loguen, Negro clergyman and
abolitionist. The material is related to the Library's Gerrit Smith collection.

.7 Comfort family.
Papers, 1803-1910. 20 ft. (2500 items). Lecture
notes, mss of George Fisk Comfort's writings, and
other papers, including the anti-slavery correspondence of Comfort's father Silas, a Methodist minister, relating to his part in the Silas Comfort Negro testimony case (1838-40) and the controversy
between the northern and southern branches of the
Methodist Church.

.8 Curto, Ernest, 1902- .
Papers, 1948-65. 16.5 ft. Lawyer and member of
the New York State Assembly. Correspondence,
bills, and legislative and other printed material,
relating to New York State political affairs, labor,
mortgages and real estate, power authority, reapportionment, the strikebreakers professional
bill, and urban renewal.

.9 Facts on Film.
Papers, 1954-67. Microfilm. Contains materials
on civil rights and race relations in the South. See
Race Relations Information Center, Nashville,
Tenn., for a full description.

.10 Hall, Francis, fl. 1895.
Letters, 1894-1900. .5 ft. Lieutenant in the military. Includes information on colonial administration in Africa.

.11 Koehler, Sylvester Rosa, 1837-1900.
Correspondence, 1877-90. 100 items. Author and
editor of the American Art Review. Persons
represented include Frederick Douglass.

.12 McKinley, William Brown, 1856-1926.
Papers, 1906-20. 9.5 ft. Illinois Congressman.
Correspondence, political records, legislative
documents, petitions, printed material and scrapbooks relating particularly to the issues and activities of the National Taft for President Bureau
during the Republican campaign for nomination of a
presidential candidate in 1912. Includes correspondence from Negro organizations regarding
terms on which the party would receive Negro
support and one letter requesting funds for projected colonization in Africa.

.13 Metcalf, George R. 1914- .
Papers, 1950-65. 24 ft. New York State senator.
Correspondence, speeches, printed material,
legislation, reports, and other papers relating to
New York State legislative hearings, discrimination, housing, education, hospital problems, and
mental health.

.14 New York State Council of Churches.
Papers, 1934-68. 4 ft. Correspondence, agenda,
minutes, memoranda and reports, dealing mainly
with legislation and social issues including abortion,
alcoholism, church and state, civil rights and
segregation, drug addiction, family relations, health
and hospitals, labor migratory workers, and por-
nography; and material related to Christian education and church planning. Restricted.

.15 Quick, George T., 1834- .
Papers, 1834-1907. 257 items. Officer of the Independent Battalion, New York Volunteers Light
Infantry, in the Civil War. Correspondence relating to family matters in Rockland Co., N.Y.,
special and general orders, accounts of courts-
martial, requisitions, muster rolls, store inventories, lists of contraband, papers relating to recruiting, and other papers are chiefly concerned
with service at Morris Island, S.C., in 1862.

.16 Rider, Fremont, 1885-1962.
Correspondence, 1831-1953. 1.5 ft. 383 items.
Librarian, editor, author, and inventor. Includes
letters collected by Rider as well as his own correspondence, the oldest letter is one written to Nat

Turner shortly before he led the slave insurrection
in Virginia.

.17 Schuyler, George W., 1895- .
Papers. ca. 6 ft. Journalist. Printed copies of
published articles and books, with some correspondence.

.18 Smith, Gerrit, 1845-1937.
Papers, 1780-1880. 77 ft. (40,000 items). Farmer
and cattle breeder. Correspondence, documents,
account books, journals and other papers of Gerrit
Smith Miller, of Peter Smith, wealthy land owner
and Indian trader, and of Smith's son Gerrit, philanthropist and reformer, relating to abolition, social reforms, and land history of New York State.
Collection is comprised primarily of letters to
Gerrit Smith from prominent persons, and includes
material on antislavery, Negro colonization movements, the American Colonization Society, Liberia,
missionary efforts in Africa, and proposals for an
African company to trade in African lands and products.

.19 Spalding family.
Ellicott-Evans-Spalding papers, 1796-1901. 1.5 ft.
Legal and financial documents, correspondence,
diaries and miscellaneous material relating to
three Western New York families, some of them
Quaker, members of which were involved with the
Holland Land Company, commercial ventures including the Erie Canal and agriculture, and in
temperance and anti-slavery movements.

NY279 SYRACUSE UNIVERSITY, ERIC CLEARINGHOUSE ON
ADULT EDUCATION. 107 Roney Lane, 13210. Tel 312
476-5541.
ERIC was established by the U.S. Office of Education to
make the educational community aware of what is taking
place within it. The ERIC Clearinghouse on Adult Education gathers and distributes information and materials
concerning adult education in formal educational systems; the organization and programs of institutions
sponsoring adult education; educational aspects of community development, and rural and urban extension
programs; literacy education for adults; educational
media in adult education; and continuing education in
the professions.

.1 ERIC Clearinghouse on Adult Education.
Reports, newsletters, pamphlets, reprints, films,
tapes, and selected curriculum materials concerning the above subjects.

NY280 SYRACUSE URBAN RENEWAL AGENCY (1964). 300 E.
Fayette St., 13202. Tel 315 473-2870. John Hildebrandt,
Cmnr. Copying, typing, inquiries answered.
The Agency plans, initiates and implements urban renewal projects. It also enforces anti-discrimination
contractual requirements on contractors and purchasers
of real estate.
Publ.: Reports, including one concerning relocation of
families in urban renewal project areas.

NY281 URBAN LEAGUE OF SYRACUSE AND ONODAGA COUNTY
(1965). 443 S. Warren St., 13202. Tel 315 472-6955.
David F. McDonald, Exec. Dir.
The League works to obtain equal opportunities for
minority group persons.

.1 Urban League of Syracuse and Onodaga County.
Files, 1965- . Records, reports, correspondence,
and other papers concerning the aims and activities
of the League.

TARRYTOWN

NY282 HISTORICAL SOCIETY OF THE TARRYTOWNS (1889). 1
Grove St., 10591.

.1 Rockwell, Charles H. 1827-1904.
Papers, 1863-65. 2 ft. (ca. 1000 items). Union
officer. Correspondence, journals, cashbooks, income tax accounts, checks, orders, traffic papers,
surveys, records of transactions with the Corps
d'Afrique, and other papers relating to Rockwell's
service in the Quartermaster Corps, U.S. Army
during the Civil War.

UTICA

NY283 COMMISSION ON HUMAN RELATIONS (1963). 1 Kennedy
Plaza, 13502. Tel 315 798-3260. Rev. Franklin J.
Upthegrove, Exec. Dir.
The Commission inquiries into incidents of tension in
the community; investigates cases of racial discrimination; makes studies in the area of human relations;
conducts educational programs to promote good intergroup relations; and attempts to eliminate discrimination through the process of conference, conciliation
and persuasion.
Publ.: Quarterly Report.

WEST POINT

NY284 U.S. MILITARY ACADEMY, CADET LIBRARY. 10996. Tel
914 938-2954. Egon Weiss, Librn. Copying, inquiries
answered.

.1 Conrad, George Bryan, 1898- .
Papers, 1907-55. 3 ft. Army officer. Collection of
papers covers most of General Conrad's Army
career. Contains some family records on the Civil
War and John Brown's raid.

.2 Flipper, Henry Ossian, 1855-1940.
Papers, and diary (1930-31). 26 items. 1st Negro
graduate of West Point (1878). Papers concern his
later business interests.

.3 Tidball, John Caldwell, 1825-1906.
Manuscript, 108 p. Commandant of Cadets, USMA,
1864. Ms of unpublished article, The Fur Seal and
the Negro, concerning western expansion during the
1840's. Tidball relates the fur seal disputes of
Western Victoria to the settlement of the slavery
question, berating President Polk for his efforts to
preserve slavery at the cost of northwestern expansion.

.4 U.S. Army, 9th Cavalry Regiment.
History, 1866-1907. 3 items. History of the 9th
Cavalry from its organization in 1866 to 1907, writ-
ten by Colonel George F. Hamilton. People and
subjects prominent in the collection include Indian
Wars in North America; Negroes in the Armed
Forces; battle of San Juan Hill (1898); and maps of
Santiago de Cuba. Prior to its organization (1866)
as a regular regiment of cavalry, the 9th Cavalry
was a USCT regiment.

.5 Whittaker, Johnson Chestnut.
Scrapbook of clippings relating to the case of Caset
Whittaker, USMA ex-1880. Whittaker was a Negro
cadet, court-martialed in a highly sensational case
at West Point, 1877. Scrapbook consists entirely
of newspaper clippings (primarily the New York
Times) concerning the case.

WESTBURY

NY285 NEGRO AIRMEN INTERNATIONAL, INC. (1967). P.O. Box
723, 11590. Tel 516 334-3873. Edward A. Gibbs, Pres.
Referrals made.
A non-profit membership organization whose objectives
are to broaden job opportunities and advancement for
Negroes in aviation, to foster recognition of the contributions to aviation made by Negroes, to encourage Negro participation in the field of aviation, and to serve
as the voice of Negro airmen universally.
Publ.: N.A.I. Newsletter, quarterly.

WHITE PLAINS

NY286 AFRO-AMERICAN CULTURAL FOUNDATION (1969). 394
Tarrytown Rd., 10607. Tel 914 761-4778. John H. Harmon, Exec. Dir. Inquiries answered, referrals made,
consultation.
The Foundation furnishes counsel and advice for those
individuals and organizations wishing to establish programs in Afro-American history; is working to establish an Afro-American book store and cultural center
which would supply books, literature curios, art objects,
and other items; furnishes speakers, lecturers, artists
and others to aid in the development of programs; encourages research and writing in the field of Afro-

American history; and seeks to disseminate material in
this field as widely as possible.
Publ.: Quarterly bulletin.

.1 Afro-American Cultural Foundation.
Materials. Books, papers, bibliographies on black
history, and programs for black history in schools
and institutions in New York State and surrounding
region.

NY287 AMERICAN JEWISH COMMITTEE, UPPER NEW YORK
STATE AREA. 48 Mamaroneck Ave., 10601. Tel 914
948-5585. Eugene DuBow, Area Dir.

NY288 AMERICAN JEWISH CONGRESS, WESTCHESTER REGION.
11 William St., 10601. Tel 914 948-1777. Jerome L.
Levinrad, Dir.

NY289 ANTI-DEFAMATION LEAGUE OF B'NAI B'RITH, WEST-
CHESTER COUNTY REGIONAL OFFICE. Room 318,
199 Main St., 10601. Tel 914 946-4831. Israel H.
Moss, Dir. Bibliographies prepared, consultation.
Publ.: Concerns of Conscience, regional newsletter;
Pamphlets on civil rights, prejudice, race rela-
tions, totalitarianism and extremism.

NY290 COMMISSION ON HUMAN RIGHTS (1965). 255 Main St.,
10601. Tel 914 949-4800. Jack P. Marash, Exec. Dir.
Speakers bureau.
The Commission investigates cases of racial discrimination and intergroup tension in the community;
makes studies in the area of human relations; conducts
educational programs to promote better intergroup relations in the community; and seeks to eliminate discrimination through the process of conferences, conciliation and persuasion.

NY291 NATIONAL CONFERENCE OF CHRISTIANS AND JEWS
(NCCJ). 175 Main St., 10602. Tel 914 946-1604.
Margaret Schwarz, Dir.

NY292 SUBURBAN ACTION (1969). 180 E. Post Rd., 10601. Tel
914 949-3326. Neil N. Gold, Dir. Inquiries answered.
Suburban Action is a nonprofit corporation for research
and action in the suburbs. It was established to explore
new courses of action for private citizens, local, state,
and federal government officials and agencies, and for
business groups, in expanding job and housing opportunities, reducing poverty, and eliminating racial discrimination and inequality.

.1 Suburban Action.
Files, 1969- . ca. 1000 items. Includes correspondence, minutes of meetings, financial records,
studies, reports, investigations and other material
dealing with the aims, history and programs of
Suburban Action.

NY293 URBAN LEAGUE OF WESTCHESTER COUNTY, INC. 6
Depot Plaza, 10606. Tel 914 949-1174. William Wolfe,
Exec. Dir.
The League works for "interracial cooperation for
better living."

NY294 WHITE PLAINS PUBLIC LIBRARY (1908). 115 Grand St.,
10601. Tel 914 946-8700. May V.K. Valencik, Library
Dir. Interlibrary loan, bibliographies prepared, literature searches, copying, inquiries answered, referrals
made, consultation.
Publ.: The Negro in America, periodically.

.1 Negro history.
Books, filmstrips, photographs, periodicals, phonorecords, pamphlets, government documents, newspaper and clipping file. Includes local and county
biographical files, and local newspaper (1926- .),
and subjects such as urban planning, renewal and
regional planning.

YONKERS

NY295 YONKERS COMMISSION ON HUMAN RIGHTS (1963). City
Hall, 10701. Tel 914 403-3980. Charlotte M. Baker,
Exec. Dir. Inquiries answered, referrals made, con-
sultation.
The Commission investigates cases of racial discrimi-

nation and intergroup tension in the community; makes studies in the area of human relations; conducts educational programs to promote better intergroup relations in the community; and seeks to eliminate discrimination through the process of conference, conciliation and persuasion. It has a subpoena power to facilitate investigations.

NORTH CAROLINA

BOILING SPRINGS

NC1   GARDNER-WEBB COLLEGE, LIBRARY. Box 836, 28017. Tel 704 434-2211. Mrs. Royce M. Ellis, Librn.

.1 Dixon, Thomas, Jr., 1864-1946.
Papers. Author, lawyer, and playwright. Includes books (ca. 1400), correspondence, paintings, and mss on such subjects as the South; slavery, Reconstruction, and the Ku Klux Klan. Dixon was the author of The Clansman, which became a stage play and subsequently "The Birth of a Nation," a movie directed by D.W. Griffith.

CHAPEL HILL

NC2   UNIVERSITY OF NORTH CAROLINA, CENTER FOR URBAN AND REGIONAL STUDIES (1957). Evergreen House, 27514. Tel 919 933-2282. F. Stuart Chapin, Jr., Dir. The Center was established to enable faculty in various fields to collaborate in urban research of both fundamental and practical significance. Focal areas of work include studies of activity patterns of various socioeconomic groups in the urban scene in relation to community services and facilities; studies of moving behavior and residential preferences of urban residents; studies of land development processes in the expansion of existing cities and in the establishment of new towns; and the development and testing of systems for modeling and simulating urban phenomena of the kinds noted above in order to evaluate their policy implications. A program is being developed for converting research results to operational forms and put to use in the analysis of urban problems in the cities of North Carolina.
Publ.: Urban Studies Monograph Series.

NC3   UNIVERSITY OF NORTH CAROLINA LIBRARIES, LOUIS ROUND WILSON LIBRARY (1795). 27514. Tel 919 933-1301. Jerrold Orne, Librn. Interlibrary loan, copying, typing.

.1 Facts on Film.
Papers, 1954-67. Microfilm. Contains materials on civil rights and race relations in the South. See Race Relations Information Center, Nashville, Tenn., for a full description.
.2 Southern Pamphlet Collection.
Pamphlets, handbills, posters, 1820- . Chiefly from the 19th century. Subjects include the Negro (ca. 200 items) and slavery (ca. 150 items), as well as other topics in Southern history.

NC4   UNIVERSITY OF NORTH CAROLINA LIBRARIES, SOUTHERN HISTORICAL COLLECTION. 27514. Tel 919 933-1301. J. Isaac Copeland, Dir., South. Hist. Collection.

.1 The Southern Historical Collection consists of more than 4000 groups of papers from which the following collections have been selected. This listing should not be considered exhaustive nor mutually inclusive in particular subject areas. Specific information may be obtained by consulting the surveys and card catalog housed with the collection.
.2 —— Alcorn, James Lusk, 1816-94.
Papers, 1850-1949. 34 items. Planter, statesman, political leader, and Confederate Army officer. Correspondence (chiefly 1850-65) from Alcorn to his wife, Amelia Walton (Glover) Alcorn, including 15 Civil War letters

written from Mississippi and Kentucky; pre-war plantation books and Alcorn's diary (1879-80). The correspondence between Alcorn and his wife chiefly concerns political conditions before and during the Civil War and reflects Alcorn's political thinking as anti-secessionist, Confederate general, and Republican Governor of Mississippi.
.3 —— Allen, George Washington.
Papers, 1832-1932. 750 items. Resident of Opelika and LaFayette, Ala. Personal, business, political, and family correspondence relating to plantation life, national politics, and the Civil War. Chiefly letters (1839-64) to Allen from his brother, Alexander A. Allen, of Lexington and Bainbridge, Ga.
.4 —— Anderson, Edward Clifford, 1815-83.
Papers, 1813-82. 63 items. Naval officer, Confederate Army officer, planter, politician and businessman, of Savannah, Ga. Mostly letters from Anderson, friends, and relatives, to his wife, Sarah McQueen (Williamson) Anderson. Includes minutes (1813-68) of the trustees of the Chatham Academy of Savannah, Ga.; miscellaneous plantation and slave records; information on affairs and life in Savannah during the Reconstruction period.
.5 —— Ashmore, John D.
Plantation journals.
.6 —— Avery family.
Papers, 1796-1916. 1000 items. Correspondence, plantation and personal accounts, and legal documents, of Daniel Dudley Avery, his wife, Sarah Craig Marsh Avery, and their ancestors and descendants. The material relates chiefly to their Louisiana plantation, Petit Anse Island, and sugar cane.
.7 —— Bailey, James B.
Papers. Contains materials pertaining to slavery.
.8 —— Bailey, John Lancaster, 1795-1877.
Papers, 1788-1890. 500 items. Legislator, judge, and lawyer of Pasquotank Co., N.C. Correspondence and papers of Bailey, other members of his family, and the related Brownrig and Cain families concerning property, politics, war, Reconstruction, and legal matters.
.9 —— Baker, Everard Green.
Diaries and plantation notes.
.10 —— Barnes, David Alexander, 1819-92.
Papers, 1806-92. 120 items. Legislator and judge. Personal and business correspondence (chiefly 1860-92) consisting of bills, receipts, wills, and charges to juries of the North Carolina Superior Court. The legal papers concern Burgwyn and McRae family matters handled by Barnes, and include letters concerning the Burgwyn plantation, Alveston, in Occoneechie Neck, Northampton Co., N.C.
.11 —— Barnsley family.
Papers, 1838-1916. 315 items. In part, microfilm of one vol. Correspondence, diaries, plantation journal (1859-61), and other papers. Includes the Civil War diary and reminiscences of George Scarborough Barnsley (b. 1837), of Woodlands (Cass Co.), Ga.; correspondence of George's father, Godfrey Barnsley (1805-73), cotton exporter of Savannah, Ga., and New Orleans, and of his brother, Lucien Barnsley (b. 1840).
.12 —— Bassett, John Young, 1805-52.
Papers, 1822-71. 153 items. Physician of Huntsville, Ala. Medical, family, and financial correspondence of Bassett and his wife, Isaphoene Thompson Bassett, including two letters from William Gilmore Simms, editor of the Southern Quarterly Review, criticizing Bassett's article on race ethnology.
.13 —— Bayside Plantation.
Records.
.14 —— Beirne, Oliver.
Business records, 1860-86. 350 items. Planter, of Virginia and Louisiana. Includes

bills, receipts, financial records, and papers
relating to the management of the Houmas
Plantation in Louisiana.

NC4.15 —— Beman, Nathan S.S.
Papers, 1834-39. 50 items. Georgia, New
York; Presbyterian minister, president of
Rensselaer Polytechnic Institute, abolitionist
leader. Religious papers.

.16 —— Bills, John Houston.
Diaries. Contains information pertaining to
slavery.

.17 —— Bourland, Albert P.
Papers, 1899-1922. ca. 3000 items. Tennessee; professor at George Peabody College,
executive secretary of Southern Education
Board, educational leader.

.18 —— Bragg, John, 1806-78.
Papers, 1851-87. 617 items. Lawyer, legislator, judge, and planter, of North Carolina
and Alabama. Correspondence, business
papers, reports, and accounts. Includes
Bragg's correspondence as member of Congress from Alabama (1851-53) reflecting his
states rights views, business materials relating to cotton planting including reports from
overseers.

.19 —— Bratton, John, 1831-98.
Letters, 1861-65. 1 v. Transcripts (typewritten, ca. 1940) from a typewritten copy
(ca. 1916) lent by the Rt. Rev. Theodore Du-
Bose Bratton; the originals were burned in
1919. Physician, state legislator, and Confederate officer, of Winnsboro, S.C. Letters
from Bratton, an officer in the 6th South Carolina Regt., to his wife Bettie (DuBose) Bratton,
describing army life at various camps in South
Carolina and Virginia, battles in which he took
part, and Negroes who remained at home and
those who accompanied their masters in the
army. Emory University Library had a microfilm copy (negative, 10 ft.) made in 1961.
The Library of Congress has a typewritten
carbon copy of these letters, in one volume,
transcribed by the North Carolina Historical
Records Survey in 1942.

.20 —— Bromberg, Frederick George, 1837-1930.
Papers, 1738-1930. ca. 12,000 items. Lawyer, and U.S. Representative from Alabama.
Legal, business and personal correspondence
relating to Reconstruction and the activities of
the Freedmen's Bureau in Mobile, Ala.; and
Alabama politics (chiefly after 1875).

.21 —— Brown, Hamilton, 1786-1870.
Papers, 1752-1907. 2 ft. Planter, militia officer, and sheriff of Wilkes Co., N.C. Correspondence, diaries, notebooks, financial and
legal records, and other papers, of Brown and
of his family, concerning land titles, slave
titles, and the misfortunes of war and Reconstruction.

.22 —— Brown, John W.
Diary. Contains references to slavery.

.23 —— Burton-Young family.
Papers. Included are materials relating to
slavery.

.24 —— Byrd, William McKendree, ca. 1817-74.
Papers, 1832-1914. 135 items. Legislator,
jurist, and politician of Linden and Selma,
Ala. Business correspondence, deeds, commissions, and personal and political letters.
Includes letters from Byrd to his wife and his
father, William S. Byrd, concerning plantation
affairs.

.25 —— Cameron family.
Papers, 1739-1929. ca. 33,000 items. Business and personal correspondence, slave
registers, account books, farming records,
and sermons, of the Cameron family and of the
related Bennehan, Ruffin, and Mordecai families, illustrating more than a century of plantation life in North Carolina. Members of the
family include Duncan Cameron (1777-1853);
his wife, Rebecca (Bennehan) Cameron; his
son, Paul Carrington Cameron (1808-91);

Bennehan Cameron (1854-1925). Correspondents include many prominent North Caro-
linians.

.26 —— Canfield, Henry Lee, 1860-1942.
Papers, 1921-42. 325 items. Universalist
minister in Kinston and Greensboro, N.C.
Correspondence and papers dealing with the
Universalist Church, race relations, prison
reform, and other social reforms. Correspon-
dents include Frank P. Graham, Lewis E.
Laws, Frederick J. Libby, Howard W. Odum,
George Ross Pou, Mrs. Myers Sternberger,
and Gertrude Weil.

.27 —— Capehart family.
Papers, 1668-1890. 405 items. In part microfilm from originals in the possession of Mrs.
W.S. Smith and Dr. William P. Jacocks. Correspondence, and other papers. The bulk of
the correspondence consists of letters by
Susan Bryan (Martin) Capehart to her father
in Louisiana and letters from members of the
Bryan, Martin, and Capehart families of
Bertie Co., N.C. during the Civil War and Reconstruction period.

.28 —— Carter, Farish, 1780-1861.
Business records, 1806-64. 2295 items.
Planter. Business and legal papers (1825-60)
and miscellaneous account books (1835-42 and
1859-65). Material relates mostly to the
running of Carter's plantations: cotton planting, buying and hiring out of slaves, and
acquisition of more land in Georgia, Louisiana, and Florida.

.29 —— Church of Bethany, Iredell Co., N.C.
Session book, 1775-1872. Typescripts.

.30 —— Cole family.
Papers, 1707-1914. 2000 items. Business,
legal, personal, and family papers of several
generations of the Cole family of New Bern,
N.C., including the papers of James C. Cole
(d. 1864), his wife, Mary Catherine Cole (1799-
1862), and their three daughters and two sons.
Also the papers (1878-1914) of their grandson,
James Cole Taylor (b. 1855), and other mem-
bers of the Taylor family of New Bern, N.C.
Includes letters (1830-60) to relatives on an
Alabama plantation; overseers' letters from
Tennessee plantations; and Cole and Taylor
account books kept in New Bern, N.C.

.31 —— Colhoun, John Ewing, 1750-1802.
Papers, 1774-1850. 250 items. Lawyer,
planter, legislator, and U.S. Senator from
South Carolina. Plantation, legal, and business papers (1785-1802) of Colhoun, including
plantation journal (1830, 1832-33) from Mid-
way Plantation; deeds; and indentures.

.32 —— Confederate States of America. Conscript Dept.
7th North Carolina Congressional District
papers, 1862-65. 1200 items. Official papers
of the chief enrolling officers of the 7th North
Carolina Congressional District, Capt. John
M. Little and Capt. D.C. Pearson, including
correspondence, applications for exemptions,
general and special orders received from
Raleigh and Richmond, reports and lists from
each county, and papers relating to deserters,
manpower for essential industry, senior reserves, and details for men on limited service.

.33 —— Cornish, John Hamilton.
Papers, 1833-78. 77 items. Episcopal minister, of Aiken, S.C. Papers, diaries, pamphlets, and clippings relating to Cornish's service as clergyman in Aiken, S.C. Includes a
register of Negroes connected with the Church
of Messiah, North Santee, S.C., Jan. 1, 1843.

.34 —— Couper, James Hamilton.
Plantation records.

.35 —— Crenshaw family.
Papers, 1751-1875. 125 items. Papers
(chiefly, 1820-60) pertaining to financial,
plantation, and legal affairs of the Crenshaw
family of Pittsylvania Co., Va. and the related
Miller family, of Halifax Co., Va. Papers
prior to 1820 consist of deeds, wills, and
broadsides.

NC4.36 — Dabney, Charles William, 1855-1945. collector.
Papers relating to education in the South,
1796-1936. 23 ft. (ca. 20,000 items). Correspondence, reports, minutes, scrapbooks, and
other papers relating to education in the
South, educational movements in the early 20th
century, the Southern Educational Association,
the Southern Education Board, the Conference
for Education in the South, the General Education Board, and related organizations. Includes the papers (1899-1922) of Albert Pike
Bourland (1861-1927) relating to Bourland's
activities as educator, field representative of
the Peabody Education Fund, and executive
secretary of the Conference for Education and
the Southern Education Board; papers (1796-
1934) of Dabney, president of the universities
of Tennessee and Cincinnati, consisting of
copies of historical materials and other data
collected for his book Universal Education in
South (1936) and Dabney's own correspondence
with educational leaders, associations, and
organizations, especially the Southern Education Board; office correspondence files of the
associate secretary of the Southern Education
Board and other correspondence and papers
(1899-1931) of George Sherwood Dikerman
(1843-1937); papers (1900-19) of James
Yadkin Joyner (1862-1954), a North Carolina
public educator, relating to the Ogden Movement and the Southern Education Board; correspondence files of the executive secretary
and other members, minutes, reports, and
other papers (1829-1932) of the Southern Education Board; and letter book (1902-04) of
Edgar Gardner Murphy (1869-1913).

.37 — Davidson family.
Papers, 1813-1937. 72 items. Family and
business correspondence (chiefly 1835-56),
ledgers and family business records (1813-
74), account books, and daybooks of the
Davidson family of Mecklenburg Co., N.C.,
who lived at Rural Hill Plantation, 1833-90;
Ingleside Plantation, 1867-75; and Dixon
Plantation, Gaston Co., N.C., 1872-93.

.38 — De Rosset family.
Papers, 1581-1940. 3880 items. Family correspondence (1760-1940) through several
generations of the De Rosset family, of Wilmington, N.C. and the allied Curtis, Kennedy,
Lord, Meares, and Waddell families and other
papers, chiefly 1821-77, relating to family
affairs, politics, slavery, the Civil War, and
Reconstruction. Other papers consist of diaries, records of births of slaves, and records
of vessels calling at Carolina ports.

.39 — De Saussure, Louis M.
Plantation book.

.40 — Dozier, Richard, 1822-1901.
Legal papers, 1787-1900. 2545 items. Lawyer and State legislator, of Georgetown, S.C.
Papers (chiefly 1870-1900) from Dozier's law
office, including account and docket books
(1836-87), plantation accounts (1846-52), and
Dozier's diary (1857).

.41 — Eggleston family.
Papers, 1825-1905. 182 items. Family correspondence (1844-99) of Elizabeth F.
(Gildart) Eggleston, and her daughter, Mahala
P.H. (Eggleston) Roach; a diary and farm
journal (1830) of Dick Eggleston who managed
a cotton plantation in Wilkinson Co., Miss.

.42 — Elliot family.
Papers, 1698-1898. ca. 5600 items. Family
letters, deeds, legal papers, accounts with
factors, plantation records, and correspondence, relating to South Carolina and sectional
politics, planting, and personal and social
activities of William Elliot (1788-1863), of
Beaufort, S.C.

.43 — Elmore family.
Papers, 1843-1936. ca. 50 items. Letters to
Franklin Harper Elmore (1799-1850) relating
to his business as a banker and planter, and to

his political career as U.S. Congressman from
South Carolina; and family correspondence,
data, and clippings.

.44 — Erwin, William.
Diary and account books. Contain references
to slavery.

.45 — Flat River Primitive Baptist Church, Person Co.,
N.C.
Records.

.46 — Fitzpatrick, Benjamin, 1802-69.
Papers, 1819-1892. 208 items. Lawyer,
planter, U.S. Senator and Governor of Alabama.
Business, political, and personal papers of
Fitzpatrick, dated chiefly from his plantation,
Oak Grove, and Washington, D.C.

.47 — Fripp, John Edwin.
Journals and slave lists.

.48 — Gayle, Sarah A.
Journal. Typescripts. Contains references to
slavery.

.49 — Gibson family.
Correspondence, 1846-1919. ca. 500 items.
Correspondence of Tobias Gibson, planter, of
Terrebonne Parish, La.; of his daughter,
Sarah T. Gibson Humphreys, of near Versailles, Ky.; and of their family. The letters
pertain to family and business affairs, education, and financial difficulties with plantation
property and crops.

.50 — Globe Baptist Church, Caldwell Co., N.C.
Records.

.51 — Graham, Frank P.
Papers. Included is material concerning the
Southern Conference for Human Welfare,
Friends of Democracy, and the Committee to
Defend America by Aiding the Allies.

.52 — Graham, William Alexander, 1804-75.
Papers, 1750-1927. 7 ft. In part, transcripts
and microfilm. Governor of North Carolina,
State legislator, U.S. Senator, Secretary of the
Navy, and Confederate senator. Correspondence with prominent state and national political figures; a microfilm copy of a diary
(1776-86) and account book of John Graham;
Graham family papers; household accounts;
law notes; and slave lists.

.53 — Graves family.
Papers, 1815-1901. 650 items. Personal and
family correspondence, account books, and
business papers of the family, whose members
and relatives lived in Caswell Co., N.C.;
Newton Co., Ga.; and Champion, N.Y. Mainly
the papers of Iverson L. Graves, cotton
planter; his wife, Sarah Dutton Graves; and a
son, Henry L. Graves, planter, State legislator,
and member of the Farmers' Alliance. Also
includes Georgia and North Carolina merchandise and plantation accounts (1815-1919), and
minutes of the Farmers' Alliance for 1890-91.

.54 — Grimball, John Berkley, 1800-93.
Papers, 1683-1930. 1638 items and 37 v.
Planter, of Charleston, S.C. Correspondence,
diaries (1832-83), plantation records, scrapbooks, and other papers. The correspondence
pertains to Grimball's planting, property, and
finances. The material is related to the library's Manigault plantation records and
papers.

.55 — Grimes family.
Papers, 1766-1929. 22 ft. Correspondence,
diaries, accounts, plantation records, business papers, albums, and other materials of
the Grimes family of eastern North Carolina.
Many of the papers concern John Bryan
Grimes, secretary of state of North Carolina.
The collection pertains to state and local public affairs and politics (from ca. 1890), social
life, education, the Civil War, Reconstruction,
and other matters.

.56 — Gwyn family.
Papers, 1779-1938. 720 items. Correspondence, diaries, plantation records, account
books, inventories of property, land grants,
and court summonses of the Gwyn family of

Green Hill Plantation, which James Gwyn (1812-38), planter, court clerk, and merchant of Wilkes Co., N.C., inherited from his father, James Gwyn (1768-1850). Includes legal papers (1779-1834) of Wilkes Co., and personal correspondence in which there are references to property, politics, and the Civil War.

NC4.57 —— Hairston, Elizabeth Seawell (Hairston), 1855-1945.
Papers, 1805-1943. 925 items. Personal correspondence of a large family connection including letters written in Patrick and Henry Counties, Va., and various towns and country places in Virginia, Tennessee, and Mississippi, giving a picture of antebellum plantation life.

.58 —— Hairston, Peter Wilson, 1819-86.
Papers, 1773-1886. 550 items. Plantation owner, of Davie and Stokes counties, N.C., and merchant of Baltimore, Md. after the Civil War. Includes business papers of Hairston, ledgers (1784-97), and account books.

.59 —— Hamilton, Charles Eaton, 1816-55.
Papers, 1800-69. 800 items. Planter, of Granville Co., N.C. Family and business papers (1828-68) of Hamilton, including letters written by him from his plantation in Lowndes Co., Miss., and a plantation record (1837) from Mississippi. Includes business papers and account books (1800-69) of John H. and William C. Bullock, Williamsboro, N.C.

.60 —— Hampton, Wade, 1754-1835.
Papers, 1791-1908. ca. 300 items, in part transcripts. South Carolina planter. Antebellum papers of Wade Hampton (1754-1835), Wade Hampton (1791-1858), and Wade Hampton (1818-1902), relating to rice and cotton plantations in South Carolina, and sugar plantation in Louisiana. Also contains Civil War and family letters of the third Hampton.

.61 —— Harding, William Giles, 1806-86.
Papers, 1819-89. 500 items. Planter, breeder, and Confederate Army officer, of Tennessee. Correspondence and Belle Meade Plantation records (1819-51, 1879, 1882-84) of Harding; papers of Howell Edmunds Jackson (1832-95), U.S. Senator from Tennessee, Associate Justice of the U.S. Supreme Court, and brother of William Hicks Jackson.

.62 —— Hargrove, William.
Account book and slave record.

.63 —— Harrington, Henry William, 1748?-1809.
Papers, 1775-1864. 71 items. In part, transcripts. North Carolina State senator, South Carolina Militia officer, and landowner. Personal correspondence and military papers, together with a copy of a diary (1826-64) of Henry William Harrington, Jr. (b. 1793) of Richmond Co., N.C., containing scattered entries dealing with daily and plantation business.

.64 —— Harrison, James Thomas, 1811-79.
Papers, 1770-1878. 181 items. Lawyer, and member of the Confederate Congress. Legal and financial papers (1770-1824) to persons in Anson and Richmond counties, N.C.; letters (1834-38) from Harrison in South Carolina and his brother, Isham, in Mississippi discussing land speculation, the sale of slaves by rice planters in South Carolina, and the annexation of Texas; and Harrison's letters (1860-65) containing descriptions of proceedings of the Confederate government and personal observations of happenings in Montgomery, Ala.

.65 —— Haywood family.
Papers, 1752-1946. 14 ft. Correspondence, account books, Confederate hospital records, letter books, dating chiefly from 1787 to 1890, of John Haywood (1755-1827), George Washington Haywood (1802-1890), Fabius Julius Haywood (1803-80), Edmund Burke Haywood (1825-94), and Ernest Haywood (1860-1946), relating to public affairs, family and social events, planting and slavery, internal improvements in North Carolina, and the Civil War.

.66 —— Henry, Gustavus Adolphus, 1804-80.
Papers, 1804-71. 650 items. Lawyer and Confederate Senator from Tennessee. Chiefly Henry and McClure family correspondence written in the 1840's and 1950's, including correspondence between Henry and his wife while he was visiting his plantations in Mississippi and Arkansas, and letters from other relatives and friends, overseers, and a few political associates.

.67 —— Herbert, Hilary Abner, 1834-1919.
Papers, 1864-1931. 2 ft. Lawyer, author, Confederate officer, U.S. Representative, and Cabinet member. Correspondence, diaries, reminiscences, scrapbooks, clippings, speeches, and autobiography. The correspondence covers Herbert's years as Secretary of the Navy in the Cleveland Cabinet (1893-97) and the following years devoted to law practice in Washington, D.C. Includes letters of Grover Cleveland, Theodore Roosevelt, Robert Carmody, Richard Olney, and other public figures, discussing contemporary issues, political conventions and campaigns, the South's Negro problem, and Reconstruction.

.68 —— Hill, John.
Plantation diary.

.69 —— Hillhouse family.
Papers, 1775-1923. ca. 900 items. Letters received by the Porter family of Hadley, Miss., from Hillhouse relatives in Georgia; business papers of David P. Hillhouse (1756-1804) and Sarah (Porter) Hillhouse; family correspondence; plantation inventory; and other papers.

.70 —— Hobbs, Mary (Mendenhall), 1852-1930. Collector.
Papers relating to the manumission of slaves by the Society of Friends in North Carolina, 1778-1845. 124 items. Papers of Richard Mendenhall, of Guilford Co., N.C., and of others relating to the manumission activities of the Society of Friends in North Carolina. Includes Mendenhall's papers concerning arrangements for sending a group of liberated slaves from North Carolina to Haiti in 1826, under the auspices of the Society of Friends; and letter press books, minutes, accounts, and other papers of North Carolina organizations dedicated to manumission and colonization.

.71 —— Holt, Erwin A., 1873-1961.
Papers, 1955-61. 800 items. Members of Lawrence S. Holt & Sons, cotton mill owners, of Burlington, N.C. Correspondence, and printed broadsides, leaflets, etc., relating to racial segregation in the U.S. and Holt's interest in preventing racial integration. Open to investigators under library restrictions.

.72 —— Hubard family.
Papers, 1741-1907. ca. 19,000 items. Business and personal papers of Edmund Wilcox Hubard (1806-78), planter, militia officer, State legislator, and U.S. Representative from Virginia and his family in Virginia, Washington, D.C., North Carolina, Tennessee, and Florida consisting of diaries, account books, plantation accounts, slave lists, notebooks, and physicians' daybooks. Includes many phases of plantation life, welfare organizations, and the Civil War.

.73 —— Jackson, Henry, 1778-1840.
Papers, 1784-1923. ca. 5 ft. Diplomat and professor of mathematics at the University of Georgia. Antebellum correspondence pertaining to family and plantation affairs, chiefly 1811-56, of Dr. Jackson, his wife, Martha Jacquelin (Rootes) Cobb Jackson (b. 1786), and her relatives, the Rootes and Cobb families of Virginia and Georgia.

.74 —— Johnston, Thomas M.
Papers, 1839-75. 88 items. Planter, of Greensboro, Ala. Correspondence and business papers. Includes deeds and tax statements (chiefly 1846-66), concerning cotton selling, slaves, and Johnston's property in

Noxubee, Winston, and Kemper Counties, Miss., and Marengo Co., Ala.

NC4.75 —— Joiner, James Harvey, 1819-81.
Papers, 1852-81. ca. 200 items. Personal and business papers of the editor and publisher of the Democratic Watchtower in Talledega, Ala. Includes records of the purchase of slaves.

.76 —— Jones, Edmund Walter, 1811-76.
Papers, 1789-1914. 372 items. Planter at "Clover Hill" in Happy Valley, Caldwell Co., N.C. Business and family correspondence, land papers, account books. The material is related to the Library's Lenoir family, Lindsay Patterson, and Edmund Jones papers.

.77 —— Kincaid, John, 1787-1867.
Legal and papers, 1820-87. 180 items. Slave owner, agent of a gold mining company, and justice of the peace, of Burke Co., N.C. Business and legal papers, chiefly of the 1830's and 1860's, of Kincaid and business papers of Andrew Jackson Corpening (1818-1904), of Caldwell Co., N.C., administrator of Kincaid's estate.

.78 —— King, Mitchell, 1783-1862.
Papers, 1801-62. 700 items. Lawyer and jurist, of Charleston, S.C. Correspondence (business and family), diary (1852-58 and 1862), legal papers, and accounts pertaining to property in Buncombe Co., N.C., King's plantation in South Carolina, and other business papers. Includes bill of sale of slaves, deeds, memoranda, political notes, and receipts.

.79 —— King, Thomas Butler, 1800-64.
Papers, 1763-1870. 5 ft. Planter, railroad promoter, State legislator, U.S. Representative from Georgia. Correspondence and papers, chiefly 1835-68, concerning King's business and public activities, the management of Retreat Plantation, St. Simons Island, Ga., and family life.

.80 —— Leak, Francis Terry.
Diaries. Contain references to slavery.

.81 —— L'Engle, Edward McCrady, 1834-90.
Papers, 1834-97. ca. 3 ft. (5140 items). Confederate Army officer, lawyer, and railroad executive, of St. Augustine, Fla. Business, legal, and personal correspondence, chiefly 1855-79, and other papers. The ante-bellum papers consist chiefly of wills, deeds, legal papers, and family correspondence dealing with personal and plantation affairs, and of the secession movement.

.82 —— Lenoir family.
Papers. Contains material pertaining to slavery.

.83 —— Lewis, Ivey Forcman, 1833-84.
Business records, 1857-1916. 88 items. Plantation owner, of Hale and Marengo counties, Ala. Business and legal papers, lawyers' records (1870-95), and account books from seven or more plantations belonging to Lewis and his heirs. Includes records of cotton picked, of payments to and indebtedness to laborers, and of births and deaths of slaves.

.84 —— Linn, Joseph Adolph, 1810-64.
Papers, 1839-81. ca. 180 items. Farmer, businessman, and Lutheran clergyman, of Gold Hill, Rowan Co., N.C. Family correspondence, business accounts, papers concerning life insurance policies on slaves and containing some references to the Lutheran Church.

.85 —— Logan, George William, 1828-96.
Military records, 1861-65. 1600 items. Confederate officer. Correspondence, reports, orders, petitions, and other papers relating to Logan's command of the 2nd Louisiana Heavy Artillery Battalion at Fort Beauregard, La., and other places. Includes daily, weekly, and monthly company reports, ordnance reports, medical reports, and papers concerning conscripts, deserters, construction work, and the use of local slave labor.

.86 —— Mackay family.
Papers, 1743-1915. 4 ft. and 3 reels of microfilm (negative). Correspondence; plantation, mercantile, and shipping records; miscellaneous accounts; and other papers (chiefly 1800-65) of Robert Mackay (1772-1865), merchant of Savannah, Ga., his wife Eliza (McQueen) Mackay (1778-1862) and their children and relatives.

.87 —— McCollam, Andrew.
Papers, 1795-1935. ca. 3 ft. (2835 items). Planter and deputy surveyor, of Donaldsonville, La. Correspondence, chiefly 1852-84; bills, receipts, records of slaves, plantation records, scrapbook, and other papers of McCollam, his family, his descendants, and the related Slattery family.

.88 —— McCormick, John Gilchrist, 1877-1928. Collector.
Papers relating to the North Carolina Secession Convention, 1896-1900. 195 items. Replies from delegates who attended the North Carolina Secession Convention of 1861 and from relatives and friends of the delegates, to a questionnaire distributed by McCormick, giving information consisting of date and place of birth, business and profession, records of public service, attitude toward secession, and when applicable, date of death.

.89 —— McDowall, Susan (Witherspoon).
Papers, 1835-55. 113 items. Wife of William D. McDowall. Chiefly letters to Susan W. McDowall in Camden, Charleston, and Columbia, S.C., from her parents, John Witherspoon, Presbyterian clergyman, and Susan D. Witherspoon, of Hillsboro, N.C. Includes information on church matters, plantation news, slavery, and family affairs in North and South Carolina.

.90 —— McDowell, James, 1795-1851.
Papers, 1750-1865. ca. 780 items. Governor of Virginia, U.S. Representative from Virginia, and State legislator. Correspondence, speeches, notes, and miscellaneous papers of McDowell, dealing with the Virginia educational system, slavery, and Congressional bills, 1820-60.

.91 —— McDowell, Thomas David Smith, 1823-98.
Papers, 1783-1925. ca. 3 ft. (ca. 3000 items). Planter, lawyer, and State legislator, and Confederate representative, of Bladen Co., N.C. Political, business, and military correspondence, mainly 1830-70, and other papers concerning politics, law courts, the Civil War, and Reconstruction.

.92 —— Massenburg, Nicholas B.
Farm journal.

.93 —— Meares, William.
Papers, 1771-1877. 74 items. Letters (1821-38) from William B. Meares (1787-1841), lawyer of Wilmington, N.C., to his brother-in-law James Alves, of Henderson, Ky. relating to business matters, Negro disturbances, and plantation management; account books; family records; and a diary (1859-60) of Armand D. Young as a young boy on the Lyrias Plantation.

.94 —— Memminger, Christopher Gustavus, 1803-88.
Papers, 1803-1915. 250 items. South Carolina State legislator and secretary of the treasury of the Confederacy. Family, business, and Civil War correspondence, mainly 1860-68, and other papers. Includes correspondence relating to the secession of the Southern states, and papers relating to Reconstruction in South Carolina.

.95 —— Middleton, Nathaniel Russell, 1810-90.
Papers, 1761-1919. 1222 items. Plantation owner, president of the College of Charleston, treasurer of the Northeastern Railroad Company, and treasurer of Charleston, S.C. Chiefly family and personal correspondence (1827-71) and other papers. Includes a plantation account book and slave list (1785-1812) of Thomas Middleton.

.96 —— Miles, William Porcher, 1822-99.
Papers, 1760-1927. 2300 items. Planter, educator, and U.S. and Confederate Congressman. Personal and family papers; deeds, mortgages, wills, claims, notes, receipts, agreements,

and other business records. In two series.
The first (1760-1927) relates mainly to Miles'
Louisiana property and business interests,
chiefly Houmas Plantation in Ascension
Parish, and includes correspondence with
title holders and their agents, lists of Negroes,
and labor agreements. The second series
(1894-96) consists chiefly of letters concerning
Miles' business interests, politics, current
affairs, and family and personal matters.

NC4.97 —— Miles, William Porcher, 1822-99.
Papers, 1782-1907 (addition to 1760-1927
papers). 4 ft. (3263 items). Personal, political, and military correspondence (chiefly
1856-96) with many prominent national and
South Carolina political figures; diary (1867-
97); and other papers. Papers, 1782-1858,
deal with criticisms of the U.S. government,
and other national problems. Papers, 1861-65,
relate to conditions in the South. Postwar papers are concerned with Reconstruction politics, suffrage, education, and economic conditions in the South.

.98 —— Mitchell, Samuel Chiles, 1864-1948.
Papers, 1915-48. 4 ft. Professor and college
president. Correspondence, articles, and an
autobiography of Mitchell, while serving as
president of Delaware College (1912-20) and
professor of history at the University of Richmond (1920-45). Includes letters from
Mitchell's family, Virginia Congressmen, labor
leaders, and southern newspaper editors, reflecting Mitchell's interest in education, interracial relations, labor relations and unioniza-
tion in the South, the New Deal, and other social and political matters.

.99 —— Mordecai, George W., 1801-71.
Papers, 1776-1898. ca. 6 ft. (4500 items).
Lawyer and businessman, Raleigh, N.C.
Family, legal, and business correspondence,
chiefly 1840-70, relating to the American
Colonization Society, the Episcopal Diocese of
North Carolina, conditions in North Carolina
and at the front during the Civil War. Other
papers consist of diaries, accounts, estate
settlements, and a Peaksville plantation account book.

.100 —— Morrison, Columbus.
Diary. Contains references pertaining to
slavery

.101 —— Murphy, Edgar Gardner, 1869-1913.
Papers, 1869-1913. ca. 200 items. Episcopal
clergyman, publicist, executive secretary of
Southern Education Board, and amateur
astronomer. Correspondence, articles, and
clippings relating to popular education, race
relations in the South, and state and national
child labor legislation. The material is related to the library's Southern Education
Board papers.

.102 —— Nevitt, John.
Plantation journal.

.103 —— Nisbet family.
Papers, 1752-1936. 2200 items. Papers of
John Nisbet (1737-1817), general merchant and
State legislator who established his family in
Rowan and Iredell counties, N.C.; Dr. James
K. Nisbet (1768-1832), physician who moved to
Georgia; Eugenius Aristides Nisbet (1803-71);
James Taylor Nisbet (1828-94); and Nisbet
family relatives including the Cooper, Hall,
King, Mitchell, Osborne, Pharr, and Young
families. Includes correspondence, accounts,
bills, receipts, invoices, slave transactions,
estate settlements, and North Carolina ac-
count books (1771-1867).

.104 —— Norfleet, Stephen Andrews.
Diaries. Contains references to slavery.

.105 —— North Carolina Fund.
Archives, 1963-69. See North Carolina Fund,
Durham, N.C. for a full description.

.106 —— Norton family.
Papers, 1760-1926. ca. 350 items. Personal
correspondence (1815-1910) of the Norton
family and with the Chilton and Dameron fami-

lies with whom they intermarried in Virginia,
Mississippi, and New Orleans, La.; accounts
and records (1820-32) of planting and slaves;
and legal documents including wills and deeds,
accounts and receipts.

.107 —— Oaksmith, Appleton, ca. 1825-87.
Papers, 1825-88. ca. 110 items. North Carolina State representative. Correspondence and
legal papers (1884-86) of the Carolina City
Company, with which Oaksmith was connected;
letters (1874-77) from his mother, Elizabeth
Oakes (Prince) Smith (1806-93), to William J.
Spence of Long Island, N.Y., relating to the
temperance movement and race relations.

.108 —— Otey, Octavia Aurelia James (Wyche).
Papers, 1824-1900. 1 ft. Correspondence,
diary (1849-1900), account books, and other
papers, of Mrs. Otey, of her husband, William
Madison Otey, and of their family, of Madison
Co., Ala., and Yazoo Co., Miss. The papers
concern social life, education of the children,
cotton planting, plantation management, sales
and purchases, politics, and difficulties of the
time.

.109 —— Parkhill, John, 1786-1856.
Papers, 1813-91. ca. 225 items. Banker, of
Richmond, Va., and Tallahassee, Fla. Busi-
ness papers and family correspondence of
Parkhill, his sons, daughters, and grandchil-
dren, letters from a former slave (1866-75).

.110 —— Pearson, Richmond Mumford, 1805-78.
Papers, 1816-78. 372 items. Judge, of North
Carolina. Family, business, and political correspondence, wills, and notes pertaining to
family matters, plantation and legal affairs,
and issues of the Civil War and Reconstruction.

.111 —— Penn School, St. Helena Island, S.C.
Records, 1861-1964. 23 ft. In part, tran-
scripts. Administrative correspondence,
trustee minutes, accounts, reports, promo-
tional literature, photo albums, clippings, and
other papers of Penn School and of Penn
Community Services, Inc., Frogmore, S.C.
The items ante-dating 1900 include copies of
the correspondence and diary of Laura M.
Towne, copies of correspondence of Arthur
Sumner, and recollections and articles concerning the School from its beginnings in 1861.
Correspondents include Rossa B. Cooley,
Hollis B. Frissell, Grace Bigelow House,
Howard and Alice Kester, Ellen Murray,
George Foster Peabody, Courtney Siceloff, and
various prominent philanthropists, state and
federal health, education, and welfare officials,
and educators and sociologists interested in
the welfare and advancement of the rural Negro population.

.112 —— Perkins, John, 1819-85.
Papers, 1822-85. 550 items. Planter, lawyer
and U.S. and Confederate Representative from
Louisiana. Correspondence, business records,
accounts, and other papers. Includes records
of extensive plantations in Louisiana and
Texas, federal and Confederate congressional
office mail (1853-55 and 1863-65).

.113 —— Pettigrew family.
Papers, 1684-1926. ca. 11 ft. (14,000 items).
Chiefly papers of four generations of the
Pettigrew family, of Tyrrell Co., N.C., describing the political, economic, social, and
cultural life of the planter class in the South
in the 19th century, particularly, 1833-63.
The earliest papers consist of deeds, wills,
indentures, sermons, and family records. Includes papers relating to the Shephard and
Bryan families, of New Bern and Raleigh, N.C.
and to the Petigru and North families, of
Charleston, S.C.; sermons and copies of letters of the Rev. Charles Pettigrew (1743-
1807), Episcopal clergyman, first bishop elect
of North Carolina, and a planter at Bonarva
plantation; account books and records of
Magnolia and Belgrade plantations; and
memorandum books and lists of slaves.

NC4.114 — Phillips, Ulrich Bonnell.
Papers, 1900-37. 39 items and 167 typed copies. Michigan, Connecticut; historian, University of Michigan and Yale professor, educational leader and author of numerous publications concerning the South and slavery, including American Negro Slavery (1918).

.115 — Pitts, P.H.
Diary and account book. Contains references to slavery.

.116 — Price family.
Papers, 1842-1928. ca. 900 items. Correspondence, business records and other papers, the bulk of which are dated 1870-93. Includes papers concerning the congressional careers and politics of Andrew Price of Louisiana and his father-in-law Edward James Gay, operations and sugar production on Acadia plantation, Lafourche Parish, La., and other family holdings.

.117 — Prudhomme, Phanor.
Business records, 1804-78. ca. 400 items. Cotton planter of Bermuda Plantation, Natchitoches Parish, La. Correspondence (1804-76) with brokers, plantation records and accounts, pocket notebooks, and indentures of Prudhomme and of J. Alphonse Prudhomme, who succeded him in 1867. Volumes for 1861-63 are in French.

.118 — Quitman family.
Papers, 1784-1940. 8 ft. (4000 items). Correspondence and social, economic, and political papers of four generations of the Quitman family and the related Duncan, Lovell, and Turner families of Natchez, Miss., and Sewanee, Tenn. Includes a journal and other papers of John Anthony Quitman (1799-1858), soldier, planter, Governor, and U.S. Representative from Mississippi; Mississippi plantation records (1866-84) of William Storrow Lovell; and diaries and account books of other members of the family.

.119 — Roulhac family.
Papers, 1785-1935. ca. 5 ft. (7000 items). Personal correspondence, chiefly 1810-1900, diaries, account books, and family history of the Roulhac family of Hillsboro, N.C., and of members of the related Hamilton and Ruffin families, of North Carolina. The papers relate to the Civil War, Reconstruction, political, and social matters.

.120 — Ruffin, Francis Gildart, 1820-92.
Papers, 1732-1900. ca. 3 ft. (4000 items). Confederate officer and auditor of Virginia. Personal and official correspondence and business papers, chiefly 1877-92, including reports (1869) on rivers and harbors of Virginia, treasury reports, discussions on the problems of the Negro, and Virginia politics. The earlier papers consist of indentures, bonds, deeds, petitions, notes, and papers of Major Albert G. Ruffin, an attorney and planter, of Winchester, Miss.

.121 — Schenck, David, 1835-1902.
Papers, 1849-1917. 19 v. Judge, of Lincolnton and Greensboro, N.C. Diaries (1849-1901) relating to the Civil War, Ku Klux Klan, church revivals, North Carolina court system, and civic and educational activities in Greensboro, N.C.

.122 — Screven family.
Papers of the Screven, Bryan, and Arnold families, 1779-1922. 2 ft. (ca. 2400 items). Papers of Joseph Bryan, Georgia planter and U.S. Representative; papers of Bryan's daughter Georgia and her husband, James Proctor Screven, planter and mayor of Savannah; business papers, plantation journals, diaries, and letter books of Screven's son John, lawyer and businessman; plantation papers of Richard J. Arnold, a Rhode Islander who became a Georgia planter.

.123 — Shaffer, William A.
Papers, 1818-1931. 2 ft. (445 items). Plantation owner, of Houma (Terrebonne Parish), La.

Business and plantation papers (ca. 150 items) consisting mainly of bills of sale, deeds, warrants for public lands in Louisiana, and miscellaneous accounts. Other papers consist of plantation records, and scrapbooks.

.124 — Singleton family.
Papers, 1759-1911. 5205 items. Personal correspondence and business papers, chiefly 1815-54, of the Singleton family, of Manchester, S.C., reflecting plantation life and cotton growing in ante-bellum South Carolina.

.125 — Smith, Peter Evans, 1829-1905.
Papers, 1738-1944. ca. 1000 items. Farmer, surveyor, and engineer, of Halifax Co., N.C. Family and business correspondence and papers (mostly 1822-99); and to Smith's work with Gilbert Elliot on the construction of the C.S.A. ironclad Albemarle. Includes account books (1823-55), list of Negroes (1858-66), scrapbooks, and an undated diary.

.126 — Smith, William Ruffin, 1803-72.
Papers, 1772-1868. 71 items. Chiefly correspondence (1844-50) of Smith with Howell Adams, overseer of a plantation in Lowndes Co., Miss., of which Smith was executor.

.127 — Southern Tenant Farmers' Union.
Papers, 1934-59. 34 ft. Correspondence of executive officers at headquarters, legal papers, press releases, orders, reports, lists, accounts, applications, union newspapers, and mimeographed materials.

.128 — Sparkman family.
Papers. Contains materials pertaining to slavery.

.129 — Sparkman, William E.
Plantation book.

.130 — Spencer, Cornelia (Phillips), 1825-1908.
Papers, 1833-1924. 3 ft. (1000 items). In part, typescripts in 20 v., of Mrs. Spencer's correspondence and writings (1838-1919) from originals in various sources, including other departments of the University of North Carolina Library, the State Dept. of Archives and History, the State Library at Raleigh, N.C., the Historical Foundation of the Presbyterian and Reformed Churches, Montreat, N.C., and newspapers. Author, of Chapel Hill, N.C. Correspondence, diaries, articles, scrapbooks, and other material, dealing with daily life at Chapel Hill, N.C., particularly its struggle during Reconstruction days.

.131 — Thompson, John.
Plantation book. Microfilm.

.132 — Thompson, Lewis.
Papers. Contains material relating to slavery.

.133 — Thompson, Waddy, 1798-1868.
Papers, 1823-51. 83 items. State legislator, militia officer, U.S. Minister to Mexico, and U.S. Representative from South Carolina. Personal, official, and business correspondence, chiefly 1842-43. Includes correspondence dealing with the sugar and cotton industries and the slave trade in Alabama and South Carolina.

.134 — Walker, A. and A.T.
Account book. Contains information relating to slavery.

.135 — Walker, John.
Diaries. Originals of first 2 v., remainder on microfilm. Contains references to slavery.

.136 — Warmoth, Henry Clay, 1842-1931.
Papers, 1798-1934. 8 ft. (ca. 5000 items). Plantation owner, Union Army officer, railroad builder, and Governor of Louisiana. Correspondence, 12 volumes of personal diaries (1863-67, 1922-31), plantation journals (1828-1963 and 1880-1927); scrapbooks dealing with politics, and other papers. The papers, 1861-65, relate to Warmoth's personal activities; papers, 1866-78, to politics in Louisiana; and the bulk of the papers, 1879-1930, to the management of Magnolia Plantation in Plaquemines Parish, La., and to Manigault Plantation.

.137 — Weeks, Stephen Beauregard, 1865-1918. Collector.
Papers, 1746-1905. 100 items. Papers re-

lating to southern education and religion, particularly in North Carolina. Includes a diary (1746-71) of Thomas Nicholson (1715-80), a Quaker writer of Perquimans Co., N.C.; ms copy of Weeks' book Southern Quakers and Slavery, 1896.

.138 —— White, Maunsell, 1783-1863.
Papers, 1802-1912. 102 items, in part, microfilm. Planter and commission merchant, of New Orleans, La. Correspondence, chiefly of White, who operated Deer Range Plantation in Louisiana, and his son, Maunsell White, Jr., relating to their planting and business activities; plantation records (1802-33); and personal family letters.

.139 —— Wilder, Gaston H., 1814-73.
Papers, 1838-1916. 300 items. Planter and Army officer, of Johnston Co., N.C. Legal and business correspondence, accounts (1847-49) of Wilder, memorandum books, and plantation accounts (1876-80) of his wife, Mrs. Sarah E. (Hinton) Wilder.

.140 —— Williams, Willis R.
Papers, 1851-1910. 236 items. Plantation owner and State legislator, of Pitt Co., N.C. Correspondence, chiefly 1851-78, of Williams and his wife, and scrapbooks of clippings (ca. 1870-90). Most of the letters deal with plantation affairs and Williams' health.

.141 —— Wills, William Henry, 1809-89.
Papers, 1748-1921. ca. 960 items. Methodist minister and merchant, of Brinkleyville, Halifax Co., N.C. Personal correspondence, business papers, and writings (chiefly 1833-80) of Wills; together with the papers of his wife, Anna Maria Baker (Whitaker) Wills; Civil War letters from their son, George Whitaker Wills (d. 1864); correspondence of another son, Richard Henry Wills (1836-91); and other members of the Whitaker and Norman families. Letters concern the Methodist Church, plantation life, slavery, politics, North Carolina schools, and land dealings.

.142 —— Wood, Robert Crooke, 1832-1900.
Papers, 1807-1910. 2 ft. Family correspondence and business papers (chiefly 1866-1900) of Wood while he was commissioner general of the American Shipping and Industrial League, and member of the New Orleans City Council. The earliest items (1807-56) consist of Bringier family papers from New Orleans, relating chiefly to the sale of slaves.

.143 —— Wright family.
Papers, 1749-1898. ca. 2 ft. (1500 items). Family correspondence and business papers, chiefly 1840-71, of members of the Wright family, of Wilmington, N.C., and elsewhere; mainly Julius Walker Wright (1838-78), lawyer and Confederate Army soldier, his wife, Mollie (Murdock) Wright, his father, Joshua G. Wright, and his mother, Mary Ann Wright. Includes papers (1860-78) of Julius Wright pertaining to Reconstruction conditions and the practice of law in Wilmington, Del.

CHARLOTTE

NC4a   AME ZION PUBLISHING HOUSE. 401 E. Second St., 28202. Tel 704 333-5302. M.B. Robinson, Editor.
Publ.: The Star of Zion, weekly official organ of the African Methodist Episcopal Zion Church.

NC5   INSTITUTE FOR URBAN STUDIES AND COMMUNITY SERVICE (1969), J. MURREY ATKINS LIBRARY. P.O. Box 12665, 28205. Tel 704 596-5970. Norman W. Schul, Dir. Interlibrary loan, copying, inquiries answered, referrals made, consultation.

.1   Materials pertaining to Negroes.
Miscellaneous. Books and journals (ca. 370) on Negro life, civil rights, Negro history, Negro authors, and Negro psychology.

NC6   JOHNSON C. SMITH UNIVERSITY (1867), LIBRARY (1911). 28208. Tel 704 372-2370. Theodus L. Gunn, Head Librn. Interlibrary loan, inquiries answered.

.1   Afro-American Heritage collection.
Materials, 17th century- . Microfilm. 131 reels. Books, newspapers, and mss concerning the Negro American and his history. See Minnesota Mining and Manufacturing Company, St. Paul, Minn., for a full description.

.2   Afro-American Studies Collection.
ca. 1000 paperbacks. Basic books on the life and history of black Americans.

.3   Johnson C. Smith University.
Archives, 1867- . Includes correspondence, minutes of board meetings, records of admission, financial records and other materials relating to the history and administration of the University.

NC7   NATIONAL ASSOCIATION FOR THE ADVANCEMENT OF COLORED PEOPLE (NAACP) OF NORTH CAROLINA. 112 N. Irwin Ave., 28208. Tel 704 392-6775. Kelly Alexander, State Pres.

NC8   NATIONAL CONFERENCE OF CHRISTIANS AND JEWS (NCCJ). P.O. Box 4436, 1709 Fountain View, 28204. Tel 704 332-4420. Mrs. Catherine C. Huffman, Prog. Dir.

NC9   MECKLENBURG ORGANIZATION ON POLITICAL AFFAIRS, COMMITTEE ON CIVIL RIGHTS (1948). 1703 Madison Ave., 28208. Tel 704 332-7737. Dr. Reginald A. Hawkins, Chmn. Consultation.
The Organization works to achieve full rights and privileges for American Negroes.

.1   Mecklenburg Organization on Political Affairs, Committee on Civil Rights.
Files, 1948- . Includes correspondence, minutes of meetings, financial records, and other material dealing with the aims, history, and programs of the Organization.

NC10   PUBLIC LIBRARY OF CHARLOTTE AND MECKLENBURG COUNTY (1903). 310 N. Tryon St., 28202. Tel 704 376-6401. Hoyt R. Galvin, Dir. Interlibrary loan, bibliographies prepared, literature searches, copying, typing, inquiries answered, referrals made, consultation.
Publ.: The Negro in America, a selective bibliography. (1970).

.1   Harry Golden Collection.
Papers. Author, and editor of the Carolina Israelite. Mss, some books, pamphlets, and research materials. Restricted.

NC11   QUARTERLY REVIEW OF HIGHER EDUCATION AMONG NEGROES (1933). Johnson C. Smith University, 100 Beatties Ford Rd., 28208. Tel 704 372-2370. Dr. Winson R. Coleman, Editor.
Publ.: Quarterly Review of Higher Education Among Negroes, quarterly journal.

.1   Quarterly Review of Higher Education Among Negroes.
Files, 1933- . Correspondence, financial records, complete run of the Review, mss submitted and/or published, and other materials concerning the history and aims of the Review.

NC12   TEXTILES: EMPLOYMENT AND ADVANCEMENT FOR MINORITIES (TEAM) (1967). 316 Tenth St., 28210. Tel 704 333-0859. Bob Valder, Dir.
TEAM is an action-oriented agency whose purpose is to improve employment and economic conditions of black people in the textile industry of South Carolina.

.1   Textiles: Employment and Advancement for Minorities.
Files, 1967- . Records, correspondence, clippings, pamphlets, and other materials concerning the operation and programs of the organization. Included are reports such as Negroes in Western South Carolina: Some Hard Facts as a Basis for Action (1967). Restricted.

CONCORD

NC13   BARBER-SCOTIA COLLEGE, LIBRARY (1867). 145 Caba-
        mus Ave., W., 28025. Tel 704 786-5171. Dr. Sara B.
        Corderey, Sch. Archivist. Interlibrary loan, copying,
        typing, inquiries answered, referrals made.

   .1   Afro-American Heritage collection.
        Materials, 17th century- . Microfilm. 131 reels.
        Books, newspapers, and mss concerning the Negro
        American and his history. See Minnesota mining
        and Manufacturing Company, St. Paul, Minn., for a
        full description.
   .2   Afro-American Studies Collection.
        Ca. 1000 paperbacks. Basic books on the life and
        history of black Americans.
   .3   Barber-Scotia College.
        Archives, 1867- . Includes correspondence, min-
        utes of board meetings, financial records, records
        of admission, and other materials relating to the
        history and administration of the College.

DURHAM

NC14   CONGRESS OF RACIAL EQUALITY (CORE). 213½ W. Main
        St., 27701. Tel 919 682-7792. John Edwards, Dir.

NC15   DUKE UNIVERSITY (1838), WILLIAM R. PERKINS LI-
        BRARY. 27706. Tel 919 684-3372. Mattie Russell,
        Dir., Ms Div. Interlibrary loan, copying, inquiries an-
        swered.

   .1   Adams, William C.
        Diary.
   .2   Aglionby, Francis (Walker) Yates.
        Papers, 1821-1933. ca. 1000 items. Family let-
        ters from Charlestown, Jefferson County, Va., with
        many details on European travel and English life,
        as well as Virginia plantation affairs, the Civil
        War, and the Protestant Episcopal Church.
   .3   Agricultural papers, 1777-1923.
        7406 items and 93 v. Mostly plantation diaries and
        yearbooks, daybooks, and other records and papers
        of farmers and plantation owners, relating to south-
        ern agricultural activities, chiefly in the 19th cen-
        tury. Includes detailed information on the use of
        slave and free Negro labor, agricultural conditions
        in the South before, during, and after the Civil War,
        and other subjects.
   .4   Alexander, Adam Leopold, 1802-82.
        Papers, 1785-1909. ca. 360 items. Planter and
        businessman with interests in banking, railroads,
        and mercantile firms. Family correspondence,
        miscellaneous deeds, and other papers. Letters
        are in part concerning the Civil War, and Recon-
        struction; and include two letters of Edward Porter
        Alexander, brigadier general of artillery and chief
        of artillery in Longstreet's corps.
   .5   Anderson, Francis Thomas.
        Papers, 1828-1915. ca. 440 items. Miscellaneous
        letters and papers concerning the sale of slaves,
        collection of debts, rental of property, teaching,
        and school tuition; business papers pertaining to
        mining operations and Anderson's Cloverdale
        Furnace, a part of the Tredegar Iron Works.
   .6   Andrews, Charles Wesley, 1807-75.
        Papers, 1808-1901. ca. 3640 items. Protestant
        Episcopal clergyman. Correspondence, journal
        (in letter form) of travels in Europe and the Near
        East in the 1840's, and other papers relating to
        church affairs, to the American Colonization So-
        ciety, to conditions in Virginia before, during, and
        after the Civil War. Includes genealogical mate-
        rial on the Meade, Page, Custis, Fitzhugh, Robin-
        son, Mines, and Boteler families of Virginia.
   .7   Applebury, Dilmus J.
        Papers, 1810-1927. ca. 1750 items. Plantation
        owner of Fluvanna County, Va. Business, family,
        and legal correspondence, indentures, and other
        papers. Correspondents whose names appear most
        often are Pettit and Leake, a legal firm of Gooch-
        land Court House, Va., Atlantic and Virginia
        Fertilizing Company of Richmond, Va., and Apple-
        bury's nephew, Thomas A. Bledsoe.

   .8   Archer, Fletcher Harris, b. 1817.
        Papers, 1804-1900. ca. 980 items. Soldier and
        lawyer of Petersburg, Va. Correspondence, dia-
        ries, scrapbooks of poems, accounts, and other
        papers. Includes letters from Mexico during the
        Mexican War, papers relating to the Civil War and
        to Reconstruction, and sermons of Allin LeRoy
        Archer, a Methodist minister.
   .9   Austin, Benjamin.
        Papers, 1756-1879. 625 items. Papers of Benja-
        min Austin and Henry Reid, farmers and justices
        of the peace of Burke County, N.C., with a few
        family letters on Burke County politics, attitude
        toward abolition in Indiana, and blacksmithing.
   .10 Bagby, Bennette M.
        Papers, 1830-1920. 910 items. Farmer (?) and
        agent for the American Tract Society after the
        Civil War; resident of Powhatan County, Va.
        Largely the correspondence of Bagby and of his
        family and of the family of his second wife, Louisa
        B. (Flippin) Bagby. Numerous letters from
        Bagby's sons and from his wife's nieces. The pa-
        pers reflect the interests of planters, soldiers, and
        educators during the period of secession, Civil
        War, and Reconstruction, revealing the economic
        plight of the South; hardships from disease; camp
        life; and the attempts of the South at readjustment
        after the war.
   .11 Ball, John, 1760-1817.
        Papers of John Ball, Sr. and Jr., 1773-1892. 3211
        items and 26 v. Rice planters, of Charleston, S.C.
        Personal and business correspondence, papers,
        and account books, largely for 1803-54. Business
        papers include lists of slaves.
   .12 Ball, William Watts, 1868-1952.
        Papers, 1805-1952. 26,728 items and 116 v. Edi-
        tor and author. Personal and political correspon-
        dence, diary, business papers, speeches, editorials,
        notes, printed matter, personal account books,
        memorandum books, and scrapbooks. The papers
        reflect Ball's activities as editor of several news-
        papers, including The State, of Columbia, S.C., and
        the Charleston News and Courier, S.C. The
        main group is concerned with national and South
        Carolina history for the first half of the 20th cen-
        tury, and includes discussion of politics, Negro
        problems, the depression and the F.D. Roosevelt
        administration, education in South Carolina, states'
        rights, and South Carolina social life and customs.
        Correspondents include J.J. McSwain, D.C. Hey-
        ward, John G. Evans, John H. Hammond, M.F.
        Ansel, David D. Wallace, James C. Hemphill,
        Ambrose E. Gonzales, Thomas R. Waring, Nathan-
        iel B. Dial, James F. Byrnes, Ulrich B. Phillips,
        Josephus Daniels, Bernard M. Baruch, Warrington
        Dawson, Ellison D. Smith, Max Fleischman,
        Nicholas Roosevelt, Wendell Wilkie, Frederick H.
        Allen, and Archibald Rutledge. Papers partly re-
        stricted.
   .13 Barksdale, Peter.
        Papers, 1783-1895. 435 items. Tobacco farmer,
        of Halifax County, Va. Correspondence, largely
        dating from 1789-1842. The earlier letters are
        from Randolph and William Barksdale, merchants
        in Petersburg, Va., and concern the purchase of
        slaves. Among other subjects included is the
        hiring of slaves, and local politics in Virginia and
        Tennessee.
   .14 Baxter, Thomas, 1799-1878.
        Correspondence, 1845-87. 89 items. Commission
        merchant and businessman, of Petersburg, Va.
        Postwar letters are concerned with radical rule in
        North Carolina during the carpetbag era.
   .15 Bellamy, William.
        Papers of William and Joseph Bellamy, 1815-88.
        100 items. Family and business papers and corre-
        spondence of William Bellamy, evidently a planter,
        of Enfield, Halifax County, N.C., and of Joseph
        Bellamy, a lawyer, chiefly dating from 1843-69.
        Includes a few Civil War letters among others. Of
        particular interest are letters and resolutions con-
        cerning the separation of Southern Methodists from
        the Northern branch of the church in 1844.

NC15.16 Bennett, Bryant.
Papers, 1767-1902. 765 items and 5 v. Merchant
and planter. Correspondence and business papers
of Bennett and his family. Includes plantation account books containing household and farm records, lists of slaves and supplies issued to them.
Most of the collection dates from 1840-75.

.17 Bibb, Thomas, ca. 1783-1839.
Papers, 1823-92. 180 items. Planter, merchant,
State legislator, and Governor of Alabama (1820-
21). Legal papers, including mortgages on land
and slaves which Bibb bought near Thibodeaux,
La.; also a list of slaves with the ages of each.

.18 Blakey, Angus R.
Papers, 1820-88. 652 items. Lawyer. Correspondence and other papers, mainly for 1840-65,
including those of Blakey's junior partners. Includes material on slavery, free Negroes, the
Virginia secession convention, the Confederate
Army, Reconstruction, and land matters.

.19 Bolling, William, 1789-1849.
Papers, 1724-1883. 877 items. Planter, army officer, and sheriff of Goochland County, Va. Correspondence, and other papers, mainly for the period
1766-1859. Subjects and persons named include
the farming operations of Bolling.

.20 Boteler, Alexander Robinson, 1815-92.
Papers. U.S. Congressman. Diary and papers referring to the American Colonization Society.

.21 Bowen, Reuben Dean, 1859-1939.
Papers, 1857-1938. 26,672 items and 6 v. Texas
businessman, farmer, promoter of the cotton industry. Correspondence, newspaper clippings, and
pamphlets, relating to the price of slaves at Richmond (1857), social legislation, agricultural organizations, World War I, labor and labor legislation,
and U.S. politics and government.

.22 Bower, William Horton, 1850-1910.
Papers, 1870-88. 260 items. Lawyer, teacher,
and political leader of North Carolina and California. Correspondence, mainly personal, including comments on North Carolina politics, radicals
in the State, Horace Greeley, provisions for the
use of the Peabody Education Fund for public
schools, results of State and national elections of
North Carolina in 1876, and other topics.

.23 Boyd, Archibald H.
Papers, 1841-97. 46 items. Businessman, Lenox
Castle, Rockingham County, N.C. Personal and
business correspondence of Boyd and his son,
James E. Boyd, attorney and political leader, including Civil War letters commenting on living
conditions, military activities, and relating to the
region around Richmond and Petersburg, Va.; and
letters dealing with North Carolina politics in the
early 1880's when James E. Boyd was U.S. Attorney for the Western District of North Carolina.
Includes letters of Samuel R. Browning, slave
trader, of Milliken's Bend, La., commenting on the
health of various slaves, conditions of the slave
market, the effects of cholera epidemics on the
slave trade, and accounts of various transactions
in which he was engaged.

.24 Briggs, George.
Papers, 1837-1908. 164 items. Confederate
soldier and farmer of Hurdle's Mill, Person
County, N.C. Correspondence and other papers;
the ante-bellum material relates to the prices of
farm products and slaves in North Carolina, Alabama, Kentucky, and Texas. Post-war papers give
a picture of the social and religious life of North
Carolina farmers during the years 1870-1900

.25 British Political Papers, 1628-1915.
707 items and 17 v. In part, photocopies. Papers
relating to the emancipation in the West Indies, the
slave trade, and other subjects.

.26 Brodnax, John G., 1829-1907.
Papers, 1830-1929. 1389 items. Confederate
surgeon and practicing physician, of Greensboro,
N.C. Personal, professional and family correspondence, genealogical papers, and other material, of Brodnax and three generations of his family. Pre-Civil War letters refer to the sale of
slaves; wartime correspondence reflects fear of

the advancing Union forces. Postwar papers include Brodnax's appointment as assistant surgeon
general of a hospital at Petersburg, Va., and his
oath of allegiance to the U.S. Includes his letters
to Mrs. Brodnax, beginning in 1881. Many papers
concern Mrs. Brodnax's activities in patriotic
societies. Some papers deal with the settlement of
the estate of John Brodnax, Jr., after 1909; there
is also a group of sermons by James K. Burch, a
Presbyterian minister.

.27 Brodnax, Samuel Houston, 1844-1932.
Papers, 1862-1932. 918 items. Farmer and State
legislator, of Walnut Grove, Walton County, Ga.
Largely correspondence; many of the earlier letters concerned with the employment of free Negroes, state politics (1867-68), and other matters;
some wartime letters on fighting in Florida, and
lack of faith in Confederate currency. A group of
letters deals with Brodnax's campaign for the State
Legislature in 1890, and post-election appeals for
patronage and office from his supporters. Some
letters allude to temperance and Negro voting.

.28 Brookes, Iveson L.
Papers, 1831-88. 718 items. Baptist minister,
landholder, and farmer, of Hamburg, Aiken County,
S.C. Some personal and family letters refer to
plantation management. Many letters allude to
public affairs, and include a prediction by Brookes
in 1836 of the coming Civil War; accounts of activities of B.F. Butler as Military Governor of Virginia, and other matters; others deal with postwar
politics including the election of a chief justice in
South Carolina, and legislative problems during
the Wade Hampton administration there.

.29 Brotherton, William H.
Papers of William H. and James Brotherton,
1803-1910. 137 items. Correspondence, indentures, and business papers of William H. and
James Brotherton, of North Carolina and Tennes-
see. About 60 letters from William Brotherton relate his experiences as a private in the Confederate
Army. The remainder of the letters are from
James Brotherton, who moved from North Carolina
to east Tennessee, and concern the distilling of
whiskey and brandy, the Ku-Klux activities near
Lynchburg, Tenn., in 1868.

.30 Brown, George M.
Papers, 1829-81. 191 items. Physician and
farmer, of Cartersville, Cumberland County, Va.
Correspondence concerning John Brown's Raid
(1859); effects of the Civil War on noncombatants;
Reconstruction; and Brown's view on slavery, Negroes in politics, and other issues of the times.

.31 Brown, William Garrott, 1868-1913.
Papers, 1898-1917. 933 items. Historian, biographer and essayist of Marion, Ala., and Cambridge, Mass. Personal and professional correspondence and literary notes, diploma, and copy of
will. The letters concern Brown's literary work
and his friends; subjects covered include the efforts of southern liberals to make the Republican
party respectable in the South and other subjects.
Among correspondents is Booker T. Washington.

.32 Bryan, John Herritage, 1798-1870.
Papers, 1735-1926. 352 items. Lawyer, State
senator, and U.S. Representative from North Carolina. Correspondence, legal papers, and other papers of Bryan and his son, Henry Ravenscroft
Bryan, relating to politics in the Jacksonian era
and post-Civil War politics in North Carolina.
Correspondents include Otway Burns, William A.
Graham, Willie P. Mangum, William B. Shepard,
and David L. Swain.

.33 Buchanan family.
Papers of the Buchanan, Dandridge, and Thomas
families, 1711-1952. 648 items. Correspondence,
photos, cancelled checks, wills, and deeds of the
three families; many are the papers of Thomas E.
Buchanan of Williamsport, Washington County, Md.
Chief period covered is 1833-58. The letters give
information on plantation life and management in
Virginia and Maryland; on slavery and slave insurrections; and on opposition to secession in Virginia.

NC15.34 Buford, John.
Papers, 1804-98. 604 items. Railroad contractor. Personal and business correspondence, and other papers of Buford and his family, whose seat was in Bedford County, Va. Some papers include material on the sale and hiring of slaves, and state politics.

.35 Burroughs, Richard D.
Papers of Richard D. and John William Burroughs, 1807-89. 2144 items. Personal and business correspondence, and other papers of a tavern keeper and planter; and of his son, also a planter, both of Prince Georges County, Md.

.36 Burt, Armistead, 1802-83.
Papers, 1825-90. 5641 items. Planter, lawyer, and U.S. Representative, of Abbeville, S.C. Political and legal correspondence, the former dealing largely with Burt's service in Congress, and reflecting the issue of secession and other public questions of the pre-Civil War decades. Many papers relate to the policies of John C. Calhoun and his period of leadership (1832-48). Among the correspondents are Pierce M. Butler, Henry T. Clark, T.L. Deveaux, James H. Hammond, A.P. Hayne, Reverdy Johnson, Hugh L. Legare, Augustus B. Longstreet, W.N. Meriwether, James L. Petigru, Francis W. Pickens, Richard Rush, Waddy Thompson, and Louis T. Wigfall.

.37 Butler family.
Papers, 1809-1916. 1632 items. Personal and business correspondence and business papers of the Butler family, Virginia planters and teachers. Chief coverage is for 1830-86. Some papers relate to the settlement of the estate of Isaac Butler. The papers give information on the Butler family and on social and economic conditions in Illinois and Virginia.

.38 Butler, Edward George Washington, 1800-88.
Correspondence, 1778-1888. 182 items. Planter and U.S. Army officer, of Iberville, La. The correspondence deals with military matters, the Mexican War, the Civil War, slavery, Lincoln's election, politics and government, southern social life and customs, Reconstruction, and contemporary European affairs. Correspondents include Caroline D. Beauregard, Braxton Bragg, James Buchanan, Jefferson Davis, Alexander Duncan, Edmund P. Gains, Andrew Jackson, J.E. Johnston, Mary Ann R.C. Lee, Robert E. Lee, Eleanor P.C. Lewis, John P. Custis, Leonidas Polk, John Slidell, and Martin Van Buren.

.39 Cable, George Washington, 1844-1925.
Papers, 1879-1917. 43 items and 1 reel of microfilm. Microfilm made from originals owned by Walter L. Pforzheimer. Author. The letters (mainly 1885-91) are largely concerned with Cable's literary activities and reflect his gradual break with the South. Some mention is made of Cable's work as a reformer, with references to the Negro problem, to criticism of himself by southern newspapers, and other issues.

.40 Cain, Patrick H.
Papers, 1783-1940. ca. 2900 items. Merchant, tobacco salesman, land owner, distiller, and representative in the North Carolina Assembly. Correspondence, legal documents, and other papers, chiefly of a business nature, relating to the interests of the Cain family of Davie County, N.C. Includes documents giving the value of slaves, their purchase and sale prices, and after the Civil War, the wages and tenancy of freedmen.

.41 Calhoun, John Caldwell, 1782-1850.
Papers, 1765-1902. 345 items. South Carolina statesman. Correspondence and family papers concerning current politics and Calhoun's public life. Many of the letters deal with Calhoun's private affairs, particularly finances and the management of his plantations. Correspondents include Armistead Burt, John D. Gardiner, Joseph McMinn, R.J. Meigs, and Francis Wilkinson Pickens.

.42 Campbell, David, 1779-1859.
Papers of David Campbell and family, 1773-1908. 8043 items and 32 v. Military and political leader, and merchant, of Abingdon, Va. Family, business, and political correspondence, diary, journal, account books, and other papers, mainly for 1800-69. The papers reflect his political activities as Governor of Virginia (1837-40), and other activities. Includes data on religion, slavery and other public issues. An important group of papers of Campbell's nephew, William B. Campbell, concerns the latter's career as Governor of Tennessee (1851-53), Unionist during and after the Civil War, and U.S. Representative from Tennessee. Papers of Virginia T.J.C. Shelton, niece of David Campbell, discuss contemporary social matters, public events and issues, and life in Richmond while her uncle was Governor. Letters to Mrs. David Campbell from her father, Judge David Campbell, are of value for their data on early history and politics in Tennessee. Letters of John Campbell, Virginia and Alabama political leader and Treasurer of the U.S., contain observations on public affairs during the Andrew Jackson period, and other matters. Letters of James Campbell, lawyer and Tennessee legislator, contain information on history and politics in Tennessee. Correspondents include Arthur Campbell (brother of David Campbell), Adine Turner, John Bell, William Blount, O.H. Browning, William G. Brownlow, Henry Clay, J.J. Crittenden, Jefferson Davis, L.C. Draper, J.H. Eaton, Millard Fillmore, Ephraim H. Foster, Joseph Gales, Horatio Gates, William A. Graham, Felix Grundy, George F. Holmes, Andrew Jackson, Cave Johnson, William B. Lewis, Louis McLane, Bishop James Madison, Return J. Meigs, Thomas Owen, Timothy Parker, Franklin Pierce, Joel R. Poinsett, James K. Polk, William C. Preston, John A. Quitman, Thomas J. Randolph, Thomas M. Randolph, William C. Rives, Thomas Ritchie, Theodore Roosevelt, Edmund Ruffin, John Rutherfoord, Winfield Scott, William B. Sprague, Andrew Stevenson, Alexander H.H. Stuart, Zachary Taylor, Waddy Thompson, Henry St. George Tucker, Martin Van Buren, Daniel Webster, Gideon Welles, Hugh L. White, and Felix K. Zollicoffer.

.43 Carrigan family.
Papers, 1817-1901. 318 items and 2 v. Correspondence and other papers of the 11 children of James Carrigan, a Cabarrus County, N.C., planter. The letters include information on the early history of Alabama, slaveholding, social and economic life generally, and conditions during the Civil War in Arkansas and east Tennessee.

.44 Carrington, Isaac Howell, 1827-87.
Papers, 1840-1932. 705 items. Confederate officer and attorney. Correspondence, and personal and business papers relating to Carrington's duties as provost marshal of Richmond, Va., to Virginia politics, and other subjects. Among the topics mentioned in the post-war correspondence are the price of slaves, plantations in Louisiana, and other matters.

.45 Carter, Robert, 1728-1804.
Correspondence, 1772-93. 3135 items. In part, typescripts. Planter and iron manufacturer of Westmoreland County, Va. Letter books and memorandum books concerning colonial plantation life, slavery, manumission, and other matters. Includes copies of letters by Carter to Charles Carroll, Benjamin Day, William Ebzer, Thomas Fairfax, William Grayson, Patrick Henry, Ludwell Lee, Richard Lee, Peyton Randolph, George Turberville, John Turberville, and George Wythe, and letters to Carter from Alexander Campbell, Christopher Collins, Thomas Jones, Richard Lee, George Newman, John Overall and Simon Triplett.

.46 Caruthers, Eli Washington, 1793-1865.
Papers, 1821-55. 250 items. Presbyterian minister. Sermons, and an unpublished anti-slavery ms, "American Slavery and the Immediate Duty of Southern Slaveholders," written at the request of Caruthers' friends. Includes a sermon on humility preached in 1850 to a Negro congregation, and other items.

.47 Chaffin, Washington Sandford, 1815-95.
Papers, 1841-1900. 108 items and 23 v. Methodist

minister and circuit rider. Personal correspondence, diaries (1845-87), sermon notes, and bills, giving information on Reconstruction, the Freedmen's Bureau in Robeson County, N.C., northern depredations in Lumberton and Fayetteville, N.C. and the behavior of the newly freed Negroes, and other affairs.

NC15.48 Chesnut, James, 1815-85.
Papers, 1779-1872. 102 items. Lawyer, planter, political leader, and Confederate Army officer, of Camden, S.C. Papers concerning public affairs include a petition from citizens of the Marion District (S.C.) regarding agitators who aroused discontent among slaves, and other information.

.49 Chessen, William L.
Papers of William L. Chesson and family, 1783-1894. 1346 items and 4 v. Clerk of the court of Washington County, N.C. Correspondence, business and personal papers, letter book of Chesson and 6 of his brothers and sisters. Most material dates from 1806-69, and includes contracts for the hire and purchase of slaves, demands from the Freedmen's Bureau for the arrest of a person in Beaufort, N.C.; the will of Andrew L. Chesson, Negro participation in Republican politics at Edenton, and other subjects.

.50 Cheves, Rachel Susan (Bee), d. 1884.
Papers, 1846-1911. 215 items and 2 v. Housewife, of Savannah. Correspondence, including family letters, notes and memoranda; most papers date from 1861-64. Among the subjects discussed are slavery, and conditions during the Civil War and Reconstruction. A statement by Mrs. Cheves (ca. 1866) and several of her letters describe the burning of Columbia, S.C., in 1864.

.51 Christian, John Beverly, 1859-1916.
Papers, 1829-1904. 519 items and 3 v. Lawyer, of Uniontown, Perry County, Ala. Correspondence, including that of the related Christian and Storrs families; notebooks; and other papers. The papers relate to slavery and the treatment of slaves; and other subjects.

.52 Christian, William Walter.
Correspondence, 1855-62. 168 items. Trader and Confederate soldier, of Christiansburg, Roanoke County, Va. The letters cover the period preceeding the Civil War and up to the outbreak of the conflict. Subjects discussed include the John Brown raid at Harpers Ferry and the attendant excitement, southern attitudes toward a Negro uprising, and other matters.

.53 Civil War Period papers, 1837-1906.
316 items and 3 v. Papers (chiefly 1861-65) containing information about the pension system after the Civil War, the efforts of a northern man to become a Mississippi cotton planter during the War, fighting among the Sea Islands of the South Carolina coast and the life of a refugee planter, his family, and his Negroes, and other subjects. Approximately 100 items relate to Reconstruction in the South.

.54 Civil War soldiers' papers, 1831-1933.
4030 items and 36 v. Correspondence, diaries, and other papers (chiefly 1861-65) relating to Negro soldiers, soldiers' attitudes towards politics in the North, and other matters.

.55 Clark family.
Papers, 1764-1890. 174 items and 3 v. Correspondence, account books, and other papers of the family of Christopher Clark, Sr., of Albemarle County, Va., who was an early settler (ca. 1722) of the Blue Ridge area. Letters written from Georgia concern, in part, slave sales and purchases, and plantation life.

.56 Clark, Henry.
Papers, 1809-45. 632 items. Tobacco planter, of Campbell County, Va. Correspondence (business and personal), bills, receipts, legal papers, and miscellaneous business items. Subjects discussed include the hiring and sale of slaves, disposition of slaves in wills, and other affairs. Includes comments by Rice W. Wood, a member of the Virginia House of Delegates, on the Negro problem in Virginia.

.57 Clark, Henry Toole, 1808-74.
Papers, 1757-1885. 1341 items. North Carolina political leader. Political and official correspondence of Clark as Governor during the Civil War; and other materials. Includes comments on state and national politics of the ante-bellum decade, letters relating to Clark's pardon and legal aspects of Reconstruction, and other matters. Of interest are the several records of slave hire.

.58 Clay, Clement Claiborne, 1819-82.
Papers of Clement Claiborne Clay and family, 1811-1925. 8541 items and 37 v. Alabama lawyer, diplomat, planter, and public official. Diaries, personal and political correspondence, business papers, plantation records, scrapbooks, clippings, notebooks, and other papers. Material pertains also to Clay's father, Clement Comer Clay, also a lawyer, planter, and statesman. Much material pertains to the elder Clay's service as Alabama Governor (1835-37) and Member of both Houses of Congress; to the son's activity in the Senates of the U.S. and the Confederacy, and to his diplomatic, planting, and legal interests. Some papers relate to social and plantation life in Alabama, and public personalities of the times, including Charles Sumner, Stephen A. Douglas, and others. Among the correspondents are Jeremiah S. Black, E.C. Bullock, David Clopton, W.W. Corcoran, J.L.M. Curry, Jefferson Davis, Varina Davis, Benjamin Fitzpatrick, U.S. Grant, Andrew Johnson, L.Q.C. Lamar, Clifford Anderson Lanier, Sidney Lanier, Stephen R. Mallory, Nelson A. Miles, James K. Polk, John H. Reagan, R.B. Rhett, E.S. Shorter, Leroy P. Walker, Louis T. Wigfall, and William L. Yancey.

.59 Clay, Henry, 1777-1852.
Papers, 1802-52. 138 items. Kentucky statesman and political leader. Correspondence and papers (mainly for the period 1821-51) dealing with the Missouri compromise, and other public affairs. Other subjects referred to include Clay's refusal to free three of his slaves, and other matters of more personal interest.

.60 Clifton, John L.
Papers, 1784-1916. 4772 items and 11 v. Businessman, clergyman, and possibly a lawyer, of Clinton and Faison, N.C. Correspondence, legal papers, and other items, mainly from 1830-89. Legal and business papers concern the administration of various estates; these include contracts for hiring slaves, deeds for the sale of slaves, and other items.

.61 Clopton family.
Papers of the Clopton and Wallace families, 1629-1915. 11,748 items and 19 v. Family correspondence and miscellaneous papers of 4 generations of the Clopton family and 3 generations of the Wallace family, centering in Virginia. Letters to a son of John Clopton, John Bacon Clopton, Virginia judge, relate to operation of a plantation in New Kent County. Correspondence of Charles Montriou Wallace, Sr., a Richmond merchant, includes accounts of Reconstruction in the South, politics in Virginia, and other matters.

.62 Coleman family.
Papers, 1806-1921. 87 items and 2 v. Correspondence, diaries, and farm records of an Arkadelphia (Ark.) family, containing accounts of social life and customs in Arkansas during and after the Civil War. Main coverage is for 1845-95. Subjects dealt with include feelings in Virginia prior to secession, and events during the Civil War; and other matters. Letters and diary entries of the Reconstruction period relate to reaction of Negroes to Reconstruction; the labor situation during the period; and other matters.

.63 Confederate States of America.
Papers, 1821-1912. 1924 items and 4 v. Papers (chiefly 1860-65) relating to a great variety of subjects, including secession, the outbreak of the Civil War, economic problems, politics, plantation life, and others. Includes papers of John C. Breckinridge, Joseph E. Brown, Alexander R. Chisolm, Thomas S. Gholson, Stephen R. Mallory,

Christopher G. Memminger, James Seddon, Thomas J. Semmes, John G. Shorter, and Leroy P. Walker.

NC15.64 Confederate States of America.
Archives and miscellaneous records and papers, 1861-65. 8313 items and 39 v. Seven general categories: Congressional records, including originals and copies of acts and statutes, with miscellaneous papers; Executive Department records of the Justice, Navy, Post Office, State, Treasury, and War Departments, with records of bureaus under each office; Army unit records; other Army records, mainly form records; State government records of Georgia, North Carolina, South Carolina, and Virginia; State agency records; and miscellaneous non-governmental papers.

.65 Confederate Veteran.
Historical articles and mss, 1786-1933. 620 items. Unpublished articles written for the periodical Confederate Veteran, "published monthly in the interest of Confederate veterans and kindred topics" in Nashville, Tenn. (1893-1932). Some material relates to the Reconstruction period, and the Ku Klux Klan.

.66 Corbin, Francis Porteus, 1801-76.
Papers of Francis P. Corbin and family, 1662-1885. 719 items. Lawyer, planter, and businessman, of Virginia, Philadelphia, and Paris. Some of the papers include early Corbin land grants, lists of property and Negroes on plantations.

.67 Corpening family.
Papers, 1780-1922. 992 items. Personal letters, legal and commercial papers, of the Burke and Caldwell counties (N.C.) family. The earlier papers include much information concerning the valuation and general treatment of slaves.

.68 Coston, Erasmus H.
Papers, 1744-1939. 965 items and 1 v. Farmer, teacher, and public official, of Palo Alto, Onslow County, N.C. Correspondence, legal papers, and a daybook. Most material dates from 1854-69. Includes material relating to such subjects as slavery and the slave trade.

.69 Crittenden, John Jordan, 1787-1863.
Papers, 1786-1932. 1055 items and 3 v. Kentucky lawyer and statesman. Family and political correspondence, scrapbooks, letter book, and speeches relating to Crittenden's service as Kentucky legislator and Governor, as Member of both Houses of Congress, and as Cabinet officer. The papers contain information on political life and public issues of Kentucky and the nation during the ante-bellum period, with significant material concerning Crittenden's efforts to avert the Civil War by means of a compromise plan in 1861. Other papers pertain to the private life of the family. Includes unpublished letters from Thomas Hart Benton, James Buchanan, William Butler, Henry Clay, Ann M. Butler (Crittenden) Coleman, Millard Fillmore, Andrew Jackson, James Madison, John Marshall, James Monroe, Franklin Pierce, Winfield Scott, William H. Seward, Alexander H. Stephens, Benjamin Taylor, Zachary Taylor, John Tyler, and Daniel Webster.

.70 Crudup, E.A.
Plantation diary.

.71 Cunningham family.
Papers, 1740-1910. 5918 items and 44 v. Business records and some personal correspondence of 4 generations of the Virginia and North Carolina family: Robert Cunningham, Alexander Cunningham, Richard M. Cunningham, John Wilson Cunningham, and John Summerville Cunningham, merchants and planters of Petersburg, Va., and Person County, N.C. Most papers date from 1825-59. Plantation records, contracts with overseers and tenants, letters to John Garner, who managed enterprises in North Carolina and Alabama during and after the 1820's.

.72 Cushing family.
Papers, 1743-1911. 996 items and 5 v. Correspondence, account books, other financial papers, legal papers, and printed matter of the family of Nathaniel Cushing, Jr., which was based in Scituate, Plymouth County, Mass. Subjects include, in part, education of Negroes in Tennessee.

.73 Daniel, John Warwick, 1842-1910.
Papers, 1849-1910. 486 items. Lawyer, U.S. Senator and Representative from Virginia. Correspondence (chiefly 1876-1909) on the Civil War, on Reconstruction, Virginia and U.S. politics and government, and economic questions, from over 150 men, including ex-officers of the Confederate Army.

.74 Dantzler, Absalom F., d. 1862.
Papers, 1840-78. 287 items. Lawyer, minister, legislator, and Confederate officer, of Jasper County, Miss. Correspondence, largely between Absalom and Susan (Millsaps) Dantzler, especially while he was in the legislature and in the Army. Susan Dantzler's letters concern home and family matters, with occasional remarks about Negro misbehavior in the community.

.75 Davidson family.
Papers, 1748-1887. 1660 items and 14 v. Personal correspondence, diaries, legal papers, and account books. Includes twelve account books and diaries of George F. Davidson, lawyer and planter of Iredell Co., N.C., showing daily activities on his plantation; and letters concerning terms for renting land and hiring Negroes (1838).

.76 Davidson, James D., d. 1882.
Papers, 1829-78. 317 items. Lawyer, of Lexington, Va. Chiefly correspondence (legal, business, and personal), pertaining to Virginia and Virginians. The bulk of the papers dates from 1836-59. Subjects mentioned include slavery.

.77 Davis, Jefferson, 1808-89.
Papers, 1851-1938. 695 items. U.S. Representative and Senator from Mississippi, U.S. Secretary of War, and President of the Confederate States of America. Chiefly personal and official correspondence. Ante-bellum letters refer to political parties and questions, the slavery controversy, and other subjects. Correspondents include Judah P. Benjamin, Milledge L. Bonham, Braxton Bragg, John C. Breckinridge, Joseph E. Brown, James Chesnut, Caleb Cushing, Nathan Bedford Forrest, Wade Hampton, B.N. Harrison, G.A. Henry, Herschel V. Johnson, Joseph E. Johnston, Edmund Kirby-Smith, John Letcher, James Longstreet, Stephen R. Mallory, James M. Mason, Christopher G. Memminger, John H. Morgan, John J. Pettus, Frances W. Pickens, L. Polk, George W. Randolph, John H. Reagan, James A. Seddon, William Smith, Pierre Soule, Zebulon B. Vance, Thomas H. Watts, and David L. Yulee.

.78 Dearing, John J.
Papers, 1821-99. 183 items. Physician, planter, and merchant, of Covington, Ga. Correspondence, and other materials. The correspondence pertains to the settlement of the estate of William Dearing, the slave trade, and other subjects.

.79 De Saussure, Henry William, 1763-1839.
Papers of Henry William and Wilmot Gibbes De Saussure, 1788-1916. 124 items and 3 v. Correspondence, and other papers of Henry William De Saussure, Revolutionary soldier, director of the U.S. Mint, South Carolina legislator, and judge of the chancery court in South Carolina; and of Wilmot Gibbes De Saussure, South Carolina legislator and Confederate Army officer, his grandson. Subjects include conditions in the Confederacy, political phases of Reconstruction, effect of the contested election in 1877, and other matters.

.80 Deveaux family.
Papers of the Deveaux, Singleton, and Moore families, 1758-1894. 350 items and 1 v. Personal and business correspondence and other records (chiefly 1864-82) of three South Carolina planter families. The Deveaux portion of the papers consists mostly of plantation records. Included is one volume containing accounts of the estates of V.M. Deveaux and of Miss Marion S. Deveaux, and plantation records for "The Ruins" and the Oakley and Pinckney plantations.

.81 Dibble, Samuel, 1837-1913.
Papers, 1779-1910. 1672 items. Lawyer, politi-

cian, and U.S. Representative from South Carolina. Correspondence, business and legal papers, and printed matter, mostly 1855-1900, and reflecting an interest in South Carolina affairs. Post-bellum correspondence deals with such matters as the Negro in post-Reconstruction politics, Dibble's opposition to Governor Tillman, and other subjects.

NC15.82 Dimitry, John Bull Smith, 1835-1901.
Cooorespondence, 1850-1910. 580 items. Soldier, Confederate Post Office official, author, and teacher, of Jackson, Miss. Post-war correspondence refers to Reconstruction in Mississippi.

.83 Dixon, Winsor, 1802-58.
Papers of Winsor Dixon and of the Lyon family. 201 items and 1 v. School teacher and agent, of Greene County, N.C. Personal and business correspondence, and other papers, of Dixon and of the Lyon family of Edgecombe County, N.C. Postwar letters refer to the scarcity of money and to hard times in the South. Dixon's papers pertain to his purchase of slaves, and other matters.

.84 Douglass, William Boone.
Papers, 1809-1948. 1873 items and 11 v. Lawyer, engineer, and surveyor. Correspondence, memorandum books, daybooks, and other papers of Douglass and of various members of the Boone and Douglass families, especially of his father, Benjamin P. Douglass, Indiana State representative, and his son, William Boone Douglass, Jr., an official of the U.S. consular service. The letters pertain to the Kansas-Nebraska question, and other subjects. Also includes an emancipation document for some slaves in Indiana Territory.

.85 Downey, Samuel Smith, d. 1851.
Papers, 1772-1932. 3202 items and 2 v. Irish immigrant and planter, of Granville County, N.C. Correspondence, bills, and receipts, of Downey and, after 1851, of his sons, John and James. Includes information on plantation management, slaveholding, economic conditions after the Panic of 1837 and in the Confederacy, and the Civil War.

.86 Dromgoole, George Coke, 1797-1847.
Papers, 1767-1920. 4545 items and 6 v. Planter, State legislator, and U.S. Representative from Virginia. Correspondence and legal and business papers (chiefly 1823-65), largely concerning plantation life and management, including such matters as sale of slaves and commodities, and labor agreements.

.87 Du Bois, Egbert.
Correspondence, 1860-1901. 523 items. Correspondence of Egbert Du Bois, planter, of Bluffton, Beaufort County, S.C., and his son, Pierre Eugene, lawyer, of Albany, N.Y. Includes news of life, economics, and politics during the Reconstruction, references to the race situation after Reconstruction, and other subjects.

.88 Duke family.
Correspondence, 1840-84. 210 items. Personal and business correspondence of William B. Duke, Dr. James E. Duke, Napoleon Bonaparte Duke, and Walter Patterson Duke, four of the sons of Edmund W. Duke of Goochland County, Va. Includes two letters describing Ku Klux Klan activities in Tennessee, and other materials.

.89 Elliott, Benjamin P.
Correspondence, 1805-86. 179 items. Teacher, storekeeper, and physician, of New Salem, Randolph County, N.C. Letters (largely 1839-86) covering a complete generation of the Elliott family, and relating to the Civil War and Reconstruction; and other subjects.

.90 Elliott, Thomas Rhett Smith, b. 1819.
Correspondence, 1785-1891. 108 items. Rice planter, of Beaufort and Charleston, S.C. Family correspondence, revealing attitudes and problems of southerners during and after the Civil War, with references to the race problem and to life and politics during Reconstruction.

.91 Emerson, J. Milton.
Journal.

.92 Faulkner, Charles James, 1806-84.
Papers, 1815-83. 370 items and 1 v. Diplomat,

Confederate officer, and U.S. Representative from Virginia and West Virginia. Correspondence, legal papers, notes, and other papers. Some topics mentioned include slavery and slave insurrections.

.93 Findley family.
Correspondence, 1826-79. 162 items. Correspondence (chiefly 1861-65) of Alexander T., Joseph R., and William M. Findley, soldiers, of Altoona, Pa. Civil War letters comment on conditions in the Union Army, lack of wisdom in freeing Negroes, Confederate destruction of southern homes, and Negro regiments in the Union Army.

.94 Fleming family.
Correspondence, 1810-1910. 1081 items. Personal correspondence, chiefly of the Flemings, a Virginia family of educators, physicians, and soldiers. The correspondence reflects living conditions during the Civil War and Reconstruction, and other matters.

.95 Forrest, Nathan Bedford, 1821-77.
Papers, 1862-66. 393 items. Planter, slave dealer, and Confederate officer. Correspondence, orders, and other papers. Some subjects include an illness of Forrest's in 1862, and his efforts to accept the outcome of the war.

.96 Fox, John, b. 1806.
Papers, 1784-1892. 2139 items. Politician and South Carolina legislator. Correspondence and other papers (chiefly 1825-92). Correspondence concerns slave purchasing and management, crime and law enforcement in the Confederacy, Reconstruction in South Carolina, political activities of Negroes in 1872, and other matters.

.97 Fraser family.
Papers, 1780-1886. 395 items and 4 v. Correspondence, account books, memoranda, newspaper clippings, and other papers (chiefly 1800-86), of three generations of the Fraser family of Charleston, S.C. Correspondence of Mary (De Saussure) Fraser forms the larger part of the collection, and concerns life around Beaufort, S.C. (1831-41), farming, politics, clothing and equipment for slaves, and other matters.

.98 Fuller family.
Papers, 1810-95. 1322 items. Correspondence and other papers of Jones Fuller, broker and merchant, and of his son, Edwin Wiley Fuller, poet and novelist, of Louisburg, N.C.; and of their cousin, William George Thomas, physician, of Wilmington, N.C. Most of the material is for 1840-70. Correspondence comments on politics, secession, Civil War conditions in Wilmington, Reconstruction, and other matters.

.99 Fuller, Stephen, 1716-1808.
Papers, 1702-96. 42 items and 2 v. British iron manufacturer and colonial agent for Jamaica. Correspondence and other papers (chiefly 1786-96). Includes discussions of slavery, the slave trade, and the Wilberforce movement for its abolition (which Fuller opposed); and other matters.

.100 Funkhouser family.
Papers, 1786-1941. 1968 items and 13 v. Correspondence, diary, and other papers, chiefly 1836-1908, of the Funkhouser family of Virginia. Topics discussed include opposition to slavery; Civil War letters concern northern opinion, and other matters.

.101 Garland, Thomas, d. 1874.
Correspondence, 1805-1911. 944 items. Planter, of Albemarle County, Va. Personal and business correspondence, dealing with such matters as Virginia politics and agriculture, and manumission of slaves, 1820-60.

.102 Gebbart, Noah L., d. 1862.
Correspondence, 1844-1900. 116 items. Miner. Letters (chiefly 1855-64) of Gebbart and of his son, Emmanual Martin Gebbart. Emmanual Gebbart's letters mainly concern the Civil War period and include discussions of Negro troops, the Knights of the Golden Circle, and other matters.

.103 Georgia miscellaneous papers, 1727-1905.
3497 items. Correspondence and other papers relating to the history of Georgia. Papers of the period between the Revolution and Civil War per-

tain to slavery, social life and customs, and other subjects. Civil War papers refer to law enforcement, the Habeas Corpus Act, and other subjects. Post-war items relate to problems of Reconstruction, the Freedmen's Bureau, and other matters.

NC15.104 Gibbons, William, d. 1804.
Papers, 1728-1803. 807 items and 1 v. Rice planter and justice of the peace, of Chatham County, Ga. Papers of Gibbons and of his family; many relating to plantation management.

.105 Glen, Tyre.
Papers, 1820-89. 1261 items and 2 v. Slave trader, planter, postmaster, and merchant, of Surry County, N.C. Provides information on the domestic slave trade in the U.S. Includes receipts for slaves purchased for re-sale, and information on original costs, maintenance, sale prices and profits realized.

.106 Graham, William Alexander, 1804-75.
Papers, 1804-75. 55 items. Papers of a North Carolina legislator, Governor, and U.S. Senator, and of his son, William Alexander Graham, Jr. Includes discussions of the sentiments of the white population during Reconstruction.

.107 Grasty, William Clark, b. ca. 1800.
Papers of William Clark Grasty and John F. Rison, 1788-1876. ca. 8000 items and 118 v. Correspondence, account books, daybooks, fee books, invoices, memoranda books, records of sales, inventories, and letter-press copybooks, chiefly 1800-69, of three generations of general merchants, of Pittsylvania County, Va. Includes letters (1849-67) of John S. Grasty, a Presbyterian minister, referring to slave hiring, Unionist sympathy among the Dutch population of Botetourt County, Va., and other matters.

.108 Grimball, John Berkley, 1800-93.
Papers, 1727-1930. 1593 items, 5 v., and 2 reels of microfilm. Planter, of Charleston, S.C. Correspondence and other papers of Grimball, of his family, and of the Van der Horst family. The bulk of the material is for 1840-1900, and pertains to the life of a planter during the Civil War and Reconstruction. Correspondence concerns war-time depredations in South Carolina, and life and economic conditions in the South during Reconstruction. Includes letters from Confederate soldiers in the South.

.109 Hall family.
Papers, 1736-1862. 1013 items and 7 v. Papers of three generations of the Hall family. Includes material on cotton planting in South Carolina, slave insurrections, and other matters.

.110 Hampton, Frank Armfield, 1884-1957.
Correspondence, 1918-53. 117 items. Lawyer, politician, and federal official. Chiefly personal, business, and political correspondence. Topics discussed include Alfred E. Smith, Josephus Daniels, Negroes in California after 1920, disfranchisement of southern Negroes, elections in New York (1926) and North Carolina (1936), political parties and politics in the U.S. (1920-30) and North Carolina (1920's and 1930's), and the presidential election of 1928. Includes many letters of William Gibbs McAdoo.

.111 Harden family.
Papers, 1772-1940. 2305 items and 11 v. Correspondence, diaries, account books, daybooks, and legal and other papers, of Edward Harden, planter, lawyer, and politician, of Athens, Ga.; of his son, Edward Randolph Harden, lawyer and politician; and of other members of their family. The material concerns Reconstruction and economic conditions, the Republican party in the South, and other matters. Includes a diary kept by Evelyn Harden Jackson during the last months of the war referring to the general alarm preceding Sherman's activities in Georgia.

.112 Harris, Frederick A.
Papers, 1817-44. 126 items. Farmer, of New London, Campbell County, Va. Chiefly family and business correspondence of Harris, mostly from his brother, William Harris, who settled at various places in Alabama, Tennessee, and Virginia. The

papers concern slavery and slave hiring, and other topics.

.113 Harriss, Thomas Whitmel.
Papers, 1795-1891. 302 items. Tobacco planter, of Littleton, N.C. Correspondence, accounts, and other papers, of Harriss and of his family. The collection concerns slave purchase, hire, and treatment (1840-60); and other subjects.

.114 Hart, Albert Bushnell, 1854-1943.
Papers, 1890-1924. 103 items. Historian. Correspondence, pamphlets, and clippings concerning the writing and publication, under Hart's direction, of Marion G. McDougal's book, Fugitive Slaves (1891); and other matters.

.115 Hartt, Charles Frederic, 1840-78.
Papers, 1859-1906. 459 items. Zoologist and geologist. Correspondence and other papers of Hartt and of his son, Rollin Lynde Hartt, a Congregationalist minister. Includes letters of the wife of a southern carpetbagger.

.116 Hatchett, William H.
Papers.

.117 Hedrick, Benjamin Sherwood, 1827-86.
Papers, 1848-93. 6033 items and 4 v. Professor of chemistry and U.S. Patent Office official. Chiefly letters to Hedrick. Other correspondence concerns life at the University of North Carolina, Hedrick's dismissal from the University in 1856 for his Republican and anti-slavery opinions, and his life in the North during the Civil War period. Other topics include Reconstruction, the economic plight of the South, and politics, including Hedrick's attempt to win political office in North Carolina (1868).

.118 Hemphill family.
Papers, 1791-1933. 12,372 items and 28 v. Correspondence, sermons, and other papers, of William Ramsey Hemphill, Presbyterian minister, and of his sons, James Calvin Hemphill and Robert Reid Hemphill, newspaper editors. The material relates to slavery, reform movements (including anti-slavery and temperance), politics in the Confederacy, Reconstruction, the race situation, journalism, and other subjects. Correspondents include William Jennings Bryan, Andrew Carnegie, Champ Clark, Grover Cleveland, Josephus Daniels, Jefferson Davis, Francis W. Dawson, Sr., Ellen Glasgow, Carter Glass, Henry P. Grady, Wade Hampton, George Swinton Legare, William G. McAdoo, William G. McCabe, Adolph S. Ochs, George W. Ochs, James L. Orr, Walter H. Page, Joseph Pulitzer, Whitelaw Reid, William H. Taft, Benjamin R. Tillman, Joseph P. Tumulty, Oscar W. Underwood, Oswald G. Villard, Booker T. Washington, and Henry Watterson.

.119 Hendrix, Eugene Russell, Bp., 1847-1927. collector.
Papers, 1764-1914. 160 items. Methodist bishop, Kansas City, Mo. Chiefly letters of prominent American and British churchmen (mainly Methodist); a few relating to the slavery controversy within the Methodist Church. Includes an autographed poem with revisions by Charles Wesley. Correspondents include Francis Asbury, John C. Calhoun, Grover Cleveland, Thomas Coke, Booker T. Washington, and George Whitefield.

.120 Higginson, Thomas Wentworth, 1823-1911.
Letters, 1868-1906. 55 items. Minister, Army officer, author, and social reformer, of Cambridge, Mass. Letters by Higginson, mainly relating to literary and personal matters and to lectures delivered by him. Addressees include William B. Carman, Daniel C. Gilman, Julia W. Howe, Charles H. Miller, John C. Ropes, and Liard Simons.

.121 Hill, Daniel S.
Correspondence, 1796-1888. 138 items. Social reformer and politician, of Louisburg, N.C. Family and political correspondence of Hill, relating to the Whig party, secession, the Civil War, Reconstruction, and temperance.

.122 Hite, Cornelius Baldwin, b. 1842.
Papers, 1709-1918. 2341 items and 2 v. Farmer, of Winchester, Va. Personal, business, and legal papers (chiefly 1855-89) of Hite and of his family. The material pertains largely to life in Virginia

during Reconstruction. Includes copies (1709-11) of passages from the diary of Mrs. Alexander Spotswood.

NC15.123 Hobbs, James Olin.
Family papers, 1806-1916. 641 items and 14 v. Correspondence, mercantile records, and other items of Hobbs, his son James Olin Hobbs, Jr., businessman of Alleghany and Augusta counties, Va., and the Hobbs family. Subjects include economic conditions (1835-75) of western Virginia, and conditions in the Methodist Episcopal Church, South, during the early Reconstruction period.

.124 Holden, William Woods, 1818-92.
Papers, 1841-1929. 762 items and 13 v. Journalist and Governor of North Carolina. Correspondence, memoirs, business papers, legal documents, poems, and other papers (largely after 1865). Post-war correspondence concerns the North Carolina Standard, which Holden edited, Reconstruction, the Ku Klux Klan, Holden's impeachment and conviction, and life and politics in Washington during the period of Radical control.

.125 Holliday, Frederick William Mackey, 1828-99.
Papers, 1846-99. 2171 items and 20 v. Lawyer, Confederate officer, and Governor of Virginia. Correspondence, and personal, business, and political papers (chiefly 1862-95). Much of the material relates to Holliday's Civil War activities, service as Governor, and other activities. Includes material on Negro claims for emancipation, Virginia politics and race relations during Reconstruction, and other matters.

.126 Holmes, Nickels J., 1847-1919.
Papers, 1834-1927. 917 items. Presbyterian minister, lawyer, and educator, of Laurens, S.C. Family correspondence and legal papers concerning attitudes toward the South and the Negro, Reconstruction, and other subjects.

.127 Hook, John, 1745 or 1746-1808.
Papers, 1737-1889. 7382 items. In part, photocopies. Merchant and planter. Correspondence, daybooks, ledgers, mercantile records, memoranda, and other papers (chiefly 1770-1848). Includes records (1771-84) of a distillery, a blacksmith shop, and three plantations owned by Hook; and other businesses.

.128 Howerton, Philip.
Correspondence, 1817-79. 828 items. Tobacco trader and sheriff, of Halifax County, Va. Letters pertain to the tobacco firm in which Howerton had an interest, first with William Cabaniss and later with his son, William Matthew Howerton; and general labor conditions after the civil War.

.129 Hunter, Charles N., ca. 1851-1931.
Papers, 1818-1931. 2946 items and 18 v. Negro educator, of Raleigh, N.C. Correspondence, scrapbooks of clippings, and other papers. The material concerns the Negro problem shortly after the Civil War, the attitude of white people toward Negroes, temperance, Negro education, and other matters. Correspondents include Charles B. Aycock, J.W. Bailey, Thomas W. Bickett, C.S. Bingham, William E. Borah, Locke Craig, Josephus Daniels, Charles G. Dawes, John A. Logan, Lee S. Overman, Charles Sumner, Franklin D. Roosevelt, Theodore Roosevelt, Zebulon B. Vance, and Booker T. Washington.

.130 Hunton, Charles H.
Papers, 1815-96. 425 items. Business and family letters of Hunton and of his son, Henry, of Buckland, Va., concerning opposition to secession, antipathy toward such events as John Brown's Raid, and life in Virginia during Reconstruction.

.131 Jackson, Thomas Jonathan, 1824-63.
Papers, 1855-1906. 2593 items. Army officer. Correspondence, commissary papers, vouchers of Jackson's command, and other papers (chiefly 1861-65). Other topics include religious denominations opposed to war.

.132 Jarratt, Isaac A.
Papers, 1807-1918. 2201 items. Soldier, merchant, landowner, and distiller, of Huntsville, N.C. Correspondence; business, plantation, and estate records; and other papers. Subjects include the Civil War and conditions in the Confederacy, emancipation, and other matters.

.133 Johnson, Herschel Vespasian, 1812-80.
Papers, 1812-80. 829 items and 31 v. Planter, Governor of Georgia, and Confederate Senator. Correspondence, ms, autobiography (1867), speeches, essays, and newspaper clippings. The papers before 1865 are scattered and mostly concern politics, his opposition to secession, and other matters. Later papers deal with life in the South after the war, and other matters.

.134 Jones, Charles Colcock, 1831-93.
Papers, 1763-1926. 845 items and 67 v. Lawyer, Confederate soldier, and historian. Correspondence, journals, commonplace books, lecture notes on literature, natural philosophy, and physics, and other papers, many dealing with the collection of historical materials. Other subjects include Union volunteer generals of foreign birth, slavery, abolitionists, and other items.

.135 Jones, Richard.
Papers, 1797-1878. 152 items and 9 v. Plantation owner, teacher, and local official, of Campbell and Pittsylvania Counties, Va. Correspondence, daybooks, records of fees and cases, expense accounts, receipts for the purchase and sale of slaves, and other materials. Includes information on plantation maintenance, and other subjects.

.136 Jordan, Daniel W., ca. 1790-1883.
Papers, 1827-1913. 4250 items and 8 v. Planter and legislator, of Camden, S.C. Family and business correspondence, account books (1836-77), and other papers. Includes material concerning Jordan's plantation management, slavery, and other matters.

.137 Jordan, Thomas, 1819-95.
Papers, 1861-65. 236 items. Confederate officer and journalist. Correspondence and military records. Other letters relate to use of Charleston harbor, use of Negro labor, and other army affairs.

.138 Keyser, William Judah, 1821-77.
Papers, 1809-1940. 2115 items and 24 v. Florida lumber exporter. Correspondence, account books, daybook, and other business papers, and other papers of the Keyser family. Subjects include personal affairs, business affairs during Reconstruction, and other matters. Correspondents include Robert Burns, Andrew Carnegie, William McKinley, and Theodore Roosevelt.

.139 Kilby, John Richardson, 1819-78.
Papers, 1755-1919. 34,414 items and 4 v. Correspondence and legal and other papers (chiefly 1840-90), of Kilby and of his son, Wilbur John Kilby, both lawyers, of Suffolk, Va., and of members of the Riddick family. Some subjects include the case of Harriett Whitehead, whose mind was impaired by the loss of her family in the Nat Turner Insurrection (1831); freedom for Negroes, with references to the work of the American Colonization Society and to life and conditions in Liberia; Negro soldiers in Charleston; the Negro Reformatory Association of Virginia, and other matters.

.140 Knight, John, 1806-64.
Papers, 1788-1891. 1323 items and 47 v. Merchant and financier. Mainly personal letters containing information about slavery and planting, general economic conditions in the U.S.(1830-65), and other matters.

.141 La Vallette, Elie A., ca. 1790-1862.
In Navy papers, 186--1944. 500 items and 10 v. Includes some material on La Vallette, commander of the African Squadron, 1850-53.

.142 Law, William, 1792-1868.
Papers, 1761-1890. 1842 items. Planter, merchant, and militia leader, of Darlington, S.C. Correspondence, account books, daybooks, and other papers (chiefly 1802-70), of Law, of Cyrus Bacot, (a relative by marriage) and of the Du Bose family. Includes material on planting operations in Sumter District, S.C.

.143 Law, William Augustus, d. 1909.
Papers, 1771-1927. 1502 items. Planter, of

Darlington County, S.C. Personal and business correspondence, bills, receipts, and other papers (chiefly 1860-1927). Later correspondence (1868-1900) includes information about economic conditions during Reconstruction.

NC15.144 Leckie, W. Robert, d. 1839.
Papers, 1768-1906. 1872 items and 14 v. Military engineer, of Washington, D.C. Correspondence and other papers of Leckie; and correspondence, account books, and plantation records of his son-in-law, William Hendrick, planter, of Mecklenburg County, Va.

.145 Lee family.
Papers, 1780-1851. 230 items. Papers of Thomas Sim Lee as Governor of Maryland; together with papers relating to litigation between his son, Col. John Lee, and his son-in-law, Outerbridge Horsey, who had been partners in a sugar plantation which was sold for debt. Includes papers relating to Negro slaves on a sugar plantation in Lafourche, La.

.146 Lee family.
Papers of the Lee and Bonney families, 1805-1914. 596 items. Correspondence, diary, mercantile records, and other papers of the Lee family, covering the years 1805-30, and the Bonney family for later dates, the bulk of the papers covering 1860-77. Letters from northern friends discuss Daniel Webster, slavery, secession, and other issues. Papers and letters of the Reconstruction period reveal details of family efforts at reestablishment in Camden, and tell of the extreme poverty of the area.

.147 Leftwich and Clayton, Lynchburg, Va.
Records, 1802-26. 277 items. Business correspondence (with a few personal letters), bills, and mercantile accounts of Leftwich and Clayton, and of its predecessor, Brown, Leftwich and Company. Records of another firm, Brown and Clayton (after 1820) are included. Subjects mentioned include slave sales and purchases; and other matters.

.148 Leslie, Robert, ca. 1794-ca. 1879.
Papers, 1783-1934. 15,389 items. Merchant, of Petersburg, Va. Correspondence, accounts, invoices, statements, and legal papers (chiefly 1814-72) of Leslie, a member of the firm of Leslie and Shepherd. Other topics include Leslie's slaveholding and attitude toward it.

.149 Lewis, Burwell Boykin, 1838-85.
Correspondence, 1843-85. 687 items. Lawyer, U.S. Representative from Alabama, and president of the University of Alabama. Correspondence of Lewis and of his family, the Garlands, chiefly concerning family affairs. Includes references to the Civil War, Reconstruction, Alabama railroad frauds, and other materials.

.150 Long, Joseph.
Papers, 1820-1902. 209 items. Virginia Militia officer and land owner, of Stevensburg, Va. Chiefly letters (1820-60) to Long from friends and relatives who left Virginia and settled in the West. The correspondence concerns, in part, anti-slavery feeling in the old Northwest, and other matters.

.151 Longstreet, James, 1821-1904.
Papers, 1848-1904. 65 items and 1 reel of microfilm. Confederate officer. Letters and other papers, mostly written after the Civil War, relating to the war, Reconstruction, and the Republican party in the South. Correspondents include Daniel Harvey Hill and other Confederate officers.

.152 Lord, Bert, 1869-1939.
Papers, 1902-39. Letter to Lord on January 27, 1938, from the Bellville Community of Orangeburg, S.C., containing a petition with 320 signers protesting against the resettlement program which will place Negroes in the white section; they say it will cause serious labor trouble. Letter from Lord, January 28, 1938, saying that local residents should decide where the Negroes are to be located.

.153 McCall, Duncan G.
Plantation journal and diary.

.154 McCalla, John Moore, b. ca. 1785.
Papers, 1785-1871. 653 items and 4 v. Militia officer and civil servant. Papers relating to the McCalla family of Lexington, Ky. Includes material on a journal of a trip to Liberia (1860); letters from former McCalla slaves in Liberia; the American Colonization Society; and an account of the inauguration of Abraham Lincoln (1861).

.155 Mackay, Eliza Ann (McQueen), 1778-1862.
Papers, 1796-1872. 233 items and 2 v. Correspondence, tax book, and other papers (chiefly 1825-47) of Mrs. Mackay of Savannah, daughter of John McQueen and wife of Robert Mackay. The papers refer to the price of slaves in Louisiana, and other topics.

.156 McGeachy family.
Papers, 1819-99. 626 items. Personal correspondence of a North Carolina family, mainly dating from the Civil War years. The bulk of the letters were written to Catherine McGeachy, schoolteacher of Robeson County, by her brother, cousins, and friends; letters from women of the family reveal the lack of small necessities and the fear of freed Negroes. Postwar letters comment on the Reconstruction period and problems relating to free Negro labor and financial difficulties; and other matters.

.157 McKie, Thomas Jefferson.
Papers, 1825-95. 796 items and 2 v. Physician and farmer, of Woodlawn, Edgefield County, S.C. Correspondence, bills for medical services, lists of purchases (1820's), articles, advertisements, college announcements (1870-71), and other papers. The collection pertains to the Freedmen's Bureau, Reconstruction in Georgia, northern bitterness toward the South, irresponsibility of and radical influence among Negroes, racial relations, activities of white groups to regain political control, status of the Democratic party, Grant and the Radicals, the Hayes-Tilden election, Wade Hampton, and other matters.

.158 McLaurin, Duncan, 1787-1872.
Papers, 1779-1922. 1883 items and 1 v. Farmer, teacher, lawyer, and State legislator, of Richmond County, N.C. Correspondence, bills, receipts, legal and other papers, and printed matter (chiefly 1822-72), of McLaurin and of members of his family. McLaurin's papers (mainly 1822-50) relate to politics in North Carolina, South Carolina, and the U.S., economic conditions, business, the Civil War, and other matters. Correspondence of relatives in Mississippi (ca. 1830-67) concerns slavery, politics, agricultural problems, sectionalism and nationalism in Mississippi, Reconstruction conditions, and family affairs. Includes an atlas with a list of slaves.

.159 McLaurin, Lauchlin W.
Papers, 1817-1924. 454 items. Confederate tax collector and merchant, of Laurinburg, N.C. Correspondence, and legal, business, and personal papers, many of them relating to McLaurin's work as a tax collector. Includes letters from an Alabama planter after the Civil War, telling of the impact of emancipation and Reconstruction.

.160 McNeill, Hector H., d. 1871.
Papers, 1835-96. 104 items. Minister, of Robeson County, N.C. Correspondence and other papers, concerning marriage of Negro freedmen (1867), politics in North Carolina, and other matters. Includes correspondence of McNeill's son Thomas Alexander McNeill, Confederate soldier and later a North Carolina legislator.

.161 MacRae family.
Papers, 1817-1943. 4186 items and 57 v. Correspondence, diary, account books, ledgers, bills, receipts, business records, legal papers, and other material. Alexander MacRae's papers concern Florida plantations and their management. Other papers pertain to post-war business and other matters.

.162 Mangum, Willie Person, 1792-1861.
Papers, 1763-1861. 142 items and 1 v. Judge, U.S. Senator, and Representative from North Carolina. Correspondence, deeds, family Bible, and

legal and other papers, concerning Whig party affairs, and other matters.

NC15.163 Manigault, Louis, b. ca. 1829.
Papers, 1781-1883. 2034 items and 4 v. Planter, of Charleston, S.C. Correspondence, account book, memorandum book (1858), notebook (1852), prescription book (1852), plantation records, and other papers (chiefly 1840-78), of Manigault and of members of his family. The papers contain information on Charleston, S.C., including social and economic conditions; management of a rice plantation, with comments on the transition from slave to free labor; and other matters.

.164 Marshall, Joseph Warren Waldo, 1820-1904.
Papers, 1826-1940. 1488 items and 2 v. Physician, of Abbeville and Greenville, S.C. Correspondence, journal, bills, business papers, and other papers (chiefly 1870-1930) of Marshall, of Anne Eliza Marshall, and of the Marshall family. The collection concerns the Ku Klux Klan, and other matters.

.165 Maryland. Orphans' Court (Cecil County).
Records, 1789-1915. 2415 items. Papers relating to the settling of estates, the administering of the poor school fund, and the apprenticing of orphans, both white and black.

.166 Massie, William, 1795-1862.
Papers, 1766-1890. 608 items and 4 v. Planter, of Nelson County, Va. Correspondence, plantation records, indentures, deeds, inventory, and other papers, of Massie and of his father, Thomas Massie (1747-1834), and brother Thomas Massie (1783-1864). The collection concerns economic conditions, politics, and international events before the Civil War; ante-bellum education in Virginia; and other matters.

.167 Maury, Matthew Fontaine, 1806-73.
Papers. 164 items. Oceanographer and astronomer who conducted oceanographic studies of the Indian Ocean and the South Atlantic Ocean.

.168 Merritt, William H.E.
Papers, 1834-89. 212 items. Planter and legislator, of Lawrenceville, Va. Correspondence and other papers of Merritt and of his family, referring to possible use of slaves in the Confederate Army, conditions of Negroes after the war, and other matters.

.169 Miles, James Warley, 1818-75.
Papers, 1838-76. 115 items. Episcopal clergyman and librarian and professor at the College of Charleston, Charleston, S.C. Correspondence, sermons, and poems. Subjects include theological issues, slavery, and others.

.170 Minor, Peter C. and Hugh.
Notebooks.

.171 Moseley, Arthur T.
Papers of Arthur T. and William P. Moseley, 1756-1907. 1022 items and 11 v. Farmer, of Buckingham County, Va. Correspondence, account books, cashbooks, landbooks, bankbooks, receipts, memoranda, tax receipts book (1852, 1882), of Moseley and of his son, William P. Moseley. The papers are concerned with plantation economy, and other matters.

.172 Motte, Jacob Rhett, 1811-68.
Papers, 1743-1909. 305 items. Physician, planter, and Army surgeon, of Charleston, S.C. Correspondence, account book (1838-42), plantation book, and other materials (chiefly 1835-57). The papers concern slavery, economic conditions, and other matters.

.173 Munford family.
Papers of the Munford and Ellis families, 1777-1942. 12,497 items and 21 v. Correspondence and family, business, and personal papers (chiefly 1830-1900) of the Munford and Ellis families of Virginia. The earlier portion of the papers centers around George Wythe Munford and his wife, of Richmond, and concerns Virginia and Virginians from the Revolution through the Civil War. Includes materials on ante-bellum social, political, and literary life, Civil War battles in Virginia and on the Mississippi River, and Reconstruction days. Includes correspondence of Powhatan Ellis, Senator from Mississippi

.174 Muse, Battaile, d. 1803.
Papers, 1726-1891. 6918 items. Planters' agent, of Berkeley County, Va. Correspondence, account books, memoranda, and other papers. The collection concerns the treatment of slaves, the Mercer (1776-83) and Fairfax estates, and other matters.

.175 Navy papers (miscellany), 1804-1944.
445 items and 10 v. Logbooks and papers (mainly 19th century) relating to naval officers, seamen, and naval administration. Includes information on the African slave patrol, and the effect of secession on the U.S. Navy.

.176 Negroes (slave and free), 1770-1944.
881 items and 4 v. Correspondence and other papers relating to slaves and free Negroes, especially southern Negroes in the 19th century. Includes information on the manumission of slaves, slave prices, slave trading, the slave market, Quaker interest in education for the slaves, the treatment and discipline of slaves, conditions among the slaves, the treatment of free Negroes in the North and South before the Civil War, the underground railroad, slaves during the Civil War, Negroes during Reconstruction, the Wilmington, N.C. race riot, and the campaign for white supremacy in North Carolina.

.177 Noble, William Henry, b. 1813.
Papers, 1807-1913. 359 items. In part, typescripts. Lawyer and Army officer, of Bridgeport, Conn. Correspondence and other papers concerned with Noble's anti-slavery and Republican party activities, and other activities. Includes letters of William A. Willoughby of New Haven while with the 10th Regiment, Connecticut Volunteers, in South Carolina, New Bern, N.C., Petersburg, Va., and St. Augustine, Fla.

.178 Nutt, Haller, ca. 1810-1864.
Papers, 1846-1911. 722 items and 1 v. Planter, of Natchez, Miss. Plantation journal and other papers (chiefly 1853-60), mostly relating to the management of Nutt's land and slave holdings in Mississippi and Louisiana.

.179 Oglesby, Thaddeus K.
Papers, 1876-1918. 2152 items and 4 v. Journalist and book salesman, of Georgia. Correspondence and other papers, chiefly relating to Oglesby's concern for the anti-southern bias of many northern historians during the late 19th and early 20th centuries, and other matters. Includes papers relating to race relations in the South after the Civil War.

.180 Orr, John M.
Papers, 1790-1911. 9580 items and 12 v. Lawyer, of Leesburg, Va. Legal and business correspondence and papers, and other items relating to Orr's activities as meat supply agent for the Confederate Army, his interest in the southern racial problem and in colonization as a possible solution.

.181 Page, Thomas Nelson, 1853-1922.
Papers, 1739-1926. 9276 items and 2 v. Author, lawyer, and diplomat. Correspondence, legal and business papers, diplomatic dispatches, and other items (chiefly 1885-1920) relating to Page's legal and literary career, and his interest in social reform, race relations, politics, and other subjects. Correspondents include C.F. Adams, Grover Cleveland, Josephus Daniels, J.C. Harris, William D. Howells, Robert Lansing, Robert T. Lincoln, Henry C. Lodge, Theodore Roosevelt, E. Root, J.M. Stoddart, and William H. Taft.

.182 Parker, Addison B., 1869-1944.
Papers, ca. 1873-1944. 6 v. and ca. 130 items. Civic leader; member of the Republican State Committee; deputy secretary of state, New York, 1915-20; Grand Patriarch, I.O.O.F., and publisher of the Lodge Record. Papers of the Parker family of Watertown include six clipping scrapbooks and photograph albums, relating mainly to Parker's civic, political, and fraternal duties, but also containing family photographs; approximately 120 letters (December 1917-April 1919) from his son, 2nd Lieutenant Fred M. Parker, relating to his experiences with the Motor Transportation Corps of the A.E.F., giving impressions, and referring to

the service of Negro soldiers; and related printed material.

NC15.183 Pickens, Francis Wilkinson, 1805-69.

Papers, 1798-1900. 440 items and 1 v. Governor of South Carolina. Political and personal correspondence (chiefly 1809-86) of Pickens and of his family, concerning secession, and other matters. Includes one volume of plantation records (1839-64). Correspondents include P.G.T. Beauregard, M.L. Bonham, Braxton Bragg, Joseph E. Brown, Armistead Burt, Lewis Cass, W.M. Churchwell, Jefferson Davis, R.W. Gibbes, Isaac W. Hayne, J.L. Orr, and William H. Seward.

.184 Political miscellany, 1743-1934.

1196 items and 1 v. Papers relating to politics in the South, especially North Carolina, Virginia, and Kentucky, during the 19th century; and politics in Virginia during Reconstruction.

.185 Pratt family.

Papers, 1758-1903. 43 items. The bulk of the material (1853-1903) is made up of letters received by Horace L. Edgar Pratt, a Protestant Episcopal rector on Staten Island, and pertains in some way to that denomination; a civil war draft exemption certificate issued to John A. Kernochan, (September 10, 1863), and miscellaneous ms and printed items. The remainder consists of Queens County documents mainly pertaining to Joseph Lawrence and relatives and including a slave bill of sale (1770).

.186 Renwick, William W.

Papers, 1792-1948. 2396 items. Correspondence and other papers of Renwick, his wife, Rosannah Rogers Renwick, and related members of the Beard, Bothwell, Lyons, Renwick, and Rogers families, including material on South Carolina cotton planting, slavery, politics, social life, and customs; and other matters.

.187 Richardson, Davis

Papers, 1720-1885. 1657 items. Justice of the peace and State legislator. Mainly legal papers, bills, and receipts of Richardson during 1820's and 1830's when he was a member of the State legislature; and some legal correspondence concerning the sale of land and slaves; and other items.

.188 Richardson, James Burchell

Papers, 1803-1910. 4110 items. Plantation owner, of Sumter District, S.C. Family letters and business papers of Richardson and of his family, relating to the use of slave labor on roads, railroads, and Civil War fortifications; political developments in South Carolina and in the nation; conditions on South Carolina plantations before, during, and after the Civil War; post-war depression and poverty in the South; and tenant farming after the war.

.189 Riddick, Richard H., d. 1870.

Papers, 1840-79. 408 items and 1 v. Lumber dealer, of Pantego, N.C. Business correspondence, accounts, legal papers, and other materials, relating to Riddick's lumber business, a runaway slave and Riddick's attempts to recover him from Boston, and other matters.

.190 Rootes, Sarah A.

Correspondence, 1822-84. 124 items. Correspondence (mainly 1858-70). Most of the letters are from Sarah A. Rootes' brother, Thomas Reade Rootes, a Confederate soldier in Company C, 4th Texas Cavalry. The material relates to Houston, Tex., during Reconstruction; the Civil War and Reconstruction in Virginia; and other matters.

.191 Ruggles, Daniel.

Papers, 1847-65. 162 items and 2 v. Army officer. Military correspondence, telegrams, reports, and other items, relating to wartime conditions in Mississippi. Includes a diary (1845-48) of Ruggles' sister, Lucy Spooner Ruggles, with an account of a journey from Charleston, S.C., to Wytheville, Va.

.192 Rutherfoord, John, 1792-1866.

Papers, 1754-1931. 2712 items and 33 v. Lawyer, merchant, and Governor of Virginia. Correspondence, travel journals, account books, memorandum books, farm records, legal records, common-

place books, class notes, and other papers (chiefly 1781-1865), of Rutherfoord; of his son, John Coles Rutherfoord, lawyer, planter, and State legislator; and of other members of the family. The papers of John Rutherfoord relate to his career as Governor, his planting and business affairs; the return of fugitive slaves; and they include letters from Edward Coles, William C. Rives, and other of Rutherfoord's relatives by marriage, concerning agriculture and anti-slavery sentiment in Virginia, and other matters. John Coles Rutherfoord's papers relate to his work as a State legislator (1852-65), and as manager of the family estates, and other matters. Includes scattered correspondence of J.C. Rutherfoord's wife, Ann Seddon Roy Rutherfoord, referring to life in the South during and after the Civil War, and family matters. Correspondents include John Brockenbrough, Richard Claiborne, Isaac A. Coles, William M. Cooke, Staige Davis, John Floyd, William B. Giles, James L. Kemper, John H. McCue, John Marshall, Hodijah Meade, C.B. Memminger, Alexander H. Porterfield, George W. Randolph, W.C. Rives, Jr., Thomas Rutherfoord, Richard Singleton, Andrew Stevenson, John W. Stevenson, Roger B. Taney, Daniel Teasdale, John Tyler, Abraham Van Buren, John Wickham, and Henry A. Wise.

.193 Scott, William Lafayette, 1828-72.

Papers, 1847-77. 1010 items. Lawyer, teacher, Confederate officer, and politician, of Greensboro, N.C. Correspondence, speeches, and other papers (chiefly 1854-71), relating to Scott's service in the State legislature (1850's), his difficulties in and ultimate resignation from the Confederate Army, his unsuccessful campaign for Congress (1870), the Ku Klux Klan, and the Whig, American, and Republican parties in North Carolina. Some correspondents include his wife, Ella Penn Scott, and his brother, Levi M. Scott; Kemp P. Battle, W.H. Battle, R.P. Dick, J.R McLean, R.M. Pearson, John Pool, D.L. Swain, A.W. Tourgee, and Jonathan Worth.

.194 Seibert, Henry James.

Papers, 1779-1912. 16,590 items and 68 v. Lawyer, election clerk, and Virginia legislator, of Martinsburg and Hedgeville, Va. (now W.Va.). Correspondence, account books, ledgers, and other professional, business, and family correspondence (chiefly 1820-85), of Seibert and of his family. The collection relates to Virginia and national politics before the Civil War, slavery in Virginia, and other matters.

.195 Sheppard, James, ca. 1816-70.

Papers, 1830-89. 1539 items. Plantation owner, of Hanover County, Va. Correspondence, accounts, tax returns, and other personal and business papers, relating to Sheppard's plantations in Virginia, Arkansas, and Mississippi, slaveholding, social and economic conditions prior to the Civil War, and other matters.

.196 Shuford, George Adams, 1895-1962.

Papers, 1952-59. ca. 36,000 items. U.S. Representative from North Carolina. Correspondence, reports, speeches, and memoranda from Shuford's Washington office, relating to agriculture, elections, civil rights, the Constitution, education, labor, North Carolina politics, and other subjects.

.197 Sickles, Daniel Edgar, 1819-1914.

Papers, 1856-1912. 22 items and 1 v. Army officer, U.S. Representative from New York, and diplomat. Letters from Sickles to William A. Weaver of Harper's Monthly, concerning political events before the Civil War, and Reconstruction; administrative telegrams of Sickles (Jan., 1866) while military Governor of South Carolina; and a letter press book (1899-1912) with information about Sickles' role in the Civil War, Civil War veterans' activities, and other matters.

.198 Simons, Siegling, and Capplemann, Charleston, S.C.

Records, ca. 1830-1929. ca. 100,000 items and 200 v. Legal and personal correspondence and papers (1830-1921) of a law firm whose partners included James Simons, Sr., James Simons, Jr., Rupert Siegling, and John D. Cappelmann. Includes information about the legal profession in Charleston, the service of James Simons, Sr., in the South Carolina Militia at the outbreak of the Civil War, the service of James Simons, Jr., in the Confederate Army, the presidencies of Rupert Siegling and James Simons, Jr., of the Charleston News and Courier Company, the service of various members of the firm in the South Carolina legislature, local, state, and national politics, the development of the Charleston public school system, slavery in South Carolina, the Civil War, Reconstruction, and the South Carolina dispensary system.

NC15.199 Simpson, William Dunlap, 1823-90.
Papers, 1789-1914. 3699 items. Confederate officer and Congressman, Governor, and chief justice of the South Carolina Supreme Court. Legal and personal correspondence and papers of Simpson, of his law partner, Henry Clinton Young, and of Simpson's sons, relating chiefly to the Civil War and Reconstruction. Other subjects include the Masonry movement in the South, 19th century politics, economic matters, and other subjects.

.200 Singleton, Richard.
Papers, 1782-1868. 403 items. Revolutionary officer and planter, of Sumter County, S.C. Correspondence and plantation accounts (chiefly 1794-1844). Correspondents include Abraham Van Buren, Angelica Singleton Van Buren, and Martin Van Buren.

.201 Slade, William, 1807-52.
Papers, 1751-1929. 2748 items and 30 v. Planter, of Williamston, N.C. Family and business correspondence, account books, memoranda books, day-books, time books, court records, and other papers (chiefly 1800-65), of Slade and of several generations of the Slade family. The papers reflect the financial and the family affairs of a planter family of the ante-bellum South, and include plantation records, and materials related to slaveholding and post-Civil War agricultural advances. Correspondents and names mentioned include Braxton Craven, Eli Peal, Ebenezer Slade, Henry Slade, J.B. Slade, James Slade, and Jeremiah Slade.

.202 Smith, Josiah Townsend, ca. 1830-ca. 1900.
Papers, 1838-1913. 652 items and 8 v. Physician and school official, of Hertford, N.C. Correspondence, accounts, and business papers of Smith and his family, relating to the Mexican War, Smith's education in the North, his former schoolmate's fears of the sectional conflict over slavery, attitudes toward secession, North Carolina politics, and ante-bellum social life and customs.

.203 Smith, Washington M., ca. 1820-69.
Papers, 1831-1916. 8578 items. Planter, banker, and lawyer, of Selma, Ala. Business and personal correspondence and other papers of Washington M. Smith and the Smith family, containing information on Smith's interests in planting, on economic conditions in Alabama after 1840, economic conditions during Reconstruction, and other matters.

.204 Smith, Whitefoord.
Papers, 1807-93. 185 items and 8 v. Methodist minister and educator, of South Carolina. Correspondence, diaries (1849 and 1853-63), accounts, memoranda, sermons, and other papers (chiefly 1839-60), relating to the Methodist Episcopal Church in South Carolina, John C. Calhoun's views of slavery, the religious instruction of slaves, and other related topics.

.205 Smith, William, 1756-1835.
Papers, 1785-1834. 240 items. Member of Parliament. Correspondence, relating mainly to the abolition of slavery in the West Indies. Letters of William Wilberforce (24 items) discuss personal affairs, politics, abolition, and other matters. Letters from Thomas Clarkson discuss the anti-slavery movement. Letters from Smith's constituents discuss politics, social conditions, slavery in the Indies, and other matters.

.206 Smith, William Patterson, 1796-1878.
Papers, 1791-1943. 23,073 items. Merchant and planter, of Gloucester County, Va. Personal and business correspondence and other papers of

Smith; of his son-in-law, Isaac Howell Carrington, provost marshal and lawyer, of Richmond; and of their families. Other papers concern social life and customs in Tidewater Virginia, slavery, secession, life in the Confederacy, Reconstruction in Virginia, and other matters.

.207 Social reformers' papers, 1782-1914.
220 items and 3 v. Papers containing information on the movement to discourage the use of tobacco, the temperance movement, and abolitionism. Includes a few papers of Dorothea Lynde Dix.

.208 Socialist Party of America.
Files, 1900-52. 23 v. and ca. 155,000 items. Official files.

.209 Society of Friends papers, 1775-1915.
334 items. In part, typescripts. Papers chiefly relating to the Quakers in North Carolina in the 19th century. Includes information on the history of the Friends in North Carolina, social life and customs, and the North Carolina Friends during the Civil War.

.210 Somers, William D.
Papers, 1817-1907. 546 items. Physician, of Collierville, Tenn. Family and professional correspondence, partly relating to hospitals and charities in Tennessee and other Confederate States, partly family letters relating to life in Tennessee after the Civil War, poverty during Reconstruction, and family affairs.

.211 Southern Labor Archives.
Papers, 1854-1953. 23 v. and 151,000 items.

.212 Southgate, James, 1832-1914.
Correspondence, 1794-1935. 1792 items and 9 v. Educator, insurance agent, and civic leader, of Durham, N.C. Family, business, and personal correspondence (chiefly after 1851) of Southgate and of his family. The material concerns life in North Carolina, Reconstruction in North Carolina, and other matters.

.213 Stebbins, Laura W.
Correspondence, 1852-84. 800 items. Schoolmistress. Family and personal correspondence of Miss Stebbins, who taught in Mississippi during two periods before the Civil War, and who, for a time, operated her own school in Springfield, Mass. Contains information on living conditions in Ohio; discussions of the relative merits of northern and southern teachers for southern schools. A few letters from Eugene Dow, friend of the Stebbins family who was connected with the Commissary of Subsistence at Norfolk, Va., and the Bureau of Refugees, Freedmen, and Abandoned Lands, relate to the standard of living, education, and citizenship status of the Negro.

.214 Stephens, Alexander Hamilton, 1812-83.
Papers, 1822-1911. 3029 items and 3 v. Congressman and Confederate vice-president. Personal, legal, and political correspondence, together with scattered newspaper clippings related to various aspects of Stephens' career. Political and personal correspondence comprises over half of the collection. Includes information on Stephens' political views, slavery in Georgia, Stephens' part in the development of southern sectionalism, the crises of 1850, his part in the Georgia secession convention, his activities as Confederate vice-president and as leader of minority sentiment in the Confederate government, commercial and economic conditions in the South, life in the South after 1865, and Stephens' attitude toward Reconstruction and post-war politics.

.215 Taft, Harvey F.
Papers, 1862-75. 75 items. Resident of Milford, Mass. Chiefly letters (1862-63) to Taft from his sons who served in the Union Army. Subjects include the Civil War in North Carolina, Virginia, and Louisiana, Negro regiments, pro-northern sentiment in the South, and other matters.

.216 Talbott, Charles Henry, 1840-1912.
Papers, 1826-1948. 647 items and 3 v. Planter and businessman, of Richmond, Va. Correspondence, plantation records, scrapbooks, and other personal, family, and business papers of Talbott, of his son, Charles Henry Talbott (b. 1877), and

of other members of the Talbott, Munford, and Wythe families. The papers relate to planting activities, and other matters.

NC15.217 Taveau, Augustin Louis, 1828-86.

Papers, 1741-1931. 1858 items and 4 v. Planter and author, of Charleston, S.C., and Chaptico, Md. Family, personal, literary, and business correspondence and other papers (chiefly 1830-86) of Taveau, of his father, Louis Augustin Thomas Taveau, and of their family. The collection centers around Augustin Louis Taveau and relates to his career in the Confederate Army, postwar condemnation of Confederate leaders, and other activities. Other subjects include rice planting before the Civil War, planting in Mississippi and Louisiana (1850's), agriculture and scientific farming in Maryland, Charleston during the Civil War, postwar politics, and other matters. Some correspondents include Horace Greeley, Thomas S. Grimké, Robert Y. Hayne, O.W. Holmes, Andrew Johnson, James L. Petigru, William Gilmore Simms, and members of the Girardeau, Swinton, and Taveau families.

.218 Telfair, Edward, 1735-1807.

Papers, 1762-1831. 896 items and 3 v. Merchant, member of the Continental Congress, and Governor of Georgia. Personal, business, and political correspondence and other papers, concerning planting in Georgia, especially rice and tobacco, slaveholding and economic conditions in Georgia, Politics during the 1790's, Telfair's administration as Governor, and other matters. Includes scattered letters from many Georgia patriots and politicians including Abraham Baldwin, Joseph Clay, Sr., Seaboard Jones, Jr., and others.

.219 Terrasson Brothers, Philadelphia.

Records of Terrasson Brothers and papers of the Prager family, 1773-1869. 1253 items. Records of the firm of Terrasson Brothers, established in Philadelphia by Antoine and Barthelemy Terrasson as a branch of their firm, John Terrasson and Company, with headquarters in Paris and Lyons, France. Papers after 1800 concern the family of Mark Prager, members of which apparently married into the Terrasson family. The later letters contain references to family affairs, slavery, politics, and sectionalism. Ca. 100 Civil War letters describe conditions in the North.

.220 Thompson, Henry J.H., b. 1832.

Papers, 1862-65. 258 items and 2 v. Union soldier. Personal letters and diaries. Letters concern Thompson's reactions to southern institutions, the use of Negro troops, and military activities along the North Carolina coast. The diary, written mainly during the last year of the war, is similar in content to the letters.

.221 Tillinghast family.

Papers, 1765-1945. 2630 items and 21 v. Family and business letters, personal journals, and papers (chiefly 1830-1911) of William Norwood Tillinghast (b. 1831), merchant of Fayetteville, N.C.; William A. Norwood (1767-1842), judge of Hillsboro, N.C.; and of the Tillinghast and Norwood families of Massachusetts, Virginia, and North Carolina. Contains information about business and economic conditions in the South before, during, and after the Civil War, agriculture in the South Atlantic States before 1860, living conditions during the Civil War and Reconstruction, and other matters.

.222 Torrence family.

Papers, 1754-1915. 559 items. Correspondence and papers of four generations of the Torrence family. Includes records about the hiring of slaves (1853-60), and other materials.

.223 Turner family.

Papers, 1827-1929. 1313 items and 8 v. Correspondence and papers of Jesse Turner, Sr. (1805-94), lawyer, jurist, and Whig politician of Van Buren, Ark.; his wife Rebecca (Allen) Turner (1823-1917); their son Jesse Turner, Jr. (1856-1919); and other members of the Turner family, relating to political activities in Arkansas and the U.S.(1840-1900), secession in Arkansas, life during Reconstruction, and other matters.

.224 Turner, George Wilmer.

Papers, 1846-96. 1579 items. Planter of Goochland County, Va. Family and personal correspondence and legal and business papers, mostly from the post-Civil War period and concerning difficulties and poverty during Reconstruction. The letters concern family and plantation affairs; economic conditions during Reconstruction; and other affairs.

.225 U.S. Census Bureau.

Ms Census Returns for 1860, Schedule III for Georgia, Kentucky, Louisiana, and Tennessee.

.226 U.S. Presidents' papers, 1753-1935.

202 items. The Presidents referred to in the papers are: John Q. Adams, James Buchanan; Grover Cleveland; Millard Fillmore; James A. Garfield; Ulysses S. Grant; Benjamin Harrison; Rutherford B. Hayes; Thomas Jefferson; Andrew Johnson; Abraham Lincoln; William McKinley; James Madison; James Monroe; Franklin Pierce; James K. Polk; Franklin D. Roosevelt; John Tyler; Martin Van Buren; and George Washington.

.227 Vinton, John Rogers, 1801-47.

Papers, 1814-61. 236 items and 9 v. Army officer. Correspondence, journals and other papers (chiefly 1837-49). The letters concern the slavery controversy and other matters.

.228 Watson, Henry, 1810-91.

Papers, 1765-1938. 3776 items and 18 v. Planter and lawyer of Greensboro, Ala. Letters, diaries, business correspondence, and papers (chiefly 1828-69) relating to Watson's career in law, his planting activities, slavery, farming conditions in ante-bellum Alabama, and other matters.

.229 Weaver, William, 1780-1863.

Papers, 1809-85. 3387 items. Ironmaster and pioneer in scientific agriculture. Correspondence and business papers of the owner of the Bath Iron Works, Buffalo Forge, Va., containing information about the use of slaves as industrial laborers, industrial conditions in Virginia during Reconstruction, life among Weaver's workers, and other matters relating to the iron industry.

.230 Whitehead, F.L. and Lofftus, N.

Accounts of slave trading.

.231 Whitford, John N., d. ca. 1894.

Papers, 1829-1921. 988 items and 27 v. Planter, Confederate Army officer, and North Carolina State senator. Correspondence, postwar plantation records, and legal papers relating to Whitford's planting activities before and after the Civil War, and other materials.

.232 Whittingham, William Rollinson, Bp., 1805-79.

Papers, 1823-79. 12,471 items. Protestant Episcopal clergyman, religious editor, and church historian. Professional papers related to pre-1860 social reform movements, the slavery controversy within the church, the work of Whittingham's associates among emancipated slaves, and other church matters. Correspondents include Philander Chase, Richard Henry Dana, Jr., Phillip Gadsden, John McVickar, William A. Muhlenberg, William E. Wyatt, and various leaders of the church.

.233 Wilberforce, William, 1759-1833.

Letters, 1788-1872. 209 items. Philanthropist and member of Parliament. Mostly letters (1814-15) by Wilberforce, relating to his activities in the anti-slave trade and abolition movements, with references to English politics, and other matters. Includes 34 letters written to William's son, Samuel Wilberforce, Bishop of Winchester (1805-73), about missionary activities of the Church of England in East Africa and various British colonies.

.234 Willcox, James M., b. 1804.

Papers, 1831-71. 328 items. Planter and member of the Virginia House of Delegates. Letters and papers of the Willcox and Lamb families, united by the marriage of Willcox and Mary Ann S. Lamb, reflecting family ties and farming operations during the late ante-bellum, Civil War, and Reconstruction periods. Consists of correspondence (1831-39) between Dr. John Ferguson Lamb, a Frankford, Pa., physician, and his daughter, Mary Ann, concerning social life in Charles City

County, Va., Nat Turner's activities; letters from
Willcox concerning the operation of his plantations,
and political affairs of the radicals during Reconstruction; and other matters.

.235 Winn family.
Papers, 1780-1925. 2657 items and 27 v. Personal and business correspondence, papers, and
volumes, mainly of John Winn (d. 1844), farmer,
lawyer, and postmaster, and his son, Philip
James Winn, physician and postmaster of Fluvanna
County, Va. The papers of the elder Winn relate
to "Bremo," the plantation of Gen. John H. Cocke.
Includes journals, account books, letter books of
various members of the family, records of births
and deaths of slaves, and accounts of the estate of
Samuel Kidd.

.236 Wood, Samuel O.
Papers, 1847-99. 368 items and 2 v. Plantation
overseer, agent for commission merchant and
planter. Letters from James P. Tarry, owner of
the plantation in Perry County, Ala., where Wood
was employed, containing information on current
prices of slaves and repeated injunctions (1851-54)
that Wood should not whip the slaves; correspondence after 1855 relating to Wood's work in a
commission house in Cahaba, Ala., and containing
references to prices and markets for slaves and
cotton; and other materials.

.237 Woody family.
Papers, 1784-1939. 2325 items and 28 v. Business and personal letters and papers (chiefly
1835-87) relating to Newton D. Woody, merchant
and miller of North Carolina, and his flight to the
North during the Civil War; the activities of Frank
H. Woody, a lawyer in the Montana Territory after
the Civil War; the activities of Woody relatives who
had migrated to Indiana; the activities of the children of Newton and his brother, Robert Woody,
merchant and postmaster; the Society of Friends
in ante-bellum North Carolina; economic conditions in North Carolina before, during, and after
the Civil War; and Reconstruction in North Carolina. Includes legal documents, business records, and minutes of the Orange Peace Society,
Orange County, N.C.

NC16   LEARNING INSTITUTE OF NORTH CAROLINA (LINC)
(1964). 1006 Lamond Ave., 27701. Tel 919 688-8211.
Dr. Richard S. Ray, Dir. Literature searches, copying,
inquiries answered, referrals made, consultation, project development.
LINC is a research and development agency designed to
contribute to the improvement of education on all
levels through efforts like the LINC Children's Center,
Cooperative Educational Leadership Project, statewide
reading workshops, curriculum development, consultant
services, assistance grants, project evaluation, leadership in early childhood education, technical assistance
to education projects, migrant education.
Publ.: LINC Quarterly; Reports, studies.

.1   Learning Institute of North Carolina (LINC).
Files, 1964- . Correspondence, minutes of meetings, financial records, studies, reports, and
other materials dealing with the aims, history, and
programs of LINC. Also includes the Education
Research Information Center Library (microfiche),
1966- . Newspaper clippings about education, race
relations in North Carolina; films.

NC17   THE L. Q. C. LAMAR SOCIETY (1970). 2727 Spencer St.,
27705. Tel 919 489-4711. Dr. Thomas H. Naylor,
Exec. Secy.
The L.Q.C. Lamar Society is a non-profit, tax-exempt,
educational organization committed to the premise that
Southerners can find practical solutions to the South's
major problems. These problems include rural poverty, substandard housing and education, unemployment, low wages and per capita income, an increasing
rate of population growth, environmental pollution, and
inadequate planning by state and local governments.
It is named for Lucius Quintus Cincinnatus Lamar, a
Mississippian who served in the late 19th century as
U.S. Senator, Secretary of the Interior and Associate
Justice of the U.S. Supreme Court.

NC18   NORTH CAROLINA CENTRAL UNIVERSITY (1910), JAMES
E. SHEPARD MEMORIAL LIBRARY (1951). 27707.
Tel 919 682-2171. Miss Pennie E. Perry, Chief Librn.
Interlibrary loan, bibliographies prepared, literature
searches, copying, inquiries answered, referrals
made, consultation.
Publ.: Annual Reports; J E S Echoes, bimonthly.

.1   Afro-American Studies Collection.
ca. 1000 paperbacks. Basic books on the life and
history of black Americans.

.2   Anti-Slavery Propaganda Collection.
ca. 2500 pamphlets. Microcards of originals located in the Oberlin College Library. See Oberlin
College Library, Oberlin, Ohio; or Lost Cause
Press (publisher), Louisville, Ky., for more complete description.

.3   Charles D. Martin Collection.
Miscellaneous. Books (ca. 3000 v.); mementos of
Africa, dictionaries of that continent, and books
and pamphlets about Negroes in the Caribbean;
pictures of the original Christy minstrels; works
on the slavery period in the U.S. and Europe, including several items written by slaves and ex-
slaves; some African items such as robes and
spears, and other objects native to Africa.

.4   Facts on Film.
Papers, 1954-67. Microfilm. Contains materials
on civil rights and race relations in the South. See
Race Relations Information Center, Nashville,
Tenn., for a full description.

NC19   THE NORTH CAROLINA FUND (1963).
The Fund, which went out of existence in 1969, was
established to study problems of improving the education, economic opportunities, living environment, and
general welfare of the people of North Carolina of all
ages and in different parts of the State; make and
recommend grants for research, pilot, experimental,
and other projects toward the solution of such problems; make available professional services to private
and public agencies; encourage cooperative state and
community action in devising such solutions; and encourage wise use of public and philanthropic funds.

The Fund's archives have been deposited at the North
Carolina Collection and the Southern Historical Collec-
tion, University of North Carolina Library, Chapel
Hill, N.C.

.1   The North Carolina Fund.
Archives and library, 1963-69. Contains books related to poverty components and variables, such as
economics, housing, and segregation; reference
items; periodicals (ca. 50 titles) which cover education, health and public welfare, economics, social
work and other subjects; newspapers (ca. 50 titles);
pamphlets (ca. 100 file drawers) relating to problems of poverty, social work and race relations;
vf (ca. 1000); theses; correspondence (ca. 250
file drawers); clippings (50 bound notebooks);
films and tapes (ca. 250 reels); photographs
(ca. 1000); unpublished papers (ca. 100 file
drawers); bibliographies relating to social problems, urban training, poverty, community organizing, and church work in social tension areas;
study outlines on politics of poverty, government,
and the Negro community, crisis in race relations;
and reading lists for symposia, Negro history, the
South, Negro leadership and politics, and other related subjects. Persons, organizations, and subjects mentioned include the 11 Community Action
Agencies (CAA) supported by the Fund, experimental efforts bearing on problems of low-income
families; Mobility, an effort to bring together the
employer and the unemployed workers; Manpower
Improvement Through Community Action (MITCE),
total family assistance with health service, employment, education and housing; Foundation for
Community Development (FCD); Learning Institute
of North Carolina (LINC), a research and development agency started in 1964; Manpower Development Corporation (MDC); Low-Income Housing
Development Corporation (LIHDC); Legal Services
and Consumer Education Study Committee; Intergovernmental Relations Study Committee; Cogs-

well Housing Project; various research programs
such as Process Analysis Study (1967), Survey of
Low-Income Families (1966), Profiles of Community Problems, Dimensions of Poverty, etc.;
Public Information Department Project (1965),
developed materials and strategies for information
to be disseminated, gave state and national publicity to CAA, and informs, educates, and involves
persons by using films, slides, printed materials,
displays, audio-visuals, speeches, reports, newsletter, publicity releases, photos (ca. 12,000 of
poverty problems), annual reports; Community
Action Technician (CAT) Training Program, young
sub-professionals who desire work in economic
opportunity movement; Volunteers In Service To
America (VISTA) Training Program (1965), provides a six-week training program; Community
Service Consultants (CSC) Training Program, professional coordinators of community resources in
anti-poverty efforts; North Carolina Volunteer
Program, workers in community actions; Youth
Educational Services (YES), statewide program
tutoring disadvantaged children (1965); Housing
Study Committee; Committee on Manpower and
Economic Development (COMED); 1967 Summer
Intern Project; 1967-68 Curriculum Development
Project; Comprehensive School Improvement Pro-
gram (CSIP), attempts to improve the quality of
primary education; Summer 1965 "Brainstorming"
Project; United Organization for Community Improvement (UOCI); Domestics United; Winston-
Salem Police Program, special training for low-
income neighborhoods; People's Program on
Poverty (PPOP); Multi-Purpose Training Center
(MPTC); Outward Bound; North Carolina Council
of Women's Organizations' Volunteer Study; President's Task Force on Poverty; Economic Opportunity Act; WAMY, incentive grants to neighborhood
councils; Macon Program for Progress, grants for
low-income farmers; Regional Education Laboratory; Frank Porter Graham Early Childhood Development Center; North Carolina Advancement
School (1965), an experimental residential school
for under achievers; U.S. Department of Labor,
Office of Manpower, Automation and Training;
Policymaker's Seminars (1965), orientation workshops to give insight into national poverty programs; University of North Carolina Institute, encourages and supports institutions to build in and
build on programs dealing with problems of the
people; Terry Sanford; John Ehle; C.A. McKnight;
Charles F. Babcock; John H. Wheeler; George H.
Esser, Jr. and others. Among the Fund publications represented in the archives are monthly
Blueprints, on education, the poor, police and
cities; Profiles, on food prices, and blacks and
whites; monographs from Manpower Improvement
Through Community Effort (MITCE), on rural poor,
unemployment, tenant farming, surveys of low-
income areas; Annual Reports; and films. Restricted.

NC20   NORTH CAROLINA MUTUAL LIFE INSURANCE COMPANY
(1899). Mutual Plaza, 27701. Tel 919 682-9201. Murray J. Marvin, Dir. of Corporate Planning. Consultation.
North Carolina Mutual is the largest Negro-operated
financial institution in the U.S. Formerly North Carolina Mutual and Provident Association.
Publ.: The Whetstone, quarterly magazine.

.1   Kennedy, W.J.
Papers. President (1952-58) of North Carolina
Mutual Life Insurance Company. Includes articles
for publication; speeches on various subjects such
as education, Negro business, race relations; annual messages to policy owners; correspondence
with government officials, civic and civil rights
leaders.
.2   Spaulding, C.C.
Papers, President (1923-52) of North Carolina
Mutual Life Insurance Company. Correspondence
with government officials, civic and civil rights
leaders; articles for publication; speeches on various subjects such as education, Negro business,
race relations; annual messages to policyowners.

NC21   OPERATION BREAKTHROUGH, INC. (1964). P.O. Box
1470, 114 W. Parrish St., 27701. Tel 919 688-8111.
John A. Croslan, Exec. Dir. Inquiries answered, consultation.
The Operation works to assist low-income people, both
black and white, to break out of the cycle of poverty.
This is done primarily through community organization
and advocacy; secondarily through the provision of direct services.
Publ.: Breakthrough Newsletter, monthly; Annual Report; Brochures.

.1   Operation Breakthrough, Inc.
Files, 1964- . Correspondence, financial reports,
minutes of meetings, complete clipping file,
monthly program progress reports; and complete
editions of Breakthrough Newsletter, Annual Report, and Economic Opportunity Report.

NC22   UNITED PUBLIC AND SERVICE EMPLOYEES LOCAL 77.
107½ E. Parrish St., 27702. Tel 919 688-4353.
Local 77 is an independent local union of mostly black
service employees, which works closely with the
student and black movements, in the area of Durham,
N.C.

ELIZABETH CITY

NC23   ELIZABETH CITY STATE UNIVERSITY (1891), G.R. LIT-
TLE LIBRARY (1939). Parkview Dr., 27909. Tel 919
355-0551. Hobson Thompson, Jr., Head Librn. Interlibrary loan, bibliographies prepared, literature
searches, copying, inquiries answered.

.1   Afro-American Studies Collection.
ca. 1000 paperbacks. Basic books on the life and
history of black Americans.
.2   P.W. Moore Memorial Collection.
Contains pamphlets, vf, clippings, and photographs, and books in the subject areas of civil
rights, issues of the 1960's, education, literature,
and history, especially of slavery.

FAYETTEVILLE

NC24   FAYETTEVILLE STATE UNIVERSITY (1937), CHEST-
NUTT LIBRARY, 28301. Tel 919 483-6144. Mrs.
Nathalene R. Smith, Head Librn. Interlibrary loan,
bibliographies prepared, literature searches, copying,
inquiries answered, referrals made, consultation.
Publ.: Book lists.

.1   Afro-American Studies Collection.
ca. 1000 paperbacks. Basic books on the life and
history of black Americans.
.2   Fayetteville State University.
Archives, 1937- . Includes correspondence, minutes of board meetings, financial records, records of admission, and other materials relating to
the history and administration of the University
(formerly Fayetteville State College).

GREENSBORO

NC25   BENNETT COLLEGE (1873), THOMAS F. HOLGATE LI-
BRARY (1939). Macon St., 27420. Tel 919 275-9791.
Mrs. Barbara Hunt-Bryan, Librn. Interlibrary loan,
bibliographies prepared, literature searches, copying,
typing, inquiries answered, referrals made, consultation.
Publ.: Guide to African and Afro-American Materials.

.1   Afro-American Studies Collection.
ca. 1000 paperbacks. Basic books on the life and
history of black Americans.
.2   Afro-American Women's collection.
Papers, chiefly 18th and 19th century. ca. 300
items. Contains secondary and primary source
materials, including letters, mss, books, clippings,
articles, and pictures, relating to Afro-American
women outstanding in the areas of literature, art,
music, and leadership. Restricted.
.3   Bennett College.
Archives, 1873- . 3 vf and 20 v. Includes pro-

grams, biographical data, clippings, bulletins, articles, and pictures, concerning the history of Bennett College. Also 20 scrapbooks concerning college programs and achievements. Restricted.

.4 Cuney, Norris Wright, 1846-99.
Papers, 1883-96. ca. 5 ft. Negro Republican party leader and collector of the Port of Galveston, Tex. Correspondence, diaries, programs, and legal documents relating to Cuney's political activities in Texas during Reconstruction. Restricted.

.5 Negro Collection.
Books, ca. 2136. Includes selected books by and about Negroes.

NC26 CONGRESS OF RACIAL EQUALITY (CORE). 703 S. Henry Blvd., 27410. Tel 919 273-3044. Pinkney Moses, 1st V.Chmn.

NC27 GUILFORD COLLEGE (1837) AND NORTH CAROLINA YEARLY MEETING (1704), QUAKER COLLECTION (1915). 27410. Tel 919 292-5511. Dorothy Gilbert Thorne, Curator, Quaker Collection. Interlibrary loan, copying, inquiries answered, consultation. The Library provides custodial care for ms materials belonging to the North Carolina Yearly Meeting, founded in 1704.

.1 North Carolina Yearly Meeting, Meeting for Sufferings.
Papers, 1704- . ca. 250 items. Minutes and correspondence of the official body of the Quakers, which eliminated slavery within its boundaries before the Civil War, and freed and assisted in freeing other slaves through the colonization movement and underground railroad.

NC28 NATIONAL CONFERENCE OF CHRISTIANS AND JEWS (NCCJ). 102 N. Elm St., 27401. Tel 919 273-8800. Andrew William Gottschall, Jr., Dir.

NC29 NORTH CAROLINA AGRICULTURAL AND TECHNICAL STATE UNIVERSITY (1891), F. D. BLUFORD LIBRARY (1894). 27410. Tel 919 273-1771. B.C. Crews, Jr., Acting Univ. Librn. Interlibrary loan, bibliographies prepared, literature searches, copying, inquiries answered, referrals made, consultation.

.1 Africa Studies Collection.
Contains books, periodicals, vf, theses and dissertations, films, and microforms (240 rolls).

.2 Afro-American Studies Collection.
ca. 1000 paperbacks. Basic books on the life and history of black Americans.

.3 Facts on Film.
Papers, 1954-67. Microfilm. Contains materials on civil rights and race relations in the South. See Race Relations Information Center, Nashville, Tenn., for a full description.

NC30 NORTH CAROLINA COUNCIL ON HUMAN RELATIONS, INC. (1955). 233½ N. Greene St., 27401. Tel 919 273-4077. W.C. Allred, Jr., Exec. Dir.
The Council strives to improve the conditions of life of people in North Carolina on a non-discriminatory basis through research, education, and dissemination of information. Records will be deposited at the Library of the University of North Carolina at Chapel Hill after 1969.

.1 North Carolina Council on Human Relations, Inc.
Files, 1955-1969. Contains books, pamphlets (3000), vf, correspondence, and clippings of 6-8 North Carolina newspapers on race relations and other matters.

GREENVILLE

NC31 EAST CAROLINA UNIVERSITY (1907), J. Y. JOYNER LIBRARY (1954). Box 2547, ECU Station, 27834. Tel 919 758-3426. Wendell W. Smiley, Dir. of Library Serv. Interlibrary loan, copying.

.1 Anti-Slavery Propaganda Collection.
ca. 2500 pamphlets. Microcards of originals located in the Oberlin College Library. See Oberlin College, Oberlin, Ohio; or Lost Cause Press (publisher), Louisville, Ky., for more complete description.

.2 Facts on Film.
Papers, 1954-67. Microfilm. Contains materials on civil rights and race relations in the South. See Race Relations Information Center, Nashville, Tenn., for a full description.

.3 J.Y. Joyner Library.
Contains books (10,000) and pamphlets (5000) relating to race relations.

HIGH POINT

NC32 AMERICAN FRIENDS SERVICE COMMITTEE (AFSC), SOUTHEASTERN REGIONAL OFFICE (1946). 1818 S. Main St., 27260. Tel 919 882-0109. Wilton E. Hartzler, Exec. Secy.
AFSC is a Quaker organization which attempts to relieve human suffering and to seek non-violent solutions to conflicts—personal, national, and international.

KITTRELL

NC33 KITTRELL COLLEGE (1885), B. N. DUKE LIBRARY (1907). 27544. Tel 919 492-2131. Mr. Larnie G. Horton, Pres. Interlibrary loan, bibliographies prepared, copying, inquiries answered.

.1 Kittrell College.
Archives, 1885- . Includes financial records, correspondence, records of admission, minutes of board meetings, and other materials relating to the history and administration of the College.

LAKE JUNALUSKA

NC34 COMMISSION ON ARCHIVES AND HISTORY OF THE UNITED METHODIST CHURCH, LIBRARY AND ARCHIVES OF THE UNITED METHODIST CHURCH. Box 488, 28745. Tel 704 456-9433. John H. Ness, Jr., Exec. Secy. Interlibrary loan, literature searches, copying, inquiries answered, consultation. Publ.: Methodist History, quarterly magazine.

.1 The Library contains records of the Methodist Episcopal Church (1766-1939), the Methodist Episcopal Church, South (1845-1939), the Methodist Protestant Church (1828-1939), and the Methodist Church (1939-68). As a result of the 1968 union with the Evangelical United Brethren Church, it is the depository for the archives of the United Methodist Church. Restricted.

MONTREAT

NC35 PRESBYTERIAN CHURCH IN THE UNITED STATES, HISTORICAL FOUNDATION (1927). Assembly Dr., 28757. Tel 704 669-7061. Kenneth Foreman, Jr., Exec. Dir. Copying, inquiries answered, consultation.

.1 Campbell, Robert Fishburne, 1858-1947.
Papers, 1876-1946. 4 ft. Presbyterian minister. Correspondence, sermons, and other papers, chiefly relating to the organization of the Synod of Appalachia of the Presbyterian Church in the U.S., Home Missions, the First Presbyterian Church of Asheville, N.C., the Historical Foundation of the Presbyterian and Reformed Churches, the race question, people of the Appalachian Mountain area, and Campbell and Ruffner family history. The material is related to the repository's Ruffner collection.

.2 Jones, Charles Colcock, 1804-63.
Papers. Presbyterian minister. Pastor, 1st Presbyterian Church, Savannah, Ga. (1831-33); home missionary among Negroes in Liberty County, Ga. (1833-35); home missionary in Georgia (1838-48); executive secretary, Presbyterian Board of Home Missions (1850-53).

.3 Lilly family.
Papers, 1924-60. 4 ft. Papers of David Clay Lilly (1870-1939), Presbyterian minister with pastorates in Alabama, North Carolina, and Virginia; moderator of the General Assembly, Presby-

terian Church in the U.S.; field secretary for International Laymen's Missionary Movement (1913-16); secretary of the General Assembly's Executive Committee of Colored Evangelization; and organizer and chairman of the Reynolds Conferences, 1923-27; and papers of Edward Guerrant Lilly (b. 1898), Presbyterian minister with pastorates in Kentucky, Alabama, and South Carolina, contributing editor to the Charleston, S.C. Evening Post, and moderator of the Synod of South Carolina. David Clay Lilly's papers include correspondence, sermons, and material relating to the Reynolds Conferences and the International Laymen's Missionary Movement. Edward Guerrant Lilly's papers include sermons, and material relating to the judicial business of the church, and the Charleston Bible Society project.

.4 Papers relating to Negroes.
Pamphlets. Subjects include slavery, Negro work, and race problems.

.5 Presbyterian Church in the U.S.
Minutes of sessions, 1791-1957. 85 ft. The minutes include proceedings of the sessions (the governing bodies of the local churches), registers of pastors, elders and deacons, and other matters in Maryland, West Virginia, Kentucky, Missouri, Oklahoma, Texas, and all states to the south and east of these boundaries. The minutes of the mid-19th century frequently contain material pertaining to the relationship of slaves to the church.

.6 Presbyterian Church in the U.S.
Papers, 1930- . Contains histories of churches and women's work.

.7 Presbyterian Church in the U.S., Committee on Colored Evangelism.
Minutes, ?-1910.

.8 Presbyterian Church in the U.S., Executive Committee of Instruction for Training Colored Ministers.
Papers, 1876, 1883-85, 1887-91.

.9 Sheppard, William H., 1865-1927.
Papers. Presbyterian minister, graduate, Hampton Institute, Stillman Institute. Pastorates in Montgomery, Ala., and Atlanta, Ga.; first Negro missionary to Congo (1890-1910), and one of first two missionaries to Congo sent by Presbyterian Church in the U.S.

.10 Snedecor Memorial Synod and Presbyteries.
Minutes, 1816-52. Snedecor Memorial Synod was created for Negro churches of the Presbyterian Church in the U.S. and was the Afro-American Synod in 1916, composed of the presbyteries of Central Alabama, Ethel, North and South Carolina, and Central Louisiana. Name of synod changed to Snedecor Memorial Synod in 1917, dissolved in 1952.

.11 Stillman College and Institute.
Catalogs.

.12 Wilson, John Leighton, 1809-86.
Papers. Presbyterian minister; missionary to Africa (1834-60); secretary, Presbyterian Board of Foreign Missions (1861-86); secretary, Presbyterian Board of Home Missions (1863-82).

RALEIGH

NC36 NORTH CAROLINA DEPARTMENT OF ARCHIVES AND HISTORY (1903), DIVISION OF ARCHIVES AND RECORDS MANAGEMENT. Box 1881, 27602. Tel 919 829-3952. A.M. Patterson, Arch. and Records Adminstr. Copying, typing, inquiries answered, referrals made, consultation.
Publ.: Guide to Private Manuscripts in North Carolina State Archives; Guide to Civil War Records.

.1 Brock, Ignatius.
Papers, 1733-1877. 172 items. Plantation owner, of Jones County, N.C. Correspondence, grants, surveys, deeds, bills of sale, Confederate money, loans, and tax-in-kind forms, other papers, and newspaper clippings. The material concerns purchases and sales of land and slaves, the Civil War, and other matters. Persons mentioned include Edward, John, John Hill, Joseph, and William

Bryan, John M. Franck, Martin Franck, and Daniel Y. Shine.

.2 Civil War and Reconstruction papers.
1851-1935. ca. 325 items. In part, typescripts and photocopies of originals in possession of individual owners. Correspondence, diaries, reminiscences, accounts of life in Army camps, descriptions of battles, clippings, accounts, scrapbooks, and miscellaneous papers relating to the Civil War, to people prominent during the war, to Reconstruction in North Carolina, to the assassination of J.W. "Chicken" Stephens by the Ku Klux Klan, and to other matters. Some papers of Col. George Wortham, commander of the 50th North Carolina Infantry, relate to the settlement of claims for damaged property and runaway slaves.

.3 Collins family.
Papers, 1761-1892. 5 ft. Correspondence, plantation accounts, church records, and account books, relating to the Lake Company which held lands in Tyrrell and Washington Counties, N.C., and was owned by the Collins family. Subjects include land purchase, plantation business, removal of slaves to Orange and Franklin counties during the Civil War, hiring of slaves, local politics, family affairs, and social life. Family members represented include Josiah Collins (1735-1819), his son, Josiah II, his grandson, Josiah III, other grandchildren, and his great-grandchildren, Josiah IV, Arthur, and George. Correspondents include Octavius Coke, Charles Edmondston, Fordyce M. Hubbard, James C. Johnston, David A. Stone, and Hugh Williamson.

.4 Cumberland, Edgecombe, and Mecklenburg Counties.
Will books, inventories, and minute books, 1830-60.

.5 Governors' Papers, 1836-54.
Calendar for incoming and outgoing letters. Abstracts and index file for subject matter. Occasional references to runaway slaves, to crimes committed by Negroes, and to free Negroes.

.6 Grimes, Bryan, 1828-80.
Papers, 1778, 1812-1912. ca. 1500 items. Member of the North Carolina State secession convention and Confederate officer. Correspondence, Grimes' reminiscences of the war, a scrapbook of newspaper clippings relating to Gen. Grimes' murder and the trial and lynching of the alleged assassin, and other items. Grimes' correspondence relates to Civil War news, the situation in eastern North Carolina during the Civil War, and business and plantation matters.

.7 Harris, James Henry.
Papers, 1848, 1864-90. 29 items. Free Negro, prominent Republican during Reconstruction, State legislator, and newspaper editor. Included are certificate of freedom, teaching certificate, political circulars, charter for Union League of America, petition to Congress for William W. Holden, appointments as commissioner of Raleigh, elector, and member of the N.C. Agricultural Society. Also included are some letters of reference and one with political comments from John Dancy, Negro editor, 1880.

.8 Haywood, Fabius Julius, 1803-80.
Papers, 1833-1900. 174 items. Physician, of Raleigh, N.C. Correspondence, account books, and other items. Includes records of slaves purchased and hired. Some of the papers pertain to Col. Allen Rogers, of Rolesville, Wake County, N.C. and other members of his family.

.9 Heller, Calvin Boyd. Collector.
Calvin Boyd Heller collection, 1735-1923. ca. 475 items. Correspondence of Thomas D.S. McDowell, member of the North Carolina House and Senate and the Confederate Congress, relating to state and local elections (1846-61), national politics (1854, 1856, 1858), Civil War conditions in Alabama; together with papers of the estate of James Iver McKay, U.S. Representative from North Carolina, relating to the preparation for and transporting of the accounts, indentures, of the Byrne, Carmichael, and Robeson families of Bladen County, N.C.

.10 Hines, Charles W.
Papers, 1765-1869. 10 ft. of microfilm. Micro-

film copy made from originals in the possession of Albert W. Cowper, Kinston, N.C. Surveys, plats, grants, and deeds for land in Craven and Dobbs (Lenoir) counties, N.C., an account (1839) of sales of slaves, account of Jesse Moore's estate (1857), and will (1957) of Amos Heath, Jones County, N.C.

NC36.11 Historical Society of Pennsylvania.

Papers relating to North Carolina, 1760-1888. 145 items. Photocopies of originals in the Historical Society of Pennsylvania. Correspondence, certificates, appointments, commissions, bills, notes, and other papers relating to North Carolina. Includes correspondence of Richard Caswell and material relating to the Revolutionary War, a slave conspiracy in Virginia, and political issues.

.12 Holden, William Woods, 1818-92.

Papers, 1852-1930. 135 items. Governor of North Carolina. Correspondence and other papers relating to Holden's governorship, Reconstruction, the Republican victory of 1868, politics, county election irregularities, disfranchisement, nominations of justice of the peace, the Ku Klux Klan, and other matters.

.13 Lewis, Nell Battle, 1893-1956.

Papers, 1862, 1920-56. ca. 10,000 items and 5 scrapbooks. Newspaper columnist, of Raleigh, N.C. Correspondence, lectures, book reviews, articles, biographical sketches, clippings, newspaper columns and editorials for the News and Observer and for the Raleigh Times, and other papers. Includes material relating to the South, Negroes, women, social problems, labor relations, political campaigns and issues, communism in North Carolina, segregation and integration, and the Olivia Raney and Richard B. Harrison Public Libraries.

.14 Mial, Alonzo T.

Papers of Alonzo T. and Millard Mial, 1830-97. ca. 2750 items and 17 v. Correspondence, estate papers, account books, mercantile and plantation accounts, sharecropper agreements, and other papers of Mial, a lawyer and plantation owner, of Raleigh, N.C. Includes letters from the Freedmen's Bureau.

.15 Mordecai family.

Papers, 1796-1876. 173 items. Correspondence, accounts, poems, sketches, and other papers, of the Mordecai family of North Carolina and Virginia. The correspondence concerns family affairs, slave insurrections in Virginia and Wilmington, N.C., depredations in Monroe County, Va., and other matters.

.16 Newspaper collection: Negro newspapers.

Included are, from Raleigh, N.C., Danner Enterprise (May 31, 1883); Journal of Industry (v. I. #1, 1879, Oct. 9, 1880), North Carolina Republican (July 30, Nov. 12, 1880), North Carolina Gazette (Sept. 26, 1885; Oct. 24, 1891; and 65 issues, Dec. 1893-Feb., 1898); from Littleton, N.C., True Reformer (July 25, 1900); from Weldon, N.C., North Carolina Republican and Civil Rights Advocate (May 22, 1884).

.17 Nicholls, Benajah.

Papers, 1783-1834. 3 boxes. Resident of Bertie County, N.C. Correspondence, receipts, and other papers. Includes correspondence relating to the estates which Nicholls administered; business papers relating to the cotton trade; letters from relatives. Subjects include a trip to the West Indies, and the Nat Turner slave insurrection in Southampton County, Va.

.18 North Carolina under the Lords Proprietors.

Papers, 1664-74. 3 v. Correspondence of Governors Samuel Stephens and Peter Carteret including letters to and from the Lords Proprietors and the "Inhabitants of Carolina" (Valentine Bird, James Blount, Edmund Chancy, John Foster, Thomas Jarvies, John Jenkins, William Jennings, Thomas Pearce, and John Willoughby). Includes Carteret's account when in Carolina (1666-73), and his report on the plantation at Colleton Island (1663-73).

.19 Pate family.

Papers, 1815-98. 1588 items. Correspondence and other papers of the Pate family of Northampton County, N.C., and the Jackson family. Includes family and business accounts, legal papers, newspapers, and other printed matter. The materials mainly relate to Burwell Pate (1820-71) and his son, John Wesley Pate (1847-96). The younger Pate's papers include a list of white and Negro children in School District 23, Oconechee Township.

.20 Peele family.

Papers, 1723-1906. 146 items. Correspondence, accounts, receipts, and advertisements (chiefly 1790-1890), of the Peele family of Wilson County, N.C. Includes receipts for slave hire and purchase, and letters from relatives in Mississippi and Illinois.

.21 Pettigrew family.

Papers, 1772-1912. ca. 3500 items. Correspondence, account books, memorandum books, plantation records, scrapbook, bills, speeches, law reports, affidavits, military reports and orders, sermons, pamphlets, broadsides, and other materials of the Pettigrew family of Tyrrell and Washington Counties, N.C. The bulk of the collection concerns Charles Pettigrew, an Episcopal minister; his son, Ebenezer Pettigrew, planter and U.S. Representative; and his grandson, James Johnston Pettigrew, South Carolina legislator and Confederate officer. A few papers relate to Charles Pettigrew's second wife, Mary Lockhart Pettigrew, and to Ebenezer Pettigrew's sons, William Shephard Pettigrew and Charles Lockhart Pettigrew, and to his daughter, Mary Pettigrew. The papers of Charles Pettigrew include a few plantation and business papers. The papers of Ebenezer Pettigrew concern plantation operations and political matters during his term in Congress (1835-37), and include information on slave care and management, his campaign for Congress, national issues of the period, and his Tennessee lands. The papers of James Johnston Pettigrew deal with his work in the South Carolina legislature (1856-58), and his military career, and include material on the reopening of the slave trade, and his military company's role in the defense of Charleston.

.22 Pickell, James Marion.

Collection, 1896-1920. 62 items. Taught chemistry at Leonard Schools of Medicine and Pharmacy at Shaw University in Raleigh, N.C. Roll books, 1900-13; catalog, 1902-03; brochure, 1897. Other papers relate to his work as a feed chemist for N.C. Department of Agriculture.

.23 Polk family.

Papers, 1730-1897. ca. 1300 items. Correspondence, receipts, accounts, speeches, military records, circulars, newspaper clippings, and other papers of Lucy (Williams) Polk and her family, relating to pre-Civil War affluence, Reconstruction and post-Reconstruction poverty in the South, Polk's fight to prevent the secession of Tennessee, the Civil War and its effects on Nashville and Columbia, Tenn., and other matters.

.24 Pou, James Hinton, 1861-1935.

Papers, 1914-20. 206 items. Lawyer, of Smithfield and Raleigh, N.C. Correspondence, speeches, photos, newspaper clippings, pamphlets, and other papers relating to Pou's activities in civic and State affairs, particularly war work. Correspondence includes letters of appreciation from Negro leaders - C.N. Hunter, editor of The Raleigh Independent, and James E. Shephard, president of the National Training School at Durham, N.C.

.25 Reid, David Settle, 1813-91.

Papers, 1803-80. 820 items. Governor of North Carolina and U.S. Representative and Senator from North Carolina. Correspondence and other papers relating to political issues, election campaigns, fugitive slave law, the strategy and growth of the Democratic party, and other matters. Correspondents include William A. Graham and Stephen A. Douglas.

.26 Saunders, William Laurence, 1835-91.

Papers, 1775-1890. 656 items. Lawyer, journalist, Democratic party leader, historian, and secretary of state of North Carolina. Correspondence relating to political affairs (1882-88), the political strength of Democrats, Radicals, and Negroes in North Carolina, and the re-election of Zebulon B. Vance to the U.S. Senate.

.27 Skinner, McRae, Wolley, and Deberry families.
Papers, 1808-95. 40 ft. of microfilm, from originals loaned by Col. Jeffrey Stanback. Correspondence and other items for the Skinner, McRae, Wooley, and Deberry families of Montgomery County, N.C. The letters of C.W. Wooley, of Lawrenceville, N.C., addressed to Edmund Deberry, U.S. Representative from North Carolina, describe local events, the sale of slaves in Troy, N.C., and other matters.

.28 Swain, David Lowry, 1801-68.
Papers, 1763-1895. ca. 1200 items and 1 v. In part, typescripts of originals in the Southern Historical Collection at the University of North Carolina. Governor of North Carolina, president of North Carolina University, and historian. Correspondence, diary (1832), and other papers of Swain. The Swain correspondence relates to a plantation in Paulding County, Ga., and other matters.

.29 U.S. Census Bureau.
Ms Census returns for 1860, Schedule III for North Carolina.

.30 Vann, John, 1768-1850.
Papers, 1765-1888. ca. 1000 items. Planter, justice of the peace, and North Carolina legislator, of Hertford County, N.C. Correspondence relating to plantation matters, local politics, records of sales, indentures, court records, Hertford County voters' lists and precinct election returns (1856), and other matters.

.31 Waddell family.
Papers, 1755-1919. 103 items. Includes deeds, plat, will and other estate papers relating to Moorefields Plantation in Orange County, N.C.

.32 Wiley, Calvin Henderson, 1819-87.
Papers, 1755-1925. ca. 2200 items and 30 ft. of microfilm. Microfilm copy made from originals in the possession of Mary C. Wiley, Winston-Salem, N.C. Educator, lawyer, and State legislator, of North Carolina. Family and other correspondence relating to Whig politics, Negro education, war and slavery, the Holden-Worth campaign for governor, and other matters.

.33 Worth, Jonathan, 1802-69.
Papers, 1831-89. ca. 5300 items. Lawyer, legislator, State treasurer, and Governor of North Carolina. Personal, business, legal, and political correspondence relating to national, state, and local politics, secession, state and personal finances, the peace movement, military occupation, the conflict of civil and military justice, freedmen, Reconstruction, the 14th Amendment, William W. Holden, and Albion W. Tourgee. Correspondents include John A. Gilmer, William A. Graham, Augustus S. Merrimon, Richmond M. Pearson, David L. Swain, Josiah Turner, Zebulon B. Vance, and Patrick H. Winston.

NC37 NORTH CAROLINA GOOD NEIGHBOR COUNCIL (1963), RESEARCH DIVISION (1963). P.O. Box 12525, 1307 Glenwood Ave., 27605. Tel 919 829-2254. Robert S. Harrell, Asst. to the Chmn. Copying, inquiries answered, referrals made, consultation.
The Council is the state's official civil rights commission, established by executive order and in 1967 by statute. Its activities are conciliation and persuasion, and conducting surveys and studies in the areas of youth training, community organization, school desegregation, merit employment; and human relations groups.
Publ.: Good Neighbors at Work in N.C., monthly; Reports, studies, pamphlets, brochures, and monographs.

.1 North Carolina Good Neighbor Council.
Files, 1963- . Correspondence, books, periodical titles, pamphlets, clippings, films, photos, tape recordings, complete run of newsletters, depository for civil rights materials, 3 essential biennial studies of non-white employment (1964, 1966, 1968) which include questionnaires to all State

agencies and material from the State personnel office on Negro and Indian employment in government; and a research file for vocational opportunities study conducted in North Carolina in 1966, concerning non-discrimination, and other materials including all areas of race relations. Restricted.

NC38 NORTH CAROLINA STATE LIBRARY (ca. 1820). P.O. Box 2889, 27606. Tel 919 829-7121. Philip S. Ogilvie, State Librn. Interlibrary loan, bibliographies prepared, literature searches (State agencies only), copying, inquiries answered, referrals made.

.1 Confederate Imprint Collection.
Publications, 1861-65. ca. 475 publications. Includes newspapers and periodicals, and North Carolina resolution and laws, and other printed materials in areas under Confederate control, some of which relate to slavery and the status of Negroes during the Civil War.

.2 North Carolina Collection.
Miscellaneous, 1585- . Includes books and other materials about and by North Carolina authors, among them the Negro authors, H.E. Brown, James H. Boykin, John M. Brewer, John Hope Franklin, and John R. Larkins.

.3 U.S. Government and N.C. State Documents.
ca. 1800- . Includes laws, hearings, reports, and various other material relating to minority groups in the U.S. and in N.C.

NC39 ST. AUGUSTINE'S COLLEGE (1881), BENSON LIBRARY. 1315 Oakwood Ave., 27602. Tel 919 828-4451. Everett Days, Librn. Interlibrary loan, copying, inquiries answered.

.1 Afro-American Heritage collection.
Materials, 17th century- . Microfilm. 131 reels. Books, newspapers, and mss concerning the Negro American and his history. See Minnesota Mining and Manufacturing Company, St. Paul, Minn., for a full description.

.2 Afro-American Studies Collection.
ca. 1000 paperbacks. Basic books on the life and history of black Americans.

.3 Negro Collection.
Contains books (ca. 4000), periodicals, pamphlets, and various other materials by and about Negroes.

NC40 ST. AUGUSTINE'S COLLEGE, EDUCATIONAL LEADERSHIP AND HUMAN RELATIONS CENTER. 27602. Tel 919 828-4451. Dr. William A. Gaines, Dir.

NC41 SHAW UNIVERSITY (1868), SHAW LEARNING RESOURCE CENTER (1968). 730 S. Wilmington St., 27602. Tel 919 833-3812. Mr. E. LeFrancois, Dir. Interlibrary loan, copying, typing, inquiries answered, referrals made, consultation.

.1 Afro-American Heritage collection.
Materials, 17th century- . Microfilm. 131 reels. Books, newspapers, and mss concerning the Negro American and his history. See Minnesota Mining and Manufacturing Company, St. Paul, Minn., for a full description.

.2 Afro-American Studies Collection.
ca. 1000 paperbacks. Basic books on the life and history of black Americans.

.3 Shaw University.
Archives, 1868- . Scattered records, including correspondence, financial records, minutes of board meetings, records of admission, and other materials relating to the history and administration of the University.

NC42 WAKE COUNTY PUBLIC LIBRARIES (1966), RICHARD B. HARRISON BRANCH LIBRARY (1935). 1313 New Bern Ave., 27610. Tel 919 832-2942. Mrs. Mollie Huston Lee, Br. Librn. Interlibrary loan, bibliographies prepared, literature searches, copying, typing, inquiries answered, referrals made, consultation.
Publ.: A Selected List of Books by and about the Negro, 1950-56; A Selected List of Books by and about the Negro, 1957-66.

.1 Children's Book Collection.
ca. 872 v. Books by and about the Negro. The Col-

lection is designed to provide the serious student with books which will enable him to make comparative studies of the changes in text content, character portrayals, etc., found in the books which have been added to the collection each year.

.2 Negro Collection.
Miscellaneous. Books (ca. 7000), periodicals and newspapers (39 titles), pamphlets, theses, clippings (ca. 3000), photographs, phonograph records, African art objects, filmstrips, and slides. Includes materials in the areas of slavery, the history of slavery, anti-slavery movements, Emancipation Proclamation, biographical books, poetry, Africa, race relation, discrimination, segregation, desegregation, integration, and related subjects.

SALISBURY

NC43 LIVINGSTONE COLLEGE (1879), ANDREW CARNEGIE LIBRARY (1883). W. Monroe St., 28144. Tel 704 633-0818. Mrs. Louise Rountree, Librn. Interlibrary loan, bibliographies prepared, literature searches, copying, typing, inquiries answered, referrals made, consultation.
Note: The Wall Memorial Heritage Hall (1969) is a depository for rare books, manuscripts, and other papers. It will contain materials on Christian heritage, the history of the African Methodist Zion Church, history and literature about Africa, Negro history and literature, and the personal papers and contributions of the donor, Bishop William Jacobs Walls. This campus facility is expected to become a study and research center for Afro-American studies.
Publ.: The American Negro and African Studies: A Bibliography on the Special Collections in Carnegie Library, Livingstone College (1968).

.1 African Studies Collection.
Miscellaneous. ca. 300 v. Materials pertaining to Livingstone College (original name changed in 1887 to honor David Livingstone, a missionary in Africa), the African Methodist Episcopal Zion Church, Africa, and to nearly every period and discipline of interest to and concerning Negroes.

.2 American Negro Collection.
Miscellaneous. Books (many rare and first editions), pamphlets, mss, periodicals (ca. 22 titles), newspapers (ca. 7 titles), correspondence, clippings, filmstrips, photographs, tape recordings, art objects, African art, historical objects, and other materials on several ethnic groups and on the history of the race in the first half of the century. Subject areas include general histories and biographies of Negroes; slavery; the anti-slavery movement; writings on the Civil War and emancipation up to and after 1865; Negro organizations and professions; the church; the press; military affairs; politics; science and medicine; sports; Negroes in literature, art, music, and stage and drama; education; population and economic status; and major issues such as "civil rights and wrongs." Among this collection are the following materials:

.3 — African Methodist Episcopal Zion Church.
Miscellaneous. Sponsor of Livingstone College. Includes histories, sermons, catechisms, minutes, daily journals, biographical sketches, disciplines, earliest hymns and tune books, books and pamphlets, and other materials by and about A.M.E.Z. bishops, ministers, and writers. Scattered journals of the General Conference of the A.M.E.Z. Church (1880-1964); minutes of the New Jersey Annual Conference of the A.M.E. Zion Church (1874-85, 12 Sessions); official journal of the New England Annual Conference of the African Methodist Episcopal Zion Church in America (1874-91); official minutes of the Western North Carolina Conference of the A.M.E.Zion Church (1951-61); and official minutes of the Philadelphia and Baltimore Annual Conference of the A.M.E. Zion Church (1882-91). Among persons represented are Jackson A. Browne, J. Van Catledge, Joseph C. Price, Cicero R. Harris, John C. Dancy and John D. Small.

.4 (This number not used)

.5 — Afro-American Heritage collection.
Materials, 17th century- . Microfilm. 131 reels. Books, newspapers, and mss concerning the Negro American and his history. See Minnesota Mining and Manufacturing Company, St. Paul, Minn., for a full description.

.6 — Afro-American Studies Collection.
ca. 1000 paperbacks. Basic books on the life and history of black Americans.

.7 — Aggrey, James E. Kwegyir.
Papers. First African student at Livingstone (1899).

.8 — Dancy, John C., Sr.
Papers, 1898-1910. Recorder of deeds (Washington, D.C.). Includes letters of Booker T. Washington.

.9 — Ecumenical Methodist Conference.
Minutes, 1881-1956. Materials from First Session (1881); Second Session (1891); Fourth Session (1911); Fifth Session (1921); Seventh Session (1947); Ninth Session (1956); and certain published conference materials and hymnals (1842-45).

.10 — Livingstone College.
Archives, 1879- . Papers concerning administration and history of the College.

.11 — Materials pertaining to Negro organizations and professions.
Miscellaneous. Histories, essays, guidelines, and historical minutes of church groups, fraternities, sororities and professional organizations. Among groups mentioned are the National Association of Colored Women (1933), Alpha Kappa Alpha Sorority (1950), National Negro Business League (1900) and others.

.12 — Price, Joseph C.
Papers. Founder and first president of Livingstone College.

.13 — Small, John B.
Daily journal, 1872-1905. 19 v. Diaries of Small, containing historical material concerning the African Methodist Episcopal Zion Church.

.14 — Star of Zion.
Bound volumes, 1925- . Official organ of A.M.E.Zion Church.

.15 — Trent, W.J., Sr.
Papers. Fourth president of Livingstone College.

WINSTON-SALEM

NC44 AMERICAN CIVIL LIBERTIES UNION (ACLU) OF NORTH CAROLINA. P.O. Box 5362, 27103. Jane S. Patterson, Exec. Secy.

NC45 WINSTON-SALEM STATE UNIVERSITY (1892), C.G. O'KELLY LIBRARY. 27102. Tel 919 725-3563. Mrs. Lucy Hyman Bradshaw, Librn. Interlibrary loan, bibliographies prepared, literature searches, copying, typing, inquiries answered, referrals made, consultation.

.1 Afro-American Studies Collection.
Ca. 1000 paperbacks. Basic books on the life and history of black Americans.

.2 Winston-Salem State University.
Archives, 1892- . Includes correspondence, records of admission, minutes of board meetings, financial records, and other materials relating to the history and administration of the University (formerly Winston-Salem State College).

NC46 WINSTON-SALEM URBAN LEAGUE. 610 Coliseum Dr., 27100. Tel 919 725-5614. Samuel D. Harvey, Exec. Dir.

.1 Winston-Salem Urban League.
Files. Correspondence, minutes of meetings, financial records, reports, studies, and other materials dealing with the aims, history, and programs of the League.

NORTH DAKOTA

BISMARCK

ND1 STATE HISTORICAL SOCIETY OF NORTH DAKOTA, LIBRARY. Liberty Memorial Bldg., 58501. Tel 701 244-2666. Margaret Rose, Librn.

 .1 Burnham, John Winthrop, d. 1912.
  Papers. 1 box. Soldier. Biography of Burnham; papers relating to his military service with Negro troops in the Civil War and as sergeant in the 10th Minnesota Volunteer Infantry, Company C; reminiscences of war experiences; recollections of John Burnham (1749?-1843), Revolutionary War soldier; family genealogy; diary (1863) of the Sibley expedition; articles of agreement to build a store in Greenville, Minn.; and scrapbook of miscellaneous newspaper clippings.

 .2 Christianson, Adolph Marcus, 1877-1944.
  Papers, 1930-50. 5 ft. Justice of the North Dakota Supreme Court. Correspondence, reports, speeches, and mss and printed material on the Federal Emergency Relief Administration, United Service Organizations, Boy Scouts, North Dakota Council on Human Relations, and legal and welfare matters.

OHIO

AKRON

OH1 NATIONAL URBAN LEAGUE, INC., MIDEASTERN REGIONAL OFFICE. 1316 First National Tower Bldg., 44308. Tel 216 762-6233. Raymond R. Brown, Dir. Referrals made, consultation, program development, training, leadership development.

OH2 NEGRO BUSINESS DIRECTORY OF AKRON (1969). 425 Robert St., 44306. Tel 216 724-1022. Theodore R. Wilson, Editor.
 Publ.: The Christian Home; Negro Business Directory of Akron, Negro reference publication.

OH3 UNITED RUBBER WORKERS, FAIR PRACTICES DEPARTMENT. High at Mill St., 44308. Tel 216 376-6181.

BEREA

OH4 BALDWIN-WALLACE COLLEGE (1913), RITTER LIBRARY (1913). 44017. Tel 216 243-5000. David Palmer, Dir. Interlibrary loan, literature searches, copying, typing, inquiries answered.

 .1 Black Studies collection.
  Miscellaneous. Books (ca. 500) on such subjects as the arts, education, Afro-American history, African studies, contemporary Afro-American culture, literature, music, religion, social science and Negro bibliography. Also included is a select number of filmstrips, records, slide sets, tapes and transparencies. Located in Humanities Department.

CANTON

OH5 CANTON URBAN LEAGUE, INC. (1920). 415 13th St., S.E., 44707. Tel 216 456-3479. C.A. Thomas, Exec. Dir.

CINCINNATI

OH6 AMERICAN JEWISH COMMITTEE, CINCINNATI CHAPTER. Room 220, 1580 Summit Rd., 45237. Tel 513 761-7500. Mrs. Norma B. Moss, Exec. Asst.

OH6a BLACK COMMUNICATION COMMISSION (1969). 599 Blair Ave., 45229. Tel 513 751-4920. J. Wilson, Adminstr. The Commission maintains in and for the black communities of Hamilton County a newspaper and an "electronic media" (radio), which direct their editorial comments and general content toward black people and black community life.
 Publ.: Black Dispatch, bimonthly newspaper.

 .1 Black Communication Commission.
  Files, 1969- . Correspondence, minutes of meetings, financial records, studies, and other material dealing with the aims, history, and programs of the Commission. Restricted.

OH7 CINCINNATI ART MUSEUM (1881). Eden Park, 45202. Tel 513 471-5204.

 .1 Duncanson, Robert, d. 1871.
  Paintings, 1851. 2 items. Artist. Includes oil paintings entitled "Blue Hole, Flood Waters, Little Miami" and "Portrait of Nicholas Longworth."
 .2 Pippin, Horace, 1888-1946.
  Painting. 1 item. Artist. Includes oil painting entitled "Christmas Morning."

OH8 CINCINNATI HISTORICAL SOCIETY (1964) (FORMERLY HISTORICAL AND PHILOSOPHICAL SOCIETY OF OHIO, 1831), LIBRARY (1831). Eden Park, 45202. Tel 513 241-4622. Mrs. Lee Jordan, Librn. Copying, inquiries answered.
 Publ.: Cincinnati Historical Society Bulletin, quarterly.

 .1 Bean, Ira A.
  Papers, 1833-56. 28 items. Letters to and from Ira A. Bean and members of his family, Urbana, Ohio. Includes comments on banking, abolition of slavery, and U.S. politics of the period.
 .2 Berry, Gail Estelle.
  Master's thesis, 1965. 150 pp. Thesis entitled "Wendell Phillips Dabney, Leader of the Negro Protest." Written at the University of Cincinnati, Cincinnati, Ohio.
 .3 Cranch, William, 1769-1855.
  Papers, ca. 1790-1855. ca. 300 items. Jurist, of Washington, D.C. Correspondence, poems, documents, and other personal and political papers, some of which relate to the importation of slaves.
 .4 Dabney, Wendell Phillips, 1865-1952.
  Papers, 1905-64. 1 box. Materials by and about Dabney of Cincinnati, Ohio, concerning his publishing The Union, a Cincinnati Negro newspaper, from 1907 for ca. 50 years. Also includes scattered issues of the paper, (1918-52).
 .5 Foraker, Joseph Benson, 1847-1917.
  Miscellaneous, 1884-1917. Scrapbooks, correspondence, speeches, and other materials on the Brownsville, Tex. riot (1905) and over 400 letters showing reaction to Foraker's part in this affair; also miscellaneous material relating to the Negro.
 .6 Gholson, William Yates, 1807-70.
  Papers, 1795-1870. Business and personal papers of Cincinnati attorney William Y. Gholson, judge of the Superior Court of Cincinnati (1854-59), and justice of the Supreme Court of Ohio (1859-63). Included are letters of his client, Frances Wright (1795-1852), founder of the Nashoba Colony, an experiment in Negro emancipation.
 .7 Green, William, 1769-1883.
  Papers, 1775-1888. 754 items. Lawyer, and Lieutenant Governor of Rhode Island. Correspondence and other material relating to Cincinnati and Ohio history, national and Ohio politics, and social life. Correspondents include Frederick Grimké and Richard R. Ward.
 .8 Harding, Leonard.
  Master's thesis, 1967. 101 pp. Thesis entitled "The Negro in Cincinnati, 1860-70: A Demographic Study of a Transitional Decade"; written at the University of Cincinnati.
 .9 Howson, Embrey Bernard.
  Master's thesis, 1951. Thesis entitled "The Ku Klux Klan in Ohio After World War I" written at Ohio State University.
 .10 Lane Seminary.
  Papers, 1822-1951. 1 box. Letters, legal documents, programs relating to the Lane Theological Seminary, Cincinnati, Ohio. The Society also has pamphlets, books, and other ms material relating

to Lane Seminary, the Kemper, Beecher and Stowe families.

.11 Pamphlets.
ca. 800 items. Pamphlets pertaining to slavery and Negroes.

.12 Pih, Richard W.
Master's thesis, 1968. 198 pp. Thesis entitled "The Negro in Cincinnati, 1802-1841"; written at Miami University.

.13 Stevenson, Thomas B., 1803-63.
Papers, 1807-81. 1 box. Correspondence and other papers of Stevenson of Cincinnati, Ohio, Ashland, Ky., and Maysville, Ky. Letters abound in local Kentucky politics (1840's-60's), and offer then current ideas about the Whig party, the "Know-Nothings," the Missouri Compromise, slavery and it's attendant problems.

.14 Taft, William Howard, 1857-1930.
Papers, 1909. 5 pp. Ms of speech "The Outlook of Negro Education," an address delivered at the Haines Normal and Industrial School, Augusta, Ga. (January 19, 1909).

.15 Urban League of Greater Cincinnati.
Manuscript, ca. 1935. 33 pp. Ms v. of Negro Opportunities in Cincinnati.

.16 Walker, Susan, 1811-87.
Papers. 1 box. Materials concerning activities in Port Royal, S.C., during the Civil War; the Freedman's Bureau; Salmon P. Chase and his support of Susan Walker and her efforts to teach Negroes; Oliver O. Howard and the Freedman's Bureau; and Andrew Johnson.

.17 Walker, Timothy, 1802-56.
Papers, 1825-55. Correspondence, documents, printed materials of prominent persons and events in Cincinnati and pertaining to the African Education and Civilization Society, newspaper clippings on "The Slave Trial" (1855).

.18 Williams, Samuel W., 1827-1928.
Papers, 1800-1927. 7 boxes. Papers and documents relating to the Methodist Church and to surveying, among which is a memorial of the members of Allen's Chapel African Methodist Episcopal Church to the Cincinnati Conference, 1854.

OH9   CINCINNATI HUMAN RELATIONS COMMISSION (1943).
Room 158, City Hall, 45202. Tel 513 421-5700.
Virginia Coffey, Exec. Dir. Copying, typing, inquiries answered, referrals made.
The Commission works to foster mutual understanding and respect among all racial, religious and ethnic groups; to promote cooperation with governmental and non-governmental agencies or organizations having similar functions; and to make studies and investigations, hold hearings, and act as conciliator. Formerly the Mayor's Friendly Relations Committee.
Publ.: Human Relations Newsletter, monthly; Pamphlets.

.1 Cincinnati Human Relations Commission.
Files, 1943- . ca. 8 vf. Includes correspondence, minutes of meetings, financial records, studies, and reports concerning the Commission's activities. Documentation of aims, programs, and history is also included among other materials.

OH10 CINCINNATI JEWISH COMMUNITY RELATIONS COMMITTEE (1938). 906 Main St., 45202. Tel 513 241-5620.
Myron Schwartz, Exec. Dir.
The goals of the Committee are equality of opportunity, religious liberty, freedom of thought, speech, press, and association, understanding and mutual respect among religious and ethnic groups. It works primarily in areas of civil rights and intergroup relations.

.1 Cincinnati Jewish Community Relations Committee.
Files, 1938- . Includes books, pamphlets, correspondence, minutes of meetings, financial reports, and other material relating to the aims, programs, and history of the Committee.

OH11 HARRIET BEECHER STOWE HOUSE. 2950 Gilbert Ave., 45206. Tel 513 751-2773.
The Stowe House is a State memorial constructed from the family home which has been converted into a museum of exhibits on Mrs. Stowe and the Negro American.

OH12 HEBREW UNION COLLEGE, JEWISH INSTITUTE OF RELIGION, AMERICAN JEWISH ARCHIVES. 3101 Clifton Ave., 45220. Tel 513 221-1875. Dr. Jacob R. Marcus, Dir. Interlibrary loan, literature searches, copying, inquiries answered, consultation.
Publ.: American Jewish Archives, semiannually.

.1 Desegregation papers.
1957-63. 247 items. Letters, articles, and other papers relating to the desegregation activities of various rabbis. Includes proceedings (1963) of the Steering Committee of Metropolitan Houston, Tex., Conference on Religion and Race, and correspondence (1962) relating to an interfaith meeting in Wichita, Kan., to commemorate the 1954 Supreme Court desegregation decision; correspondence, sermons, and newspaper clippings (1957-58) from rabbis serving congregations in the South; together with an article (1961) by Rabbi Joseph H. Gumbiner, describing his efforts in Jackson, Miss., to end segregation. Access restricted.

.2 Frank, Emmet A.
Papers, 1958. 1 box. Rabbi, of Alexandria, Va. Letters from rabbis, ministers, and anti- and pro-segregationists, commenting on Rabbi Frank's sermon on the desegregation issue; and newspaper clippings.

OH13 HOUSING OPPORTUNITIES MADE EQUAL (HOME) COMMITTEE OF GREATER CINCINNATI, INC. (1962). 3932 Reading Rd., 45229. Tel 513 221-3353. Mrs. Marjorie Jordan, Dir. Inquiries answered, referrals made, consultation.
HOME works to promote and secure equality of opportunity for housing in Greater Cincinnati. The Committee works in neighborhoods to develop an open market and to maintain integrated housing patterns, to allay the fears of the uninformed, and to overcome the practices and attitudes which result in segregated communities. Formerly the Cincinnati Committee for Equality Opportunity in Housing.
Publ.: HOME Newsletter, quarterly; Annual Report.

.1 Housing Opportunities Made Equal Committee of Greater Cincinnati.
Files, 1962- . Includes correspondence, minutes of meetings, financial records, studies, investigations, and other material dealing with the aims, programs, and history of the Committee.

OH14 NATIONAL CONFERENCE OF CHRISTIANS AND JEWS (NCCJ). 617 Vine St., 45202. Tel 513 761-5891. Malcolm B. Chandler, Dir.

OH15 NORTH AVONDALE NEIGHBORHOOD ASSOCIATION (NANA) (1960). 3932 Reading Rd., 45229. Tel 513 221-6166. Dr. George C. Hale, Sr., Pres. Copying, typing, inquiries answered, referrals made, consultation.
The NANA works to maintain North Avondale as an integrated residential community. It sets up school and housing standards and concentrates on community involvement.
Publ.: NANA News, monthly newsletter; Materials on annual activities and integrated schools.

.1 North Avondale Neighborhood Association.
Records, 1960-69. 8 vf. Includes correspondence; history of active and inactive committees; some resource material on schools, housing, integrated communities; mailing lists; and community activities.

OH16 OHIO CIVIL RIGHTS COMMISSION, SOUTHWEST REGION. Suite 807, Schmidt Bldg., 431 Main St., 45202. Tel 513 241-6605. Arthur Layman, Regional Dir.

OH17 UNIVERSITY OF CINCINNATI (1819), UNIVERSITY LIBRARY. 45221. Tel 513 475-2533. Arthur T. Hamlin, Librn. Interlibrary loan, copying.

.1 Black studies collection.
The Library is setting up a duplicate collection on

open shelves. Includes books on black history, literature, and culture.

OH18   URBAN LEAGUE OF GREATER CINCINNATI (1948). 2400
        Reading Rd., 45202. Tel 513 721-3160. Joseph A. Hall,
        Exec. Dir. Consultation.
        The League plans, encourages, assists and engages in
        the improvement of economic, industrial, social, and
        cultural conditions of Negroes and other disadvantaged
        people and interests individuals and groups in under-
        taking to meet such needs; coordinates and cooperates
        with existing agencies and organizations to further these
        aims; promotes the improvement of race relations and
        furthers cooperation of all groups in behalf of the com-
        mon welfare. Its services include economic develop-
        ment and employment, education and youth incentives,
        housing, health and welfare services and leadership de-
        velopment.
        Publ.: Annual reports and special program reports.

    .1 Urban League of Greater Cincinnati.
        Files, 1948- . Records, reports, correspondence,
        and other papers concerning the aims and activities
        of the organization.

CLEVELAND

OH19   AFRO-AMERICAN CULTURAL AND HISTORICAL SOCIETY
        (AACHS) (1953), LIBRARY. 8716 Harkness Rd., 44106.
        Tel 216 795-3121. Icabod Flewellen, Curator and His-
        torian.
        AACHS is interested in building a national Negro history
        museum in the Cleveland area. It works to promote
        study of Negro history, achievements, and contributions
        and publicizes contributions made by the white race for
        the advancement of the Negro; furnishes speakers for
        school and civic organizations; and holds history
        classes and workshops.

    .1 Afro-American Cultural and Historical Society
        (AACHS).
        Miscellaneous, 1953- . Books (ca. 1200 v.), cor-
        respondence, minutes of meetings, financial rec-
        ords, and other materials dealing with the activi-
        ties of the Society.

OH20   AMERICAN CIVIL LIBERTIES UNION (ACLU) OF OHIO.
        1302 Ontario St., 44113. Tel 216 781-6276. Norma H.
        Coffey, Off. Mgr.

    .1 American Civil Liberties Union of Ohio.
        Files. Includes correspondence, minutes of meet-
        ings, financial records, studies, investigations, and
        documentation dealing with the aims, programs, and
        history of the Union.

OH21   AMERICAN JEWISH COMMITTEE, OHIO AREA. Suite 703,
        1220 Huron Rd., 44115. Tel 216 321-7100. Seymour
        Brief, Area Dir.

OH22   BLACK ECONOMIC UNION (BEU) (1966). 10542 Euclid
        Ave., 44106. Tel 216 229-5400. James Brown, Pres.
        Financial and technical assistance.
        BEU operates nationally to provide a program to edu-
        cate and train Negroes for the skilled jobs they seek
        and to raise funds to lend to Negroes with business
        potential. Formerly Negro Industrial and Economic
        Union.
        Publ.: Annual Report; Vanguard, monthly newsletter.

    .1 Black Economic Union.
        Files, 1966- . Includes correspondence, minutes
        of meetings, financial records, studies, reports
        and documents dealing with the aims, history and
        programs of the Union.

OH23   CLEVELAND COMMISSION ON HIGHER EDUCATION, CO-
        OPERATIVE RECRUITMENT OFFICE. 1367 Sixth St.,
        44114. Tel 216 241-7583. Ralph N. Besse, Pres.
        The Office seeks to increase black enrollments at eight
        colleges and universities in Cleveland, to develop in-
        creased financial aid for the students, and to create re-
        medial curricula.

    .1 Cooperative Recruitment Office.
        Files. Includes correspondence, minutes of meet-

ings, financial records, studies, reports, and other
materials dealing with the aims, programs, and
history of the Office.

OH24   CLEVELAND PUBLIC LIBRARY (1869). 325 Superior Ave.,
        44114. Tel 216 241-1020. Raymond C. Lindquist, Dir.
        Interlibrary loan, copying, typing, inquiries answered,
        referrals made, consultation.
        Publ.: The Open Shelf, bimonthly.

    .1 Facts on Film.
        Papers, 1954-67. Microfilm. Contains materials
        on civil rights and race relations in the South. See
        Race Relations Information Center, Nashville,
        Tenn., for a full description.
    .2 Materials relating to Negroes.
        Miscellaneous. Although not housed in a separate
        collection, the library holds in superior strength
        books, periodical titles, clippings, films, and mi-
        croforms by and about Negroes.

OH25   COMMUNITY RELATIONS BOARD (1945). 320 CTS Bldg.,
        1404 E. Ninth St., 44114. Tel 216 694-3290. Bertram
        E. Gardner, Exec. Dir. Copying, typing, inquiries an-
        swered, referrals made, consultation.
        The Board promotes amicable relations among racial
        and cultural groups within the community; coordinates
        activities of private organizations concerned with these
        relationships; assembles, analyzes, and disseminates
        data relating to interracial and intergroup relationships;
        administers fair employment legislation. The Board
        also has enforcement powers.
        Publ.: Annual Report.

    .1 Community Relations Board.
        Files, 1945- . Includes correspondence, newspaper
        clippings, minutes of meetings, financial records,
        studies, reports, catalogs, investigations, and doc-
        uments dealing with the aims, programs, and his-
        tory of the Board. In part, restricted.

OH26   THE COUNCIL ON HUMAN RELATIONS (1955). Room 278,
        The Arcade, 401 Euclid Ave., 44114. Tel 216 781-6630.
        James D. Nobel, Dir.
        The Council conducts institutes, workshops, work pro-
        jects, resources in human relations, and other activities
        to further the Council's cause. The Council has pro-
        grams in education, human relations, education, social
        attitudes, and conducts workshops to train educators,
        police, social workers, and others. Specific program
        areas are: the Elementary Age Programs; Youth Coun-
        cil Programs; Human Relations Consultation and Train-
        ing; and Community Programs.
        Publ.: High Points in Human Relations, bimonthly; Re-
            source Handbook in Human Relations; Films,
            brochures.

    .1 Council on Human Relations.
        Files, 1955- . Includes correspondence, minutes of
        meetings, financial reports, studies, reports, in-
        vestigations, and documentation dealing with "new
        approaches to the problem; and descriptions of the
        experimental efforts such as the Green Circle Pro-
        gram and the Children's Human Relations Li-
        braries."

OH27   JEWISH COMMUNITY FEDERATION (1903), COMMUNITY
        RELATIONS COMMITTEE (1946). 1750 Euclid Ave.,
        44115. Tel 216 861-4360. Howard R. Berger, Dir.,
        Community Rels. Comm.
        The Federation was established to coordinate and de-
        velop an orderly program in the field of Jewish commu-
        nity relations. It works through the subcommittee, the
        Community Relations Committee, which concerns itself
        with problems of civil rights, civil liberties, interracial
        relationships, housing and other community problems.
        The Federation is at all times in joint programs with
        the Committee planning for the purpose of spreading
        information and inducing cooperative actions.

    .1 Community Relations Committee.
        Files, 1946- . Includes correspondence, minutes
        of meetings, financial records, studies, reports,
        and other materials dealing with the aims, pro-
        grams, and history of the Committee.

OH28 LUDLOW COMMUNITY ASSOCIATION. P.O. Box 2022, Shaker Square Sta., 44120. Tel 216 296-1080. Dr. William Insull, Jr., Pres.
The Association seeks to maintain a stable integrated neighborhood.
Publ.: The Ludlow News, monthly newsletter; Annual Report; Pamphlets, brochures, and other informational materials about the Association and integrated living.

OH29 MINISTRY TO METROPOLIS PROGRAM (1966). 1850 Coltman Ave., Western Reserve University, 44106. Tel 214 368-2000. Robert H. Bonthius, Dir.
The Ministry is an internship for clergymen in the Urban Ministry to provide education for ministers in the current problems of urbanization and the decision-making processes of public administrators. The specialized curriculum focuses on problems of youth, poverty, inter-group relations, health and aging.

.1 Ministry to Metropolis Program.
Files, 1966- . Includes correspondence, studies, reports, and documents dealing with the aims, programs, and history of the Program.

OH30 NATIONAL ASSOCIATION FOR THE ADVANCEMENT OF COLORED PEOPLE (NAACP). 8409 Cedar Ave., 44106. Tel 216 231-6260. Raymond J. Mooney, Metrop. Dir. Inquiries answered, referrals made, consultation.
The NAACP conducts services to further the thrust for full equality to all minorities.

.1 National Association for the Advancement of Colored People.
Files. Includes correspondence, minutes of meetings, financial records, studies, reports, investigation, and documentation dealing with the aims, programs, and history of the program.

OH31 NATIONAL CONFERENCE OF CHRISTIANS AND JEWS (NCCJ). 302 Investment Insurance Bldg., 44114. Tel 216 241-4164. Robert L. Beda, Dir.

OH32 NATIONAL PHILLIS WHEATLEY FOUNDATION. Prospect Fourth Bldg., 44115. Tel 216 391-4443. Charles M. Hadley.

.1 National Phillis Wheatley Foundation.
Files. Includes correspondence, studies, minutes of meetings, financial reports, and other documents dealing with the aims, programs, and history of the Foundation.

OH33 OHIO CIVIL RIGHTS COMMISSION, NORTHEAST REGION (1959). 435 Perry-Payne Bldg., 740 W. Superior, 44113. Tel 216 579-2800. Joseph C. Hunter, Regional Dir.
The Commission was established to remedy discrimination based upon race, color, religion, national origin and ancestry in the areas of housing, employment and public accommodations; investigates charges filed under Ohio's laws against discrimination; and has jurisdiction in employment, housing, and public accommodations.
Publ.: Various publications concerning such subjects as employment, housing, and anti-discrimination laws.

OH34 U.S. EQUAL EMPLOYMENT OPPORTUNITY COMMISSION, CLEVELAND REGIONAL OFFICE. Room 402, Engineers' Bldg., 1365 Ontario St., 44114. Tel 216 522-4784. Chester Gray, Regional Dir. Typing, inquiries answered, referrals made, consultation.
Publ.: Annual Report.

OH35 URBAN LEAGUE OF CLEVELAND (1917). 2060 Euclid Ave., 44115. Tel 216 861-4200. Ernest C. Cooper, Exec. Dir. Inquiries answered.
The League "carries on social welfare work in all its branches among the colored people of Cleveland and vicinity—to assist them and the community to mutually adjust their lives and activities to conform to the just and proper requirements of the democratic principles upon which our institutions are created." It is a charitable and educational organization which operates as a community service agency using the tools and methods of social work to secure equal opportunity for Negroes and other disadvantaged minorities. Formerly the Negro Welfare Association.

Publ.: Newsletters, special and annual reports, and selected studies on the condition of Negro citizens in Cleveland, Ohio.

.1 Urban League of Cleveland.
Files, 1917- . Includes correspondence, minutes of meetings, financial records, studies, reports, investigations, and documents dealing with the aims, history, and programs of the League.

OH36 WELFARE FEDERATION OF CLEVELAND, HUMAN RELATIONS SERVICE (1968). 1001 Huron Rd., 44115. Tel 216 781-2944. Mrs. Lolette C. Hanserd, Dir. Inquiries answered, referrals made, consultation.
The Service is a project to assist the Welfare Federation and its member agencies in efforts to create equal opportunities for Negroes and members of other minority groups. Programs include updating agency policies relative to intergroup relations, developing guidelines for implementing such policies and developing new program and service approaches.

.1 Welfare Federation of Cleveland, Human Relations Service.
Files, 1968- . Includes correspondence, minutes of meetings, financial records, studies, reports, and documents dealing with the aims, programs, and history of the Service.

OH36a WESTERN RESERVE HISTORICAL SOCIETY (1867), LIBRARY (1867). 10825 East Blvd., 44106. Tel 216 721-5722. Kermit J. Pike, Chief Librn. Interlibrary loan, copying, inquiries answered, consultation.
Publ.: Guide to Manuscripts and Archives in the Western Reserve Historical Society (1970). Annual and special publications.

.1 Ashtabula County Anti-Slavery Society.
Records, 1835-37. 1 v. Preamble, constitution, list of members, music notes for various songs, minutes of meetings, and a list of names of memorialists for 1836. The first officers of this society were Mrs. L. Bissell, Mrs. Dr. Hawley, B.M. Cowles, and Mrs. A.C. Henderson.

.2 Blakeslee, Joel, 1787-1863
Papers, 1820-60. 1½ boxes. Personal and general correspondence and copies of speeches delivered by Blakeslee who resided in Colebrook and New Lyme, Ashtabula County, Ohio. Blakeslee, who was connected with the Ashtabula Historical Society (1850's), collected information and spoke on topics such as the early history of Ashtabula County, U.S. independence, and slavery.

.3 Bowen, George Washington, 1838-1908.
Notebook, 1851-62. 1 v. Bowen, who kept this notebook while attending the Cleveland Institute of Homeopathy, served in the 5th U.S. Colored Cavalry (1864), and later practiced medicine in Fort Wayne, Indiana.

.4 Brown, Ephraim, 1775-1845.
Papers, 1790-1887. 15 boxes, 17 v. Correspondence, land agreements, and deeds, account books, business papers, financial receipts, certificates, and court books, of Ephraim Brown of North Bloomfield, Ohio; merchant, land agent, postmaster, legislator, abolitionist, and justice of the peace, and his son, Ephraim A. Brown (1807-94), merchant. A native of Westmoreland, N.H., Brown settled in the Western Reserve in 1817; represented the Whig party in the Ohio State House and Senate, (1820's and 1830's); served as Ohio State road commissioner (1825); and participated in various business ventures, including railroad and turnpike companies (ca. 1830-43). The papers which relate to aforementioned activities, include account books relating to business enterprises; political, business, and personal correspondence (1801-45); plans and charts of the township of North Bloomfield (1814-20); docket books, (1832-43); and estate papers (1845-48).

.5 Canton Ladies Anti-Slavery Society, Canton, Ohio.
Records, 1836. 1 v. Preamble and constitution along with the minutes of three meetings.

.6 Coffinberry family.
Papers, 1767-1930. In part, transcripts (handwritten) and photocopies. Correspondence, jour-

nals, plats, maps, speeches, newspaper clippings, biographical and genealogical items, engravings, photos, pamphlets, political broadsides, memorabilia, and other papers of the relatives and ancestors of Maria Duane Coffinberry (1879-1952), a member of a prominent Cleveland family. The papers are primarily concerned with Henry D. Coffinberry (1841-1912), Civil War naval officer and Cleveland ship builder; and James M. Coffinberry (1818-91), editor and jurist. Includes references to the early settlement of Ohio and the Western Reserve, Civil War, nullification, abolitionism, secession, Reconstruction, and other topics.

OH36a.7 Fessenden, William Pitt, 1806-69.
Papers, 1837-69. ca. 1 ft. Lawyer, politician, and Cabinet officer. Chiefly letters received from friends and constituents, covering Fessenden's career as a lawyer in Portland, Me., his seven years as a member of the Maine House of Representatives, his service as a U.S. Representative and Senator from Maine, and his eight months as Secretary of the Treasury. The letters deal with the rise of the anti-slavery and temperance movements; the formation of the Republican party in Maine by anti-slavery Whigs such as Fessenden himself, the Liberty and Free Soil parties, and anti-slavery Democrats. Correspondents include Charles Francis Adams, Sr., John Appleton, Salmon Portland Chase, Samuel Cony, William George Crosby, Caleb Cushing, Neal Dow, Edward Kent, Hugh McCulloch, Anson Peaslee Morrill, Edwin M. Stanton, and Israel Washburn.

.8 Garvin, Charles H., d. 1968.
Papers, 1928-65. 5 boxes. Cleveland doctor and Negro community leader.

.9 Green, John P., 1845-1940.
Papers, 1869-1910. ca. 25 boxes. Cleveland lawyer active in local and state politics, especially the presidential campaign of William McKinley (1896), as well as an outspoken leader of the Negro community.

.10 Harmon family.
Papers, 1766-1885 (1795-1860). 14 boxes. Correspondence, diaries, financial accounts and receipts, and deeds and memoranda of sales, legal documents, estate papers, powers of attorney, tax records, notebooks, surveys, and other papers relating to the activities of various members of the family of Elias Harmon (1775-1851) who moved to the Western Reserve from Suffield, Conn. (1799) and settled in Manuta, Portage County. Papers relating to his activities include references to his interest in the Protection Life Insurance Company of Hartford, Franklin and Warren Railroad, Pennsylvania and Ohio Canal, and Independent Knights of Temperance, and in the fur trade and anti-slavery movement. Includes frequent references to state and national politics, banking policies, the anti-slavery and anti-masonic movements, and to general economic conditions, and a few references to the Millerites, and to lotteries in the 1830's and 1850's.

.11 Jackson, Andrew, II.
Account books, 1845-77. 2 v. Account book containing data on the purchase, sale, birth, marriage and death of slaves at the "Hermitage" (1845-77), and a receipt book of Andrew Jackson II and Sarah Jackson (1845-77).

.12 Jenkins, George K.
Papers, 1788-1877. 3½ boxes, 2 v. Collection of papers of George K. Jenkins, a Quaker school teacher and principal who resided in Mt. Pleasant, Ohio, including records of various yearly and monthly meetings of the Society of Friends, and of various Quaker organizations. Among Jenkins' papers are copies of speeches and other writings on topics such as slavery, tobacco, and patriotism, ca. 1830's; and a journal kept on a trip to various Quaker meetings in Ohio, West Virginia, Indiana, Michigan, and Canada, and in which Jenkins recorded his observations on these places as well as on the Wabash and Erie Canal, the Great Lakes, the St. Clair River, and the Free Soil Convention (Columbus, Ohio) April 30 to July 7, 1850. Also

includes minutes and record books of various meetings in the State of Ohio.

.13 Ladies Aid Society of Brocton, Ohio.
Records, January 14-February 15, 1866. 1 v. Minutes of meetings, a list of members, and a few poems by members of this Society, the object of which was "to furnish physical moral and intellectual aid to the colored people, who have recently been in bondage." This society was an auxiliary to the New York National Freedmen's Relief Association.

.14 Lyman, Carlos Parsons, b. 1838.
Papers, 1795-1915. 1½ boxes. Primarily letters and diaries of Lyman, who served as an officer in the 100th U.S. Colored Infantry (1861-65).

.15 Palmer, William Pendleton, 1861-1927. Collector.
Regimental papers of the Civil War. ca. 16 ft. Military and personal correspondence, muster rolls, official orders, ordnance and quartermaster reports, casualty lists, memoirs, diaries, descriptions of the engagements in which various regiments took part, and papers dealing with veterans' organizations after the war. Includes material concerned with Negro regiments enlisted in the southern states occupied by Union Armies; materials covering both sides of the war; letters and papers on slavery, abolition, the Underground Railway, plantation life, and other aspects of 19th century Negro life in the U.S.

.16 Perry, Samuel V., 1896-1968.
Papers, ca. 1920-68. Cleveland Municipal Court clerk, active in Negro organizations.

.17 Pitkin, Perley Peabody, d. 1891.
Papers, 1861-68. ca. 4 ft. Army officer. Correspondence, receipts, and other papers concerning the daily business of an assistant quartermaster for the Army of the Potomac from 1862-64. Includes papers dealing with the wages of those slaves known as "contrabands" within the Federal lines.

.18 Regimental papers of Civil War, 1861-65.
36 boxes, 17 v. Records of numerous regiments in both the Union and Confederate armies from thirty states. These include military correspondence, official orders, muster rolls, ordnance and quartermaster reports, and casualty lists. In addition to these there are also letters, diaries, and memoirs of soldiers serving in these regiments, and accounts of engagements. Among the records are those of the Cuyahoga County Military Committee (1861-68); papers of H.G. Crickmore and J.W. Paine of the 4th U.S. Colored Cavalry, and those of other Negro regiments. The bulk of the collection refers to Ohio regiments, although those from Massachusetts and Illinois are well represented.

.19 Riddle, Albert Gallatin, 1816-1902.
Papers, 1835-1901. ca. 3 ft. Author, lawyer, State representative, and U.S. representative from Ohio. Correspondence, mss of autobiographical writings, personal papers and certificates, files of law cases, newspaper clippings, souvenirs of official occasions in Washington, D.C., and other miscellaneous papers. The major part of the collection consists of letters received from many well-known Americans, including members of the government, lawyers, and prominent Ohioans. Most of these letters refer to matters of legal and political importance but some concern Riddle's books and his correspondents' opinions of them. Correspondents include Susan B. Anthony, Benjamin F. Butler, Simon Cameron, James A. Garfield, Joshua R. Giddings, Ulysses S. Grant, Horace Greeley, James Ford Rhodes, William H. Seward, and Gideon Welles.

.20 Risdon, Orlando Charles.
Papers, 1861-72. 3 boxes. Official and personal correspondence, military orders, and reports, vouchers and other financial papers, maps, photo and newspaper clippings relating primarily to Brigadier General Risdon, who helped to organize the 53rd U.S. Colored Infantry, saw action in the battles of Rich Mountain, W.Va., Middle Creek, Ky., Tazewell, Tenn., Arkansas Post, Ark., and Chickasaw, Port Gibson, Champion Hill, and Vicksburg, Miss.

.21 Robinson, Marius R., 1806-78.
Papers, 1830-65, 1877. 1 box. Correspondence, speeches and lectures, and newspaper clippings relating to the activities of Rev. Marius R. Robinson, an itinerant lecturer for the American Anti-Slavery Society of Ohio, (1836-39), and later editor of the Anti-Slavery Bugle (Salem, Ohio). Relating primarily to slavery, abolitionism, and emancipation, this collection includes copies of lectures and speeches delivered by Rev. Robinson (1830-65); a scrapbook of newspaper clippings relating to the Anti-Slavery Society of Lane Seminary, Cincinnati, Ohio, and the American Colonization Society, 1830-50; a notebook of arguments and refutations concerning theological subjects, 1834-40; correspondence between Rev. Robinson and his wife, Emily (1836-39); a journal for part of the year of 1840; and other materials such as typescript copy of article written on Rev. Robinson by Homer C. Boyle for the Daily News (Salem, Ohio), July 31, 1897.

.22 Smith, A. F.
Plantation records, 1851-52. 1 v. Including inventory of stock and implements, daily accounts and records of births and deaths of Negroes on the A.F. Smith plantation in Princeton, Miss., on which B.F. Comeggs was the overseer.

.23 Trimble, Allen, 1783-1870.
Papers, 1793-1868. 4 boxes. Personal and business correspondence, land deeds, surveys, financial records, and other personal papers of Trimble, Ohio State Representative, Senator, and Governor, and of other members of his family, including William Allen Trimble (1786-1821), soldier and U.S. Senator, and William Henry Trimble (1811-?), Ohio State Representative and soldier. These papers relate to a wide range of political and military subjects, including slavery, the Missouri Compromise, and the annexation of Texas.

.24 Western Anti-Slavery Society.
Records, 1857-64. 1 v. Minute book of the executive committee, including the bylaws and the annual reports of the executive committee, which were printed in the Anti-Slavery Bugle.

.25 Whittlesey, Elisha, 1783-1863.
Papers, 1804-63. Lawyer, U.S. Representative from Ohio, and public official. Correspondence, legal papers, accounts, receipts, deeds, and other papers relating to Whittlesey's law practice in Canfield, Ohio, and his career. Whittlesey's voluminous correspondence involves a large number of men prominent in national, state, and local affairs and is concerned with the Whig party, American Colonization Society, and other organizations.

CLEVELAND HEIGHTS

OH37   AMERICAN JEWISH CONGRESS, OHIO REGION. 2000 Lee Rd., 44118. Tel 216 321-7100. Robert Frankel, Dir. Inquiries answered, referrals made, consultation. The Congress works to foster the unity and creative survival of the Jewish people; to help Israel develop in freedom, security and peace; combat anti-Semitism and all forms of racism; to oppose communism, fascism and all forms of totalitarianism; to advance civil rights and civil liberties; to achieve full equality in a free society for all Americans; and other related objectives.

.1 American Jewish Congress, Ohio Region.
Miscellaneous. Books, pamphlets, articles, and other materials on race, prejudice, civil liberties, civil rights, anti-Semitism, and other subjects.

COLUMBUS

OH38   ANTI-DEFAMATION LEAGUE OF B'NAI B'RITH, OHIO-KENTUCKY REGIONAL OFFICE. 34 N. High St., Suite 404, 43215. Tel 614 221-5417. Hersh L. Adlerstein, Assoc. Dir.

OH39   COLUMBUS URBAN LEAGUE (1917). 1319 E. Broad St., 43205. Tel 614 252-5266. Robert D. Brown, Exec. Dir.

.1 Columbus Urban League.
Files, 1917- . Includes correspondence, minutes of meetings, financial records, reports, studies, investigations and documents dealing with the aims, history, and programs of the League.

OH40   COMMUNITY RELATIONS COMMITTEE OF THE UNITED JEWISH FUND AND COUNCIL OF COLUMBUS (1960). 34 N. High St., 43215. Tel 614 221-5417. Hersh L. Adlerstein, Dir. Inquiries answered, referrals made, film library.
The Council conducts a program of education and public relations on behalf of the Jewish community of Columbus, Ohio, in the areas of race relations, civil rights, urban affairs, political extremism, equal opportunity legislation, and other related areas.
Publ.: Newsletter, bimonthly.

.1 Community Relations Committee of the United Jewish Fund and Council of Columbus
Files, 1960- . Includes all publications of national Jewish civil rights agencies (Anti-Defamation League, American Jewish Committee, American Jewish Congress, etc.), plus several thousand books and pamphlets; file materials on race relations, civil rights and other related topics. Available for office use only.

OH41   OHIO CIVIL RIGHTS COMMISSION (1959). Room 234, 240 Parsons Ave., 43215. Tel 614 469-2785. Ellis L. Ross, Exec. Dir.
The Commission is a permanent, independent agency that works to eliminate discrimination in employment, public accommodations and housing. It receives, investigates, and initiates complaints; conciliates; issues cease-and-desist orders via the courts; arranges compliance agreements; and seeks court enforcement of its orders; conducts educational programs, issues studies; and conducts research studies of discrimination in employment, and of Ohio schools (1968-69).

.1 Ohio Civil Rights Commission.
Files of Annual reports, 1959- . ca. 10 items. Includes budget, law, complaints received, research projects, studies, reports, and materials concerning programs of the Commission.

OH42   OHIO CIVIL RIGHTS COMMISSION, SOUTHEAST REGION. Room 204, 240 Parsons Ave., 43215.

OH43   OHIO COUNCIL OF CHURCHES (1918). 18 W. Spring St., 43215. Tel 614 221-6571. Carlton N. Weber, Dir. Publ.: Reports.

.1 Ohio Council of Churches.
Files, 1967- . Includes correspondence, minutes of meetings, financial records, studies, reports, and documents dealing with the aims, history, and programs of the Council. Among the studies is Church Desegregation in a Metropolitan Area: A Study in Church and Community Linkage (1967) by Dr. Ira E. Harrison.

OH44   OHIO HISTORICAL SOCIETY (1885), ARCHIVES AND MANUSCRIPT DIVISION. 1813 N. High St., 43210. Tel 614 299-1179. David R. Larson, Chief, Arch. and Manuscript Div. Interlibrary loan, bibliographies prepared, copying, inquiries answered, referrals made, consultation.

.1 The Manuscript Department of the Ohio Historical Society contains considerable amounts of individual items or small groups of items relating to racial subjects, either separately housed or housed in vertical file folders, or as small segments of larger collections. Among the larger collections with sizable amounts of materials pertaining to the Negro are the following collections.

.2 — Bingham, John Armor, 1815-1900.
Papers, 1840-1900. ca. 2000 items (4 reels of microfilm). Republican member of U.S. House of Representatives from 1854-73, except for 1863-65; U.S. Minister to Japan (1873-85); prosecutor in trial of Lincoln murder "conspiracy;" member of Joint Committee of 15 on

Reconstruction; author of first section of 14th Amendment. Contains numerous printed speeches but relatively little else on important domestic issues. Correspondents include Benjamin F. Butler, Salmon P. Chase, Rutherford B. Hayes, John Sherman, Henry Stanberry, and Louis J. Weichmann.

OH44.3 — Bricker, John William, 1893- .
Papers, 1939-58. 132 boxes; 112 v. of clippings. His official papers as Governor of Ohio (1939-45) and as U.S. Senator (1947-59). Include correspondence folders on such race-related subjects as Wilberforce University, equal rights, segregation, and Little Rock, Ark.

.4 — Brown, John, 1800-59.
Boyd B. Stutler collection of John Brown papers, 1821-1961. 8 reels of microfilm. Microfilm copy (negative) made in 1961 from originals owned by Boyd B. Stutler. Abolitionist. Correspondence, documents, newspaper clippings, articles, speeches, radio scripts, broadsides, lithographs, and other material by or about Brown. Includes letter books (1846-50) of Perkins & Brown, wool dealers of Springfield, Mass.; family letters; letters of contemporary Americans referring to Brown; correspondence of his biographers; a typewritten bibliography of John Brown in periodical literature, 1845-1961, compiled by Stutler; notes prepared by William E. Connelley for his biography, John Brown (1900); and scrapbooks of Brown material compiled by Stutler, Connelley, Edward P. Bridgman, Franklin B. Sanborn, George L. Stearns, David N. Utter, and others. Described in Inventory and calendar of the John Brown, Jr. papers, published by the Ohio Historical Society in 1962, pp. 26-31.

.5 — Brown, John, 1821-95.
Papers, 1830-1932. 382 items. Farmer, and soldier, son of John Brown, the abolitionist. Correspondence, diaries (1858 and 1861), notes, newspaper clippings, and other papers. Subjects mentioned include the raid on Harpers Ferry (1859), farming in Ohio, sheep raising, tanning, phrenology, and spiritualism. Many of the letters are addressed to Brown's wife, Wealthy C. Hotchkiss. A letter book (1847-49) of the firm of Perkins & Brown, wood dealers of Springfield, Mass., contains 632 letters of John Brown, Sr. Other correspondents include Brown's grandfather, Owen Brown, his stepmother, Mary Ann Day Brown, his brothers, Jason, Owen, Salmon, and Frederick, his sisters, Ruth Brown Thompson, Ellen Brown Fablinger, and Annie Brown Adams, his mother-in-law, Maria P. Hotchkiss Wellman, his son-in-law, T.B. Alexander, other members of the Brown family, his school friend, George B. Delamater, fugitive slave Thomas Thomas, Orson S. Fowler, Franklin B. Sanborn, Nelson Sizer, Samuel Roberts Wells, and Jarvis J. Jefferson (regarding the remains of Watson Brown, who was killed at Harpers Ferry.)

.6 — Columbus (Ohio) Urban League, 1917- .
Files, 1917-62. ca. 50 boxes. Includes printed material, records, correspondence, minutes of meetings, and documents dealing with the aims, history, and programs of the League.

.7 — Curry, William L., 1839-1927.
Papers, 1832-1926. 14 boxes of microfilm rolls. Soldier, local office-holder, militia officer, Soldiers' Claims and Pension agent, G.A.R. leader, military historian of Ohio's part in Civil War. Includes materials on Ohio U.S. Colored Troops in the War.

.8 — Dick, Charles W.F., 1858-1945.
Papers, 1887-1928. 24 boxes and 19 letter-books. An Akron, Ohio, lawyer, Spanish American War soldier, member of U.S. House of Representatives (1898-1904), U.S. Senator (1904-11), member of Republican state and national committees. Letters, speeches, military papers. Correspondents include Joseph B. Foraker, Marcus A. Hanna, John Hay, Whitelaw Reid, Theodore Roosevelt, John Sherman, William H. Taft. Includes material on Brownsville, Tex., riot (1906) and on Republican politics, state and national (1895-1911).

.9 — Dunbar, Paul Laurence, 1872-1906.
Papers, 1873-1936. ca. 25 ft. Poet, lyricist, and author of Ohio. Correspondence, mss of Dunbar's prose, poetry, and lyrics, notebooks, financial and legal records, and scrapbooks. Correspondents include members of Dunbar's family, Edward H. Dodd, publisher, and Dr. Henry A. Tobey, friend and benefactor.

.10 — Fairbanks, Newton Hamilton, 1859-1937.
Papers, 1913-34. 1 box, 84 items. Springfield, Ohio, manufacturer and politician; brother of U.S. Vice-President Fairbanks; member of Ohio House of Representatives (1935-38), chairman of Ohio Republican State Central Committee. Correspondents include Theodore E. Burton, Harry M. Daugherty, Joseph B. Foraker, Myron T. Herrick, W.S. Scarborough, William H. Taft. Calendar of letters available.

.11 — Fess, Simeon D., 1861-1936.
Papers, 1882-1937. 39 boxes and 2 v. President of Antioch College, Yellow Springs, Ohio, U.S. House of Representatives (1913-23), U.S. Senate (1923-35). Correspondence is mainly with persons of minor importance but shows Fess's stand on issues of the day. On race, for example, Henry S. Lehr, president of Ohio Northern University (April 25, 1922), to Fess.

.12 — Free Will Baptists.
Records, 1819-1916. 1 ft. Constitution, minutes (1833-1911) of Ohio River Yearly meetings, records (1862-1915) of the Ohio River Yearly Meeting Ministers' Conference, records (1877-86) of the Meigs Quarterly Meetings, and others of the Free Will Baptists. Subjects covered in the yearly meetings include slavery and other topics.

.13 — Friends, Society of.
Papers, 1688-1937. 7 boxes. Minutes of Quaker monthly, quarterly and yearly meetings, mainly in Ohio, together with correspondence exchanged between Quaker groups. Emphasis on concern about slavery, Negroes, Indians, education, temperance and pacifism.

.14 — Garford, Arthur Lovett, 1858-1933.
Papers, 1877-1933. 72 ft. (ca. 37,000 items). Industrialist, politician, and philanthropist. Correspondence, speeches, articles, balance sheets, lists, account books, 2 scrapbooks (1912-16), a list of chairmen and officials of the Roosevelt Memorial Association, printed material, other papers, and photos., concerning the industrialization of Elyria, Ohio, financing the Republican party in Ohio, the participation of businessmen in politics, the Republican Progressive split in Ohio, 1912-16, the foreign-born and Negro voter, labor relations and labor in politics, and other related topics.

.15 — Gest, Erasmus, 1820-1908.
Papers, 1834-85. 12 v., 1 box, and 5 folders. Surveyor, engineer, and railroad magnate, of Cincinnati. Business and personal correspondence, primarily incoming; journals and diaries of trips; reminiscences; maps and mounted newspaper clippings; and printed reports, mostly of Ohio and Kentucky railroads. The material relates primarily to the development of transportation, but also covers the social, political, and economic life of Cincinnati in the late 1830's and early 1840's; abolition riots and the destruction of James G. Birney's press; and other subjects.

.16 — Giddings, Joshua Reed, 1795-1864.
Papers, 1821-66. 2 ft. (10 boxes). In part, transcripts. Ohio legislator and anti-slavery advocate. Correspondence and diaries (1838-39). Includes letters to members of Giddings' family, many of political interest; copies of four letters (1839-43) from Henry Clay; letters

(1861-66) from Giddings' son Grotius R. Giddings; and letters from political and anti-slavery leaders including Charles F. Adams, John A. Bingham, Salmon P. Chase, Thomas Corwin, Columbus Delano, William Dennison, Seth M. Gates, Horace Greeley, Joshua Leavitt, Samuel J. May, John G. Palfrey, Albert G. Riddle, Joseph M. Root, Gerrit Smith, Charles Sumner, Benjamin F. Wade, and Elisha Whittlesey. Other persons named include Lydia M.F. Child, Cassius M. Clay, Fred Douglas, Ammine Giddings, William C. Howells, Samuel May, James Mott, Theodore Parker, Thaddeus Stevens, Franklin E. Stowe, Lewis Tappan, Theodore Weld, William H. Burleigh, Garrett Davis, Henry H. Garnet, Thomas W. Higginson, Owen Lovejoy, Joseph J. Slavedealer, Israel Washburn, and others.

OH44.17 —— Gladden, Washington, 1835-1918.
Papers, 1847-1921. 62 boxes. Congregational minister in New York, Massachusetts, and at the First Congregational Church in Columbus, Ohio (1882-1918). Leader in the "Social Gospel" movement; author of many articles and books on civic, social, ethical and religious subjects. Consists mainly of sermons and lectures. Sermon subjects include "Booker Washington" and "William Lloyd Garrison."

.18 —— Hassaurek, Friedrich, 1832-85.
Papers, 1849-81. 7 boxes (ca. 1100 items). Vienna-born immigrant to Cincinnati (1849); editor and publisher of German newspapers, lawyer, Republican leader of German-Americans (1860); minister to Ecuador (1861-65); liberal Republican (1872); supporter of Tilden (1876). Letters in English and German discuss issues of the time including slavery and post-Civil War politics.

.19 —— Herbert, Thomas J., 1894- .
Papers, 1947-49. 22 boxes. Lawyer, Cleveland, Ohio; assistant attorney general of Ohio, elected Governor in 1946 (served two-year term); chairman of Federal Subversive Activities Control Board (1953-56); judge of Ohio Supreme Court (1956- .) Official governors' papers for 1947-48. Includes materials concerning segregation, the National Guard, and Wilberforce University.

.20 —— James family.
Papers, 1850-1904. 2 ft. Correspondence and other writings of John Hough (1800-81), lawyer, banker, and railroad entrepreneur, of Urbana, Ohio; John Henry James (1834-98), lawyer, inventor, businessman, and Democratic politician, of Urbana and Sandusky, Ohio; and John Henry James (1866-1950), lawyer and businessman, of Urbana and Sandusky. Includes a letter to Abraham Lincoln relating to a mutiny among Negro troops, and other subjects.

.21 —— Ku Klux Klan.
Papers, 1923-24. 1 box, ca. 120 items. Includes copies of bylaws, ritual, personnel lists, directives, notices of meetings from national and Ohio State and local offices.

.22 —— Lampson, Edward C., 1876-1957.
Papers, 1802-1930. 16 boxes (ca. 2500 items). Affiliated with the Jefferson (Ohio) Gazette for sixty years and a collector of historical materials relating to, and an amateur historian of, the Western Reserve area of Ohio. Items relating to slavery include "Andover Liberty Association," "Underground Railway," "John Brown Spoke in Jefferson" and "Black Passion" (narrative of the Sons of Liberty, 1859, in the Western Reserve).

.23 —— Lundy, Benjamin, 1789-1839.
Papers, 1821-1914. 1 box, 29 items. Correspondence and other papers by and about Lundy, including a letter by William Lloyd Garrison.

.24 —— McMillen, William L.
Papers, 1852-96. 1 box, 72 items. Colonel, 95th O.V.I. (1862-75). Includes correspondence with Salmon P. Chase, Henry Stanbery,

Charles Sumner, John Sherman, William T. Sherman, and others. Letters deal with lectures given in Columbus and Cincinnati, military affairs during the Civil War, and Louisiana politics during Reconstruction.

.25 —— Myers, George A., 1859-1930.
Papers, 1890-1929. ca. 3 ft. (ca. 4000 items). Ohio Negro politician, owner of the Hollenden Hotel Barber Shop, Cleveland, Ohio, and member of the Ohio Republican State Executive Committee. Correspondence relating to Ohio and national politics, especially to the Republican party and its candidates, conventions, campaigns, and issues; appointments and activities of the Marcus A. Hanna-William McKinley faction in the years 1892-1904; and the role and attitude of Negroes in the Republican party. Correspondents include Newton D. Baker, Jere A. Brown, Theodore E. Burton, Edward E. Cooper, Charles Dick, Marcus A. Hanna, Ralph W. Tyler, and Booker T. Washington.

.26 —— Osborne, Parker B.
Papers, 1808-50, 1877-83. 1 box (65 items). Includes the journal (1808-50) of Charles Osborne (1775-1850), his father, a Quaker preacher, abolitionist and editor of The Philanthropist (1817-18). Letters largely concerned with the father's position on abolition in The Philanthropist. Correspondents include Edward D. Mansfield, Edward Deering, Orson S. Murray, Wendell Phillips Garrison, George W. Julian, S.E. Wright.

.27 —— Parker, Daniel, 1781-1861.
Papers, 1845-47. 1 box (5 items). Typed transcript of autobiography, emphasizing life from 1805-37 in Pennsylvania, Kentucky, and Ohio. Diary of river-trip to New Orleans (1845).

.28 —— Polly, Peyton.
Papers, 1850-61. 1 box (119 items). Papers concerning the abduction case. Official correspondence and legal papers concerned with efforts to free the eight children of Peyton Polly, a free Negro, who were in 1850 kidnapped from Lawrence Co., Ohio, and enslaved in Kentucky and Virginia. Includes items by Ralph Lette, Joseph McCormick, Joel W. Wilson, and Ohio Governors Wood, Medill and Chase. Related to the William Henry Smith Collection.

.29 —— Rankin, John, 1793-1886.
Miscellaneous. 1 box. Presbyterian minister at Ripley, Ohio, whose home was a station on the "Underground Railway" for slaves escaping from across the Ohio River. Includes a typed copy of an autobiography (83 pp.), and reminiscences by members of his family about fugitives, including the "Eliza" of Uncle Tom's Cabin.

.30 —— Scott, Robert Kingston, 1826-1900.
Papers, 1849-1900. Physician and business man at Napoleon, Henry Co., Ohio. In Civil War attained rank of brigadier-general; head of Freedmen's Bureau in South Carolina. As a Republican, he was elected Governor of South Carolina in 1868; re-elected in 1870. Correspondence, accounts, a letter book, with emphasis on period 1861-72. Correspondents include D.H. Chamberlain, Martin K. Delaney, James G. Haly, T.J. Mackey, J.L. Neagle, James L. Orr.

.31 —— Siebert, Wilbur Henry, 1866-1961.
Materials on American loyalists, East Florida, and the underground railroad, ca. 1740-ca. 1860, 1911-47. 32 ft. In part, transcripts (typewritten). Professor of history at Ohio State University, Columbus, Ohio. Correspondence, transcripts of official documents and letters, excerpts and notes from articles and books, unpublished mss of writings by Siebert, and seminar papers and theses, relating to loyalists, East Florida, and the underground railroad. Almost half of the material deals with the underground railraod, the items being grouped by states.

.32 — Sun (Gus) Booking Agency, Inc.
Records, 1926-55. 40 ft. Correspondence,
payroll ledgers, theater audits, route cards,
and other papers (largely 1930-45). The
material relates to bookings of vaudeville acts,
tabloid shows, movies, and acts for county and
state fairs. Includes correspondence from
branch offices in Buffalo, N.Y.; Chicago, Ill.;
Des Moines, Iowa; Detroit, Mich.; Kansas City,
Mo.; Miami, Fla.; New York, N.Y.; Pittsburgh,
Pa.; St. Louis, Mo.; Toronto, Can.; and Berlin,
Germany, and from such performers as Louis
Armstrong and others.

.33 — Tappan, Benjamin, 1773-1857.
Papers, 1795-1873. ca. 650 items. In part,
transcripts (handwritten). Jurist and U.S.
Senator from Ohio. Correspondence, autobiography (1773-1823), journal (1839-44) kept
while a Senator, and other papers. The bulk of
the collection consists of Tappan's correspondence with his son, Eli Todd Tappan, newspaper editor and educator; his brother, Lewis
Tappan, New York abolitionist; and his law
partner, Edwin M. Stanton. The material pertains to the Ohio Democratic Party, the abolition issue, Texas annexation, the Oregon question, Tappan's work as a member of the Ohio
Canal Commission (1823-34), and other items.
Includes copies of 21 letters to Tappan from
Edwin M. Stanton.

.34 — Willis, Frank Bartlette, 1873-1928.
Papers, 1911-28. 29 boxes. Professor at Ohio
Northern University, Ada, Ohio; member of Ohio
State House of Representatives, of U.S. House
of Representatives; and Governor of Ohio
(1915-17); U.S. Senator (1921-28). Official
governor's and senatorial papers containing
many items in his campaign, patronage and
legislative files related to Negro participation
and Negro complaints, as well as Willis's
attitude on race relations.

OH45   OHIO STATE UNIVERSITY, CENTER FOR COMMUNITY
AND REGIONAL ANALYSIS (1963). 1775 S. College Rd.,
43210. Tel 614 293-3148. Henry L. Hunker, Dir.
The Center is an interdisciplinary organization which
focuses largely on research and service pertaining to
the urban community. It has worked with its parent
College of Administrative Science and a community
agency—Columbus Metropolitan Area Community Action Organization (CMACAO)—in developing a new two-
year program in business for the disadvantaged (largely
black) of the area.
Publ.: Studies and reports concerning activities of the
Center.

.1   Center for Community and Regional Analysis.
Files, 1963- . Includes correspondence, reports,
studies, investigations, and documents dealing with
the aims, programs, and history of the Center.

OH46   OHIO STATE UNIVERSITY, HUMAN RELATIONS INSTI-
TUTE. 43210. Tel 614 293-3148.
The Institute conducts studies on the minority relations
in the cities and related issues.

.1   Human Relation Institute.
Files. Includes correspondence, studies, reports,
and documents dealing with the aims, history, and
programs of the Institute. Among the studies made
is "Study of Prejudice Toward Minorities."

OH47   OHIO STATE UNIVERSITY LIBRARIES (1870), WILLIAM
OXLEY THOMPSON MEMORIAL LIBRARY (1870).
1858 Neil Ave., 43210. Tel 614 293-6152. Dr. Lewis C.
Branscomb, Dir. of Libraries. Interlibrary loan,
copying, typing, inquiries answered, referrals made,
consultation.

.1   Afro-Americana Collection.
Books (ca. 4000 v.) concerning the contributions of
the black American to American culture. Bibliography available. Restricted.
.2   Anti-Slavery Propaganda Collection.
ca. 2500 pamphlets. Microcards of originals

located in the Oberlin College Library. See
Oberlin College Library, Oberlin, Ohio; or Lost
Cause Press (publisher), Louisville, Ky., for more
complete description. Restricted.
.3   Facts on Film.
Papers, 1954-67. Microfilm. Contains materials
on civil rights and race relations in the South. See
Race Relations Information Center, Nashville,
Tenn., for a full description. Restricted.

DAYTON

OH48   AMERICAN FRIENDS SERVICE COMMITTEE (AFSC), COM-
MUNITY RELATIONS DIVISION, DAYTON REGIONAL
OFFICE. 915 Salem Ave., 45406. Tel 513 278-4225.
Matt H. Thomson, Exec. Dir.
The Committee works to provide an opportunity of service for young people and adults in the fields of community peace, education, summer work projects; develop open occupancy housing, and support service
overseas.

.1   American Friends Service Committee, Community Relations Division.
Files. Includes correspondence, minutes of meetings, financial records, studies, reports, and documents dealing with the aims, history, and programs
of the Division and Committee.

OH49   BLACK UMOJA SOCIETY. 309 N. Broadway, 45407. Tel
513 222-3591. Mrs. Thomas Herring, Pres.
The Society works to "liberate the minds of black
people from 400 years of brainwashing in the concept of
white superiority and black inferiority."

.1   Black Umoja Society.
Files. Includes correspondence, minutes of meetings, financial records, studies, reports, investigations, and documents dealing with the history,
aims, and programs of the Society.

OH50   CATHOLIC INTERRACIAL COUNCIL. 4125 Oakridge Dr.,
45417. Tel 513 263-9892. Mrs. Ethel Dillingham, Dir.

OH51   CITY OF DAYTON, HUMAN RELATIONS COUNCIL (1962).
Room 212, 11 W. Monument Ave., 45402. Tel 513 222-
3441. Edward A. King, Exec. Dir. Consultation.
The Council works to improve intergroup relations;
administers anti-discrimination policies; gathers facts
about the nature and extent of discrimination, intergroup
relations problems, population changes and movements,
employment, education and housing; investigates complaints; seeks to prevent discrimination through public
education, information, and affirmative action programs. Formerly Human Relations Commission.
Publ.: Directory of Human Relations Resources (1967);
HRC Newsletter, bimonthly; Pamphlets and
brochures.

.1   Human Relations Council.
Files, 1962- . Includes correspondence, minutes of
meetings, financial records, studies, reports, investigations, and documents dealing with the aims,
history, and programs of the Council.
.2   Intergroup Relations Collection.
Miscellaneous. Contains publications, newspaper
clippings, books, and pamphlets.

OH52   DAYTON ALLIANCE FOR RACIAL EQUALITY. 333 Westwood Ave., 45417. Tel 513 222-3591. Charles E. Tate,
Chmn.
The Alliance works "to help lay the groundwork for the
liberation struggle of black people."

.1   Dayton Alliance for Racial Equality.
Files. Includes correspondence, minutes of meetings, financial records, studies, reports, and other
documents dealing with the history, aims, and programs of the Alliance.

OH53   DAYTON COMMITTEE ON CIVIL RIGHTS. 240 Schenck
Ave., 45409. Tel 513 298-2866. D.W. Coughnour,
Chmn.
The Committee works to promote progress in the human
needs of Negroes in the areas of education, housing,

employment, police-community relations, municipal services, and health and welfare.

.1   Dayton Committee on Civil Rights.
Files. Includes correspondence, minutes of meetings, financial records, studies, reports, investigations, and documents dealing with the aims, history, and programs of the Committee.

OH54   DAYTON COUNCIL ON HUMAN RIGHTS. 3223 Hoover Ave., 45407. Tel 513 268-6869. Clarence Bowman, Pres.
The Council works "to bring diverse groups together for talk and deliberation and occasional pooling of efforts on common issues."

.1   Dayton Council on Human Rights.
Files. Includes correspondence, minutes of meetings, financial records, studies, reports, investigations, and documents dealing with the history, aims, and programs of the Council.

OH55   DAYTON URBAN LEAGUE (1947). 184 Salem Ave., 45406. Tel 513 461-5810. Charles L. Sanders, Exec. Dir.
The League promotes equal opportunity in employment, education, housing, and health and welfare. It conducts broad educational programs designed to relieve racial tension and promotes good intergroup relations; workshops, speeches, and seminars; and cooperates with other intergroup relations organization.

.1   Dayton Urban League.
Files, 1947- . Includes correspondence, minutes of meetings, reports, investigations, studies, and documents dealing with the aims, history, and programs of the League.

OH56   DAYTON VIEW PROJECT (1968). 816 Ferguson Ave., 45407. Tel 513 276-3995. Joseph D. Wine, Coordinator.
The Project was established by the City of Dayton to effect physical, civic, educational, cultural, and racial stability in the Dayton View area of the city. It conducts neighborhood conservation activities; cooperates with Multiple Motivation; includes a Federal Code Enforcement grant; and maintains a site office maintained by the City of Dayton.
Publ.: The Dayton View Keystone, quarterly newsletter; Materials on programs instituted by the Project, dealing with educational, social, racial and other issues confronting the community.

OH57   DUNBAR HOUSE STATE MEMORIAL. 219 Summit St., 45407. Tel 513 228-1495.
The Dunbar House was the residence of a Negro poet, Paul Laurence Dunbar and is furnished with his personal belongings and mss of his writings.

OH58   FREEDOM, ORGANIZATION, RIGHTS, CITIZENSHIP, EQUALITY (FORCE). 1911-15 W. Third St., 45417. Tel 513 268-1621. James C. Kickerson, Exec. Secy.
FORCE works "to unite the Negro community through organization to bring about a beneficial change in the political, economic, social and psychological areas."

.1   Freedom, Organization, Rights, Citizenship, Equality (FORCE).
Files. Includes correspondence, minutes of meetings, financial records, reports, studies, investigations, and other documents dealing with the aims, history, and programs of the organization.

OH59   JEWISH COMMUNITY COUNCIL OF DAYTON, COMMUNITY RELATIONS COMMITTEE (1948). Room 240, 184 Salem Ave., 45406. Tel 513 222-5588. Robert Fitterman, Exec. Dir.
The Council works to promote equality of opportunity, religious liberty, freedom of thought, speech, press and association; understanding and mutual respect among religious and ethnic groups.
Publ.: CRC Newsletter, monthly; JCC News, monthly.

.1   Jewish Community Council of Dayton, Community Relations Committee.
Files, 1948- . Includes correspondence, minutes of meetings, financial records, studies, reports, and documents dealing with the aims, history, and programs of the Council.

OH60   NATIONAL ASSOCIATION FOR THE ADVANCEMENT OF COLORED PEOPLE (NAACP), DAYTON. 1405 W. Third St., 45407. Tel 513 222-2172. Mrs. Miley O. Williamson, Exec. Secy.
The NAACP works to eliminate discrimination and segregation from all aspects of public life in America; to secure a free ballot for every qualified American citizen; to seek justice in the courts; to secure legislation banning discrimination and segregation; to secure equal job opportunities based upon individual merit without regard to race, religion or national origin; to end mob violence and police brutality.

.1   National Association for the Advancement of Colored People, Dayton.
Files. Includes correspondence, minutes of meetings, financial records, studies, reports, investigations, and documents dealing with the aims, history, and programs of the Association.

OH61   NATIONAL COUNCIL OF NEGRO WOMEN, DAYTON COUNCIL. 4136 Oakridge Dr., 45417. Tel 513 263-7910. Mrs. Sanford Davis, Pres.
The Council's program areas include prevention of delinquency, improvement of civil and human rights, adult education, camp opportunities, recreation facilities, Christian education, furnishing scholarships, and developing new careers.

.1   National Council of Negro Women, Dayton Council.
Files. Includes correspondence, minutes of meetings, financial records, studies, reports, and documents dealing with the aims, history, and programs of the Council.

OH62   PRESBYTERIAN INTERRACIAL COUNCIL. 3211 Lakeview Ave., 45406. Tel 513 461-5810. Rev. James I. Davis, Dir.
The Council works "to apply scriptural futherance of racial justice and integration in all phases of the church's life and in the community at large in fulfillment of the principles of our democratic society."

.1   Presbyterian Interracial Council.
Files. Includes correspondence, minutes of meetings, financial records, and other documents dealing with the aims, programs, and history of the Council.

OH63   THE UNITED METHODIST CHURCH, COMMISSION ON ARCHIVES AND HISTORY (1885), LIBRARY AND ARCHIVES OF THE EVANGELICAL UNITED BRETHREN CHURCH (1947). 601 W. Riverview Ave., 45406. Tel 513 222-3861. Miss Esther George, Librn. Interlibrary loan, literature searches, copying, inquiries answered, consultation.

.1   Commission on Christian Social Action, Evangelical United Brethren Church.
Records, 1950-68. ca. 3000 items. Includes correspondence, minutes, financial records, studies, reports and documents dealing with the aims, history, and programs of the Commission.

.2   The Evangelical United Brethren Church.
Archives, 1800-1968. Materials relating to the history of The Evangelical United Brethren Church and its predecessor bodies: The United Evangelical (1894-1922); The Evangelical Church (1922-46); the Evangelical Association (1803-1922); and the Church of the United Brethren in Christ (1800-1946). The Evangelical United Brethren began in 1946 and closed in 1968, when it combined with the Methodist Church.

DELAWARE

OH64   OHIO WESLEYAN UNIVERSITY, LIBRARY. 43015. Tel 614 363-1261. Edward S. Moffat, Librn.

.1   Finley, James Bradley, 1781-1856.
Papers, 1814-53. 1480 items and 5 v. Methodist clergyman of Ohio and missionary to the Wyandot Indians. Correspondence, diary and recipe book, addresses, articles, ms of autobiography (1853), sermons, commissions, and other papers, relating to slavery, temperance, religion, and other subjects.

FREMONT

OH65   THE RUTHERFORD B. HAYES LIBRARY (1916), 1337
       Hayes Ave., Spiegel Grove, 43420. Tel 419 332-2081.
       Watt P. Marchman, Dir. Interlibrary loan, copying,
       typing, inquiries answered, consultation.

       .1   Beecher, Henry Ward.
            Papers, 1867-86. ca. 86 items. Congregational
            clergyman. Includes papers relating to the Negro
            and related subjects.
       .2   Hayes family.
            Miscellaneous. Papers of Rutherford B. Hayes
            (1822-1893), Governor of Ohio, U.S. Congressman,
            and nineteenth President of the U.S.; Mrs. Hayes
            (d. 1889); and their children. Includes corre-
            spondence, diaries, scrapbooks, photographs,
            paintings, and Hayes' Library of Americana. The
            materials concern Reconstruction removal of the
            Union Army from Florida, Louisiana and South
            Carolina; Hayes' initiation of strong civil service
            reforms; education and schools for Freedmen,
            Peabody Education Fund, John F. Slater Fund, Lake
            Mohunk Conference; ratification of 15th Amend-
            ment, race relations, Southern Society for Promo-
            tion of Race Conditions and Problems in South,
            Civil War, slavery, and other subjects.
       .3   Materials relating to Negroes.
            Miscellaneous. Includes books (ca. 400), pam-
            phlets, periodicals, reports, and mss by and about
            Negroes.
       .4   Smith, William Henry.
            Papers, 1864-95. ca. 60 items. Ohio and Illinois
            newspaper editor, Associated Press general man-
            ager, and historian. Includes portions of an un-
            published ms on history of slavery.
       .5   Stowe, Harriet Beecher.
            Papers, 1872-90. ca. 68 items. Ohio, Massachu-
            setts, and Connecticut author and abolitionist. In-
            cludes materials concerning Negroes and the aboli-
            tion of slavery.
       .6   Thompson, Richard Wigginton.
            Papers, 1845-1945. ca. 5 ft. Attorney for the
            Chiriqui Improvement Company (1859-62); Secre-
            tary of Navy (1877-80). Personal papers and pa-
            pers of the Chiriqui Improvement Company con-
            taining material relating to the Negro. Territory
            in Western Panama was under consideration for
            resettling freed slaves early in the Lincoln admin-
            istration. Arrangements had been made for trans-
            portation, etc. Papers also include correspon-
            dence, contracts, surveys, maps, minutes books,
            and other materials.
       .7   Whittier, John Greenleaf.
            Papers, 1872-89. ca. 81 items. Massachusetts
            poet and abolitionist. Includes materials pertaining
            to Negroes and the abolition of slavery.

HUDSON

OH66   HUDSON LIBRARY AND HISTORICAL SOCIETY. 22 Aurora
       St., 44236. Tel 216 863-6658. Mrs. Virginia O.
       Grazier, Librn.

       .1   Brown, John, 1800-1859.
            Papers. Abolitionist. Includes mss and biogra-
            phies by and about John Brown.

KENT

OH67   KENT STATE UNIVERSITY, CENTER FOR URBAN RE-
       GIONALISM (1965), URBAN STUDIES LIBRARY (1969).
       Lowry Hall, 44240. Tel 216 672-2232. James G. Coke,
       Dir.
       The Center was established to assist in developing a
       regional view of urban problems, and has developed a
       research program focusing on problems of poverty and
       housing with particular emphasis on the northeast Ohio
       region.
            Publ.: Bibliographies used in University Black Studies
                 program, and resource and bibliographic materi-
                 als used by scholars of intergroup relations as-
                 sociated with the Center.

       .1   Urban Studies Library.
            The library and information service is a semi-
            automatic information retrieval system geared to
            the needs of academic and professional users.

OH68   KENT STATE UNIVERSITY LIBRARIES (1913). 44240. Tel
       216 672-2962. Hyman W. Kritzer, Dir. Interlibrary
       loan, copying.

       .1   Anti-Slavery Propaganda Collection.
            ca. 2500 pamphlets. Microcards of originals
            located in the Oberlin College Library. See Ober-
            lin Library, Oberlin, Ohio; or Lost Cause Press
            (publisher), Louisville, Ky., for more complete
            description.
       .2   Facts on Film.
            Papers, 1954-67. Microfilm. Contains materials
            on civil rights and race relations in the South. See
            Race Relations Information Center, Nashville,
            Tenn., for a full description.
       .3   Materials pertaining to Negroes.
            Miscellaneous. Monographs (ca. 5000) on history
            and accomplishments of Negroes, slavery and the
            slave trade; Negro newspapers, including all titles
            (209) listed in Library of Congress bibliography
            Negro Newspapers on Microfilm, plus 17 other
            titles including three editions of the Baltimore
            Afro-American and a complete file of the Cleve-
            land Call and Post.
       .4   Wright, Richard.
            Letters, 1938-51. Letters (ca. 10) from Richard
            Wright to Joe C. Brown; and one letter from Wright
            to Ben Burns (1951); typescript of Wright's ''I
            Chose Exile,'' n.d. (1951?), 11 pp.

MANSFIELD

OH69   MANSFIELD PUBLIC LIBRARY (1897). 43 W. Third St.,
       44902. Tel 419 524-1041. A.T. Dickinson, Jr., Dir.
       Interlibrary loan, copying, typing, inquiries answered,

       .1   Sherman, John, 1823-1900.
            Books. ca. 1000 v. Personal library of Sen. Sher-
            man. Includes contemporary published accounts
            relating to question of slavery, abolition, westward
            expansion, Civil War, Sherman biography, and other
            subjects.

MASSILLON

OH70   MASSILLON URBAN LEAGUE (1936). 412 Massillon Bldg.,
       44646. Tel 216 833-4149. Alfred J. Johnson, Exec. Dir.

MIDDLETOWN

OH71   MIAMI UNIVERSITY, MIDDLETOWN CAMPUS (1966),
       GARDNER-HARVEY LIBRARY (1966). 4200 Manchester
       Rd., 45042. Tel 513 422-2741. Virginia Brown, Head
       Librn. Interlibrary loan, copying, inquiries answered.

       .1   Papers relating to Negroes.
            Miscellaneous. ca. 25 items. Small collection of
            original materials on slavery including letters of
            Cassius M. Clay, Kentucky abolitionist. Among
            related subjects are emancipation and Liberian
            colonization.

OBERLIN

OH72   OBERLIN COLLEGE (1833), CARNEGIE LIBRARY (1833).
       Oberlin College, 44074. Tel 216 774-1221. Eileen
       Thornton, Librn. Interlibrary loan, copying.

       .1   Anti-Slavery Propaganda collection.
            Books and papers, prior to 1863 (with a few ex-
            ceptions), the earliest item being dated 1777. ca.
            2800 items. Originally the emphasis was on anti-
            slavery, although around 100 pro-slavery publica-
            tions were included. The collection is being ex-
            panded currently, with equal emphasis on both sides
            of the controversy. The collection was formed
            around a gift from the estate of William Goodell and
            many of these items have marginal annotations in

Goodell's handwriting. The collection includes books, reports, speeches, tracts, and private letters bearing upon the subjects of slavery, abolition, the underground railroad, and related topics. The pamphlets cover annual reports, proceedings, constitutions, platforms and addresses of anti-slavery societies, the moral and humanitarian arguments, and religious aspects of the controversy; slavery and the law; the economic argument against slavery; anti-colonizationism; vindication of the Negro race; vindication of abolitionist principles; collections of speeches and writings of anti-slavery men; the moderate anti-slavery point of view; travelers' observations of slavery; slave narratives; biographies of leaders of the anti-slavery movement; children's literature, poetry, songs, anthologies and gift books; newspapers and periodicals; the anti-slavery controversy in politics; slavery and the Civil War; the pro-slavery reply to the anti-slavery movement; and the British anti-slavery movement.

.2 Goodell, William. collector.
Papers. Includes anti-slavery works representing the movement from the time of its inception in the U.S. Mss and early abolitionist newspapers are also in the collection.

.3 Monroe, James, 1821-98.
Papers, 1841-98. ca. 6080 items. Professor, diplomat, and U.S. Representative from Ohio. Correspondence, account books, ledgers, notes, and other papers, pertaining to Monroe's public career, his work with the American Anti-Slavery Society, and his other activities.

OXFORD

OH73 MIAMI UNIVERSITY, ALUMNI LIBRARY (1824). 45056. Tel 513 529-2161. Charles D. Churchwell, Librn. Interlibrary loan.

.1 Anti-Slavery Propaganda Collection.
ca. 2500 pamphlets. Microcards of originals located in the Oberlin College Library. See Oberlin College Library, Oberlin, Ohio; or Lost Cause Press (publisher), Louisville, Ky., for more complete description.

OH74 MIAMI UNIVERSITY, SCRIPPS FOUNDATION FOR RESEARCH IN POPULATION PROBLEMS (1922). 218 Harrison Hall, 45056. Tel 513 529-2812.
The Foundation conducts demographic research with emphasis on local, regional and national population growth in the U.S. and the quality and distribution of population growth.

.1 Scripps Foundation for Research in Population Problems.
Files, 1922- . Correspondence, minutes of meetings, financial records, studies, investigations, reports, and other documents dealing with the history, aims, and programs of the Foundation. The Library is made up chiefly of census material.

RIPLEY

OH75 JOHN RANKIN HOUSE MUSEUM. 45167.
The Rankin House was a station on the underground railroad and home of abolitionist minister John Rankin.

SALEM

OH76 SALEM PUBLIC LIBRARY. 821 E. State St., 44460. Tel 216 332-4938. Nellie L. Glass, Librn. Interlibrary loan, copying, inquiries answered, referrals made, consultation.

.1 Anti-Slavery Bugle.
Newspaper, March 20, 1846-June 18, 1859. Includes originals and microfilm copy. Published in Salem, Ohio, usually weekly.

.2 Materials relating to Negroes.
Miscellaneous, 1849-76. Books, correspondence, and pamphlets concerning anti-slavery, Quakers, abolition, Civil War, slavery, and related subjects.

SHAKER HEIGHTS

OH77 SHAKER HEIGHTS PUBLIC LIBRARY (1938). 3450 Lee Rd., 44120. Tel 513 991-2030. Miss Margaret Campbell, Dir. Interlibrary loan, bibliographies prepared, copying, inquiries answered.

.1 Ludlow Community Association.
Records, 1964- . Newsletters, pamphlets, film and mss covering Ludlow, Moreland, and Lomond communities; newsletters of the Ludlow Community Association; a film covering the activities of the Ludlow Community and mss of Winfield G. Leathers and Saul Friedman concerning housing discrimination in Ludlow.

.2 Mandel, Bernard.
Papers, 1967- . Educator. Includes the ms of Young People's History of the United States; written for use at Rawlings Junior High School, Cleveland, Ohio, in an attempt to fill gaps in American history regarding Afro-Americans.

SPRINGFIELD

OH78 CONGRESS OF RACIAL EQUALITY (CORE). 425 S. Center St., 45506. Tel 513 322-7184. Charles Honeycutt, Chmn.

OH79 SPRINGFIELD URBAN LEAGUE. 1526 S. Yellow Springs St., 45506. Tel 513 323-4603. William L. Williams, Exec. Dir.

.1 Springfield Urban League.
Files. Correspondence, minutes of meetings, financial records, studies, reports, and other materials dealing with aims, history, and programs of the League.

TOLEDO

OH80 OHIO CIVIL RIGHTS COMMISSION, NORTHWEST REGION (1959). 410 Gardner Bldg., 506 Madison Ave., 43604. Tel 419 241-9164. Emerson E. Cole, Northwest Regional Dir. Referrals made, consultation.
The Commission takes charges, investigates, writes up, submits the cases to Columbus for a decision based on the information found during the investigation; provides help, consultation and referrals when necessary; and other activities in the fields of employment, housing, public accommodation, and other places where discrimination is present.

OH81 TOLEDO AREA INTERFAITH CONFERENCE ON RELIGION AND RACE. 401 Board of Trade Bldg., 43604. Tel 419 242-7401. Rev. Leonard E. Klippen, Exec. Dir.

OH82 TOLEDO BOARD OF COMMUNITY RELATIONS (1946). 564 N. Erie, 43624. Tel 419 255-1500.
The Board works to promote interracial cooperation within the community; to assemble, analyze and disseminate authentic and factual data relating to intergroup relationships; and exercises compliance powers in cases of employment discrimination.
Publ.: Annual Report.

.1 Toledo Board of Community Relations.
Files, 1946- . Includes correspondence, minutes of meeting, financial records, studies, reports, investigations, and documents dealing with the aims, history, and programs of the Board.

TROY

OH83 TROY HUMAN RELATIONS COMMISSION. 320 W. Race St., 45373. Tel 513 335-2035. H.N. Gourley, Chmn.
The Commission works to study problems of intergroup relations; to enlist cooperation of all racial groups and community organizations to combat prejudice and discrimination; to receive and investigate complaints in matters of education, housing, and employment.

.1 Troy Human Relations Commission.
Files. Includes correspondence, minutes of meet-

ings, financial records, studies, investigations, reports, and other documents dealing with the aims, history, and programs of the Commission.

WARREN

OH84   WARREN PUBLIC LIBRARY (1888). 120 High St., N.W., 44481. Tel 216 392-7761. Clark S. Lewis, Head Librn. Interlibrary loan, bibliographies prepared, copying, inquiries answered.

.1   Warren Urban League.
Studies, 1948, 1964. 2 items. Includes a study (1964) of the economic and cultural activities in the Warren area as they relate to minority people, by W. Robert Smalls, director; and a review of the program and activities of the Warren Urban League as it relates to the needs of the Negro population of Warren, Ohio, conducted (1948) by Warren M. Banner, director of Research and Community Projects, National Urban League.

OH85   WARREN URBAN LEAGUE. 130 Pine Ave., S.E., 44481. Tel 216 394-4316. Arthur Beeler, Exec. Dir.

.1   Warren Urban League.
Files. Correspondence, minutes of meetings, financial reports, records, studies, and other materials dealing with the aims, history, and programs of the League.

WILBERFORCE

OH86   CENTRAL STATE UNIVERSITY (1887), HALLIE Q. BROWN MEMORIAL LIBRARY (1959). 45384. Tel 513 376-6011. Mrs. Wanda L. Crenshaw, Dir., Univ. Library. Interlibrary loan, bibliographies prepared, literature searches, copying, typing, inquiries answered, referrals made, consultation.
Publ.: Index to Periodical Articles by and about Negroes (formerly Index to Selected Periodicals), annually.

.1   Afro-American Studies Collection.
ca. 1000 paperbacks. Basic books on the life and history of black Americans.
.2   Central State University.
Archives, 1887- . Includes correspondence, minutes of board meetings, financial records, records of admission, and other materials relating to the history and administration of the University. Located in Bundy Hall.
.3   Negro Collection.
Miscellaneous. ca. 5000 items. Includes materials by and about the Negro covering bibliographies, religion, sociology, science, literature, art, music, history, travel, and some subject matter pertaining to Africa.

OH87   JOURNAL OF HUMAN RELATIONS (1952). Central State University, P.O. Box 307, 45384. Tel 513 372-9261. Don Werkheiser, Editor.
The policy of the Journal of Human Relations is to apply an interdisciplinary approach to understanding of the human condition; a search for scientific enlightenment toward psychosocial awareness; and practical programs which may lead toward "better life in larger freedom."
Publ.: Journal of Human Relations, quarterly.

.1   Journal of Human Relations.
Files, 1952- . Correspondence, financial records, studies, reports, investigations. Includes complete run of the Journal, mss submitted and/or published, and other materials concerning history and aims of the Journal; and such subjects as race relations, Negroes, discrimination, and segregation.

OH88   WILBERFORCE UNIVERSITY (1856), CARNEGIE LIBRARY (1856). 45384. Tel 513 372-8074. Richard Z. Smith, Librn. Interlibrary loan, inquiries answered, referrals made.

.1   African Methodist Episcopal Church.
Records. Includes the minutes of Church confer-

ences, financial records, correspondence, lists of prominent persons in the Church since its inception, and other materials relating to the history of the Church.
.2   Afro-American Studies collection.
ca. 1000 paperbacks. Basic books on the life and history of black Americans.
.3   Arnett, Benjamin William, Bp., 1838-1906.
Papers, 1860-1900. ca. 1000 items. Encyclopedist, author, editor, politician, educator, and bishop of the African Methodist Episcopal Church. Records and minutes of the AME Church conferences, reports, addresses, articles, and books relating to the Negro.
.4   Coppin, Levi Jenkins, Bp., 1848-1923.
Papers, 1888-1920. ca. 350 items. Author, editor, and bishop of the African Methodist Episcopal Church. Includes books, pamphlets, and records of the African Methodist Episcoapl Church.
.5   Daniel Alexander Payne Collection of Negro Life and History.
ca. 4500 items. Includes books, mss, and pictures. Payne (1811-93) was a bishop in the AME Church.
.6   Hill, Charles Leander.
Papers, 1948-56. ca. 2000 items. Philosopher, theologian, author, translator, educator, and president of Wilberforce University. Correspondence, articles, programs, and other papers relating to philosophy, religion, politics, the American Negro, and the Protestant Reformation.
.7   Mills, Clarence Harvey, 1892-1949.
Correspondence, 1930-47. 43 items. Philologist and professor at Wilberforce University. Correspondence with language professors, college presidents, publishers, and friends relating to articles, trips, and books.
.8   Ransom, Reverdy Cassius, Bp., 1861-1959.
Papers, 1893-1951. ca. 1000 items. In part, transcripts. Editor, author, and bishop of the African Methodist Episcopal Church. Letters, literary mss, and clippings.
.9   Scarborough, William Sanders, 1854?-1926.
Papers, 1870-1926. ca. 1000 items. Philologist, author, president of Wilberforce University, and Negro leader. Correspondence pertaining to Negroes, mss of Scarborough's writings, citations, scrapbooks, memorabilia, photos., and a collection of Negro publications that have ceased.

WILMINGTON

OH89   WILMINGTON COLLEGE, LIBRARY (1863). 45177. Tel 513 382-0951. Dr. Willis Hall, Curator.

.1   Friends, Society of. Wilmington Yearly Meeting.
Archives, 1810-1966. ca. 26 ft. Records of births, deaths, marriages, and burial grounds, and other records of the Quarterly and Monthly Meetings which are members of the Wilmington Yearly Meeting. Prior to 1892, many of the Meetings were members of the Ohio Yearly Meeting or the Indiana Yearly Meeting. Includes much source material on Quaker history in Southwestern Ohio, slavery, abolition movement, and related subjects.

WOOSTER

OH90   BELL AND HOWELL COMPANY, MICRO PHOTO DIVISION. Drawer E, Old Mansfield Rd., 44691. Tel 216 264-6666. Larry E. Block, Mgr., Projs. Opers.
As micropublishers, the Company provides the educational community with "significant information from the most qualified sources."
Publ.: Bulletin; The Micro Photo Reader, quarterly newsletter.

.1   Bell and Howell, Micro Photo Division.
Newspapers, 1893-1968. ca. 46 titles. Microfilm copies of Negro newspapers. Among those included are Washington, (D.C.) Afro-American (1932-68); New Crusader (1940-68), Chicago, Ill.; Gary American (1927-68), Gary, Ind.; Baltimore Afro-American (1883-1968), Baltimore, Md.; New Jersey Afro-

American (1941-68), Newark, N.J.; Cleveland Call and Post (1934-68), Cleveland, Ohio; Oklahoma City Black Dispatch (1948-68), Oklahoma City, Okla.; Philadelphia Afro-American (1935-68), Philadelphia, Pa.; Dallas Express (1930-68), Dallas, Tex.; Houston Informer (1930-68), Houston, Tex.; Journal and Guide (1916-68), Norfolk, Va.

.2 Black Library in Microform.
Includes ca. 10,000 titles from the Negro Collection at Atlanta University Library, with a bibliography by fellows of the Center for African and African-American Studies.

YELLOW SPRINGS

OH91 YELLOW SPRINGS HUMAN RELATIONS COMMISSION.
Municipal Bldg., Dayton St., 45384. Tel 513 767-7202.
Russell Hollister, Chmn.
The Commission works through citizen committees established by the agency to maintain the elimination of discrimination in public accommodations, employment and housing.

.1 Yellow Springs Human Relations Commission.
Files. Includes correspondence, minutes of meetings, financial records, studies, reports, investigations, committee reports, and other documents dealing with the history, aims, and programs of the Commission.

YOUNGSTOWN

OH92 MAYOR'S HUMAN RELATIONS COMMISSION, FAIR EMPLOYMENT PRACTICES COMMITTEE (1959). City Hall, Boardman and Phelps Sts., 44503. Tel 216 744-4181.
The Committee works to process complaints concerning discrimination in employment; and to improve and develop good intergroup relations.

.1 Mayor's Human Relations Commission, Fair Employment Practices Committee.
Files, 1959- . Includes correspondence, minutes of meetings, financial records, studies, reports, and documents dealing with the aims, history, and programs of the Committee.

OH93 YOUNGSTOWN AREA DEVELOPMENT CORPORATION (1968). 1002 Central Tower Bldg., 44503. Tel 216 746-5682. J. Ronald Pittmann, Exec. Dir. Inquiries answered, consultation.
The Corporation, a non-profit agency, seeks to develop minority entrepreneurship, and to help create dynamic programs to develop low-cost housing and other programs to improve the inner-city.

OH94 YOUNGSTOWN AREA URBAN LEAGUE. 1203 Wick Bldg., 44503. Tel 216 744-8603. Clifford Gates, Exec. Dir.

.1 Youngstown Area Urban League.
Files. Records, reports, correspondence, and other papers concerning the programs and aims of the League.

XENIA

OH95 XENIA AREA HUMAN RELATIONS COUNCIL (1969). City Hall, 101 N. Detroit St., 45385. Tel 513 372-7611.
David O. McCoy, Chmn. Inquiries answered, referrals made.
The Council works to promote mutual understanding and respect among all racial, religious, cultural and nationality groups; and to discourage and prevent discriminatory practices against such groups. Formerly Xenia Human Relations Commission.

.1 Xenia Area Human Relations Council.
Files. Includes correspondence, minutes of meetings, financial records, studies, investigations, reports, and other documents dealing with the aims, history, and programs of the Commission.

OKLAHOMA

LANGSTON

OK1 LANGSTON UNIVERSITY (1897), GENERAL LAMAR HARRISON LIBRARY (1897). 73050. Tel 405 406-2281.
Laron Clark, Jr., Librn. Interlibrary loan, bibliographies prepared, copying, typing, inquiries answered.

.1 Afro-American Studies Collection.
ca. 1000 paperbacks. Basic books on the life and history of black Americans.
.2 Langston University.
Archives, 1897- . Includes correspondence, minutes of board meetings, financial records, records of admission, and other material relating to the history and administration of the University.
.3 Negro in the U.S. since 1933.
Special collection includes books, periodicals, pamphlets, theses and dissertations, and clippings.

NORMAN

OK2 UNIVERSITY OF OKLAHOMA (1890), BIZZELL MEMORIAL LIBRARY (1890). 73069. Tel 405 325-2611. Dr. Arthur M. McAnally, Dir. Interlibrary loan, copying, typing, inquiries answered.

.1 Checote, Samuel.
Papers, 1867-86. 58 items. Principal Chief of the Creek Nation. Correspondence, published speeches, published reports relating to the problems of the slaves freed by the Creeks, and other papers pertaining to Creek politics.
.2 Chickasaw Nation.
Records, 1866-1904. 3 ft. Law, leases, auditor's reports, proceedings of the National Council, and other papers relating to elections, intruders, and freedmen.
.3 Hinkel, John W. collector.
Papers, 1894-1908. 65 items. Among the correspondence are items relating to the "White Caps," a local version of the Ku Klux Klan.
.4 Holt, S.L.
Papers, 1829-70. 3 items and 2 v. Two Mississippi plantation journals and account books reflecting ante-bellum social and economic life, and a few papers relating to Negro affairs.
.5 McCoy, James Stacy, 1834-62.
Papers, 1859-65. 715 items. Confederate officer. Correspondence describing conditions in the Confederate Army; a bill of sale (1859) for 3 slaves, cattle, horses, and farming equipment purchased by members of McCoy's family, and other papers.
.6 Microfilm collection, 1774-1925.
1036 reels. Microfilm of originals in the National Archives, the Wisconsin Historical Society, and other repositories. Correspondence and other records, including records (1857-69) relating to suppression of slave trade and to Negro colonization.

OK3 UNIVERSITY OF OKLAHOMA, CONSULTATIVE CENTER FOR SCHOOL DESEGREGATION IN OKLAHOMA (1966).
Bldg. 4, South Campus, 73069. Tel 405 325-0311. Joe Garrison, Dir. Bibliographies prepared, consultation.
The Center makes available to educators, community leaders, and interested groups in Oklahoma and Texas the services of professional personnel who can assist them in dealing more effectively with instructional, administrative, and community problems associated with efforts to implement the public education portion of the Civil Rights Act of 1964.
Publ.: The Consultative Center Newsletter; Pamphlets, studies, reports.

.1 Consultative Center for School Desegregation in Oklahoma.
Miscellaneous, 1966- . Materials relative to the desegregation process, human relations curriculum and teaching the disadvantaged, Negro history in the curriculum of public schools and multi-ethnic reading materials.

OK4   UNIVERSITY OF OKLAHOMA, OKLAHOMA CENTER OF
       URBAN AND REGIONAL STUDIES. 73069. Tel 405
       536-0900.
       The Center conducts research in urban affairs and pro-
       vides professional planning services to the cities of
       Oklahoma, including comprehensive urban planning,
       social and economic studies, and specialized research
       in transportation and urbanization.

OK5   UNIVERSITY OF OKLAHOMA, THE SOUTHWEST CENTER
       FOR HUMAN RELATIONS STUDIES (1960). 1700 Asp
       Ave., 73069. Tel 405 325-0311. Donald J. Hall, Dir.
       Referrals made, consultation.
       The Center works in three areas, giving special empha-
       sis in each to the problems of intergroup relations.
       First, it does research in the behavioral sciences and
       disseminates its findings. Second, it has consultation
       with communities and organizations about problems of
       intergroup and interpersonal conflict and tension, and
       solutions for these problems. Third, it provides edu-
       cation for professionals and others concerned with in-
       tergroup and interpersonal conflict and other human
       relations problem areas. The Center sponsors a spe-
       cial human relations library, an annual human relations
       seminar, and programs in areas of school desegrega-
       tion, Indian education, leadership training, labor-
       management relations.
       Publ.: Oklahoma Human Relations News, monthly news-
            letter, restricted circulation.

       .1   The Southwest Center for Human Relations Studies.
            Miscellaneous, 1960- . General literature related
            to community and group relations; race relations
            materials in duplicated form.

OKLAHOMA CITY

OK6   CONGRESS OF RACIAL EQUALITY (CORE). 407 N.
       Durland St., 73104. Tel 405 236-5491. Archibald Hill,
       Chmn.

OK7   NATIONAL CONFERENCE OF CHRISTIANS AND JEWS
       (NCCJ). Petroleum Club Bldg., 120 N.W. Robert S.
       Kerr Ave., 73102. Tel 405 232-3861. Perry S. Lusk,
       Dir.

OK8   OKLAHOMA CITY COMMUNITY RELATIONS COMMISSION
       (1964). 412 Center Bldg., 331 W. Main St., 73102. Tel
       405 231-2445. Harry N. Tower, Exec. Dir.
       The Commission receives, negotiates, resolves com-
       plaints alleging discrimination; eliminates injustice and
       causes of community tensions; builds good relationships
       between ethnic, racial and religious groups; provides
       direct services to individuals and neighborhoods in
       securing city services.

OK9   OKLAHOMA CONFERENCE ON RELIGION AND RACE.
       P.O. Box 981, 73101. Stan Twardy, Dir.

OK10   OKLAHOMA HUMAN RIGHTS COMMISSION (1963). P.O.
       Box 52945, 73105. Tel 405 521-2360. William Y.
       Rose, Dir.
       The Commission is a permanent, independent agency
       having jurisdiction over state employment; conducts
       surveys and studies; creates advisory bodies; investi-
       gates complaints; recommends solutions; conciliates.

OK11   THIRTY FAMILIES (1966). 1525 N.E. 51st St., 73111. Tel
       405 427-6100. Jerry Studebaker, Chmn.
       Thirty Families is a neighborhood organization whose
       primary purpose is to encourage creative living in an
       integrated community. The group compiles and dis-
       seminates information about available property and
       seeks fair support from realtors for integrated
       housing; works to improve the educational environ-
       ment in the Oklahoma City area; supports community
       betterment projects; and encourages an exchange of
       ideas between all ethnic and economic groups in the
       community.
       Publ.: Monthly newsletter.

OK12   URBAN LEAGUE OF OKLAHOMA CITY, INC. (1946). 215
       N. Walnut St., 73104. Tel 405 236-8549. Frank Cowan,
       Jr., Dir.

OKMULGEE

OK13   CREEK INDIAN MEMORIAL ASSOCIATION (1923), CREEK
       INDIAN MUSEUM (1923) & COUNCIL HOUSE (1870).
       74447. Tel 918 756-2324. Mrs. Juanita Dunson, Dir.
       Literature searches, inquiries answered, referrals
       made, consultation.

       .1   Creek Nation.
            Records, 1861-99. 35 items and 2 v. In part,
            transcripts. Letters, deeds, and papers of the
            Creek Nation. Includes a copy of the stolen rolls
            of Creek Indians and freedmen.

TULSA

OK14   COMMUNITY RELATIONS COMMISSION. Room 502, 9 E.
       Fourth Bldg., 74103. Tel 918 581-5251. Mrs. Lois H.
       Gatchell, Exec. Dir.

OK15   CONGRESS OF RACIAL EQUALITY (CORE). P.O. Box
       6158, 74106. Cleophus Robinson, Chmn.

OK16   OKLAHOMA CIVIL LIBERTIES UNION. 232 Sunset Dr.,
       74114. Doris Toll, Corresponding Secy.

OK17   THOMAS GILCREASE INSTITUTE OF AMERICAN HISTORY
       AND ART (1942), GILCREASE LIBRARY. R.R. 6,
       74106. Tel 918 581-5311. G.P. Edwards, Historian.
       Copying, inquiries answered.
       Publ.: American Scene, quarterly; Gilcrease Gazette,
            quarterly newsletter; Guidebook to Manuscripts,
            annually.

       .1   Five Civilized Tribes.
            Papers, ca. 1698-1939. ca. 380 items. In part,
            photocopies and transcripts. Correspondence,
            treaties with the U.S. and the Confederate States,
            resolutions of the General Council of the Cherokee
            people, and other papers relating to such subjects
            as Cherokee, Chickasaw, Choctaw, Creek, and
            Seminole Nations, to tribal affairs and slaves
            owned by the Indians.

OK18   TULSA CITY-COUNTY LIBRARY SYSTEM (1962). 400
       Civic Center, 74103. Tel 918 581-5223. Mrs. Allie
       Beth Martin, Dir. Interlibrary loan, literature
       searches, copying, inquiries answered, referrals made.

       .1   Alfred E. Aaronson Human Relations Collection.
            Several hundred volumes on human relations and
            civil rights (1928-67). Collection includes fiction,
            non-fiction, and studies from sociological, psycho-
            logical, and political aspects. Among the subjects
            covered are urban problems, slums, and com-
            munity organization.

OK19   TULSA URBAN LEAGUE (1953). 1715 N. Peoria, 74106.
       Tel 918 587-9432. Dale F. Hogg, Exec. Dir.

       .1   Tulsa Urban League.
            Files, 1953- . Correspondence, minutes of meet-
            ings, financial records, studies, reports, and other
            material dealing with the aims, history, and pro-
            grams of the League.

OK20   THE UNITED STATES JAYCEES, PROGRAM FOR HUMAN
       RESOURCE DEVELOPMENT. P.O. Box 7, 74102. Tel
       918 584-2481. Bob Miller, Prog. Mgr.
       The Program for Human Resource Development, en-
       titled Operation Opportunity, is intended to involve the
       volunteer sector of America in constructive programs
       of human resource development concentrating on em-
       ployment, education, recreation, governmental aware-
       ness, personal development, environmental improve-
       ment, and housing.
       Publ.: Operation Opportunity Manual; Action, magazine;
            Future, magazine; Reports, bimonthly.

       .1   The United States Jaycees, Program for Human Re-
            source Development.
            Records, 1967-69. Correspondence, financial re-
            ports, annual reports, minutes and materials from
            two nation-wide seminars, manuals, fliers, slides,
            idea bank for suggested local projects, records of

local projects, case digest of sample local projects, minutes of Advisory Committee Meetings (1968-69), newspaper and magazine stories, and pictures of local project activities. In part, restricted.

OK21   UNIVERSITY OF OKLAHOMA, OFFICE OF URBAN AND COMMUNITY DEVELOPMENT (1964). 423 Mayo Bldg., 420 S. Main, 74103. Tel 918 583-5717. Cyril J. Roberts, Dir. Copying, typing, inquiries answered, referrals made, consultation.
The Office conducts research in urban affairs and performs services for the urban community. Most salient of approaches is the educational/guidance function in which the Extension teaches, assists and discovers.
Publ.: Progress Report: Urban/Community Development, quarterly; Periodic research papers.

OREGON

EUGENE

OR1   UNIVERSITY OF OREGON (1873), LIBRARY (1881). 97403. Tel 503 342-1411. Carl W. Hintz, Univ. Librn. Interlibrary loan, copying.

.1   Gordon, Robert Winslow, 1888-1961.
      Papers, 1909-34. 7 ft. In part, transcripts (typewritten). Folklorist. Includes typed material from published sources, singers, and reciters, relating chiefly to the Civil War and the South; a file of Gordon's folksong column in Adventure; Harvard class notes; and private collections of Joanna Colcord, Joseph McGinnis, Mary Newcomb, and Betty Bush Winger.

.2   Gray, James Taylor, 1852-1928.
      Papers, 1854-1950. 4 ft. Steamboat builder and pilot. Correspondence, steamboat plans, and other papers relating to the Ilwaco Steam Navigation Company, the Vancouver Transportation Company, transportation companies in Alaska, and Gray's promotion of the town of Frankfort, Wash. Correspondents include his father, William Henry Gray, Mrs. W.H. Gray, his father-in-law, Oliver Otis Howard, Mrs. O.O. Howard, other members of the Gray and Howard families, Jacob Kamm, and C.E.S. Wood.

.3   Olcott, Ben Wilson, 1872-1952.
      Papers, 1911-33. 9 v. Oregon secretary of state. Includes correspondence (1911, 1916) relating to Olcott's term as secretary of state, addresses, press releases and related correspondence (1919-22), and letters and documents concerning the Ku Klux Klan in Oregon (1922).

.4   Robinson, Avery, 1878-1965.
      Papers, 1893-1964. ca. 2 ft. Composer. Correspondence, ms, music, and published music of Robinson. Includes 2 notebooks (ca. 1893) of Negro hymns collected and annotated by Mildred J. Hill, of Kentucky.

JACKSONVILLE

OR2   JACKSONVILLE MUSEUM. 206 N. Fifth St., 97530. Tel 503 899-1322.

.1   Collection of theses.
      11 items. Included is a thesis on slavery in Jackson County, Ore.

MEDFORD

OR3   OREGON BUREAU OF LABOR, CIVIL RIGHTS DIVISION, FIELD OFFICE. 130 W. Sixth St., 97501. Tel 503 779-0181.

PENDLETON

OR4   OREGON BUREAU OF LABOR, CIVIL RIGHTS DIVISION, FIELD OFFICE. State Office Bldg., 700 S.E. Emigrant, 97801. Tel 503 276-6131.

PORTLAND

OR5   AMERICAN CIVIL LIBERTIES UNION (ACLU) OF OREGON. 311 Senator Bldg., 732 S.W. Third St., 97204. Tel 503 228-0979. Mrs. Ginna Deinum, Exec. Secy. Inquiries answered.
The ACLU works for the defense and advancement of free speech, fair procedures and equal protection of the law.
Publ.: Newsletter.

.1   American Civil Liberties Union of Oregon.
      Files, 1968- . Records, reports, correspondence, and material on local cases and projects, including testimony on civil rights legislation before Oregon State legislature.

OR6   HUMAN RELATIONS COMMISSION (1950). Room 316, City Hall, 97204. Tel 503 228-6141. Russell Peyton, Exec. Dir.
The Commission studies problems arising between groups in the city of Portland which may result in tensions or discriminations; formulates and conducts a program of public education with the object of decreasing and eliminating any such discrimination or tension; investigates any complaints of discrimination, and recommends to the City Council changes of law. Formerly Intergroup Relations Commission.

OR7   NATIONAL CONFERENCE OF CHRISTIANS AND JEWS (NCCJ). 729 Southwest Alder St., 97205. Tel 503 223-7773.

OR8   NORTHWEST REGIONAL EDUCATIONAL RESEARCH LABORATORY. 400 Lindsay Bldg., 710 S.W. Second Ave., 97201. Tel 503 224-3650.
The Laboratory focuses on developmental research in education, evaluative procedures, encouragement of promising educational innovations, education for culturally different children, instruction in small schools, and conditions for effective teaching.

OR9   OREGON BUREAU OF LABOR, CIVIL RIGHTS DIVISION (1949). 466 State Office Bldg., 97201. Tel 503 226-2161. Mark A. Smith, Adminstr.
The Division, a permanent legislative agency, conducts surveys, studies, and public education programs; creates advisory bodies; investigates complaints; holds hearings; issues cease-and-desist orders; seeks court enforcement of its orders concerning employment (private, agencies, labor, training programs), housing and public accommodations.

OR10   PORTLAND STATE COLLEGE, URBAN STUDIES CENTER (1966). 1604 S.W. Tenth St., 97201. Tel 503 226-7271. Lyndon R. Musolf, Dir. Inquiries answered, referrals made.
The Center seeks to provide an interdisciplinary academic setting for study and research in problems and ideas relating to an increasingly urban nation and world, to provide a means whereby the resources of faculty and students at Portland State and other metropolitan area colleges can be used in the Portland metropolitan area, and to help these institutions to be sensitive to their potential roles within the metropolitan community.
Publ.: Reports and studies on various urban problems.

.1   Urban Studies Center.
      Bibliographic material. ca. 150 bibliographies related to urban problems, including such subject areas as poverty, housing, urban planning, and employment. Closed to investigators.

OR11   URBAN LEAGUE OF PORTLAND (1945), MARK A. SMITH LIBRARY. Community Services Center, 718 W. Burnside, 97209. Tel 503 224-0151. E. Shelton Hill, Exec. Dir. Interlibrary loan, literature searches, referrals made.
The League works to eliminate discrimination and segregation from American life, and gives guidance and help to minorities so that they may share equally in the rewards and responsibilities of citizenship. In Portland it was established at the request of local citizens concerned about rising racial tensions resultant

from the sudden increase in non-white population em-
ployed by war industries (WW II).
Publ.: Newsletter; Annual Report; Monthly Membership
Memorandum.

SALEM

OR12   OREGON STATE LIBRARY (1905). State Library Bldg.,
97310. Tel 503 364-2171. Miss Eloise Ebert, State
Librn. Interlibrary loan, bibliographies prepared,
literature searches, copying, inquiries answered, referrals made, consultation.

    .1   Oregon Index.
Portland and Salem, Ore. newspapers, and ca. 50
Oregon periodicals. Partially indexed. Subjects
include race relations in Oregon (since early
1900's) under categories such as names of minority groups, migrant labor, and other pertinent
headings.
    .2   Smith, William Carlson.
Papers, 1924-27. Sociologist. Consists of the
files of Smith relating to a survey of race relations
on the Pacific Coast.

PENNSYLVANIA

ARDMORE

PA1   THE GATE (GET AHEAD THROUGH EDUCATION) LI-
BRARY. 33 E. Spring Ave., 19003. Tel 215 642-2464.
Charles Askew, Chmn.
GATE is co-sponsored by interested persons and by
the Ardmore Progressive Civic Association. It specializes in materials on Negro history and Negro
culture for young people.

BEAVER FALLS

PA2   GENEVA COLLEGE, McCARTNEY LIBRARY (1848). Box
2, 15010. Tel 412 946-5100. R.J. Crozier, Librn.
Interlibrary loan, copying, inquiries answered.

    .1   Covenanter Collection.
Materials. Books, pamphlets, and periodicals concerning the Reformed Presbyterian Church in Scotland, Ireland, and North America. Included are
some books and pamphlets on slavery, and articles
on slavery in the following periodicals: The
Covenanter, v. 1-18 (1846-62), Reformed Presbyterian, v. 1-26 (1837-62), and Reformed Presbyterian and Covenanter, v. 1-36 (1863-96).
    .2   McCartney Collection.
Library of Dr. Clarence Edward McCartney, Civil
War and Lincoln historian. Included are some
items on slavery.

BETHLEHEM

PA3   COLLEGE PLACEMENT SERVICES, INC. (CPS) (1964). 65
E. Elizabeth Ave., P.O. Box 2322, 18018. Tel 215 868-
1421. Andre G. Beaumont, Managing Dir. Consultation.
The CPS program focuses on developing and upgrading
the career counseling and placement services of traditionally Negro colleges through a wide range of programs and services including: limited direct financial
assistance; sponsoring a consortium for placement of
over 40 black colleges; conducting training institutes,
workshops and orientation training for placement personnel of traditionally Negro colleges; arranging review
by specialists of placement operations at black colleges; sponsorship of New Career Opportunities conferences at black colleges; sponsorship of fellowship
program for black graduate students at Duke University;
and review of career counseling and placement programs for black students at predominantly white colleges.
Publ.: Newsletter, bimonthly; Research monographs,
such as Manpower Resources of the Traditionally Negro Colleges.

    .1   College Placement Services, Inc.
Materials. Included are reports and data concerning employment trends regarding black college
graduates; surveys of employment patterns of
graduates; file of materials and studies concerning
96 traditionally Negro colleges; and reports of CPS
advisory team visits to black colleges.

CARLISLE

PA4   DICKINSON COLLEGE (1773), BOYD LEE SPAHR LIBRARY
(1784). High St., 17013. Tel 717 243-5121.
Yates Forbis, Librn. Interlibrary loan, bibliographies
prepared, literature searches, copying, inquiries answered, referrals made, consultation.

    .1   Bond family.
Papers. Includes letters and pamphlets on Ne-
groes and slavery.
    .2   Bowdle family.
Papers. Includes letters and pamphlets on Ne-
groes and slavery.
    .3   Buchanan, James, 1791-1868.
Papers, 1808-68. ca. 8 ft. President of the U.S.
Correspondence, speeches, and other papers of
Buchanan and contemporary political figures. 359
items are by Buchanan, 72 letters and legal papers
are among the other items. Included are mss and
pamphlets on Negroes and slavery.
    .4   Conway, Moncure Daniel, 1832-1907.
Papers, 1847-1907. ca. 200 items. Unitarian and
Congregational clergyman and author. Letters relating to all phases of Conway's career. Among
papers are mss and pamphlets on Negroes and
slavery.

CHESTER

PA5   CROZER THEOLOGICAL SEMINARY, MARTIN LUTHER
KING, JR., SCHOOL OF SOCIAL CHANGE, BUCKNELL
LIBRARY. 21st and Upland, 19013. Tel 215 876-5528.
E. Theodore Jones, Dir. Inquiries answered, consultation, institutes.
King School is a graduate program training persons to
become leaders in communities organizing for social
change. The emphasis is on the development of a
comprehensive analysis of political structures, community resources, and theories of change, and supervised field training. While the school recognizes the
violent nature of society, it is historically rooted in the
tradition of direct nonviolent strategy.

CHEYNEY

PA6   CHEYNEY STATE COLLEGE, LESLIE PINCKNEY HILL
LIBRARY (1913). 19319. Tel 215 399-0990. Mrs.
Marguerite L. Prioleau, Librn.

    .1   Afro-American Studies Collection.
ca. 1000 paperbacks. Basic Books on the life and
history of black Americans.
    .2   Cheyney State College.
Archives. Includes correspondence, minutes of
board meetings, financial records, records of admission, and other material relating to the history and administration of the College.

DOYLESTOWN

PA7   BUCKS COUNTY HISTORICAL SOCIETY (1880), LIBRARY
(1898). Pine and Ashland Sts., 18901. Tel 215 348-
4373. Cora B. Decker, Librn. Copying, inquiries answered.

    .1   Jenks, Michael Hutchinson, 1795-1867.
Papers, 1695-1909. 2 ft. (300 items). Surveyor,
county official, and Representative from Pennsylvania. Correspondence, deeds, wills, account
books, a docket book (1819-21), scrapbooks, and a
catalog of Jenks' library to be sold at public sale
in 1838. Includes papers pertaining to slavery,
the Nebraska bill, and politics.
    .2   Wheatley, Phillis, 1753?-1794.
Ms poems. 5 items.

EASTON

PA8   LAFAYETTE COLLEGE (1826), DAVID BISHOP SKILLMAN
        LIBRARY. 18042. Tel 215 253-6281. Clyde L. Hasel-
        den, Librn.

        .1   Facts on Film.
                Papers, 1954-67. Microfilm. Contains materials
                on civil rights and race relations in the South. See
                Race Relations Information Center, Nashville,
                Tenn., for a full description.

ERIE

PA9   ERIE HUMAN RELATIONS COMMISSION (1954). Room 508,
        Municipal Bldg., 16501. Tel 814 456-8561. James W.
        Bryant, Exec. Dir.
        The Commission has compliance powers in the areas
        of housing, employment, and public accommodations
        and therefore enforces the Erie Human Relations
        Ordinance which prohibits discrimination, resolves all
        neighborhood tension problems, and provides an educa-
        tion program to prevent prejudice. Formerly Com-
        munity Relations Commission.
        Publ.: Like It Is, bimonthly; Annual Report.

        .1   Erie Human Relations Commission.
                Files, 1954- . Correspondence, reports, studies,
                investigations, minutes of meetings, financial
                records, library of pertinent books. Among
                other items is documentation dealing with the
                aims, program, and history of the Commission.

PA10   PERRY MEMORIAL HOUSE AND DICKSON TAVERN (1963).
        201 French St., 16507. Tel 814 521-9393. John V.
        Alexick, Chmn.
        The Perry Memorial House and Dickson Tavern is an
        abolition museum of period pieces (1800-1913) similar
        to the type probably used by previous owner-occupants.
        One section of the "Underground Railroad" in the
        Tavern is exposed for public viewing.

GETTYSBURG

PA11   GETTYSBURG COLLEGE (1832), SCHMUCKER MEMORIAL
        LIBRARY (1834). 17325. Tel 717 334-3131. Mrs.
        Lillian H. Smoke, Librn. Interlibrary loan, bibliog-
        raphies prepared, copying, typing, referrals made,
        consultation.

        .1   Civil War and Reconstruction Collection.
                Books, periodicals and newspaper titles, micro-
                forms, tape recordings, phonograph records, and
                filmstrips are included.

HARRISBURG

PA12   HISTORICAL SOCIETY OF DAUPHIN COUNTY (1869). 219
        S. Front St., 17104. Tel 717 233-3462. Mrs. John
        Tillman, Curator. Inquiries answered.

        .1   Cameron, Simon, 1799-1889.
                Papers, 1861-92. 4100 items. Minister to Russia,
                U.S. Senator, and Secretary of War. Correspon-
                dence and documents.

PA13   PENNSYLVANIA HISTORICAL AND MUSEUM COMMISSION
        (1913) (1945), LIBRARY. William Penn Memorial Mu-
        seum and Archives Bldg., 17108. Tel 717 787-3051.
        Donald H. Kent, Dir. Copying, inquiries answered.

        .1   Black, John D., d. 1923.
                Papers, 1815-1923. ca. 100 items. Army officer,
                of Pennsylvania and North Dakota, and assistant
                superintendent of elections, Bureau of Refugees,
                Freedmen and Abandoned Lands in North Caro-
                lina. Correspondence (1862-1923) relating to
                military and personal matters; records of com-
                missions, appointments, discharges, orders, dis-
                ability and pension papers, and other military
                papers (1862-65).
        .2   Cameron, Simon, 1799-1889.
                Papers, 1836-92. Microfilm, 10 reels. Incoming
                letters and business papers with 13 letters or

drafts of letters by Cameron himself, totalling
about 4100 items. Chiefly politics and business
matters.
        .3   Work Projects Administration, Writers Project.
                Papers. ca. 3 boxes. Included are ms reports on
                the Negro and other ethnic groups in the Phila-
                delphia and Pittsburgh areas. Subjects covered
                include medicine, personalities, arts and culture,
                among many others.

PA14   PENNSYLVANIA HUMAN RELATIONS COMMISSION (1955).
        Fourth Floor, 100 N. Cameron St., 17101. Tel 717
        787-5010. Homer Floyd, Exec. Dir. Inquiries an-
        swered.
        The Commission works for the enforcement of the
        Pennsylvania Human Relations Act and Fair Educa-
        tional Opportunities Act. It investigates complaints
        resulting from discrimination in employment and pub-
        lic accommodations; issues injunctions in certain
        housing complaints; enforces orders through the
        courts; and carries on educational projects. Formerly
        the Pennsylvania Fair Employment Practices Com-
        mission.
        Publ.: Human Relations Report, quarterly; Annual
        Report.

        .1   Pennsylvania Human Relations Commission.
                Files, 1955- . Documentation dealing with the
                aims, history and programs of the Commission.
                Includes correspondence, minutes of meetings, fi-
                nancial reports, studies, reports and investiga-
                tions.

PA15   PENNSYLVANIA STATE LIBRARY. Box 1601, 17126. Tel
        717 787-2646. Ernest E. Doerschuk, Jr., State Librn.
        Interlibrary loan, bibliographies prepared, copying, in-
        quiries answered, referrals made.

        .1   Facts on Film.
                Papers, 1954-67. Microfilm. Contains materials
                on civil rights and race relations in the South. See
                Race Relations Information Center, Nashville,
                Tenn., for a full description.

HAVERFORD

PA16   HAVERFORD COLLEGE (1833), LIBRARY. 19041. Tel 215
        649-9600. Alice E. Whittelsey, Archivist. Interlibrary
        loan, copying, inquiries answered.

        .1   Allinson family.
                Papers, 1710-1939. 14 ft. (ca. 2014 items). Cor-
                respondence, journals, diaries, poetry, common-
                place books, deeds, marriage certificates, diplo-
                mas, legal and financial papers, scrapbooks, clip-
                pings, and other papers. Persons represented in-
                clude Samuel Allinson (1739-91), New Jersey law-
                yer and magistrate, Samuel Allinson (1808-83),
                New Jersey farmer and philanthropist, William
                James Allinson (1810-74), Frederick Theodore
                Frelinghuysen, Sarah Moore Grimké, Patrick
                Henry, Julia Ward Howe, George B. McClellan,
                Josiah Parrish, Samuel Rhoads, Marcus Lawrence
                Ward, and Theodore Dwight Weld. Subjects include
                the Burlington Company and the settlement of the
                land at Otego, N.Y., the Free Produce Association
                of Friends of Philadelphia Yearly Meeting, Indians,
                Negro slavery, New Jersey Society for Promoting
                the Abolition of Slavery, New Jersey State Home
                for Boys, Jamesburg, N.J., the New Jersey State
                Temperance Society, temperance work, and the
                woman's peace movement. Includes genealogical
                and other papers of and relating to the Carey,
                Chattin, Cooper, Hinchman, Matlack, Parker,
                Scattergood, Tatum, and Taylor families.
        .2   Baily, Joshua Longstreth, 1826-1916.
                Papers, 1835-1937. 4 ft. (ca. 700 items). Mer-
                chant, of Philadelphia. Correspondence, narra-
                tives, articles, business papers, speeches, rec-
                ords and documents, family records, and other
                papers. Includes 120 letters (1852-64) from
                Baily to his wife, Theodate (Lang) Baily, and
                mother, Elizabeth Baily, concerning personal
                and religious affairs, with a detailed account of the

Baltimore Yearly Meeting of the Society of Friends (1854) and the effects upon it and other meetings of the Wilburite-Gurneyite Separation (1845-54); miscellaneous letters (1880-1914) of Joshua Baily; approximately 350 letters from Baily's colleagues, together with business and financial records; documents (ca. 1860-1914) reflecting Baily's interest in peace movements in 1875 and 1914, in education of Negroes and Indians, support of Quaker schools, in city and state politics, in the Kansas Freedmen's Relief Association and the Friends Freedmen's Association, and in other philanthropic and civic activities. Miscellaneous mss and printed articles and papers include Loyd Baily's Narrative of a visit to Burlington (N.J.)..., (1836); a typewritten, unsigned account of contention within Philadelphia Yearly Meeting during the Wilburite-Separation; accounts of Philadelphia Yearly Meeting (1844, 1846, 1847, 1871, 1874) by Baily; speeches (1880-1914) by Baily concerning temperance, Negro education, civic and political affairs; printed announcements, memorials, and testimonials on the death of Baily; initialed holograph poem by John Greenleaf Whittier with an essay on slavery on verso; and other family letters (1837-1904) including those of Theodate (Lang) Baily to her husband. Other correspondents include Joseph Bevan Braithwaite (1818-1905), Rebecca Collins (1804-92), Elizabeth L. (Rous) Wright Comstock (1815-91), Josiah Forster (1782-1870), and other members of the Society of Friends; and James Gillespie Blaine (1830-93), writing in 1865, Gifford Pinchot (1865-1946) writing in 1910, and Booker T. Washington (1858-1915) writing 1885-1900.

PA16.3 Benezet, Anthony, 1713-84.
Letters, 1756-83. ca. 50 items. Educator. Letters discuss the slave trade and abolition; peace principles of the Society of Friends; Friends affairs; publications in which Benezet was interested; methods of teaching mathematics and grammar, and the problems of maintaining a school; question of religious tolerance, and other subjects. Most of the letters are addressed to George Dillwyn, Quaker minister. Among other correspondents is Moses Brown.

.4 Cadbury, Richard Tapper, 1853-1929. collector.
Quaker autograph letters, 1770-1829. ca. 50 items. Mainly letters to James Thornton of Philadelphia. Correspondents include Samuel Allinson (1739-91) writing in 1789; Moses Brown (1738-1836) writing (1787-91) concerning abolition of the slave trade and Friends' affairs; and others.

.5 Cope family.
Papers, 1795-1896. ca. 4 ft. (ca. 60 items). Correspondence, business papers, legal papers, minutes, a diary, logbooks, and pictures. Bulk of the papers relates to Thomas Pym Cope (1768-1854), Philadelphia merchant and shipowner. Others relate to his sons Alfred (1806-75) and Henry (1793-1865), his cousin Abigail Barker (ca. 1773-1840), of Burlington, N.J., Philip Cope Garrett (1834-1905), Thomas Garrett (1789-1871), and Thomas Pim Cope (1823-1900). Includes correspondence of Thomas Pym Cope relating to his work on a committee of the Society of Friends to help freed Negroes emigrate to Haiti (1804-25); legal papers concerning the property of Philadelphia Monthly Meeting for which Thomas Pym Cope was a trustee; a diary (1850) of Philip Cope Garrett while an undergraduate at Haverford College; letters and notes regarding the organization of the Haverford College Alumni Association (1856-57); pictures of Thomas Garrett, and letters from him to Friends in Ireland regarding his work in helping slaves to escape to Canada. Material is related to the library's Marmaduke Cooper Cope collection.

.6 Cope, Marmaduke Cooper, 1804-97.
Correspondence, 1843-74. ca. 400 items. Prominent Philadelphia Quaker. Correspondence with English and American Friends. Includes 75 letters (1843-74) from Cope, discussing Yearly Meetings of the Society of Friends in New York, Ohio, New England, and Philadelphia during the Wilburite-Gurneyite Separation, the progress of the abolition

movement, the Civil War, public and private education, and the effect of other social and political affairs on the Society of Friends; letters (1845-59) of John Allen (1790-1859), English Quaker, discussing his travels in the ministry in America, affairs in various Yearly Meetings affected by the Wilburite-Gurneyite Separation, and political matters.

.7 Disciplines of Yearly Meetings of the Society of Friends.
Records, 1689-ca. 1805. 4 ft. (17 v.). Contemporary copies, made for quarterly meeting, of periodic compilations of rules of discipline of the Society of Friends of London, New England, and Philadelphia Yearly Meetings. Concerns civil obligations such as the bearing of arms, oath taking, payment of taxes, and keeping of legal records; procedures for Yearly Meetings and other meetings, rules for ministers, observance of mourning, recording of sufferings, maintenance of schools, printing of books, arbitration of disputes, conduct toward dependent groups such as the poor, orphans, prisoners, slaves, Indians, and Negroes; and personal and family conduct. Includes 2 disciplines of New England Yearly Meeting (ca. 1760 and ca. 1780); scattered disciplines of Philadelphia Yearly Meeting (1689, 1704, 1719, 1762, 1763, 1781-90, and 1797-1805). Material is related to the library's collection of minutes of the Society of Friends.

.8 Friends, Society of. American Friends Service Committee.
Archives, 1917-63. 1155 ft. Correspondence, minutes, reports, personnel data, financial papers, publications, mimeographed serials, press releases, newspaper clippings, scrapbooks, awards, gifts, recordings, photos, glass slides, posters, and other material covering work in relief and rehabilitation (especially after World Wars I and II), refugee aid, social and technical assistance, international affairs, peace education, community relations, and youth services. Includes mss and correspondence of Henry J. Cadbury (b. 1883), and others; and the records of the Friends Service, Inc. and other organizations.

.9 Howland, Gulielma M. (Hilles)
Papers, ca. 1700-1867. ca. 12 ft. (ca. 1750 items). Letters, journals, literary mss, legal and business papers. Bulk of the material consists of personal correspondence between members of several distinguished and closely connected Quaker families (Cox, Dillwyn, Emlen, Hill, Hilles, Howland, Logan, Morris, Smith, Vaux, Wells, and Wistar) giving an account of the religious, social, and cultural life of Friends in New Jersey, Pennsylvania, Delaware, and abroad, during the second half of the 18th and the first half of the 19th centuries, and touching on the abolitionist movement among other topics. Includes a journal of Susanna Morris (1682-1755) giving an account of her travels as a Quaker minister. Material is related to the library's Edward Wanton Smith collection.

.10 Journal and diary collection.
ca. 1712-1952. ca. 53 ft. Journals and diaries containing information on Quaker life, religious attitudes, world travel, economics, and politics. Includes diaries and memoranda (1784-96) of John Parrish (1730-1807) concerning slavery.

.11 Lake Mohonk Conference.
Papers, 1885-1929. ca. 22,600 items. Includes 2 record books from the Conferences on the Negro held at Mohonk in 1890-91.

.12 Letters of members of the Society of Friends in America and Great Britain.
1652-1959. 15 ft. (ca. 1150 items). In part, transcripts and photocopies from originals in the possession of Moses Brown School, Providence, R.I.; Westtown School, Westtown, Pa.; and Isabel Ross, Westmoreland, Eng. Letters, portraits, and clippings. ca. 800 letters of American Friends (1682-1959) include those of Samuel Allinson (1739-91), Moses Brown (1738-1836), Isaac Collins (1746-1817), George Dillwyn (1738-1820), John Pemberton (1742-1813), and Thomas Wistar (1798-1876). These letters, most of them (1740-1800) concern

not only religious and spiritual affairs, but also
colonial and federal politics, commerce and social
matters, slavery, Friends' relief activities, and
travels. Letters from correspondents abroad concern the early years of the Society of Friends, relations with American Friends, and other matters.
Other correspondents include John Greenleaf
Whittier (1807-92), Thomas Wistar (1798-1876),
and Cyrus Mendenhall (1810-77).

.13 Papers relating to Negroes.
     Papers, ca. 1676-ca. 1937. ca. 200 items. In part,
     photocopies. Letters, journals, articles, essays,
     manumissions, minutes, testimonies, accounts,
     pictures, and printed items relating to the slave
     trade, slavery, abolition, freedmen's activities,
     and discrimination, primarily in the Americas.
     Bulk of the material is on the period 1775-1875.
     Includes records of the Free Produce Meeting of
     Friends (1850), the Free Produce Association of
     Friends of Philadelphia (1852-68), the Friends'
     Freedmen's Association of Philadelphia (1864-
     65), the Female Anti-Slavery Sewing Society
     (1852-54), the New Jersey Society for Promoting
     the Abolition of Slavery (1793-1809), and the
     Abington, Pa., Monthly Meeting of the Society of
     Friends (1765-84); an account entitled The His-
     tory of the Rise, Progress, and the Accomplish-
     ment of the Abolition of African Slave Trade,
     written in 1840 by Thomas Clarkson (1760-1846)
     and partly in his hand; and account (1776) of a visit
     by Issac Jackson (1735-80) to Friends who kept
     slaves; and an unpublished work entitled Friends
     and Slavery, by Isaac Sharpless (1848-1920). Cor-
     respondents include Moses Brown (1783-1836),
     Elijah Coffin (1798-1863), Josiah Forster (1782-
     1870), Jesse Kersey (1767-1845), Warner Mifflin
     (1745-98), and John Greenleaf Whittier (1807-92).
     Twenty-nine letters (1865-71) of James Evans
     Rhoads (1828-95), discuss his work, in part, for the
     Freedmen's Association. Material is related to
     the library's Nathaniel Peabody Rogers papers.

.14 Philips, William Pyle, 1882-1950. collector.
     Autographed papers of Presidents of the U.S. and
     of signers of the Declaration of Independence,
     1757-1886. 68 items. Presidential autographs
     include that of Abraham Lincoln (1860) writing in
     response to charges against him concerning his
     views on Negroes and slavery.

.15 Rhoads family.
     Papers, 1822-1913. 2 ft. (121 items). Correspon-
     dence, journals, diaries, commonplace books,
     photos, and other papers of Anne (Gibbons) Rhoads
     (ca. 1810-90) and Samuel Rhoads (1806-68), pub-
     lisher and editor of the Friends Review and a
     founder and officer of the Free Produce Associa-
     tion of Friends of Philadelphia Yearly Meeting.
     Subjects include abolition, the Free Produce Asso-
     ciation of Friends of Philadelphia Yearly Meeting,
     the Separation of 1827-28, and others. Correspon-
     dents include English Friends, and Thomas Clark-
     son (1760-1846).

.16 Rogers, Nathaniel Peabody, 1794-1846.
     Papers, 1800-1911. 3 ft. (ca. 600 items). Aboli-
     tionist editor. Correspondence; articles and about
     100 editorials by Rogers; legal documents; and
     clippings. Correspondence includes about 120
     letters from Rogers to family and friends dis-
     cussing the abolition movement and its leaders as
     well as personal matters; about 150 letters (1834-
     92) written to Rogers or, after his death, to mem-
     bers of his family concerning him, by Susan B.
     Anthony, Frederick Douglass, William Lloyd Gar-
     rison, Isaac Tatem Hopper, Elizabeth Pease,
     Charles Sumner, George Thompson, Richard Davis
     Webb (24 letters), Theodore Dwight Weld, John
     Greenleaf Whittier, and other reformers; about
     200 Rogers family letters (1809-69); and corre-
     spondence concerning a memorial to Rogers.

.17 Smiley family.
     Papers, 1885-1930. 97 ft. (ca. 22,600 items). In
     part, transcripts (typewritten). Archives of the
     Lake Mohonk Conferences for the uplifting of the
     American Indian, Filipino, Hawaiian, and Puerto
     Rican peoples, sponsored by Albert Keith Smiley

(1828-1912) and Daniel Smiley (1855-1930); private
archives (1912-30) of Daniel Smiley as a member
of the U.S. Board of Indian Commissioners; and
record books (1890-91) of the Lake Mohonk Conferences on the Negro question. Includes a few
family papers and correspondence.

.18 Tallcot, Joseph, ca. 1768-1853.
     Family papers, 1724-1857. 5 ft. (ca. 601 items).
     Farmer and prominent Friend. Correspondence,
     essays, sermons, epistles, and articles. The cor-
     respondence relates to religious education,
     Friends' schools and publications, the Separation
     of 1827-28, the Wilburite separation, the Negro
     colony at Wilberforce, Canada, and Negro slavery.
     Also includes the correspondence of Gains Tallcot
     (d. ca. 1773). Among Tallcot's correspondents are
     Moses Brown, George Dillwyn, Samuel Rhoads,
     Anna Braithwaite, and Sarah Moore Grimké

.19 Thompson family.
     Papers, 1751-ca. 1876. ca. 50 items. Papers of a
     Quaker family of Philadelphia. Includes accounts of
     expenses (1753-55) incurred by Jonah Thompson
     (1702-80), English Quaker minister and teacher, in
     securing possession of land bequeathed him in
     America; letters (1773) from his son, John Thomp-
     son (ca. 1744-1819), a teacher in Anthony Benezet's
     Philadelphia school; letters from James Thomp-
     son (1855-1955) discussing slavery, financial con-
     ditions, tariffs, Liberia, and other matters; and
     letters (1874) from John Jay Smith (1798-1881)
     and others, with comments on Philadelphia af-
     fairs. Other family names mentioned are John
     James Thompson (1815-75) and George Thompson.

.20 Wood, Anna Wharton (Smith), 1864- . collector.
     Quaker papers, 1741-1853. 55 items. Letters,
     notebooks, addresses, and other papers of Quaker
     interest, including an account of the transporting
     of Negroes to Haiti under Quaker auspices (1826);
     five notebooks, attributed to George Dillwyn (1738-
     1820) on theology, ethics, and the Society of
     Friends; and letters from Samuel Emlen (1766-
     1837) and John Pemberton (1727-95).

.21 Wood, William H.S., 1840-1907.
     Material for a book on Friends During the Civil
     War, 1860-87. ca. 100 items. In part, tran-
     scripts (handwritten). Publisher and banker.
     Letters, diaries, accounts, items extracted from
     minutes of Yearly Meetings of the Society of
     Friends, and other material collected by Wood
     for a book on Friends during the Civil War. In-
     cludes about 50 letters (1881-87) to Wood from
     Friends discussing their civil and military ex-
     periences and giving accounts of interviews with
     Edwin McMasters Stanton and Abraham Lincoln,
     and other information; extracts (1861-89) from the
     journals of John Bacon Crenshaw (1820-89), Rich-
     mond Quaker active in the relief of Friends during
     the Civil War, containing accounts of interviews
     with Jefferson Davis as well as copies of petitions
     for exemptions from military service for members
     of the Society of Friends, and others; accounts of
     experiences of southern Quakers; and minutes and
     reminiscences from Yearly Meeting of Phila-
     delphia, Pa., New York, Ohio, Baltimore, Md.,
     Indiana, New England, North Carolina and other
     places.

LANCASTER

PA17 LANCASTER CITY-COUNTY HUMAN RELATIONS COM-
      MITTEE. 432 S. Duke, 17602. Tel 717 394-4331.
      Patrick Kenney, Exec. Dir. Copying, typing, inquiries
      answered, referrals made, consultation.

PA18 LANCASTER COUNTY HISTORICAL SOCIETY (1886), LI-
      BRARY (1886). 230 N. President Ave., 17603. Tel 717
      392-4633. Mrs. Charles Lundgren, Lib'n. Copying,
      inquiries answered.
      Publ.: Journal of Lancaster County Historical Society,
      quarterly.

.1   Materials relating to Negroes.
      Miscellaneous materials, including a small
      number of slavery mss, and mss and research

data of articles from the Journal of the Lancaster County Historical Society concerning abolition movement, the Columbia race riots (1834), the local underground railway, the Ku Klux Klan in Lancaster County (1923-24), and the Christiana riot, Thaddeus Stevens and James Buchanan on slavery.

.2 Permanent collection.
Materials. Books, mss, records, diaries, newspapers, photographs, paintings, furniture, utensils, and other items used in exhibits concerning slavery, the Civil War, early local industry, domestic life two centuries ago, and many other subjects.

PA19   URBAN LEAGUE OF LANCASTER COUNTY, INC. Room 460, Coho Bldg., 53 N. Duke St., 17602. Tel 717 394-1966. Edward W. Allen, Exec. Dir.

.1 Urban League of Lancaster County, Inc.
Files. Correspondence, minutes of meetings, financial records, studies, reports, and other materials dealing with the aims, history and programs of the League.

LATROBE

PA20   ST. VINCENT COLLEGE AND ARCHABBEY (1846), LIBRARY (1846). 15650. Tel 412 537-3371. Rev. Robert J. Schuetz, Dir. Interlibrary loan, copying, typing, inquiries answered, referrals made, consultation.

.1 Anti-Slavery Propaganda Collection.
ca. 2500 pamphlets. Microcards of originals located in the Oberlin College Library. See Oberlin College Library, Oberlin, Ohio; or Lost Cause Press (publisher), Louisville, Ky., for more complete description.
.2 Negro Collection.
Books (ca. 700), periodical and newspaper titles, slavery pamphlet material on microcards (6700 units), theses and dissertations, and phonograph records by or about Negroes.

LINCOLN UNIVERSITY

PA21   LINCOLN UNIVERSITY, VAIL MEMORIAL LIBRARY (1854). 19352. Tel 215 932-8300. Emery Wimbish, Jr., Head Librn. Interlibrary loan, copying, typing, inquiries answered, referrals made, consultation.
Publ.: A Survey of the Special Negro Collection and Related Resources of the Vail Memorial Library (1964).

.1 Afro-American Studies Collection.
ca. 1000 paperbacks. Basic books on the life and history of black Americans.
.2 American Negro Collection.
Materials. 3000 v. Includes history, literature, and periodicals by and about the Negro.
.3 Hughes, Langston, 1902-67.
Materials. Author and poet. Personal library of Hughes, containing ca. 3000 items, including books by Hughes, periodicals, pamphlets and memorabilia as well as books by other authors.
.4 Lincoln University.
Archives, 1845- . Among institutional archives the letter files of the Reverend Edward Webb, financial secretary of Lincoln University from 1872 until his death in 1898, include letters to and from the Reverend Epaminondas J. Pierce, sometime missionary to the Gabon, as well as letters from Lincoln alumni in the Liberian mission field. A liberal selection from this correspondence exists in mimeographed form, as an appendix to a statement on African missions prepared in 1949 by President Honorarius Horace M. Bond, under the title God Be Glorified in Africa.
.5 Pennsylvania Colonization Society.
Minutes, 1838-1913. Includes Society's constitution and bylaws, together with rosters of officers and managers (1837-66) and a roster of life members (1882). They are supplemented with a ms volume titled Executive Committee of the Young Men's Colonization Society of Pennsylvania, which

includes lists of local colonization societies in Pennsylvania and neighboring states (1835-39); copies of invoices for supplies shipped to Bassa Cove; registers of emigrants (1834-64); and record of applicants for passage to Liberia during the years 1835-38.

MEADVILLE

PA22   ALLEGHENY COLLEGE (1815), WILLIAM EDWARD REIS MEMORIAL LIBRARY (1815). N. Main St., 16335. Tel 814 337-3251. Margaret L. Moser, Librn. Interlibrary loan, copying, inquiries answered

.1 Brown, John, 1800-59.
Papers, 1826-1958. ca. 600 items. In part, photocopies of 47 Brown letters in the possession of Atlanta University and transcripts (typewritten). Abolitionist. Correspondence, speeches, articles, photos, business and other papers relating to Brown's life in Crawford Co., Pa. (1826-35), and his farm and tannery. Includes minutes, treasurers' reports, and a membership list of the John Brown Memorial Association, New Richmond, Pa. (1924-58). Persons represented include Ernest Conrad Miller, Charles Wesley Olsen, and Boyd Blynn Stutler. Formerly part of the John Earle Reynolds collection.
.2 Tarbell, Ida M., 1896-1944.
Papers. ca. 11,000 items. Includes correspondence and literary mss relating to her writings on Abraham Lincoln, and to her other activities.

PHILADELPHIA

PA23   AMERICAN CIVIL LIBERTIES UNION (ACLU), GREATER PHILADELPHIA BRANCH. 260 S. Fifth St., 19102. Tel 215 735-7103. Spencer Coxe, Exec. Dir.

PA24   AMERICAN FOUNDATION FOR NEGRO AFFAIRS. 1714 Walnut, 19107. Tel 215 546-7770. Samuel L. Evans, Chmn.

PA25   AMERICAN FRIENDS SERVICE COMMITTEE (AFSC) (1917), COMMUNITY RELATIONS DIVISION (1948). 160 N. 15th St., 19102. Tel 215 563-9372. Barbara W. Moffett, Div. Secy.
The AFSC is a non-sectarian national service organization of the Religious Society of Friends (Quakers). The Division has programs dealing with housing, education, employment, human relations education, governmental operations, social attitudes, police-community relations, half-way houses, American Indian affairs, community development, and organization. Formerly the Race Relations Program.
Publ.: AFSC Bulletin, quarterly.

PA26   AMERICAN FRIENDS SERVICE COMMITTEE (1917), LIBRARY. 160 N. 15th St., 19102. Tel 215 563-9272. John R. Sutters, Librn. Copying, typing, inquiries answered
Publ.: Quaker Service, quarterly; Bulletins and annual reports.

.1 American Friends Service Committee Library.
Files, 1917- . Books, pamphlets (ca. 1500), theses and dissertations, correspondence, clippings, films, photographs, slides, and other materials concerning work with Negroes in the areas of employment, housing, schools, migrant workers, self-help housing, visiting lectureships by Negro professors, and in the field of the administration of justice. Included are the minutes of meetings, documentation dealing with the aims, program, and history of the Committee, and financial records. Correspondence restricted.

PA27   AMERICAN JEWISH COMMITTEE, PENNSYLVANIA-DELAWARE-MARYLAND REGION. 1500 Chestnut St., 19102. Tel 215 567-5902. Dr. Murray Friedman, Regional Dir. Inquiries answered
The Committee is an intergroup relations agency

which conducts research and community action programs.
Publ.: Studies and pamphlets.

PA28   AMERICAN JEWISH CONGRESS, GREATER PHILADEL-
PHIA COUNCIL. 1524 Locust St., 19102. Tel 215 546-
4366. Sanford Weinreb, Dir.

PA29   AMERICAN PHILOSOPHICAL SOCIETY, LIBRARY (1743).
105 S. Fifth St., 19106. Tel 215 925-9545. Dr. Whitfield J. Bell, Jr., Librn.
Publ.: Guide to the Archives and Manuscript Collections of the American Philosophical Society
(1966).

.1   Boas, Franz, 1858-1942.
Papers, ca. 1858-1942. ca. 50,000 items. Anthropologist and linguist. Personal and professional correspondence, diaries, and family papers. Includes professional materials on such
subjects as academic freedom, race, and similar
topics.

.2   Hare, Robert, 1781-1858.
Papers, 1764-1859. ca. 850 items and 3 v. Chemist and professor. Correspondence with various
persons, including his father-in-law, John Innes
Clark; lectures; letters to newspapers; and other
papers, in the form of scrolls, concerning slavery,
politics, and other subjects.

.3   Parsons, Elsie Worthington (Clews), 1875-1941.
Papers, 1835-1941. 9 ft. (ca. 11,900 items). Anthropologist and folklorist. Correspondence, 77
notebooks, drawings, mask and hat designs, ca.
600 photos, ca. 265 negatives, and other papers,
relating to folklore and ethnology of the southwest,
the southern Negro, Central America, and the West
Indies; and to Mrs. Parsons' work for the American Folklore Society and the American Anthropological Association.

.4   Price, Eli Kirk, 1797-1884.
Papers, 1820-53. 35 items. Lawyer and law reformer. Correspondence and other papers. Includes papers on legal questions and one against
slavery. Correspondents include Benjamin Armi-
tage, Elie Magloire Durand, William Maclure, and
Daniel Webster.

.5   Rafinesque, Constantine Samuel, 1783-1840.
Papers, 1808-1946. 228 items. Naturalist. Correspondence; texts, report of Rafinesque's scientific findings; letters, journal, essays, notes, and
miscellaneous pieces relating to Negroes, customs
of Americans, agriculture, and other topics.

PA30   AMERICAN SUNDAY SCHOOL UNION (1817), LIBRARY.
1816 Chestnut St., 19103. Tel 215 563-3813. Rev.
Norman B. Jerome, Dir. of Christian Lit. Literature
searches, inquiries answered.

.1   American Sunday School Union.
Papers, 1817-1954. 2500 items. Includes the official records of the Union and related organizations. Among other papers are some letters involving the slavery controversy.

PA31   ANTI-DEFAMATION LEAGUE OF B'NAI B'RITH,
PENNSYLVANIA-WEST VIRGINIA-DELAWARE RE-
GIONAL OFFICE. Suite 829, 225 S. 15th St., 19102.
Tel 215 735-4267. Samuel Lewis Gaber, Regional Dir.

PA32   BOARD OF EDUCATION, OFFICE OF INTERGROUP RE-
LATIONS (1965). Parkway at 21st, 19103. Tel 215
448-3491. Robert W. Blackburn, Dir.
The Office works to plan, coordinate and evaluate all
programs dealing with race and education in the schools
of Philadelphia, Pa. Also conducts research and disseminates information concerning intergroup education.
Publ.: Dialogue, quarterly.

PA33   CITY OF PHILADELPHIA, DEPARTMENT OF RECORDS,
CITY ARCHIVES (1952). 790 City Hall, 19107. Tel
215 686-2272. Allen Weinberg, City Archivist. Copy-
ing, inquiries answered, referrals made, consultation.
Publ.: News Letter, 3 times annually; Guide to the
Municipal Archives of the City and County of

Philadelphia (1957); The Descriptive Inventory
of the Archives of the City and County of Philadelphia (1970).

.1   City Directory.
Records, 1785. Includes the names and occupations
of free Negroes in the city of Philadelphia, Pa.

.2   Commission on Human Relations.
Files, 1954-66. 36 ft. Includes materials concerned with a wide range of the Commission's
neighborhood and community action programs, its
dealings with groups as diverse as RAM and the
American Nazi Party, and also includes minutes of
the Commission's meetings, reports, and compilations of data concerning population studies and public schools.

.3   Constable returns.
Papers, 1775, 1780. 2 v. An unindexed account of
the old city wards, a catalogue of householders'
names and occupations and free Negroes.

.4   Election returns.
1820-58. 1 v. Includes material concerning the
first Negro voters in Philadelphia. Returns at
ward level do not indicate identity of voters; may
be used with city directories and enumerations to
aid in identification of voting blocs.

.5   Philadelphia General Hospital.
Records, 1766-1939. ca. 850 v. Records of the
Guardians of the Poor (1766-1887) and the Bureau
of Charities (1887-1919) which administered the
County Alms House that has since become known
as Philadelphia General Hospital. Materials cover
all phases of outdoor relief and indigent care, and
associated hospital work; and records identifying
inmates as to race, age, and address.

.6   Registration Commission.
Annual reports, 1919-65. 47 v. Each report lists
numbers of white, black, foreign-born and native-
born voters registered in each ward and division,
and the total returns for each ward and division.

.7   Tax records.
Contain materials establishing the background of
the "free men of color" in the City of Philadelphia
as determined by population, areas of residence,
mobility, voting habits, reactions to slavery, colonization, mutual aid movements, and other similar
areas. Following categories of tax records describe the exact nature of the material:

.8   — County Tax Assessment Ledger.
Records, 1779-1854. 174 v. Includes list of
all items subject to tax in possession of each
taxable, including slaves and freedmen.

.9   — Enumeration of Taxables, Slaves, Deaf and Dumb
Persons.
Records, 1821, 1828, 1835. 10 v. Includes
list of slaves mingled with the names of taxables, by race and occupation.

.10   — Poor Tax Register.
Records, 1819-47. 56 v. Includes total as-
sessed values of taxables, including slaves as
possessions to be taxed; no method of de-
termining if slaves included in total or not.

PA34   CONGRESS OF RACIAL EQUALITY (CORE). 2229 Broad
St., 19107. Tel 215 765-2229. Bill Mathais, Chmn.

PA35   FAIR HOUSING ASSOCIATION. 20 S. 12th St., 19107. Tel
215 564-2950. William E. Cameron, Jr., Asst. Dir.

PA36   THE FREE LIBRARY OF PHILADELPHIA (1891). Logan
Square, 19103. Tel 213 686-3990. Keith Doms, Dir.
Interlibrary loan, bibliographies prepared, copying,
inquiries answered, referrals made, consultation.
Publ.: Book and film lists; Annual report; Pivot,
monthly newsletter.

.1   Music Department.
Included in the collections of the Music Department
are recordings composed by and performed by
Negro musicians, as well as sheet music directly
and indirectly related to the Negro.

.2   Philadelphia Tribune.
Newspaper, 1912-present. Negro newspaper published in Philadelphia, Pa. Complete run.

.3 Print and Picture Department.
Among other items, contains ca. 3000 prints and pictures on Negroes and Negro history (early 19th cent.- .).

PA37 FRIENDS YEARLY MEETING, LIBRARY (1961). 1515 Cherry St., 19102. Tel 215 545-0391. Eleanor B. Perry, Librn.

.1 Friends Yearly Meeting Library.
Included are materials (ca. 3000 v.) concerning civil rights, civil liberties, peace and social services.

PA38 FRONTIERS INTERNATIONAL, INC. (1936). 1307 N. 52nd St., 19131. Tel 215 477-7200. Harold L. Pilgrim, Exec. Secy.
The Corporation is an educational organization to promote intergroup harmony, primarily serving Negroes. This men's service organization is autonomous and the program is determined locally, but generally its activities include education, political action, demonstrations, and legal assistance. Formerly Frontiers of America. Publ.: The Frontiersman, quarterly.

.1 Frontiers International, Inc.
Files, 1936- . Documentation dealing with the aims, program, and history of the organization. Includes correspondence, reports, investigations, minutes of meetings, and financial records.

PA39 GERMANTOWN FRIENDS MEETING, FRIENDS FREE LIBRARY (1848). 5418 Germantown Ave., 19144. Tel 215 438-6023. Mrs. Sara Woy, Librn. Interlibrary loan, inquiries answered.

.1 Quaker history collection.
Materials, some pre-1700, chiefly 1700- . Primarily printed materials, including pamphlets, pertaining to Quaker history and containing scattered references to slavery, abolition, and Afro-American history. Included is a reproduction of a proclamation (1688) of the Germantown Friends Meeting protest against slavery.

PA40 GIRARD COLLEGE (1848), LIBRARY. Corinthian and Girard Aves., 19121. Tel 215 765-7555. Howard K. Emler, Librn. Copying, consultation.

.1 Girard, Stephen.
Papers. Material relating to the slave trade and the Negro in the 1793 yellow fever epidemic. Restricted.

PA41 THE GREEN CIRCLE PROGRAM. 1515 Cherry St., 19102. Tel 215 568-4111. Gladys D. Rawlins, Dir.
The Green Circle is a program on human relations for children of elementary school age, developed by the Race Relations Committee of the Philadelphia Yearly Meeting of Friends. It seeks to help stimulate and reinforce in children and adults positive social attitudes.

PA42 HERITAGE HOUSE EDUCATIONAL AND CULTURAL CENTER. 1346 N. Broad St., 19121. Tel 215 232-1700. Mrs. Vera Gunn, Dir.
The Center maintains a communications service, library, and black community council.

PA43 HISTORICAL SOCIETY OF PENNSYLVANIA LIBRARY. 1300 Locust St., 19107. Tel 215 735-2121. Nicholas Wainwright, Dir.

.1 African Colonization Society.
Papers, 1832-72. 1 v. Includes biographical sketches of the Society and material relating to American activities in Africa.

.2 American Negro Historical Society.
Records, 1790-1901. ca. 3000 items. Correspondence, minutes, constitutions, stock certificates, accounts, receipt books, roll books, vouchers, lectures, and debates, legal papers, deeds, bonds, ports., printed matter, and speeches. Material deals with Negro American cultural and economic advancement and the struggle for freedom. Persons named include Benjamin Banneker, Jacob C. White, Isiah C. Wears, Frederick Douglass (1870-

95), and others. Organizations and institutions represented include Daughters of Africa Society, Agricultural and Mechanic Association of Pennsylvania and New Jersey, Banneker Institute, Lebanon Cemetery, Pennsylvania State Equal Rights League, Frederick Douglass Memorial Hospital, Philadelphia, Pa.; Robert Vaux Consolidated School; the First and Second African Presbyterian Churches of Philadelphia; and Negro baseball clubs.

.3 Beverly, Robert.
Business records, 1763-1852. ca. 800 items. Accounts and receipts of a Georgetown (D.C.) financier, showing the cost of education in 1820, prices of goods, and the value of slaves; also documents connected with the litigation arising out of the settling of the George Washington estate.

.4 Biddle, Charles, 1745-1821.
Papers, 1763-1829. ca. 250 items. Merchant seaman, privateer, Revolutionary soldier, and public official. Correspondence, letter book, and autobiography. Subjects include politics, naval and military affairs, and the slave trade.

.5 Bigler, William, 1814-80.
Papers, 1836-80. ca. 5000. Pennsylvania businessman, journalist, and political leader. Correspondence, speeches, pamphlets, newspaper clippings, bills, accounts, family papers, and other material. Some items relate to Bigler's service as Governor (1851-54) and U.S. Senator (1856-61), reflecting political and social trends in the State and nation during the period of expansion. Subjects referred to include the slavery question, the Kansas-Nebraska bill, efforts to maintain the Union, and economic conditions after the Civil War.

.6 Broomall, John Martin, 1816-94.
Correspondence, 1867-68. 300 items. U.S. Representative from Pennsylvania. Letters dealing with the routine work of a Congressman, and with some material on conditions in the southern states during Reconstruction.

.7 Burleigh, Charles Calistus, 1810-78.
Anti-slavery papers, 1828-57. ca. 1000 items. Burleigh's writings on the abolition movement, moral and political essays, and other material on the slavery question. Among his essays are "The Southern Refugeeism," "Kansas," and "The Church."

.8 Butler family.
Papers, 1770-1900. ca. 3500 items. Papers of Major Pierce Butler (1744-1822), his grandson Pierce Butler (1807-67), and other members of the Butler family, relating principally to their Georgia plantations, rice and cotton crops, and management of slaves. Includes the regular reports of the plantation managers, personal correspondence, accounts, legal documents, records of rice plantations in Georgia, and other papers relating mainly to the estates.

.9 Cadwalader, John, 1742-86.
Estate papers, 1727-1838. 50 items. Papers pertaining to real estate held by John Cadwalader in Maryland. The plantations mentioned are Shrewsburg Farm, Hammond, Barbados Hall, Ward's Gift and Bodwell's Indian Neck. Includes lists of slaves, plantation accounts, lists of stock, and other papers.

.10 Chase, Salmon Portland, 1808-73.
Papers, 1824-82. ca. 15,000 items. Statesman and jurist. Diaries, journals, correspondence, letter books, memoranda, speeches, lectures, legal opinions, official documents, biographical material, and other papers, mainly bearing upon political trends, economic situations, religion, slavery, and social history before and after the Civil War. Much material reflects Chase's political activities. Includes biographical notes by J.W. Schuckers.

.11 Coles, Edward, 1786-1868.
Papers, 1762-1887. ca. 600 items. Governor of Illinois, secretary to President Madison, and abolitionist. Correspondence, documents, and business papers. Includes letters (1810-68) on Coles' political activities; an autobiographical sketch; and account books.

PA43.12 Cox, John, 1754-1847.
Papers of John Cox and family, 1600-1900. ca.
5000 items. Farmer and Quaker leader, of
Burlington, N.J. Correspondence, documents, receipt and invoice books, religious and literary mss,
reports, doctrinal materials, and other papers and
records indicative of the religious, humanitarian,
social, and economic influence of the Quakers in
American life. Many papers relate to slavery and
the abolition movement, and to agencies for the relief of Negroes; the lives of prominent Quakers;
trade with Africa and elsewhere; and other subjects. Genealogical material relating to the Cox,
Parrish, Dillwyn, Mitchell, and other families. Includes letters and other writings by, to, or concerned with Israel Pemberton, James Pemberton,
John Pemberton, Roberts Vaux, Job Bacon, Samuel
Emlen, and others.

.13 Decatur, Stephen, 1779-1820.
Letter book, 1801-05. 1 v. U.S. naval officer.
Material relating to American activities in Africa.

.14 Dreer, Ferdinand Julius. collector.
Papers, 1492-1917. 40,000 items. Capitalist and
philanthropist. It contains many series of letters
and other papers of persons prominent in the political, military, literary, religious, scientific,
musical, artistic, and business history of the U.S.
and England. Papers of prominent persons include
those of John Brown (1800-59), Pa., N.Y., and
Kansas; abolitionist.

.15 Dunbar, Elizabeth. collector.
Talcott Williams memorial papers, 1808-1936.
ca. 1000 pp. In part, transcripts (typewritten).
Mainly typewritten copies of letters, testimonials, addresses, obituary notes, tributes of
Negroes, bibliographical notes, mementoes, and
sketches gathered by Elizabeth Dunbar for her
book, Talcott Williams, Gentleman of the Fourth
Estate (1936).

.16 Dutilh and Wachsmuth, Philadelphia, Pa.
Records, 1704-1846. ca. 1000 items. Miscellaneous papers pertaining chiefly to slave trade with
the West Indies and trade with Europe; cargoes,
receipts, bills, insurance policies, bills of exchange, accounts, contracts, names of vessels,
maritime regulations, French privateers, records
of litigation in admiralty courts and courts of
equity.

.17 Edwards, Howard. collector.
Autograph letters, 1779-1883. ca. 75 items. Collection of letters of eminent English divines. Subjects mentioned include church sentiments, the
antislavery movement, and cultural trends in
England during the 18th and 19th centuries. Among
the correspondents are William Wilberforce,
Hannah More, and Elizabeth Fry.

.18 Embree, Elihu, 1782-1820.
Papers, 1814-25. 50 items. Tennessee editor and
abolitionist. Letters, addressed chiefly to John
M. Paul, Quaker merchant in Philadelphia, dealing
with commercial and domestic affairs, the abolition movement, and the publication by Embree of
the Emancipator, at Jonesboro, Tenn. (1818),
America's first abolitionist periodical. Includes a
list of subscribers to the Emancipator.

.19 Henry, Alexander, 1823-83.
Papers, 1840-76. ca. 350 items. Mayor of Philadelphia during the Civil War. Correspondence, official papers and documents, and narratives of war
events. Correspondence with prominent persons
and mayors of various cities discuss war sentiments, civic affairs, rioting, popular demonstrations, the danger of mob violence, and other matters. Includes a narrative (1864) of the sufferings
of Union servicemen captured by the Confederates.

.20 Johnston, Josiah Stoddard, 1784-1833.
Papers, 1821-39. ca. 5000 items. Lawyer and
stateman; U.S. Representative and Senator from
Louisiana. Correspondence, official and personal
papers of interest in connection with national
politics, Louisiana politics, cotton, slavery, and
many other topics.

.21 Logan, Deborah (Norris), 1761-1839.
Diaries, 1815-39. 17 v. Historian; wife of George
Logan, physician, farmer, U.S. Senator from
Pennsylvania, and friend of Thomas Jefferson.
Diary entries reflecting the social life of prominent Philadelphia families, and political, religious,
and cultural developments. Other topics include
the yellow fever epidemics, slavery, Friends
meetings, and other topics. Includes many biographical notes concerning public figures, among
them Pierce Butler, Benjamin Franklin, Stephen
Girard, and others.

.22 Menzies, John.
Papers, 1793-94. Includes narrative of the ad-
ventures and experiences of Menzies as a sailor
and traveler to Portugal, Africa, and elsewhere,
relating to American activities in Africa.

.23 Meredith family.
Papers, 1760-1888. 50,000 items and 150 v. Papers relating to the activities of four generations
of a branch of the Meredith family, founded in the
U.S. by Jonathan Meredith (1740-1811), leather
manufacturer and exporter. Subjects include
politics, shipping, law, legislation, war, banking,
land, society, Civil War, slavery, and Negro insurrection. Other family names mentioned are David
Meredith (b. 1771), William Meredith (1772-1844),
William M. Meredith (1799-1873), Sullivan Amory
Meredith (1816-74), and others.

.24 Miscellaneous materials.
Papers, 1681-1938. ca. 350 items, ca. 55 v., 8
boxes, and 4 folders. In part, photocopies. Surveys, maps, deeds, lists of property holders;
military papers of various types; diary, daybooks,
hotel register, lists of subscribers to various
enterprises; scrapbooks, clippings, memorabilia,
and other miscellaneous items; documents relating
to insurance, investments, lotteries, indentures
and redemptioners; materials on slavery, local
history.

.25 North Carolina papers.
1777-1876. ca. 300 items. Letters, orders of the
Assembly (1777), and other printed matter. Letters discuss slavery, laws, religion, local affairs,
and other topics.

.26 Papers relating to Negroes.
Miscellaneous, 16th-19th centuries. Includes
materials pertaining to slavery, reactions to
slavery, slave trade, admittance of free states to
the Union, mutual aid movements, colonization,
the Reconstruction, and similar topics. Subjects
and persons mentioned include: John Quincy
Adams, letter to E.P. Atlee (June 25, 1836); Richard
Allen, petition signed to the Select and Common
Councils of the City of Philadelphia (ca. 1795);
American Convention of Abolition Societies, minute
book (Jan. 1, 1794-Jan. 13, 1804); Jehudi Ashmun,
letter signed to the Rt. Rev. Dr. Kemp (April 22,
1827); Benjamin C. Bacon and Charles Gardner, ms
of Census Facts Collected for the Pennsylvania So-
ciety for Promoting the Abolition of Slavery (1838);
Benjamin Banneker, signed letter to Andrew Elli-
cott (May 6, 1790); Philidore S. Bell, letter signed
to Jacob C. White, Jr. (Sept. 14, 1868); Anthony
Benezet, ms will signed (June 1, 1773); Border
State Convention, Call for a National Convention to
the Colored Men of the United States (1868); John
Brown, letter signed to his wife and children from
Charlestown, Va., Prison (Nov. 30, 1859); Owen
Brown, ms of "Declaration of Liberty by the
Representatives of the Slave Population of the
United States of America" (Dec. 4, 1859); William
Wells Brown, letter signed to William Still (Feb.
2, 1865); Pierce Butler, ms catalogue of Pierce
Butler's share of slaves to be sold at auction, with
appraised prices (Feb. 21, 1859); James Carter,
ms journal of the sufferings of his family as
slaves (1807); Henri Christophe, letter signed to
Tobias Lear (Dec. 19, 1801); Thomas Clarkson,
letter signed to Roberts Vaux (Jan. 31, 1820); Paul
Cuffe, letter signed to Jedediah Morse (Aug. 10,
1816); John M. Dickey, letter signed to "Brother"
Murray (June 6, 1854); Frederick Douglass, letter
signed to Thurlow Weed (Dec. 1, 1845); William
Edward Burghardt DuBois, letter signed to
Jacob C. White (Oct. 18, 1898); Bryan Ed-

wards, letter signed to Sir Joseph Banks (Sept. 24, 1798); Benjamin Franklin, letter in the third person to James Pemberton (Aug. 28, 1788); Henry Highland Garnet, a letter signed to Jacob C. White, Jr. (May 8, 1865) and a prospectus for The First Sermon Delivered in the Hall of the House of Representatives, Washington, D.C., by an American Citizen of African Descent (1865); William Lloyd Garrison, letter signed to J. Miller McKim (Oct. 13, 1861); R.R. Gurley, letter signed to Erastus Hopkins of the Office of the Colonization Society in Washington, D.C. (Feb. 19, 1833); Hinton Rowan Helper, letter signed to Messrs. Dix, Edwards & Co. (Mar. 31, 1857) and a letter signed to Henry C. Carey (Nov. 4, 1858); George W. Kirkland, letter signed to William Macpherson (Sept. 28, 1800); Philadelphia's Lebanon Cemetery, receipt book (Dec. 29, 1848-Nov. 11, 1853); Abraham Lincoln, letter signed to Salmon P. Chase (June 9, 1859); George Logan, letter signed to Caesar A. Rodney (Dec. 19, 1822); Elijah P. Lovejoy, letter signed to Archibald Gamble (Nov. 27, 1835); Zachary Macaulay, letter signed to the Rev. Stephen Hopkins (March 21, 1795); Peter and Eugenia Marks, manumission record, bill of sale, letters of recommendation, and passes (1831-39); Benjamin and John Mifflin, series of documents such as manumission papers (Dec. 5, 1769-Oct. 15, 1772); William N. Needles, letter signed to Wendell P. Garrison (June 23, 1885); Frederick Law Olmsted, letter signed to Charles J. Stillé (Feb. 25, 1863); Marie Joseph Paul, Marquis de Lafayette, letter signed to Thomas Clarkson (Feb. 18, 1830); James W.C. Pennington, letter signed to J.M. Kebbs (Oct. 18, 1854); Petition for the Colored people of Philadelphia to ride in the cars, signed document (1866); Augustus J. Pleasanton, diary (Thursday, May 17, 1838); Pythian Base Ball Club, document of a report of the delegate to the Pennsylvania Convention of Base Ball Players (1867); David Rittenhouse, letter signed to James Pemberton (1791); Prince Saunders, letter signed to Roberts Vaux (1822); Hans Sloane, letter signed to Etienne Francois Geoffroy (1699); Social, Cultural and Statistical Association of the Colored People of Pennsylvania, ms of constitution, by-laws, roll and minutes (1860-67); Society for the Relief of Free Negroes Unlawfully Kept in Bondage, articles and minutes (1775-87); William Still, journal of fugitive slaves who passed through station No. 2 of the Underground Railroad (1852-57); Sojourner Truth, letter (as dictated to her grandson William) to William Still (1876); Vigilant Committee of Philadelphia, minute book and record of cases kept by Jacob C. White, Jr. (1839-44); Alexander Stuart Wallace, letter signed to Sen. John Scott (1871); Booker T. Washington, letter signed to William Still (1888); Isaiah C. Wears, ms of remarks before the Senate Committee on "Exodus" (1880); Angelina Grimké Weld, letter signed to Lydia Maria Child (1838); Jacob C. White, Jr., letter signed to Philidore S. Bell, secretary of the Athletics Base Ball Convention (1868); John Greenleaf Whittier, letter signed to the editor of Commonwealth, Moncure D. Conway (1851); William Wilberforce, letter signed to the Hon. William Huskisson (1814).

PA43.27 Parker, Daniel, 1782-1846.
Papers, 1800-46. Adjutant and inspector general of the War Dept. Mainly official correspondence and other papers of the War Dept. Includes Governor John Dayton's letters to Thomas Jefferson (1801-02) concerning the landing of French Negroes on the southern coasts of the Union, and other papers. Daniel Parker's correspondence (1811-45) relates to his official and financial activities, with letters of W. Rawle, Parker family, and others.

.28 Paul, Joseph M.
Business records, 1800-29. 3 v. Philadelphia merchant. Daybook, letter books, and a journal of a journey through central and western Pennsylvania (1815). Includes material on the abolition movement, legal matters, and other topics.

.29 Pemberton family.
Papers, 1641-1880. ca. 15,000 items, 56 v. Correspondence and other papers of the Pennsylvania Quaker family: Phineas Pemberton (1650-1702), Israel Pemberton, Sr. (1695-1754), Israel Pemberton, Jr. (1715-79), James Pemberton (1723-1809), John Pemberton (1727-95), and their descendants. The major portion of the collection (1641-1808) is chronologically arranged to include material on seventeenth century personalities, religious intolerance and persecution, Quaker meetings, economic and social conditions, and slavery.

.30 Pennsylvania Society for Promoting the Abolition of Slavery.
Papers, 1748-1916. ca. 12,000 items. Correspondence, legal documents, minutes, ledger accounts, letter books, and list of members of the society; also ca. 6000 manumission certificates (1765-1865); manumission books (1780-1851); indenture books (1758-1835); William Still papers (1852-1902); minutes of the American Convention (1794-1809); census books of Negro population of Philadelphia (ca. 1840-47); education and employment statistics (1849-56); material on the Philadelphia Supervisory Committee for Recruiting Colored Regiments; and 17 v. on education of Negroes, among which are extensive records of the Clarkson School (1819-61). Other items pertain to the history and activities of abolition societies and the influence exerted by Quakers and other abolitionists.

.31 Rawle family.
Papers of the William Rawle family, 1683-1915. ca. 6000 items. Correspondence and essays of William Rawle, U.S. attorney for Pennsylvania, with various other papers, including a ledger (1720-26) of Francis Rawle; and papers relating to the abolition of slavery, and other matters.

.32 Read, George C., 1787-1862.
Papers, 1846-47. 7 v. Commander of the African Squadron. Includes material relating to American activities in Africa.

.33 Records of clubs and societies.
Papers, 1775-1925. ca. 35 v., 2 boxes, and 1 package. In part, photocopies. Minute books, cashbooks, membership lists, constitutions, petitions, and other diverse items relating to relief societies, burial societies, women's organizations (professional and social), colonization societies and societies for the protection of fugitive slaves, political clubs, literary associations, patriotic societies, clerical organizations, and societies connected with churches, schools, lodges, and ethnic groups.

.34 Roberts, Jonathan, 1771-1854.
Papers, 1780-1930. ca. 3000 items. U.S. Senator from Pennsylvania. Correspondence, genealogical notes, poetry, speeches, proclamations, indentures, and newspaper clippings. The bulk of the collection relates to state and national political history (1780-1848), with material on Pennsylvania legislation, political affairs at Lancaster, Pa., the Missouri question, Texas slavery contest, and other topics. Roberts' letters to his wife (1814-47) describe economic conditions, domestic and cultural life, travel, and agricultural and industrial development. Other letters (1852-1930) are from various members of the Roberts family.

.35 Rotch, William, 1734-1828.
Papers. Prominent Nantucket and New Bedford whaling merchant. Includes material relating to American activities in Africa.

.36 Steinmetz, Mary Owen.
Papers. 200 items. Genealogist, of Reading, Pa. Notes, containing material on Berks County cemeteries, newspapers, slavery, and other subjects.

.37 Tilghman, William, 1756-1827.
Correspondence, 1772-1827. ca. 8500 items. Philadelphia lawyer and jurist. Letters from clients, friends, and members of his family. The main portion of the collection pertains to claims, controversies, suits in court, and other legal matters; accounts of the purchase and sale of slaves; and other subjects.

.38 Townsend, Washington, 1813-95. collector.
Autographed letters and documents, 1716-1863.
262 items. Letters and documents apparently
gathered for an autograph collection. Includes six
letters (1852) concerning legal efforts to free a
Negro girl, Rachel Parker. Correspondents of
Isaac Dutton Barnard include Nicholas Biddle,
James Buchanan, Simon Cameron, Susan Decatur,
and others.

.39 Unger, Charles W. collector.
Papers, 1706-1904. 44 boxes (ca. 10,000 items).
Residue of the papers of an autograph dealer, containing much material on the merchants and
shippers of the early federal period, particularly
the Philadelphia house of Dutilh and Wachsmuth.
Includes some papers of other companies.

.40 Vaux family.
Papers, 1686-1893. ca. 4500 items. Correspondence, including ca. 2000 letters to Robert Vaux,
a leader in the movement for free public schools in
Philadelphia; papers of his father Richard Vaux,
including diaries (1779-82) and an account book
(1789); papers of Richard Vaux who was mayor of
Philadelphia in 1856-57. Correspondence pertains
to social and political reform, problems of general
welfare, as well as personal affairs and local and
national political events.

.41 Woolman, John, 1720-72.
Papers, 1652-1830. 24 items and 3 v. Quaker
leader and advocate of the abolition of slavery.
Woolman's journal, ledgers, letters to his wife,
accounts as executor of the estate of Elizabeth
Woolman, and his will. Other material deals with
his Quaker activities and family matters.

PA43a HISTORICAL SOCIETY OF THE EASTERN PENNSYLVANIA
CONFERENCE OF THE UNITED METHODIST CHURCH.
326 New St., 19109. Tel 215 925-7700. Howard T.
Maag, Acting Librn.

.1 The Society holds the records of the Philadelphia Methodist Conference (1800- .), and the minutes of the
Philadelphia Preachers Meetings (1841-1942). The
records of the Conference "are especially important to the exploration of the dramatic schism
of color that brought about the formation of the
African Methodist Episcopal Church and laid the
foundations for black Protestantism. They are
also essential to a study of the changes that occurred within the ranks of Methodists which brought
their leaders into the anti-slavery and abolitionist
movement even though they originally advocated
separation of the races."

PA44 HOUSING ASSOCIATION OF DELAWARE VALLEY (1909).
1601 Walnut St., 19103. Tel 213 563-4050. Cushing N.
Dolbeare, Managing Dir. Inquiries answered.
The Association works for open housing in Philadelphia
and suburbs; works with local fair housing councils to
serve communities; assists individuals with housing
problems; and actively supports open occupancy and
open housing legislation.
Publ.: Housing Facts, monthly; Annual Report; Publication list, committee reports, and fair housing
brochures; Issues, occasionally; Special Memoranda.

.1 Housing Association of Delaware Valley.
Files, 1962- . Documentation dealing with the
aims, history and programs of the Association. Included are correspondence, investigations, studies,
minutes of meetings, financial records, and other
items. Records, 1909-62, are at Temple University Urban Archives Center. Formerly Philadelphia Housing Association and the Fair Housing
Council, which merged in 1962.

PA45 INTERFAITH, INTERRACIAL COUNCIL OF THE CLERGY
IN PHILADELPHIA. 1730 N. 22nd St., 19145. Tel 215
763-1553. Rev. W.L. Bently, Pres.
The programs of the Council include counseling on
home ownership and management, and a program to
purchase properties in North Philadelphia, rehabilitate
them and resell the homes to low income families.

PA46 JEWISH COMMUNITY RELATIONS COUNCIL OF GREATER
PHILADELPHIA (1938). 260 S. 15th St., 19102. Tel
215 545-8430. Albert D. Chernin, Exec. Dir.
The Council works to protect and enhance equal rights
and opportunities for all citizens and foster conditions
that contribute toward the dignity of the Jewish community. Its principal approaches are through social
education and social action.

.1 Jewish Community Council of Greater Philadelphia.
Files, 1938- . Documentation dealing with the
aims, history, and programs of the Council. Includes correspondence, reports, studies, investigations, minutes of meetings, and financial records.

PA47 JOB LOAN AND URBAN VENTURE CORPORATION. 2030
P.N.B. Bldg., 19107. Tel 215 568-4662. William
Zucker, Pres. Loans for minority entrepreneurship.
The Corporation has a fund to make above-average
risk loans to black businessmen in the city's ghetto
areas. It is funded by 8 Philadelphia banks and the
Southern Pennsylvania Development Fund.

PA48 KAPPA ALPHA PSI. 2320 N. Broad St., 19132. Tel 215
228-7184. Earl A. Morris, Exec. Secy.
Kappa Alpha Psi is a national Negro fraternity which
has a program of social action which coordinates civil
rights activities within chapters.
Publ.: Publication for membership.

.1 Kappa Alpha Psi.
Files. Documentation dealing with the aims, history, and program of the organization. Includes
correspondence, minutes of meetings, financial
records, and other material.

PA49 LIBRARY COMPANY OF PHILADELPHIA (1731). 1314
Locust St., 19107. Tel 215 546-3181. Edwin Wolf, II,
Librn. Interlibrary loan, bibliographies prepared,
literature searches, copying, inquiries answered, re-
ferrals made, consultation.
Publ.: Annual reports; Negro History 1553-1903 (An
Exhibition Catalogue)

.1 American Song Slips.
Many of the song slips relate to Negroes, the Civil
War, and race questions.

.2 Dillwyn, William, 1743-1824.
Correspondence of William Dillwyn and his
daughter, Susanna Emlen, 1770-1824. 1 ft. (846
items). Letters between William Dillwyn, living
in London, and his daughter Susanna living in
Burlington and Philadelphia, Pa., containing comments on family affairs, the social life of Philadelphia, politics, slavery, and other events of the
time.

.3 Du Simitiere Papers.
Papers. ca. 600 items. Natural history of West
Indies; various items concerning Jamaica and St.
Domingo; Negro uprisings; missionary ventures;
etc.

.4 McAllister, John, 1786-1877. collector.
Miscellaneous mss, 1683-1881. ca. 15,000 items.
Records of business firms, papers relating to the
Civil War, slavery, and miscellaneous papers,
collected by John McAllister, Jr., and continued by
his son John A. McAllister.

.5 Papers relating to Negroes.
Miscellaneous, 1768-1862. Includes materials
pertaining to slavery, slave trade, abolition, slave
insurrections, and similar topics. Subjects and
persons mentioned include: Benjamin C. Bacon,
Statistics of the Colored People of Philadelphia
(1856); John Dickinson, letter and draft to David
Barclay (Aug. 15, 1802); Francis Johnson, Album
of Musical Compositions (1821); Abraham Lincoln,
ms of "A Proclamation in pursuance of the sixth
section of the Act of Congress entitled 'An act to
suppress insurrection, and to punish treason and
rebellion, to seize and confiscate property of
rebels, and for other purposes'" (July 25, 1862);
Samuel George Morton, notes for his study on
"The Size of Brains in Different Races" (ca. 1835);
Benjamin Rush, an address to the inhabitants of the

British settlements in America, upon slave-keeping (1773); Granville Sharp, copy book of received letters (1768-73) and a letter signed to Benjamin Rush (Feb. 21, 1774); U.S., document signed of the convention between the U.S. and Great Britain for the suppression of the slave trade (May 24, 1824); and Phillis Wheatley, ms of poems, "America," "Atheism," and "To the Honble. Commodore Wood on his pardoning a deserter" (ca. 1774-76).

.6 Rush, Benjamin, 1745-1813.
Papers, 1762-1813. 17 ft. (ca. 6500 items). Physician. Correspondence, medical writings, 3 small notebooks containing Rush's diary for 1777-78 covering debates in the Continental Congress, journals, and daybooks. Correspondence relates to Rush's medical career, land speculation, Dickinson College, controversies with Shippen and Cobbett, and family affairs. Includes letters from Dr. David Ramsay.

.7 Works of art relating to Negroes.
1792-1874. Includes colored lithographs of the celebration of Negroes on Jubilee Day, plantation scenes, black troops' activities, and similar themes; and an oil painting by Samuel Jennings entitled "Liberty Displaying the Arts and Sciences."

PA50   NATIONAL ASSOCIATION FOR THE ADVANCEMENT OF COLORED PEOPLE (NAACP), TRI-STATE AREA OFFICE. N. 13th St., 19101. Tel 215 424-4500.

.1 National Association for the Advancement of Colored People.
Files. Documentations dealing with the history, aims, and program of the Association. Includes correspondence, reports, studies, investigations, minutes of meetings, and financial records.

PA51   NATIONAL CONFERENCE OF CHRISTIANS AND JEWS (NCCJ). 1211 Chestnut St., 19107. Tel 215 564-3776. Charles C. Benham, Dir.

PA52   NATIONAL NEIGHBORS. 5 Longford St., 19136. Tel 215 338-2905. Jean Gregg Milgram, Exec. Dir. Interlibrary loan, copying, inquiries answered, referrals made, consultation.
An agency supported by Sponsors for Open Housing Investment, which seeks to serve integrated neighborhoods.

.1 National Neighbors.
Books. ca. 250 v. Subjects include race, housing, and urban problems. Available to qualified persons.

PA53   OPPORTUNITIES INDUSTRIALIZATION CENTER INSTITUTE, INC. (1965). 3639 N. Broad St., 19140. Tel 215 236-5400. Dr. L.D. Reddick, Exec. Dir.
The Center works to motivate, train, develop and utilize the technical skills of members of the communities, regardless of race, creed, color or sex, in the art of manufacturing and industrialization to ease local unemployment problems.
Publ.: The Key, quarterly.

.1 Opportunities Industrialization Center Institute, Inc.
Files, 1965- . Documentation dealing with the aim, history, and program of the Center. Includes correspondence, minutes of meetings, financial reports, and other material.

PA54   THE PENNSYLVANIA ACADEMY OF THE FINE ARTS (1879). Broad and Cherry Sts., 19102. Tel 215 564-0219.
Publ.: Annual Report.

Among the holdings of the Academy are works by the following Negro Americans.
.1 Pippin, Horace, 1888-1946.
Painting, 1942. 1 item. Artist. Oil painting entitled "John Brown Going to His Hanging."
.2 Tanner, Henry Ossawa, 1859-1937.
Painting. 1 item. Artist. Oil painting entitled "Nicodemus."

PA55   PENNSYLVANIA HUMAN RELATIONS COMMISSION, PHILADELPHIA REGIONAL OFFICE (1955). 101 State Office Bldg., 19130. Tel 215 238-6940. Ishmael R. Johnson, Regional Supvr. Inquiries answered.

.1 Pennsylvania Human Relations Commission, Philadelphia Regional Office.
Miscellaneous. Small number of reference books and pamphlets on human relations, civil rights, segregation, and discrimination for use in connection with the Commission's anti-discrimination programs.

PA56   PEOPLE FOR HUMAN RIGHTS. 5440 Morris St., 19144. Tel 215 626-6535. Peter Contryman, Dir.
People for Human Rights works to organize liberation schools for white middle-class high school students to aid them in understanding the black community.

PA57   PHILADELPHIA COMMISSION ON HUMAN RELATIONS (1952). Room 601, City Hall Annex, 19107. Tel 215 686-4670. Clarence Farmer, Exec. Dir. Inquiries answered, referrals made, consultation.
The Commission works to administer and enforce all statutes and ordinances prohibiting discrimination; institute and conduct educational programs to promote equal rights and opportunities; receive and investigate complaints of, and initiate its own investigations of, practices of discrimination; and hold public hearings for such purposes and make public its findings. Formerly the Fair Employment Practices Commission (1948).
Publ.: Annual Report; Quarterly Bulletin.

.1 Philadelphia Commission on Human Relations.
Files, 1952- . Documentation dealing with the aims, history, and programs of the Commission. Includes correspondence, minutes of meetings, financial reports, investigations, reports, and studies.

PA58   PHILADELPHIA COUNCIL FOR COMMUNITY ADVANCEMENT (1962). Room 603, 1406 Chestnut St., 19110. Tel 215 563-9581. William E. Cameron, Jr., Exec. Dir.
The Council is an independent civic agency working in services geared to urban poor, with particular emphasis on minority (Negro) problems in the areas of housing, education, employment, and community organization. The Council also has a program in the area of Negro history.

.1 Philadelphia Council for Community Advancement.
Files, 1962- . Documentation dealing with the history, aims, and programs of the Council. Includes correspondence, minutes of meetings, financial reports, studies, investigations, and other materials related to their work.

PA59   PHILADELPHIA FELLOWSHIP COMMISSION (1941), LIBRARY (1945). 260 S. 15th St., 19102. Tel 215 545-7600. Miss M. Elizabeth Robinson, Librn. Bibliographies prepared, inquiries answered.
The Commission is a city-wide, non-governmental, tax-exempt citizens' movement. It combats discrimination, segregation, racism, and religious bigotry in the areas of education, housing, industry, and law enforcement.
Publ.: Report to the Community, bimonthly newsletter; Publication lists, pamphlets, brochures, and bibliographies.

.1 Philadelphia Fellowship Commission.
Papers, 1941- . Includes correspondence, pamphlets, reports, studies, and other materials on the activities, aims, history, and programs of the Commission. These materials are not a part of the Library but are housed elsewhere in the Commission. Not open to public.

.2 Philadelphia Fellowship Commission Library.
The Library includes books (4000), periodical and newspaper titles, pamphlets (2500), films, photographs on such subjects as Afro-American history, black power, and civil rights.

PA60   PHILADELPHIA MUSEUM OF ART. 26th St. and Parkway,
        P.O. Box 7646, 19101. Tel 215 765-0500. Inquiries
        answered.
        Publ.: Museum Bulletin, quarterly.

    .1 Brown, Samuel.
            Paintings. 6 items. Included are drawings, "The
            Lynching," "Abstraction No. 2," "Georgia Rose";
            "Seated Boy," water color; and an oil, "Self-
            Portrait."
    .2 Pippin, Horace, 1888-1946.
            Paintings. 2 items. Artist. Includes oil paintings
            entitled "The End of the War: Starting Home," and
            "A Chester County Art Critic."
    .3 Sloan, Louis, 1932- .
            Painting, 1959. "Manayunk."
    .4 Tanner, Henry Ossawa, 1859-1937.
            Painting. 1 item. Artist. Oil painting entitled
            "The Annunciation."

PA61   PHILADELPHIA URBAN LEAGUE (1907). 304 Penn Square
        Bldg., 19107. Tel 215 569-3636. Andrew G. Freeman,
        Exec. Dir. Inquiries answered, referrals made, con-
        sultation.
        The Urban League is an interracial agency which uses
        the social service method of community organization to
        create equal opportunities for Negroes and other mi-
        norities. Much of the League's work is for better jobs,
        equal housing opportunities, quality integrated public
        education, and adequate equitable health and welfare
        services. The League's role is one of negotiation,
        education, coordination, and mobilizing community sup-
        port for social change. Formerly the Armstrong Asso-
        ciation.
        Publ.: Annual and quarterly reports; Departmental
            newsletters; Brochures and pamphlets.

    .1 Philadelphia Urban League.
            Files, 1907- . Includes correspondence, minutes
            of meetings, financial records, and other materials
            and documents relating to the history, aims, and
            programs of the League

PA62   PHILADELPHIA YEARLY MEETING OF THE RELIGIOUS
        SOCIETY OF FRIENDS, COMMITTEE ON RACE RE-
        LATIONS (1928). 1515 Cherry St., 19102. Tel 215 563-
        7705. Mrs. Jane R. Cosby, Exec. Secy.
        The Committee works to improve race relations within
        the Society of Friends and cooperates with other
        groups with similar goals.
        Publ.: Race Relations Newsletter, irregular.

PA63   PHILADELPHIA YEARLY MEETING OF THE RELIGIOUS
        SOCIETY OF FRIENDS, DEPARTMENT OF RECORDS
        OF PHILADELPHIA YEARLY MEETING (1681). 302
        Arch St., 19106. Tel 215 922-2408. Mrs. Alice P.
        Allen, Secy. Genealogical searches.
        The Department of Records is a depository for the
        Minutes of the Philadelphia Yearly Meeting and its
        constituent Monthly and Quarterly Meetings; also for
        the educational work of the Yearly Meeting, including
        work with the Negroes in Philadelphia and the Indians
        in New York.

    .1 Friends, Society of. Philadelphia Yearly Meeting.
            Records, 1657- . 182 ft. In part, transcript and
            microfilm (positive). Records of the yearly,
            quarterly, and monthly meetings, and of various
            committees and associations, among which are the
            Institute for Colored Youth and the Friends Free-
            doms Association. Included are minutes of meet-
            ings and other records of Friends communities,
            1681-1954; papers relating to the opposition of
            Friends to wars of the Colonies and the U.S.; and
            records of educational work among Negroes. On
            deposit are some records of the Association of
            Friends for the Instruction of Adult Colored Per-
            sons, 1789-1904, and of the Friends Freedmen's
            Association, 1863-1935. A very small part of the
            collection consists of transcripts; there are 15
            reels of microfilm. Described in detail in Inven-
            tory of Church Archives: Society of Friends in
            Pennsylvania, prepared by the Pennsylvania His-
            torical Survey (1941). A partial description can be
            found in a list of records of Meetings constituting

the Yearly Meeting of the Society of Friends, held
at 15th and Race St., Philadelphia, Pa., (1906).
Open to investigators under repository restrictions.

PA64   PROGRESS ENTERPRISES, INC. 3600 N. Broad St., 19140.
        Tel 215 233-5460.
        Progress Enterprises is a profit-making investment
        arm of an economic-development and job-training
        program organized by the Rev. Leon Sullivan of the
        Zion Baptist Church of Philadelphia, Pa. Enterprises
        grew out of a capital pool formed by members of the
        congregation and portions of its profit goes into the
        Zion Non-profit Charitable Trust. The latter operates
        vocational and managerial training centers for Ne-
        groes, sponsors nonprofit housing, and helps Negroes
        start or strengthen their own businesses.

    .1 Progress Enterprises, Inc.
            Records. Includes correspondence, financial
            records, list of contributors, and plans for further
            business developments, documentation dealing with
            the aims, programs, and history of Progress
            Enterprises.

PA65   REDEVELOPMENT AUTHORITY OF THE CITY OF PHILA-
        DELPHIA (1947). 11th Floor, City Hall Annex, 19107.
        Tel 215 569-8245. Francis J. Lammer, Exec. Dir.
        The Authority works to eliminate blighted areas; to
        supply sanitary housing; and to provide sites for busi-
        ness, industrial, science, medical and educational
        purposes.
        Publ.: Annual reports; Brochures.

    .1 Redevelopment Authority of the City of Philadelphia.
            Files, 1947- . Documentation of the aims, his-
            tory, and program of the agency. Includes corre-
            spondence, financial records, reports, investiga-
            tions, and studies.

PA66   RESEARCH FOR BETTER SCHOOLS, INC. 121 S. Broad
        St., 19107. Tel 215 546-6050.
        The Corporation is a nonprofit organization that works
        in the areas of individual instruction, teacher educa-
        tion, relating research to educational needs, training
        research disseminators, and technology in educational
        systems.

    .1 Research for Better Schools, Inc.
            Files. Documentation dealing with the aims, his-
            tory, and programs of the agency. Includes corre-
            spondence, studies, reports, and other material
            relating to the activities.

PA67   TEMPLE UNIVERSITY, CENTER FOR COMMUNITY
        STUDIES (1961). 19122. Tel 215 787-7000. Herman
        Niebuhr, Jr., Dir.
        The Center serves as an orientation center for the con-
        duct of interdisciplinary research on urban questions
        and as a means to apply the resources of the University
        to community problems. Extension projects undertaken
        by the agency have been a study for the renewal of
        Philadelphia's skid row area, a remedial project to im-
        prove the speech patterns of disadvantaged Negro
        girls, and a school district consultation. In addition,
        the Center has begun to develop short-term, intensive
        training programs such as the VISTA training pro-
        gram, the North Philadelphia leadership training pro-
        gram, and the Upward Bound Program.

    .1 Center for Community Studies.
            Files, 1961- . Documentation dealing with the
            aims, history, and programs of the Center. In-
            cludes correspondence, reports, studies, and
            other material on the business of the Center.

PA68   TEMPLE UNIVERSITY, INSTITUTE FOR SURVEY RE-
        SEARCH. 1710 N. Broad St., 19121. Tel 215 787-7000.
        Aaron J. Spector, Dir.
        The Institute provides sampling statisticians to guide
        social scientists and organizations in sample design
        and to draw national or regional samples in subject
        areas such as urban problems and race relations.
        Study directors, interviewers, editors, coders, data
        processors and computers are also available.
        Publ.: Studies, reports, surveys.

PA69   TEMPLE UNIVERSITY, URBAN ARCHIVES CENTER (1967).
Samuel Paley Library, Berks and 13th Sts., 19122.
Tel 215 787-8257. Philip S. Benjamin, Dir. of the
Urban Arch. Copying, inquiries answered, referrals
made.
The Center serves as a depository for mss and other
records relating to urban life and development, drawing upon institutions in the Philadelphia metropolitan
area during the last century. It seeks to secure papers of organizations and individuals which will provide information on ethnic and racial groups, religion,
education, social welfare, labor conditions, housing,
crime, political activity, and economic development.

.1   American Civil Liberties Union, Greater Philadelphia
Branch
Records, 1949-60. 24 ft. Includes general correspondence, records of investigations and some
legal briefs.

.2   Greater Philadelphia Federation of Settlements.
Records, 1948-67. 38 ft. Includes papers of the
Neighborhood Youth Corps, Philadelphia Anti-
Poverty Action Committee, School Settlement
Program, Project MOVE, Cause II, and the Lan-
guage Arts Recreation Program.

.3   Health and Welfare Council of Philadelphia.
Records, 1943-65. 12 ft. Includes minutes of
various committees and departments and some
pamphlet material relating to social welfare in the
city during this century.

.4   Housing Association of Delaware Valley.
Records, 1909-62. 91 ft. of papers, ca. 350 ft. of
printed materials. Includes correspondence,
books, pamphlets, periodicals, maps, and photographs concerning urban neighborhoods, zoning,
city planning, and housing problems since the beginning of the century. Formerly Philadelphia
Housing Association.

.5   National Association for the Advancement of Colored
People, Philadelphia Branch.
Records, 1943-60. 41 ft. Includes board minutes,
financial records, correspondence, newspaper
clippings (1940's), and legal briefs in the fight to
end discrimination.

.6   Society of Friends.
Census, 1848. A copy of the census of the city's
Negro population, made by the Society.

.7   Travelers' Aid Society, Philadelphia Branch.
Records, 1904-33. 1 ft. Includes board minutes
and printed materials on assistance to migrants
entering Philadelphia.

.8   Urban League of Philadelphia.
Records, 1935-62. 6 ft. Includes board and committee minutes and the correspondence of the
executive director and department heads. Among
other materials are papers concerning the agency's
activities in housing, community services, and
Negro employment.

PA70   THE UNION LEAGUE OF PHILADELPHIA (1862), LIBRARY
(1863). 140 S. Broad St., 19102. Tel 215 563-6500.
Maxwell Whiteman, Dir. Inquiries answered, consultation.

.1   Pamphlet collection.
1863-87. ca. 300 items. Material published and
distributed by the Union League. Subjects covered
include the Civil War, slavery, Negroes, and Reconstruction.

.2   Union League of Philadelphia.
Papers, 1862- . ca. 20,000 items. Includes letters, documents, and minute books, containing
references to such subjects as the Civil War, Reconstruction, slavery, and Negroes.

PA71   UNITED PRESBYTERIAN CHURCH IN THE U.S.A., DIVI-
SION OF CHRISTIAN EDUCATION. 825 Witherspoon
Bldg., 1321 Walnut, 19107. Tel 215 735-6722. Rev.
Harold Viehman, Dir.

.1   Division of Christian Education.
Files. Correspondence, minutes of board meetings,
financial records, and other materials relating to
the Division's support of the following predominantly black colleges and universities: Barber-

Scotia College, Concord, N.C.; Johnson C. Smith
University, Charlotte, N.C.; Knoxville College,
Knoxville, Tenn.; and Mary Holmes Junior Col-
lege, West Point, Miss.

PA72   UNITED PRESBYTERIAN CHURCH IN THE U.S.A., OF-
FICE OF CHURCH AND SOCIETY. 830 Witherspoon
Bldg., 19107. Tel 215 735-6722. Rev. Leslie R. Galbraith, Res. Librn. Bibliographies prepared, inquiries
answered.
The Office conducts research service to provide
denominational units with information and resources on
social issues. Work is conducted on such topics as
black power, narcotic addiction, race relations, hunger,
racism, abortion, and income maintenance, with attention to the social involvement of the church.
Publ.: Church and Society, bimonthly journal (formerly Social Progress); Studies and bibliographies.

.1   Office of Church and Society.
Contains ca. 2500 v. with strong emphasis on sociology and its importance to the church.

PA73   UNITED PRESBYTERIAN CHURCH IN THE U.S.A.,
PRESBYTERIAN HISTORICAL SOCIETY (1852). 425
Lombard St., 19147. Tel 215 735-4433. William B.
Miller, Mgr. and Secy. Bibliographies prepared,
literature searches, copying, inquiries answered,
referrals made, consultation.

.1   Papers relating to Negroes.
Papers, 18th-20th century. Includes pamphlets,
books, mss, periodicals and newspapers, theses
and dissertations, correspondence, photographs,
and microforms on such subjects as slavery,
abolition; and the Negro's position within, and
relationship to the Presbyterian Church.

.2   Presbyterian Church in the U.S.A., New York
Presbytery.
Records of local churches, 1818-36. 40 v. Minute
books, session records, and other records of
churches located within the Presbytery of New
York. Includes extracts of the minutes of the
Second Presbytery of New York concerning the
investigation of affairs of the Lexington Avenue
Presbyterian Church and Dr. Sanderson (1871).
Among the many churches represented are Shiloh
Presbyterian Church (First Colored), and the East
Harlem Presbyterian Church.

.3   Presbyterian Church in the U.S.A., Board of Freedmen.
Records. Includes mss and published materials
concerning the Board's activities.

PA74   UNITED STATES NATIONAL STUDENT ASSOCIATION, LI-
BRARY AND STUDENT GOVERNMENT INFORMATION
CENTER (1947). 3457 Chestnut St., 19104. Tel 215
222-1106. Robert P. Robinson, Dir. Interlibrary loan,
copying.
The Association works in the areas of education, political activities, academic freedom, and civil rights.

PA75   UNIVERSITY OF PENNSYLVANIA, ARCHIVES AND REC-
ORDS CENTER. North Arcade, Franklin Field, 19104.
Tel 215 594-7024. Dr. Leonidas Dodson, Archivist.

.1   Albert M. Greenfield Center for Human Relations.
Files, 1951-69. 3 boxes. Included are doctoral
dissertations of students of the Center, financial
records and correspondence, research materials
of the staff and students, and a report of the first
five years of operation.

PA76   UNIVERSITY OF PENNSYLVANIA, HUMAN RESOURCES
CENTER (1964). 3810 Walnut St., 19104. Tel 215 594-
7818. Howard Mitchell, Dir.
The Center concerns itself with efforts to realize human potential in the overlapping areas of teaching, research, and community service. It is not only concerned about the conduct of action-oriented research
efforts but has made provision for the participation of
both undergraduate and graduate students of Pennsylvania as well as other universities in order to develop
their own potential.
Publ.: Annual Report; Newsletter, quarterly;
Pamphlets.

PA77   UNIVERSITY OF PENNSYLVANIA, INSTITUTE FOR
        ENVIRONMENTAL STUDIES (1965). 203 Fine Arts
        Bldg., 19104. Tel 215 594-5000. G. Holmes Perkins,
        Res. Coun. Chmn.
        The Institute conducts a continuing program of study
        and research focused on the nature and control of
        man's environment. Areas of interest include urban
        social planning, poverty, housing and medical health.

PA78   UNIVERSITY OF PENNSYLVANIA, UNIVERSITY CENTER
        FOR URBAN RESEARCH AND EXPERIMENT (1968).
        3812 Walnut St., 19104. Tel 215 594-6491. Robert
        Mitchell, Dir.
        The Center was established to provide services and to
        generate support for existing teaching and research
        departments in the University; efforts aimed at estab-
        lishing a climate for interdisciplinary and inter-
        departmental communications and collaboration in the
        urban area; and programs of research and experi-
        mentation that integrate the results of previous study
        and that fill gaps in the existing university pattern of
        urban-oriented activity. The Center includes a Divi-
        sion of Science and Technology Utilization with
        constituent programs in transportation and communi-
        cation and others planned; a Center for Urban
        Ethnography, a Transportation Studies Center and an
        experimental program in the development of public
        urban strategies.
        Publ.: Urban-related Research and Community Involve-
              ment Programs at the University of Pennsyl-
              vania, semiannually.

        .1 University Center for Urban Research and Experi-
            ment.
            Files, 1968- . Records, reports, research data,
            and other materials pertaining to the activities of
            the Center. Included are extensive bibliographic
            materials and a file of newspaper clippings (from
            Philadelphia papers and the New York Times) on
            the problems of race, slums, ghettos, and poverty.

PA79   UNIVERSITY OF PENNSYLVANIA, VAN PELT LIBRARY.
        3420 Walnut St., 19104. Tel 215 594-7554. Warren J.
        Haas, Dir. of Libraries. Interlibrary loan, copying,
        typing, inquiries answered, consultation.

        .1 Facts on Film.
            Papers, 1954-67. Microfilm. Contains materials
            on civil rights and race relations in the South. See
            Race Relations Information Center, Nashville,
            Tenn., for a full description.
        .2 Randall, Samuel Jackson, 1828-90.
            Papers, 1867-90. 276 boxes. U.S. Representative
            from Pennsylvania and Speaker of the House who
            codified the rules of the House and was instru-
            mental in strengthening the Speaker's power. Cor-
            respondence, pamphlets, and other papers relating
            to the 45th and 46th Congresses, tariff questions,
            the settlement of problems related to Reconstruc-
            tion, and patronage.

PA80   URBAN LEAGUE OF PHILADELPHIA. 304 Penn Square
        Bldg., 19107. Tel 215 569-3636. Andrew G. Freeman,
        Exec. Dir.

        .1 Urban League of Philadelphia.
            Files. Records, reports, correspondence, and
            other papers concerning the programs and aims of
            the organization.

PA81   THE WEST MT. AIRY NEIGHBORS (1958). 7139 Cresheim
        Rd., 19119. Tel 215 242-1196. Mrs. Ruth Steele, Exec.
        Dir. Inquiries answered, referrals made, consultation.
        The Neighbors is a community organization which
        works to further the vitality and viability of a com-
        munity which is multi-racial with a wide economic and
        education range. It works through grass-roots com-
        munity activities and services.
        Publ.: Monthly newsletter; Brochures and other in-
              formational material, about such subjects as
              techniques of stopping block-busting, processing
              concerns about city services, and volunteer
              support.

PA82   WOMEN'S INTERNATIONAL LEAGUE FOR PEACE AND
        FREEDOM. 2006 Walnut St., 19103. Tel 215 563-7110.
        Mrs. Jo Kreiner Graham, Exec. Dir.

The League works by non-violent means for political,
social, economic and psychological conditions conducive to world peace. In conjunction with other human
rights agencies, the League carries on a variety of
civil rights community projects and efforts to secure
legislation promoting civil rights.
Publ.: Four Lights, monthly; Washington Newsletter.

.1 Women's International League for Peace and Freedom.
    Files. Documentation dealing with the aims, his-
    tory, and programs. Includes correspondence,
    minutes of meetings, financial records, and other
    materials.

PITTSBURGH

PA83   AMERICAN JEWISH COMMITTEE, PITTSBURGH OFFICE.
        6315 Forbes Ave., 15217. Tel 412 421-3327. William
        Shaffer, Area Dir.

PA84   INTERNATIONAL FLORISTS ASSOCIATION, INC. 2117
        Centre Ave., 15219. Tel 412 261-9279. J. Wesley Lee,
        Exec. Secy.
        The Association, predominantly Negro, seeks to
        acquaint its membership with improved merchandising
        methods and significant trends in floral design.

PA85   NATIONAL ASSOCIATION FOR THE ADVANCEMENT OF
        COLORED PEOPLE (NAACP). 2203 Wylie Ave., 15219.
        Tel 412 471-1024. Mrs. Alma S. Fox, Exec. Secy.

PA86   THE NATIONAL ASSOCIATION OF NEGRO BUSINESS AND
        PROFESSIONAL WOMEN'S CLUBS, INC. (1935). 652
        Bryn Mawr Rd., 15219. Tel 412 682-8052. Mrs.
        Marion E. Bryant, Pres.
        The Association seeks to direct the interest of busi-
        ness and professional women toward united action for
        improved social and civic conditions. Programs in-
        clude support of a library in Liberia, scholarships,
        consumer education, and special committees and
        projects in education, health, legislation, international
        affairs, housing, African study, public affairs and
        civil defense.
        Publ.: Newsletter, monthly; President's Brief,
              monthly; Responsibility, semiannually.

PA87   NATIONAL BLACK SISTERS' CONFERENCE (NBSC) (1968).
        3333 Fifth Ave., 15213. Tel 412 683-4800. Sister
        Martin de Porres Grey, R.S.M., Pres. and Exec. Dir.
        Bibliographies prepared, copying, typing, inquiries an-
        swered, referrals made, consultation.
        The Conference seeks to evaluate the role of black
        sisters within the Church and within American society,
        in light of the nation's racial situation; to help black
        people become fully free and self-determined black
        Americans in the economic, religious, political, and
        educational areas of American life; and to determine
        more effective ways to contribute to the solution of the
        problem of white racism.
        Publ.: A Shape of Soul, semiannually.

        .1 National Black Sisters' Conference and Black Priests'
            Conference.
            Records, 1968- . Minutes of meetings; conference
            and workshop proceedings; speakers bureau and
            black skills bank materials; Conference publica-
            tions; reports; tapes from NBSC speakers, sym-
            posiums and workshops; and research in such
            areas as black sisters in the Catholic Church, and
            analysis of racism and the intercultural orientation
            of Catholic-affiliated institutions. Restricted.

PA88   NATIONAL CONFERENCE OF CHRISTIANS AND JEWS
        (NCCJ). Suite 512, 100 Fifth Avenue Bldg., 15222.
        Tel 412 281-1237. Russell L. Bradley, Dir.

PA89   PENNSYLVANIA HUMAN RELATIONS COMMISSION,
        FIELD OFFICE. Room 810, 4 Smithfield St., 15222.
        Tel 412 565-5395.

PA90   PITTSBURGH COMMISSION ON HUMAN RELATIONS (1953).
        908 City-County Bldg., 15219. Tel 412 281-3900. David
        B. Washington, Exec. Dir.
        The Commission seeks to eliminate discrimination in

employment, housing, public accommodations, and other areas of intergroup relations in the social, cultural and economic life of the city. It has subpoena power and can order compliance after hearing. Formerly the Fair Employment Practice Commission. Publ.: <u>Human Relations Review</u>, bimonthly.

.1 Pittsburgh Commission on Human Relations.
    Files, 1953- . Documentation dealing with the aims, programs, and history of the Commission. Includes correspondence, minutes of meetings, financial records, studies, reports, investigations, among other materials.

PA91 UNITED STEELWORKERS OF AMERICA, COMMITTEE ON CIVIL RIGHTS. 1500 Commonwealth Bldg., 15222. Tel 412 741-5254. Alex Fuller, Dir.
    The Committee implements the United Steelworkers of America's policies in the area of civil rights through 24 district directors and civil rights coordinators. The civil rights program provides technical assistance to local union civil rights committees; coordinates the activities of locals with the international union; and serves to improve and expedite communications between unions on all levels.
    Publ.: <u>Civil Rights Briefs</u>, quarterly; Publications, films, etc.

.1 United Steelworkers of America, Committee on Civil Rights.
    Files. Documentation dealing with the aims, programs, and history of the Committee. Includes correspondence, minutes of meetings, financial reports, studies, investigations, and other material related to its activities.

PA92 UNIVERSITY AND CITY MINISTRIES (1968). Fifth and Bellefield Ave., 15213. Tel 412 628-2751. Rev. Samuel Gibson, Exec. Minister. Copying, typing, inquiries answered, referrals made, consultation.
    University and City Ministries is an ecumenical agency which seeks to bring the church, the city, and the university into a three-way dialogue and interaction. It works through divisions in the areas of academic concerns, campus ministry, youth ministries, urban action, Community of Reconciliation, and a center for creative work with children.

PA93 UNIVERSITY OF PITTSBURGH, GRADUATE SCHOOL OF PUBLIC AND INTERNATIONAL AFFAIRS LIBRARY. 304 Bruce Hall, 15213. Tel 412 621-3500. Nicholas Caruso, Librn.

.1 Public and International Affairs Library.
    Books and other materials concerning urban affairs, black studies, and race relations, including a collection of city government publications.

PA94 UNIVERSITY OF PITTSBURGH (1787), HILLMAN LIBRARY. 15213. Tel 412 621-3500. C. Walter Stone, Dir. Interlibrary loan, bibliographies prepared, literature searches, copying, typing, inquiries answered, referrals made, consultation.

.1 Archives of Industrial Society.
    Collection of historical records of Western Pennsylvania industries and organizations, including records of business firms and organizations; personal diaries, correspondence and scrapbooks of public figures; and files of newspapers, books, periodicals, printed documents, photographs, broadsides, flyers, and ephemeral printed materials. Among the materials are records of the following organizations:

.2 — American Service Institute of Allegheny County, Pittsburgh.
    Records, 1941-61. 50 ft. Minutes and other records of committees on cultural factors in group work, volunteer visitors bureau, and human relations institutes; nationality lists and analysis; reports, unpublished studies, and other material on community projects, nationality and local organizations, population, youth, aged, civil rights, housing, immigration, customs and traditions, intergroup edu-

cation, and religious prejudice; and scripts and other public relations material for television, radio, etc.

.3 — National Association for the Advancement of Colored People, Pittsburgh Branch.
    Records, 1940-66 (additions are made to the collection at irregular intervals). 29 ft. Correspondence, reports of chapter to national headquarters; minutes of executive board meetings; reports of chapter's activities; chapter programs on segregation in labor and industry, employment, education, housing, and public accommodations; membership campaigns, cards, and recordbooks; financial statements, paid bills, and receipt books. Includes public relations information, news releases, radio broadcasts, biographical information, and miscellaneous pamphlets. Permission for use must be secured from the executive director, local chapter.

.4 — Neighborhood Centers Association, Pittsburgh.
    Records, 1890-1954. 5 ft. Correspondence (1920-49); minutes of the board of directors; reports; records of Camp Bonsall; settlement books; and miscellaneous unpublished social studies and statistics. Includes records of the Woods Run Settlement House, a predecessor of the Association, engaged in social welfare work on the north side of Pittsburgh, in what was Allegheny City before 1906.

.5 — Radical literature collection.
    Miscellaneous. Includes publications of Student Nonviolent Coordinating Committee (SNCC) and Southern Christian Leadership Conference (SCLC), among others. Materials include brochures, posters, and mimeographed publications.

.6 Harmonia.
    Records, 1853-65. 2 ft. Correspondence, minutes of meetings, addresses, and financial reports, documenting the activities of the Harmonia, a mid-nineteenth century utopian group which combined socialism and spiritualism in its philosophy and made a settlement in the valley of Kiantone Creek, partly in New York State and partly in Pennsylvania. Most of the addresses are by John Murray Spear, leader of the group. Papers relate to the society's ideas on abolition and the Civil War, government, education, business, and marriage.

PA95 UNIVERSITY OF PITTSBURGH, LEARNING RESEARCH AND DEVELOPMENT CENTER. 160 N. Craig St., 15213. Tel 412 621-3500. Robert Glaser and William W. Cooley, Co-Dirs.
    The Center conducts School-University-College-and-Community Enterprise in Educational Development (SUCCEED), teacher education projects for faculties of schools having students from poverty backgrounds; and a preschool training program.
    Publ.: Working papers, reprints, and technical report series.

.1 Learning Research and Development Center.
    Files. Documentation dealing with the aims, programs, and history of the Center. Includes correspondence, reports, studies, and other material related to its activities.

PA96 UNIVERSITY OF PITTSBURGH, SCHOOL OF SOCIAL WORK LIBRARY. 2217 Cathedral of Learning, 15213. Tel 412 621-3500. Oxanna Kaufman, Librn.

.1 Papers relating to Negroes.
    Miscellaneous. Includes case reports, pamphlets on race relations in general with emphasis on locality, and books by and about Negroes.

PA97 URBAN LEAGUE OF PITTSBURGH, INC. (1918). 200 Ross St., 15219. Tel 412 261-6010. Arthur J. Edmunds, Exec. Dir. Inquiries answered, referrals made.
    The League works to improve the conditions under which Negroes, and others similarly disadvantaged, work, live, and recreate, through programs in education and employment.

SWARTHMORE

PA98   SWARTHMORE COLLEGE (1864), FRIENDS HISTORICAL
          LIBRARY (1871). 19081. Tel 215 544-7900. Frederick
          B. Tolles, Dir. Interlibrary loan, copying, inquiries
          answered.

.1   Addams, Jane, 1860-1935.
          Papers, 1838-1959. 59 ft. Settlement worker, so-
          cial reformer, and peace worker. Correspon-
          dence, mss of writings, pamphlets, and clippings
          relating to the Women's International League for
          Peace and Freedom, social conditions, labor, Ne-
          groes, immigrants, civic conditions in Chicago,
          and the rights of women and children. Includes
          some material on the operation of Hull House. The
          material relates to the library's Women's Inter-
          national League for Peace and Freedom and Emily
          Greene Balch collections.

.2   Alston, John.
          Papers, 1797-1874. 24 items. Journals (1837?-47,
          and undated); account books and business papers
          (1821-74); and essays by Nathan Lord on Negro
          slavery and salvation (1797).

.3   Balch, Emily Greene, 1867- .
          Papers, 1893-1948. 20 ft. Teacher, author, and
          peace worker. Correspondence (on problems of
          minorities among other topics), travel journals,
          clippings, pamphlets, and typewritten, mimeo-
          graphed and printed articles and books by Miss
          Balch. The material is related to the library's
          Jane Addams and Women's International League
          for Peace and Freedom collections.

.4   Bettle, Samuel, 1810-80.
          Family papers, 1800-1955. ca. 2 ft. In part,
          transcripts (typewritten) and one facsimile. Wool
          merchant, of Philadelphia. Correspondence, bio-
          graphical clippings, and copies and extracts of
          wills, of Samuel Bettle, other members of the
          Bettle family, and others. Includes a few records
          of the Bible Association of Friends, business and
          financial papers, papers relating to slavery, and
          records and papers of other Quaker groups.

.5   Bringhurst, James, 1730-1810.
          Correspondence of James Bringhurst and of
          Elizabeth Foulke, 1780-1811. ca. 2 ft. Includes
          letters of Bringhurst, a Quaker master carpenter
          and merchant, largely religious in tone; letters to
          him from John Murray, concerning abolition,
          prison reforms, education, and other topics; let-
          ters of Miss Foulke a Quaker minister; and
          letters to Miss Foulke from Joseph Bringhurst,
          containing material on prominent Quakers and on
          Philadelphia life and customs.

.6   Codding, Ichabod, 1810-66.
          Papers, 1830-1901. ca. 1 ft. Clergyman. Ser-
          mons, speeches, and notes on slavery and on po-
          litical and religious subjects, together with printed
          matter and clippings, some mounted in scrapbooks.

.7   Evans, Joshua, 1731-98.
          Papers, ca. 1788-98. 7 v. Quaker minister and
          abolitionist. Correspondence, mostly letters
          written to Evans' wife, Ann, by Quakers at whose
          homes he stayed while on his religious visits; and
          journals of his ministry in North America. In-
          cludes copies of the journals made by George
          Churchman, and copies thought to have been made
          by Abraham Warrington.

.7a Friends, Society of. Baltimore Yearly Meeting.
          Records, 1658-? 655 v.

.8   Friends, Society of (Anti-Slavery). Indiana Yearly
          Meeting.
          Records, 1843-57. 9 v. on 3 reels of microfilm.
          Microfilm copy (positive) of originals in the Rec-
          ords Depository of the Indiana Yearly Meeting in
          Richmond. Includes minutes of the Yearly Meet-
          ing; and women's minutes of the Duck Creek
          Monthly Meeting, minutes of the Duck Creek
          Quarterly Meeting, vital records and minutes of
          the Dunkirk Monthly Meeting, and minutes of the
          Newport Monthly Meeting.

.9   Friends, Society of (Hicksite). Ohio Yearly Meeting.
          Records, 1755-1944. 97 v. Minutes (1813-1919)
          of the Yearly Meeting; and minutes (1858-64) of
          the Beaver Falls Monthly Meeting, minutes (1824-

63) of the Beaver Falls Preparative Meeting, rec-
ords of marriages and minutes (1828-51) of the
Carmel Monthly Meeting, minutes (1868-73) of the
Cope's Run Preparative Meeting, records of marriage and minutes (1817-58) of the Deer Creek
Monthly Meeting, minutes (1829-65) of the Free-
port Monthly Meeting, minutes (1824-50) of the
Grove Preparative Meeting, minutes and vital
records (1828-64) of the Middletown Monthly
Meeting, minutes (1850) of the New Garden
Monthly Meeting, minutes and vital records (1813-
98) of the Plainfield Monthly Meeting, minutes and
vital records (1755-1932) of the Salem Monthly
Meeting, minutes (1850-65) of the Salem Preparative Meeting, minutes (1828-1902) of the Salem
Quarterly Meeting, minutes and vital records
(1758-1944) of the Short Creek Monthly Meeting,
minutes (1839-1915) of the Short Creek Preparative Meeting, minutes (1828-60) of the Stillwater
Quarterly Meeting, minutes and vital records
(1818-1923) of the West Monthly Meeting, and minutes (1839-59) of the Western Quarterly Meeting.

.10 Friends, Society of. Philadelphia Yearly Meeting.
          Records, 1665-1959. 400 ft. and 500 reels of mi-
          crofilm. Minutes of men's and women's business
          meetings, minutes of the ministers' and elders'
          meetings, and registers of births, deaths, mar-
          riages and removals. Includes records of suffer-
          ings during the American Revolution and certifi-
          cates of the manumission of slaves.

.11 Hancock, Cornelia, 1840-1926.
          Correspondence, 1864-78. 1 box. In part, photo-
          copies (negative) from the annual report of the
          Association of Friends for the Aid and Elevation of
          the Freedmen. Nurse, educator, and social
          worker. Letters, many of them incomplete, from
          Miss Hancock to her relatives, written while she
          was working with Negroes in South Carolina;
          letters she received while nursing soldiers during
          the Civil War; family letters; and reference mate-
          rial used by Henrietta S. Jacquette in editing Miss
          Hancock's South After Gettysburg.

.12 Hinshaw, William Wade, 1867-1947.
          Index to Quaker meeting records, 1682-1947. ca.
          18 ft. Transcripts. Genealogist, of Washington,
          D.C. Abstracts of minutes, births, deaths, mar-
          riages, removals, and other records of Quaker
          meetings in Arizona, California, Colorado, Idaho,
          Illinois, Indiana, Iowa, Kansas, Maryland, Michi-
          gan, Minnesota, Missouri, Nebraska, New Jersey,
          Oklahoma, Pennsylvania, South Dakota, and Wis-
          consin. The abstracts were prepared for the
          projected but unpublished volumes of Hinshaw's
          Encyclopedia of American Quaker Genealogy.

.13 Howland, Emily, 1827-1929.
          Papers, ca. 1836-ca. 1929. Educator, reformer,
          philanthropist. Diaries (1917-29), small diaries
          and notebooks (1849-1921); correspondence (ca.
          1836-1929), including letters from Miss Howland
          to her parents and others from "contraband
          camp" (1863-66), two letters from Susan B.
          Anthony (1899); 7 letters from Anna Howard Shaw
          (1907-14), and letters concerning Negro schools in
          Alabama, Mississippi, Tennessee, Kentucky, North
          and South Carolina, Georgia, Virginia, Maryland,
          and elsewhere; and pamphlets, miscellaneous
          writings and other printed items concerning anti-
          slavery activities and Negro education, the WCTU,
          and the peace movement, including biographical
          and genealogical material.

.14 Jenkins, Charles Francis, 1865- .
          Autograph collection, 1681-1940. 3 ft. (450 items).
          Letters and autograph documents of personalities
          distinguished as abolitionists and reformers,
          governors of Pennsylvania, members of the So-
          ciety of Friends, poets and writers, Presidents of
          the U.S., signers of the Constitution, members of
          the Old Congress, statesmen, politicians, and
          others. Includes letters of Susan B. Anthony,
          Lydia Maria Child, Thomas Clarkson, Elizabeth
          Fry, James Logan, William Wilberforce, and
          others.

.15 Lundy, Joseph Wilmer.
          Papers, 1781-1964. 7 ft. In part, transcripts.

Correspondence, diaries, journals, mss of speeches and writings, account books, cashbooks, agreements, bonds and warrants, deeds, indentures, mortgages, promissory notes, bills, tax receipts, and other business papers, genealogical material, photos, newspaper clippings, memorabilia, and other papers of Lundy, a Quaker, who was in the plumbing and heating business in Pennsylvania, and other members of the family. Many of the papers relate to Quaker affairs. Includes diaries of Lundy's wife, Bessie Lundy; 115 letters (1900-45) by Thomas Chalkley Matlack to Lundy, chiefly relating to his preparation of a book of photos and historical sketches of Friends' meetings; and material concerning Benjamin Lundy, the abolitionist.

PA98.16 Marriage certificates, 1666-1952.
ca. 320 items. In part, transcripts (handwritten) and photocopies. Largely 18th and 19th century Quaker marriage certificates. Includes a volume (1668-1755) of originals and copies of Maryland Quaker certificates; and a marriage certificate in Quaker form of two Negroes who had been slaves, signed by John Woolman.

.17 Mead, Edwin Doak, 1849-1937.
Papers of Edwin D. and Lucia Ames Mead, 1876-1937. 9 ft. Correspondence, a journal of Lucia Ames Mead (1884-1934), writings, clippings, family scrapbooks, subject files, especially on pacifism and race relations, and miscellanea. The material is related to the library's Women's International League for Peace and Freedom records.

.18 Mott, Lucretia (Coffin), 1793-1880.
Papers, 1834-96. 2 ft. (ca. 500 items). In part, transcript. Quaker minister active in social reform movements, women's rights, antislavery, peace, and education. Correspondence, diary of Mrs. Mott's trip to England to attend the World Anti-Slavery Convention of 1840, sermons, essays, and antislavery documents. The bulk of the collection consists of correspondence of Lucretia Mott and her husband, James Mott, with members of their family, and some correspondence with other reformers such as Joseph A. Dugdale, William Lloyd Garrison, Harriet Martineau, Elizabeth Cady Stanton, and Lucy Stone.

.19 Richardson family.
Papers, 1757-1917. 7 ft. Correspondence, journals, legal and financial papers, poetry, recipes, papers relating to Indians and slavery, and other papers. Names represented include Achsah Willis Nevins (later Richardson), Elisabeth Richardson, Dr. Elliott Richardson, Sarah Richardson, and others.

.20 Rotch family.
Rotch-Wales papers, 1677-1838. 2 reels of microfilm. Microfilm made in 1961 from originals loaned by Mrs. Horatio W. Wales, Massillon, Ohio. Correspondence and documents of Elisha Bates, Thomas Coffin, Hannah Fisher, Samuel Fisher, John Heald, William Heald, Elias Hicks, James Mott, Charity Rotch, Thomas Rotch, and other members of the Rotch family, relating to the Quaker religion, slavery, wool processing technology in Ohio, business conditions, 1792-1818, and other subjects.

.21 Sharpless, Joshua.
Papers, ca. 1778-1879. ca. 1 ft. Correspondence by several members of the Sharpless family, including Aaron, Edith, Mary, Joshua, and Townsend Sharpless, and by Joseph Drinker (1778-98, 1806-77); journals (1792, 1797, 1798, 1812) kept by Joshua Sharpless, mainly concerned with visits to Quaker meetings; business papers of Joshua Sharpless (1819-37) and of others (1835, 1847); and Some Observations on the State of the Black People, by Joseph Drinker (1795).

.22 Sheppard, Moses.
Papers, 1794-1927. 2 ft. In part, transcripts. Quaker humanitarian and businessman of Baltimore. Correspondence on the subjects of antislavery, colonization in Liberia, and on personal affairs; documents relating to the American Colonization Society, and a variety of other topics;

material relating to the libel trial of William Lloyd Garrison; lists of applicants for Liberia; business papers, deeds, wills, and financial records. Correspondents include Henry Ward Beecher, Matthew Carey, and Robert S. Finley.

.23 Small collections.
4 ft. In part, transcripts and photocopies. Correspondence, manumissions, poems, and other documents. Largely correspondence of individual members of the Society of Friends, including John Bright, parliamentarian, Joseph Dugdale, abolitionist, Elisabeth Fry, English Friend active in prison reform, Stephen Grellet, Quaker minister, Edward Hicks, American primitive painter, Issac T. Hopper, abolitionist, and James Pemberton, Philadelphia merchant and political figure.

.24 Stratton, Edward F.
Papers, 1750-1961. 207 items. In part, transcripts, 3 facsimiles, and a photocopy. Businessman and custodian of records, Ohio Yearly Meeting of Friends, Salem, Ohio. Correspondence, diaries (1869, 1871) of Edward Williams, biographical sketch of Mary F. Stratton by Watson Dewees, articles by Stratton, genealogical notes on the Fisher and Heald families, deeds, legal papers, articles, minutes (1804), Quaker documents, letters and reports of Edward Williams and his wife and daughter, Hannah and Sarah, as teachers in schools for freedmen in Mississippi and Texas, printed matter, and memorabilia, relating to various Quaker meetings, Quaker affairs, schools for freedmen, and opposition to war.

.25 Strong, Sydney Dix, 1860-1938.
Papers, 1914-40. 2 ft. Congregational minister, editor, and author. Correspondence, literary mss, published writings, clippings, memorabilia and other papers, concerning civil liberties of members of the Elijah Voice Society and other persons in the Pacific Northwest. Also includes material relating to Strong's daughter, Anna Louise Strong. Among the correspondents is A. Philip Randolph.

.26 Thomas, Wilbur Kelsey, 1882-1953.
Papers, ca. 1915-34. 1 ft. In part, transcripts (typewritten). Executive secretary of the American Friends Service Committee, director of the Carl Schurz Memorial Foundation, Inc., and president of the Pennsylvania Forestry Association. Correspondence, addresses, writings, printed material, and a bibliographical leaflet, relating to Thomas, world peace, friendship, war, labor, civil rights and liberties, and the American Friends Service Committee.

.27 Whittier, John Greenleaf, 1807-92.
Papers, 1839-1913. 3 ft. (ca. 700 items). In part, transcripts and photocopies. Poet and abolitionist. Correspondence, poems, and family documents. Includes family letters and much correspondence with Elizabeth Stuart Phelps Ward and Francis J. Garrison. Other correspondents include Phillips Brooks, William Cullen Bryant, Lydia Maria Child, Caleb Cushing, Ralph Waldo Emerson, James T. Fields, William Lloyd Garrison, Paul Hamilton Hayne, Thomas Wentworth Higginson, Oliver Wendell Holmes, Lucy Larcom, Henry Wadsworth Longfellow, James Russell Lowell, Wendell Phillips, Richard Henry Stoddard, and Theodore D. Weld.

.28 Wood, Mary S. (Underhill), 1805-94.
Wood correspondence, 1784-1874. ca. 200 items. Quaker. ca. 200 letters from prominent Friends to Mary, William, and Samuel Wood, concerning abolition, the Civil War, peace, freedmen, and Quaker activities. Also includes autographs of prominent Friends.

.29 Woolman, John.
Papers, 1756-72. 4 v. New Jersey Quaker preacher and abolitionist. Materials pertaining to his career and activities.

UNIVERSITY PARK

PA99 PENNSYLVANIA STATE UNIVERSITY, FRED LEWIS PATTEE LIBRARY (1857). 16802. Tel 814 865-0401. Murray S. Martin, Librn., Collection Develop.

.1 Facts on Film.
Papers, 1954-67. Microfilm. Contains materials on civil rights and race relations in the South. See Race Relations Information Center, Nashville, Tenn., for a full description.

.2 Ruttenberg, Harold Joseph, 1914- .
Papers, 1933-67. ca. 8 ft. Industrialist and research director, of Pittsburgh, Pa. Correspondence, pamphlets, bulletins, drafts, and typescripts of books and articles, and clippings, collected by Ruttenberg while on the board of the Portsmouth Steel Company, and as a member of the U.S. War Production Board. Includes material on general labor studies, Negroes in labor, Pennsylvania Security League, Steel Workers Organizing Committee, U.S. National Labor Relations Board, and the United Steelworkers of America.

.3 United Steelworkers of America.
Records, 1946-67. 99 ft. Correspondence, petitions, agreements, statements, reports, memos, pamphlets, booklets, reprints, circulars, clippings, and exhibits comprising the union's legislative office files from Washington, D.C. concerning various labor activities. Includes congressional correspondence and other legal papers, reports, and materials. Subjects covered include the AFL-CIO, area redevelopment, budget, civil rights, depressed areas, education, government grants and loans, housing, legislation and labor, manpower utilization and training, and minimum wages.

PA100 PENNSYLVANIA STATE UNIVERSITY, INSTITUTE FOR RESEARCH ON HUMAN RESOURCES (1964). 411 Boucke Bldg., 16802. Tel 814 865-4700. Jacob J. Kaufman, Dir.
The Institute conducts research and disseminates information in the field of human resources, in the specific areas of education, employment, community organization, area development, labor market, discrimination in race and educational and other social concerns.
Publ.: Publication list, pamphlets, studies.

PA101 PENNSYLVANIA STATE UNIVERSITY, INSTITUTE OF PUBLIC ADMINISTRATION (1959). 302 Engineering E, 16802. Tel 814 865-2536. Dr. Robert J. Mowitz, Dir. Consultation.
The Institute conducts a graduate program and carries on research in a number of areas of political science. Research projects relating to urban affairs include a survey of poverty in Fayette County, Pa.; a study of community action agencies and decision-making for education in seven cities throughout the U.S.; a study of the war on poverty (OEO impact) in 5 medium-sized Pennsylvania cities; and a study of fiscal problems of metropolitan areas (central city v. suburbs).

VALLEY FORGE

PA102 AMERICAN BAPTIST CONVENTION, DIVISION OF CHRISTIAN HIGHER EDUCATION. 19481. Tel 215 768-2000. Rev. Robert E. Davis, Dir.

.1 Division of Christian Higher Education.
Files. Correspondence, minutes of board meetings, financial records, and other materials relating to the Division's support of the following predominantly black colleges: Benedict College, Columbia, S.C.; and Bishop College, Dallas, Tex.; Morehouse College, Atlanta, Ga.; Shaw University, Raleigh, N.C.; Spelman College, Atlanta, Ga.; Virginia Union University, Richmond, Va.; and Mather College, Beaufort, S.C.

PA103 AMERICAN BAPTIST CONVENTION, DIVISION OF CHRISTIAN SOCIAL CONCERN. 19481. Tel 215 768-2278. Rev. Elizabeth J. Miller, Exec. Dir.
The Division seeks to discern those areas of Christian social responsibility which should be of denominational concern, to plan programs to meet the needs of those areas, and to provide local churches with factual information concerning social problems as a basis for intelligent Christian decision and action.

PA104 AMERICAN BAPTIST HOME MISSION SOCIETIES (1835). 19481. Tel 215 768-2430. Dorothy O. Bucklin, Assoc. Exec. Secy. Copying, inquiries answered.

.1 Mather School.
Archives, 1868-1968. Correspondence, minutes of board meetings, financial records, bulletins, and other material concerning the history and administration of the School, which merged (1968) with Benedict College, Columbia, S.C.

PA105 FREEDOMS FOUNDATION AT VALLEY FORGE, LIBRARY (1949). 19481. Tel 215 933-8825. Joseph R. Fugett, Librn. Emer. Literature searches, inquiries answered, consultation.
The Foundation works to "strengthen the 'American Way of Life' by awards made to individuals, organizations, and others who have contributed significantly to any or all phases of the American Way of Life in the opinion of a national jury representative of the people."

.1 George Washington Carver Project.
Papers, ca. 1770- . Books, pamphlets, newspaper titles, clippings, films, photographs, tape recordings, phonograph records, paintings, and sculpture. Material concerns contributions of Negroes to American life and culture.

WEST CHESTER

PA106 CHESTER COUNTY HISTORICAL SOCIETY (1893), LIBRARY. 225 N. High St., 19380. Tel 215 696-4755. Miss Dorothy B. Lapp, Librn. Copying, inquiries answered.
Publ.: Pamphlets and brochures.

.1 Blackston, Samuel.
Painting. Oil painting of the Chester County Historical Society building, ca. 1940.

.2 Papers relating to Negroes.
Included are ms materials on slavery, 1688- . (ca. 500 items), among which are manumission papers; and histories and clippings of each Negro church in Chester Co., Pa.

.3 Pippin, Horace, 1888-1946.
Painting, ca. 1940. Oil painting of Paul Dague.

WEST MIDDLESEX

PA107 SHENANGO VALLEY URBAN LEAGUE. 314 Idaho St., 16159. Tel 412 981-2831. Dr. T.L. Yarboro, Pres.

.1 Shenango Valley Urban League.
Files. Correspondence, minutes of meetings, financial records, reports, studies, and other materials dealing with the aims, history and programs of the League.

WILKES-BARRE

PA108 KING'S COLLEGE (1946), LIBRARY. 14 W. Jackson St., 18702. Tel 717 824-9931. Mary Barrett, Librn. Interlibrary loan, bibliographies prepared, literature searches, copying, typing, inquiries answered, referrals made, consultation.

.1 Afro-American Heritage collection.
Materials, 17th century- . Microfilm. 131 reels. Books, newspapers, and mss concerning the Negro American and his history. See Minnesota Mining and Manufacturing Company, St. Paul, Minn., for a full description.

.2 Northeastern Pennsylvania Bibliographic Center.
As a member of the Center, King's College Library specializes in the area of Afro-American studies. The "purpose is to build a strong collection on the subject in breadth and depth, particularly primary sources." Its aim is to prepare a bibliography on this collection.

WILLOW GROVE

PA109 SUBURBAN ACTION CENTER, INC. 205 Davisville Rd., 19090. Tel 215 659-9790.
The Center seeks ways to confront and combat racism in the white community.

RHODE ISLAND

NEWPORT

RI1   NEWPORT HISTORICAL SOCIETY (1854), LIBRARY. 82
    Touro St., 02840. Tel 401 846-0813. Madeline H.
    Wordell, Librn.

    .1 Lopez, Aaron, 1731-82.
        Papers. 112 items. Merchant and slave trader of
        Newport, R.I.

PROVIDENCE

RI2   BROWN UNIVERSITY (1764), JOHN HAY LIBRARY (1910).
    02912. Tel 401 863-2146. Stuart C. Sherman, John Hay
    Librn.

    .1 Brown University.
        Archives. Included are 26 theses on Afro-Ameri-
        can subjects, 2 Independent Studies papers, and one
        Meiklejohn Lecture. A Study of the Slave Narrative
        by Charles H. Nichols and Developments of Negro
        Creative Literature by J. Saunders Redding "are
        notable for their bibliographies."
    .2 Harris Collection of American Poetry and Plays.
        Materials. ca. 250,000 items. Books, mss, broad-
        sides and sheet music (ca. 100,000 items), including
        spirituals, folk songs, jazz, minstrels and ragtime.
        Included are the works of Negro American authors
        and composers, from Phillis Wheatley to LeRoi
        Jones.
    .3 Henry, Mellinger E.
        Papers, 1910-42. 1050 items. American folklorist.
        Contains typescripts of Negro Songs from Georgia,
        Nursery Rhymes and Game Songs from Georgia,
        and a Bibliography for the Study of American Folk-
        songs.
    .4 John Hay Collection.
        Papers. Includes resources pertaining to slavery,
        emancipation, the Civil War, and Reconstruction.
    .5 McLellan Lincoln Collection.
        Papers. Includes resources pertaining to slavery,
        emancipation, the Civil War, and Reconstruction.
    .6 Metcalf Collection of Pamphlets.
        Pamphlets, ca. 1776-ca. 1865. ca. 10,000 items.
        Includes pamphlets on foreign missions, fugitive
        slave law, Massachusetts Anti-Slavery Society,
        Reconstruction, slave trade, slavery addresses
        and discourses, slavery societies, suffrage, and
        African colonization.

RI3   MOSES BROWN SCHOOL, LIBRARY. 250 Lloyd Ave., 02906.
    Tel 401 831-7350. Mrs. William Paxton, Librn.

    .1 Abolition Society.
        Papers, 1789-1830. 1 v. Records pertaining to the
        Abolition Society.

RI4   NATIONAL CONFERENCE OF CHRISTIANS AND JEWS
    (NCCJ). 221 Waterman St., 02906. Tel 401 351-5120.
    Vernon J. Lisbon, Dir.
    NCCJ is a civic organization which seeks to bring to-
    gether people of various religious beliefs and ethnic
    backgrounds in an effort to create a society of under-
    standing and respect through education and intergroup
    programs of good will.

RI5   PROVIDENCE HUMAN RELATIONS COMMISSION (1963).
    56 Washington St., 02903. Tel 401 421-3708. Charles
    H. Durant, III, Exec. Dir.
    The Commission strives to eliminate prejudice and
    discrimination against any individual or group, provides
    a medium through which citizens and elected officials
    may be kept informed of developments in community
    relations; provides services in the areas of tension
    control, public information and education, community
    education, neighborhood services, and consultative
    activities.

RI6   PROVIDENCE PUBLIC LIBRARY (1878). 150 Empire St.,
    02903. Tel 401 521-7722. F. Charles Taylor, Librn.
    Interlibrary loan, copying, inquiries answered, ref-
    rals made.

    .1 Caleb Fiske Harris Collection.
        Materials. ca. 12,000 items. Chiefly 19th cent.
        pamphlets and books concerning slavery, the aboli-
        tion movement, and the Civil War; also regimental
        histories, Union and Confederate ballads, slave
        narratives, over 80 editions of Uncle Tom's Cabin,
        and files of The Liberator and Crisis. Restricted.

RI7   PROVIDENCE PUBLIC LIBRARY, SOUTH PROVIDENCE
    BRANCH. 443 Prairie Ave., 02905. Tel 409 941-2660.
    Jean L. Nash, Librn.

    .1 Edna Frazier Memorial Collection.
        Books, ca. 900 v. Beginning collection of materi-
        als covering Negro history and literature.

RI8   RHODE ISLAND CIVIL LIBERTIES UNION. 142 Eighth St.,
    02906. Tel 401 351-4852. Mrs. Natalie Robinson, Exec.
    Secy.

    .1 Rhode Island Civil Liberties Union.
        Files. Records, reports, correspondence, legal
        briefs, and other papers concerning the activities
        and court cases of the Union.

RI9   RHODE ISLAND COMMISSION FOR HUMAN RIGHTS (1949).
    244 Broad St., 02903. Tel 401 521-7100. Donald D.
    Taylor, Exec. Secy.
    The Commission is a permanent, independent agency
    which conducts surveys and studies on employment,
    housing and public accommodations; prepares public
    information programs; creates advisory bodies;
    receives and investigates complaints; initiates com-
    plaints; conciliation; holds hearings (with subpoena
    power); issues cease-and-desist orders and orders re-
    quiring remedial action on behalf of the complainant;
    seeks court enforcement of its orders.

    .1 Rhode Island Commission for Human Rights.
        Files, ca. 1949- . Official files of the Commission
        include correspondence, reports, citizen complaints
        of discrimination, and records of remedial action.
        Restricted.

RI10   THE RHODE ISLAND HISTORICAL SOCIETY (1822), LI-
    BRARY (1822). 121 Hope St., 02906. Tel 401 331-8575.
    Albert T. Klyberg, Librn. Interlibrary loan, copying,
    inquiries answered, referrals made, consultation.
    Publ.: Rhode Island History, quarterly journal.

    .1 Brown, Moses, 1738-1836.
        Papers. Manufacturer and philanthropist of Provi-
        dence, R.I. Contains references to Anti-Slavery
        Society activity.
    .2 Ku Klux Klan.
        Materials.
    .3 Materials relating to Negroes.
        Miscellaneous. Printed accounts of raising black
        regiments in the Battle of Rhode Island in the
        Revolutionary War; occasional references to the
        slave trade, in 18th cent. ms collections; narratives
        concerning 7th Regiment, USCT, and Negro troops
        in the Army of the Cumberland (1863-65) and in
        Burnside's Corps.
    .4 Negroes in Rhode Island.
        Miscellaneous, chiefly late 19th to early 20th cen-
        tury. Notes and clippings about the Negro in Rhode
        Island.

RI11   RHODE ISLAND SCHOOL OF DESIGN (1877), MUSEUM OF
    ART (1877). 2 College St., 02903. Tel 401 331-3507.
    Daniel Robbins, Dir.

    Among the holdings of the Museum's permanent collec-
    tion are works by the following Negro artists:

    .1 Bannister, Edward M., 1829-1901.
        Oil paintings. Included are "Path through the Pas-
        ture: Evening" (1882), "Street Scene," "Study,"
        and 3 landscapes.
    .2 Pippin, Horace, 1886-1946.
        Oil painting, "Quaker Mother and Child."
    .3 Prophet, Elizabeth, b. 1890.
        Sculptures. "Discontent" (wood), "Negro Head"
        (wood), and "Silence" (marble).

RI12   URBAN LEAGUE OF RHODE ISLAND, INC. (1939). 74
    Weybosset St., 02903. Tel 401 521-5103. James N.
    Williams, Exec. Dir.

The League is a professional community service agency working to eliminate racial segregation and administration in American life, and to give help to Negroes and other disadvantaged groups so that they may share equally in the rewards and responsibilities of citizenship. Formerly Urban League of Greater Providence. Publ.: Annual Report; Quarterly bulletins.

SOUTH CAROLINA

CHARLESTON

SC1   MIRIAM B. WILSON FOUNDATION (1962), THE OLD SLAVE MART MUSEUM (1937). 6 Chalmers St., 29401. Tel 803 722-0079. Mrs. Judith W. Chase, Curator and Educational Dir. Bibliographies prepared, literature searches, copying, inquiries answered, consultation. The Museum was founded to present the history of slavery in an objective way, counteracting misconceptions about slavery and to exhibit the roots of the Negro culture. The Museum collects, preserves, and exhibits Negro arts, crafts and artifacts illustrative of this culture and is located in the "Old Slave Mart" building, which was erected in 1820 and used as a place to auction slaves and material objects. Opened as a museum in 1937.
    Publ.: Bibliographies, pamphlets, leaflets; Condensed History of Slavery by Miriam B. Wilson; Color slide lectures on Afro-American History and Art.

.1   Charleston, South Carolina.
    Miscellaneous, ?-1865. Maps, pictures, documents, swords and other weapons significant in the background of Charleston, S.C., up through the Civil War. Restricted.

.2   Harleston, E. Augustus, 1882-1931.
    Painting. 1 item. Artist. Oil painting entitled "Charleston Shrimp Man." Restricted.

.3   Materials pertaining to Negroes and slavery.
    Miscellaneous. Books (ca. 500 v.); periodical and newspaper titles (ca. 400); pamphlets; mss (200 items); correspondence (1000 items); photographs; tape recordings; phonograph records; photostats; color slides; and historical objects (1000 items) consisting of slave-made arts and crafts, artifacts used by slaves which reflect his cultural history, and other objects pertaining to and used during slavery, including African artifacts related to the Afro-American. Also included is "Banjo Boy", oil painting by runaway slave in gratitude to man who helped him escape. Restricted.

.4   Negro artists collection.
    Photo files, colonial days- . Material pertaining to Negro art, and lives of Negro and African artists. Restricted.

.5   Wilson, Miriam Belangee, d. 1959. collector.
    Files. Founder of The Old Slave Mart Museum, historian, and author. Newspaper clippings (ca. 5000 items) dealing with race relations, Negro history, African culture as related to Afro-Americans, American slavery, and similar topics. The author of Condensed History of Slavery. Restricted.

SC2   SOUTH CAROLINA HISTORICAL SOCIETY LIBRARY. Fireproof Bldg. at Chalmers St., 29401. Tel 803 723-3225. Mrs. Granville T. Prior, Secy.

.1   Allston family.
    Allston-Pringle-Hill collection, 1812-1920. 4330 items and 63 v. In part, transcripts (typewritten). Correspondence, diaries, mss, time books, and other papers of a South Carolina rice-planting family. The papers of Robert Francis Withers Allston (1801-64), Governor of South Carolina, include fragmentary personal letters, receipts and plantation records (1856-58). Papers of Elizabeth Waites Allston (Mrs. John Julius Pringle, 1845-1921), rice planter and author, includes diaries, time books, and mss of her books: A Woman Rice Planter, and Chronicles of Chicora Woods. These papers disclose information on daily life on a plantation, the low-country Negro, and related data. The correspondence of Jane Allston (Mrs. Charles A. Hill, 1850-1937) relates to social life in South Carolina and other parts of America and includes letters from Richard L. Allston. Other papers include typewritten copies of letters of "anti-Secessionist" James Louis Petigru (1789-1863).

.2   Allston, Robert Francis Withers, 1801-64.
    Papers, 1757-1929. 6 v. and 31 boxes. Planter, civil engineer, legislator, and Governor of South Carolina. Family and business letters, diaries, plantation account books, estate papers, and overseers and factor's reports pertaining to Allston's rice plantation. Papers (1809-96) relate mainly to Allston and his family. The correspondence consists primarily of letters to and from members of the Allston and Petigru families. Prominent among these are Allston's children: Benjamin Allston (1833-1900), Charles Petigru Allston (1848-1922), Adele (Mrs. Arnoldus Vanderhorst, 1842-1915), Elizabeth Waites (Mrs. John Julius Pringle, 1845-1921), and Jane Louise (Mrs. Charles A. Hill, 1850-1937). Letters concerning "anti-Secessionist" James Louis Petigru appear among the family correspondence. Includes Allston's diary (1861-63), letters from other planters and State leaders, and other material.

.3   Bacot family.
    Bacot-Huger collection, 1754-1927. 6 ft. In part, transcripts. Family, legal, and genealogical correspondence, business, legal, estate, and plantation papers, receipts, diaries, and other papers, chiefly relating to the activities of Daniel Elliott Huger (1779-1854), Cooper River planter, Charleston lawyer, and U.S. Senator from South Carolina; of Thomas Wright Bacot (1765-1834), postmaster of Charleston and president of the Bank of South Carolina; of Thomas Wright Bacot, Jr. (1795-1851), assistant postmaster; of Robert Dewar Bacot (1821-1903), Charleston commission merchant and cotton broker; and of Thomas Wright Bacot, III (1849-1927), lawyer, Democratic party leader, and South Carolina State legislator. Includes material on refugees at Society Hill, S.C. (1862-65); records; account books (1824); and minute books. Other names represented include D. Huger Bacot (1847-1920), Julius M. Bacot, and Julia Huger.

.4   Ball, John.
    Plantation books.

.5   Bennett, John, 1865-1956.
    Papers, ca. 1900-57. 6 v. and 36 boxes. Author, illustrator, and lecturer, of Charleston, S.C. Correspondence; notes on local folklore, Gullah, Negro music and folksongs; and other subjects. Correspondents include Du Bose Heyward and Hervey Allen.

.6   Broughton family.
    Papers, 1703-1854. 100 items and 5 v. Correspondence, wills, land conveyances, plats, and inventories of the Broughton family of Mulberry Plantation on the Cooper River and of St. George, Dorchester, S.C.

.7   Chestnut family.
    Chestnut-Miller-Manning papers, 1744-1900. 7 boxes. Business and personal papers of John Chestnut (1743-1818); James Chestnut (1773-1866), South Carolina legislator; James Chestnut II (1815-85), U.S. Senator from South Carolina and Confederate officer; Stephen Decatur Miller (1787-1838), Governor of South Carolina; and John Manning (1816-89), Governor of South Carolina. Papers of James Chestnut II and John Manning relate to the Civil War and to Reconstruction in South Carolina. Papers (1820-38) of Stephen D. Miller pertain to the Nullification Movement in South Carolina.

.8   Cheves family.
    Papers, 1777-1938. 44 ft. In part, transcripts. Papers of three generations of the Cheves family of South Carolina: Langdon Cheves (1776-1857), lawyer, U.S. Representative, and judge of the Supreme Court of South Carolina; Langdon Cheves (1848-1940), lawyer, historian, and genealogist; comprising several groups with a unifying theme illustrating the acquisition and management of plantations

and the impact of wars, depressions and industrialization on the agricultural society of South Carolina. The papers of the Middleton and Kinloch families are included. Plantation and family papers (1830-61) include plats, leases, indentures, and other documents pertaining to the property of Langdon Cheves I, and letters written by him to his sons and sons-in-law giving advice on plantation management. Also included are the Dulles and Lovel estate papers (1780-1883); diary (1862-66) of Sophia Lovel Haskell Cheves (1846-1922), wife of Langdon Cheves III; correspondence of members of the McCord and Miles families; and miscellaneous material.

SC2.9 Coffin, Thomas Aston.
Papers. Contain references to slavery.

.10 Family account books.
1802-99. 18 v. Account books (1802-13) of the family of John Ball, Sr. (1760-1817), planter on the Cooper River, S.C.; receipt book (1834-61) of Joseph Benjamin Hinson (1801-22), planter of Stiles Point, James Island, S.C.; and account books (1850-99) of the family of Thomas Smyth (1808-73).

.11 Gilman, Caroline (Howard), 1794-1888.
Letters, 1810-80. 109 items. Author and editor. Earliest letters of Mrs. Gilman, wife of the Rev. Samuel Gilman, of Charleston, S.C.; letters written after 1819 relate to social and political events of Charleston. Includes accounts of events in Charleston during the Secession Convention and the bombardment of Fort Sumter during the early days of the Civil War and the fire of 1861. Letters (1863), written from Greenville, S.C., pertain to hardships of the war and the raid of Union soldiers under Sherman.

.12 Heyward, Du Bose, 1885-1940.
Papers, 1880-1940. ca. 10 ft. Author. Correspondence; literary mss, and early typed versions of Heyward's novels, plays, poems, and screenplays; business papers; material relating to Heyward's family of South Carolina; photos., and other papers. The letters are mostly from Heyward to Hervey Allen (1922-40) with a few from Dorothy Heyward (his wife). Literary mss include Star Spangled Virgin, Felix Hollister, Porgy (the novel), and Porgy (the play), The Leamer Tragedy, Mamba's Daughters, Angel, Brass Ankle, and versions of Heyward's screenplays, Emperor Jones, by Eugene O'Neill, and The Good Earth, by Pearl Buck, as well as other material.

.13 Laurens, Henry, 1724-92.
Papers, 1747-96. ca. 6 ft. South Carolina merchant, planter, Revolutionary statesman, and diplomat. Material relating to Indian affairs, the Revolution, commerce, and plantation affairs, and reflecting various aspects of colonial economic history.

.14 Lee, Hutson.
Papers, 1858-65. 3 boxes. Confederate Army quartermaster, of Charleston, S.C. ca. 20 advertisements of auction sales of Negroes (1858-60).

.15 Manigault family.
Papers, 1685-1873. 443 items and 5 v. Personal and business correspondence, plantation records, and other papers of a South Carolina family, mainly of Peter Manigault (1731-73), Gabriel Manigault (1758-1809) Charles Izard Manigault (1795-1874), and Gabriel E. Manigault (1833-99); memorandum book (1861-73) pertaining to Silk Hope Plantation.

.16 Milliken, John B.
Plantation journals.

.17 Pinckney family.
Papers, 1708-1878. 2 ft. In part, transcripts (handwritten) of letters (1739-83), and photocopies. Correspondence, accounts, receipts, land, legal, estate, and other papers of Charles Pinckney (1699-1758), Elizabeth (Lucas) Pinckney (1721-93), Charles Cotesworth Pinckney (1746-1825), Harriot (Pinckney) Horry (1748-1830), Thomas Pinckney (1750-1828) and other members of the Pinckney and related families. Most of the papers belong to the second generation of Pinckneys and reflect family affairs and plantation life in South Carolina in the late 18th and early 19th centuries.

.18 Porcher, John Stoney, ca. 1830-1916.
Papers of John Stoney Porcher and allied families, 1771-1883. 88 items and 3 v. Resident of Walworth Plantation, Upper St. John's, Berkeley, S.C. Papers relating to the settlement of the Porcher, Couturier and Gaillard estates, including that of General Francis Marion; miscellaneous papers relating to land; 3 v. of account books (1826-34).

.19 St. Helena's Parish.
Records of plantations, 1800-21, 3 v. and 2 items.

.20 St. John's Parish.
Records relating to St. John's Parish, Berkeley Co., S.C., 1760-1853. 7 v. Records of the Commissioners of the High Roads of St. John's Parish include lists of property owners and minutes (1760-1836). Records (1823-40) of the Police Association of St. John's and St. Stephen's parishes are composed of the constitution of the association, treasurer's record, and other records kept intermittently, whenever danger from runaway or armed slaves seemed to call for special vigilance.

.21 St. Stephen's Parish.
Records (1823-40) of the Police Association of St. John's and St. Stephen's Parishes are composed of the constitution of the association, treasurer's records, and other records kept intermittently, whenever danger from runaway or armed slaves seemed to call for special vigilance.

.22 Smith, Daniel Elliot Huger, 1846-1932.
Notebooks. ca. 4 ft. Cotton broker and historian, of Charleston, S.C. Notebooks containing abstracts of wills and conveyances, and records of the ownership of many Charleston houses and low country plantations. 128 families are treated at length, other families are mentioned.

.23 Smith, William Loughton, 1758-1812.
Papers. 1774-1832. 2 ft. Politician, diplomat, and lawyer of Charleston, S.C. Smith's estate papers (1812-32); the accounts and estates he administered including those of Joseph Allen Smith, William Crafts, Barnard Elliot, and William Wragg (d. 1803); includes accounts of John F. Grimké, C.C. Pinckney, David Ramsey, and Thomas Sumter. Also includes letters by Smith to Edward Rutledge reflecting views on foreign and internal affairs.

.24 South Carolina Episcopal Church Records, 1694-1962.
Papers. ca. 12 ft. In part, transcripts (handwritten and typewritten). Church registers, vestry minutes, financial accounts, correspondence, and other church records, which contain occasional references to Negroes. These records are a part of the collection of the Dalcho Historical Society of the Protestant Episcopal Church of South Carolina.

.25 South Carolina Low Country Land Records, 1696-1854.
Papers. ca. 100 items and 3 v. Correspondence, conveyances, deeds, indentures, grants, surveys, plats, wills, and bills of sale of slaves.

.26 South Carolina Plantation Papers, 1748-1914.
Papers. ca. 2 ft. Plantation books, daybooks, timebooks, and journals of cotton and rice plantations on the Ashley, Cooper, Cumbahee and Peedee Rivers and in Middle St. John's, Berkeley; St. Mark's Parish, Orangeburg Co.; and Georgetown Co., S.C. Includes accounts, tax returns, lists of Negroes, household inventories, records of supplies issued to Negroes, work performed, and other miscellaneous information on plantation life. Names represented include John Ball, Jr. (1812-34), Ebenezer Coffin (1765-1816), Thomas Aston Coffin, Gaillard family, Dr. Benjamin Huger (1793-1872), Mrs. Theodore Dehon Jervey, Henry Ravenel (1739-85), Augustine Thomas Smythe (1842-1914), Dr. James Sparkman (1815-97), and Daniel Cannon Webb (1817-50).

.27 Travel Journals, Diaries, and Memoirs, 1760-1907.
Papers. ca. 2 ft. In part, transcripts (typewritten). Includes a diary (1856) of J.E. McPherson Washington written at the University of Virginia and Charleston, S.C.; mss of variants of the published version of Rice Planter and Sportsman; the Recollections of J. Motte Alston, 1821-1909 (1853); and an autobiography of the Rev. Paul Trapier describing his work as an Episcopal minister among the

South Carolina Negroes and his role in guiding the
Episcopal Church in the Confederate and post-
bellum period.

.28 Vanderhorst family.
Papers, 1736-1910. 12 boxes. Chiefly correspon-
dence to and from numerous relatives of Adele
(Allston) Vanderhorst (1842-1915). One box relates
to plantation life and to social life in Charleston,
S.C.

.29 Weston family.
Papers, 1786-1869. 216 items. Grants, deeds,
mortgages, and other land papers relating to plantations in the Georgetown District of South
Carolina, on the Peedee River. Includes rice
plantation papers, bills of sale, lists of Negroes;
papers relating to the settlement of Dr. Paul
Weston's estate; papers relating to the plantation
of Plowden Weston.

COLUMBIA

SC3   ALLEN UNIVERSITY (1941), J. S. FLIPPER LIBRARY.
1530 Harden St., 29204. Tel 803 254-1700. Mrs. Edith
R. Holmes, Admin. Librn.

.1 Afro-American Studies Collection.
ca. 1000 paperbacks. Basic book on the life and
history of black Americans.

.2 Allen University.
Archives, 1941- . Correspondence, minutes of
board meetings, financial and admission records,
and other materials concerning the administration
and history of the college.

SC4   AMERICAN FRIENDS SERVICE COMMITTEE, SOUTH
CAROLINA COMMUNITY RELATIONS PROGRAM
(1966). 704 Columbia Bldg., 29201. Tel 803 253-7159.
M. Hayes Mizell, Dir.
The Program works for racial justice, understanding,
and equal opportunity through its action-oriented programs. The Program also seeks the rapid attainment of
a quality integrated school system throughout the state,
and the participation of low-income and minority groups
in the formulation and evaluation of programs and policies at the local level.
Publ.: Quaker Service, newsletter; Your Schools,
monthly newsletter.

.1 South Carolina Community Relations Program.
Files, 1966- . Correspondence, news clippings,
pamphlets, and other materials pertaining to school
desegregation in South Carolina, including statistical information, field reports, program reports,
speeches, and materials about other agencies such
as the South Carolina Voter Education Project, and
the South Carolina Advisory Committee to the U.S.
Commission on Civil Rights (1966-68). Also included are records concerning the administration
and other activities of the Program.

SC5   BENEDICT COLLEGE (1870), STARKS LIBRARY. Harden
and Taylor Sts., 29204. Tel 803 252-6394. Mrs Mae S.
Johnson, Librn. Interlibrary loan, copying, inquiries
answered, referrals made, consultation.
Publ.: The Messenger.

.1 Afro-American Heritage collection.
Materials, 17th century- . Microfilm. 131 reels,
Books, newspapers, and mss concerning the Negro
American and his history. See Minnesota Mining
and Manufacturing Company, St. Paul, Minn., for a
full description.

.2 Afro-American Studies Collection.
ca. 1000 paperbacks. Basic Books on the life and
history of black Americans.

.3 Benedict College.
Archives, 1870- . Includes correspondence, minutes of board meetings, financial and admission
records, and other materials concerning the administration and history of the College.

.4 Mather School.
Archives, 1868-1968. Scattered records, including
records of admission, duplicate minutes of the
Mather Board, and some early alumni history and
pictures of Mather School. More complete records

are at the American Baptist Home Mission Societies, Valley Forge, Pa.

.5 Negro collection.
Includes books (ca. 6000), newspapers, periodicals,
pamphlets, clippings, and other materials covering
Negro life and history.

SC6   COLUMBIA COMMUNITY RELATIONS COUNCIL. c/o
Mayor's Office, City Hall, 29201. Tel 803 765-1041.

.1 Columbia Community Relations Council.
Files. Records, reports, correspondence, and
other papers concerning the aims and programs of
the Council.

SC7   COLUMBIA URBAN LEAGUE (1967). 1920 Blossom St.,
29205. Tel 803 256-3666. Elliott E. Franks, III, Exec.
Dir. Inquiries answered, referrals made, consultation.
The League is a professional nonprofit, non-partisan
community service agency established to help primarily the black population with problems which ad-
versely affect their social and economic well being, to
aid in community organization, and to improve living
and working conditions affecting blacks and other
similarly disadvantaged groups. The services offered
include employment, employment training, education,
health and welfare, housing and leadership development.

.1 Columbia Urban League.
Files, 1967- . Correspondence, minutes of meetings, financial records, studies, reports, and other
materials dealing with the aims, history, and programs of the League.

SC8   SOUTH CAROLINA COUNCIL ON HUMAN RELATIONS
(1954). 1330 Laurel St., 29201. Tel 803 252-3651. Paul
W. Matthias, Exec. Dir.
The Council, through educational programs, seeks to
improve economic, civic and racial conditions, and to
promote better intergroup relations in the state. The
Council conducts research and action programs in such
areas as housing, employment, and school desegregation. Affiliated with the Southern Regional Council, Inc.,
Atlanta, Ga.
Publ.: South Carolina Council on Human Relations Review, monthly.

.1 South Carolina Council on Human Relations.
Files, 1954- . Correspondence, records, reports,
program plans and evaluations, and other materials concerning the administration and activities of
the Council.

SC9   THE SOUTH CAROLINA TASK FORCE FOR COMMUNITY
UPLIFT (1967). P.O. Box 11589, 29211. A. McKay
Brabham, Jr., Chmn.
The Task Force is a biracial, volunteer organization
whose purpose is to stimulate action and racial harmony
in the community.

.1 South Carolina Task Force for Community Uplift.
Files, 1967- . Records, reports, correspondence,
and other papers pertaining to the aims and activities of the organization.

SC10 SOUTH CAROLINA VOTER EDUCATION PROJECT. 1420
Lady St., 29201. Tel 803 254-4231. James Felder.

.1 South Carolina Voter Education Project.
Files. Records, reports, correspondence, and
other papers concerning the Project.

SC11 STATE OF SOUTH CAROLINA, SOUTH CAROLINA DE-
PARTMENT OF ARCHIVES AND HISTORY (1905). 1430
Senate St., 29211. Tel 803 758-3438. Charles E. Lee,
Dir. Copying, inquiries answered, consultation.
Publ.: Publications list.

.1 Comptroller General Free Negro Roll Books.
Roll books, 1821-46. 19 v. Includes names and
addresses of free Negroes in the Charleston District.

.2 Council Journals.
1671-80, 1692, 1721-76. Includes information concerning white-Indian relations on the southern
frontier, and material relating to Negro runaways
to St. Augustine, the Stono slave revolt, and the
1749 slave revolt alarm.

.3 Governor's Letterbooks.
    1867-68, 1875-1900. 50 v. Letters sent including those concerning race relations _passim_.

.4 Journals of the Commons House of Assembly.
    Contain information concerning slavery.

.5 Legislative papers.
    Papers, legislative and executive, 1782-1877. Includes letters, messages, petitions, presentments, reports and other papers concerning slaves, free Negroes, the Denmark Vesey slave plot, freedmen, the Freedmen's Bureau, and Indians and Catawba lands.

.6 Secretary of the Province and Secretary of State.
    Miscellaneous records, 1671-1903. 190 v. Records of manumissions, bills of sale, deeds, guardianship papers, appraisements of estates, wills, certificates of free birth and freedom, and other documents.

SC12 UNIVERSITY OF SOUTH CAROLINA LIBRARIES (1801), SOUTH CAROLINIANA LIBRARY (1940). 29208. Tel 803 777-3131. E.L. Inabinett, Librn. Copying.

.1 The Library's holdings include ca. 50,000 books, pamphlets and periodical volumes, extensive files of South Carolina newspapers, maps, pictures, and mss, much of which relates to Negro history in South Carolina. The Library's ms collection, ca. 2,000,000 items, and newspaper files are described, in an abbreviated fashion, in John H. Moore's _Research Material in South Carolina: A Guide_ (Columbia, 1967). Among the collections containing material relating to the Negro are the following:

.2 — Bonham, Milledge Luke, 1813-90.
    Papers, 1771-1940. 4402 items. In part, copies. Lawyer, Army officer and statesman, of South Carolina. Correspondence, legal and business papers, and other papers relating to Bonham's service in the Civil War and as Governor of South Carolina, among other subjects.

.3 — Bull, William A., d. 1839.
    Papers, 1803-60. 153 items. Correspondence, orders and reports (1836) to Bull, and plantation and personal accounts (1848-52) of John Baxter Bull.

.4 — Cantey family.
    Papers, 1771-1913. 320 items. Chiefly correspondence and business papers relating to operations of plantations in Georgia and Alabama.

.5 — Cash, Ellerbe Boggan Crawford, 1823-88.
    Papers, 1805-1935. 80 items. Lawyer, Confederate officer, and plantation owner of Cash's Depot, near Cheraw, S.C. Chiefly business and land papers connected with the Ellerbe, Gregg, Lindsay and Tolson families.

.6 — Colhoun, James Edward, 1798-1889.
    Papers, 1806-89. 598 items. Chiefly bills, receipts, and correspondence regarding Colhoun's operation of his plantation and other business activities.

.7 — Colhoun, John Ewing, 1750-1802.
    Papers, 1769-1822, 1951. 412 items. Lawyer, planter, legislator, and U.S. Senator from South Carolina. Chiefly correspondence and business papers connected with the operation of Colhoun's plantations and his legal practice.

.8 — Coker (W.C.) and Company, Society Hill, S.C.
    Records, 1842-1932. 37 v. Letter books, cashbooks, daybooks, ledgers, bills, indexes and other accounts of a firm of merchants and planters. Includes plantation book (1868-69) of William Coker.

.9 — Confederate States of America.
    Records, 1861-65. 72 items. Letters and notes relating to labor problems and use of Negroes for work on fortifications, reports and orders regarding the defense of Charleston harbor, and payroll records of the Confederate Army engineers.

.10 — Conway, Bonds, 1763-1843.
    Papers, 1800-1905. 117 items. Chiefly papers of Negroes. Includes family records (1805-99); Camden, S.C., land conveyances; crop liens; tax receipts, miscellaneous advertisements and

newspaper clippings; letters to Epsey Conway Johnson; 21 letters (1861-65) from Sergeant Thomas Scanlon, CSA, relating to the Civil War; letters from Jesse McElroy of Henderson, Texas, relating to conditions following the war; printed matter; and other papers.

.11 — Cooper, Thomas, 1759-1839.
    Papers, 1778-1951. 136 items. Scientist and educator. Chiefly letters to the board of trustees while Cooper was president of South Carolina College. Includes notes on laws regarding the freeing of slaves.

.12 — Cross, Paul, d. 1784.
    Papers, 1768-1803. 303 items and 4 v. Papers of a slave trader and bills and receipts of his wife, Anne, a tavern keeper in Charleston, S.C.

.13 — Frierson, David Ethan, 1818-96.
    Papers, 1839-96. 272 items. Chiefly sermons, together with notes of lectures and other papers. Includes an account of the First General Assembly of the Presbyterian Church, Confederate States of America, and a catechism for Negroes.

.14 — Gary, Martin Witherspoon, 1831-81.
    Papers, 1851-1927. 518 items. Lawyer, Confederate officer and political leader, of South Carolina. Correspondence, addresses, newspaper clippings, and miscellaneous papers. The major part of the collection covers the period 1866-80 and reveals Gary's part in the Reconstruction period, particularly the campaign of 1876 and his political activities, 1876-81.

.15 — Geiger, Edwin W.
    Papers, 1736-1881. 212 items. In part, photocopies of grants, deeds, plats, and receipts of the Geiger family. Land papers, bills of sale for slaves, legal papers, receipts, inventories of estates, and other papers from Orangeburg and Lexington District, Berkeley County, S.C.

.16 — Gibbes, Robert Wilson, 1809-66.
    Papers, 1803-66 and 1931. 303 items. Physician, scientist, and historian. Chiefly business and legal papers consisting of bills, receipts, land papers, and papers relating to the sale of Negroes, and the settlement of estates of the Raoul family.

.17 — Grimball, John Berkeley, 1800-93.
    Papers, 1816-95. 87 items. Planter, of Charleston, S.C. Correspondence, relating to family, personal, and plantation affairs, and other papers.

.18 — Guignard family.
    Papers, 1761-1952. 2992 items. Correspondence, letter books, account books, land grants and titles, surveys, wills, slave inventories, plantation bills and receipts, business and professional accounts, and other papers of the Columbia, S.C., family. Chiefly papers of John Gabriel Guignard I, II, and III; and of James Sanders Guignard I, II, and III; with other papers of Gabriel Alexander Guignard. The papers are of interest in showing details of plantation management, ante-bellum southern industries, rural medical practice, Episcopal Church history, and estate settlements.

.19 — Hammond, James Henry, 1807-64.
    Papers, 1823-1920. 3000 items and 106 v. Governor of South Carolina and U.S. Senator. Chiefly personal and plantation papers centering around Hammond's work as planter and leader in the improvement of southern agriculture. Includes diaries and plantation books of a son, E. Spann Hammond (1834-1921), among many other papers.

.20 — Hampton family.
    Papers of the three Wade Hamptons, 1773-1956. 283 items. In part, photocopies. Correspondence, clippings, documents, accounts, bonds, and other papers of the Richland County (S.C.) Wade Hamptons: the first, a planter, Congressman, and Revolutionary soldier; his son, a planter; and his grandson, a Confederate soldier, Governor, and U.S. Senator. Mainly letters exchanged between members of the

family and dealing with private concerns; some possess political, military, and economic significance in the history of the state and nation. Most numerous are the papers of Wade Hampton III, which reveal conditions during the Civil War, including troop dispositions, strategy, and home-front privations. His later papers deal with the Reconstruction period, and various public issues including the Negro problem and efforts to restore the southern economy.

SC12.21 — Hopkinson, James.
Papers, 1846-1917. 402 items and 20 v. Family correspondence and legal and business papers connected with the estate of John Berwick Legare, planter of Edisto Island, S.C. Includes plantation account books and journals.

.22 — Jenkins family.
Papers, 1775-1945. 931 items. Correspondence and other papers of five generations of an Edisto Island, S.C., planter family. Included are 114 letters (1861-65) of the family presenting a picture of civilian and army life during the Civil War. The papers for 1866-1900 are mainly those of John Jenkins (1824-1905) and reveal the planter's struggle to maintain possession of his land and to adjust to a new system of agriculture.

.23 — Johnson, David, 1782-1855.
Papers, 1810-55, 1951-52. 61 items. Chiefly letters of Thomas Johnson of Columbia and Chester, S.C., realting to management of the plantation and settlement of the estate, among other subjects.

.24 — Keitt, Ellison Summerfield, 1831-1911.
Papers, 1847-ca. 1900. 58 items and 1 v. Correspondence, business papers, military commissions, reminiscences with information on Keitt's services in the Civil War, his plantation, Reconstruction in South Carolina, and scrapbook containing newspaper clippings relating to Reconstruction in South Carolina and activities of the Ku Klux Klan.

.25 — Kincaid family.
Papers of the Kincaid and Anderson families, 1767-1926. 2585 items. Correspondence, wills, school reports, land grants, receipts, account books, appraisals of estates, and other papers of two closely connected upcountry South Carolina families, covering five generations. Contains information on economic history, social and religious activities, education, the War of 1812 and the Civil War, business affairs between planter and factor, and the planter during the Reconstruction. Mainly the papers of James Kincaid, William Kincaid, Edward Kirkpatrick Anderson, Elizabeth Kincaid Anderson, and Thomas Kincaid Anderson.

.26 — Lafitte, David Montague, 1791-1869.
Papers, 1817-60. 383 items and 1 v. Physician, of Barnwell District, S.C. Chiefly bills and receipts from business firms in Charleston and Savannah including medical, household, and plantation supplies; medical account book (1817-37); and legal and business papers connected with the guardianship of Whitefield S. Murphy, and the administration of the following estates: M. Brown, John G. Kugley, John Murphy, and John A. Owens.

.27 — Law, Thomas Cassels, 1811-88.
Papers, 1770-1899. 561 items. In part, transcripts and photocopies. Resident of Darlington District, S.C. Correspondence, plantation records, slave records, photos, and other papers. Includes Civil War correspondence (1864-65) of Law's son, Hugh Lide Law.

.28 — Lawton family.
Papers, 1733-1949. 2339 items. Chiefly the business and legal papers of Joseph Lawton, justice of the peace following the Revolution, and his son, Col. Alexander J. Lawton, lawyer, planter, legislator and businessman of the Robertville section of Beaufort District, S.C. Includes bills and receipts for the sale of slaves, and for household and plantations supplies, among many other papers.

.29 — Lide family.
Lide-Coker family papers, 1827-94, 1957. 212 items. Family correspondence and journals of members of the Lide and Coker families reflecting the history of the South and the old Southwest, and covering modes of travel, social conditions, religion, health, slavery, clearing lands, farming and planting, among other subjects. Includes Caleb Coker's plantation journals.

.30 — McCrady family.
Papers, 1821-1907. 262 items. Correspondence, chiefly of the two Edward McCradys with other members of the family, and a few other papers. Contains material on the Episcopal Church, the South Carolina General Assembly and the political and social problems with which it dealt, military and civilian life during the Civil War (particularly in Charleston and South Carolina), the Reconstruction, and various military and political personalities.

.31 — Mackay family.
Papers, 1822-1926. 83 items. Chiefly family correspondence from Pocotaligo, Charleston, McPhersonville, Orangeburg, S.C., and other places. Many of the letters relate to plantation affairs and the Civil War. The letters from 1874-1926 contain comments on contracts with the Negroes, poor business conditions, schools, and family news.

.32 — McLees, John, 1812-82.
Papers, 1838-1918. 435 items. Chiefly letters and papers relating to McLees' work as a Presbyterian minister. Includes letters (1856-61) concerning work among the Negroes in Greenwood and Pickens districts, S.C., and family correspondence.

.33 — McMahan, John Joseph, 1865-1936.
Papers, 1847-1934. 41 v. Papers connected with McMahan's positions as South Carolina State superintendent of education, insurance commissioner, member of the House of Representatives from Richland County, member of the board of trustees of the University of South Carolina, his law practices and operation of his plantation in Fairfield Co., S.C.; notebooks (1893-1934) containing personal and state accounts, suggested national political reforms, descriptions of parts of conversations with various people, and business notes. Includes information on the National Education Association in South Carolina and problems of the public schools.

.34 — Manning family.
Williams-Chestnut-Manning papers, 1682-1962. 2757 items. Correspondence and other papers of the Chestnut and Manning families, together with papers of the Cantey, Hampton, Miller, Richardson, and Williams families, reflecting the social and economic life of South Carolina and containing much information on political issues. The majority of the papers are of John Lawrence Manning (1816-89) and his immediate family and relate chiefly to business, plantation, and family affairs.

.35 — Means family.
Means-English-Doby families' papers, 1828-1910. 326 items. Chiefly family correspondence reflecting the social, economic, and political history of South Carolina. One third of the collection concerns the domestic and plantation affairs and education of the family of John English, physician and planter of Richland District, S.C., and his wife, Maria Elizabeth Preston (Means) English, of Fairfield District, S.C. The bulk of the collection consists of Civil War letters written by Alfred English Doby (1840-64) to his wife Elizabeth M. (Kennedy) Doby of Camden, S.C.

.36 — Means, Mary Hart, 1835-1916.
Papers, 1837-1911. 213 items and 3 v. Chiefly family letters representing the Coalter, Davis, Bates, Means, Poelnitz and other connections, containing information on education, economic,

social and religious activities of the families and the communities in which they lived in Fairfield District, S.C., Alabama, Louisiana, Missouri, and Virginia. Includes cotton book (1858) of Thomas Coalter Means and other memorandum books from Fairfield District, S.C., containing plantation records and personal accounts.

.37 —— Motte family.
Papers, 1768-1892. 124 items. Chiefly business correspondence and papers. Includes plantation workbooks (1854-56) of J. Rhett Motte from Exeter Plantation, Berkeley County, S.C.

.38 —— Moultrie, William, 1730-1805.
Papers, 1752-1844, 1929-40. 721 items. Revolutionary Army officer and Governor of South Carolina. Chiefly bills, accounts, receipts, and other business papers for the plantation and household of Moultrie.

.39 —— Noisette family.
Papers, 1841-1939. 66 items. Legal papers from Charleston, S.C., relating to land conveyances and litigation in the settlement of the estate of Alexander Noisette. Includes manumission papers for the children of Philip Stanislas Noisette and a petition to the House of Representatives requesting the children be permitted to remain in South Carolina as free persons of color.

.40 —— O'Neil, John.
Papers, 1867-1903. 50 items. Merchant, of Charleston, S.C. Family correspondence and letters (1867-73) from John Murphy relating to claims arising out of Federal seizure of cotton, Alabama claims, the Geneva Commission and Reconstruction.

.41 —— Pickens family.
Papers, 1781-1929. 284 items. The correspondence and other papers of Francis W. Pickens form the bulk of the collection and include business papers relating to the sale of cotton and plantation supplies, account books, scrapbook, and notebook. Many of Pickens' letters written to members of his family discuss plantation affairs, family and social life, and political papers.

.42 —— Pinckney family.
Papers, 1735-1922. 315 items and 7 v. Correspondence, accounts, bills, receipts, and other business, legal, and personal papers of a South Carolina family. Includes material relating to plantation affairs.

.43 —— Porcher family.
Papers of the Porcher and Ford families, 1797-1925. 401 items and 6 v. Chiefly family correspondence from Charleston, Aiken and Abbeville District, S.C., Atlanta, Ga., and other places, containing information on social and religious activities of the family and community with occasional comments on politics; together with printed almanacs containing notes on the birth and death of slaves, and other family records.

.44 —— Porcher, Frederick Adolphus, 1809-88.
Correspondence, 1862-1922. 62 items. Historian. Chiefly family correspondence with Porcher's wife and daughters, containing comments on family affairs, the Civil War, Charleston, S.C., city politics and radical rule, trouble with Negroes, education, and other subjects.

.45 —— Porcher, John Palmer.
Papers, 1831-72. 154 items. Resident of Charleston, S.C. Business papers consisting of bills and receipts for household goods, clothing, drugs, books, pew rent in St. Paul's Church, Charleston S.C., the Protestant Episcopal Society for the Advancement of Christianity, medical services, taxes, blacksmith work, wines and liquors, and slaves working on the fortifications.

.46 —— Robinson, John Andrew.
Papers, 1858-76. 311 items. Physician of Abbeville District, S.C. Chiefly family letters

and business papers. Includes information on religious and social activities, political and financial difficulties during Reconstruction; letters (1867-73) from S. Moffatt Wylie, of Chester District, S.C., discussing his medical practice, planting interests, social affairs and politics, and nearly illegible diary (1861-65) of Robinson's Civil War service.

.47 —— Rutledge family.
Papers, 1796-1862. 84 items. Chiefly family letters from Charleston, S.C., and other places, relating to personal matters, plantation affairs, and politics in South Carolina. Includes journal (1839) of Harriott Pinckney and Harry Rutledge.

.48 —— Sams family.
Papers, 1826-1934. 30 items and 35 v. Family correspondence, business papers, and genealogical material. Includes a v. (1837-70) recording births in the family and of Negroes on the plantation; and information on schools during Reconstruction, trials of a country store, family problems, and neighborhood gossip. Places represented include Allendale, Barnwell, Beaufort, Columbia, Edgefield, and Gaffney, S.C.

.49 —— Stapleton, John.
Papers, 1790-1839. 113 items. Lawyer, of London, England. Correspondence, plantation journal, lists of Negroes, and other papers relating chiefly to Stapleton's handling of the Bull family estate on St. Helena Island, Beaufort District, S.C.

.50 —— Waller, Creswell A. C.
Papers, 1822-1918. 74 items. Correspondence, bills, receipts, wills, and other family papers from Abbeville District, S.C. Includes information on the Civil War, Reconstruction, and the Waller family of South Carolina and Virginia.

.51 —— Whaley, E. Mikell.
Papers, 1763-1887. 109 items and 3 v. Correspondence, bills, receipts, land papers, guardianship and plantation records, from Edisto Island, S.C. Includes correspondence of Julian Mitchell on legal matters.

.52 —— Witherspoon family.
Papers, 1777-1937. 262 items and 9 v. Chiefly family letters, legal and business papers of a South Carolina family. Includes Civil War letters and papers relating to recruiting, enlisting and exemptions, and plantation journal and record book (1839-54). Includes correspondence of Robert Witherspoon as State treasurer, U.S. Representative and member of the South Carolina Legislature.

DENMARK

SC13   VOORHEES COLLEGE (1897), MARIAN B. WILKINSON LIBRARY. 29042. Tel 803 793-3356. Claude Greene, Librn.

.1   Afro-American Heritage collection.
Materials, 17th century- . Microfilm. 131 reels. Books, newspapers, and mss concerning the Negro American and his history. See Minnesota Mining and Manufacturing Company, St. Paul, Minn., for a full description.

.2   Afro-American Studies Collection.
ca. 1000 paperbacks. Basic books on the life and history of black Americans.

.3   Voorhees College.
Archives, 1897- . Includes correspondence, minutes of board meetings, financial and admission records, and other materials concerning the history and administration of the College.

FROGMORE

SC14   PENN COMMUNITY SERVICES, INC. Saint Helena Island, 29920. Tel 803 524-4337. John Gadsen, Dir.
Penn Community Services trains residents of rural

southern communities in community development. The
organization also provides conference facilities for
groups working in various programs of social change.

  .1 Penn Community Services, Inc.
     Files. Records, reports, correspondence, and
     other papers concerning the aims and the pro-
     grams of the organization.

GREENVILLE

SC15 FURMAN UNIVERSITY, LIBRARY (1826). 29613. Tel 803
     246-3550. Mrs. Ollin J. Owens, Librn, Spec. Collec-
     tions. Interlibrary loan, inquiries answered, referrals
     made, consultation.

  .1 Baptist Historical Collection.
     Materials, ca. 1700's- . ca. 24,000 items and
     500,000 microform pages. Books, periodicals,
     newspapers, pamphlets, vf, theses and disserta-
     tions, correspondence, minutes, microforms, and
     mss. Collection contains the annals of the South
     Carolina Baptist Convention, the Southern Baptist
     Convention, and the American Baptist Convention,
     files of the Baptist Courier and its predecessors,
     and other materials showing the attitudes of South
     Carolina Baptists towards the Negro, especially in
     relation to his church affiliation. Also included are
     microform copies of records of individual churches
     in the 19th century concerning their dealings with
     slave membership.
  .2 —— Manly, Basil, 1798-1868.
     Papers, 1828-68. ca. 60 items. Baptist
     clergyman, of Charleston and Greenville, S.C.,
     and president of the University of Alabama.
     Correspondence relating to Manley's works in
     Charleston Baptist churches, slavery, the
     Southern Baptist Convention, the Triennial
     Baptist Convention, and the editing of the
     Southern Baptist and General Intelligence,
     among other subjects.

PAGELAND

SC16 CONGRESS OF RACIAL EQUALITY (CORE). Post Office,
     29728. Tel 803 672-7034. Rev. J.D. McManus, Chmn.

ORANGEBURG

SC17 CLAFLIN COLLEGE (1869), H. V. MANNING LIBRARY.
     College Ave., 29115. Tel 803 534-4977. Mrs. Louisa
     S. Robinson, Librn. Interlibrary loan, bibliographies
     prepared, inquiries answered, referrals made, con-
     sultation.

  .1 Afro-American Heritage collection.
     Materials, 17th century- . Microfilm. 131 reels.
     Books, newspapers, and mss concerning the Negro
     American and his history. See Minnesota Mining
     and Manufacturing Company, St. Paul, Minn., for a
     full description.
  .2 Afro-American Studies Collection.
     ca. 1000 paperbacks. Basic books on the life and
     history of black Americans.
  .3 Chaflin College.
     Archives, 1869- . Correspondence, minutes of
     board meetings, financial and admission records,
     and other materials concerning the administration
     and history of the College.
  .4 Negro collection.
     Includes books (ca. 1000), periodicals (ca. 15 ft.),
     and pamphlets covering Negro life and history.

SC18 SOUTH CAROLINA STATE COLLEGE, MILLER F. WHIT-
     TAKER LIBRARY. College Ave., 29115. Tel 803 534-
     6560. Barbara J. Williams, Chief Librn. Interlibrary
     loan, bibliographies prepared, copying, typing, inquiries
     answered, referrals made.

  .1 Afro-American Studies Collection.
     ca. 1000 paperbacks. Basic books on the life and
     history of black Americans.

  .2 Negro collection.
     Includes books, periodicals, and pamphlets con-
     cerning Negro life and history.
  .3 South Carolina State College.
     Archives, 1896- . Correspondence, admission
     records, and other materials concerning the ad-
     ministration and history of the College, including
     annuals, pictures, and school papers. Restricted.
  .4 Whitaker, Miller F., 1892-1949.
     Papers. Architect, president of South Carolina
     State College. Architectural blueprints, correspon-
     dence, and other papers reflecting the history and
     administration of the College. Restricted.

ROCK HILL

SC19 CLINTON COLLEGE LIBRARY. 29731. Tel 803 327-7402.
     Mrs. Henrietta Wilkes, Librn.

  .1 Negro in History Collection.

SC20 FRIENDSHIP JUNIOR COLLEGE (1891). Allen St., 29730.
     Tel 803 328-6667. J. H. Gouldlock, Pres.

  .1 Friendship Junior College Archives.
     Records, 1891- . Correspondence, minutes of
     board meetings, financial and admission records,
     and other materials concerning the administration
     and history of the College.

SC21 WINTHROP COLLEGE (1886), IDA JANE DACUS LIBRARY.
     29730. Tel 803 328-5334. Dr. Helen Joanne Harrar,
     Librn. and Prof. of Library Sci. Interlibrary loan,
     bibliographies prepared, literature searches, copying,
     inquiries answered, consultation.

  .1 Facts on Film.
     Papers, 1954-67. Microfilm. Contains materials
     on civil rights and race relations in the South. See
     Race Relations Information Center, Nashville,
     Tenn., for a full description.

SUMTER

SC22 AFRICAN METHODIST EPISCOPAL CHURCH, COMMISSION
     ON SOCIAL ACTION (1960). 215 W. Bartlette St.,
     29150. Tel 803 773-7729. Rev. F. C. James, Consult.

  .1 Commission on Social Action.
     Files, 1960- . Records, reports, correspondence,
     and other papers concerning the aims and activities
     of the Commission.

SC23 MORRIS COLLEGE (1908), PINSON MEMORIAL LIBRARY.
     29150. Tel 803 773-7890. Maude A. McAllister, Head
     Librn. Bibliographies prepared, literature searches,
     inquiries answered, referrals made.

  .1 Afro-American Heritage collection.
     Materials, 17th century- . Microfilm. 131 reels.
     Books, newspapers, and mss concerning the Negro
     American and his history. See Minnesota Mining
     and Manufacturing Company, St. Paul, Minn., for a
     full description.
  .2 Afro-American Studies Collection.
     ca. 1000 paperbacks. Basic books on the life and
     history of black Americans.
  .3 Morris College.
     Archives, 1908- . Correspondence, minutes of
     board meetings, financial and admission records,
     and other materials concerning the history and ad-
     ministration of the College.
  .4 Negro collection.
     Books, pamphlets, periodicals, and other materials
     concerning Negro life and history.

SC24 SCHOLARSHIP, EDUCATION AND DEFENSE FUND FOR
     RACIAL EQUALITY (SEDFRE), INC. 317 W. Bartlette
     St., 29150. Tel 803 773-2353. James T. McCain.

  .1 Scholarship, Education and Defense Fund for Racial
     Equality (SEDFRE), Inc.
     Files. Records, reports, correspondence, and
     other papers concerning the aims and activities of
     the organization.

TENNESSEE

CHATTANOOGA

TN1   ALL PEOPLE'S COMMUNITY ORGANIZATION, INC.
(APCO) (1969). P.O. Box 5176, 37406. Tel 615 629-
1081. Temple Ragland, Jr., Editor.
A.P.C.O. is designed to "express the opinions and desires of the community; to inform and serve the people"
through its organ, A.P.C.O. News.
Publ.: A.P.C.O. News, weekly newspaper.

    .1 All People's Community Organization, Inc.
Files. Correspondence, financial records, and
other materials pertaining to the activities of the
organization and its publication, A.P.C.O. News.
Restricted.

COOKEVILLE

TN1a TENNESSEE TECHNOLOGICAL UNIVERSITY (1918), JERE
WHITSON MEMORIAL LIBRARY. 38501. Tel 615 526-
0213. C.P. Snelgrove, Librn.

    .1 Facts on Film.
Papers, 1954-67. Microfilm. Contains materials
on civil rights and race relations in the South. See
Race Relations Information Center, Nashville,
Tenn., for a full description.

HARROGATE

TN2   LINCOLN MEMORIAL UNIVERSITY (1897), CARNEGIE LI-
BRARY (1945). 37752. Tel 615 869-3624. Rudolph B.
Clark, Head Librn. Interlibrary loan, copying, inquiries
answered, referrals made, consultation.

    .1 Clay, Cassius Marcellus, 1810-1903.
Papers, 1840-98. 600 items. Abolitionist and
Commissioner of Freedman's Bureau. Political
and diplomatic correspondence, a few family letters, Clay's commissions in military service, and
other papers. Correspondents include Edwin M.
Stanton, Harriet Beecher Stowe, Frederick William
Seward, Abraham Lincoln, and Henry Clay.
    .2 Howard, Oliver Otis, 1830-1909.
Letters, 1850-1909. 2 boxes. Union army officer,
politician, and founder of Lincoln Memorial University. Letters by Howard to his family, chiefly to
his daughter, Bessie Howard.
    .3 Lincoln, Abraham, 1809-65.
Papers, 1838-64. ca. 53 items. Correspondence,
documents, law briefs, and other papers of Lincoln
and Vice Presidents, Cabinet officers, generals,
and other contemporaries.
    .4 Sheet music collection.
ca. 1860-65. "One of largest collections of Confederate and Federal sheet music in the United
States."

JACKSON

TN3   LANE COLLEGE (1882), J. K. DANIELS LIBRARY (1896).
501 Lane Ave., 38301. Tel 901 424-4600. Mrs. Anna
L. Cooke, Librn. Interlibrary loan, bibliographies
prepared, copying, inquiries answered, referrals made.
Publ.: The Informer, monthly.

    .1 Afro-American Heritage collection.
Materials, 17th century- . Microfilm. 131 reels.
Books, newspapers, and mss concerning the Negro
American and his history. See Minnesota Mining
and Manufacturing Company, St. Paul, Minn., for a
full description.
    .2 Afro-American Studies Collection.
ca. 1000 paperbacks. Basic books on the life and
history of black Americans.
    .3 Lane, James F., -1945.
Papers. Son of the first bishop of the Christian
Methodist Episcopal Church, and president of Lane
College for 40 years. Unavailable until processed.

    .4 Lane College.
Archives, 1882- . Correspondence, minutes of
board meetings, financial records, records of admission, and other materials dealing with the
administration and history of the College.
    .5 Negro collection.
Books (1338), periodical and newspaper titles, pamphlets, mss, clippings, photographs, filmstrips, and
art objects by and about Afro-Americans and other
persons of African descent.

JOHNSON CITY

TN4   EAST TENNESSEE STATE UNIVERSITY (1911), SHERROD
LIBRARY. 37602. Tel 615 926-1112. Hal H. Smith,
Librn.

    .1 Facts on Film.
Papers, 1954-67. Microfilm. Contains materials
on civil rights and race relations in the South. See
Race Relations Information Center, Nashville,
Tenn., for a full description.

KNOXVILLE

TN5   AMERICAN CIVIL LIBERTIES UNION OF TENNESSEE,
INC. (1967). P.O. Box 91, 713 Market St., 37901. Tel
615 524-1787. Mrs. R.W. Childers, Exec. Secy. Inquiries answered, referrals made.
The Union works to maintain and advance civil liberties
in the State of Tennessee, including freedoms of association, press, religion, speech, due process of law, and
equal protection of the law, and takes all appropriate
action in the furtherance and defense of these rights.
Publ.: Newsletter, semimonthly.

    .1 American Civil Liberties Union of Tennessee, Inc.
Files, 1967- . Correspondence, legal briefs, minutes of meetings, financial records and other
materials concerning civil liberties and rights.

TN6   HIGHLANDER RESEARCH AND EDUCATION CENTER
(1961), HIGHLANDER FOLK SCHOOL RESEARCH LI-
BRARY (1965). Route 10, Little Switzerland Dr., 37920.
Tel 615 523-4216. Mrs. Joyce Dukes, Secy. and Res.
Librn. Inquiries answered, referrals made, consultation.
The Center is a non-profit, residential, integrated adult
education center whose chief purpose is to educate
leadership for democracy and promote the general welfare of all people in the South.

    .1 Highlander Research and Education Center.
Files, 1932- . Correspondence, financial records,
studies, reports, and other material dealing with
the aims, history, and program of the Center. Includes records of the Center's predecessor, the
Highlander Folk School (1932-61) of Monteagle,
Tenn., which was closed in 1961 by revocation of
charter and confiscation of property by the State of
Tennessee. Restricted.

TN7   HIGHLANDER RESEARCH AND EDUCATION CENTER
(1961), LASKER MEMORIAL LIBRARY (1961). 1625
Riverside Dr., 37915. Tel 615 523-4216. C. Conrad
Browne, Center Dir. Copying.
The Center is a non-profit, residential, integrated adult
education center whose chief purpose is to educate
leadership for democracy and promote the general welfare of all people in the South.

    .1 Lasker Memorial Library.
Books, current periodicals, county newsletters issued by local grassroots organizations, fiction
material by Southerners, and back issues of southern publications not available in many public libraries. Restricted.

TN8   KNOXVILLE COLLEGE (1875), CARNEGIE LIBRARY. 901
College St., 37921. Tel 615 546-0751. Mrs. Lois Clark,
Librn. Interlibrary loan, copying, inquiries answered.

    .1 Afro-American Heritage collection.
Materials, 17th century- . Microfilm. 131 reels.
Books, newspapers, and mss concerning the Negro

American and his history. See Minnesota Mining
and Manufacturing Company, St. Paul, Minn., for a
full description.

.2 Afro-American Studies Collection.
ca. 1000 paperbacks. Basic books on the life and
history of black Americans.

.3 Knoxville College.
Archives, 1875- . Correspondence, minutes of
board meetings, financial records, records of admission, catalogs, bulletins, and other materials
dealing with the history and administration of the
College.

TN9   KNOXVILLE URBAN LEAGUE. 2212 Vine St., 37915. Tel
       615 524-5521. Woodrow Z. Wilson, Exec. Dir.

.1 Knoxville Urban League.
Files. Correspondence, minutes of meetings, financial records, studies, reports, and other materials dealing with the aims, history and programs
of the League.

TN10   UNIVERSITY OF TENNESSEE (1794), JAMES D. HOSKINS
       LIBRARY, DEPARTMENT OF SPECIAL COLLEC-
       TIONS. 37916. Tel 615 974-2441. John H. Dobson,
       Spec. Collections Librn.

.1 Brown, Lucius P.
Papers, 1856-98. 3 ft. (ca. 1000 items). Chiefly
concerning Major George Campbell Brown, stock
breeder of Spring Hill, Maury Co., Tenn. Also includes records pertaining to Melrose Plantation in
Mississippi, including journals concerning slave
management.

.2 Civil Rights Collection.
ca. 3000 items. Tapes, correspondence, miscellaneous printed materials, photographs, posters,
and other materials relating to the civil rights
movement in general.

.3 —— Braden, Carl.
Papers of Carl and Anne Braden, 1947-67.
Correspondence of the Southern Conference
Educational Fund (SCEF) civil rights workers
(1947-67); newspaper clippings (1947-67); court
records (1954-59); miscellaneous related financial records, address cards, and tape recordings.

.4 —— Haynie, Charles A.
Papers, 1963-65. ca. 600 items. Concerns
voter registration in Fayette County, Tenn.
Also includes films and tapes.

.5 —— Hodes, Jane E.
Papers, 1964-66. ca. 200 items. Correspon-
dence and related materials concerning Student
Nonviolent Coordinating Committee (SNCC).

.6 —— Posey, Buford.
Papers, 1957-67. ca. 100 items. Letters,
transcripts, printed matter, pictures, tapes
concerning civil rights.

.7 —— Redmond, S.R.
Papers, 1945-50. ca. 200 items. Correspondence, legal briefs, affidavits, and related materials concerning school desegregation in St.
Louis, Mo.

.8 —— Rogers, Walter and Elizabeth.
Papers, 1924-67. ca. 150 pieces. Letters and
miscellaneous printed materials relating to
labor and civil rights movements.

.9 —— Self, Roy.
Papers, 1965-66. ca. 200 items. Letters,
legal briefs, brochures, clippings and related
materials pertaining to the Southern Christian
Leadership Conference (SCLC).

.10 —— Swisshelm, Dorothy.
Papers, 1952-66. ca. 1000 items. Concerning
civil rights activities in Americus and Albany,
Ga.; Kiononia Farm, Ga.; Back Bay Mission,
Miss.; SNCC; SCLC; and other organizations.

.11 —— Williams, Claude.
Papers, 1930-66. ca. 300 items. Correspondence and miscellaneous materials (including
tapes) concerning labor organizations and the
civil rights movement.

.12 Eaton, John, 1829-1906.
Correspondence, 1865-81. 6 ft. (ca. 2500 items).

Journalist and public official. Relates to the U.S.
Bureau of Refugees, Freedmen and Abandoned
Lands, the U.S. Bureau of Education (now the Office
of Education), the Memphis Evening Post, and personal and family matters.

.13 Facts on Film.
Papers, 1954-67. Microfilm. Contains materials
on civil rights and race relations in the South. See
Race Relations Information Center, Nashville,
Tenn., for a full description.

.14 Lenoir family.
Papers, 1803-93. 3 ft. (ca. 2500 items). Papers
of Gen. William Lenoir (1751-1839), William Ballard Lenoir (1775-1852) and others of the Lenoir
family of Tennessee. Correspondence includes
items pertaining to family land and slaves.

.15 McCalley Plantation, Huntsville, Ala.
Record books, 1840-70. 4 v. Records concerning
management of the plantation and its slaves.

MEMPHIS

TN11   CHRISTIAN METHODIST EPISCOPAL CHURCH, GENERAL
       BOARD OF CHRISTIAN EDUCATION. 1474 Humber St.,
       38106. Tel 901 948-0839. Rev. C.D. Coleman, Dir.

.1 General Board of Christian Education.
Files. Correspondence, minutes of board meetings,
financial records, and other materials relating to
the Board's support of the following colleges: Lane
College, Jackson, Tenn.; Miles College, Birmingham, Ala.; Mississippi Industrial College, Holly
Springs, Miss.; and Texas College, Tyler, Tex.

TN12   CHRISTIAN METHODIST EPISCOPAL PUBLISHING HOUSE,
       LIBRARY. 531 S. Parkway, 38111. Tel 901 947-4188.

.1 Christian Methodist Episcopal Church.
Archives, 1870- . Annual conference reports,
minute books, mss, publications, and other materials relating to the history of the denomination
(formerly the Colored Methodist Episcopal Church);
and to its educational institutions, Lane College,
Jackson, Tenn., Paine College, Augusta, Ga., and
Mississippi Industrial College, Holly Springs, Miss.

TN13   COMMISSION FOR HUMAN DEVELOPMENT, MEMPHIS
       FIELD OFFICE (1967). Room 1111, 170 N. Main, 38103.
       Tel 901 534-6631. Edward Parker, Jr., Field Rep.

TN14   LeMOYNE-OWEN COLLEGE (1870), HOLLIS F. PRICE LI-
       BRARY. 807 Walker Ave., 38126. Tel 901 948-6626.
       Mrs. Mae Isom Fitzgerald, Librn. Interlibrary loan,
       copying, inquiries answered.

.1 Afro-American Heritage collection.
Materials, 17th century- . Microfilm. 131 reels.
Books, newspapers, and mss concerning the Negro
American and his history. See Minnesota Mining
and Manufacturing Company, St. Paul, Minn., for a
full description.

.2 Afro-American Studies Collection.
ca. 1000 paperbacks. Basic books on the life and
history of black Americans.

.3 LeMoyne-Owen College.
Archives, 1870- . Correspondence, minutes of
board meetings, financial records, records of admission, bulletins, catalogs, and other materials
dealing with the history, administration, and
merger of LeMoyne and Owen colleges.

.4 Materials relating to Negroes.
Miscellaneous. Books (ca. 3000), periodical and
newspaper titles, and other materials by or about
Negroes in the areas of art, literature, music,
history, biography, social science, religion, and
others.

TN15   MEMPHIS STATE UNIVERSITY (1912), JOHN WILLARD
       BRISTER LIBRARY. Southern and Patterson, 38111.
       Tel 901 321-1201. W.W. Wicker, Librn. Interlibrary
       loan, copying, inquiries answered.

.1 Facts on Film.
Papers, 1954-67. Microfilm. Contains materials
on civil rights and race relations in the South. See

Race Relations Information Center, Nashville,
Tenn., for a full description.

TN16   MEMPHIS STATE UNIVERSITY, ORAL HISTORY OFFICE
AND THE MEMPHIS SEARCH FOR MEANING COMMIT-
TEE. 38111. Tel 901 321-0111. David Yellin, Cmt.
Chmn.
The Oral History Office and the Memphis Search for
Meaning Committee are jointly involved in a project to
compile relevant information and research material
pertaining to the Memphis garbage strike and the
events leading to the assassination of Dr. Martin Luther
King, Jr.

.1   Oral History Office.
Tape recordings. Interviews with persons involved
in the Memphis garbage strike and other civil
rights activities in Memphis.

TN17   MEMPHIS URBAN LEAGUE (1932). 546 Beale Ave., 38103.
Tel 901 527-0302. Herman C. Ewing, Exec. Dir. Referrals made, consultation.
The League is a social service agency whose program
is directed toward the problems and needs of the black
community with particular concern for members of that
community who are most disadvantaged. Programs and
projects include on-the-job training (in conjunction with
U.S. Department of Labor), job development, study of
social and economic conditions in the community, promotion of interracial cooperation and understanding,
correlation of social services with other agencies, and
community action programs.

.1   Memphis Urban League.
Files, 1932- . Correspondence, minutes of meetings, financial records, studies, reports, and other
materials dealing with the aims, history and programs of the League.

TN18   NATIONAL ASSOCIATION FOR THE ADVANCEMENT OF
COLORED PEOPLE (NAACP). 234 Hernando St.,
38126. Tel 901 525-6057. Mrs. Maxine Smith, Exec.
Secy.

TN19   NATIONAL CONFERENCE OF CHRISTIANS AND JEWS
(NCCJ). 930 Falls Bldg., 22 N. Front St., 38103. Tel
901 526-7260. Robert H. Haas, Tennessee Regional
Dir.
NCCJ is a civic organization engaged in a nationwide
program of intergroup education, involving people of all
backgrounds who work together to build better relationships. It seeks to educate and influence citizens to ap-
preciate the diversities and assume the responsibilities
of a pluralistic society.
Publ.: Newsletter, quarterly; Religious news service.

TN20   SOUTHWESTERN AT MEMPHIS COLLEGE (1848), BURROW
LIBRARY. 38112. Tel 615 274-1800. Albert M. Johnson, Librn.

.1   Topp, Robertson, 1807-76.
Papers, 1805-1929. 5 reels of microfilm (ca. 2000
items and 16 v.). Microfilm copy made by the
Tennessee State Library and archives from originals owned by Southwestern at Memphis, Burrow
Library or in the possession of Susan Ball. Tennessee State legislator and businessman. Correspondence, biographical and genealogical data,
deeds, indentures, slave bills of sale, wills, and
other papers relating to Topp's cotton trade during
the Civil War and to family matters. Includes a
journal (1805-07) of William L. Brown, uncle of
Mrs. Topp, and Tennessee Supreme Court justice.

MORRISTOWN

TN21   MORRISTOWN COLLEGE, CARNEGIE LIBRARY. 37814.
Tel 615 586-5262. Jessie Matthews, Librn.

.1   Morristown College.
Archives. Correspondence, minutes of board
meetings, financial records, records of admission,
bulletins; catalogs, and other materials dealing
with the history and administration of the College.

NASHVILLE

TN22   AFRICAN METHODIST EPISCOPAL CHURCH, DEPART-
MENT OF ARCHIVES AND RECORDS. 414 Eighth Ave.,
S., 37203. Tel 615 242-1420.
Publ.: A.M.E. Review, quarterly.

.1   African Methodist Episcopal Church.
Files. Correspondence, minutes of board meetings,
financial records. and other materials dealing with
the history and programs of the Church.

TN22a   ASSOCIATION FOR AFRICAN-AMERICAN BIBLIOGRAPHY
(1970). 3213 Orleans Dr., 37212. Tel 615 291-6969.
Walter Schatz, Acting Editor. Inquiries answered, referrals made.
The Association is made up of librarians, media specialists, and others directly involved with, or having a
substantive interest in the identification, organization,
preservation, and dissemination of materials and information about the black man in the Americas and
Africa.
Publ.: Newsletter.

TN23   CENTER FOR COMMUNITY STUDIES (1966). Box 60,
George Peabody College, 37203. Tel 615 327-8121.
Dr. J.R. Newbrough, Coordinator. Consultation, re-
search coordination.
The Center was formed as an inter-institutional
organization for the coordination of research directed
toward individual and community problems in Metro-
politan Nashville.
Publ.: Annual Report; Project reports; Family Health
Study: Annual Report.

.1   Center for Community Studies.
Files, 1966- . Correspondence, minutes of meetings, financial records, studies, reports, investigations, and other materials dealing with the aims,
history, and programs of the Center. Recent projects include "The North Nashville Descriptive
Study;" "An Organizational Study of Meharry Medical College;" "North Nashville Health Survey," a
study of new adjustments of families dislocated by
Nashville's "10th and Herman" slum razing; study
of campus riots in spring, 1967, in Nashville,
Jackson, Miss., and Houston, Tex.; and a continuing
health services and epidemiological study titled
"Family Health Study."

TN24   COMMISSION FOR HUMAN DEVELOPMENT (1967). C3-305
Cordell Hull Bldg., 37219. Tel 615 741-2424. Cornelius
Jones, Exec. Secy.
The Commission works to promote equal opportunity in
areas of employment, housing, public accommodation,
and education; assists local agencies with similar objectives; cooperates in public information programs;
and conducts studies. Formerly Commission on Human
Relations.
Publ.: Newsletter, periodically; Pamphlets; Annual reports.

.1   Commission for Human Development.
Files, 1967- . Correspondence, minutes of meetings, financial records, studies, reports, investigations, and other materials dealing with the aims,
history, and programs of the Commission.

TN25   COMMITTEE OF SOUTHERN CHURCHMEN. 818 17th Ave.,
S., 37212. Tel 615 242-2448. Will D. Campbell, Dir.
Inquiries answered.
"The Committee of Southern Churchmen was formed to
work with the largely ignored whites within the churches
who are caught up in the revolution but do not know that
the most basic fundamentals of their religious faith involve them in it."
Publ.: Katallagette: Be Reconciled, quarterly.

.1   Committee of Southern Churchmen.
Files. Correspondence, minutes of meetings, financial records, and other materials dealing with
the aims, history, and programs of the Committee.
Closed to public.

TN26   DEMONSTRATION AND RESEARCH CENTER FOR EARLY
EDUCATION (DARCEE) (1965), DARCEE LIBRARY

(1967). Box 151, Peabody College Sta., 37203. Tel 615
327-0101. Robert H. Stone, Document. Specialist.
DARCEE was designed to discover and apply new knowledge to improve the education of young deprived children, primarily those under six. This knowledge includes methods and materials in the classroom, the
antecedents of deprivation, and effects of intervention
in the family and community of the underprivileged.
Publ.: DARCEE Newsletter, monthly; DARCEE papers
and reports, occasionally.

.1 Materials relating to Negroes.
 Miscellaneous. ca. 3000 items. Books (ca. 800),
 periodicals (30), pamphlets, theses, dissertations,
 microforms, and preprint and reprints relating to
 early education of disadvantaged children, race
 relations, and Negroes.

TN27 DISCIPLES OF CHRIST HISTORICAL SOCIETY (1941), LI-
 BRARY. 1101 19th Ave. S., 37212. Tel 615 327-1444.
 Marvin D. Williams, Jr., Dir. of Library and Archivist.
 Interlibrary loan, bibliographies prepared, literature
 searches, copying, inquiries answered, referrals
 made, consultation.

.1 Bostick, Sarah Lue, 1868-1948.
 Papers. Includes materials relating to her work as
 Negro home missionary in Arkansas. Unprocessed.
.2 Jarvis Christian College.
 Miscellaneous. Included are news releases and
 promotional material.
.3 Lehman, Joel Baer, 1866-1942.
 Papers. ca. 2500 items. President of Southern
 Christian Institute, 1890-93. Correspondence, pictures, church publications, and "An Autobiographical Sketch of Jepthal Hobbs," first president of the
 Institute. Unprocessed.
.4 Materials concerning Negro churchmen and churches.
 Miscellaneous vf materials. Included are biographical sketches, clippings, pamphlets, correspondence, photos, articles, news releases, and other
 papers concerning the following Negro ministers
 and lay people: William J. Alphin (1865-1937);
 Adam Daniel Beittel, 8th president of Tougaloo
 College; Walter D. Bingham (1921- .), Cleo Walter
 Blackburn, president of Jarvis Christian College;
 Walter S. Blackburn; James Blair; Calvin Bowers;
 Raymond Edward Brown (1925- .), president of the
 National Christian Missionary Convention, 1968-
 69; John Robert Compton, director of reconciliation, general office of the Christian Church; G.
 Robert Cotton, president, Kansas Technical Insti-
 tute; Alexander Cross (1811?-54), slave, first black
 missionary to Liberia (included is transcript of
 meeting (1853) discussing purchase and support of
 Cross); Gerald L. Cunningham; Dennis James
 (1928- .), president of Nashville Christian Institute;
 Ann Elizabeth Dickerson, senior psychologist,
 Meharry Medical College; Lloyd Lincoln Dickerson
 (1900-68), president, National Christian Missionary
 Convention (NCMC); Emmett J. Dickson; Merl R.
 Eppse (1893-1967), professor, Tennessee State Uni-
 versity; Lorenzo James Evans; William Kappen
 Fox, Sr., president, NCMC; 1960-62; Blair T.
 Hunt, president, NCMC, 1950-52; Robert L. Jordan;
 Sandy Jordan; Marshall Keeble (1878-1968); Jacob
 Kenoly (1876-1911), black missionary to Liberia;
 B. MacDonald Layne; James Oliver Lyttle (1949- .);
 Rufus Charles Maloy; Eunice B. Miller; Lois Marie
 Mothershed; George A. Owens (1919- .), 9th presi-
 dent of Tougaloo College; Robert Hayes Peoples;
 Zellie M. Peoples; Theodore H. Simpson; Wesley S.
 Sims; Preston Taylor (1849-1931), president,
 NCMC; Richard D. Taylor (1896-1960); Claude
 Walker (1934- .); R. Wesley Watson, president
 NCMC, 1941-42; Charles H. Webb, president,
 NCMC, 1962-64; and Rosa Page Welch (1901- .),
 singer and active churchwoman. Also included are
 such organizational materials as convention programs, pamphlets, and minutes, from the following
 states: Alabama, Arkansas, Illinois, Kansas, Kentucky, Michigan, Missouri, North Carolina, Ohio,
 South Carolina, Tennessee, Texas, and Virginia,
 and limited materials on many Negro congregations
 throughout the U.S.

.5 Materials relating to Negroes.
 Among materials of Billy James Hargis, editor of
 Christian Echoes and Christian Crusade and Gerald
 Lyman Kenneth Smith, editor of Cross and the Flag
 and Attack, are correspondence, articles, clippings,
 publications, and promotional literature containing
 scattered references to Negroes, school desegregation, racial problems, and related subjects.
.6 National Christian Missionary Convention (NCMC).
 Records, 1917- . Included are minutes, 1917-69
 (incomplete); programs, 1919-69 (incomplete);
 special reports and programs; photograph of NCMC
 delegates (1917); constitution; promotional materials and photographs; and complete file on the 1969
 Convention.
.7 Negro church publications.
 Included are scattered issues of The Christian Dispatch (1931, Mississippi), The Christian Informer
 (1907-08, Mississippi), The Christian Messenger,
 monthly newsletter of the Texas Christian Missionary Convention (1956-63), The Christian Outlook
 (1932, Chicago, Ill.), The Christian Soldier (1911,
 Lexington, Ky.), The Messenger (1912, Hagerstown,
 Md.), The National Convention Voice (1941, St.
 Louis, Mo.), The National Evangelist (1913,
 Louisville, Ky.), and Christian Plea (1889?-1965?)
 official organ of the Negro Disciples of Christ
 (published 1889?-1924? as Gospel Plea).
.8 Pamphlet collection.
 Included are pamphlets relating to the Negro and to
 slavery, such as "An address to Disciples on the
 sin of slavery, by the churches in Trumbull County,
 Ohio, and vicinity" (1841); "Philosophy of slavery
 as identified with the philosophy of human rights"
 (1849) and "An address delivered before the pro-
 slavery convention of the State of Missouri (1885),
 by James Shannon; "A Broad Field of Labor," by
 Booker T. Washington, written for the Board of
 Negro Education and Evangelization (1896?); and
 "Christian work among the Negroes...an address
 delivered at the National convention" by Edward
 Lindsay Powell (Dallas, Tex., 1895).
.9 Southern Christian Institute.
 Archives. ca. 12 boxes. Included are materials
 relating to the Home Mission School for Negroes,
 the merger of the Institute with Tougaloo Southern
 Christian College, and Mt. Beulah Christian Center.
 Unprocessed.
.10 Taylor, Alva Wilmot, 1871-1957.
 Papers, 1893-1955. 5 ft. (1700 items). Clergyman
 of the Christian Church (Disciple of Christ). Correspondence, diaries, expense accounts, autobiography, addresses, photos., pamphlets, and other
 papers. Includes materials on the Fellowship of
 Southern Churchmen and the Southern Conference
 Educational Fund (SCEF); news reports of social
 economic, and religious conditions in the South reported in the Christian Century (1908-53); and clippings and other material relating to Taylor, and
 social and religious concerns.
.11 United Christian Missionary Society.
 Records, 1849- . Microfilm. Included are the
 proceedings of the annual meetings of the United
 Christian Missionary Society, which include reports
 from the Board of Negro Education and Evangelization, the Christian Women's Board of Missions,
 and the National Christian Missionary Convention
 of the Churches of Christ. Also on microfilm is a
 complete file of the minutes of the Christian
 Woman's Board of Missions. Through these materials can be followed the history of the Negro
 churches and educational institutions, including
 Southern Christian Institute (which merged with
 Tougaloo College), Piedmont Christian Institute
 (Martinsville, Va.), and Jarvis Christian College
 (Hawkins, Tex.).

TN28 FISK UNIVERSITY, CENTER FOR AFRO-AMERICAN
 STUDIES (1967). Box 873, Richardson House, 37218.
 Tel 615 244-7128. Dr. Tandy Tollerson, III, Dir.
 The Center develops social science research programs
 which study militancy, hostility, and political percep-
 tions in Negro ghetto areas; is making a socio-economic
 profile of the Nashville Negro community; and studies
 community development.

.1   Center for Afro-American Studies.
     Files, 1967- . Correspondence, financial records,
     studies, reports, investigations, and other materi-
     als dealing with the activities of the Center, in-
     cluding the social science research program. The
     research data are unavailable until completion of
     analysis by the Center.

TN29   FISK UNIVERSITY (1866), LIBRARY (1866). 37203. Tel
       615 244-3580. Mrs. Jessie Carney Smith, Univ. Librn.
       Interlibrary loan, bibliographies prepared, copying,
       typing, inquiries answered, referrals made.
       Publ.: Special Collections in the Erastus Milo Cravath
            Memorial Library; Brochures and guides to the
            Joplin, Chesnutt, Gershwin, and Baldridge Col-
            lections, and for the Embree and Johnson papers.

.1   Afro-American Studies collection.
     ca. 1000 paperbacks. Basic books on the life and
     history of black Americans.
.2   Alexander, Ernest A.
     Miscellaneous. Books, slave narratives, pam-
     phlets, minstrel sketches, sheet music, and other
     materials reflecting the achievements of Negroes.
     Books include Les Cenelles (1845), the first anthol-
     ogy of poetry by Negroes published in the U.S.;
     William Wells Brown's Clotel: The President's
     Daughter (1853), the first novel published by a Ne-
     gro; pamphlets (2) by Julien Raimond (ca. 1789), a
     free man of color who stressed abolition before the
     French National Assembly in Paris, one of which is
     entitled Reclamations Addresses a l'Assemblee
     Nationale, Par les Personnes de Colour, Proprie-
     taires & Cultivateurs de la Colonie Francois de
     Saint Domingue; published minstrel sketches (ca.
     200); and hundreds of pieces of sheet music com-
     posed by Negroes, including "Listen to the Mocking
     Bird."
.3   Anti-Slavery collection.
     Papers, 1698-1865. 425 items. Contains bills of
     sale, free papers, and other material pertaining to
     slaves, slavery, and abolition.
.4   Baldridge, Cyrus Leroy, 1889- .
     Paintings and drawings, 1927-28. ca. 68 items.
     Artist. Includes drawings of African types and
     African pictures which form a complete record of
     native life and native types available in America.
     Drawn and painted on West Coast of Africa.
.4a Brown, Dorothy L., 1919- .
     Papers. 1 box. Speeches, correspondence, arti-
     cles. Nashville physician, and first Negro woman
     in the Tennessee State legislature.
.5   Chesnutt, Charles Waddell, 1858-1932.
     Papers, 1857-1950. 56 ft. (ca. 6200 items). Forms
     part of the Library's Negro collection. Author and
     lawyer. Correspondence, journals (1874-85),
     scrapbooks with longhand writings (1885-1950),
     certificates and contracts, photos., and the Spingarn
     medal. Includes drafts of Chesnutt's biography of
     Frederick Douglass, and of some of his novels,
     articles, short stories, speeches, poems, and a
     play; correspondence with publishers and maga-
     zines (1885-1930); and personal correspondence
     (1873-1932, largely after 1899). The earliest doc-
     uments are the marriage certificate of Chesnutt's
     parents (1857) and two early photos. of himself
     (1864, 1874). Correspondents, personal and corpo-
     rate, include Charles W. Anderson, Atlantic
     Monthly, Newton D. Baker, Boston Evening Tran-
     script, Nayhum D. Brascher, Benjamin G. Braw-
     ley, Hugh M. Browne, Roscoe Conkling Bruce,
     George Washington Cable, Walter Camp, Century
     Magazine, The Crisis, The Critic, Doubleday Page
     & Co., William Edward Burghardt DuBois (1901-
     31), John S. Durham, Harper & Brothers, Houghton
     Mifflin Co., Jerome B. Howard, The Independent,
     James Weldon Johnson (1913-29), S.S. McClure's,
     Kelly Miller, Mary White Ovington, James Pott &
     Co., Puck, William H. Richards, Emmett J. Scott,
     Small, Marynard & Co., William Monroe Trotter,
     Albion W. Turgee, Oswald Garrison Villard, Booker
     T. Washington, Edward C. Williams, Richard
     Wright, and Youth's Companion.
.6   Cullen, Countee, 1903-46.
     Papers, 1921-47. ca. 2 ft. (111 items). Forms
     part of the Library's Negro collection. Author.

Correspondence, literary mss, a plan book from
high school classes, certificates, sheet music,
handbills, programs, a scrapbook, newspaper clippings, photos, diaries, and poems dedicated to Cullen by his pupils (Jessie Fauset, Langston Hughes,
and Leon Raines). Persons named include Arna
Bontemps, Sterling Brown, Padraic Colum, Langston Hughes, Charles S. Johnson, Georgia Douglas
Johnson, James Weldon Johnson, Willard Johnson,
Helen Keller, Alain Locke, Louis Shores, and Carl
Van Vechten.
.7   Douglas, Aaron, 1899- .
     Murals, ca. 1935. ca. 10 items. Artist. Murals
     depicting the Negro's progress from central Africa
     to present-day America; pre-slavery Africa culmi-
     nating in a long line of fettered slaves; fettered
     slaves with symbolic light of Christianity approach-
     ing (Jubilee Hall, a residence center for women
     built in 1873 with funds from Jubilee Singers); and
     seven panels on which the following subjects ap-
     pear: philosophy, drama, music, poetry, science,
     night, and day. Douglas is Professor of Art Emer-
     itus, at Fisk University.
.8   DuBois, William Edward Burghardt, 1868-1963.
     Miscellaneous, 1900-60. ca. 2500 items. Author,
     historian, and founding editor of NAACP's The
     Crisis (1911-33). Books, clippings, journals, cor-
     respondence, diaries, literary mss, notebooks,
     scrapbooks, minutes, contracts, handbills, and
     memorabilia concerning his writings, the National
     Association for the Advancement of Colored People,
     and aspects of the civil rights movement.
.9   Embree, Edwin Rogers.
     Papers, 1942-44. ca. 1000 items. Former trustee
     of Fisk University, director of Julius Rosenwald
     Fund (20-year tenure, during which time he di-
     rected the practical program of building the first
     school for southern Negro children), and chairman
     of Chicago Mayor's Commission on Human Rela-
     tions. Notes and other materials relating to his
     career and his book 13 Against the Odds.
.10 Facts on Film.
     Papers, 1954-67. Microfilm. Contains materials
     on civil rights and race relations in the South. See
     Race Relations Information Center, Nashville,
     Tenn., for a full description.
.11 Fiskiana collection.
     Miscellaneous, 1866- . Catalogs, handbooks, bul-
     letins, campus publications (current and past), cor-
     respondence, books about Fisk, histories of Fisk,
     commencement and festival programs, presidential
     reports, pictures, notebooks, scrapbooks, diaries,
     handbills, correspondence of the Jubilee Singers,
     and other material relating to Fisk University. In-
     cludes letters of Erastus Milo Cravath, Fisk's first
     president, and several copies of Die Geschichte der
     Jubilaums-Sanger, translated from J.B.T. Marsh's
     Story of the Jubilee Singers (1877).
.12 George Gershwin Memorial Collection of Music and
     Musical Literature.
     Miscellaneous. ca. 550 items. Books, musical
     mss and scores, letters, first editions, recordings,
     scrapbooks of musical history collected by Carl
     Van Vechten, correspondence, phonograph records,
     and other materials related to Gershwin's career
     and Negro musicians. Among the mss are those of
     William Grant Still, J. Rosamond Johnson, James
     Weldon Johnson, and Langston Hughes; a program
     for the concert given by Paul Robeson and Law-
     rence Brown (May, 1925); and the album of the first
     company of "Porgy and Bess," including Tod Dun-
     can and Ann Brown. Other names mentioned are
     William C. Handy and Katherine Dunham.
.13 Haynes, George Edmond.
     Papers. Sociologist and former professor of social
     science at Fisk University. Mss, reprints from
     magazines, studies, notes, and other material con-
     cerning the Negro.
.14 Heartman, Charles P.
     Pamphlets, 1808, 1818, 1834. 3 items. Materials
     relating to Negro culture. Two pamphlets deal with
     the abolition of the slave trade and the third is "an
     anecdote and memoirs of William Boen, a coloured
     man who lived and died near Mt. Holly, New
     Jersey."

TN29.15 Hope, John, II.
Papers, ca. 1939-61. ca. 10,000 items. Member,
Fisk Department of Race Relations, and the Atlanta
Regional Office of the Fair Employment Practices
Commission during World War II. Includes corre-
spondence, notes and studies, clippings, reprints,
and other papers pertaining to Negroes and Hope's
career.

.16 Hopkins, Pauline.
Papers. In part, typewritten and handwritten.
Several drafts of a musical comedy; musical scores
for the production, programs, and an essay on the
evils of intemperance.

.17 Hughes, Langston, 1902-67.
Papers, 1921- . Poet, essayist, fictionist, dramatist, and lecturer. Clippings, notices of forthcom-
ing appearances, reviews of books and plays, inter-
views, articles, greeting cards, correspondence,
ads, playbills, announcements, awards and invita-
tions, scrapbooks, and other materials relating to
his career. Persons represented are Jimmie
Lunceford, Count Basie, Bennie Moten, Frenchy's
String Band, Noble Sissle, Ferdinand (Jelly Roll)
Morton, Bessie Smith, Bobby Lecan, Lillian Glenn,
Georgia White, Alice Moore, Memphis Minnie,
Ethel Waters, Lula Whidby, Mamie Smith, Ward
Singers, Roberta Martin Singers, Rosetta Thorpe,
Edna Cooke, Josh White, Sarah Vaughan, Pearl
Bailey, Louis Armstrong, Roy Hamilton, and Mar-
ian Anderson. Included are tapes of Hughes'
various speeches and poetry readings, and of
George Washington Carver's last speech.

.18 Johnson, Charles Spurgeon, 1893- . collector.
Papers, 1870-1956. 90 ft. (3000 items). In part,
transcripts (typewritten). Correspondence, addresses, interviews, memoranda, studies, abstracts, printed matter, and other papers. Most of
the materials are for the years 1928-56, when
Johnson was head of the Social Science Dept. and
president of Fisk University. Includes Johnson's
papers, part of the correspondence of Robert E.
Park, and The Pilgrimages of Jean Veneuse, by
Rene Maran. Subjects covered include the Chicago
race riot of 1919; Negro education, housing, em-
ployment, and health, race relations, the Ku Klux
Klan, the NAACP, the Union of South Africa, the
Tennessee Valley Authority, and American slavery.
Persons mentioned and organizations named include
Will W. Alexander, American Civil Liberties
Union, American Council on Race Relations; Amer-
ican Missionary Association, Race Relations Divi-
sion; Association of Colleges and Secondary
Schools for Negroes, Ruth Benedict, Herbert
Blumer, Franz Boas, Horace Mann Bond, Earl
Brown, Ina Corrine Brown, Sterling Brown, Fred
L. Brownlee, Ernest W. Burgess, Chicago Com-
mission on Race Relations, Dai Bingham, Katherine
Dunham, Fisk University, Department of Social Sci-
ence; E. Franklin Frazier, Richard T. Greener,
Melville Herskovits, Lewis Wade Jones, Buford H.
Junker, Alfred McClung Lee, Katherine Lenrott,
National Urban League, Howard Odum, Edward
Byron Rexuter, A.A. Schomburg, Southern Re-
gional Council; U.S. Dept. of Agriculture, Bureau of
Agricultural Economics; Preston Valien, Henry H.
Walker, Willis D. Weatherford, Louis Wirth, and
John Wesley Work.

.19 Jones, Thomas E.
Papers, 1925-46. ca. 10,000 items. Correspondence and other papers relating to his tenure as
president of Fisk University.

.20 Joplin, Scott, 1868-1917.
Papers, 1899-1951. ca. 2 ft. (ca. 91 items). Forms
part of the library's Negro collection. Pianist and
ragtime composer. Correspondence, a magazine,
programs, newspaper clippings, literary mss, sheet
music, photos., and Samuel Brunson Campbell's
The Original Ragtime Kid. Concerns ragtime
music and jazz of the 1890's. Joplin is the composer of the "Maple Leaf Rag."

.21 Julius Rosenwald Fund.
Archives, 1917-48. 262 ft. (500 boxes, ca. 50,000
items). Correspondence, evaluations, mss of unpublished writings, memoranda, minutes, reports,
expense books, bank statements, and journal vouchers. Concerns various aspects of Negro life: rural
education, school construction, teacher training,
health, hospitals, race relations, and institutions
for Negroes such as Atlanta, Dillard, and Fisk
Universities, Meharry Medical College, and Flint-
Goodrich Hospital. Persons whose work is in-
volved include Will W. Alexander, Marian Ander-
son, William Alexander Attaway, James Arthur
Baldwin, Carl Becker, Lowell Howard Bennett,
Horace Mann Bond, William Stanley Braithwaite,
Ina Corrine Brown, Sterling A. Brown, Charles W.
Buggs, Ralph Bunche, Horace Roscoe Cayton, Janet
Fay Collins, Harry W. Colberth, Allison W. Davis,
Frank A. DeCosta, Anna Louise DeRamis, Charles
Dean Dixon, Owen Vincent Dodson, John Dollard,
Aaron Douglas, Charles R. Drew, William Edward
Burghardt DuBois, Katherine Dunham, Ralph Waldo
Emerson, Edwin Rogers Embree, Marshall Field,
John Hope Franklin, E. Franklin Frazier, Elizabeth
Bruce Hardwick, Robert E. Hayden, George E.
Haynes, Mozell C. Hill, Chester Bomar Himes,
Langston Hughes, Zora Neal Hurston, Robert
Hutchins, Charles S. Johnson, James Weldon
Johnson, Buford H. Junker, Jacob Armstead
Lawrence, Rayford W. Logan, Herman Hodge Long,
Elizabeth Harold Lomax, James E. Lu Valle,
Claude McKay, Kelly Miller, Bucklin Moon, Willi-
ard Francis Motley, Gordon Alexander Parks,
Benjamin Arthur Quarles, Ira De A. Reid, Lillian
Smith, William Grant Still, Willis Duke Weather-
ford, Charles Edward Weir, J. Ernest Wilkins, Jr.,
John W. Work, and Monroe N. Work.

.22 King, Slater Hunter, 1927-69.
Papers, 1959-68. 500 items. Businessman, leader
of Albany, Ga. Civil Rights Movement. Family,
personal, and business correspondence. Included
are business transactions with Black Muslims for
Georgia farm land purchase; records of Albany
Civil Rights Movement; board correspondence from
Martin Luther King Center; business records of
King and King Real Estate, mss, newspaper clip-
pings, and photographs. Among correspondents are
Dr. Martin Luther King, Jr., Mrs. Coretta Scott
King, Dr. Vincent Harding, and Malcolm (Little) X.
Restricted.

.23 LaFollette Committee Senate Hearings of 1930's.
Papers. Reports of the Committee which investigated the violations of free speech and assembly
and interference with the rights of labor to organize
and bargain collectively.

.24 Langston, John Mercer, 1829-97.
Papers, 1853-98. ca. 3 ft. (ca. 1300 items). Forms
part of the library's Negro collection. Educator,
lawyer, diplomat. Correspondence, speeches,
drafts of writings, receipts, estate papers, banking
papers, handbills, passports, minutes, a scrapbook,
and newspaper clippings. Concerns slavery in the
U.S., the abolition movement, Reconstruction,
American relations with Haiti, and the Dominican
Republic, Howard University, the War Dept., and
the Bureau of Refugees, Freedmen and Abandoned
Lands. Persons mentioned are Paul H. Bracy, J.R.
Galbraith, O.O. Howard, John Ogden, O.S.B. Wall,
John L. Waller, and Caroline M. Walls (later Mrs.
Langston).

.25 Madgett, Naomi Long, 1923- .
Papers, 1941-68. 1 box. Poetess. Books, work-
sheets, poems, clippings, correspondence to Ann
Allen Shockley. Restricted.

.26 Napier, James Carroll, 1868-1939.
Papers, 1880-1917. ca. 290 items. Nashville,
Tenn., lawyer, banker, registrar of U.S. Treasury
during Taft's Presidency; founder of the first Negro bank in Tennessee (now Citizens Savings Bank
and Trust Co.); member, city council of Nashville;
and member, board of trustees of Fisk University
and Meharry Medical College. Certificates, deeds,
financial reports, periodicals and addresses relating to Napier's career, Tennessee and U.S. history
of the Negro, and related subjects.

.27 Negro Collection.
Miscellaneous, 15th cent.- . 50 ft. (ca. 9000
items). Some special collections forming part of

the Negro Collection are cataloged separately. Correspondence; diaries; literary mss; notebooks; scrapbooks; minutes; contracts; receipts; estate papers; banking papers; certificates; passports; invitations; press notices; photos.; and books pertaining to slavery (ca. 2000), Negro biographies (ca. 1000), African history (ca. 1000); periodical and newspaper titles (ca. 150); pamphlets; sheet music; handbills; programs and memorabilia. Includes papers of E.R. Alexander, William Edward Burghardt DuBois, Angelina Weld Grimké, Pauline E. Hopkins, Langston Hughes, and James Caroll Napier; memorabilia of the Jubilee Singers; memoirs of Archibald Henry Grimké; poems of Fenton Johnson; letters of Alexandre Dumas fils; The Charge of Fort Wagner, by William H. Carney; and a minute book (1834-36) of the board of managers of the Philadelphia Anti-Slavery Society. Concerns the Negro American, slavery and ante bellum history, the Civil War and Reconstruction, American foreign trade, Negroes in arts and letters, the Negro Renaissance, Fisk and Howard Universities, and the Anna T. Jeanes Foundation (Negro Rural School Fund). Includes the Lincoln or Freedmen's Bible (presented to him July 4, 1864); an edited Bible for slaves, omitting all passages relating to freedom and including excerpts acceptable from the point of view of the slave owners; British Parliament papers on the dispersion of slavery, including "The Debate on a Motion for the Abolition of the Slave Trade in the House of Commons on Monday, the Second of April, 1792."; broadsides; a copy of Alexandre Dumas' The Progress of Democracy (1841); and slavery documents that are handwritten (such as bills of sale, birth records, insurance papers, slave labor contracts, and free papers). There are several smaller collections that are maintained as a part of the Negro Collection.

.28 Park, Robert Ezra.
Papers, 1928-46. ca. 1000 items. Professor at Fisk University, Nashville, Tenn. Mss, correspondence, notes, clippings, and related papers concerning Park's career and Negroes. Includes unpublished sociological studies.

.29 Southern Education Reporting Service (SERS).
Files, ca. 1954-67. ca. 147 vf and 14 cartons (ca. 800,000 items). Chiefly newspaper and magazine clippings collected by the SERS library, concerning such subjects as race relations in the U.S., desegregation in education, equal employment opportunities, housing, civil rights, violence, riots, sit-ins, civil rights organizations, racism, the church and race, politics, and the courts. The Fisk University Library is the depository for the records of SERS and its successor, the Race Relations Information Center.

.30 Spence, Mary Elizabeth, 1865-1962.
Papers, 1828-1960. 10 boxes, 4 filing cabinets. Professor of Greek at Fisk University. Includes materials pertaining to the University.

.31 Talley, Thomas Washington.
Papers. ca. 1000 items. Professor of chemistry at Fisk University. Personal papers, lecture notes, and mss pertaining to chemistry.

.32 Toomer, Jean.
Papers, ca. 1920-50. ca. 30,000 items. In part, typewritten and handwritten. Poet. Clippings, magazine articles, literary mss, correspondence, photos, memorabilia, notes, papers, discourses, plays, and periodicals in which his works appeared. Mss of "Eight-Day World" (ca. 1933), "From Exile and Being," (autobiographical), and others. Among the correspondents are Sterling A. Brown, Sherwood Anderson, Hart Crane, Allen Tate, Jessie Redmon Fauset, Waldo Frank, Langston Hughes, Aldous Huxley, Charles S. Johnson, James Weldon Johnson, and Lewis Mumford.

.33 Wright, Richard.
Books. ca. 40 v. Author. Copies of Wright's books in foreign translations and English.

TN30   GEORGE PEABODY COLLEGE FOR TEACHERS (1875), LIBRARY. 37203. Tel 615 327-8184. Harley C. Brooks, Jr., Librn.

.1 Peabody Educational Fund.
Papers, 1868-1931. ca. 3000 items. Letters and other papers of the trustees of the Fund. Including correspondence from Booker T. Washington of Tuskegee Institute (Ala.), and from Negro schools relative to possible financial support.

TN30a   HOPE, INC. P.O. Box 50391, 37205. Tel 615 747-0271. Tom Green, Chmn. of Board.
Hope, Inc. is a private, non-profit corporation comprised of citizens working to provide adequate housing for persons of low and moderate incomes. Hope offers services such as counseling, financial assistance, and liaison between builders, bankers, housing officials, and others.

.1 Hope, Inc.
Files. Correspondence, minutes of meetings, financial records, and other materials dealing with the aims and activities of the organization.

TN31   JOINT UNIVERSITY LIBRARIES, INC. (1936), SPECIAL COLLECTIONS DEPARTMENT (1965). 21st Ave., S., 37203. Tel 615 322-2807. Head of Spec. Collections. Interlibrary loan, bibliographies prepared, literature searches, copying, inquiries answered, referrals made, consultation.

.1 Ashmore, Henry S., 1916- .
Papers. Author, and president of the Center for the Study of Democratic Institutions, Santa Barbara, Calif. Ms materials for An Epitaph for Dixie (1958), an examination of the forces of change reshaping the South.

.2 Christian Educator.
Volumes 3 and 4. Published by the Freedmen's Aid Society of the Methodist Church (1889-1931). Contains information on the Society's educational work among Negroes and its support of institutions of higher education for Negroes.

.3 Ford, Jesse Hill.
Papers. Author. Ms of The Liberation of Lord Byron Jones (1964), a novel concerning racial problems in the South.

.4 Materials relating to the Negro.
Miscellaneous, 1810-60. Microfilm copies of mss relating chiefly to Tennessee in the period prior to 1865. These films include unpublished schedules of agricultural, slave and population census schedules for a number of the southern states.

TN32   MEHARRY MEDICAL COLLEGE (1876), ALUMNI LIBRARY. 1005 18th Ave. N., 37208. Tel 615 256-3631. Mrs. Patricia M. Strong, Librn.

.1 Afro-American Studies Collection.
ca. 1000 paperbacks. Basic books on the life and history of black Americans.

.2 Meharry Medical College.
Archives. Correspondence, minutes of board meetings, financial records, records of admission, bulletins, catalogs, and other materials dealing with the history and administration of the College.

TN33   METHODIST PUBLISHING HOUSE (1789), LIBRARY (1820). 201 Eighth Ave. S., 37203. Tel 615 242-1621. Miss Elizabeth Hughey, Librn. Interlibrary loan, copying, typing, referrals made.
The Library houses the archives of the Methodist Publishing House and other materials relating to Methodism.
Publ.: The United Methodist Periodical Index.

.1 Christian Advocate.
Records and materials on Methodism, 1882-1937. ca. 3250 items and 36 folders. Correspondence, reports, minutes of meetings, addresses, clippings, pamphlets, photos., portraits, and other material on many subjects of Methodist interest. Among topics covered are Negroes and the Ku Klux Klan, including anti-Klan material and correspondence supporting the Klan program, especially its anti-Catholic activities.

.2 Freedmen's Aid Society.
Files, 1866-1920. 54 v. Reports, correspondence, and other materials of the Society, a division of the

Methodist Episcopal Church, succeeded by the
Board of Education for Negroes. Reports 1st-54th
(1866-75, 1875-76, and 1919-20); and partial file of
the Society's organ, The Christian Educator. In-
cluded is information concerning elementary
schools and institutions of higher education for
Negroes founded and supported by the Society, such
as Meharry Medical College, Claflin University
(Orangeburg, S.C.), Clark College (Atlanta), New
Orleans University (now part of Dillard University),
Wiley University (Texas), Bennett College
(Greensboro, N.C.), Cookman Institute (now
Bethune-Cookman), Morgan College (now Morgan
State University, Baltimore, Md.), Sam Huston (now
part of Huston-Tillotson College, Austin, Tex.), and
Gammon Theological Seminary (now part of Inter-
denominational Center, Atlanta, Ga.). Also included
is information on Negro education in general,
religious life, and race relations in the U.S.

TN34   THE METROPOLITAN HUMAN RELATIONS COMMISSION
        OF NASHVILLE-DAVIDSON COUNTY (1965). 1034
        Stahlman Bldg., 37201. Tel 615 747-4385. Inquiries
        answered, referrals made, consultation.
        The Commission conducts and sponsors research pro-
        jects and studies of discriminatory practices and pro-
        gress in equal opportunity in Metro Nashville; receives
        and investigates complaints, holds hearings, recom-
        mends methods for eliminating discrimination.
        Publ.: Annual Report; Mass Media Report; Newsletter.

        .1 The Metropolitan Human Relations Commission of
            Nashville-Davidson County.
            Files, 1965- . Includes correspondence, minutes
            of meetings, financial records, studies, investiga-
            tions, and other materials dealing with the aims,
            history, and programs of the Commission.

TN35   NASHVILLE URBAN LEAGUE, INC. (1968). 1922 Church
        St., 37203. Tel 615 242-5639. Charles R. Walker, Jr.,
        Exec. Dir.
        The League is a social service agency, interracial in
        staff and leadership, which works for the equalization
        of life results between black and white Americans
        through the complete integration of the Negro and other
        minorities into the mainstream of American life.

        .1 Nashville Urban League.
            Files, 1968- . Correspondence, minutes of meet-
            ings, financial records, studies, reports, and other
            materials dealing with the aims, history, and pro-
            grams of the League.

TN35a   NATIONAL BAPTIST PUBLISHING BOARD (1918). 523
        Second Ave. S., 37201. Dr. C.W. Black, Editor.
        Publ.: National Baptist Union-Review, biweekly news-
        paper.

TN36   NATIONAL BAPTIST SUNDAY SCHOOL AND TRAINING
        UNION CONGRESS (1903). 412 Fourth Ave. N., 37201.
        Tel 615 256-3209. C.R. Williams, Exec. Secy.
        The Congress is a church organization which fosters
        and stimulates all phases of religious education, train-
        ing in church membership, evangelism, and mission
        work. An auxiliary to the National Baptist Convention,
        U.S.A., Inc.

        .1 National Baptist Sunday School and Training Union Con-
            gress.
            Files, 1903- . Correspondence, minutes of board
            meetings, financial records, and other materials
            dealing with the aims, history, and programs of the
            Congress.

TN36a   NATIONAL BAPTIST VOICE. 330 Charlotte Ave., 37201.
        Caesar Clark, Editor.
        Publ.: National Baptist Voice, official organ of the Na-
        tional Baptist Convention U.S.A., Inc.

TN37   RACE RELATIONS INFORMATION CENTER (RRIC) (1969),
        LIBRARY (1955). 1109 19th Ave. S., 37212. Tel 615
        327-1361. Robert F. Campbell, Exec. Dir. Literature
        searches, copying, inquiries answered, referrals made,
        consultation.
        The Center, a private, nonprofit organization that

gathers and distributes information about race relations
in the U.S., is the successor to Southern Education Reporting Service, an agency established in 1954 to provide accurate, unbiased information on race-related
developments in education in the southern and border
states. The Center's Special Reports are intended for
use especially by newspapers, magazines, broadcasting
stations and educational institutions.
Publ.: Special Reports; Race Relations Reporter, semi-
       monthly newsletter.

.1 Facts on Film.
    Microfilm, 1954- . ca. 230 reels (through 1967-
    68 supplement). Commercially available microfilm
    series which reproduces materials collected by the
    SERS and RRIC library. Included are news stories,
    editorial cartoons, magazine articles, SERS and
    RRIC publications, Race Relations Law Reporter,
    reports, studies and surveys, speeches, pamphlets,
    newsletters, other miscellaneous printed matter,
    and a card catalog for the entire collection, on such
    subjects as race in education, race relations, and
    compensatory education.

.2 Race Relations Information Center (RRIC).
    Files, 1969- . ca. 10 vf. Correspondence, minutes
    of meetings, financial reports, personnel files,
    Includes materials relating to the operation of the
    Center, to its publications, and to research data
    used to prepare Directory of Afro-American Re-
    sources. Subjects mentioned include Black Mus-
    lims, "soul radio," Title IV of the Civil Rights Act
    of 1964, Newark (N.J.) politics, racial protest in
    the South, United Methodist Church, school desegre-
    gation, and Cubans. Restricted.

.3 Race Relations Information Center Library.
    Files, ca. 1954- . ca. 81 vf (ca. 300,000 items) and
    ca. 800 v. Correspondence, mss, newspaper and
    magazine clippings, magazines, books, pamphlets,
    reports, surveys, laws, court decisions, speeches,
    "underground" newspapers, broadsides, micro-
    films, and card catalog. The library collects ma-
    terials on all aspects of race relations in the U.S.,
    including such subjects as school and college de-
    segregation, politics, public accommodations,
    racism, federal, state and local legislation, civil
    rights, violence, riots, demonstrations, housing,
    employment, Citizens Council, Ku Klux Klan, SNCC,
    Black Panthers, Council of Federated Organiza-
    tions, sit-ins, SCLC, and Southern Regional Coun-
    cil. Also included are complete runs of publica-
    tions of numerous civil rights organizations; mss
    and statistical data for the Statistical Summary of
    School Segregation-Desegregation in the Southern
    and Border States (1957-67) and for School Deseg-
    regation in the Southern and Border States (1967-
    68); and extensive file of government publications
    with racial topics. Back files of library materials
    are periodically sent to Fisk University Library.
    In part, restricted.

.4 Southern Education Reporting Service (SERS).
    Files, 1954-69. ca. 20 vf. Correspondence, min-
    utes of meetings, reports, press releases, mss,
    photos, galleys, page proofs, financial records,
    mailing lists, and subscription records. Included
    are materials relating to SERS publications, Facts
    on Film, Southern Schools: Progress and Prob-
    lems (1959), With All Deliberate Speed (1957),
    Ordeal of Desegregation (1966), Southern School
    News (1954-65), Southern Education Report
    (1965-69), and Statistical Summary (1957-67);
    survey research data concerning "high risk" pro-
    grams, and college attitudes; distribution records
    for Race Relations Law Reporter. Subjects men-
    tioned include school desegregation, race relations,
    the "Brown decision," politics, Negro migration,
    Negro journalists, and compensatory education for
    the disadvantaged. Among correspondents are
    various representatives of the Ford Foundation, the
    Fund for the Advancement of Education, Southern
    Education Foundation, U.S. Commission on Civil
    Rights, U.S. Office of Education, Southern Regional
    Council, and Frank Ahlgren, Charles S. Johnson,
    Stephen J. Wright, John Codwell, Luther H. Foster,
    James R. Lawson, Thomas R. Waring, Jr., Bert

Struby, Robert F. Campbell, Reed Sarratt, George N. Redd, C.A. McKnight, Don Shoemaker, Edward Ball, John Popham, Alexander Heard, and others. Restricted.

TN38 SOUTHERN BAPTIST CONVENTION, BAPTIST SUNDAY SCHOOL BOARD, DARGEN-CARVER LIBRARY (1933). 127 Ninth Ave. N., 37203. Tel 615 254-1631. Helen Conger, Librn.

.1 Aldrich, Eugene Perry.
Papers, 1919-48. ca. 15,000 items. Secretary, Department of Survey, Statistics and Information of the Sunday School Board of the Southern Baptist Convention, 1920-45. Included are materials pertaining to his publications, The New Racial Situation (1946) and While Southern Baptists Sleep (1949); and to the history of the American Baptist Theological Seminary.

.2 Annual Report of the American Baptist Home Missionary Society.
Complete run, 1832- . Microfilm, and many originals. Included is information pertaining to the Freedmen's Fund and the Society's educational and mission work among southern Negroes. History of the schools supported by the Society can be followed in these reports. Schools fully controlled by the Society were Wayland Seminary (Washington, D.C.), Benedict Institute (now Benedict College, Columbia, S.C.), Nashville Institute, Nashville Seminary, and Bishop College (now in Dallas, Tex.). Affiliated but incorporated schools were Shaw University (Raleigh, N.C.), Spelman College (Atlanta, Ga.), Virginia Union (Richmond, Va.), Morehouse College (Atlanta), Jackson College (Jackson, Tenn., formerly at Natchez, Miss.), Leland College (New Orleans, La.), and Roger Williams College (Nashville, Tenn.).

.3 Annual Report of the American Baptist Publication Society.
1862-1904. Contains social commentaries.

.4 Annuals of the Southern Baptist Convention.
Complete file, with index, 1845-1965. Includes material concerning the Convention's attitudes and actions on slavery and race relations, its work in ministerial education for Negroes, and relations with Negro churches and the National Baptist Convention. Also included is material concerning the American Baptist Theological Seminary (Nashville, Tenn.), and the Christian Life Commission (1913- ., formerly Social Service Commission). Prior to 1953, the reports of the Commission, which contain information about race relations, are indexed by subject matter and after that date they are indexed under Christian Life Commission.

.5 Baptist Home Missionary Monthly.
Complete file, 1878-1909. Contains information concerning Negro educational institutions supported by the Baptists.

.6 Christian Life Commission.
Papers, ca. 1947- . ca. 19,000 items. Official correspondence file of the Commission, 1955-60, including correspondence dealing with race relations, which provides cross section of southern opinion during the first five years following the 1954 school desegregation decision.

.7 Dargan, Edwin C.
Papers, 1893-1913. ca. 2100 items. Originals and microfilm. Contains information on the background of the establishment of the American Baptist Theological Seminary.

.8 Hays, Brooks, 1898- .
Papers, 1850-59. 4 ft. (4900 items). Forms part of a collection of papers of the Southern Baptist Convention presidents. Lawyer, and U.S. Representative from Arkansas. Chiefly correspondence relating to Hays' term as president of the Southern Baptist Convention (1957-59); together with papers from his work as vice-president of the Southern Baptist Convention (1950), and with its Christian Life Commission (1955-60). Among topics discussed is race relations.

.9 Southern Baptist Convention, Executive Committee on Program Planning Process.
Papers, 1959-65. 1533 items (ca. 5000 pp.). Con-

tain information on the Christian Life Commission and American Baptist Theological Seminary.

TN39 SOUTHERN BAPTIST CONVENTION, CHRISTIAN LIFE COMMISSION (1913). 460 James Robertson Pkwy., 37219. Tel 615 244-2495. Rev. Foy Valentine, Exec. Secy. Bibliographies prepared, literature searches, copying, typing, inquiries answered, referrals made, consultation.
The Commission works to help Southern Baptists become more aware of the ethical implications of the Christian gospel with regard to such aspects of daily living as family life, human relations, moral issues, economic life and daily work, citizenship, and related fields.

.1 Southern Baptist Convention, Christian Life Commission.
Files, 1945- . ca. 10,000 items. Correspondence, minutes of meetings, financial records, studies, reports, and other materials concerning religion and race. Restricted.

TN40 SOUTHERN BAPTIST CONVENTION, HISTORICAL COMMISSION. 127 Ninth Ave. N., 37203. Tel 615 254-1631. Davis C. Wooley, Exec. Secy.

.1 Historical Commission.
The Commission is conducting an extensive microfilming program in Baptist history in general, with special attention to Negro Baptists and race relations. Microfilmed materials include the National Baptist Voice; proceedings of 50 North Carolina Negro Baptist churches and associations; numerous theses on the Negro written in Baptist seminaries and other schools; the catalogue of Roger Williams University from 1881-93; the correspondence of Richard Furman; the sermons and papers of Basil Manly, 1826-68 (Baptist minister, president of University of Alabama, founder of Southern Baptist Convention, and defender of slavery), including a sermon "On the Emancipation of Slaves;" and official papers of Baptist state organizations, including many southern papers dating to the antebellum period. The Commission houses these microfilmed materials in the Dargan-Carver Library of the Baptist Sunday School Board, Nashville, Tenn.

TN41 STATE OF TENNESSEE, DEPARTMENT OF EDUCATION, EQUAL EDUCATIONAL OPPORTUNITIES PROGRAM (1965). 114 Cordell Hull Bldg., 37219. Tel 615 741-2328. Robert K. Sharp, Coordinator. Bibliographies prepared, inquiries answered, consultation.
The Program is designed to develop public support for and community understanding of school desegregation efforts; to assist in the promulgation of desegregation plans; to advise local school systems; to provide consultation on curriculum and on problems in human relations. It also consults with the State Commissioner of Education and Department personnel on school desegregation; reviews departmental activities; recommends policies; provides leadership; and conducts explanatory and educational programs as required to insure a desegregation policy consistent with federal objectives.
Publ.: The Negro American (1969), selected list of books, magazines and recordings for school libraries.

.1 Equal Educational Opportunities Program.
Files, 1965- . Correspondence, books (ca. 300), and periodicals on civil rights, education, and school desegregation. Included are complete runs of such periodicals as Southern School News, Southern Education Report, Race Relations Law Reporter, Race Relations Law Survey, and Integrated Education (1966- .). Restricted.

TN42 TENNESSEE COUNCIL ON HUMAN RELATIONS (1954). 818 17th Ave. S., 37203. Tel 615 256-5691. Baxton Bryant, Exec. Dir.
The Council strives to identify with the poor, minorities, and the alienated; and conduct positive communication with structured society to alleviate discrimina-

tion. Affiliated with Southern Regional Council, Atlanta, Ga.

Publ.: Newsletter, monthly.

.1 Tennessee Council on Human Relations.
Files, 1954- . Correspondence, reports, records, mss, clippings, films, tape recordings, and other materials concerning the history and activities of the Council. Included are materials from all chapters of the Council in Tennessee; materials relating to the Nashville sit-ins and the multi-ethnic textbook project; correspondence, reports, studies, and other materials pertaining to the Community Action Program, Memphis, Tenn.; and correspondence, reports, clippings, and other papers concerning the activities of the Metro Action Commission, Nashville, Tenn.

TN43   TENNESSEE STATE LIBRARY AND ARCHIVES (1854). 403 Seventh Ave. N., 37219. Tel 615 741-2451. Dr. Wilmon H. Droze, State Librn. and Archivist. Interlibrary loan, copying, inquiries answered, referrals made, consultation.

Publ.: Numerous registers and finding aids.

Archives Division

.1 — Caption Cards of Negro Regiments Organized in Tennessee During the Civil War.
Microfilm, 1 reel, of materials in the National Archives.

.2 — Compiled Records of Volunteer Union Soldiers Who Served with U.S. Colored Troops.
Microfilm, 98 reels, of materials in the National Archives.

.3 — Petition collection.
Petitions to the Tennessee State Legislature, 1796-1869. Included are petitions from individuals and groups for emancipation or manumission of slaves, for and against laws regulating slavery and slaveholders, and some from free Negroes asking for protection or for their legal rights.

.4 — Secretary of State.
Papers. Included are voter registration rolls (1867- .), containing information concerning residential patterns and the Negro in Tennessee politics; and penitentiary records, which include racial classifications.

.5 — Tennessee Confederate Pension Applications.
Records, 1891- . Applications for pension, divided according to white soldiers, Negro soldiers (ca. 285 applications), and widows, giving detailed information about a soldier's military, personal, and family history, as well as his economic or financial condition at the time the application was filed. Also includes correspondence between the applicant and the Pension Board, and letters or sworn affidavits from comrades and neighbors attesting to the veteran's character and the nature of his military service.

.6 — Tennessee Department of Education.
Records, 1867- . Included is correspondence between the State Department and the Slater, Jeanes and Rosenwald funds; and materials relating to the growth and development of Tennessee State University.

.7 Library Division.
Among the holdings of the Library are books and periodicals pertaining to Negro history; monographs on Negro, slavery and the race question in the U.S.; racist publications; pro-slavery arguments; and studies of civil rights work, such as the Cornell experiment in Fayette County, Tenn. As a federal government documents depository the Library has a collection of codes, statutes, reports, and publications of federal and state governments. Also included is a complete file of reports (1869- .) of the Tennessee Department of Education, containing statistics on Negroes and whites.

Manuscript section.

.8 — Anti-Slavery movement.
Letters, 1841-78. 1 reel (microfilm copy). Materials pertaining to the anti-slavery movement.

.9 — Audio collection.
Miscellaneous, Jan. 7, 1965. 1 tape. Governor George Wallace's speech before the 27th annual convention of the Tennessee School Boards Association.

.10 — Barnsley family.
Papers, 1825-1908. ca. 850 items. Correspondence, account books, documents, maps, and memorabilia of Godfrey Barnsley and his children, relating to the family's plantation, Woodlands, in Bartow Co., Ga. The letters contain much information on economic conditions in the South after the Civil War and other subjects. Among other papers are the Civil War letters and documents of Peter Baltzell, provost marshal in the Confederate Army.

.11 — Beeler, Roy Hood, 1882-1954.
Papers, 1936-54. 4 ft. (ca. 600 items and 11 v.). Lawyer of Knoxville, Tenn., State attorney general, and solicitor general. Correspondence, reports, and other materials relating to antilynch laws, education, public welfare, and other topics. Among other material are progress reports (1939) of the Tennessee State Planning Board; speeches of Beeler and others; and eleven scrapbooks relating to Beeler's career (1938-54).

.12 — Boone, C.H.
Papers. ca. 5 ft. Minister, St. John's Church, Nashville, Tenn. Contains materials concerning local history and the African Methodist Episcopal Church.

.13 — Bostick family.
Papers, 1861-64. 59 items (165 copies). Includes letter of Abe Bostick, a Nashville youth in Anderson's brigade, who wrote of a Negro cook in the army.

.14 — Bostwick, Easley, Guy, and Hardy families.
Genealogical data, ca. 1600-1967. ca. 30 items (200 pp., copies). Includes instructions for the treatment of slaves to the overseer of Martin Winston Guy's plantation, Memphis, Tenn., 1852.

.15 — Boyd, Nannie (Seawell). collector.
Montgomery Bell papers, 1853-1939. ca. 100 items. Correspondence (ca. 44 items) dealing with biographical facts about Montgomery Bell (1769-1855); biographical data relating to Bell's family; documents relating to Bell's colonization project in Liberia; and a few photos. and memorabilia. Among the correspondents is Carter G. Woodson (director of the Journal of Negro History).

.16 — Britt, Mary (Nichols). collector.
Nichols-Britt collection, 1771-1905. 3 ft. (ca. 2000 items). Correspondence, diary notes, documents, account books, slave records, land grants, daybooks, scrapbooks, photos., memorabilia, and other papers relating to the families of Nichols, McCown, McPhail, and Carter. The papers give much genealogical information and reflect life in Williamson and Davidson counties, Tenn., from the earliest settlements. Includes historical sketches about the Civil War by George S. Nichols.

.17 — Brown, Campbell, 1840-93.
Papers of Campbell Brown and Richard Stoddert Ewell, 1852-83. Two v. of military reminiscences of Major Campbell Brown written in 1867-69 which cover his service in the Confederate Army from 1861-63, together with a daybook of farm operations; correspondence of General Richard Ewell; and ca. 200 letters from Thomas T. Gantt, a St. Louis, Mo., lawyer and the business agent of his cousin, Lisinka Campbell Brown Ewell, mother of Campbell Brown, who married Richard Ewell in 1865. All but 29 of these letters were written to Mrs. Ewell and contain discussion of abolition, politics, education, and other topics.

.18 — Brown, Joseph, 1772-1826.
Papers. ca. 280 items. Contain correspondence regarding Negroes recovered from the Indians, 1814-16.

TN43.19 — Buckner, Mary Elizabeth (Stay).
Papers, 1818-1923. ca. 4 ft. (3000 items).
Correspondence, diaries, accounts, legal documents, religious writings, genealogical data, slave lists, newspaper clippings, and other papers. Chiefly correspondence (1912-22) of Mrs. Buckner's husband, Henry K. Buckner, of Nashville, Tenn. Includes information about the Civil War. Correspondents include Upshaw Buckner.

.20 — Buell, George Parson, 1833-83.
Papers of George P. Buell and John S. Brien, 1805-1943. ca. 15 ft. (ca. 10,000 items). Correspondence, diaries, military papers, legal documents, account books, bills, receipts, scrapbooks, photos., and memorabilia. Contains John S. Brien's papers concerning slaves (1854-60) and clippings concerning the race problem.

.21 — Cable-Chestnutt.
Correspondence, 1889-98. 50 items. 1 reel (Microfilm copy). Materials pertaining to Negroes.

.22 — Campbell, David.
Papers, 1779-1859. 18 reels, microfilm. Includes letters of Virginia Tabitha Jane (Campbell) Shelton (ca. 1818-67) containing information on slavery and other subjects.

.23 — Castner, Wilson Jacob, 1817-69.
Papers, 1826-1902. 22 items. Contain references to trouble with slaves in Tennessee in 1865.

.24 — Chapman family.
Papers, 1848-81. Chiefly correspondence of the Chapman family and their friends. Many letters concern Negroes, including mention of an outbreak of Negroes in the 1850's, farm laborers, and a Negro song.

.25 — Cheatham, Benjamin Franklin, 1820-86.
Papers, 1834-93. ca. 300 items. Army officer, superintendent of Tennessee State prisons, postmaster, and farmer. Correspondence (family, personal, and military), Confederate military reports and maps, journal (1881-84) of farming activities, miscellaneous military papers, memorabilia, and other material. Includes two letters (1842-43) written to T.H. Williams by Andrew Jackson and John Tyler with references to African slave trade and other matters.

.26 — Cherokee collection.
Papers, 1775-1878. ca. 8 ft. (3500 items and 22 v.). Correspondence, documents, claims, pamphlets, photos., books, clippings, surveys and other materials relating to the Cherokees and to John Ross (1790-1866), principal chief of the Cherokees (1826-66). Includes materials concerning slave population (1824-28, 1835, 1859); "Pins Indians" (Keetoowahs); Knights of the Golden Circle, later Southern Rights party; Cherokees' ownership of Negro slaves; John Ross as the owner of 70 Negro slaves; abolition; the Civil War; lands shared with freedmen; the secession (1861); and other subjects.

.27 — Church records, Baptist.
Included are the records of Mill Creek Baptist Church, Davidson County, Tenn., 1797-1814, containing information regarding the black brethren.

.28 — Church records, Methodist.
Records of the Methodist Episcopal Church, 1866-88, 1905-25. 2 v. Included are the minutes for the annual conferences of the Methodist Episcopal Church, and records of Clark Memorial Church. Contains information concerning development of Negro and white conferences, the history of Central Tennessee College and its successor, Walden University, and the early history of Meharry Medical College, which began as the Medical Department of Central Tennessee College.

.29 — Church records, Presbyterian.
Included are records of Mars Hill Presbyterian Church, Athens, McMinn Co., Tenn., 1823-1923, among which are membership roll (1832) and names of ministers (1823-1923). Among subjects discussed are the Negro members of the church prior to the Civil War and the Reconstruction period.

.30 — Church records, Roman Catholic.
Contains records of St. Joseph's Catholic Mission, Jackson, Madison Co., Tenn., including historical sketches of St. Joseph's Catholic Mission and its school, which were established for the local Negroes.

.31 — Civil War collection.
Confederate and Federal papers, 1858-1965. 11 ft. (ca. 4500 items and 150 v.). In part, photocopies. Letters, diaries, memoirs, autograph album, casualty lists, cemetery records, clippings, maps, orders, photos, medical and supply records, scrapbooks, sketches and other papers, relating to military personnel and units, monuments, prisons, and veterans' organizations. Includes material on campaigns and battles and on military units.

.32 — Clark, George H.
Correspondence, 1847. 1 item. Letter of Clark which describes a Negro funeral in Nashville, Tenn.

.33 — Clippings.
Files. Included are clippings pertaining to the Cumberland Presbyterian Church, Negro, 1866-94. 25 items. Clippings from the Cumberland Presbyterian dealing with congregations, general assemblies, missionaries, publications of the church.

.34 — Cockrill family.
Papers, 1782-1860. Included are two letters (1855, 1856) written by Mark Cockrill from his plantation near Vicksburg, Miss., to his son Ben F. Cockrill, giving a gloomy picture of conditions, crops, and the attitudes of and work accomplished by the Negroes.

.35 — Congregational churches.
Records, 1852-1961. 19 reels (Microfilm). Includes material relating to Negroes.

.36 — Crozier, Arthur Ramsey.
Papers, 1837-58. 26 items. Includes materials pertaining to Negroes.

.37 — Crutcher, Ernest, 1858-ca. 1948.
Papers, 1939-46. Short memoir of Dr. Crutcher of Los Angeles, Calif., about his young days in Nashville, Tenn.

.38 — Crutchfield family.
Papers, 1828-86. ca. 50 items and 1 v. Correspondence, biographical and genealogical material, clippings, wills and other legal papers of the Thomas Crutchfield, Sr. and Jr.; slave deeds and a diary (1852) kept by Thomas Crutchfield, Jr. concerning his law practice near Chattanooga, Tenn., the final settlement of his father's estate, and the treatment of slaves. The correspondence includes an 18 p. letter written by Thomas Crutchfield, Jr., regarding his position as a Unionist both before and during the Civil War.

.39 — Daughters of the American Revolution.
Papers, 1910-60. 2 v. and ca. 300 items. Included is a scrapbook compiled by the General Felix K. Zollicoffer Chapter, containing newspaper story on life of Guy Washington, then 86, a former Negro slave, telling of his experiences as a noncombatant in Hood's headquarters during the Civil War.

.40 — Dickinson, Jacob McGavock, 1851-1928.
Papers, 1812-1946. 30 ft. (ca. 40,200 items and 67 v.). Cabinet officer, jurist, and lawyer. Correspondence (family, personal, and business), speeches, briefs, reports, biographical and genealogical data, scrapbooks, clippings, photos., memorabilia, and other papers. The bulk of the material covers Dickinson's service as Secretary of War (1909-11). Includes material relating to race problems; the American Commission to Liberia; slavery; Negro firemen (1909); Robert Lincoln's letter regarding

slave marriages (1907); Lincoln Memorial University; conditions in the South (1871, 1889, 1905); the "Mink Slide" operation at Columbia, Tenn., 1946; and Dickinson's speech to the Colored Fair.

TN43.41 — Donelson, Andrew Jackson, 1800-71.
Papers, 1797-1898. ca. 150 items. Forms part of the Tennessee Historical Society collection. Lawyer, editor, Army officer, secretary to Andrew Jackson, and diplomat. Correspondence, legal documents, accounts, Arkansas and Tennessee land records, and other papers relating to national politics. Includes legal papers (1871-98) of William Alexander Donelson, records (1864) of Martin Donelson; slave deeds of William Donelson; genealogical material; and correspondence of Andrew Jackson Donelson, Jr., and Martin Donelson.

.42 — Driver, William.
Miscellaneous materials. 2 v. Diaries, memoirs, and other materials relating to Negroes.

.43 — Dunlap, Hugh W., 1798-1849.
Papers of Hugh W. and John H. Dunlap, 1824-1905. ca. 200 items. Lawyers of Henry County, Tenn. Correspondence and legal documents consist mainly of bills of sale for Negro slaves, together with summonses, indentures, deeds of trust, receipts, promissory notes, and bills of gift. About 30 of the documents belonged to Nellie Grey Toler.

.44 — Eakin, William, 1810-49.
Papers, 1828-65. 14 items and 1 v. Businessman. Memoirs (to 1846); slave deeds (1841-46), a few accounts, wills, and some genealogical material on the Eakin family.

.45 — Eppse, Merl R., 1893-1967.
Papers. ca. 134 ft. (ca. 86,000 items). Historian. Professor of history, Tennessee State University. Monographs, ephemeral material, broadsides, programs, pamphlets, and other papers concerning the history of the Negro. Partially processed.

.46 — Fergusson family.
Papers, 1864-1927. 10 ft. (ca. 7000 items). Correspondence, diaries, legal documents, genealogical data, accounts, speeches, newspaper clippings, photos, and memorabilia. The correspondence of Adam Fergusson, a claims agent and man of considerable political influence in Carthage, Tenn., relates to national and state political issues of the period preceding the Civil War. The papers (1847-1919) of Adam's son William Fergusson include Civil War material consisting of military orders, war collections, family correspondence, and correspondence on the Reconstruction in Tennessee and other southern states.

.47 — Freedmen's Bureau.
Papers. 73 reels (microfilm copies).

.48 — Freeman, Mary Barry Martin, 1882-1963.
Papers, ca. 1700-1962. ca. 9 ft. (ca. 6000 items and 20 v.). In part, transcripts. Genealogist and clubwoman of Robertson Co., Tenn. Correspondence, bills, notes, receipts, licenses, honors, photos, clippings, genealogical data, and memorabilia of Mrs. Freeman, her husband, Dr. John Shaw Freeman, Carney Freeman, Lynn B. Freeman, and other members of the Freeman family; writings, speeches, and notes of Mrs. Freeman; and papers relating to civil rights, Civil War, and local history.

.49 — Grey, Henry W.
Booklet, 1962. 12 pp. Sketch by Grey concerning Clinch Gray's son and life on a Mississippi plantation, telling of Negroes before and after the Civil War, their loyalty, and their diversions.

.50 — Guy, Martin Winston.
Papers. ca. 30 items. Included are instructions (1852) for the treatment of slaves to the overseer of the Guy's plantation in Memphis, Tenn.; and genealogical data.

.51 — Hamilton family.
Correspondence. Included are letters from Alfred T. Hamilton, a water-cure doctor practicing near Winchester, to his father in Pennsylvania, in which he comments on slavery.

.52 — Harris, George Carroll, 1836-1911.
Papers, 1836-86. ca. 250 items. Episcopal clergyman in Nashville and Memphis, Tenn., and Mt. Helena, Miss. Primarily family correspondence, genealogical data, scrapbook, and other papers of Harris and other members of the Harris family, chiefly in Louisiana. Includes information on southern life before, during, and after the Civil War, Louisiana and national politics, slave labor, the raising of cotton, farm conditions, the Civil War, the 1860 election, and Reconstruction in Louisiana.

.53 — Harris, Jeremiah George.
Letter dated February 8, 1859, deals with the Negro in bondage and freedom.

.54 — Harrison, William.
Papers, 1840-90. 20 items (photostats). Included are 7 bills of sale for slaves bought by William Harrison.

.55 — Hickman, Edwin Litton, 1875-1956.
Papers, 1801- . 30 items and 3 v. Lawyer, legislator, and judge. Correspondence (1801-74), including the price of slaves in Alabama and other subjects.

.56 — Highlander Folk School audio collection.
Tapes, 1953-63. ca. 1 ft. (ca. 250 audio discs or 154 hours listening time). Copies of original tapes of conferences held by Myles Horton, Knoxville, Tenn. Contains records of dictated correspondence; labor meetings; panel discussions and reports on integration; workshops on the United Nations, the student sit-in movement, citizenship schools, and voter registration. The great bulk of this collection deals with the integration movement (1953-63) and covers such subjects as: the 1954 Supreme Court ruling on school desegregation; the role of various persons and organizations in the movement, such as National Association for the Advancement of Colored People, Congress of Racial Equality, Student Nonviolent Coordinating Committee, Southern Christian Leadership Conference, Southern Regional Council, Martin Luther King and Roy Wilkins; the impact of civil rights demonstrations upon the white and Negro community; the role of the white liberal in the movement; non-violence as a force for action in the struggle; the threat of the Black Muslims to the entire integration movement; voter registration drives; citizenship schools, and political pressure to obtain the goals of the movement; and leadership responsibilities of the younger members of the movement. The remainder of the collection includes materials from labor meetings, correspondence dictated by Myles Horton, and background material dealing with the Highlander Folk School. Related to the library's Highlander Folk School collection and the Zilphia Horton collection.

.57 — Highlander Folk School collection.
Archives, 1932-61. ca. 7 ft. The Highlander Folk School, located in Grundy County, Tenn., was the training center for southern labor and civil rights leaders. Includes correspondence, records of attendance, planning session reports, studies, reports, investigations, and other materials dealing with the history and administration of the School. Persons mentioned include Martin Luther King, Jr.; Roy Wilkins; Myles Horton, director of the Highlander Folk School; James Bevel; L.A. Blackman; Lester Carr; Harry Golden; Rosa Parks; and others. Related to the library's Highlander Folk School audio collection and the Zilphia Horton collection.

.58 — Hollingsworth, Henry, 1808-55.
Diaries, 1836-37. Contain data concerning Negroes.

.59 — Horton, Zilphia, 1910-56. collector.
Folk music collection, 1935-56. ca. 3 ft. (ca. 1000 items). Director of music at Highlander

Folk School in Grundy Co., Tenn. Correspondence, folksongs, labor union song books, picket line songsheets; musical tapes, notes, printed items dealing with folk music, clippings, and other papers. Chiefly songs (ca. 1300) of social protest with historical information about most of the songs, the events about which the songs were written, or the composers. Includes material on folk, civil rights, and labor songs, history of folk songs, labor organizations, folk dancing, and projects of the Highlander Folk School, the leading training center for southern labor and civil rights leaders (1932-61). Related to the Library's Highlander Folk School audio collection and the Highlander Folk School collection.

TN43.60 — Johnson, Andrew, 1808-75.
Papers, 1846-75. ca. 100 items. President of the U.S. In part, transcripts and photocopy. Correspondence (7 letters), clippings, a scrapbook, a broadside, two pardons, and a commission signed by Johnson, a proclamation, and memorabilia. Correspondence includes 4 letters by Johnson to his daughter, Mary, and a letter to an East Tennessee newspaper editor containing political observations.

.61 — Jones, Alice Marie.
Dissertation, 1942. 1 reel (Microfilm copy). The Negro Folk Sermon: A Study in the Sociology of Folk Culture.

.62 — Klepper, Minnie.
Papers, 1801-97. 117 items. Includes materials concerning Negroes.

.63 — Lipscomb, John.
Journal, 1784. 1 item (ca. 50 pp.). Original ms journal kept daily as Lipscomb traversed the route from the Holston settlements to Nashville, Tenn., in the summer of 1784. Contains material concerning Negroes.

.64 — McCutchen family.
Papers, 1818-1958. ca. 1 ft. (ca. 2000 items). Correspondence primarily about family affairs; accounts; bills; inventories of estates; obituaries and funeral notices; land, marriage, school, and slave records; and other papers collected by Hildegard Smith for her book, The McCutchen Trace (1963?). Papers mainly relate to James McCutchen (1796-1864), son of Samuel and Catherine (Bell) McCutchen, and his business dealings particularly his administration of various estates, records, and other papers.

.65 — McIver family.
Papers, 1801-1929. ca. 2000 items. Family and business correspondence, diaries, and memoirs, containing some references to Negroes.

.66 — Military records concerning Negroes.
Papers, 1861-75. ca. 285, and 99 reels of microfilm. Includes Confederate pension applications; an index (98 reels) to compile service records of volunteer Union soldiers who served with U.S. Colored Troops; and caption cards (1 reel) of Negro regiments organized in Tennessee during the Civil War.

.67 — Miscellaneous documents pertaining to slavery.
Papers, 1797, 1812, and 1834. 3 items. Bills of sale for Negroes.

.68 — Mooney, William Dromgoole, 1858-1941.
Papers, 1867-1941. 12 items. Tennessee educator and founder of the Mooney Schools in Williamson and Rutherford counties. Included are writings on a variety of subjects, including Negro education.

.69 — Moore, John Trotwood, 1858-1929.
Papers, 1781-1957. ca. 40 ft. (ca. 20,000 items). Author, journalist, and librarian. Correspondence, diaries (1924-28), literary mss, speeches, notes, accounts, legal documents, indentures (1781-84), photos, scrapbooks, biographical and genealogical data, memorabilia, newspaper clippings, and other papers of Moore, State librarian and archivist of Tennessee (1919-29); his second wife, Mary Brown (Daniel) Moore (1875-1957), State Librarian and archivist emeritus of Tennessee (1929-55); his father, Judge John Moore (b. 1829); and his son, Dr. Merrill Moore (1903-57), a physician. Mss of Moore's writings include his books, The Bishop of Cottontown (1906), Hearts of Hickory (1926), Jack Ballington, Forester (1911), and A Summer Hymnal (1901), and his series "Dropped Stitches in Southern History" in Taylor-Trotwood magazine (1925-32). Includes material about the Civil War and Reconstruction; Confederate imprints and sheet music; and Chicago race riots (1919).

.70 — Nashville, Tennessee, Centennial and International Exposition.
Papers, 1895-1900. ca. 2500 items. Materials concerning the Exposition (1897) celebrating the 100th anniversary of the admission of Tennessee into the Union, including accounts of the Negro building and exhibits.

.71 — Negro slavery.
Materials. Included are 2 items consisting of a slavery protest of the Germantown (Pa.) Friends Society against slavery in 1688, and the slave laws of North Carolina and Tennessee, 1729-1806.

.72 — Newell family.
Papers, ca. 1850-ca. 1908. 1 v., 88 items. Included is a sketch by Tirza Wilson Patterson of her life during the years 1850-65, in which she tells of the effect of "John Brown and his like" on the Negroes.

.73 — Open Letter Club.
Papers, 1880's-1900. ca. 60 items. Materials of a Nashville, Tenn., organization containing items pertaining to Negroes.

.74 — Orr, Mary Hamilton Thompson. collector.
Papers, 1791-1896. ca. 1 ft. (1000 items). Correspondence, business records, legal documents, diaries, memoranda, and memorabilia of the Hamilton, Harris, House, Morgan, Overton, Thompson, and Wilson families. The letters are written from Ohio, Kentucky, Tennessee, Mississippi, and Alabama, and contain information about conditions in these areas before and after the Civil War. One letter from Russellville, Ky. (1807), contains a discourse defending slavery. Another (1865) from Okolona, Miss., written by W.H. Gordon, to Albert W. Harris, discusses Negro and white relationships in the South.

.75 — Owen, Lou Cretia.
Diary, 1918-19. 150 pp. (typed). Diary kept while Miss Owen was employed as a special service worker at Old Hickory Powder Plant, mentioning that 1300 Mexicans and 378 Negroes were employed, each having their separate compounds.

.76 — Owsley, Harriet Fason (Chappell).
Owsley charts. ca. 3 ft. (ca. 1500 pages). Historian. Charts of farm ownerships, tenancy, livestock, land improvement, products and slaves in Davidson, DeKalb, Dickson, Dyer, Fayette, Fentress, Franklin, Gibson, Grainger, Greene, Hardin, Hawkins, Haywood, Henry, Johnson, Lincoln, Maury, Montgomery, Robertson, Stewart, Sumner, and Wilson counties in Tennessee, taken from unpublished schedules I, II, and IV of censuses of 1850 and 1860, compiled under the direction of Frank Lawrence Owsley by Mrs. Owsley, Chase Curran Mooney, and Blanche Henry Clark; and charts on land, livestock, crops, population, slaves, cities, schools, literacy and other information, for all counties in Alabama, Florida, Georgia, Mississippi, and Tennessee, taken from published censuses (1840-60), compiled by Mrs. Owsley.

.77 — Patterson, Malcolm Rice, 1861-1935.
Papers, ca. 1895-1935. ca. 2000 items and 2 v. Governor of Tennessee and U.S. Representative from Tennessee. Papers contain clippings about the gubernatorial campaign of 1932 in which Patterson charged the Crump

machine with illegal registration of Negro voters.

.78 — Perkins, Theresa Green (Ewen).
Miscellaneous. 1 item. Diary containing references pertaining to Negroes.

.79 — Polk, Ophelia.
Papers, 1859. 1 item. Letter of Ophelia Polk pertaining to Negroes.

.80 — Porter, Nimrod, 1792-1872.
Papers. 1 reel, microfilm. Sheriff, Maury County, Tenn., for 29 years. Diary, 1861-72, contains material pertaining to Negroes.

.81 — Pryor, Jackson, b. 1861.
Papers, 1830-97. ca. 100 items. Farmer and businessman, of Jasper, Marion Co., Tenn. Business correspondence, accounts, bills of sale, notes, receipts, shares, deeds, licenses, wage and hour record, slave bills of sale, and other papers.

.82 — Rankin, Anne (Porterfield), 1869-1942.
Papers, 1887-1941. ca. 3 ft. (2000 items). Editor and newspaper woman. Correspondence, literary mss, galley proofs, clippings, notebooks, scrapbooks, checks, invitations, and memorabilia. Bulk of the material falls within the period 1910-30. Includes letters and material on the southern way of life, the Civil War, and other topics.

.83 — Rose, Stanley Fraxer.
Sketch, 1965. 1 item. Sketch by Rose entitled "Nashville and Its Leadership Elite, 1861-69," containing information about Negroes.

.84 — Russwurm, John Sumner, 1793-1860.
Papers, 1786-1914. ca. 900 items. Farmer, merchant, inspector general of Tennessee during tenure of Governor William Carroll; of Murfreesboro, Rutherford Co., Tenn. Correspondence, accounts, biographical and genealogical data, legal documents, wills and estate papers, land records, medical prescriptions, pension data, and clippings. Correspondence concerns slavery, emancipation, family moves, and other family matters. Included are 4 letters from John Brown Russwurm, son of John S. Russwurm's uncle by a Jamaican Negro, and who graduated from Bowdoin College (1826), was the first superintendent of public schools in Liberia, and governor of the Maryland Colony, established in Liberia under the auspices of the Maryland Colonization Society.

.85 — Sanford, Henry Shelton, 1823-91.
Papers, 1796-1901. ca. 50,000 items. These papers have been separated into several large classifications, of which the following contain materials regarding the Negro: Africa, 1870-91, ca. 3600 items; Barnwell Island, 1868-89, ca. 300 items; Oakley Sugar Plantation, 1869-90, ca. 1200 items; and special correspondence, including the letters of John Tyler Morgan, R.L. Gibson, Aaron Goodrich, and others containing information pertaining to Negroes.

.86 — Scrapbook collection.
Miscellaneous, 1800-1937. 2 v. Scrapbooks concerning Nashville, Tenn. (ca. 1800-1932), and a scrapbook (1902-37), both containing material pertaining to Negroes.

.87 — Sherman, William T.
Letter, 1866. 1 item. Letter by Sherman containing material about Negroes.

.88 — Simpson, Samuel Robert, 1823-1906.
Papers, 1862-1906. ca. 300 items. Contains newspaper clippings by Alexander K. McClure (1828-1909) in which he tells of the accomplishments of Hiram Rhodes Revels (1827-1901), Negro Mississippi State senator (1870-71) and interim secretary of state for Mississippi (1873). Also includes clipping from Nashville American (June 8, 1903) concerning Mingo Jones, body servant of Nathan Bedford Forrest.

.89 — Slatter, William.
Papers. 2 items. Letters dealing with the Negro in Liberia, 1873, 1875.

.90 — Tennessee Historical Society.
Miscellaneous files, 1688-1951. 7 ft. (ca. 3500 items). In part, photocopies (negatives). Forms part of the Tennessee Historical Society collection. Correspondence; account books; county histories; sketches; land grants and deeds; maps; commissions; data on Civil War; military records; marriage records; data relating to early Tennessee settlement and government, the Ku Klux Klan, and other subjects.

.91 — Tennesseans.
Papers, ca. 1920. 2 items. Biographical questionnaires concerning slaves.

.92 — Trousdale, William., 1790-1872.
Papers, 1803-1907. ca. 850 items. Governor of Tennessee, U.S. Ambassador to Brazil, U.S. Senator, brigadier general, U.S. Army. Contains some information regarding Negroes.

.93 — Vance, James Isaac, 1862-1939.
Papers, 1899-1941. ca. 3 ft. (600 items and 4 v.). Presbyterian minister and author. Correspondence and other writings, and scrapbooks composed of newspaper clippings, programs, notices, and other items relating to the history of the First Presbyterian Church, Nashville, Tenn., and the career of Vance as its pastor. Among correspondents is Booker T. Washington.

.94 — Whyte, Robert, 1767-1844.
Papers, 1755-1844. ca. 1200 items. Lawyer, judge, and plantation owner. Correspondence, account books, wills, indentures, agreements, briefs, notes, trial dockets and other legal documents, maps, clippings, and memorabilia. The correspondence is primarily of a legal nature but there are also family letters, letters on politics, and 22 letters relating to farm and plantation matters.

.95 — Williamson family.
Papers, 1833-74. 23 items (copies). Deeds, land grants, surveys, letters, notes, and legal documents, including deed of sale for a slave.

.96 — Winchester, James, 1752-1826.
Papers, 1787-1953. ca. 1000 items, 2 v. Includes letter of General William McIntosh mentioning that "a Regiment of Blacks sailed from Jamaica some time since for New Orleans."

.97 — Wood family.
Papers, 1833-64. 62 items (copies). Correspondence of the children of Felix Wood, Sr., and Lockey Adams Wood contains some data about the Negroes in Texas in 1864.

TN44   TENNESSEE STATE UNIVERSITY (1912), MARTHA M. BROWN MEMORIAL LIBRARY (1927). 3500 Centennial Blvd., 37203. Tel 615 242-4311. Miss Lois H. Daniel, Librn.

.1 Afro-American Studies Collection.
ca. 1000 paperbacks. Basic books on the life and history of black Americans.

.2 Tennessee State University (formerly Tennessee A & I University).
Archives, 1912- . Scattered materials, including student publications, the Faculty Journal, University bulletins, yearbooks, alumni publications, and other materials. Included is a complete run of the Broadcaster (1928- .), the official organ of the Tennessee Negro Education Association.

TN45   UNITED METHODIST BOARD OF EDUCATION, DIVISION OF HIGHER EDUCATION. Box 871, 37202. Tel 615 327-2727. Rev. Myron F. Wicke, Dir.

.1 Division of Higher Education.
Records. Included are minutes of board meetings, financial records, and other materials relating to the Division's support of the following predominantly black colleges: Bennett College, Greensboro, N.C.; Bethune-Cookman College, Daytona Beach, Fla.; Claflin College, Orangeburg, S.C.; Clark College, Atlanta, Ga.; Philander Smith College,

Little Rock, Ark.; Rust College, Holly Springs, Miss.; Wiley College, Marshall, Tex.; Morristown College, Morristown, Tenn.

TN46   VANDERBILT UNIVERSITY, RACE RELATIONS LAW SURVEY (1969). 37203. Tel 615 322-2856. T.A. Smedley, Dir.
The Survey consists of summaries of court decisions and occasional summaries of legislation and administrative rulings in which the issue of race and color is a significant factor. Formerly Race Relations Law Reporter (1955-69).
Publ.: Race Relations Law Survey, bimonthly.

.1   Race Relations Law Survey.
Records, 1956- . Correspondence, reports, studies, investigations, court decisions, administrative agency rulings, legislation, opinions of attorneys general, other materials concerning race relations and related issues. Also included is a complete set (12 v.) of former publication, Race Relations Law Reporter.

TN47   VANDERBILT UNIVERSITY, URBAN AND REGIONAL DEVELOPMENT CENTER (1967). Box 1516, Station B, 37203. Tel 615 322-3535. Dr. William Yancey, Dir.
Referrals made, consultation.
The Center concentrates on the long-term goals of research (understanding the nature of urban and regional development), education (improving the urban competence of students getting a Vanderbilt education, especially at the Ph.D. level and in the School of Law), and development (widespread dissemination of knowledge on urban processes and problems).

SEWANEE

TN48   UNIVERSITY OF THE SOUTH (1860), DUPONT LIBRARY. 37375. Tel 615 598-5931. William G. Harkins, Chief Librn. Interlibrary loan, copying.

.1   Quintard, Charles Todd, 1824-98.
Papers, 1862-98. 6 ft. Correspondence, diaries (36 v., 1864-98), clippings, and photos, including material on Reconstruction, the Protestant Episcopal Church and other denominations in the South, and other topics.

TEXAS

ARLINGTON

TX1   UNIVERSITY OF TEXAS, ARLINGTON STATE COLLEGE, LIBRARY (1917). 76010. Tel 817 275-3211. John A. Hudson, Librn.

.1   Facts on Film.
Papers, 1954-67. Microfilm. Contains materials on civil rights and race relations in the South. See Race Relations Information Center, Nashville, Tenn., for a full description.

AUSTIN

TX2   GOOD NEIGHBOR COMMISSION OF TEXAS (1947). P.O. Box 12116, 507 Sam Houston State Bldg., 78711. Tel 512 475-3581. Glenn E. Garrett, Exec. Dir.
The Commission is a permanent legislative agency established to conduct surveys and studies, receive, investigate, and initiate complaints, and establish education programs. The agency works in the areas of employment, housing, public accommodations, citizen migrants, and health facilities.

TX3   HUSTON-TILLOTSON COLLEGE, DOWNS-JONES LIBRARY. 1820 E. Eighth St., 78702. Tel 512 476-7421. Mrs. Olive D. Brown, Head Librn. Interlibrary loan, bibliographies prepared, literature searches, copying, inquiries, referrals made.

.1   Afro-American Heritage collection.
Materials, 17th century- . Microfilm. 131 reels. Books, newspapers, and mss concerning the Negro American and his history. See Minnesota Mining and Manufacturing Company, St. Paul, Minn., for a full description.

.2   Afro-American Studies Collection.
ca. 1000 paperbacks. Basic books on the life and history of black Americans.

.3   Huston-Tillotson College.
Archives, 1876- . Includes correspondence, minutes of the meetings of the board, records of admission, financial records, and other materials relating to the history of the College and the administration before and since the 1952 merger of Samuel Huston College (1876) and Tillotson College (1877).

TX4   SOUTHWEST EDUCATIONAL DEVELOPMENT LABORATORY (SEDL). 800 Brazos St., 78767. Tel 512 476-6861. Dr. Edwin Hindsman, Exec. Dir.
SEDL's region has three predominant subcultures with special educational needs: the Negro American, the French American, and the Mexican American. The major problem focus is intercultural education, and the Laboratory's 4 basic programs—Language Development/Bilingual Education, Multicultural Social Education, Mathematics Education, and Early Childhood Education—are concerned with developing instructional materials, staff development packages, parent-community involvement activities and learning ecology.
Publ.: Monographs concerning educational and social change.

TX5   TEXAS CIVIL LIBERTIES UNION. 1205-B E. 11th St., 78702. Tel 512 477-3478. Doran Williams, Exec. Dir.

TX6   TEXAS STATE LIBRARY, ARCHIVES DIVISION (1836). Archives and Library Bldg., Capitol Sta., 78711. Tel 512 457-2166. Dorman H. Winfrey, Dir. Copying, inquiries answered, consultation.
Publ.: A Preliminary Guide to the Archives of Texas.

.1   Newspaper Clippings Collection.
Newspaper clippings, ca. 19th and 20th centuries. ca. 100 cu. ft. Clippings on Texas politics and government since the 1920's. Materials cover such areas as race relations in education, housing, health and welfare, transportation, employment, Negroes, civil rights, and segregation and integration.

.2   Rouser, George. collector.
Papers on Reconstruction in Texas, 1860-84. 1 folder. Materials dealing with central Texas politics during Reconstruction, including correspondence, meeting notices, political bulletins, and newspapers. Includes a charter of the Knights of the White Camelia.

.3   State agencies.
Records. Included are records of state agencies of the Civil War and Reconstruction period; and 19th cent. education agency records showing teacher and pupil statistics.

TX7   U.S. EQUAL EMPLOYMENT OPPORTUNITY COMMISSION, AUSTIN REGIONAL OFFICE. 300 E. Eighth St., Room 574, 78701. Tel 512 475-5811. Lee G. Williams, Regional Dir.

TX8   UNIVERSITY OF TEXAS AT AUSTIN (1883), LIBRARY. 78712. Tel 512 471-3811. Fred Folmer, Univ. Librn. Interlibrary loan, copying, inquiries answered.

.1   Anti-Slavery Propaganda Collection.
ca. 2500 pamphlets. Microcards of originals located in the Oberlin College Library. See Oberlin College Library, Oberlin, Ohio; or Lost Cause Press (publisher), Louisville, Ky., for more complete description.

.2   Ballinger, William Pitt, 1825-88.
Papers, 1816-1900. 29 ft. Lawyer, and Confederate receiver at Galveston, Tex. Correspondence, letter press books, diaries (1854-86), news clippings, and other papers, including material on eco-

nomic, social and political aspects of Texas history from statehood through the Reconstruction. Correspondents include John Borden, Guy M. Bryan, James Harrison, Edmund Kirby Smith, Thomas F. McKinney, John B. Magruder, and Elisha Marshall Pease.

.3 Billingsley, James B., 1828-82.
Papers of James B. and Virginia Catherine Shaw Billingsley, 1843-1920. 4 ft. Planter of Marlin, Tex. Personal and business correspondence, diaries (1872-74), legal papers, and plantation account book (1856-94). Among other items are papers of Billingsley and his wife, Virginia Catherine Shaw Billingsley.

.4 Bryan, Moses Austin, 1817-95.
Papers, 1824-95. 1 ft. Soldier, diplomat, and veterans' leader. Correspondence, bills of sale and deeds for land, bills, receipts, a memorandum book (1832), and other papers, including material on slaves, money, and the Peach Point Plantation in Brazoria County. Correspondents include Barnard Bee and Gail Borden (1801-74).

.5 Cartwright, Matthew, 1807-70.
Papers, 1831-71. 3 ft. Merchant, farmer, and land dealer. Correspondence with Cartwright's cotton factors, principally in New Orleans, concerning cotton growing and Negroes; 17 account books of his sales and purchases, including a few of his contracts; bills and receipts; a few legal papers on the sale of slaves; a biographical sketch; and printed material.

.6 Chambers, Thomas W., d. 1855.
Papers, 1824-95. 770 items. Planter, of Bastrop, Tex. Correspondence of Chambers (1837-55) and of his wife Margaret (1856-95), bills, receipts, other financial papers, legal papers, and printed material, concerning sale of cotton, slaves and land, other business matters, and personal affairs. Correspondents include Gail Borden (1801-74), Thomas Jefferson Chambers, W.P. Chambers, and William Fields.

.7 Decherd, Mary.
Papers, 1887-1946. ca. 850 items. Educator, librarian, and church worker. Among other papers are correspondence (1915-31) with the Board of Missions of the Methodist Episcopal Church, South, and publications of the Methodist Church and humanitarian societies concerning Negroes, sharecroppers, and related subjects.

.8 Duckworth, J.D.W.
Duckworth-Smith-McPherson papers, 1835-85. 73 items. Correspondence, land papers, certificates, and other papers of Duckworth, Dr. O.G. McPherson, and Jordan Smith, and their wives; and a will (1850) of Mrs. Francis Smith. Includes material on personal affairs, social and economic conditions, land, and Negroes, in Harris, Travis, Bastrop, and other Texas counties, and in Kentucky and Mississippi.

.9 Duncan, Green C.
Papers, 1853-1910. 324 items. Planter, stock raiser, and legislator, of Wharton Co., Tex. Duncan's personal correspondence (largely before 1871), business correspondence (1871-1907), diaries of Duncan (1865), financial papers comprising account books (1865-1901), bills, receipts, a cotton book, and John B. Walker's plantation book (1861-64). Among other papers are items on stock raising and planting (especially during the late Reconstruction period), on Duncan's reaction to south central Texas, and on his experiences as legislator and as a Civil War prisoner at Johnson's Island.

.10 Facts on Film.
Papers, 1954-67. Microfilm. Contains materials on civil rights and race relations in the South. See Race Relations Information Center, Nashville, Tenn., for a full description.

.11 Frazor family.
Papers, 1784-1911. 50 items. Account books, cotton and slave records, bills, receipts, Confederate bond issues with coupons attached, notes, tax receipts, legal documents, and other papers. Persons mentioned are T.D. Frazor, Moses B. Frazor, and Daniel Frazor (d. 1819).

.12 Fulmore, Zachary Taylor, 1846-1923.
Papers, 1735-1911. 735 items. Soldier, lawyer, public official, and author. Correspondence, legal documents, a few tax statements and promissory notes, cancelled envelopes, notes, newspaper clippings relating to the administration of estates, and circulars published by the Colored Knights of Pythias, of which Fulmore was secretary. Most of the letters (1880-1911) were written to Fulmore as a lawyer in Austin, Tex., and cover such subjects as litigation, land, legal advice and questions, personal matters, cement, electric railways, genealogy, Texas history, and publications. Two letters written in 1735 concern a French fort in Spanish Territory. The letters from 1840-65 deal with land, money and business in Texas. The legal documents (chiefly after 1880) include powers of attorney, wills, land titles, court summons, contracts and land surveys.

.13 Glasgow family.
Papers, 1795-1889. ca. 1 ft. Correspondence, account books, cancelled checks, bills, receipts, invoice books, legal documents, literary material, and other papers of the Alexander M. Glasgow family, planters of Virginia. Most of the correspondence deals with tobacco, slavery, farming, land, and money. The legal documents include court summons, indentures, wills, contracts, bills of sale (of Negroes and land), and papers relating to litigation and estates. The literary material consists of essays and speeches, mostly by James B. Dorman, dealing with the condition of the U.S., problems of the South, the position of women, politics, and songs about the Civil War. Among other papers are minutes (1856) of the board of directors of the American Colonization Society relating to a colony in Liberia.

.14 Graham, Edwin S., 1831-99.
Papers, 1825-1917. ca. 2 ft. Land agent and businessman. Correspondence (1857-95), diaries (1870-72), reminiscences, daybooks, account books, tax receipts, bills, inventories, cancelled checks, legal documents, newspaper clippings, articles, broadsides, and calling cards. The legal documents include bills of sale of land and Negroes, indentures, deeds, and papers relating to litigation.

.15 Green, Thomas Jefferson, 1801-63.
Papers, 1780-1872. ca. 150 items. Planter, legislator, and soldier of North Carolina. Correspondence; documents, and notes on the Yazoo Land Company; deeds for Negroes; drafts of appointments, and pamphlets. The correspondence, largely 1835-36, concerns business, national politics, the land question, and personal matters.

.16 Groce family.
Papers, 1824-71. ca. 80 items. Correspondence, legal documents, and accounts. The legal documents (chiefly 1824-41) include deeds to land, and bills of sale. Bound with the transcript of a diary (1866-67) containing material on trading, the care of slaves, and the raising and shipping of cotton, is an inventory of Jared E. Groce's slaves. Other persons represented include C.A. Groce (Mrs. Leonard W. Groce), and Leonard Waller Groce.

CANYON

TX9   WEST TEXAS STATE UNIVERSITY, LIBRARY (1910). Box 748, WT Sta., 79015. Tel 806 655-7141. Francis M. Blackburn, Librn.

.1 Anti-Slavery Propaganda Collection.
ca. 2500 pamphlets. Microcards of originals located in the Oberlin College Library. See Oberlin College Library, Oberlin, Ohio; or Lost Cause Press (publisher), Louisville, Ky., for more complete description.

COLLEGE STATION

TX10   TEXAS A&M UNIVERSITY (1876), LIBRARY (1880). 77843. Tel 713 845-6111. John B. Smith, Acting Dir. of Libraries. Interlibrary loan, copying, typing, inquiries answered, referrals made.

.1 Ku Klux Klan Collection.
Materials. ca. 250 items. Books, broadsides, microfilm, phonograph records, newspaper clippings, and other papers, dealing with all phases of the Klan's activity.

CROCKETT

TX11 MARY ALLEN JUNIOR COLLEGE, LIBRARY (1885). 75835. Tel 713 544-2934. Mrs. Mildred David, Librn.

.1 Mary Allen Junior College.
Archives, 1885- .

DALLAS

TX12 AMERICAN JEWISH COMMITTEE, SOUTHWESTERN REGION. 1809 Tower Petroleum Bldg., 75201. Tel 214 747-3531. Gustave Falk, Regional Dir.

TX13 ANTI-DEFAMATION LEAGUE OF B'NAI B'RITH, DALLAS REGIONAL OFFICE. 908 Praetorium Bldg., 75201. Tel 214 742-5708. Joseph S. Gordesky, Dir.

TX14 BISHOP COLLEGE (1881), ZALE LIBRARY (1900). 3837 Simpson-Stuart Rd., 75241. Tel 214 376-4311. George T. Johnson, Chief Librn. Interlibrary loan, copying, referrals made.

.1 Afro-American Heritage collection.
Materials, 17th century- . Microfilm. 131 reels. Books, newspapers, and mss concerning the Negro American and his history. See Minnesota Mining and Manufacturing Company, St. Paul, Minn., for a full description.

.2 Afro-American Studies Collection.
ca. 1000 paperbacks. Basic books on the life and history of black Americans.

TX15 DALLAS PUBLIC LIBRARY. 1954 Commerce, 75201. Tel 214 741-9071. Mrs. Lillian M. Bradshaw, Dir. Interlibrary loan, copying, typing, inquiries answered, referrals made.

.1 Hill, William Ely, 1886-1962. collector.
W.E. Hill theatre collection, 18th-20th centuries. ca. 75,000 items. Letters, portraits, and photos of leading American, British, and European dramatists, actors, managers, and other persons associated with the stage or the performing arts; playbills; posters of stage plays, minstrel shows, and circuses; and newspaper and magazine clippings. The bulk of the collection consists of 19th and 20th century items.

TX16 DeGOLYER FOUNDATION LIBRARY (1957). Box 399, SMU Sta., 75222. Tel 214 363-6002. Everett L. DeGolyer, Jr., Secy. of DeGolyer Found. Typing, inquiries answered, consultation.
The Foundation Library is a research library in the history of the west and business and transportation history. It houses rare books in the field; provides reference and research facilities for students, residents of surrounding areas, and scholars across the nation; and provides detailed information in the chosen areas of concentration.

.1 Civil War Collection.
Papers. Materials on naval history and on campaigns in western states, histories of western states regiments, mss of naval logs, and Dahlgren scrapbook.

.2 Labor Collection.
Papers. Materials on labor problems in western and Mexican history; railroad, maritime and mining unions; strikes, lockouts, and the Haymarket riot.

TX17 NATIONAL ASSOCIATION FOR THE ADVANCEMENT OF COLORED PEOPLE (NAACP), REGION VI. Room 107-8, 2600 Flora St., 75204. Tel 214 747-0057. Richard Dockery, Regional Dir.

TX18 NATIONAL CONFERENCE OF CHRISTIANS AND JEWS (NCCJ). 1805 Elm St., 75201. Tel 214 741-5694. William H. Tipton, Jr., V.Pres. and Dir.

TX19 TEXAS ASSOCIATION OF DEVELOPING COLLEGES (1966). 926 Exchange Bank Tower, 75325. Tel 241 258-1591. William B. Rogers, Pres.
The Association was formed by six privately supported four-year predominantly Negro colleges as a cooperative self-help agency to share limited resources and achieve economies through joint endeavors in the areas of curriculum development, reduction of overlapping courses, joint faculty appointments, pooled purchasing, training workshops for administrators, sharing library resources, and joint fund-raising. Member colleges include: Bishop College, Dallas, Tex.; Huston-Tillotson College, Austin, Tex.; Jarvis Christian College, Hawkins, Tex.; Paul Quinn College, Waco, Tex.; Texas College, Tyler, Tex.; and Wiley College, Marshall, Tex.

TX20 U.S. DEPARTMENT OF HEALTH, EDUCATION, AND WELFARE; REGIONAL OFFICE, OFFICE FOR CIVIL RIGHTS. 1114 Commerce St., 75202. Tel 214 749-3301. Carl Flaxman, Regional Dir. Inquiries answered, consultation.
The Regional Office for Civil Rights, covering Arkansas, Louisiana, New Mexico, Oklahoma, and Texas, is responsible for assuring compliance with Title VI of the Civil Rights Act of 1964 and for assuring equal employment opportunity and nondiscrimination. It is primarily concerned with the areas of elementary, secondary and higher education; state agencies of health, education, and welfare; certification of hospitals for Medicare and of contractors having contracts with the Department of Health, Education, and Welfare.

TX21 URBAN LEAGUE OF GREATER DALLAS. 2606 Forest Ave., 75215. Tel 214 421-5361. Roosevelt Johnson, Jr., Exec. Dir. Referrals made, consultation.
The League carries on a program of social services among minority group persons; works in coordination and cooperation with existing agencies for improving economic welfare of minorities; makes studies of economic conditions among minorities; conducts a program of public education among white and Negro persons to develop more sympathetic understanding; seeks to maintain harmonious race relationships; and in general promotes and assists in work for improving economic conditions among minorities in the Dallas area. Publ.: Newsletter.

.1 Urban League of Greater Dallas.
Files. Records, reports, correspondence, and other papers concerning the aims and activities of the organization.

DENTON

TX22 NORTH TEXAS STATE UNIVERSITY, LIBRARY. 76203. Tel 817 387-4511. David A. Webb, Dir. of Libraries.

.1 Facts on Film.
Papers, 1954-67. Microfilm. Contains materials on civil rights and race relations in the South. See Race Relations Information Center, Nashville, Tenn., for a full description.

EL PASO

TX23 NATIONAL CONFERENCE OF CHRISTIANS AND JEWS (NCCJ), REGIONAL OFFICE. 1900 N. Oregon St., 79902. Tel 915 532-6637. Mrs. Mary Ponce, Regional Dir.

TX23a UPTIGHT MAGAZINE (1969). P.O. Box 2075, 79951. Z.E. Kumo, Editor and publisher.
"Uptight is an opinion magazine dedicated to an authentic point of view, and to the discovery of young and gifted writers and poets." It is "particularly interested in printing the works of black and other Third World writers whose material issue from an experience too long neglected by American publications."
Publ.: Uptight.

FORT DAVIS

TX24 FORT DAVIS NATIONAL HISTORIC SITE (ca. 1854). State Highway 17, 79734. Tel 915 426-3225. Franklin G. Smith, Supt.

The Site was a headquarters for Negro cavalrymen during the Indian wars. Housed in an 1869 reconstructed barrack, the Museum displays artifacts about and used by Negro "Buffalo Soldiers." Henry O. Flipper, the first Negro graduate of West Point, was ordered here in 1880 from Fort Sill, Okla., to campaign against Chief Victorio and the Mescalero Apache. The Site is under the direction of the National Park Service, U.S. Department of the Interior.

.1 Fort Davis National Historic Site.
   Collection of military records and photographs, 1854-91. These materials date to the period when Negro "Buffalo Soldiers" and other U.S. troops served here.

FORT WORTH

TX25 NATIONAL CONFERENCE OF CHRISTIANS AND JEWS (NCCJ), REGIONAL OFFICE. 1801 TWC-Electric Bldg., 76102. Tel 817 332-3271. Anne J. Scribner, Regional Dir. Typing, inquiries answered, referrals made, consultation.
The NCCJ conducts multi-faceted programs to educate the American public in human relations, seeking to instill commitment to the values of brotherhood.
Publ.: Pamphlets, books, articles, and reprints in the area of human relations.

TX25a SEPIA PUBLISHING COMPANY. 1220 Harding St., 76102. Tel 817 332-3313. Robert Darby, Editor.
Publ.: Sepia, monthly magazine.

.1 Sepia Publishing Company.
   Files. Correspondence, financial records, and other materials dealing with the activities of the Company and the publication of Sepia.

TX26 U.S. DEPARTMENT OF HOUSING AND URBAN DEVELOPMENT, REGION V. 819 Taylor St., 76102. Tel 817 334-2867. William W. Collins, Adminstr.

GALVESTON

TX27 ROSENBERG LIBRARY (1904). 823 Tremont, 77550. Tel 713 763-8854. John Hyatt, Librn. Interlibrary loan, copying, inquiries answered, referrals made.

.1 Affleck, Thomas, 1812-68.
   Papers, 1847-66. ca. 10 items. Planter, of Glen Blythe plantation, near Brenham, Tex. Clippings, circular letter, typescripts, photostats and photographs. Includes material pertaining to slavery.
.2 Ballinger, William Pitt, 1825-88.
   Papers, 1835-97. ca. 40 items and 26 v. Lawyer, of Galveston, Tex. Family correspondence, diaries, business papers, notebooks, and law license. Included are papers concerning slaves.
.3 Borden, Gail, 1801-74.
   Papers, 1832-82. 290 items. Surveyor and inventor. Correspondence and other papers relating to Borden's personal and family affairs, slaves and slavery, Texas land properties, and his estate.
.4 Darragh, John L., ca. 1797-1893.
   Papers, 1839-93. ca. 2100 items. Lawyer and real estate dealer, of Galveston, Tex. Business papers, deeds to property in Galveston, Tex., and papers on slave trade.
.5 Dobbins, Archibald S., 1827-ca. 1870.
   Papers, 1852-69. 46 items. Planter, Phillips County, Ark., and Mississippi; Commander, Dobbin's 1st Arkansas Calvary Brigade, C.S.A., 1862-65; Commission merchant in New Orleans (1866); refugee to Santarem, Brazil (1867-?). Letters, land deeds, will, photographs, and research paper on Dobbins. One letter concerns plans to transport his slaves to Mexico or Cuba, and some items deal with his attempts to arrange native labor in Brazil.
.6 Dyer, Joseph Osterman, 1856-1925.
   Papers, 1815-1915. Mss (324 pp.), 2 scrapbooks. Galveston, Tex., physician and local historian/collector. Includes materials on Negroes.
.7 Fellows, George.
   Papers, 1844. 1 item. Letter dated October, 1844,

Galveston, to Rev. Isaac Sawyer, mentioning treatment of Negroes and feelings about slavery.
.8 Franklin, Isaac.
   Paper, 1832. 1 item. Bill of sale for slave girl, May 10, 1832, Natchez, Miss.
.9 Freedman's Bureau.
   Papers, 1865-68. Records of U.S. War Department, Bureau of Refugees, Freedmen, and Abandoned Lands, Texas Headquarters, Galveston. Includes records, circulars, acts, general orders concerning treatment, payment and work of former slaves.
.10 Grover, George W., 1819-1901.
   Papers, 1824-96. ca. 100 items and 6 v. Businessman, politician, and soldier, of Galveston, Tex. Business correspondence, ms on Galveston history written by Grover, scrapbooks, and papers pertaining to slave trade.
.11 Kauffman, Julius, d. 1913.
   Papers, 1834-79. ca. 50 items. Galveston merchant. Business records, including 1 item relating to sale of slave, 1859.
.12 League, Thomas Massie.
   Papers, 1830-50's. ca. 15 items. Galveston merchant. Includes letters to his son, Thomas Jefferson League, some of which pertain to slavery, and a receipt record.
.13 Lockhart, John Washington, 1824-1900.
   Papers, 1830-1918. ca. 750 items and 22 v. Confederate Army surgeon, agriculturist, and businessman, of Galveston, Tex. Correspondence, diaries, business journal, deeds, receipts, clippings, and other papers, together with Confederate bonds, currency, and muster rolls. Includes letters relating to Lockhart's service in the Civil War, and slave trade.
.14 Morgan, James, 1786-1866.
   Papers, 1809-80. 1095 items. Officer in the Texas Revolution, merchant, and farmer. Correspondence, personal and family papers, including bills, receipts, and papers dealing with slave trade.
.15 Porter, Clyde H.
   Papers, 1816- . 1 v. Looseleaf scrapbook of typescripts and photostats relating to the Dresel family, early immigrants to Texas and merchants of Houston-Galveston. Contains references to slavery.
.16 Rosenberg, Henry, 1824-93.
   Papers, 1845-1907. ca. 4600 items. Swiss consul, merchant banker, and philanthropist, of Galveston, Tex. Diaries, account books, business papers, and papers relating to Rosenberg's benefactions and his estate. Included are Mrs. Mollie Rosenberg's papers on slaves.
.17 Stuart, Ben C., 1847-1929.
   Papers, 1870-1921. ca. 180 items and 10 v. Journalist and historian, of Texas. Mss of writings on Texas history, miscellaneous papers, and scrapbooks of newspaper articles. Includes items on slave trade.
.18 Thompson, Isham.
   Papers, 1830-75. 37 items. Planter. Papers relate to Thompson's estate and business affairs. Included are letters, abstracts, deeds, and bill of sale for slave (1843, Washington, Tex.).
.19 Trueheart, Henry Martyn, 1832-1914.
   Papers of Charles W. Trueheart and Henry Martyn Trueheart, 1839-1905. ca. 350,000 items. Realtor, of Galveston, Tex. Personal correspondence, memoirs of H.M. Trueheart and business account books. Includes material relating to the military service of the Trueheart brothers in Civil War, and slave trade.
.20 Wallis, Joseph Edmund.
   Papers of Joseph Edmund Wallis and John C. Wallis, 1818-99. ca. 300 items. Operator of a wholesale grocery and dry goods store, of Galveston, Tex. Family correspondence and business papers. Includes material relating to the Wallis brothers' service in the Civil War, social events of Galveston, and slaves.
.21 Williams, Austin May, b. 1835?
   Papers, 1853-61. 204 items. Son of Samuel May Williams, developer (lumber mill) on father's land in Bastrop Co., Tex. Business records, letters to

his wife and family, and other papers. Includes references to Negroes.

.22 Williams, Samuel May, 1795-1858.
Papers, 1819-65. ca. 4100 items. Pioneer of Austin's colony, merchant, and banker, of Galveston, Tex. Correspondence, bills, receipts, promissory notes, accounts, and other papers. Included are papers on slavery.

.23 Williams, William Howell, b. 1833?.
Papers, 1854-60. ca. 300 items. Son of Samuel May Williams; Galveston attorney and district judge. Papers relate to legal business and electioneering. Includes some mention of the Negro.

HAWKINS

TX28 JARVIS CHRISTIAN COLLEGE (1912), OLIN LIBRARY AND COMMUNICATION CENTER (1912). 75765. Tel 214 769-2841. Doris P. Rutherford, Dir. Interlibrary loan, copying, inquiries answered.

.1 Afro-American Studies Collection.
ca. 1000 paperbacks. Basic books on the life and history of black Americans.

.2 Negro collection.
Books (ca. 1000 v.) and other materials on such subjects as slavery, civil rights, Negro literature and Negro history.

HOUSTON

TX29 AMERICAN JEWISH COMMITTEE, HOUSTON AREA (1906). 817 Main St., 77002. Tel 713 228-0159. Milton Feiner, Area Dir. Inquiries answered.

TX30 ANTI-DEFAMATION LEAGUE OF B'NAI B'RITH, HOUSTON REGIONAL OFFICE. Suite 101, 3033 Fannin, 77004. Tel 713 524-3943. Theodore Freedman, Regional Dir. Consultation.
ADL, through its regional office of trained personnel in the field of human relations, combats anti-Semitism and all prejudice. It works to secure justice and fair treatment for all citizens and to end discrimination against any sect or body of citizens.
Publ.: Bibliographies, resource materials on new methods of teaching and meeting the needs of minorities, and pamphlets and studies in the area of human relations and black history.

.1 Anti-Defamation League of B'nai B'rith, Houston Regional Office.
Files. Materials on human relations activities, including desegregation, discrimination and extremist activities and organizations in South Texas, based on first-hand reports and summaries; and material on trends, projects and theory in the human relations field. Restricted.

TX31 HOUSTON AREA URBAN LEAGUE. 3531 Wheeler, 77004. Tel 713 526-5127. Theodore M. Hogrobrooks, Pres.

.1 Houston Area Urban League.
Files. Records, reports, correspondence, and other papers concerning the aims and activities of the organization.

TX32 HOUSTON COUNCIL ON HUMAN RELATIONS (1958). 3505 Main St., 77002. Tel 713 526-1829. Roger D. Armstrong, Exec. Dir.
The Council is a private agency that works for equality in Houston in the areas of crime correction, voter education, community organization, labor education, social attitudes, employment, education, human relations education, housing and similar instances where discrimination may occur. It is affiliated with the Southern Regional Council, Inc., of Atlanta, Ga.
Publ.: News-Letter, monthly.

.1 Houston Council on Human Relations.
Files, 1958- . Documentation dealing with the aims, programs and history of the Council. Includes correspondence, reports, studies, investigations, minutes of meetings and financial records.

TX33 HOUSTON PUBLIC LIBRARY. 500 McKinney Ave., Julia Ideson Bldg., Civic Center, 77002. Tel 713 224-5441. David M. Henington, Dir. Interlibrary loan, copying, inquiries answered.

.1 Afro-American Heritage collection.
Materials, 17th century- . Microfilm. 131 reels. Books, newspapers, and mss concerning the Negro American and his history. See Minnesota Mining and Manufacturing Company, St. Paul, Minn., for a full description.

.2 Circle M Collection.
Materials. ca. 1000 items. Publications of the Civil War period, including books, pamphlets, and official records.

TX34 NATIONAL CONFERENCE OF CHRISTIANS AND JEWS (NCCJ), REGIONAL OFFICE. 405 Main St., 77002. Tel 713 228-5081. Philip N. Libby, Jr., Dir.

TX35 RICE UNIVERSITY, CENTER FOR RESEARCH IN SOCIAL CHANGE AND ECONOMIC DEVELOPMENT (1966). 6100 Main, 77005. Tel 713 528-4141. Dr. Fred von der Mehden, Dir. of the Center. Consultation.
The Center was established at Rice University to facilitate research in the study of social change, and emphasizes social change associated with economic development. Research projects, planned by social scientists and approved by the Council of the Center, include a study of Negro social psychology in the U.S.
Publ.: Books and reports resulting from the research projects of the Center, on such subjects as violence, Negro ghetto life styles, and Negro politics in Houston, Tex.

TX36 RICE UNIVERSITY (1912), FONDREN LIBRARY (1912). P.O. Box 1892, 77001. Tel 713 528-4141. Richard L. O'Keefe, Librn. Interlibrary loan, copying.

.1 Anti-Slavery Propaganda Collection.
ca. 2500 pamphlets. Microcards of originals located in the Oberlin College Library. See Oberlin College Library, Oberlin, Ohio; or Lost Cause Press (publisher), Louisville, Ky., for more complete description.

TX37 TEXAS SOUTHERN UNIVERSITY (1947), LIBRARY. 3201 Wheeler St., 77004. Tel 713 528-0611. S. W. Mothershed, Librn. Interlibrary loan, literature searches, copying, typing, inquiries answered.

.1 Afro-American Studies Collection.
ca. 1000 paperbacks. Basic books on the life and history of black Americans.

.2 Biggers, John, 1924- .
Paintings. Artist. Includes murals representing his "social realism" and surrealism specialities.

.3 Facts on Film.
Papers, 1954-67. Microfilm. Contains materials on civil rights and race relations in the South. See Race Relations Information Center, Nashville, Tenn., for a full description.

.4 Heartman Negro Collection.
Materials, ca. 1600- . ca. 16,000 items. Collected by Charles Heartman, book dealer. Books, periodicals, pamphlets, music scores, broadsides, clippings, and other materials concerning the background and development of Negro people, their contribution to world progress, and their impact on world culture. Included are personal accounts and retrospective information pertaining to Negroes in the U.S. and in other parts of the world where Negroes have lived in concentrated numbers.

.5 Texas Southern University.
Archives, 1947- .

TX38 UNIVERSITY OF HOUSTON (1934), M.D. ANDERSON MEMORIAL LIBRARY (1949). 77004. Tel 713 748-6600. Dr. Edward G. Holley, Dir. of Libraries. Interlibrary loan, bibliographies prepared, literature searches, copying, typing, inquiries answered, referrals made, consultation.

.1 Facts on Film.
Papers, 1954-67. Microfilm. Contains materials on civil rights and race relations in the South. See

Race Relations Information Center, Nashville, Tenn., for a full description.

.2   Materials relating to Negroes.
Included are monographs on black history, theatre, and literature; complete runs (on microfilm) of the Houston Forward Times and Informer, and the Dallas Express; complete run of Crisis; and materials (on microfilm) concerning the Houston race riots of 1917.

LUBBOCK

TX39   TEXAS TECHNOLOGICAL UNIVERSITY (1925), LIBRARY (1925). Box 4079, 79407. Tel 806 742-2262. R.C. Janeway, Librn. Interlibrary loan, copying, inquiries answered, consultation.

.1   Anti-Slavery Propaganda Collection.
ca. 2500 pamphlets. Microcards of originals located in the Oberlin College Library. See Oberlin College Library, Oberlin, Ohio; or Lost Cause Press (publisher), Louisville, Ky., for more complete description.

.2   Biggers, Don Hampton, 1868-1957.
Papers, 1919-57. 2 ft. (500 items). Journalist and politician. Correspondence (1919-57), scrapbooks, newspaper clippings, photos, and samples of Biggers' writings including broadsides, pamphlets, and other material. Contains material relating to Elijah L. Shettles, James E. Ferguson, and the Ku Klux Klan.

.3   Lovejoy, Elijah P.
Papers, 1804-91. Editor and abolitionist, of Missouri, and Illinois. Materials pertaining to Lovejoy's career and his family.

MARSHALL

TX40   WILEY COLLEGE (1873), THOMAS WINSTON COLE, SR., LIBRARY (1898). 711 Rosborough Springs Rd., 75670. Tel 214 934-4761. Herman L. Totten, Librn. Interlibrary loan, bibliographies prepared, literature searches, copying, typing, inquiries answered, referrals made, consultation.

.1   Afro-American Heritage collection.
Materials, 17th century- . Microfilm. 131 reels. Books, newspapers, and mss concerning the Negro American and his history. See Minnesota Mining and Manufacturing Company, St. Paul, Minn., for a full description.

.2   Afro-American Studies Collection.
ca. 1000 paperbacks. Basic books on the life and history of black Americans.

.3   Wiley College.
Archives, 1873- .

PRAIRIE VIEW

TX41   PRAIRIE VIEW AGRICULTURAL AND MECHANICAL COLLEGE, W. R. BANKS LIBRARY (1912). 77445. Tel 713 857-3311. O.J. Baker, Librn.

.1   Afro-American Studies Collection.
ca. 1000 paperbacks. Basic books on the life and history of black Americans.

.2   Facts on Film.
Papers, 1954-67. Microfilm. Contains materials on civil rights and race relations in the South. See Race Relations Information Center, Nashville, Tenn., for a full description.

.3   Prairie View Agricultural and Mechanical College.
Archives, 1912- . Includes correspondence, minutes of board meetings, financial records, records of admission, and other materials relating to the history and administration of the College.

SAN ANTONIO

TX42   NATIONAL CONFERENCE OF CHRISTIANS AND JEWS (NCCJ), REGIONAL OFFICE. 118 Broadway, 78205. Tel 512 226-7761. W. Charles Mallory, Dir.

TX43   ST. PHILIP'S COLLEGE (1927), LIBRARY (1927). 2111 Nevada St., 78203. Tel 512 532-4211. Julia H. Taylor, Librn.

.1   St. Philip's College.
Archives, 1927- . Materials pertaining to the founding of the College, correspondence, and other items relating to the Negro.

TX44   U.S. COMMISSION ON CIVIL RIGHTS, SOUTHWEST FIELD OFFICE. Room 249, New Moore Bldg., 106 Broadway, 78205. Tel 512 223-6821. J. Richard Avena, Dir.
The Southwest Field Office covers the states of Colorado, New Mexico, Oklahoma, Texas, and Arkansas.

SAN JUAN

TX45   UNITED FARM WORKERS ORGANIZING COMMITTEE, AFL-CIO. P.O. Box 54, 78589. Tel 512 487-2995. Antonio Orendain, Exec. Dir.
The Committee represents farm laborers and packers for collective bargaining purposes. Its concentration is in the areas of civil rights and poverty.
Publ.: El Malcriado (official union publication).

SAN MARCOS

TX46   SOUTHWEST TEXAS STATE COLLEGE, LIBRARY. 78666. Tel 512 245-2111. Louis C. Moloney, Librn. Interlibrary loan, bibliographies prepared, literature searches, copying, typing, inquiries answered, referrals made, consultation.

.1   Facts on Film.
Papers, 1954-67. Microfilm. Contains materials on civil rights and race relations in the South. See Race Relations Information Center, Nashville, Tenn., for a full description.

TERRELL

TX47   SOUTHWESTERN CHRISTIAN COLLEGE, LIBRARY (1948). 200 Bridge St., 75160. Tel 214 563-3341. Mrs. Doris Johnson, Librn.

.1   Negro Life and History Collection.
Books (ca. 60) by and about Negroes in the areas of history and literature.

.2   Southwestern Christian College.
Archives.

TYLER

TX48   BUTLER COLLEGE (1905), LIBRARY. Bellwood Rd., 75701. Tel 214 593-3541. John H. Williams, Pres.

.1   Butler College.
Archives, 1905- .

TX49   TEXAS COLLEGE (1894), D.R. GLASS LIBRARY (1894). 75701. Tel 214 593-8311. Emma Patterson, Dir. Interlibrary loan, bibliographies prepared, literature searches, copying, typing, inquiries answered, referrals made, consultation.

.1   Afro-American Studies Collection.
ca. 1000 paperbacks. Basic books on the life and history of black Americans.

.2   Banks Collection.
Papers. Former president of Texas College. Included are correspondence, books, and other items.

.3   Negro Collection.
Miscellaneous. Includes books, photographs, clippings, pamphlets, manuscripts, and correspondence.

WACO

TX50   BAYLOR UNIVERSITY (1845), TEXAS HISTORY COLLECTION (1923). P.O. Box 6396, 76706. Tel 817 753-4511. Guy Bryan Harrison, Dir. Inquiries answered, consultation.

.1 Ku Klux Klan.
Records, 1940-60. 20 ft. Records of the Aryan Knights of the Ku Klux Klan, of Waco, Tex. Includes name of H.S. Sherman.

TX51 PAUL QUINN COLLEGE (1872), SHERMAN-ABINGTON LIBRARY. 1020 Elm St., 76704. Tel 817 754-5627. Mrs. Dolores P. Harris, Librn.

.1 Afro-American Studies Collection.
ca. 1000 paperbacks. Basic books on the life and history of black Americans.
.2 Paul Quinn College.
Archives, 1872- . Includes correspondence, financial records, minutes of board meetings, records of admission, and other materials relating to the history and administration of the College.

TX52 WACO-McLENNAN COUNTY LIBRARY, EAST SIDE BRANCH. 1011 E. Live Oak St., 76701. Tel 817 753-6044.

.1 Negro History Collection.

UTAH

SALT LAKE CITY

UT1 AMERICAN CIVIL LIBERTIES UNION (ACLU), UTAH AFFILIATE. 1151 Michigan Ave., 84105. Tel 801 466-1344. Dr. Richard G. Henson, Interim Pres.

UT2 INDUSTRIAL COMMISSION OF UTAH, ANTI-DISCRIMINATION DIVISION (1965). Room 418, State Capitol Bldg., 84114. Tel 801 328-5552. John R. Schone, Coordinator. The Commission works to eliminate discrimination in employment by investigating complaints, holding hearings, making studies, and issuing reports of their findings.

.1 Industrial Commission of Utah, Anti-Discrimination Division.
Files, 1965- . Correspondence, clippings, reports, speeches and writings, ephemera, minutes and financial records, and related items about the Commission's activities.

UT3 UNIVERSITY OF UTAH (1850), LIBRARIES (1874). 84112. Tel 801 322-7270. Richard W. Boss, Acting Dir. of Libraries. Interlibrary loan, bibliographies prepared, literature searches, copying, typing, inquiries answered, referrals made, consultation.

.1 Anti-Slavery Propaganda Collection.
ca. 2500 pamphlets. Microcards of originals located in the Oberlin College Library. See Oberlin College Library, Oberlin, Ohio; or Lost Cause Press (publisher), Louisville, Ky., for more complete description.

VERMONT

BURLINGTON

VT1 AMERICAN CIVIL LIBERTIES UNION (ACLU) OF VERMONT. 14 Beech St., 05701. Tel 802 658-0196.

FERRISBURG

VT2 ROWLAND E. ROBINSON MEMORIAL ASSOCIATION (1937). General Delivery, 05456.
The Association maintains and operates an abolition museum (opened 1963).

MONTPELIER

VT3 VERMONT HISTORICAL SOCIETY (1838). 05602. Tel 802 223-2311. Miss Grace Quimby, Librn. Interlibrary

loan, copying, inquiries answered, referrals made, consultation, reference assistance.

.1 Johnson, Oliver.
Papers, 1861-89. 95 items. Anti-slavery leader, newspaper editor of New York and Pennsylvania.
.2 Miscellaneous materials.
Papers concerning Vermonters involved in race relations in national affairs.
.3 Papers of anti-slavery societies.
Records, 1834-47. 4 v. Minutes of four Vermont anti-slavery societies.
.4 Smith, William Farrar, 1824-1903.
Papers, 1863-1902. ca. 2 ft. Army Officer. Correspondence, clippings, diaries, travel brochures, documents, sketches, G.A.R. resolutions, autobiographical and biographical material, scrapbook, maps of Chattanooga, Tenn. (1865), and other papers relating to the Civil War, Smith's visit to Spain in 1889, Gen. Grant's habits, Smith and Montgomery Blair, and personal affairs.

OLD BENNINGTON

VT4 BENNINGTON HISTORICAL MUSEUM AND ART GALLERY (1927). W. Main St., 05201. Tel 802 442-2180. Allen D. Hill, Librn.
The Museum collects and preserves items related to the history of Vermont and surrounding areas.

.1 Abolitionist newspapers.
Newspapers. Copies of William Lloyd Garrison's papers, The Journal of the Times and The Liberator, which project his convictions and reflections on slavery in the U.S.
.2 Schwartz, William Tefft.
Painting. Painter, of Arlington, Vt. Mural of Lemuel Haynes preaching in the pulpit of Old First Church.

VIRGINIA

ALEXANDRIA

VA1 THE GREAT STATECRAFT PROPAGANDA AND AGITATION SERVICE. Suite 201, 3515 Mount Vernon Ave., 22305. Tel 703 548-7251. Daniel Paulson, Publisher. "We are an affiliation of patriotic action groups. The specific purpose of these public safety committees is to combat the spread of Communist created anarchy and savagery." The Service works "for patriotic recruiting and organization, for anti-Communist propaganda and agitation and for physical training to better prepare our members to defend America... against the Pro-Communist S.D.S. and black power terrorists."
Publ.: Statecraft Journal of Political Education, bi-monthly.

.1 The Great Statecraft Propaganda and Agitation Service.
Files. Includes correspondence, minutes of meetings, financial records, and other documents dealing with the aims, history, and purpose of the Service.

VA2 U.S. DEFENSE SUPPLY AGENCY, OFFICE OF CONTRACTS COMPLIANCE (1965). Cameron Station, 22314. Tel 202 545-6700. Robert Shafer, Chief, Off. of Contracts Compliances.
The Office works to insure equal employment opportunity and periodically reviews government contractors to insure compliance with provisions of Executive Order 11246.

.1 U.S. Defense Supply Agency, Office of Contracts Compliance.
Files, 1965- . Includes correspondence, reports, studies, investigations and other documents dealing with the history and programs of the Agency.

ARLINGTON

VA3 NATIONAL SOCIALIST WHITE PEOPLE'S PARTY (1959),
     LIBRARY. 2507 N. Franklin Rd., 22201. Tel 703 524-
     2175. William L. Pierce, Ideological Officer. Inquiries
     answered, consultation.
     The Party is a right-wing group attacking today's
     problems by "applying those timeless principles laid
     down by Adolph Hitler which forms the basis of our
     philosophy. We are above all racial nationalists."
     Formerly American Nazi Party.
     Publ.: White Power, bimonthly; Stormtrooper; Pam-
     phlets, leaflets, records, tapes, and booklets.

  .1 National Socialist White People's Party.
      Files, 1959- . Books, periodicals, newspapers,
      pamphlets, clippings, correspondence, and other
      materials concerning such subjects as George
      Lincoln Rockwell, American Nazi Party, Aryan-
      Jewish relations, racism, Adolph Hitler, Aryan
      superiority, and Rockwell Report.

VA4 NORTHERN VIRGINIA FAIR HOUSING, INC. (NVFH) (1965).
     4444 Arlington Blvd., 22204. Tel 703 524-4452. Peggy
     Wright, Exec. Secy. Inquiries answered, housing in-
     formation service.
     The NVFH works to help Negro families buy or rent in
     neighborhoods of their choice, and is prepared to offer
     practical help through its housing information service
     and community relations advisors. NVFH works
     closely with many like-minded groups such as the
     Urban League and American Friends Service Com-
     mittee. It is also actively concerned with increasing
     the supply of low and moderate cost housing in North-
     ern Virginia.
     Publ.: Pamphlets.

  .1 Northern Virginia Fair Housing, Inc.
      Files, 1965- . Includes correspondence, minutes
      of meetings, financial records, studies, reports,
      investigations, and other documents dealing with
      the aims, history, and programs of NVFH.

BOSTON

VA5 INSTITUTE FOR AMERICAN STRATEGY, FREEDOM
     STUDIES CENTER. 22713. Tel 703 825-1776. John M.
     Fisher, Pres.
     The Institute is a tax-exempt educational institution
     which works with other educational institutions and na-
     tional organizations to improve public understanding of
     the "basic foundations of American strength and free-
     dom, the Communist challenge to American freedom,
     and how a free society can meet the Communist chal-
     lenge." The Institute maintains a Freedom Studies
     Center as a cold war citizenship training center, and
     it is sponsoring, with the American Security Council, a
     joint study commission on meeting revolutionary
     challenges to America, such as those posed by "orga-
     nizations like Students for a Democratic Society, the
     Revolutionary Action Movement and Black Panthers."

  .1 Institute for American Strategy.
      Files. Records, correspondence, reports, and
      other papers concerning the aims and activities of
      the Institute.
  .2 Joint Study Commission on Meeting Revolutionary
      Challenges.
      Files concerning the research and findings of the
      Commission.

CHARLOTTESVILLE

VA6 AMERICAN CIVIL LIBERTIES UNION (ACLU) OF CEN-
     TRAL VIRGINIA. 18 Orchard Rd., 22902. Tel 703
     293-7353. G. Sheldon Gordon, Chmn.

VA7 NATIONAL DENTAL ASSOCIATION, COMMITTEE ON
     CIVIL RIGHTS. P.O. Box 197, 22902. Tel 703 293-
     8253. Dr. Eddie O. Smith, Jr., Chmn., Cmt. on Civil
     Rights.
     The Association is a national society of Negro dentists

who work for equal access in all aspects of the dental
profession.
Publ.: The Quarterly.
  .1 National Dental Association, Committee on Civil
      Rights.
      Files. Includes correspondence, minutes of meet-
      ings, financial records, studies, reports, and
      other documents dealing with the aims, history,
      and programs of the Association.

VA8 UNIVERSITY OF VIRGINIA (1819), ALDERMAN LIBRARY,
     MANUSCRIPT DIVISION (1930). 22901. Tel 703 924-
     3025. Edmund Berkeley, Jr., Acting Curator of Mss.
     Interlibrary loan, copying, typing, inquiries answered,
     referrals made.
     Publ.: Collections in the Manuscript Division...Con-
     taining References to Slavery for the Period
     from 1820 to 1865. (1967); Annual Report on His-
     torical Collections.

  .1 Abolitionism.
      Papers, 1821-87. 1 v. Bound letters to and from
      leading British anti-slavery spokesmen.
  .2 Akerman, Amos Tappan, 1821-80.
      Letter books, 1871-76. 2 v. Transcripts (hand-
      written; autograph letterpress copies). Lawyer, of
      Cartersville, Ga.; U.S. Attorney General (1870-71).
      Official and unofficial correspondence, including
      letters of the last 6 months of Akerman's Cabinet
      service. Official letters deal with the appointment
      of Territorial judges, suppression of the Ku Klux
      Klan, amnesty for Confederate soldiers, advance-
      ment of the Republican party in the South, and
      means of insuring Negro votes for the party. In-
      cludes many personal letters, and correspondence
      with William W. Belknap, B.F. Butler, Charles
      E. Butler, George S. Boutwell, D.T. Corbin, George
      William Curtis, C. Delano, Thomas F. Fullock,
      James A. Garfield, O.O. Howard, H.R. Hulburd,
      Edwin Parsons, John D. Pope, John Sherman,
      Alphonso Taft, D.A. Walker, J.K.H. Wilcox, and
      others.
  .3 Albemarle County, Virginia.
      Papers, 1831-41. 6 ft. Includes an 1831 Atlas
      containing invoices, one for the sale of slaves
      (1841).
  .4 Alderman, Edwin Anderson, 1861-1931.
      Papers, 1881-1950. 83 ft. Educator and orator.
      Personal and official correspondence, drafts of
      speeches, scrapbooks, photo albums, pictures,
      clippings, memorabilia, and other papers. The
      correspondence relates to Alderman's career, and
      activities with the Southern Education Board and
      other organizations. Correspondents and persons
      mentioned include Walter Hines Page, George F.
      Peabody, Oswald Garrison Villard, and Booker T.
      Washington.
  .5 Alderman, George.
      Papers, 1863. 1 item. Receipt (Jan. 21, 1863), in
      Wilmington, N.C., for the purchase of a slave.
  .6 Alexander, Gustavus Brown.
      Papers. ca. 1000 items. Includes the business
      records of Alexander of King George County, Va.,
      which contains a list (1848) of dower servants.
  .7 Alexandria, Virginia, Common Council.
      Papers. 16 items. Includes a report (1847)
      of a committee about a servant abused by
      the watch; a letter (1848) by the mayor concerning
      free people of color; and depositions (1856) in a
      case of Negro brick throwing.
  .8 Ambler, Elizabeth Barbour.
      Papers, 1749-1928. 75 items. Included is a bill
      of sale (1841) for a slave boy.
  .9 Ambler family.
      Papers of the Ambler and Barbour families, 1772-
      1880. 9 ft. (ca. 12,000 items). Personal and busi-
      ness papers of families prominent in the life of
      Virginia (particularly Amherst and Orange coun-
      ties and the village of Barboursville), largely of
      John Jaquelin Ambler and of his father-in-law,
      Philip Pendleton Barbour, dealing with the estate,
      "Glen Ambler," in Amherst Co. Includes papers
      of other family members, scattered letters of
      statesmen and public figures, ledgers and planta-

tion accounts of Philip P. Barbour, overseer's reports, notes on slave sales, tax lists, and other material. Among the individual correspondents is James Barbour.

VA8.10 Anderson family.
Papers. 25 ft. Included is a one volume ledger "Negro Book" for 1847-49, listing accounts of labor done, supplies issued and other items pertaining to the up-keep of slaves.

.11 Argosy collection.
Papers. 103 items. Letters and papers (mostly handwritten and signed) and ports. of Revolutionary and 19th century statesmen. Included are four manifests of slaves being transported from Alexandria, Va., for sale by slave traders (Nov. 11, 1834; Nov. 18, 1834; Nov. 20, 1834; and Nov. 21, 1834). Subjects dealt with include slavery, agriculture, politics and government.

.12 Baldwin-Lloyd.
Papers. 162 items. Correspondence of Bliss Carman, Gladys Baldwin Barr, G.M. Johnson, John Hargon, Edward Lloyd, and George F. Brinsfield concerning the attitude toward secession in Mississippi, plantation life in Mississippi, and other subjects. Included are letters (1845-59, ca. 20) to Mr. Lloyd in Maryland, from a man in Mississippi, presumably a steward or overseer on a plantation owned by Lloyd.

.13 Bankhead, Ada P.
Papers. 12 items. Included is a letter by R. Hume, written in 1825 and mentioning slave problems; an 1829 bill of sale for two Negroes; and a letter written in 1865 describing the running off of slaves at the end of the Civil War.

.14 Bankhead, Charles L.
Book, 1813-28. 1 v. Farm account book including slave lists.

.15 Baptist Church of Christ, Criglersville, Virginia.
Records, 1822-81. Church minutes, including lists of slave members.

.16 Barbee, David R.
Miscellaneous, n.d. 2 items. Two broadsides: A Plan for the Abolition of Slavery; and To the Non-Slaveholders of the South.

.17 Barbour family.
Papers, 1672-1920. 9 ft. (ca. 1600 items). Personal and business papers of the Virginia family, whose principal plantation was at Barboursville, Orange Co. Correspondence, pamphlets, newspapers, maps, speeches, documents, reports. Chiefly correspondence of James Barbour, Governor of Virginia (1812-14), Secretary of War (1825-28), and Minister to England (1828-29); papers of his brother, Philip Pendleton Barbour, of his son, Benjamin Johnson Barbour, and of other family members, with correspondence of notable Virginia and national statesmen. Among subjects mentioned are politics, government, state rights, and plantation operations.

.18 Barbour, James, 1775-1842.
Papers, 1771-1940. 4 ft. (ca. 3000 items). Planter and statesman. Correspondence, a letter book, personal and business papers, genealogical notes, and other papers, concerning Barbour's plantation in Barboursville, Orange Co., Va., and his career as Governor, Senator, Cabinet officer and diplomat. Includes a letter discussing thirty slaves available for sale, and a slave bill of sale; and a ledger (1816-40) listing working hands, the sale of slaves, and related materials. The material is related to the library's Barbour family collection.

.19 Barnes family.
Papers, 1775-1873. 76 items. In part, transcript and microfilm (negative). Correspondence, a genealogy, an account book and other papers. Chiefly Civil War letters to Mrs. R.A. Barnes from her sons Charles F. Barnes and Edward Cook Barnes, and from Henry T. Fortson, concerning conditions in Augusta, Ga., Charleston, S.C. (1863), Manassas Junction (1861-63), Wilmington, N.C. (1862); and a race riot in West Florida (1865).

.20 Barry, William Taylor.
Letterbook, 1798-1835. 1 v. Contains references to the Barry family slaves.

.21 Bell family.
Papers, 1790-1912. 200 items. Included are two slave bills of sale.

.22 Berkeley family.
Papers, 1653-1930. 20 ft. (ca. 20,000 items). Personal correspondence, legal and business papers, agricultural ledgers, and notebooks of the Berkeleys of Barn Elms plantation, Middlesex Co., Va. (1653-1820), of Aldie, Loudon Co. (1820-82), and of Albemarle Co. (1882-1930), with papers concerning the Corbin and other families. Papers of the first Edmund Berkeley, official correspondence of Sir William Berkeley as Governor of the Virginia Colony, items pertaining to military prisons and prisoners during the Civil War, overseers' reports, accounts of slave expenses, slave lists, bills of sale for slaves, and other materials and subjects.

.23 Betts, Edwin M.
Papers, 1933-60. 13 items. Correspondence concerning Jefferson's interest in slavery and other subjects.

.24 Blackford, Launcelot Minor.
Papers. 99 items. Included is a notebook written by Mary Berkeley Blackford, "Notes Illustrative of the Wrongs of Slavery."

.25 Borden, James Woodberry.
Diary-letterbook-commonplace book, 1837-38. 1 v. A combination diary-letterbook-commonplace book with comments on the Negro in Virginia.

.26 Boyle, Sarah Patton.
Papers, ca. 1962. 1 item. Ms (395 pp) of The Desegregated Heart which contains references to the Negro, since 1865.

.27 Brady, James.
Papers, 1819-59. ca. 150 items. Mainly material relating to the slave trade between Scottsville and Richmond, Va.

.28 Bray, Thomas.
Papers, 1690-1808. ca. 1000 items. Includes reference to slavery, prior to 1820.

.29 Breckinridge, James.
Papers, 1780-1821. 150 items. Letter (1828) to Breckinridge describing slaves used as payment in a contract.

.30 British abolition movement.
Papers, 1821-87. 60 items.

.31 Brockenbough, Austin.
Papers. 2 items. Includes a letter to Brockenbough (Feb. 7, 1832), from Congressman Roane mentioning the desire of a third party to purchase Negro families.

.32 Brown family.
Papers, 1781-1903. 3 items. Brown family of Buckingham County, Va. Included are entries on slaves in family Bibles.

.33 Brown family.
Papers. 18 items. Brown family of Culpeper County, Va. Included is a contract (1824) for the sale of a Negro boy.

.34 Brown-Hunter collection.
Miscellaneous. 5 items. Included is a three-volume diary (1843-46), kept by William S. Brown. Contains comments on such events as a song and prayer meeting in the slave quarters (1843); describes the killing of one slave by another (1844); and discusses one N.H. Hove, who by his will sent slaves back to Africa (1845).

.35 Bruce family.
Papers, 1790-1865. ca. 14,000 items and 13 v. Materials of the Bruce family of Berry Hill, Va., some of which pertains to Negroes and southern plantation economy. Included are account books (1863-65), containing a list of slaves, and a "Slave Book" (1 v.).

.36 Burnet, Richard C.
Papers, 1836-65. 1 v. A notebook of articles from newspapers based on letters from Burnet discussing slaves, run-aways, and related topics in Texas.

VA8.37 Byars family.
Paper, n.d. 1 item. A sketch on Lewis Fielding, "Old Virginia Reminiscences of an Old-Time Planter by His Grandson (Dr. Archibald Taylor)."
.38 Cabell family.
Papers of the Cabell and Ellet families, 1830-1930. 6 ft. Correspondence, diaries, and other papers of Mary Virginia Ellet Cabell, her father Charles Ellet, Jr., civil engineer, of Philadelphia, Pa., and her husband, William D. Cabell, of Norwood Co., Va., relating mainly to Mrs. Cabell's career as author and civic leader. Includes approximately 1000 letters from Mrs. Cabell to her children Elvira Daniel Cabell, Margaret Cabell, Nina Cabell, and Mayo Cabell; biographical and genealogical data on the Cabell and Ellet families; and other materials. Personal correspondence contains observations on the fugitive slave law; political leaders Henry Clay, Lewis Cass, and John C. Calhoun, and conditions leading to the Civil War; and other subjects. Related to the library's William Daniel Cabell papers, Joseph C. Cabell papers, and its other Cabell collections.
.39 Cabell, William D.
Papers. 3 ft. Included are numerous references to slavery, such as slave's request that he be purchased by his wife's owner; a list (1864) of servants; a list of shoes delivered to slaves; and a valuation (1863) of one slave at $3250 by a committee of freeholders.
.40 Callaway family.
Papers. 3 items. Included is a Bible record (1824-66, 8 pp.) of slave birth.
.41 Campbell, Capt. Angus.
Will, 1809. 1 item. Includes reference to slavery.
.42 Campbell, William.
Paper, 1831. 1 item. Letter (Sept. 4, 1831), describing the Nat Turner revolt.
.43 Carlton plantation.
Papers. 13 items. Included is a slave valuation (1833) for this Albemarle County, Va., plantation.
.44 Caroline County, Virginia.
Records, 1842-70. 2 v. Included are account books of John H. Martin, listing slave births, deaths, and other vital statistics.
.45 Carr family.
Papers. 1 ft. and 1 roll. Included are references (1822-47) to the emancipation of slaves, and an estate evaluation.
.46 Carrington family.
Papers, 1866-71. 1 v. Charlotte County, Va. Plantation account book containing records of slave sales, and related materials.
.47 Carter family.
Papers, 1715-1894. ca. 3 ft. Correspondence, diary, and "corn book" (1743) of Robert "King" Carter relating to his residence "Corotoman," tobacco shipments, management of his plantations and those of his deceased sons-in-law, Nathaniel Burwell and Mann Page, the slave trade, and other business affairs. Includes correspondence of Landon Carter, executor of Robert "King" Carter; letter book of Charles Yates, of Fredericksburg, Va.; plantation records of Col. John Coles of "Enniscorthy"; legal papers; indentures and deeds to lands in Mississippi and Missouri; wills; and other papers.
.48 Carter, Landon, 1710-78.
Papers, 1659, 1740-1897. ca. 3 ft. Member of the Virginia House of Burgesses, Revolutionary, pamphleteer, and planter. Correspondence, diaries, farm records, maps, drawings, land patents, deeds, indentures, bills of sale, receipts, accounts, and other papers of Carter, Landon Carter, Jr., Robert Carter (1663-1732), Robert Wormeley Carter (1734-97), Robert Wormeley Carter (1797-1861), and other members of the Carter family. Subjects include agricultural experiments and developments at Sabine Hall, Richmond Co., Va., and other Carter properties, and social life in Virginia and Washington, D.C.
.49 Cave, Richard.
Miscellaneous, 1735-1855. 1 item. Ledger, including slave births at "Montibello" plantation.

.50 Census schedule.
Papers, 1860. 2 reels. Contains the slave population statistics for Virginia, 1860.
.51 Charlottesville Committee for Public Education.
Records, 1958-60. ca. 300 items. Correspondence, bylaws, minutes, membership lists, ballots, and pamphlets, relating to the organizing of the Committee, the election of officers, efforts to reopen the public schools, the Arlington Committee to Preserve Public Schools, and the Virginia Committee for Public Schools. Correspondents include J. Albert Roston, chairman, and Constance F. Keeble, secretary, of the Charlottesville Committee for Public Education; Fendal Ragland Ellis, public school superintendent of Charlottesville, Va.; R. Stanley Goodman, chairman of the city school board; and James Lawrence Blair Buck, president, and William M. Lightsey, executive secretary, of the Virginia Committee for Public Schools.
.52 Citters, Arnout Van.
Letter, 1686. 1 item. Includes reference to slavery.
.53 Clagett, Thomas H.
Papers, 1834-51. ca. 160 items. Included are such references to slavery as "troublesome property"; arrangements for the moving of slaves; and a slave's letter to his master asking if the master had bought his children yet.
.54 Clay family.
Papers, 1828-66. 1 reel. Includes speeches on slavery and the free states.
.55 Clay, Henry.
Papers, 1834-48. ca. 6 items. Letter (Aug. 28, 1838) to C.C. Baldwin with materials concerning slavery; and a letter to Lewis Tappan relative to efforts for the suppression of the slave trade.
.56 Cocke, John Hartwell, 1780-1866.
Papers, 1725-1931. 53 ft. Planter, publicist, reformer, and Army officer. Correspondence, diaries, account books, plantation records, genealogical information, and other papers. The material relates to Cocke's interests and activities concerning the Civil War; the American Colonization Society, and other religious and reform groups. Includes diaries of Cocke, of his wife, Louisa Maxwell Holmes Cocke, and of Lucy Cocke; letters of freedmen from Monrovia, Liberia; and family correspondence of the Cocke and other families. There are references to slavery as practiced at "Bremo" and other Cocke properties, and to the institution as viewed by Cocke. Important correspondents include Joseph Carrington Cabell, Thomas Jefferson, and others. The material is related to the library's Phillip St. George Cocke papers.
.57 Cocke, Philip St. George, 1809-61.
Papers, 1829-71. 3 ft. Agriculturist and Confederate officer. Correspondence, accounts, inventories, slave lists, military dispatch and order books (April-July, 1861), special and general orders, and other papers. The bulk of the material concerns Cocke's Civil War career and Confederate military operations, particularly at Manassas (July, 1861).
.58 Coleman family.
Papers, 1819-64. 6 items. Included is an account book kept by Ethelbert Algernon Coleman, for his ward, Jane C. Coleman Hamilton of Halifax County, Va., listing the births and deaths of her slaves.
.58a Coleman family.
Papers. ca. 1000 items. Included is a journal of Mrs. Jane Lindsay Coleman of Bedford Plantation near Augusta, Ga., containing records of the births and ages of slaves, 1832-63.
.59 Coles, Edward.
Papers, 1865. 14 items. Included is a letter written by a slave wishing to return to her master.
.60 Colored population.
Papers, 1926. 4 items. Includes statistics relating to the Negro population of Philadelphia, Pa., Lynchburg and Charlottesville, Va., since 1865.
.61 Colored schools.
Papers, 1871-1957. ca. 50 items. Includes materials relating to Negro schools.

VA8.62 Compton collection.
Papers, 1826-47. 24 items. Included is a letter (1826) in which the author indicates a willingness to part with some of his slaves in exchange for land; an estate list (1846), including slaves; and a request to see that the author's slaves get safely across a river by ferry (1847).

.63 Confederate States of America.
Papers, 1864. 1 item. Slave pass dated April 24, 1864 from the Engineering Department, Richmond, Va.

.64 Crenshaw, William G.
Papers, 1847-1910. 2000 items. Contains a few references in an account book to activities of the slaves on Crenshaw's Orange County, Va., farm.

.65 Crosby, D.F.
Contract, 1867. 1 item. Labor contract relating to Negroes.

.66 Culpeper County, Virginia.
Papers, 1818-60. 1 item. Account book of Robertson Coons, containing records of slave purchases and other farm records.

.67 Custis, John Parke.
Papers, 1790-92. 2 items. Contains reference to slavery.

.68 Dabney, Virginius.
Papers, 1949-58. ca. 5800 items. Contains reference to the Negro. Restricted.

.69 Davis, Henry.
Estate inventory, 1773. 1 item. Contains reference to slavery.

.70 D'Antignac, Munroe.
Papers. ca. 30 items. Included is a folder of letters and notes relative to the hiring and leasing of slaves; and a letter (1824) from a Petersburg, Va., Negro woman, relative to her claim as heir of a Revolutionary soldier.

.71 Dickinson family.
Papers, 1794-1932. 2 items. Genealogical material including Bible records with slave birth and death records.

.72 Dorn, Harold.
Papers, 1947. 1 item. The Health of the Negro, a report.

.73 Dyer, Martha Tabb.
Books, 1823-39. 3 v. Diaries, kept by a Calloway County, Mo., woman, with references to sewing and other cares for her slaves. Includes a typescript copy.

.74 Early, William L.
Papers, 1834-42. 4 items. Included is a tax book listing free Negroes and slaveholders, kept while Early was sheriff of Madison County, Va.

.75 Early-Davis collection.
Papers, 1817-32. 4 items. Included are records from family Bibles listing slave births.

.76 Edgehill School.
Papers, 1864. 2 items. Letters (January 10 and April 16) written from this Albemarle County, Va., school with reference to the purchase of Negroes for $11,000.

.77 Eppes family.
Papers, 1805-40. 38 items. Included is an estate division, listing slaves.

.78 Eppse, Merl.
Letter, 1939. 1 item. Includes reference to the Negro.

.79 Essex County, Virginia, Court House.
Ledgers, 1813-1903. 13 v. Contains scattered references to slavery.

.80 Fauquier County, Virginia.
Paper, 1859. 1 item. Letter (Aug. 13, 1859), from L. Allan to his son, discussing slavery and related topics.

.81 Federal Writers Project. Virginia.
Papers, 1936-40. 17 ft. Typescripts of Virginia; A Guide to the Old Dominion (1940), The Negro in Virginia (1940) and notes of folklore and ballads, compiled by workers of the project.

.82 Fitzhugh and Marye.
Papers, 1838-1868. 5 items. Papers of a law firm, including the sale of a Mrs. Thorton's slaves.

.83 Folklore, Virginia.
Papers, 1936-40. ca. 17,000 items. Contains materials with reference to the Negro.

.84 Foster, Richard.
Papers, 1773-1877. 14 items. Virginia folklore which contains materials relating to slavery.

.85 Galt, James.
Diary, 1864-76. 1 v. Contains materials referring to the Negro.

.86 Garnett family.
Business records, 1794-1904. 1 ft. Ledgers, daybooks, and journals of James Mercer Garnett, Muscoe Russell Hunter Garnett, and Robert Mercer Taliaferro Hunter of "Elmwood," "Fonthill," and "Hunter's Hill," relating to their plantation, school, legal, personal merchandise, slave, grain, mill, distillery, shop, and spindle accounts.

.86a Garnett, Muscoe R.E.
Paper, 1850. Remarks to the Virginia Constitutional Convention (1850), on a measure concerning free Negroes.

.87 Garrett, John B.
Farm journal, 1838-47. 1 item. Microfilm copy. Ash Lawn farm journal, including materials on slavery.

.88 George III of England.
Document. 1 item. Includes reference to slavery, prior to 1820.

.89 Gilliam family.
Papers, 1830-90. ca. 2000 items. Included are items (ca. 100) relative to slavery; and on topics such as tax slips (slaves held), doctors' bills "more for rainy night call," slave hiring, bills for hauling Negroes, bills of sale, lists of slaves, jailor's bill for runaway, and jury summons to inquest in slave death.

.90 Gilmer, Z. Lee.
Books, 1861-62. 2 items. Diaries, containing observations by this Charlottesville, Va., soldier on Negroes in the Confederacy.

.91 Giss, Samuel.
Inventory, 1789. 1 item. Contains references to slavery.

.92 Goochland County, Virginia.
Paper, 1834. 1 item. Receipt (Sept. 30, 1824) for the sale of a slave woman and child.

.93 Goodwin family.
Papers, 1823-65. 4 items. Family Bible containing records of slave births and other vital statistics.

.94 Goose Creek, Virginia, Baptist Church.
Papers, 1775-1853. 2 v. Church records which include lists of slave members.

.95 Graham family.
Papers, 1754-1906. 16 ft. (ca. 3100 items). Business correspondence, journals, ledgers, time books, receipts, account books, inventories, personal and other papers of the Graham and Robinson families of Virginia. Among the subjects covered is Negro labor. Included is a seven-volume Time Book (1828-52), consisting of records of Negro labor; slaves hired and at what prices; information on runaways, and related material. Persons, firms, places, organizations, and institutions named include Calvin Graham, David Graham and Son, David P. Graham, J. and L. Graham, Thomas Graham, William Graham, Graham's Forge Club, and John W. Robinson.

.96 "Gratitude."
Paper, 1866. 1 item. Clipping (May, 1866) concerning the devotion of Peter Fleming, a Virginia Negro, for his former master.

.97 Gravel Hill manuscripts.
Papers. 17 items. Included is George Hannah's "Register of My Black Family's Ages, 1800-51."

.98 Graves family.
Papers, 1811-60. 56 items. Information on slave sales included.

.99 Graves, Jeremiah White.
Papers, 1822-78. 3 items. Account book (1822-53), and diaries (1843-78), of this Pittsylvania County, Va., planter with references to slavery.

100 Grinnan family.
Papers, 1749-1899. 5 ft. Business records, cor-

respondence, and account books of the Grinnan
family of Fredericksburg, Va. Papers of the
Grinnan family include correspondence of Andrew
Glassell Grinnan, correspondence of his wife,
Georgia Screven Bryan Grinnan and of his father-
in-law, Joseph Randall Bryan, of Richmond, Va.;
papers and letters of Randolph Bryan Grinnan;
business papers of Robert Alexander Grinnan and
Mrs. Helen Grinnan; indentures, documents, and
letters of forebears of Elizabeth Grinnan Jackson;
land deeds and indentures in Patrick, Carrol,
Botetourt, Wythe, and Grayson counties in Virginia;
genealogical data on Grinnan and other families;
materials on abolitionists, secession of the border
states, and property difficulties in 1861; a letter
(ca. 1824) from a slave asking to be purchased,
a letter from a slave to his master, and a letter
referring to payment for the "hauling" of Negroes.

VA8.101 Green, Philip.
Papers, ca. 1816-66. 4 v. Bound letters, sermons, and other materials of a Methodist circuit
preacher, containing numerous references to
slavery.

.102 Gurley, Ralph Randolph.
Paper, 1860. 1 item. Letter (1860) to John B.
Minor, referring to the American Colonization
Society and to slavery.

.103 Hannah, George C.
Papers, 1843-64. ca. 22 items. Bills of sale for
slaves, Charlotte County, Va.; and other materials
with references to slavery and the Negro.

.104 Harrison, Carter H.
Diary, 1834-35. 1 v. Contains a fragment relative
to Mississippi and the regulation of the slave
trade.

.105 Hawkins family.
Papers, 1769-1849. 300 items. Included are tax
receipts, doctor's bills, and bills of sale for slaves.

.106 Hemings, Betty.
Papers, 1735-1962. 14 items. Genealogical records of the slaves at Monticello.

.107 Hench, Atcheson Laughlin, 1891- . collector.
American and English literary and historical papers, ca. 1300-1956. 5 ft. (ca. 1000 items). Professor of English at University of Virginia. Material collected for use in Hench's classes with
examples of various periods. Includes material
reflecting his interest; Civil War letters; papers
relating to Virginia history; an account of slavery
in Kansas (1857-60); a statement on the relations
between the sections on slavery; and reference to
the Negro, since 1865.

.108 Henry family.
Papers. 15 items. Included is a receipt (1823)
for the purchase of two slaves, and a letter
(1840) with reference to a slave having run away to
Canada.

.109 Hill, Dickinson & Company.
Paper, 1860's. 1 item. Printed form used by
this company for slave purchases in the 1860's.

.110 Hillyer family.
Papers, 1790-1850. 350 items. Included are a
slave bill of sale; a "Cotton Book" listing the
number of pounds picked by each hand; and a list
of slaves "Freed by Abe Lincoln's Proclamation."

.111 Holladay, Mary Jane.
Diary, 1851-61. 1 v. Later entries comment on
the burdens of owning slaves.

.112 Hook, John, ca. 1745-1808.
Business records, 1758-1870. 2 ft. (131 items).
In part, microfilm. Merchant of New London, Va.
Letter books, (1758-1884, microfilm), account
books, and other business and legal papers of Hook
and of his son-in-law, Bowker Preston of Franklin
and Bedford counties, Va. Includes ledgers (1851-
69) for general merchandise, smith's work, livestock records, and birth records of slaves; daybooks (1795-1822); and other records.

.113 Hopkins collection.
Diary, 1866-67. 1 item. Diary with reference to
the Negro.

.114 Horsley, T. Braxton.
Papers. Includes reference to the Negro, since
1865. Related to R.N. Wilburn papers.

.115 Houston, Mrs. William.
Papers. 21 items. Includes a letter (1840)
from Jesse Scott to Thomas Wilson, com-
plaining that the Negroes hadn't milked the cows
clean; letter from James Whitehead in the Kansas
territory, stating "we met the pro-slavery army";
and letter (May, 1861) expressing the author's
views on slavery and the danger from bands of Negroes during the War.

.116 Howard, William.
Book, 1782-1824. 1 item. Book of Common
Prayer recording the births of slaves of an Albe-
marle County, Va., family.

.116a Hubard, Robert Thruston, 1808-71.
Farm management papers, 1812-1900. ca. 4 ft.
(5466 items). Chiefly receipts and accounts of this
Buckingham Co., Va., plantation owner, detailing
the operation of "Rosny," Buckingham Co., and
"Tye River Quarter," Nelson Co. Accounts include general merchandise, groceries, clothes, and
such supplies and necessaries as physician's fees,
blacksmith's work, slaves, hired labor, and other
items such as leases, contracts with overseers,
and bonds. Included are several notebooks (1836-
62) in which Hubard made notes concerning his
slaves. Later material is chiefly of his son, Robert
Thurston Hubard (1839-1931). Post-Civil War
material includes many receipts of payment to
freedmen for work on the Hubard plantations.

.117 Hubard, Robert Thruston, 1808-71.
Correspondence, 1825-1913. ca. 190 items. Lawyer and member of the Virginia House of Representatives, of Buckingham Co. Correspondence
dealing with the family and business affairs, the
"abolition party," the "negro question," and
Virginia and national politics. Includes letters
from Hubard's brother, Edmund Wilcox Hubard
(1806-78), U.S. Representative from Virginia, relating to the abolitionists, and other persons;
letters from Hubard's son, James Linnaeus (or
Lenaeus) Hubard (1835-1913).

.118 Huger family.
Papers, 1773-1897. 52 items. Transcripts (handwritten), photocopies, and microfilm (negatives,
ca. 3 ft.) made from originals in the possession of
the Huger family. An account by Mary Ester Huger
of life in South Carolina, (1820-90); plantation
book (1858-61) of John Allston for Huger's plantation near Savannah, Ga.; and correspondence of
Thomas Pinckney (1750-1828). Includes some correspondence of Francis Kinloch Huger, Harriet
Lucas (Pinckney) Huger, and Mary Elizabeth
Huger.

.119 Humphreys, Fountain.
Papers, 1819-31. 1 v. Farm notebooks kept at
Palmyra, Va., 1819-20; and at Spring Hills, 1828-
31, with references to the health of slaves and related topics.

.120 Hunter family.
Papers of the Hunter and Garnett families, 1704-
1940. 24 ft. Correspondence, account books, and
other papers of the Essex Co. families, chiefly of
R.M.T. Hunter, U.S. Senator and Confederate
Secretary of State, with smaller groups of papers
of his nephew M.R.H. Garnett, lawyer and statesman, and of Garnett's grandfather, James M.
Garnett, agriculturist, legislator, and pioneer educator of women. Business records of Hunter and
Garnett, plantation and slave accounts of the
Hunter estates, "Fonthill," and "Hunter's Hill,"
and of the Garnett estate, "Elmwood." Letters of
Hunter and Garnett descendants, reflecting conditions in the Reconstruction era, and Essex Co.
farm life in the early twentieth century.

.121 Hunter, Jacob.
List of tithables, 1775. 1 item. Includes reference
to slavery.

.122 Hutchinson-Abernethy families.
Papers, 1781-1850. 3 items. Genealogical mate-
rial which include Bible records on the Isaac
Hutchinson family, and on the slaves of his son.

.123 Hutter, C.S., Jr.
Miscellaneous. 6 items and 6 v. Included
is a bill of rental for a slave (Jan. 1, 1860);

and a broadside (1841) for the sale of the Barbour family servants.

VA8.124 Interview with Ex-Slaves.
Tapes, 1937. 5 items. Interviews with five ex-slaves by the WPA Project.

.125 Irby, Richard.
Papers. 500 items. Microfilm copy. Included are slave records (1805) and plantation records with slave accounts (1847, 1854-56).

.126 Jefferson, Issac.
Papers, 1847-?. 2 items. Reminiscences of this Monticello slave.

.127 Jefferson, Thomas, 1743-1826.
Papers. American statesman, 3rd President of the U.S. (1801-09). Includes an inventory of Jefferson's estate; letters (April 20, and May 20, 1826) on the subject of emancipation; and a farm book (1820-21), containing lists of clothing issued to slaves; and other Jefferson papers containing numerous references to slaves and slavery.

.128 Johnson, William.
Paper, 1767. 1 item. Bill of sale for a slave.

.129 Johnston, James.
Business records, 1859-92. 1 ft. Ledgers, daybooks, journals, and other business records of James Johnston of North Garden, Va.; a farm journal of W.E. Sims' estate, "Eldon Plantation;" and other material.

.130 Kansas-Nebraska broadside.
1856. 1 item. A call for a free state meeting in New York City, N.Y.

.131 Kean family.
Papers, 1785-1950. 7 ft. Correspondence, diary (1861-66) and other papers of the Kean family, especially Robert Garlick Hill Kean, lawyer, Confederate official, and rector of the University of Virginia, and of his son, Jefferson Randolph Kean, Army surgeon. The papers of R.G.H. Kean relate to his services with the Confederacy as adjutant general to the Secretary of War and chief of the Confederate Bureau of War, his legal career in Lynchburg, Va., during Reconstruction, and other matters. Includes Kean's diary (1861-66) and correspondence of his ancestors. The papers of J.R. Kean deals with his career.

.132 Kemper, James Lawson, 1823-95.
Papers, 1813-1903. 10 ft. Virginia lawyer, State legislator, Confederate officer, and Governor (1874-78). Correspondence and other papers, concerned with a wide variety of personal, family, military, political, and economic topics. Papers of the ante-bellum period relate to issues before the Virginia House of Delegates during Kemper's service as a legislator, including several national and State political concerns. Material of Civil War interest includes discussions of the State's unpreparedness for war, conscription and impressment, manpower problems, troop movements, the raising and provisioning of militia units, and battles. Much material relates to the Reconstruction period, Federal troops in the West and South, education, and memorials to Civil War heroes.

.133 Kennon family.
Papers and business records of the Kennon, Heth, and Randolph families, 1808-1903. 3 ft. (ca. 950 items). Personal and business papers of William H. Kennon and his son, William U. Kennon, including autographs of prominent Virginians; plantation account books and time books for laborers at Norwook, the Randolph family estate in Powhatan Co., Va., kept by Beverly Randolph and including slave records; Kennon, Heth, and Randolph bankbooks, and other materials.

.134 Kentucky slave contract.
Paper, 1814. 1 item. Slave bill of sale.

.135 King and Queen County, Virginia.
Miscellaneous, 1819-1850. Census book (1850), listing slaves held and related statistics; and the County tax books (1819-21), 3 items.

.136 Klipstone, Philip.
Papers, 1823-68. 55 items. Included are receipts for hire of Negro women and discussion of a court case involving the ownership of slaves taken from Virginia to Kentucky.

.137 Koscuisyko, Thaddeus.
Will, 1798. 1 v. Contains reference to slavery.

.138 Ku Klux Klan.
Papers. Includes reference to Negroes, since 1865.

.139 Larimer, Robert.
Papers, 1863-65. 12 items. Included is a ms (10 pp.) entitled "The Slaveholder's Rebellion," primarily a chronological account of the secession of the southern states, to which is added a speech by the unionist Governor of Maryland.

.140 Latane family.
Papers, 1650-1942. 4 ft. Correspondence, land grants, and other papers of Lewis Latane and descendants; 10 scrapbooks (1870-1919) kept by Mr. Southworth, clerk of the County Court of Essex County, Va., on local, state and southern politics; a note book (1707-94) with agreements, accounts, genealogy, and birth and death dates of slaves; and other papers pertaining to slavery, prior to 1820.

.141 Letters of prominent men.
Papers. 11 items. Included is a letter (1857) by John Tyler, in which he comments on the African slave trade.

.142 Lewis and Washington collections.
Papers. ca. 150 items. Some mss containing reference to slavery, prior to 1820.

.143 Long, George.
Papers. 2 items. Included is a letter (1862) with references to British attitudes toward slavery and the Civil War.

.144 Lunenburg County, Virginia.
Paper, 1814. 1 item. A list of free Negroes (1814).

.145 McDowell family.
Papers. 160 items. Included are a slave bill of sale; a slave list; and an agreement by one of the individuals to become security for the hire of two slaves for one year.

.146 McGuffin family.
Papers, 1831-1904. ca. 25 ft. of microfilm (negative) (ca. 275 items). Microfilm made from originals in the possession of the McGuffin family. Family correspondence, deed, and financial receipts, of a family living in Augusta and Rockbridge Counties, Va. Includes letters (1861-65) from Charles McGuffin, John McGuffin, and George Baylor, describing their experiences with the Confederate infantry, especially the 1st Battle of Bull Run, the Shenandoah Valley Campaign (1862), and the Battle of New Market (1864) in which the 4th, 5th, 6th, 36th, and 38th United States Colored Troops were engaged.

.147 Madden family.
Papers, 1760-1870. 200 items. Correspondence, business papers, and other material of a free Negro woman and her family.

.148 Madison, James, 1751-1836.
Papers. ca. 154 items. 4th President of the U.S. (1809-1817). Includes a deed (1844) relative to slaves; a letter (Jan. 22, 1853) from John Tyler to Thomas Ritchie, concerning the emancipation of slaves and related topics; and a letter (1823) from Madison to Jedidiah Morse, answering a series of questions (not included) on slavery.

.149 Madison, James, Sr.
Account book, 1744-57. 1 v. Includes reference to slavery.

.150 Manly, William G.
Letters, 1782-1802. 3 items. Contains reference to slavery.

.151 Marshall, Captain John.
Books, 1856-57. 2 v. Contains frequent references to slaves and slave problems in the farm journal.

.152 Mason family.
Papers, 1776-1899. 73 items. Included are accounts of the sale of slaves; and a speech by T.H. Bayley of Virginia in Congress, May 16, 1848, "Slavery in the Territories."

.153 Maury, Ann Fontaine.
Book, 1827-32. 1 v. A diary containing references to the debates on slavery in the Virginia General Assembly.

VA8.154 Meikleham, Septimia Randolph.
Papers, ca. 1792-1871. ca. 200 items. Included is a Monticello slave bread list (1821) in Jefferson's hand.

.155 Mennis, Callohill.
Papers, 1767-1849. 550 items. Lawyer. Included are references to a slave purchased with a bad leg; a woman needing an overseer; the hiring out of estate Negroes and other legal matters.

.156 Minor, Dabney.
Notebook, 1808-20. 1 v. Includes reference to slavery.

.157 Minor, Lewis Willis, 1808-72.
Papers, 1772-1932. ca. 150 items. In part, transcripts (handwritten). Physician with the U.S. and Confederate navies. Correspondence, genealogical information on the Minor, Carter, and Champ families, notes, and other papers. Subjects include Minor's life and medical experiences, and Reconstruction in Virginia.

.158 Mitchell-Garnett collection.
Ledgers, 1794-1904. 20 v. Included are plantation and slave accounts.

.159 Moats, Hopie Wright.
Papers, 1889-1915. ca. 165 items. Includes reference to the Negro.

.160 Monroe James, 1758-1831.
Papers. 5th President of the U.S. (1817-25). Includes reference to slavery, prior to 1820; and letters (1829-31, 4 items) in which Monroe discusses his slaves and other related subjects.

.161 Morton, Jeremiah.
Papers, 1841. 2 items. Agreement for sale of a slave to William Hume of Orange County, Va., December 27, 1841; and a bill of sale for same.

.162 Morton-Halsey.
Papers. 10,000 items and 20 v. Included is Jeremiah Morton's personal account book (1836-1847), listing slaves for sale.

.163 Mount Edd Baptist Church.
Book, 1823-44. 1 item. Batesville, Va. The minute book which contains a list of white and Negro members.

.164 Nansemond County, Virginia.
Papers, 1676-1938. 31 items. Included is an article "The Negro in Nansemond County."

.165 Neville collection.
Papers. 8 items. Included is a marriage settlement (1834), conveying the dower right to eight slaves.

.166 Olson, Carl I.
Paper, 1851. 1 item. Typescript thesis by Olson, University of Mississippi, entitled "The Negro and Confederate Morale."

.167 Omohundra, Silas and R.H.
Book, 1857-63. 1 v. The volume contains names, prices, purchasers, and profits of slaves sold by this firm.

.168 Orange County, Virginia.
Account books, 1784-1833. 3 v. Contains reference to slavery.

.169 Pocket Plantation.
Papers. 3000 items. Included are account books with records of the estate of Henry Calloway, listing purchases for and hiring of slaves (1809-25); folder (1827) with slave valuation in estate of Ralph Smith; and medical record book kept by doctor, containing references to treatment of slaves.

.170 Quitman, John Anthony.
Papers, 1781-1867. 80 items. Included is a letter (1855) referring to efforts to keep slaves safe in Texas.

.171 Rainey family.
Papers. 4 items. Included is a letter concerning the sale of slaves in 1836, and another with reference to the treatment of slaves.

.172 Randolph, John.
Papers, 1802-35. ca. 31 items. Roanoke, Va. Included is an overseer's report with slave list; a letter (June 11, 1821) from Randolph to Walter Coles, refusing to sell one of his slaves; and other references to slavery.

.173 Randolph, Thomas Jefferson.
Memoirs, ca. 1874. 1 v. Typescript of his memoirs, including reference to slavery; and other papers with reference to the Negro.

.174 Randolph-Macon College.
Notebooks. 2 v. One volume contains notes taken in 1855, by Joseph Walker on a Dr. Smith's lectures on slavery. "Well-organized pro-slavery position, anti-slavery works used as straw-men."

.175 Redman, William Henry, b. 1840.
Papers, 1859-97. ca. 1000 items. Army officer and member and speaker of the Iowa House of Representatives. Correspondence relating to Redman's experiences during the Civil War and with Reconstruction forces in Houston, Tex., the election of 1864, Abraham Lincoln, Ulysses S. Grant, and George B. McClellan; leaves from a diary kept by Redman during the Civil War; an autobiographical sketch; and other papers. Included are letters of this Civil War soldier commenting on the Negro and manumission in Louisiana and Texas.

.176 Reid, Richard J. collector.
Papers, 1770-1910. 2 ft. (ca. 2500 items). Correspondence, accounts, receipts, ledgers, other business papers, family records, legal papers, and other papers and records of various persons, firms, and institutions of Southside Virginia, particularly of Pittsylvania, Franklin, and Halifax counties, concerning slavery, politics, the Civil War, and other aspects of economic and social life. Includes doctor's bills for treating slaves or Negroes; acknowledgement of pay for keeping a family of slaves for a year; bill of hire for Negro boy; agreement for transporting and sale of slaves.

.177 Rives family.
Papers, 1781-1945. 6 ft. (ca. 4000 items). Correspondence, diaries, reminiscences, business papers, genealogical records, literary mss, plans, drawings, and other papers of William Cabell Rives (1793-1868) on cotton and wheat crops, agricultural methods, Rives' congressional and diplomatic career, and the Civil War; of Judith Page (Walker) Rives (1802-82) on social and political affairs; of William Cabell Rives (1825-89) on farming at "Castle Hill" in Albemarle Co., Va.; of Alfred Landon Rives (1830-1903); of Robert Rives (1798-1869), his wife, Elizabeth (Pannhill) Rives (1810-95) and daughter, Cornelia (Rives) Harrison Wilborn, on family and business affairs, slaves prices in Georgia and Florida, farm economics, elections, social events, and the tangible property of Henry Rives (1799-1833). Includes power of attorney given for purchase of slaves.

.178 Richmond, Virginia, Police.
Daybook, 1834-43. 1 v. Contains entries on runaway slaves and other offenses.

.179 Riddick, Robert M.
Papers. 8 items. Included is a copy of a document (1820) exempting the estate of Riddick from taxation on two slaves.

.180 Robinson, Leigh.
Papers, 1787-1930. ca. 1000 items. Included are references to Negroes.

.181 Robinson, Thomas.
Paper, 1850. 1 item. List of Robinson's slaves (1850).

.182 Rorer family.
Papers, 1770-1865. 10 ft. Included is a "Register of Blacks, 1838-1865."

.183 Seward, Walter Merrit, b. 1860.
Papers, 1833-1928. 1 ft. (ca. 300 items). Physician of New York City and Brunswick Co., Va. Personal and family papers, a farm journal (1857-88) which includes slave vital-statistics, farm records, and other materials. Includes records of the births, deaths, and marriages of family and slaves.

.184 Shaver, David.
Paper, 1831. 1 item. Memorial to the city of Lynchburg protesting the suppression of the African Baptist Church following the Nat Turner revolt.

.185 Sherman, Harry M.
Papers, 1865, 1909. 3 items. Included are two letters by a former slave to his master's son, re-

questing to spend his last years on the old home place, and recalling the Civil War, which "broke us up."

VA8.186 Singleton family.
Papers, 1845-65. ca. 14 items. Contains reference to the Negro.

.187 Slave accounts.
Paper, 1817-27. 4 pages. Accounts of expenditures for slaves, perhaps from an old ledger.

.188 Slave trade.
Letter, 1752. 1 item. Includes reference to slavery.

.189 Smith family.
Papers. 16 items. Included are some slave valuations for 1840.

.190 Smith, Mrs. Jacob Henry.
Papers, 1814-1884. 90 items. Letters, including comments on slavery.

.191 Smith, John, 1725-76.
Papers, 1724-1923. 6 ft. Correspondence, account books, ledger (1755-56), plantation records, and legal and other papers (chiefly 1740-1880), of Smith, of his son, Ralph Smith, and of George Clement, all associated with the Pocket Plantation on the Staunton (upper Roanoke) River, Pittsylvania Co., Va. Includes legal papers relating to Albemarle Co., Va.; and material relating to the estate of Peter Jefferson, slaves, Ralph Smith's estate, and the Civil War.

.192 Strickling, Charles W.
Paper, 1965. 1 item. Includes reference to the Negro.

.193 Stuart, Alexander Hugh Holmes, 1807-91.
Papers, 1791-1928. ca. 500 items. Lawyer, U.S. Representative from Virginia, and Cabinet officer. Correspondence and other papers. Includes Stuart's letters; material relating to the Reconstruction decade; and letters of Archibald Stuart and other relatives. A mounted clipping on the Virginia Secession Convention; and a copy of the Report of the Joint Committee of the General Assembly on the Harpers Ferry Outrages (24 pp.), constituting a defense of slavery and an attack on the treatment of Negroes in the North.

.194 Stuart, David.
Papers, 1787-91. ca. 5 items. Contains reference to the Negro.

.195 Sydnor, Thomas White, b. 1816.
Papers, 1825-90. 4 ft. Baptist minister and educator. Correspondence, printed matter and other papers dealing with general, social, religious, and educational conditions in the counties of King and Queen, and Nottaway, Va., where Sydnor was superintendent of schools. Includes reference to the Negro.

.196 Taft, William Howard, 1857-1930.
Letter, 1908. 1 item. 27th President of the U.S. (1909-13). Includes reference to the Negro.

.197 Tayloe family.
Papers, 1708-1917. ca. 380 items. John Tayloe of Mt. Airy, Richmond Co., Va., member of the Virginia House of Burgesses and the Council of State; his son, John Tayloe of Octagon House, Washington, D.C., and Mt. Airy, planter; and their descendants. Correspondence of Benjamin Ogle Tayloe, George P. Tayloe, and Edward Thornton Tayloe; accounts of Stephen Lyde and his brother concerning the family estates in Richmond and King George Counties, Va., Charles Co., Md., and elsewhere; a farm journal (1850-69) containing annual slave inventories, references to runaways, etc.; items pertaining to the amnesty of Edward Thornton Tayloe; papers relating to the sale of the Octagon House; and materials on lands and local politics, social conditions, prices of slaves, records of slave illnesses, etc.

.198 Taylor, Col. A.P.
Paper, 1844. 1 item. Letter (1844) on shipment of clothes for his slaves.

.199 Taylor, Allan.
Papers. 2 items. Included is a letter (1860) by a Kentucky woman concerning the freeing of her slaves.

.200 Thomas family.
Papers, 1810-62. ca. 200 items and 5 v. Includes reference to slavery.

.201 Thomas, James J.
Papers, 1965. 1 item. "Slaves at the University (of Virginia)," an eight-page typescript article.

.202 Thurmond family.
Papers. 20 items and 3 v. Included is a plantation account book (1842-93) and a slave bill of sale.

.203 Tucker family.
Papers, 1797-1843. 6 v. Brunswick County, Va. Overseer's records (1821-26); and other materials with reference to the Negro.

.204 Tucker, Henry St. George.
Papers, 1890-91. 2 items. Includes reference to the Negro.

.205 Virginia collection.
Papers, 1791-1884. 6 items. Various mss of the State of Virginia, with reference to slavery.

.206 Virginia legislative petitions.
Papers, 1772-82. 24 items. Legislative petitions containing reference to slavery.

.207 Virginia slavery collection.
Papers. Receipts, bills of sale, and lists and evaluations of slaves.

.208 Wade family.
Book, 1808-62. 1 v. Notebook containing lists of Negroes with birth dates.

.209 Walker family.
Papers. 1300 items. Included are tax receipts and letters referring to the sale of slaves (1825) to provide cash; listing high slave prices in Missouri (1837); and discussing the need for slaves for rent in Missouri, paying double the Virginia rates (1837).

.210 Wallace family.
Papers, 1750-1864. ca. 115 items. Letters and documents relating to the commercial ventures of Scottish-American merchants, mostly from 1773-1805. Members of the family represented include Gustavus Brown Wallace (1751-1802), James Wallace (1755-91), Lettice (Wishart) Smith Wallace, Michael Wallace (1719-67), Michael Wallace (b. 1753), and William Brown Wallace (1757-1833). Includes references to slavery.

.211 Washington family.
Papers of the Washington and Lewis families, 1774-1843. 1 ft. (ca. 450 items). Correspondence, accounts, bills, indentures, and other papers, chiefly concerning the settlement of the estates of George Washington, William A. Washington, Richard Henry Lee, Arthur Lee, and Thomas Turner, and revealing connections between the Washington, Lewis, Lee, and Beverley families. Includes papers of Lawrence Lewis (199 items); Bushrod Washington (1762-1829), first president (1817-29) of the American Colonization Society (ca. 50 items); and others. Also mentioned are Negroes freed by George Washington. The material is related to the library's collection of Baltimore merchants' correspondence.

.212 Washington, Lawrence.
Paper, 1831. 1 item. Included in the estate papers (1831), are slave lists.

.213 Weaver, William, 1780-1863.
Business records, 1800-91. 9 ft. (ca. 580 items). Ironmaster and pioneer in scientific agriculture. Ledgers, daybooks, journals, time books, records of free and slave labor, provision account books, cashbooks, journals, and related records, concerning Weaver's enterprises. Some papers concern the Brady family, Weaver's business partner at the Weaver-Brady Iron Works and Grist Mill. Includes the journal volume (1830-41), devoted to Negro accounts; 1 v. (1859-66) contains a record of Negroes vaccinated; and a 5 v. "Negro Book" (1839-59), with such items as a "list of boys who came in sick."

.214 Wellford, Charles C.
Paper, 1861. 1 item. Letter (May 24, 1861) requesting the exemption of plantation overseers from military service.

.215 Whitcomb, Samuel.
Papers, 1824. 1 item. An interview (1824) with
Thomas Jefferson on slavery and other subjects.
.216 Whitehead, Robert, 1897-1960.
Papers, 1932-60. 13 ft. Lawyer and member of
the Virginia House of Representatives. Speeches
and other papers relating to Virginia politics, and
government, education in Virginia, Negro education, finances and taxation, redistricting, and civil
rights.
.217 Wilburn, R.N.
Papers, 1920-32. 69 items. Term papers, include
reference to the Negro.
.218 Windsor, Robert N.
Papers. 3 items. Two of the letters (1839) concern Windsor's shipment of slaves for another
individual.
.219 Winfield, John A.
Papers, 1794-1894. 7 items. Included are a bill of
sale for a slave boy and an estate inventory (1862),
listing slaves and their valuation.
.220 Winston family.
Papers, 1847-51. 2 items. Included is a letter
(1851) from a member of the American Colonization Society, concerning the shipping of manumitted slaves to Liberia.
.221 Wise, Henry Alexander.
Papers, 1846-57. 2 items. Included is a letter
(1846) concerning the possibility that the ship
"Frederica" was engaged in the slave trade.
.222 Woods-Belmont Farm Journals.
Journals, 1850-90. ca. 14 v. Includes references
to the Negro.
.223 Wright-Hooper.
Papers, 1759-1896. ca. 300 items and 7 v. Mss
with reference to slavery.
.224 Yancey, Charles.
Miscellaneous, 1811-56. 2 v. Volumes contain
records of Yancey's three plantations, and slave
lists.
.225 Yates and Company.
Ledgers of Yates and Co., and of J.R. Yates, 1872-
1915. 6 ft. Account books of two general mercantile establishments of Pittsylvania Co., Va., reflecting trade practices and indicating the place of
the rural merchant in the system of agricultural
tenancy during the post-Civil War period. Includes
records of dealings with Negro customers
(1907-10).
.226 Among recent additions to the Manuscript Division are
letters or mss of the following American literary
figures: William S. Braithwaite, Ralph Waldo
Emerson, Thomas Wentworth Higginson, Oliver
Wendell Holmes, Julia Ward Howe, and Harriet
Beecher Stowe.

VA9 UNIVERSITY OF VIRGINIA, BUREAU OF POPULATION
AND ECONOMIC RESEARCH. Lambeth House, 22903.
Tel 703 295-2166. Charles O. Meiburg, Dir. Inquiries
answered.
The Bureau investigates demographic, economic, and
sociological factors affecting small census areas in
Virginia and makes comparative studies; provides a
fact-finding and information service for the State.

.1 Bureau of Population and Economic Research.
Files. Includes correspondence, minutes of meetings, financial records, studies, investigations,
reports, and other documents dealing with the
aims, history, and programs of the Bureau.

FAIRFAX

VA10 FAIRFAX COUNTY PUBLIC LIBRARY (1939). 3915 Chain
Bridge Rd., 22030. Tel 703 691-2121. William L.
Whitesides, Acting Dir. Interlibrary loan, bibliographies prepared, literature searches, copying, inquiries
answered, referrals made.

.1 Sherwood Reference Center.
Special collection for literature and history of
black Americans.
.2 Virginia Room.
Virginia history collection containing local news-

papers, Fairfax County Historical Society publications, and Virginia census records which provide
information on the Negro as a part of local history.

FREDERICKSBURG

VA10a MARY WASHINGTON COLLEGE OF THE UNIVERSITY OF
VIRGINIA, DEPARTMENT OF ENGLISH, STUDIES IN
BLACK LITERATURE (1970). 22401. Tel 703 373-
7250. Raman K. Singh, Editor.
SBL is an independent journal devoted to the critical
study of Afro-American and African literature.
Publ.: Studies in Black Literature, 3 issues per year.

HAMPDEN-SYDNEY

VA11 HAMPDEN-SYDNEY COLLEGE (1776), EGGLESTON LI-
BRARY (1776), 23943. Tel 703 223-4371. Paul L.
Grier, Librn. Interlibrary loan, copying.

.1 Account books and diary of Virginians.
Papers, 1800-85. 9 v. Account books of Jacob A.
Bowly of Aakgrove (1871-72), John Worsham
Rodgers, blacksmith of Kingsville (1830-33), William Seay, sexton, Hampden-Sydney College Church
(1836-81), Andrew Reid Venable, planter and
merchant (1852-83), John M. Venable of Slate Hill
(1875-85), Richard N. Venable, lawyer and State
legislator, kept by his overseer, Hezekiah Jackson (1820-29), all of Prince Edward Co., Va.; and
a diary of William R. Carter, lawyer and Confederate officer in the 3rd Regiment, Virginia
Cavalry (1861-64).

HAMPTON

VA12 HAMPTON INSTITUTE (1868), COLLIS P. HUNTINGTON
MEMORIAL LIBRARY (1903), 23368. Tel 703 723-
6581. Fritz J. Malval, Acting Dir. and Archivist. Interlibrary loan, bibliographies prepared, literature
searches, copying, inquiries answered, referrals made.

.1 Black Studies Collection.
ca. 1000 paperbacks. Basic books on the life and
history of black Americans.
.2 Dett, Robert Nathaniel, 1882-1943.
Miscellaneous. Music composer and arranger.
Music collection, including original music mss,
sheet music, pictures, clippings, and biographical
material about Dett.

.3 Hampton Institute.
Archives, 1868- . Includes correspondence
originated and received by the various officers of
the college over the years, minutes of board meetings, records of admission, academic records of
students, financial records, bulletins, records of
donations, catalogs, and ca. 3000 photos of people
and events associated with the history of the college down through the years.

Other archival materials of Hampton Institute are
currently in several repositories, and will be
organized and cataloged in the new addition to the
Collis P. Huntington Library, where the Hampton
Archives are to be located. Among materials are
found mss of Mary McLeod Bethune, George Wash-
ington Carver, Alexander Crummell, Frederick
Douglass, W.E.B. DuBois, Jessie Fauset, Issac
Fisher, John Hope Franklin, William H. Hastie,
Luther P. Jackson, James Weldon Johnson, Martin
Luther King, Jr., John Mercer Langston, Cecil T.
Lewis, Robert Russa Moton, Booker T. Washington,
Thurgood Marshall, Walter N. Ridley, Frank N.
Snowden, and Charles T. Davis. Other materials
include proceedings of the Capon Springs Conferences (1898-1901); proceedings of the Conferences of Education in the South (1901-13); trustees,
faculty, administrative board, business committee, and educational board; annual reports;
principal and treasurer (1869- .); catalogs (1870- .);
night school record books (1888-92); graduate
rosters (1871-79, 1904-05); excerpts of letters

from graduates and ex-students (1871-1900); student rosters (1899-1900); daily reports; discipline books, Sunday School records (1890-93); visitors' registers; rosters of workers; programs of college events, anniversaries, commencements, Founder's Days, and other occasions; Hampton leaflets and tracts; Negro and the South (pamphlets on agriculture, education, slavery, and other subjects); slavery documents; press clippings on General S.C. Armstrong; pamphlet boxes containing letters to principals Armstrong and Frissell; letter books containing replies of General Armstrong, Dr. H.B. Frissell, F.C. Briggs (business agent, includes letters to Indians), William S. Dodd (concerning Negro business), William H. Scoville (secretary), John Sugden (superintendent of buildings), and others; and studies of Hampton Institute.

.4 Museum Collection.
Collection of early African masks and sculpture.

.5 Negro collection (George Foster Peabody Collection).
Miscellaneous, 1830-65. ca. 10,000 v. and 1200 pamphlets. History and literature by and about the Negro; pamphlets on slavery and the slave trade, including the arguments and debates for and against; and also contains original handbills covering the sale of slaves.

.6 Tanner, Henry O., 1859-1937.
Miscellaneous. American Negro artist. Includes six original paintings, among which is "The Banjo Lesson"; and one scrapbook of clippings concerning the life and works of Tanner.

.7 White, Charles, 1918- .
Mural. Contemporary American Negro artist. A work entitled "The Contribution of the Negro to American Democracy."

HARDY

VA13 BOOKER T. WASHINGTON NATIONAL MONUMENT (1957). Route 1, Box 195, 24015. Tel 703 483-9896. Barry Mackintosh, Historian. Inquiries answered.
The Monument is a federal area administered by National Park Service at birthplace of Booker T. Washington to commemorate his life and contributions. Publ.: Pamphlets.

.1 Washington, Booker T., 1856-1915.
Miscellaneous. Books (40 v.), correspondence, photographs, works of art (5 items), and other materials by and about Washington. Includes a 17-minute film "What's a Heaven For" emphasizing Washington's accomplishments.

LAWRENCEVILLE

VA14 ST. PAUL'S COLLEGE, RUSSELL MEMORIAL LIBRARY. 23868. Tel 703 848-3111. Mrs. Clotea C. White, Librn.

.1 Afro-American Studies Collection.
ca. 1000 paperbacks. Basic books on the life and history of black Americans.

.2 St. Paul's College.
Archives. Includes correspondence, minutes of board meetings, records of admission, financial records, and other documents dealing with the administration and history of the College.

LYNCHBURG

VA15 VIRGINIA SEMINARY AND COLLEGE, MARY JANE CACHELIN LIBRARY. 24501. Tel 703 845-0941. Dr. M.C. Southerland, Pres.

.1 Virginia Seminary and College.
Archives. Includes correspondence, minutes of board meetings, records of admission, financial records, bulletins, and other documents dealing with the history and administration of the College and Seminary.

McLEAN

VA16 THE RESEARCH ANALYSIS CORPORATION (RAC). 22101. Tel 703 893-5900. Frank A. Parker, Pres.
RAC, with the cooperation of police authorities in Baltimore, has undertaken a systematic analysis of how the police operate in the city's largely Negro Western District. The project aims to develop objective information on how the police see the ghetto as a police problem, their own function and how it is performed, the relationship of their work to social controls in the ghetto itself. RAC is also under contract to determine the Negro community's perspective of the function of the police. A comparative analysis will be conducted on data obtained from the police and the citizens in this community.

.1 The Research Analysis Corporation.
Files. Includes correspondence, studies, reports, investigations, and other documents dealing with the aims, history, and programs of the Corporation.

MADISON HEIGHTS

VA17 FELLOWSHIP FOR RACIAL AND ECONOMIC EQUALITY (FREE) (1969). 24572. Tel 703 845-2301. W. Graham Barnes, Exec. Dir. Consultation.
FREE works in the white community, seeking ways to confront and combat racism.

NORFOLK

VA18 VIRGINIA STATE COLLEGE, NORFOLK DIVISION (1935), LIBRARY. 2401 Corprew Ave., 23504. Tel 703 627-4371. James S. Miller, Library Dir. Interlibrary loan, copying, inquiries answered, referrals made, consultation.

.1 Afro-American Studies Collection.
ca. 1000 paperbacks. Basic books on the life and history of black Americans.

.2 Materials relating to Negroes.
Miscellaneous. Includes books, periodical and newspaper titles, pamphlets, clippings, phonograph records, sheet music, mss, and other materials by and about Negroes.

PETERSBURG

VA19 PETERSBURG BATTLEFIELD MUSEUM CORPORATION. Franklin St., 23803.

.1 Petersburg campaign of 1864-65.
Papers, 1864-65. ca. 2 ft. and 3 reels of microfilm. Civil War letters of participants in the fighting at Petersburg, Va., diaries, the report of Gen. Bushrod Johnson (C.S.A.) on the Battle of the Crater, and an autograph book containing letters and contemporary photos of A.P. Hill, Robert E. Lee, J.E.B. Stuart, and Richard Taylor. Restricted.

VA20 VIRGINIA STATE COLLEGE (1882), JOHNSTON MEMORIAL LIBRARY. 23803. Tel 703 526-5111. Mrs. Catherine V. Bland, Acting Library Dir. Interlibrary loan, copying, inquiries answered, referrals made, consultation.

.1 Afro-American Studies collection.
ca. 1000 paperbacks. Basic books on the life and history of black Americans.

.2 Facts on Film.
Papers, 1954-67. Microfilm. Contains materials on civil rights and race relations in the South. See Race Relations Information Center, Nashville, Tenn., for a full description.

.3 Gandy, John Manual.
Papers, 1915-40. President of Virginia State College. Includes material dealing with education of Negroes in Virginia. Unavailable for research until late 1970.

.4 Jackson, Luther Porter.
Papers. History professor at Virginia State Col-

lege. Writings on the pre-Civil War free Negro in which area Jackson is an authority. Also included are records (1940-50) relating to Negro office holders in Virginia affiliated with the Virginia Negro Voters League. Unavailable for research until 1971.

.5 Johnston, James Hugo.
   Papers. Unavailable for research until late 1970.
.6 Mitchell, Arthur W., 1883-1968.
   Papers, 1883-1968. Xerox copies of the originals located in the Chicago Historical Society. Correspondence and other papers of Arthur W. Mitchell primarily relative to his service as a Representative from Illinois in the U.S. House of Representatives from January 1935 thru January 1943. Mitchell, the first Negro Democrat to serve in the House, was elected from the second U.S. Congressional district in Chicago, Ill., the seat formerly being held by Oscar DePriest and currently (1970) by William L. Dawson. In addition to their local and national political significance, the papers also concern Mitchell's role as director of Western Division of the Colored Voters of the Democratic National Committee in 1936.
.7 Prince Edward County, Va., Free Schools.
   Papers. Includes material pertaining to the Virginia Free Schools. Material uncatalogued.
.8 Virginia State College.
   Archives, 1882- . Financial records, bulletins, catalogs, and other material dealing with the history and administration of the College.
.9 Virginia Teachers Association.
   Papers. Deposited with the College when the Association merged with the Virginia Education Association. Material uncatalogued.

RADFORD

VA21 RADFORD COLLEGE, JOHN PRESTON McCONNELL LIBRARY (1913). 24141. Tel 703 639-1671. Elmer D. Johnson, Librn.

.1 Facts on Film.
   Papers, 1954-67. Microfilm. Contains materials on civil rights and race relations in the South. See Race Relations Information Center, Nashville, Tenn., for a full description.

RESTON

VA22 NEGRO HERITAGE (1961). 11372 Links Dr., 22070. Tel 703 471-1108. Sylvestre C. Watkins, Ed. and Publisher.
   Negro Heritage is a publication which seeks to present briefly the facts regarding Negro history and current Negro activity in the U.S. to stimulate further study in this area.
   Publ.: Negro Heritage, monthly magazine.

.1 Negro Heritage.
   Files, 1961- . Records, correspondence, reports, mss of articles, and other papers concerning the publication of the magazine.

RICHMOND

VA23 ANTI-DEFAMATION LEAGUE OF B'NAI B'RITH, NORTH CAROLINA-VIRGINIA REGIONAL OFFICE. 700 E. Main St., 23219. Tel 703 649-9137. Sherman Harris, Regional Dir.

VA24 CONFEDERATE MUSEUM, REFERENCE LIBRARY (1896). 1201 E. Clay St., 23219. Tel 703 648-8133. Eleanor S. Brockenbrough, Asst. Dir. and Librn. Copying.

.1 Materials pertaining to slavery and the Negro.
   Miscellaneous, 1861-65. Includes books, magazine clippings, pamphlets (ca. 33), and a few mss such as slave bill of sale, insurance policy, deed of manumission, impressment receipt, and pass.
.2 Statutes of the Confederate States, and General Orders from Adjutant and Inspector General's Office.
   Papers. Includes references to slavery.

VA25 DEFENDERS OF STATE SOVEREIGNTY AND INDIVIDUAL LIBERTIES. 405-A E. Franklin, 23218. James R. Orgain, Dir.
   Publ.: Defenders Bulletin; Defender's News and Views.

VA26 NATIONAL CONFERENCE OF CHRISTIANS AND JEWS (NCCJ) (1928). 2317 Westwood Ave., 23230. Tel 703 359-2137. Dr. Peter Mellette, Dir.
   NCCJ works "...to promote justice, amity, understanding and cooperation among Protestants, Catholics and Jews, and to analyze, moderate and finally eliminate intergroup prejudices which disfigure and distort religious, business, social and political relations with a view to the establishment of a social order in which the religious ideals of brotherhood and justice shall become the standard of human relationships."

.1 National Conference of Christians and Jews.
   Miscellaneous. A limited number of intergroup relations films, plays, music, books, and publications.

VA27 THE PRESBYTERIAN CHURCH IN THE U.S., DIVISION OF HIGHER EDUCATION. Box 1176, 23209. Tel 703 649-9021. Rev. John B. Evans, Dir.

.1 Division of Higher Education.
   Files. Correspondence, minutes of board meetings, financial records, and other materials relating to the Division's support of Stillman College, Tuscaloosa, Ala.

VA28 RICHMOND URBAN LEAGUE, INC. (1923). 112 E. Clay St., 23219. Tel 703 643-7343. Randolph C. Kendall, Jr., Exec. Dir.

VA29 UNION THEOLOGICAL SEMINARY IN VIRGINIA (1812), LIBRARY (1806). 3401 Brook Rd., 23227. Tel 703 353-2846. Dr. H.M. Brimm, Librn. Interlibrary loan, copying, inquiries answered.

.1 Materials relating to Negroes.
   Miscellaneous. Includes books, periodical titles, theses and dissertations, and a collection of 19th century pamphlets (ca. 6 boxes) on race relations.

VA30 THE VALENTINE MUSEUM (1898), THE RESEARCH LIBRARY (1928). 1015 E. Clay St., 23219. Tel 703 649-0711. Mrs. Stuart B. Gibson, Librn. Inquiries answered.

.1 Friends, Society of.
   Records of Quaker meetings in Virginia, 1673-1844. ca. 2 ft. Transcripts (typewritten) made in 1906-07 from originals in the possession of the Baltimore Orthodox Friends. Letter book of Robert Pleasants, of Curlew, Va., relating to the abolition movement among Virginia Quakers; miscellaneous letters, journals, memorials, and other papers; and minute books and other records of Friends' and Women Friends' Meetings in Virginia.
.2 Materials relating to Negroes.
   Miscellaneous. Includes books, periodical and newspaper titles, pamphlets, theses and dissertations, clippings, photographs, and historical objects.

VA31 VIRGINIA COUNCIL ON HUMAN RELATIONS (VCHR) (1955). 214 E. Clay St., 23219. Tel 703 648-4444. Curtis W. Harris, State Coordinator. Consultation to local councils.
   The Council works to carry on in Virginia an educational program for the improvement of economic, civic and racial conditions. Affiliated with the Southern Regional Council, Inc., Atlanta, Ga.
   Publ.: The VCHR Observer, periodically.

.1 Virginia Council on Human Relations.
   Files, 1955- . Includes correspondence, minutes of meetings, financial records, and other documents dealing with the aims, history, and programs of the Council. Restricted.

VA32 VIRGINIA HISTORICAL SOCIETY (1831), LIBRARY. 428 North Boulevard, 23221. Tel 703 358-4901. John M. Jennings, Librn.
   The Society library holds in excess of 3 million mss;

thousands of books, pamphlets, newspapers, prints and engravings, broadsides, sheets of music, maps and charts, as well as large collections of original works of art and cabinet objects. When "dealing with research materials on Virginia history you are dealing in virtually all cases with research materials in some way relating to the American Negro." Therefore, "virtually all of our holdings are pertinent" to this field. The following ms collections "constitute a mere token of the magnitude of our holdings."

VA32.1 (This number not used).

.2 Allen, Robert Henderson, 1817-1900.
Papers, 1850-1910. 106 items. Farmer and local official, of Oral Oaks, Lunenburg Co., Va. Correspondence, diaries (1858-1900), account books (1850-61, 1877-1910), fiduciary books (1890-1900), judgment and execution books (1883-1900), broadsides, printed matter, family Bible, and other family papers. The material concerns Allen's farming and social activities, his positions as commissioner of accounts and justice of the peace, business accounts, Army raids in Lunenburg Co. during the Civil War, Allen's work as an agent for the Freedmen's Bureau, and other material.

.3 Bassett family.
Papers, 1693-1886. ca. 2000 items. Papers of the Bassett family, of Eltham, New Kent Co., Va., and of the Lewis family, of Hanover Co., Va. Includes a plantation account book, papers concerning the settlement of the estate of William Langborn, and other materials.

.4 Charlotte County, Virginia.
Records, 1763-1896. 1003 items. Order books, docket books and other court records, accounts, correspondence, fee books, memorandum books, register of replevy bonds filed in clerk's office, execution book, receipts book, and other records of the county clerk; real estate and personal property assessments, lists of free Negroes, and other statistics, tax lists, and county records.

.5 Claiborne family.
Papers, 1803-1954. 1060 items. Correspondence, diaries (1903-23), accounts, wills, bonds, agreements, scrapbook, genealogical notes, and other papers of the Claiborne family. Includes correspondence and accounts of Henry Coalter Cabell, diaries of Catherine Hamilton (Cabell) Claiborne Cox, material concerning the imprisonment of John Brown at Harper's Ferry, the Tredegar Co., Richmond, and secession and Reconstruction in South Carolina. Among the correspondents are Salmon P. Chase, Philip St. George Cocke, and members of the Claiborne and Cabell families.

.6 Cocke, Philip St. George, 1809-61.
Plantation records, 1854-71. 6 v. Planter. Records kept by Samuel P. Collier, John W. Talbot, and George W. Taylor, Cocke's plantation managers, in Cocke's plantation and farm instruction, regulation, record, inventory and account book (Richmond, 1852 and 1861). The material concerns daily operations, slaves, and farm equipment, at Belmead and Beldale plantations, Powhatan Co., Va.

.7 Colonization Society of Virginia.
Records, 1823-59. 2 v. Minute book (Nov. 4, 1823-Feb. 5, 1859) and account book (1849-58). The minute book was kept by Frederick Bransford, David J. Burr, Peachy R. Grattan, James E. Hearth, Thomas Calthorpe Howard, Fleming James, Benjamin B. Minor, and John O. Steger, and was approved and endorsed by presidents John Marshall and John B. Floyd; the account book was kept by Thomas Harding Ellis and William Williams. Includes records for the period when the Society was an auxiliary of the American Colonization Society.

.8 Conrad family.
Papers, 1794-1959. 392 items. Correspondence, account book, scrapbook, deeds, speeches, agreements, writings, genealogical notes and other papers, of the family of Holmes Conrad of Winchester, Va. The materials relate to service in the Virginia legislature, various Confederate leaders, John Brown's raid at Harper's Ferry, and other matters. Among the correspondents are Elizabeth Tucker Coalter Bryan, Elizabeth Whiting Powell Conrad, Holmes Conrad, Robert Young Conrad, Jedediah Hotchkiss and Edwin McMasters Stanton.

.9 Cropper, John, 1755-1821.
Papers, 1779-1820. 396 items. Army officer, and planter of Accomac Co., Va. Correspondence, accounts, polls of Accomac Co., and other papers, including material on county, State and national politics, Virginia Militia affairs, slaves and slavery, and other subjects.

.10 Edmunds family.
Papers, 1826-50. 99 items. Correspondence, account book, commonplace book, accounts, newspaper articles, slave records and other papers. Persons represented include Jane Watkins (Edmunds)Berkeley, Peyton Randolph Berkeley, Mary Dupuy (Edmunds) Dupuy, Bettie J. Edmunds, Henry Edwin Edmunds, Jane Watkins (Dupuy) Edmunds, Lucy Jane (Barksdale) Edmunds, Nannie W. Edmunds, Nicholas S. Edmunds, Susan W. Edmunds, Nicholas Edmunds Flournoy, Belle (Edmunds) Morton, Sallie Elizabeth (Edmunds) Scott, and others.

.11 Hannah family.
Papers, 1760-1967. 4721 items. Correspondence, diary, deeds to land in Charlotte Co., Va., other deeds, plats, surveys, other land papers, bonds, agreements, accounts, other financial papers, estate papers, court papers, legal papers, wills, commonplace books, commissions, military papers, powers of attorney, affidavits, price lists, essays, inventories, reports, cookbooks, and other papers, of the Hannah family, chiefly of "Gravel Hill," Charlotte Co., Va., relating in part to taxation, hiring of free Negroes, slaves, and other subjects. Includes genealogical notes on the Allen, Edmunds, Hannah, Morton and other families. Persons represented include Lucy Morton (Hannah) Atkinson, Nannie Irene (Hannah) Barringer, Anne (Atkinson) Burmeister Chamberlayne, of "Gravel Hill," Ann (Cunningham) Hannah Dabbs (1755-1825), Andrew Hannah (b. 1780), Ann Eliza (Spragins) Hannah (1824-73), George Cunningham Hannah (1817-88), George Hannah (1772?-1870), Joel Watkins Hannah (1811-85), John Spragins Hannah, of "Gravel Hill," Samuel Baldwin Hannah (1843-1921), of "Gravel Hill," William Morton Hannah (1820-93), and Mary Almira (Hannah) Worth, and others

.12 Ingle, Edward, 1861-1924.
Papers, 1858-1961. 352 items. Journalist, of Richmond, Va., and Baltimore, Md. Correspondence (1883-1923); essays (1895-1924); diary (1900), and records (1923) kept by Ingle as secretary of the Monumental Church Association, Richmond, Va.; together with papers of his wife, Mary Friend (Mayo) Ingle, including correspondence (1930-40), commonplace book (1885-90), accounts (1921-23), and poetry. Ingle's correspondence and essays deal, in part, with education of Negroes, and other social issues in the South; cotton; agriculture; and other persons and subjects.

.13 Nalle, Albert G., 1811-87.
Papers, 1773-1915. 1351 items. In part, photocopies made from originals in the possession of Albert Nalle, Philadelphia, Pa. Correspondence (1834-84) of Nalle of Orange Court House, Va., Richmond, and New Orleans, concerning the cultivation of cotton at "Panola Plantation," receipts for cotton supplied to New Orleans by Nalle; muster rolls (1813); accounts; mortgage; and other business papers. Among persons represented are Jesse Nalle and various members of the Nalle family.

.14 Picot family.
Papers, 1753-1907. 63 items. Correspondence (1830-35) of Dr. Abel Francis Picot; correspondence (1849-53) of John Poe Harrison (1832-61); correspondence (1846-67) and accounts (1863-70) of Benjamin Temple as executor of the estate of Robert Temple of "Ampthill," Chesterfield Co.,

Va.; deed, terms of sale, and list of heirs to the estate; lists (1863-67) of Negroes held by Elizabeth (Skyren) Temple, wife of Robert Temple; letters and accounts of various members of the family; and genealogical notes concerning the Robinson, Spotswood, and Temple families.

.15 Pollard family.
Papers, 1782-1907. 2743 items. Correspondence, accounts, deeds, wills, agreements, bonds, lists of delinquent taxpayers, materials concerning lawsuits and the administration of estates, broadsides, memorabilia, and other papers. Much of the collection pertains to Peter Thornton Pollard and his positions as county deputy sheriff and postmaster at King and Queen Court House, Va., the plantations there, slave trade in King and Queen Co., Va., and other subjects. Correspondents include Herbert Augustine Claiborne, Catherine R. Latané, members of the Fauntleroy, Pollard, Roy, and Spencer families, and others.

.16 Rutherfoord family.
Papers, 1811-1946. 200 items. Correspondence, diaries, memorandum book, commonplace books, speeches, military instructions, lists, plats, land grant, map, power of attorney, oath, resolutions, agreements, poem, essay, genealogical notes, and other papers, relating in part to law practice in Virginia, plantations, slaves and slavery in Virginia, Virginia and Confederate politics, service in the Virginia House of Delegates, and secession. Persons represented include Ann Seddon (Rutherfoord) Johnson, John Coles Rutherfoord (1825-66), John Rutherfoord (fl. 1824-61), of Richmond, Va., and John Rutherfoord (1861-1942), of New Rochelle, N.Y., and Richmond, Va.

.17 Snead, Robert Winn, 1822-1903.
Papers, 1860-62. 75 items. Chiefly correspondence and orders of Snead, Confederate soldier from "Woodlawn," Pedlar Mills, Amherst Co., Va. Among the correspondents are William S. Hannah, Octavia Virginia (Winn) Snead, Robert Benjamin Snead, and Aunt Peggy, a Negro slave.

.18 Trist, Nicholas Philip, 1800-74.
Papers, 1791-1836. 112 items. Diplomat and lawyer. Correspondence and other papers, concerning secession, nullification, and other matters.

.19 Waller, William M.
Papers, including materials concerning slavery.

.20 Winston, Bickerton Lyle.
Slave account book.

.21 Young, William Proby.
Papers, 1860. Physician on board the "Castilian." Diary concerning the American Colonization Society. Young's ports of call were New York, Key West, Cape Mount, Robertsport, Monrovia, Grand Bassa, and New Orleans, La.

VA33 VIRGINIA STATE LIBRARY (1828). 12th and Capitol Sts., 23219. Tel 703 770-2333. Randolph W. Church, State Librn. Interlibrary loan, copying, inquiries answered, referrals made.

.1 Asheville, North Carolina, Armory.
Records, Dec. 24, 1861-May 31, 1864. ca. 4 items. Copies of letters sent to slave owners, requesting slave labor for the Armory.

.2 Bristow, Robert, 1643-1707.
Papers, 1688-1750. 2 v. Owner of Virginia lands and London merchant. Ledger (1688-1750) and letter book (1705-37, 1746-50) of Bristow and his grandson Robert Bristow relating to their activities in Virginia trade, to their lands, to the management of the various plantations, and to purchases of tobacco and other goods.

.3 Bryan family.
Papers, 1679-1943. 2650 items. Correspondence, diaries (1827-29 and 1888), business and legal papers, addresses, poems, essays, genealogical materials, and other papers pertaining to the Bryan family. The materials concern family affairs, slavery, politics, public policy, the South,

Virginia, Jefferson Davis, Bland-Randolph, Bryan, Coalter families, and other matters. Important correspondents include John Randolph Bryan, John Stewart Bryan, Joseph Bryan (1773-1812), Joseph Bryan (1845-1908), and others.

.4 Governor and Council of the State (Virginia).
Papers, 1774-1954. ca. 126 v. and 1,892,250 items. Includes Council journals (1776-1954), executive letter books, Continental Congress papers (1774-89, ca. 4000 items), naval officers' returns (1782-89), papers relating to John Brown's raid (1859), and correspondence for most of the governors.

.5 Jerdone family.
Papers, 1749-1865. Includes Jerdone family slave book (1761-1865); a journal of Francis Jerdone (1749-60, 2 v.) and a memorandum book (1766-67).

.6 Massie, William.
Records. Includes a slave book (1836-1913?) which is "a register of Negroes ages, made out February 1836" giving name, approximate date of birth, age, how slave was obtained, value, and sometimes note of death. Later additions made include list of Massie's taxable property (1840's). Also included is a farm journal (1817-44).

.7 Papers relating to slavery.
Miscellaneous, May-September, 1861. Includes payrolls of slaves employed on defensive works, and payrolls of persons employed on Confederate fortifications during the Civil War.

.8 Virginia Legislature.
Papers. Includes petitions from Accomac, Albemarle, Alexandria, Allegheny, Amelia, Amherst, Appomatox, Augusta, Barbour, Bath, and Bedford counties which include small amounts of material pertaining to the Negro.

VA34 VIRGINIA UNION UNIVERSITY, WILLIAM J. CLARK LIBRARY. 1500 N. Lombardy St., 23220. Tel 703 355-0631. Mrs. Verdelle V. Bradley, Librn. Interlibrary loan, inquiries answered, consultation.

.1 Afro-American Studies Collection.
ca. 1000 paperbacks. Basic books on the life and history of black Americans.

.2 Lewis, Howard. collector.
Books. ca. 1800. Books by and about Negroes.

.3 Virginia Union University.
Archives. Includes correspondence, minutes of board meetings, financial records, bulletins, records of admission, and other documents dealing with the history and administration of the University.

WILLIAMSBURG

VA35 COLLEGE OF WILLIAM AND MARY (1693), EARL GREGG SWEM LIBRARY (1693). 23185. Tel 703 229-3000. William C. Pollard, Librn. Interlibrary loan, copying.

.1 Barker, David.
Barker, Cooke papers, 1820-82. 182 items. Correspondence, accounts, and other papers of David Barker of Fluvanna Co., Va., and James E. Cooke, of Powhatan Co., Va. Includes letters concerning the hiring out of slaves, one giving instructions on the operation of a plantation during the absence of the owner, and data concerning the Civil War.

.2 Blow family.
Papers, 1732-1890. Correspondence, account books, ledgers, and other papers from Tower Hill Plantation, Sussex Co., Va. Includes records of tobacco sales before 1755; letter recounting the difficulties with the Algerian pirates in 1794 and the yellow fever scare in Philadelphia (1802); lists of the white persons killed and Negroes executed in the Nat Turner Rebellion of 1831; a typewritten history of the plantation with 31 drawings, by William Nivison Blow; and genealogical material on the Blow family. Family members represented include Samuel Blow (fl. 1740), Richard Blow (fl. 1762), Michael Blow (fl. 1766), Richard Blow (fl. 1810), George Blow (fl. 1891), Robert Blow (fl. 1827), William N. Blow (fl. 1850), Col. George Blow, and George Blow, Jr., who served in the Civil War, and Lucy P. Blow (fl. 1890).

.3 Brown, Alexander, 1843-1906.
Papers, 1774-1910. 5817 items. Merchant and author, of Nelson, Va. Correspondence, business papers, and materials relating to the writing of Brown's books. Includes letters (1861-65) from Brown written while he was in the Confederate Army; family letters written while he was in the Confederate Army; family letters (1867-69); ledgers of the "Union Hall" and "Norwood" plantations, with detailed instructions for plantation management; and other matters.

.4 Brown, Charles, ca. 1772-1879.
Papers, 1792-1888. 896 items. Physician and sheriff of Albemarle Co., Va. Correspondence, accounts, legal papers, and other papers. Some of the correspondence with patients contain prescriptions, and some letters concern sick slaves. Includes correspondence of Bezabeel Brown for 1807-29, of Bezabeel J. Brown for 1854-88, and of other members of the Brown family.

.5 Brown, Coalter, Tucker families.
Papers, 1769-1919. 4276 items. Family and business correspondence, legal papers, accounts, notes, poems, and other papers reflecting life in Williamsburg, Staunton, Petersburg, Fredericksburg, and other cities and towns in Virginia, plantation life in Bedford and Gloucester counties, Va. Includes reports of John Thompson Brown from Nassau Hall, Princeton, N.J., with a list of courses (1818-20), Brown's speeches on slavery, states rights, and the growth of political parties, made as a member of the Virginia Assembly from Clarksburg, Harrison Co. (now W.Va.), and from Petersburg, Va. (1828-36); and genealogical material on the Ball, Brown, Coalter, Tomlin, Tucker, and Williamson families.

.6 Cabell family.
Papers, 1719-1839. 3491 items. Militia orders, surveyor's license, surveys of Amherst, Albemarle, and Nelson counties and the Warminister area of Virginia; list of slaves, deeds, letters, and other papers of Dr. William Cabell; his sons, Col. William Cabell, member of the House of Burgess and the Virginia State Senate, and Joseph C. Cabell, a member of the House of Burgess and the House of Delegates; and William Cabell, Jr., a major in the Revolutionary War and sheriff of Amherst Co., Va.

.7 Carter family.
Papers, 1667-1862. 8604 items. Correspondence, accounts, and other papers of a family living on plantations along the James River, reflecting the social, business, and political life of Virginia. Includes much genealogical material on the Carter family. Principal family members represented are Robert "King" Carter (1663-1732), Robert Carter, II, his son Robert "Councillor" Carter, both of "Nomini," and his grandson George Carter, Charles Carter (1707-1764) of "Cleve," Landon Carter (1710-78) of "Sabine Hall," his wife Elizabeth Carter and his son Landon Carter, Jr., Charles Carter (1732-1806) of "Shirley," Robert Wormeley Carter, Sr., Robert Wormeley Carter (1734-97) of "Sabine Hall" and his daughters Elizabeth L. and Miss C. Carter. Other persons represented include George B. Carter, John Armistead Carter, Kate Carter, and John Tayloe.

.8 Chappelear family.
Papers, 1876-1959. 425 items. Maps and surveys of portions of Fauquier, Loudoun, Clark, Warren, and Frederick counties, Va., with the surveyor's field notes on the families who owned the land; genealogical material on the Chappelear family and others; ledgers and account books of John S., Elizabeth, and Samuel Owens of "Hopewell," of John Edmonds, J. Hunter, Lewis Strother, and J. Pendleton Chappelear; and newspaper clippings on the McCue murder case (1905), the Strother murder case (1907), and the Allen murder case (1912).

.9 Dromgoole, W. Edward.
Papers, 1866-96. 69 items. Correspondence, accounts, and field notes of Dromgoole of Westward Plantation and Siggard Creek Plantation in North Carolina, and addresses that he made to local

groups; papers of Robert Dromgoole; and other material.

.10 Hope, James Barron, 1820-87.
Papers, 1790-1907. 993 items. Author and Confederate Army officer, of Norfolk, Va. Correspondence, poems, addresses, newspaper clippings, and other papers. Includes a description of the rioting in Danville, Va. (1883); accounts of Hope's activities in publishing a newspaper, The Landmark in the Reconstruction period; and letters from William B. Taliaferro and others.

.11 Jones, Warner Throckmorton, 1819-91.
Papers, 1807-91. 2674 items. Correspondence and business papers of Judge Warner T. Jones, of Warner Hall, Gloucester Co., Va., his brother Richard P. Jones, of Land's End, Gloucester Co., and his nephew, John R. Page. Many letters refer to political developments in the years immediately before the Civil War when Jones was a member of the Virginia House of Delegates. Several letters (1855) are concerned with the hiring out of Jones' slaves by an agent in Richmond, Va. Includes notes for and drafts of many of his speeches; letters (1870) from John Randolph Bryan and his son, St. George Bryan, regarding the sale of their plantation; letters from Jefferson W. Stubbs, John Tabb, and William B. Taliaferro; and other material.

.12 Luttrell family.
Luttrell, Cooke papers, 1820-1900. 442 items. Correspondence of the Luttrell and Cooke families of Culpeper and Rappahannock counties, Va. Includes correspondence; among which are several letters (1853-1859) from Missouri on the living conditions, abolitionist activities, and future prospects of the area.

.13 Myers, Gustavus A.
Papers, 1834-69. 54 items. Lawyer, of Richmond, Va. Correspondence of Myer, together with letters of Thomas G. Tabb, John T. Tazewell, John A. Washington, and L.Q. Washington, relating in part to arrangements for the sale of Mount Vernon and Reconstruction problems in the South.

.14 Watkins, Nathaniel V.
Papers, 1852-89. 528 items. Correspondence of Watkins with his brother and sister, Richard H. Watkins and Pattie (Watkins) Scott, Prince Edward Court House, Va., and with his wife, relating to his experiences with the Virginia Heavy Artillery, Company H, to the Civil War, the conditions of Negroes after the war, and the post-war period in general.

VA36   COLONIAL WILLIAMSBURG, INC., RESEARCH DEPARTMENT LIBRARY. Box C, Francis and Henry Sts., 23185. Tel 703 229-1000. Mrs. Rose K. Belk, Librn. Interlibrary loan, copying, inquiries answered.
Publ.: The Negro in 18th Century Williamsburg (research study, 1965).

.1 Blathwayt, William, 1649?-1717.
Papers, 1674-1715. 2568 items. British colonial administrator. Official papers pertaining to affairs in the American continental colonies and the British West Indies, chiefly letters written to Blathwayt in London by officials in the royal colonies and some rough drafts of Blathwayt's letters. Topics covered include illegal colonial trade and attempt to enforce the Navigation acts; the tobacco trade in Virginia; wars with the French and Spanish in Jamaica; the Negro question in the Leeward Islands; and the struggle between successive governors and the Assembly in Bermuda.

VIRGIN ISLANDS

ST. THOMAS

VI1   COLLEGE OF THE VIRGIN ISLANDS (1963), LIBRARY (1963). P.O. Box 1826, 00801. Tel 809 747-1252. Ernest C. Wagner, Head Librn. Interlibrary loan, bibliographies prepared, literature searches, copying, typing, inquiries answered, referrals made.

.1 Holstein, Caspar.
   Collection of books and papers concerning the
   African heritage of the Negro, persons of African
   descent, West Indians, and American Negroes.
.2 Newspaper Clipping Collection.
   Newspaper clippings. Clippings of Virgin Islands
   area newspapers are kept in subject files and include such subjects as West Indians and American
   Negroes, civil rights, and segregation in housing
   and employment.

WASHINGTON

OLYMPIA

WA1   WASHINGTON STATE BOARD AGAINST DISCRIMINATION
       (1949). WEA Building, 319 Seventh Ave. E., 98501. Tel
       206 753-6771. Alfred E. Cowles, Exec. Secy.
       The Board works to advance civil rights through invest-
       igating complaints of discrimination in housing, health
       services, education, labor, and welfare services.
       Publ.: Newsletter, quarterly; Annual Report.

       .1 Washington State Board Against Discrimination.
          Files, ca. 1949- . Documentation dealing with the
          aims, program and history of the Board. Includes
          correspondence, reports, studies, investigations,
          minutes of meetings and financial records.

PASCO

WA2   WASHINGTON STATE BOARD AGAINST DISCRIMINATION,
       REGIONAL OFFICE (1949). Room 11, 824 W. Lewis
       St., 99301. Tel 509 547-8321. Mrs. Isabelle G. Rosen-
       fels, Field Rep. Typing, inquiries answered, referrals
       made, consultation.
       The Board works to prevent and eliminate discrimina-
       tion in employment, housing and places of public ac-
       commodation.

SEATTLE

WA3   AMERICAN CIVIL LIBERTIES UNION (ACLU) OF WASH-
       INGTON. 2101 Smith Tower, 98104. Tel 206 624-2180.
       Margaret A. Woolf, Off. Mgr.

WA4   AMERICAN FRIENDS SERVICE COMMITTEE (AFSC), COM-
       MUNITY RELATIONS DIVISION, PACIFIC NORTHWEST
       REGIONAL OFFICE. 814 N.E. 40th St., 98105. Tel 206
       632-0502. Arthur M. Dye, Jr., Exec. Secy.
       Publ.: Quaker Service, Pacific Northwest Regional Edi-
       tion, quarterly.

WA5   AMERICAN JEWISH COMMITTEE, NORTHWEST AREA.
       1306 Second Ave., 98101. Tel 206 622-3931.

WA6   ANTI-DEFAMATION LEAGUE OF B'NAI B'RITH, PACIFIC
       NORTHWEST REGIONAL OFFICE. 1718 Smith Tower,
       98104. Tel 206 624-5750. Seymour Kaplan, Dir.

WA7   CAMBRIDGE SCHOOLS, INTERNATIONAL; SIMMONS
       INSTITUTE OF HUMAN RELATIONS LIBRARY. 15004
       Dayton St., 98133. Tel 206 263-4215. Charles M. Sim-
       mons, Librn.

WA8   CENTRAL SEATTLE COMMUNITY COUNCIL (1947). 417
       Rainier Ave. S., 98144. Tel 206 324-6668. Miss Ruth
       A. Brandwein, Exec. Dir. Copying, typing, inquiries
       answered, referrals made, consultation, community
       organization.
       The Council, created (1967) through a merger of the
       Jackson Street Community Council (formed in 1946 to
       serve the needs of the Seattle ghetto) and the Central
       Area Community Council (formed in 1962 to bring to-
       gether service organizations serving the central ghetto
       area), provides programs in recreation, housing, educa-
       tion, health and welfare and transportation for commu-
       nity improvement.
       Publ.: Annual Report; CSCC Newsletter, monthly.

.1 Central Seattle Community Council.
   Files, ca. 1964- . Books, periodical and newspaper
   titles, pamphlets, correspondence, clippings, photographs and phonograph records. Among current
   files are statistical materials for the city of Seattle
   on housing and education, transportation, minority
   population, urban renewal, and neighborhood improvements; and organization listings, chiefly for
   Seattle's minority community, covering 20 years of
   community reorganization work. The dead files
   (1947-64) of the Council are in the Manuscript Division of the University of Washington Library.

WA9   CONGRESS OF RACIAL EQUALITY (CORE). P.O. Box 299,
       98110. Tel 206 349-4415. John Cornethan, Chmn.

WA10   NATIONAL CONFERENCE OF CHRISTIANS AND JEWS
       (NCCJ). 1506 Westlake Ave., 98101. Tel 206 622-7310.
       Wilfred A. Burton, Jr., Dir.

WA11   SEATTLE HUMAN RIGHTS DEPARTMENT (1969). Room
       305, Seattle Municipal Bldg., 98104. Philip Hayasaka,
       Dir. Referrals made, consultation.
       The Department carries out programs in education,
       studies and investigates problems which may result in
       tensions or discrimination.
       Publ.: News Bulletin, monthly.

WA12   SEATTLE OPPORTUNITIES INDUSTRIALIZATION CEN-
       TER, INC. (1966). 2332 E. Madison St., 98102. Tel 206
       324-8270. Rex D. Jones, Exec. Dir.
       The Center works to recruit, train and later place in
       jobs those persons formerly classified as underem-
       ployed, unemployed and untrainable.
       Publ.: Newsletter, monthly.

WA13   SEATTLE URBAN LEAGUE, INC. (1936). 1620 Smith
       Tower, 506 Second Ave., 98104. Tel 206 622-2322.
       Jerome W. Page, Exec. Dir.
       The League seeks to assist in solving problems of race
       relations, to raise the living standards of non-whites,
       and to assist non-whites to obtain adequate employment,
       housing, health, educational, and cultural opportunities.
       It provides educational and promotional programs to
       improve interracial understanding, cooperates with
       management and labor to remove racial barriers, pro-
       vides on-the-job training, and employment, health and
       welfare referrals. It also administers tuition scholar-
       ship assistance to black students.
       Publ.: Newsletter; Annual Report; Special reports, in-
          cluding "Seattle's Racial Gap: 1968" containing
          statistics and commentary.

       .1 Seattle Urban League, Inc.
          Miscellaneous. Includes books by and about black
          Americans and intergroup relations, periodicals,
          and reprints of articles concerning race relations.
          Restricted.

WA14   UNITED GOOD NEIGHBOR-KING COUNTY, PLANNING
       DIVISION. 107 Cherry, 98104. Tel 206 682-8161.
       Roger Thibaudeau, Dir., Planning Div.
       The Division plans for work in the community with
       major programs in the areas of social policy, health,
       welfare and recreation, social attitudes, volunteer
       bureau, information and referral services.
       Publ.: Community Planning, bimonthly.

WA15   UNIVERSITY OF WASHINGTON LIBRARIES, MANUSCRIPT
       COLLECTION (1958). 98105. Tel 206 543-1879. Rich-
       ard C. Berner, Univ. Archivist. Interlibrary loan,
       bibliographies prepared, copying, inquiries answered,
       referrals made, consultation.
       Publ.: Library Leaflets.

       .1 Adams, Mary Elizabeth.
          Scrapbooks, 1860-1947. General materials, with
          emphasis on Seattle and vincinity. Contain infor-
          mation concerning Seattle's Negro community.
       .2 American Civil Liberties Union.
          Records, 1917-39. ca. 5 reels. Materials per-
          taining to the Pacific Northwest. Microfilmed from
          the ACLU archives at the Firestone Library,
          Princeton University, 1966-67.

WA15.3 Anti-Defamation League of B'nai B'rith.
Files, ca. 1942-66. 4 ft. Correspondence, reports, ephemera concerning race relations in Washington and Oregon.

.4 Asberry, Nettie J., -1968.
Papers, 1886-1966. 1 ft. Biographical sketch, correspondence, minutes, photos, reports and ephemera. Mrs. Asberry was closely associated with the Colored Women's Federation of Washington, and was the founder of the NAACP in Tacoma, Wash.

.5 Barnett, Powell S., 1883- .
Papers, 1960-67. 19 items. Civic leader. Reminiscences, ephemera, clippings, tape recording concerning family migration to Roslyn, Wash., in 1888 to mine coal, and organizations in which he was active, among them the Jackson Street Community Council, Northwest Baseball Umpire's Association, American Federation of Musicians, Washington. The tape recording is an interview with Mr. Barnett by R. C. Berner, May 31, 1967.

.6 Benson, Naomi Achenbach, ca. 1878- .
Papers, 1898-1961. 20 ft. Civic leader and teacher. Correspondence, diaries, notebooks, pamphlets, financial records, campaign materials, clippings, and other papers relating to Miss Benson's interest in liberal political organizations in King and Snohomish counties, Wash. Includes materials on American Civil Liberties Union, American Friends Service Committee, Americans for Democratic Action, Civil Rights Congress, Civil Liberties Committee, Women's International League for Peace and Freedom, and other civic organizations.

.7 Burton, Philip L.
Papers, 1950-62. ca. 1000 items. Seattle, Wash., attorney and civic leader. Correspondence and related materials about civil rights legal case work; activities as member of NAACP Executive Committee, of American Civil Liberties Executive Committee (ca. 1950-62), and as chairman of ACLU Juvenile Due Process Committee (1957-58).

.8 Caldwell, Harrison, -1964.
Papers, 1942-64. 24 items. Educator in Topeka, Kans., and Seattle, Wash., and writer. Clippings, photographs, and unpublished ms, "Studies in Negro Life," (1953), prepared at University of Kansas.

.9 Carter, Randolph Warren.
Papers, 1964-68. 2 inches. Correspondence, minutes, and tape-recorded interview. Concerning the Washington State Board Against Discrimination and the Seattle Model City Program.

.10 Caughlan, John.
Files, 1947-62. 25 ft. Civic leader and attorney. Correspondence and case files relating to civil liberties.

.11 Central Seattle Community Council.
Papers, 1946-66. 13 ft. Formerly Jackson Street Community Council. Correspondence, reports, scrapbooks, ephemera, and clippings dealing with problems of minorities of central district. University of Washington is official archives for its inactive records.

.12 Civic Unity Committee, Seattle.
Records, 1944-64. 25 ft. Chiefly correspondence of an unofficial race relations-civil rights committee, together with the complete reports of the Committee's activities and a nearly complete set of minutes. The bulk of the collection dates from 1955-64, and includes material on individual case histories. Other papers relate to the Northwest Institute of Race Relations sponsored by the Committee (1948-53) and the Washington State Committee Against Discrimination in Employment (1945-49). Correspondents include the Civic Unity Committee's presidents and executive secretaries (Arthur G. Barnett, Louise P. Blackham, Henry Elliott, John F. Gordon, Paul R. Green, George Greenwood, John H. Heitzman, Frank P. Helsell, Archie S. Katz, Ann P. Madsen, Irene Burns Miller, and Alfred J. Westberg) and the American Council on Race Relations, American Jewish Committee, American Jewish Congress, the Anti-Defamation League of B'nai B'rith, Christian Friends for Racial Equality, King County (Wash.) Intergroup

Relations Committee, the National Association of Intergroup Relations Officials, National Conference of Christians and Jews, New York (City) Commission for Human Rights, the Seattle mayor, Seattle public schools, the Urban League of Portland, the Washington Citizens Committee for Civil Rights Legislation, Washington State legislators, Washington National Guard, Washington State Advisory Committee to the U.S. Civil Rights Commission, Washington State Board Against Discrimination in Employment, and the Washington State Committee Against Discrimination.

.13 Coney, Byron.
Files, 1956-62. Attorney. Papers, notes, and correspondence relating to his work with American Civil Liberties Union.

.14 Cooper, Felix Bond.
Papers, 1943-69. 3.5 ft. Correspondence, clippings, photos, minutes, and ephemera. Materials concerning the activities of Cooper and his wife, Bella Taylor McKnight, in local and national civic affairs. Also includes material concerning the Harmon Foundation's "Portraits of Outstanding Americans of Negro Origin."

.15 DeBow, Samuel P.
Scrapbook, 1915-36. Includes letters, photos, leaflets, and clippings, relating to Washington Negroes.

.16 Devin, William Franklin, 1898- .
Papers, 1957-61. 5 ft. ca. 2000 items. Lawyer, judge, and mayor of Seattle, Wash. Correspondence, briefs, reports, negotiations, date books, scrapbooks on campaigns and other campaign materials, relating to Devin's work as Municipal Court judge, as politician, as mayor, and as a lawyer involved in a number of organizations. Included among subjects are materials relating to the Washington State Advisory Committee to the U.S. Commission on Civil Rights (1958-59).

.17 Dixon, William H.
Papers, 1898-1955. 19 items. Newspaper, ephemera, letters, reminiscences, concerning the William Gross family. Gross came to Seattle in 1859.

.18 Farquharson, Mary, 1902-
Papers, 1934-48. ca. 2000 items. Washington State senator and civic leader. Chiefly correspondence and clippings relating to Mrs. Farquharson's terms as senator (1935-42) with some papers relating to the Women's International League for Peace and Freedom and the American Civil Liberties Union.

.19 Gage, Fern, -1964.
Papers, ca. 1933-63. 8 cartons. Civic leader. Correspondence, ephemera, and related material concerning her interest in various reform movements.

.20 Gayton family.
Papers, 1900-60. .5 ft. Clippings, ephemera and memorabilia of the John T. Gayton family concerning Negroes in Washington.

.21 Gerber, Sidney, -1965.
Papers, 1943-65. 7 ft. (ca. 10,000 items). Businessman, public official, and civic leader. Correspondence, diary, speeches and writings, and case files concerning personal, legal, and financial matters and pertaining to race relations and civic work in Seattle and the state. Subjects included among materials are Washington State Board Against Discrimination (1957-62, chairman), Washington State Fair Employment Practices Committee (1946-50), Harmony Homes (1960-65), and Fair Housing Listing Service (1960-65).

.22 Hunsaker, Jane Chandler.
Papers and photographs, 1936-37. Contains material pertaining to Negroes in Washington.

.23 McAdoo, Benjamin, Jr.
Papers, 1952-66. 2 inches. Correspondence and ephemera concerning McAdoo's activities with the NAACP of Seattle and Washington State.

.24 McCabe, Eliza.
Papers, 1909-66. 3.5 ft. Correspondence, clippings and ephemera concerning race relations and civic work in Tacoma, Wash.

.25 Marple, Lorna.
Papers, 1936-61. 12 ft. Civic leader, president of

Portland, Ore., NAACP, and executive committee-man of the Democratic party in Multnomah County, Ore. Correspondence, speeches, writings, notes, minutes, agendas, and political ephemera, relating to Mrs. Marple's activities in Portland's civic affairs through the Council of Churches, Portland Public Forum Association, and the Urban League. Includes many papers relating to the NAACP and the League of Women Voters. Correspondents include John F. Kennedy, Wayne L. Morse, Maurine Neuberger, Richard L. Neuberger, Henry A. Wallace, and the National Committee of the Democratic party.

.26 Mitchell, Hugh B., 1907- .
Papers, 1945-52. 49 ft. Senator, Congressman, and civic leader. Chiefly correspondence relating to his career in industrial relations and politics. Among his correspondents are John F. Kennedy, Richard Neuberger, Harry S. Truman, Americans for Democratic Action, League of Women Voters of Seattle, and the National Association for the Advancement of Colored People.

.27 National Association for the Advance of Colored People, Seattle.
Files, ca. 1935-66. 3 ft. Correspondence, clippings, reports, speeches and writings, ephemera, minutes and financial records, and related items about the Association's activities. The University of Washington is the official archive for its inactive records.

.28 National Association for the Advancement of Colored People, Vancouver, Washington.
Records, 1945-69. Correspondence, reports, minutes, and ephemera.

.29 Negro newspapers.
Incomplete runs, and in some cases only scattered issues, of the following Washington Negro newspapers: Seattle Republican (ca. 1895-1917?), Enterprise (ca. 1920- ?), Northwest Enterprise (1933-52), Northwest Herald (1944-45), Pacific Leader (1951-56), Progressive Herald (1933), Puget Sound Observer (1954, 1957-61), Seattle Observer (1964-66), Rising Sun (1911), and Searchlight (1918, 1921).

.30 Oregon Improvement Company.
Files, 1880-96. 45 ft. Correspondence and business records relating to the coal industry. This coal mining company recruited Negroes as strikebreakers in 1890, and correspondence concerning this policy is included.

.31 Roston, James A., Sr.
Scrapbook, ca. 1897-1924. Includes letters, documents, clippings and ephemera relating to Negroes in Washington.

.32 Tape recordings.
Interviews. ca. 30 tapes. Tape-recorded interviews with persons in Seattle's black community, including Calvin Armstrong, Leonard Gayton, Virginia Gayton, Terenz Goodwin, Leola Grimes, Beula Hart, Bennie Hearst, Charles Russell, Cornelia Saunders, Robert Saunders, Edward Smith, Elihu Spearman, Vivian Spearman, Eva Strong, Charles Taylor, Ernst White, Leola Woffert, George Wright, Powell Barnett, Randolph W. Carter, Clara Fraser, John Gayton, James A. Roston, Jr. (re his father), Waymon Ware, Fred P. Woodson.

.33 Underwood, William H.
Papers, 1949-57. .5 ft. Correspondence, minutes, reports, clippings and ephemera, reflecting Underwood's activities with the West Coast Region and the Northwest area of the NAACP.

.34 U.S. Historical Records Survey.
Files, ca. 1937-40. 1 case. Correspondence and reports about the State of Washington. Included in material are records of the minority population.

.35 Urban League of Seattle.
File, 1930-65. ca. 32 ft. Correspondence, case files, ephemera, reports, and minutes. The University of Washington is official archive for its inactive records.

.36 Washington, James, Jr.
Scrapbook. Contains materials relating to Negroes.

.37 Wells, Gerald.
Papers, 1959. Includes correspondence and memoirs, relating to Negroes.

.38 Woodson, Fred Patterson.
Papers, 1900-60. 1 ft. Clippings, photographs, ephemera, and tape-recorded interview concerning Negroes in Seattle.

WA16   WASHINGTON STATE BOARD AGAINST DISCRIMINATION, SEATTLE OFFICE. 1411 Fourth Ave. Bldg., 98101. Tel 206 464-6500.

SPOKANE

WA17   WASHINGTON STATE BOARD AGAINST DISCRIMINATION, SPOKANE OFFICE. Old National Bank Bldg., 422 Riverside Ave., 99201. Tel 509 624-7277. Thomas Kennedy, Jr., Rep.
The Board works to eliminate and prevent discrimination in employment, in publicly assisted housing, and in places of public resort, accommodation or amusement.

TACOMA

WA18   TACOMA PUBLIC LIBRARY (1886). 1102 Tacoma Ave. S., 98402. Tel 206 383-1574. Joseph S. Ibbotson, Dir. Interlibrary loan, copying, typing, inquiries answered. Publ.: Negro Bibliography; Afro-Americans in Literature.

.1   The Forum.
Incomplete run, 1903-15. A newspaper which was edited (1903-15) by Negro newswoman, Ellen H. Ryan, and contained Negro interest items and critiques of local government and affairs.

.2   Lincoln Collection.
ca. 1400 items. Books, pamphlets and magazines covering Lincoln, the Civil War, and Reconstruction.

.3   Newspaper Clipping Collection.
Newspaper clippings, 1909- . ca. 44 vf. Clippings of Tacoma area newspapers are kept in a subject file and include such subjects as Negroes, civil rights, and segregation in housing and employment.

.4   Tacoma/Pierce County Council of Churches.
Records, 1883-1959. ca. 3 ft. Minutes, correspondence, publications, and other papers of the Council and its predecessors.

WA19   TACOMA URBAN LEAGUE, INC. (1968). 1704 S. Kay, 98405. Tel 206 627-1908. Thomas Dixon, Exec. Dir. The League is a community service agency committed to securing equal opportunity for black Americans and other minority groups. It is non-partisan and inter-racial in its leadership and professional staff. The League's goal is to eliminate racial segregation and discrimination in American life and to help economically disadvantaged groups to share equally the responsibility and rewards of full citizenship. Publ.: Annual Report; Pamphlets and special reports.

.1   Tacoma Urban League.
Files, 1968- . Correspondence, minutes of meetings, financial records, studies, reports, and other materials dealing with the aims, history, and programs of the League.

WEST VIRGINIA

BLUEFIELD

WV1   BLUEFIELD STATE COLLEGE (1895), LIBRARY (1895). 218 Rock St., 24703. Tel 304 325-7102. Miss Doris E. Rice, Librn. Interlibrary loan, bibliographies prepared, literature searches, copying, inquiries answered, referrals made, consultation.

.1   Afro-American Studies Collection.
ca. 1000 paperbacks. Basic books on the life and history of black Americans.

.2   Bluefield State College.
Archives, 1895- . Includes correspondence, bulletins, catalogues, records of admission, and other

documents dealing with the history and administration of the College.

CHARLESTON

WV2   CHARLESTON HUMAN RIGHTS COMMISSION (1967). 302
       Clendenin St., 25301. Tel 304 344-4862. Havard E.
       Griffith, Exec. Dir. Referrals made, consultation.
       The Commission works to provide all citizens of
       Charleston with equal opportunity for employment, equal
       access to places of public accommodations, and equal
       opportunity in the sale, purchase, lease, rental, and
       financing of housing accommodations or real property.

       .1   Charleston Human Rights Commission.
             Files, 1967- . Records, correspondence, and other
             business papers of the Commission; newspaper
             clippings with reference to Negroes in employment
             and housing; and reports, books, and pamphlets
             concerning Negroes.

WV3   WEST VIRGINIA HUMAN RIGHTS COMMISSION (1961). 2019
       E. Washington St., 25305. Tel 304 348-2616. Carl W.
       Glatt, Exec. Dir.
       The Commission conducts surveys, studies, and public
       education programs; receives, investigates, and initi-
       ates complaints; and conducts conciliations. It works
       in the areas of employment, education and public ac-
       commodations, and with racial, religious, and ethnic
       groups.
       Publ.: Annual Report.

       .1   West Virginia Human Rights Commission.
             Files, 1961. Includes correspondence, minutes of
             meetings, financial records, studies, reports, in-
             vestigations, and other documents dealing with the
             aims, history, and programs of the Commission.
             Case files and formal complaints closed to public.

HUNTINGTON

WV4   CONGRESS OF RACIAL EQUALITY. 1816 Eighth Ave.,
       25703. Tel 304 523-1284. Elizabeth A. Johnson, Chmn.

INSTITUTE

WV5   WEST VIRGINIA STATE COLLEGE LIBRARY. 25112. Tel
       304 768-3981. John E. Scott, Librn.

       .1   Afro-American Studies Collection.
             ca. 1000 paperbacks. Basic books on the life and
             history of black Americans.
       .2   West Virginia State College.
             Files, 1891- . ca. 10,000 items. Includes corre-
             spondence, minutes of board meetings, financial
             records, records of admission, and other docu-
             ments dealing with the history and administration
             of the College.

MORGANTOWN

WV6   WEST VIRGINIA UNIVERSITY, LIBRARY (1867). 26506.
       Tel 304 293-0111. Robert F. Munn, Dir.

       .1   Appleton, John W.M., 1832-1913.
             Papers, 1861-1913. 1 v. and 1 reel of microfilm.
             In part, microfilm copy (1 reel) made in
             1960 from the original memoir and letter book in
             the possession of Arnold A. Barnes. Army officer.
             Scrapbook containing official papers relating to
             Appleton's service with the 54th Regt., Massachu-
             setts Volunteer Infantry of Negro troops in the
             Civil War; commissions, family letters, photos,
             newspaper clippings, register, memoir and letter
             book. Subjects include the capture of Fort Wagner,
             Charleston harbor, and the Union encampment at
             Morris Island, S.C.; the occupation of Jacksonville,
             Fla.; and the regiment's return to Fort Warren,
             Boston.
       .2   Camden, Gideon D., 1805-91.
             Papers, 1785-1958. 91 boxes, 4 folders and 8
             items. Lawyer, Democratic politician, member of

the Virginia Convention of 1850-51, circuit judge,
and State senator, of Harrison Co., W. Va. Correspondence, and business and legal papers, dealing
with Camden's legal career and his political career. Subjects include state and national politics,
ca. 1830-88; secession crisis; Compromise of
1850; New York merchants and secession; Reconstruction in West Virginia; Methodist Church and
the slavery question; and other subjects.

.3   Campbell family.
      Papers, 1795-1901. 2 reels of microfilm (4 v. and
      4 folders). Microfilm copy made in 1959 and 1960
      from originals in the possession of Mr. and Mrs.
      James W. Campbell. Business and legal papers,
      farm records, and store accounts of James Camp-
      bell, his son, James L., and his grandson, James
      Wilson Campbell, pertaining to the management of
      the family plantation and country store located near
      Arden in Berkeley Co., W. Va.
.4   Caperton, William Gaston, 1815-52.
      Family papers, 1801-1930. 1 reel of microfilm.
      Microfilm copy made in 1961 from originals in the
      possession of Mrs. H.A. Hereford, Sr. Correspon-
      dence and miscellaneous papers of a Monroe Co.,
      W. Va., farmer and politician, his wife, Harriette
      Boswell Alexander Caperton, their daughters, Isa-
      bel and Alice Beulah, Alice's husband, Frank Here-
      ford, U.S. Senator from West Virginia, and his
      daughter, Katherine (Hereford) Stoddard. Includes
      business papers (1820-41) of Thomas Edgar; let-
      ters; and a folder on family genealogy. Subjects
      include mid-19th century life in Union, Monroe Co.,
      W. Va.; the excitement in Virginia following John
      Brown's raid; Washington, D.C., and the slavery
      controversy (1860); the secession crisis in Vir-
      ginia; impressment of material in Monroe Co. by
      Union troops; the effect of the war on the social
      and economic life of Richmond; and aftermath of
      war in Virginia.
.5   Congress of Industrial Organizations. Industrial Union
      Councils. West Virginia.
      Archives, 1939-51. 51 boxes. Correspondence,
      legal papers, reports, and printed material. Sub-
      jects include the trade unions and councils allied
      with the Industrial Union Council; the activities of
      the CIO Political Action Committee at the state and
      national level; the National Labor Relations Board;
      Labor's Non-Partisan League; Interracial Council;
      the National CIO Community Services Committee;
      and others.
.6   Davis, John James, 1835-1916.
      Papers, 1824-1953. 10 boxes. Lawyer, and U.S.
      Representative from Clarksburg, W. Va. Corre-
      spondence, business and legal papers, essays and
      speeches, clippings, and clipping scrapbooks,
      family photos, and printed material. Includes cor-
      respondence; and letters (1848-61) from his aunt,
      Margaret Steen, commenting on teaching and so-
      ciety in ante-bellum Mississippi and Arkansas.
      Subjects include the Lincoln-Douglas debates; the
      secession crisis in northern Virginia; the "re-
      organized government" of Virginia; the Recon-
      struction and Bourbon politics in West Virginia,
      (1866-95); and the Wheeling Conventions of 1861.
.7   Fox, William.
      Papers, 1762-1895. 5 folders. Correspondence
      and other papers of William Fox and Vause Fox of
      the town of Romney and Hampshire Co., W. Va.,
      mainly 1762-1859. Includes accounts for various
      goods and services; and items relating to slaves.
.8   Goff, David.
      Papers, 1826-1904. 4 boxes and 1 folder. Attorney
      and land promoter in Randolph, Harrison, and
      Tucker counties, W. Va. Mainly correspondence
      dealing with the sales of slaves, politics, Civil War
      conditions in Beverly, W. Va.; the Goff family his-
      tory; and other matters. Among the correspon-
      dents are G.D. Camden and P.G. Van Winkle.
.9   Hansford, Felix G.
      Papers, 1790-1876. 1 box and 2 folders. Kanawha
      Co., W. Va., justice of the peace, entrepreneur, and
      president of the Giles, Fayette and Kanawha Turn-
      pike Company. Correspondence, business, legal,
      and land papers. Subjects include the George Box-
      ley slave plot, 1816; the Kansas struggle, 1858;

southern reaction to John Brown's raid, 1859;
family affairs; and other matters.

WV6.10 Henderson family.
Henderson-Tomlinson families' papers, 1798-1936.
1 reel of microfilm. Microfilm copy made in 1961
from transcripts (typewritten) in the possession of
Josephine Phillips. The typescripts were copied in
1936 by Ronald Good, Historical Research Project,
National Youth Administration, from originals in
the possession of Jock B. Henderson of Williamstown, W. Va. Journals and papers pertaining to
frontier life in the Parkerburg-Marietta, W. Va.,
area. Includes a journal (1798-1803) on the settlement of Alexander Henderson's land on the Little
Kanawha; his plantation accounts; correspondence;
and other material.

.11 Historical materials.
Miscellaneous. ca. 165 items, 1 v., 2 boxes, 6 folders, and 2 rolls of microfilm. In part transcripts
(typewritten) and photocopies. Interviews (tape recordings, and transcriptions), reminiscences, letters, clippings, maps, trial records, a pardon, orders, muster rolls, a poem, historical sketches, a
broadside, photos, and pamphlets. Include material on John Brown's trial, the Civil War, politics,
and other subjects.

.12 Howard, Adolphus P.
Papers, 1850-1938. 2 boxes and 1 folder. Businessman and farmer. Family and business papers,
including papers of Howard's father, John F. Howard, and other members of the family. Some of the
1850 correspondence is to A.G. DeSellem, Port
Homer, Ohio, regarding the American Missionary
Association and anti-slavery activities.

.13 Kump, Herman Guy, 1877-1962.
Papers, 1907-57. 92 boxes and 1 v. Prosecuting
attorney of Randolph Co., W. Va., mayor of Elkins,
W. Va., judge, and Governor of West Virginia.
Correspondence, legal papers, speeches, clippings,
photos, and printed material. Subjects include the
Joseph Brown lynch case. Among his correspon-
dents is John J. Davis.

.14 Lambert, Frederick B. collector.
Papers, ca. 1809-1959. 47 reels of microfilm.
Microfilm copies made in 1959 and 1960 from originals in the possession of Frederick B. Lambert.
Original mss and typescript copies of census,
school, vital statistics, and court records; obituary
notices and cemetery readings; personal recollections and biographical sketches; notes pertaining to the Guyandotte Valley and the surrounding
Ohio Valley area. Subjects include social customs,
famous murders and hangings; slavery, the "underground railroad" and the free Negro; the Civil War;
and other subjects.

.15 Legal materials.
Miscellaneous, 1790-1926. ca. 110 items, 2 v. and
4 rolls of microfilm. In part, transcript (typewritten) and photocopies. Attorney's case book, court
records, legal decisions, certificates of incorpora-
tions, complaint, and proceedings of trials. Includes material on the trial of John Brown for the
raid on Harpers Ferry, and other trials.

.16 Lewis family.
Papers, 1825-1936. 19 boxes. Personal and business papers of the Lewis family, mainly of John D.
Lewis, Charles C. Lewis, Sr., and Charles C.
Lewis, Jr., of Kanawha Co., W. Va., including papers of the Ruffner, Dickinson, and Wilson families
of Virginia, West Virginia, Ohio, Kansas, Missouri,
and other states. Correspondence, diaries,
speeches, legal papers, newspaper clippings,
scrapbooks, and photos relating to the Civil War
and post-war conditions in Virginia, Pennsylvania,
Ohio, Kentucky, and Missouri; the purchase and
sale of slaves; and other matters.

.17 McCalla, John Moore, Jr.
Papers, 1860. ca. 87 pages. Edited typescript copy
of the journal kept on a voyage, June-December,
1860, as special agent for the U.S. government and
physician appointed by the American Colonization
Society, on board the "Star of the Union," a ship
chartered by the Society for the transportation of
"re-captured Africans" to Liberia.

.18 McNeel, Isaac, b. 1830.
Papers, 1850-1908. 9 boxes and 1 v. Correspondence, legal and business papers, mercantile records, and tax receipt books of McNeel, who operated a store at Edray and Mill Point, Pocahontas
Co., W. Va., served as sheriff of the county, operated a gristmill, raised livestock, and who was
appointed provost marshal of the county in 1862
by the Confederate Army. Includes letters, school
reports, and materials relating to slave hiring, the
Virginia Secession Convention, and post-war economic and political conditions in the Pocahontas
Co., W. Va., area.

.19 Miscellaneous materials.
Papers, 1761-1954. ca. 105 items, 5 v., 1 box, 2
folders, and 1 roll of microfilm. In part, transcripts (typewritten) and photocopies. Correspondence, radio scripts, price lists, stock certificates,
land office records, statistical charts, minute
books, execution book, tax records, cemetery records, herd books, population data, genealogical
notes, bills, broadsides, circulars, printed forms,
clippings, advertisements, photos, reports, military records, materials for local history, and
memorabilia. Includes information on the Ku Klux
Klan in West Virginia.

.20 Monroe County, West Virginia.
Archives, ca. 1772-1923. 158 v. and 97 boxes.
Court case papers, wills, deeds, surveys, and plats;
bound volumes of court records, deeds, estrays,
road and tax records, a free Negro register, and
private account books.

.21 Mullen family.
Papers, 1841-1932. 1 box. Correspondence, bills,
receipts, and memoranda books of Gordon, Gordon,
Jr., Jacob, George H., and Mrs. F.R. Mullen of
Charleston, W. Va. Includes some Ku Klux Klan
papers (1928) of Dr. A.G. Mullen of Galesburg, Ill.

.22 Personal papers and related materials.
Miscellaneous, 1758-1957. ca. 370 items, 4 v., 1
box and 26 folders. In part, transcripts (typewritten) and photocopies. Correspondence, certificates of various kinds, receipts, genealogical notes,
family papers, business papers, household accounts, wills, deeds, commissions, school notebooks, military records of various kinds, legal papers, petitions, speeches, photos, and miscellaneous printed materials. Contains information on the
Civil War, slaves, and many other subjects.

.23 Smith, Clarence E. collector.
Papers, 1787-1956. 2 boxes and 1 tape recording.
Correspondence, pamphlets, newspapers, photos,
and other materials of the Barns and Smith
families of Pennsylvania and West Virginia, including papers of the Negro Democratic Club of
West Virginia; and other material.

.24 Storer College, Harper's Ferry, W. Va.
Records, 1865-1956. 162 boxes, 14 v., and 5 reels
of microfilm. Microfilm copies made in 1959 and
1961 from originals in the possession of Mrs. John
Newcomer and the National Park Service. Correspondence, office files, faculty and student records,
Veterans Administration records, financial records, clippings, photos, scrapbooks, building blueprints, and campus plans. Includes the guest
register from the John Brown Fort Museum. Subjects include the attempts of the missionaries from
the Free Will Baptist Association to establish
schools and missions for the freedmen of the
Shenandoah Valley area.

.25 Van Winkle, Peter G., 1808-72.
Papers, 1827-72. 2 boxes and 2 folders. West
Virginia attorney, political leader, and businessman. Correspondence relating to Virginia politics;
a personal journal; and holographs of speeches and
contributions to newspapers relating to the Liberia
Colonization Society, among other subjects.

.26 Woods, Samuel, 1822-97.
Family papers, 1824-1958. 2 boxes and 1 folder.
Lawyer, judge, and teacher, of Philippi, W. Va.
Correspondence, family historical and genealogical
records, clippings, printed material, and sketches
of Woods and his son, Samuel Van Horn Woods
(1856-1937) a lawyer, Democratic politician, and

president of the West Virginia State Senate. Subjects include the secession crisis in northwestern Virginia; the Richmond Secession Convention, 1861; Civil War in Barbour Co., W. Va.; business, legal, political, and civic affairs of Samuel Van Horn Woods; and other papers of the Wood family.

.27 Writers' Program. West Virginia.
Papers, 127 boxes. Correspondence, clippings, maps, photos, and mss and typewritten materials compiled for use in projected publications, including A Fact Book, West Virginia Folklore, The Negro in West Virginia, and other published works.

WISCONSIN

BELOIT

WI1 BELOIT COLLEGE (1847), COL. ROBERT H. MORSE LIBRARY (1859). 53511. Tel 608 365-3391. H. Vail Deal, Dir. of Libraries. Interlibrary loan, bibliographies prepared, literature searches, copying, inquiries answered, referrals made.

.1 Martin Luther King Collection on Non-Violence.
Contains books by and about Thoreau, Gandhi, Addams, and Mustee. Contains materials relating to the non-violence movement, world peace, pacifism, conscientious objection, and the major figures associated with these subjects. Also includes thirty-year bound file of Fellowship, the magazine of the Fellowship of Reconciliation (Nyack, N.Y.); Crisis (magazine of the NAACP), and recent volumes of several Negro periodicals.

JANESVILLE

WI2 ROCK COUNTY HISTORICAL SOCIETY (1948). 440 N. Jackson St., 53545. Tel 608 752-4519. Richard P. Hartung, Dir. Copying, typing, inquiries answered, referrals made.

.1 Janesville Area Human Rights Council.
Files, 1966- . ca. 100 items. Includes correspondence, minutes of meetings, financial records, and documents dealing with the aims, history, and programs of the Council.

.2 Papers relating to Negroes.
Files, ca. 1895-1950. ca. 25 items. Includes materials on the Negroes who live and have lived in the Rock County area.

.3 Tallman, William Morrison.
Papers, ca. 1830-75. ca. 3000 items. Includes materials on the abolition activities of Tallman and others of Janesville, Wis.

KENOSHA

WI3 HUMAN RELATIONS COMMISSION. 4123 32nd Ave., 53140. Tel 414 658-4811. John N. Davis, Dir.

.1 Human Relations Commission.
Files. Includes correspondence, minutes of meetings, financial records, and documents dealing with the aims, history, and programs of the Commission.

MADISON

WI4 DEPARTMENT OF INDUSTRY, LABOR AND HUMAN RELATIONS, EQUAL RIGHTS DIVISION (1967). P.O. Box 2209, 53701. Tel 608 266-3131. Clifton H. Lee, Adminstr. Bibliographies prepared, literature searches, inquiries answered, referrals made, consultation.
The Division is a state agency responsible for eliminating discrimination in employment, housing, public accommodations and state contracts, and for educating the public to a greater understanding, appreciation and practice of human rights, to the end that Wisconsin will be a better place in which to live. The Division was formed by the consolidation of the Governor's Commis-

sion on Human Rights (1945) and the Equal Opportunities Division (1945).
Publ.: Special reports, pamphlets; Bibliography and Resource Guide; Information Series.

.1 Department of Industry, Labor and Human Relations, Equal Rights Division.
Files, 1945- . Includes correspondence, financial records, Equal Rights Council minutes, and publications and documents dealing with the aims, history, and programs of the Division. Materials cover such subjects as migrants, Indians, Negroes, employment, housing, public accommodations, State contracts and cases.

WI5 MADISON URBAN LEAGUE. 124 E. Main St., 53703. Tel 608 251-0277. Nelson Cummings, Jr., Exec. Dir.

.1 Madison Urban League.
Files. Records, reports, correspondence, and other papers concerning the aims and activities of the organization.

WI6 STATE HISTORICAL SOCIETY OF WISCONSIN (1846). 816 State St., 53706. Tel 608 262-9576. Charles Shelter, Librn.; Josephine L. Harper, Manuscripts Curator. Interlibrary loan, copying, inquiries answered, inventories to processed manuscript collections.
Publ.: Guide to Manuscripts of the State Historical Society of Wisconsin (1944, 1957, 1966); Wisconsin Magazine of History, quarterly.

Archives and Manuscripts Division.

.1 — Allen, William Francis, 1830-89.
Papers, 1788, 1824-1920. 1 box, in part transcripts. Classical scholar. Copy of a diary (1863-64) kept by Allen while teaching at a Negro school on the Island of St. Helena, S.C., for the U. S. Education Commission; correspondence, diplomas, class records, books, reminiscences, and other papers.

.2 — Americans for Democratic Action (ADA).
Papers, 1932-65. 409 boxes, 14 v., 2 packages. Correspondence, business records, clippings, and printed matter, organized into 8 series: administrative files of ADA and of UDA, the parent group, and chapter, convention, legislative, political, public relations, and campus division files.

.3 — Andrews, Stephen Pearl.
Papers, 1869-1925. 4 boxes. Abolitionist, reformer; of Texas, Massachusetts, and New York.

.4 — Baldwin, William Henry, 1891- .
Papers, 1922-60. 4 ft. Public relations counselor and philanthropist. Correspondence and other papers, largely relating to the programs and reports of Baldwin's firm, 1924-42, in public relations counseling; and to his interest in civic and philanthropic organization, including the National Urban League. Includes his correspondence (33 items, 1947-58) with Chester Bowles; and the correspondence (ca. 75 items, 1922-34) of Baldwin's mother, Ruth Standish Baldwin, a founder of the National Urban League.

.5 — Barland-Newlands family.
Papers, 1825-1948. 3 reels of microfilm. Correspondence between members of the families of Thomas Barland (1809-96) and Thomas Wilson (d. 1883), tracing the history of Barland and his family, and his career as farmer, preacher, teacher, and inventor, and containing a discussion of life in Wisconsin, the Civil War and Negro slavery.

.6 — Bennett, Van S., 1836-1914.
Papers, 1861-64. 6 v. Civil War diaries (1863-64), roll book (1861-62) and account book (1862-64) kept for Co. I of the 12th Wisconsin Volunteer Infantry of which Bennett was captain. The diaries contain information on the siege of Vicksburg and on Sherman's army, on the conduct of Union soldiers on and off duty, the presidential election of 1864, and conditions in the invaded South.

WI6.7 —— Bliss, Robert L., 1907- .
Papers, 1953-60. 1 package. Public relations
consultant, of New York City. Notes accompanied by pamphlets and other printed material
relating to public relations, written and collected by Bliss. Most of the papers concern
the racial crisis in Little Rock, Ark. (1957),
and the part played by the Arkansas Gazette.

.8 —— Braden, Carl and Ann.
Papers, 1928-67. 93 boxes, 35 tape recordings, 1 disc recording, and 3 reels of microfilm. Correspondence, memoranda, articles,
speeches, reports, and other records documenting the Braden's campaigns against social
injustice. Included is much material on civil
rights, as well as education, labor, politics,
and journalism. Many papers relate to the
Southern Conference Educational Fund, of
which Carl Braden is executive director, and
to other civil rights groups such as Congress
of Racial Equality, Southern Christian Leadership Conference, National Association for the
Advancement of Colored People, and Student
Nonviolent Coordinating Committee. Use of
the papers is restricted. Forms part of the
Contemporary Social Action collection.

.9 —— Bridgman, Edward Payson, 1834-1915.
Papers, 1833-1937. 1 pkg. Mainly letters and
reminiscences by Bridgman describing his life
in Kansas in 1856 and recollections of John
Brown; his service with the 37th Massachusetts Infantry in the Civil War (1863-65); and
his other experiences.

.10 —— Bridgman, Louis W., 1883-1960.
Papers, 1910-60. 2 boxes. Journalist, of Madison, Wis. Chiefly correspondence pertaining
to Bridgman's career as a reporter for the
Wisconsin State Journal (1906-13) and for the
Associated Press (1913-30), as editor for the
University of Wisconsin Extension Division
(1930-53), and to his participation in the Saturday Lunch Club of Madison, in the Lincoln Fellowship of Wisconsin, and in University of Wisconsin alumni activities. Includes correspondence with Albert H. Griffith and Boyd B.
Stutler about Abraham Lincoln and John Brown;
annotated typescripts of articles of speeches on
Lincoln written by Bridgman, Albert O. Barton,
George P. Hambrecht, Harry E. Pratt, and T.
Harry Williams.

.11 —— Brisbane, William Henry, ca. 1803-1878.
Papers, 1829-1913. 2 ft. Baptist clergyman,
physician, and editor, of Arena, Wis. The bulk
of the papers are bound in 49 vols. and include
notes copied from Brisbane's journals (1834-
42), his diaries (1844-78), pro-slavery arguments (prior to 1835), anti-slavery essays and
addresses, sermons, religious compositions,
and copies of 13 letters written (1859) to such
persons as Salmon P. Chase and Carl Schurz.
The unbound material consists of some correspondence (1861-1913), sermons, mss of
stories, and clippings.

.12 —— Booth, Sherman Miller, 1812-1904.
Papers, 1818-1908. 8 boxes and 1 reel of
microfilm (negative). Abolitionist, political
lecturer, publisher, businessman, and government clerk. Correspondence and other papers.

.13 —— Clinard, Marshal Barron, 1911- .
Papers, 1939-52. 42 boxes and 1 package.
Professor of sociology at the University of
Wisconsin. Correspondence relating almost
entirely to Clinard's dissertation on urbanization and criminal behavior (University of Chicago, 1941); notes, statistics, articles, clippings, charts, and other working papers for
both the book and the dissertation.

.14 —— Congress of Racial Equality (CORE).
Papers, 1941-67. 104 boxes. Included are
files of the director, 1945-64; assistant director, 1942-64; executive secretary, 1941-
62; national action council, 1945-65; and departments and related organizations, 1946-67.
Groups represented include CORE, New York,

N.Y., CORE, Berkeley, Calif., and Southern
Regional Council, Atlanta, Ga.

.15 —— Conover, Obadian Milton, 1825-84.
Papers, 1843-82. 1 box. Lawyer. A notebook kept by Conover while in Princeton University contain two short diaries; and records of the Wisconsin State Colonization Society (1853-54).

.16 —— Contemporary Social Action Collection.
Established in 1964 with the help of civil rights
activists, the society is assembling records
from the full range of participants in the Negro
Freedom Movement. While the project began
with civil rights, it has since expanded to include such interrelated contemporary movements as those around pacifism, civil liberties,
welfare rights, and the war in Viet Nam. The
Collection is comprised of personal papers of
individuals, such as letters, diaries, reminiscences, notebooks, ms books and articles;
papers of organizations, such as minutes of
meetings, policy level correspondence, memoranda, filed reports, policy statements, reports, newsletters and new releases, clippings,
affidavits, fliers, resolutions, agendas,
speeches, legal case files and papers, legislative files, campaign literature, information
sheets, and broadsides; Freedom School records, such as information sheets, curriculum
materials, and student compositions; photographs; tape recordings; pamphlets and miscellaneous printed publications; and local
newspapers. Included are the complete back
files of National Congress of Racial Equality
(CORE); Southern CORE, Arkansas Student
Nonviolent Coordinating Committee (SNCC)
W.E.B. DuBois Clubs, National Coordinating
Committee to End the War in Viet Nam, National Freedom of Residence, Milwaukee Citizens for Equal Opportunity, Milwaukee United
School Integration Committee, Cardijn Center,
Students for a Democratic Society, Students for
a Democratic Society Chicago JOIN Project,
Radio Tougaloo Association; the complete files
of Daisy Bates relating to the Little Rock,
Ark., school desegregation crisis of 1957; the
papers of Carl and Ann Braden; partial holdings of Appalachian Committee for Full Employment, Appalachian Economic and Political
Action Conference, Committee for Miners in
Eastern Kentucky, Fayette County (Tenn.)
Project (1963-64), Freedom Primers, Freedom
Information Service, Friends of SNCC (University of Wisconsin), Cook Campaign in New
Haven (Conn.), West Tennessee Voters' Project (1964-66), Western Regional CORE, Mississippi Freedom Democratic Party challenge
(1964), Ku Klux Klan and White Citizens' Council fliers, Rabbis' March to Birmingham
(spring, 1963), and of Student Nonviolent Coordinating Committee (1964), Tupelo, Miss.;
tape recordings of interviews with Dr. and
Mrs. Martin Luther King, Jr., and other leaders of the Southern Christian Leadership Conference, and of mass meetings (1953-63); papers of attorney Murphy Bell, Baton Rouge,
La.; White Community Project (1965), Mayersville, Miss.; Ku Klux Klan meeting taped on the
outskirts of Birmingham, Ala.; papers of Congress of Federated Organizations (1965), Gulfport, Miss.; and papers of Congress of Federated Organizations Freedom Summer volunteers of 1964, from Batesville, Biloxi, Clarks-
dale, Greenville, Greenwood, Gulfport, Hatties-
burg, Holly Springs, Indianola, Jackson, Leake
City, McComb, Meridian, Natchez, Ruleville,
and Vicksburg, Miss. Complete and partial
runs are held for civil rights newspapers such
as Arkansas Voice, Bay Area Friends of SNCC,
Benton County Freedom Train, Freedom North,
Free Student, New Orleans Free Press, New
South Student, Peace and Freedom News,
Southern Patriot, Student Voice, The Mississippi Free Press, The Voice of Prince Edward

County, Vicksburg Citizens' Appeal, Voice for Jobs and Justice; and the National States Rights Party publication, The Thunderbolt. These collections are, for the most part, unprocessed, and in many cases are restricted.

WI6.17 — Cuban Archives.

Records from the Cuban archives, 1777-1811. 4 boxes. Blueprint copies of typescripts of originals in the Archivo nacional de Cuba, Havana. Material from the Bernardo de Galvez letter books, the Florida correspondence, and other records dealing with the Spanish regime in Florida and Louisiana, containing information on the importation of slaves, and relations with the Americans. Most of the papers are in Spanish.

.18 — Davis, John Givan, 1810-66.

Papers, 1826-71. 15 items, 2 v., and 1 box. Merchant and U.S. Representative from Indiana. Correspondence, stock certificates, and a few legal documents. Bulk of the collection consists of incoming business and political correspondence. Includes letters from leaders of the Democratic party, discussing attitudes toward secession, the Civil War, and national politics; and family correspondence, partly from William P. and Eli Davis describing Texas frontier conditions and advising Davis on his stand on the Nebraska Bill, the election of Stephen A. Douglas, and the Dred Scott decision.

.19 — Davis, Moses M., 1820-88.

Correspondence, 1849-83. 1 box. Wisconsin physician and State legislator. Nearly half the collection consists of letters from Davis to Congressman John Fox Potter on the subjects of Wisconsin politics, the conduct of the Civil War, and problems of the Republican party. Before 1856 Davis received letters regarding the slavery issue from Charles Sumner, John P. Hale, Joshua Giddings, and others. The correspondence, which is almost entirely of a political nature, also includes letters from state and other national Republican leaders, among them Salmon P. Chase, James R. Doolittle, Charles Durkee, William H. Seward, Carl Schurz, C.C. Washburn, and David Wilmot.

.20 — Doolittle, James Rood, 1815-97.

Papers, 1831-1935. 15 boxes, in part transcripts. Senator from Wisconsin. Correspondence, speeches, legal memorandum books, and scrapbooks. Correspondence concerns Doolittle's early political activities in New York State, the slavery controversy, the election of 1860, political campaigns, colonization plans, Lincoln's policy towards the South, Jefferson Davis and the position of the southern states, and relations between President Johnson and the Congress.

.21 — Dutilh and Wachsmuth.

Papers. 1 box. Philadelphia, Pa., shipping merchants involved in the slave trade during the 18th and early 19th century.

.22 — Galamison, Milton A.

Papers, 1954-64. Minister. Civil rights and education leader of New York, N.Y.

.23 — Gale, Zona, 1874-1938.

Papers, 1838-1941. 18 items, 1 v., and 32 boxes. Author. Mainly literary mss, together with correspondence, notebooks and reports written by Miss Gale. Correspondence concerns her interest and promotion of woman suffrage, civil liberties, and racial relations; her opposition to literary censorship, and capital punishment.

.24 — Garrett, George A., 1888- .

Papers, 1947-60. 3 boxes. Diplomat and public official. Correspondence and memorabilia kept by Garrett as a civic leader in Washington, D.C., 1954-60. Includes letters and clippings concerning Garrett's promotion of urban redevelopment and community improvement in the District of Columbia while he was president of the Federal City Council.

.25 — Gilson, Norman Shepard, 1839-1914.

Papers, 1860-1901. 49 items. Soldier, lawyer, and public official. Military and other official papers, including muster rolls, descriptive lists, promotion and discharge papers from Gilson's Civil War service in Company D, 15th Wisconsin Volunteer Infantry and 58th Infantry Regiment, U.S.C.T., together with his appointments as Wisconsin tax commissioner, 1899 and 1901.

.26 — Heuston, Benjamin Franklin, 1823-94.

Papers, 1849-94. 1 v. and 3 boxes. Wisconsin land speculator, local historian, and public official. Correspondence, mainly letters to Heuston's wife during the Civil War service in the 23rd Wisconsin Volunteer Infantry; diaries, personal accounts, memoranda, biographical material, and speeches; and articles on the Negro.

.27 — Howe, Timothy Otis, 1816-83.

Papers, 1860-90. 1 box. Lawyer, U.S. Senator from Wisconsin, and Postmaster General. Mainly family correspondence; and a letter written by Howe to William Pitt Fessenden (August 28, 1864), discussing legislation to free the slaves in the South.

.28 — Hughes, Langston, 1902-67.

Papers, ca. 1917-63. 2 boxes. Author. Mainly versions of plays and librettos, either in unpublished or published form, including Don't You Want to Be Free?, Soul Gone Home, The Gospel Glory, and The Prodigal Son; together with a biographical sketch listing all Hughes' literary work; playbills; and memorabilia.

.29 — Johnson, Thomas S., 1839-1927.

Papers, 1787-1951. 16 boxes and 1 package. Presbyterian minister and teacher, of Beaver Dam, Wis. Mainly personal correspondence covering Johnson's career from early teaching experiences at the Blairstown Academy in New Jersey; together with diaries (1850-1909), miscellaneous account books (1823-1923), the handbook (1864-66) of the 127th Regt. of the U.S. Colored Troops; and miscellaneous articles, sermons, and clippings.

.30 — Jones, Samuel, 1734-1819.

Papers, 1760-93. 1 v. Lawyer, of N.Y. Chiefly miscellaneous legal papers and letters received by Jones as a counselor in New York City. Includes a document granting manumission to a slave in 1779.

.31 — Kiplinger, Austin H., 1918- .

Papers, 1951-59. 2 boxes. News commentator and reporter, of Chicago. Correspondence (1955-56) mainly commenting on broadcasts, with frequent references to civil rights and the Supreme Court; scripts for radio and television broadcasts, consisting of reviews of daily domestic news with some commentary, relating to Illinois and Chicago news, and civil rights.

.32 — McRae, John, fl. 1845-90.

Letter books, 1845-90. 13 v. Railroad construction engineer and plantation owner, of Camden, S.C. Correspondence after 1855 is largely personal, but it includes some letters to the manager of the McRae plantation and to merchants in Charleston, and it gives information concerning prices, slavery, economic conditions, secession, labor problems, the effect of the war on a southern family and its plantation, and adjustments after the war. Correspondence after 1870 only occasionally comments on political matters and the affairs of the plantation.

.33 — Mills, Joseph T., 1811-97.

Papers, 1856-82. 1 v., and 1 box. Lawyer and assemblyman of Wisconsin. Correspondence, a letter book, and 6 memorandum books. Memorandum books contain notes on law cases and legislative proceedings. Other papers include an account of Mills' interview with Abraham Lincoln, some correspondence relating to the Civil War and Reconstruction.

.34 —— Milwaukee County Industrial Union Council.
Records, 1938-48. 17 boxes. Forms part of
the Society's labor collection. Papers relating
mainly to the political activities of the Council
a representative body of CIO unions in Milwaukee Co., Wis. Includes letters and resolutions to Congressmen, lobbying for labor measures, housing laws, rent controls, anti-discrimination bills, and similar legislation;
correspondence with the CIO-Political Action
Committee and the Wisconsin State Industrial
Union Council; and questionnaires sent to
candidates for political office in 1948.

.35 —— Piper, Benjamin, b. 1827.
Papers, 1862-79. 11 items and 6 v. Wisconsin
farmer. Six diaries (1868-79), a letter to the
editor of the Wisconsin State Journal declaring
slavery to be the cause of the Civil War,
Piper's statement of reasons for being a Universalist, and a few receipts.

.36 —— Remsen, Peter A., 1786-1852.
Papers, 1817-52. 1 box. Cotton factor, of
Mobile, Ala. Several letters in the 1820's are
written from Marine Settlement, Madison Co.,
Ill., and other places in regard to the rescue
from kidnappers of Henry Hicks, an indentured
Negro apprentice.

.37 —— Roeseler, John Samuel, 1859-1942.
Papers, 1888-90. 2 boxes. Replies to a questionnaire issued by Roeseler to school superintendents, teachers, county officials, priests,
pastors, and others concerning foreign populations in Wisconsin. The information, covering
nearly every county of the state, varies from
brief form replies to detailed accounts of the
racial and religious backgrounds of foreign
groups and their progress in amalgamating
with the native-born population.

.38 —— Sand, Nathan, 1881-1947.
Papers, 1914-47. 4 boxes. Forms part of the
Society's collection of Wisconsin Jewish Archives. Correspondence, minutes, and related
printed papers kept by Sand, secretary of the
Milwaukee, Wis., division of the American
Jewish Congress, 1931-47. Includes papers
pertaining to the work of the American Jewish
Congress; papers relating to Milwaukee Jewish
groups interested in labor, youth, veterans, and
inter-racial relations.

.39 —— Shepard, Charles, 1822?-ca. 1865.
Papers, 1850-1958. 1 reel of microfilm, made
from originals lent by Mrs. David Crichton.
Freed slave and farmer, of Beetown Township,
Grant Co., Wis. Chiefly family correspondence
relating to living conditions, religion, and per-
sonal concerns. Includes 2 mss: "History of
the Pioneer Settlers of Grant County," and
"The Shepard Family History"; and a clipping,
"One survivor of Negro colony" from the
Dubuque Telegraph-Herald (June 1, 1958).

.40 —— Swain, Samuel Glyde, 1835-1904.
Papers, 1861-84. 2 boxes. Engineer. Personal correspondence, diaries, and other papers, relating mainly to Swain's service as
engineer in charge of constructing fortfications
at Fort McPherson, Natchez, Miss., and later
as subcommissioner of the Freedmen's
Bureau for Warren County, Miss. Includes
drawings and specifications for the fortifications, and maps of plantations which Swain
supervised as subcommissioner.

.41 —— Textile Workers Union of America.
Records, 1918-60. 166 boxes and 6 reels of
microfilm. Forms part of the Society's labor
collection. Correspondence, reports,
speeches, staff memoranda, radio scripts,
news releases, posters, leaflets, and other
printed and mimeographed material issued by
the Union, and other papers giving information
on local and national union business and politics, including its relations with the CIO, its
interest in legislation, domestic politics, education, and civil rights.

.42 —— Voice of America.
Records, 1960-61. 22 boxes. Scripts used by

the Central Services Division (May 31 to June
29, 1960) and news copy from the International
Broadcasting Service (1960-61), for the Voice
of America radio program. The news copy is
strictly reportorial and includes daily logs and
indexes. The scripts elaborate on news,
giving comments and analysis, and also describe features of American life, such as the
status of the Negro.

.43 —— Walling, William English, 1877-1936.
Papers, 1871-1962. 3 boxes. Author, lecturer,
and civic leader. Correspondence, dealing
primarily with family affairs; typewritten
copies of a few of Walling's articles and
speeches on labor, the national economy,
racial problems; newspaper clippings; and
miscellaneous materials pertaining to Walling's career. Includes letters discussing the
race riots in Springfield, Ill. (1909), the Socialist party and its problems prior and during
World War I, the Negro and trade unions
(1929).

.44 —— Webster, Daniel, b. 1833.
Correspondence, 1859-65. 3 boxes. Letters
from a captain of the 1st Battery, Wisconsin
Light Artillery, to his fiancee Gertrude Moore,
most of which were written during his Civil
War service in the Mississippi River theater.
The letters describe battles in Kentucky and
Tennessee, camp life, the status of the Negro,
in the Union armies, Vicksburg after the sur-
render of 1863. During the period 1864-65
Webster was stationed in New Orleans and
Baton Rouge, La.

Library Division.

.45 —— Among the holdings of the Library are a collection
of American Negro newspapers; materials (ca.
2000 books and pamphlets) on the American
Negro, slavery, civil rights, and the contemporary black movement in the U.S.; and the
following collection:

.46 —— Anti-Slavery Propaganda Collection.
ca. 2500 pamphlets. Microcards of originals
located in the Oberlin College Library. See
Oberlin College Library, Oberlin, Ohio; or
Lost Cause Press (publisher), Louisville,
Ky., for a more complete description.

WI7   UNIVERSITY OF WISCONSIN, CENTER FOR LAW AND
BEHAVIORAL SCIENCE (1963). Social Science Bldg.,
53706. Tel 608 262-2083. Prof. Jack Ladinsky, Dir.
The Center conducts research on the legal process and
interrelations of law and social structure. Representation research includes studies of political processes in
cities, role of law in defining limits of freedom of expression, literary censorship, aid to dependent children,
popular democracy and judicial independence, impact of
garnishment and bankruptcy proceedings on wage earn-
ers, law and poverty, the limits of effective legal action,
social origins of lawyers, and the role of the legal profession in the provision of legal services to the poor.
The Center holds semimonthly seminars for interested
law and social science faculty members of the University and a summer institute in behaviorial science and
law for graduate social science students and law students. Formerly Russell Sage Foundation Sociology and
Law Program.
Publ.: "Law and Society" section of Wisconsin Law Review, quarterly; Working paper series.

.1   Center for Law and Behavioral Science.
Files, 1963- . Correspondence, financial records,
studies, reports, and other materials dealing with
the aims, programs and history of the Center.

WI8   UNIVERSITY OF WISCONSIN, INSTITUTE FOR RESEARCH
ON POVERTY (1966). Social Science Bldg., 53706. Tel
608 266-6358. Harold W. Watts, Dir. Bibliographies
prepared, literature searches.
The Institute works to foster basic research into the
nature and causes of poverty and the means to combat
it.
Publ.: Discussion Papers, Institute series; Studies, surveys, reports.

WI9   UNIVERSITY OF WISCONSIN, THE MEMORIAL LIBRARY
        (1850). 728 State St., 53706. Tel 608 262-3521. Louis
        Kaplan, Dir.

        .1   Facts on Film.
                    Papers, 1954-67. Microfilm. Contains materials
                    on civil rights and race relations in the South. See
                    Race Relations Information Center, Nashville,
                    Tenn., for a full description.

        MILWAUKEE

WI10   ANTI-DEFAMATION LEAGUE OF B'NAI B'RITH, WISCON-
        SIN-UPPER MIDWEST REGIONAL OFFICE. 623 N.
        Second St., 53203. Tel 414 276-7920. Saul Sorrin, Dir.

WI11   CITIZENS' GOVERNMENTAL RESEARCH BUREAU, INC.
        (CGRB) (1913). 125 E. Wells St., 53202. Tel 414 276-
        8240. Norman N. Gill, Exec. Dir. Inquiries answered,
        referrals made, consultation.
        CGRB is a non-profit civic research agency devoted to
        better government in the Milwaukee metropolitan area.
        Its two main functions are: to assist public officials in
        improving the operations of local government and
        schools in the area; and to keep the public informed
        about local public affairs. CGRB's activities include:
        factual studies of revenues, expenditures, and ser-
        vices; presentation of facts at daily public hearings of
        public bodies; suggestion for administrative surveys as
        needed; preparation of Research Bulletins and reports
        of analyses of civic problems requiring citizen and of-
        ficial action; and cooperation with officials and major
        private business, service and welfare organizations who
        use findings for community progress.
        Publ.: Citizens' Governmental Research Bureau Bulle-
        tin; Special reports and pamphlets.

WI12   CONGRESS OF RACIAL EQUALITY (CORE). 2981 N.
        Teutonia Ave., 53204. Cecil Brown, Jr., Dir.

WI13   DEPARTMENT OF INDUSTRY, LABOR AND HUMAN RE-
        LATIONS, BUREAU OF ENFORCEMENT. 819 N. Sixth
        St., 53203. Tel 414 224-4384.

WI14   GREATER MILWAUKEE CONFERENCE ON RELIGION
        AND URBAN AFFAIRS. 1933 W. Wisconsin Ave., 53233.
        Tel 414 276-9050.

WI15   MARQUETTE UNIVERSITY, MEMORIAL LIBRARY. 1415
        W. Wisconsin Ave., 53233. Tel 414 224-7414. Dr. Wil-
        liam A. Fitzgerald, Dir.

        .1   Facts on Film.
                    Papers, 1954-67. Microfilm. Contains materials
                    on civil rights and race relations in the South. See
                    Race Relations Information Center, Nashville,
                    Tenn., for a full description.

WI16   MILWAUKEE ART CENTER. 750 N. Lincoln Memorial Dr.,
        53202. Tel 414 271-9508. Tracy Atkinson, Dir. In-
        quiries answered, referrals made, consultation, art
        works loaned.

        .1   Hunt, Richard, 1935- .
                    Art works, 1966-67. Welded steel form (1967), and
                    untitled lithographs (1966).
        .2   Tanner, Henry Ossawa, 1859-1937.
                    Paintings, 1910-11. 2 items. Artist. Includes oil
                    paintings entitled "Sunlight Tangiers" (1910) and
                    "Moonlight Hebron" (ca. 1910/11).

WI17   MILWAUKEE COMMISSION ON COMMUNITY RELATIONS
        (1944). 200 E. Wells St., 53202. Tel 414 276-3711.
        Calvin W. Beckett, Exec. Secy.
        The Commission inquires into causes of intergroup
        tension and discriminatory practices and initiates
        studies and investigations in areas of housing, employ-
        ment, education, and public accommodations. Formerly
        the Milwaukee Commission on Human Rights.
        Publ.: Newsletter, bimonthly.

        .1   Milwaukee Commission on Community Relations.
                    Files, 1944- . Includes correspondence, minutes
                    of meetings, financial records, and documents

dealing with the aims, history, and programs of the
Commission.

WI18   MILWAUKEE COUNTY HISTORICAL SOCIETY (1935), DIVI-
        SION OF RESEARCH COLLECTION (1935). 910 N.
        Third St., 53203. Tel 414 273-8288. Robert G. Car-
        roon, Curator of Res. Collections. Bibliographies pre-
        pared, literature searches, copying, inquiries answered,
        referrals made, consultation.
        Publ.: A Preliminary Survey of Manuscript and Archival
        Collections of the Milwaukee County Historical
        Society (1967); The Negro in Milwaukee, A His-
        torical Survey (1968).

        .1   Dorsey, James W., 1897-1966.
                    Papers, 1930-66. 1 ft. (1 box). Negro attorney.
                    Personal and business correspondence, speeches,
                    election campaign circulars, clippings, and photo-
                    graphs relating to his career.
        .2   Hall, Cornelius Mack.
                    Records of Milwaukee's Inner City Development
                    Project, 1965-66. 25 ft. of microfilm (530 items).
                    Microfilm made from originals in the posses-
                    sion of Mr. Hall or in the files of the Inner
                    City Development Project. Community organization
                    specialist. Correspondence and data on Milwau-
                    kee's antipoverty organizations and lists of Negro
                    churches and organizations in Milwaukee; corre-
                    spondence, notes, and statements of the Inner City
                    Development Project's advisory boards for neigh-
                    borhood youth and adult poverty programs; case
                    studies of clients; consultation reports of meetings
                    with other agencies; a training guide for the Negro
                    area unit of I.C.D.P.; and the 1965 report and his-
                    tory of the project. Includes general correspon-
                    dence and biographical sketches of Mr. Hall.
        .3   Jacobson, Thomas.
                    Papers, 1962-65. 1 roll of microfilm. Lawyer.
                    Correspondence relating primarily to legal work
                    done for the Milwaukee Congress of Racial Equality
                    and other civil rights organizations in Wisconsin.
                    Restricted to 1986.
        .4   Materials relating to Negroes.
                    Miscellaneous. Books, periodical titles, pamphlets,
                    mss, microfilms, one art object by an 1850's Mil-
                    waukee Negro, and several dresses worn by pioneer
                    Negro women.

WI19   MILWAUKEE NEGRO EDUCATIONAL-CULTURAL PRO-
        JECTS, INC. (1966). 800 W. Wells St., 53206. Tel 414
        374-3097. Bennie E. Graham, Dir.
        The Projects emphasize contributions made by Negroes,
        past and present, to the cultural fabric of America.

        .1   Milwaukee Negro Educational-Cultural Projects, Inc.
                    Files, 1966- . Includes correspondence, minutes of
                    meetings, films, financial records, and documents
                    dealing with the aims, history, and programs of the
                    Projects.

WI20   MILWAUKEE URBAN LEAGUE. 936 W. Center St., 53206.
        Tel 414 374-5850. Wesley L. Scott, Exec. Dir.

        .1   Milwaukee Urban League.
                    Files. Records, reports, correspondence, and
                    other papers concerning the aims and activities of
                    the organization.

WI21   NATIONAL CONFERENCE OF CHRISTIANS AND JEWS
        (NCCJ). 759 N. Milwaukee St., 53202. Tel 414 273-
        6746. Maurice H. Terry, Dir.

WI22   UNITED NEGRO TOUR ASSOCIATION, INC. (UNTA) (1967).
        1319 W. Center, 53206. Tel 414 562-4580. Theodore W.
        Thomas, Pres. and Treas.
        The Association represents a group interested in estab-
        lishing a travel agency designed to promote good will
        and relieve the anxieties and apprehensions that the
        traveling Negro feels as to when he is welcome and what
        kind of reception he will receive.
        Publ.: Travel guide.

        .1   United Negro Tour Association, Inc.
                    Files, 1967- . Includes correspondence, minutes
                    of meetings, financial records, and documents deal-
                    ing with the aims, history, and programs of the
                    Association.

WI23 UNIVERSITY OF WISCONSIN-MILWAUKEE, DEPARTMENT OF URBAN AFFAIRS (1963). 53201. Tel 414 964-4751. Warner Bloomberg, Jr., Chmn.
The Department offers a master's degree program for individuals seeking careers as change agents in urban areas, emphasizing social planning, institutional change, community development and organization, innovative programming and administration, and related research. It is multi-disciplinary and faculty and students engage in research and action projects in such areas as poverty and racial issues.

.1 Department of Urban Affairs.
Files, 1963- . Includes unpublished studies, investigations, reports, and other materials dealing with the work of the Department in the areas of racial conflicts, poverty, and other city problems.

WI24 UNIVERSITY OF WISCONSIN-MILWAUKEE, INSTITUTE OF HUMAN RELATIONS (1964). 3273 N. Maryland Ave., 53211. Tel 414 228-4821. Dr. Victor Hoffmann, Dir.
The Institute conducts research on minority problems and social conflict, including examination of nature, goals and drives of minority groups, their relationships with the majority, effects of specific actions on these groups and individuals within them and study of development and resolution of social conflict which arises out of conditions of denial and discrimination against minorities.
Publ.: Blueprint for Action.

.1 Institute of Human Relations.
Files, 1964- . Correspondence, financial records, studies, reports, and other materials dealing with the aims, history, and programs of the Institute.

WI25 WISCONSIN CIVIL LIBERTIES UNION. 1840 N. Farwell Ave., 53202. Tel 414 272-4032. Edward McManus, Exec. Dir.

RACINE

WI26 DOMINICAN COLLEGE, LIBRARY (1937). 5915 Erie St., 53402. Tel 414 639-1211. Sister Mary Helen, Librn.

.1 Negro history collection.

WI27 NATIONAL ASSOCIATION FOR THE ADVANCEMENT OF COLORED PEOPLE (NAACP), RACINE CHAPTER (1947). 815 Silver St., 53402. Tel 414 632-6951. Julian Thomas, Pres.
Publ.: The Black Book (1969).

.1 National Association for the Advancement of Colored People, Racine Chapter.
Files, 1947- . Includes correspondence, minutes of meetings, clippings, financial records, and other documents dealing with the aims, history, and programs of the Association.

WI28 RACINE ENVIRONMENT COMMITTEE, INC. (1967). 820 Sixth St., 53403. Tel 414 637-8893. Joseph Nelson, Exec. Dir.
Publ.: Record, monthly.

.1 Racine Environment Committee, Inc.
Files, 1967- . Includes correspondence, minutes of meetings, financial records, and other documents dealing with the aims, history, and programs of the Committee.

WI29 RACINE PUBLIC LIBRARY (1896). 75 Seventh St., 53403. Tel 414 633-8281. Forrest L. Mills, Librn. Interlibrary loan, copying, typing, inquiries answered, referrals made.
Publ.: The American Negro (1963), a selected bibliography.

.1 Papers relating to Negroes in Racine, Wisconsin. Miscellaneous, 1949-69. Reproductions of material on Negro history, Negro biography, housing,de facto school segregation, racial problems. Publications of Mayor's Commission on Human Rights, Racine Environment Committee, Urban League, NAACP. Clippings on civil rights questions from local papers.

WI30 URBAN LEAGUE OF RACINE, INC. (1963). 818 Sixth St., 53403. Tel 414 637-8532. Wilbur Johnston, Exec. Dir.

.1 Urban League of Racine, Inc.
Files, 1963- . Includes correspondence, minutes of meetings, financial records, ledgers, and other documents dealing with the aims, history, and programs of the League.

WHITEWATER

WI31 WISCONSIN STATE UNIVERSITY-WHITEWATER (1868), HAROLD ANDERSEN LIBRARY (1868). W. Main St., 53190. Tel 414 473-4000. Stith M. Cain, Dir. of Libraries. Interlibrary loan, copying, inquiries answered.

.1 Facts on Film.
Papers, 1954-67. Microfilm. Contains materials on civil rights and race relations in the South. See Race Relations Information Center, Nashville, Tenn., for a full description.

WYOMING

CHEYENNE

WY1 WYOMING DEPARTMENT OF LABOR AND STATISTICS. 304 State Capitol Bldg., 82001. Tel 307 777-7261. Paul H. Bachman, Cmnr.
The Department is empowered to investigate, initiate and act on complaints of discrimination in employment.

.1 Department of Labor.
Files. Records, correspondence, reports, statistics, and other papers concerning equal employment opportunity programs and other activities of the Department in the area of job discrimination.

BIBLIOGRAPHY

BIBLIOGRAPHY

Alert Americans Association. First National Directory of "Rightist" Groups, Publications and Some Individuals in the United States (and Some Foreign Countries). Los Angeles: 5th Edition, 1965. 54 pp.

Allswang, John, and Patrick Bova. editors and annotators. NORC Social Research 1941-1964: An Inventory of Studies and Publications in Social Research. Chicago: National Opinion Research Center, The University of Chicago, 1964. 80 pp.

Alpha Kappa Alpha Sorority. Negro Women in the Judiciary. Heritage Series # 1. Chicago: August, 1968. 24 pp.

———. Women in Politics. Heritage Series # 2. Chicago: July, 1969. 35 pp.

American Association of School Librarians, Treatment of Minorities in Library Books and other Instructional Materials Committee. Multi-Ethnic Media: Select Bibliographies. American Library Association, (1969?). 12 pp.

American Oil Company. American Traveler's Guide to Negro History. Chicago: 3rd. edition, 1967. 58 pp.

Amistad Research Center. Packet on the Negro In America: Prepared for Secondary Teachers of History, Civics, Government and Problems of Democracy. Nashville, Tennessee: 1969. 102 pp.

Amistad Research Center and Race Relations Department, American Missionary Association. Pamphlets, Periodicals, Audio-Visual Aids, and Articles: 24th Annual Institute of Race Relations. (1967). Nashville: June, 1967. 38 pp.

———. Pamphlets, Periodicals, Audio-Visual Aids, and Articles: 25th Annual Institute of Race Relations. (1968). Nashville: June, 1968. 37 pp.

———. Pamphlets, Periodicals, Audio-Visual Aids, and Articles: 26th Annual Institute of Race Relations. (1969). Nashville: June, 1969. 43 pp.

———. Selected Bibliography: Books, 24th Annual Institute of Race Relations. (1967). Nashville: June, 1967. 36 pp.

———. Selected Bibliography: Books, 25th Annual Institute of Race Relations. (1968). Nashville: June, 1968. 31 pp.

———. Selected Bibliography: 26th Annual Institute of Race Relations. (1969). Nashville: June, 1969. 43 pp.

Andrews, Regina M. Intergroup Relations in the United States: A Compilation of Source Materials and Service Organizations. New York: The National Council of Women of the United States, 1959. 74 pp.

Ash, Lee, and Denis Lorenz. compilers. Subject Collections: A Guide to Special Book Collections and Subject Emphases as Reported by University, College, Public, and Special Libraries in the United States and Canada. New York: R.R. Bowker Co., Third Edition, Revised and Enlarged, 1967. ix + 1221 pp.

The Association for the Study of Negro Life and History, Inc. Bibliographical Suggestions for the Study of Negro History. Washington, D.C., n.d. (196?). 11 pp.

"The Availability of Negro Source Material in Philadelphia." The Negro History Bulletin, Volume 32, No. 3, March 1969. P. 17.

Baker, Joseph V., Associates, Inc. editors. When They Meet: A Convention and Conference Guide, Twelfth Edition, 1970. Lancaster, Pennsylvania: Hamilton Watch Company, 1970. 46 pp.

Baxter, Katherine. The Black Experience and the School Curriculum: Teaching Materials for Grades K-12: An Annotated Bibliography. Philadelphia: Wellsprings Ecumenical Center, 1968. 52 pp.

Beers, Henry Putney. Guide To The Archives of the Government of the Confederate States of America. Washington, D.C.: The National Archives, 1968. ix + 536 pp.

Bergman, Peter M. The Chronological History of The Negro In America. New York: The New American Library, 1969. 698 pp.

Bicknell, Marguerite E. Guide to Information About the Negro and Negro-White Adjustment. Memphis: Brunner Co., 1943. iv + 39 + iii pp.

Bontemps, Arna. "Special Collections of Negroana." The Library Quarterly, Volume 14, No. 3, July, 1944. Pp. 187-206.

Broadwater, Aloha. Data Relating To Negro Military Personnel In the Nineteenth Century. Washington, D.C.: Preliminary Draft Prepared for the Conference on the National Archives and Statistical Research, May, 1968. 14 pp.

Brode, John. The Process of Modernization: An Annotated Bibliography on the Sociocultural Aspects of Development. Cambridge: Harvard University Press, 1969. x + 378 pp.

Bronner, Terre, and Mimi Grindon. Discrimination Today in the U.S.A. Tools for Research: Directory To Human Relations Agencies and Bibliography on Human Rights. Purchase, New York: Social Action Secretariat, Manhattanville College of The Sacred Heart. Social Action Series 1, No. 8, 1961. 28 pp.

Brown, Carol. compiler. Afro-American History. Focus: Black America Bibliography Series. Bloomington, Indiana: Indiana University, Summer, 1969. 43 pp.

Brown, Henry D. "A Brief Survey of the Holdings of Michigan Institutions and Activities in the Field of Negro Life and History." The Negro History Bulletin.

California State Department of Education. The Negro in American History Textbooks: A Report of a Study of the Treatment of Negroes in American History Textbooks Used in Grades Five and Eight and in the High Schools of California's Public Schools. Sacramento: June, 1964. 25 pp.

California Fair Employment Practices Commission. A Directory of City and County Human Relations Commissions in the State of California. San Francisco: April, 1968. 36 pp.

California Fair Employment Practices Commission. A Directory of City and County Human Relations Commissions in the State of California. San Francisco: June, 1969. 37 pp.

Cameron, Colin, and Anila Bhatt. compilers. Hard-Core Unemployment: A Selected, Annotated Bibliography. Madison, Wisconsin: The University of Wisconsin, Institute for Research On Poverty, (1969?). 18 pp.

Cassidy, Maureen P. editor. A Directory of Intergroup Relations Agencies. 1969. New York: Brotherhood-In-Action, Inc., 1969. vii + 160 pp.

Chapman, Abraham. The Negro in American Literature and A Bibliography of Literature By and About Negro Americans. Oshkosh, Wisconsin: Wisconsin Council of Teachers of English, 1966. 135 pp.

Chappelle, L. Lucille. compiler. Selected Bibliography On The Negro - Fourth Supplement. New York: National Urban League, 4th Edition, September, 1968. 50 pp.

Citizens' Governmental Research Bureau. Services and Studies in Social Action for Milwaukee's Negro Community. Milwaukee, Wisconsin: Citizens' Governmental Research Bureau, Vol. 56, No. 7, May 4, 1968. 12 pp.

Claspy, Everett. The Negro in Southwestern Michigan: Negroes in the North in a Rural Environment. Dowagiac, Michigan: Everett Claspy, 1967. 112 pp.

Collins, L.M. Books by Black Americans. Nashville, Tennessee: Institute on the Selection, Organization, and Use of Materials By and About the Negro. Fisk University, Summer, 1970. 53 pp.

Combined Paperback Exhibit. Red, White and Black Minorities in America: A Collection of Paperbacks with a Selected List of Bibliographies. Briarcliff Manor, New York: The Combined Book Exhibit, Inc., June, 1969. 33 pp.

—————. Red, White and Black (and Brown and Yellow) Minorities in America. Briarcliff Manor, New York: The Combined Book Exhibit, Inc., 1970. 31 pp.

Committee on Civil and Human Rights of Educators of the National Commission on Professional Rights and Responsibilities. An Index to Multi-Ethnic Teaching Materials and Teacher Resources. Washington, D.C.: National Education Association, 1967. 18 pp.

—————. The Negro American in Paperback: A Selected List of Paperbound Books Compiled and Annotated for Secondary School Students. Washington, D.C.: National Education Association, 1967. 28 pp.

—————. The Negro American in Paperback: A Selected List of Paperbound Books Compiled and Annotated for Secondary School Students. Washington, D.C.: National Education Association, Revised Edition, 1968. 45 pp.

Connecticut Inter-Racial Commission. Selected Bibliography for Inter-racial Understanding. Hartford: June, 1944. 36 pp.

Copenhave, Christina, and Joanne Boelke. compilers. Library Service To The Disadvantaged: A Bibliography. Bibliography Series # 1. Minneapolis: Educational Research Information Center Clearinghouse for Library and Information Sciences, December, 1968. 19 pp.

Council of Community Services. Starting Points For Those Who Need Help: A Guide To Information About Health and Welfare Services in Metropolitan Nashville and Davidson County, Tennessee. Nashville: July, 1968. 20 pp.

Davis, John P. editor. The American Negro Reference Book. Englewood Cliffs, New Jersey: Prentice Hall, Inc., 1966. xxii + 969 pp.

—————. editor. The Public Library and Reference Material on the American Negro. New York: Phelps-Stokes Fund, 1963. 39 + iii pp.

Davison, Ruth M., and April Legler. compilers. Government Publications on the Negro in America 1948-1968. Focus: Black America Bibliography Series. Bloomington, Indiana: Indiana University, Summer, 1969. 27 pp.

Dayton, Ohio. Human Relations Council. Directory of Human Relations Resources. Dayton, Ohio: n.d. (1967?). 44 pp.

Donald, David. The Nation In Crisis, 1861-1877. New York: Appleton-Century-Crofts, Goldentree Bibliographies, c1969. xv + 92 pp.

Downs, Robert B. American Library Resources: A Bibliographic Guide. Chicago: American Library Association, 1951. 428 pp.

—————. editor. Resources of Southern Libraries: A Survey of Facilities for Research. Chicago: American Library Association, 1938. xii + 370 pp.

Drotning, Phillip T. A Guide to Negro History in America. Garden City, New Jersey: Doubleday and Company, Inc., 1968. xiv + 247 pp.

DuBois, W.E.B. Encyclopedia of the Negro. New York: Phelps-Stokes Fund, 1946. 2nd edition. 215 pp.

—————. editor. A Selected Bibliography of the Negro American. Atlanta: Atlanta University Press, 1905. 71 pp.

Duignan, Peter. Handbook of American Resources for African Studies. San Francisco: Hoover Institute on War, Revolution, and Peace, 1966. xvi + 218 pp.

Ebony, Editors of. compilers. The Negro Handbook. Chicago: Johnson Publishing Company, Inc., 1966. 535 pp.

Educational Research Information Center Clearinghouse On Early Childhood Education. Bibliography On Race and Minorities, Supplement II. Urbana, Illinois: June, 1967. 17 pp.

English, Thomas H. Roads to Research: Distinguished Library Collections of the Southeast. Athens: University of Georgia Press, 1968. xiii + 116 pp.

Erastus Milo Cravath Memorial Library. A List of Published Books by Members of the Fisk Faculty and Alumni Since 1955. Nashville: Fisk University, April, 1962.

Everly, Elaine. Statistical Records Among The Records of the Bureau of Refugees, Freedmen, and Abandoned Lands. Washington, D.C.: Preliminary Draft Prepared for the Conference on the National Archives and Statistical Research, May, 1968. 10 pp.

Farnsley, Nancy, and Charles Farnsley. Lost Cause Press Microcard Collection: Anti-Slavery Propaganda in the Oberlin College Library. Louisville: Lost Cause Press, November, 1968. 101 pp.

Fisk University Library. Charles Spurgeon Johnson: A Bibliography. Nashville, Tennessee: November 7, 1947. 16 pp.

Forbes, Jack D. Afro-Americans in the Far West: A Handbook for Educators. Berkeley: Far West Laboratory for Educational Research and Development, 1968. 106 pp.

The Ford Foundation. Grants and Projects Related to the Development of the American Negro (All Fiscal Years Through June 10, 1966). New York: n.d. (1966?). 60 pp.

Frank, Virginia. compiler. Higher Educational Opportunities for Southern Negroes. Atlanta: Southern Education Foundation, 1967. 32 pp.

The Free Library of Philadelphia. To Be Black in America: A Selected Bibliography. Philadelphia: n.d. (1970?). 33 pp.

Freeney, Mildred, and Mary T. Henry. A List of Manuscripts, Published Works and Related Items in the Charles Waddell Chesnutt Collection of the Erastus Milo Cravath Memorial Library. Nashville: Fisk University, 1954. 32 pp.

Friends of the Florida State University Library. Catalog of the Negro Collections in the Florida Agricultural and Mechanical University Library and the Florida State University Library. Tallahassee: 1969. 80 pp.

Gale Research Company. Encyclopedia of Associations. Detroit: 5th Edition, 1968. 392 pp.

George Cleveland Hall Branch Library. The Special Negro Collection at the George Cleveland Hall Branch Library. Chicago: 1968. 6 pp.

Gibson, Gail M. compiler. Directory of Pennsylvania Historical Organizations and Museums: 1966. Harrisburg: Pennsylvania Historical and Museum Commission, 1966. 90 pp.

Giles, H.H. "The Present Status and Programs of Private Intergroup Relations Agencies." The Journal of Negro Education, Volume 20, No. 3, Summer, 1951. Pp. 408-424.

Goldwater, Walter. Radical Periodicals in America 1890-1950: A Bibliography With Brief Notes. New Haven: Yale University Library, 1966. xv + 51 pp.

Graham, Hugh Davis. A Selected Bibliography of 20th Century Southern History with Special Emphasis on Racial Relations, Especially Since 1954. Palo Alto, California: Stanford University, Department of History, March, 1967. 16 pp.

Grambs, Jean Dresden. Intergroup Education: Methods and Materials. Englewood Cliffs, New Jersey: Prentice-Hall, Inc., 1968. viii + 199 pp.

Gravely, William B. Report on Summer Project, 1967. Atlanta: Interdenominational Theological Center Library, 1967. 8 pp.

Greene, Lorenzo J. "Manuscripts." The Negro History Bulletin, Vol. 30, No. 6, October, 1967. Pp. 14-15.

————. "Negro Manuscript Collections In Libraries." The Negro History Bulletin, Volume 30, No. 3, March, 1967. P 20.

Guzman, Jessie P. editor. Negro Year Book, 1941-1946. Tuskegee Institute, Alabama: Department of Records and Research, Tuskegee Institute, 1947. xv + 708 pp.

————. editor. Negro Year Book, 1952. New York: William H. Wise and Co., Inc., 1952. xxi + 423 pp.

Guzman, Jessie P., and Woodrow W. Hall. editors. Desegregation and the Southern States 1957: Legal Action and Voluntary Group Action. Tuskegee Institute: The Department of Records and Research, 1958. 59 pp.

Hackman, Martha. A Library Guide to Afro-American Studies. Los Angeles: John F. Kennedy Memorial Library, California State College, April, 1969. 13 pp.

Hamer, Philip M. editor. A Guide to Archives and Manuscripts in the United States. New Haven: Yale University Press, 1961. xxiii + 775 pp.

Harris, M.A. ("Spike"). A Negro History Tour of Manhattan. New York: Greenwood Publishing Corporation, 1968. xiii + 113 pp.

Harvard College Library. Afro-American Studies: A Guide to Resources of the Harvard University Library, Preliminary Edition. Cambridge: 1969. 38 pp.

————. Resources of the Harvard University Library For Afro-American and African Studies. Cambridge: 1969. 21 + vi pp.

Havrilesky, Catherine, and Preston Wilcox. A Selected Bibliography on White Institutional Racism. New York: Afram Associates, Inc., July 1, 1969. 7 pp.

Hesterberg, Ann, and Mary Bricker. revised by. Discrimination Today in the U.S.A. Lunch Counters: The Sit-Ins, A Nonviolent Youth Movement. Purchase, New York: Social Action Secretariat, Manhattanville College of the Sacred Heart, Social Action Series 1, No. 7, 1961. 42 pp.

Hicks, Richard, Carol Tullis, and Robert Swisher. compilers. Black Americans in Public Affairs/Black American Biography/Black American Scientists. Focus: Black America Bibliography Series. Bloomington, Indiana: Indiana University, Summer 1969. 52 pp.

The Interracial Council for Business Opportunity of New York. A Directory of Negro-Owned and Operated Businesses in New York City. New York: n.d. 17 pp.

Irvin, Betty Jo, and Jane A. McCabe. compilers. Fine Arts and the Black American/Music and the Black American. Focus: Black America Bibliography Series. Bloomington, Indiana: Indiana University, Summer, 1969. 33 pp.

J.K. Daniels Library, Lane College. Negro Collection: A Bibliography. Jackson, Tennessee: 1965. 20 pp.

Jackson, Giovanna R. compiler. Afro-American Religion and Church and Race Relations. Focus: Black America Bibliography Series. Bloomington, Indiana: Indiana University, Summer, 1969. 18 pp.

Jefferson, Marjorie, et.al. The Role of Racial Minorities in the United States: A Resource Book for Seattle Teachers. Seattle: Seattle Public Schools, 1968. 203 pp.

Johnson, Charles S., and Associates. Directory of Agencies in Race Relations. Chicago: Julius Rosenwald Fund, 1945. 124 pp.

Johnson, Clifton H. American Missionary Association Archives: As a Source for the Study of American History. New York: American Missionary Association of the United Church Board for Homeland Ministries, n.d. 32 + vii pp.

————. "Some Archival Sources on Negro History in Tennessee." Tennessee Historical Quarterly, Volume 28, Winter, 1969. Pp. 297-416.

Joint Committee of the American Library Association Children's Service Division, and The African-American Institute. Africa: An Annotated List of Printed Materials Suitable for Children. New York: Information Center on Children's Cultures, United States Committee for UNICEF, 1968. iv + 76 pp.

Kaiser, Ernest. "Public, University and Private American Library Holdings on the Negro." In Black America. edited by Patricia Romero. Washington, D.C.: United Publishing Corporation, c1969. Pp 332-343.

Katz, William Loren. Teachers' Guide to American Negro History. Chicago: Quadrangle Books, 1968. 192 pp.

Kelley, Clarice Y. Where It's Happening: A Selective Guide to Continuing Programs Funded by the United States Office of Education. Garden City: Doubleday and Company, Inc., 1968. 58 pp.

Kentucky Commission on Human Rights. Black Business in Louisville. Louisville, Kentucky: 1969. 24 pp.

Knobbe, Mary L., et.al. Directory: Planning, Building and Housing Libraries, United States and Canada. College Park, Maryland: 1969. 36 pp.

Kobitz, Minnie W. The Negro in Schoolroom Literature: Resource Materials for the Teacher of Kindergarten through the Sixth Grade. New York: Center for Urban Education, February, 1967. iii + 68 pp.

Kruzas, Anthony T. editor. Directory of Special Libraries and Information Centers, Second Edition. Detroit: Gale Research Company, c1968. 1048 pp.

Kuncio, Robert A. Negro History, 1553-1903: An Exhibition of Books, Prints, and Manuscripts from the Shelves of the Library Company of Philadelphia and the Historical Society of Pennsylvania, April 17 to July 17, 1969. Philadelphia: The Library Company of Philadelphia, 1969. v + 83 pp.

Lawrenz, Marguerite Martha. Bibliography and Index of Negro Music. Detroit: The Board of Education of the City of Detroit, 1968. 52 pp.

Leach, MacEdward, and Henry Glassie. A Guide for Collectors of Oral Traditions and Folk Cultural Material in Pennsylvania. Harrisburg, Pennsylvania: Pennsylvania Historical and Museum Commission, 1968. 70 pp.

Lewinson, Paul. compiler. A Guide to Documents in the National Archives: For Negro Studies. Washington, D.C.: American Council of Learned Societies, 1947. x + 28 pp.

Link, Arthur S., and William M. Leary, Jr. compilers. The Progressive Era of the Great War, 1896-1920. Goldentree Bibliographies. New York: Appleton-Century-Crofts, c1969. x + 85 pp.

Lipscombe, Mildred. The Education of the Afro-American: A Selected Bibliography. Newark: Newark Public Library, 1968. 8 pp.

McAllister, Dorothy M. "Library Resources for Graduate Study in Southern Universities for Negroes." The Journal of Negro Education, Volume 23, No. 1, Winter, 1954. Pp. 51-59.

McCabe, Jane A. compiler. Education and the Afro-American. Focus: Black America Bibliography Series. Bloomington, Indiana: Indiana University, Summer, 1969. 26 pp.

McCabe, Jane A., Robert S. Wood and Wilmer H. Baatz. compilers. Black Entertainers and the Entertainment Industry/Black American Athletes. Focus: Black America Bibliography Series. Bloomington, Indiana: Indiana University, Summer, 1969. 23 pp.

McConnell, Roland C. "Importance of Records in the National Archives on The History of the Negro." The Journal of Negro History, Volume 34, 1949. Pp. 135-152.

McDonough, John. "Manuscript Resources for the Study of Negro Life and History." Washington, D.C.: The Quarterly Journal of the Library of Congress, Volume 25, Number 3, July, 1969. Pp. 126-148.

McWorter, Gerald A. The Political Sociology of the Negro: A Selective Review of the Literature. New York: Anti-Defamation League of B'nai B'rith, 1967. 31 pp.

Maida, Peter R., and John L. McCoy. The Poor: A Selected Bibliography. Washington, D.C.: U.S. Department of Agriculture, Miscellaneous Publications No. 1145, Government Printing Office, May, 1969. ii + 56 pp.

Mansfield, Stephen. compiler. Collections In the Manuscripts Division, Alderman Library, The University of Virginia, Containing References to Slavery For The Period From 1820 to 1865. Charlottesville, Virginia: Alderman Library, The University of Virginia, August, 1967. 178 pp.

Meyer, Jon K. Bibliography on the Urban Crisis: The Behavioral, Psychological, and Sociological Aspects of the Urban Crisis. Washington, D.C.: National Institute of Mental Health, Public Health Services Publication No. 1948-1969. vii + 452 pp.

Michalak, Thomas J. compiler. Economic Status and Conditions of the Negro. Focus: Black America Bibliography Series. Bloomington, Indiana: Indiana University, Summer, 1969. 21 pp.

Michigan Civil Rights Commission. Directory of Civil Rights and Human Relations Agencies In Michigan. Detroit: May, 1967. 23 pp.

Michigan Department of Education. The Heritage of the Negro in America, a Bibliography: Books, Records, Tapes and Filmstrips. Lansing, Michigan: 1969. 48 pp.

————. Bibliography for Educators: The American Negro. Lansing, Michigan: May, 1968. 8 pp.

Michigan-Ohio Regional Educational Laboratory. Racism and Education: A Review of Selected Literature Related to Segregation, Discrimination, and Other Aspects of Racism in Education. Detroit: May, 1969. vii + 93 pp.

Michigan State Library. Negroes in Michigan: A Selected Bibliography. East Lansing, Michigan: February, 1968. 4 pp.

Miller, Elizabeth W. compiler. The Negro In America: A Bibliography. Cambridge: Harvard University Press, 1966. xvii + 190 pp.

Milwaukee County Historical Society. A Preliminary Survey of Manuscript and Archival Collections of the Milwaukee County Historical Society. Milwaukee, Wisconsin: March, 1967. 20 pp.

Murden, Kenneth W., and Henry Putney Beers. Guide to Federal Archives Relating to the Civil War. Washington, D.C.: The National Archives, 1962. x + 721 pp.

Murphy, Nancy. Discrimination Today In the U.S.A. Civil Rights, The Right To Vote. Purchase, New York: Social Action Secretariat, Manhattanville College of The Sacred Heart, Social Action Series I, No. 9, 1961. 29 pp.

Murray, Florence. The Negro Handbook, 1942. New York: Malliet and Co., 1942. 269 pp.

————. The Negro Handbook, 1944. New York: Current Reference Publications, 1944. 283 pp.

————. The Negro Handbook, 1946-1947. New York: Current Books, Inc., 1947. viii + 392 pp.

————. The Negro Handbook, 1949. New York: Macmillan, 1949. 368 pp.

National Association for the Advancement of Colored People, Education Department. Integrated School Books: A Descriptive Bibliography of 399 Pre-school and Elementary School Texts and Story Books. New York: 1967. 55 pp.

National Association of Intergroup Relations Officials. Directory of Intergroup Relations Agencies with Paid Professional Personnel: 1959. New York: 1959. 82 pp.

————. NAIRO Directory. Washington, D.C.: 1967. 75 pp.

National Council of Churches, Division of Christian Education. Negro Heritage Resource Guide: A Bibliography of the Negro in Contemporary America. New York: Council Press, 1967. 21 pp.

National Council on Crime and Delinquency. Selected Reading List in Delinquency and Crime. New York: 1966. 38 pp.

National Opinion Research Center. Bibliography of Publications, 1941-1960: Supplement, 1961 - December, 1967. By Subject and Author. Chicago: National Opinion Research Center, The University of Chicago, January, 1968. 78 pp.

National Service Secretariat. Directory of Service Organizations. Washington, D.C.: 1968. 49 pp.

National Urban League, Research Department. A Partial List of Community Studies on the Social and Economic Conditions of Minority Population in Various Cities: 1940-1967. New York: n.d. 8 pp.

————. Selected Bibliography on the Negro. New York: Revised Edition, September, 1939. 47 pp.

————. Selected Bibliography on the Negro. New York: Fourth Edition, June, 1951. 124 pp.

————. Selected Bibliography on the Negro, Supplement to Fourth Edition. New York: September, 1958. 48 pp.

————. Second Supplement to the Selected Bibliography on the Negro, Fourth Edition, June, 1951. New York: November, 1963. 36 pp.

————. Third Supplement to the Selected Bibliography on the Negro, Fourth Edition, June, 1951. New York: April, 1966. 51 pp.

Negro Book Club, Inc. Negro Book Club's Guide to African American Books, Records, Visual Aids, Maps, Film Strips and Art. New York: Negro Book Club Inc, 1969. 64 pp.

New Hampshire Library Association. Special Collections and Subject Area Strengths in New Hampshire Libraries. Henniker, New Hampshire: June, 1969. 38 pp.

New York City, The Department of Commerce and Industry. A Representative Sampling of Minority Owned Manufacturing and Service Establishments in New York City. New York: n.d. 17 pp.

Nobel, J.D. editor. Resource Handbook In Human Relations. Cleveland: The Council On Human Relations, 1959. 75 pp.

Oakland Public Schools. Cultural Diversity: Library and Audio-Visual Materials for In-Service Education. Oakland, California: March 18, 1964. iv + 39 pp.

————. Cultural Diversity: II, A Supplement. Library and Audio-Visual Materials for In-Service Education. Oakland, California: November 20, 1964. iv + 21 pp.

————. Cultural Diversity: III, A Supplement. Library and Audio-Visual Materials for In-Service Education. Oakland, California: May 10, 1967. iv + 42 pp.

Osborn, Francis H., Jr. compiler. Resource Handbook in Human Relations. Cleveland: The Council on Human Relations, 1959. 75 pp.

Pennsylvania Historical and Museum Commission. Preliminary Guide to the Research Materials of The Pennsylvania Historical and Museum Commission. Harrisburg, Pennsylvania: 1959. 58 pp.

Phinazee, Annette Hoage. editor. Materials By and About American Negroes. Atlanta: Atlanta University School of Library Services. 1967. ix + 111 pp.

Pinkett, Harold T. "Recent Federal Archives As Sources for Negro History." Negro History Bulletin, Volume 30, No. 8, December, 1967. Pp. 14-17.

Plans For Progress. Directory of Predominately Negro Colleges and Universities in the United States of America (Four-Year Institutions Only). Washington, D.C.: January, 1969. 91 pp.

Ploski, Harry A., and Roscoe C. Brown, Jr. The Negro Almanac. New York: Bellwether Publishing Company, Inc., 1967. xii + 1012 pp.

Porter, Dorothy B. "Library Sources for the Study of Negro Life and History." Journal of Negro History, Volume 5, Number 2. Pp. 232-44.

————. The Negro in the United States: A Selected Bibliography. Washington, D.C.: Library of Congress, 1970. x + 313 pp.

————. compiler. A Working Bibliography on The Negro in The United States. Ann Arbor, Michigan: University Microfilms, 1969. 202 pp.

Potts, Alfred M., II. editor. Knowing and Educating The Disadvantaged: An Annotated Bibliography. Alamosa, Colorado: The Center For Cultural Studies, Adams State College, Cooperative Research Project No. S-173, 1965. v + 460 pp.

Pratt Center For Community Improvement. Community Information Manual, Central Brooklyn Edition. New York: Pratt Center for Community Improvement, Pratt Institute, 3rd Edition, December, 1966. vi + 93 pp.

Prentice-Hall Editorial Staff. compilers. Educator's Complete ERIC Handbook. Englewood Cliffs, New Jersey: Prentice-Hall, Inc., 1967. x + 862 pp.

Preschel, Barbara M. "The Information Center on Crime and Delinquency." Special Libraries, January, 1968. Pp. 40-46.

Prince George's County Memorial Library, Oxon Hill Branch. Selective List of Government Publications About The American Negro. Oxon Hill, Maryland: February, 1968. 8 pp.

————. Selective List of Government Publications About the American Negro. Oxon Hill, Maryland: February, 1969. 26 pp.

Quarles, Benjamin. "What the Historian Owes the Negro." Saturday Review, September 3, 1966. Pp. 10-13.

Race Relations Department, American Missionary Association. Selected Articles, Audio-Visual Aids, Pamphlets, and Periodicals, 17th Annual Institute of Race Relations. (1960). Nashville: June, 1960. 46 pp.

————. Pamphlets-Periodicals, Audio-Visual Aids, and Articles: 18th Annual Institute of Race Relations. (1961). Nashville: June 1961. 52 pp.

————. Pamphlets and Periodicals, Audio-Visual Aids, and Articles: 19th Annual Institute of Race Relations. (1962). Nashville: June, 1962. 51 pp.

————. Pamphlets, Periodicals, Audio-Visual Aids, and Articles: 20th Annual Institute of Race Relations. (1963). Nashville: June, 1963. 54 pp.

————. Pamphlets, Periodicals, Audio-Visual Aids, and Articles: 21st Annual Institute of Race Relations. (1964). Nashville: June, 1964. 51 pp.

————. Pamphlets, Periodicals, Audio-Visual Aids, and Articles: 22nd Annual Institute of Race Relations. (1965). Nashville: June, 1965. 60 pp.

————. Pamphlets, Periodicals, Audio-Visual Aids, and Articles: 23rd Annual Institute of Race Relations. Nashville: June, 1966. 41 pp.

————. Selected Bibliography: 17th Annual Race Relations Institute. (1960). Nashville: June, 1969. 27 pp.

————. Selected Bibliography: (Books), 18th Annual Institute of Race Relations. (1961). Nashville: June, 1961. 34 pp.

————. Selected Bibliography: (Books), 19th Annual Institute of Race Relations, June 25-July 7, 1962. Nashville: June, 1962. 36 pp.

————. Selected Bibliography: (Books), 20th Annual Institute of Race Relations, June 24-July 6, 1963. Nashville: June, 1963. 41 pp.

————. Selected Bibliography: (Books), 21st Annual Institute of Race Relations, June 29-July 11, 1964. Nashville: June, 1964. 38 pp.

————. Selected Bibliography: (Books), 22nd Annual Institute of Race Relations, June 28-July 10, 1965. Nashville: June, 1965. 35 pp.

————. Selected Bibliography: (Books), 23rd Annual Institute of Race Relations. (1966). Nashville: June, 1966. 31 pp.

Randolph, H. Helen. Urban Education Bibliography: An Annotated Listing. New York: Center for Urban Education, April, 1968. 97 pp.

Reddick, L.D. Bibliography: The Afro-American Experience. Nashville: Fisk University Workshop on Negro Culture, August, 1969. 5 pp.

———. "Library Resources for Negro Studies in the United States and Abroad." New York: Encyclopedia of the Negro, 2nd edition, 1946. Pp. 171-190.

Richard B. Harrison Public Library. A Selected List of Books By and About the Negro: 1950-1956. Raleigh, N.C.: 1956. 26 pp.

Richard J. Bernhardt Memorial Library. A Guide to Resources for Antipoverty Programs: A Selected Bibliography. New York: Federation Employment and Guidance Service, April, 1965. 24 pp.

Rose, Peter I. editor. Research Bulletin on Intergroup Relations, 1962. New York: Anti-Defamation League of B'nai B'rith, January, 1962. 30 pp.

———. editor. Research Bulletin on Intergroup Relations, 1963. New York: Anti-Defamation League of B'nai B'rith, 1963. 48 pp.

Rountree, Louise M. compiler. The American Negro and African Studies: A Bibliography on the Special Collections In Carnegie Library. Salisbury, North Carolina: Carnegie Library, Livingstone College, 1968. 78 pp.

Rudwick, Elliott M. W.E.B. DuBois: A Study in Minority Group Leadership. Philadelphia: University of Pennsylvania Press, 1960. 382 pp.

Ryan, Pat M. compiler. Black Writing In the U.S.A.: A Bibliographic Guide. Brockport, New York: Drake Memorial Library, 1969. v + 48 pp.

St. John, Nancy Hoyt, and Nancy Smith. Annotated Bibliography on School Racial Mix and the Self Concept, Aspirations, Academic Achievement and Interracial Attitudes and Behavior of Negro Children. Cambridge: Harvard Research and Development Center on Educational Differences, 1967. 81 pp.

Salk, Erwin A. compiler and editor. A Layman's Guide to Negro History. New York: McGraw-Hill Book Company, 1966. xviii + 170 pp.

———. compiler and editor. A Layman's Guide to Negro History. New York: McGraw-Hill Book Company, new, enlarged edition, 1967. xviii + 196 pp.

Sawyer, Frank B. editor. U.S. Negro World: 1967 Negro Press Edition. New York: U.S. Negro World, 1967. 40 pp.

Schein, Irving, and George A. Taylor, Jr. A Port Royal Experiment and the Afro-American. Hartford, Connecticut: Curriculum Research and Development, Hartford Board of Education, 1969. 46 pp.

Schermer, George. Guidelines: A Manual for Bi-Racial Committees. New York: Anti-Defamation League of B'nai B'rith, 1964. 96 pp.

Science Information Exchange. Notices of Research Projects. Washington, D.C.: Smithsonian Institution. (Data through July 13, 1967).

Sinclair, Donald A. general editor. New Jersey and The Negro: A Bibliography, 1715-1966. Trenton: New Jersey Library Association, 1967. 196 pp.

Sinder, Leon. editor. Research Bulletin On Intergroup Relations, 1963-1964. New York: Anti-Defamation League of B'nai B'rith, 1964. 48 pp.

Singh, Raman K. editor. Studies in Black Literature, Volume I, Number 1. Fredericksburg, Virginia: Mary Washington College of the University of Virginia, Spring, 1970. iii + 116 pp.

Sloan, Irving J. The Negro in Modern American History Textbooks. Washington, D.C.: American Federation of Teachers, AFL-CIO, 2nd Edition, December, 1967. 95 pp.

———. The American Negro: A Chronology and Fact Book. Dobbs Ferry, New York: Oceana Publications, Inc., 1965. xii + 84 pp.

Smith, Jessie Carney. The Research Collections In Negro Life and Culture At Fisk University. An Unpublished Paper delivered at the Workshop on Bibliographic and Other Resources for a Study of the American Negro held at Howard University, July, 1968. 26 pp.

———. Survey of Manuscript and Archival Collections for the Study of Black Culture. An Unpublished Manuscript, n.d. (1969). 110 pp.

Southern Association of Colleges and Schools, The Education Improvement Project Staff. Selected Titles on Afro-American and African Culture. Atlanta: 1969. 52 pp.

Southern Education Reporting Service. Facts on Film. Nashville: Tennessee Microfilms, 1957-1968.

Southern Regional Council. Organizations Supporting The Student Protest Movement. Atlanta: Report L-28, November, 1961. 4 pp.

———. Special Report: Organizations and Personnel Engaged In Human Relations Activities in the South. Atlanta: November 25, 1957. 8 pp.

Spangler, Earl. compiler. Bibliography of Negro History. Minneapolis: Ross and Haines, Inc., 1963. vii + 101 pp.

Spivey, Lydia L. editor. The Negro in America: A Selective Bibliography of Material in the Public Library of Charlotte and Mecklenburg County. Charlotte, North Carolina: 1970. 46 pp.

State Historical Society of Missouri. Published Negro Material. Columbia, Missouri: n.d. (1969?). 12 pp.

Steiner-Prag, Eleanor F. compiler. American Library Directory: 1968-1969. New York: R.R. Bowker Co., 26th Edition, 1969. xiv + 1071 pp.

Stetler, Henry G. compiler. Inter-Group Relations Bibliography: A Selected List of Books, Periodicals, and Resource Agencies in Inter-group Relations, Including a Special Section Devoted to Connecticut Studies. Hartford: Connecticut State Inter-Racial Commission, 1947. 82 pp.

Storen, Helen F. Readings in Intergroup Relations. New York: National Conference of Christians and Jews, Revised Edition, October, 1959. 53 pp.

Suchman, Edward A., John P. Dean, and Robin M. Williams, Jr. Desegregation: Some Propositions and Research Suggestion. New York: Anti-Defamation League of B'nai B'rith, 1958. 128 pp.

Sweet, Charles E. compiler. Sociology of the American Negro. Focus: Black America Bibliography Series. Bloomington, Indiana: Indiana University. Summer, 1969. 53 pp.

Sweet, Charles E., and Giovanna R. Jackson. compilers. The Negro and the Establishment: Law, Politics and the Courts/Black Nationalism. Focus: Black America Bibliography Series. Bloomington, Indiana: Indiana University, Summer, 1969. 28 pp.

Swisher, Robert, and Jill A. Archer. compilers. Black American Literature/Black American Folklore. Focus: Black American Bibliography Series. Bloomington, Indiana: Indiana University, Summer, 1969. 25 pp.

Swisher, Robert A., and Charles E. Sweet. compilers. Psychology of the Black American/Biological Aspects of Race. Focus: Black America Bibliography Series. Bloomington, Indiana: Indiana University, Summer, 1969. 26 pp.

Teachers Professional Library, San Francisco Unified School District. A Selected Bibliography on Human Relations. San Francisco: December, 1963. 28 pp.

Tennessee Department of Education, Division of School Libraries. compilers. The Negro: A Selected List of School Libraries of Books by or About the Negro in Africa and America. Nashville: 1935. 22 pp.

Tennessee Department of Education, Equal Educational Opportunities Program. The Negro American: A Selected List of Books, Magazines, and Recordings for School Libraries. Nashville: October, 1969. 14 pp.

Tennessee State Library and Archives. Indian Materials in the Manuscript Section. Nashville: Tennessee State Library and Archives, 1969. 2 pp.

———. Negro Materials in the Manuscript Section. Nashville: Tennessee State Library and Archives, 1969. 2 pp.

Thompson, Edgar T., and Alma Macy Thompson. Race and Region: A Descriptive Bibliography Compiled with Special Reference to the Relations Between Whites and Negroes in the United States. Chapel Hill: The University of North Carolina Press, 1949. xii + 194 pp.

Tumin, Melvin M. editor. Research Annual on Intergroup Relations: 1965. New York: Anti-Defamation League of B'nai B'rith, 1966. 176 pp.

———. Segregation and Desegregation: A Digest of Recent Research, 1956-1959. Supplement. New York: Anti-Defamation League of B'nai B'rith, 1960. 32 pp.

Tumin, Melvin M., and Cathy S. Greenblat. editors. Research Annual on Intergroup Relations, 1966. New York: Frederick A. Praeger, 1967. 338 pp.

Turner, Darwin T. compiler. Afro-American Writers. New York: Appleton-Century-Crofts, 1970. xvii + 117 pp.

United Nations Educational, Scientific and Cultural Organization. Research on Racial Relations. Amsterdam, Holland: 1966. 265 pp.

U.S. Civil Service Commission Library. Equal Opportunity In Employment: Personnel Bibliography. Washington, D.C.: Series Number 29, December, 1968. 122 pp.

U.S. Commission on Civil Rights. Civil Rights Directory. Washington, D.C.: October, 1968. vii + 168 pp.

———. Directory of National Private Organizations with Civil Rights Programs. Washington, D.C.: 1966. 71 pp.

U.S. Department of Commerce. A Guide To Negro Marketing Information. Washington, D.C.: September, 1966. v + 50 pp.

U.S. Department of Health, Education, and Welfare, Office of Education. Federal Research and Demonstration Programs Benefiting the Disadvantaged and Handicapped. Washington, D.C.: Government Printing Office, January, 1968. 53 pp.

———. Office of Education Programs for the Disadvantaged. Washington, D.C.: Government Printing Office, January, 1969. 49 pp.

U.S. Department of Housing and Urban Development. Housing and Planning References. Washington, D.C.: U.S. Government Printing Office, New Series, No. 26, September - October, 1969. 109 pp.

U.S. Department of Housing and Urban Development, HUD Clearinghouse Service. Selected Information Sources for Urban Specialists. Washington, D.C.: U.S. Government Printing Office, June, 1969. iv + 43 pp.

U.S. Department of Housing and Urban Development Library. Equal Opportunity: A Bibliography of Research on Equal Opportunity in Housing. Washington, D.C.: U.S. Government Printing Office, April, 1969. 24 pp.

U.S. House of Representatives, Committee on Un-American Activities. Guide to Subversive Organizations and Publications (and Appendixes). Washington, D.C.: U.S. Government Printing Office, December 1, 1961. v + 245 + xxxviii pp. Revised edition, to supersede Guide published on January 2, 1957. Includes index. Prepared and released by the Committee on Un-American Activities, 87th Congress, 2nd Session, House Document No. 398.

U.S. House of Representatives, Committee on Un-American Activities, 90th Congress, 1st Session. Subversive Influences in Riots, Looting, and Burning, Part I. Washington, D.C.: U.S. Government Printing Office, 1968. iv + 715-922 + xii.

———. Subversive Influences in Riots, Looting, and Burning, Part 2. Washington, D.C.: U.S. Government Printing Office, 1968. iv + 923-1121 + ix. pp.

———. Subversive Influences in Riots, Looting, and Burning, Part 3. (Los Angeles - Watts). Washington, D.C.: U.S. Government Printing Office, 1968. iv + 1128-1312 + x pp.

U.S. House of Representatives, Committee on Un-American Activities, 90th Congress, 1st Session. Subversive Influences in Riots, Looting, and Burning, Part I. Washington, D.C.: U.S. Government Printing Office, 1968. iv + 715-922 + xii. (cont.).

—————. Second Session. Subversive Influences in Riots, Looting, and Burning, Part 3-A. (Los Angeles-Watts). Washington, D.C.: U.S. Government Printing Office, 1968. iv + 1815-1850 + xi pp.

—————. Subversive Influences in Riots, Looting, and Burning, Part 4. (Newark, New Jersey). Washington, D.C.: U.S. Government Printing Office, April, 1968. iv + 1851-1983 + x pp.

—————. Subversive Influences in Riots, Looting and Burning, Part 5. (Buffalo, New York). Washington, D.C.: U.S. Government Printing Office, April, 1968. iv + 1987-2048 + vi pp.

—————. Subversive Influences in Riots, Looting, and Burning, Part 6. (San Francisco-Berkeley). Washington, D.C.: U.S. Government Printing Office, June, 1968. iv + 2048-2195 + xiv pp.

U.S. Joint Economic Committee. A Directory of Urban Research Study Centers. Washington, D.C.: Government Printing Office, August, 1967. x + 77 pp.

U.S. Library of Congress. Folk Music: A Catalog of Folk Songs, Ballads, Dances, Instrumental Pieces, and Folk Tales of the United States and Latin America on Phonograph Records. Washington, D.C.: U.S. Government Printing Office, 1964. 107 pp.

—————. The National Union Catalog of Manuscript Collections, 1959-1961. Ann Arbor, Michigan: J.W. Edwards, 1962. xiii + 1061 pp.

—————. The National Union Catalog of Manuscript Collections, 1962. Hamden, Connecticut: The Shoe String Press, Inc., 1964. x + 532 pp.

—————. The National Union Catalog of Manuscript Collections, 1963-1964. Washington, D.C.: 1965. xv + 500 pp.

—————. The National Union Catalog of Manuscript Collections, 1965. Washington, D.C.: 1966. xxiii + 701 pp.

—————. The National Union Catalog of Manuscript Collections, 1966. Washington, D.C.: 1967. xxv + 920 pp.

—————. The National Union Catalog of Manuscript Collections, 1967. Washington, D.C.: 1968. xxv + 525 pp.

—————. The National Union Catalog of Manuscript Collections, 1968. Washington, D.C.: 1969. xxv + 811 pp.

—————. Negro Newspapers on Microfilm: A Selected List. Washington, D.C.: The Library of Congress Photoduplication Service, 1953. 8 pp.

U.S. Library of Congress, National Referral Center for Science and Technology. A Directory of Information Resources in the United States: Federal Government: With a Supplement of Government Sponsored Information Resources. Washington, D.C.: U.S. Government Printing Office, June, 1967. vii + 411 pp.

—————. A Directory of Information Resources in the United States: Social Sciences. Washington, D.C. U.S. Government Printing Office, 1965. v + 218 pp.

U.S. National Archives and Records Service, General Services Administration. Selected Series of Records Issued by the Commissioner of the Bureau of Refugees, Freedmen, and Abandoned Lands, 1865-1872. Washington, D.C.: 1969. 8 pp.

U.S. President's Council on Youth Opportunity. Bibliography On Youth Programs. Washington, D.C.: May, 1968. 13 pp.

United States National Student Association, Southern Student Human Relations Project. Resources for Race Relations: Work, Study, Involvement. Atlanta: July, 1964. 7 pp.

University Microfilms, Inc. Selected Pre-Twentieth Century Periodicals on the Negro in America. Ann Arbor: n.d. 3 pp.

University of North Carolina, Scholarship Information Center. College Opportunities For Southern Negro Students. Chapel Hill: YMCA-YWCA Human Relations Committees, Second Edition, September, 1966. 106 pp.

University of Pennsylvania Center For Urban Research and Experiment. Urban Related Research and Community Involvement Programs At the University of Pennsylvania. Philadelphia: March, 1969. 35 pp.

The Urban Institute. A Directory of University Urban Research Centers. Washington, D.C.: 1969. 141 pp.

Viet, Jean. compiler. Selected Documentation for the Study of Race Relations. Paris, France: UNESCO, International Committee for Social Sciences Documentation, June, 1958. 81 pp.

Watt, Lois B. compiler. Literature for Disadvantaged Children: A Bibliography. Washington, D.C.: Office of Education, U.S. Department of Health, Education and Welfare, August, 1968. 16 pp.

Waxman, Julia. Race Relations: A Selected List of Readings on Racial and Cultural Minorities in the United States with Special Emphasis on Negroes. Chicago: Julius Rosenwald Fund, 1945. 47 pp.

Weinberg, Meyer. Research on School Desegregation: Review and Prospect. Chicago: Integrated Education Associates, 1965. 39 pp.

—————. editor. School Integration: A Comprehensive Classified Bibliography of 3,100 References. Chicago: Integrated Education Associates, 1967. iv + 137 pp.

Welsch, Erwin K. The Negro in the United States: A Research Guide. Bloomington: Indiana University Press, 1965. xiii + 142 pp.

West, Earle H. compiler. A Bibliography of Doctoral Research on the Negro: 1933-1966. Ann Arbor: University Microfilms, 1969. vii + 134 pp.

White, Carl Milton. Sources of Information in the Social Sciences. Totowa, New Jersey: Bedminister Press, 1964. xii + 498 pp.

Whiteman, Maxwell. A Century of Fiction by American Negroes, 1853-1952: A Descriptive Bibliography. Philadelphia: Alber Saifer, 1968. 64 pp.

Wilcox, Laird M. Guide to the American Left. Kansas City, Missouri: United States Directory Service, 4th Edition, September, 1969. 59 pp.

————. compiler. Guide To The American Left, Fifth Edition. Kansas City, Missouri: U.S. Directory Service, February, 1970. 59 pp.

Williams, Edwin Everitt. Farmington Plan Handbook. Bloomington, Indiana: Association of Research Libraries, 1953. v + 170 pp.

Williams, Daniel T. compiler. Tuskegee Institute: Social Science Research: Listing of File Cabinets and Boxes. Tuskegee Institute, Alabama: Tuskegee Institute Library, June, 1967. 32 pp.

Winchell, Constance Mabel. Guide to Reference Books. Chicago: American Library Association, June, 1967. 8th Edition. 741 pp.

Wirth, Louis. Directory of Agencies in Intergroup Relations. Chicago: American Council on Race Relations, 1948.

Wisconsin Department of Industry, Labor and Human Relations, Equal Rights Division. Bibliography and Resource Guide: An Aid to Understanding in Intergroup Relations, Negro History and Aspiration, the Civil Rights Struggle and the Crisis in our Cities. Madison: April, 1968. 7 pp.

Wittenberg, Rudolph M. A Brief Survey of the Major Agencies in the Field of Intercultural Education. New York: Department of Scientific Research, American Jewish Committee, 1949.

Work, Monroe N. A Bibliography of the Negro in Africa and America. New York: Wilson, 1929. xxi + 698 pp.

————. Negro Year Book, 1912. Tuskegee Institute, Alabama: Tuskegee Institute, 1912. 215 pp.

————. The Negro Year Book, 1913. Tuskegee Institute, Alabama: Negro Year Book Company, 1913. 348 pp.

————. The Negro Year Book, 1914-1915. Tuskegee Institute, Alabama: Negro Year Book Company, 1915. 448 pp.

————. The Negro Year Book, 1916-1917. Tuskegee Institute, Alabama: Negro Year Book Company, 1917. 488 pp.

————. The Negro Year Book, 1918-1919. Tuskegee Institute, Alabama: Negro Year Book Company, 1919. 520 pp.

————. The Negro Year Book, 1921-1922. Tuskegee Institute, Alabama: Negro Year Book Company, 1922. 494 pp.

————. The Negro Year Book, 1925-1926. Tuskegee Institute, Alabama: Negro Year Book Company, 1925. vii + 544 pp.

————. The Negro Year Book, 1931-1932. Tuskegee Institute, Alabama: Negro Year Book Company, 1932. xiv + 543 pp.

————. The Negro Year Book, 1937-1938. Tuskegee Institute, Alabama: Negro Year Book Company, 1937. xiv + 575 pp.

Yale University. Exercises Marking the Opening of the James Weldon Johnson Memorial Collection of Negro Arts and Letters. New Haven: Yale University, 1950. 19 pp.

Yearbook of International Organizations (annual). International Publications, 12th Edition, 1969. 1220 pp.

Yelton, Donald C. A Survey of the Special Negro Collection and Related Resources of the Vail Memorial Library of Lincoln University. Lincoln University, Pennsylvania: Lincoln University Library, February, 1964. 15 pp.

INDEX TO DIRECTORY ENTRIES

INDEX TO DIRECTORY ENTRIES

AAA see Agricultural Adjustment Administration

AACHS see Afro-American Cultural and Historical Society

AAI see AFRAM Associates, Inc.

AAUP see American Association of University Professors

AAUP Bulletin. DC3

ABCD see Action for Boston Community Development

ACHR Newsletter. AR6

ACLU see American Civil Liberties Union

ACNS see American Council for Nationalities Service

ACT see Associated Community Teams

ADA World. DC14

ADL see Anti-Defamation League of B'nai B'rith

ADL New Materials Bulletin. IL16

AFDC see Aid to Families with Dependent Children

AFL-CIO see American Federation of Labor and Congress of Industrial Organizations

AFRF see American Freedom of Residence Fund

AFRF News. IL10

AFSC see American Friends Service Committee

AFSC Bulletin. PA25

AFSC Reporter. CA108

AIA see American Institute of Architects

AJC see American Jewish Committee

AJC Newsletter. NY73

AMA see American Medical Association

AME see African Methodist Episcopal Church

AME Review. TN22

AMEZ see African Methodist Episcopal Zion Church

AMSAC see American Society of African Culture

AMSAC Newsletter. NY80

ANA see American Nurses Association

ANA in Action. NY79

APCO see All People's Community Organization, Inc.

A.P.C.O. News. TN1.1

API see Amalgamated Publishers, Inc.

A. Phillip Randolph Educational Fund. NY57

A. Phillip Randolph Institute. NY58

ARCH see Architects Renewal Committee in Harlem

ASM see Afro-American Student Movement

ATC see Action Training Coalition

A.T. Jeanes Foundation. NJ31.3

AVC see American Veterans Committee, Inc.

AVC Bulletin. DC13

ABBEVILLE, S.C. NC15.36, 164

ABBEVILLE District, S.C. SC12.43, 46, 50

ABBEY, Richard (1805-?). MS17.1

ABELL, G.W. KY8.1

ABELL, William (Dr.). NY46.3

ABELL family. NY46.3

ABERDEEN, Miss. MS17.33; MS28.12

ABERDEEN County, Miss. MS17.24

ABERNATHY, Ralph D. (Rev.). GA33.13, 15, 19; NY146.1

ABERNETHY family. VA8.122

ABINGDON, Va. NC15.42

ABINGTON, Pa., monthly meeting of the Society of Friends. PA16.13

ABOLITION Convention (1794). MD14.1

ABOLITIONIST and anti-slavery activities

See also Anti-slavery societies; Freedmen; Slaves and slavery-Fugitive slaves; Underground railroad

Abolition Society of Delaware. DE6.1

Abolition Society (Providence, R.I. 1789-1830). RI3.1

Adams, President John, comments of. IL28.182

American Antislavery Society. DC176.7

American Anti-Slavery Society. MI11.1, 8; NH1.5

American Convention of Abolition Societies. PA43.26

American Reform Tract and Book Society. IL29.1

Anti-Slave Treaties of U.S.A. DC172.7

Anti-Slavery Bugle (Salem, Ohio). OH36a.21, 24; OH76.1

anti-slavery coins. NY78

Anti-Slavery Reunion, 1874 (Chicago). IL28.70

Anti-Slavery Society (Providence, R.I.). RI10.1

Ashtabula County (Ohio) Anti-Slavery Society. OH36a.1

Auburn, N.Y. NY46.68

British and Foreign Anti-Slavery and Aborigines Protection Society. DC176.21

British and Foreign Anti-Slavery Society. NY46.12

British correspondence. VA8.1

broadsides. NY46.42; VA8.16

Canton (Ohio) Ladies Anti-Slavery Society. OH36a.5

correspondence. IL28.26, 28, 29; KY1.1; MA39.17, 20, 34, 42, 55, 58, 65, 76, 87, 104; MA46.4, 21, 24; MA47.2; MA56.6, 8; MA72.5; MA76.2; MI9.4, 33, 34; MI19.12; TN43.8

correspondence and records (microfilmed). OK2.6

Emancipator. PA43.18

England. PA43.17

Exeter Hall, meetings in. NY46.32

first editions collection. IL72.3

Friends of Freedom. DC176.58

general collections. DC48.35; GA32.1, 14; IL90.17; IN26.1; IN33.2; MD14.1; MD24.1; MA8.1, 5; MA14.1; MA32.1; MA39.50, 82; MA40.3; MA56.4; MA58.1; MA63.1; MA74.1; MI81.1; NJ8.2; NY46.1; NY210.63; NC42.2; OH72.1, 2; PA16.13; RI6.1; TN29.3, 24

Germantown (Pa.) Friends Meeting. PA39.1; TN43.71

Harmonia (utopian community). PA94.7

Harpers Ferry Investigating Committee. KS10.4

Illinois. IL28.26

Ithaca, N.Y. NY46.67

Janesville, Wis. area. WI2.3

Lancaster County, Pa. PA18.1

Lincoln, Abraham, relations with. IL28.110

Louisiana. LA17.4

Maine. MN22.56

Massachusetts. MA76.6

Massachusetts Anti-Slavery Society. NY206.7

ALBANY (Ga.) Movement, 1962. DC28.257, 262, 344; GA33.8, 11, 19; TN29.22

ALBANY (Ga.) Urban League. GA2.1

ALBANY Institute of History and Art. NY2

ALBANY, N.Y. NY46.4; NY276.2; NC15.87

ALBANY, N.Y., Interracial Council. NY3; NY46.26

ALBEMARLE County, Va. NC4.125; NC15.55, 101; VA8.3, 22, 43, 76, 116, 177, 191; VA33.8; VA35.6

ALBERT, Emily. MD19.5

ALBERT M. Greenfield Center for Human Relations. PA75.1

ALBION, Ill. IL28.77

ALCOHOLIC beverages. SC12.45

ALCORN, Amelia Walton (Glover). NC4.2

ALCORN, James Lusk. MS17.2; NC4.2

ALCORN Agricultural and Mechanical College. MS17.20; MS23; NY210.57

ALCORN family. MS17.2

ALCOTT, Abigail May. NY272.2

ALCOTT, Louisa May. MA46.21

ALDEN, George J. DC172.97

ALDERMAN, Edwin Anderson. VA8.4

ALDERMAN, George. VA8.5

ALDIE Plantation, Loudon County, Va. VA8.22

ALDIS, Arthur Taylor. IL90.1

ALDIS, Graham. IL90.1

ALDIS and Company. IL90.1

ALDIS family. IL90.1

ALDRICH, Eugene Perry. TN38.1

ALDRICH, J. Frank. IL28.70

ALDRICH, James Franklin. IL28.3

ALDRICH, Nelson W. DC176.143

ALDRICH, Thomas Bailey. CA179.10, 13

ALDRIDGE, Amanda Ira. NY210.2

ALDRIDGE, Ira Frederick. IL28.4; MA39.105; NY210.2, 60

ALEXANDER, Adam Leopold. NC15.4

ALEXANDER, Clifford L., Jr. DC28.3

ALEXANDER, E.R. TN29.27

ALEXANDER, Edward Porter. NC15.4

ALEXANDER, Ernest A. TN29.2

ALEXANDER, Felton S. DC28.4

ALEXANDER, Fred. DC28.5

ALEXANDER, Gustavus Brown. VA8.6

ALEXANDER, Kelly. DC28.6

ALEXANDER, Sadie T.M. DC28.7

ALEXANDER, Sidney. DC28.8

ALEXANDER, T.B. OH44.5

ALEXANDER, Titus. CA63.1

ALEXANDER, Will. GA19.9

ALEXANDER, Will W. TN29.18, 21

ALEXANDER Collection. CA179.1

ALEXANDER Gumby Collection on the American Negro. NY100.1

ALEXANDRIA County, Va. VA33.8

ALEXANDRIA, Va. OH12.2; VA8.11

ALEXANDRIA, Virginia, Common Council. VA8.7

ALFRED E. Aaronson Human Relations Collection. OK18

ALFRED P. Sloan Foundation. NY62

ALGER, Russell A. CA188.7

ALGREN, Nelson. NY278.4

ALINSKY, Saul. DC28.9

ALL People's Community Organization, Inc. (APCO). TN1, TN1.1

ALLAN, L. VA8.80

ALLEE family. DE1.3

ALLEGHENY College. PA22

ALLEGHANY County, Va. NC15.123; VA33.8

ALLEN, Alexander A. NC4.3

ALLEN, Charles B. MS17.19

ALLEN, Cleveland G. NY210.3

ALLEN, Ernie. DC28.10

ALLEN, Frederick H. NC15.12

ALLEN, George Washington. NC4.3

ALLEN, Henry W. MS17.10

ALLEN, Hervey. SC2.5, 12

ALLEN, Ivan. DC28.11

ALLEN, John. PA16.6

ALLEN, Joseph. MA57.1

ALLEN, Joseph (Mrs.). MA57.1

ALLEN, Michele Paul (Mrs.). DC28.12

ALLEN, Richard. PA43.26

ALLEN, Robert. DC28.13

ALLEN, Robert Henderson. VA32.2

ALLEN, Samuel Clesson. DC176.86

ALLEN, William Francis. WI6.1

ALLEN, William V. NB3.6

ALLEN family. VA32.11

ALLEN Murder Case (1912). VA35.8

ALLEN University, Columbia, S.C. DC1.1; SC3, SC3.2

ALLENDALE Plantation, La. MS17.10

"ALLEN'S National News Bureau." NY210.3

ALLIANCE for First Amendment Freedoms. IL112, IL112.1

ALLIANCE of Norman. NB3.6

ALLINSON, Samuel (1739-91). PA16.1, 4, 12

ALLINSON, Samuel (1808-83). PA16.1

ALLINSON, William James. PA16.1

ALLINSON family. PA16.1

ALLSTON, Benjamin. SC2.2

ALLSTON, Charles Petigru. SC2.2

ALLSTON, John. VA8.118

ALLSTON, Richard L. SC2.1

ALLSTON, Robert Francis Withers. SC2.1, 2

ALLSTON family. SC2.1, 2

ALMA Lutz Collection on Church and Slavery. MA30.1

ALPHA Kappa Alpha Sorority. DC28.336; IL7, IL7.1; NC43.10

ALPHA Kappa Mu National Honor Society. AL35.7

ALPHA Phi Alpha. IL8

ALPHIN, William J. TN27.4

ALSTON, Charles. CA63.2

ALSTON, Charles Henry. NY149.1

ALSTON, Harry. DC176.106

ALSTON, John. PA98.2

ALTADENA Human Relations Center. CA1a

ALTERNATIVE Press Index. MN16

ALTON, Ill. IL28.176

ALTOONA, Pa. NC15.93

ALVAREZ, —. NY210.4

ALVES, James. NC4.93

ALVESTON Plantation, Occoneechie Neck, N.C. NC4.10

ALVORD, Wm. CA12.1

AMADOR, Monico. DC28.14

AMALGAMATED Publishers, Inc. (API). NY63

AMATRUDA, Catherine. DC176.61

AMBLER, Elizabeth Barbour. VA8.8

AMBLER, John. DC176.6

AMBLER, John Jaquelin. VA8.9

AMBLER family. VA8.9

AMELIA County, Va. VA33.8

AMENIA Conference. DC48.50

AMERICA First Committee. CA187.1

AMERICAN. TN43.88

AMERICAN Academy of Arts and Letters. NY64, NY64.2, 4

AMERICAN Agent for Liberated Africans. DC172.61

AMERICAN Alliance for Labor and Democracy. NY100.20

AMERICAN and Foreign Anti-Slavery Society. MA39.88

AMERICAN Anthropological Association. PA29.3

AMERICAN Antiquarian Society. MA76, MA76.2

AMERICAN Anti-Slavery Society. DC176.7; MD14.1; MA32.1; MI11.1, 8; NH1.5; NY46.49; OH36a.21; OH72.3

AMERICAN Art Review. NY278.11

AMERICAN Association of Group Workers. MN22.14

AMERICAN Association of Junior Colleges. DC2

AMERICAN Association of Social Workers. MN22.14

AMERICAN Association of University Professors (AAUP). DC3, DC3.1

AMERICAN Baptist Convention. PA102, PA102.1; PA103; SC15.1

AMERICAN Baptist Historical Society. NY267

AMERICAN Baptist Home Mission Societies, Valley Forge, Pa. PA104; SC5.4

AMERICAN Baptist Theological Seminary. TN38.1, 4, 7, 9

AMERICAN Bible Society. NJ31.5

BLAIRSTOWN Academy, New Jersey. WI6.29

BLAKE, Lillie Devereux. NY46.37

BLAKESLEE, Joel. OH36a.2

BLAKESLEE, S.U. CA12.1

BLAKEY, Angus R. NC15.18

BLANCHARD, Jonathan. IL124.1; MA58.1

BLANCHARD, Rufus. IL28.20

BLAND-Randolph. VA33.3

BLATHWAYT, William. VA36.1

BLATNIK, John A. MN22.52

BLEASE, Cole. NY210.10, 42

BLEDSOE, Thomas A. NC15.7

BLEWITT, Charles H. MS28.16

"BLIND Beggars." NY149.8

BLISS, Calvin. AR7.1

BLISS, Charles M. NY46.74

BLISS, Robert L. WI6.7

BLOODY Williamson. IL28.7

BLOOMFIELD Congress of Racial Equality. CT1

BLOOMINGDALE Neighborhood Conservation Association. NY86

BLOUNT, James. NC36.18

BLOUNT, William. NC15.42

BLOW, George. VA35.2

BLOW, George (Col.). VA35.2

BLOW, George, Jr. VA35.2

BLOW, Lucy P. VA35.2

BLOW, Michael. VA35.2

BLOW, Richard. VA35.2

BLOW, Robert. VA35.2

BLOW, Samuel. VA35.2

BLOW, William N. VA35.2

BLOW, William Nivison. VA35.2

BLOW family. VA35.2

BLUE, M.J. NB3.5

BLUE and White Bus Company. CA48

BLUE Hills Civic Association. CT5

BLUE Hills News. CT5

BLUE Ridge, N.C. NC15.55

BLUEFIELD State College. WV1, WV1.2

BLUEPRINT for Action. WI24

BLUEPRINT for Negro Literature. IL30.5

BLUEPRINTS. NC19.1

BLUFFTON, S.C. NC15.87

BLUMER, Herbert. TN29.18

BLUNT, James G. (General). KS10.8; IL28.145

BLYDEN, Edward. NY210.42

BLYDEN, Edward Wilmon. DC48.46

B'NAI B'rith. NY52.1; NY210.47

See also Anti-Defamation League of B'nai B'rith

B'NAI B'rith Women. DC39

BOARD of Education. PA32

BOARD of Education for Negroes. TN33.2

BOARD of Education of the City of New York. NY16, NY16.1

BOARD of Higher Education. IN20; MO39.1

BOARD of Mediation and Conciliation. DC172.9

BOARD of Negro Education and Evangelization. TN27.8, 11

BOAS, Franz. PA29.1

BOCHFORD, Amos. IL28.174

BODWELL'S Indian Neck. PA43.9

BOEN, William. TN29.14

BOGERT, Jacob C. NY278.3

BOGERT, John A. NY278.3

BOGERT, Willie. NY278.3

BOGHOSSIAN, Alexander. CA63.2

BOGUE,Chitto Community. AL12.1

BOK, Edward W. MN22.31

BOLDRICK, Samuel J. KY8.30

BOLIN, Jane (Justice). NY210.50

BOLIVAR County, Miss. MS17.4

BOLLING, William. NC15.19

BOLTON, William C. DC172.25

BONAPARTE family. CA188.5

BONARVA Plantation. NC4.113

BOND, H. Julian. DC28.54; GA33.1

BOND, Horace M. PA21.4

BOND, Horace Mann (Dr.). GA33.1; TN29.21

BOND, Horace Mann (Mrs.). GA33.1

BOND, Hugh Lennox. MD19.3

BOND, John. MD19.2

BOND, Thomas. MD19.2

BOND, Thomas Emerson. MD19.2

BOND family. MD19.2, 3; PA4.1

BONGA, George. MN22.4

BONHAM, M.L. NC15.183

BONHAM, Milledge L. DC176.119; NC15.77

BONHAM, Milledge Luke. DC176.119; SC12.2

BONHAM, Milledge Luke (Governor). IL28.16

"BONJA Song." IL28.131

BONNEY family. NC15.146

BONTEMPS, Arna Wendell. CT24.23; GA19.10; NY210.66, 67; NY278.4; TN29.6

BOOK clubs. NY195

BOOK of Common Prayer. VA8.116

BOOK of Resemblances. MO53.1

BOOK publishers

Alabama. AL22.1

Birmingham Publishing Company. AL6

BOOKER, Charles A. DC48.19

BOOKER T. Washington National Monument. VA13

BOOKS by Negro Authors. NY250

BOOKS for Brotherhood. NY165

BOOKSTORES. CA34; NY183; NY250

BOONE, C.H. TN43.12

BOONE, Richard (Rev.). DC28.55

BOONE family. NC15.84

BOOTH, Edwin. MD19.7

BOOTH, John Wilkes. MD19.7

BOOTH, Mary. DC28.56

BOOTH, Sherman Miller. WI6.12

BORAH, William E. MO4.15; NC15.129

BORDEN, Gail. LA16.3; TX8.4, 6; TX27.3

BORDEN, James Woodberry. VA8.25

BORDEN, John. TX8.2

BORDER State Convention. PA43.26

BORGMAN, Albert Stephens. MA39.10

BOSSAGE, Edward. DC176.169

BOSTICK, Abe. TN43.13

BOSTICK, Sarah Lue. TN27.1

BOSTICK family. TN43.13

BOSTON Athenaeum. MA13

BOSTON Evening Transcript. TN29.5

BOSTON Guardian. GA19.23

BOSTON Herald. MS4.2

"BOSTON Hymn." MA39.55

BOSTON, Mass. NY46.74

Public Hospital. MA39.75

Public Library. MA14

University. DC28.133, 488; MA15; MA16, MA16.5

BOSTON School Committee. MA46.21

BOSTON Transcript. NY46.77

BOSTWICK families. TN43.14

BOSWORTH, Francis. NY210.50

BOTELER, Alexander Robinson. NC15.20

BOTELER family. NC15.6

BOTETOURT County, Va. NC15.107; VA8.100

BOTHWELL family. NC15.186

BOTSFORD, Amos. IL28.109, 161

BOTTS family. KY8.64

BOURLAND, Albert Pike. NC4.17, 36

BOURNE, George. MA8.5

BOUTWELL, George S. DC176.169; IL90.17; VA8.2

BOWDITCH, Henry. DC48.8

BOWDLE family. PA4.2

BOWDOIN College. ME2

BOWEN, George Washington. OH36a.3

BOWEN, J.W.E. GA32.5; NY210.42

BOWEN, Reuben Dean. NC15.21

BOWER, William Horton. NC15.22

BOWERS, Calvin. TN27.4

BOWIE, Harry. DC28.57

BOWIE State College. MD26

BOWLER, Elizabeth (Caleff). MN22.8

BOWLER, James Madison. MN22.8

BOWLER, Joseph. MN22.8

BOWLES, Chester. WI6.4

BOWLY, Jacob A. VA11.1

BOWMAN, Mary E. NY46.37

BOWRING, John. LA16.3

"BOXER." NY149.2

BROTHERHOOD of Sleeping Car Porters. DC28.368; IL28.22; NY89, NY89.1; NY210.66

BROTHERLY and Paternal Order of Elks. DC28.272

BROTHERS and Sisters of Purity. MO2.8

BROTHERTON, James. NC15.29

BROTHERTON, William N. NC15.29

BROUGH, Charles Hillman. AR1.1; AR7.2

BROUGHTON family. SC2.6

BROWN, Abiel. GA19.6

BROWN, Albert G. MS17.17

BROWN, Alexander. VA35.3

BROWN, Ann. NY152.2; TN29.12

BROWN, B. Gatz. MO4.6

BROWN, Benjamin D. DG28.67

BROWN, Benjamin G. MO2.32

BROWN, Bezabeel. VA35.4

BROWN, Bezabeel J. VA35.4

BROWN, Campbell. TN43.17

BROWN, Charles. VA35.4

BROWN, Charlotte (Hawkins). MA46.5

BROWN, Cora. MI27.4

BROWN, Edward. DC28.68

BROWN, Emma V. NY46.37

BROWN, Ephraim. OH36a.4

BROWN, Ephraim A. OH36a.4

BROWN, Ethan Allen. DC176.148

BROWN, Ewart. DC28.69

BROWN, Frederick. OH44.5

BROWN, George Campbell (Major). TN10.1

BROWN, George M. NC15.30

BROWN, Grafton T. CA100.1

BROWN, Hamilton. NC4.21

BROWN, Homer M. MO4.4

BROWN, Ina Corrine. TN29.21

BROWN, J.E. MS17.17

BROWN, James. MO4.4

BROWN, James (of New York City). MS17.19

BROWN, James (of Oxford). MS17.17

BROWN, James F. NY206.2

BROWN, Jason. GA19.6; OH44.5

BROWN, Jere A. OH44.25

BROWN, Joe C. OH68.4

BROWN, John. CA179.26; DC176.22; GA19.6, 23; GA32.14; IL28.195, 196; IL87.2; IL90.17; KS6.6; KS10.4, 7; MA14.1; MA23.3; MA39.12, 38, 75; MA47.1; NY46.37; NY100.22; NY120.2; TN43.72; VA32.5; WI6.9, 10; WV6.13

death of. MN22.34; NY46.44

Harper's Ferry raid. KY6.8; NY284.1; NC15.52; VA32.8; VA33.4; WV6.4, 9

papers of. GA19.6; IL28.23; KS10.1; OH44.4; OH66.1; PA22.1; PA43.14, 26

trial of. IL28.136; WV6.11, 15

BROWN, John (Mrs.). MA47.1

BROWN, John (Senator). KY8.14

BROWN, John, Jr. MA47.1; OH44.4, 5

BROWN, John, Sr. OH44.5

BROWN, John Mason. NJ12.3

BROWN, John Thompson. VA35.5

BROWN, John W. NC4.22

BROWN, Joseph. TN43.18

BROWN, Joseph E. DC176.142; GA4.3; NC15.63, 77, 183

BROWN, Lawrence. TN29.12

BROWN, Lucius P. TN10.1

BROWN, M. SC12.26

BROWN, Mary Anne (Day). GA19.6; OH44.5

BROWN, Moses. PA16.3, 4, 12, 13, 18; RI10.1

BROWN, Oliver. GA19.6

BROWN, Orlando. KY8.14

BROWN, Orlando, Jr. KY8.14

BROWN, Otis, Jr. DC28.70

BROWN, Owen. OH44.5; PA43.26

BROWN, Raymond Edward. TN27.4

BROWN, Robert. KY8.14

BROWN, Salmon. OH44.5

BROWN, Samuel. PA60.1

BROWN, Sarah. MA47.1

BROWN, Sterling A. CT24.23; NY210.44; TN29.6, 21, 32

BROWN, Theodore. DC28.71

BROWN, Watson. OH44.5

BROWN, William. IL28.183

BROWN, William Garrott. NC15.31

BROWN, William H. IL28.118

BROWN, William L. TN20.1

BROWN, William S. VA8.34

BROWN, William Welles. NY210.42

BROWN, William Wells. NY210.41; PA43.26; TN29.2

BROWN, Willie L. DC28.72

BROWN and Clayton. NC15.147

BROWN family. KY8.14; MA47.1; NC4.21; VA8.32, 33; VA35.5

BROWN Farm, North Elba, N.Y. NY46.27

BROWN-Hunter Collection. VA8.34

BROWN, Leftwich and Company. NC15.147

BROWN University. DC176.73; RI2, RI2.1

BROWN vs. Board of Education (1954). NY210.64

BROWNE, Hugh M. TN29.5

BROWNE, Jackson A. NC43.4

BROWNE, John. DC28.73

BROWNELL vs. Civil Rights Congress. NY210.13

BROWNING, A.F. (Lt. Col.). IL28.16

BROWNING, O.H. NC15.42

BROWNING, Samuel R. NC15.23

BROWNING, Silas W. DC176.23

BROWNLEE, Fred L. TN29.18

BROWNLEE, Frederick Leslie (Rev.). LA16.5, 7, 16

BROWNLEE, Ruth. LA16.16

BROWNLOW, William G. NC15.42

BROWNRIG family. NC4.8

BROWNSVILLE, Tex. MI11.6; OH8.5; OH44.8

BROWNSVILLE (Tex.) riot (August, 1906). DC172.48

BRUCE, Blanche Kelso (Senator). DC48.6; NY210.10

BRUCE, Charles. DC176.24

BRUCE, Elvira. DC176.24

BRUCE, James. DC176.24

BRUCE, John E. DC176.168

BRUCE, John Edward. NY46.77; NY210.10, 60

BRUCE, Roscoe Conkling. DC48.18; TN29.5

BRUCE, William Henry. DC48.19

BRUCE family. DC176.24; VA8.35

BRUNSWICK County, Va. VA8.183, 203

BRYAN, Edward. NC36.1

BRYAN, Elizabeth Tucker Coalter. VA32.8

BRYAN, Guy M. TX8.2

BRYAN, Henry Ravenscroft. NC15.32

BRYAN, John. NC36.1

BRYAN, John H. MO4.14

BRYAN, John Herritage. NC15.32

BRYAN, John Hill. NC36.1

BRYAN, John Randolph. VA33.3; VA35.11

BRYAN, John Stewart. VA33.3

BRYAN, Joseph. NC4.122; NC36.1

BRYAN, Joseph (1773-1812). VA33.3

BRYAN, Joseph (1845-1908). VA33.3

BRYAN, Joseph Randall. VA8.100

BRYAN, Moses Austin. TX8.4

BRYAN, St. George. VA35.11

BRYAN, W.J. NB3.2

BRYAN, William. NC36.1

BRYAN, William J. NH1.1

BRYAN, William Jennings. IL87.11; NC15.118

BRYAN family. MO2.2; MO4.14; NC4.27, 113, 122; VA33.3

BRYANT, Baxton. DC28.74

BRYANT, Dabney S. IL28.24

BRYANT, Ethel C. DC28.75

BRYANT, William Cullen. IL87.2; NY100.8; PA98.27

BRYANT, Willie. NY210.50

BUARD, Alexandre. LA11.1

BUARD, Suzette (Mrs. L.A.). LA11.1

BUCHANAN, Bessie A. NY210.5

BUCHANAN, James. DC176.94; NY46.44, 69; NC15.38, 69, 226; PA4.3; PA18.1; PA43.38

BUCHANAN, James M. MI11.1

BUCHANAN, Robert Christie. MD19.4

BUCHANAN, Thomas E. NC15.33

BUCHANAN family. NC15.33

BUCK, — (Captain). DC193.1

BUCK, Alfred E. GA4.3

BUCK, E.S. NY46.63

CARTER, Kate. VA35.7

CARTER, Landon. VA8.47, 48; VA35.7

CARTER, Landon, Jr. VA8.48; VA35.7

CARTER, Randolph W. WA15.32

CARTER, Randolph Warren. WA15.9

CARTER, Robert. IL28.93, 128, 151, 175

CARTER, Robert (1663-1732). VA8.48

CARTER, Robert (1728-1804). IL28.32; NC15.45

CARTER, Robert, II. VA35.7

CARTER, Robert "Councillor." VA35.7

CARTER, Robert "King." VA8.47; VA35.7

CARTER, Robert L. DC28.90

CARTER, Robert Wormeley (1734-97). VA35.7

CARTER, Robert Wormeley (1797-1861). VA8.48

CARTER, William. CA63.2

CARTER, William R. VA11.1

CARTER, Yvonne. CA100.1

CARTER family. TN43.16; VA8.47, 157; VA35.7

CARTER "Nomini" (plantation). VA35.7

CARTER G. Woodson Reference Collection. NY49.1

CARTERET, Peter. NC36.18

CARTERSVILLE, Ga. VA8.2

CARTERSVILLE, Ga. Court of Inquiry, 1871. GA30.9

CARTERSVILLE, Va. NC15.30

CARTHAGE, Ill. NY46.72

CARTOONS

Anti-Beauregard. NY46.16

Chicago Tribune, editorial. MS4.2

CARTWRIGHT, Marguerite Dorsey. LA16.8

CARTWRIGHT, Matthew. TX8.5

CARUTHERS, Eli Washington. NC15.46

CARVER, George Washington. AL34.4; AL35.4; DC172.12, 131; DC176.161, 168; IA1.1; IA9.1; MA56.5; MS17.7; MO1.1; NY100.1; NY210.50, 67; TN29.17; VA12.3

CASE, — (Union officer). DC172.70

CASE, Ebenezer. IL28.98

CASEY, James V. NB3.5

CASH, Ellerbe Boggan Crawford. SC12.5

CASH'S Depot, Cheraw, S.C. (plantation). SC12.5

CASKIN, John L. (Dr.). DC28.91

CASLER, G.V. NB3.5

CASS, Lewis (General). IL28.66; NC15.183; VA8.38

CASSELL, Charles. DC28.92

CASSITY, H.T. MS17.4

"CASTILIAN." VA32.21

CASTLE, Henry A. MN22.49

"CASTLE Hill," Albemarle County (farm). VA8.177

CASTNER, Burton. DC176.61

CASTNER, Wilson Jacob. TN43.23

CASWELL, Richard. NC36.11

CASWELL County, N.C. NC4.53

CATALOG of Urban Corps Programs. NY251

CATAWBA Islands. SC11.5

CATHCART Collection. DC48.7

CATHER, Willa. NB3.2

CATHOLIC

See also Churches

Adult Education Center. IL28.30

Archdiocese of St. Louis, Commission on Human Rights. MO32

Board for Mission Work Among the Colored People. NY92, NY92.1

Charities, Diocese of Brooklyn, Social Action Department. NY20, NY20.1

Church, Negro in. CT24.23; MD16.1

Council on Working Life. IL28.30

Dioceses of Wilmington, Office for Inner-City Development. DE4

education. MD22.1

Foreign Mission Society of America (Maryknoll). NY52

Interracial Council. OH50

Interracial Council of Chicago. IL21; IL28.30, 33, 196

Interracial Council of New York. NY92a

Interracial Council, San Jose, Calif. DC28.315

University of America. DC20

CATHOLIC Scholarship for Negroes, Inc. MA66

CATHOLICISM. AL37.4; GA32.10; MN22.13; NB3.5

CATLEDGE, J. Van. NC43.4

CATLETT, Elizabeth. GA19.18; IL61.1

CATLETTE, John, Jr. IL28.175

CATT, Carrie Chapman. DC176.151; MA46.1; MA56.6

CATTON, Douglas M. DC28.110

CAUGHLIN, John. WA15.10

CAUSE II, Philadelphia. PA69.2

CAUSES and Prevention of Violence, President's Commission on. DC172.150

CAVE, Richard. VA8.49

CAVETT, E.D. MS28.1

CAYTON, Horace R. IL28.137

CAYTON, Horace R. (Dr.). DC28.93

CAYTON, Horace Roscoe. TN29.21

CAZENOVIA, N.Y. NY46.41

CEMETERY records. MS17.15

CENSUS, 1850. GA64.6; TN43.76

CENSUS, 1860 (schedules I, II, IV). TN43.76

CENSUS, 1880. GA64.6

See also Population

CENSUS Facts Collected for the Pennsylvania Society for Promoting the Abolition of Slavery (1838). PA43.26

CENTENARY College, La. LA37

CENTER for Advanced Study in the Behavioral Sciences, Inc. CA186, CA186.1

CENTER for African and African-American Studies. OH90.2

CENTER for Applied Linguistics. DC21

CENTER for Community Studies, Nashville, Tenn. TN23, TN23.1

CENTER for Emergency Support. DC22

CENTER for Extending American History. CA53

CENTER for Law and Behavioral Science Program. WI7.1

CENTER for Real Estate and Urban Economics. CA14

CENTER for Research Libraries. IL22

CENTER for Research on Social Organization. MI4.1

CENTER for the Study of Democratic Institutions. CA183; GA49.1; TN31.1

CENTER for the Study of Metropolitan Problems in Education. MO24, MO24.1

CENTER for the Study of Racial and Social Issues. CA54

CENTER for Urban Education. NY93; IL17

CENTER for Urban Encounter. MN19, MN19.1

CENTER Forum. NY93

CENTER Magazine. CA183

CENTRAL Brooklyn Neighborhood College. NY21

CENTRAL Christian Advocate. GA32.3

CENTRAL High School, Ark. DC28.174

CENTRAL Michigan University. MI81

CENTRAL Midwestern Regional Educational Laboratory, Inc. MO27

CENTRAL Seattle Community Council. WA8, WA8.1; WA15.11

CENTRAL State University (Ohio). OH86, OH86.2

CENTRAL Tennessee College. TN43.28

CENTURY Magazine. TN29.5

CENTURY with the Negroes of Detroit: 1830-1930. MI79.3

CERF, Bennett. NY46.11; NY270.5

CERTIFICATES of Freedom. MD2.3

CHACE, Lydia. MA14.1

CHADICKS, W.D. AL37.9

CHAFFIN, Washington Sanford. NC15.47

CHALFANT, James. GA32.9

CHALLENGER. NY29.1

CHALMERS, Allan Knight. MA16.5

CHAMBER of Commerce of the United States of America, Community and Regional Development Group. DC23; DC24

CHAMBERLAIN, D.H. OH44.30

CHAMBERLAIN, James F. NY46.43

CHAMBERLAYNE, Ann (Atkinson) Burmeister. VA32.11

CHAMBERLIN, T.W. MO40.4

CHAMBERS, Margaret. TX8.6

CHAMBERS, Thomas Jefferson. TX8.6

CHAMBERS, Thomas W. TX8.6

CHAMBERS, W.P. TX8.6

CHAMP family. VA8.157

CHAMPION, George. MA39.15

CHAMPION, Newton E. DC28.94

FREELAWN. FL26.1

FREEMAN, Carney. TN43.48

FREEMAN, John Shaw (Dr.). TN43.48

FREEMAN, Lynn B. TN43.48

FREEMAN, Mary Barry Martin. TN43.48

FREEMAN, Orville. DC28.156

FREEMASONRY. MS17.23; NY210.63; NC15.199

FRELINGHUYSEN, F.T. IL90.17

FRELINGHUYSEN, Frederick Theodore. PA16.1

FREMONT, John C. MO40.9

FREMONT, John Charles. IL28.26; NY46.31, 44

FREMONT Human Relations Commission. CA29

FRENCH-American subculture. TX4

FRENCH forts. TX8.12

FRENCH National Assembly, Paris, France. TN29.2

FRENCH West Indies. MD28.3

FRENCHY'S String Band. TN29.17

FRIEDMAN, Saul. OH77.1

FRIENDS and Slavery. PA10.13

FRIENDS Committee on National Legislation. DC41

FRIENDS During the Civil War. PA16.21

FRIENDS Freedoms Association. PA63.1

FRIENDS in Ireland. PA16.5

FRIENDS of Freedom. DC176.58

FRIENDS of SNCC (University of Wisconsin). WI6.16

FRIENDS Review. PA16.15

FRIENDS Society, Germantown, Pa. TN43.71

FRIENDS, Society of. OH44.13; VA30.1

See also Quakers; Society of Friends

American Friends Service Committee. PA16.8

Indiana Yearly Meeting. PA98.8

Ohio Yearly Meeting. PA98.9

Philadelphia Yearly Meeting. PA98.10

Wilmington Yearly Meeting. OH89.1

FRIENDS Yearly Meeting Library. PA37, PA37.1

FRIENDSHIP Baptist Church. CA189

FRIENDSHIP House, Chicago. IL28.30, 33, 80, 196; IL44, IL44.1

FRIENDSHIP House, N.Y.C. IL28.80

FRIENDSHIP House of Harlem. NY210.25

FRIENDSHIP House, Portland, Ore. IL28.80

FRIENDSHIP House, Washington, D.C. IL28.80

FRIENDSHIP Junior College. SC20

FRIERSON, David Ethan. SC12.13

FRIPP, John Edward. NC4.47

FRISSELL, H.B. (Dr.). VA12.3

FRISSELL, Hollis B. NC4.111

"FROM Exile and Being" (essay). TN29.32

FROM the State Capitals. NJ1

FRONTIER life, Parkersburg-Marietta, W.Va. WV6.10

FRONTIERS International, Inc. PA38, PA38.1

FRONTIERSMAN. PA38

FROST, Edward. DC176.59

FROST, Robert. NY46.11; NY278.5

FROST, Wm. G. KY1.5

FROTHINGHAM, Octavius Brooks. DC176.127; IL28.81

FROUDE, James A. MN22.36

FRY, Elizabeth. PA43.17; PA98.14, 23

FUGITIVE Slave Law. DC172.50; GA32.10; NY46.7, 46, 74

FUGITIVE Slaves (book). NC15.114

"FUGITIVE Song." IL29.1

"FUGITIVE'S Song." IL28.164

FULHAM Palace Archives. DC176.60

FULLER, Edwin Wiley. NC15.98

FULLER, Erasmus Q. GA32.3

FULLER, Hoyt. MI29.9

FULLER, Jones. NC15.98

FULLER, Margaret. MA39.32

FULLER, Stephen. NC15.99

FULLER family. NC15.98

FULLOCK, Thomas F. VA8.2

FULMORE, Zachary Taylor. TX8.12

FULTON, D.B. NY210.60

FUND for the Advancement of Education. TN37.4

"FUNERAL Sermon" (painting). NY18.1

FUNERALS. TN43.32

FUNKHOUSER family. NC15.100

FUNN, Dorothy Kelso. NY210.47

FUR Seal and the Negro. NY284.3

FURMAN, Richard. MA6.1; TN40.1

FURMAN University. SC15

FURNAS, R.W. NB3.2

FUTURE. OK20

FUTURE of the American Negro. IL.28.187

GAR see Grand Army of the Republic

G.A.T.E. (Get Ahead Through Education) Library. PA1

GIA see Group Investigation Associates

GIA Newsletter. MA67

GT&EA Reporter. GA31

GTEA see Georgia Teachers and Education Association

GTEA Herald. GA31

GABON (mission). PA21.4

GADSDEN, Phillip. NC15.232

GAFFNEY, S.C. SC12.48

GAFFORD, Alice. CA63.2

GAGE, Fern. WA15.19

GAILLARD, E.W. NY210.60

GAILLARD estate. SC2.18

GAILLARD family. SC2.26

GAINES, Edmund P. DC176.117; NC15.38

GAINES, H.T. IL28.73

GAINES, Irene McCoy. IL28.83

GAINES, Jennie Bell. MO4.11

GAINES family. MO4.11

GALAMISON, Milton A. WI6.22

GALBRAITH, J.R. TN29.24

GALE, George W. NY46.58

GALE, Zona. WI6.23

GALE Memorial Library. MA57

GALES, Joseph. NC15.42

GALLAGHER, Buell. AL30.5

GALLAGHER, James. IL28.84

GALLATIN, Albert. MN22.31

GALLATIN, Tenn. NB3.3

GALLAWAY, Wiley. IL28.84

GALLWEY, Sydney Hollingsworth. NY46.27

GALT, James. VA8.85

GALVESTON, Port of, Tex. IL28.178

GALVESTON, Tex. NC25.4; TX8.2; TX27.4, 6, 10, 11, 12, 13, 15, 10, 19, 20, 23

GAMBLE, Archibald. PA43.26

GAMBLE, Hamilton. MO2.5

GAMBLE, Hamilton R. MO40.9

GAMBLE family. MO2.2

GAME Songs From Georgia. RI2.3

GAMMON Theological Seminary. GA32.3, 7; TN33.2

GANDHI, M. IL90.2; WI1.1

GANDY, John Manual. VA20.3

GANNETT, Ezra Stiles. NY272.2

GANNETT, William Channing. NY272.2

GANO, John Allen. MO4.12

GANS, Curtis. DC28.157

GANT, Danny. DC28.158

GANTT, Thomas T. TN43.17

GARDINER, John D. NC15.41

GARDNER, Charles. PA43.26

GARDNER, Frederick D. MO4.15

GARDNER, James. GA30.20

GARDNER-Webb College. NC1

GARFIELD, James A. DC176.159; LA16.1; NH1.1; NC15.226; OH36a.19; VA8.2

GARFIELD, James H. NB3.2

GARFORD, Arthur Lovett. OH44.14

GARLAND, August H. DC176.142

GARLAND, Thomas. NC15.101

GARLAND family. NC15.149

GARLOCK, William Bryan. IL28.85

GARMAN, Betty. DC28.159

GARNER, James Wilford. IL121.3

GARNER, John. NC15.71

GARNETT, Henry Highland. DC48.24, 45; NY210.16, 42; PA43.26

GARNETT, James Mercer. VA8.86, 120

GARNETT, Muscoe R.E. VA8.86a

GARNETT, Muscoe Russell Hunter.
    VA8.86, 120

GARNETT family. VA8.86, 120

GARRETT, George A. WI6.24

GARRETT, John B. VA8.87

GARRETT, Philip Cope. PA16.5

GARRETT, Thomas. DE6.6; PA16.5

GARRISON, Agnes. MA56.4

GARRISON, Eleanor. MA56.4

GARRISON, Ellen Wright. MA56.4

GARRISON, F.J. NY210.70

GARRISON, Francis J. PA98.27

GARRISON, Francis Jackson. MA46.9;
    MA56.4

GARRISON, Frank Wright. MA56.4

GARRISON, George Thompson. MA56.4

GARRISON, Lloyd. DC48.29

GARRISON, Theresa H. NY210.70

GARRISON, Wendell P. PA43.26

GARRISON, Wendell Phillips. MA39.33;
    MA56.4; OH44.26

GARRISON, William Lloyd. CT14.5;
    DC48.11, 19; DC176.166, 141, 169;
    GA32.14; IL28.189; IL90.17; LA16.3;
    MA8.5; MA14.1; MA18.5; MA39.10, 50;
    MA46.12, 20; MA56.4, 6; NH1.1;
    NY206.7; NY210.5, 26, 42, 63, 70;
    OH44.23; PA16.16; PA43.26; PA98.18,
    22, 27; VT4.1

GARRISON, William Lloyd, Jr. MA39.38;
    MA56.4

GARRISON, William Lloyd, Sr. MA39.33,
    38; MA56.4

GARRISON family. MA39.33, 64

GARVEY, Amy Jacques. NY210.5

GARVEY, Marcus. AL35.12; DC176.104;
    NY210.10, 42, 54

GARVIN, Charles H. OH36a.8

GARVIN, S. KY8.32

GARVIN, Sidney W. IL28.16

GARY, Martin Witherspoon. SC12.14

GARY American (newspaper). OH90.1

GARY Commission on Human Relations.
    IN13

GARY, Ind. NY191.1

GASTON, A.C. DC28.160

GASTON, William. IL28.86

GATE City Guardian (newspaper). MA1.2

GATES, Horatio. NC15.42

GATES, Merrill Seth. MI11.1

GATES, Seth M. OH44.16

GAUTIER, Andrew. IL28.75

GAY, Allan. NY100.8

GAY, Edward James. NC4.116

GAY, Sarah. NY100.8

GAY, Sydney Howard. NY100.8

GAY family. NY100.8

GAYARRE, Charles E.A. LA35.4

GAYLE, Sarah A. NC4.48

GAYTON, John. WA15.32

GAYTON, John T. WA15.20

GAYTON, Leonard. WA15.32

GAYTON, Virginia. WA15.32

GEBBART, Emmanual Martin. NC15.102

GEBBART, Noah L. NC15.102

GEIGER, Edwin W. SC12.15

GEIGER, Joseph H. DC176.159

GEIGER family. SC12.15

GENEALOGICAL data, Robertson County,
    Tenn. TN43.48

"GENEALOGY of the Lincoln-Dayton-
    Staples Family." MN22.51

GENERAL Accounting Office Records.
    DC172.146

GENERAL and Specialty Contractors Asso-
    ciation, Inc. CA99; CA153, CA153.1

GENERAL Board of Christian Education.
    TN11.1

GENERAL Council of the Congregational and
    Christian Churches of the United States.
    MA8.2

GENERAL Education Board. AL35.12;
    DC176.161; NY125, NY125.1; NC4.36

GENERAL Hospital (Farmville, Va.).
    DC172.104

GENERAL Hospital 13 (Richmond, Va.).
    DC172.105

GENERAL Hospital 21 (Richmond, Va.).
    DC172.105

GENERAL Hospital 24 (Richmond, Va.).
    DC172.105

GENERAL Orders from Adjutant and In-
    spector's General Office. VA24.2

GENERAL Records of the U.S. Government.
    DC172.7

GENEVA College. PA2

GENEVA Commission. SC12.40

GENIUS of Liberty (newspaper). IL28.70

GENIUS of Universal Emancipation. MD14.1;
    MI9.4

GEOFFROY, Etienne Francois. PA43.26

GEORGE III, of England. VA8.88

GEORGE, E.H. GA25.5

GEORGE, Henry. MA56.4

GEORGE Edmund Haynes Memorial Collec-
    tion. NY55.1

GEORGE Foster Peabody Collection.
    VA12.5

GEORGE Gershwin Memorial Collection of
    Music and Musical Literature. TN29.12

GEORGE Peabody College for Teachers.
    NC4.17; TN30

GEORGE Washington Carver National Monu-
    ment, Research Library. MO5

GEORGE Washington Carver Neighborhood
    Center. MO13

GEORGE Washington Carver Project.
    PA105.1

GEORGE Washington University. DC42

GEORGETOWN County, S.C. SC2.26

GEORGETOWN, D.C. PA43.3

GEORGETOWN District, S.C. SC2.29

GEORGETOWN, S.C. NC4.40

GEORGIA. GA4.4; NC4.15, 28, 69, 73, 122;
    NC15.55, 64, 179, 218; PA98.13;
    VA8.177

    census returns. GA64.6; NC15.225

    civil rights court cases. GA64.5

    Council of Human Relations. GA29

    Department of Archives and History.
        GA30

    general collections. GA25.6; NC15.103

    Governor of. DC176.142

    historical documents. CT24.24; MI11.7;
        NC4.53, 79; NC15.133; PA43.8;
        SC12.4

    Historical Society. GA66

    history. GA4.3, 5; GA15; GA17.3;
        NC15.103, 111, 157

    Methodist Episcopal church in. GA32.9

    slavery in. NY46.51; NC15.214

    State Legislature. DC28.54, 67

    University of. DC28.433; GA4; GA5;
        GA6; GA7

GEORGIA Congress of Colored Parents and
    Teachers. GA28

GEORGIA Council Newsletter. GA29

GEORGIA family. GA28

GEORGIA Lynching Campaign. NY210.47

"GEORGIA Rose" (drawing). PA60.1

GEORGIA Teachers and Education Associa-
    tion (GTEA). GA31, GA31.1

GERBER, Sidney. WA15.21

GERE family. NB3.2

GERMANTOWN Friends Meeting. PA39,
    PA39.1

GERRIT Smith Collection. NY278.6

GERVAIS, John Lewis. DC176.85

GESCHICHTE der Jubilaums-Sanger.
    TN29.11

GESELL, Arnold Lucius. DC176.61

GESELL Institute of Child Development.
    DC176.9, 61

GEST, Erasmus. OH44.15

GET Ahead Through Education (GATE) Li-
    brary. PA1

"GET Along Black Man!" (song). IL28.131

GETTYSBURG Address. DC176.89

GETTYSBURG College. PA11

GETTYSBURG, Pa. GA25.4

GEYER, Henry S. MO2.5

GHETTO redevelopment. MI50.1

GHOLSON, Thomas S. NC15.63

GHOLSON, William Yates. OH8.6

GIBBES, R.W. NC15.183

GIBBES, Robert Wilson. SC12.16

GIBBONS, Herbert. NJ31.12

GIBBONS, William. NC15.104

GIBBS, Jonathan. DC48.45

GIBBS, Jonathan C. DC48.59; NY197.1

GIBERN, — (Rev.). IL28.32

GIBSON, John. DC28.161; IL28.75

GIBSON, R.L. TN43.85

GIBSON, Tobias. NC4.49

GIBSON County, Tenn. TN43.76

GIBSON family. KY6.5; KY8.35; NC4.49

GIBSON-Humphrey family. KY6.5

GIDDINGS, Grotius, R. OH44.16

GIDDINGS, J.R. MA39.65

GIDDINGS, Joshua. WI6.19

GIDDINGS, Joshua R. OH36a.19

GIDDINGS, Joshua Reed. DC176.62; OH44.16

GIFFORD, Henry. NY46.69

GILBERT, General. NY46.31

GILBERT, Olive. MD30.1

GILCREASE Gazette. OK17

GILES, Fayette, and Kanawha Turnpike Company. WV6.9

GILES, Henry. MA55.1

GILES, William B. NC15.192

GILLESPIE, James A. LA5.6

GILLESPIE family. LA5.6

GILLETTE, James Jenkins. DC176.63

GILLETTE, William. MA46.2

GILLIAM family. VA8.80

GILLIS, John A. MN22.18

GILMAN, Caroline (Howard). SC2.11

GILMAN, Charlotte Perkins. MA46.3

GILMAN, Daniel C. NC15.120

GILMAN, E.W. CA12.1

GILMAN, Robbins. MN22.19

GILMAN, Samuel (Rev.). SC2.11

GILMER, John A. NC36.33

GILMER, Z. Lee. VA8.90

GILMORE, Thomas. DC28.162

GILSON, Norman Shepard. WI6.25

GIRARD, Stephen. PA40.1; PA43.21

GIRARD College. PA40

GIRARDEAU family. NC15.217

GIRAUD, Daniel. MD19.24

GISS, Samuel. VA8.91

GIVENS, Cornelius. DC28.163

GIVENS, Spencer H. MO4.13

GIVVON and Company. IL28.4

GLADDEN, Washington. OH44.17

GLASER, William A. NY99.4

GLASGOW, Alexander M. TX8.13

GLASGOW, Ellen. NC15.118

GLASGOW family. TX8.13

GLASS, Carter. NC15.118

GLASSBORO State College. NJ8

GLEN, Tyre. NC15.105

"GLEN Ambler" Estate, Amherst County. VA8.9

GLEN Blythe Plantation, Brenham, Tex. TX27.1

GLENN, Lillian. TN29.17

GLENN family. MN22.19

GLENWOOD Lake Association. NY56

GLIDDON, George R. DC176.140

GLOBE Baptist Church, Caldwell County, N.C. NC4.50

GLOUCESTER, James N. DC176.93

GLOUCESTER County, Va. NC15.206; VA35.5

GLOVER, Robert. CA100.1; IL61.1

GLOVER, Samuel Taylor. DC176.18

GOD Be Glorified in Africa (book). PA21.4

GODDARD family. MA46.21

GODWIN, Parke. LA16.3

GOFF, David. WV6.8

GOFF, Helen. NB3.6

GOFF, Regina. DC28.164

GOFF family. WV6.8

"GOING To Work" (gouache). NY32.1

GOLD Hill, Rowan County, N.C. NC4.84

GOLDBLATT, —. NY201.1

GOLDEN, Harry. TN43.57

GOLDEN State Mutual Life Insurance Co. CA63

GOLDMAN, Emma. IL2.2

"GOLGOTHA" (watercolor). NY145.3

GOMILLION, Charles G. DC28.166

GOMPERS, Samuel. IL2.2

GONZALES, Ambrose E. NC15.12

GOOCHLAND County, Va. NC15.19, 88, 224; VA8.92

GOOCHLAND Court House, Va. NC15.7

GOOD, Ronald. WV6.10

GOOD Earth (screenplay). SC2.12

GOOD Neighbor Commission of Texas. TX2

GOOD Neighbors at Work in N.C. NC37

"GOOD Shepherd" (painting). NJ24.1

GOODALE, Warren. MA23.4

GOODELL, William. KY1.6; MA39.34; MI11.1; OH72.1, 2

GOODENOW, Samuel. MA57.1

GOODLETT, Carleton B. DC28.165

GOODLOW, William A. DC176.159

GOODMAN, Paul. IN30.2

GOODMAN, R. Stanley. VA8.51

GOODRICH, Aaron. TN43.85

GOODSELL, Bishop. GA32.3

GOODWIN, Terenz. WA15.32

GOODWIN family. VA8.93

GOOSE Creek, Va., Baptist Church. VA8.94

GORALEIGH (works of art by). NY210.4

GORDEN, John F. WA15.12

GORDON, Charles. DC176.99

GORDON, Charles U. MS28.16

GORDON, James. MS17.9

GORDON, John. KY6.6

GORDON, John B. DC176.142; GA4.3; GA25.6

GORDON, Neal McDougal. KY6.6

GORDON, Robert. MS17.9

GORDON, Robert Winslow. OR1.1

GORDON, W.H. TN43.74

GORDON family. KY6.6

GOSPEL Glory (play). WI6.28

GOSPEL Plea (publication). TN27.7

GOTCHER, Henry. IL28.102

GOULD, Jay. DC176.40

GOULD, John Stanton. NY46.28

GOULD, Stephen Wanton. NY46.29

GOULD, William P. AL21.4

GOULD family. NY46.28

GOVERNMENT Contracts, President's Committee on. DC172.150

GOVERNMENTAL Employment Policy, President's Committee on. DC172.150

GOVERNOR'S Commission on the Los Angeles Riots. CA72.1

GOVERNOR'S Human Rights Commission. MN24.1

GOVERNOR'S Interracial Committee of Minnesota. MN10.1

GOVERNOR'S Letterbooks. SC11.2

GRABILL, Levi. CA179.11

GRADY, Henry P. NC15.118

GRAHAM, Calvin. VA8.95

GRAHAM, David. VA8.95

GRAHAM, David P. VA8.95

GRAHAM, Edwin S. TX8.14

GRAHAM, Frank P. DC28.167; NC4.26, 51

GRAHAM, Hugh. IL28.42

GRAHAM, John. NC4.52

GRAHAM, L. VA8.95

GRAHAM, Thomas. VA8.95

GRAHAM, William. VA8.95

GRAHAM, William A. NC15.32, 42; NC36.25, 33

GRAHAM, William Alexander. NC4.52; NC15.106

GRAHAM, William Alexander, Jr. NC15.106

GRAHAM family. NC4.52; VA8.95

GRAHAM'S Forge Club. VA8.95

GRAINGER County. TN43.76

GRAMBLING College of Louisiana. LA7

GRAMBS, Blanche. NY210.4

GRAND Army of the Republic (G.A.R.). IL87.8; OH44.7

See also Army; Civil War; U.S.-Army

Department of Illinois. IL28.82

Department of the Gulf. IL28.49

GRAND Gulf, Miss. MS17.10

GRAND Order of the Orient. MO2.10

GRAND Rapids, Mich. MI9.18; MI67

GRAND United Order of Odd Fellows. MO2.9

GRANDISSIME: A Story of the New Orleans Creoles. MA39.14

GRANGER, Lester B. DC28.168; NY102.2

GRANGER Movement. MN22.13

GRANITE Freeman (newspaper). NH1.6

GRANT, Abraham. DC176.161

HAWES, Andrew. IL28.24

HAWKINS, Augustus F. DC28.199

HAWKINS, Eugene. CA100.1

HAWKINS County, Tenn. TN43.76

HAWKINS family. VA8.105

HAWKINSVILLE, Ga. GA30.1

HAWKS, Ester H. DC176.72

HAWKS, J. Milton. DC176.72

HAWTHORNE, Nathaniel. CA179.10

HAY, John. DC176.89; MN22.28, 36; OH44.8

HAY, John Milton. DC176.73; IL116.8, 9

HAYCOCK, William F. NB3.5

HAYDEN, Lewis. DC48.8

HAYDEN, Palmer. CA100.1

HAYDEN, Peyton R. MO2.5

HAYDEN, Robert E. TN29.21

HAYES, Dean Dixon Roland. NY152.2

HAYES, Roland. NY210.50

HAYES, Rutherford B. NC15.226; OH44.2; OH65.2

HAYES (Rutherford B.) Administration. DC176.134

HAYES family. OH65.2

HAYES' Library of Americana. OH65.2

HAYES-Tilden Election. NC15.157

HAYGOOD, Bishop. GA32.3

HAYLEY, William. MA39.19

HAYLING, Robert B. DC28.200

HAYMAKER Plot. GA19.6

HAYMARKET Riot, Chicago, Ill. IL87.11; TX16.2

HAYNE, A.P. NC15.36

HAYNE, Isaac W. NC15.183

HAYNE, Paul H. DC176.142

HAYNE, Paul Hamilton. PA98.27

HAYNE, Robert Y. NC15.217

HAYNE, William. IL116.10

HAYNES, George E. DC172.1; TN29.21

HAYNES, George Edmond. TN29.13

HAYNES, George Edmund. DC176.106

HAYNES, Lemuel. NY210.16, 30

HAYNIE, Charles A. TN10.4

HAYS, Arthur Garfield. IL2.2

HAYS, Brooks. TN38.8

HAYS, Richard. KS19.1

HAYS, Robert. IL28.101

HAYWOOD, Edmund Burke. NC4.65

HAYWOOD, Ernest. NC4.65

HAYWOOD, Fabius Julius. NC4.65; NC36.8

HAYWOOD, George Washington. NC4.65

HAYWOOD, John. NC4.65

HAYWOOD County, Tenn. TN43.76

HAYWOOD family. NC4.65

HAZARD, Ben. CA100.1

HAZELHURST, Samuel. MD19.10

HEAD Start. CA3.1; GA33.12

HEALD, John. PA98.20

HEALD, William. PA98.20

HEALD family. PA98.24

HEALTH. SC12.29

See also Hospitals; Medical Care

legislative action agencies. TX2

Medical Committee for Human Rights. DC59

Negroes. TN29.18, 21; VA8.72

New York City. NY110.1

periodicals concerning. NC19.1

research centers. MA43; MN11.1

HEALTH and Welfare Council of Philadelphia. PA69.3

HEALTH and Welfare Council of the National Capital Area, Inc. DC44

HEALTH of the Negro (report). VA8.72

HEALTH Rights. DC59; NY147

HEARD, Alexander. TN37.4

HEARST, Bennie. WA15.32

HEARTH, James E. VA32.7

HEARTMAN, Charles. TX37.4

HEARTMAN, Charles P. TN29.14

HEARTMAN Negro Collection. TX37.4

HEARTS of Hickory. TN43.69

HEATH, Amos. NC36.10

HEATH, Gordon. NY152.2

HEBREW Union College. OH12

HECHINGER, John. DC28.201

HECTOR Davis and Company. IL28.58

HEDGEMAN, Anna Arnold. DC28.202; LA16.10

HEDGES, John. KY8.76

HEDGES family. KY8.64

HEDGEVILLE, Va. NC15.194

HEDRICK, Benjamin Sherwood. NC15.117

HEFFERNAN, Elaine. DC28.203

HEFLIN, James Thomas. AL37.4

HEILER, Calvin Boyd. NC36.9

HEITZMAN, John H. WA15.12

HELM, MacKinley. NY210.67

HELM, Thomas E. MS17.19

HELPER, Hinton R. DC176.157

HELPER, Hinton Rowan. PA43.26

HELSELL, Frank P. WA15.12

HEMINGS, Betty. VA8.106

HEMPHILL, James C. NC15.12

HEMPHILL, James Calvin. NC15.118

HEMPHILL, Robert Reid. NC15.118

HEMPHILL, William Ramsey. NC15.118

HEMPHILL family. NC15.118

HEMPSTEAD, Stephen. MO40.14

HENCH, Atcheson Laughlin. VA8.107

HENDERSON, A.C. (Mrs.). OH36a.1

HENDERSON, Alexander. WV6.10

HENDERSON, Jock B. WV6.10

HENDERSON, John B. MO4.6; MO40.9

HENDERSON, Leroy W. CA100.1

HENDERSON, Lloyd. DC28.204

HENDERSON, Mae. DC28.205

HENDERSON, Thelton E. DC28.206

HENDERSON family. WV6.10

HENDERSON, Ky. NC4.93

HENDERSON, Tex. SC12.10

HENDRICK, William. NC15.144

HENDRIX, Eugene Russell (Bishop). NC15.119

HENLEY, Donald. IL28.144

HENNEPIN County Anti-Slavery Society. MN22.46

HENRICI Waitresses Case. IL90.20

HENRY, Aaron. DC28.207

HENRY, Alexander. PA43.19

HENRY, Anson J. IL116.11

HENRY, Anthony R. DC28.208

HENRY, Clifton W. DC28.209

HENRY, G.A. NC15.77

HENRY, Gustavus Adolphus. NC4.66

HENRY, Mellinger E. RI2.3

HENRY, Milton. NY210.66

HENRY, Patrick. NC15.45; PA16.1

HENRY, Sarah W. Syme. KY8.56

HENRY, Theodore. DC28.210

HENRY County Female Anti-Slavery Society. IN26.1

HENRY County, Tenn. TN43.43, 76

HENRY County, Va. NC4.57

HENRY E. Huntington Library and Art Gallery. CA179; DC176.74

HENRY family. VA8.108

HENRY Street Settlement, New York. NY100.11

HENRY W. Sage Collection. NY46.35

HENSON, — (Father). GA32.14

HENSON, Matthew J. MD20.4

HENTOFF, Nat. NY210.66

HERALD (ship). MA64.1

HERALD of Freedom (newspaper). NH1.5, 6

HERBERT, Hilary Abner. NC4.67

HERBERT, Thomas J. OH44.19

HEREFORD, Frank. WV6.4

HEREFORD, H.A., Sr. (Mrs.). WV6.4

HERITAGE House Education and Cultural Center. PA42

HERITAGE Series. IL7

"HERMITAGE" (plantation). OH36a.11

HERNANDEZ, Aileen C. DC28.211

HERNDON, William. CA179.17

HERNDON, William Henry. DC176.74

HERNDON case. CA79.1

HERNDON-Lamon collection. IN11.3

HERNDON-Weik collection. DC176.15; 74; IN11.3

"HERO Construction" (sculpture). IL18.1

HEROINES of Jericho (lodge). MO2.11

JORDAN, Robert L. TN27.4

JORDAN, Sandy. TN27.4

JORDON, Louis. NY152.2

JORDON, Thomas. NC15.137

JORDON, Vernon. DC28.250

JOSEPH G. Brin Memorial Collection of Human Relations Literature. MA15.1

JOSEPHINE Wilson Bruce Collection. DC48.6

JOSEPHITE Fathers. MD16, MD16.1

JOSEPHSON Collection. KS6.4

JOURNAL. NY242

JOURNAL and Guide (newspaper). OH90.1

JOURNAL of Black Poetry. CA157

JOURNAL of Health and Social Behavior. DC12

JOURNAL of Human Relations. OH87, OH87.1

JOURNAL of Industry (newspaper). NC36.16

JOURNAL of Intergroup Relations. DC67

JOURNAL of Negro Education (periodical). DC46.1; IL30.3; MD22.1; NY55.1

JOURNAL of Negro History (periodical). DC18.1; IL30.3; MA40.4; MD22.1; MI3.1; MN22.4; NY55.1

JOURNAL of Negro Life and History (periodical). DC176.168

JOURNAL of Religious Education of the A.M.E. Church. GA32.3

JOURNAL of Research in Crime and Delinquency. NY176

JOURNAL of the Kuklux Committee. DC172.123

JOURNAL of the Illinois State Historical Society. IL116

JOURNAL of the Lancaster County Historical Society. PA18.1

JOURNAL of the Times (publication). VT4.1

JOURNALISM. DC205

JOURNALISTS. TN37.4

See also Black Journalists

JOURNALS of the Commons House of Assembly, S.C. SC11.4

JOURNALS see Diaries

JOYES, Patrick. KY8.46

JOYES, Thomas. KY8.46

JOYES family. KY8.46

JOYNER, James Yadkin. NC4.36

JUBILEE Day. PA49.7

JUBILEE Hall. TN29.7

JUBILEE Singers. TN29.7

JUDAISM. CO8.1

JUDAISM. NY76

JUDD, Walter H. MN22.52

JUDGE Advocate General's Office (Navy). DC172.118

JUDGE Advocate General's Office (War). DC172.128

JUGGER—Washington Case. NY210.34

JULIA Davis Collection. MO47.2

JULIAN, George W. DC48.8; DC176.62; IN26.4; OH44.26

JULIUS Rosenwald Fund. NY210.50; MN11.9; TN29.9, 21

"JUNEY at the Gate." (song). IL28.164

JUNIOR College Journal. DC2

JUNKER, Buford H. TN29.18, 21

JUVENILE and family courts. NY176

JUVENILE delinquency. DC146.1

K.A.M. Temple, Chicago, Ill. IL28.185

KCLU see Kentucky Civil Liberties Union

KKK see Ku Klux Klan

KAERCHER family. NY46.79

KALAMAZOO, Community Relations Board. MI72

KAMM, Jacob. OR1.2

KANAWHA County. WV6.9, 16

KANE, Thomas Leiper. CA188.4

"KANSAS" (essay). PA43.7

KANSAS. IL28.23, 172; MN22.6; NY46.69; TN27.4; VA8.107

Civil Liberties Union. KS4

Commission on Civil Rights. KS9

Freedmen's Relief Association. PA16.2

State College of Pittsburgh. KS7

State Historical Society. DC176.110; KS10

struggle (1858). WV6.9

Technical Institute. TN27.4

Territory. MO2.34

University of. KS6

KANSAS City American. MO2.31

KANSAS City Call (newspaper). MO2.31

KANSAS City, Mo. NY191.1; OH44.32

Commission on Human Relations. MO17, MO17.1

KANSAS City Sun (newspaper). MO2.31

KANSAS Free State. KS6.5

KANSAS Historical Quarterly. KS10

KANSAS-Nebraska Act. DC176.118, 142, 156, 160; MO2.5; NY46.74

KANSAS-Nebraska Bill. IL28.168; NY46.39, 74; PA43.5

KANSAS-Nebraska broadside. VA8.130

KANSAS-Nebraska problem. NC15.84

KANSAS Volunteers. MA47.1

KANSAS West Conference of the United Methodist Church. KS18

KANTER, Sam. NY210.13

KAPP, Friedrich. DC176.81

KAPPA Alpha Psi. PA48, PA48.1

KASTENMEIR, Robert W. DC28.251

KATALLAGETTE: Be Reconciled. TN25

KATZ, Archie S. WA15.12

KAUFFMAN, Julius. TX27.11

KAUFMAN, Elayne Jones. NY210.66

KAUNDA, Kenneth. NY210.66

KAZIN, Alfred. NY210.66

KEAN, Jefferson Randolph. VA8.131

KEAN, Robert Garlick Hill. VA8.131

KEAN family. VA8.131

KEARNY, Stephen W. MO4.1

KEATS, Ilene. MI27.3

KEBBS, J.M. PA43.26

KEEBLE, Constance F. VA8.51

KEEBLE, Marshall. TN27.4

KEELE family. MO2.2

KEESON, John W. KS19.2

KEETOOWAHS ("Pins Indians"). TN43.26

KEEVER, C.M. DC28.252

KEITH, Ellison Summerfield. SC12.24

KEITH, William (Sir). IL28.104

KELLER, Helen. TN29.6

KELLER, James. NB3.5

KELLER, Rosa. DC28.253

KELLEY, Albert. NY100.11

KELLEY, Caroline B. NY100.11

KELLEY, Florence. NY100.11

KELLEY, John Bartram. NY100.11

KELLEY, Lloyd W. NB3.5

KELLEY, Margaret Dana. NY100.11

KELLEY, Nicholas. NY100.11

KELLEY, Thomas. CA101.1

KELLEY, William Darrah. NY100.11

KELLEY family. NY100.11

KELLIE, Luna E. NB3.6

KELLIE, — (Miss). NB3.6

KELLOGG, William Pitt. IL28.3

KELLY, Edward J. IL28.186

KELLY, Harry F. MI80.3

KEMP, — (Rt. Rev. Dr.). PA43.26

KEMPER, James L. NC15.192

KEMPER, James Lawson. VA8.132

KEMPER County, Miss. NC4.74

KEMPER family. OH8.10

KENDRICK, John F. IL28.105

KENNEDY, Albert J. MN11.5, 10

KENNEDY, Jay Richard. MA16.9

KENNEDY, John Fitzgerald. MA29.1; MS28.8; WA15.25, 26

KENNEDY, Joseph H. DC28.254

KENNEDY, Stetson. NY210.35

KENNEDY, W.J. NC20.1

KENNEDY Administration. MA29.1

KENNEDY family. NC4.38

KENNON, William H. VA8.133

KENNON, William U. VA8.133

KENNON family. VA133

KENOLY, Jacob. TN27.4

KENT, Edward. OH36a.7

KENT State University. OH67; OH68

KENTUCKY. IL28.72, 78; IN11.2; KY8.31; NY46.3, 31; NY206.6; NC4.2; NC15.24, 69, 225; OH44.15, 27, 28; PA98.13; WV6.16

census records. KY8.47

churches in. NC35.5; TN27.4

PERKINS and Brown. OH44.4, 5

PERKINS family. CT14.2

PERQUIMANS County, N.C. NC4.137

PERRY (free Negro). MI9.26

PERRY, Matthew. (Commodore.). IL104.4

PERRY, Matthew C. DC172.25; DC176.115

PERRY, Samuel V. OH36a.16

PERRY County, Ala. NC15.51, 236

PERRY Memorial House and Dickson Tavern. PA10

PERSHING, John Joseph. DC176.116

PERSKY, Stan. MO53.1

PERSON County, N.C. NC4.45; NC15.24, 71

PERSONAL Recollections of the Civil War (ms). MI9.5

PETAL Paper (newspaper). MA16.7

PETERS, Charles H. DC48.19

PETERS, Joe. DC28.356

PETERS, Solomon. NY210.52

PETERS, Thomas. DC48.9

PETERSBURG Battlefield Museum Corporation. VA19

PETERSBURG Campaign of 1864-65. VA19.1

PETERSBURG, Va. NC15.8, 13, 14, 23, 26, 71, 148; VA8.70; VA35.5

PETERSON, C. Petrus. NB3.5

PETERSON, James E. DC28.357

PETERSON, Kennith P. MN22.55

PETERSON, Val. NB3.5

PETERSON family. DE1.3

PETIT Anse Island, La. NC4.6

PETITION for the Colored People of Philadelphia to Ride in the Cars (1866). PA43.26

PETRY, Ann. DC48.38

PETTEGREW, John. IL28.144

PETTIGREW, Charles. NC4.113; NC36.21

PETTIGREW, Charles Lockhart. NC36.21

PETTIGREW, Ebenezer. NC36.21

PETTIGREW, James Johnston. NC36.21

PETTIGREW, Mary. NC36.21

PETTIGREW, Mary Lockhart. NC36.21

PETTIGREW, William Shephard. NC36.21

PETTIGREW family. NC4.113; NC36.21

PETIGRU, James L. NC15.36, 217

PETIGRU, James Louis. SC2.1, 2

PETIGRU family. NC4.113; SC2.2

PETITION Collection. TN43.3

PETTIT and Leake (legal firm). NC15.7

PETTUS, John J. NC15.77

PETTUS, O.H. IL28.181

PETTWAY, Hinckey. IL28.101

PEYTON, Polly. OH44.28

PFEIFFER, Dorothy S. NY46.51

PFORZHEIMER, Walter L. NC15.39

PHARR family. NC4.103

PHELPS, A.A. MA14.1

PHELPS, A.J. MS17.35

PHELPS, Amos A. DC176.169

PHELPS, Amos Augustus. MA8.5

PHELPS, Anson G. LA16.3

PHELPS, Elizabeth Stuart. MA46.21

PHELPS family. MS17.35

PHELPS-Stokes Fund. AL35.14; NY225, NY225.1, 2

PHENIX, Roger. DC28.358

PHI Alpha Theta Collection. MS28.9

PHI Beta Sigma Fraternity, Inc. NY26

PHILADELPHIA Afro-American (newspaper). OH90.1

PHILADELPHIA House of Dutilh. PA43.39

PHILADELPHIA House of Wachsmuth. PA43.39

PHILADELPHIA; Pa. DC28.7; IL28.78, 188; NJ12.3, 11, 13; NY206.9; NC15.66; PA13.3; PA16.1, 19; PA33.4, 7, 8, 9, 10; PA43.19, 21, 28, 30, 37, 40; PA49.2; PA69.7; PA98.4, 5, 23; VA8.60; VA35.2

Anti-Poverty Action Committee. PA69.2

Commission on Human Relations. PA57, PA57.1

Council for Community Advancement. PA58, PA58.1

Fellowship Commission. PA59, PA59.1

Female Anti-Slavery Society. NY46.38

General Hospital. PA33.5

Lebanon Cemetery. PA43.26

Museum of Art. PA60

Supervisory Committee for Recruiting Colored Regiments. PA43.30

Tutorial Service. DC28.269

Yearly Meeting of the Religious Society of Friends. PA16.2, 7; PA62; PA63, PA63.1

PHILADELPHIA Terminal employees. DC172.2

PHILADELPHIA Tribune (newspaper). PA36.2

PHILANDER Smith College, Ark. AR11; TN45.1

PHILANTHROPIST (publication). MI11.1; MO14.1; OH44.26

PHILBRICK, Edward. DC48.8

PHILIPPI, W.Va. WV6.26

PHILIPS, William Pyle. PA16.14

PHILLEO, Calvin Wheeler. CT7.4

PHILLEO, Prudence Crandall. CT25.1

PHILLIPS, Channing. DC28.359

PHILLIPS, Josephine. WV6.10

PHILLIPS, Marshal. IL28.149

PHILLIPS, P.B. DC28.360

PHILLIPS, Philip. DC176.118

PHILLIPS, Ulrich Bonnell. CT24.24; NC4.114; NC15.12

PHILLIPS, Vel. DC28.361

PHILLIPS, W. GA32.14

PHILLIPS, Wendell. DC176.41, 169; MA14.1; MA39.10, 38, 39, 62, 65, 69; MA55.1; MA56.4; NH1.2; NY206.7; PA98.27

PHILLIPS, William. MS17.10

PHILLIPS, William Hallet. DC176.118

PHILLIPS County, Ark. TX27.5

PHILLIPS family. DC176.118

PHILLIPS Gallery. DC98

PHILLIPS Library (Salem, Mass.). MA64

PHILLIS Wheatley Branches of YWCA. NY260.1

PHILLIS Wheatley Home for Girls, Chicago, Ill. IL90.23

PHOENIX Commission on Human Relations. AZ4

PHOENIX Urban League. AZ5

PHONOGRAPH record collection. MN15.1

PHONORECORD collection. MI10.1

PHOTOGRAPH collections. AL35.15; CT24.22; NY149.10, 12; NY151.1; NY210.53

PHILLIS Wheatley Settlement House, Minneapolis. MN22.42

PHYLON, A Review of Race and Culture. GA18

PIATT, Donn. DC176.159

PICKARD, Samuel T. MA39.70

PICKARD-Whittier Papers. MA39.70

PICKELL, James Marion. NC36.22

PICKENS, Francis W. NC15.36, 77; SC12.41

PICKENS, Francis Wilkinson. DC176.119; NC15.41, 183

PICKENS, Israel. AL21.5

PICKENS, William. DC176.104; IL28.63; LA16.5; NY210.54

PICKENS District. SC12.32

PICKENS family. SC12.41

PICOT, Abel (Dr.). VA32.14

PICOT family. VA32.14

PIEDMONT Christian Institute, Martinsville, Va. TN27.11

PIERCE, Epaminondas J. (Rev.). PA21.4

PIERCE, Franklin. IL28.141; NY46.69; NC15.42, 69, 226

PIERNAS, Pedro. IL28.142

PIERPONT, John. IL28.143

PIERRE Chouteau, Jr. and Company. MO40.16

PIH, Richard W. OH8.12

PIKE, Charles B. IL28.144

PIKE, Zebulon. IL28.144

PIKE County, Miss. MS17.32

PILGRIM Baptist Church. MN22.32, 34

PILGRIMAGES of Jean Veneuse. TN29.18

PILLOW, William. KS19.2

PILLSBURY, A.E. DC48.18

PILLSBURY, John S. MN22.28, 36

PILOT. IL68.1

PILSBURY, Parker. MA56.4

PINCHBACK, P.B.S. DC48.6, 37; NY210.42

PINCHOT, Gifford. MO4.15; PA16.2

PINCKNEY, C.C. SC2.23

PINCKNEY, Charles. SC2.17

PINCKNEY, Charles Cotesworth. DC176.91; SC2.17

PINCKNEY, Edward R. NY278.1

PINCKNEY, Elizabeth (Lucas). SC2.17

PINCKNEY, Gustavus M. MD19.8

PINCKNEY, Harriott. SC12.47

PINCKNEY, Thomas. MO2.33; SC2.17; VA8.118

PINCKNEY family. SC2.17; SC12.42

PINCKNEY Plantation. NC15.80

PINE Street Anti-Slavery Society of Boston. MA23.2

PINEY Woods College (Piney Woods, Miss.). MO34.1

PINEY Woods Country Life School. MS26, MS26.1

PINKNEY, William. MD19.19

"PINS Indians" (Keetoowahs). TN43.26

PIONEERS, Negro. CO17.6

PIPER, Benjamin. WI6.35

PIPPIN, Horace. MI24.1; NY32.1; NY149.11; OH7.2; PA54.1; PA60.2; PA106.3; RI11.2

PIRATES, Algerian. VA35.1

PIRTLE, Alfred. KY8.65

PIRTLE, Henry (Judge). KY8.66

PIRTLE family. KY8.66

PISCATAWAY Township, N.J. NJ12.8

PITKIN, Pearly Peabody. OH36a.17

PITT County, N.C. NC4.140

PITTS, P.H. NC4.115

PITTS, Thomas Henry. GA25.9

PITTSBURG Human Relations Commission. CA112, CA112.1

PITTSBURGH Courier (newspaper). IN9.2; KY4.3; MD31.3; MA1.2; MA40.1

PITTSBURGH, Pa. OH44.32; PA13.3; PA99.2

    Commission on Human Relations. PA90, PA90.1

    University of. PA44; PA93; PA94.1; PA95, PA95.1; PA96

PITTSYLVANIA County, Va. NC4.35; NC15.107, 135; VA8.176, 225, 191

PIVOT. PA36

PLACE, Enoch. NY2.1

"PLAIN Facts About Some Virginians." MD19.22

PLAINFIELD Human Relations Commission. NJ28

PLAN for the Abolition of Slavery (broadside). VA8.16

PLANNED Communities, Inc. (P.C.). NY226, NY226.1

PLANNERS for Equal Opportunity (PEO). NY227

PLANTATION books and journals

    Ball, John, S.C. SC2.4

    Bassett family, Va. VA32.3

    Coker, Caleb. SC12.29

    Coker, William, S.C. SC12.8

    collection. DC176.5

    Dupree, H.T.T., Raymond, Miss. MS17.6

Florida. MO40.12

Hammond, James Henry. DC176.67

Hill, John. NC4.68

Huger's Plantation, Savannah, Ga. VA8.118

Means, Thomas Coalter, Fairfield District, S.C. SC12.36

Milliken, John B., S.C. SC2.16

Motte, J. Rhett, Exeter Plantation, Berkeley County, S.C. SC12.37

Mount Ararat Plantation, Church Hill, Miss. MS17.14

Osborn, Samuel George, Hinds County, Miss. MS17.21

Panther Burn Plantation, Percy, Miss. MS17.22

Randolph, William B. DC176.121

Sims, W.E., Va. VA8.129

Walker, John B., Wharton County, Tex. TX8.9

PLANTATION papers and records

    Affleck, Thomas, Brenham, Tex. TX27.1

    Allendale Plantation, Baton Rouge, La. MS17.10

    Allston family, S.C. SC2.1, 2

    Arcadia Plantation, Lafourche Parish, La. NC4.116

    Argyle Plantation, Ga. GA66.4

    Arnold, Richard J., Ga. NC4.122

    autobiographical accounts, Miss. MS17.27

    Bacot and Huger family, S.C. SC2.3

    Barbour family, Va. VA8.17, 18

    Barker, David, Fluvanna County, Va. VA35.1

    Barnsley family, Bartow County, Ga. TN43.10

    Bayside Plantation, N.C. NC4.13

    Belgrade Plantation, N.C. NC4.113

    Belle Meade Plantation, Tenn. NC4.61

    Berkeley family, Barn Elms Plantation, Va. VA8.22

    Bermuda Plantation, Natchitoches Parish, La. NC4.117

    Billingsley, James B., Marlin, Tex. TX8.3

    Bird and Ulmer families, Jefferson County, Fla. FL26.1

    Blow family, Tower Hill Plantation, Sussex County, Va. VA35.2

    Broughton family, Dorchester, S.C. SC2.6

    Brown, Alexander, Nelson, Va. VA35.3

    Bruce family, Staunton Hill Plantation, Charlotte County, Va. DC176.24

    Bryan, Moses Austin, Brazoria County, Tex. TX8.4

    Bull, John Baxter, S.C. SC12.3

    Butler family, Ga. PA43.8

    Cadwalader, John, Md. PA43.9

    Campbell, James, Berkeley County, W.Va. WV6.3

    Cantey family, Ga. and Ala. SC12.4

    Clark, Charles, Doro Plantation, Bolivar County, Miss. MS17.4

    Clinch family, Ga. DC176.33

    "Clover Hill," Caldwell County, N.C. NC4.76

    Cocke, Philip St. George, Powhatan County, Va. VA32.6

    Cockrill family, Vicksburg, Miss. TN43.34

    Colhoun, James Edward, S.C. SC12.6

    Collins family, N.C. NC36.3

    Cooke, James E., Powhatan County, Va. VA35.1

    Deer Range Plantation, La. NC4.138

    Dixon Plantation, N.C. NC4.37

    Doar, Stephen D. DC176.42

    Dozier, Richard, Georgetown, S.C. NC4.40

    Dunbar, William, Adams County, Miss. MS17.5

    Elliot family, Beaufort, S.C. NC4.42

    general collection, Miss. MS17.19

    "Glen Ambler," Amherst County, Va. VA8.9

    Graves family, Caswell County, N.C. NC4.53

    Graves family, Newton County, Ga. NC4.53

    Green Hill Plantation, N.C. NC4.56

    Grimball, John Berkley, Charleston, S.C. NC4.54

    Grimes family, N.C. NC4.55

    Guignard family, S.C. SC12.18

    Guy, Martin Winston, Memphis, Tenn. TN43.14

    Guy family, Memphis, Tenn. TN43.50

    Hairston, Peter Wilson, N.C. NC4.58

    Hamilton, Charles Eaton, Granville County, N.C. NC4.59

    Hammond, James Henry. SC12.19

    Hannah family, Va. VA32.11

    Harrington, Henry William, Jr. NC4.63

    Hill of Howth Plantation. AL21.4

    Hillhouse family, Ga. NC4.69

    Holt, S.L., Miss. OK2.4

    Hopkinson, James, Edisto Island, S.C. SC12.21

    Houma Plantation, Terrebonne Parish, La. NC4.123

    Houmas Plantation, Ascension Parish, La. NC4.96

    Houmas Plantation, La. NC4.14

    Hubard family. NC4.72

    Hunter family, Va. VA8.120

    Ingleside Plantation, N.C. NC4.37

    Irby, Richard, Va. VA8.125

    Jemison family. AL37.5

    Jenkins family, Edisto Island, S.C. SC12.22

    Johnson, David, S.C. SC12.23

    Keitt, Ellison Summerfield. SC12.24

    Killona Plantation, Miss. MS17.12

TOLONO, Ill. IL28.45

TOLSON family. SC12.5

TOMLIN family. VA35.5

TOMLINSON, Joseph, Jr. NY46.59

TOMLINSON family. NY46.59; WV6.10

TOMPKINS County, N.Y. NY46.15, 27

TOOMER, Jean. CT24.23; TN29.32

TOPEKA Interfaith Council for Racial Justice. KS11

TOPP, Mildred S. MS28.16

TOPP, Robertson. TN20.1

TORBET, James M. AL21.8

TORGERSON, Torger A. MN18.4

TORIAN, Wm. KY8.89

TORONTO, Canada. OH44.32

TORRENCE family. NC15.222

TORREY, Charles Turner. MA8.5

TOUGALOO College. IN20.1; LA16.5; MS30; NY242.1; TN27.11

TOUGALOO Southern Christian College. TN27.9

TOURGEE, Albion W. NC15.193; NC36.33

TOUSSAINT, Pierre. NY207.10

TOUSSAINT L'Ouverture, François Dominique. CT7.1; DC176.124; MA39.39, 89; NY210.42

TOWER Hill Plantation. VA35.1

TOWN, Henrietta (Larson). MN22.28

TOWNE, Laura M. NC4.111

TOWNS, George Alexander. GA19.28

TOWNSEND, Edmund. AL37.9

TOWNSEND, James B. KY8.14

TOWNSEND, Samuel. AL37.9

TOWNSEND, Washington. PA43.38

TOWNSEND, Willard E. NB3.5

TOYLER, Nellie Grey. TN43.43

TRACY, Octavius. DC28.445

TRADE Union Congress. MS28.13

TRAINING-Within-Industry Service in the War, Manpower Commission. DC172.143

TRANSACTIONS on the Plantation of William Dunbar (journal). MS17.5

TRANSPORTATION, U.S. Department of, Office of Civil Rights. DC167.1

TRAPIER, Paul (Rev.). SC2.27

TRAVEL
commentaries on. SC12.29
discrimination against passengers. DC175

TRAVEL agencies
United Negro Tour Association Inc. WI22.1

TRAVELER'S Aid Society. PA69.7

TRAVELERS Research Publishing Company, Inc. IL79, IL79.1; IL90.28

TRAVIS County, Tex. TX8.8

TREADWELL, Jefferson. MI9.34

TREADWELL, Jerome. MI9.34

TREADWELL, Seymour Boughton. MI9.33, 34

TREASURY Department. DC172.102; NY210.54

TREAT, John Henry. MA39.90

TREDEGAR Company. VA32.5

TREDEGAR Iron Works, Cloverdale Furnace. NC15.5

TREDGOLD, J.W. NY46.12

TRENDS in Housing. NY161

TRENT, W.J, Sr. NC43.14

TRENTON, N.J. DC28.217
Free Public Library. NJ36

"TRENTON Six." NY210.13, 34

"TRIAL of the 12." NY210.13

TRIALS.
Brown, John. WV6.15

TRIENNIAL Baptist Convention. SC15.2

TRIMBLE, Allen. OH36a.23

TRIMBLE, Isaac Ridgeway. MD19.21

TRIMBLE, Robert Wilson. AR7.9

TRIMBLE, William Allen. OH36a.23

TRIMBLE, William Henry. OH36a.23

TRINITY College. CT15; DC107

TRIPLETT, Simon. NC15.45

TRIST, Nicholas Philip. DC176.155; VA32.18

TRI-STATE Bank of Memphis. DC28.272

TRI-STATE Defender. DC28.377

TRI-STATE NAACP. DC28.398

TROTTER, Geraldine. DC48.32

TROTTER, Monroe. GA19.23

TROTTER, William Monroe. DC48.32; MA8.6; MA39.91; TN29.5

TROUSDALE, William. TN43.92

TROUTMAN, Francis. KY6.12

TROUTMAN, John Michael. KY6.11

TROUTMAN family. KY6.11

TROWBRIDGE, Luther Stephen. MI9.35

TROY, N.Y. NY276.2
Human Relations Commission. OH83, OH83.1

TROY, N.C. NC36.27

TRUD! NJ7

TRUE American. KY8.27

TRUE Reformer. NC36.16

TRUEHEART, Charles W. TX27.19

TRUEHEART, Henry Martyn. TX27.19

TRUMAN, Harry S. MO4.18; MO6.2, 7; NY210.47; WA15.26

TRUMBULL, James Hammond. MI11.2

TRUMBULL, Lyman. DC176.89, 141, 156

TRUTH, Sojourner. MA39.92; MI9.20; PA43.26

TRUTH Seeker. DC176.169

TUBMAN, Harriet. NY46.71; NY210.68

TUCKER, D.M. MO4.28

TUCKER, Henry St. George. NC15.42; VA8.204

TUCKER, J.H. MO4.28

TUCKER, Sterling. DC28.288, 446

TUCKER County, W.Va. WV6.8

TUCKER family. VA8.203; VA35.5

TUCSON Commission on Human Relations. AZ8

TUFTS University. MA49; MA50

TUGWELL, Rexford G. MN22.58

TULANE, Victor H. DC176.161

TULANE University. LA30; LA31

TULSA City-County Library System. OK18

TUMULTY, Joseph P. NC15.118

TUPELO, Miss., SNCC's March to. WI6.16

TURBERVILLE, George. NC15.45

TURBERVILLE, John. NC15.45

TUREAUD, A.P. DC28.447

TURGEE, Albion W. TN29.5

TURNER, Adine. NC15.42

TURNER, Edward Walter. DC48.53

TURNER, George Wilmer. NC15.224

TURNER, Henry McNeal. DC48.54; GA32.3

TURNER, Jesse. DC28.448

TURNER, Jesse, Jr. NC15.223

TURNER, Jesse, Sr. NC15.223

TURNER, Josiah. NC36.33

TURNER, Nat. NY210.63; NY278.16; NC15.234; NC36.17; VA8.42
See also Nat Turner Revolt

TURNER, Rebecca (Allen). NC15.223

TURNER, Thomas. VA8.211

TURNER family. NY46.72; NC4.118; NC15.223

TURNER Theological Seminary. DC1.1

TURNPIN, Walter E. CT24.23

TUSCALOOSA, Ala. NY102.1

TUSKEGEE, Ala. AL35.19; DC28.15, 252, 374
City Council. DC28.77, 345, 425

TUSKEGEE Civic Association. DC28.304

TUSKEGEE Collection. AL35.19

TUSKEGEE Experimental Station. DC172.131

TUSKEGEE Institute. AL34; AL35, AL35.3, 9, 12, 18, 20; AL36, AL36.1; DC28.73, 131, 166, 248, 249, 327, 360, 425, 428, 481; DC172.12, 58; DC176.109, 161, 175; KY19.1; MA39.60, 96; MN22.29; NY210.70

TUTTLE Collection. GA19.29

TUTWILER Southern History Collection. AL5.3

24th U.S. Infantry. DC176.114; IL28.105

29th Connecticut Volunteers. MI11.6

TWIN City Federation of Settlements. MN22.14

"TWO Disciples at the Tomb" (painting). IL18.3

"TYE River Quarter," Nelson County. VA8.116a

TYLER, Al. IL61.1

TYLER, Gerald. GA19.22

TYLER, John. NC15.69, 192, 226; TN43.25; VA8.141, 148

TYLER, Ralph W. OH44.25

TYRRELL County, N.C. NC4.113; NC36.3, 21

TYSON, Thomas. IL28.5

TYUS, Wyomie. DC28.449

URBAN Leagues (cont.)
DC206, DC206.1, 2; FL20; FL28, FL28.1;
GA2; GA19.14; GA20, GA20.1; IL4, IL4.1;
IL28.50; IL34; IL90.4, 9; IL100, IL100.1;
IL111; IL118, IL118.1; IL122; IN1; IN4;
IN10, IN10.1; IN16; IN27, IN27.1; IN31,
IN31.1; IN37, IN37.1; KS17, KS17.1; KY7,
KY7.1; LA33; MA62, MA62.1; MA71,
MA71.1; MD9; MI9.9, 13, 23; MI14,
MI14.1; MI31, MI31.2; MI66; MI68; MI76,
MI76.1; MI83, MI83.1; MI87; MN13;
MN22.9, 34, 42; MS21, MS21.1; MO25;
MO51, MO51.1; NB3.4, 5; NB10, NB10.1;
NJ5, NJ5.1; NJ6; NJ11; NJ14; NJ26,
NJ26.1; NY1, NY1.1; NY33, NY33.1;
NY100.16; NY210.47, 53; NY252; NY273;
NY281, NY281.1; NY293; NC46, NC46.1;
OH5; OH8.15; OH18, OH18.1; OH35,
OH35.1; OH39; OH55, OH55.1; OH70;
OH79, OH79.1; OH85, OH85.1; OH94,
OH94.1; OK12; OK19, OK19.1; OR11;
PA19, PA19.1; PA61, PA61.1; PA69.8;
PA80.1; PA97; PA107, PA107.1; RI12;
SC7, SC7.1; TN9, TN9.1; TN17; TN35,
TN35.1; TX21, TX21.1; TX31, TX31.1;
WA13; WA15.12, 25, 35; WA19, WA19.1;
WI5, WI5.1; WI20, WI20.1; WI29.1; WI30;
VA28

URBAN Research Corporation. IL91

URBAN Research Library Collection.
CT30.2

URBAN Research News. CA19

URBAN Research Report. CT30

URBAN Review. NY93

URBAN Studies Collection. MO48.1

URBAN Studies Institute. MD21.1

URBAN Studies Monograph Series. NC2

URBAN Training Center for Christian Mission. IL92

URBAN West. CA175

URBANA, Ohio. OH8.1; OH44.20

URBANEWS. IN27

USSERY, Wilfred T. DC28.451

UTICA Junior College. MS31, MS31.1

UTOPIAN groups
Harmonia (19th century). PA94.6

UTTER, David N. OH44.4

VCHR see Virginia Council on Human Relations

VCHR Observer. VA31

VISTA see Volunteers in Service to America

VALE, Gilbert. MD30.1

VALENTINE Museum. VA30

VALIEN, Preston. TN29.18

VALIEN, Preston and Bonita. LA16.15

VALLAD, Paul. IL28.72

VALLANDIGHAM, Clement Laird. IL28.179

VALLE, Felix. IL28.180

VALLEY of the Lower Mississippi.
DC172.66

VALTMAN, Edmund S. MS4.2

VAN, Slater. CA100.1

VAN Alstyne family. NY51.1

VAN Buren, Abraham. NC15.192, 200

VAN Buren, Angelica Singleton. NC15.200

VAN Buren, Martin. DC176.18, 158;
IL28.72; KY8.66; MD19.24; NC15.38, 42,
200, 226

VAN Buren, Ark. NC15.223

VANCE, James Isaac. TN43.93

VANCE, Letitia Thompson. KY8.36

VANCE, William L. KY8.36

VANCE, Zebulon B. NC15.77, 129;
NC36.26, 33

VAN Cortlandt, Jacobus. NY206.9

VANCOUVER Transportation Company.
OR1.2

VANDERBILT, Cornelius. MN22.31

VANDERBILT University. TN46; TN47

VANDERCOOK, Roy C. MI9.36

VANDERHORST, Adel (Allston). SC2.28

VANDERHORST, Arnolous (Mrs.). SC2.2

VAN der Horst family. NC15.108

VANDERHORST family. SC2.28

VANDERPOEL, —. NY46.73

VAN Der Zee, James. NY149.12

VANGUARD. IN39; MI52; OH22

VAN Horn, Benjamin. KS10.8

VAN Jackson, Wallace. GA19.10

VAN Kleek, —. MA56.12

VAN Liew, John D. NJ12.12

VAN Liew family. NJ12.12

VANN, John. NC36.30

VANSANDT, Christopher. IL28.104

VanSANT, Samuel R. MN22.28

VAN Schaick family. NY46.4

VAN Vechten, Carl. CT24.7, 22; DC176.180;
NY207.11; TN29.6, 12

VAN Vorhis, John. DC48.13

VAN Winkle, P.G. WV6.8

VAN Winkle, Peter G. WV6.25

VAN Zandt, Gerrit. NY2.1

VARDAMAN, James K. NY210.10

VASHON, George B. DC48.24, 59

VAUGHAN, Sarah. TN29.17

VAUGHN, George. DC176.169

VAUGHN, Jackie. NY210.66

VAUGHN, Royce H. CA100.1

VAUX, Richard. PA43.40

VAUX, Robert. PA43.26, 40

VAUX, Roberts. PA43.12, 26

VAUX family. PA16.9; PA43.40

VENABLE, Andrew Reid. VA11.1

VENABLE, John M. VA11.1

VENABLE, Richard N. VA11.1

VENICE, Fla. NY46.48

VERMONT Historical Society. VT3

VERMONT State Legislature. MA2.1

VERMONTERS. VT3.2

VERNON, Robert. NY210.66

VERSAILLES, Ky. NC4.49

VERTICAL file collection. FL24.1

VESEY, Denmark. NY210.63

VESEY, Paul. DC48.38

VEST, George G. MO4.1

VETERANS Administration. DC172.11;
DC197.1

See also U.S. Veterans Administration

VICK, Burwell. MS17.35

VICK, Gray J. MS17.35

VICK, Henry W. MS17.35

VICK family. MS17.35

VICKSBURG and Warren County Historical
Society. MS32.1

VICKSBURG Citizen's Appeal. WI6.16

VICKSBURG, Miss. MS17.31, 37

battle of. CA179.6; OH36a.20; MN22.8;
MS32.1; WI6.6

VICKSBURG Riot, 1874. MS17.3

VICKSBURG, Va. IL101.2

VICTOR Gruen Foundation for Environmental Planning. CA89

"VICTORIAN Interior" (oil painting).
NY149.11

VIETNAM war. MS28.9

SCLC resolution opposing. GA33.19

VIEWPOINT Magazine. IL96

VIGILANCE Committee. NY206.7

VIGILANT Committee of Philadelphia.
PA43.26

VILLARD, Henry. NY46.74

VILLARD, Oswald Garrison. DC48.29;
DC176.104, 161; IL28.23; MA39.43, 93;
MN11.9; MN22.58; NY46.14; NY100.22;
NC15.118; TN29.5; VA8.4

VINCENNES, Ind. IL28.45

VINCENT, Stenio (The Hon.). NY210.60

VINTON, John Rogers. NC15.227

VIOLENCE. KS7.1

VIOLENCE

See also Civil disorders and riots; Slave
revolts

research center. MA73

VIRGIN Islands. DC172.41; DC176.104;
VI1.2

College of the. VI1

St. Croix. NY46.58

VIRGINIA. IL28.78, 172; MS17.37; NY46.75;
NY206.11; NC4.72, 73, 90, 106, 120;
NC15.6, 33, 42, 56, 61, 62, 64, 66,
71, 73, 86, 92, 94, 100, 101, 112, 123,
125, 166, 173, 192; PA98.13; SC12.36;
TN27.4; VA8.48, 216

British colonial period. VA36.1

business records from. NC4.14;
NC15.37, 76

Civil War and post-war period. GA25.4;
NY46.21; NC15.122, 130, 206, 215,
229; WV6.4, 16

General Assembly. CA179.29; IL28.32;
VA8.153

Governor of. NC15.28; VA33.4

historical collections. VA8.205, 207;
VA32.1

House of Burgesses. VA8.48

House of Delegates. VA8.132; VA32.16

WHITE, Hamilton. NY46.75

WHITE, Hugh. NY46.76

WHITE, Hugh. MS28.16

WHITE, Hugh L. NC15.42

WHITE, J.A. MS28.16

WHITE, Jacob C. DC48.59; PA43.2, 26

WHITE, Jacob C., Jr. PA43.26

WHITE, John R. MO4.31

WHITE, Josh. TN29.17

WHITE, Mamie M. MN22.34

WHITE, Maunsell (1783-1863). NC4.138

WHITE, Maunsell, Jr. NC4.138

WHITE, Newman Ivy. MA39.100

WHITE, Walter. DC48.33; DC176.104, 145; MA39.101; NY210.5, 50, 60

WHITE, Walter F. CT24.21

WHITE, William (Rev.). IL28.188

WHITE, William Pierrepont. NY46.76

WHITE Americans to Support Black Legislation. NY255

WHITE Attitudes Toward Negroes. DC172.142

"WHITE Caps," Ku Klux Klan. OK2.3

WHITE Citizens Council. DC176.105; GA12.1; GA13.1; MS28.3, 7; NV5.2; NY210.66; WI6.16

WHITE Collection. CT14.4

WHITE Community Project, Mayersville, Miss. WI6.16

WHITE Ethiopian. MA39.99

WHITE House. DC28.399; GA19.27

WHITE Panther Party. MI13

WHITE Plains Public Library. NY294

WHITE Power. VA3

WHITE Sentinel. FL5

WHITE supremacist groups. NV5.2

See also Extremist Movements Collection; Right-wing organization; groups by name for fuller listing and for others not included below

Aryan Knights of the Ku Klux Klan (Waco, Tex.). TX50.1

Citizen's Councils. MS28.3, 7; TN37.3

Citizens Councils of America. MS9

Congressional committee hearings. MI60.6

general collection. CO4.2; IA11.2; NV5.2

Great Statecraft Propaganda and Agitation Service. VA1.1

Ku Klux Klan. AR1.4; DC176.55; GA19.23; GA30.9, 14; GA49.3; KS18.1; MD19.3, 4; MA39.48; MN22.20; MO4.9; NY210.35, 47, 54; NC1.1; NC4.121; NC36.2, 12; PA18.1; RI10.2; TN29.18; TN33.1; TN37.3; TX10.1; TX39.2; TX50.1; VA8.2, 138

Ku Klux Klan (Ala.). MO40.18

Ku Klux Klan (Colo.). CO17.2, 5

Ku Klux Klan (Galesburg, Ill). WV6.21

Ku Klux Klan (Ill.). IL28.7

Ku Klux Klan (Noxubee, Miss.). MS28.1

Ku Klux Klan (Ohio). MO4.17; OH8.9; OH44.21

Ku Klux Klan (Oregon, 1922). OR1.3

Ku Klux Klan (S.C.). SC12.24

Ku Klux Klan (W.Va.). WV6.19

National Socialist White People's Party. VA3

National States Rights Party. GA67.1

North Carolina. NC15.176

New Society. NJ7.1

research center on. MA67.1

United Klans of America. AL33

"White Caps" (Okla.). OK2.3

White World Distributing Company. LA34

WHITE World Distributing Company. LA34

WHITEFIELD, George. NC15.119

WHITEHALL, Pa. IL28.34

WHITEHEAD, F.L. NC15.230

WHITEHEAD, Harriett. NC15.139

WHITEHEAD, James. VA8.115

WHITEHEAD, Lofftus N. NC15.230

WHITEHEAD, Robert. VA8.216

WHITELAW, Reid. OH44.8

WHITFORD, John N. NC15.231

WHITLEDGE, T.B. MO4.6

WHITNEY, Anne. MA74.2

WHITNEY, Henry. NJ12.13

WHITNEY, Henry Austin. MA39.102

WHITTAKER, Johnson Chestnut. NY284.5

WHITTAKER, Miller F. SC18.4

WHITTELSEY family. MI9.24

WHITTIER, John Greenleaf. CA179.10, 13, 30; DC48.18; DC176.149; MN22.56; MA13.3; MA39.70; MA56.8; MA63.4; NH1.2, 8; NY100.9; OH65.7; PA16.12, 13, 16; PA43.26; PA98.27

WHITTINGHAM, William Rollinson. NC15.232

WHITTLESEY, E.W. DC176.148

WHITTLESEY, Elisha. OH36a.25; OH44.16

WHITTLESLEY, E. DC48.24

WHO Riots? A Study of Participation in the 1967 Riots. NY99.3

WHYTE, Garret (art works by). IL61.1

WHYTE, Robert. TN43.94

WICHITA, Kans. OH12.1

WICHITA State University. KS16

WICKERSHAM Commission. DC172.6

WICKHAM, John. NC15.192

WICKLIFFE, Charles Anderson. KY8.56

WIDEN, Raphael. IL28.118

WIDENER Library. MA40

WIER, Roy William. MN22.55

WIGFALL, Louis T. NC15.36, 58

WILBERFORCE. PA16.18

WILBERFORCE, Samuel. NC15.233

WILBERFORCE, William. CA179.21; MA14.1; NJ12.14; NY210.63; NC15.205, 233; PA43.17, 26; PA98.14

WILBERFORCE Movement. NC15.99

WILBERFORCE University. DC1.1; DC48.51; DC172.28; OH44.3, 19; OH88; OH89.6

WILBORN, (Rives) Cornelia Harrison. VA8.177

WILBUR, Julia A. NY46.37

WILBURISM. NY46.37

WILBURITE-Gurneyite Separation. PA16.2, 6, 18

WILBURN, R.N. VA8.114, 217

WILCOX, J.K.H. VA8.2

WILCOX, Preston. DC28.469; NY60

WILCOX Collection of Contemporary Political Ephemera. KS6.7

WILCOX family. MO2.2

WILD, — (Union officer). DC172.70

WILD, Edward A. MA16.16

WILDER, Burt Green. NY46.77

WILDER, Charles Baker. CT24.27

WILDER, Gaston H. NC4.139

WILDER, Sarah E. (Hinton) (Mrs.). NC4.139

WILEY, Calvin Henderson. NC36.32

WILEY, George. DC28.470

WILEY, Mary C. NC36.32

WILEY College, Marshall, Tex. TN45.1; TX19; TX40, TX40.3

WILEY University, Tex. TN33.2

WILIE, E.L. KS19.2

WILKERSON, Doxey A. NY210.44

WILKES County, N.C. NC4.21, 56

WILKESON, Samuel. NY29.2

WILKINS, J. Ernest, Jr. TN29.21

WILKINS, Roger. DC28.471

WILKINS, Roy. DC176.104; NY102.2; TN43.56, 57

WILKINSON, Henry B. NY210.60

WILKINSON, James. MD19.11, MO2.33

WILKINSON County, Miss. NC4.41

WILKS, Gertrude. DC28.472

WILLARD, A.L. NY46.74

WILLARD, Frances E. MA56.6

WILLARD, Samuel. IL28.198

WILLARD Library. IN7

WILLCOX, James M. NC15.234

WILLCOX family. NC15.234

WILLERS, Diedrich. NY46.78

WILLEY, Austin. MN22.56

WILLEY, Samuel Hopkins. CA12.1

WILLIAM Allan Neilson Library, Sophia Smith Collection. MA56

WILLIAM Beaumont (book). MO40.6

WILLIAM Henry Smith Collection. OH44.28

WILLIAM L. Moore Foundation. MD25

"WILLIAM Lloyd Garrison." OH44.17

WILLIAM Wyles Collection. CA184.2

WILLIAMS, Archibald P. KY8.45

WILLIAMS, Aubrey Willis. NY45.4

WILLIAMS, Austin May. TX27.21

WILLIAMS, Bert. MI29.1

WILLIAMS, Bert. IL61.3

WILLIAMS, Campbell A. MS28.17

WILLIAMS, Claude. TN10.11

WILLIAMS, Daniel Hale. DC48.60; DC172.38; IL76.1

WILLIAMS, David. IL28.133

WILLIAMS, David Reichard. LA10.3

WILLIAMS, Edward. PA98.24

WILLIAMS, Edward C. TN29.5

WILLIAMS, Edward H. MN22.57

WILLIAMS, Edwin Anderson. MD19.22

WILLIAMS, Egbert Austin. NY210.74

WILLIAMS, Francis. NY210.60

WILLIAMS, Fred Hart. MI27.3; MI29.9

WILLIAMS, George W. DC48.46

WILLIAMS, Hannah. PA98.24

WILLIAMS, Harry T. WI6.10

WILLIAMS, Hattie P. NB3.5

WILLIAMS, Horton. KS19.1

WILLIAMS, Hosea. GA33.19; NY146.1

WILLIAMS, Howard Yolen. MN22.58

WILLIAMS, J.C. MN22.57

WILLIAMS, James O. DC28.473

WILLIAMS, John A. DC28.474

WILLIAMS, Judy. IL28.190

WILLIAMS, Louise. MN22.57

WILLIAMS, Otho Holland (Gen.). MD19.15, 23

WILLIAMS, Paul. NY210.50

WILLIAMS, Robert. NY210.66

WILLIAMS, Rodney E. DC28.475

WILLIAMS, Ruth Hale. MN22.57

WILLIAMS, Ruth J. MN22.58

WILLIAMS, Samuel McKeehan. MN22.56, 57

WILLIAMS, Samuel May. TX27.21, 22, 23

WILLIAMS, Samuel W. OH8.18

WILLIAMS, Sarah. MN22.57; PA98.24

WILLIAMS, T.H. TN43.25

WILLIAMS, Talcott (memorial papers). PA43.15

WILLIAMS, Thomas Hale. MN22.57

WILLIAMS, Walter. DC194.4

WILLIAMS, Wesley. KY8.92

WILLIAMS, William. VA32.7

WILLIAMS, William Howell. TX27.22

WILLIAMS, William Taylor Burwell. AL35.21

WILLIAMS, Willis R. NC4.140

WILLIAMS family. MN22.57; MS28.17; MO4.22; SC12.34

WILLIAMSBORO, N.C. NC4.59

WILLIAMSBURG. VA35.5

WILLIAMSON, Harry A. NY210.38, 75

WILLIAMSON, John. IL28.8

WILLIAMSON, Thomas P. IL28.49

WILLIAMSON County, Ill. IL28.7

WILLIAMSON County, Tenn. TN43.16, 68

WILLIAMSON family. NY210.38; TN43.95; VA35.5

WILLIAMSPORT, Md. NC15.33

WILLIAMSTON, N.C. NC15.201

WILLIAMSTOWN, W.Va. WV6.10

WILLIS, Frank Bartlette. OH44.34

WILLIS, George H. MA66.16

WILLIS, John. MS17.22

WILLIS, M.F. IL28.8

WILLIS, Nathaniel. MA8.5

WILLISTON Memorial Library. MA65

WILLKIE, Wendell. NC15.12

WILLOUGHBY, Benjamin. MI29.6

WILLOUGHBY, John. NC36.18

WILLOUGHBY, William A. NC15.177

WILLOUGHBY family. MO2.2

WILLS, Anna Maria Baker (Whitaker). NC4.141

WILLS, George Whitaker. NC4.141

WILLS, P'lla. CA63.2

WILLS, Richard Henry. NC4.141

WILLS, William Henry. NC4.141

WILMINGTON College. OH89

WILMINGTON, Del. NC4.143

WILMINGTON, Ga., District Court records. GA64.4

WILMINGTON, N.C. NC4.38, 93, 143; NC15.98; VA8.5, 19

   race riot in. NC15.176

   slave insurrections in. NC36.15

WILMORE, Gayraud S. DC28.476

WILMORE, Jacques. DC28.477

WILMOT, David. WI6.19

WILSON, Alpheus Waters. GA25.11

WILSON, Butler. DC48.18

WILSON, Butler R. DC48.17

WILSON, D.L. MO4.15

WILSON, E. NY210.4

WILSON, Fred R. CA100.1

WILSON, Halena (Mrs.). IL28.22

WILSON, Henry. DC176.166; IL90.17; MA16.8; NY46.35

WILSON, Joan. NY99.1

WILSON, Joel W. OH44.28

WILSON, John. GA19.18; IL61.1

WILSON, John Leighton. NC35.12

WILSON, Miriam Belangee. SC1.5

WILSON, Olander W. IL90.22

WILSON, Samuel Mackay. KY6.12

WILSON, Susan B. GA25.11

WILSON, Thomas. VA8.115; WI6.5

WILSON, William J. DC176.93

WILSON, Woodrow. DC176.11, 113, 152; MD19.8

WILSON County, N.C. NC36.20

WILSON County, Tenn. TN43.76

WILSON family. TN43.74; WV6.16

WILSON Tariff Reform Bill. MN22.48

WILTBERGER, Christian. DC176.167

WIMBISH, Christopher C. IL28.191

WIMBISH family. IL28.191

WINCHESTER, James. TN43.96

WINCHESTER, Miss. NC4.120

WINCHESTER, Va. NC15.121; VA32.8

WINDOM, William. MN22.28

WINDSOR, Robert N. VA8.218

WINFIELD, John A. VA8.219

WINGER, Betty Bush. OR1.1

WINKS, Robin W. NY210.73

WINN, John. NC15.235

WINN, Philip James. NC15.235

WINN family. NC15.235

WINNSBORO, S.C. NC4.19

WINSOR, Justin. MN22.36

WINSTON, Bickerton Lyle. VA32.20

WINSTON, Patrick N. NC36.33

WINSTON County, Miss. NC4.74

WINSTON family. VA8.220

WINSTON-Salem, N.C., Police Program. NC19.1

WINSTON-Salem, N.C., State University. NC45, NC45.2

WINTERS, Lawrence. NY152.2

WINTHROP, Robert Charles. MA55.1

WINTHROP College. SC21

WIRTH, Louis. IL87.12; NY210.44; TN29.18

WIRTZ, Willard. DC28.478

WISCONSIN. IL28.69

   Civil Liberties Union. WI25

   Conference of Social Work. NY45.4

   foreign-born groups. WI6.37

   State Colonization Society. WI6.15

   State Historical Society of. KY19.1; OK2.6; WI6

   State Industrial Union Council. WI6.34

   State Legislature. DC28.34

   state politics. WI6.19

   State University. WI31

   22nd Regiment of Wisconsin Volunteers. NY46.31

   22nd Wisconsin Infantry, Company E. NB3.3

   University of. DC28.103; WI7; WI8; WI9; WI23, WI23.1; WI24, WI24.1

WISCONSIN Jewish Archives. WI6.38

WISCONSIN Law Review. WI7

WISCONSIN Magazine of History. WI6

WISCONSIN State Journal (publication). WI6.10, 35

WISE, Henry A. DC176.22; IL28.23, 172; MD19.24; NC15.192; VA8.221

WISE Men of the U.S.A. MO2.26

WISTAR, Thomas. PA16.12

WISTAR family. PA16.9

WITHERELL, Benjamin Franklin Hawkins. MI29.10

WITHERSPOON, John. NC4.89

WRIGHT, Martha Coffin Pelham. MA56.4

WRIGHT, Mary Ann. NC4.143

WRIGHT, Michael. DC28.481

WRIGHT, Mollie (Murdock). NC4.143

WRIGHT, Richard. CT24.23; IL30.5; IL104.5; OH68.4; NV5.5; TN29.5, 33

WRIGHT, Robert E. DC28.482

WRIGHT, S.E. OH44.26

WRIGHT, Stephen J. LA16.16; TN37.4

WRIGHT, William. MA14.9

WRIGHT, William H. De Courcy. MD19.24

WRIGHT family. MA56.4; MN22.59; NC4.143

WRITERS

　See also Poets; persons by name for fuller listing and for others not included below

　Adamic, Louis. NJ31.4

　Allen, Cleveland G. NY210.3

　Ashmore, Harry S. TN31.1

　Atkins, James A. CO17.1

　Baker, Ray Stannard. MA39.5

　Baldwin, James. NV5.5; NY64.1

　Bontemps, Arna Wendell. NY278.4

　Boykin, James H. NC38.2

　Braithwaite, William Stanley. NY210.8

　Braithwaite, William Stanley Beaumont. NY278.5

　Brawley, Benjamin Griffith. DC48.5

　Brewer, John M. NC38.2

　Brown, H.E. NC38.2

　Brown, Orlando. KY8.14

　Bruce, John Edward. NY210.10

　Chandler, Elizabeth Margaret. MI9.4

　Chase, D.A. MI9.5

　Chesnutt, Charles Waddell. TN29.5

　Clark, Kate (Upson). MA56.3

　correspondence among. MA39.11

　Cullen, Countee. TN29.6

　Davenny, Wilson Imbrie. MI9.8

　Dixon, Thomas, Jr. NC1.1

　DuBois, William E.B. NY64.2; NY210.19; TN29.8

　Ellison, Ralph. NV5.5; NY64.3

　Emerson, Ralph Waldo. CA179.9; MA47.2

　Faulkner, William. NJ31.10

　Ford, Jesse Hill. TN31.3

　Franklin, John Hope. NC38.2

　Frazier, E. Franklin. DC48.16

　general collections. CA179.10, 13

　Gilbert, Olive. MD30.1

　Golden, Harry. NC10.1

　Grimké, Angelina Weld. DC48.17

　Grimké, Archibald Henry. DC48.18

　Harris, James Henry. NC36.7

　Hathaway, Clarence A. MN22.24

　Heyward, DuBose. SC2.12

　Higginson, Thomas Wentworth. CA179.13; NY64.4

　Himes, Chester Bomar. TN29.21

　Howe, Julia (Ward). MA46.17

　Hughes, Langston. CT24.12; IL30.2; NV5.5; NY64.5; NY210.31; PA21.3; TN29.17; WI6.28

　Johnson, James Weldon. CT24.13

　Killens, John Oliver. MA16.10

　Larkins, John R. NC38.2

　Lawrence, Jacob. NY64.6

　Lea, Henry Charles. MA39.49

　Lincoln, C. Eric. GA19.16

　Locke, Alain. NY210.36

　McKay, Claude. CT24.14

　Martin, Margaret Nickerson. MI9.20

　Parton, James. MA39.67

　Rollins, Bertie. MS17.24

　Saxon, Lyle. LA30.6

　Semmes, John Edward. MD19.10

　Spencer, Cornelia (Phillips). NC4.130

　Spingarn, Joel Elias. DC48.50

　Terrell, Mary Church. DC48.52

　Thurman, Wallace. CT24.19

　Toomer, Jean. TN29.32

　Vale, Gilbert. MD30.1

　Van Vechten, Carl. NY207.11

　Voorhees, Lillian Welch. LA16.16

　White, Walter F. CT24.21

　Wright, Richard. IL30.5; IL104.5; NV5.5; TN29.33

　Yerby, Frank. MA16.17

WRITER'S Program. WV6.27

　See also Work Projects Administration

WRITERS' workshops. IL75.2

WURF, Jerry. DC28.483

WYANDOT Indians. OH64.1

WYATT, William E. NC15.232

WYETH, S.D. MD19.10

WYLIE, S. Moffatt. SC12.46

WYLLY and Montmollin (Savannah, Ga.). MA14.9

WYMAN, Lillie Buffam Chase. DC48.17, 18

WYMAN family. MN22.17

WYNES, Charles E. GA19.31

WYOMING. CA179.1

WYOMING Department of Labor and Statistics. WY1

WYTHE, George. NC15.45

WYTHE County, Va. VA8.100

WYTHE family. NC15.216

Xchange Newsletter. MA27

XAVIER University. LA35

XENIA Area Human Relations Council. OH95.1

YES see Youth Educational Service

YES Newsletter. CA176

YMCA see Young Men's Christian Association

YWCA see Young Women's Christian Association

YALABUSHA County, Miss. MS17.19

YALE Clinic of Child Development. DC176.61

YALE University. CT24; DC28.316; NC4.114

YANCEY, Charles. VA8.224

YANCEY, P.Q. DC28.484

YANCEY, William Lowndes. AL21.10; NC15.58

YARBROUGH, J.W. GA32.9

YARDLEY, Richard Q. MS4.2

YATES, Andrew. NY276.2

YATES, Charles. VA8.47

YATES, Charles E. CA100.1

YATES, J.R. VA8.225

YATES, Richard. DC176.166; IL28.149

YATES and Company. VA8.225

YATES County, N.Y. NY46.5

YAZOO City, Miss. MS17.31

YAZOO County, Miss. MS17.1, 31; NC4.108

YAZOO Land Company. TX8.15

YEARGANS, Hartwell. CA100.1

YEARLY Meetings of the Society of Friends. PA16.6, 21; PA63.1

　See also Society of Friends

YEATMAN, James E. MO40.9

YELLOW Fever Epidemic of 1793. PA40.1

YELLOW Springs Human Relations Commission. OH91, OH91.1

YEPEZ, Dorothy. LA16.18

YERBY, Frank. MA16.17

YERGAN, Max. NY210.47

YERGER, William. MS17.4

YESHIVA University. NY257

YIVO Institute for Jewish Research. NY258

YONKERS Commission on Human Rights. NY295

YORTY, Sam. DC28.75, 393

YOUNG, Andrew. DC28.485; GA33.13, 19; NY146.1

YOUNG, Armand D. NC4.93

YOUNG, Charles. DC176.168

YOUNG, Clement Calhoun. CA188.3

YOUNG, Henry Clinton. NC15.199

YOUNG, John Clarke. KY8.88; MI11.1

YOUNG, Pauline. DE6.9

YOUNG, Pete. DC28.486

YOUNG, Whitney M., Jr. DC176.106; MN10.1

YOUNG, William Proby. VA32.21

YOUNG Democrats. DC28.260

YOUNG family. LA10.2; NC4.23, 103

YOUNG Men's Christian Association (YMCA). IL90.31; IL96, IL96.1; MD19.5; MN22.31; NY100.20; NY175.1; NY259

　See also National Council of YMCA's of U.S.A.

YOUNG People's History of the United States. OH77.2

PERSONNEL INDEX

PERSONNEL INDEX

Abajian, James de T. CA148
Abbott, John C. IL101
Abbott, Sidney. NY227
Abernathy, Ralph. GA46
Abner, Willoughby. DC73
Abramowicz, Dina. NY258
Achtenberg, Gail W. MO10
Acosta, J. Wesley, Jr. NY263
Adams, John Quincy. MS15
Adelman, Libby. NY75
Adelsperger, Robert J. IL90
Adler, Harold. NB4
Adlerstein, Hersh L. OH38, OH40
Ahlschwede, Arthur M. MO39
Alderfer, William K. IL116
Alderman, Harry J. NY73
Aleshire, Robert A. DC62
Alexander, Kelly. NC7
Alexick, John V. PA10
Alford, Thomas E. MI15
Alfsen, Wendy. CA173
Alinsky, Saul. IL49
Alix, Ernest K. IL1
Allen, Alexander J. NY190
Allen, Alice P. PA63
Allen, Edward W. PA19
Allen, Joseph. NY274
Alleweit, Millicent. NY277
Allred, W.C., Jr. NC30
Althoff, Joseph M. MI56
Alverson, Madeline. CA149
Amato, Salvatore J. NY5
Ames, Margery L. CA22
Anderson, John F. CA172
Anderson, Joseph P. NY160
Andrews, Louis R. DC101
Andrews, Paul E. MA64
Applebaum, Harold. NY43
Aptheker, Herbert. NY71
Arana, Luis R. FL22
Aries, Leonard P. DC77
Armstrong, Robert D. NV5
Armstrong, Roger D. TX32

Arnett, Alvin Jones. DC16
Artner, Gail M. MI27
Aschenbrenner, Lawrence. MS12
Ashford, Freddye B. MO7
Ashford, Laplois. NY273
Ashmon, Martha. LA38
Askew, Charles. PA1
Atkinson, Tracy. WI16
Atkisson, Arthur A. CA85
Atwood, Robert H. MI63
Avena, J. Richard. TX44
Axelrod, Nancy. CA14

Bachman, Paul H. WY1
Bailey, Bill. MO35
Bajema, Bruce. CA181
Baker, Charlotte M. NY295
Baker, O.J. TX41
Baldinger, Mary Alice. DC74
Banks, W.C. FL23
Baragwanath, Albert K. NY152
Barbour, Hubert U., Jr. NJ3
Barcley, Julius P. CA188
Barker, Paul G. NY164
Barksdale, Edith. DC76
Barksdale, Gaynelle. GA19
Barkstall, Vernon L. IL4, IL122
Barndt, Joe. CA97
Barnes, Carl B. DC124
Barnes, Clarence. MI87
Barnes, Fannie. GA22
Barnes, Francis M. CA160
Barnes, John T. NJ23
Barnes, W. Graham. VA17
Barnett, Thomas H. IN28
Barny, Clarence L. LA33
Barrett, Mary. PA108
Barry, David. NY204
Barry, Marion. DC100
Barton, Judith. NY99
Battle, Robert, III. MI52
Bayliss, John F. IN38
Beach, Robert F. NY239

Beaumont, Andre G. PA3
Bebout, John E. NJ13
Beck, Bertram M. NY150
Becker, William. CA154
Beckett, Calvin W. WI17
Becks, Edward R. CA113
Beda, Robert L. OH31
Bedenfield, Clara L. MS7
Bee, John C., Jr. CA175
Beeler, Arthur. OH85
Belding, Maxwell M. CT8
Belk, Rose K. VA36
Belknap, Robert. NY101
Bell, Derrick A., Jr. CA86
Bell, Whitfield J., Jr. PA29
Bellow, Gary. DC111
Benedict, Donald L. IL39
Benford, Robert. MN3
Benham, Charles C. PA51
Benjamin, Philip S. PA69
Benne, Kenneth D. MA15
Bennett, Edwin G. NY117
Bennett, Fay. NY188
Bennett, L. Howard. DC132
Benson, Carl A. IN12
Bently, W.L. PA45
Benton, Charles. IL10
Benton, David H. MA57
Berger, Howard R. OH27
Berhel, Martha M. FL3
Berkeley, Edmund, Jr. VA8
Berman, Daniel M. DC52
Bermingham, Grace Joyce. NY105
Berner, Richard C. WA15
Bernstein, Janice. CA67
Berry, Margaret E. NY180
Berthel, John H. MD14
Besig, Ernest. CA135
Besse, Ralph N. OH23
Bihn, Mark C. CA177
Bishop, M.S. AL18
Bittirsch, Charles. DC103
Bjorke, Wallace S. MI10

Black, C.W. TN35a
Black, Nannie E. MI46
Blackburn, Francis M. TX9
Blackburn, Robert W. PA32
Blair, James H. NJ21
Blake, Elias, Jr. DC51
Blanchard, J. Richard. CA25
Bland, Catherine V. VA20
Bledsoe, Geraldine. MI42
Block, Larry E. OH90
Blue, Eleanore. MO9, MO14
Bodell, Harry L. CA35
Bodem, Dennis R. MI80
Bogucki, David. DC93
Bogucki, S. David. MI67
Bogue, Donald J. IL86
Bohanon, M. Leo. MO44
Bold, Frances Ann. MA52
Bond, William H. MA39
Bonthius, Robert H. OH29
Boon, Ina. MO41
Boone, Richard W. DC26
Boone, William H. CA1a, CA109
Boorkman, Charles J. CA40
Border, Virgil L. MO43
Borgeson, Earl C. MA42
Borom, Lawrence. MO51
Bosch, Johanna. NY264
Bosma, Boyd. MI41
Boss, Richard W. UT2
Bostick, John Welsey. FL4
Bosworth, Karl A. CT30
Botnick, A.I. LA13
Bousfield, H.G. NY17
Bowden, Marion A. DC113
Bowman, Clarence. OH54
Bowman, Junius A. AZ5
Bowman, Paul H. MO15
Bowman, Willard L. AK1
Bova, Patrick. IL70
Bowles, Elinor. NY80
Bowles, Robert O. CT23
Boyd, Leroy H. NY159

Nichols, Nelson H. NY33
Niebuhr, Herman, Jr. PA67
Nobel, James. OH26
Nolan, Fred. MS21
Nolan, Walter H. MA22
Norris, Elizabeth. NY260
Nugent, Randy. NY59
Nunnally, U.Z. AL28
Nurney, Geraldine L. CA178

O'Connor, Elizabeth. NY266
O'daniel, Therman B. MD19a
Oganovic, N.J. DC116
Ogilvie, Philip S. NC38
O'Hare, Robert W. CA37
O'Keefe, Richard L. TX36
Oliver, William H. MI53
Olivero, Jack J. NY247
Ollander, Joel. IL12
Olson, Bernhard E. NY165
Olsson, Helen. NJ24
O'Neil, B.W. CA41
O'Neil, James E. NY45
O'Neill, Richard W. DC179
Orendair, Antonio. TX45
Oresen, L.V. NY110
Orgain, James R. VA25
Orgel, Alexandra. MO30
Orne, Jerrold. NC3
O'Rourke, James R., Sr. KY4
O'Rourke, Martha L. AL32
Orr, Mary Mark. KS19
Orr, Robert W. IA1
Ortique, Revius O., Jr. LA14, LA22
Overton, L. Joseph. NY198
Owens, Olin J. SC15
Owens, Sebastian C. CO19

Page, Jerome W. WA13
Palmer, Charles F. DC200
Palmer, David. OH4
Pansini, Francis D. CA20
Parker, Edward, Jr. TN13
Parker, Frank. VA16
Parker, Wyman W. CT17
Parsons, Irene. DC197
Paterson, Robert. MO3
Patterson, A.M. NC36
Patterson, Emma. TX49
Patterson, H.R. AL8
Patterson, Jane S. NC44
Paul, Sarah. NY143
Paul, Tamar. MD6
Paulson, Daniel. VA1
Pavela, Jean. KS2
Pawley, James A. NJ26

Paxton, William. RI3
Payne, F. Dana. DC177
Payzs, Tibor. MI54
Peabody, Malcolm E. MA20
Peckham, Howard H. MI11
Pemberton, Lounneer. MO25
Penn, William H., Sr. MI44
Perkins, G. Holmes. PA77
Perkins, Madelyn E. NY62
Perlmutter, Philip. MA10
Perlstein, Norman H. NY88
Perry, Eleanor B. PA37
Perry, George M. NY184
Perry, Pennie. NC18
Peters, Francis Warren. MI28
Peterson, Pattie. LA1
Peyton, Russell. OR6
Pharr, William L. AR10
Phillips, Donald E. AZ6
Phillips, Paul. MI68
Phillips, Treadwell O. MI7
Phinnie, Lucille. IL54
Pierce, Wendell H. CO12
Pierce, William L. VA3
Pierport, Robert Joe. NY256
Pifer, Alan. NY91
Pike, Kermit J. OH36a
Pilgrim, Harold L. PA38
Pin, Dorothy. CA61
Pinkston, Garland. DC88
Pinkus, Craig Eldon. IN23
Pirie, James W. MI65
Pittmann, J. Ronald. OH93
Pitts, Raymond J. CA111
Pius, Mary, O.S.P. MD22
Plank, Betty. IL44
Pollard, William C. VA35
Ponce, Mary (Mrs.). TX23
Poo, Riva. MA7
Pope, Jan. MO27
Porter, Dorothy B. DC48
Porter, Scipio, Jr. CA5
Post, Suzanne K. KY9
Potter, Charles A. MA63
Pouissant, Alvin F. AL26
Pratt, Helen E. MI70
Pratt, John M. CA57
Prejean, Charles. GA27
Preston, Carey B. IL7
Price, Paxton P. MO47
Printis, Marvin L. CA110
Prioleau, Marguerite L. PA6
Prior, Granville T. SC2
Psarakis, Emanuel N. CT6
Pugh, Sally. CA136

Pumphrey, Muriel W. MO54

Purdy, G. Flint. MI58
Putnam, Roger L. MA66

Quijano, Carla. NY52
Quimby, Grace. VT3
Quinn, Frank. CA174

Raab, Earl. CA155
Radelet, Louis A. MI62
Radoff, Morris L. MD2
Ragland, Temple, Jr. TN1
Ralph, Arthur. NY63
Ramage, David, Jr. NY171
Rand, Larry. MS14
Randall, F.S. IL2
Randall, J.H. IL71
Randolph, Carl. KS3
Rassoull, Abass. IL57
Rausch, George J., Jr. IA4
Rawlins, Earl A. NY202
Rawlins, Gladys D. PA41
Ray, Richard S. NC16
Raymond, George M. NY27
Redd, Charles. IN10
Reddick, L.D. PA53
Reeves, Norman V.A. MD25
Regulus, Homie. GA63
Renfro, Jenifer W. IL67
Renner, Gerald A. IL66
Reynolds, Fred J. IN9
Reynolds, James F. CO10
Reynolds, W.E. MD25a
Rhoads, James B. DC172
Rice, Doris E. WV1
Richardson, Paul E. NY3
Richmond, Al. CA168
Richmond, Robert W. KS10
Ridley, Rachel. IL41
Riessman, Frank. NY216
Riley, Stephen T. MA23
Risk, Richard E. MO8
Roach, Jeannetts C. MS30
Robb, Felix C. GA45
Robbins, Daniel. RI11
Robbins, Warren M. DC40, DC60
Roberts, B.J. DC54
Roberts, Clark G. IL81
Roberts, Cyril J. OK21
Robin, Fred. MD4
Robinson, Cleophus. OK15
Robinson, Cleveland. NY194
Robinson, Dorothy W. IL73
Robinson, Louisa S. SC17
Robinson, M. Elizabeth. PA59
Robinson, Milton J. MI14, MI66
Robinson, Natalie. RI8
Robinson, Robert P. PA74

Robinson, Ted. MD5
Robison, Joseph B. NY74
Robles, Tom E. NM4
Rochell, Carlton C. GA17
Rodgers, Carolyn. IL75
Rodgers, Curtis E. MI26
Rodriguez, Richard J. NM5
Rogers, David B. MI89
Roos, Joseph. CA65
Root, John O. IL96
Rose, Margaret. ND1
Rose, William Y. OK10
Rosen, A. Abbot. IL16
Rosenfels, Isabelle G. WA2
Ross, David C., Jr. IL6
Ross, Ellis L. OH41
Rounds, Joseph B. NY30
Rountree, Louise. NC43
Rovelstad, Howard. MD28
Rowley, Philip D. CO1
Rubenstein, Lewis C. NY50
Rogers, Ruby. AR2
Ruffle, Evelyn. NH4
Rush, N. Orwin. FL26
Rushing, Lawrence. GA48
Russell, John R. NY272
Russell, Mattie. NC15
Rustin, Bayard. NY57, NY58
Rutherford, Doris P. TX28
Rutledge, Edward. NY161
Ruttenberg, Charles B. DC180
Ryan, Emily S. MO33
Ryweck, Morton W. MO29

Sachs, Perry. IL13
Sacks, Albert M. MA61
Sadik, Marvin S. DC194a
Sadofsky, Stanley. NY215
Saladin, Al. IL51a
Samuel, Patricia A. DC207
Sandberg, Neil. CA43
Sanders, Charles L. OH55
Sandweiss, Sherwood. MI21
Sardeson, Charles T. CT13
Sass, Morris S. NY82
Sasse, Mary Angela. IN8
Sawyer, David A. DC166
Scanlon, Bill. CA32
Scannell, Francis X. MI79
Schacter, David. IL53
Schatz, Walter. TN22a
Scheiner, Samuel L. MN5
Schell, A.R. CA93
Schell, Edwin. MD24
Schietinger, E.F. GA50
Schilling, Howard S. DC183
Schlitt, Jacob. DC119

Schloss, Marjorie. NY81
Scholes, William E. NY172
Schon, Donald A. MA45
Schone, John R. UT1
Schoneman, Ruth E. IL18
Schreiber, Evelyn. MO28
Schuetz, Robert J. PA20
Schul, Norman W. NC5
Schultz, Charles R. CT18
Schulze, Albert. DC115
Schwab, Leona. NY40
Schwarz, Margaret. NY10, NY291
Schwartz, Myron. MO1
Schwartz, Myron. OH10
Schwarzschild, Henry. NY140
Scott, Irving. FL19
Scott, John E. WV5
Scott, Wesley L. WI20
Scribner, Anne J. TX25
Scriven, Margaret. IL28
Seabron, William M. DC121
Seale, Bobby. CA8
Seaver, James. KS4
Seder, Norman. IN22
Seeman, Isadore. DC44
Segal, Robert E. MA21
Selden, David. DC9
Sells, Lucy. CA17
Semel, Max. CA170
Sengstacke, John H. IL69
Senn, Milton A. CA45
Sewell, C.W. AL3
Shade, Camile S. LA6
Shafer, Robert. VA2
Shaffer, William. PA83
Shannon, Lyle W. IA10
Shapiro, J.L. NY96
Sharp, Robert K. TN41
Shelton, Edward. DC165
Shelton, Robert M. AL33
Shephard, George W., Jr. CO18
Sherizen, Sanford. IL34
Sherman, Stuart C. RI2
Shetler, Charles. WI6
Shinert, Gregory E. KY5
Shooshan, Harry. DC163
Showell, Franklin C. MD18
Shull, Anne W. DC105
Shull, Leon. DC14
Siegle, Peter E. MA31
Silverman, Jason. DC15
Silverman, Sidney H. IL20
Silverson, Reuben D. DC24
Simmons, Charles M. WA7
Simmons, Dondra. AL28
Simmons, Henry. IL32

Simmons, Samuel J. DC144
Simmons, W.J. MS9
Simms, Paul B. NY97
Simms, Robt. H. FL17
Simonson, James W. IN32
Sinclair, Donald A. NJ12
Sinclair, John. MI13
Singer, Richard. AL38
Singh, Raman K. VA10a
Singley, Elijah. AL20
Sisson, John P. LA23
Skipper, James E. CA15
Slaiman, Donald. DC7
Slate, Ted. NY222
Slawson, Robert. CT27
Slayton, William L. DC201
Slive, Zoya. MA34
Small, Louise. NB3
Smallwood, Audrey Y. MD15
Smallwood, Kenneth W. NY248
Smedley, T.A. TN46
Smiley, Wendell W. NC31
Smith, Earnest A. DC109
Smith, Eddie O., Jr. VA7
Smith, Franklin G. TX24
Smith, Gordon M. NY32
Smith, Hal H. TN4
Smith, Herman B., Jr. GA37
Smith, Hermon Dunlap. IL103
Smith, Jessie Carney. TN29
Smith, John B. TX10
Smith, Laura H. MA48
Smith, Leonard E. GA40
Smith, Mark A. OR9
Smith, Maxine. TN18
Smith, Nathalene R. NC24
Smith, Ralph V. MI91
Smith, Richard Z. OH88
Smith, Samuel C. DC84
Smith, Virginia. AL17
Smith, Wilbur J. CA83
Smoke, Lillian H. PA11
Snelgrove, C.P. TN1a
Snyder, Edward F. DC41
Solomon, Victor. NY113
Soltow, Martha Jane. MI61
Sompter, Beverly. MI12
Sorin, Saul. WI10
Southerland, M.C. VA15
Spector, Aaron J. PA68
Speiser, Lawrence. DC4
Spiegal, John P. MA73
Sporleder, James H. MO37
Sprug, Joseph W. CO13
Spyers-Duran, Peter. MI75
Stack, Norman A. MO38

Stadler, Frances H. MO40
Staley, Harold E. DC27
Stanley, Frank L. CA75
Starr, Edward C. NY267
Starr, Louis M. NY102
Station, Alice E. NB7
Stavis, Morton. NY138
Steele, Charles T. KY15
Steele, Percy H., Jr. CA141
Steele, Ruth. PA81
Steelman, Alan. DC188
Stein, Hannah. NY167
Stein, William S. NY146
Steinhauser, Sheldon. CO8
Stephen, Charles S., Jr. NB1
Stern, Arthur W. NY25
Sterns, Marshall W. NY130a
Stevens, Christine N. MS31
Stevens, George. CA131
Steward, Luther C., Jr. DC127
Stewart, Bryon L. NM1
Stewart, Maxwell S. NY229
Stiefel, Harry. NY90
Stilger, Robert. MN16
Stone, C. Walter. PA94
Stone, Robert H. TN26
Strader, Curtis. MI69
Strickler, George M., Jr. LA20
Strong, Patricia M. TN32
Stuck, Bernard J. NJ33
Studebaker, Jerry. OK11
Sturgis, Gladys Marie. MO26
Suelflow, Aug R. MO34
Sullivan, David W. NJ28
Sullivan, Donald F. DC78
Sullivan, John. NJ7
Sutters, John R. PA26
Swanson, Bert A. NY12
Swanson, Dorothy. NY220
Switzer, Mary E. DC140

Talbert, Henry A. CA78
Tanis, Norman. CA95
Tate, Charles E. OH52
Tate, Horace E. GA31
Tavel, William S. DC149
Taylor, Betty Kaye. NY189
Taylor, Clark E. IL110
Taylor, Donald D. RI9
Taylor, F. Charles. RI6
Taylor, Harold C. MI74
Taylor, Julia H. TX43
Taylor, Kanardy L. DC134
Taylor, Lynnette. DC33
Teitelbaum, Arthur N. FL12
Templeton, Furman L. MD9
Tennelly, J.B. DC30

Terry, Maurice H. WI21
Thibaudeau, Roger. WA14
Thiele, Karl. IN39
Thomas, C.A. OH5
Thomas, Carl E. NY145
Thomas, Charles. CA54
Thomas, Charles H., Jr. DC187
Thomas, Elaine F. AL34
Thomas, George B. MA38
Thomas, George L. CA58
Thomas, James E. CA127
Thomas, Julian. WI27
Thomas, Mary L. NY51
Thomas, Theodore W. WI22
Thompson, Enid T. CO17
Thompson, Hobson, Jr. NC23
Thompson, Leroy. FL16
Thomson, Matt H. OH48
Thorne, Dorothy Gilbert. NC27
Thornley, Fant Hill. AL5
Thornton, Eileen. OH72
Thrasher, Margaret. MD30
Throckmorton, Robert. NV2
Tidwell, Kenneth W. GA44
Tiger, Edith. NY179
Tillman, John. PA12
Tipton, William H., Jr. TX18
Tobias, Susan. IL38
Todd, Sally Lou. MN8
Tolan, Edwin K. NY276
Tolefree, Shirley. AR11
Toll, Doris. OK16
Tollerson, Tandy, II. TN28
Tolles, Frederick B. PA98
Tomlin, Ian. MS10
Toombs, Kenneth E. LA10
Totten, Herman L. TX40
Tower, Harry N. OK8
Towner, Lawrence W. IL72
Townley, Joyce. IL40
Towns, Rose Mary. CA116
Travis, Dempsey J. IL80
True, Douglas G. DC173
Tucker, Harold W. NY49
Tucker, Lynette V. NY16
Tucker, Sterling. DC89
Tudiver, Miss L. NY19
Turnbow, Carri. MA60
Twardy, Stan. OK9
Tydings, J. Mansir. KY11
Tyner, Jarvis. IL94
Tyler, Robert R. CA124
Tyler, Sara. KY2

Upthegrove, Franklin J. NY283

Vail, Edward O. CA69
Valder, Bob. NC12
Valencik, May V.K. NY294
Valentine, Foy. TN39
Vanden Bosch, August H. FL15
Van Why, Joseph S. CT14
Venable, A.S. DC129
Vieham, Harold. PA71
Von Der Mehden, Fred. TX35
Vorspan, Albert. NY108

Wade, Lyndon A. GA20
Wagman, Frederick H. MI6
Wagner, Ernest C. VI1
Wainwright, Nicholas. PA43
Waiter, Francis X. AL31
Walker, Charles R., Jr. TN35
Walker, Donald C. IL93
Walker, John L. NM3
Walker, Lucius, Jr. NY133
Walker, R.H. DC42
Walton, Clyde C. IL98
Walton, John. MS33
Wamer, William. GA2
Ward, Douglas Turner. NY196
Ward, Francis. IL43
Ward, Wardell. CA107
Warner, Robert M. MI9
Washington, David B. PA90
Washington, George L. DC29
Washington, Kenneth S. CA50
Watkins, Mary Lou. DC135
Watkins, Sylvestre C. VA22
Watkins, Ted. CA90
Wattel, Harold. NY44
Watts, Daniel. NY61
Watts, Harold W. WI8
Waugh, Charles E. MI82
Waymon, Carrol W. CA129

Webb, David A. TX22
Webb, Muriel. NY118
Webb, William H. CO4
Webber, Jean Y. DC8
Webber, Malcolm C. CT19
Weber, Carlton N. OH43
Weber, J. Robert. NY176
Weinberg, Meyer. IL51
Weinreb, Sanford. PA28
Weinstein, Jerry B. CA34
Weiss, Egon. NY284
Weitting, June. IL124
Welch, Nat. GA16
Welch, Robert. MA5
Wellington, David H. CA33
Wendel, George D. MO48
Werkheiser, Don. OH87
Wesley, Charles H. DC18
Whaley, Leon E. CA56
Wheeler, Marcia. IN7
Wheeler, Wayne. NB11
Whickam, Katie E. DC71
White, Clotea C. VA14
White, Wilford L. DC49
White, Woodie W. DC110
Whitehill, Walter Muir. MA13
Whitelock, Alfred. IN29
Whiteman, Maxwell. PA70
Whitesides, William L. VA10
Whittelsey, Alice E. PA16
Wicke, Myron F. TN45
Wicker, W.W. TN15
Wickline, Lempi L. DC182
Wickman, John E. KS1
Wilburn, A.P. MS25
Wilcox, Preston. NY60, NY157
Wiley, George A. DC91
Wilkes, Henrietta. SC19
Wilkins, Roy. NY141, NY158
Williams, Barbara J. SC18

Williams, C.R. TN36
Williams, Daniel T. AL35
Williams, Doran. TX5
Williams, Eddie N. DC161
Williams, Elizabeth. AL30
Williams, Franklin H. NY107
Williams, Gordon R. IL22
Williams, James D. DC118
Williams, James N. RI12
Williams, Jim. NY15
Williams, Joe N. NB8
Williams, John H. CA38
Williams, John H. TX48
Williams, Julius E. MO19
Williams, Kale. IL11
Williams, Lee G. TX7
Williams, Marvin D., Jr. TN27
Williams, Percy H. DC128
Williams, William L. OH79
Williamson, Miley O. OH60
Willitts, Gail. NJ2
Wilmore, Gayraud, Jr. NY245
Wilmore, Jacques. NY246
Wilson, Arnold. MO55
Wilson, J. OH6a
Wilson, M.L. NY144
Wilson, T.G.G. NY147
Wilson, Theodore R. OH2
Wilson, Woodrow Z. TN9
Wimbish, Emery, Jr. PA21
Wine, Joseph D. OH56
Winfrey, Dorman H. TX6
Winge, Edwin N. DC164
Winston, Gertrude E. DE2
Winston, Oliver C. NY47
Winters, Wilma E. MA19
Wittenstein, Charles F. GA12
Wolf, Edwin, II. PA49
Wolf, Heken M. FL5

Wolfe, William. NY293
Wolohan, Juliet. NY6
Wood, Clarence N. AL7
Wood, Daniel. NY93
Woodruff, Elaine L. DC117
Wooley, Davis C. TN40
Woolf, Margaret A. WA3
Woolfenden, W.E. MI24
Woolsey, Theodore D. DC133
Wordell, Madeline H. RI1
Woy, Sara. PA39
Wright, Arthur D. NY92a
Wright, Charles H. MI35
Wright, Clarence S. DC181
Wright, Herbert. CT1
Wright, M.E., Jr. LA27
Wright, Peggy. VA4
Wright, Penelope L. DC67
Wyke, Joseph H. NJ14

Yancey, William. TN47
Yanich, Yosef I. FL21
Yarboro, T.L. PA107
Yasui, Minoru. CO9
Yates, Waverly. CT26
Yellin, David. TN16
Yenawine, Wayne S. KY20
Yoder, Theodore O. CO15
Young, Laurence T. IL8
Young, Wallace L., Jr. LA19, LA21
Younge, Samuel L. GA56

Zack, Jane N. DC145
Zand, Walter. FL11
Zeides, Solomon. NY257
Zobeir, Talib M. NY22a
Zorach, Margaret B. NY18
Zucker, Milton. CT20
Zucker, William. PA47